AMERICA
The Glorious Republic

*How little do my countrymen know what precious blessings they
are in possession of, and which no other people on earth enjoy!*

THOMAS JEFFERSON, *writing to James Monroe from Paris, June 17, 1785*

AMERICA
The Glorious Republic

Henry F. Graff

Professor of History
Columbia University

Houghton Mifflin Company   BOSTON

Atlanta   Dallas   Geneva, Ill.   Hopewell, N.J.   Palo Alto   Toronto

Cover: Watercolor rendering by Elizabeth Moutal of wood carving by John Haley Bellamy.
Half-title: Watercolor rendering by Alfred H. Smith of wood carving by William Beal.
Frontispiece: "Genesee Scenery," by Thomas Cole. **Page 7:** Portuguese vessel, 16th century.
Page 8: "Spirit of '76." **Page 9:** Irish immigrants, mid-19th century. **Page 10:** Railroad poster.
Page 11: Fourth of July celebration, 1916. **Page 12:** Flag raising at Iwo Jima. **Page 13:** Space
shuttle. **Page 15:** Map of North and South America, 1596.

Printed in the U.S.A.
ISBN: 0-395-33992-8

BCDEFGHIJ-D-93210/898765

To
Molly Ann Morse
and
Elizabeth Graff Morse,
splendid young women
of the
Glorious Republic

AUTHOR

HENRY F. GRAFF is a noted historian and teacher of history. For many years he has been on the faculty of Columbia University, having risen through the ranks of the Department of History to full professor and serving a term as Chairman. He has also lectured on scores of campuses throughout the country. For six years he was a member of the National Historical Publications Commission, having been appointed by the President. A specialist in the history of the presidency and of United States diplomatic relations, Dr. Graff has published extensively on both subjects. His previous textbooks for high school and junior high school classes have been widely acclaimed. Renowned for the elegance and liveliness of his lectures, he has been honored with Columbia's Great Teacher Award and with the coveted Mark Van Doren Award, bestowed by the student body of Columbia College for distinguished teaching and scholarship.

SUSAN A. ROBERTS, who prepared the study material for *America: The Glorious Republic*, is a teacher at Del Norte High School, Albuquerque, New Mexico.

READERS

TOM ALLEN, Irving Independent School District, Irving, Texas.

ARLENE DAWSON, George High School, Atlanta, Georgia.

LINDA FRANCIS, Fort Bend Independent School District, Stafford, Texas.

BALTAZAR GARCIA, Nogales High School, Nogales, Arizona.

NORMAN McRAE, Detroit Public Schools, Detroit, Michigan.

VIRGINIA DRIVING HAWK SNEVE, Flandreau, South Dakota.

GEORGE TURNER, Northeast High Schocl, Philadelphia, Pennsylvania.

Contents

UNIT **6**

CRUSADING AT HOME AND ABROAD   **505**
1865–1920

ATLAS AND REFERENCE SECTION

Features

Eyewitness to History

Documents of Freedom

Achievements in Technology

Life in America

Maps

(continued)

Maps *(continued)*

Graphs and Charts

A LETTER

from the author...

Dear student:

The American past is full of fascinating people, events, and deeds — even a master novelist could not have invented them. A true account of American history, then, has all the surprises, twists and turns of plot, and variety of characters that people expect to find in a good story. In *America: The Glorious Republic* I have sought to tell the history of the United States as it deserves to be told. To my account I have brought knowledge accumulated through years of experience in reading and teaching about America (I made up my mind when I was in grade school that I would one day be an historian).

As you read and study this book, I trust you will enjoy its style and content, addressed especially to Americans like you who are now young and who will live most of their lives in the twenty-first century. In that not-so-far-off time you will need to know and value the formative landmarks of the country's past. From this book you can acquire historical background to help you face public issues that Americans today may not have even guessed will then be before the nation.

To enrich your understanding, I have enhanced my own words with original documents, first-hand accounts, direct quotations, song lyrics, and revealing anecdotes. These materials permit you to see close up some of the footprints that earlier Americans have left on the paths they took in meeting the problems of *their* day. To help make the successive eras of America's history vivid and memorable, my publisher has brought to these pages a matchless array of illustrations drawn from hundreds of collections. Good pictures, as you know, enable the past to remain forever alive.

Each unit of the book will draw your attention to the technological innovations that altered America's course or outlook. Ingenuity has always been an American characteristic, and recognizing its impact is indispensable to understanding the nation's development.

The maps in the book, taken together, constitute a built-in historical atlas. They will enable you to locate precisely — as you should — every American place name mentioned in the text. In addition, the many graphs, charts, and time lines will assist you in fixing firmly in your mind important facts and significant points. Summaries at the end of each chapter will allow you to review conveniently what you have read.

Finally, because the book offers a modern view of America, its history is presented in the context of events taking place in the world at large. A "World Scene" feature in every chapter will help you view American history in the tumultuous international setting in which it has unfolded.

When you have come to the end of the book, you may want to ponder the immense journey the nation has been on since Columbus' men first shouted "Land! Land!" in 1492. You will, I hope, be pleased that through your knowledge of American history you have grown in your ability to make judgments about the dilemmas and concerns of your own time. If this proves to be the case, I will feel well rewarded for my efforts to make the book accurate and interesting. No less important than your personal pleasure and satisfaction, however, will be your ability to take your place in a new generation of voters and officeholders more fully appreciative of what it means to be an American.

Henry B. Graff

UNIT 1

BEGINNINGS

1000 – 1775

I believe that the earthly paradise lies here, which no one can enter except by God's leave. I believe that this land which your Highnesses have commanded me to discover is very great, and that there are many other lands to the south, of which there have never been reports.

JOURNAL OF CHRISTOPHER COLUMBUS

CHAPTER 1

America Known and Unknown

1000 – 1550

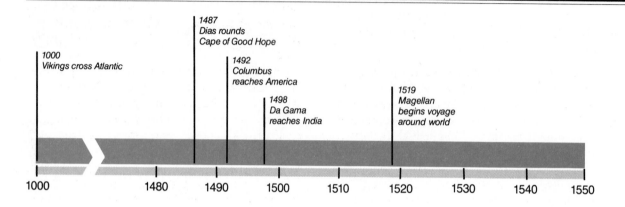

1000
Vikings cross Atlantic

1487
Dias rounds
Cape of Good Hope

1492
Columbus
reaches America

1498
Da Gama
reaches India

1519
Magellan
begins voyage
around world

1000   1480   1490   1500   1510   1520   1530   1540   1550

CHAPTER OUTLINE

1. European explorers search for a water route to Asia and find America.

2. Europe's knowledge of the world increases.

3. Europeans find a variety of peoples in the Americas.

The United States shines among the nations as the "land of opportunity." Simply stated, the phrase means that Americans enjoy the freedom to pursue individual goals. As we study United States history, we quickly learn that this freedom was built into American life from the start. The quest for opportunity gave vitality to the settlement of North America. It has been the magnet drawing immigrants to the American continent ever since.

In the 1400's Europe was emerging from the Middle Ages. A new era, characterized by discovery and change, was slowly taking shape. The oceans were no longer seen as forbidding barriers; instead, they came to be viewed as avenues for contact with other lands. Merchants and bankers were gaining influence throughout Europe and helping their monarchs finance expeditions to unknown shores. Then, as countries grew powerful through discoveries and the setting up of colonies, a spirit of enterprise stirred even ordinary Europeans to dream of having a chance for advancement on the other side of the Atlantic.

Adventurers such as Christopher Columbus, Ferdinand Magellan, and John Cabot opened the way across the oceans. These trailblazers were followed by brave pioneers willing to settle permanently in North America. Out of these beginnings a society emerged in America unlike any other — energetic and, above all, gloriously free.

1 European Explorers Search for a Water Route to Asia and Find America

During the 1300's and 1400's Europe's seafarers gradually reached a revolutionary conclusion: that all the oceans are connected, making it possible for all countries with seacoasts to be in touch with one another. As a result, European civilization took on new life and made its influence felt throughout the world as no other civilization ever before had done.

Prince Henry of Portugal encourages exploration. Portuguese mariners were among the first to become interested in overseas exploration. In this enterprise they were encouraged by a member of the royal family of Portugal, Prince Henry. In 1415 Prince Henry had participated in the Portuguese capture of the Muslim city of Ceuta (SAY-oot-ah) on the northern coast of Africa. There he learned from merchants about a trade in gold along routes that led across the Sahara to powerful West African kingdoms. If Portugal could get control of these sources of gold, Henry reflected, it would have immense power, for Europe was suffering from a shortage of the precious metal.

Henry's desire for gold was matched by his desire to make contact with a mysterious Christian ruler said to control a vast empire in East Africa. Henry believed that if he could find Christian allies in Africa, together they could defeat the powerful Muslims. The eagerness to destroy Muslim power grew out of envy of the profits Muslim merchants of North Africa earned on the trade in goods brought overland from Asia.

Henry decided that to become a powerful country, Portugal needed to strengthen its navy. To that end, he established on the Portuguese coast a school where he gathered leading geographers, map makers, and students of *navigation* (the science of sailing ships).

As the geographers and mariners learned more about the oceans, they challenged myths and superstitions about boiling seas and hideous monsters. Soon, many sailors felt bold enough to sail into unknown waters along the west coast of

Portuguese explorers of the late 1400's set out from Lisbon harbor, pictured below, in search of a sea route to Asia.

Africa. Henry also set up supply stations on islands off the African coast — the Madeiras and the Canaries. These bases could be used by crews who intended to push farther to the south.

By 1460, the year of Henry's death, Portuguese navigators had reached the Gold Coast of Africa (map, page 32). John II of Portugal carried on Henry's work, and Portuguese mariners continued southward along the African coast. In time, a rich trade in gold and slaves developed between Portugal and various African kingdoms.

Portugal seeks a water route to India. Sometime after the middle of the fifteenth century the Portuguese found another reason for carrying on their journeys south. They were eager to take over the spice trade with Asian lands. Throughout Europe practically no fresh food — except milk and cream — was available after the fall harvest until the following year. Spices — especially pepper and cloves — were valuable in hiding the bland or rancid taste of many foods, especially meat which had been stored for a long time.

The use of spices grew and grew until well-to-do Europeans regarded them as a necessity and developed a well-organized trade. From the East Indies and from the city of Calicut in India, spices were shipped to ports in the eastern Mediterranean. Muslim traders then sold the spices to Christian merchants based in Venice.

The Portuguese envied the riches that flowed into the hands of the Italians — as indeed into the hands of the Muslims along the way. Why, reasoned the rulers of Portugal, could not ships sail around Africa, go to the source of the spices, and bring them back to Portugal directly?

The Portuguese sail around Africa to India. In 1487 John II dispatched Bartholomeu Dias (DEE-ahs) with three ships to sail around Africa. Caught in a violent storm as he passed southwest Africa, Dias was blown off course. When the winds died down, he discovered that they had carried his ship all the way around Africa. The king, when he learned the news, named the southern tip of Africa the Cape of Good Hope — because of the high promise it held that eventually his subjects would reach India by sea.

In 1497 a new Portuguese king sent another sea captain, Vasco da Gama, with four vessels to sail around Africa and seek spices. Da Gama easily rounded the Cape of Good Hope and then sailed northward. Along the East African coast he met a man from India, an experienced sailor, who guided him across the Indian Ocean. By May, 1498, Da Gama's ship was riding at anchor off the coast of India. Within a few years, Portugal began to participate actively in the spice trade.

Even though Portuguese sailors had cut away the mystery of navigation to the south, they did not try sailing to the *west* across the Atlantic. In that direction lay more mysteries than they were ready to cope with.

The Vikings cross the Atlantic. Few Portuguese would have suspected that five hundred years earlier European sailors *had* ventured westward. Around the year 1000, seafarers from northern Europe called Vikings had set forth on voyages that took them across the Atlantic. They may have been following the lead of even earlier adventurers, Irish fishermen, who were said to have sailed far to the west and found strange islands in the Atlantic.

The Viking voyages took place after a Norwegian named Eric the Red was banished to Iceland for a crime he had committed. (Iceland had been reached and colonized by the Vikings in the ninth century.) Deciding to sail still farther to the west, Eric eventually reached Greenland, where he built a settlement.

About the year 986, another Norwegian, Bjarni Herjulfson, set out from Iceland to join Eric's settlement in Greenland. Through an error in navigation Herjulfson missed his intended destination and sailed on and on, finally reaching a flat, forested country not at all like Greenland. Herjulfson and his sailors, no doubt dismayed, quickly sailed away. Unknowingly, they had "discovered" North America.

Leif Ericsson, a son of Eric the Red, was fascinated by the account Herjulfson gave of the land he had happened upon. With a crew of 35, Ericsson sailed westward from Greenland in about the year 1003. After a long trip the expedition landed, probably on the coast of what is now Newfoundland and, later on, at what is now Nova Scotia. They may even have reached land farther south, for they described a country where grapes were growing and where cattle could graze all winter. The visitors called the land Vinland (Wineland).

Viking settlements in North America fail to thrive. In the next few years two of Leif Ericsson's brothers made separate trips to Vinland. Other explorers followed, and eventually settlements were started. Contact with Vinland probably continued on and off for two more centuries, but gradually the settlements died out. Possibly there were too few settlers to make a Viking colony a success. Possibly also the climate became too harsh, or perhaps political troubles at home caused contacts with Norway to grow weaker.

Europeans misjudge the distance to Asia. Although the Vikings had reached America, knowledge of their exploits was not widespread. If a few educated Europeans heard about Vinland, they probably assumed it was an island. In fact, the Atlantic Ocean was thought to be full of islands.

Still, at the beginning of the fifteenth century certain important facts were known to European geographers. One was that the earth is round and that by traveling due west from Europe a sailor ought to be able to reach Asia. The other was that two fabulously rich countries were in the part of the world Europeans called "the East": China and Japan.

Most European geographers believed, however, that Asia was much closer to Europe than it actually is. They had read the work of Ptolemy (TAHL-uh-mee), an ancient Greek scholar, who had underestimated this distance. Moreover, the most highly regarded geographer of the 1400's, an Italian physician and map maker named

The seal of the city of Bergen, Norway, shows the kind of ship the Vikings used in their long-distance voyages many centuries ago.

Toscanelli, declared that China was only 5,000 nautical miles from Europe by sea. (In reality it lies more than twice as many miles away.)

Marco Polo describes the riches of Asia. European interest in Asia was first aroused at the end of the thirteenth century by the exploits of an Italian adventurer named Marco Polo. His account was — and remains — the most influential travel story that has ever been written.

From 1271 to 1295 Marco Polo, a citizen of Venice, traveled in Asia. He even became an official in the service of Kublai Khan, whose immense power as emperor of China was based not only on military exploits but also on his fostering of commerce and the arts. When Marco Polo returned to Venice and began to describe the riches he had seen, the report caused a sensation. Polo's written account was widely circulated throughout Europe and remained popular long after his death. One man who owned a copy was Christopher Columbus.

Christopher Columbus plans to sail west to Asia. Columbus, the son of a weaver, was born in 1451 in Genoa, Italy. As a youth he practiced his father's craft. Soon, however,

The Caravel

In the 1400's the Portuguese developed rugged sailing vessels for exploring the coast of Africa. These ships, called caravels, were distinguished not only for their sturdy hulls but also for their remarkable speed.

The caravel's rig — the arrangement of masts and sails — was responsible for its good performance. The rig consisted of one or two forward masts that carried large square sails which made for efficient sailing when the wind was blowing from behind. There was also a rear mast with a triangular, or lateen, sail which enabled the ship to sail into the wind.

The hull design of the caravel was characterized by built-up sections in the bow and the stern. Called the forecastle and the sterncastle, they provided protection for the crew from the large waves of the open sea. It was this kind of vessel that enabled European explorers to make their successful voyages across the Atlantic.

he became a sailor, traveling as far north as Iceland and as far south as the Gold Coast of Africa.

No one knows when Columbus decided that he could reach Asia by sailing west. He may have been influenced by a brother who is said to have sailed with Dias on his trip around the Cape of Good Hope. Columbus was impressed by Toscanelli's certainty that China was within easy reach of a well-supplied European fleet. But who would put up the money for such a journey? When Columbus failed to interest anyone in his native city of Genoa, he set out for Portugal to present his ideas at the Portuguese court and to seek support for his "Enterprise of the Indies." John II, however, turned him down too. Columbus then went to Spain to present his case.

After waiting six years for an answer, Columbus finally obtained the backing of King Ferdinand and Queen Isabella for the scheme. No doubt the Spanish monarchs were moved by a feeling of rivalry with their neighbor Portugal, then beginning to grow rich from trade with West Africa.

Columbus begins his voyage. Columbus was 41 years old in 1492. Tall, with red hair turning to gray, he was an impressive figure. In the harbor of the Spanish port of Palos, he rounded up ships and crews. He acquired three vessels, the *Niña*, the *Pinta*, and the *Santa Maria*. Ninety experienced men were assembled to serve as crews. None could have known that they were embarking on a voyage that would be a supreme turning point in history.

Before dawn on August 3, 1492, Columbus ordered the ships to set sail from Palos. He headed first for the Canary Islands, intending to travel westward along their latitude by using the winds that blew in the late summer. After taking on fresh water, meat, and wood, and making repairs — all of which took a month — the three vessels were on their way again.

As anticipated, the winds were favorable and the ships made excellent time. Columbus, mindful that the crew had misgivings about the trip, kept two records: one for himself in which he stated the dis-

tances covered, and one for the men in which he understated the distances. He feared that the crew might panic — or even mutiny — if they learned how far from Palos they had actually sailed.

As the days passed, the crew became increasingly jittery. Aboard the *Santa Maria* serious trouble was brewing. After being at sea for thirty days, the crew was threatening to throw Columbus overboard if he did not turn back.

Columbus reaches America. As the expedition continued westward, tension rose higher. Then one day flocks of birds were sighted overhead. There was soon another sign that land was near: branches of trees and shrubs were drifting about in the water. On October 11, thirty-three days out of the Canaries, there was a cry from the *Pinta*: "*Tierra! Tierra!* Land! Land!" It was no false alarm.

The land proved to be a small island where the people were, as Columbus said, "poor in everything." The inhabitants were Taino (TY-noh) Indians, friendly and gentle. Columbus named the island San Salvador — "Holy Saviour." (It lies in the Bahamas, southeast of Florida.) The people living there had always called it "Guanahani," but that name, like the names of other islands and territories that Europeans came upon, would quickly be forgotten.

Continuing his search for China or Japan, which he felt must be nearby, Columbus set sail and in fifteen days reached another island. He sent ashore a delegation headed by Luis de Torres, a Jew converted to Christianity who had knowledge of several languages. It was expected that Torres would be able to converse at the court of any ruler. Also in the group was Rodrigo de Jeres (heh-RAYS), who had once been sent to the court of an African ruler and presumably understood how to deal with an unfamiliar culture. Nothing the men found on the islands, however, persuaded them that they were in Asia.

The first Spanish settlement in America is started. Columbus's concern was increasing. For three months he traveled around the Caribbean Sea, sailing along the coasts of two other islands, Cuba and Hispaniola. On Christmas Eve the *Santa Maria* went aground off the northern coast of Hispaniola. As the ship began to break up in the pounding surf, the crew removed the supplies and salvaged the timber. Out of the wood the men constructed a few dwellings for themselves. Without planning to, they had established the first European settlement in the Americas since the days of the Viking explorers.

Columbus returns to Europe. When Columbus set sail again, it was to return to Spain as soon as possible with news of his "discovery." He had found, he was sure, a group of islands never before visited by Europeans, lying off the mainland of China. In

---

EYEWITNESS TO HISTORY

With Columbus in the Caribbean

In 1493, a Spanish physician named Chanca sailed with Columbus on his second voyage across the Atlantic. Chanca's narrative, in which he calls Columbus "the Admiral," is the only personal account of the voyage that has survived.

> About dawn on the first Sunday after All Saints Day, namely the third of November, a pilot on the flagship cried out, "I see the land." The joy of the crew was so great that it was wonderful to hear their cries and exclamations of pleasure. They had good reason to be delighted for we had been at sea since September 25, and I felt that everyone had seen enough of the water.
>
> On that morning we saw lying before us an island, and soon on the right another appeared. The first was high and mountainous, the other low and very thickly wooded. As soon as it became lighter, other islands began to appear on both sides, so that on that day, there were six islands to be seen lying in different directions, and most of them of considerable size.
>
> We directed our course towards the island which we had first seen, and, reaching the coast, we proceeded along in search of a port where we might anchor, but without finding one. When we found that there was no harbor, the Admiral decided that we should go to the other island. At length we found a good harbor where we saw both people and dwellings. There the Admiral, accompanied by a great number of men, landed with the royal banner in his hands and took formal possession on behalf of their Royal Majesties.

Christopher Columbus

> This island was filled with an astonishing thick growth of wood; the variety of unknown trees, some bearing fruit and some flowers, was surprising. The inhabitants fled at the sight of our men and the Admiral ordered soldiers to search the houses. Various household articles had been left behind, as were two large parrots, quite different from any we had seen before. They also found a great quantity of cotton prepared for spinning.
>
> After completing our exploration, we set sail for the island of Hispaniola, where a party of men from the first voyage had been left.

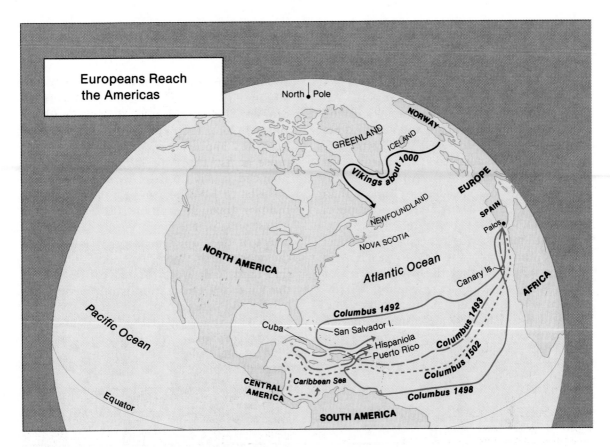

Europeans Reach
the Americas

North Pole

NORWAY
GREENLAND
ICELAND
Vikings about 1000
NEWFOUNDLAND
NOVA SCOTIA
EUROPE
SPAIN
Palos
NORTH AMERICA
Atlantic Ocean
Canary Is.
AFRICA
Columbus 1492
Cuba
San Salvador I.
Hispaniola
Puerto Rico
Columbus 1493
Pacific Ocean
Columbus 1502
CENTRAL
AMERICA
Caribbean Sea
Columbus 1498
Equator
SOUTH AMERICA

Christopher Columbus, believing that the world was much smaller than it really is, thought he could reach Asia by sailing west. Not only is the globe bigger than Columbus thought, but America lies west of Europe, blocking the way to Asia. What lands did Columbus reach on each of his voyages?

marked contrast to the outward journey, the trip home was full of terrible storms. At last, on March 15, 1493, the battered expedition arrived at Palos.

During the trip Columbus had written a report for Ferdinand and Isabella. It told of beautiful islands off the coast of Asia full of spices and, above all, gold. The inhabitants were friendly, Columbus added, eager to work, and ready to receive the Christian gospel. He was misleading his sovereigns just as he had misled his crew with the false journal. He had prevented his men from mutinying; now he had to persuade Ferdinand and Isabella to finance another voyage.

Columbus continues his search for Asia. In the years that followed, Columbus made three more trips across the Atlantic (map, above). On those voyages he explored Cuba,

Hispaniola, Puerto Rico, and Jamaica. He also sailed along the coasts of South America and Central America. Columbus continued to his dying day to insist that he had found Asia.

SECTION REVIEW

1. Vocabulary: *navigation*.
2. (a) Why were the Portuguese interested in explorations along Africa's coast? (b) Why did they seek a water route to India? (c) How successful were they?
3. (a) What Europeans sailed across the Atlantic around the year 1000? (b) What lands did they find? (c) What happened to the settlements they started?
4. (a) What led Columbus to believe that it was possible to reach Asia by sailing west? (b) What were the results of his exploration?

2 Europe's Knowledge of the World Increases

News of Columbus's voyages across the Atlantic fascinated the Portuguese, and the competition between Spain and Portugal became livelier. Within a few years after Columbus's first voyage, Da Gama had reached India (page 24). Another Portuguese expedition, headed by an Italian navigator named Amerigo Vespucci (veh-SPYOO-chih), set out in 1499 to explore the South American coast. Vespucci believed that the only way to reach Asia was by sailing around the southern tip of South America. Vespucci's exploits so impressed a leading German map maker that he decided to name the new lands *America* after the explorer. Other map makers followed his example, and America soon became an accepted name.

Spain and Portugal divide the world. In keeping with tradition, Spain and Portugal, as exploring countries, sought the Pope's approval for their claims to any land that might be "rescued" from non-Christian peoples. Spain, eager to exploit the products and people of the new territories across the Atlantic, applied for exclusive rights to those lands. The Pope, a Spaniard, was influenced in his decision by Ferdinand and Isabella. In 1493 he drew a north-south line running through a point 100 leagues (300 miles) west of the Cape Verde Islands. The effect of the Pope's decision was to divide the world into two halves. All non-Christian lands that were located to the east of this Line of Demarcation would henceforth belong to Portugal. All non-Christian lands located to the west of the line would now belong to Spain.

Portugal raised objections to this arrangement made by the Spanish Pope, and

Baptista Agnese, a Venetian map maker, included Magellan's voyage on this 1540 map. What does the map tell you about Agnese's knowledge of the Americas?

the Hohokam people disappeared, probably merging with other groups who lived in the same region.

The Anasazi, who lived in the area where Arizona, Utah, Colorado, and New Mexico now join, were once a wandering people dependent on the hunting of animals and the gathering of food. They raised their crops on flat-topped hills called **mesas.** Below the mesas the Anasazi built pit houses, so called because the floors of the houses were a few feet below ground level. In about the year 750, the Anasazi left their pit houses and began to live in dwellings — actually rectangular rooms with flat roofs — built very close together and then one on top of the other. The Spanish later gave this kind of house the name *pueblo,* their word for "village."

For hundreds of years the Anasazi people thrived. Then, a long dry period began in 1276 and lasted till the end of the century. By then the surviving Anasazi had migrated to other regions. Their descendants,

the Pueblo Indians, remained in the area, however, becoming one of the largest Indian groups by the time of the Europeans' arrival.

The Indians are divided into many culture areas. By 1492 Indians were living throughout the Americas. It is useful to think of the Native Americans as living in *culture areas* where, despite significant variations among the different tribes, ways of living were generally similar.

Plains. The Indians of the Plains culture area depended on the buffalo for practically all their needs. They ate buffalo meat, used buffalo hides for clothing and shelter, and turned buffalo horns into weapons and tools. Because the buffalo was indispensable, the tribes, including the Sioux, Pawnee, and Comanche, sent out hunting parties in summer to pursue and slay the huge beasts. In those months the Indians lived in tepees, which they could move as required. For most of the year,

Mandan, Indians of the Plains culture area, lived in villages like this one on the [Miss]ouri. Here, Mandan women bring firewood across the river.

in 1494 a new arrangement was worked out (map, page 32). This time the line was moved 370 leagues (1,110 miles) to the west of the Cape Verde Islands. Thus, when a Portuguese expedition commanded by Pedro Cabral (kuh-BRAHL) reached the coast of Brazil in 1500, Portugal claimed the land because it fell east of the revised Line of Demarcation.

Magellan continues the search for a westward route to Asia. European explorers continued to look for a way to reach Asia by sailing west. One explorer who carried on the search was Ferdinand Magellan. Magellan had been reared in the Portuguese court and had served in Portuguese India and Morocco. He fell into disfavor, however, after accusations that he had mishandled royal property. When the king of Portugal rejected his proposal to reach Asia by sailing west, Magellan went to Spain where he received support for his plan.

Magellan hoped to find a water passage through South America that would make possible a direct route from Spain to the East Indies. With five well-worn vessels and a crew made up mainly of prisoners released for the journey, Magellan set out from Spain in September, 1519. Without major incident the expedition reached the coast of Brazil and turned south, looking for the strait that would lead through the continent. They found no such entranceway. As winter set in, Magellan and his crew pitched camp in a region afterward called Patagonia.

In that bleak setting, fear mounted, as the crew began to believe they would never see home again. Some of the men plotted a mutiny which Magellan quashed by killing two of the ringleaders.

Magellan finds a passage around South America. Magellan had by now lost two ships — one that was wrecked and another that deserted and went back to Spain. Nevertheless, he pressed on, despite the pleas of many of his men to return home. Near the tip of the South American continent, Magellan found the strait that today bears his name (map, page 32). With marvelous skill he led his expedition through the stormy

320-mile passageway. Then he came into a sea which he named the *Pacific* (meaning "peaceful"), because its calmness contrasted with the turbulence of the Atlantic.

From this point on, however, the journey across the Pacific Ocean proved to be a nightmare. For more than two months the expedition sighted no land. The drinking water spoiled and the food ran out. The survivors ate rats and even leather from the ships' riggings.

On March 16, 1521, the expedition reached the Philippines. Magellan knew that the East Indies lay only a few hundred miles to the south, but he did not live to complete his voyage. He lost his life in fighting that broke out between his men and the people of the islands.

Magellan's voyage proves the earth is round. The expedition pushed on without Magellan, and one vessel, commanded by Juan Sebastián del Cano (CAH-noh), completed the journey, limping back to Spain in September, 1522. On the way, the ship had picked up a cargo of cloves, the sale of which paid for the cost of the expedition. The voyage of Magellan and his crew, however, had had more than commercial importance. It had showed, for one thing, that Asia was much farther west of Europe than previously supposed. In addition, it had established by actual testing that the earth was round. Magellan, in brief, had completed the connection between the achievements of Columbus and those of Da Gama.

The English also search for a route to Asia. The passage from Europe to Asia that Magellan had found was too long and dangerous for merchant vessels to follow. Ambitious explorers, therefore, began searching for a short cut through the American land mass.

In about 1495, an Italian mariner named Giovanni Caboto traveled to England from Spain, where he had heard about Columbus's journeys and discoveries. This man, known to the English as John Cabot, convinced Henry VII and English merchants that he could reach Asia by heading in a more northwesterly direction than Columbus had taken.

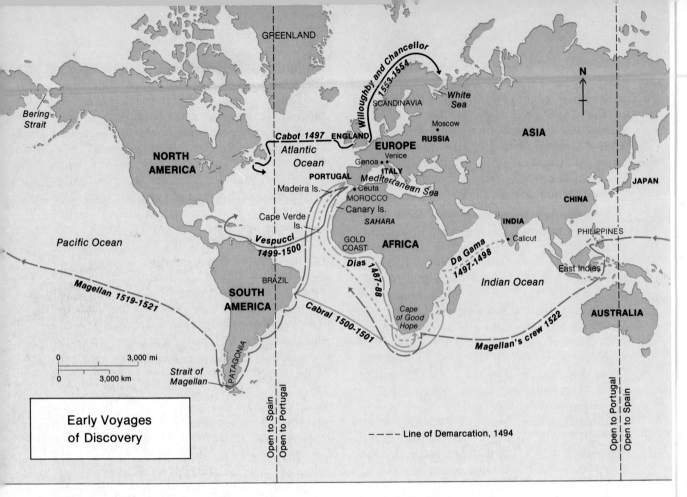

Early Voyages of Discovery

The Line of Demarcation enabled Spain to claim most of the Western Hemisphere.

In May, 1497, in a small ship called the *Matthew*, Cabot sailed west. On this expedition he may have landed at Newfoundland, for on his return to England his crew told of finding a spectacular abundance of fish. Cabot reported to his English backers that he had reached the outskirts of China! They were sufficiently convinced by his tale to send him out again, this time accompanied by his young son, Sebastian. Little is known about Cabot's second voyage, though he may have sailed as far south as the coast of what is now the United States. At any rate, his voyages — considered failures at the time for not having tapped Asia's wealth — established a basis for England's later claims in North America.

The English eagerness to find a northwest passage to Asia was for a time matched by their zeal to find a north*east* passage. In 1553 Sir Hugh Willoughby and Richard Chancellor journeyed north of Scandinavia in such a search. Chancellor had been inspired by Sebastian Cabot, who had himself become a noted explorer. Willoughby died en route. Chancellor managed to reach the White Sea after passing through treacherous Arctic waters. He then traveled south across Russia to Moscow, where he met with the Russian czar (known in history as Ivan the Terrible). His meetings with that ruler opened the way for the establishment of trade relations between England and Russia.

SECTION REVIEW

1. How did the Pope settle the rival land claims of Spain and Portugal?
2. (a) What was Magellan's purpose in sailing west? (b) What was the significance of the voyage completed by Magellan's crew?
3. (a) What routes to Asia did explorers sent out by England search for? (b) What success did they have?

3 Europeans Find a Variety of Peoples in the Americas

Columbus had been so certain his voyages had taken him to the East Indies that he called the people he encountered *Indians.* (We still use that term today or, sometimes, the term *Native Americans.*) Actually, most historians believe that the first inhabitants of America had come from Asia thousands of years before the arrival of the first Europeans. The basis for this belief is the theory that a broad area of land once connected Asia and the Americas and that people made their way across it as they hunted animals. According to this theory, the "land bridge" between the two continents was created by huge glaciers which tied up so much water that the sea level was more than 300 feet lower than it is today. When the glaciers began to melt, the seas rose once again and the land bridge disappeared beneath the waters of the Bering Strait.

The first inhabitants of North America are hunters. The people who crossed the land bridge probably formed themselves into small bands, surviving by hunting for their food and using animal hides for shelter and clothing. Their tools were crude at first, consisting of flat stones for cutting, scraping, and pounding. Then, these early Americans learned to chip stones to produce sharp points. The stone points could be bound with leather strips to the ends of wooden spears, which were used to hunt big game. (One kind of point is called the Clovis point after the name of the New Mexico town near which many were unearthed.) The knowledge of how to make and use these sharp points spread rapidly through the Americas. The Clovis point, for example, has been found from the plains of North America to the tip of South America.

Agriculture is developed. As the Native Americans confronted different environments — ranging from freezing cold in the north to tropical heat at the equator — they learned how to adapt their surroundings to meet their needs. It was the Indians of central Mexico who were the first people in the

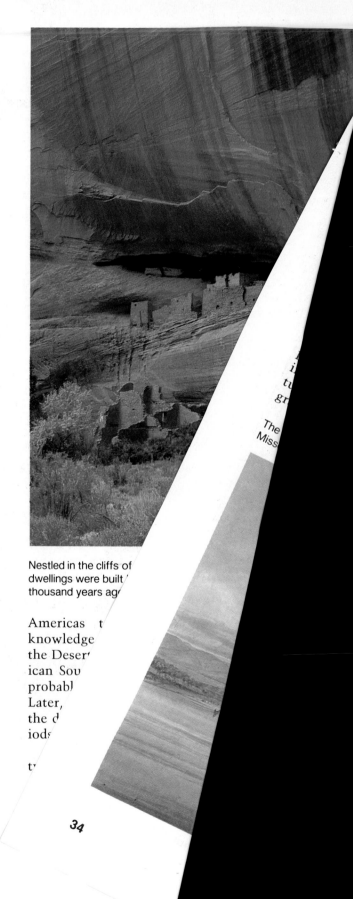

Nestled in the cliffs of
dwellings were built
thousand years ag

Americas
knowledge
the Deser
ican Sou
probabl
Later,
the d
iods

t

34

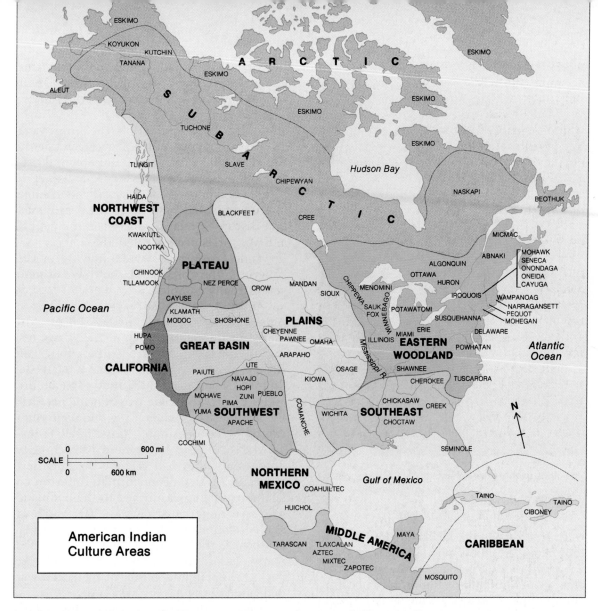

At the time of the arrival of the first Europeans, there were hundreds of Indian tribes in North America. The most important tribes are shown on the map above.

though, the Plains Indians lived in villages near rivers and streams where they cultivated corn and other crops.

Eastern Woodland. In the Eastern Woodland culture area lived such tribes as the Chippewa and Menomini of Minnesota and Wisconsin and the Algonquin and Huron, who made their homes north of the Great Lakes. The tribespeople lived in villages surrounded by fields in which they raised corn, squashes, beans, and pumpkins. In addition to farming, these Indians hunted and fished extensively.

South of the Great Lakes and extending to the east were the Iroquois, the best known of the Eastern Woodland tribes. The Iroquois were, in fact, a confederation of tribes: the Mohawk, Seneca, Onondaga, Oneida, and Cayuga. By joining together, these tribes could exercise considerable military power since most other tribes preferred to stand alone.

The Iroquois developed an advanced form of government, including a council made up of representatives of the tribes. Women had considerable authority. They

One of the mighty achievements of Maya culture was the construction of high stone pyramids like this one at Tikal, in what is now Guatemala.

siderable skill in astronomy and mathematics and excelled in architecture. Their weaving and jewelry were superior in design and quality.

In the 700's and 800's the impressive centers of Maya culture were suddenly abandoned for reasons still unknown. Possible explanations for this odd development include a sudden epidemic, a severe change in climate, some kind of political upheaval that disrupted relations between the people and the priests who ruled the society. By the time Europeans started arriving in the Americas, the collapse of the Maya empire was virtually complete.

Aztecs. North of the Mayas the Aztecs came to power in the 1200's. Formerly an impoverished nomadic group living in northern Mexico, the Aztecs had slowly migrated south. Through effective diplomacy and much luck they gained allies and began to dominate neighboring peoples. By about 1325, when they founded their capital, Tenochtitlán (tay-NOHCH-tee-TLAHN), on the site where Mexico City now stands, they had become the mightiest power in Mexico. Tenochtitlán, built on an island in a lake, was linked to the mainland by three huge causeways — the work of skilled engineers. One of the largest urban centers in the world at that time, it had many shops and markets and handsome parks. The religious center of the island was dedicated to the Aztecs' war god.

Incas. In what is today the South American country of Peru, a third vigorous Indian empire emerged — that of the Incas. Like the Aztecs, the Incas were poor people who had slowly come to establish control over neighboring societies.

The Incas' strongest weapon was their genius for organization and engineering. Their emperor was head of a tightly run government that required instant obedience from all people. All property belonged to the state. The only beast of burden they had was the llama. Still, the Incas constructed massive public buildings without any of the equipment — including wheeled vehicles — that present-day engineers would regard as indispensable. Their extensive highway

were regarded as the heads of families, and they chose the chiefs who led the tribes.

Southeast. In the Southeast culture area were a number of important tribes, including the Choctaw, Chickasaw, Creek, Seminole, and Cherokee. These Indians lived in towns surrounded by stockades constructed of tree trunks. An agricultural people, they raised vegetables and also cotton for making cloth.

Empires are formed in Mexico and South America. Far to the south, still other Indian societies arose. Some of them were more complex than many of those we have been describing.

Mayas. One of the first Indian empires was created by the Mayas of Yucatán and Central America. The Mayas had established a well-structured government and society based on a religion distinguished by elaborate ritual. They had developed con-

system was another engineering marvel, as were their terraced fields, ingeniously linked together at many levels high in the mountains.

Indians and Europeans come into contact. When the first Europeans arrived in America, they knew nothing about Indian life. They soon learned, however, about the Indians' deep respect for the natural environment. The settlers also discovered that the Indians had developed a remarkable group of agricultural products completely unknown to Europeans. By crossbreeding and cultivation of wild plants, the Indians had produced corn or "maize," white and sweet potatoes, peanuts, pumpkins, squash, tomatoes, a variety of beans and berries, and cacao. These agricultural products account for more than half the edible crops grown in the world today.

Europeans who came to America in the 1500's and 1600's often owed their very survival to the Indians. From the Indians, the newcomers learned how to cultivate American crops. The Indians showed the settlers efficient methods of hunting and fishing and instructed them in the crafting of canoes, snowshoes, moccasins, hammocks, and other useful items. Indians were also able to pass on their valuable knowledge of the medicinal uses of many plants.

A lively trade developed between Indians and the Europeans who came to America. In exchange for food, seeds, and furs, the newcomers provided weapons and tools made from iron. In heavy demand were European cooking utensils, fishhooks, traps, needles, knives, and guns. Grain crops from Europe (wheat, barley, rye, and oats) and livestock (pigs, cattle, chickens, goats, and sheep) were also introduced into the Americas. So, too, was the horse, which altered the Plains Indians' way of life. After the Spanish brought horses to the American continent, the Plains Indians developed new ways of hunting buffalo.[1]

---

[1] The horse had once existed in America but had become extinct many years earlier — along with the mammoth, mastodon, camel, and other animals.

Conflicts develop. The exchange of goods and ideas between the Europeans and Indians did not, however, remain harmonious. Conflicts arose, often brought about by differing views about the ownership of land. The Indians believed that land could not be bought and sold by individuals but rather was the common property of an entire tribe, to be held as such forever. When Europeans took possession of land and claimed it as their own, the Indians were deeply angered. As settlers occupied more and more territory, fierce struggles between Indians and Europeans broke out.

A further consequence of the coming of Europeans was that Indian tribes were gradually forced out of their traditional lands and pushed westward. Eastern Indians who moved west entered the domains of other tribal groups. These intrusions, upsetting well-established divisions of territory, led to a number of wars among Indian tribes.

The arrival of Europeans also had an impact on the Indians' motives for hunting. An enormous demand for furs in Europe encouraged the Indians to seek skins and pelts for sale abroad. Animals that once had been plentiful began to disappear, stepping up the competition and strife among Indian tribes.

As time went on, the Indians became increasingly concerned about the presence in America of all Europeans. Seeing the Spanish arrive, then the French, and then the English, most Indians realized that a profound change was afoot, one that they would be unable to reverse.

SECTION REVIEW

1. Vocabulary: *irrigation, mesa, culture area.*
2. How did Indian tribes in each of the following culture areas get their food? (a) Plains (b) Eastern Woodland (c) Southeast
3. (a) In what areas did the Maya, Aztec, and Inca empires arise? (b) What were the major characteristics of each?
4. (a) What did Europeans who came to America learn from the Indians? (b) What did the Indians acquire from the Europeans? (c) How did differing views lead to conflict between Indians and Europeans?

Chapter 1 Review

Summary

By the 1400's changes in Europe had led to a search for new sources of trade. European seafarers came to believe that regions of Africa and Asia possessing gold and spices could be reached by sea. Prince Henry of Portugal was eager for his country to capture control of the African gold trade and also to spread Christianity to distant regions. With these purposes in mind, he started a school for the study of geography and navigation. Portuguese navigators soon began exploring the African coast, and in 1487 Bartholomeu Dias sailed around the southern tip of Africa. Eleven years later Vasco da Gama succeeded in reaching India by sea, thus opening the spice trade for Portugal.

Few Europeans knew that nearly 500 years earlier, other mariners had sailed westward across the Atlantic. Vikings from northern Europe sailed first to Iceland and then to Greenland and Newfoundland, and eventually to the northern coast of North America. These voyages, however, led to no permanent settlements.

Inspired by Marco Polo's tales about the riches of Asia, and convinced he could reach them by sailing west, an Italian seafarer named Christopher Columbus set forth in 1492 under the flag of Spain to search for a water route to China and Japan. After a long and suspenseful voyage, Columbus reached what he thought were islands off the coast of China. In reality what Columbus had found were the islands of the Caribbean Sea. With this discovery he opened the door on a whole new area for European exploration and expansion.

Columbus's account of what he had found startled Europe and encouraged other expeditions to cross the Atlantic. A keen rivalry developed between Spain and Portugal, as the two European powers both rushed to claim territory in the Western Hemisphere. Finally, a Line of Demarcation was proclaimed by the Pope to divide the world between Spain and Portugal.

In due course, Europeans came to realize that the lands across the Atlantic were not Asia. They were, in fact, the American continents and inhabited by peoples who had been unknown to Europe. Called Indians by Columbus at the time of his arrival in 1492, the Native Americans had formed a variety of culture areas throughout the Americas. In Mexico and South America, mighty Indian empires — those of the Mayas, Aztecs, and Incas — had also come into being.

Vocabulary and Important Terms

1. navigation
2. Vinland
3. San Salvador
4. Line of Demarcation
5. land bridge
6. Clovis point
7. irrigation
8. mesa
9. pit house
10. pueblo
11. culture area
12. Tenochtitlán

Discussion Questions

1. (a) Why were spices important to Europeans? (b) Before the Portuguese established a water route to India, how were spices brought to Europe, and who profited from the spice trade? (c) As they became involved in the spice trade, what did Portuguese sailors contribute to geographic knowledge?
2. (a) What places in North America might the Vikings have reached? (b) What might have been the reasons for the dying out of the Viking settlements in North America?
3. Why was Marco Polo's account of his travels in Asia so important?
4. (a) What important facts were known to European geographers at the beginning of the fifteenth century? (b) What mistaken belief did most geographers hold regarding the distance between Europe and Asia? (c) What effect did that belief have on Christopher Columbus and his voyages?
5. (a) Why did King Ferdinand and Queen Isabella decide to finance Columbus's expedition? (b) For what reason did Columbus keep two records during his first voyage westward? (c) What lands in the Americas did Columbus explore?
6. (a) What passage from Europe to Asia did Magellan find? (b) Where did other explorers then begin to search for passages through the American land mass?
7. (a) Compare the attitudes of Europeans and Indians regarding land. (b) What were the consequences of European settlement upon Indian ways of living?

Relating Past to Present

1. European sailors in the 1500's challenged legends and mysteries by sailing into unknown waters along the coast of Africa and, later, by sailing to the west. What unknown areas remain to be challenged in today's world? Explain your answer.
2. The desire to participate in the spice trade encouraged European explorers to brave the unknown.

Spices are still in demand today, but the reasons for their use have changed since the 1400's. From what countries do Europe and the United States now import spices?

Studying Local History

What Indians lived in your region at the time of the Europeans' arrival in the Americas? What ways of living did they follow, and what special customs or ceremonies were important to their culture? Under what circumstances did they first come into contact with European settlers? How did the ways in which the Indians lived change as a result of that contact?

Using History Skills

1. *Reading maps.* Study the maps showing the voyages of Christopher Columbus and Ferdinand Magellan on pages 29 and 32. (a) How many voyages did Columbus make to the Americas? (b) What was Columbus's original goal, and why did he never fulfill that goal? (c) Why were Columbus's voyages important? (d) Use the map to describe the route Magellan and his crew followed. (e) What did Magellan's voyage show about the distance between Europe and Asia? (f) What other fact about the world did Magellan's voyage establish?

2. *Comparing.* What personal characteristics and accomplishments made each of the following an important explorer? (a) Vasco da Gama (b) Leif Ericsson (c) Christopher Columbus (d) Ferdinand Magellan (e) John Cabot

3. *Writing a report.* Indian cultures had an impact on European settlers and on the ways in which the newcomers lived. Use an encyclopedia or general accounts of Indian cultures to find out more about that impact. Write a report based on this information.

4. *Making connections.* On page 31 you read that Magellan "completed the connection between the achievements of Columbus and those of Da Gama." What was that connection? Explain the relationship among these three great expeditions.

WORLD SCENE

Travelers Before Columbus

The voyages of Columbus and Magellan were considered by Europeans to be extraordinary. Unknown to them, however, other travelers elsewhere in the world were also reaching distant places.

A journey to Arabia. In 1307 a young man named Mansa Musa (MAN-suh MOO-sah) became emperor of the great empire of Mali in West Africa. Under his rule, Mali reached even grander heights. In order to promote Mali's reputation and enhance his own fame, Mansa Musa planned a pilgrimage to the Islamic holy city of Mecca in Arabia.

In 1324 he set out on the journey that would take him nearly 4,000 miles across Africa to his destination. His caravan made an unforgettable impression. It consisted of thousands of attendants clothed in silks and brocades. A hundred camels, each burdened with bags of gold dust, trudged in the procession. Mansa Musa himself sat astride a magnificent charger, preceded by 500 slaves armed with staffs of gold. The lavish gifts Mansa Musa left along the route made him and his people a legend long before he arrived at last at the object of his striving.

Cheng Ho's expedition. In 1405 the emperor of China appointed a warrior named Cheng Ho to command a series of naval expeditions designed to develop trade and extend the country's influence. These expeditions were more elaborate than any that a country of Europe could have launched. The first of them consisted of 62 large ships, 255 smaller ones, and almost 28,000 merchants, clerks, soldiers, and sailors. When this fleet sailed into a port, people believed it to be an invasion force!

The various voyages that Cheng Ho commanded carried China's banner through the South China Sea to the Indian Ocean, and from there into the Arabian Sea and down the coast of East Africa. Expeditions visited Java, Sumatra, Ceylon, India, Arabia, and various Muslim ports in East Africa. The ships took back to China valuable products as well as tribute — "gifts" of respect.

The expense of the fleets, and the need to deal with troubles along China's western and northern borders, led to the end of overseas expeditions in 1431. The emperor forbade Chinese ships to leave coastal waters, and China became increasingly isolated.

Explorers and New Settlers

1500 – 1685

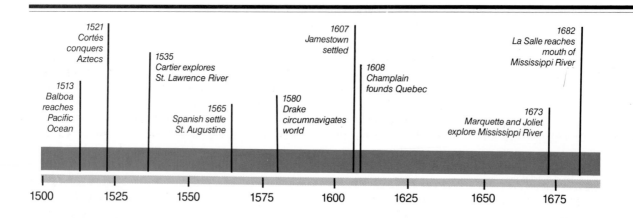

1513
Balboa reaches Pacific Ocean

1521
Cortés conquers Aztecs

1535
Cartier explores St. Lawrence River

1565
Spanish settle St. Augustine

1580
Drake circumnavigates world

1607
Jamestown settled

1608
Champlain founds Quebec

1673
Marquette and Joliet explore Mississippi River

1682
La Salle reaches mouth of Mississippi River

1500 1525 1550 1575 1600 1625 1650 1675

CHAPTER OUTLINE

1. Spain builds a great empire.

2. Spanish civilization takes hold.

3. France takes an interest in starting American colonies.

4. England starts colonies in North America.

The European discoveries of the American continents brought about a new understanding of the size of the world. This accomplishment was made possible by the enormous energy and ambition of western European nations — and the superiority of their technology, which included new weapons that no other peoples of the world could match at that time.

Spain and Portugal, the first European nations on the scene, boldly assumed they could divide the world between them. They did not, however, have the field alone for long. France also sought gold and then a foothold in North America. Few in number, the French attached themselves to the Indians and turned the Indians' skill as hunters and trappers into a new industry based on furs and skins.

To the early explorers America had been a frustrating obstacle on the road to Asia. Then it became a remarkable source of treasure, especially for Spain. No one had yet considered that America could be a brilliant setting in which humanity would have a "second chance," an opportunity to start over by avoiding the mistakes of Europe. Unwittingly the English undertook this greatest of challenges. They did it by starting colonies made up of English families who slowly adapted their ways to the American environment and went on to create a land of freedom and opportunity like none other in the world.

1 Spain Builds a Great Empire

The immense land masses as well as the tiny islands that the Spanish explorers had found were like gift boxes still unwrapped. What lay inside them? What surprising scenes would excite the imagination or depress the spirit? The answers came only gradually.

Spanish explorers search for "glory, God, and gold." In the years just after Columbus's death in 1506, Spain established the pattern of its activities in the Americas. The Spanish invaders called themselves *conquistadors*, or conquerors. The leaders of the various expeditions acted like kings in miniature. They had absolute power over the men they commanded and over the people they conquered. The conquistadors, however, served under the Crown of Spain. The Spanish monarch licensed them to enlist recruits and purchase the equipment they required. The conquests were accomplished at practically no cost to the monarch — even though the monarch received one fifth of all the gold that was discovered.

The conquistadors were sworn to bring the Christian gospel as well as the king's law to the conquered land, and missionaries were part of every expedition. The purposes of the conquistadors, therefore, were sometimes summed up as "glory, God, and gold."

Balboa journeys to the Pacific. After the first excitement of hunting for gold on Hispaniola was over, many Spaniards turned to other enterprises. Ambitious, grasping men, they began to take Indians as slaves in raids on the Bahamas, seek treasure on other islands, and explore coastlines not yet visited by Europeans. The West Indies became the base from which most of the expeditions were launched.

It was on one such expedition from Hispaniola that a debt-ridden planter named Vasco Nuñez de Balboa (bal-BOH-uh) fled to the Isthmus of Panama (then called the Isthmus of Darien). He had himself nailed into a barrel and stowed with the ship's provisions in order to escape his creditors. Upon his arrival in Panama, Balboa heard from an Indian chief that beyond the mountains lay an immense ocean washing a

Within fifty years of Hernando Cortés's arrival in Mexico, Spain ruled an immense empire and had become Europe's richest and most powerful nation.

VERACRVZ. N 2

41

region "flowing with gold where you may satisfy your great greed for it."

Balboa set out to find the ocean and the gold. On September 25, 1513, after crossing the Isthmus of Panama, he approached the crest of a mountain ridge with his party, which included 190 Spaniards, several hundred Indians, and 50 Africans. While his followers waited below, he went alone to the summit and from there he beheld "the great South Sea," as he named it. He fell to his knees, thanking God and claiming the vast body of water and the shores it washed in the name of the king of Spain. (The name did not stick. Map makers preferred "Pacific," which is what Magellan called it.)

Spain claims Florida. The same year that Balboa reached the Pacific, Juan Ponce de León (POHN-say day lay-OHN) became the first Spaniard to set foot on what is now United States soil. A former governor of Puerto Rico, he was granted permission to sail northward and colonize a place called Bimini. An incidental purpose was to find a spring or river said to flow in Bimini, the waters of which could restore youth to the aged. Landing in the Easter season, he named the new land Florida (from the Spanish *Pascua florida*, meaning "Easter").

Ponce de León did not find the magic water he had been looking for. Nevertheless, he returned in 1521 to start a settlement and to find out if Florida was an island. He appears to have tried to start a colony near what is now called Tampa Bay, but he could not deal successfully with the Indians in the region. In a fierce battle, he lost many men and was himself mortally wounded.

The Spanish never really colonized Florida, owing to Indian resistance as well as to the absence of gold and silver there. In 1565, however, they founded St. Augustine in order to protect Spain's claim in Florida. The oldest city in the United States, St. Augustine was started more than forty years before the first English settlers came to Jamestown. Spain's chief interest in building St. Augustine was to control the Straits of Florida, through which Spanish vessels sailed from Mexico to Europe.

Cortés invades the mainland. Six years after Ponce de León's journey to Florida, and in the very year Magellan began his epic voyage around the world (page 31), Hernando Cortés set forth on history's greatest march of conquest. Ever since the Spanish arrived in the Caribbean area, they had heard rumors about a powerful Indian empire located inland. In truth, this country, the land of the Aztecs (page 36), was in Mexico, only a few hundred miles from Cuba.

In 1519 the Aztec emperor's hold on his people seemed to be slipping. The empire was filled with the news that a white god named Quetzalcoatl (kayt-sahl-KOHT-al), who had gone into exile five hundred years earlier, was about to fulfill his promise and return from the east. Reports were circulating in Mexico that he and his followers had been sighted.

Still, no legend or rumor had prepared the Aztecs for what they soon were called upon to face: powerful armed men led by Hernando Cortés. Cortés, now 34 years old, had spent the previous fifteen years in America. He had participated in the conquest of Cuba and, like other Spaniards, was deeply disappointed not to have found gold there. When he was appointed to open trade with the Aztecs, gold-hungry adventurers rushed to join his expedition.

Cortés conquers the Aztecs. With a band of 600 soldiers Cortés left Cuba. After landing in Yucatán (a peninsula of eastern Mexico), Cortés had the luck to rescue a Spaniard who had been captured by the Mayas and had learned their language. Cortés also acquired a female slave — soon baptized Marina — who spoke both Maya and Aztec. Through the rescued man and Marina, Cortés was able to communicate with the people of Mexico.

The Aztecs, hearing of Cortés's approach, became convinced the conquistador was indeed Quetzalcoatl. Cortés, a magnetic and imaginative leader, encouraged this misconception. The Spaniards rewarded the

Aztec emperor for welcoming them as descendants of Quetzalcoatl by putting him in prison. Cortés then engaged the Aztec warriors in battle.

Cortés's boldness led to the quick defeat of the Aztecs. The Aztecs were brave fighters and excellent archers, but their weapons were no match for the steel swords and artillery of the invaders. Moreover, being mounted, the Spanish seemed invincible. The Aztecs, who had never before seen horses, thought that each rider and his horse were one terrifying creature.

With the help of Indian enemies of the Aztecs, Cortés and his tiny band had conquered the mighty empire by 1521. The gold and silver that Cortés soon was sending across the Atlantic made Spanish officials begin to think for the first time that colonies in the Americas could be of value.

Indians resist the Spanish invaders. Not all the Indian peoples succumbed as readily to the invading Spaniards as the Aztecs did. In Yucatán and nearby Guatemala small groups of Mayas resisted the conquistadors in fierce and costly warfare that lasted for many years. The people of those regions were not finally subdued and brought under control until the 1530's. Some Maya Indians resisted the Spanish invaders for almost a hundred years.

Pizarro conquers Peru. Only one other conquistador rivaled Cortés in finding large quantities of precious metals. He was Francisco Pizarro (pih-ZAHR-oh), who conquered the great Inca empire, in what is now Peru, between 1532 and 1536. Pizarro, following Cortés's method, captured the Inca emperor, Atahualpa (ah-tah-WAHL-pah), after deceiving him with friendly words. Atahualpa was promised his release upon payment of a huge ransom — a room filled with gold. His people did not understand the demand because they did not use money. They employed gold only for decorative purposes. Although the treasure was collected, Atahualpa was not set free. Instead the Spanish soldiers placed him on trial, charged him with crimes, and executed him.

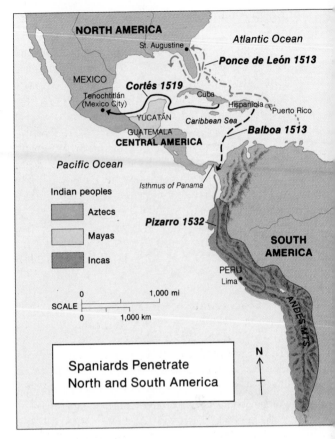

In their search for "glory, God, and gold," the Spanish conquistadors found three highly developed Indian societies in the Americas. Use the key to locate the areas of those societies on the map.

The precious metal was distributed among Pizarro's followers after one fifth had been set aside for the Spanish king. In dividing the spoils, the greedy Pizarro — greedy even by the standards of the conquistadors — quarreled with his associates. They assassinated him.

The Indians fall victim to European diseases. The impact of Spanish military force on Indian cultures in the Americas, as we have seen, was overwhelming. No less devastating, however, were the fatal epidemics produced by diseases the European conquerors brought to America. These epidemics of measles, influenza, and smallpox exacted a terrible toll, since the Indians had no natural immunity to them. The Indian population on the Gulf and Pacific coasts of

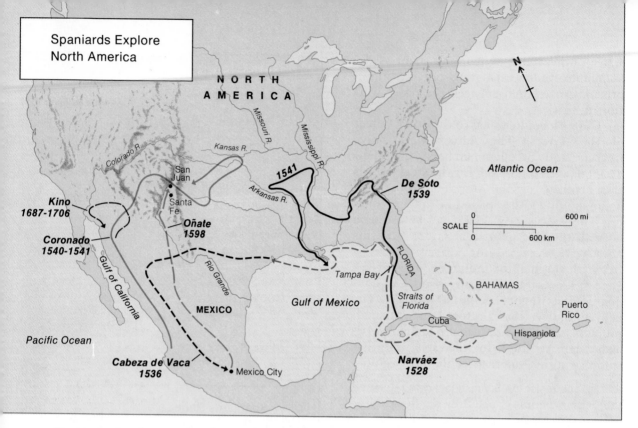

NORTH
AMERICA

Atlantic Ocean

Missouri R.

Mississippi R.

Kansas R.

Colorado R.

San
Juan

Santa
Fe

1541

Arkansas R.

De Soto
1539

**Kino
1687-1706**

**Oñate
1598**

**Coronado
1540-1541**

Gulf of California

Rio Grande

MEXICO

Tampa Bay

FLORIDA

BAHAMAS

Straits of
Florida

Puerto
Rico

SCALE

0   600 mi

0   600 km

Cuba

Hispaniola

Gulf of Mexico

Pacific Ocean

**Cabeza de Vaca
1536**

Mexico City

**Narváez
1528**

The travels of explorers such as Coronado and De Soto gave the Spanish knowledge
of the geography of a large part of North America.

Mexico was all but wiped out. Some areas in the Mexican interior were said to have lost up to 80 percent of their people. In the area of present-day Lima, Peru, people died so quickly that, it is estimated, in a relatively few years only 20,000 Indians out of about two million were left.

The Spanish expand into the borderlands. Far north of Mexico City the Spanish *borderlands* also drew the attention of would-be conquistadors. In those days the borderlands region spread across northern Mexico into what are now the states of Texas, New Mexico, Arizona, and California. Florida was also part of the borderlands.

After Ponce de León's visit to Florida, several Spanish sea captains explored the Florida coastline. One of them, Pánfilo de Narváez (nar-VAH-ayss) landed on the Gulf coast near present-day Tampa Bay with 6 ships and 400 people. One mishap after another befell the group. Hearing of a rich land farther west, Narvaez sent his vessels

ahead to await him. They never met. Narváez and his dwindling band followed the coastline on foot, suffering terribly in the swamps and forests and then in the frost of winter. Finally, like wandering skeletons they continued their cruel journey in leaky rafts they built themselves. Off the coast of Texas, treacherous currents swamped four of the boats and Narváez drowned. The survivors reached the mainland, where they were captured by Indians and held as slaves for five years. In 1534 a Spaniard named Cabeza de Vaca (kah-BAY-sah day VAH-kah) and three others, including an African named Estevanico (ays-tay-VAH-nee-koh), managed to escape. They traveled westward to the Gulf of California and from there made their way to Mexico City in 1536.

De Soto searches for the "seven cities." Once in Mexico City, Cabeza de Vaca proceeded to tell stories he had heard about the incredibly rich "seven cities of Cibola," said to be built of solid silver and lying far to the north of Mexico. One of those fired with ambition by Cabeza de Vaca's reports was Hernando de Soto. De Soto had been with Pizarro in Peru and became governor of Cuba in 1539. He obtained the king's permission to explore what is now the southeastern part of the United States. It was De Soto's hope not only to find a wealthy Indian empire but also to locate an all-water route linking the Atlantic and Pacific oceans. Geographers were so sure such a waterway existed that they had a name waiting to affix to it: the Strait of Anian.

De Soto's expedition landed at Tampa Bay in 1539 and advanced into the interior. De Soto treated the Indians he met with great cruelty. He made a practice of capturing a local chief and holding him hostage in order to obtain the services of the tribe. Those Indians he forced to travel with him were chained together with iron collars. Wandering from village to village, De Soto heard of an Indian empire governed by a woman. In 1540 he found the woman who, it turned out, did not rule an empire but a tiny settlement. Frustrated over his failure to discover Indian riches, he took her captive.

De Soto and his men continued to march westward, on and on. He seemed unimpressed by the fact that his journey had brought him to the Mississippi River and that he was the first European to see and cross the Father of Waters. He pressed on, going as far as present-day Oklahoma. He returned to the Mississippi, crestfallen that he had not found what he sought and, stricken by fever, died soon afterwards. His men secretly dropped his body into the mighty river he had found, lest the Indians he had abused learn of his death and rejoice.

Coronado learns more about North America. Cabeza de Vaca's account of the "seven cities" had also excited Antonio de Mendoza, the Spanish governor at Mexico City. To find out more about the rich cities, Mendoza organized an expedition under the command of Francisco de Coronado. The guide with the advance party was Estevanico, Cabeza de Vaca's old companion. Unfortunately, Estevanico was slain by Indians just as he neared what he believed to be the fabled empire. What he was approaching, it turned out, were the pueblos of the Zuni Indians in what is now New Mexico.

Later, while the Coronado party wandered along the banks of the Rio Grande, they heard stories of a place called Quivira, where everyone was said to eat out of golden bowls and drink from golden jugs. Coronado and his men headed north to find Quivira. On the way they came upon huge herds of buffalo. For as far as the eye could see, hundreds of thousands of animals filled the scene, "nothing but cows and sky," as one of the Spaniards later reported. When at last Coronado's party reached Quivira, they were dumbstruck by what they found. Quivira was merely a collection of grass huts on the banks of what is now called the Kansas River. The chief of the tribe was wearing a copper necklace; there was no gold at all.

Oñate leads an expedition north of the Rio Grande. In an effort to strengthen Spain's claims to the territory north of the Rio Grande, Juan de Oñate (ohn-YAH-tay) in 1598 led an expedition of 83 wagons with over 700 men, women, and children and 7,000 head of cattle north from Mexico City. When the Spaniards reached the Rio Grande, they established a small settlement. The group then continued north and took possession of an Indian town, renaming it San Juan. Using this settlement as a base, Oñate and a band of soldiers spent three years exploring the territory to the east and west, all the time hoping to find gold and other treasure.

Santa Fe is settled. Oñate's interest in finding gold caused him to run through all his funds and brought him into disfavor. Oñate was recalled in 1607 and returned to Mexico in disgrace. Meanwhile, the scattered settlers from Oñate's expedition began moving to a site a short distance from San Juan, where they founded the town of Santa Fe in 1609.

For years Santa Fe remained an isolated outpost, primarily attracting Spanish missionaries intent on converting the Indians. In 1680 the Pueblo Indians rose up against the Spanish and killed 400 of them. Those who escaped fled south. The Spanish did

Exploring the Spanish Borderlands

In 1598, a wealthy mine owner named Juan de Oñate received a commission from the viceroy of New Spain to explore and colonize the land north of the Rio Grande. A year later, Oñate wrote to the viceroy, telling about the Indians he had encountered on his travels.

> Here and in the other provinces there must be, by conservative reckoning, sixty thousand Indians. Their towns are like ours with houses built around rectangular plazas.
> The dress of the Indians consists of cotton blankets, well decorated with white or black designs. It is very good clothing. Others dress in buffalo skins, of which there is a great abundance. These furs have a beautiful wool; I am sending you some samples of what the Indians make of it.
> This land is plentiful with the meat of the buffalo, sheep with huge antlers, and native turkeys. There are many wild animals and beasts, and the Indians tan and use their skins. The Indians' corn and vegetables, as well as their salt deposits, are the best to be found in the world. There is a great abundance and variety of ores which

A Spanish conquistador

> are very rich. There are fine grape vines, rivers, and forests with many oaks and some cork trees.
> The people are as a rule of good disposition, generally of the color of those of New Spain, and almost the same in custom, dress, grinding of meal, food, dance, songs, and in many other respects. This is not true of the languages, which here are numerous and different from those in Mexico.

not regain control of Santa Fe until a military force overcame Indian resistance in 1697.

Father Kino extends Spanish influence. While Santa Fe was under the control of the Indians, an Italian-born missionary named Father Eusébio Kino (KEE-noh) set out from Mexico for what is now Arizona with a group of missionaries and a herd of cattle and horses. Described by his fellow Spaniards as "merciful to others but cruel to himself," the energetic Father Kino explored and mapped much of southern Arizona beginning in the 1680's. By the time of his death in 1711, Father Kino had founded some two dozen missions, converted over 4,000 Indians, and traveled thousands of miles through territory previously un-

known to Europeans. Known as the Apostle of Arizona, Father Kino's kindness to the Indians and knowledge of their traditions contributed much to Spanish influence in this region.

SECTION REVIEW

1. Vocabulary: *borderlands*.
2. How did the expression "glory, God, and gold" reflect the aims of the Spanish conquistadors?
3. How did Balboa and Ponce de León contribute to European understanding of the Americas?
4. What part did Cortés and Pizarro each play in the growth of Spain's American empire?
5. What region did each of the following explore? (a) Pánfilo de Narváez (b) Cabeza de Vaca (c) Hernando de Soto (d) Francisco de Coronado (e) Eusébio Kino

2 Spanish Civilization Takes Hold

Even as the extraordinary era of Spanish exploration drew to a close, riches from Mexico and Peru were making Spain the most powerful country in Europe. At the same time, Spain continued to send soldiers and administrators to America to run the ever-growing empire.

Spain's new empire is immense. Spain eventually controlled a vast area extending from what is now the southwestern United States and Florida through Central America and south along almost the entire west coast of South America. This domain was divided into two *viceroyalties* — New Spain and Peru. Each viceroyalty was ruled by a *viceroy,* a colonial governor named by the king and responsible only to him. New Spain's viceroy was situated in Mexico City; Peru's, in Lima. The towns of the empire had councils that could deal with matters of strictly local importance. Beginning in 1530, however, Charles V forbade the councils to meet without his specific approval, which he rarely gave.

The viceroys had immense power and prestige. They administered tax laws, meted out justice, and regulated the conditions of labor. Spain had a Council of the Indies to make laws for its American possessions, but the distance from the scene kept the Council weak. In practice, most laws were made on the spot by the viceroys and their advisory bodies, called *audiencias* (ow-DYEN-syahss).

Spain gains wealth from its empire. Gold and silver from the Americas made Spain wealthy. The discovery of new mines in Peru and Mexico led to a flow of silver into Seville, making it the richest city in Europe. The Spanish Crown, however, squandered the treasure on new explorations and on wars in Europe that kept government expenses higher than income. Further, while the Spanish colonies at first were a market for such manufactured goods as wool and silk cloth, the colonies themselves were soon producing those goods.

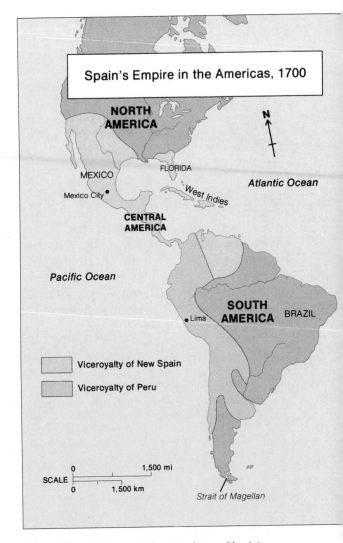

Spain's Empire in the Americas, 1700

NORTH AMERICA

MEXICO

FLORIDA

Atlantic Ocean

Mexico City

West Indies

CENTRAL AMERICA

Pacific Ocean

SOUTH AMERICA BRAZIL

Lima

☐ Viceroyalty of New Spain

☐ Viceroyalty of Peru

SCALE 0 — 1,500 mi 0 — 1,500 km

Strait of Magellan

N

New Spain and Peru were the two viceroyalties into which Spain's immense American empire was divided. Which viceroyalty included areas of what is now the United States?

To make up the constant shortfalls in the royal treasury, the king sold government jobs in the colonies to the highest bidders. He also sold for large sums the exclusive rights to ship certain commodities to America, including gunpowder, salt, and slaves. Of these monopolies, the *asiento* (ah-see-AYN-toh) became the most famous. Under the *asiento* system, contractors paid the king a fee for every slave they transported from Africa to the colonies. African slaves began to be sold in the Americas when the deaths of so many Indians created a severe labor shortage.

The Indians are forced to work for the Spanish. The society that replaced the simple Indian agricultural life was based on extensive land grants, or *encomiendas* (en-koh-MYEN-dahs), made to royal favorites who were called *encomenderos* (en-koh-men-DAY-rohs). The *encomenderos* were placed in charge of groups of Indians numbering between fifty and a hundred. The aim was not only to convert the Indians to Christianity but also to make them work for the Spanish on farms or in mines. The *encomienda* Indians were, in general, mistreated. Those who escaped and were caught sometimes were made slaves as punishment. Cut off from their families and villages, the *encomienda* Indians lost many of their old skills as hunters and artisans. They became almost entirely dependent on the Europeans for their living.

The Spanish themselves also were badly affected by the system. To demonstrate their authority, they refused to do manual labor. This insistence on not working made relations tense between *encomenderos* and their Indian and black workers. Among the *encomenderos* there was always fear of an uprising by the laboring people.

By 1575, approximately five million Indians were living in *encomiendas*. These basic units of the Spanish empire were located around some 200 towns, which were the homes of roughly 160,000 Europeans. Spain's control was so great that its people effectively imposed their language, laws, and culture on the huge, sprawling empire. In time the mixture of races in the Spanish empire included Americans of Indian and Spanish background, Americans of Spanish and African background, and Americans of

In areas where gold or silver was discovered, the Spanish put the Indians to work in the mines. At this Bolivian silver mine, painted in about 1584, Indians dug ore from the mountain and then prepared it for smelting.

African and Indian background. For centuries, however, the people of European origin would dominate all the others.

The Indians are made Christians. The work of Europeanizing the Indians was carried on by dedicated priests, working in settlements called *missions.* Missions usually began as simple chapels around which Indians were gathered. Gradually the little structures were added to as their influence developed, becoming in time schools as well as religious centers. While their chief purpose was to teach the Roman Catholic faith, the mission priests also taught Indians Spanish ways of farming.

In teaching new methods of farming, the Spanish introduced food crops never previously grown in America, such as wheat, barley, rye, chickpeas, and lentils. Under the priests' supervision, citrus fruits, as well as apricots, almonds, walnuts, chestnuts, apples, mulberries, and cherries were also raised in the Americas for the first time.

The Spanish brought farm animals to the Americas too. The most dramatic changes in the Indians' ways of living resulted from the widespread appearance of mules and horses. Thirty years after Cortés left Mexico, horses were roaming America at will. A sixteenth-century writer observed that the Indians "blessed the beasts which relieved them from burden-bearing."

Spain's empire suffers from a lack of unity. Until the nineteenth century, more imposing buildings, universities, and cities were found in the Spanish colonies than anywhere else in America. Still, for all their wealth the Spanish colonies never became unified. This was partly due to the great distances, as well as the terrain, which prevented people from being in close touch with one another. Moreover, owing to the wide gulf between the handful of rich people and the vast mass of poor people that the Spanish system created, Spanish-American society had built-in strains and conflicts. In addition, the sharp divisions that existed between the races interfered with the establishment of representative government.

SECTION REVIEW

1. Vocabulary: *viceroyalty, viceroy, mission.*
2. (a) What role did the viceroys play in governing Spain's American empire? (b) Why were they more powerful than the Council of the Indies?
3. What effects did the discovery of gold and silver in America have on the Spanish government?
4. (a) What was the *encomienda* system? (b) What effect did that system have on the Indians in Spain's empire? (c) What was the purpose of the missions?
5. What factors contributed to a lack of unity in Spain's empire?

3 France Takes an Interest in Starting American Colonies

By the time that Spain had conquered Mexico, France was also becoming a strong country. The energetic young ruler of France, Francis I, was not willing to sit idly by while Spain and Portugal divided the world. Francis was stirred by the news of Magellan's voyage to enter the search for a direct route to Asia.

Early French explorers stake out claims. French sailors had already been in North America. By the early 1500's, French fishermen were dragging their nets off the Grand Banks of Newfoundland and supplying northern France with cod. The market was immense, for Catholic France had 153 days a year on which the eating of meat was forbidden. In time the Grand Banks became known as the "silver mines of the Atlantic," a tribute to the sleek fish that were found there in such quantity.

Francis, however, had something other than fish in mind. He needed a source of wealth to pay for the wars he was conducting against his rival, Charles V of Spain. An all-water route to Asia might provide the riches Francis sought.

Verrazano searches for a route to Asia. A Florentine sailor living in France named Giovanni da Verrazano (vehr-rah-ZAH-noh) came to Francis's attention. Francis commissioned him to find a route to Asia by

49

crossing the Atlantic. After an uneventful seven-week voyage early in 1524, Verrazano landed on the coast of what is today North Carolina. Following the shoreline of the Atlantic Ocean, he sailed northward, constantly searching for a strait that would cut through the continent. He reached the mouth of the Hudson River, which leads to one of the most beautiful valleys in the world. We do not know how much of it Verrazano saw, but he had reached the present site of New York City. He likely sailed very near where the Statue of Liberty now stands.

Verrazano saw Cape Cod and sailed to Newfoundland along what we call the New England coast. When Verrazano returned to France, he was full of big talk and deceit. He even insisted that Pamlico Sound, off the North Carolina coast, was the gateway to Asia. Nevertheless, although he had clearly failed to find a passage to Asia, Verrazano had established France's first claims to North America.

Cartier explores the St. Lawrence. Francis persisted. He decided to send Jacques Cartier (car-TYAY), a French harbor pilot, to look for a route to Asia. Cartier's first expedition took him to the Gulf of St. Lawrence, where he claimed the surrounding land for his king in 1534. Cartier found the Indians friendly and eager to trade for metal tools.

There were no apparent treasures in the region and surely no ready route to the East. Still, Francis was sufficiently encouraged by Cartier's reports to send him back on a second expedition in 1535. Francis was more eager than ever for results. While Cartier was exploring the St. Lawrence, Pizarro was plundering Peru, sending back to Europe great quantities of gold and silver.

Cartier was lured by reports of two rich cities, Stadacona and Hochelaga, even as De Soto and Coronado had been enticed by accounts of the "seven cities of Cibola." Like the Spaniards, he was doomed to disappointment. The "rich cities" proved to be Indian villages. One day, however, the forbidding fortress of Quebec would stand on the site of Stadacona, and the city of Montreal would rise where Hochelaga stood.

Cartier and his men wintered at Stadacona. Many in the party died of scurvy. The survivors returned to France, taking with them several Indians. The returned Frenchmen gave fresh assurance to the Crown that another Mexico or Peru was within easy reach of where they had explored.

Champlain pushes into the interior. Shortly after Cartier's expeditions to North America, religious and civil wars in Europe began to occupy the attention of France's rulers. Not until the early 1600's could the French again pursue their interest in exploration. At that time Samuel de Champlain, the greatest of all French explorers, came to North America in search of furs. Furs were needed to make the wide-brimmed beaver hats that had become the delight of well-dressed Europeans. The first Frenchmen to deal in furs were fishermen who traded for them with the Indians.

Between 1604 and 1607 Champlain traveled and mapped the area that later became New England. Then in 1608 he started a French settlement at Quebec, on cliffs overlooking the St. Lawrence River. Since the river narrows there, the settlement could be easily defended.

Champlain used Quebec as a base from which to push farther west. He hoped to reach the Pacific Ocean and then Asia from this base. What he thought was the Pacific, however, was actually Lakes Ontario and Huron. He conducted expeditions in the vicinity of those lakes, as well as to the lake that now bears his name. Jean Nicolet, one of his most trusted lieutenants, explored Lakes Huron and Michigan in 1634–1635.

The fur trade brings profits. As the French reached into more and more land previously unknown to Europeans, the development of the fur trade kept pace. Trading in furs came to depend on two new types of Frenchmen. One was the *coureur de bois* (koo-RUR deh BWAH), literally "runner-of-the-woods," who traded and hunted in the forest. The other was the *voyageur* (voy-ah-GEHR), who traveled in search of furs even beyond the wooded areas, onto the plains. Both types learned Indian ways and often married Indian women.

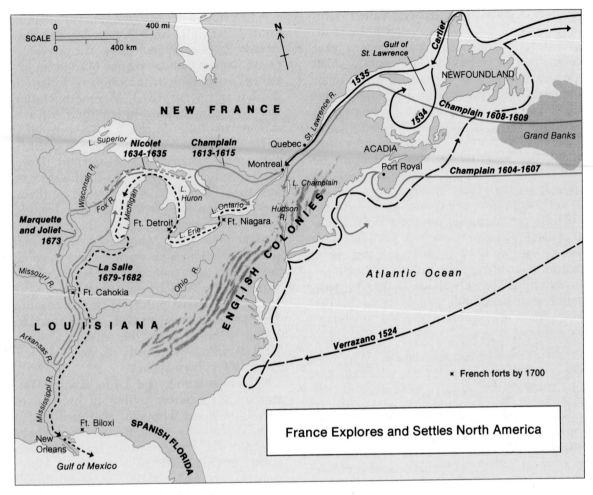

The St. Lawrence and the Mississippi were the two waterways by which French explorers penetrated the North American continent.

Despite the success of the fur business, the dream of reaching Asia did not die. When Nicolet explored the Great Lakes, he carried a handsome ceremonial robe of cloth decorated "with flowers and birds of many colors." He intended to put it on when he greeted Chinese officials! Until the early 1700's, every path and every stream continued to hold the possibility of being the long-sought passage to Asia.

Farming is unprofitable in New France. By the time Champlain's career had come to an end, other Frenchmen were making plans to start permanent colonies in New France, as the large domain claimed by the French had come to be called. One such planner was Cardinal Richelieu (REESH-eh-loo), who in 1624 became the chief adviser to the French king. Richelieu wanted to consolidate French possessions in a powerful empire. With that aim in mind, he established the Company of New France. The partners, who put up money, were granted control over the fur trade. They also hoped to convert the Indians to Christianity.

Richelieu had the idea that he could establish in America the kind of society that existed in France. He created an order of nobles called *seigneurs* (sen-YURS) to live in America on land grants known as *seigneuries* (sen-yur-EEZ) along the lakes and rivers of New France. The *seigneurs* were expected to bring settlers to farm their land.

Seigneurs paid no rent to the Crown for their land, but had to acknowledge the authority of the king's representative at Quebec. *Seigneurs* were also liable for military service. The settlers, called *habitants* (ah-bee-TAHNTS), were obliged to give forced labor each year. Once a year they also had to pay the *seigneurs* a small sum of money and a quantity of grain or poultry. The presenting of the annual payments was a social occasion for the entire community.

Relations with the Indians were generally good. Nevertheless, for protection — and to offset the terrible loneliness — the French located their *seigneuries* close together. Still, the chief interest lay in fur trading, not farming. By 1663 only a few thousand acres of land had been cleared, and as late as 1712 there were only about ninety *seigneuries*. The population of New France then was only about 17,000. Of that number about 3,000 people lived in the three main towns of Quebec, Montreal, and Port Royal.

New France attracts few settlers. Why was the population of New France so small? For one thing, non-Catholics were kept out of the region. Second, many people who left France chose to settle on islands in the Caribbean and set up sugar plantations. By the 1660's, for instance, Haiti had about 15,000 French settlers. Finally, the natural increase of population in New France was slow. Most of the *habitants* and all of the soldiers were single. Unmarried French women had constantly to be encouraged to set out for New France. Frequently groups of orphaned girls were shipped to America where they quickly became brides. Generous sums were paid to young men and women who married at an early age, and handsome sums of money were paid to couples who had large families.

Marquette and Joliet explore the Mississippi. Louis XIV, who became the most powerful of French kings, assumed complete control of the French government in 1661. One of the monarch's aims was to make New France strong enough to rival Spain's empire. He sent his personal representative, Jean Talon, to New France. Talon, working closely with Jesuit missionaries, hoped to extend French influence westward and claim for France the Mississippi Valley.

To explore the Mississippi, Talon chose Louis Joliet (JOH-lih-ET), a trader who may already have traveled near the river. A priest named Father Jacques Marquette obtained permission to accompany Joliet. In the late spring of 1673, Marquette, Joliet, and five companions began their voyage, starting at Lake Michigan. They paddled down the Fox and Wisconsin rivers until finally they reached the Mississippi. Here, they must have thought, was finally the passage to Asia. Gradually it dawned on them, however, that the great river flowed south. After arriving at the place where the Arkansas joins the Mississippi, they met Shawnee Indians who warned them to go no farther lest they fall into the hands of the Spanish. The Frenchmen wrote, "Beyond a doubt, the Mississippi River discharges into the Florida or Mexican Gulf, and not to the east in Virginia or to the west in California." Heeding the words of the Shawnee, the explorers turned back.

Upon reaching the Ohio River, Marquette gave a letter telling of his trip to friendly Indians who said they had traded with Europeans. Marquette may have thought the letter would reach Spanish priests or perhaps English priests in Maryland. As it turned out, the letter fell into the hands of an English settler in Virginia. In ways like this, geographical information sometimes quickly ceased being secret.

La Salle claims Louisiana for France. Nine years later, early in 1682, a French nobleman named Robert Cavelier, Sieur de la Salle, completed the journey that Marquette and Joliet had not dared to finish. With a party of 54 Indians and Frenchmen, La Salle traveled down the entire course of the Mississippi until he reached the river's mouth. There he claimed for his king the river itself, all the rivers entering it, and all the land washed by them. In honor of Louis XIV he named the territory Louisiana.

La Salle had even grander aims. He dreamed of creating a permanent French settlement near the mouth of the Mississippi. It would anchor in the south the French empire he envisioned running in a gigantic arc across the continent. La Salle's

Near the beginning of his journey to the mouth of the Mississippi, La Salle reached one of the natural wonders of North America. This painting, by the American artist George Catlin, shows La Salle's party gazing at Niagara Falls.

colony would also cut off the Spaniards in Florida from those in Mexico. Returning to France, La Salle obtained financing for the scheme and in 1684 sailed into the Gulf of Mexico with his party. However, he failed to see the mouth of the Mississippi, sailed past it, and wound up instead on the coast of Texas. La Salle landed his colonists, but the settlement they started failed to prosper, and La Salle lost his life in a fight. Not until 1718 did the French build New Orleans at the mouth of the Mississippi.

SECTION REVIEW

1. (a) Why did Francis I send Verrazano across the Atlantic? (b) What did Verrazano accomplish for France?
2. (a) What region did Cartier explore? (b) Why did Champlain journey to North America? (c) Describe the area he explored.
3. (a) Why did Cardinal Richelieu establish the Company of New France? (b) Why was New France unable to attract large numbers of settlers?
4. (a) Describe the explorations of Marquette and Joliet. (b) What was the object of La Salle's exploration? (c) What role did those explorers play in establishing French claims in America?

4 England Starts Colonies in North America

England lagged behind Spain and France in sending explorers and settlers to North America. Once the English arrived, however, they more than made up for their late start.

England grows strong. An island country, England had always been a land of sailors. The discovery of the Americas and the new activity on the oceans gave the English a sense that they had an important role to play in world affairs. They were powerfully inspired by their queen, Elizabeth I, who had come to the throne in 1558. Elizabeth made Spain her enemy, even turning down an offer of marriage from the Spanish king, Philip II. During Elizabeth's reign, English vessels raided Spanish coastal towns in Central and South America and plundered Spanish galleons bound for home with treasure.

The most successful of the English raiders was Francis Drake. In 1577, with the queen's connivance, Drake planned to

53

Queen Elizabeth I, respected and loved by her people, ruled at a time when England was taking fresh interest in America.

attack Spanish possessions in South America. A superb seaman, he sailed safely through the Strait of Magellan in his little ship, the *Golden Hind.* Moving northward along the western coast of South America, he looted unprotected ports and treasure ships, filling the hold of his vessel with silver. Afraid to travel south again lest the Spanish catch him, he looked for a waterway to the Atlantic through the continent — a north*east* passage. Finding none, he put in for repairs and provisions near San Francisco Bay. From there he sailed west, passing the Philippines and the Spice Islands and then going around the Cape of Good Hope. He arrived at Plymouth, England — home at last — in September, 1580. His cargo netted his sponsors, including the queen herself, a fortune.

Drake, the first Englishman to sail around the world, was received at home as a hero. When Queen Elizabeth came aboard his vessel to make him a knight, the challenge to Spain was clear. English strength was rising. William Shakespeare, the outstanding poet and playwright of the day, caught the spirit of his land when he had

one of his characters boast, "The world's mine oyster, which I with sword will open."

Most people in England are Protestants. A number of factors, aside from boldness and nerve, were causing England to challenge Spain and France. One of the most important was that England had become a Protestant country, breaking with the Church of Rome in 1534. This meant that the English monarch, rather than the Pope, now was the head of the church in England. The newly established church became known as the Anglican Church, or the Church of England. The differences in religious doctrine led to hostility between Protestant England, on the one hand, and Roman Catholic Spain and France on the other. In that religious age European conflicts were readily carried into the Americas.

English manufacturing and trade are on the rise. The beginning of manufacturing was also influencing English life. England did not yet have factories in the 1500's, but the future was already being glimpsed. Iron, glass, and pewter were being produced in ever-increasing amounts. English shipyards were busy too, building vessels for the growing seaborne trade. New industries producing paper, soap, copper, and brass were giving steady employment to large numbers of people.

As a result of this activity the towns of England were probably growing faster than any others in Europe. They were places in which the ambitious could find enterprise to satisfy their appetite. Moreover, the pace of life was quicker in English towns, the outlook more optimistic, and the chances to get ahead greater. More and more English goods were seen on the world's trading routes, and Englishmen felt they were every bit as good as the Dutch and Spanish traders they met in the major ports of the world.

The English defeat the Spanish Armada. English people also had a strong sense of national pride, acquired earlier than in other nations. The Hundred Years' War (1337–1453), fought against France, had given England self-confidence. Playwrights worked hard to keep alive stories of English heroes of that struggle.

During the second half of Elizabeth's reign, Spain was the feared enemy of the English Crown. Responding to the raids of Francis Drake and others on Spanish shipping, Philip II sent a mighty fleet, known as the Spanish Armada, against England in 1588. Bold English mariners sailed their ships against the Armada in the English Channel and smashed the enemy fleet.

The Spanish defeat marked a turning point in European history. It made the English eager and feisty. England was a small country, but its inhabitants came to see themselves as a folk tightly bound together with a glorious destiny in store. All English people, anywhere in the world, felt they were a vital part of what Shakespeare called "this land of such dear souls, this dear, dear land."

The English become interested in starting colonies. The stunning victory over the Spanish Armada convinced the English that the time had come to take on the enemy in the Americas too. But how should they do this? A popular writer of the time, Richard Hakluyt (HAK-loot), had attracted attention in 1584 when he prepared a pamphlet for his friend Sir Walter Raleigh with the intriguing title *A Discourse Concerning Western Planting.* Hakluyt argued that the time had come for England to start colonies. Overseas colonies, he said, would serve as sources for various raw materials that the English had been buying from other nations. Colonies would also, he wrote, prevent the Spanish "from flowing over all the face . . . of America." Hakluyt proposed too that orphaned English children as well as the outcast and downtrodden be sent to America, "and there be raised again and do their country good service."

England had already developed a form of business organization for overseas undertakings. This was the *joint-stock company.* Run by a board of directors, such a company was owned by a group of investors who had put up money for shares in the company. The shares were called *stock.*

Most joint-stock companies were organized to carry on trade in distant parts of the world. The Muscovy Company, formed in 1555, conducted commerce with Russia. The Levant Company traded with Turkey and surrounding countries. ("The Levant" was the term then used for the eastern shore of the Mediterranean and nearby lands, including Turkey.) The Barbary Company controlled trade with North Africa; the Guinea Company, with West Africa. The most powerful of the joint-stock companies, with 218 founders, was the East India Company. Started in 1600, it was designed to compete with the Dutch for trade with the Spice Islands in the East Indies.

The profits realized by these new companies stirred English life. The news of a ship's arrival or of a new privilege acquired by English traders abroad became as important in daily conversation among business people as was the latest gossip from the royal court. Where landowners had once dominated English life, merchants were now becoming influential too.

Early efforts at colonization fail. The first Englishman to start a settlement in America was Sir Humphrey Gilbert. A good friend of

Queen Elizabeth and a shareholder in the Muscovy Company, he received permission to claim for England lands not already the property of any Christian ruler. Gilbert did not know much about America. He long believed that it was an island and that by sailing around it, he would find the way to Asia.

After an unsuccessful first voyage, Sir Humphrey set sail in 1583 with a small band of settlers. They landed at Newfoundland, but soon realized that they were not prepared to live in such a forbidding place. On their voyage back to England, Gilbert was lost at sea.

The first English colonies in America were started on these royal grants. Notice that the grants of the Plymouth group and the London group overlapped.

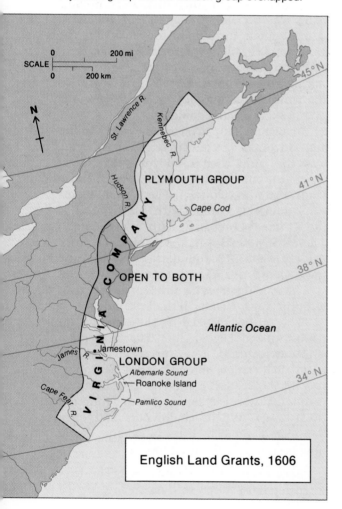

English Land Grants, 1606

Gilbert's rights in North America now passed to Sir Walter Raleigh, his half brother. Raleigh, immensely influenced by Hakluyt's writing and eager to make his fortune, had a high goal for America: "I shall yet live to see it an English nation." Seeking to avoid Gilbert's mistakes, he planned a settlement on a warmer part of the Atlantic coast. In 1584 Raleigh sent an expedition to have a look at Spanish defenses in the Caribbean and to spy out a suitable location for a colony. His men were attracted by the area around Albemarle Sound in what is now North Carolina, and they landed on Roanoke Island before heading back to England. Raleigh was very pleased with the account of the site that had been chosen. In honor of the queen he named it Virginia.

In June of the following year an expedition arrived at Roanoke. Badly advised on how to deal with the Indians, the English made enemies of them. Then an especially severe winter followed. Near starvation, the settlers had the good luck to have Francis Drake, fresh from a raid against Spanish shipping, stop on his way home to see how they were faring. They persuaded him to take them back to England.

Among the "experts" Raleigh sent to America were John White, an artist, and Thomas Hariot, a writer. When the colonists returned, Hariot published an account of the Roanoke site, for which White drew the illustrations. The pamphlet enticed more than one hundred people to sign on for the next expedition to Virginia, which set out in 1587. Among the hundred were the first English women and children to come to America. The hardy souls must have guessed that they could survive only if supplies arrived from home steadily. John White, who had been made governor of the colony, soon returned to England to arrange for food and other supplies to be sent.

Unhappily, war broke out between England and Spain, and no supply ships could be sent to the colony. Not until 1590 did White return to Roanoke. When he reached Roanoke he could not find a trace of the settlers — among them his daughter and his granddaughter, Virginia Dare, the first English child born in America. To this day no one knows for certain what happened to the settlers of the "lost colony."

Further attempts are made at colonizing. Raleigh would not give up. He tried to get businesspeople to invest money in the colony in return for trading rights. In 1603, however, he was arrested and accused of treason. Three years later the investors with whom he had been negotiating received from King James I a *charter,* or license, of their own to set up a colony in America. They quickly organized a joint-stock company called the Virginia Company.

The king made two grants of land to the Virginia Company. To one group of stockholders — the London group — he gave the land lying between the 34th and 41st parallels of north latitude. To the other group — called the Plymouth group — he gave the land lying between the 38th and 45th parallels. These grants overlapped by three degrees (map, page 56), but the groups were instructed not to occupy land within a hundred miles of each other.

The English settle at Jamestown. As the looseness of the grants indicates, the Virginia Company had no understanding of what settling America would be like and no clear idea of how the colonists would make a living. The London group sent out the first settlers. Three ships, carrying a hundred men under Captain Christopher Newport, left London in December, 1606. When the expedition finally reached the Virginia coast in May, 1607, the loveliness of the scene encouraged the exhausted travelers. The countryside was abloom, and strawberries were ripe enough to be picked. The settlers went ashore about fifty miles upriver, naming the place Jamestown in honor of their sovereign. Their ranks included fifty gentlemen. (These were men who, according to the definition of the time, did no work with their hands.) There were also four carpenters, twelve laborers, two bricklayers, a blacksmith, a mason, a tailor, a surgeon, a sailmaker, various other artisans, a drummer, and four boys.

Captain Newport returned home heartened and full of talk. He told people that the settlers had found copper and gold deposits, and even shellfish rich in pearls. His tales did not help the poor settlers, of whom too much was already expected. Although the leaders of the London group had not known what they would find in their colony, they now looked for quick profits on their investment. Upon hearing of the gold, they sent additional men across the Atlantic to Jamestown. These included assayers (specialists in judging the quality of precious metals) and goldsmiths, who could work the ore into jewelry and other objects. They also sent tailors and perfumers, because this was going to be, after all, a society of rich people!

The newcomers quickly began digging for gold. What they found, however, proved to be "fool's gold" — a yellow mineral that has no great value. The settlers might better have devoted themselves to building shelters and preparing food for the winter. Things soon went from bad to worse, and starvation and disease began taking a heavy toll.

To survive, the colony would need strong leadership, a way for the people to make a living, and fresh inspiration. Furthermore, new ways of thinking, different from those of Spain and France, seemed required. No one yet dreamed that individual liberty would be the key to that thinking. No one yet imagined that English families could form the foundation of a country richer than Mexico and Peru had ever been.

SECTION REVIEW

1. Vocabulary: *joint-stock company, stock, charter.*
2. (a) What were Francis Drake's achievements? (b) How did those achievements influence national sentiment in England? (c) What other factors led to rivalry between England and Spain?
3. What role did each of the following play in England's attempts to start colonies in North America? (a) Richard Hakluyt (b) Sir Humphrey Gilbert (c) Sir Walter Raleigh
4. How did the English start a colony at Jamestown?

Chapter 2 Review

Summary

During the century following Columbus's voyages, Spanish adventurers explored and conquered a great expanse of land in the Americas. Among the bold Spaniards were Balboa, the first European to approach the Pacific Ocean by land, and Ponce de León, the first European to explore Florida. Hernando Cortés, who conquered the mighty Aztec empire in Mexico, built Mexico City as the center of a vast Spanish domain. To the north, in the borderlands region extending from California to Florida, such men as Cabeza de Vaca, Hernando de Soto, and Vasquez de Coronado led important explorations. Meanwhile, far to the south a second wealthy Indian empire — the Inca empire of Peru — was conquered by Spanish conquistadors.

Spain's empire in America extended from what is now the southwestern United States through Central America to include almost the entire west coast of South America. The territory was divided into the viceroyalties of New Spain and Peru, each ruled by a viceroy appointed by the king. The Spanish established large farms called *encomiendas* on which Indians and African slaves were forced to work. The *encomienda* system created tensions between the races and between rich and poor settlers, contributing to a lack of unity in the empire.

French exploration in eastern North America led to claims over a broad territory and to a thriving fur trade. Early French claims were made by Giovanni da Verrazano and by Jacques Cartier. Those explorers were followed by Samuel de Champlain, who mapped much of the area that became New France. Later French expeditions took Marquette and Joliet to the Mississippi. La Salle completed their work by traveling south to the mouth of the river, where France eventually founded the settlement of New Orleans in 1718.

England, though late to enter the competition for land in the Americas, eventually was the most successful. The English sought colonies as sources of raw materials and also as expanded markets for trade. Early English efforts to start colonies in America ended in failure. Sir Humphrey Gilbert tried to start a settlement in Newfoundland, but the site was soon abandoned. Sir Walter Raleigh started a colony at Roanoke, but the settlers disappeared. Then, in 1607 an ill-prepared expedition was sent to a promising site named Jamestown. The settlers soon learned that they would have to overcome many difficulties if they were to survive.

Vocabulary and Important Terms

1. conquistador
2. St. Augustine
3. borderlands
4. viceroyalty
5. viceroy
6. *asiento*
7. *encomienda*
8. mission
9. Quebec
10. *coureur de bois*
11. *voyageur*
12. New France
13. *seigneurie*
14. Anglican Church
15. Spanish Armada
16. joint-stock company
17. stock
18. charter
19. Virginia Company

Discussion Questions

1. (a) Why have the aims of the Spanish conquistadors been summarized as "glory, God, and gold"? (b) How successful were the conquistadors in fulfilling those aims?
2. Describe the ways in which Spanish military force, European diseases, and the *encomienda* system affected the Indians.
3. (a) What happened to the great wealth that Spain took from its American colonies? (b) What steps did Spain's rulers take to make up for shortfalls in the royal treasury? (c) How did the *encomienda* system benefit Spanish landowners in the colonies?
4. What factors contributed to the development of strains and conflicts in Spanish-American society?
5. (a) For what reasons were the French interested in starting colonies in the Americas? (b) How completely did the development of New France fulfill the hopes of French colonial leaders?
6. (a) Explain why the population of New France was relatively small. (b) What steps did French colonial leaders take to encourage population growth?
7. What factors in the 1500's enabled England to challenge Spain and France?
8. Why, according to Richard Hakluyt, had the time come for England to start colonies?
9. (a) For what reasons did the Jamestown colony nearly fail? (b) What did that colony and other English colonies need in order to survive?

Relating Past to Present

1. The explorers of the 1500's and the 1600's added greatly to geographic knowledge of the world. Today people are exploring many other fields of knowledge. Who are some of the "explorers" of today, and what contributions to knowledge have they made in recent years?

2. Superior weapons helped make it possible for Europeans to conquer the Americas. How did the introduction of other new kinds of technology change ways of living in the Americas?

Studying Local History

What influence, if any, did the Spanish or French have on the state in which you live? Did they influence your state's legal system or the architectural styles of public or private buildings? Is Spanish or French influence present in the names of your state's cities, rivers, or mountains? Are there other indications of the early presence of the Spanish or French in your state? Explain your answer.

Using History Skills

1. *Reading maps.* Look at the map showing Spanish explorations of North America on page 44. (a) Which Spanish explorer journeyed through much of what is today the southeastern part of the United States? (b) Which Spanish explorer traveled through much of what is now the American Southwest, reaching as far north as the Kansas River? (c) Why can the expeditions of these two Spaniards be considered both successes and failures?

2. *Reading source material.* Study Juan de Oñate's description of the Spanish borderlands on page 46. (a) How did Oñate describe the Indians' towns? (b) Their clothing? (c) What similarities and differences did he find between the Indians living north of the Rio Grande and those in New Spain? (d) In your opinion, would the viceroy have found prospects for colonization north of the Rio Grande encouraging or discouraging? Give reasons for your answer.

3. *Organizing information.* Make a chart with three columns. In the first column list the explorers you read about in this chapter. In the second column identify the area covered by each explorer. In the third column describe the significance of the explorer's findings.

WORLD SCENE

The Lure of Mysterious Lands

The legend of the seven cities of Cibola was only one of many reports about "golden" lands that drew explorers into unknown territory.

The quest for Prester John. Ever since the 1300's, rumors had circulated in European royal courts about a mysterious Christian ruler in eastern Africa, called Prester John. Some people claimed to have read a letter he had written to a European king. Supposedly the letter told about the wonders of his empire, including rivers of gold and silver.

Prince Henry hoped that the Portuguese voyages along the coast of Africa would lead to contact with Prester John. The Portuguese were fascinated by the reports of Prester John's wealth, but they also wanted to enlist him in their struggle against Muslim power. Other European rulers began to sponsor voyages of exploration, too, hoping somehow to make contact with this shadowy man.

When Portuguese seamen reached Ethiopia in eastern Africa and discovered that the people were Christian, they believed they had at last found the land of Prester John. Ethiopia contained no rivers of gold, however, and European fascination with the fabled ruler soon came to an end.

The legend of El Dorado. When Spanish explorers first arrived in South America, they heard tales about El Dorado (doh-RAH-doh), an Indian king somewhere in the interior of South America. El Dorado, it was told, would cover himself with fine gold dust every morning. Then, according to the story, he would float on a raft to the middle of a sacred lake and there cast offerings of gold and emeralds into the waters. In the same place he would ceremonially wash the gold dust from his body.

As the legend was passed from explorer to explorer, the name *El Dorado* came to refer not to a man but to a place where immense treasure and plenty could be found. Many Europeans, including Pizarro's half brother Gonzalo and the English adventurer Sir Walter Raleigh, ventured into the interior of South America hoping to find El Dorado. No one succeeded, however.

Upon returning home, Raleigh wrote a book about his search. The book spread the legend of El Dorado throughout Europe, and the name found its way onto maps.

CHAPTER 3

Founding England's First Colonies

1600 – 1700

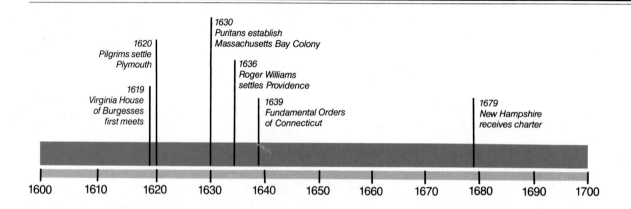

CHAPTER OUTLINE

1. Virginia becomes England's first successful colony.

2. Pilgrims and Puritans seek a new life in America.

3. Other settlers start colonies in New England.

The first true English leader in America was John Smith. Born around 1580, Smith lived a life of high adventure. Before arriving in Virginia in 1607, he had fought as a soldier in France and Holland and in eastern Europe against the Turks. Then, while in England in 1604, he met people who had been in America — "and all their talk was of its wonders." Smith signed on to see Virginia for himself.

Once in America, Smith became a member of the Council of Seven, a group that ruled the Jamestown colony. He soon became its dominant figure. To end the quarreling that had begun even before the settlers had landed, he started to enforce discipline. He ordered the building of a blockhouse to serve as protection from Indian raids. He even forced the gentlemen-settlers to clear fields and plant crops. Jamestown needed a strong manager like Smith. Under his guidance, the colony began to take hold.

Meanwhile, in 1620, far to the north of Virginia on the rocky shores of New England, a small group of brave men and women came ashore. Seeking a land where they would be free to worship as they pleased, these determined people started a settlement they called Plymouth. Out of Jamestown and Plymouth grew England's first permanent colonies in America.

1 Virginia Becomes England's First Successful Colony

In England the Virginia Company recognized the need to get "wife, children and servants to take hold and root in [Virginia]." Getting the Jamestown settlement solidly under way, however, was far from easy. Only after years of hard work did Virginia become a successful colony.

Jamestown survives the "starving time." The early years at Jamestown were filled with danger. The winter of 1609–1610 was so terrible for Virginia that it was long remembered as the "starving time." During that winter the colonists sorely missed the leadership of John Smith, who, injured in an accident, had returned to England.

The misery of the colonists can hardly be imagined today. Newly arrived settlers did not bring sufficient supplies with them. They became an additional burden on the struggling colony. There was so little food that people ate rats and mice and dried-up roots. Famine claimed hundreds of lives.

Those who survived the "starving time" were near the end of their rope. Some of them must have recalled the fate of the Roanoke experiment (page 56), and trembled over what their own might be. Just when the colonists had decided to abandon their settlement, however, the acting governor of the colony, Thomas Gates, arrived at Jamestown. His ships, the *Deliverance* and the *Patience*, sailed up the James River in May, 1610 — a welcome sight to the sixty remaining settlers. Soon thereafter, Virginia's new governor, Lord Delaware, appeared with a relief party and supplies. He persuaded the downcast colonists to try to dig in once again. Success finally rewarded their efforts, giving the English a permanent foothold in North America.

The Virginia settlers discover the benefits of the new land. The colonists remained in close touch with England, of course, and for a long time continued to think of it as "home." The attractions of America, nevertheless, were unmistakable. To be sure, the winters were harsher and the summers hotter than in the old country, but so much seemed bigger and better. Cattle, it was early reported, grew "to a far greater bulk of body" than in England. On cleared land, wheat, oats, barley, and rye grew more

Jamestown was England's first successful colony in North America. In this view, settlers are bargaining in the village marketplace.

abundantly than at home. Wild turkeys were so numerous that when a flock took to the skies, it could blot out the sun. Seafood, more varied than on the other side of the Atlantic, included oysters, crabs, sturgeon, bass, cod, eels, shad, trout, and salmon. The berries that the local woods displayed dazzled the newcomers: raspberries, blackberries, gooseberries, cranberries, and strawberries. Upon tasting strawberries for the first time an English minister could not contain himself. "Doubtless God could have made a better berry," he exclaimed, "but doubtless God never did." Finally, from the Indians the settlers learned about Indian corn, squashes, pumpkins, cucumbers, sweet potatoes, tomatoes, and onions.

Settlers move inland. Clearing the land and starting farms was very hard work. The forests were an obstacle that had to be removed tree by tree. To judge the amount of labor that was spent in settling America, we might consider the physical energy required

to uproot millions of trees by hand. Some trees were destroyed, Indian-fashion, by girdling them with deep cuts and allowing them to die. Others were brought down by sturdy pioneers wielding their axes with strength and skill. After felling the trees, the settlers began digging up the roots and turning over the hard-packed soil.

The natural features of Virginia were another hurdle for the early settlers. The Appalachian Mountains were a forbidding barrier. Indeed the Virginians were at first hemmed in between the coastline and the mountains. (Not for a hundred years would there be English settlements on the other side of the Appalachians.) Furthermore, the rivers of that region flow from west to east. The coastal plain, or *tidewater,* extends inland between fifty and a hundred miles, being wider in the south. West of the plain is the *piedmont* region (literally "the foot of the mountains"). At the place where the piedmont joins the plain is the *fall line* of the rivers, where waterfalls become a serious hindrance to navigation.

Representative government begins. In 1624 James I canceled the charter of the Virginia Company, thus making Virginia a royal colony. From then on the king would appoint the colony's governor and councilors. Five years before, however, the Company had made a lasting contribution to government in America by granting Virginia a legislature. The House of Burgesses, as the legislature was called, first met on July 30, 1619, in a little church in Jamestown to write the laws of Virginia. At that time there were eleven settlements in the colony. Each of them elected two burgesses, as representatives were called.

The House of Burgesses remained in existence even after James I took control of Virginia. The right of colonists to govern themselves in local matters was clearly recognized. This initial step in the long process of establishing representative government in America was only one of the many changes in the Company's original plan that had never entered the minds of the colony's founders.

The first English settlements in Virginia were started east of the fall line, on the wide coastal plain known as the tidewater.

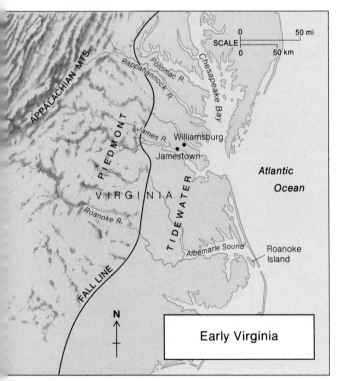

Early Virginia

Representative government got its start in America when Virginia colonists met in their legislature, called the House of Burgesses, in 1619.

Tobacco cultivation assures Virginia's success. Another unanticipated development was the discovery that raising tobacco was a profitable way to make a living. Indians living near the colonists had long raised tobacco, but the Europeans did not like its taste. In 1612 a tropical variety, possibly from Trinidad, was introduced to Virginia by Captain John Rolfe. Rolfe, like other Englishmen, had learned to enjoy puffing on a pipe. (Smoking tobacco had become popular in England after John Hawkins, an associate of Drake's, had brought some leaves from Florida forty years earlier.) Rolfe's tobacco found a waiting market in London. The first crop arrived there in 1614. By the late 1630's Virginia was sending to England 1.5 million pounds annually — the level of production maintained for the rest of the century. Rolfe, a widower who fell in love with the Indian princess Pocahontas and married her in 1614, deserves a place beside John Smith as a maker of Virginia's success.

The cultivation of tobacco required vast acreage. The "weed" quickly wore out the land, and the steady search for new acres was instrumental in pushing settlement farther and farther west. Because rivers were required for shipping the crop, the banks of the Potomac, the James, and the Rappahannock rivers soon were lined with tobacco farms. So completely did tobacco take up people's lives in Virginia that no large towns developed as centers of commerce and culture.

The town of Williamsburg was the political hub of the colony. It became Virginia's capital in 1699 after Jamestown was destroyed by fire. The leaders of the colony met there to debate governmental matters. We may be sure that besides land questions and tobacco prices they discussed another subject of grave concern: where to get cheap labor to work the land.

Indentured servants come to America. Sweeping changes in England suggested one solution to the labor problem. Many people had been driven off the land by what was called the enclosure movement. Millions of acres of farmland were fenced, or "enclosed," to permit the raising of sheep.

63

Some of the poor, of course, found jobs in England's cities. Others, however, were without work and lived on the verge of starvation. To get across the Atlantic to Virginia became for them a stirring hope.

The cost of crossing the Atlantic was, however, beyond the means of these people. Out of the need for labor in America came a solution: the *indenture system.* Under that system, a farmer in America would gladly agree to pay the ship passage of an immigrant. The immigrant would, in turn, agree in writing to serve that farmer for a specified number of years, varying from four to seven.

After the period of indenture was over, the worker became a free man or woman again, often receiving land to take up farming. Many indentured servants quickly sold the land they had obtained and moved to the edge of settlement — that is, to the frontier. There they cleared new land, farmed it, and perhaps headed on again. Sometimes a frontier family did this two or three times in their working lifetime. It may be said, therefore, that the indenture system helped to speed up the westward movement of Virginians.

The indenture system had its drawbacks, however. Many servants, once they had arrived in America, resented their condition and worked unwillingly. Some of them farmed their masters' land so carelessly that it wore out even more quickly than expected. Many indentured servants ran off to escape having to fulfill the obligations they had accepted.

Slavery is introduced. Among the early indentured servants were people who did not come to America willingly. These were Africans who had been taken from their homelands and sold into slavery. The first Africans in Virginia arrived in 1619. Brought by a Dutch ship, they were sold as indentured servants to work in the tobacco fields. For the next thirty years or so, Africans were generally treated like indentured servants from Europe. They were able to obtain land when they had "worked off"

The tidewater of Virginia was devoted primarily to tobacco plantations. Slaves picked the tobacco leaves, dried them, and loaded them onto ships bound for England.

their cost. By 1651 there were about 300 Africans in Virginia's population of 15,000.

Still, the English settlers regarded black people from the beginning as inferior — a notion that had already developed in Europe. By 1640 some black servants were forced to serve their indentures for life. Within twenty years slavery was recognized in the laws of Virginia, and intermarriage between the races was forbidden. Soon, blacks were being treated more like property than people. Slaveholders were given increasing control as the personal and civil freedom of black people was more and more restricted. Finally, as the 1700's opened, the English were becoming heavily involved in the profitable slave trade, until then a monopoly of Spain.

Relations with the Indians are tense. At the same time that Africans began arriving in Virginia, the cultivation of tobacco and the continuing demand for new land were putting terrible pressure on the Indians. At first the Indians had been weakened by the infectious diseases that the Europeans brought. Indeed, between 1617 and 1619 the Indian people along the Virginia coast were almost wiped out by epidemics. The anger of the Indians finally boiled over in 1622 when they attacked the English settlements along the James River. About one third of the settlers, including John Rolfe, lost their lives.

Some of the Virginia leaders blamed themselves for the attack, declaring that they had dealt badly with the Native Americans. The general conclusion, however, was that Indians were permanent enemies and that it was not the business of English people to "civilize" and Christianize them. So believing, the colonists did not hesitate to seize land from the Indians. They chose to forget how much they had learned from the Indians in getting settled.

Again in 1644, the Indians rose up furiously against the settlers. At the cost of hundreds of lives, the Virginians thoroughly defeated the Indians. Thereafter, all the land of the coastal tribes was taken over by the Virginia colony.

SECTION REVIEW

1. Vocabulary: *tidewater, piedmont, fall line, indenture system.*
2. (a) What difficulties did the early Jamestown settlers face? (b) How did they overcome those difficulties?
3. (a) What were some of the attractions of life in the Virginia colony? (b) What natural obstacles did the colonists encounter?
4. (a) What was the House of Burgesses? (b) What is its significance in American history?
5. What role did the cultivation of tobacco play in the history of the Virginia colony?
6. (a) What was the indenture system? (b) How did it differ from slavery?
7. Describe the relations that existed between the Jamestown settlers and the Indians who lived along the Virginia coast.

2 Pilgrims and Puritans Seek a New Life in America

The experience of the Virginians in America quickly became known in England. People learned from the account of the "starving time" not to leave for America without making proper plans. Everybody knew now that a successful colony required a good deal of money and the steady encouragement of its backers.

The Council for New England provides land grants. In 1620 the Plymouth group (page 57) was reorganized, becoming the Council for New England. Consisting of forty aristocrats, the Council had the power to make land grants, start plantations, and write laws. The group was to do its colonizing in the territory lying between the fortieth and forty-eighth parallels and stretching indefinitely westward. (The area was labeled New England by John Smith, who in 1614 had explored the North Atlantic coast in the service of other London merchants.) Although the Council failed to start any settlements of its own, it provided the initial grants for the New England colonies of Massachusetts Bay, New Hampshire, Maine, and Connecticut.

A band of English Separatists moves to Holland. The first permanent settlement of Europeans in New England was started by a group of English people known as Puritans. The Puritans' story began shortly after England broke away from the Roman Catholic Church in 1534. In time, many English people became convinced that the new Anglican Church was dominated by too much ritual and ceremony. They believed that the church must be simplified — *purified* was the word they used. The Puritans rejected ranks for clergymen. They believed true religion was based on the word of God as revealed in the Bible.

The Puritans considered showiness of any kind to be wrong. They denounced dancing and public entertainment as sinful. Every person, the Puritans preached, had two "callings." The first was to serve the Lord. The other was to labor earnestly at a craft or in the home. Puritans drew inspiration from these words in the Bible: " Seest thou a man diligent in his business? He shall stand before kings," and "Go to the ant, thou sluggard. Consider her ways and be wise."

Some Puritans feared that the Anglican Church could never be "purified." Among them were a band of humble folk from Nottinghamshire, in central England, who called for a total break with the Anglicans. For that reason they were called Separatists.

Persecuted by their neighbors, the Separatists fled England in 1607 and 1608 — just when Jamestown was getting started — and sought refuge in Holland. Their leaders were William Brewster, a bailiff; William Bradford, a well-to-do farmer's son; and John Robinson, the minister. In 1609 these people settled in the Dutch town of Leyden. They were soon joined by other Separatists.

The Separatists search for a new homeland. For eleven years the Separatists flourished in Holland, some pursuing their trades as weavers and manufacturers of cloth, others finding work as day laborers. Once again, however, the Separatists felt forced to move. The reasons seemed compelling. First of all, their children were becoming too Dutch, losing their use of the English language. Second, the children were drifting from the strict religious standards of the Separatists and were picking up the ways of the general community. In so doing, as William Bradford later wrote, they were "getting the rein from their necks, and departing from their parents. Some became soldiers, others embarked on far voyages by sea, and others on some worse courses . . . to the great grief of their parents and dishonour of God." Third, war between Holland and Spain seemed sure to disrupt daily life. In order, then, to protect themselves as a group, most of the Separatists decided to

The Pilgrims sailed to America aboard the *Mayflower* in 1620. This painting shows the *Mayflower* lying at anchor in what is now Provincetown harbor, in Massachusetts.

The Mayflower Compact (1620)

We, whose names are underwritten, . . . having undertaken for the glory of God, and advancement of the Christian faith, and the honor of our King and country, a voyage to plant the first colony in the northern parts of Virginia; do by these presents, solemnly and mutually in the presence of God and one another, covenant and combine ourselves together into a civil body politic; for our better ordering and preservation; and furtherance of the ends aforesaid . . . do enact, constitute, and frame such just and equal laws, ordinances, acts, constitutions, and offices from time to time as shall be thought most [proper] and convenient for the general good of the colony unto which we promise all due submission and obedience. In witness whereof we have hereunto subscribed our names at Cape Cod the eleventh of November, in the year of our sovereign lord King James of England . . . *anno domini* 1620.

leave Holland for a haven "devoid of all civil inhabitants." The Separatists became Pilgrims — wanderers in search of a new homeland.

Various "wild coasts" were discussed as possible areas of refuge, but finally Virginia met with general approval. Representatives of the Pilgrims met with Thomas Weston of the Virginia Company and arranged to settle on its lands in America. The new colonists agreed to work as a group for the Company over a period of seven years. They expected after this time to divide any profits with the investors in England and then to be on their own. King James I promised that he would allow the Pilgrims to live without interference from the Crown.

The Pilgrims sail to America. On a leaky ship misnamed the *Speedwell*, 35 brave souls left Holland for the English port of Southampton. There a larger vessel, the *Mayflower*, was waiting. Many of the *Mayflower's* passengers were not Separatists. They had little interest in the religious purpose of the voyage.

In August, 1620, the two vessels set sail. Shortly the *Speedwell* proved unseaworthy and had to turn back. Taking on the *Speedwell's* passengers, the *Mayflower* continued alone across the Atlantic. Among the 102 people aboard, some stand out. One was William Brewster, still a model for the

flock; another was Miles Standish, a soldier destined to become the military leader of the colony; and there was William Bradford, who would serve as governor for thirty years. Bradford's history of the settlement is our chief source of knowledge about its first years.

The Mayflower Compact is drawn up. The crossing went smoothly. Near the end of November the *Mayflower* came to what is now Provincetown harbor at the tip of Cape Cod (map, page 71). Although the group was within the grant of the Council for New England, the non-Separatists threatened to leave because the land was not in the jurisdiction of the Virginia Company. To overcome the difficulty, 41 of the 44 men aboard the vessel signed an agreement while the *Mayflower* rode at anchor in Provincetown harbor. In the agreement, known as the Mayflower Compact, the settlers pledged that they should live together in a peaceable and orderly manner and make "such just and equal laws . . . as shall be thought most [proper] and convenient for the general good of the colony." The agreement was a covenant, intended to set up a temporary government. It was not meant to be a constitution. Still, because the colonists never were able to obtain a charter, the Mayflower Compact was the only constitution the Pilgrims would ever have.

67

The Pilgrims establish Plymouth. After the Mayflower Compact had been agreed to, a landing party, led by Miles Standish, went ashore to select a suitable place for the Pilgrims' first winter in America. We can imagine the anxiety aboard the anchored ship. The warm English weather of August was only a memory. The long trip had been trying. There were now thirty children aboard: "Oceanus" had been born en route; "Peregrine" (from the Latin word for Pilgrim) was born as the passengers waited for Standish to return.

Standish and his scouts soon made their decision. The people would come ashore at a site across Cape Cod Bay and make ready to stay. They would not be going south to Virginia. Bradford afterward described the scene and the prospects: "It was winter, and they that know the winters of the country know them to be sharp and violent. . . . What could they [the Pilgrims] see but a hideous and desolate wilderness . . . ?" They settled in an abandoned Wampanoag Indian cornfield, naming the place Plymouth.

Indians help the Pilgrims. The hardships of that first winter in Plymouth defy description. By springtime half the Pilgrims had died. We can only guess at their anguish as the once-hopeful families and the once-spirited children trudged again and again to the burial ground. Sometimes only a handful of the Pilgrims were up and around. Bradford wrote later that the able-bodied admirably cared for the sick. They "spared no pains, night or day . . . fetched them wood, made them fires, [cooked] their meat, made their beds, washed their loathsome clothes, clothed and unclothed them. . . . "

Still, the Pilgrims met with some good fortune too. They were befriended by Squanto, an Indian who had been kidnapped by an English ship captain a few years earlier. Sold in Spain, Squanto had managed to get to England, and then sailed across the Atlantic several times on English ships. Squanto was introduced to the Pilgrims by Samoset, a Wampanoag who had learned some English from Europeans fishing in American waters. Squanto, it is said, taught the Pilgrims to plant corn by placing seed in the ground with herring as fertilizer.

The Pilgrims celebrate the first Thanksgiving. The Pilgrims who survived the first winter had a chance to leave on the *Mayflower* when it sailed back to England in April, but not a single person did so. The stouthearted men and women of Plymouth

Plymouth, rebuilt today, continues to be a symbol of the faith, hard work, and determination required of all pioneers who sought a better life in America.

worked all spring and summer building houses and tending their crops. By autumn a satisfactory harvest rewarded their labor. They held a Thanksgiving feast that Indian friends attended. It consisted of roasted venison, wild duck, clams, and cornbread.

Progress at Plymouth is slow. Handicapped by poor soil, the Plymouth settlers still had to depend on supplies from home. Trade in furs, nevertheless, helped the colony pay its debts. Whenever the London partners sent a shipload of supplies to Plymouth, the Pilgrims would fill the ships with a valuable cargo of skins for the return voyage.

A shortage of food persisted in Plymouth until about 1623. At that time, land that had been held in common was divided into family farms. With each family knowing it was responsible for its own livelihood, food production began to increase. The London people remained dissatisfied, however, with the return on their investment. In 1626 they sold their interest to the Pilgrims.

Plymouth was never a wealthy or powerful colony. In 1637 its population totaled only 549. Bradford's history allows us to know more of its beginnings, however, than those of any other colony.

The Puritans plan to settle in Massachusetts. While the Pilgrims struggled to farm their unwilling soil, a larger group of Puritans were making plans of their own to leave England. Where the Pilgrims had been mostly poor people, this second wave of colonists consisted of people who had wealth. These people had hoped to "purify" the Anglican Church by remaining within it. When James I died in 1625, however, they became alarmed that they faced a "general calamity." James's successor, Charles I, had declared his intention of crushing Puritan ideas. America loomed as a haven for these people who felt unwelcome in England.

By now, of course, the North American continent was becoming better known. Hundreds of sailors had visited the tiny American settlements or from sea had seen the houses of English people on the Atlantic seaboard. The excitement of what was tak-

John Winthrop led thousands of his fellow Puritans to New England, where they started the Massachusetts Bay Colony in 1630.

ing place in America remained, even if the uncertainty of how to start a colony was disappearing.

The concern of the Puritans in England was relieved when the Massachusetts Bay Company was granted a charter in 1629. The Bay Company's grant lay within the holdings assigned to the Council for New England, but the Council was never able to get the Massachusetts charter annulled.

The Massachusetts Bay Company contained people of various religious opinions, but the Puritans were in control. Their leader was a lawyer named John Winthrop. Heavily in debt, he had found it increasingly difficult to make a living in England when his non-Puritan clients stopped coming to him. A deeply religious man, he said his prayers and sang psalms as he went about the day.

The "Great Migration" begins. In March, 1630, Winthrop led a large Puritan group to North America. His wife, expecting a baby, would come later. He soon wrote her, "Be of good courage, it shall go well with thee and us . . . therefore raise up thy thoughts, and be merry in the Lord."

Winthrop, having studied the experience of the earlier colony-builders, knew that fresh provisions would immediately be required. With that need in mind, he sent the ship *Lyon* back to England with the understanding that it would return as quickly as possible. It returned none too soon, for starvation and disease had begun taking a heavy toll.

Winthrop was at the head of the first large-scale migration in American history. Even as Virginia had to struggle to find colonists, 11 ships brought 1,000 colonists to Massachusetts in the summer of 1630 alone. In the next few years the colony grew at a remarkable rate. By 1641, three hundred vessels had carried 20,000 passengers across the Atlantic.

The settling of Massachusetts has appropriately been called the "Great Migration." Boston became the chief town of the colony, although the neighboring villages of Roxbury, Charlestown, Dorchester, Newtown (later Cambridge), and Watertown also had substantial populations.

Puritan ministers have great power in Massachusetts government. The first settlers in the Massachusetts Bay Colony had been allowed to take their charter with them. This charter enabled them to govern the colony themselves. Nowhere were religion and politics more intertwined. Ministers spoke with authority; their word was enforced as law. Only *freemen* enjoyed the right to hold office and vote for the governor and members of the General Court, as the legislature was called. Freemen were, at first, the stockholders of the Massachusetts Bay Company. Later, all male church members were given freeman status.

Town government gives people more say in government. Those in the colony who did not belong to the Puritan Church were denied the right to vote. Still, the New Jerusalem, as the leaders of Massachusetts regarded their settlement, contributed powerfully to the idea of citizen participation in government. Responding to the ready availability of land and yet wanting to retain control of their expanding settlements, the Puritan leaders established a *township system.* Under this system, the General Court would designate a group of freemen to be owners of a new town. Each town was six miles square and built around a village center where land was set aside as common pastureland for livestock. Nearby, suitable places for the village school and church were chosen. The remaining land was divided up, with lots assigned to each freeman. Some land was unassigned and held for later settlers. Each freeman was also granted a strip of land on the edge of town for cultivation — a way of securing and marking the town's boundaries. Each resident could also obtain wood at the common woodlot.

The affairs of the town were discussed at the *town meeting.* There the men of the town "selected" town officials known as selectmen. These officials were in charge of such governmental functions as organizing the defense of the town when needed. At the town meeting the delegates to the General Court were also chosen. While some townsmen were not allowed to vote, everybody could take part in the meeting. So it was that the free discussion of public issues early became an honored practice in Massachusetts.

Many people who could not vote, nevertheless, were displeased. Some of them sought to overcome their lack of political and religious freedom by moving west. Just as the cultivation of tobacco propelled farmers westward in Virginia, so the quest for greater freedom led people in Massachusetts to push away from the coastal towns.

SECTION REVIEW

1. Vocabulary: *freeman, township system, town meeting.*
2. (a) Why did Puritans in England call for reform of the Anglican Church? (b) Who were the Separatists? (c) Why did they flee to Holland? (d) Why did they later go to America?
3. (a) What was the Mayflower Compact? (b) Why was it drawn up?
4. (a) What hardships did the Pilgrims face at Plymouth? (b) How were the Pilgrims helped by Indians?
5. (a) Why did John Winthrop emigrate to America? (b) What colony did he establish? (c) How was that colony organized and governed? (d) What groups were not allowed to hold office or vote?

3 Other Settlers Start Colonies in New England

For fifty years the Puritan ministers kept strict control of Massachusetts Bay. Men and women of independent spirit, however, sometimes chafed under the tight yoke. A number of them broke away and established colonies in other parts of New England.

Roger Williams flees from Massachusetts. The best-known opponent of the Puritans was a young pastor named Roger Williams. A warm person, Williams became a good friend of John Winthrop. His views, however, soon were out of harmony with those of the ruling ministers. He preached, for instance, that the Anglican Church could not be "purified," that a complete separation from it was needed. He also held the view that Massachusetts land belonged to the In-dians and that the settlers had no right to take it from them without paying. He further questioned the right of government to interfere with any individual's religious views or practices.

In 1635 the Massachusetts authorities, believing Williams's ideas to be dangerous, banished him from the colony. They were willing to allow him to remain throughout the winter if he stopped his unacceptable preaching. Williams would not remain silent, however, and the General Court decided to ship him to England. Before the authorities could act, he fled south to the Narragansett Bay area where Indians took him in and gave him shelter. (His friend Winthrop had apparently steered him toward the Narragansett Indians.) Nearby he founded the village of Providence in 1636. Williams had had no intention of being a colonizer, but friends joined him and he soon found the role thrust upon him.

From Boston and its neighboring communities (see inset map), Massachusetts colonists set out to start other settlements in New England.

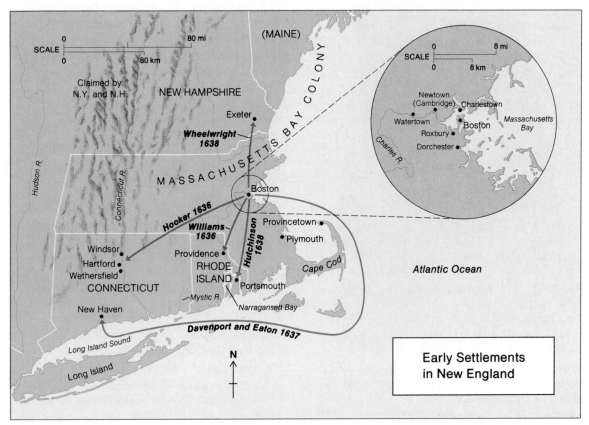

Early Settlements in New England

Under Roger Williams's leadership, settlers in Providence were given liberty of conscience, that is, freedom to worship God in their own fashion. In time this freedom became a glory of the American republic. Williams deserves the credit for being its original advocate in America.

Anne Hutchinson is banished from Massachusetts. Anne Hutchinson also caused the Puritan ministers trouble. Like Williams she made friends easily and gave readily of her help to anybody who needed it. She quickly came to know many people after her arrival in Massachusetts in 1634.

Anne Hutchinson liked to discuss the sermons she had heard and held a weekly

When Anne Hutchinson challenged the authority of the Puritan clergy, she was brought to trial and forced to leave Massachusetts.

meeting in her house for that purpose. She believed that being filled with the Holy Spirit was more important than attending church or heeding the instructions of a minister. The Puritan leaders were upset by these ideas. If such views took hold, the ministers felt, they could not maintain the strict moral behavior of the colony. Anne Hutchinson's popularity was taken as a serious threat to the community, and the Massachusetts leaders quickly took steps to stop her meetings.

Brought to trial, Anne Hutchinson was convicted of "slandering the ministers," and banished from Massachusetts in 1637. Along with some of her followers she went to what is now Rhode Island. There she established the town of Portsmouth.

Rhode Island is started. Portsmouth and other settlements organized by people forced to leave Massachusetts gradually joined together. Then, in 1643 the people of Rhode Island sent Roger Williams to England to obtain a royal charter from King Charles I. He arrived to find that a civil war had broken out in England. Before it was over, the people had beheaded the king, and Parliament was in charge of the nation. In 1644 Parliament granted Williams the charter he sought.

In such a manner Rhode Island came into being. Although its government was modeled on that of Massachusetts, there were important differences. Rhode Island men did not have to be church members in order to vote. Moreover, individual towns could reject laws passed by the legislature.

Pioneers settle Connecticut. Some of the settlers who left Massachusetts were simply looking for better economic opportunity. Particularly alluring was the fertile land of the Connecticut River valley.

By 1635 a number of Massachusetts pioneers, having received a grant from the Council for New England, had started settlements in the Connecticut Valley. In that year the Council sent out John Winthrop, Jr., the eldest son of the Massachusetts founder, to be their governor. The Council wanted to protect the land from encroach-

In search of a freer system of government and more fertile land, Thomas Hooker and his followers set out for the Connecticut Valley in the summer of 1636.

ment by the Dutch who were settling nearby New Amsterdam.

Winthrop was soon joined in Connecticut by the Reverend Thomas Hooker of Newtown, Massachusetts. Hooker and his followers had felt crowded by the steady influx of people into Massachusetts. In 1636 Hooker led his flock of 100 settlers to a new location at Hartford.

In May, 1637, people living in the communities of Hartford, Windsor, and Wethersfield formed a self-governing colony. They established a General Court like that of the Bay Colony. Two years later the General Court drew up a document called the Fundamental Orders. The Fundamental Orders gave all men in Connecticut the right to vote. This document was the first written constitution to create a government on the continent of North America.

If any of the new settlements gave satisfaction to the strict Puritans of Massachusetts Bay, it must have been New Haven. Located on Long Island Sound, New Haven was started by a group of settlers under their minister, John Davenport, and a wealthy London businessman, Theophilus Eaton. Davenport had become distressed over the treatment of Roger Williams and Anne Hutchinson, and had decided to leave Massachusetts. The colony at New Haven was severe in its rules. Only church members could vote and there was no trial by jury for people accused of crimes.

In 1662 John Winthrop, Jr., sailed for England. He intended to persuade Charles II to grant Connecticut all the land from the border of Massachusetts to Long Island Sound — and westward to the Pacific. Successful in his quest, Winthrop returned and was elected governor for eighteen terms in a row. The king also permitted the colony to continue to govern itself under the Fundamental Orders. To the distress of some of its inhabitants, New Haven also became part of Connecticut. Winthrop, beloved figure to the people of his colony, must be regarded as having been as influential as his father in planting New England firmly on the North Atlantic coastline.

New Hampshire and Maine are started. Massachusetts settlers also moved north, starting communities in New Hampshire and Maine. One community was founded in 1638 at Exeter, New Hampshire, by the Reverend John Wheelwright, brother-in-law of Anne Hutchinson. Wheelwright had taken Anne Hutchinson's side in her famous conflict with the Puritan authorities (page 72) and had also been banished from Massachusetts. As towns grew up in New Hampshire, however, their people disagreed so much on religious issues that they could not easily join together. For many years they remained under the influence of Massachusetts Bay and sent representatives to the Massachusetts General Court. Still, they persisted in their desire to be separate from Massachusetts, and in 1679 New Hampshire was made a royal colony by Charles II.

Maine's history was also, in the beginning, a story of relatively weak settlements. Massachusetts claimed the Maine settlements and took control of them one by one during the 1650's. When Massachusetts received a new charter in 1691, Maine became a part of Massachusetts and lost its identity as a separate colony.[1] Maine remained part of Massachusetts until 1820.

Indian wars break out. The civil war that had ended with the beheading of Charles I (page 72) absorbed so much energy and attention in England that the colonies had to fend for themselves. One of the colonists' greatest challenges was how to deal with the Indians. Problems had continually arisen as the English settlements grew. The Indians were frightened and angered by the settlers' encroachments on their territory. The Puritans, for their part, looked on the Indians with scorn.

The Puritans never understood what the growing settlements were doing to Indian culture and self-respect. Indians eagerly sought certain items, particularly iron tools, from the English. Although a few tribes adopted Christianity and were known as "praying Indians," most Native Americans held fast to their own cultures. They steadfastly refused to adopt English religion and English governmental forms.

Although European diseases had weakened most of the Indian tribes of New England, the Pequots were strong and vigorous. They sought to join with the Narragansetts to stem the English advance. As we have seen, however, Roger Williams was a great friend of the Narragansetts. So the Pequots, though powerful, had no allies.

In the summer of 1636, when a trader from Boston was killed, the leaders of Massachusetts put the blame on the Pequots. The Pequots apparently were not guilty, but cruel warfare broke out the next year.

In May, 1637, the English and their Mohegan allies surrounded and surprised a Pequot village on the Mystic River in Connecticut. They practically destroyed the entire Pequot tribe, burning the village and killing hundreds of people. The remaining Pequots were later executed or sold into slavery.

This Indian-language Bible, printed in 1685, was one of the first books published in America.

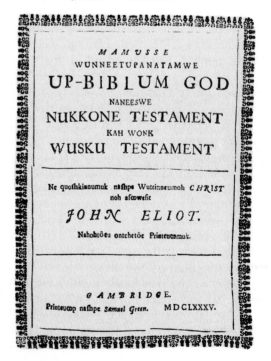

MAMUSSE
WUNNEETUPANATAMWE
UP-BIBLUM GOD
NANEESWE
NUKKONE TESTAMENT
KAH WONK
WUSKU TESTAMENT

Ne quoſhkinnumuk naſhpe Wuttinneumoh *CHRIST* noh aſoowefit

JOHN ELIOT.

Nahohtôeu ontchetôe Printeuenemuk.

CAMBRIDGE.
Printeuꝏp naſhpe *Samuel Green.*   MDCLXXXV.

---

[1]Another provision of the 1691 charter united the Massachusetts Bay Colony and Plymouth under the name of Massachusetts.

A Call for Indian Unity

Miantunnomoh (mee-AHN-tuh-NOH-moh) was a Narragansett Indian who befriended the early English settlers. As more and more Europeans arrived in New England, however, Miantunnomoh became alarmed by what was happening to the land of his people. In 1642 he pleaded for all Indians to unify against the white settlers. Here, he addressed a delegation of Indians from Long Island.

Brothers, we must be one as the English are, or we shall all be destroyed. You know our fathers had plenty of deer and skins and our plains were full of game and turkeys, and our coves and rivers were full of fish. But, brothers, since the Englishmen have seized our country, they have cut down the grass with scythes and the trees with axes. Their cows and horses eat up the grass, and their hogs spoil our beds of clams; and finally we shall starve to death. Therefore, stand not in your own light, I ask you, but resolve to act like men. All the sachems [chiefs] both to the east and the west have joined with us and we resolved

A Narragansett Indian

to fall upon them, at a day appointed, and therefore I come to you secretly, because you can persuade your Indians to do what you will.

In 1675 warfare broke out again. This time the Wampanoag Indians, under their able chief, King Philip, attacked settlements all along the New England frontier. More than a thousand colonists were slain, and twelve towns were destroyed. The English were too numerous, however, and too well armed to be defeated. King Philip was killed in 1676, and a treaty was signed two years later.

When the immediate struggle to survive had ended, the New England colonists felt self-assured in the land they were now calling home. They took to heart what one minister preached on the subject of New Englanders: "God hath sifted a nation, that he might send choice grain into this wilderness." More successfully than either the Spanish or the French, the English believed they had shown that America could be home — a beloved home — to Europeans.

SECTION REVIEW

1. For what reasons did Puritan leaders banish Roger Williams and Anne Hutchinson from Massachusetts Bay?
2. How did the Rhode Island system of government differ from that of Massachusetts Bay?
3. (a) For what reasons was Connecticut settled? (b) What was the significance of the Fundamental Orders of Connecticut? (c) What other New England colonies were started?
4. (a) Why did problems arise between the Indians and the English colonists? (b) What outbreaks of violence resulted?

Chapter 3 Review

Summary

After a difficult beginning, Jamestown became the first permanent English settlement in America. Colonists soon moved inland to clear land for farming after discovering that tobacco could be grown. The widespread cultivation and profitable export of tobacco assured Virginia's success. Indentured servants, and then slaves, were brought to Virginia to work on tobacco plantations. Meanwhile, the Indians of Virginia who resisted seizure of their lands were defeated in battle.

To the north, English colonists landed on the Massachusetts coast in 1620 to start the tiny settlement of Plymouth. This group of Pilgrim colonists came to North America to establish a community where they could practice their religious beliefs. Never wealthy or powerful, Plymouth was soon overshadowed by the fast-growing Massachusetts Bay Colony, settled in 1630 by a large group of Puritans led by John Winthrop.

In Massachusetts Bay, the Puritan ministers had great authority. Participation in government was broadened as the township system, with its town meetings, developed. Yet the power of the colony's religious leaders challenged men and women of independent spirit. Roger Williams and Anne Hutchinson were foremost among those who left Massachusetts Bay to establish communities permitting greater freedom.

Under Roger Williams's leadership, first Providence and then the colony of Rhode Island grew up. Connecticut, to the west and south of Massachusetts Bay, was settled by colonists seeking greater freedom and economic opportunity. To the north, settlements were started in New Hampshire and Maine. As the number of English settlers grew, relations between the colonists and the Indians of the region worsened. Fighting broke out with the Pequots in 1636 and with the Wampanoag Indians in 1675, both times resulting in important victories for the English.

Vocabulary and Important Terms

1. tidewater
2. piedmont
3. fall line
4. House of Burgesses
5. indenture system
6. Council of New England
7. Puritans
8. Separatists
9. Mayflower Compact
10. Massachusetts Bay Company
11. Great Migration
12. freeman
13. General Court
14. township system
15. town meeting
16. selectman
17. Fundamental Orders of Connecticut

Discussion Questions

1. How did John Smith help make it possible for Jamestown to survive and become the first permanent English colony in the Americas?
2. How did the Virginia House of Burgesses influence the development of colonial government in America?
3. (a) How did the indenture system promote colonization in America and provide needed labor? (b) In what ways did the indenture system not work well in America?
4. (a) What attitudes did most English settlers have toward black people and Indians? (b) How did those attitudes affect the treatment received by black people and Indians in the English colonies?
5. (a) Why did the Separatists leave England for Holland and some years later leave Holland for America? (b) Compare the hardships faced by the settlers at Plymouth with those suffered by the first Jamestown colonists.
6. In what way did the experience of earlier colony-builders contribute to the success of the Puritan colony at Massachusetts Bay?
7. (a) By what means did the Puritans of Massachusetts Bay limit both political participation and religious freedom? (b) How did the Puritans contribute to citizen participation in government through their township system?
8. What contributions did the early settlers of Rhode Island make to the concepts of self-government and freedom of religion?
9. Describe how the Fundamental Orders of Connecticut differed from the Massachusetts plan of government?

Relating Past to Present

1. Why did some people move farther west after they had arrived in the early English colonies? For what reasons do Americans move today? Compare the problems faced by Americans on the move today with those of Americans who moved during the period of early colonization.
2. Town meetings were one way in which citizens participated in government in the early New England

colonies. Today there are many more opportunities for citizen participation in political affairs. How is your community governed? What opportunities are there for citizens to participate?

3. How did the cultivation of tobacco play a part in Virginia's early history? Find out if there is any crop or product that is today of similar importance to the economy of your state or community.

Studying Local History

Representative government got its start in the English colonies at Jamestown with the meeting in 1619 of the Virginia House of Burgesses. How did the first settlers in your state govern themselves? What was the first seat of government? Was that seat of government a different town or city from your state's capital today?

Using History Skills

1. *Reading maps.* Look at the map of New England on page 71. (a) What settlements were started in the vicinity of Boston? (b) What settlements were founded by people who left Massachusetts? (c) Why did these people leave Massachusetts and start new communities?

2. *Writing a report.* Roger Williams believed that the land of New England belonged to the Indians and that the English settlers had no right to take it from them. Do research to find out how Williams came to settle on Indian land in Rhode Island. Also find out about other dealings Williams had with the Indians. Include your findings in a report.

3. *Reading source material.* Study Miantunnomoh's address on page 75. (a) What is the main idea of the speech? (b) Which sentence contains the main idea? (c) What arguments support the main idea?

4. *Writing a summary.* A summary is a restatement, in brief form, of the main ideas of a speech or piece of writing. Reread Section 3 of this chapter, "Other Settlers Start Colonies in New England," and write a short summary of the reasons given for the settlement of Rhode Island, Connecticut, New Hampshire, and Maine. You will find the headings helpful as clues.

WORLD SCENE

Expansion of Empire

At the same time that England was establishing colonies in America, Europeans were starting footholds on other continents as well.

The Dutch in southern Africa. In the 1600's the Dutch East India Company was shipping goods to Europe from India and East Asia. The Dutch needed a supply base where their vessels could replenish food and water supplies and make repairs. They found the harbor at the Cape of Good Hope on the southern tip of Africa an ideal place for this need. The Company set up a supply station there in 1652, calling it Cape Town.

Dutch settlers, attracted by southern Africa's temperate climate, flocked to the area and started permanent settlements. To entice Dutch people to Cape Town, the Company provided free passage from Europe and fertile farmland. The colony prospered and for more than a century it was part of the Dutch Empire.

The English in India. While the Dutch East India Company was getting started, an English company with a similar name was seeking trading posts in India. The Mogul emperor Jahangir gave the English company permission in 1608 to set up a commercial base at the Indian port of Surat. By 1647 the East India Company had expanded its operations to include 27 such posts, located primarily along the coast. Cities began to grow up around these places, among them Bombay, Madras, and Calcutta.

From their posts the East India Company courted Indian princes to gain trading rights. The English were competing with Dutch and French traders also participating in the rich commerce in textiles, jewels, and tea. Competition among the Europeans made the traditional rivalry among the Indian rulers keener than ever. As a result, Company officials often acted like government authorities. By the end of the 1600's the Company was negotiating treaties, acquiring territory, and even fighting wars. Although the Company had extensive political power, it did not represent the British government. Its only interests were trade and profit. In pursuit of those interests, however, the Company eventually involved Britain deeply in Indian life.

A Variety of English Colonies

1600 – 1775

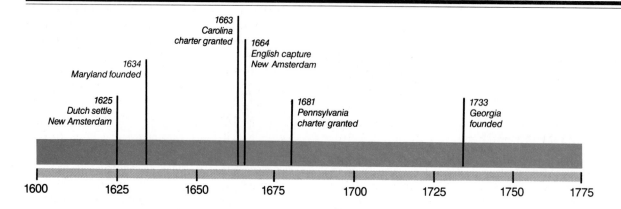

1663
Carolina
charter granted

1664
English capture
New Amsterdam

1634
Maryland founded

1625
Dutch settle
New Amsterdam

1681
Pennsylvania
charter granted

1733
Georgia
founded

1600   1625   1650   1675   1700   1725   1750   1775

CHAPTER OUTLINE

1. More colonies are settled in the South.

2. European rivalry leads to settlement of the Middle Colonies.

3. Colonial patterns of living and working take shape.

Nearly 130 years after the founding of the English colony at Jamestown, the colony of Georgia was established. This completed a continuous arc of thirteen English colonies that stretched along the Atlantic coast from northern New England to Spanish Florida. During this period a variety of personal and religious motivations, as well as changing political realities in England itself, prompted thousands of people to brave the risky ocean voyage and settle in the new land.

Although distinct in climate, geography, and economic organization, the thirteen colonies developed a markedly American outlook. More than just a land of immigrants, the colonies were populated by a new breed of British subject. Tied to England by language, custom, and government, the American colonists occupied a unique position which demanded new considerations.

As the resources of North America and the energy of its inhabitants became evident, the importance of the thirteen colonies was gradually understood by the English Parliament and monarch. How England chose to deal with its overseas possessions would set the tone for the development of the American colonies and would determine the path of future colonial relations.

1 More Colonies Are Settled in the South

In the years that followed the establishment of Jamestown, other colonies were started along the southern Atlantic coast. These colonies drew heavily on the experience of the Virginians. While the origins of each were unique, all the Southern Colonies came to resemble one another in the ways their people lived and worked.

MARYLAND

Maryland is the first proprietary colony. The guiding hand in founding Maryland was Sir George Calvert, a friend of King James I. For a number of years Calvert had served at the royal court. When he announced in 1625 that he had become a Roman Catholic, however, he was forced to resign his position. Still, he and the king remained on good terms. The king gave him the title of Baron of Baltimore, and he was called Lord Baltimore.

Lord Baltimore dreamed of carving out a great landed estate for himself in America. He hoped also to create a refuge for Catholics, who were discriminated against by English laws. With those ends in mind, he helped his son Cecilius obtain a grant on the upper reaches of Chesapeake Bay from Charles I, who became king in 1625. Lord Baltimore named his colony Maryland, in honor of the queen, Henrietta Maria.

The first settlers set out for Maryland in 1633 aboard ships called the *Ark* and the *Dove.* Among the settlers, Catholic gentlemen-adventurers were in the minority. The newcomers were mostly Protestant laborers and craftworkers. The good reports now reaching England from the Virginians and the Pilgrims had made it comparatively easy to get people to try their luck in Maryland.

Meanwhile, Cecilius, second Lord Baltimore, remained at home. There he was known as Lord Proprietor of Maryland, because he was the *proprietor,* or owner, of the colony. Maryland, controlled by one man with privileges from the king, was known as a ***proprietary colony.***

Cecilius Calvert had named his brother, Leonard, governor of Maryland. The goal was to create a family-controlled domain on which the Calverts would have the power to appoint and dismiss officials and receive all profits from the land. The Calverts were not yet familiar enough with America to imagine how completely their ambitious plans would be changed.

Named after the founder of Maryland, Baltimore looked like this in 1752. The people made a living by fishing and by shipping grain and tobacco to England.

Maryland offers religious toleration. Leonard Calvert and his party reached the Potomac River in March, 1634, landing on a tiny island they called St. Clements. There Father Andrew White celebrated the first Catholic mass in English-speaking America.

The colonists dug in at a settlement they named St. Marys. Everybody was delighted with the location, but troubles soon developed. Virginians living nearby claimed that the Marylanders were occupying their land. Moreover, conflicts between Protestants and Catholics led to the establishment of a Protestant town, called Annapolis. The constant bickering between the two groups led to the passage in 1649 of the Toleration Act. This important document guaranteed religious freedom to all Christians living in the colony.

The Calverts had laid out Maryland in huge estates, each of which was run by relatives and friends. From these specially created "lords of the manors" the Calverts named a council to advise them on running their colony. Within only fifteen years, however, this assembly had in fact begun to make the laws of Maryland.

During the English Civil War (page 72), Lord Baltimore lost his colony, but after the monarchy was restored in 1660, he was put back in control. Sadly, in spite of the Toleration Act, many Protestants resented having a Roman Catholic as head of the colony. In 1689 a group of Protestants took over Maryland. The Baltimores were allowed to keep only their own property. The Church of England soon became the established church of the colony, and the capital was placed at Annapolis. When the fifth Lord Baltimore himself became a convert to the Church of England, the doubts about the family's loyalty began to fade and in 1715 the colony was restored to the family's proprietorship.

THE CAROLINAS

Proprietors settle Carolina. Throughout the 1600's, as they expanded their reach into America, the English started colonies in the Caribbean to protect their sea lanes and to keep a watchful eye on the Spanish.

To strengthen English control along the Atlantic seaboard, Charles II in 1663 granted to eight of his favorites the huge area between Virginia and Florida. In honor of the king they named the region "Carolina," *Carolus* being the Latin word for Charles.

One of the newly named proprietors of Carolina had recently returned from Barbados, in the Caribbean, where he had been a planter. Another had been governor of Virginia. Adventurous Englishmen of that time moved readily from one part of the empire to another.

The grant to the proprietors of South Carolina gave them absolute control over their territory. They were granted power, for instance, to create titles of nobility. They were allowed, moreover, to extend freedom of religion even to those people who did not accept the Church of England. Nevertheless, their aim, specifically stated, was to have a government free of the dangers of "a numerous democracy."

Carolina never became unified politically or economically. Swamps and thick forests, as well as the flow of rivers from west to east, prevented the parts of the colony from feeling connected to one another. By the time the proprietors first arrived, a fair number of discontented Virginians had been living for some years along the Chowan River in what is now North Carolina. Another group of people, from New England, had established themselves along Cape Fear. (Carolina was the only southern colony settled at the start by English men and women who came from other colonies instead of directly from Europe.)

The largest community of Carolina was Charles Town (later called Charleston), which became the capital after 1680. Magnificently situated, it proved in time to be the most important southern port on the Atlantic coast.

By 1700 rice was being cultivated in Carolina. Introduced into the colony by a New England sea captain who brought the seed from Madagascar, rice grew well in the humid Carolina climate. In addition to rice, pitch and tar from the colony's pine forests were shipped from Charles Town's excellent harbor.

Life in Colonial South Carolina

Eliza Lucas and her family settled in Charles Town, South Carolina, in 1739 when she was sixteen years old. Her family soon started a plantation, which Eliza visited often and assisted in supervising. In letters to friends and family, Eliza described her life in South Carolina.

I will set down a short description of the world I now inhabit. South Carolina is a large and extensive country near the sea. Most of the settled part of it is very flat — the soil near Charles Town is sandy, but inland it becomes clay and swampy. It abounds with fine navigable rivers and great quantities of fine timber. About a hundred and fifty miles from Charles Town, the country becomes very hilly. The soil is fertile and there are very few European or American fruits or grains which do not grow here. The staple crop is rice and it is the only thing exported to Europe. Beef, pork, and lumber are sent to the West Indies.

The city of Charles Town is a neat pretty place with streets and houses regularly built. St. Phillips church in Charles Town is a very elegant one, and much frequented. There are several more places of public worship in this town, and most of the people are of a religious turn of mind.

In general I rise at five o'clock in the morning, read until seven, then take a walk in the garden or field, see that the servants are at work, then have breakfast. The first hour after breakfast is spent at my music, the next in recalling something I have

A southern plantation

learned, such as French or shorthand. After that I devote time to our little sister Polly and two black girls I am now teaching to read. If I have the permission of my father, I intend to be the school mistress for the rest of the black children.

By the way, I have planted a large fig orchard and hope to export the dried fruit. I calculated my expenses and intend to make a tidy profit. I find that I have a good mind for business and love raising vegetables and fruits.

North and South Carolina break apart. Gradually, differences grew up between the northern and southern parts of Carolina. For a while they were governed separately. Then, beginning in 1691, they had a single governor. Finally, in 1712 they broke apart — this time for good. North Carolina made its living from tobacco-raising and from the lumber and naval stores it produced. South Carolina, heavily dependent upon slaves, cultivated rice in its lowlands. In 1729 both North Carolina and South Carolina became colonies and were ruled directly by the Crown.

GEORGIA

Georgia is founded by James Oglethorpe. The work of defending the English colonies against the Spanish fell to Georgia, the last colony to be established. Georgia lay between the Savannah and Altamaha rivers, on land that the Carolina proprietors had unsuccessfully tried to colonize.

The remarkable genius who settled Georgia was James Oglethorpe. As a member of Parliament, Oglethorpe had served on a committee investigating conditions in England's debtor prisons. Appalled by what he learned, he decided to establish a colony where such unfortunate prisoners could start their lives afresh. In June, 1732, a group of 21 trustees under Oglethorpe's leadership received a charter for this purpose. The colony was this time called Georgia, in honor of King George II.

A committee of trustees was named to govern Georgia for its first 21 years, after which the Crown would take over the colony. Parliament donated a large sum of money to help assure the success of the undertaking. This was the first time the English government had made an outright gift to help establish a colony. Meanwhile, the project was well advertised. Ministers in England even spoke of it in their sermons. Oglethorpe sought out deserving poor people, both in and out of prison. He also made his plans known to persecuted Protestants in various Catholic countries of Europe.

At last, the ship *Anne* sailed for Georgia late in 1732, bearing more than 120 people. In January, 1733, it put in briefly at Charles Town, where Carolinians welcomed the newcomers and cheered them on. Restocked with food, the *Anne* set forth again, landing the next month on the Savannah River. There the passengers started to build the town of Savannah, laying it out with great care.

Persecuted Europeans move to Georgia. The colony grew rapidly. Religious wars were being fought in Europe, and the knowledge that America was a refuge gave reassurance to thousands of people who had courage and ambition. At Ebenezer a settlement was made by Lutherans from Salzburg, a town in the Austrian Alps. In the first summer of Georgia's existence some forty Portuguese Jews arrived. They were at first denied admission because the trustees had instructions to keep out Jews and Catholics. Oglethorpe, however, insisted that the newcomers remain. The group included a medical doctor, whose services were quickly in demand. Before long, a sprinkling of Catholics were also living in the colony.

When James Oglethorpe returned to England in 1734, he took with him a group of Indians who had sold him land. This painting shows a meeting between the Indians and English investors in Georgia.

Georgia continued for some time to attract idealists and reformers. Among them were John Wesley, later the founder of the Methodist Church, and his brother Charles, who was a secretary to Oglethorpe. Oglethorpe's reports on Georgia's excellent progress also attracted a group of Scottish highlanders. After landing in the colony, they founded the town of New Inverness.

The experiment fails to meet expectations. Despite the trustees' imaginative plans, Georgia failed to carry out its stated aims. One problem the Georgians faced was that the land did not prove as fertile as anticipated. Also, the proprietors of the colony forbade the introduction of black slaves. As a result, some settlers moved to South Carolina, where slavery had become widespread. The trustees, however, stuck to their ideas and ruled with an iron hand. Furthermore, they made no arrangement for representative government.

In 1749 slavery was finally permitted in Georgia, and restrictions that earlier had been placed on importing rum were lifted. By then Georgians had also been at war with the Spanish. Oglethorpe had led a joint expedition of Georgians and South Carolinians in a siege of St. Augustine that proved to be unsuccessful. In the summer of 1742, Oglethorpe managed to defeat a Spanish effort to destroy Georgia.

Militarily Georgia was a success; financially it was a disappointment. When repeated attempts to raise silkworms and citrus fruits failed, the proprietors became discouraged. They gave up their rights to Georgia in 1751, and shortly afterward it became a royal colony.

SECTION REVIEW

1. Vocabulary: *proprietor, proprietary colony.*
2. (a) What were Lord Baltimore's aims in founding Maryland? (b) What difficulties in the colony led to passage of the Toleration Act?
3. (a) How was Carolina settled? (b) Why did it finally become two separate colonies?
4. (a) Why did James Oglethorpe decide to establish Georgia? (b) In what ways did Georgia fail to carry out Oglethorpe's aims?

2 European Rivalry Leads to Settlement of the Middle Colonies

During the 1600's Spain and France were not England's only rivals in starting colonies. An important contest took place between England and Holland as well.

NEW YORK AND NEW JERSEY

Hudson establishes a Dutch claim to America. The Dutch East India Company had been organized in 1602 to win for Holland a share of the trade with Asia. Like other Europeans, the Dutch were eager to find a shorter passage to the East. The Company hired, therefore, an experienced English navigator, Henry Hudson, to sail on a mission of discovery. Hudson had already spent time seeking for England a route to the East Indies in the frozen reaches of the North.

In 1609, sailing in a small Dutch ship, the *Half Moon,* Hudson again headed northeast of Europe. Making no progress because of the wind and ice, he turned west instead and crossed the Atlantic. He at last reached North America and, after sailing along the Atlantic coast, came upon the magnificent river that now bears his name. Thinking he had finally found the Northwest Passage, he followed the river to the present site of Albany, New York.

The Indians Hudson encountered were friendly. They eagerly exchanged beaver, otter, and mink pelts for metal tools. Still, Hudson was disappointed when he realized that the river was clearly not a passage to Asia. Before setting sail for home, he headed southward and entered Chesapeake Bay. He may well have glimpsed the struggling band of English settlers at Jamestown.

Stopping in England on his return, Hudson was arrested for having sailed under a foreign flag. His report, nevertheless, reached his Dutch employers. It told of friendly Indians in a region rich with furs. The Dutch eagerly claimed the land along the Hudson River. Within five years they were sailing that river with valuable cargoes.

The Dutch found New Netherland. By 1614 Dutch trading establishments had been started on Manhattan Island. In addition to creating markets for their manufactured goods, the Dutch hoped to win converts to Protestantism. Meanwhile, government officials were eager to set up posts in America from which to harass Spanish treasure ships.[1]

To consolidate their toehold and encourage colonization, the Dutch authorities granted a charter in 1621 to an organization called the Dutch West India Company. They gave it a monopoly of trade on the eastern coast of America and the western coast of Africa.

The Company named its new American colony New Netherland and in 1624 sent settlers not only to Manhattan but also to Fort Orange, near present-day Albany. Still other settlers were dropped off at a site on the Delaware River. There they built Fort Nassau, opposite the location of present-day Philadelphia.

In 1625, a group of Dutch settlers began work on a fort on the southern tip of Manhattan Island. Called Fort Amsterdam and constructed of logs, it guarded forty houses. Together the houses formed a town known as New Amsterdam, later the capital of New Netherland.

Population grows slowly. The Dutch settlements were handicapped by the prosperity of Holland itself. Most Dutch people were too pleased with conditions at home to venture to America in quest of improvement. Besides, there were only two million people in Holland, and many Dutch adventurers were already located far from home on four continents.

The strict policies of the Dutch West India Company also discouraged settlement in New Netherland. All settlers became employees of the Company and had to agree to live for six years on land assigned to them. They were expected to raise crops designated by the Company's representatives. In addition, the Company required that settlers belong to the Dutch Reformed Church.

One of the first directors of the Company was a shrewd, capable man named Peter Minuit. He maintained generally good relations with the Indians, and he is best remembered for having "purchased" Manhattan Island for about $24 worth of trinkets. Minuit also established cordial relations with the Pilgrim colony at Plymouth. Still, he made enemies among his own people and in 1631 was recalled to Holland to answer charges of mismanagement.

The patroon system is set up. To try to stimulate immigration to America, Company officials worked out a plan similar to the one the French were trying in Canada. The Dutch had the same lack of success. Under their system, a large estate was given to an appointee called a patroon, who was required to persuade fifty adults to settle on his land within four years. Each patroonship extended approximately sixteen miles along one bank, or eight miles along each bank, of a navigable river. It would also reach as far inland as the owner could establish control. The settlers would, in feudal manner, pay dues to their patroon and agree to use his mill for grinding their flour. The patroon would supply the required tools, animals, and buildings.

Just five patroonships were set up. The only successful one was called Rensselaerswyck, owned by Kiliaen Van Rensselaer, a director of the Company, who was a wealthy diamond and pearl merchant. His estate, in the vicinity of present-day Albany, was enlarged by purchases from Indians so that eventually it covered most of three present-day counties of New York. Van Rensselaer never came to America. He ruled through an agent, like an absentee monarch. Company ships had to pay a tariff when they passed through his domain. They even had to salute his personal flag! Such arrangements, however, could not produce a satisfactory way of life in America. Even when the Dutch modified the patroon system in 1640 to allow for the establishment

---

[1]The Dutch, most of whom were Protestant, had declared their independence from Spain in 1581.

of smaller estates, not many people left Holland to move to America.

The real rulers of New Amsterdam were the burghers, or town dwellers, whose warehouses on Manhattan Island bulged with tobacco from Virginia, furs from nearby forests, and choice goods from home. For a long time the burghers tried to recapture the look of the Dutch landscape, even building windmills. They constructed their houses of brick and tile, as in Holland.

Dutch leadership is weak. The political leaders of New Netherland were arrogant and unimaginative. The third governor, William Kieft, almost brought the colony to a disastrous end. He failed dismally in his relations with the Algonquin Indians of the Hudson Valley. These Native Americans had sought refuge among the Dutch during a dispute with their enemies, the Mohawk. Kieft treacherously gave orders to attack and slaughter the embattled, frightened Indians. The reprisal of the Algonquins against the Dutch was ferocious. Practically all the settlers south of Fort Orange had to seek refuge in New Amsterdam. They barricaded themselves behind a stockade, or wall, that Kieft had ordered built along the southern tip of Manhattan Island. The place where that stockade once stood is now Wall Street, the world's leading financial center.

The Dutch take over New Sweden. If the Dutch were on bad terms with their Indian neighbors, they also were on the outs with their fellow Europeans in America. One such group had come from Sweden.

In 1638 an expedition sent out from Sweden landed at Delaware Bay, a region the Dutch had already claimed. By luck the Swedes had obtained the services of Peter Minuit. They benefited greatly from his wide experience in North America.

The Swedes built Fort Christina on the site of what is now Wilmington, Delaware. The settlement was named for Christina, the twelve-year-old queen of Sweden. Christina's father, Gustavus Adolphus, hoped that the American settlement would prove to be the "jewel" of his kingdom. There were not more than 400 people in New Sweden, however, when the aggressive Dutch leader Peter Stuyvesant (STY-vuh-sant) conquered the colony in 1655 and attached it to New Netherland.

Although the Swedish colony was not a success, a permanent legacy of New Sweden is the log cabin. This type of dwelling, which originated in northern Europe, became the ideal frontier home and later came into general use on the fringes of the American forest. When, well into the nineteenth century, Daniel Webster, the Massachusetts senator, apologized to an audience for not having been born in a log cabin, he was revealing how important it had become as a symbol of American life.

Tension between Holland and England grows. By the beginning of the 1660's New Amsterdam was a thriving port of 2,500 people. (Of all the towns on the Atlantic seaboard only Boston was larger.) New Amsterdam's prosperity attracted the envy of English merchants and settlers. Already the global rivalry between England and Holland was reflected in America.

The Dutch had taken advantage of the English Civil War (1642–1649) to build up their trade. Dutch ships entered English colonial ports and sold hardware, dry goods, and spirits at cheap prices. They received American tobacco in exchange. The prosperity of Holland reached new heights.

The English resented the Dutch behavior. In retaliation, Parliament passed the so-called Navigation Act of 1651. The measure was designed to stop the Dutch from carrying on trade between England and other countries. It provided that goods from Asia, Africa, or America might enter England or its colonies only if they were shipped in English vessels. Products from Europe might enter English or colonial ports in foreign ships only if the vessels bore the flags of the countries in which the goods were made or grown. As an example of how this arrangement worked, the Portuguese and the Spanish, who had no merchant vessels, were now forced to transport their wine and olives to English ports on English ships. They were no longer permitted to use Dutch ships.

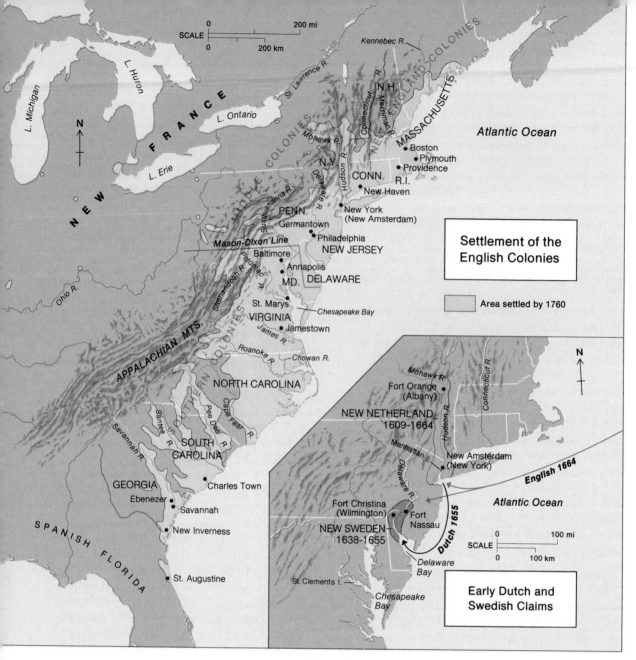

The thirteen English colonies stretched along the Atlantic coast. Early settlements were near the ocean, and inland areas were largely unknown to the settlers.

The English take New Amsterdam. Angry feelings between England and Holland in Europe finally led to the expulsion of the Dutch from North America. The English were helped in this endeavor by dissatisfaction in New Netherland with Peter Stuyvesant, governor of the colony after 1647.

Only 37 years old when he came to New Netherland, Peter Stuyvesant had been wounded while fighting the Portuguese in the West Indies. He wore an artificial leg decorated with silver bands and nails, and so was known as "Old Silver Nails." The burghers found him a humorless, hot-tempered tyrant. He warned that if anyone protested his iron-handed rulings, "I will make him a foot shorter, send the pieces to Holland and let him appeal in that way."

In 1664, the showdown between the English and the Dutch came to a head. England sent four frigates into New Amsterdam harbor and demanded the colony's surrender. Stuyvesant made frenzied attempts to prevent an attack. When the English commander ordered him to surrender, Stuyvesant refused, screaming, "I'd rather be carried a corpse to my grave!" He had no support from his people, however, whom he had so often offended. Moreover, the Dutch had practically no ammunition. Stuyvesant surrendered without firing a shot. The English renamed the colony New York in honor of the Duke of York whose brother, King Charles II, had made him proprietor of the former Dutch possession.

New Jersey is founded. New Netherland had included the region between Delaware Bay and the Atlantic that became known as New Jersey. In 1664 the Duke of York granted this tract to Lord Berkeley and Sir George Carteret. (These men were also proprietors of the Carolinas.) The tract was already inhabited by Swedish, Dutch, English, and Finnish people. Still, it was thinly settled, and the proprietors announced that they would welcome newcomers. To encourage settlement, they promised freedom of religion and representative government. New Jersey was soon drawing Puritans from New England and immigrants from Scotland and Northern Ireland.

PENNSYLVANIA

William Penn develops strong religious views. Pennsylvania had the benefit of the experience accumulated by American settlers in the previous three quarters of a century. The man who started the colony was William Penn, the son of an admiral who was a close friend of King Charles II. Young Penn infuriated his father when, in his early twenties, he changed the direction of his life and became a Quaker, a member of the Society of Friends. His outraged father threw him out of the family house.

The Society of Friends had grown up in seventeenth-century England under the leadership of George Fox. The Quakers went further than any other religious group in rejecting the doctrines of the Church of England. They believed that people did not require any ceremony or minister to be in touch with God. A person need only be guided by his or her "inner light."

The Quakers preached in the streets, something unheard-of in those days. The most extreme of the leaders trembled, or "quaked," when they offered their message. The devoutness of the Quakers often astonished their fellow-citizens. Many suffered punishment at the whipping-post and in jail, and were even willing to die for their cause. They steadfastly refused to pay taxes to the king or to the Church of England. As a result, English jails were filled with Quakers. Even William Penn had been imprisoned.

The Quakers also preached the equality of individuals — and tried to practice that belief. They would not remove their hats in the presence of "superiors." They believed, furthermore, that men and women were equal and that it was wrong to own slaves. They used *thee* and *thou* in speaking, words usually employed only in addressing friends, children, and social inferiors.

The king repays a debt. King Charles did not like Quakers, but he had good relations with the Penn family. At the time that Admiral Penn died, Charles owed him many thousands of pounds. In 1681 the king paid off his debt to the son in the form of a huge grant of land in America. The land was named Pennsylvania ("Penn's woods"), in honor of Admiral Penn. The next year the Duke of York added to the grant the territory known as Delaware. (Delaware was organized as a separate colony in 1704, but remained under the control of the Penn family until the American colonies won independence.) Unfortunately Pennsylvania's southern border was not clearly drawn, and for many years the colony quarreled with Maryland over conflicting land claims. The dispute was not settled until the 1760's when surveyors named Mason and Dixon drew a precise boundary between Pennsylvania and Maryland. The Mason-Dixon Line lives in history as the dividing marker between the American North and South.

Penn makes plans for his "Holy Experiment." Penn quickly set about making real his dream of building a refuge in America for Quakers. He wrote a Frame of Government to guide his "Holy Experiment." In it he stated that "any government is free to the people under it where the laws rule and the people are a party to those laws." Under the Frame of Government the governor would be assisted by a council to be elected by freeholders, that is, by property owners. The freeholders would also elect an assembly. Meeting in 1682 for the first time, the assembly passed what is now known as the Great Law. It gave all Christians in the colony full freedom of worship.

Penn also made careful plans for the chief town of the colony — Philadelphia — the "city of brotherly love." Streets were laid out in an orderly checkerboard pattern. Particularly handsome trees were left standing. The city hall was placed at the city's geographical center. Penn's attention to detail reflected the growing interest in England in improving urban living.

Indian relations are based on mutual respect. In his relations with the Indians Penn also broke original ground. Even before he arrived in America, he wrote the following letter to the Delaware Indians: "The King of the country where I live, hath given me a great province therein, but I desire to enjoy it with your love and consent, that we may always live together as neighbors and friends. . . . " Penn made up his mind to try to learn the Delaware language so that in dealing with the Indians he would not need an interpreter. For the first time an English colony's official policy was to treat Indians as human beings.

There is a story that Penn and the Indians drew up "a great treaty" under an elm tree in Philadelphia in which the parties pledged to respect each other. Even if all the details cannot be proved, the story reflects the excellent relations the Quakers and Indians sought to have. Sadly, along with the tools, blankets, kettles, and mirrors that Penn brought to America, he also included guns, ammunition, and alcohol. He could not, apparently, refuse to provide the Indians with these destructive goods that they by now had learned to want.

Pennsylvania becomes a prosperous colony. Penn remained in Pennsylvania for only 22 months on his first visit. Still, he accomplished much in setting the colony on the road to success. Within ten years Philadel-

Shortly after he arrived in Pennsylvania, William Penn made a treaty of friendship with the Indians of the region. According to legend, Penn and Tamenend, chief of the Delaware Indians, exchanged gifts under the elm tree shown below.

The Thirteen Colonies

Colony	Original Charter	Date of Charter	First Settlement
Virginia	joint-stock	1606	Jamestown 1607
New Hampshire	proprietary	1622	Portsmouth 1623
Massachusetts	joint-stock	1629	Plymouth 1620
Maryland	proprietary	1632	St. Marys 1634
Rhode Island	proprietary	1644	Providence 1636
Connecticut	proprietary	1662	Hartford 1636
North Carolina	proprietary	1663	Albemarle Sound 1650
South Carolina	proprietary	1663	Charles Town 1670
New York	proprietary	1664	New York (New Amsterdam) 1625
New Jersey	proprietary	1664	Fort Nassau 1623
Pennsylvania	proprietary	1681	Philadelphia 1682
Delaware	proprietary	1682	Wilmington (Fort Christina) 1638
Georgia	proprietary[1]	1732	Savannah 1733

[1]Administered by group of trustees

phia could count a population of 4,000. The city was already larger than New York. Because the Quakers came well-prepared and because they received help from the Dutch and the Swedes nearby, they never had to endure a "starving time." Moreover, Pennsylvania was practically untouched by the Indian wars that other English colonies had experienced.

Pennsylvania profited from its central location on the Atlantic seaboard. Many of the lanes of commerce flowed in all directions through Philadelphia. The colony also benefited from Penn's persuasive advertis-

ing in Europe. Many non-English groups came to Pennsylvania, drawn by the attractions of prosperity and religious liberty.

Among the arrivals were eighty German Quakers from Frankfurt, Germany, who came with their pastor, Francis Daniel Pastorius, aboard the *America*. Pastorius called the vessel his "Noah's Ark." In 1683 Pastorius founded Germantown, a short distance from Philadelphia. In the first part of the eighteenth century a second wave of Germans arrived. The German influence in Pennsylvania was so strong that for many years the Pennsylvania legislature published its record of proceedings in the German language as well as in English.

Pennsylvania attracted other non-English families, including people from Wales who settled west of Philadelphia. There were also large numbers of Scotch Presbyterians who had earlier moved from Scotland to Ireland. Known as Scotch-Irish, they quickly earned a reputation in western Pennsylvania as imaginative and tough frontierfolk.

SECTION REVIEW

1. (a) Where did the Dutch claim land in North America? (b) What was the basis of their claim?
2. (a) Why did the population of New Netherland grow slowly? (b) What did Dutch officials do to encourage immigration to America? (c) How successful were they?
3. What steps led to the English takeover of New Netherland?
4. (a) Why did William Penn establish Pennsylvania? (b) In what ways did Pennsylvania prove to be a successful colony?

3 Colonial Patterns of Living and Working Take Shape

Once they were well dug in, most of the English colonies grew very fast. In 1641 there were 50,000 settlers in English America. By 1700, the colonial population was nearly 275,000. Sixty years later that figure had grown to more than 2,000,000.

SYSTEMS OF LABOR

The colonies experience a shortage of workers. Throughout the colonial period the shortage of labor persisted. Because there were never enough hands to do everything, wages were higher than in Europe. Skilled workers who were drawn to the colonies by the prospect of high wages found, however, that they could also buy land cheaply. Many of them left their craft and took up farming. The percentage of people who owned their own land was far greater in America than in England.

Colonial officials tried to ease the combined impact of high pay and shortage of workers by setting wages. There was no common arrangement among the colonies, however, on this matter. It was not unusual for workers to move from one colony to another to improve their lot. As a result, the fixing of wages and prices ended by the close of the eighteenth century.

The apprentice system is widespread. Until the end of the eighteenth century, much labor was provided by *apprentices.* Apprenticing was used by many families to ensure that their children learned a trade and by communities that needed help in caring for orphans. A parent or guardian would arrange for a child to work for a skilled person for a period of from four to seven years. Apprenticeships usually ended at age 21 for boys and 18 for girls.

Apprentices lived in the homes of skilled workers. There they learned a trade and received a rudimentary education. One apprentice agreement pledged to teach a girl "house-wifery, knitting, spinning, sewing, and such like exercises as may be fitting and becoming her sex." Apprentices were expected to be willing, obedient, and respectful. They were also taught that work was ennobling and idleness sinful. Despite the usefulness of the apprentice system, there were many examples of young people running away.

Indentured servants ease the labor shortage. As you have read (page 64), thousands upon thousands of adults came across the Atlantic as indentured servants pledged to redeem by their labor the cost of their passage. The agent who signed up these people sold their indentures to a ship's captain. The captain often imprisoned the emigrants aboard his vessel until sailing time in order to protect his investment. When the ship arrived in America, the captain resold the indentures he held on his passengers to eager would-be employers waiting on the wharf.

Parliament authorized that about 50,000 convicts be sent to America as indentured servants. Most of them went to Virginia and Maryland. Despite the angry protests of some colonial governments, the convicts were quickly snapped up by labor-hungry farmers, particularly on the frontier. Some convicts, like Anthony Lamb, remade themselves in America. Sentenced to labor in Virginia in 1724 for theft, Lamb later made mathematical instruments in Philadelphia. His son John became a leading American Patriot, reaching the rank of general in the Continental Army.

The demand for slaves increases. Another response to the labor shortage was the importation of African slaves. By the 1660's slavery was well-established in Virginia and Maryland and was spreading to the other colonies. Black children now inherited the condition of their mothers: a child, in other words, would be free or slave according to whether the mother had been free or slave.

Slave trading itself mocked the high ideals on which so many of the colonies had been founded. An eyewitness described what life aboard a slave ship was like: "The sense of misery and suffocation was so terrible in the 'tween-decks — where the height sometimes was only eighteen inches — that the unfortunate slaves could not turn round. In their frenzy some killed others in the hope of procuring more room to breathe." For the suffering slaves the torment was often made worse by the fact that they came from different parts of Africa. Thrown together for the trip across the Atlantic, they could not even communicate with one another.

Some Africans tried to escape their misery by starving themselves to death aboard the ships. Others jumped overboard. Because the death rate on the Atlantic crossing was high and so many bodies were thrown overboard, sharks, it was said, followed every slave ship.

Those Africans who survived the Atlantic crossing were quickly taken in hand and taught the tasks they would have to perform in America. Accustomed to agricultural work in Africa, they became indispensable to the colonial economy. Still, they soon found out that while America was a land of opportunity for white people, for blacks it meant giving up familiar ways of life to face a future without hope.

Most slaves in the colonies, like this son of a Mendi chief, came from the western coast of Africa.

THE COLONIAL COMMUNITY

Living conditions vary. People throughout the colonies had many things in common, but there were also important differences in ways of living. Life in the Southern Colonies, for instance, differed notably from life in the North. First of all, many southern farmers raised such cash crops as tobacco, indigo, and rice to provide a source of income. Most New Englanders, on the other hand, were subsistence farmers, raising only what they required for their own families or for local consumption. Second, the South relied heavily on indentured servants and slaves to work the fields. Third, some southern plantations were hundreds, even thousands, of acres in size. "King" Robert Carter, a planter in Virginia, owned a plantation that covered 333,000 acres. Most farms in New England were small enough to be run by a single family.

Planters and merchants live comfortably. Throughout the English colonies, people of wealth lived well. Some large southern landholders lived like European nobles. William Fitzhugh, who arrived in Virginia in 1670, was able a few years later to entertain guests with a violinist and an acrobat. Rich people like Fitzhugh and Carter acquired

When Martha Custis married George Washington in 1759, she was one of the wealthiest women in Virginia. In this view of the wedding ceremony we see the handsome young couple surrounded by friends and family.

the kinds of possessions that rich Europeans enjoyed. They used pewter plates and cups, and on festive occasions they sat down to silver tableware. Their homes were adorned with furniture hewn by craftworkers.

The wealthiest people had their clothes made abroad. Men wore linen shirts with bone or metal buttons, shoes with buckles of silver or brass, and brightly colored broadcloth coats and waistcoats. Women wore dresses imported from England. Many women carried fans, perhaps to suggest that the hands that carried them did no work. Some wealthy men and women wore wigs in the European style. Some even had wigs made for their slaves.

Such a show of wealth could be found in the North too. In New York, for instance, the Schuylers, Van Cortlandts, Beekmans, and others lived lavishly on large estates, in houses ornamented with elegant and beautiful objects. These people of wealth felt under no pressure, however, to keep acquiring land. Instead, they increasingly invested their money in commerce. As their wealth grew, they built elegant mansions in town. These they embellished with Chinese wallpaper, cabinets and tables made of walnut and mahogany, and chairs upholstered in silk cloth. In Boston the mansions of the Faneuils, Bromfields, and Hancocks were adorned on the outside with spectacular formal gardens in the best tradition of the English manor. Even in Philadelphia, where Quakers continued to pride themselves on plain dress and simple furnishings, some families kept ornate homes containing furniture designed in England by Thomas Chippendale and other cabinet-makers.

Colonists work hard to better themselves. In the colonies people could rise from very humble beginnings to positions of wealth and distinction. Benjamin Franklin, for example, arrived penniless in Philadelphia from Boston at the age of seventeen. The tenth son of a candlemaker, the brilliant Franklin advanced through hard work to become an author, inventor, philosopher, and diplomat.

Although Franklin's accomplishments were extraordinary, he had friends who also rose from humble status. William Parsons, for instance, started his career as a shoemaker and ended as surveyor general of Pennsylvania. This kind of story seemed commonplace. In Massachusetts, John Hull farmed as a boy with his father. Helped by a brother, young Hull then became a goldsmith. In a few years he was in charge of minting the colony's coins, the most famous of which was the so-called pine-tree shilling. For every twenty shillings Hull and his partner produced, they received one for themselves. Within a few years Hull was a leading merchant, trading furs with England and France and bringing into the colony molasses, tobacco, cocoa, and sugar from the Caribbean islands. He even had a farm in the West Indies where he raised and sold horses. When his daughter Hannah was married at the age of eighteen to Samuel Sewall (later an important judge in Massachusetts), her father, it is said, gave the couple as a gift her weight in pine-tree shillings.

Although opportunity was abundant, most colonists did not rise to positions of wealth. They were, instead, hard-working people who labored with their hands. The vast majority of Americans, as we have seen, were farmers who lived on their own land. Others were people trained in special skills. Carpenters, weavers, blacksmiths, cabinetmakers, barrelmakers, and glassblowers lived in the towns and often ran one-family shops.

Some colonists struggled to make a living on the frontier. Known as "squatters," they actually functioned as small-time speculators. They improved the land by doing the backbreaking work of tearing out the trees and turning the soil in order to grow a crop. Then they sold the land to a new family and moved on.

In the villages and towns there were poor people too. These men — and some women — worked as dockhands, farm hands, or handymen. Because their skills were limited, they could not enter the trades. In the coastal towns, large numbers of unskilled colonists went to sea. The long voyages of many months, and sometimes of several years, made family life difficult. Work, for those who did manual labor, was exhausting. This explains the lack of entertainment or recreation in the colonies.

The colonies provide for education. Opportunities for education in the early colonies were limited. Some schools were started, nevertheless, mostly to preserve the culture brought across the Atlantic from Europe. People long feared that the isolation of life in America might lead their young to become savages. A New Englander, writing in the 1660's, explained: "We in this country being far removed from the more civilized parts of the world [must] use utmost care and diligence to keep up learning and all helps to education amongst us, lest barbarism, ignorance, and irreligion do by degrees break in upon us."

The Puritan clergy in New England constantly reminded their congregations that

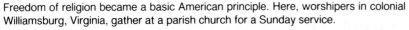

Freedom of religion became a basic American principle. Here, worshipers in colonial Williamsburg, Virginia, gather at a parish church for a Sunday service.

Satan would try to keep them from "the knowledge of scriptures." Massachusetts, as a result, provided more elementary schools than any other colony. A Massachusetts law of 1647 required all towns of fifty families or more to hire an instructor to teach children reading and writing. Only boys attended these early schools. Most girls who learned to read and write did so at home, though some might be sent each day to a neighborhood woman who conducted a "dame school" in her home.

In the Middle Colonies schooling was left almost entirely to religious groups. In 1638, for instance, the Dutch Reformed Church opened the first school in New Amsterdam. In Philadelphia the Friends' School was chartered in 1697. Jesuit priests set up Maryland's earliest schools.

In the South, some white boys learned reading, writing, and ciphering (as arithmetic was called) while serving as apprentices. Of the handful of schools that were set up, some were started by rich planters. On his death in 1634, Benjamin Syms of Virginia left two hundred acres along the Chesapeake River for the establishment of a local school.

Throughout the colonies the children of well-to-do parents were taught by private tutors. Sometimes children of the very rich were sent abroad to school. One such student was Charles Carroll of Maryland, who was enrolled in a French school in 1748 at the age of eleven. Well-trained youths like Carroll — himself destined to sign the Declaration of Independence — could look forward to careers as lawyers and elected officials.

Indians and blacks had almost no chance to learn reading or writing. Some New Englanders, to be sure, initially encouraged the education of Indian youths and the translation of the Bible into Indian languages. In other colonies the teaching of Indians was done by missionaries. Occasionally free black children attended school with whites. For the most part, however, the education of blacks was largely ignored.

Colleges are founded. As colonial life became more secure, the beginnings of a vital intellectual tradition emerged. Harvard College, the first institution of higher learning in the colonies, was founded in Massachusetts in 1636. Colonists started the school because they feared they would not have any educated ministers to replace the ones who died.

In Connecticut, Yale College came into being in 1701. It was named in honor of Elihu Yale, an official of the East India Company who was born in New England. The College of New Jersey (now Princeton) was founded in 1746. Its purpose was to train Presbyterian clergy — ministers of the branch of Protestantism that began in Scotland. In 1754 King's College (now Columbia) was started in New York City. Chartered by the New York colonial authorities, it forbade the barring of "any person of any religious denomination . . . on account of . . . religion."

In the South, Virginia placed a special tax on tobacco in order to create the College of William and Mary in 1693. It too aimed to train ministers, in this case clergy for the Anglican Church. An additional purpose was to encourage young Virginians to stay at home rather than go to school in Europe.

COLONIAL TRADE

The importance of colonial trade grows. Rich colonists, as you have read, made much of their money from the land. Business people soon found, however, that trade was becoming another significant source of profit. Colonial trade first developed around products from the sea. Fishing was the earliest colonial occupation, and the Grand Banks off Newfoundland (page 49) the choicest place. The best fish were shipped to the Catholic countries of Europe in exchange for salt and wine. The lowest-grade fish were sold to the West Indian sugar islands, where they were fed to slaves.

Another sea-going activity was whaling. Whales provided oil for lamps, whale bone and ivory for buttons, and ambergris for perfume. The work of the whaler was dangerous. Not only were whales known to capsize ships, but the boiling pots used to reduce whale fat to oil could set the deck afire. The centers of the whaling industry were in New England. In 1775 Nantucket Island alone had 150 whaling ships at sea. Connecticut encouraged whaling by exempting whalers, as well as cod fishers, from paying taxes.

Merchants also came to recognize the importance of the lumber industry. The forests of America freed England from its dependence on northern Europe for ship masts and naval stores — tar, pitch, rosin, and turpentine. Agents of the Crown roamed through the forests of English America. They marked the tallest and healthiest pines with a broad arrow in order to reserve them for the masts of the royal navy. The white oak of the Middle Colonies was particularly useful for barrels and ship timber. Yellow pine from the Southern Col-

onies supplied naval stores for the navy and merchant fleet.

England had still other uses for the products of America's forests. Timber, for example, was required for the manufacture of iron. Charcoal, obtained by burning wood in special ovens, was used to feed the fires with which iron was produced. Cabinetmakers, moreover, were increasingly busy making fine furniture. They welcomed walnut, cherry, and red maple wood from America. There was also a lively market for potash, which is extracted from wood ash. Potash was necessary for washing wool.

Colonial industries develop. England also required large quantities of pig and bar iron, and encouraged the colonies to produce those goods. (It prohibited, however, the

LIFE IN AMERICA

Colonial Crafts

Skilled workers were in great demand in colonial America. Pewterers and wheelwrights could make a good living. Colonial women, meanwhile, used their leisure to create fancy needlework.

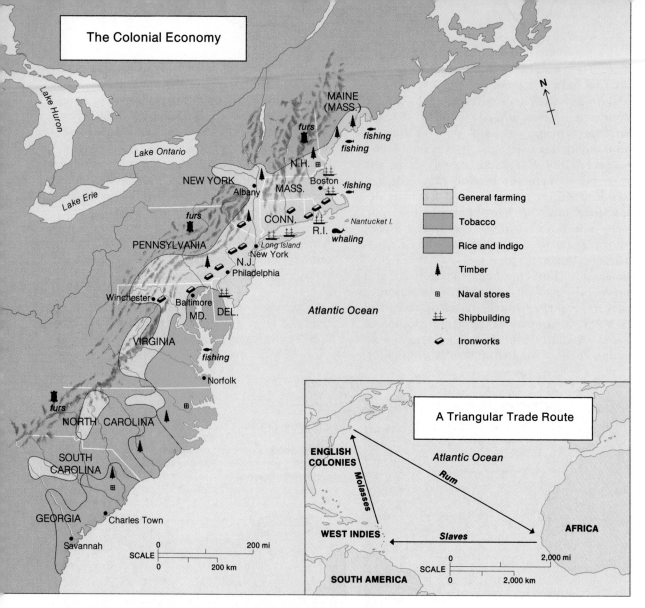

The Colonial Economy

Lake Huron

Lake Ontario

Lake Erie

MAINE
(MASS.)

furs

fishing

fishing

N.H.

NEW YORK

Boston

fishing

Albany

MASS.

furs

CONN.

Nantucket I.

R.I.

PENNSYLVANIA

whaling

Long Island

New York

N.J.

Philadelphia

Winchester

Baltimore

MD.

DEL.

Atlantic Ocean

VIRGINIA

fishing

Norfolk

furs

NORTH CAROLINA

SOUTH
CAROLINA

GEORGIA Charles Town

Savannah

	General farming
	Tobacco
	Rice and indigo
♠	Timber
⊞	Naval stores
⚓	Shipbuilding
◆	Ironworks

SCALE

| 0 | 200 mi |
| 0 | 200 km |

A Triangular Trade Route

Atlantic Ocean

ENGLISH
COLONIES

Rum

Molasses

AFRICA

WEST INDIES

Slaves

SOUTH AMERICA

SCALE

| 0 | 2,000 mi |
| 0 | 2,000 km |

The American colonies produced a variety of goods for trade with England and other parts of the world. A major source of income for colonial merchants was from a triangular trade involving Africa, the West Indies, and the colonies.

manufacture of finished products in America.) By 1775 America had more blast furnaces and forges than England and Wales combined. A typical ironmonger was Isaac Zane, Jr. The son of a wealthy Quaker craftworker from Philadelphia, Zane set up a smelter and forge near an iron mine just south of Winchester, Virginia. He produced bar iron for use in making plows and various household implements.

England regulates colonial trade. The restrictions placed on the American iron industry grew from Parliament's belief that the colonies should first and foremost serve the interests of England. Indeed, some experts on public affairs believed the only reason for the colonies' existence was to strengthen England. To that end, beginning in the mid-1600's the English government passed a series of laws to regulate colonial trade.

You have already read (page 85) how the Navigation Act of 1651 was passed to keep Dutch ships from carrying goods bound for the English colonies. A second Navigation Act, passed in 1660, named certain goods that the colonists had to ship first to England before they could be sold anywhere else. These specially designated items, known as *enumerated goods,* were sugar, cotton, tobaccco, indigo, ginger, and dyewoods. The list was later expanded to include rice, naval stores, furs, iron, and lumber.

A third Navigation Act was passed in 1663. It stated that all European cargoes headed for America had to be sent to England first and reshipped from there in English vessels. Then the Navigation Act of 1696 was passed to strengthen the previous laws. It gave colonial customs officials the power to seize unlawfully shipped goods. Also, merchants accused of smuggling were to be tried in special colonial courts without juries, because colonial juries tended to be sympathetic to such law-breaking.

The Navigation Acts are unpopular. The colonists came to resent the system of dependence that the Navigation Acts produced. It hurt their pride as well as their pocketbooks. They were taking instructions from home, like children, and were unable to seek their own, perhaps more profitable, markets in Europe. Adam Smith, the leading English political thinker of the day, wrote: "To prohibit a great people from making all that they can of every part of their own produce . . . is a manifest violation of the most sacred rights of mankind."

Still, the colonists could not overlook the advantages the Navigation Acts provided, even long after Holland ceased to be a threat. First, under the laws England paid a *bounty,* or subsidy, for some products such as indigo. Such crops could not have been grown without the special bounties. Second, the producers of tar and tobacco enjoyed a near monopoly of the English market. Third, colonial shippers had the protection of the British navy. This was a valuable assurance in a time when pirates took a heavy toll of shipping. Fourth, the Navigation Acts bound the portions of the British Empire closely together. In so doing, they enlarged the dignity and self-assurance many colonists felt as loyal Britons.

Triangular trade patterns emerge. The variety of products and the restrictions placed by the Navigation Acts on colonial trade helped create distinctive patterns of commerce known as the *triangular trade.* Molasses, rum, and slaves were all involved in one example of triangular trade (map, page 96). West Indian colonies sent molasses to Boston. From molasses New Englanders manufactured rum, which slave traders then carried to the western coast of Africa. There they bartered the rum for slaves. The African slaves were transported to the West Indies to raise new crops of sugar and make more molasses.

A spirit of nationhood is slowly developed. By 1750 most colonists still felt keen loyalty to their own colony. Although lines of trade bound the colonies loosely together, very few people thought of themselves as Americans. They were Yorkers or Virginians or whatever else their colony called its inhabitants. At times people even thought of their colony as their country. Some farsighted colonists could see, however, that the colonies might be strengthened by joining together. An inspiring preacher named Jonathan Edwards declared proudly that Providence had chosen America "as the glorious renovator of the world." A leading South Carolinian expressed the hope of many people: "There ought to be no New England men, no New Yorkers, etc., known on this continent, but all of us Americans." The rise of such a national feeling, however, would have to await the coming of the next generation.

SECTION REVIEW

1. Vocabulary: *apprentice, enumerated goods, bounty, triangular trade.*
2. (a) Why did the colonies experience a continuing labor shortage? (b) What three systems of labor were established in an effort to relieve that shortage?
3. In what ways did the Northern and Southern Colonies differ?
4. How was colonial education provided for?
5. What were some of the most important goods exported by the colonies?
6. (a) Why did England seek to regulate colonial trade? (b) In what ways did the Navigation Acts limit trade? (c) How did the colonies benefit from the Navigation Acts?

Chapter 4 Review

Summary

Colonies were established in the South as English proprietors received land grants from the Crown and then sent groups of settlers to America. The owners of the first of these colonies, Maryland, hoped to acquire great estates for themselves and also to provide a refuge for English Catholics. Conflicts arose between Catholic and Protestant colonists in Maryland, however, leading to passage of the Toleration Act, a measure that gave freedom of religion to all Christians.

The territory between Virginia and Florida gradually developed into the colonies of North Carolina, South Carolina, and Georgia. The Carolinas, with Charles Town as an important seaport, prospered by shipping abroad rice and lumber. Georgia was established under the leadership of James Oglethorpe to provide a fresh start for impoverished people from England. Immigrants from other European countries also contributed to Georgia's early development. Economically, however, Georgia failed to reward its proprietors.

As a result of the explorations of Henry Hudson, Holland started the colony of New Netherland. The Dutch set up trading establishments on Manhattan Island and built forts near present-day Albany and on the Delaware River. Rising tensions with the English led to open conflict over New Netherland. Unwilling to support their tyrannical governor, Peter Stuyvesant, the Dutch in New Amsterdam surrendered to an English naval force in 1664. The English renamed the colony New York.

In 1681 William Penn founded the colony of Pennsylvania as a haven for his fellow Quakers. Well-planned, and well-provided for, the colony grew quickly, in harmony with its Indian neighbors.

The chief economic problem facing the English colonies was a shortage of labor. The apprentice system, the indenture system, and the importation of slaves from Africa were all attempts to increase the supply of workers, both skilled and unskilled.

While wealthy planters in the South and successful merchants throughout the colonies enjoyed luxuries, the great majority of colonists worked hard to meet daily needs. The colonies provided, nevertheless, impressive opportunities for people with talent and persistence to rise in the world. Trade and manufacturing became ways by which some colonists prospered.

Beginning in the mid-1660's, British trade regulations prevented colonial merchants and manufacturers from expanding as they wished. Most managed to prosper in spite of the restrictions. At the same time, influential colonists began slowly to develop a spirit of nationhood.

Vocabulary and Important Terms

1. proprietor
2. proprietary colony
3. Toleration Act (1649)
4. Dutch West India Company
5. patroon
6. Quakers
7. apprentice
8. subsistence farmer
9. squatter
10. naval stores
11. enumerated goods
12. bounty
13. Navigation Acts
14. triangular trade

Discussion Questions

1. (a) Why was Maryland founded? (b) To what extent did Maryland fulfill the dreams of its founders, the Calverts? (c) Why was Carolina established? (d) Why did it split into two separate colonies?
2. (a) In what way was the founding of Georgia different from that of any other colony? (b) Why might the founders of Georgia have considered their colony to be both a failure and a success?
3. Why did the English want to take over New Netherland?
4. (a) What was William Penn's dream for his colony in America? (b) What factors contributed to the development of Pennsylvania into a prosperous colony?
5. Describe the different systems of labor that grew up in the English colonies as a response to the shortage of workers.
6. What ways of living were shared by people of wealth throughout the colonies?
7. What educational opportunities existed in colonial America?
8. Describe the different ways in which colonial Americans earned a living.
9. (a) What actions were taken by Parliament to regulate colonial trade? (b) How did the colonists react to these regulations, and what advantages, if any, did these regulations provide the colonists?

Relating Past to Present

1. The log cabin, first built in North America by Swedish colonists, gradually became an important symbol of American life. What do you think causes

certain things to become symbols of a nation's way of living? What are some symbols of American life today?

2. Compare the educational opportunities in colonial America with those that exist today. Why is it an accepted belief in our society that children should be educated?

Studying Local History

Most of the colonists in English America were farmers. Find out what kind of farming was done by the earliest settlers of European origin in your state. How large were their farms? What were some of the crops they grew?

Using History Skills

1. *Reading maps.* Study the map showing the colonial economy on page 96. (a) What crops were grown in the Southern Colonies? (b) What crops were grown in the Middle Colonies? (c) In what section were fishing and whaling major sources of income? (d) Compare the economies of the New England, Middle, and Southern Colonies. Which of the three sections had the most varied economy? Explain your answer in a short paragraph of two or three sentences.

2. *Writing a report.* Use an encyclopedia or a history of the colonial period to learn more about the imprisonment and trial of John Peter Zenger, a publisher charged with criminal libel for printing articles which criticized the governor of New York. In your report describe Zenger's defense, and tell how his acquittal paved the way for the establishment of an important principle — freedom of the press in America.

3. *Reading source material.* Study Eliza Lucas's description of colonial South Carolina on page 81. (a) What was the main crop grown in colonial South Carolina and why was it important? (b) What evidence was there that most of the people of Charles Town were of a ''religious turn of mind''? (c) If you had been a farmer thinking of moving to South Carolina, which part of the colony would you have found most attractive? Explain your answer.

WORLD SCENE

A Refuge for Religious Minorities

Following the establishment of colonies in North America, oppressed groups in Europe saw them as places of refuge.

French Huguenots. During the last half of the sixteenth century, religious rivalry between French Catholics and Protestants was ferocious. A group of Protestants known as Huguenots suffered terrible persecution. While Henry IV, a Protestant, was on the throne, however, he extended religious rights to the Huguenots by issuing the Edict of Nantes in 1598. Thereafter, an uneasy peace prevailed for almost a century. Then, during the long reign of Louis XIV (1643 – 1715), persecution of the Huguenots resumed. When Louis XIV revoked the Edict of Nantes in 1685, thousands of Huguenots fled France. Some settled in other European countries, but many crossed the ocean and began new lives in the English colonies.

The Huguenots contributed notably to colonial development. Many French family names — such as Revere and Faneuil in Boston, Minuit in New York, and Manigault in Charleston — are a permanent reminder of the Huguenot heritage in America. George Washington noted with pride that one of his Virginia ancestors was Nicholas Martiau, a Huguenot.

Jewish exiles. The marriage of Isabella of Castile and Ferdinand of Aragon in 1469 produced a political union strong enough to unite almost all of Spain under their control. To guarantee the unity they desired, Isabella and Ferdinand demanded that all their subjects convert to Christianity. In 1492 the monarchs decreed that all Jews who continued to practice their religion were to be expelled from Spain. About 150,000 Jews chose exile rather than conversion. Aware of greater religious toleration in the colonies of Portugal, many refugees made their way to these outposts. A community of Jews settled in Brazil and lived there until 1654, when the Portuguese ordered them to leave. A group of them sailed in that year to the Dutch settlement of New Amsterdam, where they established the first Jewish community in North America.

UNIT 1 REVIEW

Important Dates

1000 Vikings cross Atlantic.
1487 Dias rounds Cape of Good Hope.
1492 Columbus reaches America.
1498 Da Gama reaches India.
1513 Balboa reaches Pacific Ocean.
1519 Magellan begins voyage around world.
1565 Spanish settle St. Augustine.
1607 Jamestown settled.
1608 Champlain founds Quebec.
1609 Santa Fe settled.
1619 Virginia House of Burgesses first meets.
1620 Pilgrims settle Plymouth.
1639 Fundamental Orders of Connecticut.
1664 English capture New Amsterdam.
1682 La Salle reaches mouth of Mississippi River.
1733 Georgia founded.

Review Questions

1. (a) How did the Spanish, the French, and the English view the American Indians? (b) What impact did each of these European groups have on the Indians? (c) Which European settlers, if any, lived in harmony with their Indian neighbors? Explain your answer.

2. (a) What were Spain's goals in building an empire in the Americas? (b) What was the extent of the Spanish empire? (c) What was the main value to Spain of its colonies? (d) Describe the kind of society the Spanish created within their empire.

3. (a) Why did the French build an empire in North America? (b) What was the extent of France's American empire? (c) How successful were France's colonization efforts?

4. (a) Why did the English become interested in starting colonies in the Americas? (b) From 1580 to 1607 who settled the early English colonies? (c) How successful were they?

5. (a) Why were the colonies at Plymouth and at Massachusetts Bay started? (b) Which of the two colonies was more successful? Give reasons for your answer.

6. (a) Why was the concept of freedom of religion important in the English colonies? (b) Which of the original thirteen colonies offered some degree of religious freedom to its inhabitants?

7. (a) Where did representative government get its start in English America? (b) To what extent were the English colonists free to govern themselves?

8. (a) What opportunities for a better life existed in England's thirteen American colonies? (b) Which groups in the colonial population did not share in these opportunities?

9. (a) Why did England want to regulate colonial trade? (b) How did England's trade regulations foster a spirit of nationhood within the American colonies by 1750?

Projects

1. Keep a diary as if you were a member of an expedition led by one of the following explorers: (a) Cabot, (b) De Soto, (c) Coronado, (d) Cartier, (e) La Salle. In your diary make note of such matters as the purpose of the expedition, the dangers and hardships encountered, points of interest, and the expedition's accomplishments. Include in your diary a map of the expedition route.

2. On an outline map of the world indicate what European geographers knew about the world by the mid-1400's. Then show on that map how the voyages of Columbus and Magellan added to Europeans' knowledge of the world. Write on the map the names of places reached during the voyages of those two explorers.

3. Find out more about early Spanish settlements in what is now the United States — namely, in Florida, New Mexico, California, Arizona, and Texas. Choose one of these areas and use the library to find out how the Spanish settled there. Report on your findings to the class.

4. Find a book in the library about the settling of the Jamestown or Plymouth colonies. Write a book report explaining the difficulties encountered by the early English settlers at Plymouth or Jamestown. In your book report tell why notable individuals, such as William Bradford or John Smith, were important to the founding of permanent English colonies in America.

5. Write a newspaper article that might have appeared at the time of the founding of one of the thirteen English colonies. In the article include details on each of the following topics: (a) the colony's founders, (b) the reason for the colony, and (c) where the colony was located.

6. Write a script for a debate between a supporter and an opponent of Roger Williams's beliefs before his expulsion from the Massachusetts Bay Colony. In writing your script, try not to favor one side over the other.

A NEW PEOPLE

1750 – 1800

The sun never shone on a cause of greater worth. It is not the affair of a city, a country, a province, or a kingdom; but of a continent. . . . It is not the concern of a day, a year, or an age. . . . Now is the seedtime of continental union, faith, and honor.

THOMAS PAINE, "COMMON SENSE"

CHAPTER 5

The Road to Independence

1754 – 1775

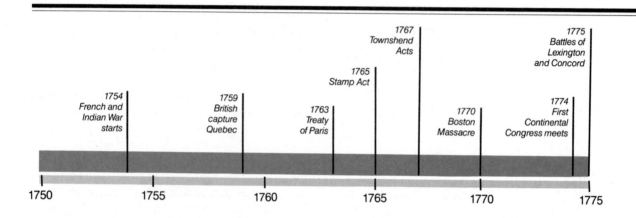

CHAPTER OUTLINE

1. Britain triumphs over France in the struggle for North America.

2. New policies anger the American colonists.

3. Britain uses a firmer hand.

4. Fateful blunders lead to open warfare.

By the beginning of the eighteenth century, England clearly had become the most successful colonial organizer of all the European nations with settlements in America. Spain was never able to obtain goods from its colonies, except for gold and silver, that it did not produce itself. France continued to be short of people willing to take a chance in the Americas. Holland had been eliminated as a rival to the other powers in North America by 1680.

England's colonial success, however, brought with it responsibility. As their economic value increased and their population expanded, the English colonies could no longer be limited to the narrow coastal plain of eastern North America. Trappers, pathfinders, and intrepid farmers were already moving inland and building outposts on the frontier. This inevitable westward expansion meant that a showdown with France over the territory beyond the Appalachian Mountains was in the making.

To organize and administer England's new colonial empire effectively, informed and thoughtful leadership was required. Unfortunately, those in power showed themselves to be short-sighted, arrogant, and naively unaware of the complex problems England faced. Their failure to comprehend the realities of the situation in North America altered the course of history.

1 Britain Triumphs over France in the Struggle for North America

The likelihood of conflict between the French and the English had grown noticeably as the 1600's ended and the 1700's dawned. For one thing, the mainland colonies were becoming more valuable every year. As suppliers of food, lumber, and horses to the increasingly prosperous sugar and tobacco islands of the West Indies, they were worth fighting over. Keen rivalry had also developed in the Great Lakes region over the fur trade and in the area of Newfoundland over the fisheries that supplied southern Europe and the West Indies. Still, the English-French friction did not become heated until after 1689, when William and Mary came to the English throne. The new English monarchs believed the time had come to challenge the scheme of Louis XIV to dominate Europe (page 52). They also wanted to show France it could not hold the American interior without challenge.

France and England each have advantages. As the competition warmed up, France had some notable advantages. First, the French had excellent relations with the Indians, especially the Hurons and Algonquins, maintaining a string of alliances from Maine to Wisconsin. Moreover, through the *coureurs de bois* the French had a scout system extending deep into the forests that the English could not match.

On the other hand, the English had a much larger population in America than the French. The English navy, moreover, was a powerful guardian of the sea lanes. Furthermore, British manufactured goods could be invaluable in efforts to woo the Indians from the French.

Early conflicts are inconclusive. Beginning in 1689, England and France periodically went to war over their American possessions. The pattern of the fighting was always about the same. The French and their Indian allies would attack English frontier settlements, aiming to halt the relentless westward movement of the English. The English, in retaliation, would hit hard at the French fortress towns, which were a source of support to the Indians. Several times the two enemies seized substantial chunks of each other's territory. Then they

Engravings like this one kept colonists informed about the fighting with France. Entitled ''Britain's Glory,'' it shows the capture of Louisbourg in 1758 (page 106).

would make peace by giving back the territory they had seized.

For many decades neither side was able to overwhelm the other. In King William's War (1689–1697), France sought to conquer New York. New York was centrally situated so that its capture would break the line of English settlements in two. The war ended, however, inconclusively.

In 1701 hostilities started once more. This time, in what is known as Queen Anne's War (1702–1713), New England bore the brunt of the fighting. The war ended with Britain in possession of Newfoundland, Nova Scotia, and Hudson Bay.

During these years, relations between the Spanish and the British were also badly strained. The treaty ending Queen Anne's War had given Britain a monopoly of the slave trade in the Spanish colonies. The British seized upon the opportunity to smuggle goods into the Spanish possessions. Spanish vessels were powerless to stop the practice, although occasionally they seized a British ship, adding to the tensions. As a result, France and Spain were brought into a virtual alliance against England.

In 1744 a third colonial war — King George's War — broke out. Again Britain and France fought for control of the seas and possession of colonies. In North America, British and colonial soldiers captured the powerful French fortress of Louisbourg on Cape Breton Island. Britain threw away the costly victory, however, by returning Louisbourg to France in the 1748 treaty ending the war.

The French and Indian War begins in the Ohio Valley. Three wars had not settled the struggle between Britain and France in North America. The race to control the Ohio Valley opened the final bout, which became known as the French and Indian War. The immediate cause of the conflict was the French move into the disputed area.

Virginia promoters had organized the Ohio Company in 1749 to encourage settlement of the Ohio River valley. Settlers were soon on their way west to take up tracts in the grant of thousands of acres that the king had made to the Company.

The Marquis of Duquesne (doo-CANE), who had recently become governor of New France, believed it was his duty to stop the westward flow of English settlers. With that aim in mind, he constructed a line of forts from Lake Erie to the Ohio River. Two of them were Fort Le Boeuf and Fort Venango.

Britain interpreted this activity as a new sign of France's effort to destroy the British Empire. Other parts of the empire, in India and Africa, were also coming under pressure from French forces. France, for its part, recognized that as far as America was concerned, it was now or never. The population of Britain's American colonies was well over a million. New France, on the other hand, contained only a twentieth of that number. Furthermore, the British colonial population, because it contained far more families, was growing at a much faster rate.

The Albany Plan of Union is rejected. Although the English colonists vastly outnumbered the French, this fact alone could not guarantee the outcome of the struggle for control of North America. The colonists were not prepared to work together, let alone fight together. Each colony was prepared to defend its own frontier, not the frontier of all of them. The French troops, moreover, were well-trained. The English colonies had no military force that could match what they might soon have to face.

Concerned about the lack of colonial unity, British officials called a meeting at Albany in 1754 to try to get the colonies to work together. Seven colonies sent representatives to Albany to debate a plan proposed by Benjamin Franklin of Philadelphia. They were joined by representatives of the Six Nations, the powerful Iroquois Confederation of central New York that had allied itself with the British.

Franklin had been deeply impressed by the example of the Iroquois Confederation. In his Albany Plan of Union he proposed a similar loose confederation among the colonies. The plan would have provided for a permanent council of defense chosen by the colonies, along with a president-general to be appointed by the king. The council would manage relations with the Indians and have control over various problems of mutual defense, subject to approval by the president-general and the Crown.

The Albany Congress accepted Franklin's proposal. The colonial assemblies, however, either rejected the plan or ignored it. The colonists simply refused to recognize any need for a strong central authority. The British, for their part, thought the plan put too much power into the hands of the colonists. The Albany Plan was ahead of its time. Twenty-two years later, when the colonists faced the wrath of George III, many people recalled the wisdom of Franklin's idea that the colonists needed to work together. Meanwhile, the thirteen separate colonies faced the French without a common plan.

Britain objects to the building of French forts. Concern in Virginia over French fort-building on the frontier was intense. The colony's able lieutenant governor, Robert Dinwiddie, reacted sternly. In 1753 he sent a message to the commander of the new French forts. The message, carried by a 21-year-old Virginian named George Washington, expressed "concern and surprise" that the French were there on British soil. The British were really using polite language to say "Get out!"

Washington was unable to persuade the French to leave. After he returned home, a number of Virginians decided to build a fort at the place where the Allegheny and Monongahela rivers come together, forming the Ohio River. The French, however, drove the Virginians out and finished the fort themselves. They named it Fort Duquesne in honor of their governor (page 104).

Dinwiddie, not knowing that the fort was already lost, sent Washington out with a small force to protect it. On the way a French scouting party attacked the Virginians, sending them into retreat. Wisely guessing that the main French force was in the vicinity, they hastily constructed a strong point named Fort Necessity.

The French soon found the troops from Virginia, and the makeshift fort surrendered to them on July 4, 1754. Washington and his little party were permitted to go

The French and Indian War began when George Washington, a young militia officer, tried to drive the French away from the forks of the Ohio River.

home. The opening skirmish of the French and Indian War had been fought. July 4 would one day have a happier association for the people of the colonies.

The British try to force the French from the Ohio Valley. In 1755 the colonists welcomed with joy the arrival of British regulars to help in the fight against France. The troops were commanded by General Edward Braddock, a veteran of European campaigns. Operating in the style he knew in Europe, Braddock set out with large numbers of wagons and pack animals. He soon had to take George Washington's advice to travel light in order to speed up his movement. With 300 axmen hacking a road through the forest, the general advanced on Fort Duquesne, accompanied by 1,400 of his own proud troops and 450 Virginia militiamen under Colonel Washington.

Braddock's force was ambushed by the French and Indians just seven miles from Fort Duquesne. Washington watched from nearby where he lay ill, stricken with a sudden fever. The scene made an indelible impression on the young Virginian. Marching through the forest in their brilliant uniforms as the fife and drum corps played the "Grenadier's March," Braddock's troops met 900 French and Indian fighters in a quick, bloody engagement on July 9, 1755. The British, in red coats, made perfect targets. They died by the hundreds. Braddock himself, after four horses had been killed under him, was fatally wounded.

French successes continue. Braddock's defeat was only the first in a series of reverses that the French inflicted on the British. Fort Oswego, on Lake Ontario, fell to the French in 1756, and Fort William Henry, on Lake George, in 1757. Fighting raged on other continents too. In Europe, Frederick the Great of Prussia, Britain's ally, was menaced by the armies of Russia, Austria, Sweden, and France. British and French forces in India were also locked in deadly embrace.

William Pitt helps turn the tide. As the French gained control of the Great Lakes area, more and more Indians came to their side. It was one of the darkest moments

Britain had ever known. At this grave time Parliament chose a new prime minister. He was William Pitt, known as the Great Commoner for his brilliance as a member of the House of Commons. Before taking his high office, Pitt had confidently declared, "I believe that I can save this country and that no one else can." He was a moody man, sometimes exuberant and excitable, sometimes gloomy and listless. He had a grand strategy to win the war, however, and he pursued it purposefully.

First of all, Pitt sent strong military support to Frederick of Prussia. This move tied down French troops otherwise destined for North America. Second, by his speeches Pitt raised the morale of the English people. He made English merchants see that by expanding the navy Britain could gain prosperity as well as the admiration of the world. Third, he sent two outstanding commanders to America. Jeffrey Amherst was one of them. Placed in charge of all British forces in North America, Amherst captured Louisbourg in 1758, giving Britain its first great victory of the war. The other commander was James Wolfe. Only 31 years old in

After early British reverses, fighting during the French and Indian War centered around the capture of key French fortresses. By what routes did British forces advance toward Quebec and Montreal?

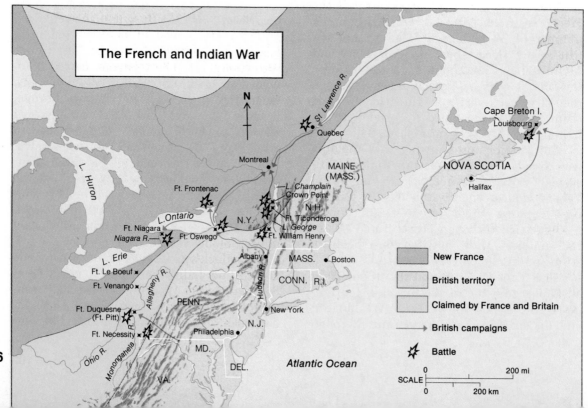

106

1758, the bold Wolfe was already an experienced campaigner. Amherst and Wolfe were a match for France's superb military leader, General Louis Montcalm, another veteran of Europe's wars.

The fall of Louisbourg gave Britain control of the St. Lawrence River. Shortly afterward, a British unit under Lieutenant Colonel Bradstreet seized Fort Frontenac on Lake Ontario, sealing off the western end of the St. Lawrence. The French then abandoned Fort Duquesne to the British, who rebuilt it and named it Fort Pitt in honor of the resourceful prime minister who had revived their cause. (On its site, the city of Pittsburgh would later rise.)

The British take Quebec. As 1759 began, France no longer controlled the Mississippi and Ohio valleys. Disaster lay ahead for the French. In July, British troops under General Amherst forced the French out of their forts at Crown Point and Ticonderoga, while another British unit defeated French forces at Fort Niagara. Meanwhile, General Wolfe was leading a mighty British fleet up the St. Lawrence to attack Quebec, the capital of New France.

Quebec was built on high, steep cliffs above the river. The French, commanded by General Montcalm, were confident that enemy troops could not scale those cliffs. They did not reckon on the determination of General Wolfe. One night in September he led his troops up the forbidding rocky approach along a path just north of the city. At daybreak Montcalm faced his foes on an expanse of land that was called the Plains of Abraham.

A sensitive man, Wolfe recited Gray's "Elegy Written in a Country Churchyard" before the battle began. He said to some of his soldiers, "Gentlemen, I had rather be the author of that poem than take Quebec." Surely he must have pondered the line, "The paths of glory lead but to the grave." A little later, as his troops were overwhelming the French, Wolfe perished in the battle. Within a few hours Montcalm also lay dead. Before a week was over, Quebec surrendered. In 1760 British forces under Amherst moved upon Montreal, which they easily captured. The contest in North America between France and Britain had finally come to an end.

Britain triumphs throughout the world. In that same year George II died. He was succeeded by his grandson, George III, who sought to end the war. Pitt wanted to continue fighting until France was defeated everywhere in the world, but he was forced out of office. The momentum was too great, however, to alter the course of British advances. On the sea France's Atlantic and Mediterranean fleets were destroyed. In Africa, British success halted the French traffic in slaves. In India, English victories ended French influence.

In 1762 Spain unwisely decided to enter the war on the side of France. One after another, Spanish islands in the West Indies, including Cuba, fell to Britain. A British force from India took the Philippines, Spain's possession in the Pacific. On the European continent, the British continued to help Frederick until he had disposed of all of his enemies. A popular author, Horace Walpole, reflected the satisfaction of the British when he wrote, "It is necessary to inquire every morning what victory there is, for fear of missing one."

France is expelled from North America. The global conflict was formally brought to a close by the Treaty of Paris in 1763. Under its terms New France became a mere memory in North America, as Britain acquired Canada and all French holdings east of the Mississippi River. The Caribbean sugar islands of Guadeloupe and Martinique were restored to France. The French also retained the tiny fishing islands of St. Pierre and Miquelon, off Newfoundland.

To reward Spain for its faithfulness, France turned over to it New Orleans and the enormous area west of the Mississippi known as Louisiana. In exchange for East and West Florida, Britain returned Cuba and the Philippines to Spain. The map of North America had been remade. A new era in world history was opening.

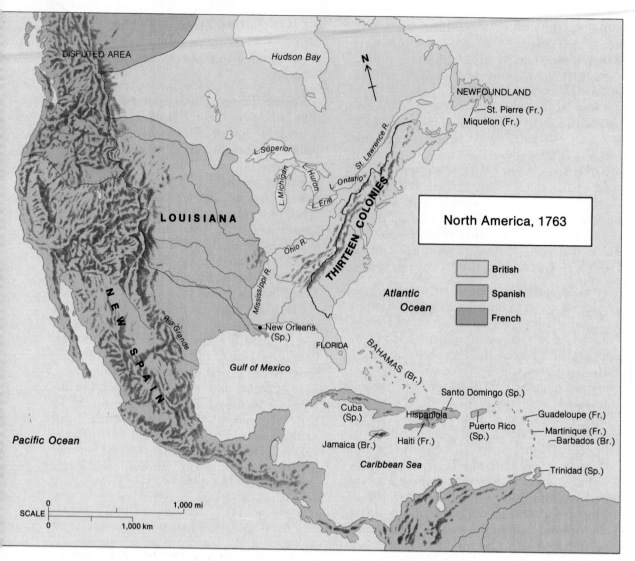

DISPUTED AREA

Hudson Bay

N

NEWFOUNDLAND

—St. Pierre (Fr.)
Miquelon (Fr.)

L. Superior

L. Michigan

Huron

L. Ontario

L. Erie

St. Lawrence R.

LOUISIANA

THIRTEEN COLONIES

Ohio R.

North America, 1763

Mississippi R.

Atlantic
Ocean

British

Spanish

French

N E W   S P A I N

Rio Grande

• New Orleans
(Sp.)

FLORIDA

BAHAMAS (Br.)

Gulf of Mexico

Santo Domingo (Sp.)

Cuba
(Sp.)

Hispaniola

Guadeloupe (Fr.)

Puerto Rico
(Sp.)

Martinique (Fr.)

Pacific Ocean

Jamaica (Br.)

Haiti (Fr.)

Barbados (Br.)

Caribbean Sea

Trinidad (Sp.)

SCALE

0   1,000 mi

0   1,000 km

Under the terms of the Treaty of Paris, France gave up its holdings on the mainland of
North America to Great Britain and Spain. Great Britain had clearly become the
dominant power in North America.

SECTION REVIEW

1. (a) Why were the British and French rivals in North America? (b) In their competition for control over North America, what were the main advantages of the British? (c) Of the French?
2. (a) What was the purpose of the Albany Plan of Union? (b) Why was it rejected?
3. (a) What dispute led to the outbreak of the French and Indian War? (b) What were some of France's early successes? (c) How did William Pitt turn the tide? (d) What battle determined the outcome of the war?
4. What were the main terms of the Treaty of Paris?

2 New Policies Anger the American Colonists

With the defeat of France and Spain, Britain became the most farflung empire in the history of the world. Horace Walpole boasted, "I shall burn my Greek and Latin books. They are the histories of little people."

Weak leaders govern Britain. The growth of the empire brought new issues and new concerns. How was Britain to go about the military, economic, and political rearranging that the times required? Britain's prime ministers proved sadly inadequate. Pitt was gone from power and the men who followed him lacked his vision and energy. The new king proved to be another terrible handicap. George III was different from the first two Georges. Where George I, being German, spoke no English and George II only spoke it badly, George III spoke it perfectly — and too much. He hoped to take an active part in ruling the country, but he had neither the good sense nor the right temperament to succeed. A man who threw tantrums when he felt frustrated, George III took any criticism of the monarchy or any suggestion for reform as a personal affront. On top of everything he suffered from an illness that led increasingly to periods of insanity.

King George insisted on appointing and dismissing his own ministers. One group in the House of Commons that called itself the "King's Friends" slavishly yielded to the monarch's wishes without argument. Since Britain did not yet have a party system, it was hard for other members of Parliament to oppose the king.

The British fail to plan an overall colonial policy. Victory can make a nation overconfident and arrogant. In Britain's case, its leaders did not believe they needed to make any more concessions to the colonies now that the French threat had been ended. Again and again, for more than 75 years, the British had made concessions. Now in possession not only of the thirteen original colonies but also of Canada and the land from the Appalachians to the Mississippi, Britain made plans. The new policies the British contemplated would have to take care of the needs of a broad range of colonists — merchants, land speculators, fur traders, West Indian sugar growers, and pioneers surging ever more determinedly westward. The Indians, who had lost their powerful French friends, would have to be dealt with too.

Britain made efforts to establish a satisfactory land policy, regulate trade, and make the colonies pay their share of the cost of government. Those efforts, however, eventually shook the empire to its foundations. The American colonists were in no mood to be governed more tightly. They had come to enjoy controlling their own political affairs.

Patrick Henry attacks the Crown. Two court cases soon arose, indicating that the colonies would resent interference from Britain. The first occurred in Virginia. Under Virginia law, Anglican clergymen were usually paid in tobacco. In 1755 and again in 1758 poor crops drove up the price of tobacco, making the clergymen unexpectedly wealthy. In response, the House of Burgesses passed the Two Penny Act. That act provided that the clergy be paid in paper money, which had lost value. Parliament, however, disallowed the law in 1759.

When a clergyman sued to recover his back salary, a 26-year-old defense lawyer named Patrick Henry represented the Virginia taxpayers. Although the law was clearly on the side of the minister, Henry stirred up the community with his argument that the Crown had violated the sacred right of Virginia's freemen to govern themselves. The jury, in sympathy with Henry's fiery charges, granted the clergyman an award of only one penny. Henry's impassioned oratory in the case (known as the Parson's Cause) made him famous.

James Otis protests the writs of assistance. In Massachusetts another young lawyer, James Otis, similarly attacked the Crown in 1760. Representing 63 Boston merchants, he protested the issuance of *writs of assistance.* The writs, which had first appeared in the colonies in 1751, were search warrants. They gave customs officials the right to search anywhere for suspected illegal goods. (Ordinary warrants permit searches only in specified places.)

During the French and Indian War, British customs officials had obtained writs of assistance to try to cut off illegal trade that the colonies were carrying on with Canada and the West Indies. The writs had aroused little opposition at that time. Then, when George III became king, all the old writs

Patrick Henry's arguments in the case of the Parson's Cause were applauded by colonists who resented British interference in America.

issued in his grandfather's name expired. New ones were now required.

Like Patrick Henry in the Parson's Cause, Otis had no strong legal grounds for opposing the writs. He relied, therefore, on emotional arguments. A courtroom observer named John Adams described Otis as "a flame of fire." Arguing that a man's home is his castle, Otis denounced the writs as a violation of the people's natural right to liberty. Adams later wrote, "American independence was then and there born; the seeds of patriots and heroes were then and there sown." Otis lost his case, but what had been a dispute over search warrants had been elevated into a keen discussion of personal liberty. (Eventually a prohibition of writs of assistance was written into the United States Constitution.)

The British decide to enforce trade regulations. Getting the colonies to obey trade regulations became a sore point in Great Britain's relations with the colonies. Absentee English landlords objected strenuously to the trade carried on between French planters in the West Indies and merchants in New England. In 1733 the landlords had obtained passage of the Molasses Act, which placed a high duty on molasses and sugar shipped into the colonies from the French and Spanish islands. The act would have hurt the Northern Colonies very badly if it had ever been strictly enforced, but it was largely ignored. The profits from smuggling enabled New Englanders to purchase the manufactured goods they wanted — to the delight of English merchants. For thirty years Parliament behaved as if it did not notice the disregard of the Molasses Act.

When smuggling continued during the French and Indian War, however, British leaders vowed one day to bring the colonies to heel. As soon as hostilities ended, Parliament ordered all customs officials to their posts in America. Until then officials had usually appointed colonists to serve as their deputies, or substitutes. These deputies were rarely willing to crack down on the smugglers.

The Sugar Act angers the colonists. To curb the illegal trade with the French islands, Parliament passed the Sugar Act in 1764. Under the Sugar Act the *duty,* or tax, placed on molasses entering the colonies was reduced from sixpence to threepence a gallon. At the same time duties were raised on sugar and certain other luxuries imported by the colonies. The British made known their intention that in all cases the law was to be strictly enforced.

The enforcement of the Sugar Act quickly put a brake on New England trade. New Englanders, distressed by the new law, admitted that the *regulation* of trade was the business of Parliament. They regarded *taxation*, however, as exclusively their own affair. They denounced the act as a monstrous tax law masquerading as an effort to regulate trade.

Britain closes the frontier in 1763. The Middle and Southern Colonies were also aroused by a plan the British had adopted for dealing with the Indians west of the Appalachians. Relations with the Indians had been troubled ever since a determined Ottawa chief named Pontiac had persuaded the tribes of the Great Lakes region to join together to halt the westward movement of American pioneers. The Indians also sought to put an end to the cheating of English fur traders and land speculators. In 1763 Pontiac's forces captured all of Britain's west-

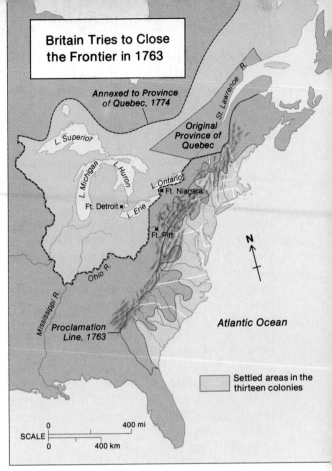

As a result of Pontiac's Rebellion, the British prohibited settlement west of the Proclamation Line.

Pontiac, an Ottawa chief, led the Indians of the Great Lakes area in a plan to destroy frontier settlements.

ern outposts except Forts Niagara, Pitt, and Detroit. For a year the entire western frontier was aflame with war. By the time that peace was restored in 1765, hundreds of Indians and settlers had been killed.

Pontiac's Rebellion, as the Indian uprising was known, was put down by colonial troops recruited and financed by the colonists themselves. Before the fighting ended, British authorities came up with a plan to prevent future troubles. In 1763 they drew a line on the map along the crest of the Appalachians — the Proclamation Line of 1763 — and forbade settlement west of it. Commissioners in charge of Indian affairs would govern the area. Land would gradually become available for settlement as it was acquired from the Indians by purchase.

In the Middle and Southern Colonies land speculators were furious. These included many leading people, among them George Washington and Benjamin Franklin.

Some colonial assemblies denounced the Proclamation of 1763 for interfering with their western land claims. Frontier settlers were outraged because they would not be able to move freely westward to take up new acres.

A new mood begins to develop. The colonists, it must be noted, were feeling greater self-assurance every year. Their ability to defend themselves against Pontiac, for instance, made them bolder in their disagreements with Great Britain. Most Americans were still proud to live as British subjects. Yet time was starting to alter that once-universal sentiment. More and more Scotch-Irish and German immigrants were arriving, bringing with them a keen anti-British point of view. Furthermore, as the number of colonists born in America increased, the ties of devotion to Great Britain were stretched thinner and thinner. Some Americans were even beginning to imagine that they could get along without guidance from London.

SECTION REVIEW

1. Vocabulary: *writs of assistance, duty.*
2. How did Britain's attitude toward its American colonies change once the French threat was ended?
3. What rights did Patrick Henry defend in the Parson's Cause?
4. (a) What were the provisions of the Sugar Act? (b) Why did it anger New Englanders?
5. (a) Why did the British issue the Proclamation of 1763? (b) Why did the colonists oppose it?

3 Britain Uses a Firmer Hand

By 1763 the British had already tackled the problems of enforcing trade regulations and of western settlement and were ready to go further. George Grenville, prime minister from 1763 to 1765, took on the problem of reducing Britain's crippling national debt. Grenville, who was William Pitt's brother-in-law, understood finance well. He was, however, stubborn and heavy-handed. To his surprise, his efforts to raise revenue in the colonies met stiff resistance up and down the Atlantic seaboard.

The Stamp Act is passed. Grenville was determined that the American colonies should pay at least half the annual cost of administering and defending themselves. To raise the needed revenue, he proposed a scheme to levy a tax within the colonies, through the sale of stamps. Stamps would have to be purchased and placed on newspapers, pamphlets, all kinds of legal documents, and even on playing cards and dice.

The idea of a stamp duty was not a new one. Stamps had already been in use for tax purposes in England, and some colonial legislatures had imposed stamp taxes too. The Stamp Act of 1765 produced, nevertheless, a storm of protest in the colonies. The British seem not to have calculated that the burden of the tax measure would fall on the most vocal colonists. Newspaper editors, merchants, and lawyers led the opposition because they were the ones most immediately affected.

The colonists oppose taxation without representation. The Stamp Act provoked the colonists because Parliament had seen fit to tax them directly, even though this right had always been reserved to the colonial legislatures. James Otis (page 109) denounced what he called "taxation without representation." He claimed that Parliament had no right to tax the American colonies since colonists were not represented in that body. This argument particularly annoyed the British. They insisted that Parliament passed laws for the entire empire, therefore giving the colonies what was called "virtual" representation. A Maryland attorney, Daniel Dulany, denounced the notion of virtual representation as "a mere cob-web, spread to catch the unwary and entangle the weak." He said the Stamp Act was not an ordinary bill, but one placing an *internal* tax on the colonies.

In Virginia's House of Burgesses, Patrick Henry, laying the blame on the king, used bold language. "Caesar had his Brutus," he exclaimed, "Charles the First his Cromwell, and George the Third. . . . "

The assemblage gasped, and voices interrupted with cries of treason. Henry, unruffled, continued "... may profit by their example! If this be treason, make the most of it."

Opposition to the Stamp Act mounts. Some colonists seemed ready to resist the tax with open rebellion. They organized themselves into groups called Sons of Liberty and Daughters of Liberty to protect what they regarded as their rights. In Boston a mob threatened to kill Andrew Oliver, the Massachusetts stamp distributor. Other protesters ransacked the mansion of Chief Justice Thomas Hutchinson, destroying many of his belongings, including his magnificent collection of books. Some Americans who had applied for posts as stamp agents quickly changed their minds. The New Hampshire stamp agent resigned after being bullied by an angry crowd: "Some were for cutting off my head, others for cutting off my ears and sending them home with my commission."

The Stamp Act Congress meets. James Otis now proposed that the colonists begin to act together. As a result of his efforts, the Stamp Act Congress met in New York in October, 1765. Nine colonies sent representatives to it. These 27 delegates made up the most important intercolonial gathering yet assembled. The Congress produced a declaration to the king and a petition to Parliament to repeal the Stamp Act, claiming the "undoubted right of Englishmen, that no taxes be imposed on them without their consent." The tone of the protest was respectful, even including a statement of affection for the king and of loyalty to Britain. Still, the delegates agreed that the colonies would *boycott,* or refuse to buy, all British goods until the law was repealed.

The Stamp Act is repealed. Meanwhile, Grenville and George III had had a falling out. A new prime minister, Lord Rockingham, now had to deal with the American colonies. The pressure from British merchants immediately complicated Rockingham's work. Their business had dropped sharply because of the colonists' boycott, and many of them were finding it difficult to collect debts owed them by American importers.

The British merchants pleaded with Parliament to repeal the Stamp Act. Rockingham, hoping to win friends on both sides of the Atlantic, finally agreed. The Stamp Act was lifted in 1766, but the repeal was accompanied by a face-saving law called the Declaratory Act. That measure asserted Parliament's right to tax the colonies if it chose to. The colonists, busy celebrating the repeal of the Stamp Act, ignored the new law.

The Townshend Acts reopen the quarrel. Since the need for revenue remained, Parliament took the advice of Charles Townshend, the new finance minister. He suggested laying import duties on a long list of products important to the colonies. The Townshend Acts, passed in 1767, placed taxes on all glass, paper, lead, tea, and paints entering the colonies. The money collected would be used to help with the cost of colonial administration. Any surplus funds would pay for the stationing of British troops in America.

Townshend did not understand how obstinate the Americans had become. He recognized that the colonists had objected to the Stamp Act as "internal taxation" (duty collected within the colonies). He mistakenly concluded, however, that the Americans would accept the "external taxation" provided for in the Townshend Acts. The truth that escaped Townshend and most members of Parliament was that the colonists did not want any taxes — internal *or* external — levied on them from London.

The Townshend Acts bring forth new protests. Opposition to Parliament's new plan was immediate. British authorities were ready to deal with it. When colonists used violence against customs commissioners in Boston, the warship *Romney* was sent to ride at anchor in that city's harbor. Parliament wanted the colonists to understand that this time there would be no repeal of unpopular tax legislation.

Some colonists insisted on stepping up the pressure. An attractive opportunity arose when the *Romney* seized the sloop

John Hancock, shown with his wife Dorothy Quincy, was a leader in the struggle for independence.

Liberty. The vessel, carrying a smuggled cargo of Madeira wine, happened to be owned by John Hancock, a leading Boston merchant. Hancock had vowed that he would never drink a drop of wine "polluted by the payment of duties." When a group of Boston youths learned of the capture of the *Liberty*, they attacked the customhouse and drove the customs officials out of the city.

The new revenue laws and the *Liberty* incident produced a fresh war of words, waged in newspapers and pamphlets. A widely influential set of arguments appeared in *Letters from a Farmer in Pennsylvania*, written by a well-to-do lawyer named John Dickinson. In these essays Dickinson argued that external taxes to regulate trade were legal, but that external taxes to raise revenue were illegal without the approval of the colonial assemblies. Dickinson's essays contained no call for rebellion or violence. Their author was an advocate of moderation, and he expected that Parliament would eventually adjust its views.

Many colonists, however, were not content with words alone. They revived the method that had worked so well in their opposition to the Stamp Act: the boycott. By agreeing not to buy English goods, they sought once more to bring British merchants to their knees. Again the colonists succeeded. Exports from Britain to the colonies soon fell by 38 percent.

The Townshend Acts are revised. In April, 1770, Parliament repealed all of the Townshend Acts except the one on tea. This tax was retained in order to show that Parliament still claimed the right to tax the colonies. Shortly, the return of general prosperity in Britain as well as in the colonies helped quiet both sides in the struggle. Neither side wanted further upset.

Colonial merchants especially wanted to restore calm at home. Non-importation associations had been formed throughout the colonies to enforce the boycott. The merchants had observed that the associations seemed to encourage some people to enjoy the strong-arm methods and excitement of mob activity. Clearly, society itself would be in danger if the mobs got out of hand and undermined *all* public authority.

In England even loyal supporters of the colonists were distressed by the breaking of British law in America. One English newspaper said it was time to teach the colonists, and especially the people of Boston, "their insignificance." Some colonists, nevertheless, favored continued resistance to Britain. Known as Patriots, they were eager to keep alive the embers of revolt. British authorities were in need of great wisdom to prevent further troubles.

The Boston Massacre strengthens opposition. Following the *Liberty* incident, British authorities had sent two regiments of troops to Boston to help keep order. The arrival of these troops greatly irritated the colonists. Some 10,000 British soldiers were already in North America, stationed there permanently since the end of the French and Indian War. A bill had been passed in 1765 requiring homeowners to provide these soldiers with housing. Many colonists did not understand why, if the frontier required defending, the soldiers had to be in the cities along the seacoast. To the local population the soldiers looked like an army of occupation.

The presence of troops who had been sent to maintain order in Boston only made things worse. There were at least twenty incidents in which a redcoat out alone was attacked and beaten. One mob even threw stones at troops marching in formation. Meanwhile, radical colonial leaders were constantly reminding Bostonians that the troops represented British tyranny pure and simple. The most influential of these leaders was Samuel Adams, a graduate of Harvard College. Adams had never ceased to believe that his father had lost his money as a speculator because of British policies. He worked tirelessly to keep alive the spirit of rebellion by instilling courage in others who were more cautious and by stirring up the young people who did most of the brawling.

The critical moment came on March 5, 1770. A gang of ruffians stood at the customhouse and taunted the soldiers with gibes like, "Come on you rascals, you bloody-backs, you lobster scoundrels, fire if you dare!" Some of the group began to hurl snowballs at the redcoats on duty. The captain of the guard, apparently thinking the troublemakers were bent on seizing the customs receipts, tried to restore calm. Then, as the unruly Bostonians closed in on the soldiers, the word "Fire!" was heard. In the confusion that followed, five colonists were killed. One of the victims was Crispus Attucks, a runaway slave. He and the other victims became heroes to many people in the colonies. Patriots began referring to the incident as the Boston Massacre. Colonists everywhere were now more sour than ever about the stationing of British troops in the colonies.

Following the Boston Massacre, the British soldiers were put on trial and charged with murder. The commanding officer and six of his men were acquitted, while two others were found guilty of manslaughter. One of the defense attorneys was John Adams. A second cousin of Sam Adams, he undertook the unpopular task out of a sense of duty, he said, to see that innocence was protected.

Patriot leaders organize opposition to Britain. Sam Adams kept up his attacks on British policies in brilliantly written pamphlets. He skillfully drew farmers, artisans, and merchants to the Patriot cause. One merchant with whom he worked closely was John Hancock. Hancock, the orphan of a poor minister, had been adopted by a childless uncle who was the richest merchant in Boston. At the age of 27, Hancock inherited his uncle's huge business and a fortune in money. A vain man of good manners and expensive tastes, Hancock enjoyed being a popular idol in the Patriot cause.

Events kept the quarrel with Britain in the public eye. In June, 1772, the British customs schooner *Gaspée* ran aground while pursuing another vessel near Providence, Rhode Island. A band of citizens boarded the *Gaspée*, shot the captain, removed the crew, and set the ship afire. The outraged British vowed to find the culprits, but an extensive search failed to turn them up — even though there had been eight boatloads of men involved.

The Committees of Correspondence are formed. Sam Adams soon persuaded fellow Patriots in Boston to appoint a committee to make contacts with similar groups in other Massachusetts towns. The purpose of the committees was to discuss such events as the *Gaspée* incident and to plan new steps. Within a year all the colonies except Pennsylvania had similar committees. This Patriot network effectively linked the activities of people like Sam Adams in Massachusetts with those of people like Patrick Henry in Virginia.

The Tea Act causes more trouble. A new crisis shortly gave the Committees of Correspondence an opportunity for joint action. The cause of the crisis was, of all things, tea. Tea was usually smuggled into the colonies on Dutch ships. The legally imported tea came on vessels of the British East India Company, a private company that was closely tied to the British government. Partly because of a surplus of seventeen million pounds of tea, the East India Company was in extreme financial difficulty.

In May, 1773, Parliament moved to help the East India Company by passing the Tea Act. This measure granted the Company a monopoly of the tea trade with America. It also allowed the Company to ship tea to the colonies without payment of the regular export tax in Britain. The Company, moreover, would sell tea directly to favored agents in the colonies. Even with the Townshend duty, the tea could be sold in the colonies for less than the smuggled tea from Holland.

The scheme seemed ideal. The colonists, it was thought, would snap up the inexpensive tea, and the East India Company would be rescued from its troubles. At the same time, the colonists would, in effect, be acknowledging the right of Parliament to levy taxes in America, while the tea smugglers would be badly hurt.

The Patriots caught on quickly. They knew that if the tea were sold, they could no longer say that the colonists would refuse to pay taxes laid on them by Britain. The Patriots, therefore, sought to prevent the tea from coming ashore. In their plans they had the support of local merchants. Many merchants were more distressed by the monopoly than by the tax. They were afraid that if a monopoly on tea could be given to one company, other goods might soon be marketed in the same way. All free enterprise would then be in danger.

Boston holds a tea party. The memory of what had happened to the collectors of the stamp tax was still fresh in the colonial cities. Tea agents appointed in New York, Philadelphia, and Charles Town promptly resigned their places. The tea sent to New York and Philadelphia was returned to England. The tea shipped to Charles Town was stored in a warehouse so it would not be sold.

Things were different in Boston — as usual. Governor Thomas Hutchinson was determined that the tea be landed. He wanted to defend the king's cause, of course, but he had another interest too: two of his sons and a nephew had been appointed tea agents. Hutchinson was sure that this time Sam Adams and his associates would have to yield.

Meanwhile, Adams and his colleagues had been making plans. They were spreading word that the Company's tea was no good, because it had been "sweating" for several years in a warehouse. What they meant was explained by one colonist: "Do not suffer yourself to sip the accursed, dirtied stuff. For if you do, the devil will immediately enter into you, and you will instantly become a traitor to your country!"

The Patriot leaders went further than simply spreading propaganda. Meeting on the night of December 16, 1773, a band of fifty or sixty men, disguised as Indians,

Colonists disguised as Mohawk Indians dumped cargoes of tea into Boston harbor in 1773 to protest "taxation without representation."

boarded the three vessels of the East India Company in Boston harbor. They proceeded to dump the Company's tea into the water as thousands of sympathizers watched from the shore.

When news of the Boston Tea Party reached London, people were stunned and dismayed. Many of those who had long sympathized with the colonists were friends no longer. Many Americans were also shocked by this deliberate destruction of property. A few towns even disbanded their Committees of Correspondence.

SECTION REVIEW

1. Vocabulary: *boycott.*
2. (a) What was the Stamp Act? (b) What arguments were used by the colonists who opposed it? (c) What events led to its repeal?
3. (a) How did taxation called for in the Townshend Acts differ from that of the Stamp Act? (b) How did colonists show their opposition? (c) What changes did Parliament make in the Townshend Acts?
4. What was the Boston Massacre?
5. Why did the colonists form Committees of Correspondence?
6. (a) Why did the Tea Act cause more trouble in the colonies? (b) How did Patriot leaders in Boston respond?

4 Fateful Blunders Lead to Open Warfare

The Boston Tea Party put Parliament in a mood of vengeance. Its members recognized that their authority was being challenged brazenly. Only a firm crackdown, they concluded, would prevent even more serious defiance.

Parliament punishes the city of Boston. In early 1774 Parliament passed four laws called the Coercive Acts. The colonists quickly dubbed them the Intolerable Acts. One of the acts ordered the port of Boston to be shut down until the East India Company had been paid for its tea. A second provided that any British official accused of committing a serious offense in enforcing

the laws in Massachusetts would be tried in another colony or in England. Under a third act, soldiers would be quartered, or housed, in the colonies whenever they were needed to suppress disorder. Still another act limited the right of self-government in Massachusetts by weakening the power of the legislature and making it necessary to obtain the governor's permission to hold a town meeting.

The Intolerable Acts strengthen the Patriots. An unplanned result of the Intolerable Acts was to draw the colonies even closer together. The punishment of Boston was so severe — in effect cutting off all the city's trade — that colonists everywhere were stunned. Moreover, when General Thomas Gage, the commander-in-chief of British forces in America, was named governor of Massachusetts, everybody could see that Britain meant business.

Parliament chose this time to pass yet another law that outraged the colonists. This was the Quebec Act of 1774. Providing for the civil government of Canada, the law extended the boundaries of Quebec south to the Ohio River and west to the Mississippi (map, page 111). The effect was to wipe out the western land claims of the thirteen colonies. Land speculators in Virginia, Pennsylvania, Massachusetts, and Connecticut were indignant. Their exasperation added powerful fuel to American opposition to British policy. The Quebec Act also granted religious toleration to Roman Catholics in Quebec, a position that alarmed the inhabitants of the seaboard colonies (who were mostly Protestant).

The new laws persuaded people throughout the colonies that Britain's actions were unjust. A successful planter and lawyer in Virginia named Thomas Jefferson, only 31 years old, wrote a convincing pamphlet. He argued that Britain had no right to tax the colonies, and indeed had no right to exercise any control over them at all. In Pennsylvania a talented Scottish immigrant, James Wilson, wrote a pamphlet in which he came to the same conclusion as Jefferson. In New York another recent arrival, Alexander Hamilton, only seventeen years old, dropped out of King's College in order to aid the Patriots' cause with his lively pen. Hamilton was inclined to defend the king even as he attacked the doings of Parliament.

At the same time that these pamphlets were being circulated, the Committees of Correspondence went into action, urging support for the suffering people of Boston. Help came in a torrent from the other colonies. New York's Sons of Liberty promised enough food to permit Boston to withstand a siege of ten years. Connecticut sent sheep; Pennsylvania, flour; and the Carolinas, rice. Bostonians jeered at Britain, boasting that the supplies had come in greater quantity than the people could readily use.

The First Continental Congress assembles. The royal governor of Virginia was so exasperated by Patriot sentiment that he dissolved the House of Burgesses. Its members promptly reassembled and issued a call for a Continental Congress to discuss the plight of the colonies. People in Virginia and Massachusetts took the lead in organizing such a meeting. Every colony except Georgia chose delegates.

The First Continental Congress met in Carpenters' Hall, Philadelphia, on September 5, 1774. John Adams later described the gathering as a "nursery of American statesmen." In London, William Pitt called it the "most honorable assembly of statesmen since those of ancient Greeks and Romans." The delegates varied in outlook, from would-be rebels like Patrick Henry to moderates like Joseph Galloway of Pennsylvania.

A leading figure was George Washington. He had been slow to join the opposition to British policy. He knew, however, that the actions of Parliament denied him rights that he would have had if he lived in England. In July, 1774, he wrote that the time for petitioning Parliament for relief was past. He explained simply, "We have already tried it in vain." Washington's presence in Philadelphia was important because he was well known and widely respected. He helped reassure wavering colleagues that boldness was what the moment required.

After all, opponents of the Continental Congress were calling the delegates such names as "croakers of calamity."

Sam Adams was clearly the most rebellious of the Patriots. He was tireless in his efforts to get the Congress to support a clean break with Great Britain. Joseph Galloway wrote of him, "He eats little, sleeps little, drinks little, thinks much, and is most decisive and indefatigable in the pursuit of his objects."

The moderates hoped for a peaceful settlement of their differences with Great Britain. They supported a plan put forward by Galloway. The plan, somewhat like the Albany Plan of Union (page 104), would have provided for an American Parliament to be paired with the British Parliament, both to serve under the Crown. Galloway's plan failed by only one vote to be adopted.

The delegates sound the call for strong action. Now the Patriots took over. They were determined to be free of Parliament's control. In a measure written by John Adams, the delegates once again declared that Parliament had no authority to legislate for the colonies without their consent. The delegates also avowed that the colonies must not obey the Intolerable Acts. At the same time, they approved a respectful appeal for reason to the people of Great Britain. This appeal was written by John Jay, a young, well-liked lawyer from New York.

Finally, the First Continental Congress adopted an intercolonial agreement establishing another boycott against Britain. This agreement, known as The Association, also called for encouragement for manufacturing — as if to make ready for a prolonged shortage of British factory goods. The agreement discouraged, in addition, every type of extravagance and public spectacle — like horseracing, cockfighting, and other entertainments. Truly, the delegates seemed to be getting ready for the somber times that wartime might require.

The Patriots created watchdog committees to spy on businesses to see if they were violating The Association. These committees went so far as to ask questions about suspicious transactions. They even handed

Minutemen at the Ready

Spring of 1775 was a tense time in Massachusetts. Abigail Adams was well aware of the dangerous situation since her husband, John Adams, was on his way to the Second Continental Congress in Philadelphia. In a letter, she informed him of an incident that took place on May 24, in their town of Weymouth, just south of Boston.

I suppose you had a formidable account of the alarm we had Sunday morning. When I awoke about six o'clock, I was told that the drums were beating, that three alarm guns were fired, and that the Weymouth bell was ringing. I immediately went out to find the reasons for the alarm and saw the whole town in confusion. Three British sloops and one cutter had come out of Boston and dropped anchor just below Great Hill.

A report came that 300 men had landed and were marching to town. The alarm flew like lightning, and men from all parts came flocking down till 2,000 were collected. It turned out that the British troops were heading for Grape Island to seize Levet's hay. It was difficult for our men to get out to the island since there were no boats. But the sight of such an assemblage of armed men prevented the British from getting more than three tons of hay.

At last a sloop came around from Hingham and some of our men got to the island. They quickly set fire to Levet's barn and destroyed over 80 tons of hay, thus keeping it out of the hands of the British.

A statue of a minuteman

We expect there to be continual alarms until something decisive takes place. We wait with longing expectation in hope of hearing good news from you about union and harmony among the colonies.

out punishment to merchants they believed had acted disloyally to the Patriot cause. The actions of these committees alarmed many people. They wondered if the tyranny of their fellow-colonists had not simply replaced the tyranny of the British.

The Congress agreed to meet again in May, 1775, if British wrongs had not been set right. Meanwhile, the Patriots prepared for war. John Adams wrote Patrick Henry, "I expect no redress, but, on the contrary, increased resentment and double vengeance. We must fight." Henry agreed heartily. Patriot leaders were more and more certain that the colonies were caught in a conspiracy against their liberties that only they themselves could break.

Parliament refuses to back down. America's few supporters in Parliament were still trying to achieve conciliation with the rebellious colonies. Lord Chatham introduced a bill to remove the redcoats from Boston, but it was too late. Benjamin Franklin, who was in London representing Massachusetts, wrote that the motion was treated by the

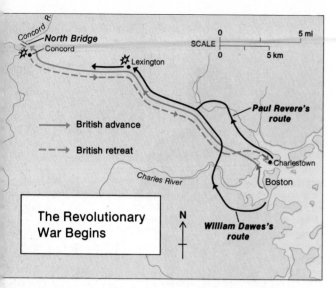

Fighting at Lexington and Concord marked the beginning of the American Revolution.

members "with as much contempt as they could have shown to a ballad offered by a drunken porter." George III, meanwhile, had written, "The New England governments are in a state of rebellion, [and] blows must decide whether they are to be subject to this country or independent."

The colonists prepare to fight. Patriot militiamen in Massachusetts were beginning to store arms and ammunition to fight the British. They were confident that they could count on help from the other colonies. General Gage knew that when the "blows" fell, Massachusetts would not be fighting alone. He had seen at first hand how fiercely independent in outlook the American colonists had become. Passions in Britain also ran hot. As the king explained, "The spirit of the British nation [is] too high . . . to give up so many colonies which she has planted with great industry, nursed with great tenderness . . . and protected and defended at much expense of blood and treasures."

On February 9, 1775, Parliament declared Massachusetts to be in open rebellion. The New England colonies were forbidden to trade anywhere in the world except with Britain, Ireland, and the British West Indies. New England's fishing fleets were banned from the waters off New-

foundland. In April these restrictions were extended to five other colonies.

British authorities believed they could end the revolt by arresting Sam Adams and John Hancock and bringing them to trial in England. The prime minister, Lord North, guessed that most colonists found the Boston Patriots annoying and would enjoy seeing them taken down a peg or two.

Lord North, who had mismanaged American affairs since 1770, received much bad advice. The head of the British navy had informed him, for instance, that American troops were "raw, undisciplined, cowardly men [and that] the very sound of a cannon would carry them off." In Parliament, Lord North often dozed through important speeches. Seeing the prime minister napping during one session, Edmund Burke, an admirer of America, expressed the hope that the "government was not dead, but only asleep."

The first shots of the American Revolution are fired. The British could not remain idle while Massachusetts Patriots defied the government by gathering arms. General Gage decided, therefore, to move on the village of Concord to seize a supply of arms that local Patriots had hidden there. He also hoped to capture Sam Adams and John Hancock, who were at nearby Lexington.

Patriots in Boston were expecting the British to take action, and they kept a constant eye on the redcoats. A well-known engraver and silversmith named Paul Revere arranged a signal to inform the countryside of any British move. He explained it later: "If the British went by water, we would show two lanterns in the North Church steeple; and if by land, one as a signal."

Shortly before midnight on April 18, 1775, Gage sent his men toward Lexington. Quickly, Revere was on his way to give warning. He rowed across the Charles River, his oars muffled by an old petticoat. He found Adams and Hancock in Lexington and sped them on their way to safety. As the sun rose, Adams turned to Hancock and whispered, "What a glorious morning this is!" He added, with a chuckle, "I mean for America."

The militiamen, called *minutemen* because they were pledged to be ready to fight on very short notice, rushed to the Lexington village green just as the redcoats approached. British officers called out, "Throw down your arms and you shall come to no harm." There came immediately from the rebel ranks the clear voice of Captain John Parker: "Don't fire unless fired upon. But if they want a war, let it begin here." Ignoring an order to disperse, the Americans held their ground. Shots were exchanged, and in minutes eight Americans lay dead and ten had been wounded.

The British now swept on toward Concord. Neither Revere nor William Dawes, a Patriot companion, had been able to alert the Concord minutemen. Dr. Samuel Prescott got through, however, and when the British reached Concord, they were met by a large force of minutemen who had poured in from nearby towns and villages. The men held North Bridge against the redcoats, who now fled back to Boston in disarray. Years later Ralph Waldo Emerson immortalized the engagement with the lines:

> Here once the embattled farmers stood,
> And fired the shot heard round the world.

As the reports of American bravery and success sped from colony to colony, a strong sense of unity developed. Each day more and more people could understand the true meaning of Patrick Henry's words, "The distinctions between Virginians, Pennsylvanians, New Yorkers and New Englanders are no more. I am not a Virginian, but an American." A group of frontier settlers in Kentucky decided to name their town Lexington, in honor of the victory their fellow Americans had won in Massachusetts.

A woman in Philadelphia boldly wrote a friend, a captain in the British army in Boston, that she was ready to make her contribution to the cause of liberty. Her only brother had already joined the rebel army. She was sorry, she said, that she did not have twenty brothers and sons who could also go. She herself had stopped drinking tea and buying new clothes since the Battle of Lexington. She had now learned to knit,

Paul Revere won fame for carrying news to Lexington of the approach of the British and for warning Samuel Adams and John Hancock of their danger.

she continued, and was "making stockings of American wool for my servants." She concluded, "I know this, that as free I can die but once, but as a slave I shall not be worthy of life. I have the pleasure to assure you that these are the sentiments of all my sister Americans."

We do not know what the captain thought when he read these defiant words. They hint, however, at the mighty burden resting on the American rebels: they would have to make the outcome of the struggle ahead justify the sacrifice and high ideals of their supporters.

SECTION REVIEW

1. Vocabulary: *minuteman*.
2. (a) What were the Intolerable Acts? (b) Why were they passed? (c) What effect did they have on the Patriots?
3. (a) Why did Patriots in Virginia issue a call for a Continental Congress? (b) What action did the Congress take?
4. (a) What was General Gage's aim in sending British troops to Lexington and Concord? (b) What happened as a result? (c) What was the reaction in the other colonies?

Chapter 5 Review

Summary

Beginning in 1689, Britain and France fought a series of wars over their American possessions. The final bout in the struggle, known as the French and Indian War, started in 1754 when the French tried to tighten control of the Ohio River valley. That war ended with the capture by Generals Amherst and Wolfe of the French fortresses of Quebec and Montreal. The Treaty of Paris (1763) gave Britain control over Canada and all the French land east of the Mississippi, as well as Florida. France turned over New Orleans and Louisiana to its ally, Spain.

Once the British had triumphed over France in the struggle for North America, relations with the American colonists quickly began to deteriorate. British efforts to establish a new land policy, regulate trade, and make the colonies pay a larger share of the cost of government were major points of conflict. Some of the most heated debate surrounded the Stamp Act, a measure that raised the question of whether Parliament had the right to tax the colonies. Outspoken colonists denounced the Stamp Act as "taxation without representation." They formed groups called Sons of Liberty and Daughters of Liberty, and led boycotts of British goods.

After Parliament repealed the Stamp Act, it passed new tax measures known as the Townshend Acts. Colonial opposition to the Townshend Acts was just as vehement. In 1770 Parliament again backed down, repealing all the acts except for the tax on tea. Many colonists, wanting peace, were content to have friendly relations restored. Some Americans, on the other hand, favored resistance to British authority. Following the Boston Massacre, Committees of Correspondence were formed in almost every colony to strengthen the Patriot cause.

After colonists dumped the East India Company's tea into Boston harbor in December, 1773, to protest a new Tea Act, Parliament made up its mind to punish Massachusetts. It passed the Coercive (or Intolerable) Acts for that purpose. As a result, anti-British sentiment became more widespread. Patriots played a leading role in organizing the First Continental Congress, which voted to deny Parliament's authority to legislate over the colonies without their consent. The Congress also passed measures urging the colonies to prepare for possible warfare. Angered, Parliament enacted further punitive measures and ordered troops in Massachusetts to seize arms that had been gathered by local Patriots. Fighting at Lexington and Concord resulted, and the American Revolution had begun.

Vocabulary and Important Terms

1. Albany Plan of Union
2. French and Indian War
3. writs of assistance
4. Sugar Act
5. duty
6. Proclamation Line of 1763
7. Stamp Act
8. boycott
9. Declaratory Act
10. Townshend Acts
11. Patriot
12. Boston Massacre
13. Committees of Correspondence
14. Tea Act
15. Boston Tea Party
16. Intolerable Acts
17. Quebec Act
18. First Continental Congress
19. minuteman

Discussion Questions

1. (a) What was the immediate cause of the French and Indian War? (b) What was William Pitt's grand strategy for defeating the French, and how successful was this strategy? (c) How did the outcome of the French and Indian War remake the map of North America?

2. (a) Why did Britain's leaders believe they did not have to make any more concessions to the colonies after the French and Indian War? (b) What events were advance signs that the colonies would resist interference from Britain?

3. (a) Why did British authorities issue the Proclamation of 1763 and pass the Sugar Act in 1764? (b) How did the colonists react to these new laws? (c) Why was a new mood of self-confidence beginning to develop in the colonies at this time?

4. (a) Why did George Grenville propose the Stamp Act? (b) Why did James Otis denounce the Stamp Act as "taxation without representation"? (c) What was the British response to this argument?

5. (a) In what ways did the colonists show their opposition to the Stamp Act? (b) What form of colonial protest caused the repeal of the Stamp Act? (c) Why at the same time did Parliament issue the Declaratory Act?

6. (a) Why did Charles Townshend propose the Townshend Acts? (b) What mistaken belief did Townshend have about the willingness of the colonists to be taxed? (c) What new colonial protests did the Townshend Acts bring forth? (d) In repealing most of the Townshend Acts, why did Parliament retain the tax on tea?

7. (a) Who emerged as leaders of the Patriot opposition to Britain? (b) Why were Committees of Correspondence formed, and how effective were these committees?

8. (a) Why did the British think that the Tea Act would be an ideal scheme of taxation? (b) What arguments were used by colonists opposed to the Tea Act?

9. (a) What unplanned effect did the Intolerable Acts have on the colonies? (b) Why did the Quebec Act further outrage the colonists?

10. What actions taken by the First Continental Congress showed that the colonists were determined to be free of Parliament's control?

11. Why did fighting break out between British forces and Patriot minutemen at the towns of Lexington and Concord?

Relating Past to Present

One of the actions taken by delegates to the Stamp Act Congress was to send a petition to Parliament asking for repeal of the Stamp Act. When and for what reasons are petitions used in our society today? In what other ways can we communicate our wishes, concerns, and beliefs to government leaders?

Studying Local History

What effect, if any, did the struggle for control of North America have on your state? What country other than the United States once claimed the territory that made up your state?

Using History Skills

1. *Classifying.* Make a chart with two columns. In one column list arguments in support of Parliament's belief that it had the right to govern the colonies in any way it pleased. In the other column list arguments that supported the Patriots' belief that Parliament did not have that right. Use the information in your chart to prepare for a classroom debate on the topic of Parliament's right to exercise full control over the colonies.

2. *Writing a report.* Two of the most outspoken Patriot leaders were Samuel Adams and Patrick Henry. Use an encyclopedia or history of early America to find out about the lives of these two men after the Revolution. Write a report based on this information.

WORLD SCENE

Far-flung Wars

After they started colonies, European nations came into conflict outside of Europe. The French and Indian War, for instance, was only one phase of a worldwide contest.

The war in Europe. From 1689 to 1763 France and Britain were engaged in a series of wars to determine which would be the dominant colonial power in the world. The struggle led to British involvement in a brutal war in Europe from 1756 to 1763, even as redcoats were fighting the French and Indians in America. The Seven Years' War, as it is known, grew out of competition between Prussia and Austria for dominance of Central Europe. Since France was allied with Austria, which had assistance from Russia and Sweden, Britain gave its support to the Prussian side.

The king of Prussia at this time was Frederick the Great, who began the war in 1756 with a surprise attack on Saxony, a minor ally of Austria. He went on to win a number of important victories over the forces of Russia, Sweden, and Austria. As the war progressed, however, Prussia's ability to combat these combined armies declined. Just when it seemed Prussia would be overwhelmed, the ruler of Russia died and her successor, an ad-

mirer of Frederick the Great, ended Russian participation in the war. Unable to defeat Prussia without Russian support, Austria agreed to a peace settlement.

The war in India. While the Seven Years' War was dragging on in Europe, French and British armies were also fighting in India. British and French trading companies had long been rivals for the profitable trade with India. At the beginning of the fighting in 1756, the French joined forces with the ruler of the state of Bengal, and together they captured the British garrison in the city of Calcutta. The ruler of Bengal locked up the British survivors in a small cell. By the next morning over half of them had suffocated.

When the British heard the news of the "Black Hole of Calcutta" (as it has been known ever since), they were outraged. A force made up of British troops and their Indian allies recaptured Calcutta. Soon afterwards, at the Battle of Plassey (1757), the combined force overwhelmed a large army of French and Bengali troops. After this battle, the French could no longer block British expansion in India. The battle marked the end of French influence in India.

CHAPTER **6**

Winning the American Revolution

1775 – 1783

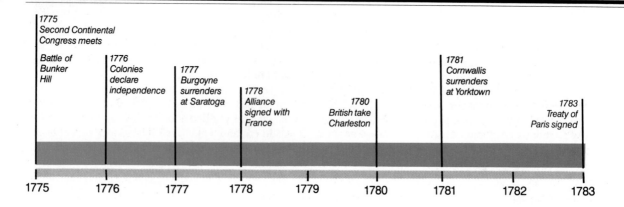

1775
Second Continental
Congress meets

Battle of
Bunker
Hill

1776
Colonies
declare
independence

1777
Burgoyne
surrenders
at Saratoga

1778
Alliance
signed with
France

1780
British take
Charleston

1781
Cornwallis
surrenders
at Yorktown

1783
Treaty of
Paris signed

1775   1776   1777   1778   1779   1780   1781   1782   1783

CHAPTER OUTLINE

1. The American colonies declare their independence.

2. The Americans struggle against heavy odds.

3. The fight for independence continues.

4. American victories win the Revolutionary War.

In the spring and summer of 1775 the "embattled farmers" of the American colonies responded to a call to arms that would pit them against one of the most highly trained and best-equipped armies in the world. Eventually the British would have 50,000 of their troops stationed in America, as well as 30,000 mercenaries. The Patriot army, on the other hand, would rarely have 5,000 men. By all standards, moreover, the rebel troops would be ill-supplied, badly organized, and poorly trained. Encounters such as the Battle of Bunker Hill, however, proved that the colonists were willing to stand and fight.

The idea of struggling against heavy odds was not new in the experience of the colonists. The constant uncertainties of frontier existence, the extraordinary labor required to turn forests into farms, and the tragic encounters with the Indians had formed their outlook. It had also provided them with lessons and inspiration. Thinking over their history, now more than 150 years long, they could justifiably credit self-reliance and individual initiative for their record of overcoming obstacles.

The work, nonetheless, was unfinished. For such a people as they were, it was only "common sense," as Thomas Paine put it, to form a free and independent nation. Drawing on their past and their faith in themselves, the American colonists knew they had the courage and stamina to do what was required in order to win the prize of liberty.

124

1 The American Colonies Declare Their Independence

When the First Continental Congress adjourned in the autumn of 1774, the delegates agreed to reassemble in the following spring if colonial grievances remained. All during the winter of 1774–1775 tensions increased between the colonies and Great Britain, and in April, militiamen and redcoats fought in Massachusetts (page 121). News of the fighting reached Philadelphia just before the delegates to the Second Continental Congress met on May 10, 1775.

The Second Continental Congress discusses colonial grievances. The members of the Second Continental Congress recognized that hopes for reconciliation with Britain were growing dim. The mood of the delegates, moreover, was more radical in outlook than that of the First Continental Congress. The body included many individuals with strong views. Benjamin Franklin and John Adams were there. So were other notable names of the recent struggles, including Sam Adams and John Hancock from Massachusetts and Patrick Henry and Thomas Jefferson from Virginia.

A few optimistic, moderate delegates still believed it possible to patch up the differences with Britain. The majority, however, argued that military force alone could win concessions. A number of the delegates had already concluded that complete independence was the only realistic goal. Nevertheless, those favoring a break with Britain had to proceed cautiously in seeking to carry their colleagues with them.

Congress petitions George III once more. While continuing to assert that colonial rights had been trampled on, the Congress made one more conciliatory gesture to King George III. It offered what came to be known as the Olive Branch Petition. The work of John Dickinson (page 114), and

After the Americans inflicted heavy losses on the British at the Battle of Bunker Hill, General Gage reported to his superiors in London, "These people show a spirit and conduct against us they never showed against the French."

BOSTON

CHARLES TOWN

signed "your faithful colonists," the petition urged the king to protect the colonists from the harsh policies of Parliament.

George III had already decided he must use force to defend British authority in America. "When once these rebels have felt a smart blow, they will submit," he declared. He refused even to receive the Olive Branch Petition.

The Patriots take the offensive. Until the late spring of 1775, American military action had been defensive only. Now the Patriots went on the attack. On Lake Champlain, in northeastern New York, British army posts guarded the military road to Canada. A ragtag group of volunteers called the Green Mountain Boys, from what is now Vermont, seized the posts at Crown Point and Fort Ticonderoga. Ethan Allen, a New Hampshire land speculator, led the small Patriot band that captured Ticonderoga. When the British commander demanded to know on what authority the Patriots were acting, Allen responded, "In the name of the Great Jehovah and the Continental Congress."

Meanwhile, in June, 1775, Patriot troops gave a good account of themselves on another battlefield. After the British retreat to Boston, Patriot forces surrounded the city. They began to occupy the heights in Charlestown, from which artillery could command Boston. Before the Americans could dig in, however, General Gage attacked and the Battle of Bunker Hill was under way. (Fighting took place on Breed's Hill, but the engagement is named for nearby Bunker Hill.) After two costly British assaults, the Patriots were finally driven off. The British, nevertheless, had suffered heavy losses. Gage wrote home that the casualties were "greater than we can bear."

Congress establishes an army. Congress now decided to form a Continental Army to assist Massachusetts in driving the redcoats from Boston. The delegates chose George Washington, the most celebrated soldier in the colonies, to lead the Patriot forces. Washington journeyed north from Virginia, reviewing several companies of volunteers along the way. He arrived in Philadelphia wearing his blue and buff uniform as a colonel in the Virginia militia. He may have put on the uniform to show the delegates that Virginia, the most important southern colony, was ready to join the fight.

John Adams had helped push the selection of Washington as commander of the army. Adams did not yet know Washington's character. He had a troubling thought or two that a victorious general might make himself king of an independent America. Another Massachusetts leader, though, had more generous feelings: "I pity our poor general, who has a greater burden on his shoulders than I think should fall to the share of so good a man." After John Adams's wife, Abigail, met Washington, she reported graciously, "The gentleman and the soldier look agreeably blended in him."

Washington takes command in Massachusetts. Washington took command of the Patriot army at Cambridge, outside of Boston, on July 3, 1775. In the months that followed, the Patriots were unable to drive the British from Boston. Then, early in 1776, Washington was immensely strengthened by the arrival of cannon captured at Ticonderoga. These heavy weapons had been

After the Patriots fortified Dorchester Heights with cannon dragged overland from Fort Ticonderoga, the British decided to evacuate Boston.

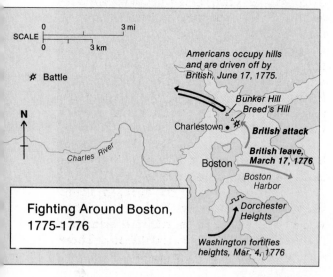

SCALE

0 ——— 3 mi
0 ——— 3 km

✳ Battle

N

Charles River

Americans occupy hills and are driven off by British, June 17, 1775.

Bunker Hill
Breed's Hill

Charlestown

British attack

British leave, March 17, 1776

Boston

Boston Harbor

Dorchester Heights

Washington fortifies heights, Mar. 4, 1776

Fighting Around Boston, 1775-1776

dragged part of the way to Boston on sleds drawn by oxen. The guns helped the Continental Army to fortify Dorchester Heights, which overlooked Boston.

The British, meanwhile, had concluded that General Gage was too timid a commander. They replaced him with Sir William Howe, a brave officer who had led the first party of men up the cliffs of Quebec during the French and Indian War (page 107). Recognizing the price they would have to pay to dislodge the Americans now armed and dug in around Boston, the British decided to withdraw to Halifax, in Nova Scotia. With General Howe in command, the troops left Boston on March 17, 1776.

So high were anti-British feelings in Boston that over a thousand colonists loyal to the king fled with Howe, fearing for their safety if they remained behind. Many of these Loyalists, as they were called, assumed that Britain had lost the war. Preferring to live under the Crown, they wanted no part of an independent America.

Fighting breaks out elsewhere. Britain knew that Loyalist sentiment was strong in many colonies. Policymakers were relying on the Loyalists, or Tories as they were called in the South, to bring the rebellious colonists to their senses. At the same time, Britain believed that sending powerful naval forces to America as a display of strength would effectively frighten the rebels.

British hopes for military help from the Loyalists were dashed in early 1776, however, when rebels defeated a unit of Tories at Moore's Creek, North Carolina. The Patriots took 800 prisoners. Only a few weeks later, having secured Boston, Washington moved his army to New York and set up headquarters there.

Three great British expeditions were now moving across the Atlantic. One was bound for Quebec, one for Charleston, and one for New York. The expedition to Quebec was under orders to protect that fortress city from ambitious Americans who hoped to seize Canada. Late in 1775 General Richard Montgomery and an American force had attacked and captured Montreal. When Montgomery and Colonel Benedict Arnold, one of the heroes of Ticonderoga, tried to take Quebec, however, they failed. Montgomery was killed in the fighting, and Arnold and his troops were forced to camp outside the city as winter closed in. In the spring of 1776 a British army led by Sir Guy Carleton pushed Arnold back to Lake Champlain.

The British attack Charleston. The second British naval expedition, under orders to attack Charleston, was led by Admiral Sir Peter Parker. After the long Atlantic crossing, the fleet arrived in June, 1776. It met the inspired resistance of Colonel William Moultrie and 600 militiamen. The Americans pounded the British ships from behind a partially built fort (later named for Moultrie). Aboard Parker's ships were 2,000 British troops under the command of Sir Henry Clinton. The ships were badly battered by the cannon fire, which caused heavy British casualties. The vessels turned tail and headed for New York, with only one of the ships still seaworthy. A British sailor wrote sadly, "We never had such a drubbing in our lives."

The campaign for New York begins. The third British expedition, a mighty fleet on its way to New York, was under the flag of Admiral Richard Howe, brother of the general who had replaced Gage at Boston. The colonists, it was assumed, would be intimidated by the very sight of the vessels and would quickly surrender. If the show of force failed to have an effect, then the British intended to seize New York City and sail up the Hudson River, cutting off New England from the rest of the colonies. New England, considered to be the heart of the rebel conspiracy, was still the main target of British wrath.

The naval attack on New York was to be coordinated with a powerful assault on land. According to the plan, General Howe's troops would be brought south from Halifax to New York City. They would land and move northward along the Hudson River valley toward Albany. There they would join Carleton's troops.

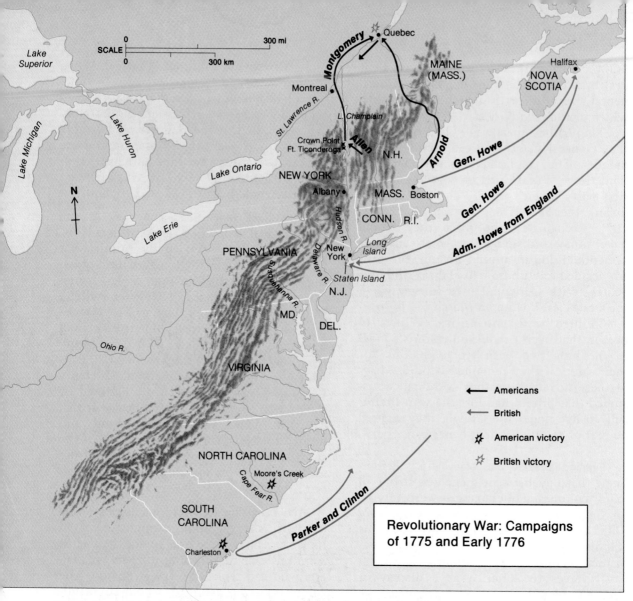

The first year of the war was discouraging for the Patriots. Despite two victories in the South and the withdrawal of British forces from Boston, the American plan to capture Quebec failed. A strong British force, meanwhile, occupied New York City.

Anticipating the Howes' strategy, General Washington moved his soldiers to the western end of Long Island. On July 2, General Howe came ashore at New York. He and his brother commanded the largest fighting force that the American continent had ever seen. It included over 32,000 experienced soldiers and more than 350 ships manned by 10,000 sailors.

Congress debates the call for independence. The Howes arrived just as a momentous political event was taking place — one that would change forever the history of the world. For fourteen months the Continental Congress had held back from making a clean break with Britain. Not all the colonists were as aflame for rebellion as the people of Boston. Even Sam Adams saw that independence could not be rushed, that it was necessary to "wait till the fruit is ripe before we gather it." When the time came, he knew, it would be necessary that the colonies work together. Benjamin Franklin put it bluntly: "We must all hang together, or assuredly we shall all hang separately."

Thomas Paine's "The Crisis" (1776)

These are the times that try men's souls. The summer soldier and the sunshine patriot, will, in this crisis, shrink from the service of their country; but he that stands by it *now* deserves the love and thanks of man and woman. Tyranny . . . is not easily conquered; yet we have this consolation with us, that the harder the conflict, the more glorious the triumph. What we obtain too cheap, we esteem too lightly; it is dearness only that gives everything its value. Heaven knows how to put a proper price upon its goods; and it would be strange indeed, if so celestial an article as *freedom* should not be highly rated. Britain, with an army to enforce her tyranny, had declared that she has the right, not only to tax, but "to *bind* us in *all cases whatsoever*"; . . . if being bound in that manner is not slavery, then there is not such a thing as slavery upon earth.

. . . Not a place upon earth might be so happy as America. Her situation is remote from all the wrangling world, and she has nothing to do but to trade with them. . . . I am as confident as I am that God governs the world, that America will never be happy till she gets clear of foreign domination.

By his actions, George III had helped Patriot leaders complete the work of unifying colonial opinion. In October, 1775, for instance, the king announced that he intended to hire foreign troops, or **mercenaries,** to fight the Americans. The very idea of buying the services of troops from other European countries infuriated the rebels.

By the beginning of 1776, colonial leaders were asking harder questions: How will we govern ourselves now that royal authority has collapsed? Is the Continental Congress to be permanent? What is the army fighting for? How can we get the foreign military assistance we need? Colonial leaders knew that France would do almost anything to separate Britain from its American colonies. French aid could only come, however, after the colonies themselves had broken their ties with Great Britain. Many people could see that a declaration of independence must be the first move toward securing foreign help.

Thomas Paine stirs public opinion. In January, 1776, a pamphlet was published that made the case for independence seem more appealing than ever. Appearing at just the right moment, *Common Sense* immediately achieved enormous influence. It was the work of Thomas Paine, an Englishman who had only recently arrived in America.

Paine attacked the monarchy and especially George III, calling him "the Royal Brute of Great Britain." Paine's words had wide influence. "Everything that is right or natural pleads for separation," he asserted. "Even the distance at which the Almighty hath placed England and America is a strong and natural proof that the authority of one over the other was never the design of heaven." Reconciliation, he argued, would be the ruin of America. People who already favored a clean break with Britain now seemed happier than ever to champion that course. (Above is reprinted a famous passage from *The Crisis*, a pamphlet written by Thomas Paine in December, 1776.)

The Declaration of Independence is prepared. By May, John Adams was writing that "every post and every day rolls in upon us Independence like a torrent." Fervent Patriots were gaining control in most of the colonies. The time for decisive action seemed at hand.

129

On June 7, 1776, Richard Henry Lee of Virginia introduced three resolutions in the Continental Congress. The first proposed that "these United Colonies are, and of right ought to be, free and independent States. . . ." The second proposed that the colonies seek at once to arrange foreign alliances. The third proposed that the colonies form themselves into a confederation.

A committee made up of Thomas Jefferson of Virginia, Benjamin Franklin of Pennsylvania, John Adams of Massachusetts, Roger Sherman of Connecticut, and Robert R. Livingston of New York had already been appointed to prepare a declaration of independence. The men agreed on the declaration's general content. Jefferson was then designated by the others to write the draft. Jefferson's eloquence and skill at argument had already been demonstrated in several important Virginia documents.

When Jefferson sat at the portable desk he had brought to Philadelphia, he understood his task. He must write, in uplifting language, a statement that would present the arguments for independence so well that they would seem beyond dispute. Jefferson's handiwork proved a stunning success. Aside from minor changes proposed by Adams and Franklin, the Declaration of Independence is entirely the great Virginian's creation. Lee's reaction to the finished product was typical: "The thing is in its nature so good, that no cooking can spoil the dish for the palates of freemen."

The colonies declare their independence. The moderates in Congress could no longer delay the movement for independence. Lee's first resolution — the one calling for independence — was debated briefly and adopted on July 2. Despite this remarkable action, it was July 4, 1776, that would be remembered forever by all people who love freedom.

July 4 dawned as an ordinary day. In the morning Jefferson occupied himself by ordering gloves for the women of his family. It was, however, no ordinary day for America. In the afternoon the Congress enthusiastically approved and adopted the Declaration. John Hancock of Massachusetts, president of the Congress, signed it with bold strokes. Other members of the Congress put their names to it at a formal ceremony on August 2. In the meantime, the text of the Declaration was rushed to the legislatures of the newly created states, so that its words could become known to all Americans.

On July 4, 1776, the members of the Second Continental Congress approved the Declaration of Independence.

The Declaration proclaims human liberty. The text of the Declaration of Independence can be found at the back of this book. The document is divided into two parts. The first part is a general statement of principles. It expresses the idea that people are entitled to certain rights that government cannot take from them. "We hold these truths to be self-evident," states the Declaration, "that all men are created equal, that they are endowed by their Creator with certain unalienable rights, that among these are Life, Liberty, and the pursuit of Happiness." This immortal sentence named the rights that have ever since been the goals of good government for all peoples.

The principles stated in the Declaration reflect ideals, not realities. Since 1776 many generations of Americans have sought to bring their laws and institutions into harmony with these ideals. As Abraham Lincoln said, many years later, of Jefferson and other of the nation's founders, "They meant to set up a standard maxim for a free society, which could be constantly looked to, constantly labored for, and even though never perfectly attained, constantly approximated."

In another shining phrase, Jefferson declared his perfect faith that only upon "the consent of the governed" can a just government be based. He had offered humanity the vision of a government more responsive to its people than any had ever been before. In so doing, the purpose of the struggle with Britain was now greatly enlarged.

The second part of the Declaration is a list of specific grievances against George III. Jefferson heaped much abuse on that weak but essentially humane man in order to personify "the enemy." To attack a single individual seemed a much better tactic than to attack Parliament, composed of many individuals. Besides, it was British tradition to attack the Crown, not Parliament. It may also have been in Jefferson's mind that if the rebellion failed, the colonists would have to make peace with Parliament, not with the king. It would be wise not to anger the members in advance.

No one could yet estimate the price that Americans would have to pay to achieve their goals of independence and self-government. Even as the Declaration was before the Congress, however, the Patriots glimpsed the promise of the future. John Adams wrote to his wife, "I am well aware of the toil, and blood, and treasure, that it will cost us to maintain this declaration and support and defend the States. Yet through all the gloom I can see the rays of ravishing light and glory."

SECTION REVIEW

1. Vocabulary: *mercenary*.
2. (a) What final step did the Second Continental Congress take to try to settle its dispute with Great Britain? (b) What was the response of George III?
3. (a) How did Patriot forces capture Boston? (b) Where else did fighting between Patriots and British troops take place early in the war?
4. What was Britain's three-part strategy for putting an end to the American Revolution?
5. (a) Why were the delegates to the Second Continental Congress at first reluctant to declare independence? (b) For what reasons did they finally decide to break ties with Britain? (c) What three proposals were presented by Richard Henry Lee to the Congress?
6. Describe the two main parts of the Declaration of Independence.

2 The Americans Struggle Against Heavy Odds

The road ahead for America would be long, hard, and, for some time, lonely. To win, the rebels required organization, money, foreign assistance, and unbreakable will. These elements did not come together until there had been many setbacks and disappointments.

Maintaining a Patriot army is difficult. Large numbers of Americans were in favor of the struggle against Britain. Only a tiny fraction of the population, however, served in the Continental Army. Mostly the colonies relied on their militias and on men serving short-term enlistments.

The Patriots never had a large army of regulars. They relied instead on militiamen, like these North Carolinians who rallied to expel the British from their state in 1780.

Discipline in the army was a constant problem at first. Most of the officers were elected by their men. Rank, therefore, often was proof of popularity rather than of military ability. To ensure obedience, General Washington worked hard to eliminate the easy friendship existing between officers and enlisted men.

Desertion and absence without leave were also problems. Soldiers tended to disappear in the spring at planting time and in the fall at harvest time in order to help at home. It has been estimated that up to 25 percent of the men of the Continental Army were absent without leave at one time or another. Still, shocking as that figure seems, it was considerably lower than the usual rate in European armies of the time.

No reliable count of casualties[1] in the Revolutionary War was ever made. Disease probably killed ten times more Patriot soldiers than did enemy bullets. The Continental Army in 1777 had three to five times as many soldiers in hospitals as the British. The hospitals were badly run, and the sick and wounded were crowded together. Only patients who could pay had adequate food. Benjamin Rush, surgeon general of the Continental Army, wrote after the war, "Most of the suffering and mortality in our hospitals were occasioned not so much by actual want or scarcity of anything as by the ignorance, negligence, etc., in providing necessaries for them."

Conditions were harsh for the soldiers. Officers and men alike were expected to bring their own firearms when they enlisted. Officers had to buy not only their own uniforms but also all their own food. Although soldiers were issued clothing, a deduction was made each month from their meager wages until the clothing had been paid for. Blankets were so scarce that soldiers who brought their own were granted a small money allowance.

Yet more significant than all the problems was the quality of the troops who stood and fought. They sustained their morale by keeping before them the justice and purpose of the war — a fact attested to in the many diaries that soldiers kept. Their determination was reflected in how they fought. A French officer who served with the Continentals said, "It is incredible that soldiers composed of men of every age,

---

[1]*Casualties* refers to soldiers injured, killed, captured, or missing in action.

even children of fifteen, of whites and blacks, almost naked, unpaid, and poorly fed, can march so well and withstand fire so steadfastly." Many British officers also admired the fortitude of the Americans.

Not all Americans support independence. The Americans most immediately hurt by the outbreak of the fighting were the Loyalists. They comprised a very significant portion of colonial society. Many of them were people whose social and business connections made them directly dependent upon the Crown. These included career military officers, appointees of the royal governors, and lawyers whose work was chiefly in behalf of the king's interests. Many landowners and merchants also remained loyal to the Crown, as did the Anglican clergy, whose church recognized the king as its head.

As a group, the Loyalists probably were no richer or poorer than the Patriots. Most of them were ordinary people, in full agreement with the argument "no taxation without representation." However, they refused to agree with the rebels that the king and Parliament were engaged in a conspiracy against their liberties.

Ardent Patriots found the Loyalists a potential danger to the cause. The Continental Congress persuaded the states to pass treason laws and other statutes describing crimes against the Revolution. These crimes included giving military information to the British, spreading demoralizing rumors, and even speaking kindly of the king.

To be a Loyalist in some parts of the country was harder than in others. In New England, Loyalists were a lonely minority, making up only about 10 percent of the population. In three states — New York, Pennsylvania, and South Carolina — Loyalists were probably in the majority. Being unorganized, however, they were unable to protect themselves from their Patriot neighbors, who sometimes showed more hostility toward them than toward the British. The 1700's were violent times, and it was not unheard of for people to be tarred and feathered or driven from their homes. The threat of such treatment could guarantee

good behavior on the part of most Loyalists.

Tragically, the issue of loyalty sometimes split families. A brother of William Hooper, who signed the Declaration of Independence for North Carolina, was a Loyalist. So was Benjamin Franklin's son, William Franklin, who served as the royal governor of New Jersey.

By the end of the American Revolution, about 100,000 Loyalists had left the country. Some of them went to Nova Scotia; others sailed for England. Those who fled to England were generously treated by the British government. Still, they were homesick for America, and many grew increasingly disillusioned and unhappy with the British military effort across the water. Most of them never returned to America. Joseph Galloway (page 118) fled to England in 1778 and became the spokesman there for Loyalists. His estate in America had been confiscated and he had to live on a small British pension. Even as late as 1793, Pennsylvania refused him permission to return, and Galloway died in exile.

The Patriots have some advantages. Despite the odds facing the Americans, they had several advantages in the struggle. First, they were fighting for their own future. Having declared themselves for independence, they knew there could be no turning back. Defeat would mean disaster — personal as well as public. Second, they were masters of the forest and frontier. As a result, they were well-prepared for the physical conditions they would have to face. Third, although the Americans had no experienced officer corps, as the enemy did, they did have veterans of the French and Indian War who could train the recruits. Fourth, the Americans quickly learned that their long rifle was a more accurate weapon than the smoothbore musket used by the British.

That George Washington was the American commander gave an advantage to the Patriots that many people only recognized gradually. A man of iron will, Washington supplied the patience, virtue, and courage to inspire victory. Despite disappointments that would have overwhelmed a weaker leader, Washington, through his character and spirit, strengthened the American cause at every critical moment. At one low point Washington wrote, "The long and great suffering of the army is unexampled in history." He never lost his faith that everything would come right in the end, however, and he managed to convey this faith to his troops.

Women support the Patriot cause. American women were not bystanders in the fight for independence. A teenager, for instance, wrote to her cousin in England that while she might not be able to lead an army into battle, she could, nevertheless, have an effect on the outcome. She would knit, she said, and turn homespun into garments. Many women chose to accompany their husbands to the army, and faced enormous hardships in doing so. They served as doctors, nurses, seamstresses, cooks, guides, and spies. Those who stayed behind had the duty of holding their families together in spite of disorder, disease, and the possibility of enemy invasion. Rumors that the British were coming would often force women to gather their families and flee.

A handful of women were actively involved in the fighting. Having disguised herself as a man, Deborah Sampson fought in the Continental Army for a considerable time. A Georgia woman named Nancy Hart is still remembered for her singlehanded capture of a band of Tories.

A major mobilization of women's energies began in Pennsylvania under the leadership of Esther Reed, the wife of a prominent publisher. Pennsylvania women were asked to contribute money for the troops. "The offering of the ladies," as the effort was called, was a success. The idea was soon copied by the other states.

Some women saw in the Revolution an opportunity to advance the cause of women's rights. Abigail Adams urged her husband and other members of the Continental Congress to "remember the ladies" in the "new Code of Laws" about to be drawn up. "Be more generous and favorable to them than your ancestors," she wrote. "Do not put such unlimited power into the hands of the husbands." She could foresee another kind of American "revolution": "If particular care and attention is not paid to the ladies, we are determined to foment a rebellion, and will not hold ourselves bound by any laws in which we have no voice, or representation."

Blacks join the Continental Army. Black Americans took part in the fighting right from the start. Blacks fought with distinction as minutemen at Lexington, Concord, and Ticonderoga. At the Battle of Bunker

A patriotic American sets fire to her wheat fields, rather than let them fall into the hands of an approaching British army.

Hill, Peter Salem, a slave from Massachusetts, fired the shot that killed Major John Pitcairn, the officer who had commanded the British at Lexington. Salem Poor, another black minuteman, was praised in the official report of the battle as a "brave and gallant soldier." By September, 1775, however, the Congress ordered the discharge of all blacks from the army. Members feared that the arming of black people could threaten the slave system, a point of view understood by General Washington, a plantation owner himself.

The Congress quickly reversed itself when the British started to offer freedom to slaves who agreed to fight for the king. On December 31, 1775, Washington announced that black soldiers would be welcome in the Patriot ranks. By the end of the war about 5,000 blacks, both free and slave, had served in the Continental Army. Black soldiers, furthermore, had taken part in every major battle.

The Patriots seek foreign aid. Cut off from trade with the British Empire, the Patriots needed arms and financial aid from other countries. As soon as the Congress declared independence, it sent a diplomatic mission abroad to seek foreign aid. In response, France, Spain, and Holland secretly began sending supplies to the Americans. The Patriot diplomats who arrived in France in 1776 also recruited a number of foreign officers to serve the American cause. Perhaps the best known was the Marquis de Lafayette. The nineteen-year-old Frenchman soon earned the affection of the Continental Army and of George Washington, who treated him like a son.

Another foreign recruit was Baron Friedrich von Steuben, a Prussian officer. Von Steuben arrived in America dressed in a magnificent scarlet uniform and accompanied by his greyhound. Speaking his own mixture of French, German, and English, he gave his full energy to organizing and drilling the Continental Army.

Two officers from Poland also joined the Patriot forces. Casimir Pulaski (poo-LAH-ski), a cavalry officer, saw much action and died in battle at Savannah.

Thaddeus Kosciusko (kos-ee-US-koh) designed the fortifications at West Point.

The Americans receive help from France and Spain. After a decisive victory at Saratoga in 1777 (page 138), the Patriot cause looked more promising to European nations. As a result, the United States and France entered into a treaty of alliance in 1778. It was largely the work of Benjamin Franklin. Franklin had an international reputation as an inventor, scientist, and diplomat. He charmed the French, as he charmed everybody, with his wit and lively conversation.

Under the terms of the treaty of alliance, the French agreed to fight at the side of the Americans until full independence was achieved. The French were, of course, serving their own ends by aiding a rebellion against their old enemy, Great Britain. As their foreign minister commented, "The power that first recognizes the independence of the Americans will be the one that will reap the fruits of the war."

Spain, too, was an enemy of Great Britain, but the Spaniards feared the effects of American independence on their own colonies in the Americas. When Spain finally entered the war, in 1779, it did so as France's ally, without committing itself to fighting for American independence. The Patriots, however, had an ally in Bernardo de Galvez, the commander of Spanish troops stationed in Louisiana. During the early years of the Revolution, Galvez supplied the frontier militia with arms and supplies. Later, after Spain had entered the war, he fought in the South, capturing British outposts at Baton Rouge, Natchez, Mobile, and Pensacola.

SECTION REVIEW

1. Why was it difficult to maintain the Continental Army?
2. (a) What groups of colonists were Loyalists? (b) How were they affected by the Revolution?
3. What were the Patriots' chief advantages during the American Revolution?
4. (a) Describe the contributions of women during the struggle for independence. (b) What role did blacks play? (c) How did foreign nations help?

3 The Fight for Independence Continues

When General Washington received a copy of the Declaration of Independence two days after its adoption, he was in New York, gravely worried about General Howe's landing (page 128). Washington was concerned that some of his soldiers might desert, now that the purpose of the struggle had changed. On July 9, however, he ordered his brigades drawn up on the parade ground to listen to a reading of the document. Cheers went up from the ranks when the reading was done. That night, some of the troops joined a crowd of civilians who pulled down a statue of George III and broke off the head.

Admiral Howe makes a final attempt at a truce. In spite of the Declaration of Independence, the Howe brothers hoped to end the war without further fighting. Acting on instructions from Parliament, they were ready to talk peace with the Americans. In September, Admiral Howe met with three negotiators appointed by the Congress — John Adams, Benjamin Franklin, and Edward Rutledge — to discuss a truce. This final peace effort fell apart, however, when Admiral Howe revealed that he was not authorized to deal with the three Americans until the Continental Congress and its army had been disbanded.

The arrest soon afterward of Captain Nathan Hale of Connecticut dramatized the fierce emotions on both sides. Hale, only 21 years old, was caught spying on the British on Long Island. He may have been betrayed by a Tory cousin. Without hesitation, General Howe ordered that Hale be executed by hanging. As Hale faced death, his last words were said to have been, "I only regret that I have but one life to lose for my country."

The British take New York City. After arriving at the mouth of the Hudson, General Howe crossed to Long Island, where he defeated the Americans decisively at the Battle of Brooklyn Heights on August 27, 1776. In September, as Howe took over New York City, Washington withdrew to the north. The Loyalists in the city felt saved. Indeed, Manhattan Island became a refuge for Loyalists throughout America as the British turned it into the center of their military and naval operations.

Just as the British were celebrating their victory in New York, a fierce fire broke out, destroying almost 500 dwellings. The British, furious, were hard pressed to house their troops. Possibly a Patriot had been at work. General Washington concluded, "Providence, or some good honest fellow, has done more for us than we are disposed to do for ourselves."

Washington retreats to New Jersey. After a sharp battle at White Plains, north of New York City, Washington retreated across the Hudson River with the main body of his troops. Howe, waiting for reinforcements instead of pursuing Washington, let a chance to end the war slip away. Two weeks later, however, Howe's troops captured Fort Washington and Fort Lee, on opposite sides of the Hudson River, taking 2,800 prisoners. It was a low point for the Patriot cause. Tom Paine was now writing, "These are the times that try men's souls."

Washington's troops had not only been defeated — they were also in tatters. Numbering only 6,000, they withdrew across New Jersey. Still, a British officer wrote that these ragged troops "will neither fight nor totally run away. We are always a day's march from them. We seem to be playing at bo peep."

The Patriots strike at Trenton and Princeton. On Christmas night, 1776, Washington found a chance he had been looking for — to catch the enemy by surprise. Safely crossing the ice-filled Delaware River near Trenton, New Jersey, he fell upon and defeated an encampment of Hessian mercenaries.[2] Washington luckily came upon the Hessians as they were sleeping off the effects of their Christmas celebration. Almost 1,000 men and officers surrendered to the Americans, who scarcely needed to fire their

---

[2]Many, but not all, of the mercenaries fighting for the British came from the German state of Hesse-Kassel. Hence they were called Hessians.

One of the turning points of the war was the Battle of Princeton, shown in this work by William Mercer, son of an American general who was killed in the fighting.

weapons. The Patriots suffered just four casualties — two killed, two wounded. One of the wounded, Lieutenant James Monroe of Virginia, would later become the fifth President of the United States.

Washington then swept on toward Princeton, where he surprised the British general, Lord Cornwallis. The Americans won a stunning victory, smashing the redcoat garrison on January 3, 1777. As the British troops retreated from Princeton, they looted and set fires on the way to New York.

Benjamin Rush wrote to Richard Henry Lee about the destruction in Princeton: "You would think it has been desolated with the plague and an earthquake as well as with the calamities of war. The College and church are heaps of ruin. All the inhabitants have been plundered." Rush's father-in-law, Richard Stockton, who had been a signer of the Declaration of Independence for New Jersey, may have been singled out for special treatment. The enemy put the torch to his furniture and personal belongings and carried off all his cattle, horses, hogs, sheep, and grain.

By clearing New Jersey of the enemy, the Continental Army gave the Patriots renewed hope. Meanwhile, Washington and his troops went into winter quarters at Morristown, New Jersey.

The British plan a three-pronged attack. The British military strategists had not abandoned their early plan to seal off New England from the rest of the colonies (page 127). On instructions written by George III himself, they now prepared to have three British armies meet in the vicinity of Albany. One of the armies, under General John Burgoyne, would come south from Canada. The second, under Colonel Barry St. Leger, would proceed east from Lake Ontario, through the Mohawk Valley. The third, a detachment of Howe's troops in New York, would march north along the Hudson River to join the other two.

From the start, the complicated operation went wrong. St. Leger, first of all, encountered far stiffer resistance than had been expected. After the bloody Battle of Oriskany (or-ISS-kuh-nih), his forces retreated to Fort Oswego (map, page 139), abandoning their drive toward Albany. General Howe, meanwhile, made his own plans. He thought he could capture Philadelphia, the "rebel capital," and still be able to send enough men to join the other forces at Albany. Howe took Philadelphia, even though Washington's troops stubbornly resisted him in battles at Brandywine Creek and Germantown. Despite their gallant fighting, the Patriots could not stop Howe. Beginning in December, 1777, Washington and his troops once again went into winter quarters — this time at Valley Forge. Howe, meanwhile, was never able to send help to Burgoyne.

The Patriots are victorious at Saratoga. While Howe was preparing to move toward Philadelphia, Burgoyne had succeeded in capturing Fort Ticonderoga, a heavy loss to the Americans who had so dramatically taken it in 1775 (page 126). The road to Al-

bany now seemed open to the British. Burgoyne, however, proved to be his own worst enemy. In European style, he was traveling with large quantities of baggage, loaded onto hundreds of burdensome wagons. Even so, Burgoyne's baggage did not include enough supplies for his army. When a strong detachment of Hessians and Loyalists was sent into Vermont in August, 1777, in search of supplies, it was overwhelmed by Patriots at Bennington.

As Burgoyne's weakened troops finally reached the vicinity of Saratoga, they faced more than 7,000 troops under General Horatio Gates of Virginia. There was a brief but bloody fight on Freeman's Farm, and Burgoyne's forces halted their advance, having suffered heavy losses.

EYEWITNESS TO HISTORY

Burgoyne's Close Call

In 1775 eighteen-year-old Simeon Alexander responded to a call-to-arms and joined the Massachusetts militia. Two years later Simeon was with a contingent of militiamen that was sent to New York to halt General Burgoyne's invading army. In this narrative Simeon relates some of his experiences in that campaign.

An American cannon crew

I was stationed at a place called Scheider's Mills very near the Hudson River. That night I had guard duty and heard some people approaching. I challenged them and called the officer of the guard. Two horsemen were brought in and questioned by Captain Merriman and then allowed to proceed. They proved to be carrying orders from General Gates to General Baily to march up the river and cut off General Burgoyne's retreat in that quarter.

We were soon marched down the river to a place opposite to where Burgoyne was located. Here an incident occurred which I will relate. . . . There was a small red house situated on a hillside just across from our position. This house was just out of musket-shot range and an officer observed "Who knows but maybe Burgoyne is in that house?" "We will try it and see," said

another officer. So they brought up a cannon to bear on the house and fired. We heard the cannonball strike the house, and immediately a number of men who looked like British officers ran out of it.

During the following night a cease-fire was agreed upon. The next day some of the British soldiers came over into our camp, and one of them told me that Burgoyne and his officers were holding a council of war in that house at the time our cannonball passed through it. Soon after Burgoyne surrendered his entire army.

Following several weeks of indecisive fighting, the British launched a major attack on American positions. Benedict Arnold made a daring assault, however, forcing Burgoyne back toward Saratoga. On October 17, 1777, Burgoyne, badly outnumbered, surrendered his entire army of 5,700 men to the Patriots.

The American victory at Saratoga was a turning point of the war. In Britain, Lord North had to face a call that he resign. France, which had secretly been aiding Americans with money and supplies, now decided to aid the rebel cause openly (page 135).

Americans harass the British at sea. One effect of the successful American diplomacy in Europe was that Britain, fearing a French-Spanish invasion, kept a significant portion of its navy in home waters. If the entire navy had been able to *blockade,* or seal off, the colonies, Patriot resistance might very early have been smashed. A truly effective blockade might also have stopped American *privateers* (privately owned vessels authorized to attack enemy ships) from going to sea and harassing the British navy. The privateers caused far more damage to the British than did the tiny Continental Navy. By the end of the war, American privateers had cost Britain about 600 ships lost, with cargoes worth over $18 million. The Continental Navy captured or destroyed about 200 vessels.

Meanwhile, John Paul Jones was helping to begin a tradition of valor for the United States Navy. In 1777, Jones took a brand-new eighteen-gun ship, named *Ranger,* from Portsmouth, New Hampshire, to a port in France. After the treaty with France became a fact, he sailed his vessel along the British coast, setting fire to buildings on the water's edge. Jones was later given another vessel by the French king, an old merchant ship refitted for battle. The ship was renamed the *Bonhomme Richard* in honor of

In 1777 the Patriots won their most dramatic victory at Saratoga but were forced to suffer the hardships of Valley Forge.

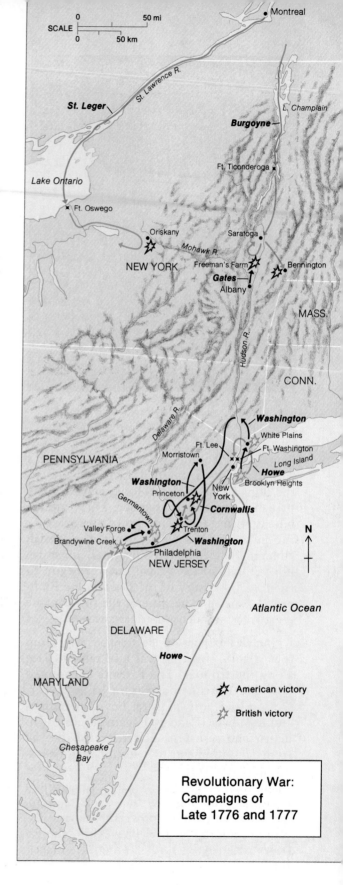

Revolutionary War:
Campaigns of
Late 1776 and 1777

The skill and courage of John Paul Jones helped to establish the traditions of the young American navy.

Hundreds of Indian families starved or froze to death during the following winter. Those who survived continued to aid the British.

Meanwhile a young Virginian, George Rogers Clark, aimed to put an end to British activity beyond the Appalachians. Early in 1778 Clark and a small force of volunteers made their way from Fort Pitt to the Mississippi. They seized the British posts at Kaskaskia and Cahokia in what is now Illinois, and Vincennes in what is now Indiana. As time passed, however, Clark lost much of what had been gained. The Americans were never able to muster the strength required to control the region. It would be some years after the war before the United States finally ousted the British completely from the Northwest.

Benjamin Franklin, whose *Poor Richard's Almanac* was a colonial favorite. Aboard the *Bonhomme Richard*, Jones captured the British *Serapis* in September, 1779, after a bloody three-and-a-half hour struggle. At the height of the battle, when the British commander demanded surrender, Jones replied in defiance, "I have not yet begun to fight." The victory of the *Bonhomme Richard* — especially because of the ship's name — stirred up much American pride.

Americans fight on the frontier. Far from the Atlantic, fighting was also taking place along the frontier. The Patriots confronted not only British troops from bases at Fort Detroit and Fort Niagara, but also Indians and Loyalists. Time and again forces of Indians and pro-British settlers destroyed frontier settlements in western Pennsylvania and New York.

In 1779 Washington sent a force under General John Sullivan to attack the Iroquois, Britain's most powerful Indian ally. Moving through central New York, the Patriots destroyed forty Iroquois villages, forcing the Indians toward Fort Niagara.

SECTION REVIEW

1. Vocabulary: *blockade, privateer.*
2. (a) Why was Admiral Howe unable to bring the war to a halt? (b) What event revealed the angry feelings on both sides?
3. (a) Describe the opening campaign of the Revolution in 1776–1777. (b) Why were victories at Trenton and Princeton especially important to the Patriots?
4. (a) Describe the British plan of attack in 1777. (b) Why did it fail? (c) What was the result?
5. (a) What success did the Americans have in fighting at sea? (b) On the frontier?

4 American Victories Win the Revolutionary War

The defeat of the British army at Saratoga gave an enormous boost to the Patriot cause. The British plan to cut off New England had been thwarted. The French, and later the Spanish, were not only providing arms and other supplies but were openly taking part in the fight against the British. Still, many battles lay ahead, and continued hardship faced the Americans.

Washington's men suffer through the winter at Valley Forge. The American troops had spent the winter of 1777–1778 at Valley Forge (page 138), outside of Philadelphia. There they underwent terrible suffering. While General Howe's troops in nearby Philadelphia were well fed and comfortable, Washington's forces were enduring cold, hunger, and disease. The Patriot soldiers were desperately short of meat, clothing, blankets, and soap. Their encampment was located in fertile farmland, but the area had been stripped of cattle and grain during the recent fighting. Some of the local people, furthermore, had found it more profitable to sell their supplies to the British army than to the Americans. Another cause of the suffering was a lack of wagons and drivers to deliver goods to the soldiers.

By the end of 1777, Washington reported to Congress that nearly 3,000 of his men were "unfit for duty because they were barefoot and otherwise naked." Many of the shivering soldiers despaired of relief and deserted the army. Even officers resigned or threatened to resign.

To improve the distribution of supplies, the Congress appointed Nathanael Greene of Rhode Island to be in charge of provisions. The son of a Quaker, Greene had been expelled from the sect because he approved of armed resistance to Great Britain. He brought boundless energy to his new post, and the shortages began to abate.

Despite the terrible winter, by the spring the army's morale was restored. The training and drill imposed by Baron von Steuben had helped make the troops confident once again of their ability. Kitty Greene and Martha Washington, the wives of the military commanders, were also at Valley Forge, and were organizing entertainment for the men.

The British move back to New York. In late June, 1778, the British army, now under the command of Sir Henry Clinton, withdrew from Philadelphia and marched toward New York City. On a blistering hot day they encountered Washington's refreshed American forces at Monmouth, in New Jersey. During the fighting at Monmouth, Mary Ludwig Hayes, the wife of an artillery man, brought water to the parched troops and earned undying fame as Molly Pitcher. When her husband was overcome by the heat, Molly Pitcher bravely took his place at the cannon for the remainder of the day.

After the fighting at Monmouth, the British continued their march across New Jersey. Washington followed them to New York, setting up headquarters in White Plains. Washington, however, could only keep watch on Clinton. He lacked the power to dislodge him from the British stronghold at New York City.

Fighting shifts to the South. The fighting in the North soon bogged down in stalemate, and for the remainder of the Revolution there was little action there. From the close of 1778 to the end of the war, nearly all the fighting was in the South.

In June, 1780, Clinton placed southern operations in the hands of General Charles Cornwallis, his second-in-command. The British expected quick victories. They relied on support from the Tories, who were numerous in the southern states. They also

While Howe's army spent the winter of 1777–1778 in Philadelphia, twenty miles away at Valley Forge, Washington and his men had inadequate shelter and little food.

foresaw an easy time in occupying southern seaports.

By the summer of 1780, Cornwallis was apparently making good progress. Savannah fell in December, 1778, and a large force of Americans surrendered at Charleston in May, 1780. Then, just three months later, Cornwallis inflicted a disastrous defeat on a small American army led by General Gates, at Camden, South Carolina. Shortly, all of South Carolina and Georgia were under redcoat control. Not everything, however, went Britain's way. At Kings Mountain, along the ridge extending between North and South Carolina, the Patriots crushed a largely Tory force, which lost over a thousand soldiers.

Greene replaces Gates. Gates's defeat at Camden led to his replacement by Nathanael Greene. Greene divided his command into small units that could move swiftly and avoid being trapped. (Today, such groups are called guerrilla bands.) Early in 1781, Daniel Morgan, who excelled at this kind of warfare, defeated part of Cornwallis's force at Cowpens.

In March, 1781, after Greene received reinforcements, he engaged the British at Guilford Courthouse in North Carolina. There Cornwallis inflicted a severe defeat on the Americans, forcing Greene to retreat. The British, nevertheless, had taken such heavy losses that they had to withdraw from North Carolina.

George Rogers Clark's victories strengthened American claims to the Northwest. In the South, meanwhile, the British retreated to Yorktown.

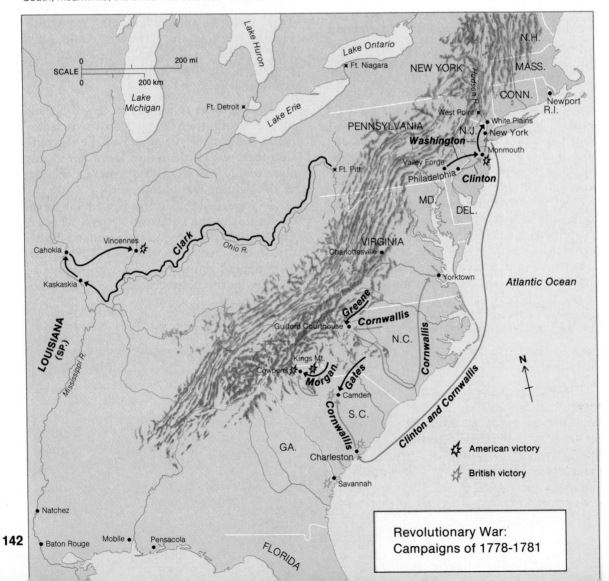

Revolutionary War:
Campaigns of 1778-1781

Cornwallis pulled back to Virginia, leaving Greene to set about reconquering South Carolina and Georgia. Even with the aid of the guerrilla fighter Francis Marion (known as the "Swamp Fox"), Greene found the fighting costly.

Cornwallis carries the fight to Virginia. Meanwhile, General Clinton ordered Cornwallis to take up positions in Virginia. Cornwallis was reinforced there by other British troops sent from New York. The British had already been busy in Virginia. Their raiders were operating under the command of Benedict Arnold, who had shocked his fellow Americans a year earlier by going over to the British side.

An ambitious man who thought himself unappreciated, Benedict Arnold had been dissatisfied with his salary and slow advance in rank. In 1780 Washington had given him command of West Point. Shortly thereafter, in exchange for a money bribe, Arnold prepared to turn the fortress over to Clinton. The plot was foiled when Major John André, the British officer with whom Arnold was dealing, fell into rebel hands. When incriminating papers were found in André's shoes, Arnold's treason was revealed. Benedict Arnold remains the most reviled name in American history, a synonym for what Nathanael Greene called "treason of the darkest dye."

The British succeeded so well in their operations in Virginia that they almost captured the capital at Charlottesville. Thomas Jefferson, whose term as governor had just ended, barely escaped. Washington quickly sent several regiments south under Lafayette, and this force stopped Cornwallis's campaign. In a defensive move Cornwallis fortified Yorktown and Gloucester on both sides of the York River. Military attention now centered on these operations.

Cornwallis is caught in a trap. France's intervention, meanwhile, began to be felt on land and on sea. Cornwallis had settled in on the peninsula between the James and York rivers in Virginia. Washington now made his boldest move. He laid plans with Count de Rochambeau (roh-shahn-BOH), the commander of the French forces aiding

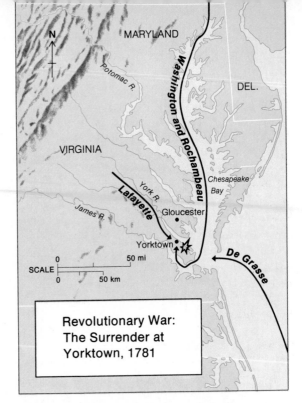

Revolutionary War: The Surrender at Yorktown, 1781

Cornwallis was trapped at Yorktown by American and French land forces and by a French fleet.

the Patriots. A shrewd, tactful, and experienced military man, Rochambeau had led some 7,600 soldiers to America, reaching Newport, Rhode Island, in July, 1780. In the following year a magnificent fleet under Admiral De Grasse, a huge, energetic man, put in at the French West Indies. In August, 1781, Washington received word that De Grasse would be sailing northward for Chesapeake Bay by the middle of the month. Rochambeau's men had joined Washington's troops north of New York City, and both commanders were very pleased. They knew they could not defeat Clinton. Cornwallis, however, was another matter.

Secretly, Washington led the joint army from New York to Virginia. Meanwhile, De Grasse had moved into Chesapeake Bay and defeated a British squadron bringing help to Cornwallis. Surrounded by enemy forces on three sides, Cornwallis was caught. A Patriot general wrote, "We have got him handsomely in a pudding bag." Cornwallis had no choice but to surrender.

Cornwallis surrenders at Yorktown. Mortified, Cornwallis could not bear to be

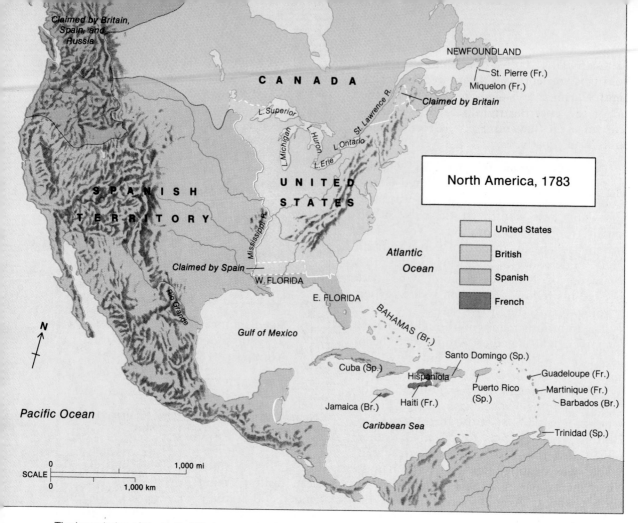

The boundaries of the United States were set by the Treaty of Paris, signed by the Americans and British on September 3, 1783.

present for the ceremony of surrender, which took place at Yorktown on October 19, 1781. A Patriot officer reported that "the British officers in general behaved like boys who had been whipped in school. Some bit their lips; some pouted; others cried." Tradition says that the British band played the tune "The World Turned Upside Down." The British would have preferred to surrender to the French, whom they considered worthy opponents, rather than to the ragtag Continentals they despised. Washington, however, would have none of it. To add to the British humiliation, Lafayette ordered the band to strike up "Yankee Doodle" to remind the redcoats that the Americans had earned the triumph.

Almost two years would pass before a treaty of peace would be signed, but independence for America was now an indisputable fact. When Lord North heard the news from Virginia, he could only say, "It is all over," and repeat the words again and again. The king's ministers agreed that "it would be madness not to conclude peace on the best possible terms we can obtain."

The British and Americans negotiate a peace treaty. To negotiate peace terms with the British, the Congress sent the best diplomats the new nation could choose. They consisted of Benjamin Franklin, the wily old Philadelphian; John Jay, an astute New York lawyer; and John Adams, fresh from concluding a treaty in which Holland recognized American independence. A fourth negotiator was Henry Laurens of South Carolina, who had been captured by the

British while on his way to Holland. He was held prisoner in the Tower of London for eighteen months and was exchanged in 1781 for Lord Cornwallis. By the time Laurens was released, the treaty was almost concluded.

Fortunately for the Americans, Lord North had been replaced by Lord Shelburne. The new prime minister sought to serve his country's interest above everything else. Still, as an old friend of the colonies, Lord Shelburne believed it was his duty to secure American good will.

In entering into its alliance with France in 1778, the Congress had pledged not to make a separate peace with Great Britain. In the first days of negotiation, therefore, the Americans kept the French informed about their talks with the British. One day, however, John Jay found out that France was secretly negotiating with the British without consulting the United States. France, it turned out, was hoping to divide the area west of the Appalachians among Britain, Spain, and the United States and thus, as Franklin said, "coop us up." Jay saw quickly that America could count on nobody "except on God and ourselves," as he put it. As a result, the Americans signed a separate preliminary treaty with the British. The French were angry, but Franklin, through his skill and graceful manner, was able to smooth over what he called "this little misunderstanding."

The Treaty of Paris confirms American independence. In September, 1783, at a little hotel in Paris, the Americans signed a treaty in which Britain recognized the independence of the United States. Because of Britain's desire for a quick end to the war, the United States also won a generous territorial settlement. America's boundaries were set at Canada on the north and at the Mississippi River to the west. To the south the limits were set at the northern frontiers of Spanish Florida. The exact Florida boundary remained in dispute for some time, however, as did the boundary between Maine and Canada (map, page 144).

The United States gained other important concessions in the Treaty of Paris. One gave the Americans the right to fish in Canadian waters. Many people in Britain had wanted to deny this right, as a particularly deserving punishment for the New Englanders. John Adams, however, was insistent. He could finally write, "Thanks be to God that our Tom Cod are safe in spite of the malice of enemies, the finesse [tricks] of allies, and the mistakes of Congress."

Another thorny question discussed at Paris was what to do about the debts that Americans owed to people in Britain. After much wrangling, the negotiators agreed that British merchants should be able to recover legitimate debts. The treatment of Loyalists also presented difficulties and led to long and often sharp disputes among the negotiators. The British wanted reimbursement for any property taken from Loyalists during the war. The final treaty, however, merely recommended that confiscated properties be returned to the owners.

The treaty opened the door to new possibilities and opportunities for Americans. Washington wrote, "With our fate will be the destiny of millions involved." He was referring to the destiny not only of Americans but of all peoples, for the United States was the first new nation in modern times. It represented the first tear in the fabric of Europe's system of overseas colonies. It was the first modern nation of any size, moreover, to choose to be governed without a monarch. Everywhere kings and queens felt threatened, and everywhere people seeking liberty saw America as a beacon lighting the way.

SECTION REVIEW

1. (a) Describe the difficulties that the American troops at Valley Forge faced in the winter of 1777–1778. (b) How were conditions improved?
2. (a) For what two reasons did the British expect easy victories in the South? (b) What success did the British have? (c) How did the Patriots fight back?
3. (a) How was Cornwallis trapped at Yorktown? (b) What was the outcome of his surrender?
4. (a) Who were the American negotiators at Paris? (b) Why did they enter into secret talks with the British? (c) What were the chief provisions of the Treaty of Paris?

145

Chapter 6 Review

Summary

The Second Continental Congress, which convened in May, 1775, organized a Continental Army and chose George Washington of Virginia to be its commander. Military encounters with the British took place all through the next year, culminating in Washington's forces driving the British from Boston. By June, 1776, British harshness, combined with the inspiring writings and speeches of the more determined Patriots, led many Americans to demand complete separation from Great Britain. On July 4, 1776, the Congress adopted the Declaration of Independence.

The Patriots faced numerous obstacles in attaining their goals of independence and self-government. Disease and lack of discipline plagued the army. Money for food, uniforms, and arms was scarce. In addition, many Americans remained loyal to George III. Above all, the well-trained and well-equipped British troops greatly outnumbered the Patriot forces. The Patriots, however, enjoyed several advantages. They were fighting on familiar ground. They won the support of powerful European allies. They had a natural leader in George Washington. Most important, the Patriots were fighting for a mighty cause.

When the Declaration was issued in the summer of 1776, Washington and his troops faced a powerful British army and navy in New York. The Patriots were soon forced back from New York City, which became a British stronghold. Retreating across New Jersey, Washington was able to surprise and defeat the British and their Hessian mercenaries at Trenton and Princeton. The next year a major British attack plan was thwarted when Burgoyne's army was stopped at the Battle of Saratoga. As a result of this stunning victory, France and Spain began to support the American effort openly.

Washington and the troops spent a grim winter at Valley Forge in 1777–1778, before moving toward New York, to keep an eye on the British forces occupying the city. Skirmishes and raids continued, meanwhile, on the frontier. At the same time, General Clinton and his deputy, General Cornwallis, carried the battle to the South. Cornwallis was finally pinned down in Virginia and surrendered at Yorktown, on October 19, 1781.

French and American diplomats carried on lengthy peace negotiations with Great Britain. Benjamin Franklin, John Adams, John Jay, and Henry Laurens protected American interests. In the Treaty of Paris, signed in 1783, the victorious Patriots gained a generous territorial settlement and confirmation of their nation's complete independence.

Vocabulary and Important Terms

1. Second Continental Congress
2. Olive Branch Petition
3. Continental Army
4. Loyalist
5. mercenary
6. Declaration of Independence
7. *Common Sense*
8. Saratoga
9. blockade
10. privateer
11. Valley Forge
12. guerrilla
13. Yorktown
14. Treaty of Paris, 1783

Discussion Questions

1. (a) What was the mood of the delegates to the Second Continental Congress? (b) How did this outlook differ from that of the First Continental Congress?
2. (a) Why did the Second Continental Congress form the Continental Army and choose George Washington to lead the Patriot forces? (b) What personal characteristics helped make Washington an outstanding leader?
3. Why was Thomas Paine's *Common Sense* such an important publication?
4. How did the Declaration of Independence change the purpose of the colonists' dispute with Britain?
5. (a) What obstacles did the Patriots encounter in their fight to achieve separation from Great Britain? (b) What groups of people made major contributions to the American victory?
6. (a) What effect did successful American diplomacy have on Britain's use of its navy? (b) What role did foreign nations play in America's fight for independence?
7. Why can the American victory at Saratoga be called a turning point in the war?
8. What factors played a part in helping the United States gain a favorable peace treaty?

Relating Past to Present

George Washington was a great Patriot hero. How is he regarded by the American people today, and how is he best remembered? What reminders are there in our everyday life of Washington's place in the hearts of Americans?

Studying Local History

What Revolutionary war battles, if any, took place in your state? What effect, if any, did they have on the outcome of the war? If no battles took place in your state, find out if there are cities, towns, or counties named after Revolutionary heroes or battles.

Using History Skills

1. *Reading maps.* Study the map showing the campaigns of late 1776 and 1777 on page 139. (a) What battles did the Americans win in New Jersey? (b) What battles did the British win in Pennsylvania? (c) How does the map indicate the failure of Britain's military strategists to cut off New England from the other colonies?

2. *Ranking.* Read through the list of colonial grievances against King George III in the Declaration of Independence. Then select the five points that you think best express the complaints the colonists had against British rule. (You may want to review the protests of the colonists in Chapter 5 before making your selection.) Then rank the five grievances in order, beginning with the one you consider to be the colonists' most serious objection to British rule.

3. *Writing a report.* A shortage of money was one of the problems faced by the Americans in their struggle for independence. Use an encyclopedia or a history of the Revolutionary War to find out how the shortage of money handicapped the young American nation. Also find out how the Americans financed their war effort. Write a report based on this information.

4. *Placing events in time.* Look back through the chapter and find five important battles that led to American independence. Make a time line showing those battles.

WORLD SCENE

The Spirit of Revolution

In the final decades of the 1700's, the story of the American Revolution gave encouragement to other peoples fighting for liberty.

The Polish struggle for freedom. For many years a lack of strong leadership and a series of wars had weakened the Polish nation. In 1772 Poland's more powerful neighbors — Russia, Austria, and Prussia — took advantage of this condition and seized Polish territory. In 1793, Russia acquired another large section of eastern Poland, and Prussia gained most of the western part.

Aroused by this aggression, the Polish people rose up against their foreign tormentors. The leader of the rebellion was Thaddeus Kosciusko, a Polish general who had come to America during the Revolutionary War to contribute what he could as an engineer and soldier. The Polish patriots fought with unbounded courage. In the end, however, they went down to defeat before the superior forces of Russia and Prussia.

Poland was now completely swallowed up by the victors and Kosciusko was sent to prison. When he was released, he journeyed to the United States to be welcomed as a hero by his old friend George Washington.

Venezuelan independence. During the American Revolution, people in the Spanish colonies of South America were also talking about gaining independence. Francisco de Miranda, a Venezuelan who had been an officer in the Spanish army, traveled to North America soon after the victory at Yorktown. In the United States, he met many American patriots and learned how strong can be the power of a people determined to be free.

Miranda's dream was to free Venezuela from Spanish control. With support from sympathetic Americans, Miranda put together a small army in 1806 and attempted an invasion of Venezuela. His meager force was quickly dispersed, and Miranda fled to London where he lived in exile.

In 1810 a group of young revolutionaries *did* succeed in overthrowing the Spanish government in Venezuela. One of the rebels went to London to invite Miranda to return home. On July 5, 1811, Venezuela announced its independence from Spain and chose Miranda to be the leader of South America's first republic. The individual traveling to London was Simón Bolívar, who would later play a major role in liberating other South American countries.

Forging the Republic

1775 – 1788

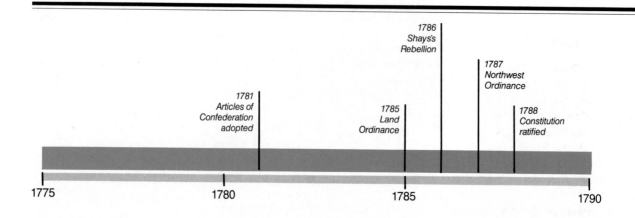

| 1781 Articles of Confederation adopted | 1785 Land Ordinance | 1786 Shays's Rebellion | 1787 Northwest Ordinance | 1788 Constitution ratified |

1775   1780   1785   1790

CHAPTER OUTLINE

1. The states search for a new form of national government.

2. The Confederation proves to be a weak government.

3. The Constitution is written.

4. The Constitution is ratified.

The compelling forces that had united the colonies during the Revolutionary War disappeared with victory over Great Britain. Even before the fighting ended, old differences and disputes had risen to the surface. Most Americans continued to feel loyalty to their state or their particular section of the country, rather than to the idea of a national union. When asked about his allegiance, one New Englander remarked, "My affections still flow in what you will deem their natural order — towards Salem — Massachusetts — New England — the Union at large."

After the peace treaty, Benjamin Rush, a signer of the Declaration of Independence, stated, "The American war is over, but this is far from being the case with the American Revolution." The "revolution" Rush had in mind was the transformation of the diverse American population into a united entity, loyal to a central government. The first attempt at such a union, the Articles of Confederation, was not successful. The Confederation proved to be only a stage, however, in the process of nation-building. In 1787 American delegates overcame what seemed like irreconcilable differences at the Constitutional Convention in Philadelphia. They created a Constitution that was later called "the most wonderful work ever struck off at a given time by the brain and purpose of man."

1 The States Search for a New Form of National Government

The Declaration of Independence had made the thirteen colonies "free and independent States." Immediately, Americans started to form state governments. In all the states, constitutions were drawn up to define the powers of those new governments.

LEGAL AND SOCIAL CHANGES

The states adopt constitutions. Understandably, the politicians who wrote the new state constitutions were deeply influenced by the struggle with Britain. To insure individual freedom, many of the state constitutions included a detailed bill of rights. Each bill of rights contained guarantees of personal liberties, among them freedom of speech and press, a prohibition of unjust imprisonment, and the right of trial by jury. These guarantees reflected a determination to prevent the same offenses that Britain had been blamed for before the Revolution.

The states did not, however, extend political rights to women. Except for the notable case of New Jersey, where the law gave qualified "inhabitants" the right to vote, nowhere did women obtain the vote or the privilege of holding office. New Jersey women voted in state elections until 1807 when the constitution was changed to limit voting rights to free white men.

In every state, factions vied with one another for control of the government. Men of greater wealth believed they needed protection from their less affluent neighbors. These people of means, therefore, argued for a system similar to that in Britain, where only those who owned property or had an income of a certain value could vote

By the end of the Revolutionary period, most of the states had adopted the principle of separation of church and state. Here, Reverend Lemuel Haynes, who fought at Concord and Ticonderoga, preaches to a New England congregation.

or hold office. Ownership of property, they said, gave a person a more permanent stake in the community and prompted a willingness to contribute to the common good. Large property-holders insisted that people without property would be a danger in public office, stating bluntly that "a legislature of beggars will be thieves."

Less prosperous groups also made demands. There were insistent calls, for instance, for easier access to officeholding, annual elections, and increased representation for the western parts of the states. (People living in the newer western communities had long considered themselves at the mercy of the longer established Easterners.)

Still, on one thing everybody seemed to agree: the power of government should rest in the hands of representatives elected by the people. In their constitutions, the states always provided that the executive be subordinate to the legislature. As colonists, Americans had learned to fear any kind of government they could not control directly. They had become suspicious of governors and judges, since those officials had previously been appointed by the king, without the say of the people.

The availability of land creates new opportunities. The new constitutions went into effect at a time when many older "aristocratic" practices were disappearing. The changes taking place helped open new opportunities for Americans.

One change was that more people could own good land. Land that had belonged to Loyalists was taken over by the states. These properties were divided into smaller parcels which then were sold to help pay the states' share of the war's cost or to compensate soldiers for their service. Some of the land was sold directly to small farmers. Most of the states, however, sold land in large blocks to speculators, who often profited handsomely from reselling it piece by piece. Either way, the number of small landowners increased.

Certain old-fashioned features of the land laws were abolished. The laws of *entail* and *primogeniture*, for example, were ended. They were survivals of feudal times, originally designed to make society stable by keeping land in the same family for generation after generation. Entailed land was land that legally could not be subdivided but had to be passed intact from father to son. Primogeniture was the legal requirement that the eldest son must inherit all of his father's real estate when the father died.

Some of these practices had already been modified by the time of the Revolution. By 1790 entails had practically been ended everywhere and primogeniture abolished completely. In North Carolina and New Jersey, however, daughters were not placed on equal footing with sons in the inheritance of property.

Church and state are separated. The Revolution brought notable changes in the position of the churches too. Since churches were among the largest buildings in any community, many had been used as hospitals or barracks. The Old South Church in Boston became a riding-school for the redcoat cavalry. In New York City some Presbyterian churches were made into stables or military prisons.

The physical damage to religious institutions was matched by more fundamental changes. When the war began, there were established churches — those officially supported by colonial governments — in nine of the thirteen colonies. By 1787, this support had been cut off in all the states except Massachusetts, New Hampshire, and Connecticut. Thus, church and government, or, as we say, church and state, had been separated. The support of religious institutions would now have to depend entirely on the voluntary contributions of their members.

In Virginia, the best-known advocate of the separation of church and state was Thomas Jefferson. He was the author of the Statute of Religious Freedom, adopted by the Virginia legislature in 1785. Jefferson came to believe that among the achievements of his life, only the writing of the Declaration of Independence was more important than his drafting of this law. The Statute declared that nobody could be forced to support any church, or suffer in any way for his or her religious beliefs.

Although not rigorously enforced, religious qualifications continued to bar Roman Catholics from holding office in five states and Jews in nine. These restrictions were only gradually abolished. (During the Revolution the presence of friendly French troops — almost all of them Catholics — helped somewhat to lessen anti-Catholic feelings.)

The question of slavery is considered. The uplifting ideals of the Revolution also affected attitudes towards slavery. When the Revolution began, there were about 500,000 slaves in the colonies. The phrase in the Declaration of Independence stating that "all men are created equal" was a constant rebuke to the Patriots who owned slaves. Countless Americans must have shared John Jay's view that as long as slavery existed, "prayers to Heaven for liberty will be impious."

Five days before the Battle of Lexington in 1775 a group of Quakers in Philadelphia formed "The Society for the Relief of Free Negroes Unlawfully Held in Bondage." The Society declared that the freeing of black slaves should always be the duty of Christians, "but more especially at a time when justice, liberty, and the laws of the land are the general topics among most ranks and stations of men." Similar societies were soon organized in a number of states.

During the Revolution the states passed various laws limiting slavery. By 1786 all the states except Georgia had banned the importation of slaves. Most northern states took steps to abolish slavery entirely. In the South, where slavery was more deeply rooted, the problem was more difficult. In 1782 Virginia passed a law allowing a slave owner to free slaves, but only after guaranteeing that the freed blacks would not become public charges. Slavery continued to exist in the South, but the ideals of the Revolution had severely shaken the conscience of many slaveholders.

THE MARKS OF WAR

Economic problems plague the new states. During the Revolution the Patriots had tightly enforced the boycotts imposed by The Association (page 118). As a result, the states suffered a severe shortage of English manufactured goods, including linen, glass, paper, and ironware. Each year the prices of these and other scarce commodities rose higher. To make matters worse, all the states busily printed their own paper currencies. Specie (gold and silver coins) soon disappeared from circulation. In an effort to gain control of the situation, which had resulted in severe *inflation* (a continuing rise in prices), the Congress tried without success in 1777 to persuade the states to stop this ruinous printing of money.

The paper currency of a state usually did not circulate in any other state. Only the money put out by the Congress — the Continental dollar — circulated everywhere. Because these dollars could not be exchanged for equivalent amounts of gold and silver in the Treasury, however, their value kept dropping. More and more dollars were needed to pay for a given amount of goods. By the beginning of 1780 the Congress had issued about $250 million in paper money. Another $200 million or so had been printed by the states. Money circulated at a ratio of forty paper dollars to one dollar in metal coin.

In an attempt to control the value of the dollar, the New England states passed laws in 1776 fixing wages and prices. The Congress quickly accepted the idea of regulation, and urged the other states to follow New England's example. New York, New Jersey, and Pennsylvania took the advice, but it was very difficult to enforce such legislation. In the end, efforts to fix wages and prices by law failed.

Laws were also passed requiring merchants to accept paper currency in payment of debts. The merchants insisted that their liberty included the right to refuse to take the paper bills. They did not want to receive money worth far less than the value printed on it. As a result, many of them sold their goods in a "black market" where they were paid in coin.

Wages, of course, increased as prices rose, but wages always lagged behind prices. Some town workers became desperate to make ends meet. In 1779, as inflation soared, a mob laid siege to a house in Philadelphia in which a group of wealthy men were meeting. Those in the house included James Wilson and Thomas Mifflin, signers of the Declaration. The mob, clamoring for a reduction in prices, was finally dispersed by militia.

The states have trouble raising money. The states' financial problems might have been held in check if the Congress had been able to levy taxes. The struggle with Great Britain, however, had made the word *tax* a bad one. The work of raising money by collecting taxes had been left to the individual states; but they preferred to borrow money instead. One result of this practice was to make it harder for the Congress to borrow money. As Benjamin Franklin explained, "The Agents from our different States running all over Europe begging to borrow Money at high Interest, has given such an Idea of our Poverty and Distress as has exceedingly hurt the general Credit."

Moreover, the Congress was unable to get the states to contribute to a national treasury. In 1783 somewhat less than 15 percent of the $10 million requested by the Congress had been paid by the states. Robert Morris, a leading financier, said that sending requests for money to the states was like preaching to the dead.

THE ARTICLES OF CONFEDERATION

The states have little experience working together. The idea of loyalty and devotion to the United States grew only slowly. Most people still felt that their prime duty was to their state or the particular section in which they lived. Jefferson almost despaired that the sections would ever come together. Speaking of the East and the West, he declared, "God bless them both and keep them in union, if it be for their good, but separate them, if it be better." Even within the states there were serious divisions between citizens living along the coast and those in the interior. Some states, aiming at greater harmony among their people, moved their capitals farther inland.

The Articles of Confederation are proposed. How would the independent nation govern itself in the face of so little unity? When Richard Henry Lee introduced his resolution for independence in 1776, he also made another proposal. He suggested that the Continental Congress prepare "a plan of confederation" which would give the United States a permanent government. Congress appointed a Committee of Thirteen — one member from each state — to produce the plan. In a month the committee presented a charter of government under the title "Articles of Confederation."

The Articles drew heavily on a proposal Franklin had submitted to the Continental Congress the previous year, which in turn had been a rewriting of his Albany Plan of Union (page 104). Franklin was a life-long advocate of a system in which state governments would manage day-to-day affairs while a national government wrestled with the larger problems affecting all people in all the states.

The Articles were chiefly the work of John Dickinson (page 114), who called the government he had designed "a firm league of friendship." He envisioned an alliance in which the national government would be dependent upon the states for support. Dickinson was responding to the widespread fear of a strong national government that was a legacy of British policies toward the colonies.

Under the Articles, the powers of the national government were strictly limited. All powers not expressly granted to it were left to the states. The new Congress was given the power to wage war and make peace, send diplomatic representatives abroad, and arrange treaties. It was forced to rely, however, on the states for money and soldiers. Furthermore, while it might authorize the floating of loans, it could not levy taxes. The Congress, moreover, had no power over interstate commerce (although it could regulate trade with the Indians). It could establish the value of money, but could not control the issuing of paper money by the states.

The new Congress that the Articles proposed would be so weak that it would not

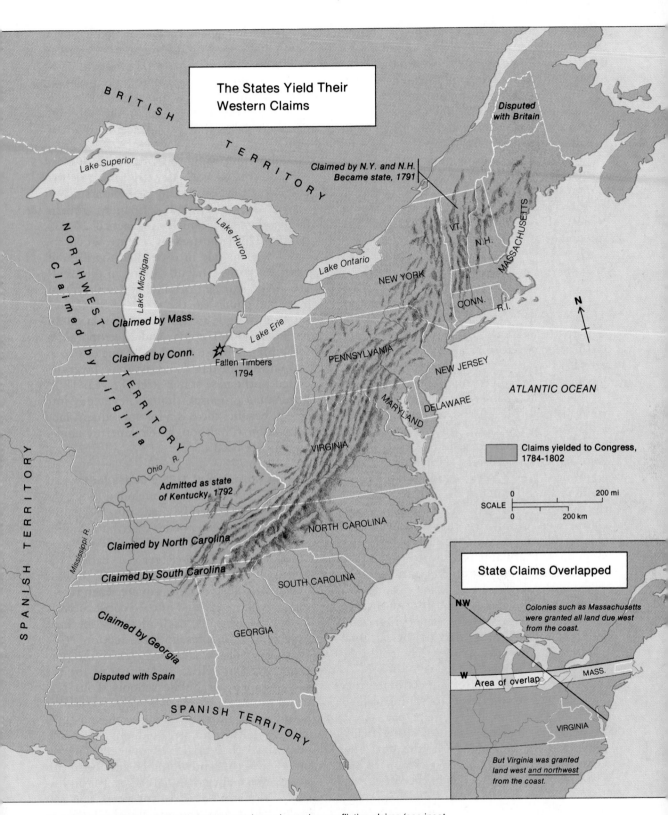

The States Yield Their Western Claims

BRITISH TERRITORY

Lake Superior

Disputed with Britain

Claimed by N.Y. and N.H. Became state, 1791

NORTHWEST Claimed by Virginia

Lake Michigan

Lake Huron

Claimed by Mass.

Lake Ontario

VT.

N.H.

MASSACHUSETTS

NEW YORK

Claimed by Conn.

Lake Erie

CONN.

R.I.

N

★ Fallen Timbers 1794

TERRITORY

PENNSYLVANIA

NEW JERSEY

Ohio R.

MARYLAND

DELAWARE

ATLANTIC OCEAN

SPANISH TERRITORY

VIRGINIA

Admitted as state of Kentucky, 1792

Claims yielded to Congress, 1784–1802

Mississippi R.

Claimed by North Carolina

NORTH CAROLINA

0   200 mi

SCALE

Claimed by South Carolina

SOUTH CAROLINA

0   200 km

Claimed by Georgia

GEORGIA

Disputed with Spain

State Claims Overlapped

NW

Colonies such as Massachusetts were granted all land due west from the coast.

W   Area of overlap

MASS.

SPANISH TERRITORY

VIRGINIA

But Virginia was granted land west and northwest from the coast.

The land grants made in colonial charters overlapped, causing conflicting claims (see inset map). Once the states had ceded their western claims, the way was paved for ratification of the Articles of Confederation.

be able to force a state to obey its laws. Even though a state could send not fewer than two and not more than seven delegates to the Congress, each state would have only one vote there. The delegates would be paid not by the Confederation but by their states, and the states would have the power to call them home at any time.

The Articles did not provide for an executive or for a system of courts. When the Congress was not in session, a "Committee of the States" would take over. It would consist of a member from each state. The agreement of nine members was required to reach a decision. All thirteen members had to approve amendments to the Articles.

The Articles of Confederation are ratified. After months of debate the Articles were sent to the states in November, 1777, for *ratification,* or formal acceptance. The approval of *all* the states would be required for the Articles to go into effect.

Five years passed before the Articles were ratified. The reason for the delay was a dispute over western lands. On the basis of their colonial charters, Connecticut, Georgia, Massachusetts, North and South Carolina, New York, and Virginia all claimed huge stretches of territory beyond the Appalachians. The states *without* land claims were afraid that they would remain weak and small in comparison with their neighbors. Maryland refused to accept the new frame of government until all the states with western land claims surrendered them to the Confederation, "for the good of the whole." The western lands, Maryland insisted, must become part of the national domain so that eventually they could be carved into new states.

Early in 1781, after much dickering, Virginia agreed to give up its claims to land north of the Ohio River (map, page 153). Maryland immediately ratified the Articles, putting them into effect. In the next few years six other states also gave up to the Confederation their claims in the West.[1]

---

[1]The cession of western lands was not completed until 1802.

Jefferson proposes a new land policy. The new government under the Articles agreed that states carved out of the western territories would be admitted to the Union on a basis of equality with the original thirteen. The fertile mind of Thomas Jefferson originated the plan that would accomplish this end.

Jefferson's proposed Ordinance of 1784 divided the western domain into ten districts, each eventually to become a state. A district would form a permanent government when its population reached 20,000. It would be admitted as a state when the number of people in it equaled the number of free persons currently living in the smallest of the thirteen original states. Jefferson even had names for the states-to-be, including such tongue-twisters as Pelisipia, Dolypotamia, Assimisippia, and Metropotamia. Imagining a future America no one else foresaw so well, he dared suggest that slavery be ended in the new states after the year 1800. Jefferson's proposal, though never put into effect, became the basis for subsequent land legislation — although the fanciful names were never used.

The Ordinance of 1785 provides for the sale of land. Having now concluded how the western land would be made into states, the Congress arranged for its distribution. The Ordinance of 1785 provided that the area north of the Ohio River — called the Northwest Territory — would be divided into townships six miles square. Each township would be divided into 36 consecutively numbered sections, each of them one mile square, or 640 acres, in size. Section 16 in every township was to be given to the people to rent or sell in order to pay for the establishment of public schools. Four sections would be reserved for the use of the national government, along with one third of the wealth from any gold, silver, or copper mines that might be opened. The remainder of the land would be auctioned off, in lots no smaller than 640 acres, for no less than a dollar an acre. In the years that followed, the size of the lots and the price per acre were from time to time changed.

In practice the Land Ordinance of 1785 was ignored. Pioneers simply did not have the $640 that was the minimum required to purchase land. As a result, land companies took over. The Congress, needing money, was pleased to sell large tracts to these groups of speculators at reduced prices. The speculators could then sell small parcels to prospective farmers at a price they could afford.

The Northwest Territory is organized. Anticipating that the land companies would readily dispose of their holdings, the Congress adopted in 1787 another great land law. Called the Northwest Ordinance, this law built on ideas Jefferson had proposed earlier. It established for the Northwest Territory a plan of government that would, in time, be applied to all the land included in the national domain.

Under the Northwest Ordinance at least three, but not more than five, states would be carved out of the territory. The area would at first be administered by a governor, a secretary, and three judges chosen by the Congress. As soon as there were 5,000 free adult males in the territory, a territorial legislature would be formed. When the population of a given area had grown to 60,000 free inhabitants, it could become a state "on an equal footing with the original states in all respects whatsoever." Other provisions of the ordinance guaranteed the inhabitants freedom of worship, civil liberties, and free

The Ordinance of 1785

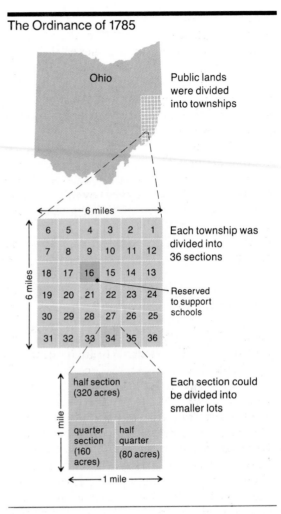

Public lands in the new territories were divided as shown by this diagram. Within a few years frontier towns had sprung up, including Cincinnati on the Ohio River, a thriving community by 1800.

The Northwest Ordinance (1787)

... The following articles shall be considered as articles of compact between the original States and the people in the said territory, and forever remain unalterable, unless by common consent, to wit:

Article 1. No person ... shall ever be molested on account of his mode of worship or religious sentiments. ...

Article 2. The inhabitants of the said territory shall always be entitled to the benefits of *habeas corpus,* and of trial by jury. ... No man shall be deprived of his liberty or property, but by the judgment of his peers or the law of the land. ...

Article 3. Religion, morality, and knowledge being necessary to good government and the happiness of mankind, schools and the means of education shall forever be encouraged. The utmost good faith shall always be observed toward the Indians; their lands and property shall never be taken from them without their consent. ...

Article 4. The said territory, and the States which may be formed therein, shall forever remain a part of ... the United States of America. ...

Article 5. There shall be formed in the said territory, not less than three nor more than five States.

Article 6. There shall be neither slavery nor involuntary servitude in the said territory, otherwise than in the punishment of crimes. ...

public education. Also, with admirable foresight, the Northwest Ordinance prohibited the introduction of slavery.

SECTION REVIEW

1. Vocabulary: *inflation, ratification.*
2. (a) How did the new states provide for individual rights? (b) For land-ownership? (c) What changes were made in the relationship between church and state? (d) What steps were taken against slavery?
3. (a) What financial problems faced the new states as the Revolutionary War came to an end? (b) What efforts were made to deal with these problems?
4. (a) What powers were granted to the national government under the Articles of Confederation? (b) What powers were left to the states?
5. (a) What dispute delayed ratification of the Articles of Confederation? (b) What was the outcome of this dispute?
6. (a) What were the terms of the Ordinance of 1785? (b) In what way were the land-sale terms of this Ordinance ignored? (c) What were the chief provisions of the Northwest Ordinance of 1787?

2 The Confederation Proves to Be a Weak Government

The government of the Confederation had other problems besides organizing and settling the Northwest Territory. They were brought on, in part, by the limited powers granted to the new central government. Both in its ineffectual dealings with nations abroad and in its failure to solve problems at home, the Confederation revealed its shortcomings.

FACING THE WORLD

American trade grows. Confronted by hard times in the 1780's, American merchants looked for new places to sell their goods. In 1784 a group of businessmen, probably including Superintendent of Finance Robert Morris, acquired a vessel that was renamed the *Empress of China.* They sent the ship to Canton, China, from New York with a cargo of ginseng (a plant used as a medicine). The return load of tea and silks proved so profitable that other merchants copied the New York group. The resulting China trade remained small, but it soon brought the American flag into Asian waters on a regular basis.

Foreign countries lack respect for America. Other routes of commerce were also opened during the 1780's. The United States signed favorable trade treaties with France, Sweden, Prussia, and Holland. Still, the American government was not able to command the respect required to settle some of its difficulties in foreign affairs.

Before independence, American ships had sailed the Mediterranean under the protection of the British navy. With that protection now absent, American vessels and their crews were subject to seizure by the Barbary pirates of North Africa (map, page 214). The United States gave Morocco $30,000 to ensure that American ships could sail the Mediterranean freely. Algiers, Tunis, and Tripoli set their prices so high, however, that the United States could not meet them. American merchant ships were captured and hundreds of American sailors imprisoned. Many years would pass before the United States was strong enough to end the humiliation it endured at the hands of the Barbary pirates.

The British remain hostile. Relations with Great Britain, however, were the most irritating and frustrating. The first minister[2] to England, John Adams, suffered the embarrassment of representing a weak country. On one occasion an Englishman sneeringly inquired of him, "Do you represent one country or thirteen?" At a public reception George III turned his back on him. Moreover, the British showed their contempt for the former colonies by sending no diplomatic representative to America.

In 1783 a new British prime minister, William Pitt the Younger, came under the influence of politicians determined to put the Americans in their place. One of these was the influential Lord Sheffield. In a widely read pamphlet Lord Sheffield maintained that Americans would have to trade with Britain whether they liked it or not, for England was their best market and their only source of manufactured goods. The British, he said, could conduct that trade on their own terms. "America," he wrote, "cannot retaliate. It will not be an easy matter to bring the American States to act as a nation. They are not to be feared as such by us." Acting upon this judgment, Britain closed Canadian and West Indian ports to

---

[2]A **minister** is authorized to represent his government in diplomatic dealings with other governments, usually ranking below an ambassador. The United States did not exchange ambassadors with other countries until the early twentieth century.

Following the profitable trading voyage of the *Empress of China*, the American flag was soon flying with those of other nations above the harbor at Canton.

American trading ships in 1783. Secretary of Foreign Affairs John Jay found a ray of hope: "The more we are ill-treated abroad, the more we shall unite and consolidate at home."

The United States is denied the Northwest posts. Britain's most glaring offense was its refusal to turn over the trading posts that ran from Lake Champlain to Lake Superior and were within American territory. Britain had agreed to evacuate the posts in the Treaty of 1783. Now it sought to hold on to them in order to give Canadian fur traders time to strengthen their alliances with the Indians of the Northwest. Another bone of contention was Britain's refusal to compensate American slaveholders for some 3,000 slaves they had helped to freedom during the Revolution.

The British found excuses for not carrying out the treaty agreements. They pointed out that Americans had failed to pay debts owed in England and had also failed to restore to the Loyalists property taken from them during the Revolution. John Jay was gloomy about the long-term effects of British stubbornness: "[The English] may hold the posts, but they will hold them as pledges of enmity; and the time must and will come when the seeds of discontent, resentment, and hatred . . . will produce very bitter fruit." Meanwhile, Americans could not make use of the Great Lakes.

Navigation rights on the Mississippi are refused. Relations with Spain were equally unfriendly. At the end of the Revolutionary War, the Spanish had come into possession of East and West Florida. This development gave Spain control of the mouth of the Mississippi River, an indispensable waterway for many Americans living west of the Appalachians. American farmers depended on the river to ship their goods to market. The Spanish, however, refused to allow Americans to use New Orleans as a port without paying a tax. In addition, Spain refused to give up the city of Natchez, which was well within the limits of territory ceded to the United States.

John Jay tried to negotiate a settlement. Still, he knew that eastern merchants wanted to keep their commerce with Spain. He refused, therefore, to anger the Spanish by pressing them to open the Mississippi to western farmers.

In time the Americans would have the strength they needed to deal with other countries. Now, however, having disbanded their army, they were unable to seize from Britain or Spain what they regarded as rightfully theirs. Thomas Jefferson, always looking on the bright side, wrote from Paris, where he was representing the United States government, that Europe's internal quarrels would eventually work to America's advantage. "Those . . . who have influence in the new country," he said, "would act wisely to endeavor to keep things quiet till the western parts of Europe shall be engaged in war."

PROBLEMS AT HOME

The Congress lacks authority at home. The inability of the Congress to deal with the nation's problems showed itself more and more as the 1780's advanced. The national government was powerless even to prevent conflicts between the states. It was so weak that some Vermonters were trying to attach their region to Canada. At about the same time James Wilkinson, who had been an officer in the Revolution, was apparently working to attach Kentucky to Spain's Louisiana territory.

Harsh economic times bring hardships. The well-known optimism of Americans was being sorely tested. When the Revolution ended, business leaders had been hopeful. To help serve their needs, the Bank of North America was founded in 1781, followed by the Bank of Massachusetts and the Bank of New York. Banks were also planned for other leading cities. All of them could be useful in helping American manufacturing enterprises get started.

The anticipated boom, however, did not develop. People were eager for factory goods unavailable during the Revolution. The demand at war's end was quickly met by English merchants who dumped products in America at low prices that American manufacturers could not match. The cash

The Conestoga Wagon

After the Revolutionary War, American settlers began to move into the lands west of the seaboard colonies. Pioneers were aided in their efforts to open up this region by the Conestoga wagon, which had its origin among the Pennsylvania Dutch about 1750. The Conestoga wagon was a large, sturdily built vehicle with broad wheels that were well-suited to dirt roads. When necessary, the wheels could be removed and the wagon used as a boat to cross deep rivers. The Conestoga wagon's roomy body was elevated at both ends to prevent its contents from spilling out as the wagon went up and down hills. A white canvas top, which could be rolled up for better ventilation, protected the passengers and cargo.

Life on the Frontier

John Bernard was an English actor who toured frontier communities west of the Appalachians in the late 1700's. In his journal, Bernard recorded his impressions of some of the individuals he encountered.

> There appears to have been three kinds of settlers who penetrated the western woods. The first were the pioneers, shaped in frame and spirit to sustain the dangers and difficulties of their undertaking. With a gun, a dog, and a wagon, perhaps with a cow and a pig, they pursued their lonely path through stream and prairie to some inviting spot. There they felled trees for a log hut and cleared space to raise a few vegetables. Their guns, traps, and fishing lines supplied them with abundant provisions.
>
> The second class were the adventurers, generally with more imagination than courage. They had thought back in the city that some state of primitive happiness could be realized in the woods. Their funds were chiefly spent in the purchase of animals which they believed would do all the work. When their dwellings were half up, however, and their cattle had strayed or died, these adventurers would then turn over the whole affair to whoever would supply them enough dollars to return home.
>
> On their heels came a third and more substantial group. These people brought knowledge and decision which swept away all difficulties. They speedily converted their well-stocked farms into growing settlements.
>
> On our way to Pittsburgh we met with various specimens of backwoodsmen, and I must say that, when clad in their green hunting shirts, with deerskin caps and leggings, their height fully displayed in the free handling of their long rifles, they presented the most picturesque appearance I had ever seen.

A backwoodsman

> I soon perceived in them some decided characteristics, such as a sharp insight into character, a ceaseless suspicion, and a quiet humor. They had a way of leaning on their guns and surveying a stranger which struck me as singularly intelligent. Their look said, not "Who are you?" but "I know you."

that Americans paid for these foreign goods, moreover, could not readily be replaced. The barring of New Englanders from trading with the British West Indies led to a collapse of the distilling industry. Southern growers not only lost the custom-ary market for their goods but also missed the bounties they had received from Britain for growing indigo and producing tar, pitch, and turpentine. On top of everything else, tobacco was overproduced after 1781 and began wearing out the soil. The more prosperous planters moved westward to better land. Those unable to move faced declining prices and, in many cases, bankruptcy.

A difficulty facing farmers everywhere was that they received very little gold and silver for their crops. The scarcity of hard money led to much bartering of goods and services. North Carolina businesses, for instance, for a while accepted whiskey in place of money. Nevertheless, taxes and other obligations had to be paid in specie. Lacking gold or silver when times turned bad, farmers demanded that their states either issue paper money or enact laws postponing the payment of obligations. Because people were imprisoned for not paying debts, prisons from 1785 on were filled to overflowing.

Shays's Rebellion alarms the nation. Hoping to prevent further imprisonment for debt, farmers in western Massachusetts tried to stop the local courts from holding sessions. The farmers were infuriated when the Massachusetts legislature adjourned in July, 1786, without remedying their desperate situation.

The leader of the farmers was Daniel Shays. Now 39 years old, he had been recognized for bravery at Bunker Hill. Near the end of the war Lafayette had presented him with a magnificent sword honoring his gallantry. Within a few years, however, Shays was so poor that he had to sell this treasured memento.

The climax of the rebellion came in the fall of 1786 when Shays led a band of men that forced the court at Springfield, Massachusetts, to adjourn. Unable to control his followers, who seemed bent on seizing the Springfield arsenal, Shays aroused the fury of the authorities. The governor of Massachusetts declared him and his followers to be outlaws. State militia were sent to put down the rebellion, and Shays fled to Vermont.

Eventually all of the rebel farmers were pardoned, including Shays. Although they had not achieved their stated purpose, they aroused a good deal of sympathy. Baron von Steuben, that old friend of American independence, watched these events from retirement on the Mohawk River in New York. He observed simply, "When a whole people complains . . . something must be wrong."

Shays's Rebellion was only a protest, not the first salvo of a new revolution. Still, many people were frightened by it. Was this episode evidence that the monarchs of Europe were right, that the American experiment was destined to fail? George Washington was in despair. If someone had told him in 1781, he said, that he would live to see "such a formidable rebellion against the laws and constitutions of our own making . . . I should have thought him a [lunatic], a fit subject for a madhouse."

Opinions as to the cause of Shays's Rebellion varied. To some the uprising was proof that the government under the Articles of Confederation was too weak. On the other hand, for many friends of liberty there was nothing to be concerned about. Wrote Jefferson from Paris, for example, "I hold it, that a little rebellion, now and then, is a good thing, and as necessary in the political world as storms in the physical."

SECTION REVIEW

1. Vocabulary: *minister.*
2. (a) How was trade with China started? (b) What problem did American ships have when sailing in the Mediterranean Sea?
3. (a) What matters continued to be disputed between the United States and Britain in the 1780's? (b) Why were American relations with Spain unfriendly?
4. (a) What economic problems continued to trouble the United States in the 1780's? (b) Which of these problems specifically led to Shays's Rebellion? (c) Why were many Americans seriously concerned by this outbreak of protest?

3 The Constitution Is Written

Thoughtful people believed that whatever the cause of the restlessness revealed by Shays's Rebellion, the nation sorely needed a new form of government. Such a government, many of them asserted, should be able to issue currency (and protect its value), wage war when required, regulate commerce, and settle disputes between states. To set up a government with these powers became a challenge to some of the most prominent Americans of the day.

Preliminary meetings lead to the Philadelphia Convention. In 1784 Virginia and Maryland were quarreling over navigation on the Potomac River. This river, which forms the boundary between the two states, was a waterway to the western lands. George Washington was personally interested in bettering transportation to the West because he owned considerable acreage there. In 1785 he invited representatives of the two states to meet at his estate, Mount Vernon, in Virginia, to discuss the future use of the Potomac. At this conference the representatives agreed to hold another meeting the following year. They planned to include Delaware and Pennsylvania, and to discuss commercial problems.

The Virginia legislature went even further. It issued a call to *all* the states to meet at Annapolis, Maryland, in 1786. Only five states, however, sent representatives to the Annapolis Convention. The small atten-dance was a disappointment to the convention's leaders, James Madison of Virginia and Alexander Hamilton of New York.

Fascinated by government, James Madison studied history with an eye to understanding why some peoples managed their affairs better than others. Although Madison was responsible for the calling of both the Mount Vernon and the Annapolis conventions, the real leader at Annapolis was Alexander Hamilton. Not yet thirty years old, Hamilton had been born in the West Indies. He was an outsider seeking a high place in society. Never one to court popular approval, however, he freely spoke his mind. His genius lay in being able to organize the machinery of government and draw supporters to it.

Hamilton drafted the report issued by the Annapolis meeting. It recommended that a convention gather at Philadelphia the following May to discuss amendments to the Articles of Confederation that could strengthen the central government. The Congress accepted the proposal. In doing so, it emphasized that the purpose was to *revise*, not *discard* the Articles. Still, we may guess that some of the men who would go to Philadelphia were disguising their purpose. Having masterminded the enor-

Mount Vernon, George Washington's home, was the site of one of the meetings that led to the Philadelphia Convention.

mous political change called independence, this generation of leaders was about to effect another change no less far-reaching. They would peacefully reshape the government in order to make it work.

Distinguished Americans meet at Philadelphia. The delegates who came together in Philadelphia in May, 1787, understood their task. Madison believed that the Convention's goal was nothing less than "to decide forever the fate of republican government." Gouverneur Morris, a delegate from New York who would play a powerful role, predicted flatly: "The whole human race will be affected by the proceedings of this Convention."

The scene in Philadelphia was one of activity and expectancy. Philadelphians knew they were witness to a historic moment. The heroes of the Revolution were coming together to deal once again with America's problems. A number of them stayed at the Indian Queen, a lodging house only two blocks from the State House — now known as Independence Hall — where the meetings would take place. George Washington, a delegate from Virginia, was a guest of Robert Morris, who owned the handsomest house in the city.

Jefferson called the gathering "an assembly of demigods." Even when we recognize that the delegates were human beings like ourselves, we can see them as a remarkably talented group of men. Who were they?

Of the 55 delegates who were present, all except 8 had been born in America. The eldest was the irrepressible Benjamin Franklin, now 81 years old. The youngest, only 26, was Jonathan Dayton of New Jersey. Twenty-one of the delegates were under forty. Almost half of them were college graduates, in a time when higher education was rare. Madison, for instance, had been graduated from the College of New Jersey (now Princeton University); Alexander Hamilton and Gouverneur Morris had studied at King's College (now Columbia); and George Wythe (pronounced WITH) had been educated at William and Mary College in Virginia. Thirty-four of the delegates were lawyers.

All of the delegates had served or would serve in significant positions. Eighteen of them had been officers in the Continental Army. Eight had signed the Declaration of Independence. Sixteen had been or would be governors. Two future Presidents were in the group, as was one future Vice President. Two would be unsuccessful candidates for the presidency; one would run for the vice presidency.

Two of the delegates held the respect of all Americans. George Washington, America's most honored figure, brought leadership to the Convention. Many friends recognized that he was risking his reputation by re-entering national service. Washington had, however, what Madison called "a zeal for the public interest." His quiet strength would prove invaluable as the debates heated up. Benjamin Franklin was the wise elder of the Convention. Having pondered the requirements for good government almost all his adult life, he had much to offer. Like Washington, he was a harmonizer of disputes. Moreover, as an internationally famous symbol of the United States, his enthusiastic approval of whatever document the Convention produced would bring it wide support.

A number of leading figures were not present. Richard Henry Lee refused to be a delegate from Virginia, fearing that the Articles of Confederation were going to be discarded. Patrick Henry stayed away too. A leading defender of the rights of states, he said he "smelt a rat." Thomas Jefferson and John Adams did not attend because they were in Europe.

George Washington is elected chairman. The first session of the Convention opened on Monday, May 14, 1787. The Convention could not get down to business, however, because delegates from seven states had still not arrived in town. Within a few weeks all the states were represented except Rhode Island — which did not send delegates.

At the first meeting, on May 25, George Washington was elected chairman of the Convention. Although this meant he could not make speeches or take sides, Washington would play an important role behind

The Constitutional Convention assembled in Philadelphia, the largest city in the nation.

the scenes. When ballots were taken, moreover, he could participate as a representative of Virginia.

The sessions of the Convention were conducted in private. The delegates had realized that if knowledge of the issues being debated became public, pressures from outside the meeting hall might unfairly influence the discussions. Washington himself was so careful that even his diary gives no hint of what went on during the historic proceedings.

The delegates debate the Virginia Plan. On May 29 Governor Edmund Randolph of Virginia "opened the main business." Randolph, whose melodious speaking voice intrigued his listeners, proposed what has come to be known as the *Virginia Plan*, also called the large-state plan. It was the work of the seven Virginia delegates, even though its guiding genius was James Madison.

The Virginia Plan provided for a national legislature of two houses. The lower house would be elected by qualified voters, while members of the upper house would be chosen by the lower house. The total number of members would be divided among the states according to the free population of each state. This national legislature would make laws about matters that

affected all the states. It could also overturn state laws that were judged to be contrary to the national constitution. There would be a "National Executive" possessing most of the executive powers held by the Congress of the Confederation. There would also be national courts.

The Virginia Plan, we now see, contained the nucleus of the Constitution as it gradually emerged. The proposal clearly was more than a mere revision of the Articles of Confederation. It provided, in Edmund Randolph's words, for "a *national* government . . . consisting of a *supreme* Legislature, Executive and Judiciary."

Gouverneur Morris, described by one observer as a flamboyant speaker who "charms, captivates, and leads away the senses of all who hear him," took Randolph's side. Contemplating what he regarded as the political disorder developing in America, he declared, "We had better take a supreme government now, than a despot twenty years hence — for come he must." Rather than revise the Articles, therefore, the delegates set about creating an entirely new framework of government. The meeting, as a result, became known as the Constitutional Convention.

The small states — Delaware, Connecticut, New Hampshire, and New Jersey — were less afraid of a despot than of being dominated by the large states. This, they believed, would happen if the Virginia Plan were adopted and seats in the legislature were apportioned according to population. As the debate developed, some important changes unrelated to the objection of the small states were made. One gave state legislatures the right to elect the upper house. Another made the executive a single individual with the power of veto. In addition, it was proposed that the completed document be submitted to specially chosen state conventions for ratification. The intense discussion of the Virginia Plan, however, did not end the fierce opposition to it on the part of the small states.

The New Jersey Plan calls for a one-house legislature. On June 15 an alternative proposal, known as the *New Jersey Plan*, or small-state plan, was introduced by William Paterson of New Jersey. Paterson, in effect, offered an attack on the Virginia Plan. Seeking only to patch up the Articles of Confederation, Paterson suggested adding to the powers of Congress the right to levy taxes and to regulate foreign and interstate commerce. He also proposed a plural executive, that is, one consisting of several individuals. In addition, he called for a national court system.

The small-state plan aimed to strengthen the government by designating as "the supreme Law of the respective States" all laws passed by Congress and all treaties made with foreign powers. The central element of Paterson's plan, however, was a one-house legislature in which each state would be equally represented without regard to the size of its population.

The Great Compromise breaks a deadlock. The sharp disagreements between the large and small states over the two plans came close to breaking up the Convention. At this point Franklin proposed that "prayers imploring the assistance of Heaven . . . be held in this Assembly every morning." Hamilton, it is said, opposed the motion, possibly out of fear that the public would hear news of the discord.

Good sense won out. Possibly a turn in the weather from being unbearably hot to being comfortably cool helped put the members in a better frame of mind. On July 16 there emerged what is called the Great Compromise, offered by Connecticut's three delegates. One of the most determined of them was Roger Sherman. It was said of him "no man has a better heart nor a clearer head."

The Great Compromise provided for a two-house legislature. To satisfy backers of the Virginia Plan, representation in the lower house, or House of Representatives, would be based on population. Members would be elected every two years. They alone would have the right to originate money bills. To satisfy backers of the New Jersey Plan, the states would be represented equally in the upper house, or Senate. Each state could elect two senators, who would vote individually and who would serve for six years.

Other compromises are reached. When the question was raised as to how slaves were to be counted in determining the size of a state's population, another keen debate began. Northerners asked why slaves should be counted at all, since they were not permitted to vote or hold office. Another compromise was made. Three fifths of the slaves would be counted in determining a state's population. Direct taxes would be levied on the same basis.

The slave trade was another vexing matter for the delegates. Northerners maintained that Congress ought to be able to pass navigation laws, levy taxes on imports and exports, and regulate the foreign slave trade. Southerners, as producers of tobacco, rice, and indigo for foreign markets, wanted no export tax. Moreover, the delegates from South Carolina and Georgia threatened to leave the Convention if Congress were given the power to control the slave trade. In the end yet another compromise was struck. Congress was given the power to regulate interstate and foreign commerce but not to levy taxes on exports. In addition, Congress was forbidden to interfere with or abolish the slave trade before 1808.

The legislative and judicial branches are set up. The Convention gave Congress the power "to lay and collect taxes" and "to regulate commerce with foreign nations and among the several states." Congress was also assigned the power to "raise and support armies." All of these powers the Congress under the Articles had lacked. Moreover, the Constitution includes what is now called the elastic clause. This provision simply states that in addition to the powers enumerated in Article I, Section 8, Congress may pass such other laws as may be "necessary and proper" to carry out its stated powers. Through the years, Congress and the courts have used the elastic clause to make government flexible enough to meet changing needs.

Concerning the establishment of the judicial branch, there was almost no dispute.

The Virginia and New Jersey plans both recognized the need for a court system. The Convention provided for the creation of a Supreme Court, to be appointed by the President with the advice and consent of the Senate. The delegates also gave Congress the power to organize lower courts.

The executive branch is provided for. The problem of the executive was a thorny one. Some of the delegates, as you have read, preferred a plural executive. James Wilson, a Pennsylvania delegate whose Scottish burr riveted the attention of his hearers, disagreed. He maintained that only a single executive could give the necessary "energy, dispatch and responsibility to the office."

Wilson's argument carried the day. Now that the delegates had created a single executive not dependent on the legislature, however, they agreed that he could be *impeached*, that is, accused of acting unlawfully or misusing power. The Senate could then try the President. If found guilty by a two-thirds majority, the President would be removed from office. The delegates also agreed that the executive's veto could be overridden by a two-thirds vote of Congress.

Not until the end of August, after most other matters had been agreed upon, did the delegates decide how the President was to be chosen. Direct election by the voters, they recognized, would give the advantage to the large states. Election by Congress would build into the office an unacceptable dependence of the President on Congress. The Convention turned the problem over to a committee for solution. The committee brought forth the idea of having *electors* choose the President. (As a group the electors were called the electoral college.) The electors would be selected in each state in any way the state legislature directed. Each state would have as many electors as the number of its representatives and senators in Congress.

While the large states would have an advantage under this electoral system, the delegates assumed that "nineteen times in twenty" — as one of them said — no individual would win a majority of the votes cast. The choice would then be up to the House of Representatives, with each state having one vote.

As for the length of the term a President would serve, that too was the work of compromise. Six or seven years was taken as an acceptable length for a single term (although Alexander Hamilton, out of tune on this question, proposed that the President be elected for life). Four years was eventually agreed upon, with no limit placed on re-election.

The Constitution breaks fresh ground. The completed Constitution is sometimes called a "bundle of compromises" because it reconciled so many conflicting ideas among the delegates. In the end, however, it was the product of the best eighteenth-century thinking on the nature of good government. It provided, most important of all, for separate legislative, executive, and judicial branches in the government. This system is called *separation of powers.* The Constitution also set up a system of *checks and balances* so that one branch could counter but nor paralyze the actions of another. For instance, the President may veto a bill passed by Congress; Congress may check the President's action with a two-thirds vote in favor of the bill; and the Supreme Court has the right to try cases arising from laws passed by Congress. (See diagram, next page.)

Fundamental to the success of the new frame of government, finally, was the establishment of a new relationship between national (or federal) power and state power. The kind of government the Constitution set up, in which a union of states recognizes the sovereignty of a central government while retaining certain governmental powers, is called a *federal system.* The Constitution and all the laws made under it were declared to be "the supreme Law of the Land." This phrase, which significantly altered Paterson's phrase "the supreme Law of the respective States" (page 165), must be regarded as showing that the power of the Constitution flows from *all* the people and not from the states. It cements the Union together by making the laws of Congress apply everywhere. It also gives the Supreme

The System of Checks and Balances

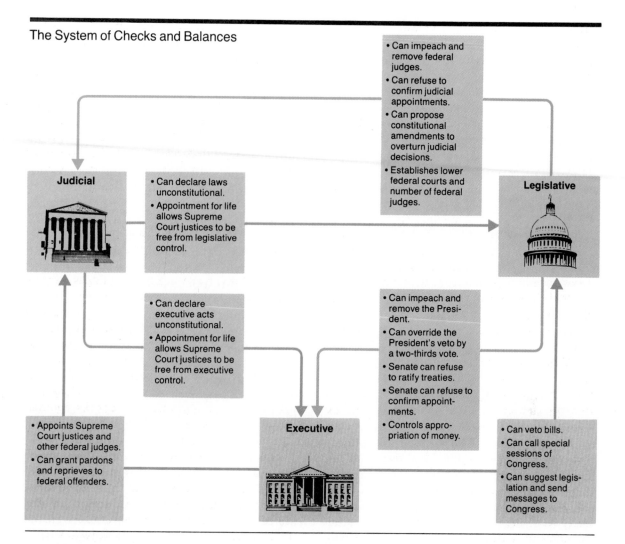

Judicial

- Can declare laws unconstitutional.
- Appointment for life allows Supreme Court justices to be free from legislative control.

- Can impeach and remove federal judges.
- Can refuse to confirm judicial appointments.
- Can propose constitutional amendments to overturn judicial decisions.
- Establishes lower federal courts and number of federal judges.

Legislative

- Can declare executive acts unconstitutional.
- Appointment for life allows Supreme Court justices to be free from executive control.

- Can impeach and remove the President.
- Can override the President's veto by a two-thirds vote.
- Senate can refuse to ratify treaties.
- Senate can refuse to confirm appointments.
- Controls appropriation of money.

- Appoints Supreme Court justices and other federal judges.
- Can grant pardons and reprieves to federal offenders.

Executive

- Can veto bills.
- Can call special sessions of Congress.
- Can suggest legislation and send messages to Congress.

The framers of the Constitution divided the government into three separate branches and gave each branch certain checks over the other two.

Court the basis for its power to declare laws — state or national — unconstitutional. It is the means by which the federal government may pass laws that act directly on the people, without necessarily having to do its work through the states.

The delegates' work is completed. By September the delegates were tired. Some of them were growing impatient with the changes their fellows were proposing in unimportant matters. Irritated, several of them announced that they would not sign the completed document. Still, the enthusiasm for finishing the work was overwhelming. On Saturday, September 8, the Convention established a Committee of Style to put the language of the Constitution into its final form. The leading participant was Gouverneur Morris, whose gift of language was much admired.

The most powerful change the Committee made was to have the *preamble*, or opening statement, begin with the words "We the people of the United States" instead of "We the people of the States of New Hampshire, Massachusetts, etc." The delegates were making clear their intention that the national government would act in the name of the people and not the states.

By the following Thursday the Convention was able to go over the document, article by article, and put the finishing touches to it. On September 17, 1787, the Convention gathered for the last time. Thirty-nine delegates, representing twelve states, signed the completed work.

Benjamin Franklin was especially pleased. Aware that no one regarded the completed instrument as perfect, he urged each delegate to imagine himself mistaken about his objections and sign the document anyhow. Madison recorded the following in notes that he kept during the proceedings:

> Whilst the last members were signing it, Doctor Franklin, looking toward the President's chair, at the back of which a rising sun happened to be painted, observed to a few members near him, that painters had found it difficult to distinguish in their art a rising from a setting sun. "I have," said he, "often and often in the course of the Session . . . looked at that [sun] behind the President without being able to tell whether it was rising or setting; but now at length I have the happiness to know it is a rising and not a setting Sun."

The delegates adjourned shortly after signing the document and made their way to the City Tavern. There they took dinner, bade one another goodbye, and departed for their homes. The Convention had agreed that special state conventions, rather than the state legislatures, would be elected to ratify or reject the Constitution. The belief was that this arrangement would allow for the fullest expression of public sentiment.

SECTION REVIEW

1. Vocabulary: *impeach, elector, separation of powers, checks and balances, federal system, preamble.*
2. (a) What meetings led up to the Philadelphia Convention? (b) Who were some of the best-known delegates at that Convention? (c) What American leaders did *not* attend?
3. (a) What were the key terms of the Virginia Plan? (b) Of the New Jersey Plan? (c) Of the Great Compromise?
4. (a) What powers did the Constitution grant to Congress? (b) What was the elastic clause?
5. What provisions were agreed upon for the method of electing the President?
6. By what process was the Constitution to be ratified?

4 The Constitution Is Ratified

The Constitutional Convention had done more than most Americans had imagined it could do. Yet not many delegates felt certain that the Constitution would ever go into effect, or that if it did, the new government would succeed. Indeed, when the Convention had ended, a woman asked Franklin: "Well, Doctor, what have we got, a republic or a monarchy?" "A republic," he replied, "if you can keep it." What he meant was that a *republic* — a government whose highest officials are elected by the people and responsible to them — requires the constant vigilance of its citizens.

The public's opinion of the new frame of government was soon tested as the scene shifted to the states. The approval of nine of the thirteen states was required to ratify the Constitution. No single state would be able to hold up ratification, the way Maryland had delayed approval of the Articles of Confederation a few years earlier.

Some Americans oppose the Constitution. Heated opposition in the states was expected, because approval of the new government would result in a reduction in the states' powers. Moreover, the failure to include a bill of rights was already arousing much concern and suspicion. Such a bill had been omitted because those rights already belonged to the people, and had not been regarded as the business of the central government. Besides, most state constitutions already contained a bill of rights. Still, many people were unwilling to allow these liberties to be taken for granted in the new federal document.

At Philadelphia there had been broad agreement among the delegates on what they deemed the requirements of the day: a stronger central government, a barrier to the irresponsible issuing of paper money, and the national regulation of commerce. Not all Americans were convinced that a strong government capable of providing these conditions was required. The dissenters, who soon were known as Antifederalists, simply had not been represented in Philadelphia in 1787. They were at home, waiting to spring into action when the campaign for ratification opened.

The Federalists and Antifederalists campaign for support. Argument and counterargument filled the air during the remainder of 1787 and most of 1788. The supporters of the Constitution, called Federalists, had a big advantage over the Antifederalists. Their ranks included a large number of Revolutionary War veterans, esteemed clergymen, and influential business leaders. Madison observed correctly, "The weight of abilities and of property is on the side of the Constitution." No less important, the Federalists supported something positive, a document that could be read and discussed. Their opponents, who also recognized the need for change, had no alternative proposal.

On the other hand, opponents of the Constitution regarded the very idea of a *new* frame of government as an illegal seizure of power. The Philadelphia Convention, having been called to revise the Articles, had not submitted its work to the Congress of the Confederation. To submit the Constitution to state conventions rather than to the state legislatures, furthermore, was a revolutionary step.

Pamphlets, handbills, and papers were issued by both sides. The most persuasive document was a series of 85 essays in support of the Constitution, called *The Federalist*, that appeared in New York newspapers. Signed "Publius," the essays were actually written by Madison, Jay, and Hamilton. They remain today the best commentary ever written on the Constitution. Nevertheless, the most compelling argument for ratification proved to be the public's belief that without the new Constitution the Union would probably fall apart.

Ratification of the Constitution begins. The small states, reassured by the Great Compromise, quickly ratified the Constitution. Delaware's state convention led off with a vote of unanimous approval on December 7, 1787. New Jersey, Connecticut, and Georgia also ratified with little hesitation.

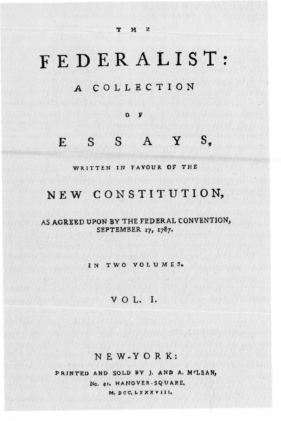

THE

FEDERALIST:

A COLLECTION

O F

E S S A Y S,

WRITTEN IN FAVOUR OF THE

NEW CONSTITUTION,

AS AGREED UPON BY THE FEDERAL CONVENTION,
SEPTEMBER 17, 1787.

IN TWO VOLUMES.

V O L. I.

N E W - Y O R K:
PRINTED AND SOLD BY J. AND A. M'LEAN,
No. 41, HANOVER-SQUARE.
M, DCC, LXXXVIII.

The essays in *The Federalist* offered convincing arguments in favor of the Constitution.

The real struggle came in the states with large populations.

The first sign of important opposition was in Pennsylvania. Delegates at the Pennsylvania convention approved the Constitution on December 12, by a two-to-one majority. Still, outraged Antifederalists charged that the convention had been called hastily in order to prevent opponents from being fully represented.

Massachusetts gave the Federalists cause for worry. Opposition to the Constitution was ferocious. Farmers were still seething over the events that had led to Shays's Rebellion. Moreover, two of the state's most popular heroes, Sam Adams and John Hancock, were opposed to the Constitution. Hancock was silenced, however, by being made chairman of the ratifying convention. It was also hinted that he might become the first Vice President of the United States. By a vote of 187 to 168,

Massachusetts ratified the Constitution in February, 1788. The Massachusetts Antifederalists were satisfied by a promise that a bill of rights would shortly be added to the document.

Maryland ratified the Constitution in April, and South Carolina in May. In June, New Hampshire became the ninth state to accept it. The Constitution was now in operation. In practical terms, however, the new government could not function until the large states of Virginia and New York were in the fold.

Virginia and New York approve the Constitution. In Virginia both sides had their best people in the state convention. The Federalists claimed Washington, Madison, and young John Marshall. On the Antifederalist side were Patrick Henry, Richard Henry Lee, and George Mason. Madison defended the Constitution article by article, as no other person in the land was able to. For the Antifederalists, Patrick Henry spoke with his customary liveliness. He denounced the new position of "great and mighty President," for it sounded to him as if a power-

James Madison was a key leader in the campaign to secure ratification of the Constitution.

ful monarch were in the making. As he spoke, a summer storm broke over the meeting hall with thunder and lightning punctuating his words. At last, after recommending that a bill of rights be added to the Constitution as Massachusetts had done, Virginia ratified it by the narrow margin of 89 to 79.

Of the large states only New York now remained outside the ranks. The Antifederalists were led by Governor George Clinton, a determined fighter. The Federalists, however, had prepared their ground well. Indeed, *The Federalist* had been published in New York City in order to counteract Clinton's support elsewhere in the state. Moreover, the delegates at the convention were greatly influenced by the persuasive speeches of Alexander Hamilton, who, like Madison, believed passionately in the new frame of government. Working hardest for the Federalists was the fact that the Constitution would go into effect, regardless of what New York decided to do. By three votes the ratification resolution squeaked through New York in late July, 1788.[3]

The Bill of Rights is adopted. Almost as soon as the new Congress met in 1789, James Madison offered a group of amendments to safeguard the rights of the individual. These first ten amendments to the Constitution, known as the Bill of Rights, went into effect in 1791. They guarantee to Americans the rights that are indispensable to enjoying "the blessings of liberty." Among other things, the Bill of Rights guarantees to American citizens that Congress will make no laws abridging (1) freedom of religion, speech, press, assembly, and petition; (2) freedom from unauthorized search; (3) fair trial by jury; (4) protection of life, liberty, and property; and (5) protection from cruel and unusual punishment.

Madison knew well that the Bill of Rights had completed the work done at Philadelphia. "In framing a government,"

[3]North Carolina and Rhode Island, both dominated by Antifederalists, did not join the reshaped Union until after its establishment. The new government was launched without them.

he wrote, "you must first enable the government to control the governed; and in the next place oblige it to control itself."

The nation celebrates. After New York's ratification of the Constitution, Congress decided that elections should be held to choose representatives, senators, and presidential electors. The elections were held, and when the electors assembled they announced that George Washington and John Adams had been chosen President and Vice President. Meanwhile, Americans had been celebrating the adoption of the Constitution with festivals in the chief cities. The biggest of the parades was a "federal procession" held in Philadelphia. It was organized and directed by Francis Hopkinson, a signer of the Declaration of Independence for New Jersey, now living in Pennsylvania. The elaborate floats and the elegantly costumed horsemen who rode alongside them depicted notable events of the Revolutionary era that had led to this triumphant moment. The most striking float, however, was a huge dome supported by thirteen columns. It represented "The Federal Edifice," now ready for use.

Present also, glorying in the day, was Benjamin Rush (page 132). He was pleased that this parade, unlike the processions in Europe that honored individuals, honored all Americans without regard to their place in society. He reported that in the crowds lining Philadelphia's streets "every countenance wore an air of *dignity* as well as pleasure. Every tradesman's boy in the procession seemed to consider himself as a principal in the business." He also offered another observation on that bright day: "The Rabbi of the Jews locked in the arms of two ministers of the gospel was a most delightful sight. There could not have been a more happy emblem contrived of that section of the new Constitution which opens all its power and offices alike not only to every sect of Christians but to worthy men of *every* religion."

———

The framers of the Constitution had brought forth a blueprint creating a central

In New York, where the Constitution was ratified by a margin of just three votes, Federalists held a parade to celebrate the event.

authority while safeguarding individual liberty. But would the new government succeed? People in every part of the world watched and waited for the answer, some in great fear, many in eager hope. At home Americans could reflect on the truth of the motto on the banner that carpenters carried in the Philadelphia procession: "Both buildings and rulers are the work of our hands."

SECTION REVIEW

1. Vocabulary: *republic*.
2. What were the two main reasons for opposition to the Constitution?
3. How did *The Federalist* papers play a part in the campaign to win ratification of the Constitution?
4. (a) What states were most willing to approve the Constitution? (b) How was ratification achieved in Virginia and New York?
5. (a) Why was the Bill of Rights added to the Constitution? (b) What rights does it protect?

Chapter 7 Review

Summary

Having declared their independence from Britain, the colonists set about establishing new state governments. Features most of the states had in common included constitutions insuring individual rights, new laws abolishing entail and primogeniture, the separation of church and state, and, in many cases, restrictions on slavery.

The Revolutionary War, which had disrupted manufacturing and trade, had caused a severe shortage of goods. As wartime austerity gave way to peacetime demand, prices rose dramatically. To make matters worse, there was no central control over the supply of money; nor was the Congress able to levy taxes.

To find a remedy for this situation and to establish a national government, representatives from the thirteen states approved a framework called the Articles of Confederation. The Articles were little more than a weak league of states. There was no provision for a national court system or for a Chief Executive.

A dispute over the status of the western domain delayed ratification of the Articles of Confederation for five years. To handle the question, ordinances were adopted that provided for the sale of land, and established conditions for admitting new states to the Union.

Disputes between states, revenue and currency problems, economic hardships, and problems with other countries soon tested the strength of the new government. An angry protest by Massachusetts farmers, known as Shays's Rebellion, made it clear that a stronger central government should be considered.

In 1787 delegates met in Philadelphia to review the Articles of Confederation. A sense of common purpose and compromise produced the Constitution. The new system granted power to a central government without destroying the authority of the states. The government was made up of three parts, each with checks on the other. Ten amendments, known as the Bill of Rights, were adopted soon after the Constitution was ratified. They provided for the protection of basic liberties.

The Federalists, backers of the Constitution, were able to organize support for the new frame of government and bring about its ratification. By 1790 all thirteen states had approved, and the new government was securely in operation.

Vocabulary and Important Terms

1. inflation
2. Articles of Confederation
3. ratification
4. Ordinance of 1785
5. Northwest Ordinance
6. minister
7. Shays's Rebellion
8. Mount Vernon Conference
9. Annapolis Convention
10. Virginia Plan
11. New Jersey Plan
12. Great Compromise
13. impeach
14. elector
15. separation of powers
16. checks and balances
17. federal system
18. preamble
19. republic
20. Antifederalists
21. Federalists
22. *The Federalist*
23. Bill of Rights

Discussion Questions

1. After the Revolution, what changes in American society reflected a trend toward greater opportunity?

2. (a) What kind of government did John Dickinson think would emerge under the Articles of Confederation? (b) How was the power of the national government under the Articles limited?

3. What proposals were made by Thomas Jefferson in his Ordinance of 1784?

4. Why was the plan of government established by the Northwest Ordinance so significant?

5. (a) How did foreign countries show their lack of respect for the United States during the Confederation period? (b) What internal problems showed the weakness of the national government in the 1780's?

6. (a) What was Shays's Rebellion? (b) How did opinions as to the meaning of that rebellion vary?

7. (a) How did meetings at Mount Vernon and Annapolis help point the way to the convention at Philadelphia? (b) What was the original purpose of the Philadelphia Convention, and how did that purpose change once the Convention was under way?

8. (a) What was the key issue dividing the large states and the small states at Philadelphia? (b) How was the argument resolved? (c) Over what matters did Northerners and Southerners disagree?

9. How did the system of government established under the Constitution differ from the system of government under the Articles of Confederation?

10. Why did the supporters of the Constitution have an advantage over those who opposed the new form of government?

Relating Past to Present

1. The intent of the Bill of Rights was to guarantee that the federal government would not interfere with the rights that are indispensable to enjoying "the blessings of liberty." Is the Bill of Rights as important to Americans today as it was when it went into effect in 1791? What rights guaranteed in the Bill of Rights are most often in the public eye today?

2. Thomas Jefferson called the gathering at Philadelphia "an assembly of demigods." What personal characteristics and professional accomplishments made the delegates to the Philadelphia Convention so outstanding? If a convention were held today to discuss constitutional matters, what Americans might be asked to serve as participants?

Studying Local History

What role, if any, did people from your state play in the deliberations that took place at the Constitutional Convention in Philadelphia?

Using History Skills

1. *Placing events in time.* Make a time line of the events that highlighted the history of the United States during the 1770's and the 1780's. Include on your time line such events as the following: Shays's Rebellion; ratification of the Articles of Confederation; Cornwallis's surrender at Yorktown; the Northwest Ordinance; and the Constitutional Convention.

2. *Stating both sides of an issue.* The debate between the Federalists and the Antifederalists over ratification was heated. Use an encyclopedia, a history of the United States, or a copy of *The Federalist,* to find out more about the arguments that were advanced for and against the Constitution. Use this information to write a script for a debate between a supporter and an opponent of ratification.

3. *Organizing information.* Make a chart in which you list (a) the powers granted the national government under the Articles of Confederation and (b) the powers granted the national government under the Constitution.

WORLD SCENE

Exploring the Pacific Northwest

Trade with China prompted both Britons and Americans to explore the coastline of the Pacific Northwest.

The voyages of Captain Cook. In 1776 the British government sent Captain James Cook on an expedition to find a water passage from the Pacific Ocean through North America to the Atlantic. The English hoped that the discovery of such a route would significantly shorten the sailing time from Britain to China.

Cook had established a reputation with his earlier voyages. He had explored the St. Lawrence River, surveyed the coast of Newfoundland, and sailed throughout the South Pacific, mapping the entire coast of New Zealand and the eastern seaboard of Australia. During these journeys, Cook experimented with his crew's diet and found that fresh fruit and vegetables would control scurvy, a disease that had always plagued sailors on long voyages.

Cook's visit to America's northwest coast uncovered no passageway through the ice-bound Arctic Ocean. The expedition was, however, the first from Europe to land on the Hawaiian Islands. Cook called them the Sandwich Islands in honor of an English diplomat, the Earl of Sandwich, said to be the creator of the first sandwich.

The explorations of Captain Gray. As accounts of Captain Cook's voyages circulated in the United States, they were read with interest by merchants eager to share in trade between the Pacific Northwest and China. One of the first Americans to undertake such a voyage was Captain Robert Gray.

Gray reached the Oregon coast in 1788 and continued across the Pacific to China. After leaving China, he sailed westward through the Indian Ocean, and made his way back to Boston in 1790. Gray was the first American to sail around the world.

Gray made a second voyage to Oregon, arriving in 1792. Although primarily interested in trade, Gray explored the coastline of present-day Washington and Oregon. On this expedition Gray sailed into a magnificent river that he claimed for the United States. He named it after his ship, the *Columbia.*

CHAPTER 8

Under the First Presidents

1789 – 1800

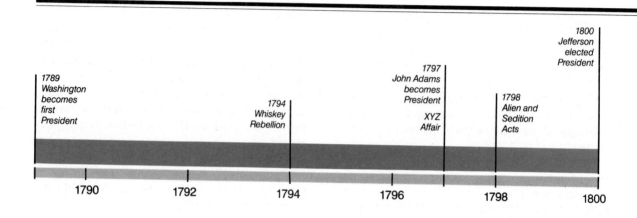

1789
Washington
becomes
first
President

1794
Whiskey
Rebellion

1797
John Adams
becomes
President

XYZ
Affair

1798
Alien and
Sedition
Acts

1800
Jefferson
elected
President

1790   1792   1794   1796   1798   1800

CHAPTER OUTLINE

1. The new government is launched.

2. Hamilton tackles the nation's money problems.

3. Political parties are formed.

4. Federalist power declines.

George Washington was the most trusted man in the United States. Unanimously elected President in April, 1789, he gave the new government respectability even before it was fully organized. Still, the work that lay ahead was a challenge no one had ever faced.

Differences between the northern and southern states had showed themselves at the Philadelphia Convention. Business leaders and farmers were not in agreement on the policies the new nation should pursue. Americans on the frontier were so far from the seat of government that they found it hard to feel involved in the changes taking place.

In spite of such uncertainties, the people's energies were turned to making the Constitution work. The architects of the new government had understood that at the Philadelphia Convention they had written only an outline of the new government. Indeed, people called it "the frame of government." What was now needed was the enthusiasm of men and women who would give it life and direction.

April 30, 1789, the day that the nation began its life under a President, was notable in the history of the world. A country not ruled by a king or queen was so novel that for many years people everywhere would refer to the United States as the "American experiment." No one could know for sure if the experiment would succeed. Few could imagine that its features would become a model for other nations for centuries to come.

1 The New Government Is Launched

The task of getting the country off on the right foot was taken on by the group that had been enthusiastic for the ratification of the Constitution. The goal of the Federalists was now one of making the new government effective and respected.

George Washington is inaugurated. In the spring of 1789, the President-elect left Mount Vernon for New York City, where he would be inaugurated. The journey took eight days over roads muddy from rain. It was a triumphant procession. In every town and village George Washington passed through, thousands of people greeted him with speeches, banners, and flowers. They treated him like a Roman hero, even building triumphal arches in his honor. Many veterans who had served under his command in the Revolution were on hand to greet him and wish him well. Already the nation was coming together under Washington's leadership.

Washington had not wanted to return to public life. "My movements to the chair of government," he wrote, "will be accompanied by feelings not unlike those of a culprit who is going to the place of his execution." His beloved Martha was also distressed by his re-entry into the limelight. She agreed only reluctantly to uproot herself again from their Virginia home.

Martha Washington missed her husband's triumphant entry into New York City. He crossed the Hudson River aboard a special barge decorated in red, white, and blue with everything in thirteens to symbolize the thirteen states. When Martha Washington traveled north to join her husband a month later, she too was cheered along the way to New York. Then Washington crossed the Hudson from New York to fetch her. When they landed in Manhattan, guns boomed in salute.

George Washington was sworn in as President at Federal Hall in New York City.

As First Lady, Martha Washington presided with dignity and grace. Still, she sometimes complained of feeling like a "state prisoner."

On April 30, 1789, Washington took the oath of office on the balcony of Federal Hall. The strain of the occasion showed, for his hands trembled and his voice could hardly be heard. A senator in the audience observed, "This great man was agitated and embarrassed more than ever he was by the leveled cannon or pointed musket." Washington was dressed in a dark brown suit of American manufacture, but he also wore a sword and white stockings, in the fashion of court ceremonies in Europe. When the ceremony was over, the crowd below cheered, shouting "Long live George Washington, President of the United States."

Both Washington and the American people would have to learn how to deal with this new office, the presidency. A heated discussion had already taken place in the Senate as to how a President should be addressed. One participant suggested "His Highness the President of the United States

of America and Protector of their Liberties." Another proposed "His Elective Highness." Yet another offered "His Patriotic Majesty." Finally it was agreed that the Chief Executive was to be called simply "President of the United States."

Washington was not eager for a fancy title, but he was not a "man of the people" either. Naturally aloof and reserved, he never shook hands as President. On social occasions, moreover, he always greeted guests while standing on a raised platform.

Happily, the spring and summer brought no crisis and so the new government was launched under favorable conditions. The country was experiencing general prosperity, furthermore, and people were pleased to credit the new government for the good times.

Washington chooses a Cabinet. At the outset the only other member of George Washington's administration was Vice President John Adams of Massachusetts. Adams and the President were not friendly, however, and they could not work closely together. For advice, the President turned to the heads of the executive departments. Those departments, set up by Congress in 1789, included State, Treasury, and War, and the office of the Attorney General. Together, the heads of these departments came to be known as the *Cabinet.* Even though the word *Cabinet* does not appear in the Constitution, Cabinet members have become recognized as a group of official advisers to the President.

Washington chose his Cabinet with great care. To be Secretary of State he selected Thomas Jefferson, a fellow Virginian. At the time, Jefferson was serving as minister to France. He would bring to the new office not only his considerable experience of the world, but a sense of the revolutionary stirrings that were beginning to reshape Europe. The appointment of Jefferson was also aimed at winning the loyalty of those people, like Jefferson himself, who had not thought the United States needed the new Constitution at all.

Washington named Alexander Hamilton to be Secretary of the Treasury. Only in his mid-thirties, Hamilton had already devoted much time to working for a strong national government.

The Secretary of War was General Henry Knox of Massachusetts. Knox had headed the War Department under the Confederation government. Weighing over three hundred pounds, he had been a leading artillery officer during the Revolution. Now he was a symbol of continuity with the previous government.

The post of Attorney General went to Edmund Randolph, another Virginian. Randolph had at first been uncertain about the Constitution, but after deciding to support it he had helped to obtain Virginia's ratification.

Congress establishes courts. One of the first acts of the new Congress, as required by the Constitution, was to pass a law establishing the Supreme Court and other federal courts. The Judiciary Act of 1789 provided for a Supreme Court made up of a Chief Justice and five associate justices.[1] It also established three circuit courts and thirteen district courts.

In filling the Supreme Court, President Washington had the privilege no other Chief Executive would have — that of naming all the members. He chose three justices from the North and three from the South, all of them staunch defenders of the Constitution. The first Chief Justice was John Jay of New York, one of the authors of *The Federalist* essays.

Rival groups emerge in the administration. In making decisions, President Washington sought all the facts, relying upon advice offered by his Cabinet and by the Chief Justice. He also turned to help from Congress, where James Madison, a member of the House from Virginia, was one of his most trusted friends and advisers.

Because there were no political parties, Washington depended on people in government who had been active in seeking ratification of the Constitution. He assumed that these people would be united in the com-

This picture shows President Washington meeting with Cabinet members Alexander Hamilton, Henry Knox, Thomas Jefferson, and Edmund Randolph.

mon goal of working for harmony in the government. The President's hopes soon vanished, however, as two rival groups developed in the administration. One group found its leader in Jefferson; the other, in Hamilton. Each man became a symbol of ideas that had become current in America in the years since the writing of the Declaration of Independence.

Jefferson and Hamilton hold contrasting views. Jefferson believed that the ideal American nation should be one consisting of farmers who owned their own land. He thought that farmers were the most noble of all people. Jefferson also believed that people were by nature good. The purpose of government, therefore, should be to provide a free atmosphere in which individuals might pursue their personal goals without interference.

America, Jefferson maintained, should not try to become an industrial nation. Having seen "the mobs of great cities" in Europe, he was eager that his own beloved country avoid them. Instead of building large factories, he thought it possible for Americans to develop household manufacturing. At Monticello, his home in Virginia, he had set up a small nail factory run by slave children.

Despite his views on industrialization, Jefferson believed strongly in the will of the majority. He held that if people wished to live in cities and establish factories, their

---

[1]The number of associate justices is now eight.

Thomas Jefferson believed that the future of the United States depended on its continuing to be a land of small farmers.

leaders must not stand in the way of those goals. Above all, government must constantly merit the approval of its citizens.

Hamilton, on the other hand, maintained that people needed a strong government. Government, he said, must be energetic and efficient. By this he meant that it must exert its power boldly in order to operate properly. He was convinced that by using without hesitation the powers granted it, the new government would prove vigorous and respected. It would benefit all the people, because they would be able to obtain every advantage they wanted.

The two contrasting viewpoints resulted in clashes over policies within the Washington administration. Jefferson wanted to leave most governing to state and local governments. He had particular confidence in the state legislatures, because they reflected readily the will of the people. Still, he held firmly to the view that "that government is best which governs least." Hamilton, on the other side, wanted a strong

government led by a strong President. He also supported policies that would benefit people of wealth. Such policies, he believed, would lead to the prosperity of the rest of the people.

It is wrong to think that Jefferson and Hamilton were personal enemies. Indeed, Jefferson kept a marble bust of Hamilton in the entranceway of his home. Their hostility was over policies, and it grew only slowly. Hamilton took office in September, 1789. Jefferson did not return from Paris to assume his post until the following spring. By then, Jefferson, who hoped to be a good Secretary of State, especially wanted to be on good terms with the Secretary of the Treasury. For his part, Hamilton, who did not meet Jefferson until 1790, greatly respected him for his reputation and accomplishments.

Neither Jefferson nor Hamilton had at first a clear sense of the views of the other. Still, their views soon were the driving forces in a struggle for power within the new government. By 1792 Washington was pleading with each of them to be tolerant of the other, lest their differences "tear the machine asunder" and destroy the new union of states.

1. Vocabulary: *Cabinet*.
2. Name the four members of Washington's Cabinet, and tell which position each held.
3. (a) What courts were established by the Judiciary Act of 1789? (b) Who was appointed Chief Justice?
4. (a) Compare Jefferson's and Hamilton's views on the role and purpose of government. (b) Why were the differences between Jefferson and Hamilton important during Washington's presidency?

2 Hamilton Tackles the Nation's Money Problems

Of all the members of the Washington administration, Alexander Hamilton had the clearest ideas of what the new government should do. He was especially determined to establish the credit of the United States. He wanted, therefore, to pay off the large debt the new government had inherited from the Confederation.

Hamilton studies the financial situation. Hamilton had a remarkable grasp of financial affairs. He believed the country should view the national debt as a means of making the union solid. He maintained that people who were owed money by the government would want to see it succeed and would support its policies. The debt could, therefore, be turned into an indispensable "public blessing."

The debt consisted of three parts. One was the sum owed to European nations. Totaling about $12 million, it had been run up during the Revolution and under the Confederation when the successive Congresses had borrowed from abroad.

The second part of the debt was money owed to private citizens within the country.

This domestic debt amounted to about $40 million, and consisted of a bewildering assortment of obligations incurred by various national government agencies, among them the military branches. Most of the money had been borrowed by the government through the sale of *bonds.* A bond is a certificate issued in exchange for a loan of money. The certificate states when the money will be repaid and contains a pledge to pay a specified amount of interest.

The third part of the debt was money that the states had borrowed from private citizens during the Revolution. The state debt totaled some $21 million, also incurred through the sale of bonds.

Hamilton proposes a program for settling the nation's debts. In January, 1790, Hamilton sent to Congress his first Report on the Public Credit. In it he proposed that the entire national debt — foreign, domestic, and state — be combined and paid by the federal government. People who had bought government bonds of any kind could expect to receive payment on them in full, plus

Alexander Hamilton's crowning achievement as Secretary of the Treasury was the establishment of a strong financial basis for the new republic.

interest, when they fell due. Hamilton believed that the sum could be paid by the new government in gradual, regular installments.

A storm of opposition arises. Merchants and bondholders were delighted with Hamilton's plan, but almost immediately protests arose in Congress. It is easy to see why. Practically no one questioned that the national honor required paying off the entire foreign debt with interest. The idea of having the federal government pay off the domestic and state debts, however, aroused heated opposition.

Southerners particularly objected to paying off the domestic and state bonds at full value. During the Revolution, bonds were very low in value. Speculators were able, therefore, to buy many of the bonds from the original purchasers at low prices. Most of the speculators lived in New York, Boston, and Philadelphia. These people stood to profit handsomely if the bonds they held were paid in full. Southerners, angry that they had felt forced to sell their bonds cheaply, resented the idea of wealth flowing into northern cities — at their expense, they believed. They came to resent the North, which they viewed as a stronghold of support for Hamilton.

If all the states had been in debt, the story might have been different; but some states, including Virginia, had already paid most of their obligations. Representatives from these states demanded to know why their people should now be taxed to help states like Massachusetts and New York pay their debts.

One of the severest critics of Hamilton's plan was James Madison. Because Madison was considered the "Father of the Constitution," his words were listened to closely. He was all for paying the entire public debt, but he insisted on doing justice to the original holders of the bonds. He proposed redeeming the bonds at market value and paying the original purchasers the difference between that value and the face value of the bonds.

Hamilton strikes a bargain. The opposition of Madison and others made it difficult for Hamilton to get his plan through Congress, especially the part providing for the assumption of the domestic debt. He was helped by Jefferson, however, who had returned from France just as the debt plan was getting bogged down in debate. The split in Congress was almost even. Pennsylvania, it was generally believed, would have the deciding votes.

The deadlock was broken by crafty domestic diplomacy. At a dinner held in Jefferson's house, Hamilton, Jefferson, and Madison reached a bargain. The two Virginians would round up enough southern votes to pass Hamilton's bill. In return, Philadelphia would become the temporary capital of the United States (a decision designed to flatter Pennsylvanians), and in ten years a site on the Potomac River would become the permanent capital. Actually a Potomac-Philadelphia bill was already on its way to passage in Congress. Yet people still give credit to Hamilton, Jefferson, and Madison for what may be called the Compromise of 1790.

Hamilton proposes a national bank. In December, 1790, Hamilton submitted a report calling for the establishment of a Bank of the United States under a charter to run for twenty years. The bank would begin operations with $10 million, of which the federal government would furnish $2 million. The remaining money would be raised by selling capital stock to private citizens. They could pay for the stock with specie or with United States bonds. The bank would be authorized to issue paper money to help meet the money needs of the nation. The paper money could be used to pay taxes and debts to the government. Currency would have the same value throughout the country.

Debate over the bank bill reveals sharp differences. Under Hamilton's bank plan, the government and the bank would be bound together inseparably. In addition, people of wealth would be further tied to the federal government. Hamilton's opponents became alarmed. A strong centralized government seemed to be in the making. James Madison argued that a bank such as the one proposed would be unconstitutional, because the

Planning for the nation's new capital began after George Washington had chosen a site on the Potomac River in 1791.

Constitution did not specifically provide for a bank. Nevertheless, the bill incorporating the Bank of the United States was passed by Congress in February, 1791.

President Washington, troubled by the harsh criticism of the bank bill, hesitated to sign it. Being a man who took pride in reaching important decisions only after careful consultation, Washington turned to Jefferson for advice.

Jefferson took the same position as Madison. He believed that a bank, though likely to be convenient and helpful, could not be established under the Constitution. Nowhere in the Constitution was the power to set up such an institution "clearly enumerated." Furthermore, all of Congress's powers, he declared, could be carried out without creating a bank. Jefferson was interpreting the Constitution narrowly. His interpretation became known as *strict construction* of the Constitution.

Washington now sought Hamilton's opinion. Hamilton wrote one of his greatest papers in order to persuade the President to sign the bank bill. In the paper the Secretary of the Treasury reminded Washington that the Constitution gave Congress the powers "necessary and proper" for carrying out its functions. A bank, he pointed out, would enable the government to carry out such functions as collecting taxes, regulating trade, and providing for the nation's defense. Hamilton was interpreting the Constitution broadly. This interpretation is known as *loose construction* of the Constitution. In time this view would be the basis for the steadily widening activities of the federal government.

The national bank is established. Hamilton's strong arguments convinced Washington that he should sign the bank bill. Accordingly in February, 1791, a charter

181

was granted, setting up the bank. The Bank of the United States almost immediately proved its usefulness to the whole country. Still, many people complained that it served the interests of business people while ignoring those of farmers.

Hamilton proposes a tax plan. Hamilton completed his financial arrangements for the country by proposing a new system of taxes. These taxes would be placed, first of all, on goods entering the country. This kind of tax is called a *tariff*. Hamilton also recommended internal taxes on the sale of certain products. The opposition to these *excise taxes* was fierce, because one tax Hamilton proposed was to be on whiskey distilled within the United States. The whiskey tax placed a severe hardship on farmers who lived in the western counties of Pennsylvania, Maryland, Virginia, and North Carolina. These farmers converted surplus grain into whiskey because bad roads made it difficult to transport anything as bulky as corn or rye.

The Whiskey Rebellion fails. By 1794, farmers in western Pennsylvania were flatly refusing to pay the tax on whiskey and were sometimes resorting to violence. This so-called Whiskey Rebellion was the first direct challenge to the authority of the new government. Washington agreed with Hamilton that troops must be used to end the defiance. The President himself led a force of 13,000 militiamen into Pennsylvania before the resisting taxpayers gave up their struggle. At the President's side, also in uniform, was Hamilton.

The expedition into Pennsylvania had shown the power of the federal government, but the action had made Hamilton many enemies. His critics called him a tyrant who lorded it over fellow-citizens. Frontier settlers turned to Jefferson as their champion, and they became the core of his political support.

Hamilton foresees the emergence of American industry. The differences between Hamilton and Jefferson had already been

The Whiskey Rebellion was an early test of the use of federal power. Here, President Washington reviews troops assembled to put down the disturbances.

highlighted in 1791 by Hamilton's third and final report to Congress. Called the Report on Manufactures, it was Hamilton's most farseeing work. In it Hamilton called for the development of factories in America. He proposed a system of tariffs in support of them, government subsidies to encourage agriculture, and a network of roads and canals to make the movement of goods easier. Tariffs would be placed on products imported from Europe, making them more expensive than similar goods produced in the United States. In that way the market for American manufacturers would be protected from foreign competition, and manufacturing would flourish in the United States.

Congress took no action on Hamilton's proposal. The United States was still overwhelmingly agricultural, and few people could imagine the kind of world that Hamilton was describing. Most Americans must have felt sympathy with ideas expressed by Jefferson: "While we have land to labor then, let us never wish to see our citizens occupied at a work-bench. . . . For the general operation of manufacturers, let our workshops remain in Europe."

The new policies promote prosperity. Hamilton's report was the blueprint by which the United States in time became the greatest industrial power in the world. Hamilton's immediate aim, however, was to guarantee the prosperity and security of the country. Paying the foreign debt strengthened the nation's reputation abroad. At home, people had fresh confidence in the future. Nearly bankrupt in the 1780's, the nation now basked in increasing prosperity.

In their debates over the nation's policies, Hamilton and Jefferson seemed to be at opposite poles. Hamilton foresaw a nation where factories would hasten prosperity. Jefferson could see a nation of free farmers prizing individual liberty as much as their fertile soil. In actuality the land of thriving farms that Jefferson envisioned and the land of creative factories that Hamilton sought have both come to pass. The rich values of both worlds are woven together in the American tradition.

SECTION REVIEW

1. Vocabulary: *bond, strict construction, loose construction, tariff, excise tax.*
2. (a) What were the three parts of the national debt? (b) What was Hamilton's proposal for settling this debt?
3. (a) Why did some people object to Hamilton's proposal for settling the debt? (b) How did Congress resolve this problem?
4. (a) What were the terms of Hamilton's plan to establish a Bank of the United States? (b) Who objected to the bank? (c) For what reasons?
5. (a) What circumstances led to the Whiskey Rebellion? (b) What was its outcome?
6. (a) What ideas were expressed in Hamilton's Report on Manufactures? (b) Why was little action taken on these ideas at the time?

3 Political Parties Are Formed

By 1792 the dispute over Hamilton's program had led to the creation of political parties. The supporters of Jefferson and Madison were called Democratic-Republicans, or simply Republicans. (This name should not be confused with the present-day Republican Party, which was organized in the 1850's.) The Republicans could be found chiefly in the rural parts of the North and South and in the frontier regions. The supporters of Hamilton came to be known as Federalists. They included business and manufacturing people located in the East.

Washington is re-elected. Although President Washington hated the idea of political parties, his sympathies lay with the Federalists. Still, he was such a towering figure that both Hamilton and Jefferson urged him to run for re-election in 1792. He was again chosen unanimously by the electoral college, with John Adams once more named Vice President. Meanwhile, Jefferson and Hamilton were growing increasingly restless in the Cabinet. Jefferson resigned in 1793, and Hamilton left a year later. Each began making plans for the 1796 election.

News of the French Revolution reaches America. The outbreak of revolution in France had a greater effect on American politics than Hamilton's programs. The French Revolution began on July 14, 1789. On that day a Paris mob stormed the Bastille, a political prison that was a hated symbol of royal oppression, and freed the prisoners.

This event, taking place only a little more than ten weeks after Washington's first inauguration, was greeted with enthusiasm by some in the United States. The French people, it appeared, were following the American lead in striking at tyranny. Lafayette sent Washington the key to the Bastille as a symbol of how the two revolutions were connected. Some Americans were so enthusiastic about developments in France that they took on the new French habit of addressing one another as "Citizen" and "Citizeness," instead of "Mr." and "Mrs."

Almost from the start, however, there were Americans who feared that discontented people in their own country might be made rebellious by too much of what was termed "Bastille fever." Then, in January, 1793, the Revolution took a fearful turn. Its leaders beheaded Louis XVI, America's friend in sending aid during the Revolutionary War. A few months later they executed Queen Marie Antoinette.

Jefferson, who had been an eyewitness to the storming of the Bastille, had been delighted when the Revolution broke out in France. By 1793 he was writing, "All the old spirit of 1776 is kindling." Although he was upset over the bloody Reign of Terror that had developed, he was certain that in the end liberty, as well as order, would triumph.

Everywhere people reminded themselves that Frenchmen had died fighting for American independence. Many people believed the United States ought to send aid to France. As a prominent Westerner put it, "If kings combine to support kings, why not republics to support republics?" Besides, did not the United States have a treaty that obliged Americans to help France?

Federalists and Republicans disagree over France. As time went on and the French Revolution became more extreme, a growing number of Americans had a change of heart. They believed France was now devoted to mob rule and massacre. They were also made uneasy by the French revolutionary attack on social position and religion.

Because the success of Hamilton's program depended heavily on continued trade with England, Hamilton and the Federalists were generally pro-Britain and anti-France. Americans who opposed Hamilton's program, mostly followers of Jefferson, tended to be pro-French in sympathy. They did not share the concern of business people who feared that if the United States aided France, the British navy would destroy America's ships and overseas trade. They still thought the United States should help revolutionary France.

The United States remains neutral. By this time France and Britain were at war, and the United States was facing its first crisis in foreign policy. Washington, as he had in the past, consulted his Cabinet. After much discussion he backed the position favored by Hamilton. On April 22, 1793, he issued a paper that has become known as Washington's Neutrality Proclamation. In it the President pointed out that war with France or with Britain would be equally disastrous. He assured foreign nations that the United States would be "friendly and impartial" to both sides in the war. In other words, the United States would stay *neutral.*

Many Republicans were unhappy. One of them complained that "the cause of France is the cause of man, and neutrality is desertion." Unwilling to attack Washington himself, the Republicans blamed Hamilton. They regarded him as the "evil counsellor" responsible for the Proclamation.

Genêt stirs up controversy. The decision to remain neutral was soon tested by the arrival in America of "Citizen" Edmond Genêt (zhuh-NAY), the new French minister to the United States. Genêt's mission was to convince Americans to support their "sister republic" across the Atlantic. Hoping to dramatize his arrival, Genêt landed in Charleston, South Carolina, rather than in the federal capital of Philadelphia. He assumed that by traveling northward, through areas where the Republicans were strong, he would be well received.

Genêt was not mistaken. Everywhere he was greeted with enthusiasm. Only thirty years old, he was a witty man, polished in manners, and skilled in languages, including English. A close student of the American Revolution, Genêt was fascinated by the experiments in government now under way on both sides of the Atlantic.

When Genêt arrived in Philadelphia, the atmosphere was much different from that in the South. Washington greeted him coolly. Since Hamilton was very friendly with the British ambassador, Jefferson took Genêt into his confidence. Genêt misunderstood the friendship. Already he had tried to fit out an American privateer to be sent against the British from an American port. Now he tried to appeal for American support over the head of the President. Washington quickly asked France to recall Genêt.

Jefferson breathed a sigh of relief. Genêt, he had to conclude, showed "no judgment" and was "disrespectful and even indecent to the President." Jefferson was afraid that if Genêt continued his activities, he would "sink the Republican interest." In fact, Genêt had become an embarrassment to Jefferson's followers.

These developments took place in the late summer of 1793, just when a fearful epidemic of yellow fever was breaking out in Philadelphia. As thousands of people fell ill, and as thousands died within a short time, the government practically ceased to function. Washington, and others who were able to, fled the city. The eerie silence seemed to be broken only by the mournful call of the cartman on his rounds: "Bring out your dead." No one knew what had caused the disease; no one knew how to cure it. John Adams believed that it was the outbreak of the epidemic alone that prevented the United States from coming to the side of France.

The United States has trouble with Britain. Although relations with Britain were stormy during Washington's presidency,

By calling on the United States to side with France in its war with Great Britain, Edmond Genêt put American neutrality to the test.

the Federalists' policy was to settle disputes by negotiation. The most serious issue for the Americans was the continued British refusal to give up the trading posts in the Northwest (page 158). Ten years after the Treaty of Paris ended the American Revolution, the Union Jack still flew over these little forts. The commander of the British fort at Niagara even refused to permit Americans to view Niagara Falls!

The British were able to hold on because they had won the nearby Indians to their side. Britain hoped to create an Indian barrier to the continued westward expansion of the Americans. To carry out their plan, they supplied the Indians with gifts and small arms. This scheme, the British believed, would protect Canada from the Americans as well as preserve the valuable fur trade for Britons.

From 1783 on, fighting raged between Indians and white settlers in the Northwest. The British overplayed their hand, however, and underestimated the Americans. In 1794 a large force of Shawnee, Ottawa, and Chippewa were defeated at the Battle of Fallen Timbers by an army under the command of "Mad Anthony" Wayne, a Revolutionary War hero. Following the battle, the Indians agreed to sign peace treaties with the victorious Americans.

The British navy seizes American ships. On the high seas, too, Britain treated America scornfully. The British had gone to war against France in 1793. Britain ordered any neutral ship carrying foodstuffs bound for France stopped and turned away from French ports. Neutral vessels trading with French islands in the Caribbean were to be similarly diverted. Since the United States was the principal country concerned, British naval authorities soon were seizing American ships and imprisoning their crews.

Most Federalists did not feel directly threatened by the continued British pressure in the northwestern posts. The frontier people who were affected were mostly Republicans. The brutal interference with American vessels, however, made Federalists in the shipping communities of New England and the Middle States denounce Great Britain too. Thus, British policies had the effect of helping unite the country.

Hamilton condemned the calls for war with Britain that were heard in some quarters. The success of his financial program depended heavily on the tariffs paid on English manufactured goods. It helped when Britain agreed to pay for the cargoes it seized, for this step temporarily quieted American business people. Jefferson's supporters, however, wanted England to take further steps, including giving up the posts. To satisfy the Republicans, the administration agreed to send a special representative to Britain to negotiate.

John Jay negotiates with the British. The Republicans were dismayed when the President chose Chief Justice John Jay to represent the United States. In addition to being a dyed-in-the-wool Federalist, Jay was rumored to be an ardent friend of Britain. Jay had hardly arrived in London when he was received by the queen of England. In the gentlemanly fashion of the day, he bowed low before her and kissed her hand. When the news reached America, the worst fears of the Republicans seemed confirmed. Screamed one furious Republican, "John Jay, ah! The arch traitor — seize him, drown him, burn him, burn him alive! Men of America, he betrayed you with a kiss!"

When the terms of Jay's Treaty were made public in 1794, the Republicans were even more outraged. Still, the treaty may have been the best that any negotiator could have obtained. The British agreed, as they had agreed eleven years earlier, to turn over the forts along the Great Lakes to the United States. (This time Britain kept its word.) Other issues, such as the boundary line between Maine and Canada, the pre-Revolutionary War debts, and payments for recent losses on the high seas were left to arbitration by British-American commissions to be appointed later.

A member of General Anthony Wayne's staff painted this picture of the Indian leader Little Turtle surrendering after the Battle of Fallen Timbers.

Washington's Farewell Address (1796)

A solicitude for your welfare which cannot end with my life . . . urges me on an occasion like the present . . . to recommend to your frequent review some sentiments which are the result of much reflection. . . .

The name of American, which belongs to you . . . , must always exalt the just pride of patriotism. . . . You have in a common cause fought and triumphed together. The independence and liberty you possess are the work of joint councils and joint efforts, of common dangers, sufferings and successes. . . . Every portion of our country finds the most commanding motives for carefully guarding and preserving the union of the whole. . . .

This government, the offspring of our own choice, . . . completely free in its principles, in the distribution of its powers, uniting security with energy, and containing within itself a provision for its own amendment, has a just claim to your confidence and your support. Respect for its authority, compliance with its laws, acquiescence in its measures, are duties enjoined by the fundamental maxim of liberty. . . .

Against the insidious wiles of foreign influence, the jealousy of a free people ought to be *constantly* awake, since history and experience prove that foreign influence is one of the most baneful foes of republican government. . . . The great rule of conduct for us in regard to foreign nations is in extending our commercial relations to have as little political connection as possible. . . . It is our true policy to steer clear of permanent alliances, with any portion of the foreign world. . . .

In postponing the settlement of these issues, America gained an advantage. As the nation grew stronger, it could make a more forceful case for itself. In providing for arbitration, the treaty broke fresh ground. The arbitration of international disputes was a new idea that may be said to have begun with Jay's Treaty.

The Senate ratifies Jay's Treaty. For Jay to have satisfied the Republicans he would have had to obtain British concessions on every issue. Clearly that was impossible. The Republicans denounced the treaty because it failed to provide compensation for slaves carried off by the British during the Revolution. The treaty also said nothing about the British plotting with Indians along the frontier.

Although quieter than the Republicans, many Federalists were also unhappy. The treaty had not mentioned the seizure of

United States sailors by the British navy, nor did it fully open up trade with the British West Indies. For example, it prohibited American vessels from carrying molasses, sugar, coffee, cocoa, and cotton from the West Indies to any other part of the world.

The Senate ratified Jay's Treaty in 1795, but only after long debate. President Washington's influence was indispensable in achieving the required two-thirds majority. Washington knew that the country needed a long period of peace so that it could expand and develop. The treaty could help provide such a breathing spell.

Pinckney's Treaty settles differences with Spain. Both the Federalists and the Republicans were pleased with a treaty that Thomas Pinckney negotiated with Spain. Spain had extended an invitation to open talks with America after it had learned of Jay's Treaty. The Spanish feared that an

Anglo-American alliance was in the making, one that might endanger Spain's American colonies.

Pinckney's Treaty, ratified unanimously by the Senate in 1796, gave United States citizens the right to travel freely on the Mississippi. Americans also acquired the right of deposit — that is, the right to store goods at New Orleans for later reshipment. Finally, Spain and the United States agreed to the boundary between Georgia and Florida. Each party pledged to restrain the Indians within its jurisdiction from raiding the territory of the other.

Americans living on the frontier were delighted. They regarded Pinckney, who became a western hero, as a much better diplomat than Jay. The truth was, nevertheless, that Spain, afraid of war with Britain, had eagerly sought American good will by making concessions. The fledgling United States had learned to take whatever advantages came its way on the treacherous seas of international relations.

Washington retires. By 1796 Washington was ready to retire from politics. He had been worn down by quarrels between the Federalists and Republicans. Washington was also in declining health. He had undergone serious surgery on his thigh early in his administration. Uncomplainingly he had accepted a second term in 1792. Now exhausted, he deserved an easier life. He was, he said, eager to have dinner alone with his wife, something he had not enjoyed for twenty years.

Before leaving office, Washington issued a "Farewell Address" to his fellow citizens. In it he gave wise advice on a number of subjects. He warned against the dangers of political parties. He emphasized the need for neutrality, urging the nation "to steer clear of permanent alliances." He made a strong case that religion and morality are "indispensable supports" of good government. He also called upon the people to be alert to the abuse of power by public officials. Washington's Farewell Address, portions of which are printed on page 187, has come to be regarded as one of this country's most important public documents.

portions of which are printed on page 187

SECTION REVIEW

1. Vocabulary: *neutral.*
2. (a) What was the initial reaction of many Americans to news of the French Revolution? (b) What effect did the growing violence of that Revolution have on American opinion?
3. (a) Compare the views of Federalists and Republicans on the question of American aid to France. (b) What course did Washington choose to follow?
4. (a) What problems with Britain angered Americans in the early 1790's? (b) What positions did the two political parties take on these issues?
5. (a) What were the provisions of Jay's Treaty? (b) How did the treaty benefit the United States? (c) Why were some Americans not pleased with it?
6. (a) How did Pinckney's Treaty settle problems with Spain? (b) What motivated Spain to sign the treaty?
7. What advice did Washington give the American people in his Farewell Address?

4 Federalist Power Declines

John Adams, who had been Vice President during Washington's two terms of office, was elected President in 1796. Thomas Jefferson, who received the second highest number of votes in the electoral college, became Vice President. The new administration now had a Federalist President and a Republican Vice President.

John Adams takes office. Adams had long been jealous of President Washington. He regarded the general as unintelligent and uneducated. The luck and fame that Washington had enjoyed irritated him as undeserved. When Adams took the oath of office, dressed elegantly in a gray broadcloth suit, he resented that all eyes were on Washington. Adams wrote to his wife, Abigail, that even at the moment of the oath-taking, Washington appeared "to enjoy a triumph over me. Methought I heard him say, 'Ay! I am fairly out and you fairly in! See which of us will be happiest'." Still, the incredible development was that the presidency had been peacefully transferred from one man to another. Such a transfer, which

John Adams was the first President to live in the White House. It was unfinished when he and his wife moved in, and they suffered many inconveniences. Here, Abigail Adams watches a servant hang out clothes in the unfinished East Room.

seems so normal today in America, was almost without precedent. As Adams wrote, "The sight of the sun setting . . . and another rising (though less splendid), was a novelty."

Adams was a hard man to please. He found that the President's house in Philadelphia, only sparsely furnished by the Washingtons, was not comfortable. Adams complained, "There is not a chair fit to sit in. The beds are in a woeful pickle." Soon, however, Adams had bigger concerns. The United States was facing serious foreign problems.

The XYZ Affair angers Americans. France had been unhappy when the United States signed Jay's Treaty with Great Britain. To retaliate, the French government refused to receive the new United States minister, Charles Cotesworth Pinckney of South Carolina, a devoted Federalist. He had been appointed to succeed James Monroe, whose open support of the French Revolution had irritated many Federalists.

In 1797 Adams sent three Americans to Paris to negotiate with France over the Pinckney problem. The three were Pinckney, John Marshall of Virginia, and Elbridge Gerry of Massachusetts. French officials,

however, refused to meet with the Americans. Ready to leave, the diplomats were suddenly approached by three visitors from the French foreign ministry. Later identified by Adams only as X, Y, and Z, the visitors said they could arrange to reopen diplomatic relations. In return, they demanded a bribe of $240,000. France was to be given, in addition, a loan of $2 million, while the President was to apologize for some recent harsh words about France.

The Americans, astounded, responded angrily that there would be no payment, no loan, no apology. "No! No! Not a sixpence!" shouted Pinckney. When news of the demands reached the United States, the clamor against France could be heard everywhere. People demanded war, crying, "Millions for defense, not one cent for tribute!"

In the surge of national feeling that followed this XYZ Affair, one of America's first patriotic songs was born. Composed by Joseph Hopkinson, it was called "Hail, Columbia!" Its rousing opening lines are:

> Hail! Columbia, happy land!
> Hail! Ye heroes, heaven-born band,
> Who fought and bled in freedom's cause. . . .

In writing the anthem, Hopkinson aimed to bring together the Federalists, who were so insistently anti-French, and the Republicans, who were no less anti-British. Both groups, said Hopkinson, must now think of themselves as Americans first of all.

Relations with France worsen. Undoubtedly Adams could have led the country into a popular war against France, but he resisted the opportunity that many Federalists were urging him to take. They seem not to have asked how the United States could have engaged France in battle. Except for three frigates, there was no American navy. As for the army, it consisted of only about 3,500 officers and troops scattered across the frontier.

By 1798 French privateers, operating along the Atlantic coast, were wreaking havoc on American shipping. Congress, alarmed, appropriated money for a navy and an increase in the army. Some people even wanted to bring Washington out of retirement and place him in charge of the troops. Nevertheless, although France was hurting the United States, Adams held firm. He would not ask the country formally to go to war because he considered it unnecessary. Years later, still defending himself, he declared, "I desire no other inscription over my gravestone than: 'Here lies John Adams, who took upon himself the responsibility of peace with France in the year 1800'." At the time, however, even many of the President's strongest supporters called him spineless. The Republicans, moreover, showed no gratitude at all for John Adams's policy of restraint.

Congress passes the Alien and Sedition Acts. As the dispute with France reached its

Following the XYZ affair, feelings against France were at their height. Fighting broke out at sea, and the Americans began to build a navy. In this picture, work proceeds on the construction of the hull of the *Philadelphia*.

The Death of Washington

Samuel Goodrich, the son of a minister, grew up in a small town in the hills of western Connecticut. When George Washington died in December, 1799, Samuel Goodrich was a young boy. Years later he recalled the sorrowful event.

I remember the death of Washington, which took place in 1799 and was commemorated all through the country by the tolling of bells, funeral ceremonies, orations, sermons, hymns, and dirges. It was attended by a mournful sense of loss and seemed to cast a pall over the entire heavens.

In our town, the meeting-house was dressed in black. Lieutenant Smith came over every day to our house to talk about the event, and to bring to us the proceedings in different parts of the country. He brought us a copy of the *Connecticut Courant* which gave us the particulars of the rites and ceremonies which took place in Hartford.

One memorial service for George Washington was the performance of the celebrated hymn written for the occasion by Theodore Dwight. This hymn became a

A memorial to George Washington

part of the cherished lore of my childhood — here is a stanza:

Hear, O Most High! our earnest
  prayer —
Our country take beneath Thy care;
When dangers press and foes draw
  near,
Let future Washingtons appear.

---

height, the Federalist-controlled Congress passed laws that it claimed would unite the country. Observers quickly pointed out, however, that the laws would also restrict the growth of the Republican Party. Many Federalists were convinced that a victory for the Republicans in the next national election would be a victory of evil over good. They had also been annoyed by criticism of Adams's policies in Republican newspapers.

The Naturalization Act of 1798 was the first anti-Republican measure. It increased from five to fourteen years the length of time required for an immigrant to become a citizen. Many immigrants who came to this country tended to be Republican in sympa-

thy. By delaying citizenship for them, the Federalists could prevent them from voting for a number of years.

The Alien Act of 1798 was directed at specific foreigners, or aliens. It gave the President the unheard-of power to expel from the United States any foreigner he deemed "dangerous to the peace and safety of the United States." Some Federalists wanted to deport a number of Republican newspaper editors and party leaders who had been born abroad. Other Federalists feared that the thousands of French immigrants who had come to the United States were about to revolutionize the country. Most of the newcomers actually were opposed to the French Revolution and would willingly have returned home to live in peace if they could have.[2]

The Sedition Act, passed in July, 1798, was designed to stifle criticism of the Federalists. It made it a crime, severely punishable, for citizens or aliens to join together to oppose the execution of laws. It also forbade, among other things, "false, scandalous, and malicious" remarks — spoken or written — about the President or Congress.

The Alien and Sedition Acts were a tragic mistake. The Sedition Act was an especially serious threat to American liberty. Even Hamilton was frightened by its possibilities. "Let us not," he warned, "establish a tyranny." The Federalists, so eager to protect President Adams and other federal officeholders from Republican attack, made no effort to protect Vice President Jefferson from attack by Federalists. Jefferson, indeed, was subjected to merciless slanders in Federalist newspapers. How strange that Adams, who feared that war would damage American liberties, had signed these bills so readily.

The Virginia and Kentucky Resolutions are offered. The Republicans vigorously opposed the Alien and Sedition Acts as attacks on American liberty. Madison and Jefferson were convinced that if the Federalists smashed the Republicans in their "American Reign of Terror," the United States might slip into tyranny. They decided that if the states did not come to the rescue, the Constitution would be destroyed. The states, they concluded, must be given the right to decide whether or not laws are constitutional.

To Madison and Jefferson the Sedition Act was clearly unconstitutional, because it violated the First Amendment guarantees of freedom of speech, press, assembly, and petition. Very worried, they wrote resolutions late in 1798 that were adopted by the legis-

latures of Virginia and Kentucky. The people, said Jefferson, required protection against "the passions and powers of a majority of Congress." The states, he went on, must have the right to declare acts of Congress "null and void" (that is, not in force) if they violate the Constitution. Madison, expressing the same idea, said that the states have the right "to interpose" (that is, to step in) when Congress acts contrary to the Constitution.

In a short time the anti-Republican fever died down. The ideas expressed in the Virginia and Kentucky Resolutions, however, did not disappear. In the years that followed they became the basis of the *states' rights* argument. This was the theory upholding the power of the states as opposed to the power of the central government.

The Republicans win the 1800 presidential election. As Vice President, Thomas Jefferson had been unable to play an effective role in shaping policies. He had presided over the Senate with dignity and grace, but mostly he had pursued personal interests. He even took time to view an elephant herd at an exhibition in Philadelphia. Jefferson claimed that he did not seek to be President: "I have no ambition to govern men; no passion which would lead me to delight to ride in a storm." Nevertheless, although he liked Adams personally, their conflicting ideas had widened the gulf between them. By 1800 they were political enemies.

In the 1800 presidential election the Federalists renominated John Adams, with Charles Cotesworth Pinckney this time the candidate for Vice President. The Republican candidates for President and Vice President were Thomas Jefferson and Aaron Burr, a New York politician.

The contest was heated. The Federalists painted Jefferson as "Mad Tom," shouting that if he became President he and his friends would destroy all the good works of the previous decade. The public credit and confidence in the new government, insisted the Federalists, would be shattered beyond repair.

---

[2]It must be said that the Republicans also feared immigration — from Britain. They were concerned that when George III finally died, many English people would want to move to America and, of course, vote Federalist.

While the excitement of the campaign was mounting, the federal government was moving to its permanent home on the banks of the Potomac. The presidential mansion (later to be known as the White House) was still unfinished when John Adams moved in. Abigail Adams did not arrive until November 16, 1800. Meanwhile, Adams had written her the words that today are inscribed over the fireplace of the great state dining room: "I pray heaven to bestow the best of blessings on this house and on all that shall hereafter inhabit it. May none but honest and wise men ever rule under this roof."

Thomas Jefferson becomes President. When the electoral votes were counted, Jefferson and Burr were tied for first place. Each had received 73 votes. Adams ran third. He had carried New England and New York, while most of the South had backed the Republicans. The Constitution did not then provide for separate voting for President and Vice President. Everybody knew, however, that people meant for Jefferson to be the Chief Executive and for Burr to have the second place. When Burr refused to step aside, the election was thrown into the House of Representatives. There a struggle took place that did not end until Inauguration Day was practically at hand.

In a remarkable twist of history, it was Hamilton's decision that gave the election to Jefferson. Hamilton simply concluded that he disliked Burr, whom he regarded as totally without principles, even more than he disliked what Jefferson stood for. Hamilton believed that, despite his feelings about the great Virginian, "the public good must be paramount to every private consideration," and he threw his support to Jefferson.[3]

On March 4, 1801, Jefferson took the oath as President while Republicans rejoiced and celebrated. Adams was not in at-

---

[3]The confused election of 1800 led to the ratification, four years later, of the Twelfth Amendment. It provided that electors cast separate votes for President and Vice President.

REPUBLICANS

Turn out, turn out and save your Country from ruin !

From an *Emperor*—from a *King*—from the iron grasp of a *British Tory Faction*—an unprincipled banditti of British speculators. The hireling tools and emissaries of his majesty king George the 3d have thronged our city and diffused the poison of principles among us.

DOWN WITH THE TORIES, DOWN WITH THE BRITISH FACTION,

Before they have it in their power to enslave you, and reduce your families to distress by heavy taxation. Republicans want no Tribute-liars—they want no ship Ocean-liars—they want no Rufus King's for Lords —they want no Varick to lord it over them—they want no Jones for senator, who fought with the British against the Americans in time of the war.—But they want in their places such men as

Jefferson & Clinton,

who fought their Country's Battles in the year '76

A handbill reveals the heated emotions of American politics in the early 1800's.

tendance. His son Charles had died suddenly in New York and the second President had left Washington. Some Republicans said that Adams had refused to be present, but he had, in fact, sent a note to Jefferson wishing him "a quiet and prosperous administration."

Many people regarded Jefferson's coming to power as "the revolution of 1800." Yet his election as President represented only a change of party and a change of viewpoints. One of Jefferson's first acts was to place portraits of Washington and Adams in his bedroom. Jefferson recognized that the peaceful change of leadership was no less important to the stability of the republic than particular policies and programs.

SECTION REVIEW

1. Vocabulary: *states' rights.*
2. What was the outcome of the 1796 presidential election?
3. (a) What happened in the XYZ Affair? (b) How did the American people react? (c) What was Adams's policy toward France?
4. (a) What were the terms of the Naturalization, Alien, and Sedition acts? (b) In what way did the Virginia and Kentucky legislatures show their opposition to those laws?
5. (a) Describe the roles of John Adams, Thomas Jefferson, Aaron Burr, and Alexander Hamilton in the election of 1800. (b) What was the outcome of the election?

Chapter 8 Review

Summary

The responsibility for launching the government under the Constitution and making it work fell to the Federalists and to the first President, George Washington. The Federalists developed a workable government by setting up executive departments and by creating a system of federal courts.

Two members of Washington's Cabinet, Thomas Jefferson and Alexander Hamilton, held opposing views about the nation's future. Jefferson favored the development of small towns and farms with limited government interference. Hamilton, on the other hand, wished to encourage manufacturing and urban growth. He also called for a strong central government.

As Secretary of the Treasury, Hamilton was in a position to put his ideas to work. He proposed that the federal government pay the entire national debt, and he called for the creation of a central bank. He also framed a program of taxes to encourage domestic industry and to raise revenue. Under Hamilton's guidance the economy of the new nation got off to a strong start.

Diverging interests led to the formation of political parties. By 1792, two parties had appeared: the Republican Party, which embraced Jefferson's ideals; and the Federalist Party, which supported Hamilton.

The Federalists recognized the necessity of avoiding war with foreign powers and adhered to a policy of strict neutrality. They were able to keep the United States out of the European conflicts touched off by the French Revolution. Tensions with Britain over possession of forts in the Northwest, furthermore, were eased by a treaty negotiated by John Jay. Thomas Pinckney's negotiations with Spain gained for Americans the right to navigate the Mississippi River and to use the port of New Orleans.

In 1796 John Adams succeeded Washington as President, with Jefferson becoming Vice President. Relations with France became increasingly tense following the XYZ Affair. Adams avoided war with France, but the Federalist majorities in Congress passed the Naturalization, Alien, and Sedition acts to control opposition to Federalist policies. Republicans protested that these acts violated the liberties of American citizens. As discontent with Federalist rule grew, the Republicans benefited. They were able to score an electoral victory in 1800 with Thomas Jefferson becoming the nation's third Chief Executive.

Vocabulary and Important Terms

1. Cabinet
2. Judiciary Act of 1789
3. bond
4. strict construction
5. loose construction
6. tariff
7. excise tax
8. Whiskey Rebellion
9. Republicans
10. Federalists
11. French Revolution
12. neutral
13. Battle of Fallen Timbers
14. Jay's Treaty
15. Pinckney's Treaty
16. Washington's Farewell Address
17. XYZ Affair
18. Alien and Sedition Acts
19. Virginia and Kentucky Resolutions
20. states' rights

Discussion Questions

1. What factors contributed to a strong beginning for the government under the Constitution?
2. (a) How did the contrasting viewpoints of Thomas Jefferson and Alexander Hamilton affect policies within the Washington administration? (b) In what sense have both men's dreams of the nation's future come to pass?
3. (a) What objections were raised to Hamilton's proposals for having the federal government pay off the debt? (b) For establishing a national bank? (c) For levying excise taxes on such goods as whiskey? (d) How was each of these issues resolved?
4. (a) What divisions in American public opinion were caused by the French Revolution? (b) Why did Washington decide that the United States should remain neutral?
5. How did continued British presence in the Northwest and British interference with American merchant vessels help unite the United States?
6. (a) What was the reaction of the American public to Jay's Treaty? (b) What advantages did the United States gain in the treaty? (c) How did Jay's Treaty affect the negotiation of a treaty with Spain?
7. (a) What developments made it difficult for John Adams to adhere to George Washington's policy of neutrality toward France? (b) Why did Adams resist leading the United States into war?
8. (a) Why did the Federalist-controlled Congress pass the Alien and Sedition Acts? (b) Why did the Republicans oppose those acts, and how did they express their opposition? (c) What ideas expressed in the Virginia and Kentucky Resolutions became the basis of the states' rights argument?
9. Why was the transfer of power after the presidential election of 1800 so notable?

Relating Past to Present

1. George Washington was a reserved and aloof individual who brought formality to the office of President. Do research to find out the extent to which more recent Presidents have followed Washington's example.
2. For advice, President Washington turned to the heads of his executive departments. How has the Cabinet changed over the years? How large is it today? From what other experts do Presidents seek advice today?

Studying Local History

If your state had entered the Union by 1800, find out which political party it supported that year. If it joined the Union later, which political party did it support in the early years of statehood?

Using History Skills

1. *Evaluating.* American historians rank George Washington as a great President. Prepare a report evaluating the personal characteristics and presidential actions that made Washington so effective.
2. *Classifying.* Make a chart with two columns in which you list differences between the Federalists and the Republicans. Include the following information for each party: (a) party leaders; (b) sections of the country in which the party was strong; (c) groups of people who supported the party; (d) party views about the power of government, the Constitution, and foreign affairs.
3. *Reading source material.* Study Samuel Goodrich's recollection of the death of Washington on page 191. How does the passage indicate the high regard in which Washington was held by his countrymen?

WORLD SCENE

Recognizing the New Nation

Holland, in 1782, was the first government to recognize the independence of the new American nation. Other governments soon followed. Before long, the United States was exchanging ministers with other countries, some in distant places.

Ties with China. In 1784 the emperor of China announced the opening of trade with Europe and the United States. The trade would, however, be strictly regulated. Merchants would be forced to remain in an area outside of Canton. They could not trade directly in Chinese markets but would have to deal with one of thirteen *hongs*. These were Chinese firms that paid the imperial government for the right to handle transactions with foreign countries.

Within the limits of these rules, the Chinese in 1784 cordially welcomed an American vessel shrewdly named *The Empress of China*, commanded by Samuel Shaw of Boston. Shaw later wrote, "We were treated by them in all respects as citizens of a free and independent nation. They styled us 'The New People'."

In 1786 Shaw made another trip to Canton, this time as the first United States trade representative to China. At a dinner given in his honor by the other foreign merchants in China, the room was decorated with bird cages. At a signal the hosts cried "liberty," whereupon the bird-cage doors popped open and the freed birds soared into the air.

Ties with Russia. From 1762 to 1796 Russia was ruled by a ruthless, ambitious woman known as Catherine the Great. A brilliant student of politics, Catherine refused to choose sides in international disputes if Russia would not benefit from such action. In the early spring of 1779, for instance, George III asked Catherine to provide him with 12,000 troops to help put down the rebellion in America. Catherine refused to oblige her fellow-monarch. Nor did the cause of American independence appeal to her. In 1780 the Congress sent Francis Dana to win Russia's support. He remained in Russia for two years, but Catherine refused to receive him or recognize America's claim to independence.

After independence was won, American merchants established a thriving trade with Russian ports along the Baltic Sea. Not until after Catherine's death, however, was an American diplomat received at the Russian court. In 1809 John Quincy Adams was dispatched to Russia as the official representative of the United States.

UNIT 2 REVIEW

Important Dates

1763   Treaty of Paris.
1765   Stamp Act.
1767   Townshend Acts.
1770   Boston Massacre.
1773   Boston Tea Party.
1774   First Continental Congress meets.
1775   Battles of Lexington and Concord.
1776   Colonies declare independence.
1777   Burgoyne surrenders at Saratoga.
1778   Alliance signed with France.
1781   Cornwallis surrenders at Yorktown.
1783   American independence recognized.
1786   Shays's Rebellion.
1787   Northwest Ordinance.
1788   Constitution ratified.
1789   Washington becomes first President.
1791   Bill of Rights added to Constitution.
1794   Whiskey Rebellion.
1796   Adams elected President.
1798   Alien and Sedition Acts.
1800   Jefferson elected President.

Review Questions

1. (a) How did the attitude of Britain's leaders toward their North American colonies change after the French and Indian War? (b) Why did this change in attitude put the British on a collision course with the colonists?

2. (a) In what sense did British policies in the 1760's and 1770's have the unplanned effect of uniting the colonies? (b) Why was colonial unity important in the struggle against British actions?

3. (a) What disagreement about taxation led to the colonies' break from Great Britain? (b) What issues besides taxation finally caused the colonies to declare their independence in July, 1776?

4. What factors enabled the American colonists to win the Revolutionary War?

5. (a) Why was the creation of the United States, the first new nation in modern times, so important? (b) In the 1780's, how was the new nation threatened by internal and external problems? (c) Why did the government set up under the Articles of Confederation find it impossible to solve these difficult problems?

6. (a) What disagreements at the Constitutional Convention had to be settled by compromise? (b) On what matters did most of the Convention delegates agree?

7. List the individual liberties guaranteed by the Bill of Rights.

8. (a) How did the disagreement between Alexander Hamilton and Thomas Jefferson affect the rise of political parties in the United States? (b) What stand did each party take on the question of American neutrality?

Projects

1. Write a newspaper article, as it might have appeared at the time, on one of the following subjects: (a) colonial resistance to the Stamp Act, (b) the Boston Massacre, (c) the Boston Tea Party, (d) the meeting of the First Continental Congress, (e) the fighting at Lexington and Concord, (f) the surrender of the British at Yorktown.

2. Keep a diary as if you were one of the delegates to the Second Continental Congress. In your diary include entries that note such matters as colonial preparations for war, the selection of George Washington as commander-in-chief of the Continental Army, and the debate over the resolution by Richard Henry Lee calling for independence.

3. Read a book on one of the Patriots. Then write a book report explaining the Patriot's background and the role he or she played in the movement to secure independence.

4. Do research to find out about the writing of your state constitution. Be sure to answer questions such as these: (a) Where and by whom was your state constitution written? (b) In what year was it ratified? (c) What did it originally say about such matters as voting requirements and, if applicable, the status of slavery, the status of a state-supported church, and officeholding requirements? (d) What are some of the most important changes that have been made in your state's constitution?

5. Learn the Preamble to the Constitution. Be sure to look up the meaning of any words you do not know.

6. Write a script for a debate between a supporter and an opponent of Hamilton's financial program. In writing your script, try not to favor one side over the other.

7. Create a set of six handbills, three each for the Federalist and the Democratic-Republican parties at the time of the election of 1800. On these handbills include such information as the strengths of each party's presidential candidate and the position of each party on the important issues facing the United States.

A SHORT SURVEY OF
AMERICAN HISTORY TO 1800

BEGINNINGS

THE AGE OF EXPLORATION

Columbus reaches America. In the last decades of the fifteenth century there was lively interest among Europeans in finding water routes to Asia. Portuguese navigators sailed around Africa, and by the early 1490's they had opened up a rich trade in spices. At the same time, an Italian mariner named Christopher Columbus became convinced that he could reach Asia by sailing westward from Europe. Columbus petitioned Queen Isabella and King Ferdinand of Spain for money, ships, and a crew so that he could prove his theory. Jealous of the riches accumulating in Portugal, the Spanish monarchs agreed to back Columbus's expedition. After more than two months at sea, Columbus reached America in 1492.

Later explorations revealed the true nature of Columbus's achievement. When a ship from Ferdinand Magellan's fleet succeeded in voyaging around the world, this confirmed the belief held by Columbus that Asia could be reached by sailing west. Magellan's expedition and those that followed also showed, however, that the globe was much larger than Columbus had thought it to be. Europeans eventually realized that Columbus had actually found a land mass previously unknown to them.

Spain establishes an American empire. Columbus died frustrated because he failed to reach Asia and its expected treasure of spices. Not until later expeditions revealed that the inhabitants of Central and South America had vast quantities of gold and silver objects did the Spanish rulers show keen interest in the Americas. The conquest of Mexico by Hernando Cortés and of Peru by Francisco Pizarro crushed great Indian civilizations and brought Spain enough precious metals to make it the richest and most powerful nation in Europe. By the sixteenth century, Spanish explorers and conquistadors lay claim to a vast American empire. It stretched, finally, from the southern portion of North America to the tip of South America.

Spain's wealth proves costly in human terms. The European "discovery" of America was actually a *rediscovery* since the ancestors of the people mistakenly called Indians had arrived there first, migrating from Asia. The Indians developed a variety of cultures — from simple hunting societies to complex empires. Throughout the Americas, the Indians had learned to cultivate a variety of agricultural products. The knowledge they passed on to the Europeans who settled in America enabled the newcomers to adjust to their surroundings.

The arrival of the Spanish and other Europeans spelled tragedy for the Native Americans. Countless Indians died from diseases for which they lacked immunity. As the newcomers pushed inland, many Indians were killed in warfare.

The work of Europeanizing the Indians was undertaken by Spanish missionaries. These dedicated priests set up schools for Indians and taught them new methods of farming. The Spanish also introduced farm animals to the Americas.

When Indian workers became scarce, the Spaniards turned to African slaves. Slave ships carried captive human cargoes across the Atlantic to the Americas. Africans who survived the cruel voyage outnumbered other workers in the West Indies and provided a substantial part of the labor force in Spain's provinces on the mainland.

France establishes colonies in America. Not to be outdone by his energetic Spanish foes, France's king, Francis I, decided to join the quest for a shorter route to Asia. His first claim to American territory resulted from the explorations in 1524 of Giovanni da Verrazano, an Italian sailing under the French flag. Jacques Cartier claimed the Gulf of St. Lawrence for France in 1534. French adventurers seeking a passage to Asia then explored the St. Lawrence River and the Great Lakes. This region was called New France. In 1682, La Salle claimed the entire Mississippi River valley for King Louis XIV and named the surrounding territory Louisiana in his honor.

England is a latecomer in settling North America. England's claim to territory in the Western Hemisphere went back to 1497 when John Cabot reached the North American coast. Nearly a century passed, however, before England was ready to establish colonies. Meanwhile, it grew strong from manufacturing and trade. More and more English ships traveled the world's trading routes, successfully competing with other European merchants. When the English king broke with the Roman Catholic Church in 1534, hostility grew between England and the continental powers — especially the Catholic countries of Spain

and France. Under Queen Elizabeth I, England began to plunder Spain's treasure ships. Then, England defeated the Spanish Armada in 1588. Many English people were convinced that their country ought to be starting colonies in America too.

THE AGE OF ENGLISH COLONIZATION

Early attempts to establish colonies meet with failure. Sir Humphrey Gilbert, a friend of Queen Elizabeth, was the first Englishman who obtained a grant to start a colony in North America. In 1583 he and a small band of followers tried to establish a settlement in Newfoundland. They abandoned the undertaking when they realized that they had chosen an unsuitable place. Gilbert died on the return voyage, and his rights passed to Sir Walter Raleigh.

In 1584 an expedition under Raleigh chose Roanoke Island off the North Carolina coast as the site for a colony. Raleigh named the region Virginia and sent the first settlers to Roanoke the next year. The settlement on Roanoke Island failed.

A colony is started at Jamestown. In 1606, King James I granted investors a charter to establish colonies along the Atlantic coast between present-day New England and North Carolina. The investors set up an enterprise named the Virginia Company and divided it into two trading groups: the London group and the Plymouth group.

The London group founded the first permanent English settlement in America. In 1607, a hundred men landed at a place they called Jamestown in the present-day state of Virginia. At first they sought gold, neglecting preparations for the winter months. The result was a heavy loss of life from starvation, disease, and other misfortunes. Then Captain John Smith, a member of the governing council, took charge. The discipline Smith enforced saved the colony. Another colonist, John Rolfe, introduced a tropical variety of tobacco, and in time its cultivation became the chief business of the colonists.

Jamestown seeks workers. A leading problem for the colonists was the acute shortage of labor. An arrangement known as the indenture system was developed to provide workers. Under this system, men and women could pay for their passage across the Atlantic by working for a number of years as indentured servants. At the end of their terms of service, they received land of their own. When a few captive Africans arrived in Jamestown in 1619, they also served as indentured servants. By 1660, however, the colony's black population had been reduced to slavery.

A representative legislature is established. In 1619 the Virginia colonists organized the House of Burgesses, the first representative legislature in America. By 1699, when Williamsburg became the capital, plantations lined the rivers in the tidewater region, and smaller farms had been cleared in the western foothills. Virginia was a flourishing colony.

Pilgrims start a colony at Plymouth. The first successful New England colony was begun in 1620 at Plymouth. Its founders were a religious group known as Puritans because they had joined with others in England to "purify" the Anglican Church. Some Puritans, however, gave up hope of reforming the Church of England and decided to separate from the main body of Puritans. Driven out of England, these Separatists, or Pilgrims, searched for a safe place for their community. First they went to Holland, where they enjoyed full toleration. When their children began losing their Separatist beliefs and their English ways, the Pilgrims then decided to go to America. There, they believed, they and their descendants could be fully Separatist and English. They were given a land grant by the Virginia Company and set out on the voyage across the Atlantic.

On their journey the Pilgrims' ship, the *Mayflower*, went off course and reached what is now Provincetown harbor at the tip of Cape Cod. Before going ashore, the Pilgrims prepared a document, and 41 of the 44 men present signed it. They agreed to live together in an orderly manner and to "make just and equal laws" for the good of all. This agreement, the Mayflower Compact, helped to make the idea of self-government under majority rule a basic principle of American political life.

The Pilgrims chose for their permanent settlement a site already cleared by the Indians across Cape Cod Bay. Like the Virginians to the south, the newcomers had to struggle before achieving a measure of self-sufficiency.

Massachusetts Bay Colony is settled by Puritans. The succession to the English throne in 1625 of Charles I alarmed the main body of Puritans from which the Pilgrims had separated. The new king seemed determined to crush Puritan ideas. With Plymouth as an example, America loomed as a haven for thousands of English subjects unwilling to abandon their religious principles.

In 1629 the Massachusetts Bay Company was granted a royal charter. The next year, a devout Puritan lawyer, John Winthrop, led what became the first large-scale migration in American history. Within a decade, more than 300 vessels had carried 20,000 passengers to Boston and other Massachusetts villages.

Other colonies are started in New England. Various opponents of Puritan rule in Massachusetts were denied political and religious freedom, and sought haven outside the Bay Colony. Roger Williams was expelled from Massachusetts and founded Providence as a refuge for religious dissenters. Providence was the first settlement to allow full religious freedom — which became a basic principle of American life. Another dissident, Anne Hutchinson, founded Portsmouth. Eventually, these settlements were joined with others to form the colony of Rhode Island.

Economic factors also lured settlers out of Massachusetts. The fertile Connecticut River valley attracted farmers to settlements at Hartford, Windsor, and Wethersfield. Later, these towns joined with others to form the colony of Connecticut. In 1639 the settlers drew up the Fundamental Orders of Connecticut, the first written constitution creating a government on the North American continent.

Colonists from Massachusetts settled land to the north as well. New Hampshire was chartered in 1679 as a separate colony. Settlements along the Maine coast joined with the Pilgrim colony at Plymouth to become part of Massachusetts in 1691.

Lord Baltimore starts Maryland. The founding of Maryland resulted from the efforts of Sir George Calvert, a Roman Catholic who was later given the title Lord Baltimore. Seeking a great estate for himself and a haven for Catholics, Calvert died before he could obtain a charter from his friend, King Charles I. Calvert's son, the second Lord Baltimore, received from the king a huge domain in North America. He named the colony Maryland, in honor of Queen Henrietta Maria. Maryland was first settled in 1634 and from the beginning had more Protestants than Catholics. Conflicts led in 1649 to the passage of the Maryland Toleration Act, granting religious freedom to all Christians.

Colonies are founded in the South. In 1663, Charles II granted the region between Spanish Florida and Virginia to eight friends as a proprietorship. In his honor, the huge territory was named Carolina. By the time the proprietors arrived, discontented Virginians had for years been living in what is now North Carolina. This portion of the territory consisted of small farms on which tobacco was raised. Its forests were a source of lumber, tar, and other naval stores. Farther south, where the climate was hot and humid, large rice plantations were developed. Conflicts split the two colonies apart in 1712. In 1729, North and South Carolina became separate royal colonies.

The region south of the Carolinas became the colony of Georgia. It was established in 1733 by the reformer James Oglethorpe. Oglethorpe wished to give the persecuted and downtrodden people of England a chance for a better life. He received a charter for this purpose from King George II, in whose honor the colony was named. Private investments were obtained to finance colonization, but Parliament also contributed funds to advance the colony's lofty goal — the first time the English government had contributed money to help establish a colony.

New Netherland becomes New York. Inevitably, other European nations were also lured to North America in the race for empire. In 1609, Henry Hudson, an Englishman sailing for the Dutch, explored the river now bearing his name. Soon, Dutch ships were navigating the Hudson and Delaware rivers to trade with the Indians for furs. Trading posts were established at the southern tip of Manhattan Island, at Fort Orange near present-day Albany, and at Fort Nassau across the Delaware River from the site of present-day Philadelphia. In 1625 a fort and a few houses were built on Manhattan Island. The tiny settlement became New Amsterdam, later the capital of New Netherland (as the Dutch colony was called).

New Amsterdam's merchants grew wealthy through trade, but the colony was not well governed. Though the town attracted settlers of many different faiths and nationalities, the intolerance of its leaders, notably Governor Peter Stuyvesant, caused frequent disputes. No resistance was offered when, in 1664, the English took over the colony. It was renamed New York in honor of its new proprietor, the Duke of York, brother of King Charles II.

New Jersey is founded. The surrender of New Netherland also gave the Duke of York proprietorship over the region that became known as New Jersey. Among his new subjects were some 400 Swedes whose main settlement at Fort Christina (now Wilmington, Delaware) had been captured by the Dutch.

In 1664 the Duke of York granted New Jersey to Lord Berkeley and Sir George Carteret. To encourage settlement, they promised freedom of religion and representative government. Into New Jersey came New England Puritans, immigrants from Scotland and northern Ireland, and others.

William Penn starts a colony in Pennsylvania. One of the greatest colonizers was William Penn. As a young man, Penn joined a religious group called the Quakers. Charles II had no use for Quakers, but he owed the

Penn family a large sum of money. When Penn's father died, the king paid the debt to the son with a huge grant of land in America. It was named Pennsylvania ("Penn's woods"). Shortly, Delaware was added to it.

Penn planned his colony as a "Holy Experiment" in which people would live in freedom under the rule of law. He carefully laid out Philadelphia, the "city of brotherly love," as the chief town of his colony. Penn dealt with the Indians on a basis of mutual respect, proclaimed religious freedom for all Christians, and encouraged representative government.

Colonists develop distinctive ways of life. By 1760, England's American colonies had more than two million people. Most people were prosperous by European standards, and many worked their own land. In the towns, artisans and unskilled workers earned high pay because of the shortage of labor. Apprentices, indentured servants, and slaves were widely used in the fields and workshops, but the labor shortage was always serious.

Educational opportunities were limited throughout English America. The New England Colonies, however, generally provided enough public education to teach the "basics" of that time and to encourage a knowledge of the Scriptures. In the Middle Colonies education was left almost entirely to religious groups, while in the South schooling was usually the responsibility of individual families. In every colony the children of the rich were privately tutored, and college attendance was limited to the sons of wealthy families. Few educational facilities existed for girls and young women. The education of slaves was generally ignored.

Trade regulations favor England. The colonial economy was dependent on exports. Fish, whale oil, forest products, iron, and furs were shipped from the New England Colonies. Farmers in the Middle and Southern Colonies exported tobacco, grain, beef, pork, and other products.

Parliament, convinced that colonies should above all serve the interests of England, began in the mid-1600's to pass Navigation Acts. These laws required that colonial exports be shipped first to England before their sale on the European continent. In similar fashion, European goods destined for the colonies had to be shipped through England. These acts were unpopular because the colonists resented being told how to conduct their business.

The French and English clash for empire. Rivalry between Great Britain and France in Europe inevitably affected their American colonies. Beginning in 1689, Great Britain and France fought a series of wars that sought to end for all time the competition for empire. The outcome of the wars fought in America — King William's War (1689–1697), Queen Anne's War (1702–1713), and King George's War (1744–1748) — brought neither side complete victory.

In 1749 a group of Virginians formed the Ohio Company to promote settlement of the Ohio River valley. To halt the westward flow of English settlers, the French then constructed a series of forts from Lake Erie to the Ohio River. Conflict was inevitable.

The French and Indian War began in 1754. In that year Virginia militiamen, led by young George Washington, were defeated by the French at Fort Necessity in southwestern Pennsylvania. For a number of years the war raged on, with one British fort after another falling to the French. Then in 1758 the British sent two outstanding military commanders — Jeffrey Amherst and James Wolfe — to America. The tide of the war now began to turn. French forts in western Pennsylvania, as well as French strongholds along the St. Lawrence River, fell to the British. When Quebec, the capital of New France, was captured in 1759 and Montreal surrendered the following year, the war was over.

In the Treaty of Paris of 1763, France turned over to Britain all of Canada, except for two tiny fishing islands off the coast of Newfoundland, as well as all the French holdings east of the Mississippi River. New Orleans and the vast Louisiana territory went to France's ally, Spain, while the British acquired Spanish Florida.

THE AMERICAN REVOLUTION

Relations between Britain and the colonies grow tense. With the French threat removed, the colonies and the British government were more and more at odds. British leaders no longer felt that they had to give in to the colonial legislatures. This clash of wills had already come to a test in 1760 when Parliament vetoed a Virginia law regulating the payment of clergymen. Patrick Henry boldly attacked the action as a violation of the colony's sacred right of self-government. In Massachusetts that same year, James Otis protested the use of writs of assistance, or general search warrants, as a violation of the people's liberty.

Great Britain tightens its control. As soon as the French and Indian War was over, Parliament decided to end violations of its Navigation Acts and to enforce trade restrictions on colonial trade. The British also sought to halt the fighting between colonists and Indians on the western frontier by issuing a proclamation that prohibited settlement beyond the Appalachian Mountains. Americans regarded these actions as designs to suppress their own freedom.

New taxes are imposed. To raise revenue in the colonies, the British passed the Stamp Act of 1765. This law required that tax stamps be purchased and placed on newspapers, pamphlets, legal documents, playing cards, and dice. The stamp tax was an internal tax rather than a customs duty; internal taxes before this time had been enacted only by the colonial legislatures.

Immediately the cry went up that the Stamp Act was an example of "taxation without representation." Colonists organized groups such as the Sons of Liberty to protest the measure. A colonial boycott on imported goods distressed British merchants so much that Parliament withdrew the Stamp Act.

In its place, Parliament in 1767 passed the Townshend Acts. These measures imposed taxes on glass, paper, lead, tea, and paints. The new taxes were external taxes that British leaders thought the colonists would accept. Moreover, these taxes would be used to pay for the administration and defense of the colonies. The colonists, however, protested the new taxes as vigorously as they did the stamp tax. Once again a boycott was organized, forcing Parliament to repeal all of the Townshend Acts except the tax on tea.

Violence breaks out in Boston. Boston was the center of opposition to British regulations. After British customs officials had been run out of town, the troops already stationed in Boston were reinforced. The presence of the soldiers irritated the Patriots, who regarded them as an army of occupation. In March, 1770, a large crowd began taunting British soldiers at the customhouse. In the fighting that developed, five colonists were killed. This incident, known as the Boston Massacre, further aroused anti-British feelings. Committees of Correspondence were formed throughout the colonies to coordinate protests against British policies.

Tea now became the focus of discontent. In May, 1773, Parliament gave the British East India Company a monopoly on the tea trade with America. Even with the Townshend tax still in effect, the tea would sell in the colonies at a lower price than smuggled tea. The colonists objected to the monopoly, however, since they understood that their purchases of the cheap tea would automatically confirm Britain's right to impose a tax on them. In Boston, a band of Patriots dressed as Indians boarded three tea ships and dumped the cargoes of tea into the harbor. Parliament's response to the Boston Tea Party was to pass a series of harsh laws known as the Intolerable Acts.

The Revolutionary War begins. Boston's plight drew the colonists even closer together. Patriots in Virginia called for the holding of a Continental Congress. Every colony except Georgia was represented when the delegates met in Philadelphia on

September 5, 1774. The First Continental Congress, declaring that Parliament had no right to enact laws for the colonists without their consent, appealed to the king and the British people for reason. When it became clear that neither Parliament nor the king was willing to make concessions, the colonists started arming themselves. Fighting between colonial minutemen and British regulars began in Lexington and Concord, near Boston, on April 19, 1775. Then, in preparation for an attack on Boston, the colonists began to fortify Breed's Hill in nearby Charlestown. The British, after suffering heavy losses, dispersed the Patriots in June, 1775, in the Battle of Bunker Hill.

Meanwhile, the Second Continental Congress assembled at Philadelphia. The Congress decided to form a Continental Army to oust the British from Boston and chose George Washington to lead it. For almost a year, Washington's forces surrounded Boston. Finally, in March, 1776, the British evacuated the city and sailed to Nova Scotia. Washington then moved to New York, where he expected a major British invasion.

The Declaration of Independence is written. Sentiment in favor of American independence was growing, meanwhile, in the Continental Congress. On June 7, 1776, Richard Henry Lee of Virginia introduced three resolutions in the Congress. The first called for independence, the second for foreign alliances, and the third for a confederation uniting the colonies. A committee was formed to prepare a declaration of independence, and Thomas Jefferson was named to write it. The Congress adopted Lee's first resolution on July 2, officially ending all ties with Great Britain. Two days later, it approved the Declaration of Independence.

The Declaration of Independence was a stirring proclamation of human liberty. "All men," Jefferson wrote, "are created equal." Among their "unalienable Rights" are "Life, Liberty, and the pursuit of Happiness." Free people, Jefferson continued, also possess the right to change or overthrow any government that denies them their liberties. The document then listed the grievances that had led the colonists to separate from Great Britain.

Americans fight for freedom. Declaring independence proved easier than winning it. The thirteen colonies faced Europe's greatest military power. Americans had to raise and organize a fighting force and find capable officers. They needed supplies and foreign aid. Their conviction that they were fighting for their freedom had to be transformed into a determination to push on until victory was achieved.

Washington's prediction that the British, after evacuating Boston, would attempt to take New York proved correct. Forces led by General William Howe captured New York City in 1776 after defeating Washington in the Battle of Brooklyn Heights. Later, following a retreat across New Jersey, Washington defeated the British and their Hessian mercenaries at Trenton and Princeton.

The main British strategy in the Revolutionary War was to divide the colonies by sealing off New England. For this purpose, Britain's General John Burgoyne led an army south from Canada to join a detachment of Howe's army that was to march up the Hudson River from New York City. A third force, commanded by Colonel Barry St. Leger, would proceed east from Lake Ontario. This complicated operation proved unsuccessful from the start. St. Leger's forces met stiff opposition and retreated to Fort Oswego. Howe's troops were diverted to Philadelphia, leaving Burgoyne alone to face American forces under General Horatio Gates. After several weeks of fighting, Burgoyne surrendered his entire army at Saratoga in October, 1777.

The American victory at Saratoga was a turning point of the war. Following news of the British defeat, France decided to ally itself openly with the Americans. Burgoyne's surrender, moreover, gave Americans a needed taste of victory and the determination to fight on.

American independence is won. Having failed to defeat the Patriots in the North, the British targeted their attack on the South. They took Savannah and Charleston and defeated the Americans at Camden, South Carolina. Then they moved north to Yorktown, Virginia, only to discover that a French fleet had moved north from the Caribbean to Chesapeake Bay. American and French troops stationed in the North moved quickly to Yorktown. They prevented a British force under the command of Lord Cornwallis from escaping by land, while French ships blocked an evacuation by sea. Cornwallis's surrender to Washington on October 19, 1781, convinced the British that further fighting was useless.

In the Treaty of Paris of 1783, Great Britain recognized American independence. The boundaries of the United States were set at Canada on the north, the Mississippi River to the west, and Florida on the south. Free at last from the tyranny of kings, the United States was the first modern nation to be founded on the principle that government exists to serve the governed.

THE ARTICLES OF CONFEDERATION

The states enact reforms. The end of British rule and the spread of republican sentiment encouraged the former colonists to make changes in their laws and governments. Determined to preserve individual liberty, the states included bills of rights in their new constitutions. They also increased the authority of their legislatures at the expense of the governors.

Reforms governing the ownership of property were made. Slavery also came under attack. By 1786, all the states except Georgia had banned the importation of slaves. Most northern states took steps to abolish slavery, while many southern slaveholders freed individual slaves. Everywhere there was a growing awareness that slaveholding violated the ideals expressed in the Declaration of Independence.

A confederation of states is established. The colonial experience had made Americans fearful of strong central government. They saw local self-government as a safeguard against tyranny and looked with suspicion on proposals for a strong central government.

When Richard Henry Lee proposed independence in 1776, he also called for "a plan of Confederation" to give the United States a permanent government. A committee soon presented a charter of government called the "Articles of Confederation." Adopted by the Congress in 1777, it was finally ratified by all the states in 1781. Until 1789, the Articles of Confederation provided a central government for the thirteen states.

The government under the Articles of Confederation had little power. The states regarded themselves as separate political entities, able to manage their own affairs. As a result, they strictly limited the powers of the Congress to wage war, conduct foreign affairs, and make treaties. Though the Congress could grant loans, it could not levy taxes and had to rely on the states for money. The Congress could not regulate trade or control the issuing of paper money by the states. It could not resolve disputes among the states. Since the new government was a "league of friendship" among sovereign states, each state — regardless of its population — had a single vote in the Congress. There was no executive power to enforce obedience to national laws and no judges to decide their meaning.

Despite its weaknesses, the Confederation achieved important results. It concluded the Revolutionary War and negotiated the Treaty of Paris. It also made plans for the sale of western land and the organization of new states.

In the original debate over the Articles, an agreement was reached providing that states with western land claims cede them to the national government. In 1785, the Congress passed a law that set up a plan by which the land north of the Ohio River, called the Northwest Territory, was to be surveyed, subdivided, and sold. In the Northwest Ordinance of 1787, Congress provided for the political organization of the territory. Slavery would be banned from it, and its inhabitants would enjoy full religious freedom and other rights. The territory would eventually be divided into five new states, each with the same rights as the original thirteen.

The weaknesses of the Confederation government are revealed. Throughout its existence, the Confederation government was plagued by foreign problems. Britain closed ports in Canada and the West Indies to American shipping and refused to evacuate forts on American soil. Spain blocked American use of its port facilities at New Orleans. In the Mediterranean, Barbary pirates were stopping American ships, seizing the crews, and demanding payment of tribute. In each case, the United States lacked the power to take appropriate action.

To make matters worse, economic conditions were bad. Inflation had sent prices sky-high while wages lagged, causing widespread discontent. The Congress proved unable to stop the states from printing paper money which fed the inflation and which many merchants refused to accept in payment of debts. Prisons were filled with debtors unable to meet their obligations. Disorders broke out, and debt-ridden farmers in western Massachusetts seized a courthouse. This protest, called Shays's Rebellion, was quickly crushed by the state militia but nevertheless caused great alarm throughout the country.

THE CONSTITUTION

A stronger national government is sought. Concerned over a dispute regarding navigation on the Potomac River, George Washington in 1785 invited representatives from Virginia and Maryland to meet at his home, Mount Vernon, to talk over their differences. At this conference, the representatives agreed to invite other states to join them at a meeting the following year to resolve various commercial problems. In the end, all the states were invited to send delegates to the gathering which assembled at Annapolis, Maryland, in September, 1786. The sponsors were disappointed that only five states participated. Their conclusion was important anyway. They agreed that the Articles of Confederation needed revision and strengthening. Alexander Hamil-

ton, a brilliant young lawyer from New York, wrote the report issued by the convention. It was approved by the Congress and sent to all the states with a proposal that a convention be held in order to amend the Articles.

The Philadelphia Convention meets. In May, 1787, a group of distinguished Americans assembled at Independence Hall in Philadelphia. According to James Madison of Virginia, a leading figure at both the Mount Vernon and Annapolis meetings, the purpose of the convention was "to decide forever the fate of republican government." The delegates chose George Washington as their presiding officer. Meetings were held in secret to discourage outside pressure and to permit open debate.

Several broad principles of government met with wide acceptance from the beginning of the Convention. Almost all the delegates wanted a national government with limited powers but with enough strength to gain obedience at home and respect abroad. These powers, the delegates believed, should be stated clearly and should define the authority of the central government. Powers not specifically delegated to the central government should remain with the states. To insure liberty under the law, the delegates supported the principle of checks and balances. This principle involved the separation of governmental powers and their assignment to the legislative, executive, or judicial branches. Each of these branches would have sufficient authority to carry out its functions while checking the other two branches.

Compromises are made. Much time was devoted at the Convention to reconciling opposing points of view. A major difficulty confronting the delegates was the question of representation in the national legislature. Large states favored the Virginia Plan, which would base representation on population. Small states favored the New Jersey Plan, which would give all states equal representation (as under the Articles of Confederation). A proposal for a two-house Congress offered by Roger Sherman of Connecticut broke the deadlock. This plan called for a Senate in which the states would have equal representation and a House in which representation would be based on population. Sherman's recommendation was so crucial to the success of the convention that it became known as the Great Compromise.

Before finishing their work, the participants at Philadelphia made some far-reaching decisions. Although they had assembled to propose amendments to the Articles of Confederation, the delegates decided to disregard their instructions and prepare a new framework of government. The Constitution, moreover, would derive its power not from the states but from the people. The result would be a federal system in which the people ruled through both the state and national governments. Accordingly, the delegates directed the states to elect special conventions to consider ratification of the Constitution. They agreed that the Constitution would be put into effect whenever nine states had ratified the plan.

The Constitution is ratified. The framers of the Constitution were not at all sure that their work would be approved. When the document was made public, it was bitterly attacked in some places. Its opponents, called Antifederalists, charged that the proposed national government was too strong and that too much power had been taken from the states. The Antifederalists, furthermore, deplored the absence of a bill of rights. They argued that the increased power of the national government made the protection of individual rights even more essential than ever.

The Federalists, supporters of the Constitution, pointed out that the nation's most admired leaders — among them Washington and Franklin — favored the new government. In a series of essays called *The Federalist*, James Madison, Alexander Hamilton, and John Jay wrote persuasive arguments defending the Constitution.

In December, 1787, Delaware became the first state to ratify the Constitution. New Jersey, Georgia, and Connecticut quickly followed. The important state of New York delayed ratification because of the Antifederalist sentiments of such leaders as Governor George Clinton, but it finally voted approval. In June, 1788, New Hampshire became the ninth state to ratify the Constitution, putting the new government into effect.

Since several states had urged the addition of a bill of rights when they ratified the Constitution, the first Congress moved quickly to propose appropriate amendments. In 1791, the first ten amendments, called the Bill of Rights, won state approval and became part of the Constitution. They provided for basic freedoms — speech, press, religion, assembly, and petition. The Tenth Amendment made it clear that powers not given to the national government were reserved to the states or to the people.

Early in 1789 the first national elections took place in the United States. Citizens voted for members of the House of Representatives while the state legislatures chose senators and presidential electors. On April 6, the electoral votes were counted and, as expected, George Washington was elected President. On the last day of April, at Federal Hall in New York City, George Washington took the oath of office. A new era had begun.

THE FIRST PRESIDENTS

Washington takes command. Universally respected, Washington assumed national leadership at a time of general prosperity. This created good will for the new government, helping Washington to form his administration with popular approval. His closest advisers were the heads of the executive departments, which were created by Congress. Nominated by the President with Senate approval, these advisers eventually became known as the Cabinet.

Congress soon created the Supreme Court, consisting, at that time, of a Chief Justice and five Associate Justices. Washington named John Jay of New York as the first Chief Justice. Two additional Northerners and three Southerners were appointed to the Court — all of them staunch defenders of the Constitution.

Different views give rise to political parties.

By 1792 two major political parties had arisen in the United States — the Federalist Party and the Democratic-Republican Party (often called at that time the Republican Party). Their origin lay in the different political philosophies that evolved in the face of major problems. Their leaders were Washington's principal advisers, Alexander Hamilton and Thomas Jefferson.

Jefferson and Hamilton disagreed about the nation's future and the role that government should play in the lives of the people. Jefferson regarded farmers who worked their own land as the most dependable of citizens. A nation of independent farmers, he believed, would make for general happiness. He maintained that cities are a hindrance to a good society and, above all, that America should not try to develop industry. Jefferson argued that "that government is best which governs least."

Hamilton, on the other hand, wished to encourage manufacturing and the growth of cities. America, he believed, would prosper through industry and trade. Hamilton was convinced that a strong central government would insure national growth. Merchants, manufacturers, and bankers rallied around Hamilton.

Hamilton strengthens the nation's finances.

As Secretary of the Treasury, Hamilton had an opportunity to put his ideas into effect. His first goal was to establish the credit of the United States. Hamilton proposed that the government assume the wartime foreign and domestic debts of the Continental Congress and of the states. Some southern states objected to the assumption of state debts because they had already paid their own obligations. To gain their support for his plan, a deal was finally struck. It was agreed that the permanent national capital be built on the Potomac River, on a site to be selected by President Washington. To win the votes of Pennsylvania's representatives, it was agreed to move the capital from New York City to Philadelphia temporarily.

Hamilton's other proposals were also far-reaching. He persuaded Congress, for instance, to pass a tariff act that encouraged domestic manufacturing while raising revenue. Since additional revenue was needed, Hamilton called for an excise tax on whiskey.

Western farmers protested this tax because they made whiskey from surplus grain, and in 1794 serious disturbances broke out in western Pennsylvania. Washington mobilized a large force of militiamen to put down the so-called Whiskey Rebellion. By threatening to use force, if necessary, the new government showed that it was strong enough to enforce its laws, thus adding to its prestige.

Hamilton recommends a national bank.

Hamilton's proposal that Congress charter a national bank provoked a major conflict with Jefferson and the Republicans. Hamilton argued that such a bank was needed to safeguard the government's funds, to make loans to the government, and to issue notes that would provide a sound national currency.

Hamilton used a broad, or loose, interpretation of the Constitution in arguing that Congress had the power to charter the bank. Jefferson disagreed, calling for a narrow, or strict, interpretation of the Constitution. The government, he insisted, should not assume powers not expressly granted to it. According to Jefferson, Congress would be violating the Constitution by chartering a bank.

Washington gave his support in this matter to Hamilton, recognizing the need for a national bank. In 1791, Congress chartered a national bank which did much to stabilize the nation's money system and to facilitate the payment of the national debt.

Foreign affairs trouble the Washington administration.

In the months before assuming his duties, Secretary of State Jefferson had witnessed the opening events in the French Revolution. Like many others who remembered French support during America's Revolution, he felt sympathy for those who were seeking to end tyrannical government in France.

As the French Revolution grew more extreme and led to war between France and Great Britain, many Americans had a change of heart. They feared that mob rule in France would inspire similar behavior in America. They wished, moreover, to safeguard America's substantial trade with Great Britain. Washington decided that any involvement in European affairs might jeopardize America's hard-won freedom and ruin its recovery and growth. In 1793 he issued a Proclamation of Neutrality, pledging American impartiality in the war between France and Britain.

Agreements are reached with Great Britain and Spain. Meanwhile, America's postwar differences with the British remained unresolved. The northern border was in dispute, and British posts on American territory still had not been evacuated. The British, moreover, had cultivated the friendship of the Indians in an effort to halt America's westward expansion and to monopolize the fur trade.

Tensions between the United States and Great Britain increased in 1793 when Americans tried to protect neutral rights on the sea while warfare was going on in Europe. American ships were seized by the Royal Navy, and their crews were forced to serve aboard British naval vessels.

In 1794, Washington sent John Jay to London to reach a settlement with Great Britain. He persuaded the British to give up their posts on American territory. America, moreover, gained some trading privileges with the British Empire. Other issues, such as the Maine boundary, the pre-Revolutionary War debts, payments for recent losses on the high seas, and impressment, were left to joint arbitration commissions.

Americans fared well in a treaty with Spain concluded in 1795 by Thomas Pinckney. Pinckney's Treaty gave Americans unlimited use of the Mississippi River and the right to transfer goods to ocean-going vessels at the port of New Orleans.

Washington leaves office. Before Washington left the office of President at the end of his second term in 1797, he had a few words of advice to give the young nation. In his "Farewell Address," Washington urged his fellow citizens "to steer clear of permanent alliances" with other nations. He also warned against the dangers of political parties and the abuse of power by public officials.

President Adams maintains peace. Soon after taking office as America's second President, John Adams faced serious problems with France. Angered over American neutrality and Jay's Treaty, the French government refused to receive the new American minister. Instead, American diplomats were asked for a bribe by men sent by the French foreign minister. The Americans refused and returned home.

When news of the XYZ Affair was made known in America, a cry went up for war with France. Realizing that the United States was still too weak to engage in a war, Adams resisted. In 1798 the French began attacking American ships, and American frigates and privateers reciprocated. Not until 1800 did the two governments settle their differences.

The Federalists pass a "gag" law. Meanwhile, to silence critics of the administration and to stop immigrants from joining the Republican Party, the Federalist Congress passed a series of laws known as the Alien and Sedition Acts. The Alien Act authorized the President to deport foreigners he regarded as dangerous. The Sedition Act, which made it a crime to speak out against the President, was intended to end criticism of Adams's policies by Republican newspaper editors. Jefferson and the Republicans countered the Alien and Sedition Acts by drawing up the Virginia and Kentucky Resolutions. They declared that the states should have the right to decide if laws are constitutional. The ideas expressed in the Virginia and Kentucky Resolutions became the basis of the states' rights argument.

Jefferson becomes President. In the election of 1800, Thomas Jefferson won the presidency while Aaron Burr was elected Vice President. The nation had earlier accepted without incident the installation of a new President upon Washington's retirement. Jefferson's election meant still another new President, but it also meant a change of party and a change of viewpoint.

A NATION OF SECTIONS

1801 – 1860

*I know no South, no East, no West, to which I owe any allegiance.
The Union, sir, is my country.*

HENRY CLAY, SENATE SPEECH, 1848

The Age of the Jeffersonians

1801 – 1815

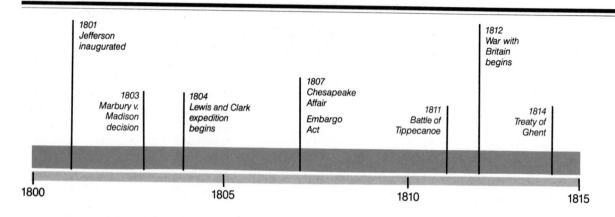

1800   1805   1810   1815

1801
Jefferson inaugurated

1803
Marbury v. Madison decision

1804
Lewis and Clark expedition begins

1807
Chesapeake Affair

Embargo Act

1811
Battle of Tippecanoe

1812
War with Britain begins

1814
Treaty of Ghent

CHAPTER OUTLINE

1. The Republicans come to power.

2. The United States gains a vast territory west of the Mississippi.

3. Jefferson seeks to defend America's neutral rights.

4. Britain and America fight again.

On March 4, 1801, Thomas Jefferson was sworn in as our nation's third President. After taking the oath of office, Jefferson began to read his address. The audience may have missed some of what he was saying because he was a poor public speaker. His words, however, proved imperishable.

On the previous day Jefferson had given a copy of the speech to a Washington newspaper editor. Before the swearing-in ceremony was over, boys were selling newspapers that contained the full text of the speech. This news leak, unusual for the time, enabled people to read Jefferson's words almost immediately.

Jefferson began by saying, "We are all Republicans, we are all Federalists." By this he meant that both parties agreed on the basic principles of the government, even though they often disagreed on how to implement them. Calling the United States government the "world's best hope," Jefferson offered his view on what the young republic yet required: "Kindly separated by nature and a wide ocean from the exterminating havoc of one quarter of the globe . . . possessing a chosen country, with room enough for our descendants to the thousandth and thousandth generation . . . with all these blessings, what more is necessary to make us a happy and prosperous people?" The answer was simple: A wise government that leaves people "free to regulate their own pursuits of industry and improvement, and shall not take from the mouth of labor the bread it has earned."

1 The Republicans Come to Power

Despite the soaring phrases of Jefferson's speech, the republic, though well begun, required further crafting. Nothing symbolized its condition better than the recently built home of the President in the new capital at Washington, D.C. When Jefferson moved in, the slate roof still leaked a little. Most of the furnishings were odds and ends that Washington and Adams had used in Philadelphia. Jefferson set about completing work both on the government and on the presidential mansion. He was to learn what all Chief Executives have learned: that neither task is ever wholly done.

Jefferson reassures the Federalists. Having been fearful that a Republican victory would mean the end of the new republic, the Federalists were reassured by Jefferson's inaugural address that revolutionary changes were not planned. Most Americans, moreover, were satisfied that Jefferson's Cabinet was first-rate.

For Secretary of State, Jefferson chose James Madison. Madison was a close friend of the President, although some years younger. Twice a year Madison and his wife Dolley paid long visits to Jefferson at Monticello. A woman who saw the men in close conversation declared, "I do believe father never loved son more than Mr. Jefferson loves Mr. Madison." Their work together has been called "the great collaboration."

The Secretary of the Treasury was Albert Gallatin. Born in Switzerland, he came to America when he was nineteen years old. Only recently naturalized, he spoke English with a Swiss-French accent. As a member of Congress from western Pennsylvania, he quickly rose to a position of leadership in the House. He became Jefferson's most trusted adviser on matters of finance.

Jefferson appointed two Massachusetts men to the Cabinet, hoping to win support in New England where the Federalists were strong. Determined, however, to avoid the political bickering he had experienced in Washington's administration, he refused to name a Federalist to the official family. In fact, in appointing people to federal jobs he almost always chose Republicans. He was resolved to introduce Republican policies. His opponents charged that despite the theme of unity in his inaugural, he was out to punish his opponents. Actually, Jefferson tried to walk a narrow path between gain-

Throughout his years of public service, Thomas Jefferson welcomed the opportunity to return to Monticello, the home he designed and built in Virginia.

Jefferson preferred informality over the more aristocratic manners of the Federalists.

at the White House. They were denying themselves the company of one of the most talented individuals who has ever occupied the presidency. In addition to his brilliant gifts as a writer and political philosopher, Jefferson was also an architect, inventor, surveyor, mathematician, and student of languages.

A widower, Jefferson frequently called upon Dolley Madison to be his hostess when entertaining guests. Her devotion to Jefferson was complete. Jefferson might have enlisted the help of his daughters, Patsy and Polly, but they were at home in Virginia with their young families. Their husbands, both members of the House of Representatives, lived at the White House when Congress was in session. They shared the generous table that Jefferson spread, for he loved good food. He introduced macaroni and ice cream to America, serving both at the executive mansion.

Jefferson challenges Federalist control of the courts. One of Jefferson's first steps in office was to obtain repeal of the Judiciary Act of 1801. That act, passed shortly before John Adams left office, had established a number of new positions for judges. Adams had promptly appointed Federalists to be the judges. Because he filled these positions just as he was stepping down, the nominees became known as "midnight judges."

The Republicans angrily charged that, having failed to keep control of the presidency and Congress, the Federalists were trying to put a stranglehold on the court system. Control of the courts was very important because judicial decisions affected land claims, disputes over bankruptcy, and other questions concerning property rights. Since many Federalists were large property-holders, Republicans feared that Federalist judges would be unfriendly on issues dear to the Jefferson administration.

Jefferson rightly believed that the midnight appointees could cripple his programs for the country. He quickly took action. The appointments had been confirmed by the Senate and signed by the President before Adams's term ended. Nevertheless, the commissions (the documents that made the

ing the support of Federalists and keeping the good will of his own backers.

Jefferson introduces an informal style to the presidency. One of Jefferson's most important contributions to the country was in matters of style and outlook. Jefferson was the first Chief Executive to shake hands. (Washington and Adams had merely bowed when meeting someone.) Informality was his trademark. People in the nation's capital were delighted, as well as amazed, for instance, when they saw the President taking a nephew shopping to buy school clothes.

In line with his desire for republican simplicity, Jefferson would not permit presidential birthday celebrations — or even tell friends the date of his birthday. In greeting visitors at the White House, he took no account of differences in rank. He regarded all persons as "perfectly equal, whether foreign or domestic, titled or untitled, in or out of office."

Many Federalists were offended by the President's manners. Some political opponents even declined his invitations to dine

appointments official) had not yet been delivered. Madison, whose responsibility as Secretary of State was to deliver the commissions, withheld a number of them, thus preventing the men claiming them from taking office.

One of the "midnight judges" was William Marbury, who had been appointed justice of the peace in the District of Columbia. Along with three other disappointed nominees, Marbury went to the Supreme Court and asked for a *writ of mandamus*[1] ordering Madison to hand over the commissions. They based their case on the Judiciary Act of 1789, which had authorized the Supreme Court to issue writs to the executive branch of government.

John Marshall establishes judicial review. In this way began the court case of *Marbury v. Madison.* The remarkable decision that emerged from it had the effect of making the judiciary more powerful than either Adams or Jefferson would have guessed possible. The ruling by the court was shaped by John Marshall, who had been appointed Chief Justice by John Adams in 1801. Though a distant cousin of Jefferson's, Marshall was a staunch Federalist.

Marshall was in a difficult position. He knew that if he issued the writ that Marbury sought, Madison would ignore it. Yet if the Court failed to issue it, the Republicans would claim victory. Marshall found a way out. He declared that Marbury and the others were indeed entitled to the writ they sought. The Chief Justice said, however, that the Court did not have the power to issue it. The reason, he said, was that the section of the Judiciary Act of 1789 authorizing writs conflicted with the Constitution and was, therefore, not valid.

This decision was the first in which the Supreme Court declared a law passed by Congress unconstitutional. The power to declare acts of Congress and of state legislatures unconstitutional is called *judicial review.* More than half a century would pass before the Court exercised this power again.

---

[1]A *writ of mandamus* is a court order compelling a public officer to perform a particular duty.

Nevertheless, the establishment of judicial review was a landmark in American history. It made the Supreme Court the capstone of the system of checks and balances. It also made the power of the judiciary as strong in legislative matters as that of Congress or the President.

Jefferson never accepted the principle of judicial review. Like other Republicans he denounced the boldness of the Supreme Court. Still, in a narrow sense, Jefferson had won the case. He did not have to seat the "midnight judges." A new Judiciary Act in 1802, more acceptable to the Republicans, provided for only six circuit courts — to which Jefferson named Republican judges.

Some Federalist policies are reversed. Jefferson proceeded with his work. He pardoned those who had been imprisoned under the Alien and Sedition Acts (page 190), including many who were his friends. He also obtained repeal of the Naturalization Act, which had been aimed at Republicans.

Jefferson was not merely following a strictly partisan course. The policies he pursued in all matters of government reflected his deepest convictions. He was firmly committed, for example, to reducing the cost of government. Not only were taxes lowered, but the national debt went from $83 million in 1801 to $57 million in 1809. Unlike Hamilton and the Federalists, Jefferson did not believe that "a public debt is a public blessing." He considered public indebtedness an obligation to be reduced by regular payments, in much the same way that a farmer pays off a mortgage.

Some of the budget cutting was done at the expense of the navy. The Republicans believed an ocean-going navy was a waste of money. Besides, a large military and naval establishment, they said, would be oppressive and tyrannical.

In order to protect coastal shipping, the President naively authorized the building of small gunboats that could be hauled ashore when not in use at sea. The scheme proved unsuccessful. After one of the vessels was washed aground during a heavy storm, a critic of Jefferson jeered, "If our gunboats are of no use upon the water, may they at least be useful upon the land."

Jefferson defends American rights in the Mediterranean. Events taught Jefferson to value armed strength. Early in his administration he had to fight an expensive war far from American shores. The enemy were the Barbary pirates, who preyed on American merchant vessels in the Mediterranean Sea (page 157). For many years the Muslim states of Morocco, Algiers, Tunis, and Tripoli had been seizing ships and crews sailing along the Barbary Coast, as that part of North Africa was called. The crews were imprisoned and held for ransom. Year after year the names of American hostages, including those of youths who had signed on as cabin boys, were read aloud on Sundays in hometown churches. Some countries, including the United States, had avoided attacks by agreeing, from time to time, to pay annual tribute to the Barbary States. This the new President refused to do.

The United States fights the Barbary pirates. Almost as soon as Jefferson took office, he

American tribute to Tripoli ended in 1803 but continued to other Barbary States until 1816.

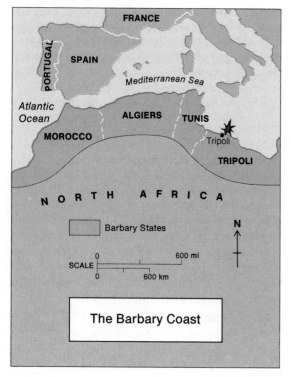

The Barbary Coast

sent ships of the navy to the Mediterranean. They were there in May, 1801, when Tripoli declared war on the United States by cutting down the flagpole in front of the American consulate. From the ensuing Tripolitan War — which went on until 1805 — a national hero emerged. He was Lieutenant Stephen Decatur, a gallant young Marylander. Decatur courageously avenged the humiliation of seeing Tripolitans in charge of the American frigate *Philadelphia*, which had accidentally become stranded in Tripoli's harbor in 1804. Having captured a small Tripolitan vessel, which he renamed the *Intrepid*, Decatur ran it alongside the *Philadelphia*. Taken by surprise, the Tripolitan crew was swept overboard by the attacking Americans, and the *Philadelphia* was set afire. In twenty minutes the daring boarders were gone, unharmed despite fire from shore batteries. Decatur was immediately promoted to captain. Admiral Nelson, the English naval giant of that time, called Decatur's exploit "the most bold and daring act of the age."

Despite this display of fearlessness, the Americans paid $60,000 to ransom the crew of the *Philadelphia*, languishing in Tripoli's prisons. Not until 1816 was the United States able to force Algiers to accept a treaty ending the pirates' raids. How odd it must have seemed to a Virginia planter like Jefferson to be defending American honor in a place as distant as North Africa. From the earliest days, however, American Presidents have had to think beyond domestic politics to the defense of the nation's place in the world.

SECTION REVIEW

1. Vocabulary: *judicial review.*
2. (a) How did Jefferson reassure the Federalists once he became President? (b) What Federalist policies were reversed?
3. (a) Why did William Marbury bring suit against James Madison? (b) What was Justice Marshall's decision in the case? (c) What has been the lasting importance of that decision?
4. (a) Why did President Jefferson send ships to fight in the Mediterranean? (b) How was the question of the prisoners from the *Philadelphia* finally resolved?

2 The United States Gains a Vast Territory West of the Mississippi

As President, Jefferson had to modify many of his plans. His scheme to scrap the navy had given way to more realistic thinking. Similarly he decided not to interfere with the Bank of the United States or with the rest of Hamilton's financial program. Moreover, despite Jefferson's hopes, the judiciary remained in the hands of Federalists. The Republicans did try to remove from the Supreme Court, by impeachment, Justice Samuel Chase of Maryland, but Chase was acquitted in a sensational trial in the Senate. In sum, Jefferson would have had little to show for his first four years in office had it not been for a remarkable accomplishment, the purchase of the Louisiana Territory.

France makes plans to restore its American empire. The history of Louisiana was closely tied to the struggle for power in Europe. At the close of the French and Indian War in 1763, France had ceded Louisiana and the port city of New Orleans to its ally, Spain (page 107). When the French Revolution got under way, though, many people in France began to think seriously of rebuilding their American empire. Louisiana would be indispensable in any such plans. Americans, anticipating the success of their new government, also hungrily eyed the western territory. Jedidiah Morse, the father of American geography, wrote in 1789, "We cannot but anticipate the period, as not far distant, when the American empire will comprehend [contain] millions of souls, west of the Mississippi."

As the 1790's drew to a close, events in Europe heightened French interest in Louisiana. Napoleon Bonaparte's powerful armies had already won control of much of continental Europe. His grand goal was to defeat Great Britain by seizing Egypt and then India. The British ended this dream, however, when they decisively defeated his forces on the Nile River in 1798.

Still seeking worlds to conquer, Napoleon made up his mind to recover Louisiana. He hoped to revive the memory of Louis XIV, for whom the region had been named. In addition, if Napoleon succeeded, he would be able to strike at Britain by moving against Canada.

Americans understood that in planning for a new empire, the French considered Louisiana and the Caribbean islands a unit. Louisiana would supply the foodstuffs and timber that the tropical holdings required. Haiti was the chief French possession in the West Indies (map, page 144). It would serve as the naval base from which Louisiana would be defended.

France regains Louisiana. Through delicate maneuvering begun in 1800, Napoleon got Spain to sign a secret treaty giving Louisiana back to France. Spain was in fact keen to be rid of the trans-Mississippi territory because of the high cost of administering it. In return for Louisiana, Napoleon agreed to give a small Italian kingdom to the Spanish king's son-in-law. Suspecting for a long time that Napoleon would not go through with this promise, Charles IV of Spain did not sign the agreement to transfer Louisiana until 1802.

In the two years that elapsed, rumors of the impending swap spread across the United States. Tension rose because Spain had just cut off the right of deposit at New Orleans, as agreed to under the Pinckney Treaty (page 188). If Napoleon were in charge of the region, he might even forbid Americans the use of the Mississippi itself!

Jefferson decides to act. When news of the transfer of Louisiana to France reached Jefferson, the President responded immediately. He declared that from the moment France gained control of New Orleans, "we must marry ourselves to the British fleet and nation."

Jefferson knew that he would have to act before the Federalists made political gains among the Westerners. Already some Westerners were hinting that they would march on New Orleans and seize it. Federalists were encouraging them in such mischief. In order to keep the Westerners quiet — and to allow time for negotiations with France — the President hinted that he

Jefferson considered access to the port of New Orleans essential because it was a transfer point for cargo from Mississippi riverboats to ocean vessels.

might seek an alliance with Britain. The aim was to frighten the French and Spanish diplomats in the United States. The Spanish took the bait and quickly restored the right of deposit, although the administration did not immediately learn of the turn-about.

Jefferson offers to buy Louisiana. Jefferson had already instructed Secretary of State Madison to find out from the United States minister to France, Robert R. Livingston, what price France wanted for New Orleans and West Florida. (Officials in Washington mistakenly believed West Florida had also been transferred to France.) Early in 1803, Jefferson sent James Monroe to Paris to help Livingston. Monroe and Livingston were instructed to buy New Orleans and West Florida for $2 million (though they had the authority to go as high as $10 million). Jefferson told his envoys that on the results of their mission "depend the future destinies of this republic."

Napoleon's American ambitions now began to cool. In spite of what the United States believed, Spain had refused to turn over West Florida to the French. Without it, Louisiana, the anchor of the planned empire, would be at the mercy of Britain and America. More devastating to Napoleon than even the rebuff by Spain was the news from Haiti. The people of that island colony, under their valiant leader Toussaint L'Ouverture (too-SAN loo-ver-TYOOR), had risen against the French. An army of 30,000 troops commanded by General Le Clerc, a brother-in-law of Napoleon, was sent to the island. Heavy fighting and yellow fever wiped out thousands of French soldiers, including Le Clerc.

France sells all of Louisiana. Napoleon, far from that scene of disaster and suffering, sulked in his imperial palace. Disturbed by events in Europe as well as in Haiti, he lost his appetite for an American empire. He decided to sell Louisiana — all of it.

When Livingston learned of Napoleon's decision, the American was stunned with disbelief. His wildest dreams had not included the *whole* of Louisiana. He was joined the next day by Monroe, just arrived in Paris. Together the diplomats accepted the offer, and began to dicker over the price. In making the deal, they vastly exceeded their instructions. They obtained not only the city of New Orleans, but also 900,000 square miles of land (map, page 219). The Americans agreed to pay France about $15 million.

The Louisiana Purchase was a magnificent bargain. While Napoleon returned once more to remaking the map of Europe, Americans could see that they had remade their own map too. Livingston predicted, as he signed the treaty, "From this day the United States take their place among the powers of the first rank."

The Louisiana Purchase is ratified. Most Americans welcomed the news of the Louisiana Purchase and wanted the treaty ratified. Not surprisingly, however, some opposition developed. Federalists called the deal unconstitutional, pointing out that nowhere in the Constitution is the federal government authorized to add land by purchase. They were using the strict construction arguments that Jefferson himself had used to oppose the Bank of the United States in 1791 (page 181). Federalists in the Northeast were especially offended by the Purchase. They envisioned many agricultural states being carved out of the new territory. They could see themselves as a minority in a much larger Union than they had ever anticipated, outvoted in Congress by sugar planters and fur trappers.

Jefferson was troubled by the Federalist arguments. Nevertheless, he justified the Louisiana Purchase under the Constitution's treaty-making and war-powers clauses. He was sure the country had been made stronger by the Purchase and that in time his judgment would prove right. In October, 1803, the Senate ratified the treaty. The President had allowed common sense to overcome his conscience.

The Louisiana Purchase was a dividing line in American history. Before it, America faced out across the Atlantic Ocean and saw English trade as its principal source of prosperity. Now eyes were turned westward, with confidence that America's future greatness lay in that direction. Jefferson's administration, with a mighty assist from Napoleon, had opened the door on a new epoch in American history.

Jefferson seeks information about the Louisiana Territory. Jefferson himself had never traveled more than fifty miles west of Mon-

ticello. The vision of an America extending even beyond Louisiana, however, was already in his mind. In January, 1803, just a week before Monroe's appointment as special envoy to Paris, the President asked Congress for $2,500 to send a small expedition as far as the Pacific coast.

Jefferson chose his private secretary, Meriwether Lewis, a 29-year-old Virginian, to head the expedition. Lewis, in turn, selected as his companion William Clark, a lieutenant in the army and a younger brother of George Rogers Clark. William Clark had red hair, like many of his family. This distinguishing feature made him stand out when he was among the Indians, who came to know him as "Red Head."

Knowing the frontier well, Lewis and Clark made a perfect pair as they began a journey that would link their names inseparably in American history. Though they were unalike in temperament, each supplied qualities the other lacked. Clark, an inspiring leader, could also draw fish and birds beautifully and make superb maps.

Toussaint L'Ouverture led the Haitian people against French forces when Napoleon attempted to gain complete control over Haiti.

Lewis was a reliable organizer and administrator. They developed a strong friendship based on mutual respect. Their mission was to trace the Missouri to its source and to find a water route to the Pacific. Moreover, they were instructed to make notes about the plant and animal life of the region, to record information about its geography, and to collect information about its inhabitants.

The Lewis and Clark expedition gets under way. After months of preparation Lewis and Clark and a party of 48 others set out from a point near St. Louis in May, 1804, traveling up the Missouri River in three boats. No brief account of the travels can do justice to the dangers the party faced almost daily, to their excitement at seeing natural wonders, or to their nagging uncertainty as to whether they would survive. Still, a sergeant named Charles Floyd was the only member of the expedition to lose his life. His companions buried him on a bluff close to what is now Sioux City, Iowa, and named the nearby river for him.

Late in 1804, Lewis and Clark reached the villages of the Mandan Indians in what is now North Dakota. There they built Fort Mandan and spent the winter. From the fort, Lewis wrote letters to his family and to Jefferson. This was the last news anyone had from Lewis for a year and a half.

By the time the expedition set forth again in April, 1805, it had been joined by a remarkable Shoshone guide and interpreter named Sacajawea (SAK-uh-juh-WEE-uh). Sacajawea had been captured by a war party when she was twelve years old and had lived with the Sioux for some time. Now married to a French Canadian trapper, Sacajawea provided the expedition with the necessary bridge of languages: English to French to Siouan to Shoshonean.

By July, 1805, Lewis and Clark had reached the Great Falls of the Missouri, at the edge of the Rockies. Sacajawea then led the party to her own tribe, the Shoshone, who showed openhanded hospitality. One of them, Lewis wrote, "gave me a piece of roasted salmon. This was the first salmon I had seen and perfectly convinced me that we were on the waters that flowed to the Pacific Ocean." The Shoshone supplied Lewis and Clark with horses and provisions, and also gave them directions for journeying to the Columbia River.

The Lewis and Clark expedition, shown here descending the Columbia River to the Pacific Ocean, yielded important geographical information about the western lands.

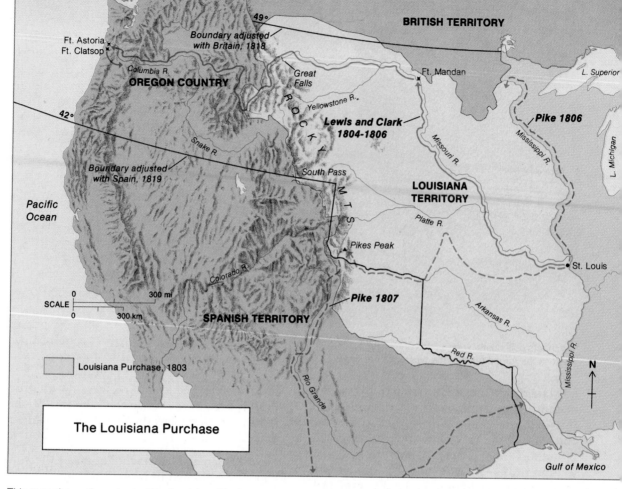

This map shows the extent of the Louisiana Territory and the routes traveled by Lewis and Clark and Zebulon Pike in their explorations.

Lewis and Clark reach the Pacific. In November, Lewis and Clark traveled down the Columbia River to the Pacific, "the object of all our labors, the reward of all our anxieties." There they established Fort Clatsop, named, like Fort Mandan, for the Indians that welcomed them. They had crossed the continent by navigating two of its great rivers, the Missouri and the Columbia. Clark carved on a tree, "By Land from the U. States in 1804 & 1805." Nineteen months had passed since the party started out.

After spending their second winter near the mouth of the Columbia, Lewis and Clark returned to St. Louis in September, 1806, to learn that they had been given up for lost. Their reports proved invaluable to future settlers. Appropriately, Lewis served as governor of the Louisiana Territory from 1807 to 1809.

Pike explores the Southwest. Other adventurers were also beginning to probe the new territory. One of them was Zebulon Pike, a young army lieutenant who led an expedition in 1805 to find the headwaters of the Mississippi. His party explored the upper Mississippi but failed to locate the true source of the river.

The next year Pike headed into the southwestern part of the Louisiana Purchase. Untrained for the work of scientific exploration, Pike nevertheless gave America its first description of the Great Plains and the Rockies. During a side trip to the Colorado country, Pike unsuccessfully tried to scale the mountain peak that bears his name today. Pike's journey provided Americans with much useful information.

Fur traders head west. The work of exploring the northern and central Rockies

Merchants built posts, such as this one in Iowa, for the trade of staples and other goods in exchange for the pelts of the western fur trappers.

fell largely to fur traders and trappers. For instance, a fur trader named Robert Stuart found South Pass, a broad, level valley that cuts through the Rocky Mountains. The mountains only slowly yielded their secrets to Americans. In 1806 John Colter, a Virginian discharged from the Lewis and Clark expedition, joined a group of trappers headed by Manuel Lisa, born in New Orleans. With only a gun and a thirty-pound pack, Colter had made his way alone for five hundred miles through the lower Missouri River. He told the trappers about painted canyons, incredibly treacherous waterfalls, gushers periodically bursting from the earth, and boiling water atop an ice-covered lake. The area he described later came to be known as Yellowstone Park.

When Lisa returned to St. Louis in 1808, he had made up his mind that only large companies could effectively exploit the fur trade in such a vast region. He and others formed the Missouri Fur Company in 1809, a company that for the next few years controlled the fur trade of the northern Rockies.

In the Pacific Northwest a German immigrant named John Jacob Astor founded the American Fur Company in 1808. Astor later operated a chain of trading posts running westward from the Great Lakes to the Pacific. His headquarters were located at Fort Astoria, on the same Columbia River that Lewis and Clark had so recently visited and explored.

Jefferson is re-elected. Thomas Jefferson had said he hoped to retire after one term in office, but what he called "the abominable slanders of my political enemies" made him decide to run again. He wanted "a verdict from my country" on how well he had performed. He was handily re-elected in 1804, with a new Vice President, George Clinton of New York.

That Clinton succeeded Aaron Burr was one outcome of the fierce politics of this era. Earlier the same year Burr, incensed by hostile words that Alexander Hamilton had written, challenged him to a duel with pistols. Hamilton was not eager to fight but on principle refused to withdraw his remarks. In the duel each man fired a single shot. Hamilton missed, perhaps deliberately. Burr's shot found its target and Hamilton fell, fatally wounded. Burr completed his term in office, but the disgrace of killing a political opponent ruined his career.

Burr is involved in a conspiracy. Burr soon was in another scrape. Rumors were heard that he was engaged in a treasonous plot to separate the western territories from the

United States and join them, under his leadership, to Spain's possessions. The extent of Burr's involvement was unclear. In any case he was working closely with General James Wilkinson, the commander of the American troops in Louisiana and one always ready to sell his services to the highest bidder. Wilkinson, however, turned against Burr in 1806 and wrote to Jefferson, giving him an account of Burr's activities. At first Jefferson would not believe the tale, but in November, 1806, he ordered Burr's arrest.

Presiding over Burr's trial was Jefferson's old enemy, Chief Justice Marshall. Jefferson was certain Burr was guilty, but the Court acquitted him. The decision distressed many of Jefferson's supporters, who saw it as a rebuke of the President. Still, Marshall was on solid ground. He pointed to the definition of treason in the Constitution. Burr was found innocent because he would not confess, and because the government could not find two witnesses willing to testify "to the same overt act." Despite the unpopularity of his decision, Marshall won fresh respect for the Constitution.

SECTION REVIEW

1. (a) For what reasons did France want to regain control of Louisiana? (b) Why did Napoleon change his mind and agree to sell Louisiana to the United States?
2. (a) Why did the Federalists oppose the purchase of Louisiana? (b) How did Jefferson justify it?
3. (a) For what reasons were Lewis and Clark sent to explore the Louisiana Territory? (b) What regions were explored by Zebulon Pike?
4. (a) Why did Aaron Burr's political career end in disgrace? (b) In what conspiracy was he later involved?

3 Jefferson Seeks to Defend America's Neutral Rights

Despite Jefferson's deep interest in the West, in his second term his attention was turned once more to international affairs. Again, an American President found himself trying to keep the United States free of turmoil that was convulsing Europe.

France and Britain resume warfare. The fighting between Napoleon and other European nations had entered a new, more violent phase in 1803. Napoleon had reopened hostilities with Britain in that year, just after selling Louisiana to the United States. Britain and France continued to do battle, and Napoleon appeared to be on his way to gaining control of the entire European continent.

American trade prospers. The resumption of fighting at first proved a windfall for American merchants. Their ships, being from a neutral country, readily moved in and out of European ports. Britain, however, was understandably angered by the way the Americans were growing prosperous on trade ordinarily conducted by English vessels. Having driven French merchant ships from the seas, the British were not going to allow Americans to take their place.

Tension with Britain mounts. The British were particularly offended by the American disregard of what they had come to call the Rule of 1756. This principle, devised during the French and Indian War, said that trade closed in time of peace could not be opened in time of war. This meant, particularly, that American merchants could not sell sugar from the French West Indies, since trade with the French West Indies was not open to Americans in peacetime. British ships began to stop and seize American vessels that broke the rule. Americans were infuriated by what they considered as a disregard of their rights as neutrals.

Jefferson, a man of peace, felt frustrated by his inability to overcome this abuse. He earnestly believed "that a just and friendly conduct on our part will procure justice and friendship from others." Still, the claws of the British lion grew sharper as England faced fiercer and fiercer pressure from Napoleon.

The British seize American sailors. The most outrageous British response was the practice of *impressing,* or drafting by force, the hands they needed to help man the Royal Navy. It was bad enough that Britons

The impressment of American seamen by the British reached a climax when the *Chesapeake* was attacked.

were seized for involuntary naval service. Americans, however, were now being made victims too. Because American merchant crews were paid higher wages than British sailors, desertions from the Royal Navy were common. Armed impressment parties began boarding American ships to arrest sailors they deemed deserters. Fighting a life-and-death struggle with Napoleon, the searchers did not make a fine distinction between deserters and American citizens.

The British were deaf to American protests. When Americans argued that the boarding of ships on the high seas was a violation of the rights of neutrals and, in fact, of their very territory, the British dismissed the protests as nonsense. In seizing and impressing recently naturalized Americans, whom they identified by their accents, the British held to the principle "once an Englishman, always an Englishman." They even had the impertinence to commit their mischief on American ships in American home waters.

Both Britain and France erect blockades. In October, 1805, the British fleet, commanded by Lord Nelson, decisively defeated the French in the Battle of Trafalgar, off the coast of Spain. The war went on, however, with Napoleon seemingly invincible on land. To cut off the trade of Napoleon and his allies, the British in 1807 issued a series of commands called Orders in Council. These Orders authorized the seizure of any vessel that tried to trade in ports on the continent of Europe unless it first had obtained British permission. In response, the French tried to blockade the British Isles. In a number of decrees, they said they would seize all neutral ships trading with the British. The French even threatened to seize neutral ships that allowed themselves to be searched by British cruisers.

American ship captains were in a dilemma. Outside any continental port they were subject to seizure by the British if they had not stopped first in England. Inside, they were subject to seizure by the French if they *had*.

The Chesapeake Affair arouses anti-British feeling. More than American commerce appeared to be at stake; American dignity itself seemed in the balance. The limit appeared to have been reached on June 22, 1807. On that day the British warship *Leopard*, pursuing some alleged deserters, opened fire on the United States frigate *Chesapeake*, ten miles out of Norfolk, Virginia. Twenty-one crew members were killed or wounded. The British removed four men they said were deserters, three of whom were actually Americans.

When the battered *Chesapeake* limped back to Norfolk and the crew reported the attack, the news spread like wildfire. Jefferson wrote, "Never since the Battle of Lexington have I seen this country in such a state of exasperation as at present." War might have come immediately if the United States had been prepared for it.

As angry as Jefferson was, he still wanted to keep peace, just as the Federalists had done when they were in charge. He sensed that American power was gradually growing, and that a new test with Britain should be delayed. Twenty years of peace, he believed, would be a rich blessing for the young nation. The President put it this way: "At the end of that period, we shall be twenty millions in numbers, and forty in energy, when encountering the starved and rickety paupers and dwarfs of English workshops."

Congress passes an embargo. If the United States did not go to war, what was the solution to the dispute with Britain? Congress, harking back to the methods of pre-Revolutionary days, had passed a Non-Importation Act in 1806. The boycott, however, did not shake Britain from its oppressive behavior.

As a principal architect of the Revolution, Jefferson continued to have faith in the methods that had worked in the old days. Under his direction Congress passed the Embargo Act of 1807. This act forbade trade between the United States and *all* foreign countries. If American ships stayed in home ports, Jefferson reasoned, they would be safe from seizure.

The embargo fails. Jefferson's Embargo Act did not work as planned. Britain and France felt little effect from the stoppage of American supplies. They were not as dependent on American food as American farmers had believed. Moreover, while smugglers flourished, business in the United States ground to a halt. In every port city, ships lay at anchor, idle. Urban unemployment, moreover, became widespread.

After a trip home to Virginia, Jefferson reported, "I have been happy in my journey through the country to find the people unanimous in their preference of the embargo to war." If he had traveled in New England, however, he would have found deep and growing hostility. Merchants in that region — most of them Federalists — were suffering from the embargo, and many claimed that Jefferson had set out deliberately to destroy them. They argued that trade should not be regulated by the government, and that the merchants alone ought to judge the risks of overseas trade.

The truth was that the embargo could not work without full public support.

Moreover, the embargo was actually helping Britain and France. The British gained because American commercial competition had been removed from the seas. The French gained because they could now seize American vessels that were ignoring the embargo and smuggling goods into Europe. The French argued that these surely could not be *American* ships; they must be British ships flying false flags! So frustrating were these conditions that some Americans came to think that war against Britain *and* France would be the only way to set things right.

Jefferson repeals the embargo before leaving office. Just before Jefferson's second term expired on March 4, 1809, he signed the Non-Intercourse Act. It repealed the embargo and reopened trade with all the nations of the world except Britain and France. The act also provided that if either Britain or France stopped violating American rights, the United States would open trade with that country once again.

The economic effects of the Embargo Act of 1807 are shown on this graph by the decrease in trading activity.

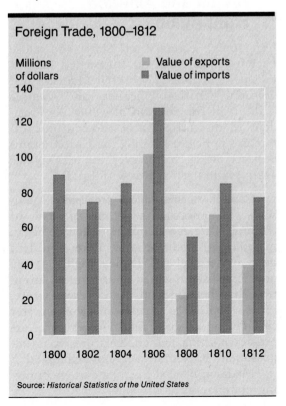

Foreign Trade, 1800–1812

Millions of dollars

Value of exports
Value of imports

Source: *Historical Statistics of the United States*

This was Jefferson's final official act. Jefferson yearned to be back home at his beloved Monticello. Now almost 66 years old, he suffered from rheumatism and the severe headaches that had plagued him during much of his life. In his letters he sometimes described himself as a sailor weary of the sea. At other times he said he felt like a prisoner about to be released from his chains. He did not seek a third term.

SECTION REVIEW

1. Vocabulary: *impress*.
2. (a) What effect did the resumption of warfare in Europe between Britain and France have on American trade? (b) What was the British response?
3. (a) Why did Britain and France each erect trade blockades? (b) How did these actions affect the United States?
4. What was the Chesapeake Affair?
5. (a) What was the purpose of Jefferson's embargo? (b) Why was it a failure?

4 Britain and America Fight Again

Jefferson's Secretary of State and close friend, James Madison, succeeded him as President on March 4, 1809. Madison had defeated Charles Pinckney and George Clinton in the election of 1808. As President, Madison tried his best to continue Jefferson's policy of keeping the United States at peace. By 1812, however, the nation once again found itself at war with Britain.

Madison inherits difficult problems. Madison's inauguration was not a day of triumph. Pale and trembling when he began his address, Madison grew more confident only as he read on. Dolley Madison, the new First Lady, seemed to draw more attention than her husband. An observer wrote, "Mrs. Madison is a handsome woman. Her complexion is brilliant . . . her face expresses nothing but good nature. It is impossible to be with her and not be pleased."

Madison needed a strong and encouraging companion at his side, because, as he said in his address, the country faced a situation "without parallel." When the Non-Intercourse Act expired in 1810, Congress passed yet another law designed to bring Britain and France to heel. Known as Macon's Bill No. 2, it opened trade with all countries for one year. If either Britain or France stopped interfering with America's rights as a neutral — and the other failed to do so within three months — the Non-Intercourse Act would go back into effect against the offending country. In desperation the United States was offering itself to the higher bidder — a shameful way to conduct foreign policy. Madison himself called the law a "miserable, feeble Puff."

Britain and France treated the United States with contempt. Napoleon went so far as to fool Madison into believing that France had ended its blockade of Britain. Joyfully the President reopened trade with France before he discovered, to his immense embarrassment, that he had been tricked. The British, for their part, sent to Washington an anti-American ambassador named Francis James Jackson. He was known as "Copenhagen" Jackson because in recent fighting in Europe he had ordered the British navy to destroy the Danish capital. An insufferable critic of American life, he found fault with the quality of the food Madison served at the White House and described Mrs. Madison as "fat and forty, but not fair." When it proved impossible to negotiate with Jackson, the State Department asked London to recall him.

Anti-British sentiment continued to run strong in the United States. In November, 1811, Madison told Congress that America's very survival was at stake. Referring to Britain's "hostile inflexibility in trampling on rights which no independent nation can relinquish," the President requested that Congress "place the country into an armor and an attitude demanded by the crisis."

The Northwest Indians are defeated at Tippecanoe. Far from the sea the British were also engaged in hostilities against Americans. On November 7, 1811, Americans under William Henry Harrison, governor of the Indiana Territory, defeated a force of

Indians at the junction of the Tippecanoe and Wabash rivers. Although he was not present at the battle, the leader of the Indians was the impressive Shawnee chief Tecumseh (teh-KUM-sah). Tecumseh had formed a confederacy of Indians who had joined together to make a unified stand against white settlement. After the Battle of Tippecanoe, however, the power of the confederacy was broken.

Most Americans believed that Britain had encouraged the Indians to fight. Indeed, some of the weapons left behind after the Battle of Tippecanoe had clearly been supplied by the British. Westerners now joined their voices with those of Easterners who had felt the force of British maritime policies. The cry spread across the country, "Look at the Wabash, look at the impressed seamen!"

The War Hawks move the United States closer to war. The Congress that assembled in 1811 contained many members who thought that war with Britain was inevitable, even desirable, to save American honor and nationhood. This group included Henry Clay from Kentucky, John C. Calhoun of South Carolina, and Felix Grundy from Tennessee.

The older leaders who had made the Revolution a success were passing from the scene. Those honored Americans, like Jefferson and Adams, had presented their ideas thoughtfully in letters. The new leaders came to national attention because of powerful speeches they made in Congress. At their head was Henry Clay. A representative of the "new West," Clay was elected Speaker of the House, a position more powerful in setting policies than it is at present.

These new southern and western leaders were dubbed "War Hawks" because they believed that war with Great Britain was necessary. Without a substantial navy, however, how would the nation wage war against Britain? The answer seemed obvious: conquer the nearby British colony of Canada.

Some Southerners also had their eyes on Florida. Escaped slaves sometimes found safety in that Spanish territory, and Indians occasionally launched attacks from it. Madison had already taken advantage of a revolt against Spanish rule in West Florida to proclaim it part of the United States in 1810. Now, Southerners were demanding East Florida too. Since Spain was an ally of Britain, expansionist Southerners and expansionist Westerners shared common aims.

Still, the desire for land was not the War Hawks' chief goal. Both Southerners and Westerners were eager primarily to punish Britain and uphold the honor of the nation. Andrew Jackson of Tennessee, rising to leadership in the army, wrote in March, 1812, that "we are going to fight for the re-establishment of our national character, misunderstood and vilified at home and abroad."

Some Americans oppose war with Britain. New Englanders, especially those in the port cities, were less eager for war than people in other parts of the country. They feared being bombarded from the sea, as Copenhagen had been. It was said that one could tell how keen people were for war by how far they lived from the coast. Many New Englanders also resented the political strength of the western "foresters," as they called them. The growing population of the new states was weakening the power of the eastern states.

Congress declares war. By the beginning of 1812, British merchants had begun to feel the effects of the loss of American trade. British factories had closed, and food prices in Britain were beginning to rise. In response, Parliament repealed the Orders in Council on June 16, 1812. Congress, unaware of this favorable turn, was already considering President Madison's request for a declaration of war.

Madison's long effort to avoid war had grown, in part, out of his knowledge that the country was not prepared for it. Nevertheless, he had gradually come to accept the need to fight. Even an important London newspaper had observed that the peace-at-any-price policy had forced the United States "either to surrender their independence, or maintain it by war."

Early in June, 1812, Madison asked Congress to declare war on Great Britain. He listed four main grievances in his request. They were (1) the impressment of American sailors, (2) the violation of American rights on the sea, (3) the British Orders in Council, and (4) the incitement of the Indians. On June 18, 1812, just two days after the British repealed the Orders in Council, Congress agreed to the President's request, and hostilities formally began.

Madison wins re-election. In the presidential election that year, Madison won a second term. His opponent was De Witt Clinton of New York, a peace candidate. The President's backing was chiefly in the South and West. During the campaign the Federalists snarled that the War of 1812 was "Mr. Madison's war." In fact, it could also have been called "Mr. Clay's war" or "Mr. Calhoun's war." Many could see that it was truly "America's war."

The United States wages war clumsily. American strategy in the War of 1812 was to capture Canada and hold it until Britain recognized American neutral rights or to exchange it for any United States territory the British might seize. Unfortunately, the United States had only 7,000 poorly trained troops in the regular army, even though Congress had authorized a force of 35,000. The scheme to conquer Canada was further handicapped by weak American military leadership. The inept Secretary of War, William Eustis, was a surgeon who had served at Bunker Hill. He spent much of his time

---

EYEWITNESS TO HISTORY

On Board an American Privateer

During the War of 1812 the American navy depended on privateers to challenge the formidable sea power of Great Britain. Noah Jones, an officer of a famous American privateer, the *Yankee*, kept a journal in which he described the capture of a British vessel off the coast of Africa in November, 1812.

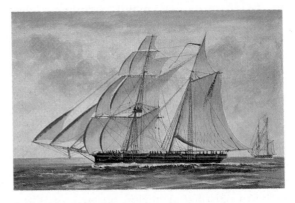

An American privateer

At six in the morning a sail was sighted bearing N.E. at a distance of about three leagues. All sails were set to give chase. The wind was light and the sea calm — we were able to overtake the vessel quickly. All hands were called to quarters and the decks cleared for action.

Our quarry was identified as a sloop flying British colors at the masthead. A gun was fired and our commander hailed her and ordered her to strike her colors and surrender. The sloop did so immediately and we sent over a boat with a boarding party. We found our prize to be the sloop *Mary Ann* out of London, Captain Stewart Sutherland in command with a crew of nine persons bound home with a cargo of gold, ivory, tropical wood, and palm-oil.

The English captain was given quarters with the officers in their cabin and the rest of the British crew were also well provided for. Conscious that it is a sufficient misfortune for our enemies to lose their ship and become prisoners of war, we feel it our duty to render their suffering as light as possible. We do not war against individuals; we have no private revenge to gratify; we know the peculiar hardships of the present war, and we wish to soften its rigor as far as it is consistent with our commission. We are instructed to burn, sink, and destroy, which compelled us to set fire to the *Mary Ann*. But we never have, nor I trust we never shall, deprived an unfortunate mariner of his private property or baggage.

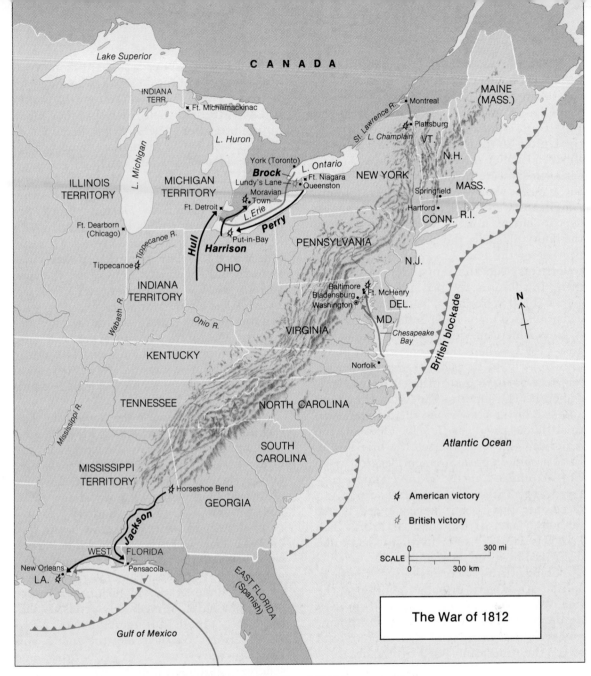

The British had an early and decisive advantage in the War of 1812 because of their naval strength. Their naval blockade put military and economic pressure on America.

poring over newspapers to see where he could buy hats and shoes and other supplies for the troops. The senior general was Henry Dearborn. He too had earned fame in the Revolution some thirty years earlier.

To make matters worse, the country, as we have seen, was not united. Even in regions where people supported the war, enthusiasm was not high. As in the French and Indian War and the Revolution, moreover,

some Americans did not hesitate to trade with the enemy. The British commander-in-chief happily reported at one point that most of his men were eating American beef.

Finally, while people bravely shouted "On to Canada!" Congress did not have the courage to levy taxes to finance the war. Congress authorized the borrowing of $11 million, but the Treasury Department never sold out the bond issue it offered the public.

Americans win victories at sea. Although no match for the formidable British navy, the Americans scored some stunning triumphs at sea in the early months of the war. To face the awesome power of Britain, the United States had just three frigates and thirteen smaller ships. Nevertheless, American officers were capable professionals, and the sailors were eager volunteers. Many Americans were attracted by the chance to capture enemy merchant ships and share in the booty. (Usually the government took 50 percent of the booty, leaving 32.5 percent to officers, and the remainder to enlisted men.) In addition, 185 privateers set sail.

In the first round of battle, the Americans captured eight English merchant ships. A great American victory took place in August, 1812, when the *Constitution* (later known as "Old Ironsides") met the British frigate *Guerrière* and inflicted heavy damage on it. The superior American firepower and size of the crew made the difference in this fierce naval battle. In October the American ship *Wasp* seized the brig *Frolic*. In that same month Stephen Decatur (page 214), commanding the *United States*, captured the British frigate *Macedonian*. In December the *Constitution* slugged it out with the *Java* off the coast of Brazil. The *Java* was damaged so badly that it had to be destroyed by its own crew.

These stirring victories raised American spirits. An American ballad contained the line, "We dare their whole navy to come to our coast." The British were confident, however, that in the end their navy would sweep the American vessels off the ocean.

The invasion of Canada fails. On land it was a different story for the Americans. As part of the plan to capture Canada, the American command decided to invade what is now Ontario. General William Hull, governor of the Michigan Territory from 1805 to 1812, was ordered to Detroit to prepare the invasion. Within a few days of having crossed into Canada, however, he withdrew to American soil, fearful that Indian attacks might cut his lines of communication. A short while later, Hull surrendered Detroit to Isaac Brock, an able English general who had led British troops westward from York (present-day Toronto). Brock was aided by Tecumseh (page 225), whose fighting ability had so impressed the British that they made him a brigadier general. The surrender of Detroit won Brock immediate fame in England, and he was made a knight.

The United States had no such hero, and would not have one for some time. After his triumph at Detroit, Brock defeated American troops under Stephen Van Rensselaer on the Niagara River at Queenston. Van Rensselaer, the fifth in direct descent from Kiliaen Van Rensselaer, the first patroon in New Netherland, was a Federalist who had at first opposed the war with Britain. In northern New York, meanwhile, General Dearborn was preparing to invade Canada along Lake Champlain. The effort ended in failure when the New York State militia refused to cross into Canada to fight.

The Americans regain the Northwest. The second year of the war, 1813, brought a remarkable American naval victory on the Great Lakes. The Americans were led by Oliver Hazard Perry, a handsome, 28-year-old naval lieutenant, who at the age of 15 had fought against the Barbary pirates. Perry defeated a British force at Put-in-Bay on Lake Erie. Carpenters had built Perry's ships right on the lake, using fir trees felled in the nearby forests. The crews were local recruits, some of whom had never before been on a ship. Immediately after his victory, Perry sent an unforgettable message to his superior: "We have met the enemy and they are ours; two ships, two brigs, one schooner, and one sloop."

In the fall of 1813, General William Henry Harrison, by now renowned as the hero of Tippecanoe, was able to retake Detroit. Harrison's forces, pursuing the British and their Indian allies into Canada, defeated them at Moravian Town on the banks of the Thames River. Tecumseh was killed in the fighting. With Tecumseh gone and the British in retreat, the threat to the Northwest was ended. Still, Forts Michilimackinac and Dearborn (now Chicago) remained in British hands. Furthermore, in December, 1813, the British captured Fort

The British avenged themselves for the Americans' burning of York, the capital of Upper Canada, by setting fire to many government buildings in Washington.

Niagara. They appeared to be taking revenge for the action of American troops who had put several Canadian towns to the torch, including York.

The British attack Washington, D.C. The year 1814 saw the end of fighting in Europe. Napoleon's scheme to dominate the continent had been smashed at the Battle of Waterloo. Now the United States felt keen anxiety as experienced British soldiers were transferred from European battlefields to America.

The British, angry that their American "cousins" had caused them so much trouble during the desperate years of struggle against Napoleon, were determined to punish the United States. Blockading the Atlantic coast, they carried out hit-and-run attacks against American seaports and fishing villages.

One such assault was launched from Chesapeake Bay in August, 1814, against Washington, D.C. The city was practically without defense. Government clerks hastily hid public records before joining other citizens fleeing the scene. All available soldiers rushed to Bladensburg, Maryland, hoping to make a stand there against the invaders. As soon as the makeshift army of defenders saw the veteran British soldiers, however, most of them turned and ran.

President Madison left Washington for Maryland as the British approached the city. Dolley Madison remained at the White House, supervising the packing of household furnishings and official papers. At last on August 24 she was urged to flee, for the British had entered the city. As she was about to depart, Dolley Madison remembered her promise to Martha Washington's grandson: the Gilbert Stuart portrait of Washington must never fall into British hands. She ordered the frame broken and the irreplaceable canvas removed.

Meanwhile, the British set fire to the Capitol. Then they hurried to the White House to continue the destruction. The

British commander sat down and ate the meal still on the table, and drank scornfully "to Jemmy's health" — the only way he ever referred to the President. His men later piled furniture in the center of the parlor and set it afire. The enemy soldiers completed their work by putting the torch to the Navy Yard, the bridges across the Potomac, and other government buildings.

Heavy rains pelted the stricken capital and added further to the gloom that had overtaken the people. The downpour helped, however, to extinguish the flames, which could be seen for miles.

Baltimore withstands a British assault. After leaving Washington, the British forces moved up Chesapeake Bay to attack Baltimore. Troops who had been sent ashore to seize Fort McHenry, however, encountered stiff resistance. The British decided to hold up the assault until their fleet could bombard the fort and "soften" it up.

Luck was with the American defenders this time. The water was too shallow to allow the British ships to do their work properly. On the day after the bombardment, a young lawyer from Washington, Francis Scott Key, saw the Stars and Stripes still flying over the fort. Inspired by the thrilling sight, he wrote "The Star-Spangled Banner," setting the words to an old English tune. His song afterward became the national anthem. It has given generation after generation of Americans the sense of Key's satisfaction that in the attack on the fort "the rockets' red glare, the bombs bursting in air, gave proof through the night that our flag was still there."

British advances are stopped. Happily, Madison, whose reputation had sunk to a new low, soon had the benefit of a fresh group of American army officers and some historical luck to restore his stature. Even as the British were making ready the assault on Washington, General Jacob Brown, a Pennsylvania Quaker, led a final American invasion of Canada. At the Battle of Lundy's Lane, Brown faced superior British forces and fought them to a draw. The Americans soon retreated, however, leaving the British in control of Canada.

In September, 1814, the British tried to cut New England off from the rest of the Union with an army they sent south along the Lake Champlain route. The issue was decided in favor of the United States. American vessels under the command of Thomas Macdonough, a veteran of the Tripolitan War, defeated the enemy at the Battle of Plattsburg and ended the British threat in the region.

Peace talks lead to the Treaty of Ghent. By 1814 both sides were seeking a quick end to the costly and discouraging struggle. At about the time Washington was being put to the torch, an American delegation arrived at the Belgian town of Ghent to talk peace with the British.

There were five American peace commissioners at Ghent. One was John Quincy Adams, an experienced diplomat and the son of John Adams. Another was Albert Gallatin (page 211), who had joked that as a "foreigner with a French accent" he would have advantages in European diplomacy. A third commissioner was James Bayard of Delaware, whose vote in the House of Representatives had made possible Jefferson's election over Burr. Henry Clay, who had helped bring on the war, and Jonathan Russell, the American minister to Sweden and Norway, completed the group.

The commissioners had instructions that the British would have to accept certain terms. They must stop the impressment of American sailors, respect the rights of neutrals on the high seas, and pay America for the damages they had caused before and during the war. The Americans were also instructed to try to obtain Canada.

The British came with terms too. They wanted to keep all the United States territory they were occupying at war's end. They also sought to slice off a piece of Maine and attach it to Canada.

The Treaty of Ghent, signed on Christmas Eve, 1814, was unusual in that neither side won or lost anything. The document provided for an end to hostilities, the release of prisoners, and the mutual restoration of occupied territory. It made no mention, however, of impressment or of the rights of neutrals. Time would have to take care of those problems.

Jackson defeats the British at New Orleans. The news that the war was over had not reached America by the time the British attacked New Orleans early in 1815. The Americans there were under the command of Andrew Jackson, a senator from Tennessee and a general in the state militia. During the early years of the war Jackson had directed an American campaign against the Creek Indians in the Mississippi Territory. In March, 1814, he had crushed the Creeks at the Battle of Horseshoe Bend and obtained from them a treaty that opened up the Southwest to settlement. Jackson had next marched into Florida to prevent the British from using the Spanish base at Pensacola against the United States. Then, arriving in New Orleans, he found himself face to face with 8,000 seasoned British troops. Jackson's forces included volunteers from Tennessee and Kentucky, two battalions of free blacks, Cherokee Indians, sailors, and even some pirates.

The Americans, though greatly outnumbered, were able to inflict a fearful defeat on the British. The enemy suffered over 700 killed (including the British commander), compared with just 8 American fatalities. The battle was the most important American victory since Yorktown.

The Hartford Convention proves damaging to the Federalists. The triumph at New Orleans not only rescued Madison's administration from disgrace but produced in the person of Andrew Jackson a new American hero as well. Jackson's deed wiped out the effects of an unhappy episode on the home front: the Hartford Convention.

In the despair following the burning of Washington, Massachusetts Federalists had called upon their neighbors to meet at Hartford, Connecticut, in December, 1814. All the New England states sent representatives. They were so upset at Madison that they talked of the need for New England to *secede*, or withdraw, from the Union. In the end they were content to suggest new amendments to the Constitution. Because they blamed the country's troubles on the Presidents from Virginia, the New Englanders proposed limiting a Chief Executive to one term and barring a state from providing a President twice in succession. Following the lead of Jefferson and Madison in the Virginia and Kentucky Resolutions (page 192), the delegates also proposed that a state be allowed to declare unconstitutional any law it thought interfered with its citizens' liberties.

The Hartford Convention sent "ambassadors" — Federalists, of course — to Washington to present the resolutions. They had hardly arrived when the city learned of the victory at New Orleans. Then on February 14 came the news, no less satisfying, of the Treaty of Ghent. The Federalists quietly slipped out of Washington.

The Federalist Party never recovered from the effects of the ill-timed meeting at Hartford. Jefferson commented that under any other government, the members of the Hartford Convention would have been hanged for treason. "We let them live," he wrote, "as the laughing stocks of the world, and punish them by the torment of eternal contempt." Madison could afford to give the Federalists of Hartford "the silent treatment." He could see that what Dolley Madison was calling "the bustle and noise" of an America once again at peace foretold an era of growth and prosperity.

SECTION REVIEW

1. Vocabulary: *secede.*
2. (a) Why were southern and western leaders in Congress so bitterly opposed to British policies? (b) What stand did representatives from New England take?
3. For what reasons did the United States declare war on Britain in 1812?
4. (a) In what ways was the United States unprepared for war in 1812? (b) Why did the American invasions of Canada fail?
5. What was the outcome and significance of each of the following battles? (a) Tippecanoe (b) Baltimore (c) Lake Champlain (d) New Orleans.
6. (a) What were the terms of the Treaty of Ghent? (b) Why was it an unusual treaty?
7. (a) What was the Hartford Convention? (b) What amendments to the Constitution did the delegates at this convention propose?

Chapter 9 Review

Summary

Following his election as the first Republican President, Thomas Jefferson tried to calm the fears of the Federalists. He allowed the foundation of Hamilton's financial system — the Bank of the United States — to remain in operation. Even though he challenged Federalist control of the courts, he did not meet with notable success. He had to accept John Marshall's decision in the *Marbury v. Madison* case, a decision that set a landmark precedent by establishing the Supreme Court's power of judicial review.

Jefferson's presidency was marked by a reduction of the national debt, an informal style in the White House, and a drawn-out naval contest with the Barbary States. The purchase from France of the vast Louisiana Territory was Jefferson's chief accomplishment. This tract included the city of New Orleans and 900,000 square miles of land. Jefferson sent Meriwether Lewis and William Clark to explore the new territory. Other explorers reported on the Rocky Mountains and the Great Plains.

Throughout his presidency, Jefferson tried to protect America's neutral rights on the high seas. During his second term of office those rights were threatened when war resumed between Britain and France. Harassment of American shipping, including the impressment of American sailors into the British navy, angered the United States. A British attack on the *Chesapeake* in 1807 led to an American embargo on all foreign trade. Intended to hurt the British, the embargo instead proved harmful to the United States. Meanwhile, support for a declaration of war against Britain was growing in Congress. The demand for war was led by the War Hawks, many of them Westerners and Southerners who wanted to conquer Canada and Florida. Congress finally declared war on Britain in June, 1812.

Militarily unprepared, and lacking unified support on the home front, the United States was unable to achieve the quick victories the War Hawks had anticipated. Efforts to invade Canada, for instance, ended in failure. The American navy scored several important victories, however, both on the inland lakes and at sea. By 1814 both sides, weary of the struggle, met in the Belgian city of Ghent to arrange a peace treaty. Signed on December 24, 1814, the treaty restored the prewar boundaries but made no mention of the causes of the hostilities.

One final battle was fought at New Orleans after the peace treaty had been signed. Andrew Jackson emerged a military hero, and the stage was set for a return to growth and prosperity.

Vocabulary and Important Terms

1. *Marbury v. Madison*
2. judicial review
3. Tripolitan War
4. Louisiana Purchase
5. Burr conspiracy
6. impress
7. Chesapeake Affair
8. Embargo Act of 1807
9. Non-Intercourse Act
10. Macon's Bill No. 2
11. Battle of Tippecanoe
12. War Hawks
13. Treaty of Ghent
14. Battle of New Orleans
15. Hartford Convention
16. secede

Discussion Questions

1. (a) How did Jefferson as President prove more moderate than he had once sounded? (b) What contributions to the republic did Jefferson make in matters of style and outlook?

2. (a) Why did Jefferson seek to repeal the Judiciary Act of 1801? (b) How did he try to block the "midnight judges" from taking office? (c) How was the *Marbury v. Madison* case resolved?

3. (a) Why was New Orleans so important to the United States? (b) How did Jefferson respond to the news of Louisiana's transfer to France? (c) Why did Napoleon finally decide to sell Louisiana to the United States?

4. (a) Why did some Americans oppose the Louisiana Purchase? (b) How did Jefferson justify the purchase? (c) Why has the Louisiana Purchase been called "a great divider" in American history?

5. (a) What were the goals of Lewis and Clark's expedition? (b) What did the expedition accomplish? (c) What areas of the Louisiana Territory did Zebulon Pike explore? (d) How did fur traders and trappers help explore and develop the West?

6. (a) Why did the resumption of fighting in Europe between France and Britain prove at first to be a windfall for American shipping? (b) What subsequent British actions aroused anti-British feelings in the United States? (c) Why did Jefferson support the idea of a trade embargo? (d) Why did it fail?

7. (a) Why did both the Non-Intercourse Act of 1809 and Macon's Bill No. 2 fail to preserve America's neutral rights? (b) For what reasons did the War Hawks favor war with Britain? (c) What four main grievances against Britain did Madison list in his war message to Congress?

8. To what extent was the United States unprepared for the War of 1812?

9. (a) What were some of America's important victories during the war? (b) What major setbacks did America suffer?

10. (a) What hopes did the American and British peace commissioners have when they arrived at Ghent? (b) What did the treaty actually provide?

Relating Past to Present

1. Thomas Jefferson enacted a trade embargo in 1807 to protect America's neutral rights. Find out how embargoes have been used in recent years. (Consider, for instance, the 1973–1974 Arab embargo on petroleum to the United States or this nation's embargoes on goods to unfriendly nations.) What differences do you see between Jefferson's embargoes and more recent embargoes?

2. Review the way in which the United States finally declared war on Britain in 1812. How might modern means of communication have changed the way the war began? The way in which it ended?

Studying Local History

If the expeditions of Lewis and Clark or Zebulon Pike passed through your state, trace the route on a detailed map of the state. Look in an encyclopedia or a history of the West to find what information about your state these explorers gathered.

Using History Skills

1. *Reading maps.* Study the map showing the Louisiana Purchase on page 219. (a) What made St. Louis a good starting place for American explorers? (b) What lands were explored beyond the Louisiana Purchase? (c) Compare this map to a map of the United States today. What states in whole or in part were carved out of the Louisiana Territory?

2. *Reading graphs.* Study the graph showing American foreign trade on page 223. During the years shown on the graph did the United States generally export or import more goods? Explain your answer.

3. *Ranking.* Many American historians rank Thomas Jefferson as one of our greatest Presidents. Prepare a talk describing the personal characteristics and presidential actions that made Jefferson an effective leader.

WORLD SCENE

World Rivalry

The War of 1812 was the American part of a titanic struggle between Napoleon and most of the other European powers. At issue was Napoleon's ambition to dominate Europe.

The Battle of Trafalgar. One of the decisive battles of the Napoleonic Wars was the Battle of Trafalgar. This naval engagement between Britain and France took place in 1805 off the coast of Spain. Napoleon knew that to undertake an invasion of Britain he had first to deal with the formidable British navy. To do this he organized a combined French and Spanish fleet of 33 ships. As Napoleon's fleet left the Mediterranean en route to Britain, it made contact with a British force commanded by Lord Horatio Nelson. Nelson's battle order to his ships and their crews was simply, "England expects that every man will do his duty."

Although outnumbered, Nelson surprised the enemy by maneuvering his ships so as to cut through the French-Spanish battle line in two places. Twenty French ships were captured in the battle and the remainder destroyed or scattered. The British navy won the Battle of Trafalgar without the loss of a single ship. Lord Nelson, however, was fatally wounded in the action. The disastrous defeat at Trafalgar ended Napoleon's dream of invading Britain.

The Congress of Vienna. At the little town of Ghent in Belgium in 1814, British and American diplomats worked out agreements ending the War of 1812. The arrangements for a peace settlement in Europe after the Napoleonic Wars were more complicated. The five major European powers — Austria, Britain, Prussia, Russia, and France — gathered at a meeting known as the Congress of Vienna, held in Austria, from September, 1814, to June, 1815.

The diplomats' main business was to restore the authority of the royal dynasties that Napoleon had toppled and establish a new balance of power. It was hoped that the new arrangement would prevent any one nation from dominating Europe as France had done under Napoleon.

The balance of power established by the Congress of Vienna succeeded in preventing a major European war for 100 years. The men of Vienna, however, failed to recognize the rising force of nationalism, and revolutions broke out periodically during the nineteenth century.

10

Shaping a National Spirit

1816 – 1828

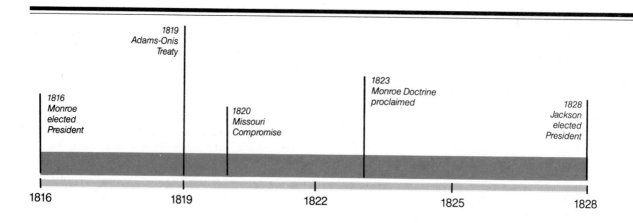

1819
Adams-Onís
Treaty

1816
Monroe
elected
President

1820
Missouri
Compromise

1823
Monroe Doctrine
proclaimed

1828
Jackson
elected
President

1816   1819   1822   1825   1828

CHAPTER OUTLINE

1. A spirit of nationalism sparks American life.

2. American foreign policy reflects national pride.

3. Sectional differences check the growth of nationalism.

4. Sectional rivalry becomes more intense.

In the aftermath of the War of 1812, a new America emerged. Having endured what many people called the Second War of Independence, the United States felt fresh confidence in the future. Albert Gallatin noticed the change in people: "They are more American; they feel and act more like a nation."

Still flushed with what it considered *its* victory in the war, the Republican Party in 1816 was able to elect to the presidency another Virginian, James Monroe. Soon after taking office, Monroe left Washington, D.C., to tour the North. He was pleasantly surprised by the warm reception he received. A Federalist newspaper in Boston, commenting on the festivity that marked the President's visit to the city, talked of the "Era of Good Feelings." In time the name was used to characterize Monroe's years as President.

The "Era of Good Feelings" was not an altogether accurate description of American life from 1817 to 1825. Although Americans shared a rich feeling of national pride, differences between the sections were also growing stronger. On the surface, nevertheless, national politics seemed calm.

Monroe himself became a fatherly symbol of national unity. Tall and erect, he looked something like George Washington. For many people he was a warm reminder of the Revolutionary days, the last of the generation that had created the republic. Having served as a senator, governor, and diplomat, he seemed well prepared to be President.

1 A Spirit of Nationalism Sparks American Life

After the War of 1812, Americans' pride in their young nation was more noticeable than ever. Observers could see that the spirit of *nationalism* — devotion to one's country — was affecting all aspects of American life.

PRIDE OF COUNTRY

Symbols remind Americans of the nation's glories. Americans were surrounding themselves with tangible evidence of their national heritage. History textbooks emphasized the superiority of the United States, contrasting it sharply with "worn-out" Europe. Spellers and readers, like those first published by Noah Webster in the 1780's, earnestly preached patriotism. Just as important was Webster's dictionary, which first appeared in 1806. It modified the British spelling, usage, and pronunciation of many words, helping to create a distinctly *American* language.

Whereas language was the strongest bond of union Americans had, they were also moved by various symbols of the nation. One was the flag itself. First flown during the American Revolution, the flag's design was changed several times before 1818. In that year Congress agreed to set the number of stripes at thirteen and to add a star each time a state joined the Union.

Uncle Sam, as a representation of the United States, had first appeared during the War of 1812. The original Uncle Sam was a meat-packer from New York named Sam Wilson, who supplied local troops. The earliest cartoon of Uncle Sam — a hard-working figure who was incredibly strong — did not appear until 1853. Long before then, "Uncle Sam" had come into common use as a synonym for "the United States."

The bald eagle, adopted as the national bird in 1782, came more and more into use as a decoration for such items as chinaware, furniture, magazines, watch chains — for almost everything. Likenesses of this large, powerful bird were stamped on the country's coins, too, "to encourage a national spirit and to foster national pride."

The Liberty Bell was another hallowed emblem. It was tolled in 1776 to announce the adoption of the Declaration of Independence. Later, its peal was reserved for occasions of patriotic significance.

The Fourth of July was an intangible but no less significant symbol. It reminded the nation each year of the sacrifices of the

After the War of 1812, Americans felt great confidence in their nation. Citizens of a small New Hampshire town displayed their pride in a Fourth of July parade.

Revolutionary generation. Americans celebrated the "glorious Fourth" with feasts and parades. Even amid the dangers of their journey through the Louisiana Territory, Lewis and Clark took time to celebrate Independence Day with "a sumptuous dinner of fat saddles of venison."

The nation also acquired fresh heroes just as the giants of the Revolution were passing from the scene. The most important was Andrew Jackson, a new kind of patriotic model. His affectionate nickname, "Old Hickory," attested to the fact that he came from the frontier, not from the comforts of the East. His triumph at New Orleans in 1815 had rescued the nation from frustration. He had offered living proof that an iron will can overcome all obstacles.

Signs of the nation's growth are a source of pride. Americans had only to look about them to see examples of their country's rapid growth. The population, which had stood at 5,300,000 in 1800, was almost twice that number in 1820. The cities of Boston and New York doubled in size during that same period. Western towns such as Pittsburgh, Cincinnati, Louisville, and New Orleans expanded even more rapidly. The steady growth of urban communities foretold the future, even though the nation would long remain almost entirely rural. In 1820 only four cities could boast more than 50,000 people. Well over 90 percent of the population lived in rural areas.

Despite the spread-out population, new technological developments were starting to link the parts of the country together. The most important invention was the steamboat. Until it appeared, most river traffic could not travel other than downstream. Only by means of sails or towlines, or by poles pushed into the river bottom, was a keel boat able to go upstream. Through incredible exertions, for example, a crew of about 30 could take such a boat the 975 miles up the Mississippi from New Orleans to Cairo, Illinois. A journey like this could take three months. Because it was so hard to travel upstream, flatboats were usually sent down the Mississippi, unloaded, and sold for wood at New Orleans. The captain

and the crew would then return home on foot or horseback.

The steamboat brought about a revolution in transportation. The first successful one — Robert Fulton's *Clermont* — had chugged up the Hudson River in 1807. Soon it was possible to travel the ninety miles from New York to Philadelphia in thirteen hours. During the War of 1812, the *Vesuvius* journeyed from Pittsburgh to New Orleans in nine and a half days. On a visit to Savannah, Georgia, in 1819, James Monroe went on a day's excursion aboard a steamboat, the first President to ride on one. Passengers were by then traveling on vessels that provided dining facilities and other comforts. While thousands of flatboats continued in operation for fifty years, steamboats dominated the waterways.

The nation's expanding postal service took advantage of the steamboats to help Americans in the West keep their connections in the East. In 1802 the country had fewer than a thousand post offices; by 1817 there were 3,459. In 1801 there were 25,000 miles of post roads; by 1817 there were twice as many. Moreover, by the end of the War of 1812, post roads were being laid west of the Mississippi.

These striking developments went hand-in-hand with the increasing size of the Union itself. During Washington's presidency, the term "western states" meant only Kentucky (admitted in 1792) and Tennessee (admitted in 1796). Now, however, new states were entering the Union with astonishing frequency. Ohio joined in 1803, Louisiana in 1812, Indiana in 1816, Mississippi in 1817, Illinois in 1818, and Alabama in 1819. By then the flag bore 22 stars.[1]

THE VOICE OF NATIONALISM

Marshall's Court interprets the Constitution. While the nation was growing physically, the Constitution was being strengthened through a series of Supreme Court decisions. Under Chief Justice John Marshall's

---

[1] Vermont, finally settling a long-standing dispute with New York over territorial jurisdiction, had entered the Union as the fourteenth state in 1791.

Impressions of the Nation's Capital

As a young man eager to learn more about his country, Arthur Singleton left Boston in 1814 and toured the United States. His travels brought him to Washington, D.C., which he described in a letter to his brother.

Since Congress is still in session, I shall tarry two or three weeks. This little district, of ten miles square, whose name is an honor paid to the great Columbus, is the proud jewel in the ample ring of the Union. How ennobling to the feeling of an American President to stand upon Capitol Hill and to cast his thoughts northward, and southward, and westward, over our vast and free continent, and to reflect that he is the chosen leader of all he surveys, and whose right there is none to dispute.

I went for a number of days into the galleries of the Senate chamber and the hall of Representatives, where strangers listen to the debates. The heart is impressed with an emotion of awe and noble pride when one beholds this venerable body, legislating for the good of the country. In the balcony are seen rows of ladies and gentlemen sitting up and observing the goings-on below. Down in the body of the House, you behold, from all points of the compass, individuals with diverging minds gathering for a common purpose.

Capitol Hill

One subject discussed in the House while I was present was how to encourage manufacturing in America. It was debated whether it would not be a good idea for Congress to require that the legislatures of each state oblige their members to wear domestically made suits. The rationale offered was that when great men present a good example, the little men will soon follow their lead and purchase clothing manufactured in our country.

bold direction, the supremacy of the national government over the states was irreversibly established.

Marshall, who had been appointed Chief Justice in 1801, served until 1835 when he was in his eightieth year. By his far-reaching decisions he showed that the Constitution was a living document, capable of being adapted to the changing size and needs of the nation.

Despite his lack of training as a lawyer, Marshall had the ability to write decisions in clear, precise language. His decisions were often criticized, but their logic was solid. A fellow Virginian, angry over one of them, growled, "All wrong, all wrong, but no man in the United States can tell why or wherein."

The Supreme Court declares a state law unconstitutional. In 1803 Marshall rendered his famous decision in *Marbury v. Madison* (page 213), when the Supreme Court asserted the power to declare unconstitutional a law passed by Congress. In 1810, in the case of *Fletcher v. Peck*, Marshall again broke fresh ground. These are the facts the Court faced: In 1795 Georgia's legislature had made a grant of the state's western land to four land companies. The following year, finding that fraud had been involved in the transaction, the legislature annulled the grant. Did the legislature have the right to do this, in effect breaking a contract?

Marshall unhesitatingly answered no. The legislature's act of annulment, he asserted, was unconstitutional. He sidestepped the issue of the fraud involved, saying that to look into "the corruption of the sovereign power of a state" would be "indecent." By his shrewd decision Marshall had upheld the sanctity of contract, which is necessary to the proper conduct of business. He had also paid respect to the independence of state authority, establishing at the same time the right of the Supreme Court to declare a state law unconstitutional. In 1816, in *Martin v. Hunter's Lessee*, the Supreme Court affirmed its power also to overturn the decision of a state court.

Marshall defends the sanctity of charters. In 1819, in the case of *Dartmouth College v. Woodward*, Marshall went further in defending the sanctity of contracts. Dartmouth College, situated in New Hampshire, had been chartered by the British king in 1769. In 1816 the state of New Hampshire sought to alter the terms of the charter and reorganize the college. Could the charter be changed? Again the Court decided firmly. It asserted that a charter is a contract, "the obligation of which cannot be [altered] without violating the Constitution of the United States." Later, the Dartmouth College decision would have immense significance for the growth of American corporations, which depend on rights granted in charters.

The Supreme Court upholds the national bank. Marshall rendered yet another momentous decision in 1819. This one upheld the power of Congress to legislate on any subject it deemed necessary. In 1818 Maryland had passed a law requiring each bank engaged in business within the state, even if not chartered by it, to pay an annual tax of $15,000. Two years earlier, Congress had chartered the Second Bank of the United States which had opened a branch in Baltimore. The cashier of the Baltimore branch, James McCulloch, refused to pay the tax. Maryland sued to collect it.

In this case, *McCulloch v. Maryland*, Marshall had to answer two questions. (1) Did Congress have the power to incorporate a bank? (2) Was Maryland's tax on the Bank of the United States constitutional?

To the first question Marshall replied that the establishment of the bank was "necessary and proper" for the exercise of the powers granted to Congress in the Constitution. To the second question Marshall replied with no less certainty. A state, he said, may not tax an agency of the federal government. He used these words: "The power to tax involves the power to destroy. . . . The power to destroy may defeat and render useless the power to create." All governments are limited, Marshall declared, but Congress must have "that discretion . . . which will enable [it] to perform the high duties assigned to it, in the manner most beneficial to the people."

To a large extent, Marshall relied on Hamilton's 1791 arguments on the bank (page 181). So long as a law was constitutional, Marshall concluded, the federal government could use any legitimate means to carry out the law's purposes.

Marshall deals with interstate commerce. In 1824 another case leading to an influential decision came to the Supreme Court. The case involved the all-important commerce clause of the Constitution. In 1808 the New York legislature had given Robert Livingston and Robert Fulton the exclusive right to navigate the waters of New York State by steamboat. Livingston and Fulton, in turn, granted a man named Aaron Ogden sole permission to run steamboats between New York and New Jersey. Thomas Gibbons refused to accept Ogden's monopoly. Could he operate competing boats?

In deciding the case, *Gibbons v. Ogden*, Marshall said that the monopoly granted by New York was illegal. He pointed out that Congress alone had the power to regulate interstate and foreign commerce. The importance of this decision was enormous. Within a few years both steamboats and railroads were helping bind the nation tightly together, without the restrictions of old-fashioned state monopolies.

Marshall expresses national sentiment.
Some of Marshall's opinions have been modified or discarded, but their effect has been lasting. Marshall spoke for nationalism at a time when states' rights sentiment was strong. To him the Supreme Court was a platform from which he could proclaim the authority of the nation. At the heart of his decisions was the principle that the Constitution is not a mere compact of convenience among the states, but a permanent agreement of the *people.* To act on behalf of the people as a whole is the work of the federal government. Marshall gave voice to this view in the case of *Cohens v. Virginia* (1821), when he upheld the right of citizens to appeal convictions in state courts to the federal judiciary. "In war we are one people," he wrote. "In making peace we are one people. . . . In many other respects the American people are one, and the government which is alone capable of controlling and managing their interests in all these respects is the government of the Union."

SECTION REVIEW

1. Vocabulary: *nationalism.*
2. What symbols of national unity became important to Americans in the early 1800's?
3. (a) How did the nation and its cities grow in population from 1800 to 1820? (b) What important improvements were made in transportation?
4. What states entered the Union from 1803 to 1819?
5. What was the decision of the Supreme Court in each of the following cases? (a) *Fletcher v. Peck* (b) *Dartmouth College v. Woodward* (c) *McCulloch v. Maryland* (d) *Gibbons v. Ogden* (e) *Cohens v. Virginia*
6. What was the long-lasting significance of John Marshall's court decisions?

2 American Foreign Policy Reflects National Pride

Even as Marshall's decisions were helping create a powerful sense of nationhood, dealings with other countries were also strengthening American patriotism.

Troubles arise with Spain. Florida had long been a trouble spot in American relations with Spain. Madison, in 1810, had issued a proclamation authorizing occupation of part of West Florida (page 225). At that time Spain was too deeply involved in the war against Napoleon to do anything to stop the Americans.

During the War of 1812, Congress annexed another portion of West Florida. By 1816 it appeared that East Florida too would soon become American, and negotiations with Spain began. Spain's ability to maintain order in Florida had notably declined. Revolutions for independence in Spain's other American colonies had forced the Spanish to withdraw some of their soldiers from Florida. Seminole Indians now took to raiding across the border into Georgia. The Seminoles were in an angry mood because their Creek kinfolk, having been driven out of Georgia, had been forced to find refuge in Seminole territory in Florida. Georgians themselves were irate that runaway slaves were escaping to Florida.

Andrew Jackson invades West Florida. Late in 1817 the Georgia-Florida frontier became inflamed by conflict between Indians and white settlers. Andrew Jackson was appointed commander of American forces on the border. The hero of New Orleans was instructed to proceed to Fort Scott, on the Apalachicola River, to put an end to the fighting. His orders permitted him to pursue the Seminoles into Florida if necessary. Jackson also had in mind driving the Spanish out of Florida. He wrote President Monroe, "Let it be signified to me . . . that the possession of the Floridas would be desirable to the United States and in sixty days it will be accomplished."

The Monroe administration neither approved Jackson's aggressiveness nor discouraged it. Considering the official silence to be approval to act, Jackson marched into Florida and seized the Spanish fort at St. Marks in April, 1818. He captured several other towns, including Pensacola, and claimed the surrounding territory for the United States. He even seized two British subjects, Alexander Arbuthnot and Robert

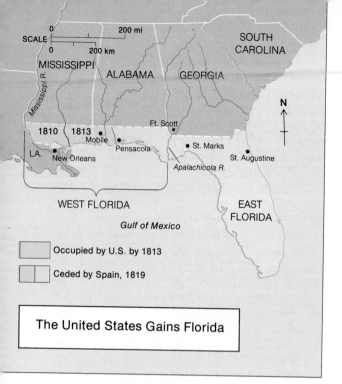

The United States Gains Florida

When Spain ceded Florida in 1819, the United States gained additional river outlets to the Gulf of Mexico.

Ambrister, whom he charged with inciting the Seminoles to raid American territory. After a speedy trial, Jackson had the two men executed.

Jackson's high-handed behavior was severely criticized in Congress. Still, when Jackson returned to Tennessee after less than two months in the field, he was welcomed as a hero. A popular toast expressed local feelings: "The Floridas — ours without sixteen years of negotiations."[2]

A storm of protest broke out in Spain and Britain. In both countries there was much talk of going to war to avenge the misdeeds of the Americans. The President and his entire Cabinet, with one exception, agreed that Jackson had indeed misbehaved. Secretary of State John Quincy Adams, on the other hand, vigorously supported the general. Jackson's actions, he said, had been necessary in order to defend the United States. Adams told Spain that if it could not maintain order in Florida, it must cede the

---

[2]Many Americans believed that the United States had actually acquired Florida years earlier in the Louisiana Purchase and had vainly been negotiating with France and Spain to make good the title to it.

territory to the United States. For the time being, the austere Adams and the flamboyant Jackson were in agreement.

The Adams-Onís Treaty gives the United States control of Florida. Because of trouble it was having in its other American colonies, Spain yielded. Following extensive negotiations, the Adams-Onís Treaty was signed on Washington's Birthday in 1819. Under the terms of the treaty, Spain gave up all claim to West Florida (already in American hands anyway) and turned East Florida over to the United States as well. The *western* limits of the Louisiana Purchase were also defined, producing the zigzag line shown on the map (page 219). Adams had, in effect, yielded American claims to Texas, but in return he had acquired Spain's claim to the Oregon Country — the land north of the 42nd parallel. The United States, for its part, agreed to pay the claims of its citizens against Spain (about $5 million).

Adams joyfully signed the treaty document, for he had won a great triumph in American diplomatic history. He knew that the United States had entered a new era of territorial growth.

The settlement took on added importance because in the Convention of 1818 the United States and Britain had agreed to occupy the Oregon Country jointly for ten years. At the same time, the border between the United States and British North America had been fixed along the 49th parallel, from the Lake of the Woods to the Rockies. In this way, the *northern* boundary of the Louisiana Purchase was established.

Spain loses its American colonies. The sale of Florida was another step in the shrinking of Spain's American empire. While the wars with Napoleon were going on in Europe, successful independence movements had been launched in most of Spain's colonies. Americans naturally sympathized with these revolutions. By 1818 some members of Congress were urging the Monroe administration to grant formal recognition to the newly created republics. Monroe refused, however, until the Adams-Onís treaty was formally ratified by Spain — lest

Spain back out of the agreement. In 1822, when the Spanish government finally acted, the United States quickly recognized the independence of Mexico, Peru, Chile, Colombia, and Argentina.

European nations threaten the Americas. The crowned heads of Europe were frightened by the events in Spain's American possessions. They saw the revolutions as evidence that the Spirit of '76 was still spreading. When peace was restored in Europe in 1815, many people believed that Spain would try, with the help of France, or perhaps even Russia, to recover control of its former colonies. What made the possibility of such a threat to America seem believable was that Russia, Prussia, Austria, and Great Britain had formed an alliance (later joined by France) to preserve peace and resist all revolutionary movements. The stated intentions of this alliance aroused deep concern in the United States.

Americans' fears were reinforced by events on the Pacific coast. In September, 1821, Czar Alexander I extended Russian claims in North America southward into the Oregon Country (map, page 322). All foreign ships were ordered to keep out of the region. Russian influence extended even farther south. Just north of San Francisco, at Fort Ross (map, page 327), Russian settlers had been operating an iron foundry for many years, producing iron for plows and bells.

John Quincy Adams felt he was a good judge of Russia's intentions. At the age of fourteen he had served as the secretary to the United States minister in Russia. In 1809 he himself had become minister. In occasional walks with the czar, he had become familiar with the monarch's thinking. Adams was ready to be as firm in his dealings with the Russians as he had been with the Spanish. In July, 1823, he warned the Russian ambassador that the United States would "contest the right of Russia to *any* territorial establishment on this continent." Furthermore, Adams added, "the American continents are no longer subjects for *any* new European colonial establishments." These blunt words were an assertion that a new power among nations was coming into its own. How, though, could the United States make its position heard in the world at large?

Britain proposes joint action. An opportunity appeared in the following month. Great Britain and the United States had a common aim regarding Spain's former colonies. Both countries desired a larger share in the valuable trade with the new republics than they had previously been allowed by Spain. Both feared, in addition, that France, through helping Spain, might once again try to gain territory in the Americas. In August, 1823, therefore, George Canning, the British foreign secretary, made a remarkable proposal to Richard Rush, the United States minister to London. Canning suggested that the United States join Britain in a warning to the powers of Europe that any attempt to help Spain recover its colonies would be opposed by force.

President Monroe was wary of Canning's proposal, recalling George Washington's advice to keep out of "the toils of European ambitions." Monroe decided to seek the opinions of former Presidents Jefferson and Madison. They responded quickly that now was a good time to stand with Britain. With Great Britain "on our side," Jefferson said, "we need not fear the whole world." Madison echoed this sentiment. When the Cabinet met in November, however, it was Adams's view that prevailed. Adams insisted that the United States should act alone. He argued, in words that became famous, "It would be more candid, as well as more dignified, to avow our principles explicitly to Russia and France, than to come in as a cockboat in the wake of the British man-of-war."

Adams had other reasons for not joining Britain in a declaration against European intervention. Canning had also proposed that neither Britain nor the United States take over any former Spanish colonies. Adams believed that one day Cuba or Texas might ask for annexation to the United States. He wanted to be sure that a blast against any new European meddling in the Americas be understood to apply to Britain too.

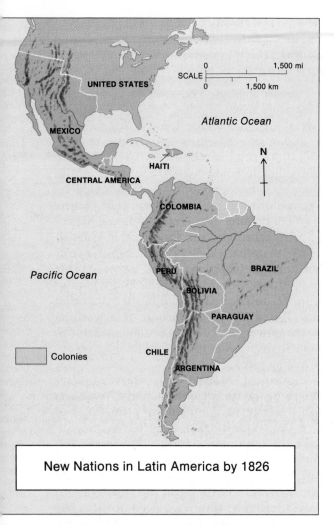

New Nations in Latin America by 1826

By 1826, a number of Spanish colonies had succeeded in breaking away from Spanish rule and establishing their independence. Brazil had declared its independence from Portuguese rule in 1822.

The Monroe Doctrine is proclaimed. Having persuaded his colleagues that his judgment was right, Adams had its substance included in President Monroe's annual message to Congress on December 2, 1823. The message contained four main points: (1) The American continents were "henceforth not to be considered as subjects for future colonization by any European powers." (2) The United States would oppose any attempt to extend the European system of monarchy to the Americas. (3) The United States would not interfere with existing European colonies in the Americas. (4) The United States would not interfere in the internal affairs of European countries.

Monroe's words, long afterward labeled the Monroe Doctrine, in time became respected as the keystone of United States foreign policy. When this policy was issued, however, it made little impression in Europe. The Russian ambassador declared that it merited "only the most profound contempt." Years would pass before other nations would listen intently to the words of American Presidents.

Monroe's words were a statement not of defiance, but of America's intention to isolate itself from Europe. The Doctrine was a second Declaration of Independence. The original Declaration had been directed only at Britain; this one was directed at all of Europe on behalf of all the Americas. Its bold language appealed to national self-esteem. In a tone of pride, a Boston newspaper boasted that if the European powers tried "to control the destinies of South America, they will find not only a lion, but an eagle in the way."

Although European monarchs ridiculed Monroe's proclamation, they knew the British navy would back up its principles. They made no attempt, therefore, to restore Spain's American colonies. Spain eventually recognized the independence of those former colonies, while Russia and the United States signed a treaty in 1824 fixing the southern boundary of Alaska at 54°40'. The director of the Russian foundry at Fort Ross expressed his disappointment. He had assumed, he said, that Russia had the right to annex "the whole continent up to the Rocky Mountains."

In spite of its interest in supporting the Latin American republics, the United States did not make common cause with them. When Simon Bolívar, the "Liberator" of South America, tried to form a federation of republics in 1824, he invited the United States to the founding conference. The Americans, however, refused to participate. Defenders of slavery in the United States feared the effects on the slave population if American delegates sat down with delegates from the black republic of Haiti.

1. (a) What situation along the Georgia-Florida border was Andrew Jackson sent to resolve? (b) How did Jackson go beyond his orders?
2. (a) What were the terms of the Adams-Onís Treaty? (b) Describe the borders of the United States after that treaty was signed.
3. (a) What was the reaction of the United States to the efforts of Spain's American colonies to win independence? (b) Why was the United States suspicious of both Spanish and Russian intentions in the Americas?
4. (a) Why did John Quincy Adams reject Britain's proposal for joint action against other European powers? (b) How did the Monroe Doctrine reflect Adams's views on foreign policy?

3 Sectional Differences Check the Growth of Nationalism

The Federalist Party, disgraced by the Hartford Convention (page 231), had nominated in 1816 what proved to be its last candidate for President, Senator Rufus King of New York. The party then disappeared, as Federalist merchants, manufacturers, and bankers discovered that their needs were being met by the Republicans. Ironically, the measures Alexander Hamilton had once advocated — a national bank, government encouragement of manufacturing, a tariff, and a strong army and navy — were now pet projects of the Republicans. The Republicans, a New Englander observed, had "out-Federalized Federalism."

The Republicans adopt Federalist policies. In 1816 the Republicans enthusiastically chartered the Second Bank of the United States. All government funds would be deposited in it for safekeeping. The bank would be subject to the scrutiny of Congress, which had the power to revoke its charter. In return for its charter, the bank would pay a bonus of $1.5 million into the United States Treasury. Not all sections agreed that the bank was a good thing. Many Westerners opposed it, believing that a bank located in the East would not respond to their needs for credit.

Like the bill to renew the bank, the Tariff of 1816 also grew out of the nationalistic enthusiasm that followed the War of 1812. Hamilton would have chuckled to know that Madison himself had recommended the tariff bill to Congress! Moreover, members of Congress from every section of the country voted for it. They believed that Britain was trying to stunt the growth of American manufacturing by flooding American markets with low-priced goods.

Southerners, like John C. Calhoun of South Carolina, voted for the bill, thinking that a tariff might yet encourage his section to develop manufacturing. Westerners too

The Capitol, devastated in the War of 1812, was restored by 1819. Members of Congress in the ensuing years faced serious sectional disagreements.

243

were agreeable to the bill. Recognizing the high costs of transporting goods into the interior states, they could foresee the building of factories inland. They also understood that as domestic industry grew, the market for farm products would expand. Americans were, in short, accepting the coming of industry as a benefit to all.

A Republican split develops. After the disappearance of the Federalists, only the Republicans were a national party. Even they, however, split into two factions which developed into two new parties.

One faction consisted of those who remained faithful to the views of the early Republicans. They still argued, as Madison had in the 1790's, for strict construction of the Constitution and for economic principles fashioned by the Jeffersonians. These older Republicans continued to envision an America of free farmers, small shopkeepers, and independent craftworkers.

The other faction was made up of those young Republicans who had accepted the idea of a strong national government. They insisted that the national government encourage economic development.

The leader of the young Republican faction was Henry Clay. Clay had a picture in his mind of the nation bound together by economic ties as well as by those of patriotic sentiment. Unlike the old Republicans, however, he foresaw a country whose future lay in the West. The nation, he believed, would one day extend westward to the Pacific and southward to the Rio Grande. Clay saw this vision being realized through *internal improvements* — the building of roads and canals financed by federal money.

Sectional differences arise. Although the two groups of Republicans disagreed sharply in their political views, they both continued until 1823 to call themselves Republicans. As a result, many Americans believed the nation had just one party. This fact added to the general feeling of harmony during Monroe's presidency. Nevertheless, the idea of internal improvements — the program of the young Republicans — was causing disagreements among the sections.

People in the Middle Atlantic states could see that a system of internal improvements would give them better means of transportation to the interior. Many New Englanders, however, were less enthusiastic and therefore less eager to pay taxes to provide for internal improvements. They could see themselves increasingly cut off from the rest of the nation as it expanded west. Moreover, improved transportation might drain away the labor supply so badly needed in the port cities and in the factories now appearing in Massachusetts. Southerners were divided in their opinion. Those who lived on the coast did not think they would benefit from canals and roads built west of the fall line. Those in the interior, however, could see themselves aided significantly in getting their products to market.

Sectional rivalry also became an issue when hard times struck the country in 1819. Many farmers in the South and West, unable to borrow money, blamed the bank — "the Monster," as they called it. Eastern business leaders, however, defended the bank because it aided their activities.

The admission of Missouri starts a conflict over slavery. The differences between the sections were further highlighted by a sharp disagreement that arose in 1819. The occasion was the application of Missouri to enter the Union. The debate in Congress that followed was destined to shake the nation to its foundations, for underlying the controversy was the question of slavery.

When Missouri submitted its application to enter the Union as a slave state, many antislavery Northerners were angered. Under an unwritten agreement in Congress, the number of slave states had been kept equal to the number of free states. Illinois had entered as a free state in 1818, creating an imbalance in the North's favor which Alabama's admission, in 1819, had corrected. Missouri's statehood, however, would throw the balance off again.

Tallmadge's compromise is rejected. In response to this knotty subject, Representative James Tallmadge of New York offered an amendment to the bill calling for Missouri's admission. The amendment would

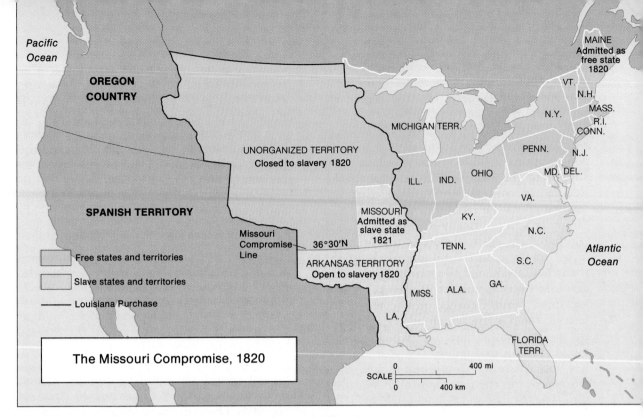

The Missouri Compromise maintained the balance of sectional power in the Senate.

have prohibited the entry of slaves into Missouri. Moreover, the amendment provided that the children of slaves already in Missouri would be freed upon reaching the age of 25. Tallmadge hated slavery, and he was urging a step he believed could prevent slavery from crossing the Mississippi. Immediately, however, the country was in an uproar. Wrote Monroe, "I have never known a question so menacing to the tranquility and even the continuance of our Union as the present one."

Monroe, in a way, reflected the nation's dilemma on the subject of slavery. Like many otherwise humane people, he owned slaves. His response to the slavery question was to support the American Colonization Society, a group that favored the establishment in Africa of a colony to which black Americans could be sent. The colony, started in 1821, was called Liberia — "land of liberty." Liberia honored the President by naming its capital Monrovia.

Tallmadge's bill to admit Missouri passed the House but met defeat in the Senate. The issue came up again at the end of 1819 when a new Congress had gathered.

Fierce arguments ensued over the question of Congress's power to prohibit slavery in a new state. What especially troubled Southerners was that in the House of Representatives the free states already had 24 more seats than the slave states. The balance still held in the Senate, but the admission of Missouri as a free state would give the North the advantage in that body too. If Congress could bar slavery in one state, the South asked, what could prevent it from voting abolition in all the states?

The Missouri Compromise is accepted. The deadlock was broken by a compromise. Maine had just applied for admission as a free state. Senator Jesse B. Thomas of Illinois proposed that both Maine and Missouri be admitted to the Union. Maine, it was understood, would be free, and Missouri, slave. Slavery, however, was to be barred in the rest of the Louisiana Territory north of the parallel 36°30'. The balance of power in the Senate would be maintained, with twelve free and twelve slave states.

In completing the compromise, Henry Clay, a keen defender of national unity, played a crucial part in persuading his colleagues in Congress to accept the measure. Somewhat unwillingly, Monroe signed the bill containing what was known thereafter as the Missouri Compromise. He believed that limiting the spread of slavery was unconstitutional. John Quincy Adams also supported the compromise reluctantly, believing, in contrast to Monroe, that any "bargain between freedom and slavery" was "morally and politically vicious." Jefferson compared the entire debate to the sounding of a fire alarm in the middle of the night, for it had awakened the nation to the dangerously divisive subject of slavery. A congressman from Georgia prophesied, "You have kindled a fire which all the waters of the ocean cannot put out, which seas of blood can only extinguish!"

The Missouri Compromise had been worked out in the new Capitol in Washington. The House and Senate each held sessions in its own rectangular wing of the structure, rebuilt after the British destroyed it in 1814. The restored House chamber was hung with scarlet silk curtains, as much for their elegance as to muffle annoying echoes. Some people thought that they and the canopy which framed Speaker Clay's chair were too regal for a republican country. Still, the House — and the Senate, no less handsomely adorned — now became the center of national political life. What was said there soon rumbled across the country as words to be listened to and heeded. Speeches that became famous would be quoted again and again. Students in school would learn some of them by heart. Because of the silver-tongued oratory that characterized the next forty years, the period has been called America's Silver Age.

The sections debate the tariff. In 1820 the popular Monroe was re-elected, winning all but one vote in the electoral college. Even Monroe, however, could not prevent the growing tendency of the sections to pull apart from one another. The tariff was a principal cause of southern dissatisfaction. By 1820, the South had concluded that a tariff to protect manufacturing was damaging to the section's interests. The South clearly was not going to be a manufacturing region. It would need to import, therefore, at as low a price as possible, factory goods produced elsewhere.

Western farmers and eastern business leaders, however, kept up the pressure for a higher tariff. Henry Clay, his heart set on becoming President, tried to form a political alliance made up of these two groups, and become its leader.

Clay proposes the American System. Henry Clay called his program for achieving this goal the "American System." Manufacturers would get a protective tariff on foreign goods. This protection would allow eastern manufactured goods to be sold in the South and West. In return, these areas could provide foodstuffs and raw materials to the workers of the North and East. Westerners would get internal improvements, paid for, in part, by the increased customs receipts. The American System was a plan, in sum, that would bind the nation together economically, making the United States self-sufficient in war and peace.

Despite southern opposition, Congress passed a new protective tariff in 1824. Clay's American System, however, was never fully enacted into law. Most of the costs of internal improvements were left to the states or to private individuals.

SECTION REVIEW

1. Vocabulary: *internal improvements*.
2. (a) What happened to the Federalist Party after 1816? (b) What policies formerly supported by the Federalists were taken up by the Republicans?
3. What differences of opinion began to divide the Republicans into two factions?
4. (a) What disagreements developed between the sections of the country over the spending of government money on roads and canals? (b) Over the Bank of the United States?
5. (a) For what reasons did Missouri's application to enter the Union stir up controversy? (b) What were the terms of the Missouri Compromise?
6. (a) Why had the tariff become a point of sectional disagreement? (b) What was Henry Clay's American System, and what part did the tariff have in that plan?

4 Sectional Rivalry Becomes More Intense

In 1824, the Marquis de Lafayette, on Monroe's invitation, returned to the United States after an absence of forty years. A highlight of his journey through America came in December when Congress officially received him, making Lafayette the first foreigner to speak before a joint meeting. His presence in the refurbished House chamber thrilled the members. What satisfaction he must have felt to see a republican legislature flourishing in such a splendid setting. Nevertheless, forces were at work below the surface that would show how fragile the national unity really was.

The 1824 campaign is a sectional contest. Soon after Lafayette's nostalgic visit, the United States was embroiled in a presidential election campaign. Each section had at least one candidate. All of the candidates were Republicans.

John Quincy Adams had the strong backing of his native New England. He believed the White House was rightfully his because he had served as Secretary of State. Each of the Virginia Presidents except Washington, he could note, had stepped up from that office.

The West had two candidates: Henry Clay and Andrew Jackson. Clay hoped his American System would bring to his side enough New Englanders who otherwise would support Adams. Jackson, beloved son of the frontier, aimed to be strong outside his own section too. He emphasized his southern birth and presented himself in the North as a friend of the protective tariff. (He also had important critics — like Jefferson, who considered him totally unfit for the White House.)

William H. Crawford of Georgia was the southern candidate. Crawford had strong backing in other sections as well. In 1823, however, he suffered a crippling illness that effectively ended his candidacy. John C. Calhoun, "the young men's candidate," was also available. He finally agreed not to run for the presidency but to be a candidate for Vice President.

John Quincy Adams becomes President. When the returns were in, Jackson had 99 electoral votes, Adams had 84, Crawford had 41, and Clay had 37.[3] A majority (131 votes) was needed for election. Under the terms of the Twelfth Amendment the names of the top three candidates were sent to the House of Representatives, where the election would be decided.

Clay was in the position of being able to choose the next President by throwing his support to either Adams or Jackson. He persuaded his followers in the House to vote for Adams, because Adams backed the

---

[3]Calhoun, who had run on both the Jackson and Adams tickets, received a majority of the electoral votes for Vice President.

Although Jackson had the greatest number of electoral votes in the election of 1824, the contest was finally decided in the House of Representatives. The fate of the Jackson steamboat in this cartoon indicates the outcome of that election.

John Quincy Adams, son of the second President, continued a family tradition of government service.

American System. Moreover, Clay had long disliked Jackson, whom he regarded as lacking in political experience.

When the House voted, in February, 1825, Adams was elected President by a paper-thin margin. The deciding vote, which gave New York to Adams, was cast by Stephen Van Rensselaer, whom last we met in the War of 1812 (page 228). Van Rensselaer later told how he had bowed his head and prayed for divine guidance on how to vote. When he opened his eyes, he saw at his feet a ballot with Adams's name on it. He knew, he said, what he had to do.

Jackson's supporters boiled with rage on hearing that their man had been denied the presidency. When it became public that Clay had been appointed Secretary of State, the cry of "bargain and corruption" went up. In the politics of that day words were used as powerful weapons. Congressman John Randolph of Virginia, for instance, was known for his sarcasm. He once described an opponent as "a man of splendid abilities, but utterly corrupt. He shines and stinks like rotten mackerel by moonlight." Randolph now complained so heatedly about Clay's and Adams's "corrupt bargain" that Clay challenged him to a duel with pistols. Fortunately, when the duel took place, both men missed their target.

John Quincy Adams spends an unhappy term as President. Adams was 59 years old when he was elected President. Yet in many ways he belonged to the generation that had made the Revolution. As John Adams's son, he had met the giants of the age when only a boy. Like those men, he did not seek the popular acclaim that politicians now believed they needed. He once wrote, "I am a man of reserved, cold, austere [stern], and forbidding manners." Never modest, for more than fifty years Adams faithfully kept a diary that he was sure could become "next to the Holy Scriptures, the most precious and valuable book ever written by human hands." The diary reveals a man who could hate and love with passion. He felt no love more intensely than his love of the country he served.

Adams's administration opened under a dark cloud of distrust. In his inaugural address Adams admitted he was "less possessed of your confidence . . . than any of my predecessors." He promised an honest and dutiful term, but the Jackson people continued their assault on his integrity.

Adams worked hard as President. He usually rose between four and six o'clock, took a walk around the city, returned to the White House, lit the fireplace, and had breakfast. Then he was ready for work. His day ended late in the afternoon when he began writing his diary or reading important papers.

Adams had golden dreams for America. He hoped to see a national university and a national astronomical observatory established. He wanted the western territories to be held in trust by the federal government and slowly developed. He also desired that Congress promote the arts and sciences and standardize weights and measures.

In his first annual message to Congress, Adams advocated a vast expansion of road-

and canal-building with federal aid and a protective tariff. His program, which would have led to a strengthened national government, became caught in the cross-currents of sectional rivalry. The proposals alienated many Southerners and Westerners who believed that Adams had designed them chiefly to aid eastern business interests. Congress acted on few of Adams's recommendations.

Adams faced more savage attacks than his father, the nation's second President, had ever experienced. The son's opponents sneered, "The cub is a greater bear than the old one." The President confidently wrote, however, that his policies would "outlive the blast of faction and abide the test of time."

Jackson's supporters prepare for the 1828 election. Adams's energetic efforts were thwarted by the determination of Jackson's people to make their hero President in 1828. Indeed, they turned Adams's presidency into a four-year-long presidential campaign for their man. The administration's supporters were soon known as the National Republicans. The friends of Jackson, considering themselves the true heirs of Jefferson, took the name Democratic-Republicans, later shortened to Democrats.

The Democrats made the new tariff bill that came before Congress in 1828 their chief interest. Their complicated strategy was to propose so high a tariff that all sections of the country, even New England, would be against it. The blame for defeat of the tariff could then be placed upon President Adams (who was expected to veto it). To the surprise and embarrassment of many people, however, Congress passed this so-called "Tariff of Abominations," and Adams signed the bill. The South, resentful that tariff duties had been pushed so high, pledged revenge.

Andrew Jackson is elected President. Jackson and Adams faced each other again in the election of 1828. Jackson, "the people's choice," easily emerged victorious. He won every state west of the Appalachians and south of the Potomac and also captured Pennsylvania. John Calhoun was re-elected Vice President.

Andrew Jackson came into office accompanied by the thunderous cheers of Americans who felt that the White House was occupied at last by a people's President. The inaugural celebration turned into a mob scene. Crowds pressed into the White House to catch a glimpse of "Old Hickory." Women fainted in the crush, while crystal glasses and china table service were trampled upon. Men in muddy boots stood on the elegant furniture, purchased only a few years earlier by the Monroes and brought from Paris. In an attempt to lure people out of the mansion, an enormous punchbowl was placed on the White House lawn.

Adams had refused to attend the inauguration. He felt insulted that Jackson had ignored the practice of calling at the White House after the election to pay his respects. Adams could never fully accept Jackson's victory. When Harvard College decided to give Jackson an honorary Doctor of Laws degree in 1837, Adams was incensed at this act of his alma mater. He indignantly wrote that he would not "be present to witness [Harvard's] disgrace in conferring its highest honors upon a barbarian who could not write a sentence of grammar and hardly could spell his own name." Most Americans, however, were becoming accustomed to changes afoot in the nation. The president of Harvard might have been speaking in their behalf when he said of the award to President Jackson, "As the people have decided that this man knows law enough to be their ruler, it is not for Harvard College to maintain that they are mistaken."

SECTION REVIEW

1. (a) Who were the candidates in the 1824 presidential election? (b) How did John Quincy Adams become the winner?
2. (a) What were some of Adams's hopes for the nation? (b) Why did Adams fail to win support for his programs?
3. How did Jackson's supporters try to use a tariff bill in their campaign against Adams?
4. What was the outcome of the 1828 presidential election?

Chapter 10 Review

Summary

As the nineteenth century began, a new spirit of nationalism captured the feelings of Americans. These patriotic sentiments fostered national unity and created symbols around which citizens could rally. The flag, the bald eagle, the Liberty Bell, and the annual celebration of the Fourth of July all contributed to popular appreciation of the uniqueness of America's history and of its republican form of government.

The dynamic growth of the nation could be witnessed in the doubling of its population from 1800 to 1820. This growth was paralleled by the increasing vigor of the federal government. Under Chief Justice John Marshall, the Supreme Court made decisions which established the supremacy of the national government.

Americans' pride in their nation was also strengthened by dealings with other countries. Andrew Jackson's invasion of Florida led to the signing of the Adams-Onís Treaty in 1819. John Quincy Adams's firm stand against further European expansion into the Americas resulted in the proclamation of the Monroe Doctrine in 1823. Henceforth, the United States would oppose any further colonization or interference by European powers in the Western Hemisphere.

The spirit of national unity also appeared in politics, as the Republican Party adopted many of the views of the Federalists. Republicans were now sympathetic to the need for a national bank, a tariff, and encouragement of manufacturing. The Republicans did not, however, remain totally of one mind. Two factions developed — one favoring a rural economy with a limited federal role, the other advocating a strong national government and expansion into the western territories.

Sectional rivalry, in fact, was on the rise, and by the 1820's politicians were heatedly debating such subjects as internal improvements, tariff proposals, and the re-establishment of the Bank of the United States. The most divisive issue of all — that of slavery — was temporarily resolved by the Missouri Compromise.

Sectional differences became obvious in the presidential election of 1824 when each section of the country offered its own candidate. John Quincy Adams won the election, but supporters of Andrew Jackson were outraged, charging that a "corrupt bargain" had led to Adams's victory. Four years later the two candidates were rivals again, and this time Jackson was elected President.

Vocabulary and Important Terms

1. nationalism
2. Adams-Onís Treaty
3. Convention of 1818
4. Fort Ross
5. Monroe Doctrine
6. Second Bank of the United States
7. Tariff of 1816
8. internal improvements
9. American Colonization Society
10. Missouri Compromise
11. American System
12. Democratic-Republicans
13. Tariff of Abominations

Discussion Questions

1. Explain how evidence of a growing sense of nationalism could be seen in (a) Noah Webster's dictionary, (b) the American flag, (c) decisions of the Supreme Court, (d) the American System.
2. What belief about the Constitution was at the heart of John Marshall's Supreme Court decisions?
3. (a) Why was Spain unable to maintain order on the Georgia-Florida border? (b) Why did Andrew Jackson's actions in Florida cause trouble both abroad and at home? (c) How did John Quincy Adams use Jackson's actions to negotiate a treaty with Spain? (d) Why was the Adams-Onís Treaty a great American diplomatic victory?
4. (a) What factors made a European threat to America seem believable in the early 1820's? (b) How did the United States respond to that threat?
5. In what sense was the Monroe Doctrine a second Declaration of Independence?
6. (a) Why did the Federalist Party disappear? (b) What split then occurred within the Republican Party, and in what ways did the two factions differ from one another?
7. (a) Why did sectional differences arise over the issue of internal improvements? (b) How did the hard times that struck the country in 1819 further add to sectional rivalries? (c) What other disagreements added to the growth of sectional tensions?
8. (a) How was the election of 1824 a sectional contest? (b) Why did John Quincy Adams's administration open under a dark cloud of suspicion? (c) How successful was Adams as President?
9. Why did the election of Andrew Jackson as President in 1828 signify a shift in American politics?

Relating Past to Present

1. After the War of 1812 a growing sense of national unity swept the United States. To what extent

do Americans today have strong feelings of national unity? What are this country's strongest bonds of union?

2. How do the speeches of our nation's leaders today compare with the silver-tongued oratory of the years from 1820 to 1860? (Consider changes in methods of communication.)

Studying Local History

1. How does your community celebrate the Fourth of July? Are there annual events in your community that in other ways celebrate the national spirit? If so, what are they?

2. What did the flag of the United States look like at the time your state entered the Union? What symbols are part of your state flag?

Using History Skills

1. *Comparing maps.* Compare the map of Latin America on page 242 with the Atlas map of the world at the back of the book. (a) What new nations have appeared in South America since 1826? (b) Which Latin American colonies won their independence after 1826?

2. *Making connections.* Compare the three Presidents discussed in this chapter. How was James Monroe a reminder of the giants of Revolutionary days and Andrew Jackson a new kind of patriotic model? To which generation of American leaders did John Quincy Adams belong? Why?

3. *Reading source material.* Study the description of Washington, D.C., on page 237. How does Arthur Singleton make clear his pride in the United States?

WORLD SCENE

The Inspiration of Independence

The success of the United States in establishing a republic helped arouse in Mexico and South America the desire for independence from Spain.

Revolt in Mexico. In Mexico the independence movement started in 1810 with an Indian rebellion led by a priest named Miguel Hidalgo. Although successful in liberating several towns, his ill-equipped rebels were no match for the Spanish army sent to put down the revolt. Hidalgo was taken prisoner and executed, but the revolution did not end. For years the Mexican Indians continued to fight the Spanish from bases in the mountains.

When a revolt occurred in Spain itself in 1820, the Creoles (people of European descent born in Spanish America) saw an opportunity to take over Mexico for themselves. An ambitious Creole army officer named Agustín de Iturbide tricked the Mexican Indians into supporting the Creole cause. Then, after routing the Spanish garrison at Mexico City, he set himself up as emperor of Mexico. Those who had fought so long to establish a republic, however, soon forced him to flee. In 1824 a federal republic was at last brought into being in Mexico.

South American independence. Simón Bolívar, born to a wealthy Creole family in Caracas, was a leader in the struggle for Venezuelan independence. When the Spanish regained control of that country in 1814, Bolívar fled to Jamaica. By 1819 he had returned to Venezuela and assembled an army. Avoiding the strong Spanish force in Venezuela, Bolívar crossed the Andes and surprised the Spanish in Colombia. Over the next several years Bolívar freed Colombia, Venezuela, Ecuador, Panama, Bolivia, and Peru from Spanish rule. His efforts on behalf of South American independence earned him the title of "Liberator."

Meanwhile, in the south another liberator was winning battles against the Spanish. José de San Martín, like Bolívar, believed that no country in South America would be secure until Spanish authority had been completely eliminated. With a gallant army of patriots, San Martín left his native Argentina in 1817, crossed the high Andes, and defeated Spanish forces in Chile. In 1821 San Martín and his army entered Lima, Peru, and helped the former land of the Incas achieve independence. Later, his forces were united with those of Bolívar. In 1824 the two armies defeated the last strong Spanish forces at the Battle of Ayacucho (ah-yah-KOO-choh). Independence for all of Spanish South America had finally been won.

CHAPTER 11

The Jacksonians in Power

1829 – 1845

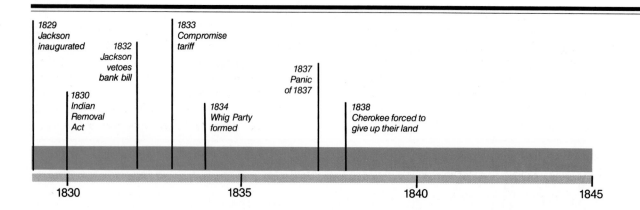

1829 Jackson inaugurated		1833 Compromise tariff			
1832 Jackson vetoes bank bill			1837 Panic of 1837		
1830 Indian Removal Act		1834 Whig Party formed		1838 Cherokee forced to give up their land	

1830   1835   1840   1845

CHAPTER OUTLINE

1. Jackson exercises strong powers as President.

2. Jackson kills the Bank of the United States.

3. The Jacksonian Era comes to an end.

4. The American people gain a larger share in the government.

5. The Whigs win the presidency.

Andrew Jackson was a man of contradictions. He was a Southerner, born in the Carolinas, who made his home in Tennessee. Yet he became the voice of politicians in the Northeast. He was one of the largest landholders of his state and a favorite of southern plantation owners. Yet he remained a frontiersman in spirit, holding many prejudices against people of wealth. He was set in his ways. Yet he became the beloved and fiery leader of a new political movement. Jackson himself once said, "I know what I am fit for. I can command a body of men in a rough way: but I am not fit to be President." Yet "Old Hickory" is regarded as one of the nation's most dynamic Presidents.

Jackson was the first American President born in poverty. On his own from the age of fourteen, he became a self-made man, living a life of action and achievement. When he came to Philadelphia in 1796 as Tennessee's first congressman, he wore the rough garb of the West. His hair, long in the back, was tied in a ponytail, frontier-style. No one could have guessed that 33 years later he would be President. Over the years, however, Jackson's reputation grew. A splendid soldier, he had begun his service as a mere boy in the Revolution, spending a brief time as a captive of the British. After he became a victorious general at New Orleans in 1815, he was never again out of the public eye.

1 Jackson Exercises Strong Powers as President

When he entered the White House in 1829, Andrew Jackson had no well-defined program of action. As one who felt it his duty to carry out the will of the people, however, he was not slow to tell Congress what he thought was best for the country.

Jackson depends on the advice of his "kitchen cabinet." President Jackson chose a Cabinet which included representatives from the groups in the country that had made his election possible. The most important figure in the Cabinet was Martin Van Buren, the Secretary of State. Van Buren was sometimes called "Old Kinderhook" (after the name of the village where he was born). He was a wily politician who could hide his aims so well that it was said he "rowed to his object with muffled oars." Jackson appreciated Van Buren's talent as a politician, and Van Buren quickly had the President's confidence.

The President depended upon Van Buren, but he rarely turned to the rest of the Cabinet for advice. He relied instead on an informal group of newspaper editors and northern politicians who had worked for his election. They came to be labeled the "kitchen cabinet." The most important member was Amos Kendall of Kentucky. Once a tutor to Henry Clay's children, Kendall, for personal reasons, had turned against his former employer and was now eager to help Jackson however he could.

Andrew Jackson, shown here at the Battle of New Orleans, exercised equally strong and vigorous leadership when he became President of the United States.

Rachel, Andrew Jackson's wife, suffered from the vicious attacks of his enemies. She fell ill and died only a few weeks before Jackson took office.

Kendall became known as "the moving spring of the administration; the thinker, the planner, the doer." Another member of the kitchen cabinet was Francis Preston Blair, a slight, sharp-eyed little man who weighed scarcely a hundred pounds. He had the task of editing the Washington *Globe,* a newspaper expressly established to praise the Jackson administration and its policies. Still another member was Major William B. Lewis of Tennessee. Lewis had worked for years to make Jackson, an old friend, President. While a member of the kitchen cabinet, Lewis lived at the White House.

The Eaton affair reveals divisions within the administration. It was the *official* Cabinet which raised a storm that came close to tearing the administration apart. Jackson had appointed an old friend, John H. Eaton, to be Secretary of War. Eaton's new bride was Peggy O'Neale, daughter of an innkeeper in Washington. Eaton, like Jackson, had occupied rooms at O'Neale's inn years before. Peggy O'Neale had acquired a bad reputation, however, and the other Cabinet wives, led by Floride Calhoun, wife of the

Vice President, refused to have anything to do with her. Jackson was enraged. Possibly he was reminded of how his own wife, Rachel, had once been slandered as a woman of low morals. Jackson would not allow this to happen to another woman he regarded as being under his protection. He battled his Cabinet so intently on Peggy O'Neale's behalf that soon he could not even meet with it. A story is told that Jackson visited Floride Calhoun in order to insist she return a call Peggy O'Neale had made upon her. Mrs. Calhoun, it was reported, ordered the President out of her house.

Calhoun and Van Buren maneuver for position. Jackson made up his mind that the cause of the trouble was Vice President Calhoun himself. Jackson's suspicion of Calhoun was kept alive by Martin Van Buren. A widower, Van Buren could entertain Peggy O'Neale without raising objections from members of his family. In so doing he gained favor with the President. Van Buren had already set his mind on becoming Jackson's successor in the White House.

Van Buren cleverly found a face-saving formula to settle the Eaton affair. He resigned from the Cabinet, aware that as Secretary of State and therefore the senior member, his stepping down would prompt other members to do likewise. When they followed Van Buren's lead, the President reformed his administration with fresh appointments. Having a harmonious official family at last, Jackson appointed John Eaton to be governor of the Florida Territory and Martin Van Buren to be minister to Great Britain.

Van Buren, a schemer, was delighted. He foresaw that in the party battles ahead he would be off the scene, but able to return to the United States just in time to become President himself. Calhoun, however, tripped him up. When Van Buren's appointment came to the Senate, there was a tie vote. Since a tie can only be broken by the Vice President, Calhoun was able to ruin Van Buren's plan by voting against him, declaring gleefully to a friend, "It will kill him, sir, kill him dead. He will never kick, sir, never kick."

Calhoun, realizing that he could not be the "heir apparent" himself, resigned as Vice President. He went home to South Carolina, which promptly elected him to the United States Senate. Quickly he was in the thick of things again as the South's leading defender of states' rights.

South Carolina protests against the tariff. Calhoun and Jackson now were mortal enemies. Their chief disagreement was over the tariff. Congress, you will recall, had passed the Tariff of Abominations in 1828 (page 249), a bill regarded as objectionable by every section of the country. Southerners, more aware than ever that their future lay with agriculture, felt especially injured by this tariff. They had, in fact, already come to the conclusion that *all* tariffs were bad for their region.

Calhoun, 48 years old in 1830, was a vastly different man from the one in 1816 who had advocated a strong national government active in promoting business (page 243). He was now filled with fervor to defend the South. He had developed an intense style of arguing public questions that irritated many people, even those inclined to agree with him.

In 1828, without being identified as the author, Calhoun had written a pamphlet entitled *Exposition and Protest.* In the pamphlet, issued by South Carolina's legislature, he called the Tariff of Abominations "unconstitutional, oppressive and unjust." He asserted that Southerners were becoming "the serfs of the system." The states, he insisted, had created the national government and, therefore, had the power to resist oppression by it. He argued, as Madison and Jefferson had argued in the Virginia and Kentucky Resolutions (page 192), that a state could refuse to enforce within its borders any law of Congress it regarded as unconstitutional. If three fourths of the states believed such a law to be unconstitutional, Calhoun went on, it would be null and void. This was Calhoun's statement of *nullification.*

In his annual message to Congress in 1830, Jackson supported the principle of protection contained in the tariff of 1828.

The young John Calhoun is shown here. He served as Vice President under two Presidents, John Quincy Adams and Andrew Jackson.

He made no mention of the doctrine of nullification. South Carolinians were disappointed because they had looked forward to Jackson's response to Calhoun. The dispute was, of course, more than just a confrontation between two strong-willed men. At bottom lay the question of slavery. The people of South Carolina, a state with a large slave population, feared that if Congress could impose a tariff on them, it could also free the slaves. The issue of slavery was becoming the special lens through which the South viewed all political questions — not least of all, the nature of the Union itself.

Webster and Hayne debate states' rights. The issue of the Union's powers came before the nation in 1830 during a Senate debate. Robert Y. Hayne, the other senator from South Carolina, took the side of those who wanted a federal government with limited powers. He pointedly reminded his opponents that New Englanders had taken a stand for nullification at the Hartford Convention sixteen years earlier.

Senator Daniel Webster of Massachusetts, sometimes known as "Black Dan" in

A renowned orator, Daniel Webster is the focus of this painting of the famous debate in 1830. Arguing for states' rights in that debate was Senator Robert Hayne.

tribute to his deep-set dark eyes, rose to answer Hayne. The best orator of his generation, Webster could rivet an audience's attention as no one else of the time could, holding them enthralled for hours on end. Alternating between a calm presentation of facts and electric emotional outbursts, he could send shivers down people's spines. On days when he was going to speak, he wore a double-breasted blue coat with brass buttons. These clothes reminded listeners of the Revolutionary heroes, making Webster's appearance even more dramatic.

Now 48 years old, Webster was at the height of his powers. His argument was that the Union was created by the people and could not be dissolved. "It is, Sir," he declared, "the people's Constitution, the people's government, made for the people, made by the people, and answerable to the people." The federal government, he was saying, manifests the will of the people, not of the states. The interest of the nation, he was sure, must be much greater than the interest of any state or section. Then he delivered words that several generations of young Americans would learn by heart in school:

When my eyes shall be turned to behold for the last time the sun in heaven, may I not see it shining on the broken and dishonored fragments of a once glorious Union. . . . Let their last feeble and lingering glance, rather, behold the glorious ensign of the Republic . . . bearing for its motto no such miserable interrogatory [question] as, "What is all this worth?" Nor those other words of delusion and folly "Liberty first, and Union afterwards"; but everywhere, spread over all in characters of living light . . . that other sentiment, dear to every true American heart — Liberty *and* Union, now and forever, one and inseparable!

Webster's reply to Hayne was impressive, but the question of whether or not a state could nullify a law had not been settled. Webster's stirring phrases, nevertheless, had captured the emotions of millions of Americans who had tied their hopes to a permanent Union.

Calhoun challenges Jackson on the issue of states' rights. A month after Webster's speech, at a Democratic dinner celebrating the anniversary of Jefferson's birth, southern leaders hoped to advance their ideas on states' rights. President Jackson came to the festivities prepared for battle. Being the leading guest, he spoke first. Standing ramrod straight and staring directly at Calhoun, he offered a toast: "The Federal Union — it must be preserved!" The noisy gathering was suddenly silent. The President had hurled a challenge that supporters of the South Carolina position could not leave unanswered.

Eyes now turned toward Calhoun. He rose from his seat to respond. Facing the President, he offered a toast of his own: "The Union — next to our liberty, the most dear." Jackson and Calhoun had now come to a complete break.

South Carolina threatens nullification. The continued hostility of the two men mingled with the growing concern over nullification. Jackson said to a member of Congress who was returning home to South Carolina, "Tell them [the nullifiers] from me that they can talk and write resolutions and print them to their heart's content. But if one drop of blood be shed there in defiance of the laws of the United States, I will hang the first man of them I can get my hands on to the first tree I can find." Still, Jackson tried to be conciliatory. He recommended in December, 1831, that the tariff be reduced, and Congress followed his suggestion the next year. The South Carolina legislature, however, was not satisfied, complaining that the rates were still too high. It declared the tariff acts of 1828 and 1832 null and void, and prohibited the collection of duties within the state after February 1, 1833. It also made clear that if the federal government used force to collect the duties, South Carolina would no longer consider itself a part of the Union. Jackson told a friend who had been with him at New Orleans, "If this thing goes on, our country will be like a bag of meal with both ends open. Pick it up in the middle or endwise, and it will run out. I must tie the bag and save the country."

With the intention of honoring his presidential oath to defend the Constitution, Jackson made preparations to call up the army. He *hoped* it would not be necessary to fight, for he could not be certain how much support for military action he would find among other Americans. Still, he quickly obtained from Congress a Force Bill, authorizing him to use troops against South Carolina if it resisted federal customs officials.

A compromise is reached. Both sides, meanwhile, were searching for a compromise. The movement to break the deadlock was led by Henry Clay. Once before, in the crisis over Missouri, Clay had helped save the Union by seeking a compromise (page 245). Now he worked out the Compromise Tariff of 1833, a bill providing for the immediate removal of duties on certain goods. The measure also called for a gradual lowering of the duty on other items until, in 1842, the rates reached the levels of 1816.

The Jacksonians at first were suspicious of Clay's motives. His bill, nevertheless, was a genuine compromise. South Carolina felt it had won the argument because Congress had agreed to lower the tariff. On the other hand, Jackson had also won because he had forced South Carolina to back down on its threat to leave the Union. The President could write James Buchanan of Pennsylvania, a former congressman whom he had recently appointed to be minister to Russia, "I met nullification at the threshold." Jackson's firmness in this dark hour for the Union remains a standard for presidential action in moments of national crisis. Still, no one could doubt the truth of Calhoun's comment: "The struggle, so far from being over, is not more than fairly commenced."

SECTION REVIEW

1. Vocabulary: *nullification.*
2. (a) What was Andrew Jackson's "kitchen cabinet"? (b) How did antagonism develop between Jackson and Calhoun? (c) How did the tariff dispute add to ill feeling between the two men?
3. (a) What were Calhoun's arguments in favor of nullification? (b) By what argument did Daniel Webster deny that principle?
4. (a) What action did the South Carolina legislature take as a way of opposing the tariff laws of 1828 and 1832? (b) What was Jackson's reaction? (c) How was the issue resolved?

2 Jackson Kills the Bank of the United States

President Jackson's attack on the Bank of the United States raised another political storm. The first bank had been started as part of the economic plan of Alexander Hamilton (page 180). The second bank was chartered at the end of the War of 1812 (page 243). It had quickly become unpopular, however, and had been blamed for the hard economic times that struck the nation in 1819.

Jackson opposes the bank. Like many Westerners who speculated in land, Jackson distrusted banks. Banks had no customer services as they do today. Ordinary people did not write checks. Mainly, banks were in business to lend money. But many local banks, called "wildcat banks," issued their loans in the form of paper money that could not be fully exchanged for gold and silver. Much of this paper money did not circulate far from the bank, for few people outside

Nicholas Biddle of Philadelphia served as president of the Bank of the United States and sought to recharter it in 1832, thus arousing Jackson's wrath.

the area it served would accept the bills at their face value.

Although the Bank of the United States was a well-run and profitable institution, it aroused the President's anger. By its policies, the bank affected financial matters throughout the country, loosening up credit when the economy was lagging and tightening it when it was booming. Jackson believed, however, that the bank favored eastern business interests at the expense of southern planters and western farmers.

The bank seemed beyond attack after the case of *McCulloch v. Maryland* (page 238). Jackson's supporters found important new reasons, however, for criticizing "the Monster." Many farmers and land speculators blamed it whenever there was a shortage of money. Some Easterners said it was responsible for inflation. The bank's policies were especially distrusted in the West. The paper money it issued tended to drive out of circulation the notes of the less secure state banks in that region. The national bank was, therefore, a threat to the very existence of the local banks. A supporter of Jackson in the Senate concluded that "all the flourishing cities of the West are mortgaged to this money power." One of the most influential newspaper editors of the country, Hezekiah Niles, said that the bank "had more power than we would grant to any set of men unless responsible to the people."

The president of the bank was Nicholas Biddle, appointed to that position in 1823. A literary person, Biddle was the author of the official history of the Lewis and Clark expedition. As head of the bank, this witty and sentimental man proved to be a domineering manager. Many people referred to him as "Czar Nicholas," in mock comparison to the oppressor on the throne of Russia. Biddle regarded himself as possessing influence equal to that of the President of the United States. He tried to befriend Jackson, but "Old Hickory" refused to change his mind that the bank was an enemy. He insisted that the bank discriminated against his supporters and did not play fair with them when they sought loans. Once when Biddle had his pocket picked in the entranceway to his bank, Jackson people snickered. They said the incident was nothing more than a sample of how the bank itself normally did business.

Jackson vetoes the bank bill. Jackson was obviously not going to renew the bank in 1836, when its charter expired. Therefore, in 1832, four years earlier than necessary, Henry Clay and Daniel Webster — both political opponents of Jackson — persuaded Biddle to apply immediately for a new charter and make the bank an issue in the presidential campaign.

The day Congress approved the bill to renew the bank's charter, Jackson, who was ill in bed, was roused to fury when Van Buren brought him the news. "The Bank," he told Van Buren, "is trying to kill me, *but I will kill it.*" The President promptly vetoed the bill and wrote a stinging message of explanation. In it he said that the bank was unconstitutional, existing only to aid "the rich and the powerful." A pro-Clay newspaper denounced the President's words as "a mixture of the demagogue and the despot, of depravity, desperation and feelings of malice and vengeance." Daniel Webster, personally in debt to the bank, called the President's words an effort to "inflame the poor against the rich." The President's friends praised the message, however, as a forceful statement of his belief that small businesses should have easy access to economic opportunity through bank credit.

Jackson wins re-election. The presidential campaign of 1832 had just one issue: the bank. The Democrats, of course, named Jackson again, although he was in poor health. For the vice-presidential candidate they chose Martin Van Buren. The Republicans nominated Henry Clay, who received financial help from the bank.

Jackson drew intense personal hatred from his opponents, who dubbed him King Andrew the First. An editorial in a Boston newspaper denounced him this way: "There is one comfort left: God has promised that

Jackson's withdrawal of federal funds from the bank ushered in its downfall, which is portrayed in this cartoon. Biddle, viewed by some as a despot, is here represented as a creature of evil.

the days of the wicked shall be short; the wicked is old and feeble, and he may die before he can be elected." Clay's supporters, however, misjudged the extent of the President's popularity. Jackson's victory in 1832 was overwhelming.

Government funds are removed from the bank. Jackson took his re-election to mean that the people wanted him to continue his war against the bank. At the beginning of his second term, he made up his mind to destroy the bank even before its charter had run out. He decided to withdraw the government's funds from the bank. Nicholas Biddle could tamper with the nation's economy no more.

Although Jackson had to remove his Secretary of the Treasury because he refused to carry out the administration's policy, the new Secretary, Roger B. Taney (TAWN-ee) of Maryland, cooperated. Secretary Taney deposited the federal money in selected state banks. These became known as "pet banks," because people considered them favorites of the government. The "pet banks" promptly did what the Jacksonians expected they would: they expanded their

Jackson's bold use of executive authority and the presidential veto provoked opposition. He was frequently satirized by antagonistic newspapers, as in this cartoon showing him dressed as "King Andrew."

loans, creating credit for speculation. Soon the West had the appearance of prosperity as land prices rose to dizzy heights. Revenues poured into the federal Treasury, wiping out the federal debt and creating a surplus. In 1836, Congress passed a distribution bill, dividing the surplus among the states.

Inflation becomes a problem. The Bank of the United States, without the federal deposits, was now severely crippled. It survived, however, until its charter expired in 1836. Meanwhile, the easy-credit policies of the "wildcat banks" led to inflation that could not easily be controlled. To apply a brake to the chaotic economic growth, Jackson issued an order called the Specie Circular in July, 1836, even though it cost him the support of some western friends. The Specie Circular provided that public lands could henceforth be paid for only in gold or silver.

The Specie Circular had a disastrous effect. Western land speculation was reduced, as gold and silver were drained eastward. A financial crisis in Britain in early 1837 caused a further drain on American supplies of gold and silver as bankers sought to convert their investments into specie. The continued demand for specie put a heavy burden on state banks everywhere, and large numbers of them very soon drifted into bankruptcy.

Jackson leaves office. Jackson returned to private life when his second term ended on March 4, 1837. In his farewell address he spoke to the needs of his fellow Americans, those rural and city people without substantial wealth who made up what he called "the bone and sinew of the country." He urged continued attacks on paper money, reckless speculation, and unfair business practices.

To the end, Jackson was both loved and hated. An influential New Yorker called Jackson's presidency "the most disastrous in the annals of the country." A New England minister had another view. He said that he knew "of nothing that a people may reasonably expect from good government, but that the United States have enjoyed under [Jackson's] administration." Regardless of any individual's opinion, Jackson had left a permanent mark on the nation's politics.

SECTION REVIEW

1. (a) What was the main business of local banks in the early 1800's? (b) Why were people unwilling to accept the paper money issued by wildcat banks? (c) How did the existence of a national bank affect the smaller banks?
2. (a) How did the national bank become the most important issue in the 1832 presidential election? (b) When re-elected, what action against the bank did Jackson take?
3. (a) How did Jackson's bank policies lead to inflation? (b) What effect did the Specie Circular have on the economy?

3 The Jacksonian Era Comes to an End

The Democrats expected to stay in power even though their unsurpassed leader had left office. Jackson's choice as his successor in the 1836 election was Vice President Martin Van Buren. The "Crown Prince," as he was known, had become the chief architect of the Democratic Party structure. Van Buren understood, better than anyone else, the role of public opinion and careful organizing in the winning of elections. In working out his techniques to serve Jackson, Van Buren had become, in fact, the first national politician able to influence local party activities on behalf of a President. Jackson was so grateful to Van Buren that he had given thought to resigning during his second term in order to allow the Vice President to move immediately into the presidency.

A new party is formed. The Republicans looked forward to defeating Van Buren in 1836. They had earlier been heartened when, in continued distrust of Jackson, the Calhoun people had formed an alliance with them. The three great Senate leaders — Clay, Webster, and Calhoun — were now linked together politically. In 1834, reflecting this unity, a new political party was formed. The party adopted the name Whig.[1]

The new party had strength among a number of groups. In the East, Whigs included lawyers, factory owners, merchants, and skilled workers. In the Ohio Valley, Whigs tended to be people who speculated in canal-building and land schemes, as well as farmers seeking internal improvements. In the South, Whigs were commercial and banking people who had deserted Jackson on the bank and on other money issues. Combining with these anti-administration Southerners were the big cotton, tobacco, and sugar planters — those who owned perhaps two thirds of the slaves in the South.

They were anti-Jackson because of the President's stand on states' rights and nullification. Finally, the Anti-Masonic Party threw in its lot with the Whigs. This small group opposed secret societies and prided itself on its open meetings. Its leader, Thurlow Weed, made the Whigs a powerful national party. A New York journalist, he became a master political manager and manipulator.

Despite the varied composition, the Whigs were held together by certain political principles. Most Whigs supported Clay's American System (page 246). Most of them believed in putting the good of the nation as a whole above sectional interests, although they sometimes talked about states' rights to please southern Whigs. Above all, the Whigs agreed that President Jackson was a symbol of what was wrong with the country. They saw him as an uneducated, irresponsible man with an explosive temper who allowed emotion, rather than reason, to control his actions.

The furious political hatred of the time was illustrated by an attempt on Jackson's life in 1835 while he was visiting the Capitol. A house painter named Richard Lawrence fired two pistols at Jackson at close range. Both weapons misfired. Jackson, utterly fearless, took after his assailant with cane upraised, before being restrained by an aide. Jackson felt sure that this first attempt to assassinate a President was the work of a Whig senator from Mississippi. An investigation, however, cleared the man. Other Whigs suggested that the whole episode had been staged. How could two pistols have failed, they asked? Lawrence, in any event, was declared mentally disturbed.

Van Buren defeats the Whigs. In an overheated atmosphere, the presidential campaign of 1836 got under way. Because the Whigs could not agree upon a national candidate, each section was represented by a "favorite son." New England Whigs backed Daniel Webster, while southern Whigs supported Senator Hugh White of Tennessee. Whigs in the Northwest put up William Henry Harrison of Ohio, the elderly, revered hero of Tippecanoe (page 224). It was

---

[1] Jackson's political enemies took the name Whig from the Whigs in England, the party that had opposed George III, just as the anti-Jacksonians were now resisting "King Andrew."

expected that Van Buren would fail to receive a majority in the electoral college. The election would then have to be decided by the House of Representatives once again.

The Vice President endured merciless slander. Davy Crockett's words are a sample: "When [Van Buren] enters the Senate chamber in the morning, he struts and swaggers like a crow in the gutter." The youthful William Seward of New York, emerging as a Whig leader, described him as "a crawling reptile."

Van Buren never lost confidence in the outcome. When the electoral votes were being counted, Henry Clay remarked to him, "It is a cloudy day, sir." Van Buren answered, "The sun will shine on the Fourth of March, sir." So it did. Van Buren won more electoral votes than all of his opponents combined, a thumping endorsement of Jackson's policies. At the inauguration, Jackson, who left a sickbed to be present, was cheered enthusiastically.

Prosperity ends in the Panic of 1837. In his inaugural message Van Buren gave assurance that America's prosperity was sound. No sooner had he settled into the White House, however, than the nation was caught up in the Panic of 1837. Fear swept the country as people worried about severe financial problems. The situation was made worse by a drop in the price of cotton. A shortage of specie also developed as foreigners, struck by hard times themselves, stopped investing in American enterprises. It was easy for critics to blame Jackson's financial policies as the cause of the trouble.

By September, 1837, nine tenths of the country's factories had closed their doors. Unemployment rose sharply and many people in the cities suffered great hardship. In New York the police had to be called to put down a flour riot. People became desperate when winter arrived and they could not pay their rent or buy fuel. As the decline in business activity and jobs grew sharper, the nation was said to be in a *depression*.

Van Buren sets up the Independent Treasury. The Whigs lost no time in blaming the administration for the trouble. Still,

Van Buren's opponents could not agree on a plan for coping with the economic disaster. The southern Whigs were opposed to a national bank, the tariff, and internal improvements. The northern Whigs favored all three.

Van Buren, though tempted to let the depression run its course, proposed a new way of handling government funds. He asked Congress to withdraw federal deposits from the "pet banks" and put them in the treasury in Washington, the vaults of the mint, or branch treasuries located in the principal cities. He hoped that by this method the federal government could control the issue of paper money and so prevent inflation in the future. The banking community and most Whigs regarded Van Buren's system, called the Independent Treasury, as an outrage. A policy of separating banking from the government seemed to them the first step toward national disaster. Hamilton's arguments of old were heard again: the national government and the interests of American business must be tied together.

Van Buren's administration limped to an unimpressive close. The Independent Treasury finally became law in 1840, but the Democrats had little else to claim as an achievement. A notable action was an executive order, issued in 1840, limiting to ten hours the workday of all laborers on federal projects. This move was an important bow to the wishes of working people.

Relations with Britain take a turn for the worse. Van Buren's administration ended amid a threat of war with Great Britain. In 1837, in the worst days of the economic crisis, a rebellion against the British authorities had broken out in Canada. Eager to be helpful, American sympathizers sent aid to the rebels. Late in December, 1837, the British set fire to an American steamer, the *Caroline*, that was carrying supplies across the Niagara River. Many Americans immediately called for revenge, while the British denounced the interference in Canadian affairs and demanded it be stopped.

Van Buren succeeded in quieting both sides. He reminded Americans that despite their love of freedom, they had no business invading a friendly neighbor. Also he sent General Winfield Scott to patrol the Canadian border. Britain, however, refused to apologize or pay for the loss of the *Caroline*.

The *Caroline* issue simmered until 1840. Then a Canadian was arrested in New York for having taken part in the *Caroline* affair. The British announced that if he were hanged there would be war. The man was acquitted. Still, the United States and Britain had come dangerously close to hostilities. Lord Ashburton, the British ambassador to the United States, then began a new policy of conciliation. Shortly afterward, Daniel Webster, now Secretary of State, accepted a British apology for the *Caroline* affair.

Webster and Ashburton had succeeded in reducing tensions between their countries in part because they got along well personally. Webster, like many New England Whigs, was sympathetic to Britain and wanted peace. Ashburton had married an American from a wealthy Philadelphia family. His affection for the United States — as well as his sense of humor — made him an ideal person to negotiate with Webster.

The Webster-Ashburton Treaty is signed. The two men also worked to reach a peaceful settlement on the question of the boundary line between Maine and Canada. For more than fifty years this matter had troubled relations between the United States and Great Britain. In 1832 America refused to accept a line drawn by the king of the Netherlands, who had been asked to settle the issue. In 1838, when Canadians entered the Aroostook Valley in Maine to cut timber, Maine called out the militia. President Van Buren again dispatched General Scott to the scene of border trouble. He was ordered to arrange a truce in this so-called "Aroostook War."

In 1842 the negotiators reached a compromise over the Maine boundary. By the Webster-Ashburton Treaty, the United States received about 7,000 of the 12,000 disputed square miles (somewhat less than the king of the Netherlands had earlier pro-

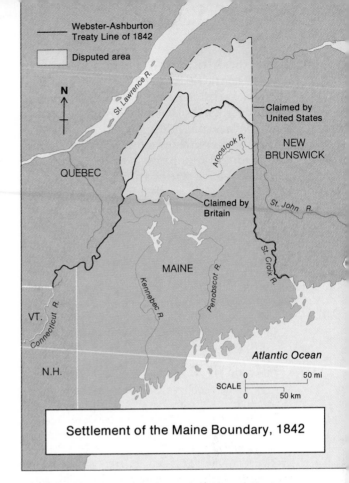

Settlement of the Maine Boundary, 1842

Before it was settled by the Webster-Ashburton Treaty, the boundary between New Brunswick and Maine had been in dispute since the Treaty of Paris of 1783.

posed). The British also agreed to adjust in America's favor a boundary line in the vicinity of Lake Champlain. The treaty, in addition, defined the northern boundary of the United States as far west as the 1818 boundary settlement (map, page 219).

Disagreement over the slave trade almost forced Webster and Ashburton to break off their negotiations. The United States and Great Britain had made it illegal for their citizens to engage in the international slave trade after 1808. Having abolished slavery throughout its colonies in 1833, Britain now wanted all nations to enforce the ban on the slave trade. Illegal American slave traders, however, refused to allow the British on their vessels, insisting that a neutral vessel could not be searched in peacetime. In the end, Webster and Ashburton were able to agree that their countries would each maintain a squadron to patrol the African coast in order to put a halt to the traffic in human beings.

The Webster-Ashburton Treaty had its opponents on both sides of the Atlantic. Andrew Jackson boldly tagged it "disgraceful, and disreputable to our national character." Domestic politics, however, does not always coincide with national needs and interests. The Webster-Ashburton Treaty was an outstanding piece of diplomacy — for both sides.

SECTION REVIEW

1. Vocabulary: *depression.*
2. (a) What were some of the groups within the Whig Party? (b) What were the special concerns of each? (c) What brought members of this party together?
3. (a) Who were the candidates in the 1836 election? (b) What was the outcome?
4. (a) What economic problems caused serious trouble in the early days of Van Buren's presidency? (b) How was the Independent Treasury supposed to help solve the nation's economic problems?
5. (a) What boundary disputes were settled by the Webster-Ashburton Treaty? (b) What other issue was dealt with in that treaty?

4 The American People Gain a Larger Share in the Government

The period between 1820 and 1840 witnessed a broadened acceptance of the idea of democracy.[2] Andrew Jackson was not personally responsible for this development, but he was the first Chief Executive to understand and use it in managing the country's affairs.

The idea of political equality becomes accepted. The basis for the changes in the ideas about democracy lay in the growth of free public schools and newspapers, which made people better able to form opinions about public issues. The result was a demand for increased participation of all white men in the governing of the country. The view also became accepted that any man could hold public office without special education. More than previous Presidents, Jackson used the *spoils system* — the practice of making party loyalty the chief basis for political appointment.

Furthermore, "artificial distinctions," the Jacksonian term for privilege, were brought under constant attack. The new western states that were entering the Union refused to set property qualifications limiting the ballot. Their constitutions usually provided that all white males were entitled to *suffrage* (the right to vote) upon reaching the age of 21. Gradually the older states followed suit, dropping property requirements for voting.

New political practices develop. As out-of-date styles of government gave way, new and unanticipated ones took their place. The role of the President itself changed in the time of Jackson. Differing from his predecessors in the conduct of his lofty office, "Old Hickory" made full use of the enormous power the President can wield. The President and the people, furthermore, were in much closer touch than ever before. Jackson's messages were intended for the mass of voters as much as for Congress, to whom they were officially addressed. Voters were also allowed now to select the presidential electors who, under the Constitution, choose the President.

The national nominating convention made its appearance during this period, becoming one of the most innovative and exciting features of American political life. Presidential candidates formerly had been chosen by party caucuses, or meetings, of political leaders in Congress. "King Caucus," however, was discredited as "undemocratic" in the campaign of 1824. The first convention of delegates ever held was that of the Anti-Masonic Party in 1831. Not to be outdone, the Republicans and the

[2] *Democracy* is a philosophy of government that recognizes the right of the people to take part directly or indirectly in controlling their political institutions. The word *democratic* describes such a government. It also describes practices of society as a whole that enlarge opportunities for people and that place emphasis on the dignity of the individual.

The spirit of the "common man" is a celebrated theme in the paintings of George Caleb Bingham. This work by the Missouri artist is entitled "Canvassing for a Vote."

Jacksonian Democrats quickly followed the Anti-Masons' lead.

Among other political innovations was logrolling — the practice by which legislators exchange favors by voting for or influencing the passage of one another's bills. Logrolling originally was a frontier word. It referred to the occasion, usually in the spring, when neighbors gathered to clear away fallen trees that hindered farming.

Another new practice was gerrymandering, the irregular redrawing of an electoral district's lines so that one party acquires an unfair advantage in elections. Elbridge Gerry of Massachusetts gave his name to this process after he had redrawn the electoral map of his state. A friend, seeing the result, sketched a head, wing, and claws on one misshapen district, and declared, "That will do for a salamander." "No!" shouted a bystander. "Gerrymander!"

Still another practice that developed in the Age of Jackson was lobbying — the pressuring of members of a legislature by nonmembers to vote for or against certain bills. The word *lobbying* was first used in 1832. It came from the common habit that lobbyists (those who lobby) followed of buttonholing legislators in the lobby of their meeting place.

Hand in hand with the new political ways went the belief that the voters as a whole must be heeded. Calhoun might insist that "the will of the majority is the will of a rabble," but never again could the majority be ignored. This period of American history is said to have witnessed "the rise of the common man."

The American people gain more economic freedom. On the economic side, the most important change of the era was the freeing of ordinary citizens to engage in business. Up-and-coming business people were aided by the easier credit that new banking laws made possible. Even risky enterprises found encouragement. States passed bankruptcy laws enabling the owners of failed businesses to settle their debts as best they could, without being hauled off to debtors' prison. By the beginning of the 1840's, most states no longer imprisoned debtors.

Democratic advances do not affect all Americans. One of the foundations of Jacksonian democracy was the belief that government belonged to all people who could vote. The Jacksonians' faith in the good sense of the people is found in the words of the poet of democracy, Walt Whitman. Whitman wrote,

> With the noble democratic spirit — even accompanied by its frauds and its excesses — no people can ever become enslaved; and to us all the noisy tempestuous [stormy] scenes of politics witnessed in this country — all the excitement and strife, even — are *good* to behold. They evidence that *the people act.*

Still, the achievements of the Jacksonian Era did not apply to all Americans. Women still played no role in politics and most did not expect to. Harriet Martineau, an English author who traveled in the United States in 1834, said that a main feature of America was the "political non-existence of women." Women, upon marriage, yielded all control of their property to their hus-

Free blacks met frequently in convention during the 1830's and 1840's, struggling to secure the rights of citizenship and education.

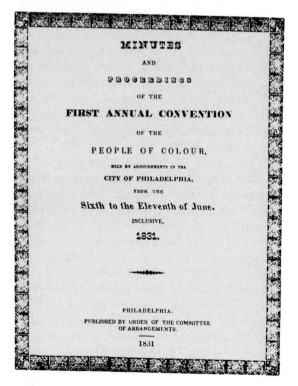

bands. Women were often treated with courtesy and gallantry, but this public show of respect did not make up for the complete legal subordination that was their lot.

Black slaves, more numerous in these years than ever, could not hope to share in the privileges of democracy. Free blacks, who could vote in many states after the Revolution, had their suffrage rights gradually taken from them. By the end of the Jacksonian Era, free blacks could vote only in Maine, New Hampshire, Vermont, Rhode Island, and Massachusetts.

The relocation of the Indians continues. During the Jacksonian Era the policy of removal — the forced relocation of Indian tribes — was expanded and intensified. The practice of removing tribes from their traditional homelands had become an active policy after the War of 1812 and was a primary consideration in Indian treaties negotiated after that time.

In 1825 President Monroe had sent a message to Congress proposing a policy that would persuade all remaining tribes in the East to relocate west of the Mississippi. Besides pressure from land speculators and farmers who wanted the Indians' land, the major reason for relocating tribes to those remote territories was the widely held belief that Indian and white populations could not peacefully live near one another. Many Americans were concerned about the welfare of Indians and were convinced that relocation was the only way to save Native Americans from ultimate extinction.

Jackson strengthens removal policies. When Andrew Jackson took office, he let it be known that he favored an accelerated policy of Indian removal. Jackson's background as a frontiersman and Indian fighter gave him a hard attitude toward the Indians. He thought Indians should not be dealt with by the federal government as tribal units, but rather as individuals like everyone else in the country. Jackson believed this would help those Indians who wanted to break away from the customs of the tribe and adopt the ways of white settlers. Traditionally, however, Indian tribes had been regarded by the government

A Frontiersman's Conscience

A well-known hunter and pathfinder, Davy Crockett was elected to Congress from Tennessee in 1829. One of the leading issues of the day, the Indian Removal Act, soon placed Crockett in opposition to his old friend President Andrew Jackson. Davy Crockett explained the situation in this passage from his journal.

Davy Crockett

I was elected to Congress in 1829 by an overwhelming majority; and soon after this I saw that it was expected of me that I would bow to the name of Andrew Jackson, and follow him in all his motions, and windings, and turnings, even at the expense of my conscience and judgment. Such a thing was new to me, and a total stranger to my principles. I knew well enough, though, that if I did not "hurrah" for his name, the hue and cry was to be raised against me, and I was to be sacrificed, if possible.

Jackson's famous, or rather I should say infamous, Indian Bill was brought forward, and I opposed it from the purest motives in the world. Several of my colleagues got around me, and told me how they admired me, and how I was ruining myself. They said this was a favorite measure of the President, and I ought to go for it. I told them I believed it was a wicked, unjust measure, and that I should go against it, let the cost to myself be what it might.

I was willing to go with General Jackson in everything that I believed was honest and right; but, further than this, I would not go for him, or any man in the whole of creation. I would sooner be honestly and politically condemned than go down in history as a hypocrite.

---

as "nations" separate from American society. They had long been viewed, furthermore, as having some property rights by virtue of their long-standing possession of certain lands. The federal government had always gone through the process of negotiating treaties with each of the Indian tribes, much as was done with foreign countries. The Indian Removal Act of 1830 authorized President Jackson to set up districts in areas west of the Mississippi that would be designated as territory to be occupied by Indians only. The President could then negotiate treaties with individual tribes that would provide for the exchange of Indian lands in the East for "permanent homelands" in the West. In addition, the act provided for the payment of compensation to the Indians, assistance in relocation, and protection from harassment in their new location. During Jackson's presidency 94 treaties providing for relocation were negotiated with Indian tribes.

Some Indians resist relocation. Not all Indians peacefully accepted this policy of exchanging their homelands for unknown territory in the West. The Sauk and Fox Indians were relocated from their lands in southern Wisconsin and northern Illinois to an area in the Iowa Territory. Unhappy with their new circumstances, they tried desperately to return to their original homes. Under the leadership of their chief, Black Hawk, they fought against the United States Army but were defeated in 1832. The

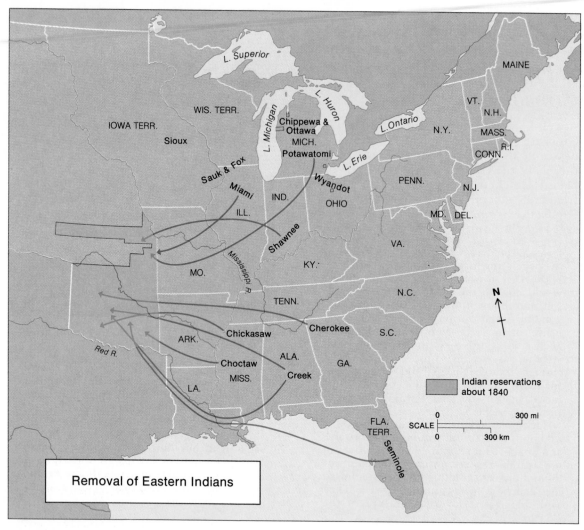

The forced migration of eastern Indians is outlined on this map. Note the areas designated as reservations for the resettlement of the Indians.

Seminole Indians of Florida had been defeated by Andrew Jackson many years earlier (page 239). In 1832 they agreed in a treaty to move westward across the Mississippi within three years. Most of the tribespeople, however, led by the young chief Osceola (os-ee-OH-lah), resisted relocation with great bravery. Many women left their children in order to fight alongside the men. Only after thousands of lives — United States soldiers and Indians alike — had been lost, was a treaty concluded in 1842 ending the costliest and cruelest Indian war ever fought. The Seminoles were then removed to lands in the West.

The Cherokee struggle to keep their homelands. One of the saddest chapters in this tragic story was the fate of the Cherokee people who lived in Georgia. More than any other group of Indians the Cherokee had adopted the ways of white society. They had developed a written language, published a newspaper, and established their own schools, factories, and plantations. In addition, they had a constitution that provided for a legislature, a judicial system, and a militia. None of these accomplishments made the slightest difference to white settlers and land speculators, especially after gold was discovered in Georgia.

The state legislature of Georgia declared that the Cherokee claim to their ancestral lands was no longer valid. The Cherokee were classified as mere tenants on state land and subject to the state's laws and authority. Therefore they could be legally forced to relocate.

The Cherokee took their case to the Supreme Court in a valiant effort to retain their land. In 1832, Chief Justice John Marshall ruled that Georgia had no jurisdiction to interfere with the rights of the Cherokee and that forceful removal from their lands violated Cherokee treaties with the federal government. President Jackson, however, had no intention of honoring this decision. He was reported to have remarked, "John Marshall has made his decision, now let him enforce it."

After this disappointment, some Cherokee gave up and moved west. Most, however, continued to resist removal. In 1838 General Winfield Scott and a unit of federal troops rounded up the 15,000 Cherokee left in Georgia, and during the cold and rain of winter forced the Indians to march to their assigned lands in the West. To the Cherokee people this journey became known as the Trail of Tears, since nearly one quarter of the tribespeople died along the way of disease, starvation, and exposure to the bitter cold.

What was the Jacksonian legacy? Jackson's attitude toward the Indians was not so different from that of most white Americans of his time. Nor would he have seen any contradiction in the denial of political and legal rights to blacks and women. Nevertheless, in the Age of Jackson the chance for white men to rise on the economic ladder may have been greater than at any previous time in the nation's history. An observant French traveler, Alexis de Tocqueville, saw this fact everywhere he went. He phrased it simply: "In America most of the rich men were formerly poor." If much of the work of extending democracy remained undone, the Jacksonians left an enduring legacy of the *possibilities* for personal liberty that only a free society can offer.

SECTION REVIEW

1. Vocabulary: *democracy, spoils system, suffrage.*
2. (a) In what way did the spoils system reflect the Jacksonian idea of democracy? (b) How did the new western states lead the way in expanding the number of voters?
3. What new political practices developed during the Jackson years?
4. What changes resulted in greater economic freedom?
5. (a) What groups did not share in the expansion of political equality during the Jacksonian period? (b) What was Jackson's policy toward the Indians?

5 The Whigs Win the Presidency

The depression that followed the Panic of 1837 hurt Van Buren's chances for re-election in 1840. The Whigs were certain that they could now capture the White House if only they could agree on a candidate. Henry Clay was eager to be that man. Upon hearing that the nominating convention had turned away from him, he exclaimed angrily, "My friends are not worth the powder and shot it would take to kill them! I am the most unfortunate man in the history of parties; always run by my friends when sure to be defeated, and now betrayed for a nomination when I, or anyone, would be sure of an election." William Henry Harrison, who had no program but no enemies either, was nominated. As consolation to Clay's southern supporters, the Whigs nominated John Tyler of Virginia to be Harrison's running mate.

The Whigs capture the White House. Harrison had the advantage of a remarkable build-up by his party followers. He was made into a kind of Whig Jackson — a military hero who spoke the language of humble people. The Whigs took advantage of a Democratic taunt that Harrison would be happy in a log cabin with a pension and a barrel of hard cider. They made their symbols a log cabin and hard cider, and their

The victory of the Whig Party and William Henry Harrison in the election of 1840 was no doubt aided by the colorful and boisterous "log cabin" publicity campaign.

slogan "Tippecanoe and Tyler too." A Whig jingle about Harrison ran:

> He lives in a cabin built of logs
> Drinks nothing but hard cider too,
> He plows his own ground, and feeds his
>   own hogs,
> This fellow of Tippecanoe.

It did not matter that, in fact, Harrison lived in a 22-room mansion on a farm of 2,800 acres and never drank hard cider.

The Whigs ridiculed President Van Buren without mercy. They claimed he slept in a luxurious, imported bed, preened himself before mirrors framed in gold, and used the same perfume as young Queen Victoria of England. "Van, Van is a used-up man," they chanted again and again. They joked that Van Buren would give working people "fifty cents a day and French soup," while the Whigs would provide "two dollars a day and roast beef."

The election of 1840 was the first one full of noisy public fanfare. Huge parades, accompanied by torchlights and heralded by the firing of cannon, advertised the candidates. American party politics had become a form of public entertainment.

Van Buren, in the end, could not overcome the harmful effects of the depression.

When the returns were in, Harrison had won an electoral vote of 234 to 60, although the popular vote was much closer — 1,275,017 to 1,128,702. The Liberty Party, calling for an end to slavery, had entered a candidate for the first time, James G. Birney. He received fewer than 7,000 votes.

Vice President Tyler succeeds to the presidency. General Harrison, 68 years old when he was inaugurated, was the last President to have been born under British rule. On March 4, 1841, wearing no gloves or overcoat in the freezing weather, he rode a white horse up Pennsylvania Avenue to take the oath of office. His address, which lasted two hours, was the first inaugural ever sent immediately to several parts of the country by railroad. People in Philadelphia were able to read the speech that same evening. Forty years earlier it had been remarkable that Jefferson's speech was made available locally.

During what proved to be a brief presidency, Harrison was completely dominated by the Whig leaders, Webster and Clay. Webster became Secretary of State after Clay declined the position. Clay, who preferred to be the power behind Harrison, pressed his opinions so hard that Harrison exclaimed to him on one occasion, "Mr. Clay, you forget that I am President."

President Harrison was immediately besieged by officeseekers. He tried to do everything that was expected of him — and more. He soon suffered in health, caught a cold, and died just a month after his inauguration. John Tyler, the Vice President, was notified immediately of Harrison's death. He hurried from his home in Virginia to become the nation's tenth Chief Executive. Tyler was the first Vice President to move up to the White House under such circumstances. Some people seriously doubted whether he was in fact President, considering him only to be "Acting President." Others, like John Quincy Adams, regarded him as "Vice President acting as President." Adams even questioned "whether the Vice President has the right to occupy the President's house, or to claim his salary." No framer of the Constitution was alive to say what the delegates at Philadelphia had had in mind for such a situation. No one, it turned out, could prevent Tyler from becoming President and assuming the powers of the office. The precedent he set has never since been challenged.

Tyler quarrels with the Whigs in Congress. The Whigs were uncomfortable with Tyler, a former states' rights Democrat. On the critical questions of the bank and the tariff, he remained in sympathy with the Democrats. Because he had broken with Jackson over the nullification issue and become a Whig, the Democrats rejected him too, calling him "Turncoat Tyler." Tyler knew that he would have to make his own way and not let himself be controlled by anybody. He spoke bluntly to the Cabinet he inherited from Harrison: "I shall be pleased to avail myself of your counsel and advice. But I can never consent to being dictated to as to what I shall or shall not do. When you think otherwise, your resignations will be accepted."

The Whigs in Congress in 1841, led by Clay, introduced resolutions representing Whig policy. They called for the repeal of Van Buren's Independent Treasury (page 262), the creation of a new Bank of the United States, and an increase in tariff rates.

The Independent Treasury was repealed, and the federal government once again began depositing its funds in "pet banks." Tyler, however, vetoed a bill that would have set up a third national bank. Clay had pleaded with him to accept it, but the President turned aside all arguments in its favor. Angered by the veto, the entire Cabinet, except Webster, promptly resigned.

The only other Whig measure Tyler signed was the Tariff of 1842. Faced by a shortage of revenue, the President agreed to raise the rates to the level of the Tariff of 1832 (page 257).

Clay and the Whigs in general took advantage of the fact that Tyler was a President without a party. A Whig leader in New York, Philip Hone, wrote in his diary, "Poor Tippecanoe! It was an evil hour that 'Tyler too' was added to make out the line. There was rhyme but no reason in it." Some Whigs took pleasure in privately referring to the President as "His Accidency."

The Democrats had hoped they could profit from the shameful struggle between the President and the people who had helped elect him, but they too were divided. The northern wing of the party still looked to Van Buren as their leader. The southern wing leaned toward Calhoun. Clay, distressed by his dealings with Tyler, resigned from the Senate in 1842 and went home to his estate, "Ashland," in Kentucky. The following year, when he spoke in Ohio, over 100,000 people turned out, possibly the largest crowd that had ever heard an American politician. Clay believed that his time had come, that in 1844 he would be elected President at last.

SECTION REVIEW

1. What factors contributed to Harrison's victory over Van Buren in 1840?
2. What precedent was set after President Harrison's death in office?
3. (a) On what issues was Tyler at odds with other Whigs? (b) What action of Tyler's caused his Cabinet to resign?

Chapter 11 Review

Summary

A man of the frontier, Andrew Jackson brought a fresh perspective to the White House in 1829. Ignoring the politicians who made his election possible, Jackson relied on a "kitchen cabinet" of old cronies and on his feeling for the "will of the people" in deciding what was best for the country.

The first major issue to confront Jackson centered on the tariff question. Southern states felt threatened by the federal government's imposition of a national tariff. They felt the next step would be federal interference with slavery. The crisis came to a head when South Carolina threatened to nullify the tariff law. A compromise was reached, but the issue of states' rights was left unresolved.

Jackson's next battle was over the Bank of the United States. Like most Westerners, he distrusted banks, feeling they served only the interests of wealthy Easterners. When Congress in 1832 made a campaign issue out of a bill to renew the bank's charter, Jackson did not hesitate to use his veto. Then, seeing his re-election in 1832 as a popular mandate against the bank, Jackson vowed to destroy it. He withdrew government funds from the bank and distributed them to selected state "pet banks." The financial dislocations caused by this tactic brought about an economic crisis several months after Jackson left office.

The 1836 election was hotly contested. The Democratic nomination went to Jackson's Vice President, Martin Van Buren. Hostility to Jackson's administration was so intense, however, that many voters left the Democratic Party and joined the recently formed Whig Party. Van Buren won the election, but was soon confronted with the Panic of 1837. The new President was never able to deal effectively with this serious financial problem.

The years spanning Jackson's and Van Buren's presidencies witnessed profound changes in the nation's ideas about democracy. The spoils system, national nominating conventions, and lobbying were among the practices that accompanied greater citizen participation in the political process. This colorful era came to a close when the Whig candidate, William Henry Harrison, defeated Van Buren in the 1840 election.

Vocabulary and Important Terms

1. "kitchen cabinet"
2. nullification
3. Force Bill
4. Compromise Tariff of 1833
5. Specie Circular
6. Panic of 1837
7. depression
8. Independent Treasury
9. Aroostook War
10. Webster-Ashburton Treaty
11. democracy
12. spoils system
13. suffrage
14. lobbying
15. Indian Removal Act of 1830
16. Trail of Tears

Discussion Questions

1. (a) What kind of leadership did Andrew Jackson exercise as President? (b) Why has Jackson sometimes been called "the maker of the modern presidency"?

2. (a) Who did President Jackson rely on for advice? (b) What caused the split between Jackson and his Vice President, John C. Calhoun? (c) What became of Van Buren after he resigned from office during Jackson's first administration?

3. (a) Why did Southerners object to the Tariff of Abominations of 1828? (b) What arguments against the tariff and for nullification did Calhoun offer in the *Exposition and Protest* pamphlet? (c) What arguments for national unity did Daniel Webster advance in his debate with Robert Y. Hayne?

4. (a) How did Jackson respond to South Carolina's declaration that the tariff was null and void? (b) How was the nullification crisis finally resolved?

5. (a) Why did Jackson distrust all banks in general and the Bank of the United States in particular? (b) What arguments against the bank did Jackson offer in vetoing the bill to renew its charter?

6. (a) Why was Van Buren the logical person to succeed Jackson as President? (b) What effect did the Panic of 1837 have on the nation and on Van Buren's term as President?

7. (a) Why was the Whig Party formed, and who belonged to it? (b) What basic political principles did the Whigs rally around?

8. (a) What were the causes of the tense relations between the United States and Great Britain? (b) How did Daniel Webster and Lord Ashburton succeed in reducing tensions between the two countries?

9. (a) What profound changes in the nation's ideas about democracy occurred in the period between 1820 and 1840? (b) During this same period how did the American people gain more economic freedom?

10. (a) Why was the appearance of the national nominating convention such an important innovation in American political life? (b) What other political practices developed during the Jacksonian Era?

11. Why can it be said that the achievements of the Jacksonian Era did not apply to all Americans?

12. (a) Why was the presidential campaign of 1840 unique, and why did William Henry Harrison win the election? (b) What was the significance of Harrison's death in 1841 and the succession of John Tyler to the presidency?

13. (a) Why were the Whigs uncomfortable with Tyler in the White House? (b) Why were the Democrats unable to profit from the struggle between Tyler and the Whigs in Congress?

Relating Past to Present

1. Andrew Jackson's years as President are sometimes called the Age of Jackson. Is it possible for an individual today to stamp his or her image on an entire age in the same manner as Jackson? Who in the United States today might have such an impact?

2. During the 1830's and 1840's the major political parties were made up of a variety of groups who often had different political goals. To what degree are our major political parties today made up of political factions?

Studying Local History

1. Find out about the advance of voting rights in your state. When did your state drop property requirements for voting? Religious qualifications?

2. When were women first given the right to vote in your state?

Using History Skills

1. *Classifying.* Make a chart with two columns in which you show the arguments for and against the concept of nullification. In one column place the arguments expressed by John C. Calhoun and Robert Y. Hayne in favor of nullification. In the other column place the arguments expressed by Andrew Jackson and Daniel Webster against that idea. Use these arguments to prepare for a classroom debate.

2. *Reading source material.* Study the passage from Davy Crockett's journal on page 267. (a) When was Crockett elected to Congress? (b) What was his opinion of the Indian Removal Act? (c) What evidence is there that during the debate over removal Crockett remained true to his principles?

WORLD SCENE

Reform and Revolution

While reforms during the Jacksonian Era were giving more Americans a fuller voice in government, people in other countries were also striving for a larger political role.

The British Reform Bill. In the early 1800's Parliament was still controlled by rich landowners, and the right to vote was denied to the middle class as well as to farm and factory workers. To provide a remedy, Parliament passed the Reform Bill of 1832 after years of agitation. The act lowered the property qualification required to vote. Middle-class men thus received the ballot, although workers would still have to wait for it.

The Reform Bill was a landmark in British history. It brought a shift in political power of vast consequence. As a result of the maneuvering to pass the act, the House of Commons became the dominant branch of Parliament, replacing the House of Lords — the traditional domain of the landed aristocrats. Henceforth, Parliament would recognize the interests of business and manufacturing.

Greek independence. The struggle of the Greek people to have a government of their own was another stirring story. For centuries Greece had been dominated by the Ottoman Turks. In 1821 Greeks rose in rebellion against the Turks. The ensuing war for independence was supported by many Americans and Europeans who had studied and admired classical Greek culture.

The Greek rebels took on a large Turkish army that fought ferociously to suppress the revolt. On one Greek island the Turks massacred nearly 20,000 inhabitants. When this news reached the outside world, people were outraged.

In 1827 the governments of Britain, France, and Russia agreed that they must help the Greeks. When the Turks refused to halt the fighting, the powers combined to force the Turkish army out of Greece. By 1830 Greek independence had been won. To maintain their influence in Greece, the European monarchs designated a German prince named Otto to be the new king.

The North:
Enterprise and Freedom

1790 – 1860

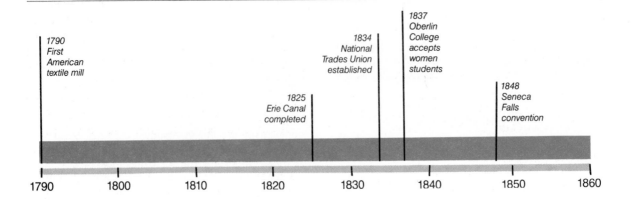

1790
First
American
textile mill

1825
Erie Canal
completed

1834
National
Trades Union
established

1837
Oberlin
College
accepts
women
students

1848
Seneca
Falls
convention

1790   1800   1810   1820   1830   1840   1850   1860

CHAPTER OUTLINE

1. Manufacturing and trade transform the North.

2. Workers respond to the growth of an industrial society.

3. Reformers seek to improve American life.

4. Northern cities expand as immigration surges.

5. New means of transportation unite the North.

Every American early was conscious of living in a particular section of the country. To be a Northerner meant living in New England, the Middle Atlantic states, or that part of the West located north of the Ohio River.

The people of New England occupied a notably demanding setting. The winters were long and harsh, and the soil rocky and stubborn. Many New Englanders moved west and south, seeking a more agreeable environment. Those who remained developed an uncommon devotion to the country as a whole, keeping in touch with children and other relatives elsewhere in the land.

The Middle Atlantic states were more generously endowed than New England. Being richer in resources, and having a somewhat milder climate, the region had a more robust economy. By 1820, the ports of New York and Philadelphia were the gateway cities to the West. The people could not avoid being connected to the rest of the country in every direction. Being centrally located, they valued their ties to the Union and strengthened them steadily.

The West was also influenced by its location. The Great Lakes stretching eastward and the Mississippi flowing southward served as giant straps holding the West tightly to the rest of the Union.

Despite differences in ways of making a living, the regions of the North were dependent on one another. Their need for a flourishing Union riveted them together.

1 Manufacturing and Trade Transform the North

By the 1830's the North was still mainly agricultural. The appearance of smoke-stacks in many northern towns, however, foretold the direction in which the United States was heading.

The first factories are started. Interest in building factories in the United States had been slowly gathering force since the early 1790's, when Hamilton's Report on Manufactures had been debated (page 183). The growth of industry was encouraged by the enterprise of a handful of business people, by the increasing supply of skilled workers, and by the confidence of private investors. Moreover, seeing the advantages that Great Britain was gaining from factories, Americans aimed to follow England's lead.

The most immediate push to the building of factories had come at the time of the War of 1812. With the country cut off from European goods, some ambitious Americans began to go into manufacturing on this side of the Atlantic. Much trial and error was required, because factories had been chiefly a British development, and manufacturers in Britain jealously guarded the secrets of their methods. They kept watch especially on the design of the power-driven machinery they used for producing cloth. Elsewhere in the world, thread was still being made at home on spinning wheels, and cloth was being woven on hand looms.

Samuel Slater builds textile machinery. The first American factory was built in Pawtucket, Rhode Island, in 1790. It was the work of Samuel Slater, who had been the general overseer of the making of machinery in an English cotton mill. When Slater learned of prizes being offered in the United States for cloth-making machines, he decided to enter the competition. He slipped away from Great Britain in 1789 in disguise, because anyone with his knowledge was forbidden to leave the country. Landing in New York, he was invited to Rhode Island by a Quaker merchant named Moses Brown. Brown hired Slater, who built from memory a factory like the one he had left in England.

Slater's mill, which began hiring workers in 1791, was located beside a waterfall. (All early factories depended on the

After Slater's mill was built in Rhode Island, factories were started in many northern states, providing cheap, machine-made goods for a growing population.

force of rapidly flowing water to turn huge wheels that provided power.) At first the machines just spun thread, which was then distributed to home weavers who turned it into cloth. The owners of Slater's mill discovered, however, that home weaving was not a satisfactory way to get reliable cloth production. They wanted looms installed in the factory itself and driven by water power. A partner of Slater pointed out in 1809 that "a hundred looms in families will not move so much cloth as ten constantly employed under the immediate inspection of a workman."

The first power loom is built. A Boston merchant named Francis Cabot Lowell responded to the cry for power looms. Convinced that national wealth and greatness depended on the building of factories, Lowell formed the Boston Manufacturing Company at Waltham, Massachusetts, in 1812 and soon teamed up with a mechanical genius named Paul Moody. Moody was fascinated by machines and what they could do. His expert knowledge, combined with Lowell's money and business experience, produced the first power loom in America.

It is hard today to imagine the novelty of a machine like the power loom. Such machines were just beginning to reveal how human toil could be reduced — just beginning, therefore, to open a new era in human achievement. A leading investor in Lowell's firm later wrote about the Lowell-Moody loom: "I well recollect the state of admiration and satisfaction with which we sat by the hour, watching the beautiful movement of the new and wonderful machine, destined as it evidently was, to change the character of all textile industry." When the machines were finally set up at Waltham in 1813, Lowell had the first factory in the world that combined all the operations for converting raw cotton into finished cloth.

Experiments are made with conveyor belts and steam. Even in the first days of industrialization, some Americans looked forward to endless supplies of manufactured goods produced in factory towns all over the country. Such a man was Oliver Evans, the son of a Delaware farmer. In 1780 Evans began working on a series of improvements in flour-mill machinery. Five years later his equipment was ready. He had devised a way, through a series of gears and vertical belts, of "applying the power that drives the millstone to perform all the operations which were hitherto effected [carried out] by manual labor, namely from receiving the grain from the wagon or ship until manufactured into superfine flour, ready to be packed into barrels." The conveyor belt — the kind used today on production and assembly lines everywhere — was Evans's lasting contribution to factory operation.

Evans, looking beyond even this accomplishment, wanted to build engines powered by steam so that factories would not have to be built on rivers. By 1802 Evans had such an engine working in his mill. Soon he started a business as a builder of high-pressure steam engines.

Other inventors, in America and abroad, were also experimenting with steam engines. Meanwhile, Evans looked forward to the day when vehicles would be powered by steam. He wrote in 1812:

> The time will come when people will travel in stages [coaches] moved by steam engines, from one city to another, almost as fast as birds fly, fifteen to twenty miles in an hour. . . . A carriage will set out from Washington in the morning, and the passengers will breakfast at Baltimore, dine in Philadelphia, and sup at New York the same day.

Production is aided by the use of interchangeable parts. Factories also quickly took advantage of an important discovery made by Eli Whitney, an inspired tinkerer and inventor. In the late 1790's Whitney had built a factory in Connecticut that produced muskets. Instead of making each gun from start to finish by hand, his workers first manufactured quantities of the various parts. They turned them out so precisely that the parts fitted perfectly with one another to make a gun. In short, any of the triggers worked with any of the barrels, and so on. Whitney put on a demonstration of *interchangeable parts* before President John Adams and Vice President Jefferson. He disassembled ten muskets, scrambled the parts, and then quickly put them together again — to the amazement of the onlookers.

Whitney's technique, ideally suited to the making of metal products, was seized upon by industries springing up throughout the North. The procedure was soon improved and made to work faster and more economically. Europeans came to the United States to observe what came to be called admiringly "the American method."

New England takes an early lead in manufacturing. The advances brought about by Slater, Lowell, Moody, Evans, Whitney, and many other talented people made New England the first part of the country to feel the impact of factory life. The rest of the North, however, did not lag far behind.

By the 1830's most New Englanders were still farmers, but momentous changes were in the making. The building of canals and railroads was tying together the Northeast and regions west of the Appalachians. As a result, New England farmers began to face stiff competition from agricultural products that poured in from the more fertile West.

Discouraged, many New Englanders left their farms altogether. Others limited their farming to specialized production, like dairy farming or market gardening (the raising of fruits and vegetables), to supply the needs of the new factory towns. By 1850 New England had become a food-importing

EYEWITNESS TO HISTORY

Early Mills in New England

By the 1830's and 1840's many young women had found jobs in New England's textile mills. In a letter home, a young woman from a New Hampshire farm described her experience working in a Lowell, Massachusetts, mill.

When I left home, I told you that I would write and let you know my impression of Lowell. Well, I went into the mill, and was put to learn with a very patient girl. You cannot think how odd everything seemed to me. They set me to threading shuttles, and tying weaver's knots, and such things, and now I have improved so that I can take care of one loom.

At first the hours seemed very long, but I was so interested in learning that I endured it very well. When I went out at night, the sounds of the mill were in my ears — all mingled together in strange discord. It makes my feet ache and swell to stand so much, but I suppose I shall get accustomed to that too. The right hand, which is used in stopping and starting the loom, becomes larger than the left, but in other respects the factory is not detrimental to a young girl's appearance.

Mill workers

These mills are not such dreadful places as you imagine them to be. You think them dark damp holes. They are no such thing. They are spacious, well-built edifices, with neat paths around them and beautiful plots of greenery and flowers. Inside, the rooms are high, very light, kept nicely whitewashed, and extremely neat, with many plants in the window seats. The machinery is very handsomely made and painted, and is placed in regular rows, presenting a beautiful and uniform appearance.

region, dependent on the West for most of its provisions.

Factories seek workers. As New Englanders built more and more factories, larger numbers of laborers were needed to work in them. One method of obtaining factory hands was to hire whole families. Husband, wife, and children would be put to work in the same factory and would live in houses provided by the factory owner.

Another source of labor was the Irish people fleeing the starvation that followed the failure of the potato crop beginning in 1845 (page 291). To work in a factory was a chance for many Irish immigrants to make a new start in life.

Young women, no longer needed at home to spin cotton and wool cloth, also began to seek factory work. As an observant minister of the time wrote, there was occurring a shift from "mother-and-daughter power to water-and-steam power." In the factories young women were starting to turn out the very products they had formerly made by hand at their mothers' sides.

The Waltham System flourishes. Young women were first employed on a large scale at the Waltham, Massachusetts, factory of Francis Lowell. Kept under close supervision, they were housed in dormitories as if they were schoolgirls. A man who lived in the 1830's wrote enthusiastically about the Waltham System, as it was known. He said that the manufacturers' sincere concern for the employees' well-being "gained the confidence of the rural population, who were no longer afraid to trust their daughters in a manufacturing town."

The Waltham System spread to several other factory towns, including Lowell, Massachusetts. When the English novelist Charles Dickens visited Lowell in 1842, he was delighted to see how the workers lived. "I cannot recall," he wrote, "one fact that gave me a painful impression." Indeed, the best of motives lay behind the system. The Massachusetts investors were eager to avoid the horrors of factory life in England, about which Dickens had written so effectively. The young women of Lowell even pub-lished an impressive literary periodical called *The Lowell Offering.* It was the first magazine produced by American women.

American trade expands. At the same time that industry was growing, American ships were carrying on trade all over the world. Even before 1800, Yankee vessels were on every sea. In 1784, as you remember (page 156), the first American ship had set sail for China. In the years that followed, American merchants constantly expanded trade with Europe, while opening up new opportunities in the ports of the East Indies, the Philippines, and India. Americans also traded with ranchers in California, then under Spanish control.

By 1850 the Middle Atlantic states dominated the country's foreign commerce. At the beginning of the 1840's, New York City's totals for merchant-marine tonnage and foreign-ship arrivals surpassed Boston's for the first time and were never thereafter challenged. By mid-century, New York exported $47.5 million worth of goods — $9 million more than New Orleans, its rival.

Water transportation improves. Sailing ships called packets, designed to provide cargo space, safety, and comfort, were a familiar sight at the wharves of American port cities in the early 1800's. Isaac Wright established the Black Ball Packet Line in 1818, which made regular runs between the United States and England. The trip took about forty days each way. Competition with other lines quickly became lively, and four packet ships sailed in each direction every month.

In 1836 the new Dramatic Line — so called because its ships were named for famous actors — was founded by Edward Knight Collins. The line was barely established, however, when steam power revolutionized transatlantic shipping. In 1838 the *Sirius* and the *Great Western*, British steamships, reduced the transatlantic journey to about fifteen days. Collins rose to the challenge. "I will build steamers," he told a friend in 1840, "that shall make the passage from New York to Europe in ten days or less." Ten years later he fulfilled his pledge.

Clipper ships, like the ones shown here, were known for their sleek beauty and speed. Their presence in harbors around the world demonstrated America's increasing participation in international trade.

It was the graceful clipper ship that made the American flag — "the starry blue banner," as one German saw it in his port — familiar everywhere on the seven seas. Shipbuilders had always said it was possible to have speed or cargo capacity in a vessel, but not both. After considerable experimentation, the clipper ship — slender and sharp-bowed and carrying abundant billowing sail — proved that statement wrong. Under the right conditions, clippers could run faster than steamships.

The clippers brought the American port cities in closer touch with one another than ever before. In 1851, for instance, Donald McKay's *Flying Cloud* made its maiden voyage from New York to San Francisco, around the tip of South America, in 89 days. The clippers were also used successfully in trade with Europe and Asia.

Trade strengthens the North. The clipper's heyday was brief. The coming of the steamship, a temporary slowing of immigrant traffic, and increased competition from Europe brought a decline in clipper shipping. Between the mid-1840's and 1860, nevertheless, American trade continued to increase. Commerce brought to the port cities, and through them to the entire North, new ideas and new vigor as well as an endless variety of goods. The bustling commercial activity helped give the North a speedy tempo of life which constantly astonished visitors. A writer of the day was in despair over the traffic on New York's Broadway: "Look up and down the street," he said, "and then run for your life." New York City, with nearly 620,000 people by 1850, had already become a symbol everywhere of the driving energy of the North — and of America.

SECTION REVIEW

1. Vocabulary: *interchangeable parts.*
2. What technological advances were brought about by each of these innovators? (a) Samuel Slater (b) Paul Moody (c) Oliver Evans (d) Eli Whitney
3. (a) Why was New England the first section of the country to feel the impact of industrial growth? (b) What kinds of people worked in the New England factories? (c) What was the Waltham System?
4. (a) How did American trade expand in the first half of the nineteenth century? (b) What advances in transportation aided this growth?

279

2 Workers Respond to the Growth of an Industrial Society

As time went on, the factory system was clearly altering life in the North. Most immediately it affected the people who worked in the plants. Although conditions in American factories were generally better than those in Europe, the lot of many American laborers was hard.

Working conditions deteriorate. By the 1830's and 1840's American factory owners were in stiff competition with one another. To gain an edge, they kept wages as low as possible and imposed long hours on their employees. The Panic of 1837 (page 262) made conditions worse for workers because jobs became scarce. Employers, moreover, expected their hired hands to increase their output. If a worker did not meet a fixed quota, a new hand who might prove more cooperative was hired.

The change in conditions is suggested by the words of a factory owner: "I regard my work-people just as I regard my machinery. So long as they can do my work for what I choose to pay them, I keep them, getting out of them all I can." The so-called "slavers," the recruiting wagons that went about the countryside of Vermont and New Hampshire, found it impossible any longer to promise young women that they could "dress in silks and spend the day reading." The change in working conditions made even Waltham a less rosy place.

Workers were generally paid only four times a year, and often in company-store coupons rather than in cash. The company stores — owned by the employers — often charged high prices. The workers usually had no choice but to shop in them because they could not get credit elsewhere. Besides, other stores seldom honored the coupons.

Before industrialization, items were hand-crafted in small shops. As manufacturing grew, workers made goods in mechanized factories with less pleasant conditions.

A reformer named Seth Luther wrote in 1832 of another problem: the maltreatment of child laborers. He described "whipping rooms," where young children were lashed with cowhide straps to make them work faster. Luther saw "instead of rosy cheeks, the pale, sickly, haggard countenance of the ragged child." To its credit, Massachusetts passed the first American child-labor law in 1842. This law limited to ten hours a day the working time for children under twelve.

The first labor unions are formed. Some working people believed that by organizing unions they would improve factory conditions. The earliest American unions had been formed in the 1780's. They were really associations of master craftworkers who sought to maintain prices and standards of quality. When these skilled workers joined together, however, they usually were seeking only to win an argument of the moment, not to create a permanent union.

By the beginning of the 1800's the wages of unskilled workers had generally risen. The steady demand for laborers to build roads and canals helped to push up the level of pay. Because these laborers were also provided with shelter and food, their wages often exceeded those of skilled workers.

Consequently, skilled workers — tailors, carpenters, shipwrights, cabinetmakers, shoemakers, weavers, and barrelmakers — began to join together according to their trade or craft. Sometimes they banded together merely for companionship or to provide life-insurance benefits for members. More and more, however, the organizations — called *craft unions* — focused their efforts on boosting pay.

Resistance to unions is strong. The opposition of employers and the courts to unions was intense. In 1806, for example, a strike by the shoemakers of Philadelphia for higher wages ended in court. The trial judge lectured the jury on the evil of unions, saying that they tended to produce "public mischief and private injury." His widely shared view was in keeping with the old English tradition that a combination of workers was illegal.

By the early 1800's the habit of opposing oppression — political or economic, real or imagined — was deeply ingrained in Americans. Recognizing that their strength lay in uniting, the skilled workers of Philadelphia in 1827 joined their craft unions in the Mechanics' Union of Trade Associations. For the first time, the members of more than one trade were brought together in a single organization.

Workers' political organizations are short-lived. A new phase of labor history began in 1828 when workers in the North formed political parties. These parties were able to affect the outcome of some local elections. The labor party in Philadelphia called for free education for everyone, the abolition of imprisonment for debt, laws to protect workers against bankrupt or dishonest contractors, and the abolition of the Bank of the United States. In New York a labor party made similar demands. It also complained that working people were underrepresented in the state legislature, charging that people of wealth controlled its actions. In 1832 a workers' tune admonished that:

Mechanics, cartmen, laborers
Must form a close connection,
And show the rich aristocrats
Their power at this election.

For a number of reasons the labor parties disappeared by the mid-1830's. First, some of their ideas were taken over by the major parties and incorporated into American life as part of Jacksonian democracy. Second, the local labor parties were unable to join together and become a national force. Third, the leadership was more and more assumed by people who themselves were not workers and did not know how workers felt. Fourth, without the support of unskilled laborers, a workers' party could not expect to be powerful at the polls.

The first national union is formed. As the factory system spread through the Northeast, union organizing — rather than direct political activity — became labor's way. In 1834 representatives of trade unions from six cities met in New York City and established the National Trades Union. It was

Because of worsening conditions in the shoe industry, a strike of shoeworkers spread through New England in 1860. These women marched in Lynn, Massachusetts.

the country's first national union. The National Trades Union agreed on a program to improve working conditions, but its leaders were convinced that they must stay out of politics. As one of them said, they "belonged to no party; they were neither disciples of Jacksonism nor Clayism, Van Burenism nor Websterism, nor any other ism except workeyism."

Early labor makes few gains. The membership of the National Trades Union grew rapidly — from 26,250 in 1834 to about 300,000 in 1836. As labor activity intensified, workers began to call for recognition of their right to organize unions and to bargain collectively. (*Collective bargaining* refers to discussions between a union and an employer to decide such things as employees' hours, wages, and working condi-

tions.) Unions used the *strike,* or the refusal of employees to work, as a means for winning their demands. Several hundred strikes were called between 1833 and 1837, the chief demand being a ten-hour day for the same pay that was then being given for a twelve-hour day.

Unions in this early period had few successes. Then, in the face of the Panic of 1837, the National Trades Union collapsed. Members either dropped out because they were unemployed or because they feared antagonizing their employers, on whose favor they depended.

Nevertheless, in 1842 labor made an important gain in a Massachusetts courtroom. The case of *Commonwealth v. Hunt* had arisen when Boston bootmakers agreed among themselves not to work for any employer who fired a member of their union.

The decision held that the bootmakers' refusal to work under this condition was not an illegal action. In other words, labor unions were recognized as legal organizations, not conspiracies as courts had previously ruled. The full force of this decision was not felt, however, until several more decades had passed.

Other responses to the growth of industry are offered. Not all efforts to deal with the effects of industrialization came about through unions. Some people insisted that the best way for laboring people to overcome their difficulties was to return to the land. In the 1840's an organization called the National Reform Association made an appeal to working people with its slogan "Vote yourself a farm." Few factory hands, however, had the means to switch easily to agriculture.

Reformers were also looking for ways to remove the evils they saw in the changing scene. One of the best-known reformers was Robert Owen, who had built a model village for his mill workers in Scotland.

Owen came to the United States in 1824 to set up a *utopian*, or ideal, community. On invitation, he addressed a huge audience which included President Monroe. In speaking about his plans, he said that enterprises he intended to establish would relieve workers of the drudgery of factory labor. He especially counted on music, dancing, and relaxation to restore his people's spirits. They would work no more than eight hours a day.

In 1825 Owen and his son, Robert Dale Owen, established the community of New Harmony, Indiana. There the Owens planned to settle 2,400 people. Every able-bodied person would work at some trade or occupation and accumulate credit for food and other goods at the public store. The elder Owen owned the community and took all the financial risks.

Despite these optimistic plans, New Harmony was doomed to fail. It lacked economic self-sufficiency and was always short of skilled labor. Moreover, some of Owen's assumptions did not prove valid. Not only was there constant bickering among the members of the colony but, one visitor reported, "young ladies and gentlemen of quality will not mix with the common sort." Possibly there was too much dancing and music and too little food and work. In spite of the failure of New Harmony, other utopian experiments were started. One of the most publicized experiments, also short-lived, was at Brook Farm, near Boston.

SECTION REVIEW

1. Vocabulary: *craft union, collective bargaining, strike, utopian.*
2. (a) What problems did factory workers of the 1830's and 1840's face? (b) Why did some workers try to form unions?
3. (a) What was the aim of political parties formed by workers in the early 1830's? (b) Why did these parties disappear within a few years?
4. (a) What was the National Trades Union? (b) How successful was it?
5. What was the importance of the case of *Commonwealth v. Hunt*?
6. What was Robert Owen's plan for solving the problems of working people?

3 Reformers Seek to Improve American Life

By the mid-1800's, the comparatively simple life of rural America was yielding ground to the more complex, impersonal ways introduced by factories. Yet it was sometimes said that to a larger extent than ever in the past, people in these years were sure they would see a golden age in America in their own lifetime. To assure its coming, many Americans understood that they must take steps to preserve the principle of the dignity of the individual. The resulting crusades to overcome obstacles to the flowering of democracy were, taken together, known as the reform movement.

Several factors give energy to the reform movement. The reform movement that marked the years between 1830 and 1850 was based chiefly in the North. The South had comparatively few friends of reform during this period.

Evangelical doctrine and ideas about reform were preached at large camp meetings.

The reforming urge was the result of a number of elements which seemed to have come together at the same time. The first was the spread of evangelical religion, such as Methodism, which emphasized that it was an individual's duty to work for righteousness in himself and in others. Preachers who traveled from community to community — circuit riders, they were called — distributed books and pamphlets emphasizing this obligation. It made people take to heart the teaching of the Bible that they were their "brother's keeper."

A second element was the outpouring from Britain of ideas about reform. Reformers on this side of the Atlantic followed the lead of British reformers in working for greater opportunities for women and for the abolition of slavery.

A third element was provided by the Panic of 1837 — the first economic downturn that significantly affected cities. With sailing ships lying idle at the docks, with foundries, shoe factories, and textile mills shut down, the suffering of working people was great. The unemployed had no place to turn for assistance. Surely, many thoughtful people were saying, it ought to be possible to learn the root cause of the disaster and do something about it. In the meantime they could help out by "doing good."

The demand for public education grows. The movement for tax-supported public education typified the spirit of this period of reform. Its hero was Horace Mann, who once said, "In a republic, ignorance is a crime." Mann worked tirelessly to promote the establishment of public schools. Even his vacations were devoted to touring other states and countries to learn about education systems. In 1837 he became secretary of the newly organized board of education in Massachusetts and opened the first teacher-training school in that state two years later. He campaigned for better school buildings, textbooks, libraries, and equipment. Mann explained the concern of all educational reformers: "If we do not prepare children to become good citizens, if we do not develop their capacities, if we do not enrich their minds with knowledge, then our republic must go down to destruction, as others have gone before it."

Horace Mann was not alone in working for improved public schools. Henry Barnard carried on similar work in Connecticut and Rhode Island. Samuel Read Hall, a Vermont minister and a teacher, published in 1829 the nation's first book on education.

Tax-supported public schools are established. At first the movement for public schools met the resistance of voters who refused to approve the necessary taxes. Some people objected to the idea of public education itself, thinking it might make working people too independent. As the benefits of education became clear, however, the idea of supporting schools through taxation took hold. By the mid-1800's most white children in northern states could obtain a free elementary education. The 1850 census reported that the country had about 80,000 primary schools, attended by almost 3,500,000 young people.

In 1821 Boston established the first public high school. As the demand for high schools spread, their number grew, not only in Massachusetts but also in such states as Ohio and New York. Some high schools admitted young women, although in most places boys and girls were enrolled in separate schools.

Higher education makes advances. Tax-supported higher education was also a new idea. A growing number of states, beginning with North Carolina in 1789, had established their own universities. The College of the City of New York, chartered in 1847, was the trailblazer among colleges financed by cities.

Women seek their rights. Some reformers regarded the most glaring deficiency in American life to be the denial of opportunities for women. American Quakers had granted women privileges in worship that the other religious groups did not allow. Not until Frances Wright came to this country in 1818 from Scotland, however, did the movement for women's rights begin to take hold.

A friend of Lafayette, Frances Wright accompanied the Revolutionary hero on his triumphal tour of the United States in 1824 (page 247) and shared in the idolizing that he experienced. Closely associated with Robert Dale Owen in the New Harmony experiment, she condemned the lack of legal rights for married women. Frances Wright was roundly attacked for her views by most women as well as men. What drew the sharpest criticism was her practice of making speeches in public. Such behavior was practically unheard-of and considered impermissible. Still, she drew listeners, chiefly out of curiosity, and won converts to her point of view.

Other leaders of the 1830's joined in the struggle for women's rights. In 1835 Lydia Maria Child published her *History of the Condition of Women in Various Ages and Nations*. That book, together with Frances Wright's lectures, gave women leaders the arguments they needed. John Quincy Adams, who was elected to the House of Representatives after his term as President, fervently defended the right of women to send petitions to Congress. Possibly he recalled the words of his mother, Abigail Adams: "If we mean to have heroes, statesmen, and philosophers, we should have [well-educated] women."

Further encouragement to women came from Margaret Fuller, the remarkable editor

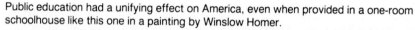

Public education had a unifying effect on America, even when provided in a one-room schoolhouse like this one in a painting by Winslow Homer.

The Seneca Falls Declaration (1848)

When in the course of human events, it becomes necessary for one portion of the family of man to assume among the people of the earth a position different from that which they have hitherto occupied, but one to which the laws of nature and nature's God entitle them, a decent respect to the opinion of mankind requires that they should declare the causes that impel them to such a course.

We hold these truths to be self-evident: that all men and women are created equal; that they are endowed by their Creator with certain inalienable rights . . . that to secure these rights governments are instituted, deriving their just powers from the consent of the governed. . . .

The history of mankind is a history of repeated injuries and usurpations on the part of man toward woman, having in direct object the establishment of an absolute tyranny over her. . . .

Now, in view of not allowing one half the people of this country to vote, of their social and religious degradation . . . and because women do feel themselves aggrieved, oppressed, and fraudulently deprived of their most sacred rights, we insist that they have immediate admission to all the rights and privileges which belong to them as citizens of the United States.

In entering upon the great work before us, we anticipate mistaken ideas, misrepresentations, and ridicule; but we shall make every effort within our power to secure our object.

of a journal, the *Dial*, to which the best New England minds subscribed. She could say truthfully, "I find no intellect comparable to my own." She, too, wrote an important book, called *Women in the Nineteenth Century*. As the first woman correspondent of an American newspaper, she covered the Italian revolution of 1848 for the *New York Tribune*. While in Italy she married an Italian nobleman. As she was returning to America with her husband and infant son, the three were lost at sea in a shipwreck. She has long been remembered for her mighty words in support of equal rights: "We would have every path laid open to woman as freely as to man."

The first women's rights convention is held. Another pioneer of the women's movement was Elizabeth Cady Stanton. Along with Lucretia Mott, a Quaker reformer, Mrs. Stanton organized the first women's rights convention. It was held at Seneca Falls, New York, in July, 1848. In her opening address Mrs. Stanton presented a "Declaration of Sentiments." She began, "We hold these truths to be self-evident: that all men and women are created equal." A long list of grievances followed, with "man" filling the place that George III had had in the Declaration of 1776. When Mrs. Stanton offered the startling proposal that women be given the vote, even Mrs. Mott was shocked. "Why, Lizzie," she said, "thou will make us ridiculous." Still, most delegates agreed that the vote was what women needed in order to advance the cause of equal rights. The resolution passed, and the women's suffrage movement had begun.

Opportunities for women remain limited. In spite of the work of these reformers, there was little to show for their efforts until after 1850. By the 1860's a number of states had passed laws providing that married women could own property. Legal equality for women, however, was a long way off. Meanwhile, education was the first professional area in which a handful of women were able to prove themselves.

Most schools for girls and women beyond the primary schools provided further training only in such subjects as music, dancing, and sewing. Then, in 1821, a principal named Emma Willard opened a new kind of institution, the Female Seminary at Troy, New York. The girls enrolled in this school studied subjects previously considered too difficult for them. To the surprise of many people, girls had no more difficulty understanding geometry, Greek, or philosophy than boys did.

As other schools like Emma Willard's were opened, Oberlin College in Ohio broke fresh ground in 1837 by enrolling four women students. They were the first women ever to work toward college degrees. Slowly, very slowly, professions opened to women. The first woman to earn a medical degree was Elizabeth Blackwell. Graduating at the head of her class in 1849 at a small medical school in New York State, Dr. Blackwell went to Paris to complete her studies. A sister-in-law, Antoinette Brown Blackwell, completed work for the ministry at Oberlin in 1850. Her difficulties in getting a license to preach probably discouraged other women from following in her footsteps.

Better care is given the mentally ill. Another dedicated reformer was Dorothea Lynde Dix. She had discovered her life's work one dreary Sunday in 1841 when she came upon mentally ill people herded together in a Massachusetts prison. Aroused, she investigated conditions in asylums elsewhere. To her horror she learned that the mentally ill were locked up, as she wrote, "in cages, closets, cellars, stalls, pens! Chained, naked, beaten with rods, and lashed into obedience!" This gentle and delicate woman became a tiger in the cause of improving the treatment of the unfortunate people she championed. As a result of Dorothea Dix's efforts, Massachusetts and other states began to provide public institutions for the mentally ill.

Temperance leaders oppose the use of alcohol. Still other reformers became involved in the *temperance movement,* a campaign against the consumption of alco-

The graduation class at Oberlin College in 1855 included a black woman. Many teachers and students at Oberlin spoke out for an end to slavery.

hol. These crusaders believed that the use of alcohol robbed people of their self-respect and pride. Heavy drinking also interfered with the success of democracy, they argued, because citizens in a democratic nation must be able to make thoughtful decisions.

The crusade against alcohol found many supporters. Some people, however, fought back, asserting that outlawing alcohol was an invasion of people's private lives. Still, Neal Dow led a campaign in Maine calling for the prohibition in that state of intoxicating drinks. With the passage of the "Maine Law" in 1846, declaring the sale of liquor illegal, Dow achieved his goal. The Maine law became a model for similar laws in other states and communities.

This song honoring the abolitionist Frederick Douglass dates from 1845, the same year in which Douglass published his autobiography.

Reformers seek to abolish slavery. Of all the reformers, none were more devoted to their purpose than the *abolitionists,* those people who worked in the movement to abolish, or do away with, slavery. The American abolition movement had begun in the eighteenth century, when leaders like Benjamin Franklin condemned slavery. Franklin felt deeply the contradiction between the existence of slavery and the lofty words of the Declaration of Independence.

Some abolitionists believed that slavery would gradually die out — particularly after the foreign slave trade was banned in 1808. Others backed the goals of the American Colonization Society (page 245), which sent small numbers of black Americans to Liberia in West Africa. Colonization, however, did not work out well. A group of free blacks in Philadelphia spoke for many who opposed the Society: "We have no wish to separate from our present homes for any purpose whatever." By the late 1820's this point of view was accepted by many white reformers, who now saw that slavery would never be wiped out by sending black Americans to Africa. These reformers issued a call for the abolition of slavery.

Garrison demands abolition. Certain leading abolitionists, like Benjamin Lundy, the publisher of an abolitionist newspaper in Baltimore, continued to count on colonization as the solution. Lundy's assistant, William Lloyd Garrison, disagreed. Garrison, a young printer from Massachusetts, insisted that slavery must be abolished at once. To delay, he maintained, served only to protect the interests of slaveholders. Garrison was arrested and sent to jail when one of his editorials denounced slave auctions in Baltimore. Upon his release, he left Lundy's employ and went to Boston. There in 1831 he founded a new abolitionist newspaper, *The Liberator.* Garrison expressed in these words his firm intention to fight slavery: "I am in earnest — I will not equivocate — I will not excuse — I will not retreat a single inch — *and I will be heard.*"

Abolitionists spread their antislavery views. In the 1830's abolitionist fervor burned with a new intensity in the North. This development took place in part because both Mexico and Great Britain had recently freed their slaves and in part because the South's prosperity now depended on the *permanence* of slavery. Garrison and a handful of followers organized the New England Antislavery Society in 1831. Two years later they joined with reformers from areas outside New England to found the American Antislavery Society. Through their writing and lecturing they carried on a nation-wide campaign to spread their views.

One of the American Antislavery Society's most important lecturers was Frederick Douglass, a slave who had escaped bondage in 1838. Sojourner Truth was another well-known black abolitionist. A freed slave, she became a persuasive speaker not only for antislavery but also for women's rights. She traveled throughout New England and the western states, inspiring listeners with her message. Samuel Cornish and John Russwurm were other black abolitionists. In 1827 they published the first black newspaper, called *Freedom's Journal*. Still another black abolitionist was Henry Highland Garnet, pastor of a mostly white Presbyterian church in Troy, New York. Garnet helped edit an antislavery newspaper, *The National Watchman*, and later published his own newspaper, the *Clarion*.

A few powerful individuals who preached antislavery ideas came from southern slaveholding families. One was James G. Birney, a planter in Alabama. Birney had failed in an attempt to persuade the framers of Alabama's first constitution to provide for the gradual freeing of slaves. In 1834, shortly after freeing his own slaves, he became a leader in the American Antislavery Society. As you have read (page 270), when the abolitionist Liberty Party was organized in 1840, Birney became its presidential candidate.

Two South Carolina sisters, Sarah and Angelina Grimké, left their mark on the abolitionist movement. Their antislavery speeches attracted much attention because the Grimké sisters were members of a prominent family of slaveholders. In 1838, when Angelina Grimké was already nationally known, she married an abolitionist minister, Theodore Dwight Weld. Weld was deeply influenced by the reform spirit of his day. In the 1820's he was a spokesman for the temperance movement in western New York. From the 1830's on, he gave his energy to the antislavery cause.

A modest man, Weld permitted none of his writings to be published under his name, and he refused to speak when reporters from newspapers were present. His effectiveness, nonetheless, was unquestioned. Among the influential people he converted to the cause of abolition were Harriet Beecher, famous later as Harriet Beecher Stowe, and Edwin Stanton, who later served in Abraham Lincoln's Cabinet. Finally, Weld persuaded John Quincy Adams to open a campaign in the House of Representatives against slavery. Weld's most lasting contribution to the antislavery cause may have been his role in organizing the Liberty Party. By so doing he brought abolition into politics, where it stayed until the Thirteenth Amendment put an end to slavery altogether.

SECTION REVIEW

1. Vocabulary: *temperance movement, abolitionist.*
2. (a) What factors contributed to the spirit of reform in America between 1830 and 1850? (b) What advances were made in public education during this period?
3. How did each of the following contribute to the broadening of opportunities for women? (a) Frances Wright (b) Lydia Child (c) Margaret Fuller (d) Elizabeth Cady Stanton (e) Emma Willard (f) Elizabeth Blackwell
4. (a) How did Dorothea Dix bring about changes in the treatment of the mentally ill? (b) What arguments were used by those who supported the temperance movement?
5. (a) How did William Lloyd Garrison work for the cause of abolition? (b) Why did abolition win new support in the 1830's? (c) What other individuals took leading roles in the abolition movement?

4 Northern Cities Expand as Immigration Surges

Another aspect of the transformation of America into an industrial society was the rise of cities. In 1830 New York City had about 215,000 people. Within the next twenty years its population nearly tripled. During the same period the population of Philadelphia and Boston doubled.

Technology spurs the rise of cities. A number of technological developments help explain the phenomenal growth of urban America. The most important of these changes revolutionized the way houses were built. The availability of cheap machine-made nails, along with standard sizes of sawn lumber, for the first time made possible the construction of inexpensive wood houses. A carpenter and a helper could now "frame out" a house in a couple of days by nailing together the pieces of lumber — the two-by-fours, the two-by-sixes, and the two-by-eights. No longer did a house have to be put together laboriously by many skilled workers cutting grooves to hold the beams tight. The first of these dwellings — sometimes called balloon-frame houses — was constructed in 1837 by Augustine Taylor, a Hartford, Connecticut, carpenter.

Another technological development was the introduction of macadam, a type of road surface able to withstand heavy traffic in all kinds of weather. First used in Great Britain and named for its pioneer, John McAdam, macadam consists of thin layers of crushed rock bound together by a mixture of stone dust and water. Dirt roads could now be paved and turned into thoroughfares.

The emerging cities also gained from new networks of transportation and commerce that were transforming family life. Many of the items required by the American family were now "store-bought." Once, practically everything would have been made or grown at home. It is said that by 1830 no American farmers even bothered to make their own brooms, one of the easiest tools to put together in spare moments. With factories making more and more

Many streets in New York City were planned and built between 1830 and 1850 when the city was growing very rapidly. This scene shows Broadway in 1855.

goods, many people could leave the farms without being missed and move to cities.

Many immigrants come to America from Ireland and Germany. Immigration brought increasing numbers of people to the North, particularly to northern cities. Two shattering events in Europe contributed to the rising tide of immigration.

The first of these events was the "Great Hunger" in Ireland, a famine caused by the failure of the potato crop. Almost half of the people of Ireland, the most densely populated country in Europe at that time, lived on plots of land less than five acres in size. In normal times an acre and a half of land could grow enough potatoes to support a family. With the surplus the family might buy a hog, a cow, or some chickens.

Beginning in 1845, a plant disease destroyed a series of potato crops in Ireland, bringing unspeakable suffering. Thousands of Irish people fled their homeland. Many of them arrived in Boston, where a clergyman named Theodore Parker declared, "Boston is a young Dublin!" In 1848 half of the school children in Boston were foreign-born, probably two thirds of them Irish.

A second event in Europe propelled a large number of Germans to the United States. This was the failure in 1848 of several revolutions led by reformers who wanted to establish republican governments in the German states. Among the "Forty-Eighters," as these newcomers were called, were editors, scholars, and professional people. Usually arriving with more money than the Irish immigrants, the Germans settled not only in eastern cities but also in towns and farms throughout the West. Cities like Cincinnati and Milwaukee quickly had large German populations.

A good number of Jews were among the "Forty-Eighters," forlorn that their hopes for more tolerance in their homeland had been dashed. Arriving without a trade or training, many of the men became peddlers. Based in the cities where they bought their stock of goods, they carried their backpacks into rural areas, providing an important link between the expanding factories and the farmers who wanted manufactured

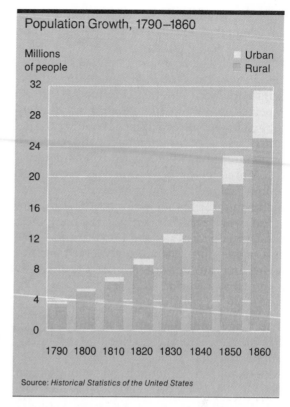

Much of the growth in urban population after 1830 was due to European immigration.

goods. As the peddlers accumulated savings, they bought horses and wagons and opened shops. Some of America's leading department stores today were founded by German Jews who started out as peddlers.

In the waves of immigrants were important religious leaders. One was Carl F. W. Walther, who organized the Missouri Synod as a stronghold of orthodox Lutheranism. Another was Rabbi Isaac Mayer Wise. Wise made Cincinnati the center of the Reform Judaism he preached. His goal was to reconcile the ancient traditions of Judaism with the eagerness of newly arrived German Jews to merge with the general population.

Immigration has an impact on American life. The stream of immigration, which brought somewhat fewer than 650,000 persons to America in the 1830's, became a torrent of almost 3,000,000 people in the 1850's. The Middle Atlantic states led by far the rest of the Union in the number of new arrivals. Of the 5,450,000 immigrants who came to

America from 1820 to 1860, more than two thirds entered by way of the port of New York City.

Most of the immigrants remained in the big cities of the North, crowded into ethnic neighborhoods. The fact that most of them expected a better life for their children rubbed off on all Americans. Looking to the future, rather than longing for the past, became more than ever a national characteristic. Moreover, immigration was creating a unique society. Herman Melville, best remembered for his novel *Moby Dick*, understood what was happening. He compared the United States to "the flood of the Amazon, made up of a thousand noble currents all joining into our one. We are not a nation so much as a world."

Some Americans oppose the foreign-born. The huge numbers of newcomers sometimes created new irritations. Some immigrants fell into street crime, causing other Americans to denounce all foreign-born people. The fact that most of the new arrivals were Roman Catholics occasionally aroused prejudice among Protestants. Some native-born Americans, ignoring the poverty that forced so many immigrants to dwell in overcrowded and unsanitary buildings, concluded that foreigners preferred such quarters.

The newcomers contribute to the nation's growth. On the other hand, many citizens could see that immigrants also benefited the nation. For one thing, as members of the work force, immigrants contributed substantially to rapid industrial growth in the North. In addition, the millions of newcomers became valuable consumers of goods. Owners of vessels that carried cotton and grain to Europe found it profitable and advantageous to transport immigrants on the return voyage. (Transatlantic fares from Liverpool to New York fell, as a result, from about $50 in 1816 to about $12 in 1846.) It was recognized, too, that each newcomer usually brought to America a small sum of money. Even if the sum was small, the immigration of the 1850's may have transferred to the United States as much as $100 million in European capital.

Most of all, immigrants carried to this country a desire to put down roots and prosper in a land of freedom. Fulfilling these aspirations meant working hard to make a decent living. *The New York Tribune* pointed out in 1851, "Europe pours her surplus millions in armies upon our shore and their first cry is for Work!" The North, spurred by the growth of industry, was able to supply it.

SECTION REVIEW

1. What technological developments played a part in the growth of cities in the 1830's and 1840's?
2. What circumstances brought increasing numbers of immigrants from Ireland and from Germany?
3. (a) Why did some native-born Americans look down on immigrants? (b) In what ways did the newcomers contribute to the nation?

5 New Means of Transportation Unite the North

At the same time that industry and trade were expanding in the Northeast, improvements in transportation were also taking place. The building of roads and canals strengthened the links between the eastern and western sections of the nation. The rise of railroads soon made it easier for farmers to send their crops to market and for manufacturers to sell their goods.

Turnpikes are built. Before 1812 the states along the eastern seaboard were joined by a haphazard system of roads. As time went on, roads were built west. The most important of these was the National, or Cumberland, Road. Authorized during Jefferson's presidency, the National Road connected Cumberland, Maryland, with Wheeling on the Ohio River (map, page 293). Completed in 1818, it was later extended to Vandalia, Illinois, becoming the chief route for settlers heading west.

During the War of 1812 the British blockade of coastal shipping forced Americans to rely heavily on land transport. Many of the roads they employed followed routes

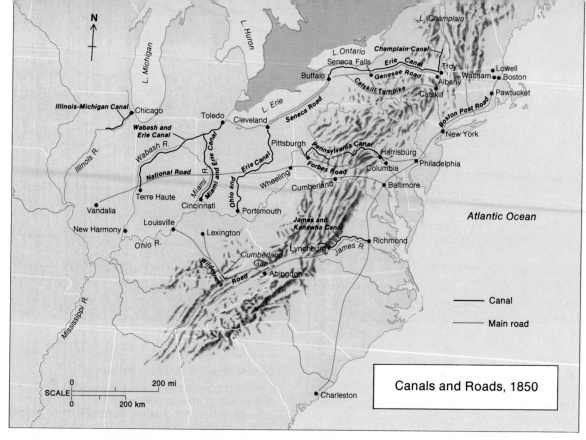

The importance of the National Road dwindled as canals were built.

used since colonial times. Some of them were *turnpikes,* highways on which tolls were collected at various points. Overland travel, however, was discouraging. Seventy-five days were needed, for instance, for a wagon loaded with goods to make a trip from Massachusetts to South Carolina. Roads were unpaved, and spring thaws flooded them and turned them into mud. In summer, travelers were choked by the dust. Still, roads continued to be built during the 1820's and 1830's.

In the 1840's planks — laid crosswise, side by side — were introduced to improve the turnpikes' surfaces. Wet weather rotted the wood and often made travel dangerous. The ready availability of wood, nevertheless, made planks half the cost of macadam.

Canals offer cheap water routes. Both eastern manufacturers and western farmers needed some means of transportation that was cheaper and more efficient than the turnpikes. Canals proved the most satisfactory answer.

So many canals were built from 1825 to 1840 that people called this period the Canal Era. The best-known of these waterways was the Erie Canal, begun in 1817 and completed after eight years of extraordinary labor. Financed by New York State, it made possible an all-water route from New York City to the Great Lakes. The longest canal in the world, it was a demonstration of American enterprise and engineering skill. It was also a monument to its forceful backer, Governor De Witt Clinton, whose imaginative project had initially been laughed at as "Clinton's Big Ditch."

The success of the Erie Canal was immediate. The cost of moving goods between New York City and Buffalo dropped from $100 a ton to $10. Moreover, the travel time was cut from twenty days to eight. Buffalo, Albany, and other cities along the Erie Canal grew rapidly as expanded commerce made them prosperous. New York City's population doubled within ten years. The Erie Canal was so heavily used that it paid for itself in just nine years.

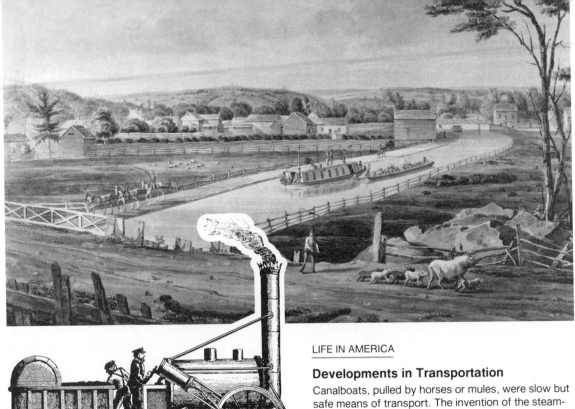

Developments in Transportation

Canalboats, pulled by horses or mules, were slow but safe means of transport. The invention of the steam-powered locomotive heralded the coming of the railroad. Until a transcontinental railroad was built, people traveled westward by overland stage.

Almost immediately a canal-building frenzy gripped the nation. Cities and legislatures throughout the country announced plans to build canals. Between 1826 and 1834, Pennsylvania constructed a system of canals linking Pittsburgh with towns and cities in eastern Pennsylvania. While this system never threatened the supremacy of the Erie Canal, it enabled Philadelphia to continue to compete with New York for trade. Extensive canal construction ultimately made it possible to travel by internal waterways from New York to New Orleans. By the time the Panic of 1837 put an end to the canal boom, some 3,300 miles of canals had been built, mostly in the North.

The steam locomotive marks a new era. At the same time that canals were being dug, railroads were making their first appearance in this country. As early as 1813, Oliver Evans had predicted that steam could be used to move vehicles (page 276). Enthusiasm, however, did not develop overnight. A Boston editor wrote that a railroad from his city to Albany would prove "as useless as a railroad to the moon."

American interest quickened after an Englishman, George Stephenson, invented the steam-driven locomotive in 1825. Just five years later, Peter Cooper's steam engine, the *Tom Thumb*, made a successful trial run out of Baltimore, fulfilling Evans's prediction. Thereafter, the "iron horse," as the steam locomotive was soon called, came into heavy use. Nevertheless, railroad building was haphazard. New Haven and Hartford were linked in Connecticut before a line tied New Haven to New York City. In 1833, 136 miles of track joined Charleston and the small town of Hamburg, South Carolina. For a short time it was the longest railroad in the world.

Railroads spread rapidly. Railroads became the most important method of transportation by the mid-1800's. In 1840 the country had 2,800 miles of railroad track; in 1850, about 9,000 miles. By 1860, this figure had risen to more than 30,000 miles. The effect was felt everywhere. Henry David Thoreau was fascinated by the coming of the railroad. In his book *Walden*, he wrote, "when I hear the iron horse make the hills echo with his snort like thunder, shaking the earth with his feet, and breathing fire and smoke from his nostrils ... it seems as if the earth had got a race now worthy to inhabit it." Railroads speeded up life itself. "Do [people] not talk and think faster in the depot than they did in the stageoffice?" Thoreau asked. Moreover, the need to keep trains on schedule affected everybody, making people more time-conscious than ever before.

The nation enjoyed the excitement of building new lines, and thousands of people invested their money in them. As they awaited their profits, investors could glory in the opening of the road. An entire town, moreover, could know keen satisfaction when the first train pulled in, bearing people, mail, goods — and ideas — from elsewhere.

The canal and turnpike interests, of course, fought the coming of the railroads. One canal agent called the railroad "the Devil's own invention, compounded of fire, smoke, soot, and dirt, spreading its infernal poison throughout the countryside." Such opposition, however, was quickly drowned in a chorus of demands for more railroads.

Railroad networks unify the North. Consolidation of shorter lines into giant railroad systems began to take place in the 1850's. The New York and Erie was the first such line to link the Atlantic seaboard with the Great Lakes. By 1851 its trains were running from New York City to Dunkirk, New York, on Lake Erie. The completion of that line was hailed as the "Work of the Age." The merging of a number of smaller lines between Albany and Buffalo marked the beginning in 1853 of the New York Central system. In that same year, the Baltimore and Ohio reached Wheeling, on the Ohio River. In 1854 the Pennsylvania Railroad connected Philadelphia and Pittsburgh.

As you can see from the map on page 297, most railroad lines built before 1860 ran from east to west. In addition, lines connecting the northern states were more numerous than elsewhere. These lines were simply following natural channels of trade. Eastern factory owners found their best markets in the West, while western farmers sent their goods to Atlantic ports for shipment abroad.

Nowhere were the effects of the improvements in transportation felt more strongly than in the West. The building of turnpikes, canals, and railroads caused that section to grow rapidly. By 1840 its three and a half million people made the region more populous than New England. Within ten years it had well over five million people. Lake and river cities blossomed: Cincinnati, Cleveland, Toledo, Detroit, and Chicago. New states were formed in the region too. Michigan came into the Union in

The Iron-Truss Railroad Bridge

In the 1840's and 1850's railroad lines were constructed along the Atlantic seaboard and across the Appalachian Mountains. The building of these long-distance railroad networks would have been impossible without a means of crossing the many rivers and valleys that characterized the American landscape. New designs and techniques developed by American engineers led to the construction of iron bridges capable of spanning considerable distances and of bearing the enormous weight of locomotives. These railroad bridges were designed so that the burden of weight was equally distributed over a series of triangular-shaped frameworks called trusses. The earliest such bridges were built with cast iron. Later, a stronger, less brittle kind of iron, known as wrought iron, was used.

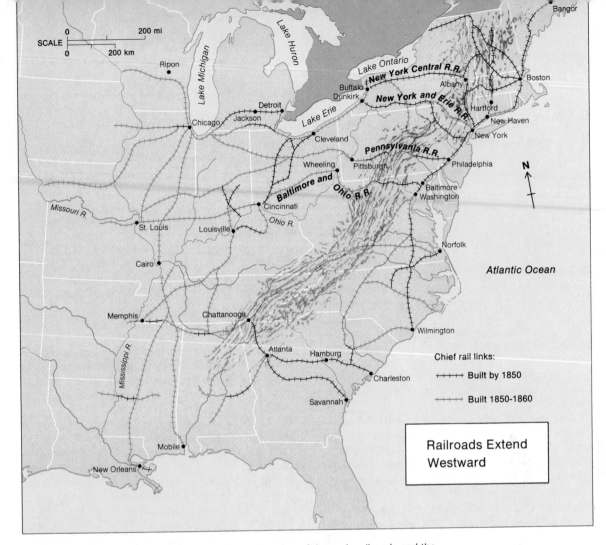

Easily identified on this map are the east-west orientation of the early railroads and the later development of north-south connections.

1837. Iowa was admitted in 1846 and Wisconsin followed two years later. With Minnesota's admission in 1858, the entire west bank of the Mississippi had been carved into states.

The western states were, for the most part, agricultural. By the end of the 1840's, however, their forests were yielding great quantities of lumber, and the iron and copper deposits found along the Great Lakes foretold future industrial development.

The lives of Northerners, then, were more and more influenced by the hum of factory machines and the endless beat of commerce coursing along the canals and railroads. The North seemed to be a section in constant motion. It was unified by an unbounded faith in the future and in the unlimited possibilities open to free people.

SECTION REVIEW

1. Vocabulary: *turnpike.*
2. (a) Why had the need for better roads become important? (b) What was the National Road?
3. (a) Why were canals built? (b) What was the importance of the Erie Canal?
4. (a) Why were Americans enthusiastic about railroad-building in the 1840's and 1850's? (b) How were railroad lines consolidated into systems?
5. What effects did transportation development have on the West?

Chapter 12 Review

Summary

By the beginning of the 1800's farsighted Americans realized the importance of developing manufacturing. Secrets of British industrial technology were leaked to the United States, and factories — especially textile mills — soon appeared. Conveyor belts, steam power, and Eli Whitney's method of using interchangeable parts contributed to rapid industrial growth in the Northeast.

The growth of manufacturing was a fortunate development for New Englanders since their principal occupation, farming, was suffering from competition with the more fertile lands in the West. Yankee business leaders built mills which attracted workers from rural areas and from Europe. The need for workers occasioned a great influx of young New England women into factory towns. As steam-powered vessels and rapid clipper ships were developed, the eastern seaboard became a flourishing center for trade.

Stiffer competition and economic depressions led many factory owners to impose longer working hours and lower wages by the 1830's and 1840's. To protect their interests, some skilled workers organized unions. These labor organizations were weak, however, and met with little notable success. Other responses to the growth of industry included calls for a return to farming and for the creation of utopian communities.

By the mid-1800's an active reform movement had developed in the United States. Reformers advocated tax-supported public education, equal rights and opportunities for women, better care for the disadvantaged and mentally ill, and laws against the consumption of alcohol. Another key area of reform was the abolitionist movement, the effort among blacks and whites to end slavery.

Changes in construction methods and the development of new networks of transportation and commerce contributed to the growth of cities. Agricultural disasters and political repression in Europe led great numbers of people to seek a new life in America, with many settling in the growing cities of the North. Immigrants, while resented by some native-born Americans, made important contributions to the expansion of the nation.

Growth in the North was also spurred by the building of turnpikes, canals, and railroads. In the 1850's, the shorter railroad lines began to be consolidated into large systems that linked East and West, speeding population growth in the lands west of the Appalachians.

Vocabulary and Important Terms

1. interchangeable parts
2. Waltham System
3. craft union
4. National Trades Union
5. collective bargaining
6. strike
7. *Commonwealth v. Hunt*
8. utopian
9. reform movement
10. Seneca Falls convention
11. temperance movement
12. abolitionist
13. *The Liberator*
14. National Road
15. turnpike
16. Erie Canal

Discussion Questions

1. (a) What factors encouraged the early growth of industry in the United States? (b) What technological advances led to improvements in factory production? (c) How did industrial growth affect life in the North?

2. (a) What sources of labor were tapped to obtain the large numbers of workers needed by new factories? (b) What working conditions were present in factories that followed the Waltham System? (c) What working conditions were present in most American factories by the 1830's and 1840's?

3. (a) What was happening to American trade at the same time that industry was growing? (b) What improvements were made in water transportation? (c) How did the expansion of American trade affect life in the North?

4. (a) Why did skilled workers begin to form labor unions in the early 1800's? (b) What demands did workers make, and what methods did they use to try to win those demands? (c) Why did labor parties in this early period have few successes? (d) Why did labor unions likewise fail?

5. (a) What did Horace Mann believe to be the proper concern of all educational reformers? (b) What problems did the movement for tax-supported public education face? (c) What advances were made in public education and higher education by 1850?

6. (a) Who were some of the leading reformers in the movement for women's rights? (b) What were their goals? (c) What opportunities were available for women in American society during this period?

7. (a) When did the abolition movement get its start in America? (b) By the late 1820's, what point of view concerning slavery was accepted by many reformers? (c) How did abolitionists spread their views and their influence in the 1830's and 1840's?

8. (a) What events in Europe contributed to the rising flow of Irish and German immigrants into the United States? (b) What impact did the Irish, Germans, and other immigrants have on American life, and what benefits did they bring to the nation?

9. (a) What improvements in transportation were taking place at the same time that industry and trade were expanding in the Northeast? (b) What impact did these improvements in transportation have on commerce? (c) On the distribution of population?

Relating Past to Present

1. The reform movement flourished in the North from 1830 to 1850. What kinds of reformers are active in American society today? What aspects of American life do they believe are in need of improvement, and what are their goals?

2. The mid-1800's was a period when significant changes in factory methods were taking place. What are some of the major technological improvements taking place in American industry today?

Studying Local History

Find out what effect, if any, the movement for public education had in your state. Who were the leaders? Find out about the state's first public high school and the first institution for higher learning.

Using History Skills

1. *Comparing maps.* Study the maps on pages 293 and 297. (a) What forms of transportation are shown on these maps? (b) Which section of the country had the best system of transportation? (c) What two sections were brought closer together by the growth of transportation?

2. *Comparing.* Find out what made each of the following an effective reformer: (a) Elizabeth Stanton, (b) Dorothea Dix, (c) Theodore Weld.

3. *Classifying.* Make a chart with two columns. In one, list the goals of the movements for women's rights and abolition. In the other, list their accomplishments by 1860.

WORLD SCENE

Migration

The first half of the nineteenth century saw great migrations of peoples in several parts of the world. The movement of Europeans to the northern cities of the United States was one such migration. Other people found their way to the interior of Africa or to Australia.

The Great Trek. One of the most celebrated movements of people took place in Africa. Cape Colony — the territory at the southern tip of Africa — had been settled in the 1600's by Dutch farmers, known as Boers. After the region fell into the hands of Britain, the British imposed restrictions on the Dutch people there. Infuriated, many Boers resolved to leave the Cape. Between 1835 and the early 1840's, nearly 14,000 Boers traveled northeast into the region known as Natal (nah-TAHL). The difficult journey, undertaken on foot and in ox-drawn wagons, became known as the Great Trek.

In Natal, the Boers encountered Zulu tribespeople whom they defeated at the Battle of Blood River in 1838. The political troubles of the Boers, however, were not over. In 1843 the British annexed Natal and forced the Boers to move again, this time to the areas that became the Orange Free State and the Transvaal. Finally, after a three-year war the British defeated the Boers in 1902. Eight years later, Britain joined together Cape Colony, Natal, the Orange Free State, and the Transvaal to form the Union of South Africa.

Australian settlement. The first European settlers in Australia were not pioneer farmers but convicts and their guards. Great Britain, like other European countries of the eighteenth century, often rid itself of criminals by shipping them to distant colonies. In keeping with that policy, Captain Arthur Phillip in 1788 landed at the newly claimed British territory of New South Wales with 730 prisoners. Over the next 80 years, more than 150,000 convicts from the British Isles were sent to Australia.

In 1793 the British government began to allow free settlers to emigrate to Australia and by 1840 free settlers outnumbered the convicts. These settlers demanded political rights and put pressure on Britain to cease exporting its convicts to Australia. They believed that as long as the Australian colonies were heavily populated by convicts, they would not be granted self-government. In 1867 the shipments of prisoners ceased, and three years later all the Australian colonies had gained representative government.

CHAPTER 13

The South: Expansion and Slavery

1780 – 1860

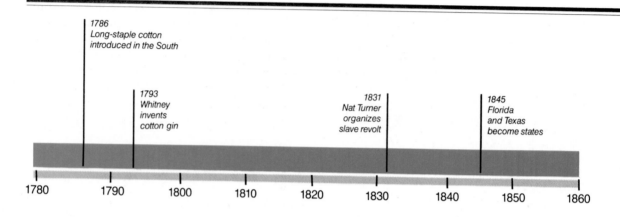

1786
Long-staple cotton
introduced in the South

1793
Whitney
invents
cotton gin

1831
Nat Turner
organizes
slave revolt

1845
Florida
and Texas
become states

1780   1790   1800   1810   1820   1830   1840   1850   1860

CHAPTER OUTLINE

1. Plantation crops shape the southern economy.

2. Cotton comes to dominate the South.

3. The South rallies around slavery.

4. The North and South grow further apart.

Throughout the early 1800's, ways of living and working in the South were becoming more distinct from those of the North. Slavery appeared to be shaping the outlook of Southerners just as the factory system was shaping the outlook of Northerners.

The idea of progress — so important to Northerners — was largely absent in the slave states, as white Southerners resisted any suggestion of change. More and more, southern life was modeled on aristocratic life in western Europe, a way of life that was itself already dying out. Southerners loved to read the novels of Sir Walter Scott, especially *Ivanhoe*, because the stories were set in an age when distinctions between the classes had been sharp and clear. One northern book dealer said he shipped Scott's works to the South by the truckload.

In southern society, tense because of fears for the future, the sharpest resentment was reserved for Northerners who criticized slavery and offered advice on what to do about it. In 1841 a southern member of Congress, himself a critic of the slave system, stated that the South would not accept northern interference. "The cause of the abolitionists," he declared, "has riveted the chains of slavery with double and triple bolts of steel."

1 Plantation Crops Shape the Southern Economy

Ever since the arrival of the first European settlers, the South had been a farming region. By the 1770's a small and tightly knit planter aristocracy had developed on the rich land stretching inland from the Atlantic coast. Tobacco, the most important crop, was raised on large plantations in Virginia, North Carolina, and Maryland, and indigo and rice were cultivated in South Carolina.

The Revolutionary War damages the southern economy. During the American Revolution, many southern planters suffered heavy losses. The struggle with Britain disrupted the colonial economy and cut off markets in Europe for American crops. The war also interrupted the slave trade, raising the cost of black field hands needed to work the plantations.

After the Revolution, the planters attempted to regain their former prosperity. In addition to indigo, rice, and tobacco, they planted wheat and corn, hoping that these crops could be sold abroad and bring new profits. However, disappointment was in store for them. The indigo market in Europe did not recover, and, without the bounty Britain had paid colonial farmers for growing it, indigo was no longer a profitable crop. The market for rice picked up only slowly. Not until 1820 was rice growing again as prosperous as it had been before the war.

The market for tobacco recovered somewhat more quickly, although the American share in the trade was never again as large as it had been earlier. American growers now had to compete with planters in South America and Asia, and the industry in America boomed only when a new curing method was introduced in the 1840's.

White Southerners debate the future of slavery. By the 1820's the agricultural economy of the South was in trouble. Prospects for farming in the states along the Atlantic coast were discouraging. Some Southerners now believed that with less need for farm

In contrast to the North which was undergoing industrialization, the South in the mid-1800's was dependent upon agriculture, including plantation crops.

Eli Whitney's cotton gin prompted planters to concentrate more and more on growing cotton.

hands, the time had come to put an end to the slave system. A number of leading planters, moreover, questioned whether owning slaves was right. Patrick Henry said of slavery, "I cannot justify it." Jefferson, deeply troubled, declared, "I tremble for my country when I reflect that God is just, that His justice cannot sleep forever."

During Jefferson's presidency the importation of slaves was officially ended. In a message to Congress, Jefferson congratulated the nation on ending "those violations of human rights which have been so long continued on the unoffending inhabitants of Africa. . . . " Slavery, however, continued to be in force. Jefferson, for his part, was not in favor of general emancipation. A few planters, including John Randolph, upon their death freed their slaves by will. George Washington left his slaves to his wife but provided that upon her death they "shall have their freedom."

Meanwhile, a wider interest in freeing the slaves grew. Quakers, Baptists, and Methodists, in keeping with their religious outlooks, were increasingly calling for abolition. In 1831 and 1832, the Virginia legislature even debated abolishing slavery in

that state, though no action was taken. In 1834, a Tennessee constitutional convention admitted in a report that, in its view, slavery was wrong. Yet, the report lamented, "To prove it to be evil is an easy task, but to tell how that evil can be removed is a question that the wisest hearts have not been able to answer in a satisfactory manner."

Even among abolitionists there was confusion as to what the future would hold for the slaves once they were freed. Various plans were devised. One such plan, proposed by the American Colonization Society (page 288), had many adherents. The Society had been organized not by northern reformers, but by slave owners in Virginia, Maryland, and Kentucky.

Southern planters seek a new crop. New developments were taking place in southern agriculture, meanwhile, that would boost the economy, revive the need for field hands, and encourage the expansion of the slave system once again. By the late 1700's, many planters and small farmers had begun experimenting with a new cash crop — cotton. The British had recently begun using steam-powered machines to spin cotton yarn and weave cotton cloth. The result — cloth cheaper than ever before — started a revolution in the amount and variety of clothing people could buy. The market for inexpensive cotton fabric seemed unlimited, provided there was enough raw cotton to feed the mills.

The cotton Americans produced was mainly sea-island, or long-staple, cotton.[1] The sea-island seed had been introduced in the United States from the Bahama Islands in 1786. The American crop was an excellent product, but it would only grow near the coast. Short-staple, upland cotton, on the other hand, would grow anywhere, but its clinging green seeds had to be removed laboriously by hand. An experienced laborer could clean only about a pound of short-staple cotton a day.

If planters could find a way to supply short-staple cotton quickly and profitably

---

[1]Long-staple cotton is cotton with long fibers.

to Britain's hungry factories, Southerners believed that their region would come out of its economic slump. The Georgia legislature even offered a prize for a machine that could effectively pick the seeds from short-staple cotton.

Eli Whitney invents the cotton gin. The mechanical genius who found the answer was Eli Whitney (page 277). In 1792 Whitney, recently graduated from Yale College, accepted a place as tutor with a family in South Carolina. On his way south he met the widow of General Nathanael Greene, the Revolutionary War hero. Catherine Greene invited Whitney to spend the winter at her family home in Savannah, Georgia.

Listening to a conversation in Savannah about the need for a device to clean "upland cotton" of its seeds, Whitney, who had never before seen a cotton plant, was intrigued. In ten days he built a model of a cotton-cleaning machine. Whitney's cotton gin was a wooden box filled with stiff wire teeth. When the teeth brushed against the cotton, they picked up the cotton fiber and left the seeds behind. By April, 1793, Whitney had produced an engine, or *gin*, capable of cleaning fifty pounds of cotton a day.

Cotton revives the southern economy. Whitney did not get rich from his invention because the gin was too easy to copy. It cost very little to make, and planters everywhere hurried to build their own machines. The rush was on to take advantage of the huge market for cotton waiting in Great Britain. By the late 1790's planters were producing three million pounds of short-staple cotton each year.

Cotton soon became the South's most important crop. Cotton plantations gradually spread from South Carolina and Georgia into North Carolina and Tennessee. As the price of cotton rose in response to the needs of the growing textile industry, planters devoted more and more land to its cultivation. Cotton wore out the land, to be sure, but there was always new land farther west, or so it seemed. With the rapid development of cotton as a plantation crop, the South's prosperity seemed guaranteed.

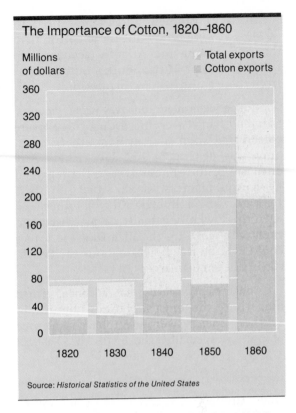

The Importance of Cotton, 1820–1860

Source: *Historical Statistics of the United States*

By 1860, cotton had become the United States' leading export. About 75 percent of the entire cotton crop was grown for foreign trade.

SECTION REVIEW

1. How did the American Revolution affect agriculture in the South?
2. What support was there in the South for the abolition of slavery?
3. (a) What technical problem did the cultivation of short-staple cotton present? (b) How was this difficulty overcome? (c) What impact did cotton have on the southern economy?

2 Cotton Comes to Dominate the South

The steadily increasing need for new land for cotton brought state after state into the Union — Louisiana in 1812, Mississippi in 1817, Alabama in 1819, and Missouri in 1821. Later, other southern states would be added — Arkansas in 1836, and Florida and Texas in 1845.

By 1830, the new states along the Gulf of Mexico were producing more cotton than the states along the Atlantic seaboard. In fact, 75 percent of the South's output came from these southwestern plantations.

Cotton cultivation requires many laborers. So many hands were necessary to cultivate cotton that soon the entire southern economy was dependent on slave labor. Any criticism of the system came to be regarded by cotton planters as an attack on their right to earn a living. Many Southerners, even those who personally despised slavery, eventually gave up the idea that the slaves could ever be freed. Throughout the South, slavery became an accepted fact.

Cotton planters hold great influence. For a long time, the most important figures in southern society were the tobacco and rice planters, especially those in the eastern coastal states. They and their families were often well-educated and cultured. They lived in elegant homes and entertained lavishly, and some were even widely traveled. They formed a small but powerful group, and set a style of life which became the accepted picture of the South to Northerners and to visitors from abroad.

In the early 1800's the old planters were joined by a new class of Southerners, the cotton planters, who were to become the dominant political group in the South. The life the cotton planters led was to some degree lacking in the graciousness that one could find on the old plantations, but the cotton barons did not mind. In their world a person's wealth was measured by the number of acres under cultivation and by the number of slaves one owned.

Actually the number of cotton planters with large slaveholdings was relatively low.

Cotton cultivation, begun in the states along the eastern seaboard, spread southwest to newer states along the Gulf of Mexico and the Mississippi River.

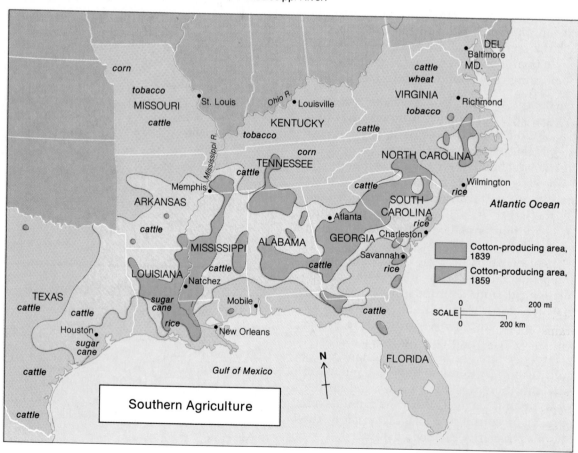

Southern Agriculture

In 1860 only about 2,000 white Southerners owned more than 100 slaves each, with just 11 people owning more than 500. Only one white family in four owned slaves.

Other groups form the bulk of the white population. Three fourths of all white Southerners owned no slaves at all. Nevertheless, almost all of them favored the slave system because, in one way or another, they depended upon it economically. These whites made up several distinct groups.

One group consisted of merchants and professionals — doctors, lawyers, ministers, and teachers. Their livelihood was in large part based on service to the families on the large estates. From these southern white professionals came many of the books and articles defending slavery.

Next below the professionals on the social ladder were the independent farmers of the South. They made up the largest single class of white Southerners. The small farmers worked hard on their few acres, tilling and planting the land and harvesting their crops. They raised enough food for themselves and set aside some acres for cotton or tobacco crops that they could sell.

Like the merchants and professionals, some of the small farmers owned a slave or two. Those who did so worked beside their slaves in the fields. Yet these farmers maintained strict social distinctions between the races. They feared that if slavery were abolished, they would be thrown into economic competition with blacks.

Most independent farmers admired and envied the plantation owners. If some farmers aimed to reach that class themselves, however, few succeeded. They simply could not accumulate enough money.

Below the small farmers on the social ladder were people called "poor whites." They lived, for the most part, in the mountains and in the less fertile "pine-barrens" (timbered land scattered amid richer lands).

The poor whites were really frontier people, encountering all the rigors faced by settlers on the western frontier. On a few acres per family, they grew corn and vegetables. They also raised horses and mules, and some were able to sell hogs for a profit.

Slave Owners, 1850

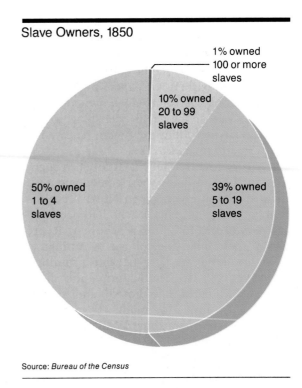

1% owned 100 or more slaves

10% owned 20 to 99 slaves

50% owned 1 to 4 slaves

39% owned 5 to 19 slaves

Source: *Bureau of the Census*

Almost 90 percent of all slaveholders owned fewer than twenty slaves. Those who owned large numbers of slaves were very influential.

Free blacks are a part of southern life. Still another group in southern society consisted of the free blacks. Many had been liberated by their owners for humanitarian reasons, or out of appreciation and affection. Thousands of others had simply run away from bondage and were never found by their former owners.

For some blacks, freedom could be a reward for distinguished public service. A fund collected in Mobile, Alabama, for instance, bought the freedom of Pierre Chastange in 1819 after he had courageously aided people during a yellow fever epidemic.

In 1790, there were about 60,000 free blacks in the South; by 1860 that figure had grown to approximately 260,000. As slaves grew more valuable, however, most states after 1830 restricted or prohibited their release. Free blacks were regarded as a threat to slavery because their very presence was a constant reminder to black people that freedom was possible.

Free blacks frequently earned their livelihood as domestic servants or as hired farm workers. In towns, most were laborers. Some were also skilled at crafts, working as shoemakers, barbers, or paperhangers. Some 3,600 free blacks themselves owned slaves. In many cases, they had been able to buy their relatives, whom they were required by law to maintain as slaves.

A very few free blacks attained recognition in the South for their achievements in the arts and in business. In North Carolina, John Chavis, a free black who had been educated at Princeton, ran a school that prepared young men for college. A number of his white students later became prominent officeholders. In Charleston, John Jones owned one of the best hotels, and in New Orleans, Thomy Lafon made a fortune from his real-estate operations. William Johnson, another free black, owned 1,500 acres of good farmland near Natchez, Mississippi.

Laws restrict free blacks. Free blacks, however, lived uncertain lives. Many feared being kidnapped and sold once again into slavery. If arrested and fined a sum they could not pay, moreover, they could be sold in order to discharge the debt.

During the 1830's, more and more local and state laws were enacted to restrict the movement of free blacks. By 1835, black people had lost the right of assembly everywhere in the South, and numerous other restrictions were placed upon them. In North Carolina, free blacks were no longer permitted to preach freely, to sell goods without a license beyond the county in which they lived, or to own a shotgun without a license. In most states, a free black could not testify against a white person in court. Black Southerners, finally, were often forced to leave their home state upon becoming free.

Most black Southerners are held in bondage. By 1860, nearly four million black Southerners labored as slaves. The treatment of slaves differed from one part of the South to another. Planters who had few slaves and knew them well were inclined to treat them kindly. In other cases, many slaves rarely saw their owners. For instance, some hands worked on rice plantations in the lowlands of South Carolina, which their masters, who lived in Charleston, only visited about once a year.

In the fertile, newer portions of the South where cotton lands were being opened up, slaves were most numerous. There they were generally treated more harshly. They greatly outnumbered the whites in these places and, because escape on the frontier was thought to be easier, were more closely guarded. In the border slave states, the mere threat of being "sold down the river" was said to act as a control on blacks. They understood that conditions were severe on the sugar plantations of Louisiana and on the recently established cotton plantations.

Work on cotton plantations is hard. No matter what treatment slaves received, plantation work in itself was exhausting. On the larger plantations, a bell was rung or a horn sounded before dawn to awaken the slaves. When the sun was well up, a second bell or horn was sounded, and all hands

Planters in the large cotton-producing states transported their cotton by riverboat to ports along the Gulf of Mexico for export to Europe.

The South was overwhelmingly agricultural. The majority of southern farmers lived and worked on small farms, like this one in Texas, rather than on large plantations.

were expected to be in the fields. The work day for the field hands ended only as the sun was setting.

Special techniques were required for the growing of tobacco, rice, and sugar, but the routine of work was about the same as for cotton growing. The hands worked in "gangs," each of which labored under the eyes of a black "driver." Drivers could administer punishment — sometimes with the whip — because they, too, were subjected to beatings if production did not meet expectations.

The particular tasks varied with the season. When the crop had been harvested in the fall, the land itself required attention. Fences had to be repaired, drains cleared, tools sharpened, and wood cut. During the winter, the chores included clearing new land and doing some of the preparatory work for the next growing season.

The least demanding situation for plantation slaves was service in the household. The slaves in the "big house" often bore responsibilities for the well-being of the owner's family and for rearing the children.

Ultimately, no words could hide the nature of slavery. Frederick Douglass, a leading black abolitionist (page 289), wrote of what it was like to be a slave:

> The slave is a human being divested [stripped] of all rights — reduced to the level of a brute — a mere "chattel" [an article of property]. . . . In law the slave has no wife, no children, no country, and no home. He can own nothing, possess nothing, acquire nothing, but must belong to another. He toils [so] that another may reap the fruit . . . he labors in chains at home, under a burning sun and biting lash, that another may ride in ease and splendor . . . he is sheltered only by the wretched hovel [in order] that a master may dwell in a magnificent mansion; and to this condition he is bound down as by an arm of iron.

SECTION REVIEW

1. (a) What was the most important social class in southern society? (b) How did the small white farmers live? (c) Who were the "poor whites"?
2. (a) How did some black Southerners earn their freedom? (b) What restrictions did they face?
3. What work did plantation slaves do?

3 The South Rallies Around Slavery

As the number of blacks — both slave and free — increased in the early 1800's, state and local governments in the South enacted hundreds of laws to restrict or regulate their lives and actions.

Town laws regulate slaves. Although the southern economy was mainly agricultural, a small number of manufacturing industries had been started in town and cities. Some slaves were hired out to these businesses by owners who had no immediate need for their services. Richmond, for example, had not only the Tredegar Iron Works — the South's largest foundry — but tobacco factories as well. At the foundry and in the factories, slaves did practically all the work.

Southern towns passed laws requiring slaves working in local businesses to live either on the premises of their owner or on those of the owner's representative. The penalties for violating these restrictions

---

EYEWITNESS TO HISTORY

A Slave Woman's Story

Linda Brent lived in South Carolina as a slave until the age of 27. In 1844 she escaped and made her way to New York. In this passage from an account of her life as a slave, she told how the strict codes of slavery kept her from marrying the man she loved.

There was in the neighborhood a young black carpenter — a free-born man. We became mutually attached, and he proposed to marry me. But when I reflected that I was a slave, and that the laws gave no sanction to the marriage as such, my heart sank within me.

My suitor wanted to buy my freedom; but I knew that Dr. Flint [Linda Brent's owner] was too willful and arbitrary a man to consent to that arrangement. From him, I was sure of experiencing all sorts of opposition, and I had nothing to hope from my mistress. Like so many others, she seemed to think that slaves had no right to any family ties of their own; that they were created merely to wait upon the family of the mistress.

The man I loved was intelligent and religious. Even if he could have obtained permission to marry me while I was a slave, the marriage would give him no power to protect me from my master. It would have made him miserable to witness the insults I should have been subjected to. And then, if we had children, I knew they must "follow the condition of the mother." What a terrible blight that would be on the heart of a

A woman held in slavery

free, intelligent father! For his sake, I felt that I ought not to link his fate with my own unhappy destiny.

He was going to Savannah to see about a little property left him by an uncle; and hard as it was to bring my feelings to it, I earnestly entreated him not to come back. I advised him to go to the free states, where his tongue would not be tied and where his intelligence would be of more avail to him. He left me, still hoping the day would come when my freedom could be bought.

were severe. A slave required a "ticket," properly signed, in order to live elsewhere, even temporarily. Enforcement proved difficult, however, and at times slaves were on their own, out of the reach of supervisors. They found rooms in every part of town, usually taking the poorest dwelling available. Nevertheless, these arrangements allowed slaves relative freedom. A southern editor complained in the 1840's that blacks living apart from their owners were proving "a great source of the corruption and discontent of our slaves."

As the races were increasingly separated in the social structure, a form of public control was exercised over all blacks — free as well as slave. In cities and towns, restaurants and hotels would not serve black people. New Orleans, for example, began to provide separate cars for black passengers on its street railway. In some cities, black pedestrians could not use certain streets. *Segregation* thus became part of urban life, with separate cemeteries, prisons, poor houses, and hospitals.

Plantation slaves find ways to protest. On plantations, there were a number of unstated ways for slaves to resist the system of bondage. Owners understood that frequently there would be deliberate loafing on the job. From time to time, slaves would protest more directly the harshness of their lives by damaging crops, injuring livestock, destroying tools or machinery, or by stealing from the main house.

Slave revolts are difficult to organize. Open revolt was yet another method of resistance, but one not lightly undertaken. While successful slave revolts had broken out in such places as Haiti (page 216), they were rare in the South. One reason was that blacks were a minority of the population in all of the southern states except South Carolina and Mississippi. The number of slaves on a given plantation was also relatively small, unlike, by contrast, the slave populations on the great sugar plantations of the Caribbean. Slave owners were usually able to keep all their slaves under constant surveillance, and punishment for slaves who re-

Resisting their bondage, some black Southerners made desperate attempts to escape to freedom in the North, not always with success.

belled was sure to be swift. Slaves also had little experience with firearms and, knowing that whites could use them with skill, feared the consequences of resistance.

Another reason that revolts were rare in the South was that there was a steady westward movement of slaves, as they were taken to the new cotton plantations on the frontier. This shifting of people westward disrupted the ties of friendship between blacks, preventing the kinds of close bonds out of which conspiracies could develop. In addition, slaves regarded as troublemakers by their owners could readily be sold before they created problems.

A number of slave uprisings take place. Still, some ferocious uprisings broke out, all the more remarkable for the odds against their occurrence. One, known as Cato's Revolt, took place in 1739 near Charleston. Thirty whites were killed before it was harshly suppressed. Forty-four blacks either died in the fighting or were executed later.

White slaveholders were frightened when they heard about the slave revolt in Haiti in the early 1790's. Their fears seemed justified when, in 1800, Gabriel Prosser and Jack Bowler gathered a thousand slaves outside of Richmond, Virginia, with the intention of marching on the city. The planned revolt was quickly crushed, however, after two slaves tipped off the authorities. James Monroe, then Virginia's governor, had called out the state militia, which quickly put down the uprising.

In the following decade, tension was high in Virginia and in North Carolina. From time to time slaves would be hanged for taking part in what were said to be conspiracies. Then, in 1811, several hundred armed Louisiana slaves set out for New Orleans. On the way they set fire to several plantations and killed a number of whites. The uprising was smashed well before it reached its destination. The following year New Orleans was the scene of a revolt, and 82 slaves were captured and executed.

In 1822, as many as 10,000 slaves were involved in a plot in Charleston. They were led by Denmark Vesey, a former slave who had purchased his freedom with money he won in a lottery. With the cooperation of a blacksmith who made weapons — daggers and pikes — and a barber who fashioned wigs and beards for disguises, an uprising designed to take over Charleston was planned for a summer Sunday. The plot was crushed, however, after an informer alerted local authorities. Thirty-seven blacks were hanged and many others banished from the state. Four whites who had aided the plot were fined and sent to jail.

Although every precaution was taken to prevent further uprisings, many slave owners were gloomy about the prospects of keeping their slaves under control. They became especially alarmed when copies of an abolitionist pamphlet entitled *Walker's Appeal to the Colored Citizens of the World* appeared in 1829. Published by a free black, David Walker, it was widely circulated among the slaves and inflamed the fears of white Southerners.

Nat Turner's revolt inspires fear. In 1831 an insurrection in Virginia startled and terrified slave owners everywhere. This uprising was led by Nat Turner. Turner, a slave, had been taught to read by one of his owner's sons. When the white boys were sent to school and Turner was sent to work in the fields, however, he became deeply embittered. Encouraged by his mother, Turner grew up to be a preacher of considerable ability. He came to believe that he had a divine mission to deliver black people from bondage.

Turner was able to gather together a band of slaves and organize a revolt. The uprising, first planned for the Fourth of July, was postponed when Turner fell ill. Turner and his band finally attacked a number of white homes on August 21, 1831. Before the end of the rebellion, about 160 people of both races had been killed. Turner and nineteen others were caught and hanged.

Slave codes are strengthened. Nat Turner's Rebellion had a profound effect throughout the South. It immediately put an end to the South's abolition societies and the talk among Southerners of eventual emancipation. For years, Virginia in particular was in a state of near panic, fed by constant rumors of new trouble.

In some parts of the South, laws required that black people wear tags identifying them as slave or free.

Young adults were especially in danger of being sold away from their families because they were capable of hard labor, a quality that slaveholders valued.

Laws restricting the conduct and activities of slaves were already in effect throughout the South. Now these *slave codes,* as they were called, were made tighter. When violators were caught, punishment was swift and cruel.

Under the slave codes, blacks could no longer serve as ministers. It was feared that black ministers might preach passages from the Bible that, for example, described the Israelites' flight from slavery in Egypt. Slaves could only attend their owners' churches and hear sermons based on the theme of obedience. Strict nighttime curfews were also enforced. A slave needed a pass to be away from a plantation, and from time to time slave quarters were searched for weapons. Other parts of the codes carefully regulated relations between the races. Even a small gathering of slaves, without the presence of a white, was considered to be an "unlawful assembly."

One provision of the codes, however, was frequently neglected in practice. Whites were prohibited from teaching slaves to read or write. One state law, for example, warned that "the teaching of slaves to read and write has a tendency to excite dissatisfaction in their minds, and to produce rebellion that injures the citizens of this state." Yet a southern editor remarked that he had never heard of a slave who wanted to read who had been prevented from doing so. The southern abolitionist Sarah Grimké (page 289), knowing that she was risking a large fine, taught one of her family's slaves to read. She described a typical lesson: "The light was put out, the keyhole screened, and, flat on our stomachs, before the fire, with the spelling-book under our eyes, we defied the laws of South Carolina."

Slaves suffer the breakup of families. Perhaps the cruelest aspect of slavery was the forced separation of families. Slaves were traded or sold at auctions with little regard for family relationships. One man explained what had happened to him when he was a little boy:

> My brothers and sisters were sold off first, and one by one, while my mother held me by the hand. Her turn came, and she was bought by a man named Isaac Riley. Then I was offered to the assembled purchasers. . . . She fell at Riley's feet, entreating him to spare her one, at least, of her little ones. Can it be believed that this man freed himself from her with such violent blows and kicks as to reduce her to the necessity of creeping out of his reach?

Ways of escape are developed. Even though many slaves were miserable in their bondage, it was very hard for them to escape. Once in a while a slave would hide for a time in a nearby swamp, possibly only to avoid punishment. Soon, however, the slave would be hunted down or would surrender out of fear or hunger.

Beginning in the 1830's, some slaves were helped to freedom by the development of the Underground Railroad. The "Railroad" was a series of stopping places, beginning near the cotton-growing states and extending northward, that made it possible for slaves to find safety in the North or in Canada. It was established by abolitionists and operated mostly by free blacks.

One of the best-known organizers of the Underground Railroad was Levi Coffin, a Quaker abolitionist who made his house in Indiana one such stopping-off station. Coffin always kept a horse and wagon ready to help a runaway. Many people considered him to be "President" of the Underground Railroad, because he helped more than 3,000 slaves to escape. Another "conductor" of the escape route was Robert Purvis, a black Philadelphian. Purvis had helped organize the American Antislavery Society. He was also the first head of the mostly white Pennsylvania Antislavery Society. Like similar groups elsewhere, this organization raised money to aid slaves who escaped to freedom. One of the bravest "conductors" was John Fairfield, whose family owned slaves in Virginia, but who himself detested slavery. Wearing various disguises, Fairfield traveled south, seeking out and reuniting slaves with their relatives or friends who had reached the North or Canada.

Harriet Tubman, a former slave, was another leading "conductor." In her own escape from a plantation in Virginia, she had been guided only by the light of the North Star. Tubman, who was called "Moses" by her people, went back into the South at least nineteen times during the 1850's to rescue her parents, her children, her sister, and hundreds of other slaves. Her special technique was to return north on Saturday and Sunday, when most newspapers did not publish. She would thus have two days to travel before the owners could advertise for the return of their runaways.

White Southerners defend slavery. The Underground Railroad was just one way in which Northerners interfered with the slave system. Soon, pressure from northern abolitionists caused new anxieties in the South. White Southerners were beginning to fear that their "peculiar institution" was endan-

Harriet Tubman urged that fugitives make their way to Canada to assure their freedom.

gered and began to present new arguments in its favor.

One of the most influential advocates of the slave system was Thomas Dew. The son of a Revolutionary War veteran, Dew had been an army captain in the War of 1812. Later, he became a teacher at the College of William and Mary in Virginia.

Dew developed the argument that, since slaves were mentioned in the Bible, slavery was approved by divine authority. He disputed the argument of the Declaration of Independence that "all men are created equal." Instead, Dew used passages from the Scriptures to insist that people were unequal — some fit only to do manual labor and others clearly qualified to be the managers of society.

As agitation by northern abolitionists increased, the arguments put forward by the defenders of slavery became sharper. A Virginia lawyer named George Fitzhugh built a proslavery reputation in the 1850's. He argued that the North increasingly would be forced to deal with labor strikes and deteriorating conditions among its workers. The only solution for these expected labor problems, as he saw it, was for northern industrialists to adopt slavery. "Slavery," he predicted, "will everywhere be abolished or everywhere be reinstituted."

Once, when Fitzhugh was traveling in the North, he was taken to see how well free working people lived. He nonetheless refused to change his belief that the slave system was superior, insisting that blacks were better off in bondage. "The Southerner is the Negro's friend, his only friend," he said. "Let no intermeddling abolitionist dissolve this friendship."

Some Southerners remain critical of slavery. A number of white Southerners, however, refused to accept these defenses of slavery, knowing that they contradicted the principles of liberty on which the nation had been founded.

Among the southern critics of slavery was James C. Birney (page 270). To champion abolition, as Birney did, required uncommon courage. Birney broke with his father and other members of his family over the issue of slavery. Even as he lay dying, in 1857, he refused to see his sister because she still owned slaves.

The critic of slavery who most outraged his fellow Southerners was Hinton Rowan Helper of North Carolina. In 1857 he expressed his views in a book published in New York, *The Impending Crisis of the South: How to Meet It.* Slavery, Helper insisted, was impoverishing the small farmers of the South. Moreover, he claimed, planters were constantly using their surplus money to expand their cotton fields instead of using the capital to build factories. Slavery, according to Helper, was making Southerners the economic prisoners of the North:

> If you would, fix your mind on a southern "gentleman." Observe the routine of his daily life. See him rise in the morning from a northern bed, and clothe himself in northern apparel; see him walk across the floor on a northern carpet. . . . See him uncover a box of northern powders, and cleanse his teeth with a northern brush. . . . See him at the breakfast table saying grace over a northern plate, eating with northern cutlery, and drinking from northern utensils. . . . See him riding to his neighbor's in a northern carriage, or furrowing his lands with a northern plow. His labors, his talents, his influence, are all for the North, and not for the South. . . .

What angered the planters and made them regard Helper as particularly dangerous was that he aimed his words to the great majority of white Southerners — those who owned no slaves. In some places in the South, a person could be arrested for possessing a copy of *The Impending Crisis.*

SECTION REVIEW

1. Vocabulary: *segregation, slave codes.*
2. Describe some of the laws that regulated slave life in southern towns and cities.
3. (a) In what ways did slaves protest their condition? (b) Why were slave revolts hard to organize? (c) What slave revolts did take place?
4. (a) What was the Underground Railroad? (b) Who were some of its organizers?
5. (a) What arguments did southern defenders of slavery put forward? (b) What arguments did southern opponents of slavery use?

4 The North and South Grow Further Apart

By the 1850's, as attacks on slavery were heard less frequently in the South, criticism of other social evils also died out. The spirit of reform that was stirring in the North was rarely felt in the slave states.

Social reform is slow in the South. For most white Southerners, reform of any kind was associated with abolition. For years, southern postmasters had censored incoming mail, to dam up the flow of abolitionist propaganda. In so doing, they kept out other reform literature as well, fearing its effects on the South. The leading southern politicians, furthermore, were absorbed in national affairs, to the considerable neglect of local matters — including social reform. Thus, in defending slavery, Southerners were closing the door to useful social im-provements and to new thinking on public problems.

Still, while Southerners were opposed to introducing the "isms," as they called them, of northern reform, they were working hard to establish what they called "Christian justice." In particular, they worked to reform the criminal justice system. Between 1815 and 1850, Southerners eliminated many of the harsh methods of punishment that had existed from colonial times — branding, flogging, and confinement to stocks. The number of crimes for which death was the penalty was reduced in all the southern states.

The South also made notable advances in improving prison conditions. The Auburn system of providing separate cells for prisoners, which had begun in New York, was widely copied. Dorothea Dix brought to the South her crusade to improve conditions for the mentally ill. Under her influence, the southern states built asylums to

A canal built in 1830 enabled boats to bypass the falls of the Ohio River and brought about a great increase in river traffic. As a result, Louisville grew rapidly in the 1830's and 1840's, reaching a population of 43,000 by mid-century.

keep mentally ill patients separate from criminals.

River towns and ports show rapid growth. A number of southern towns and cities, meanwhile, were growing in size. River towns, such as Louisville, St. Louis, and New Orleans, gained from the new steamboat trade and expanded rapidly. In Tennessee, the city of Memphis grew from a population of 8,800 in 1850 to more than 22,000 in 1860. Atlanta also, mushroomed, mostly as a result of railroad building.

The South was fortunate to have good harbors. New Orleans was its most important port, and by 1850 that city was a bustling center of about 150,000 people. Each year, thousands of flatboats carrying farm products sailed down the Mississippi to New Orleans. To it also came cotton and sugar from the plantations of the Gulf states, to be loaded on ships and sent to northern cities or Europe.

The second-ranking southern port was Mobile, Alabama, and after it came Savannah, Georgia. Charleston, a leading port since early colonial days, declined after cotton became the South's most important crop. Charleston was not situated on a river that could easily receive cotton from plantations in the interior.

Industrial development lags in the South. Despite the expansion of agricultural production and the growth of some towns and cities, little industrial progress was made in the South. Some attempts at manufacturing were made, particularly in Virginia, but the value of the goods produced was small. Railroads, moreover, were not as numerous in the South as in the North because the money required to build them was not available. The railroads that were built usually failed to link the South to the rest of the Union. A rail line between Charleston and Cincinnati, which had once been proposed, might have created closer economic ties between western farmers and the planters of the South. It was never built, however. The farmers of the western regions, meanwhile, were becoming more and more dependent on their markets in the North.

In foreign commerce, too, the South lagged far behind the North. Exports from the busy ports were not sufficient to make the economy boom. Imports into southern harbors were valued far below the value of outgoing cargoes. New Orleans, for instance, usually received imports amounting to only about 25 percent of its exports. Ships returning from Europe brought their wares to northern ports instead, where merchants gained profits by selling the manufactured goods to their southern customers. As Hinton Helper pointed out (page 313), Southerners reinvested much of their money in slaves, putting little into the development of merchandising, insurance, banking, or other commercial businesses. These profitable enterprises were almost always owned by people in the big cities of the North. Southern cotton planters were usually in debt to Northerners for long-term loans, very much as tobacco planters had been in debt to English merchants before the Revolution. For this reason many Southerners were inclined to consider themselves in the spiteful grip of a new "Lord North."

A few southern writers tried vainly to encourage the building of more railroads and factories and the opening of more direct trade with Europe. By the 1850's, however, the South's economic life was staked on the continuation of cotton prosperity. Most Southerners believed, in fact, that the North's prosperity, no less than that of the South, was dependent on cotton. They cheered in agreement when Senator James Hammond of South Carolina thundered on the floor of the Senate, "You dare not make war on cotton — no power on earth dares make war on it. Cotton is King!"

SECTION REVIEW

1. (a) Why was the movement for social reform slow in the South? (b) What steps toward social reform were taken?
2. (a) What southern ports became important urban centers? (b) How did the South compare with the North in railroad construction, growth of industry, and foreign commerce?

Chapter 13 Review

Summary

After the Revolutionary War, the agricultural economy of the South declined and southern planters began looking for a new crop to bring about a return of prosperity. Then, as a result of the invention of the cotton gin in 1793, cotton cultivation spread throughout the region.

In the years before 1830, many Southerners deplored the institution of slavery. Reform-minded religious groups called for its abolition. Even some southern states debated its merits. As cotton became the South's most important crop and as the need for field hands grew, however, many of these voices were stilled. Increasingly, cotton and slavery came to dominate southern life.

Slaveholding cotton planters, though a minority of the southern population, became the most important social and political force in the region. Other whites supported the institution of slavery even if they owned no slaves themselves. Some believed it essential to the South. Others feared the competition for jobs if slaves were freed. Free blacks, meanwhile, formed another segment of southern society. Most lived and worked in towns, where they were strictly regulated by local laws.

Most black Southerners labored as slaves. The condition of slavery varied from place to place, but no matter what treatment they received, the slaves' lot was a hard one. Some slave revolts took place, and white Southerners, fearing the disruption of their "peculiar institution," enforced strict slave codes. The Underground Railroad, nevertheless, enabled some slaves to escape to freedom in the North and in Canada.

After 1830, as abolitionist sentiment grew in the North, southern defenders of slavery became more outspoken. A southern critic named Hinton Helper pointed out, however, that it was slavery itself that was holding back the economic development of the South. In those years, while railroads were beginning to crisscross the North and while northern factories and trade with Europe flourished, little industrial growth took place in the South.

Vocabulary and Important Terms

1. short-staple cotton
2. cotton gin
3. segregation
4. slave codes
5. Underground Railroad
6. *The Impending Crisis of the South*
7. Auburn system

Discussion Questions

1. (a) What was the condition of the South's agricultural economy by the 1820's? (b) Why did some Southerners believe that the time had come to put an end to slavery?
2. (a) Why did planters and small farmers begin experimenting with cotton in the late 1700's? (b) What were the results of their experiments?
3. (a) Once cotton had become the South's main crop, why did the plantation system spread rapidly into new areas? (b) What new states entered the Union as a result of more land being placed under cultivation for cotton? (c) How did cotton production in the new states compare to that of the older states?
4. How did the cultivation of cotton affect the slave system and the attitude of most white Southerners about the future of that system?
5. (a) Into what social classes was southern society divided? (b) How did the life of planters differ from that of other white Southerners?
6. (a) Why were free blacks regarded as a threat to the slave system? (b) How did local and state laws reflect the concerns of white Southerners about free blacks?
7. (a) In what ways did the slaves lead hard lives, and what was perhaps the cruelest aspect of slavery? (b) What effect did Nat Turner's Rebellion have throughout the South?
8. (a) In response to criticisms of slavery, what new arguments in favor of slavery did white Southerners begin to present? (b) Why did some Southerners, such as Hinton Helper, remain critical of slavery?
9. (a) By the 1850's, why did Southerners consider themselves to be in the grip of a new "Lord North"? (b) What did they mean when they proclaimed "Cotton is King"?

Relating Past to Present

1. By 1850 the southern economy depended upon the cultivation of cotton. What crops do southern farmers raise today? What different kinds of industry has the South developed to go along with its agriculture?
2. By the 1850's the North and the South had developed as two distinct regions. In what ways, if any, have the North and the South retained distinctive ways of living?

Studying Local History

By the mid-1800's, cotton had become "king" in the South. Has any crop similarly dominated the agricultural economy of your state or region? What crops do the farmers of your state or region produce for sale today?

Using History Skills

1. *Reading maps.* Study the map of the South on page 304. (a) In what states was cotton grown by 1839? (b) In what other states was it grown by 1859? (c) In what southern states was little or no cotton grown? How can you account for the variations in cotton agriculture?

2. *Reading graphs.* Study the graph showing the economic importance of cotton on page 303. (a) What was the approximate value of exported cotton in 1820? (b) In 1860? (c) Why might the 1860 figure have convinced Southerners that cotton would always be "king"?

3. *Comparing sources.* Study Frederick Douglass's account of slavery on page 307. (a) According to Douglass, what specific rights was a slave denied? (b) How does Linda Brent's account of her experience on page 308 reinforce Douglass's description of slavery?

4. *Writing a report.* Find out more about the life of Eli Whitney. Study his personal background and learn about other devices he invented besides the cotton gin. Write a short report on your findings.

WORLD SCENE

Plantation Agriculture

By the early 1800's plantation agriculture was thriving not only in the American South but also in other parts of the world. Two notable areas of plantation agriculture were Egypt and Brazil.

Egyptian cotton. Mohammed Ali, the Ottoman governor of Egypt from 1805 to 1848, introduced the plantation system of agriculture into the Middle East. An ambitious young officer, Mohammed Ali, sought to establish a dynasty in Egypt. To finance his plans — which included modernization, industrialization, and military expansion — he looked for a cash crop that could be produced by peasant labor. He found that cotton was a suitable crop. Between 1824 and 1830 alone, he increased by eightfold the amount of land devoted to cotton cultivation in Egypt.

Mohammed Ali made the large-scale production of cotton possible by having peasants extend the irrigation system used since ancient times. He then ordered that cotton be sold only to the government. The treasury quickly filled as the government bought the high-quality cotton from the peasants and sold it to Europeans at a substantial profit.

Egypt prospered during the mid-nineteenth century, helping to supply the raw material for England's cotton mills. Cotton prices skyrocketed during the American Civil War, but the end of the war marked the end of the boom in the "white gold." By 1876 Egypt was bankrupt.

Brazilian plantations. Brazil, like the American South, attracted European colonists because it contained magnificent tracts of land suitable for the cultivation of cash crops. The only major obstacle to cultivation was a severe shortage of labor. Brazil overcame this obstacle through the importation of African slaves.

The first Brazilian plantations, begun with slave labor in the mid-1500's, produced sugar. Sugar had been known in Europe since the time of Alexander the Great, but only as an item of luxury. Sugar cane flourished in the climate of Brazil and was grown there in such quantity in the 1500's and 1600's that prices fell, and sugar became a common part of European diets.

In the 1700's cotton outstripped sugar as Brazil's main export. Then, in the early 1800's the cotton gin came into use in the United States, and American plantations soon moved ahead of Brazil's in cotton production. At that point the Brazilian government, newly independent from Portugal, began to encourage planters to cultivate a new luxury crop — coffee. By the late 1800's coffee had become the nation's main export. Brazil remains today one of the leading producers of coffee in the world market.

UNIT 3 REVIEW

Important Dates

1803 *Marbury v. Madison* decision.
Louisiana Purchase.
1804 Lewis and Clark expedition begins.
1807 Embargo Act.
1811 Battle of Tippecanoe.
1812 War with Britain begins.
1814 Treaty of Ghent.
1819 Adams-Onís Treaty.
1820 Missouri Compromise.
1821 First public high school (Boston).
1823 Monroe Doctrine proclaimed.
1825 Erie Canal completed.
1830 Indian Removal Act.
Webster-Hayne debate.
1831 Nat Turner organizes slave revolt.
1832 Jackson vetoes bank bill.
1834 National Trades Union established.
1837 Oberlin College accepts women students.
1848 Seneca Falls convention.

Review Questions

1. (a) The statement "Europe's distresses were America's diplomatic successes" has been used to explain the achievements of the young republic in its foreign relations. What diplomatic successes did the United States have in its relations with France and Spain in the years between 1801 and 1819? (b) Describe the relations between the United States and Great Britain during this same period. What diplomatic successes, if any, did the United States enjoy?

2. (a) In what sense was the War of 1812 a second struggle for American independence? (b) What effect did the war have on the American people and their sense of national unity? (c) In what ways did that national unity soon become apparent?

3. (a) The Monroe Doctrine has been called America's second Declaration of Independence. What events led up to its announcement, and why did the United States decide to act alone? (b) What are the Doctrine's major points?

4. (a) How did the decisions of the Marshall Court strengthen both the power of the Supreme Court and the power of the national government? (b) Which decisions by the Marshall Court did Presidents Jefferson and Jackson dispute? Why?

5. What contributions did Jefferson and Jackson each make to the concept of the American presidency?

6. (a) By the 1820's sectionalism was on the rise. How were the dispute over Missouri's admission to the Union and the election of 1824 evidence of this sectionalism? (b) How did the different sections divide over the issues of the tariff, internal improvements, and the Bank of the United States?

7. (a) What sources of labor were tapped to work in the northern factories and on southern plantations? (b) Under what conditions did factory and plantation workers labor, and to what extent was each group able to show its discontent with these conditions?

8. (a) What advances were made in American transportation by 1860? (b) For what reasons did cities grow, both in the North and the South?

Projects

1. Write a report on one of the leading "War Hawks" in Congress. Find out about the individual's background, his reasons for encouraging war against Great Britain, his role in moving the country toward war, and his life and career after the War of 1812.

2. Participate in a classroom debate on the issue of the protective tariff. Some members of the class should take the northern position and support the tariff. Others should take the southern position and oppose it.

3. Form a classroom panel to examine the American reform movement that began in the 1820's. The panel should identify the various reform movements and their goals, outstanding reform leaders, the ways in which reformers worked toward their goals, and the reformers' accomplishments. Panel members should also discuss whether the goals of the reform movements were reasonable, whether the methods of the reformers were effective, and whether the accomplishments of the reformers were meaningful.

4. Write a book report on Alexis de Tocqueville's *Democracy in America* or on Francis J. Grund's *Aristocracy in America*. In your book report, note the key observations made about American society. Also tell why the book is important to the study of American history.

5. Make a bulletin board display in which you illustrate the differences that had developed by 1860 in ways of living and working in the North and the South.

6. Find out more about one of the means of transportation that revolutionized Amerian society during the first half of the 1800's and report on it. Possible subjects are steamboats, packet ships, clipper ships, or steam engines. You might include with your report a model or drawing of your subject.

4

UNION AND DISUNION
1820 – 1877

"A house divided against itself cannot stand." I believe this
government cannot endure permanently half slave and half free.
I do not expect the Union to be dissolved; I do not expect the
house to fall; but I do expect it will cease to be divided. It will
become all one thing, or all the other.

ABRAHAM LINCOLN, 1858

From Sea to Sea

1820 – 1855

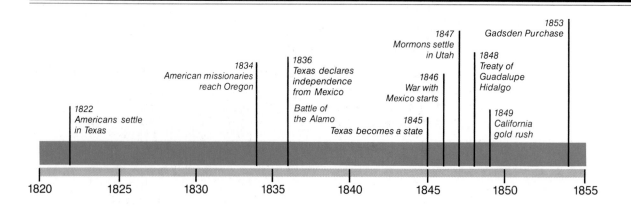

CHAPTER OUTLINE

1. American settlers move to Oregon and the Great Basin.

2. Americans become interested in California and the Southwest.

3. The United States acquires Texas and Oregon.

4. The United States fights a war with Mexico.

5. Gold seekers rush to California.

To every generation of English-speaking settlers, "the West" has had a different meaning. The first colonists to move a few miles inland from the Atlantic coast "moved west." At the beginning of the 1700's, pioneers who journeyed to the far side of the Appalachians had "moved west." By the end of the century the West was Kentucky and the Ohio River valley. Finally, by 1820 the ever-changing West had reached the Mississippi River.

For some fifty years hardy pioneers believed that the land between the Mississippi and Missouri rivers and the Rocky Mountains was a Great American Desert, "almost wholly unfit for cultivation," as one traveler put it. People heading west, therefore, made their way to the fertile Pacific Coast. In struggling to reach the Pacific, they were motivated by the idea that Providence had intended America to extend its authority to its geographical limits. The editor of the *Democratic Review*, a magazine, coined the phrase "manifest destiny" in 1845 to describe this westward push.

Many Americans believed that the nation's destiny was to spread its form of government not only across the continent but to the far shore of the Pacific as well. A powerful spokesman for manifest destiny was a Missourian, William Gilpin. Wrote Gilpin: "The democratic republican image of North America is . . . predestined to expand and fix itself to the continent; to control the oceans on either hand, and eventually the continents beyond them."

1 American Settlers Move to Oregon and the Great Basin

Although many Americans were thinking grand thoughts about spreading the nation's form of government abroad, immediate attention centered on the Oregon Country. Interest in Oregon had been growing for a long time.

Britain and the United States claim Oregon. Oregon first came to American attention in 1788 when a Boston sea captain, Robert Gray, sailed into the area of Vancouver Island, off the northwest coast of the continent. In 1792 Gray became the first American to sail into the mouth of the Columbia River. A number of years later a ship owned by John Jacob Astor's American Fur Company retraced the route Gray had traveled around South America, and in 1811 Astor established his trading post at the mouth of the Columbia (page 220). This voyage became the basis for the claims of Astor's Company and of the United States to the Pacific Northwest. Britain, however, also laid claim to the region, based on the early exploration there of an English sea captain.

The rich Oregon Country had once been claimed by France, Spain, and Russia. France gave up its rights when it sold Louisiana to the United States in 1803. Spain surrendered its claim when it sold Florida to the United States in 1819. In 1824 Russia yielded its claim (page 242).

The region now belonged to the United States and Britain — or to whichever could make its claim stick. In 1818 the two countries agreed to occupy the Oregon Country jointly for the next ten years. Under this arrangement, British and American settlers alike could enjoy the use of the Columbia River valley. In 1827, after again failing to reach a permanent compromise on ownership of the land, the United States and Britain renewed the joint occupation for an indefinite period.

The Pacific Northwest begins to attract Americans. To most Americans, Oregon was too

Rugged pioneers made their way westward along such routes as the Oregon Trail, shown in this painting by Albert Bierstadt.

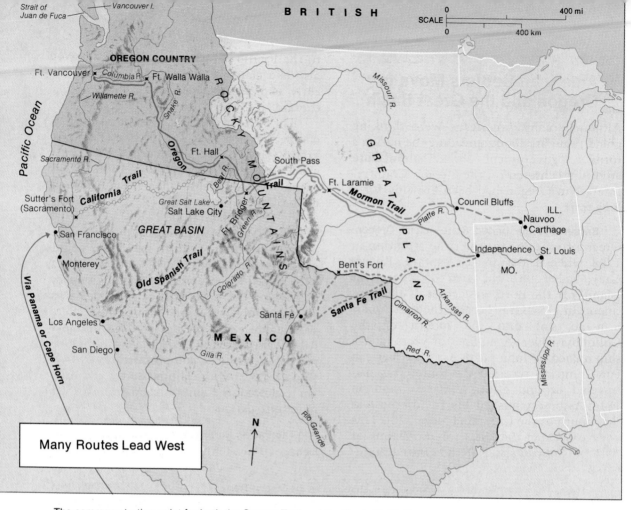

Many Routes Lead West

The common starting point for both the Oregon Trail and the Santa Fe Trail was Independence, Missouri, as shown on this map.

far away to be of interest or concern. A few foresighted Americans could predict, however, that Oregon would one day be valuable to the United States. One of these was Dr. John Floyd, a member of Congress from Virginia. Floyd was a friend of William Clark (who with Meriwether Lewis had explored the Louisiana Territory). Floyd kept the Oregon question before Congress when, from 1821 on, he introduced bills to organize the Oregon Country. They were all voted down because most congressmen could not yet envision American settlements on the Pacific shore.

Pioneer farmers, however, gradually created an interest in Oregon that Easterners could not ignore. The people were lured to the region by reports of its beauty and rich natural resources. One early spokesman for Oregon was a Boston school-teacher named Hall Jackson Kelley. Kelley read the reports of Lewis and Clark with much excitement and became obsessed with the idea of American settlement in Oregon.

Kelley was himself unequal to the task of managing a colonizing expedition to Oregon, but he succeeded in interesting others. Among them was Nathaniel Wyeth, a Massachusetts ice merchant who, it was said, had invented every tool used in the ice industry. Wyeth organized a company to develop resources along the Columbia River. His little band of 31 men first practiced frontier living on an island in Boston harbor, garbed in uniforms featuring broad belts from which dangled the tools they thought they would need — bayonets, knives, and axes. Starting overland from Boston for the Pacific Northwest in 1832, they sent their heavy provisions around

South America by ship. These supplies unfortunately never arrived. After reaching Oregon, Wyeth returned to Boston with a handful of his original party.

Although the effort to establish a trading company was a failure, Wyeth kept a journal recording this first trip of Americans along what later was called the Oregon Trail (map, page 322). This pathway to the Pacific Northwest became world-famous. It rolled across the prairies and mountains from Independence, Missouri, through the South Pass entry into the Rockies in Wyoming. Then it passed Fort Hall, constructed by Wyeth on the Snake River, and ended 2,000 miles from its beginning at Fort Vancouver on the Columbia River in Oregon.

Wyeth made a second effort to colonize Oregon. It too failed, and for a similar reason: supplies sent around South America did not catch up with the Bostonians. Still, Wyeth had demonstrated that traveling to Oregon by land was not beyond endurance.

Missionaries establish posts among the Indians. The British were well served in the Oregon Country by Dr. John McLoughlin, who represented the Hudson's Bay Company, an English fur-trading firm. Possessed of a fierce temper, McLoughlin nevertheless established excellent relations with the Indians, who fondly called him "White Eagle." McLoughlin gave shelter to the first American missionaries to arrive in the Pacific Northwest.

One of these missionaries was Marcus Whitman, from the state of New York. Whitman, 32 years old in 1834, had practiced medicine for a time in Canada. In 1834 he and his brother were operating a sawmill in New York, when Marcus decided to answer a call for Protestant missionaries to work among the Oregon Indians. On a visit there he met with groups of Snake, Nez Perce, and Cayuse Indians who apparently welcomed the founding of a mission settlement in their country.

Whitman came back to New York, recruited a small party for his important work, and was married. He returned to Oregon with his wife, Narcissa — the first non-Indian woman to live in the Pacific Northwest. The Whitmans set up a mission near Fort Walla Walla in what is now the state of Washington.

On a trip home in 1842, Whitman visited the Secretary of War in Washington, D.C., hoping to persuade him to establish supply stations along the Oregon Trail for pioneers. Shortly, Whitman returned to Oregon, little dreaming of the fate awaiting him and his family.

In 1847 a measles epidemic broke out in Oregon. As a doctor-missionary, Whitman tried vainly to halt the disease. White children who caught measles generally recovered, but most Indian children, having no immunity, died. The Cayuse Indians came to the conclusion that Whitman had poisoned their children as part of a scheme to wipe out the Indians. In a rage they massacred Marcus and Narcissa Whitman, along with twelve other settlers.

A Jesuit missionary, Father Pierre Jean de Smet, had meanwhile begun to work in Oregon in 1841. A friend of the Indians, Father de Smet succeeded in settling disputes between the tribes and the white settlers over land rights. By working in the Pacific Northwest and by calling on their churches back East for support, Christian missionaries like the Whitmans and Father de Smet helped expand knowledge of the Oregon Country.

Immigration to Oregon swells. By 1840 only about 400 Americans, mainly missionaries and retired trappers, had reached the Pacific Northwest. Soon, however, a trickle of prospective settlers, increasing each year, flowed across the continent. The Panic of 1837 (page 262) had caused deep distress among families in the Mississippi Valley. Oregon's rich river valleys beckoned, offering new opportunities and access to the markets of Asia, where furs could be traded for silk, tea, and other goods.

Interest was heightened also by the reports of navy lieutenant Charles Wilkes, who visited the Northwest Coast in 1841. Wilkes had been leading a great American scientific expedition to the Pacific Ocean and Antarctica (where he gave his name to Wilkes Land). In Oregon he sent out a land party that traveled extensively in the area. He himself explored the Willamette Valley.

During his travels Wilkes lost one of his vessels at the treacherous entrance to the Columbia River. In his published report, as a result, he reserved his praise for harbors along the Strait of Juan de Fuca to the north. Many Americans now wanted to take control of the region, but the strait lay in a part of Oregon dominated by the British.

You will recall that in 1842 Secretary of State Webster and the British ambassador to the United States, Lord Ashburton, had concluded a treaty settling the northeastern boundary of the United States (page 263). The British had hoped that the two negotiators could clear up the Oregon question too, but the long-patient Ashburton was old and tired. Vexed by the intense heat and humidity of Washington, D.C., in summertime, he returned home. The United States saw no point in pressing Britain at this time. In a few years 10,000 Americans would be in Oregon, with many thousands more preparing to go there. American diplomats would then be in a strong position to seek a final settlement of the Oregon issue, one that might even place the valuable Strait of Juan de Fuca under United States control.

Trappers and traders explore the Great Basin. Meanwhile, tough and self-reliant mountain men — trappers and traders who made the Rockies their home and helped many wagon trains on their way to Oregon — were exploring the Great Basin, a desert region lying between the Rocky Mountains and the Sierra Nevada. In 1825, Jim Bridger, one of the most famous of the mountain men, traveled extensively in the Great Basin. At one point he came upon a remarkable lake some 80 miles long and 50 miles wide. He was probably the first non-Indian to gaze upon the Great Salt Lake, the largest lake west of the Mississippi River.

The Mormons seek a permanent home. Hard times in settled areas had usually stirred people to move westward, but the group of pioneers who settled the Great Basin were motivated by religion. They were Mormons, members of the Church of Jesus Christ of Latter-Day Saints. The land they chose to settle was one of the most demanding and difficult regions in the United States. How they started a new home in the Great Basin is a dramatic story of leadership and perseverance.

The Mormon movement had been started in 1830 in western New York by Joseph Smith, a native of Vermont. In 1827, Smith announced that he had found a set of golden plates containing sacred scriptures. Three years later he published the scriptures as the Book of Mormon.

Smith was just one of a number of preachers active on the New York frontier. Even though the area was not hospitable to the Mormons, the movement grew, aided by the organizing genius of its leader.

Smith and his followers relocated several times in the next years, in search of a more congenial home. In 1831 they settled in Ohio. Converts flocked in, and the group prospered. Shortly, however, the Panic of 1837 took a heavy toll of the Mormons' assets and membership. Smith moved the remnant of his following to Missouri, but there the Mormons encountered hostility from their neighbors. The Mormons were considered "outsiders," and their prosperous ventures aroused much envy.

Under intense pressure, the Mormons fled to western Illinois in 1839, where they established the town of Nauvoo. Mormon missionaries were winning converts in such large numbers that Nauvoo's population in 1844 reached 15,000, making the city the largest in Illinois at that time. Smith, however, drew furious opposition by maintaining that no law of Illinois could apply in Nauvoo without his permission. He also declared that the Mormon Church would allow polygamy (having more than one wife at a time). In July, 1844, Joseph Smith and his brother Hyrum were imprisoned in Carthage, Illinois, to protect them against threatened violence. A mob, nevertheless, battered its way into the prison and murdered the Smiths. Joseph Smith became a martyr to his people.

Brigham Young leads the Mormons to the Great Basin. The new leader of the Mormons was Brigham Young, a man of spiri-

Brigham Young and his Mormon followers wintered along the Missouri River before continuing their westward migration in 1847.

tual fire and administrative skill. Under his leadership, the Mormons prepared once again to head westward. With 3,700 wagons, 30,000 cattle, and large numbers of sheep, hogs, and chickens, they migrated to a place along the Missouri River opposite Council Bluffs, Iowa. By the autumn of 1846, 12,000 Mormons were dug in to spend the winter.

In the spring of 1847 Young set out with a "pioneer band" of 146 people to find a permanent homeland. They journeyed into the mountains and through the South Pass, arriving at Fort Bridger. There they consulted with Jim Bridger, who recommended heading toward the Willamette or Bear valleys. As for the Great Basin region, Bridger was certain it was a barren wasteland. The Mormons, however, followed their own instincts. Young led the pioneer band into the valley of the Great Salt Lake on July 24, 1847 — a day ever since celebrated in Utah as Pioneer Day. In the next year the main body of Mormons followed the pioneer band into the chosen place.

Success came only gradually to the Mormons at Salt Lake City. The land itself was forbidding. Before anything could be grown, the soil needed irrigation. Wood had to be searched for and carried long distances. The period from 1847 to 1849 was the Mormons' "starving time," like that of the Jamestown colonists long before. The pioneer band of Mormons was reduced at one point to eating animal hides.

Many hands working together were required to make the desert bloom. The Mormons became expert at desert farming. The population grew as thousands of European converts came to join the Mormons.

In 1849 the Mormons formed a state they called Deseret. They planned for it to include present-day Utah and parts of California, Arizona, New Mexico, Colorado, Wyoming, Idaho, and Oregon. *Deseret* was a word used in the Book of Mormon, meaning "honeybee." Although the name was eventually dropped, the beehive remains a Mormon symbol.

Deseret quickly encountered strong opposition because of the Mormons' continued unorthodox ways — especially the practice of polygamy. When Deseret sought to enter the Union in 1850, its request was not granted. Instead, Congress established the Utah Territory, which extended far to the east and west of present-day Utah (map, page 349). During the 1860's parts of the Territory were given to Nevada, Wyoming, and Colorado. Finally, in 1896 Utah was admitted to the Union as the forty-fifth state.

SECTION REVIEW

1. (a) On what basis could Great Britain and the United States each justify its claim to the Oregon Country? (b) What early efforts did Americans make to settle the region?
2. (a) What contributions did the Whitmans and other missionaries make to the settlement of the Pacific Northwest? (b) What role was played by mountain men?
3. (a) Why were the Mormons forced to move west? (b) Why did they settle in the Great Basin? (c) Describe their activities after they arrived at the Great Salt Lake.

2 Americans Become Interested in California and the Southwest

While the Oregon Country and the Great Basin were being opened up, reports of other areas in the West attracted Americans. Still, the push westward involved dangers Americans had never before faced. One group of pioneers, the Donner party, set out for California from Illinois in 1846. Slowly the party made its way across the western prairies and desert, only to be stranded in the deep snow of the Sierra Nevada. Following a fearful winter, only 45 of the 79 members who entered the mountains were finally rescued. After safely reaching California, a thirteen-year-old girl who lived through the disaster wrote to a cousin in Illinois, "It is a beautiful country. It ought to be a beautiful country to pay us for our troubles in getting to it."

The Spanish are the first Europeans in California. Some 300 years earlier, in 1542, the Spanish explorer Juan Rodriguez Cabrillo

(cah-BREE-yoh) came upon California. He was the first European to sail into San Diego Bay. Much of the colonization of California was the work of Junípero Serra, a Spanish Franciscan priest. Father Serra first arrived in California as a member of a military expedition led by Gaspar de Portolá. Spanish authorities in Mexico City had sent Portolá to California to keep it from falling into the hands of the Russians. Russian traders had been pushing steadily southward along the North American coast in search of seal pelts.

In 1769 Serra founded a mission at San Diego, the first of nine that he established. He and the fourteen Jesuits who worked with him left a deep impression on life in California. Through Serra and the missionaries, European cattle were brought to California and European methods of farming were introduced. Large numbers of Indians converted to Christianity. (See the map on page 327 for the missions Serra founded.)

In the same year that Serra founded the San Diego mission, Portolá set out to the north for Monterey Bay, which he had heard about from earlier reports. Arriving there in October, 1769, he was disappointed with what he found. The shallow bay lacked shelter and was unfit for large naval vessels. Portolá's men pressed northward. On November 1, 1769, they reached a harbor so large that it could have contained not only the ships of Spain but the naval vessels of all of Europe as well. This was San Francisco Bay. Work was begun in 1776 on a *presidio*, or fortress, to guard the area where San Francisco now stands.

Throughout the late 1700's other California settlements were established. In 1781 the town of Los Angeles was begun, its site having been visited by Portolá twelve years earlier. California remained under Spanish control until 1821, when Mexico won its independence. As an outlying province of Mexico, California was very isolated. Its means of communication with Mexico City were severely limited.

Opportunities lure Americans to California. While these developments were taking place in the West, a new nation — the

United States — was being born in the eastern part of North America. Gradually, its people began to make contact with California. Some of them, having sailed around South America, stopped at California's harbors to get supplies and make repairs. Others entered the growing trade in cattle and hides with Mexican ranchers. In 1832, a party led by Joseph Walker, a mountain man transplanted from Tennessee, entered California from the east. Walker became the first white man to find a route across the Sierras.

Like Oregon, California had its boosters who described its good points in books and pamphlets and in letters sent back home. The most important of these was a book written by Richard Henry Dana, entitled *Two Years Before the Mast*. It detailed Dana's experiences as a sailor on a trip around Cape Horn to California from 1834 to 1836. His account was so gripping that his adventures still make lively reading today. His enthusiasm for that rich and beautiful land proved contagious to his readers.

Another leading figure in publicizing California was a merchant named Thomas Larkin. Originally from Massachusetts, Larkin arrived at Monterey by sea in 1832. On shipboard he had met his future wife. Their children were the first born in California whose parents were both English-speaking Americans. Larkin soon became an active trader. He designed and built California's first large flour mill. He exchanged goods with Mexico and the Sandwich Islands (now Hawaii), supplying not only flour but also potatoes, beaver and sea-otter pelts, and horses. As United States consul (official representative) from 1844 to 1848, he looked out for the interests of American sailors and immigrants. Constantly he promoted activities to pave the way for the eventual transfer of California to the United States.

By 1845 about 500 Americans were living in California, most of them in the Sacramento Valley. The leading figure there was John Sutter, a native of Germany who had come to California after sojourns in New York, St. Louis, Santa Fe, Oregon, and the Sandwich Islands. In California he estab-

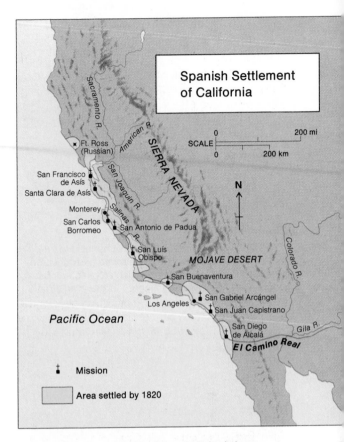

The nine missions of Father Serra stretched along *El Camino Real*, which means "the royal highway."

lished a ranch, located where the American and Sacramento rivers come together. Local Indians helped clear the land, dig irrigation ditches, and build a fort. Sutter was a kindly man who welcomed new settlers to the Sacramento Valley. His place became a center for Americans who hoped that California one day would belong to the United States.

Merchants and traders journey to New Mexico. Before Mexico became independent in 1821, Americans were not welcome in the region that later became known as New Mexico and Arizona. Zebulon Pike (page 219) was imprisoned by the Spanish when he entered New Mexico in 1807. The Spanish jealously guarded their monopoly of trade in Santa Fe, a center of commerce established in 1609 (page 45).

Shortly after Mexico became independent, Americans began to gain a toehold in the Santa Fe trade. The Mexicans were less wary of their American neighbors than the

Spanish Heritage

Spaniards brought horses and horsemanship to America, giving rise to words like *rodeo* and *buckaroo*. Spanish life also introduced mission architecture: thick adobe walls, with Spanish arches, surrounding a patio where people could gather.

Spanish had been. In 1821 an American named William Becknell took a load of goods from Missouri into Santa Fe and sold it at a profit. This trip marked the beginning of the extensive Santa Fe trade. One of James Monroe's last acts as President was to approve a grant of money in 1825 for marking a wagon route to New Mexico. The resulting survey created the Santa Fe Trail.

Almost immediately merchants, packing their wares in canvas-covered "prairie schooners" to keep them dry and in place,

were gathering at Independence, Missouri — and then heading toward Santa Fe. For protection they traveled the rugged Santa Fe Trail within sight of one another. The heat of the desert, the constant danger of sandstorms, and the fear of a wagon accident or an Indian raid made the journey tense and its outcome a gamble.

The new trade provided the residents of Santa Fe with a ready supply of iron, cutlery, various gadgets and notions, and American-made cloth. For Americans the

On the Trail to Santa Fe

When Josiah Gregg's doctor prescribed a trip to the plains to help him recover from a long illness, he signed on as a bookkeeper with a wagon train leaving Independence, Missouri, bound for Santa Fe in May, 1831. The 800-mile journey restored Gregg's health and so fascinated him that he wrote a best-selling book about the Santa Fe Trail.

Along the Santa Fe Trail

As we were proceeding on our march, we observed a horseman approaching us, who excited at first considerable curiosity. His picturesque costume soon showed him to be a Mexican *cibolero* or buffalo-hunter. These hardy devotees of the chase usually wear leather trousers and jackets and flat straw hats, while swung upon the shoulder hangs their quiver of bow and arrows. The long handles of their lance are set in a case and suspended by the side with a strap from the pommel of the saddle, leaving the point waving high over the head with a tassel of colored streamers dangling at the tip of the scabbard.

The *cibolero* saluted us with demonstrations of joy, nor were we less delighted at meeting with him, for we were now able to obtain information from Santa Fe, from where no news had been received since the return of the caravan last fall. Traders clustered around the new visitor and everyone who could speak a word of Spanish had questions to ask.

The *cibolero* was anxious to sell us some provisions which were welcome enough, for most of the company were out of bread, and meat was very scarce. Our visitor returned to his camp and with several of his *compadres* afterwards brought us an abundance of dry buffalo meat and bags of coarse oven-toasted bread much used by Mexican travelers.

profits were high. Becknell, for instance, sold his first cargo at five times what it would have brought in St. Louis. No less important, the trade with New Mexico drew attention to another area that might one day be added to the Union.

SECTION REVIEW

1. (a) Who was the first European to reach California? (b) Describe the activities of Father Serra and of Portolá in that region.
2. (a) What attracted Americans to California? (b) Describe the settlements started by Larkin and Sutter.
3. (a) Why did Americans become interested in Santa Fe? (b) What was the result?

3 The United States Acquires Texas and Oregon

Yet another portion of Mexico in which Americans were settling was Texas. The United States originally had claimed Texas as part of the Louisiana Purchase. Then, in the treaty of 1819 with Spain (page 240), it had given up the claim. Ever since, many Westerners had criticized President Monroe for making that agreement.

Texas attracts attention. A resolute American named Moses Austin opened the way for Americans to settle in Texas when, early in 1821, he received permission from Spanish authorities to locate 300 families in the province. Austin was an enterprising man who had been a dry goods merchant in Philadelphia, a mine owner in Virginia, a judge in the Louisiana Territory, and a banker in Missouri. He had large-scale dreams for his Texas project, but he died before he had barely started it.

When Mexico won its independence in 1821, the new Mexican government confirmed the grant the Spanish had made to Austin. His devoted son Stephen vowed to fulfill his father's dream. In 1822 Stephen Austin brought a group of settlers to Texas. Known later as the "Old Three Hundred," they became dutiful citizens of Mexico and adopted the Roman Catholic faith, in accordance with the laws of Mexico.

Less than 10 years later, more than 20,000 Americans were living in Texas.

Texans who had wrested control of their land from Mexico fought against Santa Anna's attacks in 1836.

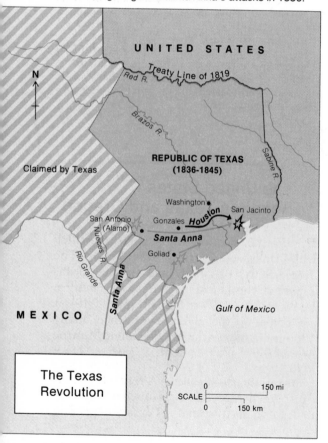

The Texas Revolution

Some of the later arrivals, in disregard of Mexican law, had brought slaves with them. Many of these newcomers, Americans at heart, were beginning to talk of breaking away from Mexico. Mexico grew alarmed at the possibility that this valuable land would slip out of its control.

Texans seek to establish a republic. One Texan, Haden Edwards, organized a rebellion in 1826 to establish what he called the "Republic of Fredonia." The uprising was sparked by a dispute over rights to land that Edwards had been granted. Edwards was not generally supported by other Americans in Texas, however, and the revolt was suppressed in 1827 without bloodshed.

Stephen Austin worked hard to calm Mexico's fear that the province was becoming too American. In the meantime, the Mexican government tried to tighten control over the Texans. In 1830 it restricted further American settlement of Texas. Things went from bad to worse after General Antonio Santa Anna came to power in 1833 as the dictator of Mexico. Santa Anna appeared eager to take from the Texans what they considered to be their rights.[1]

The Americans rose in revolt late in 1835. This time their leader was Sam Houston, a hard-driving Virginian who had served in the United States Army under Andrew Jackson during the War of 1812. When Monroe was President, Houston had been a government agent to the Cherokee. Later, he became governor of Tennessee at the age of 34. Flamboyant, shrewd, and experienced in frontier ways, Houston was an ideal leader for Americans living under the Mexican flag.

Texas fights for its independence. As a result of several clashes with Mexican forces, Texans had taken control of Gonzales, Goliad, and San Antonio (map, this page) by the end of 1835. Santa Anna was now determined to make the Texans submit to him. With 5,000 troops, he attacked an old mission in San Antonio called the Alamo. In-

---

[1]The settlers' specific grievances included the absence of trial by jury, the use of Spanish in legal and commercial transactions, and burdensome customs regulations.

Outnumbered about fifteen to one, Texan defenders fought to their deaths inside and atop the walls of the Alamo. The courage of these soldiers inspired Texas patriots to persist in their fight for independence from Mexico.

side were fewer than 200 Texans. The defenders included Lieutenant Colonel William B. Travis, commander of the rebels; Jim Bowie, second-in-command; and frontiersman Davy Crockett, who had arrived with a dozen volunteers from Tennessee. On February 24, 1836, with the Alamo under siege, Travis bravely wrote a message addressed "to the people of Texas and all the Americans in the world." He wrote, "I call on you in the name of liberty, of patriotism and everything dear to the American character to come to our aid with all dispatch. . . . If this call is neglected, I am determined to sustain myself as long as possible and die like a soldier who never forgets what is due to his own honor or that of his country. Victory or death!"

The heroic Texans held out desperately. Finally, on the morning of March 6, 1836, Santa Anna ordered his buglers to blow the terrifying *degüello*, indicating that he would give no quarter to the rebels inside the building. The defenders of the Alamo died in fierce hand-to-hand battle. On March 27 several hundred Texans were put to death by Mexican soldiers after having surrendered at Goliad.

Texas wins its independence. At the time that the defenders of the Alamo were holding off the Mexicans, 59 delegates met at the little hamlet of Washington-on-the-Brazos. On March 2, 1836, they declared Texas an independent republic. Within a few weeks, a battle was fought that would gain that independence. On April 21, 1836, Sam Houston's small Texas army attacked Mexican soldiers at San Jacinto (juh-SIN-toh). The Texans struck crying above the din of battle "Remember the Alamo! Remember Goliad!" In eighteen minutes the struggle was over.

Santa Anna himself was discovered and taken prisoner the next morning. Houston resisted the demands of some Texans that the Mexican chief be executed. To gain his release, Santa Anna agreed that Mexican troops would retreat south of the Rio Grande and that his government would recognize the independence of Texas. After Santa Anna was freed, the Mexican government refused to accept the treaty. Still, Mexico made no effort to win back the Texans, who now gloried in their independent state, and soon raised the Lone Star flag of the Republic of Texas.

Sam Houston, a hero of the Texas revolution, served two terms as president of the Republic of Texas, became a United States senator after Texas was annexed, and was elected governor of that state in 1859.

Americans consider annexation. Many Americans, filled with the spirit of manifest destiny, had long set their hearts on bringing Texas into the Union. Now, they thought, the time had come to act. The question of slavery proved, however, to be a stumbling block. Many Southerners — including the powerful Senator Calhoun — were in favor of admitting Texas because it would add another slave state to the Union. Northerners were equally determined, for the same reason, to keep Texas out. Some antislavery people expressed fear that Texas, once admitted, might be cut up into five or more slaveholding states.

President Jackson would have liked the satisfaction of adding the star of Texas to the flag, but despite the earnest pleas of his friend Sam Houston, Jackson resisted making the effort. The day before he left office, Jackson formally recognized Texas as an independent country and exchanged diplomatic representatives with it. Britain also formally recognized the Republic of Texas,

having concluded that it would be a good market for English goods and a reliable supplier of cotton. The British may also have looked on Texas as a barrier to further southward advance by the expansionist Americans.

When Martin Van Buren succeeded Jackson as President, he came under immediate pressure to *annex,* or add, Texas to the Union. Van Buren, too, was cool to the idea, wanting to avoid splitting the Democratic Party. Feelings ran high.

John Tyler, who came to the presidency in 1841, was more friendly to annexation than his predecessors had been. A man of independence and spirit, he was often at odds with his colleagues. Still, he was determined not to offend northern Whigs who had agreed to serve in his Cabinet. Fate, however, soon took a hand.

On a February day in 1844, a group of leading politicians boarded the U.S.S. *Princeton,* a new propeller-driven steam frigate on an inspection trip down the Potomac River. During the trip the vessel's twelve-inch cannons were fired to show off their power. One of the cannons exploded, killing Secretary of State Abel P. Upshur, Secretary of the Navy Thomas W. Gilmer, and others. Following the tragic accident, Tyler acted quickly to fill the vacancies and reorganize the entire Cabinet — appointing not a single Northerner or Whig. Calhoun, who came out of retirement to serve as Secretary of State, agreed with Tyler that Texas must be brought into the Union. Northerners, however, remained hostile to the idea. They made sure that Tyler's treaty of annexation, submitted to the Senate in the spring of 1844, was defeated.

Annexation becomes an election issue. Meanwhile, the issue of Texas was affecting the presidential campaign of 1844. Former President Van Buren seemed likely to win the Democratic nomination, while Clay was the front runner for the Whigs. Van Buren had visited Clay's home in Kentucky in 1842, and the two rivals appear to have agreed to keep the Texas question out of the campaign. Both subsequently went on record as opposing immediate annexation.

Texas Declaration of Rights (1836)

All men, when they form a government, have equal rights, and no man or group of men is entitled to special privileges.

All political power comes from the people, and all free governments are founded on their authority. At all times they have the right to change their government in such a manner as they think proper.

No preferences shall be given by the law to any religious group or any mode of worship over another. Every person shall be permitted to worship God according to the dictates of his own conscience.

Every citizen shall be at liberty to speak, write, or publish his opinion on any subject, but is responsible for abusing that privilege.

The people shall be secure in their persons, houses, papers, and possessions from all unreasonable searches and seizures.

A person accused of committing a crime shall have the right of being heard by himself or by a lawyer. In all prosecutions, he shall have the right to a speedy and public trial by an impartial jury.

No citizen shall be deprived of privileges, outlawed, exiled, or in any manner denied the right to vote, except by due course of the law.

No title of nobility or hereditary honors shall ever be granted or conferred in this republic.

No unreasonable bail should be set nor shall the writ of *habeas corpus* be suspended except when the public safety may require it.

Excessive fines shall not be imposed, or cruel or unusual punishment inflicted.

No person shall be imprisoned for debt, even if he cannot pay.

No person's services shall be demanded, nor property taken by the government for public use, unless by his own consent, without just compensation being made according to the law.

Every citizen shall have the right to bear arms in defense of himself and the republic. The army shall at all times be controlled by the government of the people.

This stand cost Van Buren the support of his old friend Jackson, who wanted to see Texas in the Union before he died.

When the Democrats gathered for their convention at Baltimore, southern delegates refused to support Van Buren. Northerners, for their part, would not accept Calhoun. The deadlocked delegates finally turned to James K. Polk of Tennessee, a former Speaker of the House of Representatives. Polk was the first "dark horse" nominee for President. (A "dark horse" is a candidate who unexpectedly wins support at a convention or in an election.)

The Whigs, as expected, nominated Clay. On the Texas question Clay said he was in favor of annexation if it could be achieved with the agreement of all sections of the country — and without provoking Mexico into war. He did not say how these conditions could be met. The Whig platform, moreover, ignored the subject.

Polk did not hesitate to announce his strong support of annexation. The Democratic platform was outspokenly expansionist, calling for the "re-annexation of Texas and the re-occupation of Oregon." This catchy phrase implied that Texas had really been a part of the Louisiana Purchase all along and that the treaty with Britain providing for joint occupation of Oregon might be annulled.

People had matters other than Texas in mind when they went to vote. A number of antislavery Whigs in New York deserted Clay in favor of James G. Birney, the candidate of the Liberty Party. The shift of their votes caused Clay to lose that key state and, with it, the election. During the campaign, the Whigs made believe they had never heard of Polk, taunting, "Who is James K. Polk?" They now had the answer: Polk was President of the United States!

Texas becomes a state. Tyler was convinced that the voters wanted Texas in the Union. In the last days of his term he decided to use an unusual method to admit Texas: a joint resolution of Congress. A joint resolution could be passed by a simple majority in each house, whereas a treaty would require the approval of two thirds of the Senate. Duly passed, the resolution was signed by Tyler just before he left office. On July 4, 1845, Texas delegates met in a convention and voted to accept statehood.

Polk becomes President. Polk, at 49 years of age, was the youngest President to date. He was a hard-working man, who only once during his term accepted an invitation to have dinner at a private home. Later, when he died soon after leaving office, many people believed that he had literally worked himself to death.

Sarah Polk, the President's wife, was frequently referred to as "the Presidentress." Deeply interested in politics, she has been called "the first working-wife First Lady." A stickler for tradition, Mrs. Polk nevertheless saw the installation in the White House of gaslights, which had only recently become available.

The United States acquires Oregon. James Polk had ambitious plans for the country's future. Having run on a platform calling for the annexation of both Texas and Oregon, he could concentrate on Oregon now that Texas had been taken care of. Almost immediately after taking office, Polk took steps to end the joint occupation of Oregon. He declared in his first message to Congress in 1845 that he could not compromise on the question. Although seriously irritated by Polk's warlike tone, the British were in fact ready to give up the Columbia River region because the fur trade there was played out and no longer profitable. Moreover, the British were beginning to recognize that the United States was the best customer for the products of English factories and that its friendship was valuable.

The British proposed a settlement that would divide Oregon at the 49th parallel of latitude. Polk was not satisfied that the United States had acquired enough of the Oregon Country. Still, the arrangements were contained in a treaty accepted by the United States in the late spring of 1846.[2] Polk's campaign promise — to acquire Texas and Oregon — had been fulfilled.

SECTION REVIEW

1. Vocabulary: *annex.*
2. (a) How did Americans first come to settle in Texas? (b) Why did they decide to seek independence from Mexico?
3. (a) What was meant by "Remember the Alamo"? (b) How did the Texans secure their independence?
4. (a) Why did some Americans oppose the annexation of Texas? (b) How did the question of annexation become an issue in the election of 1844? (c) How was annexation finally accomplished?
5. How did President Polk reach a settlement with Great Britain over Oregon?

4 The United States Fights a War with Mexico

Late in 1844 confidential word reached Washington that Mexico was prepared to sell California to the United States. The idea appealed to Polk; as soon as he was inaugurated, he sent a negotiator to Mexico to arrange for the purchase. A new government had been installed in Mexico, meanwhile, and it refused to receive the negotiator. Some Americans concluded that this refusal insulted the United States and that Mexico deserved to be punished.

California settlers proclaim a republic. About the same time, an American army officer and explorer named John C. Frémont, arrived in California with a force of 62 men. Frémont, already known as the "Pathfinder of the West," explained that his mis-

---

[2]Part of the Oregon Territory was admitted to the Union as the state of Oregon in 1859.

sion in California was to find routes suitable for overland travel. Not surprisingly, the Mexican authorities did not welcome these men in uniform. Besides, they knew that Frémont, then 32 years old, was the son-in-law of Thomas Hart Benton, an ardently expansionist senator from Missouri and a man close to President Polk. The Mexican officials ordered Frémont and his party to leave California immediately. After a show of defiance, Frémont withdrew to Oregon — temporarily.

In May, 1846, Frémont and his soldiers returned to California. Frémont knew that if he remained in uniform, Mexico might blame the Polk administration for causing trouble in California. Therefore, he resigned from the military service so that he could act as a private citizen. He joined forces with a group of American settlers at Sonoma who proclaimed their own government, calling it the Bear Flag Republic. The name came from the design of their flag, dominated by a grizzly bear facing a red star.

Trouble with Mexico heats up. Meanwhile, war was brewing between the United States and Mexico. The Mexican government had refused to recognize the recent annexation of Texas by the United States. Mexico also claimed that the Nueces River formed the Texas-Mexico border, not the Rio Grande as the Texans insisted.

Polk again decided to send a representative to Mexico to settle differences between the two countries. Designating John Slidell of Louisiana as special envoy to Mexico, Polk authorized him to deal with three matters: (1) the monetary claims of American citizens against the Mexican government, (2) the acquisition of California, and (3) the Texas boundary. Slidell's instructions were to agree to have the United States take over the claims in return for recognition of the Rio Grande boundary. He was also authorized to offer $5 million for New Mexico and as much as $25 million for California. Plainly no Mexican leader could have yielded so much territory and retained enough popular support to stay in office. When Mexican officials refused to meet

with Slidell, Polk came to the conclusion that only war could settle the issue.

Immediately after Texas accepted annexation, Polk had sent General Zachary Taylor to defend the new state. Taylor set up camp at the mouth of the Nueces River. When Polk heard that Slidell had been snubbed by the Mexicans, he ordered Taylor to take up a position on the Rio Grande, a move certain to anger the Mexicans. On May 9, 1846, Polk told his Cabinet that he was prepared to ask for war. Only the Secretary of the Navy, the distinguished historian George Bancroft, objected. He believed that the nation should wait until Mexican troops attacked.

The United States declares war. Before another meeting of the Cabinet could take place, word arrived in Washington that Mexican troops had crossed the Rio Grande and attacked Taylor's troops. On May 11, therefore, Polk sent a war message to Congress in which he asserted that American blood had been shed "upon the American soil," and that a state of war existed "notwithstanding all our efforts to avoid it." War, the President concluded, "exists by the act of Mexico herself." In a sense he was right. Mexicans had been offended at the annexation of Texas. They, therefore, had looked on Taylor as an invader wrongfully encamped on Mexican territory.

Some Americans oppose the Mexican War. When Congress declared war on Mexico two days later, the action had the support of most Americans. The historian William Prescott had recently published *A History of the Conquest of Mexico*, a popular account of the adventures of Cortés. Reading it, many Americans saw themselves as successors to the conquistadors of long ago. In many cities posters appeared with such rallying cries as "Mexico or Death!" and "Ho, for the halls of Montezuma!"[3]

Still, strong opposition to the war developed. Henry Clay called the war with Mexico "unnatural . . . lamentable." Daniel Webster called it "unconstitutional in its

---

[3]Montezuma referred to the Aztec ruler at the time of the Spanish conquest.

origin," believing that Polk had involved the nation without adequately consulting Congress. Before long, Clay and Webster each lost a son in the war. John Calhoun, who had favored annexation of Texas, had pleaded with his colleagues in the Senate to vote against passing the resolution for war. He could see that by conquering Mexico the door would open to a searing dispute between Northerners and Southerners over whether the new areas gained would be free or slave.

Another opponent of the war was Representative Abraham Lincoln of Illinois. He tried to make Polk admit that the place or "spot" where the shooting started was actually in Mexico. An Illinois newspaper began referring to the lanky new congressman as "spotty Lincoln."

The United States invades Mexico. With much of the public behind him, Polk set about achieving his goal. He was determined to obtain for the United States all Mexican land lying between Texas and the Pacific Ocean. In Zachary Taylor the President had a general whom he considered equal to the task. Now 61 years old, Taylor had been a soldier for almost forty years, with much of his career spent fighting Indians. Because Taylor did not like to parade in a dress uniform, preferring to go around in shirt sleeves, his men called him "Old Rough and Ready."

Almost immediately after the declaration of war, Taylor pushed the Mexican forces back beyond the Rio Grande. Following them as they retreated, he took the town of Matamoros. In September, 1846, he

General Scott's forces sailed from New Orleans, landed at Veracruz, and then moved inland to Mexico City. Important battles also took place in California.

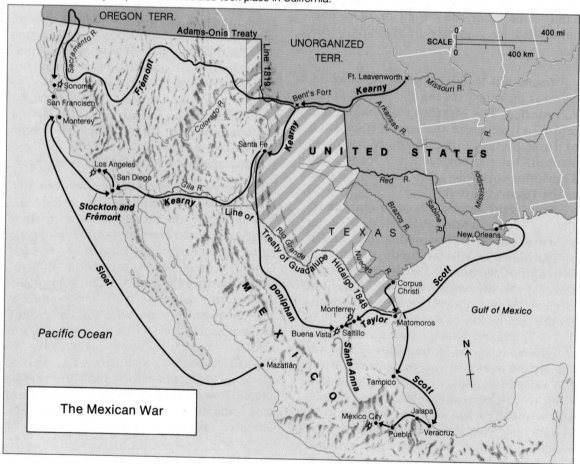

The Mexican War

In their efforts to capture the Mexican capital, United States forces fought well-armed Mexican troops. This battle occurred at Molino del Rey, outside Mexico City.

reached the stronghold of Monterrey, which fell after just three days of fighting. The march to Monterrey, however, was costly, and Taylor allowed the Mexican garrison there to get away. The Mexicans, moreover, considerably outnumbered his own forces and fought bravely for their homeland. Taylor looked forward to taking Mexico City but lacked the supplies needed to make the long march.

California and New Mexico are conquered. Soon after the war began, John Frémont and the other leaders of the Bear Flag Republic went into action in California. They hastened to cooperate with United States naval forces under Commodore John D. Sloat, who landed at Monterey, south of San Francisco. Then, forces led by Frémont and Commodore Robert Stockton moved against Mexican troops in southern California.

New Mexico had already fallen to the United States. In early summer, Colonel Stephen W. Kearny had set out from Fort Leavenworth, Kansas, for Santa Fe. After capturing Santa Fe without a struggle, Kearny pressed westward to southern California. Despite stiff resistance from Mexi-

can settlers near San Diego, Kearny completed the American takeover of California by capturing Los Angeles in early 1847.

Polk's territorial claims had now been satisfied. The war might have ended there if Mexico had been willing to admit to its people that it could not recover its lost provinces. But no nation — however desperate it may be — will yield its territory without a struggle.

Taylor defeats the Mexicans at Buena Vista. Polk, fearing that Taylor's growing popularity might make him a political rival, ordered him to remain in a defensive position at Monterrey while most of his troops were sent to join General Winfield Scott at Veracruz. There an assault was being launched that was intended to end with the capture of Mexico City.

The drama shaping up was intense. The Mexican forces were once again under the command of that old American nemesis, General Santa Anna. By luck, Santa Anna came upon a letter to Taylor ordering the American general to send all but 6,000 of his troops to the coast. Suspecting that Taylor would be vulnerable with such reduced

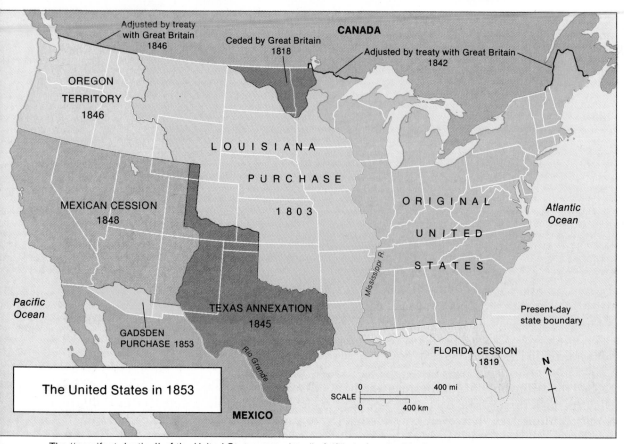

The map shows:

Adjusted by treaty with Great Britain 1846

Ceded by Great Britain 1818

CANADA

Adjusted by treaty with Great Britain 1842

OREGON TERRITORY 1846

L O U I S I A N A

P U R C H A S E

1 8 0 3

O R I G I N A L

U N I T E D

S T A T E S

Atlantic Ocean

MEXICAN CESSION 1848

Mississippi R.

Pacific Ocean

GADSDEN PURCHASE 1853

TEXAS ANNEXATION 1845

Rio Grande

Present-day state boundary

FLORIDA CESSION 1819

The United States in 1853

N

SCALE 0 — 400 mi / 0 — 400 km

MEXICO

The "manifest destiny" of the United States was virtually fulfilled after the Mexican Cession of 1848. The nation then reached to the Pacific shore.

ranks, Santa Anna decided the time was ripe to attack "Old Rough and Ready." Then he would turn and proceed against Scott without fear of being attacked from the rear.

Taylor, meantime, had defied the orders of the President. He had moved many of his soldiers — including a detachment under Colonel Alexander Doniphan who had come south from Santa Fe — into exposed positions south of Monterrey, aiming to take the town of Saltillo seventy miles to the southwest. Learning that Santa Anna was on his way, Taylor pulled his troops into the little town of Buena Vista in February, 1847, and prepared to face an attack. In the first part of the battle that followed, the Americans were badly mauled. Taylor, however, quickly rallied his forces. Among the units that fought heroically that day was the "Mississippi Rifles" under the command of Taylor's son-in-law, Jefferson Davis.

The Americans won a gigantic victory at Buena Vista. Badly beaten, the Mexicans suffered nearly 1,800 casualties before retreating. Santa Anna hurried back to help defend Mexico City. Scott had taken Vera-cruz in a brilliant victory and was on his way toward the Mexican capital.

Although Scott, like Taylor, was a Whig, the similarity between the two generals ended there. Scott was a stickler for discipline and details. He also enjoyed wearing his dress uniform. The troops referred to him as "Old Fuss and Feathers." Now general-in-chief of the army, his long career had brought him practically every military honor. President after President had relied upon him: Madison had offered him the position of Secretary of War, Jackson had put him at the head of the troops sent to South Carolina during the nullification controversy, and Van Buren had sent him to the troubled Niagara region in 1837.

Scott fights his way to Mexico City. The landing of Scott's men at Veracruz in March, 1847, was the first amphibious operation in American military history. In 16 hours about 10,000 troops were put ashore. Speed was essential during the campaign because Scott knew he had to get to Mexico City before yellow fever destroyed his ranks. By the end of April, Scott and his men were in Jalapa. From there they struggled to Puebla, Mexico's second largest city. By now the American troops were plagued by inadequate supplies. They were also being badly hurt by illness. Nevertheless, the road to the "halls of Montezuma" — Mexico City — now lay open.

Scott rebuilt his army at Puebla during the summer of 1847 and prepared for the final fighting. After crushing a Mexican force led by Santa Anna, he approached Chapultepec, at the western outskirts of the city. Against the advice of many of his officers, Scott went ahead with plans to capture this fortress by assault.

Chapultepec was the home of the National Military Academy of Mexico. During the fierce hand-to-hand struggle, the cadets, some of them mere boys, fought to the death rather than surrender. About 2,000 of the defenders were killed or wounded in the encounter. They are still remembered as heroes by the Mexican people.

On September 14, 1847, American soldiers at last entered Mexico City. Scott rode into the center of the city on a beautiful horse. The sight was so splendid, observers reported, that even the Mexican onlookers cheered. Yet underneath this showy pageant lay tragic facts. Of the 100,000 Americans who served in uniform, 1,500 fell in battle and 11,000 died of disease and exposure. Even those figures do not tell the whole story. Half the men who survived to return home died within a few years of diseases contracted during the war.

The United States gains a vast territory. In February, 1848, Mexico accepted peace terms. The treaty that ended the fighting was signed at Guadalupe Hidalgo, a suburb of Mexico City. In the treaty the Mexicans gave up all claims to Texas, as well as to a huge area called the Mexican Cession. (The Mexican Cession contained the present states of California, Nevada, and Utah, and parts of Arizona, Wyoming, Colorado, and New Mexico). In addition, Mexico accepted the Rio Grande as the southern boundary of Texas. The vast region ceded by the Mexicans (including Texas) added 1,200,000 square miles to the national domain. The United States agreed to pay the defeated Mexican government $15 million and also to pay American citizens $3,250,000 which the Mexican government owed them.

The Treaty of Guadalupe Hidalgo all but completed the present-day southwestern boundary of the United States. Five years later, in 1853, the United States agreed to pay Mexico $10 million for a strip of land in what is now New Mexico and Arizona. The land, known as the Gadsden Purchase, was needed to construct a southern transcontinental railroad. The acquisition was arranged by the American minister to Mexico, James Gadsden.

SECTION REVIEW

1. How was the Bear Flag Republic established?
2. (a) How did the annexation of Texas by the United States lead to war? (b) What American political leaders opposed the Mexican War?
3. (a) What military action followed the declaration of war? (b) What part in the fighting was played by Taylor, Scott, Kearny, and Frémont?
4. (a) What were the terms of the Treaty of Guadalupe Hidalgo? (b) What land acquisition completed this nation's southern boundary?

5 Gold Seekers Rush to California

Whig abolitionists had maintained all along that southern Democrats had brought on the war with Mexico chiefly to acquire new slave territory. They believed that this was especially the purpose in seeking California. The poet James Russell Lowell put it this way: "They just want this Californy so's to lug new slave states in."

The discovery of gold opens new vistas. A remarkable occurrence changed the course of events in California in the late 1840's. Early in 1848, gold was discovered on the property of John Sutter (page 327). One of his workers, James Marshall, noticed some pea-sized flecks of bright metal in a stream where a sawmill was being built. What happened next was described years later by a soldier named William T. Sherman, who was to become a famous general during the Civil War:

> After picking up about an ounce, [Marshall] hurried down to the fort to report to Captain Sutter his discovery. Captain Sutter himself related to me Marshall's account, saying that as he sat in his room one day in February or March, 1848, a knock was heard at his door, and he called out, "Come in." In walked Marshall, who was a half-crazy man at best, but then looked strangely wild. . . . Marshall inquired if anyone was within hearing, and began to peer about the room, and look under the bed, when Sutter, fearing that some calamity had befallen the party up at the sawmill and that Marshall was really crazy, began to make his way to the door demanding of Marshall to explain what was the matter. At last he revealed his discovery, and laid before Captain Sutter the particles of gold he had picked up in the ditch.

Suddenly the nation was stirred into a frenzy of excitement and activity. Fortune hunters deserted their farms and their families and rushed west to try for a lucky strike in the gold fields. Some came by prairie schooner, braving desert hazards and Indian attacks. It is estimated that 45,000 people came over the Sierra Nevada in 1849 alone.

Large numbers of **forty-niners,** as they were called, came by ship around South America — a journey that could take many months, varying with the season. Others took ships to the Isthmus of Panama, where they crossed to the Pacific and sailed north. Some who ventured along these southern routes never made it, succumbing to tropical fevers and other hazards.

Many of the gold seekers came from Mexico, China, South America, or Europe. All were determined to pan for gold and to find it. The Americans among them sang words that expressed the hopes of the forty-niners:

> I'll scrape the mountains clean, my boys,
> I'll drain the rivers dry,
> A pocketful of rocks bring home,
> So brother don't you cry.

Californians lead a rough life. Most of the gold seekers were young people who quickly changed the look of California with their energy and ambition and greed. San Francisco, which had been a quiet port town, was transformed in one year into a roaring metropolis unable to control vice and crime. Hotels and rooming houses could not contain the influx of people, and tents and shanties soon sprang up, adding to the state of disorder.

The language was soon enriched by new phrases: *strike it rich, pan out, clean up, hit pay dirt, hit it lucky, cash in, stake out.* For a prospector who found gold, the returns could be enormous — anywhere from $500 to $5,000 a day. One soldier on a short leave boasted that he had made as much money from mining as he would earn in his whole enlistment. The miners were often called *argonauts* — after those who accompanied Jason, the hero in Greek mythology who searched for the golden fleece. Unlike Jason, however, most miners were unsuccessful. Many who arrived singing "Oh California that's the land for me" soon gave up. They prepared to go home, singing — if they sang at all — "Oh carry me back to old Virginia, to old Virginia's shore."

In the long run the people who profited most were the merchants, traders, land speculators, and restaurant and hotel owners. The gold rush also brought prosperity to the Mormon community at Salt Lake City, the last stopping-off place for supplies before California. The prospectors may, indeed, have unwittingly been responsible for the survival of the Mormon colony.

The slavery issue is reopened. The population of California grew so rapidly following the gold rush that the territory was soon ready to enter the Union. However, the prospect of making California a state, along with the annexation of other areas from

The gold deposits mined in California in the early days were mixed with sand and gravel. Miners developed washing techniques such as panning to separate the gold. Later, lode mining was developed to extract gold from rock formations.

Mexico, had already revived the quarrel over slavery.

One summer evening in 1846, a little-known congressman from Pennsylvania named David Wilmot was speaking on the floor of the House of Representatives. Before the House was a bill that would have provided funds for the purchase of territory from Mexico. Wilmot, allotted only a few minutes, used his time to write his name indelibly in history. He offered a *proviso,* or condition, to the bill. The proviso was that slavery be banned forever from any territory that might be acquired by treaty from Mexico. Wilmot had voted for the admission of Texas even though slavery was allowed there. But, he asserted, if free territory were acquired, "God forbid that we should be the means of planting this institution upon it."

Northern state legislatures immediately voted resolutions supporting the Wilmot Proviso. With equal heat, Southerners denounced it. Although the Wilmot Proviso was voted down by Congress, everybody could see that a new era of strife had opened. A Boston newspaper said of the Wilmot Proviso, "As if by magic, it brought to a head the great question which is about to divide the American people." How deep that division would be no one could have imagined.

SECTION REVIEW

1. Vocabulary: *forty-niner, proviso.*
2. (a) Why did people rush to California after 1848? (b) What routes did they follow? (c) How did the surge of newcomers affect life in California?
3. (a) What was the Wilmot Proviso? (b) Why did it lead to controversy between North and South?

Chapter 14 Review

Summary

By the early 1800's Americans had come to believe that the nation would inevitably spread its influence across the continent and beyond. Trappers, missionaries, and pioneers began the long trek westward to the Oregon Country, which was claimed jointly by Britain and the United States.

Another area in the West was settled by Mormons, a religious group seeking a permanent home. When their founder Joseph Smith was murdered in Illinois, Brigham Young took charge, leading the Mormons to the Great Basin, where they established prosperous farming communities.

In California the first Europeans were the Spanish, who built missions and forts along the coast as far north as San Francisco. By the 1800's California's rich soil and excellent climate began to lure Americans west. The commercial center at Santa Fe, in New Mexico, also attracted American merchants and traders.

In the 1820's a group of Americans led by Stephen Austin established a community in Texas, then part of Mexico. Texans, under the leadership of Sam Houston, revolted against Mexican rule in 1836 and set up the Republic of Texas. The Texans were victorious at the Battle of San Jacinto and achieved independence.

Texas soon sought admission to the Union, but Americans were divided on the issue, with abolitionist Northerners opposed to annexation and proslavery Southerners supporting it. President Tyler, by a joint resolution of Congress, annexed Texas in the last days of his administration. Tyler was succeeded by James Polk, who had campaigned on a promise to annex Texas and Oregon. With Texas already in the Union, Polk reached a settlement with Britain dividing the Oregon Country.

Mexico, angered by the Texas annexation, attacked General Zachary Taylor's troops stationed just north of the Rio Grande. In May, 1846, Polk asked Congress for a declaration of war against Mexico. Despite political opposition to the war, and despite heavy losses in the ensuing fighting, the American army forced the surrender of Mexican troops at Mexico City. The Treaty of Guadalupe Hidalgo greatly increased the territory of the United States and settled all claims between the two countries. The southwest boundary of the United States was finally completed in 1853 by the Gadsden Purchase.

The discovery of gold in 1848, meanwhile, caused the population of California to grow dramatically. As the area became settled, California too sought admission to the Union. Meanwhile, the slavery question had been raised again, this time by the Wilmot Proviso.

Vocabulary and Important Terms

1. manifest destiny
2. Oregon Trail
3. Great Basin
4. Deseret
5. Santa Fe Trail
6. Battle of San Jacinto
7. Republic of Texas
8. annex
9. Bear Flag Republic
10. Nueces River
11. Treaty of Guadalupe Hidalgo
12. Mexican Cession
13. Gadsden Purchase
14. forty-niner
15. proviso

Discussion Questions

1. Describe the role played by (a) missionaries and (b) mountain men in the American settlement of Oregon.
2. (a) Describe the early years of the Mormon settlement at the Great Salt Lake. (b) Why did strong opposition to the Mormon state of Deseret develop? (c) Under what circumstances was the area of Mormon settlement finally added to the Union?
3. How were each of the following involved in the American settlement of California? (a) Richard Henry Dana (b) Thomas Larkin (c) John Sutter
4. Why was the growth of the Santa Fe trade important both to New Mexico and to American expansion westward?
5. (a) Why did disagreements arise over the question of Texas's admission to the Union? (b) How did President Tyler interpret the outcome of the election of 1844, and why was Texas admitted to the Union by a joint resolution of Congress?
6. (a) Why did President Polk send John Slidell to Mexico, and what was Slidell authorized to do? (b) How did Polk react to the news that Slidell had been rejected by the Mexicans?
7. (a) What were the results of the Mexican War? (b) Why did the United States buy additional land from Mexico in 1853?
8. (a) What parts did John C. Frémont and Stephen W. Kearny play in the American takeover of California? (b) Why was California ready to enter the Union so quickly?
9. (a) What problem was opened by California's request for admission to the Union? (b) How did the debate over the Wilmot Proviso contribute to the controversy?

Relating Past to Present

1. Settlers rushed to California following the discovery of gold there in 1848. What factors or trends today cause people to move from one part of the country to another?

2. Find out what memorials there are in Texas that honor the brave men and women who fought for Texas independence.

3. In the 1840's America expanded westward to the Pacific Ocean with a sense of destiny. Is the United States today pursuing any endeavors with similar fervor? Explain your answer.

Studying Local History

Locate your state on the map on page 338. Is your state shown as part of the original United States? If not, by which territorial acquisition did your state or region become part of the United States? What present-day states are not shown on this map?

Using History Skills

1. *Reading maps.* Study the map on page 322, noting the trails settlers followed as they headed west. (a) At what point did the Oregon Trail begin? (b) Where did it end? (c) What trails did Americans follow to California? (d) In what ways does the map help explain why the journey west was a difficult one?

2. *Reading source material.* Study the Texas Declaration of Rights on page 333. The delegates who wrote this famous document set down the rights they believed a free people should have. Make a list of the rights contained in this document. Then look for similarities between the Texas Declaration of Rights and the Bill of Rights of the United States Constitution.

3. *Placing events in time.* Look back through this chapter and find events that were important in the settlement of California. Make a time line showing those events.

WORLD SCENE

Expansion

In the first half of the nineteenth century, while the United States was expanding across North America, European nations were building empires in Asia and Africa.

The British in India. At the end of the 1700's the British, recognizing the growing importance of Indian trade in their economy, took steps to protect their interests in India. First, Parliament moved to limit the power of the East India Company. Next, British leaders began to change their role in Indian politics. Instead of merely trying to keep the peace among the Indian princes for the purpose of maintaining favorable trade conditions, the British began to build an empire in India.

By 1850 the British had brought large areas of India under their control. Some of these territories were placed under direct British rule; others were allowed to remain independent in name, but were in fact controlled by Britain.

Many Indians resented the presence of the British and their well-meant but clumsy attempts to reform Indian life. In 1857 these resentments exploded in a bloody revolt by Indian soldiers serving in the British army. The Sepoy Rebellion shocked the home country and sealed the fate of the East India Company. The following year the British government annexed the Company's Indian holdings and made India part of the British Empire.

The French in Algeria. Algeria, on the Barbary coast of the Mediterranean Sea, was the scene of French activity. In the early nineteenth century, Algeria was part of the Turkish Empire, but it was so far from Constantinople that its rulers could operate with a high degree of independence.

Piracy against foreign ships was a major source of income for the Algerians. European countries as well as the United States had been plagued by the Barbary pirates. In 1830 France's anger at Algeria boiled over when the Turkish governor at Algiers, the capital, struck the French consul with a fly whisk during a dispute over an old French debt. The French king, Charles X, responded by invading Algeria. He defended his action as a move to wipe out piracy. Three weeks later the offending governor surrendered. In addition to Algiers, the French took control of other coastal towns. Resistance in the interior of the country, however, continued on and off throughout the century.

Algerians found themselves treated as a conquered people. French was made the national language, property was confiscated from former rebels, and immigration from Europe was encouraged.

CHAPTER 15

The Quest for Compromise

1848 – 1860

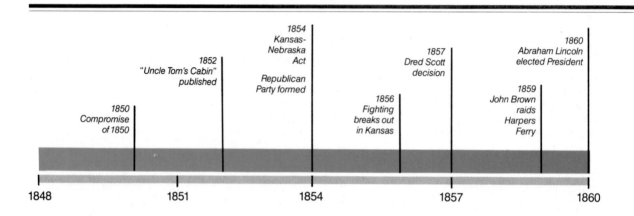

1850
Compromise
of 1850

1852
"Uncle Tom's Cabin"
published

1854
Kansas-
Nebraska
Act

Republican
Party formed

1856
Fighting
breaks out
in Kansas

1857
Dred Scott
decision

1859
John Brown
raids
Harpers
Ferry

1860
Abraham Lincoln
elected President

1848   1851   1854   1857   1860

CHAPTER OUTLINE

1. The Compromise of 1850 is adopted.

2. The Kansas-Nebraska Act stirs up an angry debate.

3. Sectional differences are sharpened.

4. The South breaks away from the Union.

Ever since 1836, Congress had prohibited the discussion of bills and petitions concerning slavery. The repeal of this "gag rule" then became a goal of the abolitionists. Their leader in Congress was former President John Quincy Adams, who had come back to Washington to represent his Massachusetts district in the House. Holding that the gag rule violated the Constitution, Adams caused an uproar every time he rose to read an antislavery petition. Finally, while the nation's attention was riveted on the war with Mexico, Adams achieved his goal: the House agreed to lift the ban on the discussion of slavery. By then Adams was known to antislavery people as "Old Man Eloquent" and "the Representative of the whole Nation."

On February 21, 1848, Adams collapsed in his chair in the House and died two days later. At the funeral, a speaker asked, "Where could death have found him but at the post of duty?" All the dignitaries of Washington, including President Polk, attended the services. As Speaker of the House in 1836, Polk had once ruled Adams out of order for trying to open the subject of slavery. Now everybody was speaking on the subject — and Polk's annexation policies had brought it to the fore. What effect the argument over slavery would have on the Union no one could predict. John Calhoun, anxious about the nation's future, said, "The curtain is dropped and the future closed to our view."

1 The Compromise of 1850 Is Adopted

With victory over Mexico, the United States had all but completed its continental expansion. Yet the acquisition of new lands promised to open a new political debate between the North and South. Tension between the sections was already high during the presidential campaign of 1848.

The parties choose their candidates in 1848. In the late 1840's successful generals again became appealing candidates for President. Zachary Taylor, the hero of Buena Vista, let it be known in 1847 that he expected to be nominated by both major parties and, like George Washington, to become President without opposition! In 1848 the Whigs nominated Taylor at their convention in Philadelphia, with Millard Fillmore of New York as his running mate. Fillmore, who had begun his career as an apprentice in a clock-making mill, was a lawyer and a former member of Congress. An early Whig, he had increasingly come to have antislavery views. On the Whig ticket he balanced Taylor, a Louisiana slaveholder.

The Whigs presented no platform because they had no program that could appeal to people in all sections. The party was said to be held together by a cotton thread running from one end of the country to the other. This witty comment was a way of pointing out that cotton planters in the South and cotton manufacturers in the North were the Whigs' strongest supporters. Some people described these two groups as "the lords of the lash and the lords of the loom."

The Democrats, ignoring Taylor, chose as their standard-bearer Lewis Cass of Michigan. Then 65 years old, Cass was proud of having once supported Jefferson and Jackson. Cass had been a general in the War of 1812, governor of the Michigan Territory, and a United States senator. Like many politicians, he had a proposal for dealing with the problem of whether there

When Congress convened in 1849, senators and representatives debated the question of slavery and sought to preserve the Union by means of compromise.

should be slavery in the new territories. He called his idea *popular sovereignty.* By this he meant that the voters in a territory, not Congress, would decide for themselves if they wanted to permit slavery.

Slavery becomes a campaign issue. Popular sovereignty was fresh fuel in the debate over slavery. Now that the territories in the West were beginning to ask for admission to the Union, the issue was no longer only a subject to be agitated by abolitionists. It had also become the business of politicians seeking to gain additional voting power in Congress. But who had a solution?

The Democrats were, in fact, badly split on the question. The "Barnburners," a New York faction, angrily pulled out of the nominating convention in Philadelphia and named Martin Van Buren as their candidate. (This group, which got its name because its members were willing to "burn down the barn" in their antislavery zeal, had emerged in the campaign of 1844.) Later in the summer of 1848, they and other antislavery Democrats joined with the Liberty Party and with a number of so-called "Conscience" Whigs to form the Free-Soil Party. Meeting at Buffalo, New York, the new party firmly supported the Wilmot Proviso (page 341) and adopted the slogan "Free soil, free speech, free labor, and free men."

Taylor is elected President. General Taylor won in November by a narrow margin. The Free-Soilers failed to capture a single state. Van Buren, nevertheless, took enough votes from the Democrats in New York to give the electoral votes of the state and the election to Taylor.

Zachary Taylor was a man of strong principles and deep feelings. He looked, it was often said, "like a man born to command." His wife, Margaret Smith Taylor, was the daughter of a Maryland planter. As an army wife, she had accompanied Taylor for forty years from one post to the next. Their six children were born in four different states and territories. Taylor once said of her, "You know, my wife was as much of a soldier as I was."

Taylor's lack of practical political experience threatened to be a handicap. Before his election he had never voted. Yet he was confident he could win support. His favorite horse, Old Whitey, had the freedom of the White House lawn, a constant reminder to visitors of Taylor's battlefield glory.

Taylor opposes the spread of slavery. When Polk left office in March, 1849, he had recommended that California and the rest of the new land acquired from Mexico be organized as territories. But what would be the fate of slavery in these territories? Even moderate Southerners seemed ready to break up the Union if slavery were banned in them.

President Taylor's idea for dealing with the question seemed straightforward. He believed that slavery where it already existed ought to be defended. Beyond that, he urged the people of California and New Mexico to apply immediately for statehood, without first being organized as territories. Everybody understood that the new states would be free states.

Southerners were astonished and infuriated. They had considered Taylor to be one of their own. Taylor, however, had fallen under the influence of William Seward, the Whig senator from New York. Seward had a reputation as a humanitarian and as an outspoken abolitionist. His sway over the President had become obvious by the summer of 1849, when Taylor said, "The people of the North need have no apprehension of the further extension of slavery."

California, with its population approaching 100,000, acted quickly on the President's suggestion that it become a state without delay. At a convention in Monterey, delegates adopted a state constitution banning slavery. The constitution was soon ratified by a large majority.

Taylor's strong stand against slavery in the western lands had united the slave states in their opposition. Southerners held that if California came into the Union as a free state, the South deserved something in return. Many Southerners began to oppose a number of northern actions. They were bitter that Northerners protected runaway slaves, despite laws requiring their capture and return. Moreover, they were angry that many Northerners were now calling for an end to the slave trade in the District of Columbia.

Taylor came more and more to think that the South was to blame for the disagreement threatening the Union. Upon learning that some Southerners wanted to spread slavery by moving the boundary of Texas, a slave state, westward at the expense of New Mexico, the President used his power. He sent troops to guard the Texas-New Mexico border. Then, hearing people say that army officers would refuse to act against Texans, Taylor replied forcefully. If he found men in rebellion against the Union, he roared, he would hang them with less hesitation than he had hanged "deserters and spies in Mexico"!

Congress meets amidst controversy. The Senate, which took up the question of California statehood in the autumn of 1849, contained an impressive number of well-known statesmen. Among them were Clay, Calhoun, and Webster.

Henry Clay of Kentucky had been reelected to the Senate in 1848 after seven years away from Washington. Having lost the Whig nomination to Taylor at the convention in Philadelphia (page 345), he knew he would never be President. Earlier, when he had failed to get the Whig nomination in 1840, Clay and his wife had wept in each other's arms. Perhaps now he could show what he had meant when he once responded to a critic, "Sir, I would rather be right than President." He was returning to Congress, he said, intending to "be a calm and quiet looker on."

Calhoun was deathly ill. Racked by tuberculosis, he coughed constantly. His eyes still showed some of their old fire but they seemed sunken in his emaciated face. He was so feeble that he had to be helped up the steps of the Capitol and led to his seat.

The third of the old notables was Daniel Webster of Massachusetts. His steely stare had lost none of its power to hold listeners. Webster was also ill, however, and near the end of his brilliant career.

The presence of these majestic figures called to mind some of the dramatic struggles of the Age of Jackson. Other men from

Henry Clay (center), Daniel Webster (left), and John Calhoun (right) met in the Senate for the last time to debate the Compromise of 1850.

that time were also in the Senate. Thomas Hart Benton of Missouri was there. A senator since 1821, Benton had once opposed the restriction of slavery in Missouri. More recently, he had come to favor gradual abolition. Present also was Sam Houston from Texas, handsomely dressed in a waistcoat of panther skin. Houston was becoming a strong supporter of the Union and was increasingly at odds with most of his southern colleagues.

A new generation of powerful voices could also be heard. William Seward, as we have learned, was already playing a part. Stephen A. Douglas of Illinois was also making a name in the Senate. Short, but with a large head and broad shoulders, Douglas was known as the Little Giant.

Some of the finest spokesmen of the South were in the House of Representatives. Alexander Stephens, a conciliatory Georgian, was proslavery but also pro-Union. Stephens, nevertheless, identified strongly with the South. "Her fate is my fate; and her destiny is my destiny," he declared. Another clear voice was that of Robert Toombs, also from Georgia. A huge man with a hearty laugh, he was eloquent and well-educated. Yet another Georgian was Howell Cobb, a burly man who owned 1,000 slaves. He had just been elected Speaker of the House.

Clay offers his last compromise. During the summer of 1849 Clay did not seem to be following the Senate debates closely. His desire to be only a bystander, however, soon gave way to his instinct for compromise, a talent which he had amply demonstrated in the past. He prepared to make another effort — his last, it proved — for the unity of the nation.

In spite of his physical frailty and a hacking cough, Clay called at Webster's home one day near the end of January, 1850. His purpose was to seek support from his old friend for a compromise he intended to present to the Senate. Both men, long disappointed in their presidential ambitions, now knew they would have to persuade extremists on both sides to give ground. In describing his plan to Webster,

Clay was mindful that there was no new slave state to offer the South in exchange for California's admission to the Union as a free state. He hoped, nevertheless, that Southerners would be willing to accept a solemn promise that their property would be protected.

Working on this understanding, Clay, on January 29, 1850, introduced in the Senate a number of resolutions that, taken together, have become known as the Compromise of 1850. The resolutions called for (1) the admission of California as a free state; (2) the organization of the rest of the territory acquired from Mexico without any restriction on slavery; (3) the assigning to New Mexico of the vacant land in dispute along the Texas border, in return for the federal government's assumption of the pre-annexation debts of Texas; (4) the abolition of the slave trade — but not of slavery — in the District of Columbia; and (5) the passage of a stricter fugitive slave law.

Congress debates the Compromise of 1850. Clay defended these proposals in the Senate a week later. Hundreds of spectators in the overheated Senate chamber added to the drama.

Clay began by warning that this was no time for fancy words or "decoration of speech." He intended simply to appeal to reason and patriotic feeling. California, the Kentuckian pointed out, had already drawn up a free-state constitution. As for the rest of the land that Mexico had ceded, many people did not believe slavery could be profitable in that area anyway. Therefore, to arouse the South by taking a stand on the question did not appear necessary. He appealed to Northerners not to put pressure on the South. "What more do you want?" he asked. "You have got what is worth more than a thousand Wilmot Provisos. You have nature on your side — facts upon your side — and this truth staring you in the face, that there is no slavery in those territories."

The gallery was almost entirely on Clay's side, but most Southerners had other views. In the debate that followed, their ar-

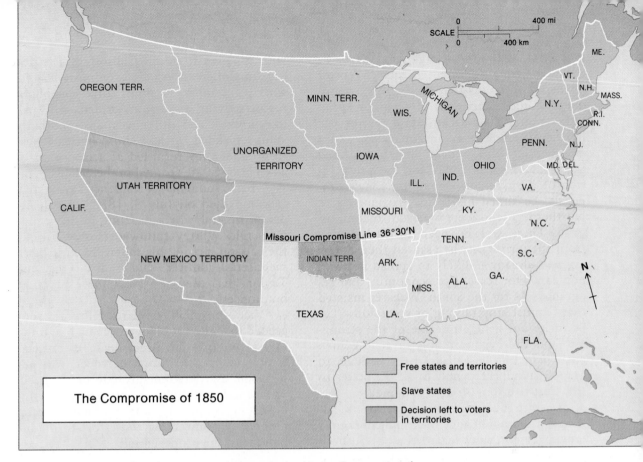

Free states and territories	
Slave states	
Decision left to voters in territories	

The Compromise of 1850

Political leaders thought that the agreement they worked out in the Compromise of 1850 would settle the dispute over slavery in the territories.

guments were fully aired. Calhoun, too weak to deliver his words himself, sat wrapped in blankets as his friend, Senator James Mason of Virginia, read the South Carolinian's carefully prepared speech.

Calhoun began by arguing that to answer the question "How can the Union be preserved?" it was necessary to ask first "What is it that has endangered the Union?" He thereupon attacked the North, which, he pointed out, now dominated the federal government, having a majority of the states and a majority of the population.

The South, Calhoun went on, had yielded ground time after time to the North — in the Northwest Ordinance, in the Missouri Compromise, in Oregon. Now the South was being asked to yield in the case of the territory obtained from Mexico too. The question, he said, was not whether the South would suddenly secede and wreck the Union. Ties that held the Union together were *already* breaking. The Protestant

churches had split on North-South lines and the political parties could not remain national much longer. This tearing apart of the nation would continue, he predicted, "until nothing will be left to hold the states together except force." Calhoun gave the North an ultimatum. The North must extend to the South the right to take slaves into the territories and it must approve laws protecting that right.

When Mason had finished speaking, Calhoun returned to his boarding house exhausted, but cheered by the knowledge that his words had left a memorable impression. He never again appeared in the Senate. Before the month was over, he was dead.

Webster delivers his "Seventh of March" speech. Webster's turn to speak came on March 7. He had put on the blue and buff suit he traditionally wore when he spoke on grand occasions (page 256). His plea was in sharp contrast with Calhoun's remarks. In what was afterward always referred to as the "Seventh of March" speech, Webster opened with words that generations of students would memorize: "I wish to speak today, not as a Massachusetts man, nor as a northern man, but as an American, and a member of the Senate of the United States. . . . I speak today for the preservation of the Union." Defending Clay's proposals, he aimed his words particularly at Northerners who were opposed to compromise. There was no need to ban slavery from the territories, he assured them. Slavery was already unlikely to spread into the new lands for reasons of economics and geography. As for the South, Webster insisted that it must stop talking of secession: "Let us make our generation one of the strongest, and the brightest link in that golden chain which is destined, I fully believe, to grapple [bind] the people of all the states to this Constitution, for ages to come."

Despite the high level of Webster's language, it did not change the minds of Southerners. Taylor, now regarded as a southern President with northern ideas, opposed Clay's proposals. He was convinced that anybody who was against California's admission as a free state was a traitor.

Northern abolitionists were angrier than ever and took out their rage on Webster. John Greenleaf Whittier, the "good gray Quaker poet," wrote sadly of the change he detected in the "god-like Daniel." He penned these lines about Webster:

. . . from these great eyes
The soul has fled:
When faith is lost, when honor dies,
The man is dead!

Many northern radicals found comfort in Senator Seward's speech on the Clay resolutions. Seward declared himself opposed to compromise, because compromise, he said, meant a surrender of "judgment and conscience." He refused to believe that the Constitution was intended to defend slavery. No, he asserted, there is a *higher law* than the Constitution that decent people must obey: the law of God.

Death alters the scene. President Taylor, ignoring Clay's resolutions, went ahead with his plan to admit California. The debate in Congress became even more heated and, as tempers flared, some members began arriving at sessions armed with pistols, knives, and other weapons. Southern Whigs pleaded with Taylor to turn back from what they regarded as a mad course. The nation's fate seemed in the balance.

Then, suddenly, President Taylor fell sick and died on July 9, 1850. The President's funeral was a dazzling military display. Old Whitey followed closely behind the caisson bearing his fallen rider. A Massachusetts admirer said sadly, President Taylor "has died too soon for everybody but himself."

Vice President Millard Fillmore succeeded to the White House. He had no military glamour and, in fact, had little of the fighter in him. Fillmore, however, was dependable and gentlemanly. He put himself on the side of Webster and Clay. Clay by now was completely exhausted and Senator Douglas was directing the effort to obtain passage of the proposed bill.

Congress passes the Compromise of 1850. In September, 1850, Congress approved Clay's resolutions (page 348). Immediately there were torchlight processions in support of the Compromise of 1850, and patriotic people could cry with one voice, "The Union is saved!" Clay went home to Kentucky to be greeted by the cheers of his neighbors. His public work was done. Meanwhile, Stephen Douglas had expressed his firm intention: "I have determined never to make another speech on the slavery question."

SECTION REVIEW

1. Vocabulary: *popular sovereignty.*
2. How did the political parties approach the slavery issue in the election of 1848?
3. (a) Why did California's request for statehood lead to controversy? (b) What was President Taylor's solution to the problem? (c) How did the South view Taylor's position?
4. (a) What were the main provisions in the compromise proposed by Clay? (b) How were they viewed by Calhoun? (c) By Webster? (d) By Seward?

2 The Kansas-Nebraska Act Stirs Up an Angry Debate

The public, although relieved that an open break between North and South had been prevented, was not enthusiastic about the Compromise of 1850. On both sides, fire-brands saw the settlement as a "sellout," and tension between the free and slave states stayed high.

The North defies the Fugitive Slave Act. Southerners now looked to the new Fugitive Slave Act to protect their property. In the North, at the same time, every effort to enforce the law seemed only to make radicals out of moderates. In a town not far from Philadelphia, a slave owner trying to recover a fugitive was slain in 1851 by a group of black men. One of the most celebrated cases of the time involved Anthony Burns, a slave who at the age of twenty escaped from Richmond, Virginia, by ship. When he was arrested in Boston, a stronghold of abolitionist feeling, people were said to be more outraged than at any time since the Boston Massacre. They besieged the courthouse to which Burns was taken and were finally turned away only by federal marshals and state troops. Eventually Burns was returned to his owner but at a cost to the federal government estimated at $100,000.

Wisconsin, which had a large population of former New Englanders, went even further in defying the law: its highest court declared the Fugitive Slave Act unconstitutional. These examples of the North's attitude were proof to many Southerners that the institution of slavery itself, not simply the extension of slavery into the territories, was in danger.

***Uncle Tom's Cabin* provokes a storm.** Neither Northerners nor Southerners were prepared for the furor caused by a new book entitled *Uncle Tom's Cabin, or Life Among the Lowly.* Its author, Harriet Beecher Stowe, wrote with the zeal of a reformer. Her father was a leading antislavery preacher, and five of her brothers were also

This advertisement for *Uncle Tom's Cabin* illustrates a scene from the story.

ministers. She grew up to feel moral causes deeply, and she wrote about them vividly.

Uncle Tom's Cabin, which had been published first as a serial in an antislavery newspaper, came out as a book in 1852. It was an instant success. Before the year was out, over 300,000 copies had been sold. It was quickly translated into many languages and read the world over. Millions more saw it enacted on the stage and wept for the slave, Uncle Tom, when he was flogged to death, and for Eliza, when she tried to escape from the bloodhounds.

Harriet Beecher Stowe had had no first-hand knowledge of slavery — a fact that especially infuriated southern defenders of the system. She had heard accounts from escaped slaves, however, and she had felt deeply offended by the Fugitive Slave Act. She had taken to heart the words of a sister-in-law: "Now, Hattie, if I could use a pen as you can, I would write something which would make this whole nation feel what an accursed thing slavery is."

Franklin Pierce wins the election of 1852. As the election of 1852 approached, political moderates on both sides of the Mason-Dixon Line tried to win broad support. President Fillmore had said he would not seek election in his own right. The Whig Party was badly divided. Having won with Taylor in 1848, it finally decided to run the other hero-general of the Mexican War, Winfield Scott. Still, many southern Whigs objected to Scott because, like Taylor, he had become associated with Seward, the antislavery senator from New York. They feared that Scott held free-soil notions too.

The Democrats met in Baltimore to pick their candidate. Avoiding the most famous names of the party, they cast 49 ballots before finally settling on Franklin Pierce of New Hampshire. A tense man, Pierce had served as a United States senator and as a general in the Mexican War. Pierce was a graduate of Bowdoin College in Maine. A fellow student had been Nathaniel Hawthorne, the noted author who remained a lifelong friend. Hawthorne wrote a biography of Pierce that helped draw public attention to him as a possible President.

Pierce won an overwhelming victory. Scott took only four states. The Whig Party never recovered from the defeat. The Free-Soil Party also attracted many fewer votes than four years earlier. Since the Democratic platform had accepted the Compromise of 1850, Pierce's election seemed to show that the public desired moderation.

Douglas introduces the Kansas-Nebraska bill. During Pierce's term of office the nation was struck by a new political storm that the President was ill-equipped to handle. The upheaval resulted from the actions of Stephen A. Douglas, senator from Illinois. Douglas, who had promised never again to talk about slavery in the territories, broke his word. Without warning, he reopened the question on January 23, 1854, by introducing a bill to organize the Kansas and Nebraska territories on the principle of popular sovereignty. The bill also provided for the repeal of the Missouri Compromise. This meant that the latitude of 36°30′, agreed upon in the Missouri Compromise (page 245), would no longer divide slave states from free states. Douglas, with the help of Jefferson Davis, persuaded President Pierce to back his bill, and so made it a Democratic Party measure.

People have long debated Douglas's motives in proposing such controversial legislation. Douglas may honestly have believed that popular sovereignty was the only fair way to settle the question of slavery in the territories. He was also eager to promote the building of a northern transcontinental railroad with its eastern starting point in Chicago, in his own state of Illinois. Leaders in New Orleans, Memphis, and St. Louis favored a southern route, and they were competing to make their city the eastern terminus. Douglas may have felt that he could get the South's support for the northern route by opening the Kansas and Nebraska territories to slavery. Some observers believed, also, that Douglas was simply trying to turn attention from the dull Pierce administration and to put the spotlight on himself as a national leader.

Sectional tensions are inflamed by Douglas's legislation. The North responded with fury to the Kansas-Nebraska bill. Salmon P. Chase, an antislavery senator from Ohio, denounced it as "a gross violation of a sacred pledge . . . as part and parcel of an atrocious plot." Northerners had been watching with dismay what they considered to be the growth of southern influence in government. They regarded Pierce as a "doughface," a term applied to a Northerner with southern principles. Northern farmers were upset, furthermore, that Southerners had prevented Congress from passing legislation for a more generous way of distributing western land. Douglas's proposal, said farmers, only opened the West to further southern "meddling."

To the charge that he was a traitor to the North, Douglas had a ready reply. He said that the Missouri Compromise had, in fact, been repealed by the Compromise of 1850, which supported popular sovereignty. He argued, furthermore, that whenever Congress tried to interfere with slavery, trouble followed immediately. The time had come, he advised, to let the people decide. Douglas fought hard to gain support for the new legislation. With solid southern support, Congress passed the Kansas-Nebraska Act. On May 30, 1854, President Pierce signed it into law.

A few days earlier, Seward, in a speech to the Senate said angrily, "Come on then,

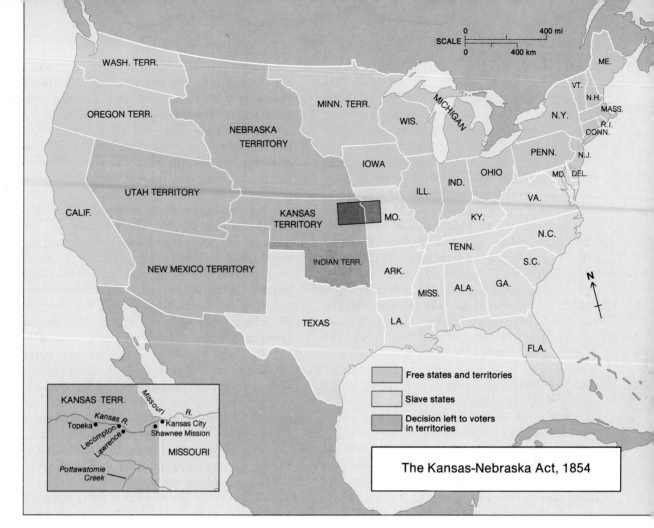

The Kansas-Nebraska Act, 1854

Free states and territories

Slave states

Decision left to voters in territories

After passage of the Kansas-Nebraska Act, control of Kansas was bitterly contested by antislavery and proslavery factions.

gentlemen of the slave states, since there is no escaping your challenge, I accept it in behalf of the cause of freedom. We will engage in competition for the virgin soil of Kansas, and God give the victory to the side which is stronger in numbers as in right." The forecast proved astonishingly correct.

SECTION REVIEW

1. How did the North respond to the new Fugitive Slave Act?
2. (a) What was Harriet Beecher Stowe's purpose in writing *Uncle Tom's Cabin*? (b) Describe the novel's effect on public opinion.
3. (a) What was the intent of the Kansas-Nebraska Act? (b) What might have been Douglas's motives in proposing it? (c) Why did many Northerners oppose it?

3 Sectional Differences Are Sharpened

The movement of Americans westward had continued throughout the 1840's and early 1850's. People were recognizing that the vast region between the Mississippi River and the Rockies — once considered too dry for cultivation — could be rich farmland. Northern farmers already felt the pull of Kansas and Nebraska as places where they might take up land.

Free settlers and slaveholders struggle over Kansas. Tragic events were soon to overtake Kansas. Eli Thayer, originally a school principal in Massachusetts, took upon himself the work of making Kansas a free-soil state. He formed the Massachusetts Emigrant Aid Society. The organization attracted wide support, appealing to land speculators as well as abolitionists, and within three years Emigrant Aid had brought about 2,000 people to Kansas.

Southerners had not ignored the challenge. A similar movement was under way to find settlers who favored slavery. Proslavery politicians in neighboring Missouri had an opportunity to help out on November 29, 1854, when an election took place to select a delegate to represent the Kansas Territory in Congress. Several hundred armed men streamed across the border from Missouri and voted illegally for a proslavery candidate. When a territorial legislature was chosen the following March, 5,000 men — nicknamed "Border Ruffians" — crossed into Kansas to vote.

In the fraudulent March election, a proslavery legislature was chosen. Soon afterwards it met at Shawnee Mission, Kansas, and began enacting laws protecting slavery. Free-Soilers in Kansas refused to accept the government at Shawnee Mission and established their own government at Topeka. In October they held a convention, drew up a free-state constitution, and asked for admission to the Union. President Pierce at once denounced the Topeka government as "revolutionary" and illegal.

Kansas now had two governments. As the rest of the country debated the "Kansas question," the impact on the shaky Democratic and Whig parties was profound.

The Republican Party emerges. Throughout the North, people who opposed the extension of slavery and were distressed by the Kansas-Nebraska Act began to cut their ties to both the Whig and the Democratic parties. Many voters who considered themselves good Democrats would not forgive President Pierce for having supported Douglas in the Kansas debate. Similarly, many Whigs who had hoped that their party could become a national antislavery party were also disheartened by recent events.

In 1854, during the debate on the Kansas-Nebraska Act, groups of antislavery Democrats, Whigs, and Free-Soilers came together in several places to express their views. At one such meeting in Ripon, Wisconsin, members chose the name *Republican* and decided to organize a party opposed

The violence in Kansas caused people to refer to that territory as "Bleeding Kansas." The free-staters won this battle at Hickory Point in 1856.

to the extension of slavery. The first convention of a Republican state party was held in Jackson, Michigan, on July 6, 1854. In the elections of 1854 the new party sent many members to Congress and won control of several state governments.

The Know-Nothing Party is formed. For a time in 1854 many people assumed that the most powerful new political party would not be the Republicans but yet another group, the Know-Nothings. This party grew out of a secret organization of native-born Americans who solemnly pledged never to vote for any foreign-born or Roman Catholic candidate for office. When questioned about their organization, members responded "I know nothing," an answer that furnished the party with its name.

The Know-Nothings attracted native-born Americans in both the North and South who felt threatened by the heavy immigration from Ireland in the late 1840's (page 291). Many Northerners considered the immigrants to be proslavery because they often tried to break up abolitionist meetings. The newcomers, mostly unskilled people, were afraid they would have to compete with freed blacks for jobs. Southerners, for their part, looked upon immigrants as an antislavery force, because most of the new arrivals settled in the North.

Know-Nothing candidates won several state offices in New England, where opposition to the Irish was strong in factory towns. The party also had victories in California, where anti-Chinese feeling ran high. In 1856, former President Millard Fillmore became the Know-Nothing candidate for President. However, the party, by then divided on the slavery question, had lost much of its strength. Fillmore carried only one state and the party soon disappeared.

"Bleeding Kansas" draws wide concern. As the presidential campaign of 1856 got under way, terrible things were taking place in Kansas. Civil war had broken out in that tormented land.

In May, "Border Ruffians" and proslavery Kansas men pillaged and burned the free-soil town of Lawrence. They were determined to "give distinct notice that all

who do not leave immediately for the East, *will leave for eternity.*" Two people lost their lives in the assault and the entire community was terrorized.

John Brown, a fanatical abolitionist, made up his mind to avenge the attack on Lawrence. For many years this Connecticut-born zealot had devoted time to helping black people. Now, in 1856, he believed that he was an instrument of God, selected to crush sin in the world. With seven other men, including four of his sons, Brown raided a proslavery settlement near Pottawatomie Creek in Kansas. The attackers brutally murdered five men. In the months that followed, the fighting in "Bleeding Kansas" took the lives of more than 200 men and women before federal troops could restore order.

Sumner is attacked in the Senate. Newspapers kept the public inflamed and prepared for further violence. Meanwhile, the struggle in Kansas led to a shameful event on the floor of the Senate. In May, 1856, Republican Senator Charles Sumner of Massachusetts delivered a fiery speech in which he attacked the South and Senator Andrew Butler of South Carolina. Butler was absent at the time. Two days after the address, Preston Brooks, a House member from South Carolina and Butler's nephew, approached Sumner, who was working at his desk in the Senate. Brooks began beating Sumner with a cane and continued until the senator lost consciousness.

Brooks immediately resigned his seat, but his district quickly re-elected him. From all over the South, "Bully" Brooks received new canes. Sumner, for his part, would suffer fierce head pains for the rest of his life. Over the next three years he did not appear in the Senate, his empty seat a silent but eloquent reminder that violence had threatened representative government itself.

The Democrats nominate Buchanan in 1856. The election of 1856 took place in the midst of this state of affairs. The very words being used — the "sack" of Lawrence, the "massacre" at Pottawatomie, the "assault" on Sumner — had aroused the nation.

Violence in the Kansas Territory

For Victoria Clayton, a native of Alabama, each new free state admitted to the Union seemed to present a threat to the southern way of life. In her memoirs she told about the efforts of the Clayton family to defend the "old regime" of the South and assure the extension of slavery to Kansas.

A raid in Kansas

It was in 1856 that the Kansas Territory was seeking admission into the Union as a state. All the southern people were interested in having it admitted as a slave state and consequently desirous of sending out emigrants to settle there. A considerable amount of money was contributed for this purpose by the states of Alabama and Georgia. This money was entrusted to my husband for the purpose of taking out a group of Southerners and settling them in the territory so as to secure their vote for the South in the coming election.

We left Alabama in early August, gathering emigrants as we journeyed westward. When at last we reached Kansas City, Missouri, the greatest excitement prevailed there. Men were coming from all over to form an army to expel a band of men whose leader was John Brown, later of Harpers Ferry renown. Brown's band was marching from home to home in the Kansas Territory, destroying property and turning women and children out homeless on the prairies, because of differences in politics. They too were interested as to how the territory should come into the Union, and were using these means for the accomplishment of their purpose.

My husband and his men at once offered their services to these Missourians who were determined to put a stop to the outrages being committed by these disturbers of the peace. They were immediately outfitted with red flannel shirts, corduroy pants, canteens, and cartridge boxes, then sent out on the trail of Brown's lawless band.

The Democrats, who still considered themselves a national party, sought a candidate not identified with the Kansas question. They refused to renominate President Pierce, therefore, or to support the ambitious Senator Douglas. On the seventeenth ballot they chose James Buchanan of Pennsylvania, another "doughface."

Buchanan, a bachelor, was the son of an Irish immigrant. Although America was humming to the sounds of the telegraph, the factory, and the railroad, Buchanan was an old-fashioned man. He wore a long black coat, to which he had become accustomed during his recent service as United States minister to Great Britain. Formal in manner, he allowed few people to address him by his first name. Even his niece, Harriet Lane, who served as First Lady after he became President, always called him "Mr. Buchanan" in public.

While in England, Buchanan had won friends in the South. With President Pierce's secret approval, he had met at Ostend, Belgium, in October, 1854, with the United States ministers to Spain and France. They had drawn up and submitted to the Secretary of State a document that came to be known as the Ostend Manifesto. It declared that the United States should purchase Cuba from Spain, "with as little delay as possible." The paper argued that if Spain should refuse to sell the island, then the United States would have the right to seize it. The publication of the Ostend Manifesto raised a storm in the North. The Pierce administration quickly denied any responsibility for the document. Still, critics called it a disgrace: manifest destiny, once seen as a way of spreading America's democratic system, had apparently been turned into a call for military aggression.

Buchanan defeats John Frémont. The Republican Party, meeting at Philadelphia in 1856, unanimously chose John C. Frémont, the "Pathfinder of the West" (page 334), as its candidate for President. Now 43 years old, Frémont was one of the youngest men ever to run for that office. He was a free-soiler, although not an abolitionist. The Republicans chanted their campaign slogan: "Free speech, free press, free soil, free men, Frémont, and victory!"

The Republican platform supported the right of Congress to make decisions on slavery in the territories. It also expressed approval of a transcontinental railroad and condemned the Ostend Manifesto. The Republicans did not hesitate to say they were the party of "the laboring people." They jeered at Buchanan as "Ten-cent Jimmy" because he had said that ten cents a day ought to be enough for any worker.

The Democrats played on the public's deep concern that the Union was in danger of splitting apart. As a result, when Buchanan won the election, many people took the victory as evidence that Americans wanted the Union, above everything else, to hold together. A significant fact, however, was the sectional division of the vote. Frémont carried New England and many other northern states, while Buchanan's support was mainly in the South.

SECTION REVIEW

1. (a) Explain how Kansas became a battleground between free settlers and slaveholders. (b) How did Kansas come to have two governments?
2. (a) What new political parties were formed in the 1850's? (b) What were the goals of each?
3. What was meant by "Bleeding Kansas"?
4. (a) What candidates ran for President in 1856? (b) How did the outcome of that election reveal sectional divisions?

4 The South Breaks Away from the Union

In his inaugural address in March, 1857, "Old Buck," as people called Buchanan, made a plea for popular sovereignty. He hoped, he said, that its meaning would be agreed upon and that the slavery question would then cease tormenting the country. The Supreme Court, the President continued, was about to hand down an important decision on the subject. He pledged to accept the decision "cheerfully, whatever this may be." Buchanan was actually being crafty; he had already been told what it would be.

The Dred Scott case causes a furor. Two days after the inauguration, the Supreme Court decision was announced. It concerned the status of a slave named Dred Scott. Scott, born in Missouri, had been taken by his owner, Dr. John Emerson, to Illinois, a free state, and then into Wisconsin Territory (a part of the Louisiana Territory declared free by the Missouri Compromise). After four years on soil where slavery was prohibited, Scott was returned to Missouri. In 1846 he brought a lawsuit for his freedom on the grounds that his residence on free soil had made him free.

The first court to hear the case was in Missouri. It agreed with Dred Scott, saying that he was indeed entitled to his freedom. Then, in 1852 the Missouri state supreme court overruled the lower court. The case was finally taken to the United States Supreme Court, where it was **argued** in December, 1856. In their deliberations the justices concerned themselves with three crucial questions: (1) Was Scott a citizen of Missouri and therefore entitled to sue in a federal court? (2) Had his stay on free soil given him freedom, and if so, did he retain that freedom upon returning to Missouri? (3) Was the Missouri Compromise, which had banned slavery in the Louisiana Territory north of 36°30′, constitutional?

The Court decided against Scott by a vote of seven to two. Chief Justice Roger B.

Taney, who wrote the majority opinion, asserted that Scott was not a citizen and, moreover, that *no* slave or descendant of a slave was a citizen under the Constitution. Therefore, the Court ruled, it had no jurisdiction in the case.

If the Court had gone no further, it might have prevented the general outcry that followed. It also held, however, that the time Scott had spent on free soil did not make him free in Missouri, a slave state, because as a resident of Missouri he was governed by its laws. The most sensational part of the Court's decision was that the federal government was obliged to protect slaves as property wherever their owners chose to take them. Slavery, in short, could exist anywhere — even in the territories. The Missouri Compromise, therefore, which had limited the area of slavery, was unconstitutional, even though it had been the law of the land since 1820.

Southern defenders of slavery were delighted with Taney's stand. The Court had affirmed their long-held view that slavery could exist anywhere in the country except where forbidden by state law. The Republicans were beside themselves with rage. The Boston *Atlas* labeled the decision "the deadliest blow which has been aimed at the liberties of America since the days of Benedict Arnold."

A new controversy grips Kansas. An immediate effect of the Dred Scott decision was to cut the ground from under the Republican Party's opposition to the extension of slavery. The Democrats were also badly hurt because popular sovereignty, which it had been advocating, had been rendered meaningless. Just how meaningless became clear in Kansas, where new events set the stage for more controversy.

Meeting in Lecompton, Kansas, early in 1857, a proslavery convention drew up a new state constitution, one that protected slavery. President Buchanan supported the Lecompton Constitution, saying that it represented the feelings of the majority of Kansans. Senator Douglas was irate. He recognized that events in Kansas had destroyed his doctrine of popular sovereignty.

He made up his mind to have it out with the President.

In a face-to-face confrontation with Douglas, President Buchanan remained unmovable. He warned Douglas against trying to defy a President of his own party. Douglas, however, vowed that he would have his way through a fair vote in Kansas on the constitution or "fall in the attempt." When the constitution as a whole was submitted to the voters in 1858, it was overwhelmingly rejected. (Kansas remained a territory until 1861, when it entered the Union as a free state.) Meanwhile, the Democratic Party was torn by the struggle over the Lecompton Constitution, and Douglas had lost standing among former supporters in the South.

Douglas runs against Lincoln for the Senate. Douglas was up for re-election to the Senate in 1858. Not only did he receive no support from the White House, but he had to face a formidable Republican challenger, Abraham Lincoln. Douglas viewed the race as the means to put himself in position for the presidential nomination in 1860. He had recently remarried, and his bride, Adele Cutts, a grandniece of Dolley Madison, was as ambitious as the Little Giant himself.

Douglas had to walk a tightrope in the campaign. He had to win the support of Illinois voters who opposed the extension of slavery. At the same time, with his eye on the 1860 Democratic ticket, he had to satisfy his backers in the South who had cheered the Dred Scott decision.

When Douglas heard that Lincoln would be his rival for senator, he told friends, "I shall have my hands full. He is the strong man of his party — full of wit, facts, dates — and the best stump speaker, with his droll ways and dry jokes, in the West."

Lincoln, a tall, gangling Springfield lawyer, was a self-made man. Born in a log cabin in Kentucky, he had moved to Illinois, where he served in Congress from 1847 to 1849. Since then he had had little success in politics. Lincoln's interest in politics was rekindled by the Dred Scott decision. He viewed slavery as a terrible wrong because he believed in the words "all men are created equal." Still, he did not know how to uproot the system. His immediate hope was to confine slavery and prevent it from spreading.

The power of Lincoln's mind, his gift of language, and his uncommon political skills were known only to a few people at the time he began his campaign for the Senate. After Douglas accepted Lincoln's challenge to a series of debates, however, the campaign captured the attention of voters not only in Illinois but throughout the nation.

The Lincoln-Douglas debates attract wide attention. As the candidates debated, the contrasts between them in appearance and style impressed their audiences. Douglas — short, handsome, and self-confident — spoke in a deep, melodious voice. Lincoln spoke somewhat awkwardly in a high-pitched voice, and wore rumpled clothes that seemed too small for him. Words, however, were what the prairie crowds in Illinois had come to weigh and compare.

At Freeport, Illinois, Lincoln raised a difficult question: "Can the people of a United States territory, in any lawful way, against the wish of any citizen of the United States, exclude slavery from its limits prior to the formation of a state constitution?" Lincoln was asking Douglas to choose between what the Dred Scott decision said — that slavery could not be banned anywhere — and his earlier support of popular sovereignty. Douglas responded with what seemed to be a shrewd reply. He said that despite the Supreme Court ruling, slavery could be excluded from a territory if local protection for it was not adequate.

The Illinois voters were satisfied by this Freeport Doctrine, as it came to be called, and returned Douglas to the Senate. Douglas's stand, however, angered the South. His defense of popular sovereignty would cost him southern support for the presidential nomination in 1860.

Although Lincoln lost the election to Douglas, he had become a national figure. People could see that the attempt to extend slavery, as Douglas had provided for in the Kansas-Nebraska Act, would only aggravate the problem. The answer for now seemed to lie not in the abolition of slavery but in the refusal to let it spread. Such a position, Lincoln believed, would put slavery on the road to "ultimate extinction."

John Brown leads a raid on Harpers Ferry. Onto the troubled scene now stepped John Brown, leader of the "Pottawatomie Massacre" (page 355), who decided to act against slavery in the South. Brown confided his plans, but not the details, to six abolitionist

Douglas is seated on Lincoln's right during their fourth debate. Douglas charged that Lincoln altered his position on slavery to suit his Illinois audiences.

Abolitionist John Brown was tried for treason and for criminal conspiracy. Before his execution, he wrote that slavery "will never be purged away but with blood."

leaders, and they provided him with the money he needed. His scheme was to establish an outpost in the mountains of Virginia and turn it into a military base from which he would free slaves all over the South.

Brown planned to attack the federal arsenal at Harpers Ferry, Virginia, and seize enough guns to arm the slaves. On the night of October 16, 1859, Brown and eighteen followers set out from their camp in Maryland to begin the operation. As the town of Harpers Ferry slept, Brown took over the arsenal. Some men moved into the countryside to kidnap slave owners and hold them hostage. After two days of fighting, however, it was clear that Brown had overreached himself. A detachment of marines, under Colonel Robert E. Lee, arrived from Washington. In the struggle that followed, ten raiders, four residents of Harpers Ferry, and one marine died.

John Brown is executed. After his capture, Brown looked forward to becoming a martyr to the cause of abolition. He must

have been disappointed that not one slave had voluntarily joined him in his scheme. He remained unshaken, however, and his words at his trial moved many people everywhere. "Now if it be deemed necessary that I should forfeit my life for the furtherance of the ends of justice," he said, "and mingle my blood further with the blood of my children and with the blood of millions in this slave country whose rights are disregarded by wicked, cruel, and unjust enactments, I say, let it be done." Sentenced to death, he was hanged in December, 1859.

Abolitionists were shocked by Brown's execution. The Boston minister Theodore Parker declared Brown to be "not only a martyr but also a saint." The poet Ralph Waldo Emerson said that the hanging of Brown would "make the gallows glorious like the Cross." No one approved of the death and destruction that Brown had caused, but as the poet James Russell Lowell put it, "they who blamed the bloody hand forgave the loving heart."

As church bells tolled for Brown in the

North, people in the South became more anxious than ever, fearing further raids. The Charleston *Mercury* wrote that Southerners now knew that "there is no peace for the South in the Union."

Among Southerners who saw Brown mount the scaffold were at least three people whose names would come to the fore again: Thomas J. Jackson (later known as "Stonewall"); Edmund Ruffin, a leading expert on southern agriculture and an ardent defender of slavery; and a promising young actor named John Wilkes Booth. We can only guess at the thoughts that crossed their minds on that cold day in December.

Sectional differences split the Democrats. The year 1860 promised to be a fateful one in American history. The spirit of suspicion between the sections had turned into outright hostility. The time was past when a politician could appeal successfully for moderation. William Seward, the leading

Republican candidate for the nomination in 1860, had earlier spoken of an "irrepressible conflict" in the making.

In this atmosphere, the Democratic convention of 1860 opened in Charleston, South Carolina, late in April. The southern wing of the party wanted a platform calling clearly for the protection of slavery in the territories. Douglas's northern supporters, still favoring popular sovereignty, would not agree to such a call. The southern delegates, thereupon, walked out and the convention soon broke up. (Douglas had had the support of more than half the delegates, but in those days a two-thirds vote was required for nomination.)

In June, Democrats from the North and the border states went to Baltimore, where they nominated Douglas. The Southerners met at a separate Baltimore convention and nominated John C. Breckinridge of Kentucky for President on a platform that supported slavery in the territories. The

Shapers of Conscience

Famous writers influenced nineteenth-century reform movements. Ralph Waldo Emerson (right) favored abolition as did Henry David Thoreau, who wrote *Walden*. The fiction of Nathaniel Hawthorne (bottom center) focused on good and evil in human nature, while *Uncle Tom's Cabin,* by Harriet Beecher Stowe (bottom right), drew popular support for abolition.

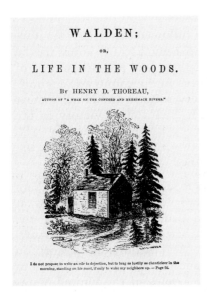

question of slavery had finally split the Democratic Party.

The Constitutional Union Party nominates Bell. A new party offered a candidate for President in 1860. A handful of former Whigs and Know-Nothings had formed the Constitutional Union Party. They nominated John Bell of Tennessee and denounced sectional parties. The party, urging Americans to support the Constitution and the Union, took no stand on slavery.

Lincoln wins the Republican nomination. Meanwhile, the Republicans were meeting in Chicago. Seward, the front-runner, was too closely associated with the abolitionists to be the party's choice. Besides, moderates did not want to believe that conflict with the South was certain, as Seward predicted, even though they hotly opposed the extension of slavery.

In February, Abraham Lincoln had traveled east to visit his son Robert, who attended school in New Hampshire. Being low on funds, Lincoln accepted an invitation to speak at Cooper Union Institute, in New York City, for a $200 fee. While in New York, Lincoln called at the photographic studio of Mathew Brady and had a picture taken that would be widely circulated in the Northeast. Lincoln was no longer the uncomfortable-looking man he had seemed to be in 1858. Now, smartly dressed, he looked every inch the competent politician he was.

On February 27, 1860, Lincoln made his speech at Cooper Union. It was a snowy night, but 1,500 people — "the best of the intellect and culture of our city," according to the *Tribune's* editor, Horace Greeley — braved the weather to hear "the Westerner." With his words and thoughts, reported an eyewitness, "Lincoln held the audience in the hollow of his hand."

In the address Lincoln rejected northern extremism as well as popular sovereignty. He repeated what he had said so often: slavery is wrong and there must be no extension of it. He pleaded that the people not be frightened by the talk of disunion. "Let us have faith," he urged, "that right makes might, and in that faith, let us, to the end, dare to do our duty as we understand it." The hall rang with applause. Lincoln was surprised but delighted with his reception.

Lincoln knew that he was the delegates' second choice at the Republican convention. If Seward could not win on the first ballot, Lincoln would get the nomination. He wanted it badly, telling a friend, "The taste *is* in my mouth a little." On the third ballot Lincoln's hopes were realized, and he was nominated. Lincoln received the news by telegraph in Springfield while he was playing ball. (Not until much later in history did important candidates attend conventions that nominated them.) Lincoln excused himself to share the message with his wife, Mary Todd Lincoln.

Lincoln leads the Republicans to victory. The division in the Democratic Party greatly aided Republican chances for victory. Douglas made speeches in the North and the South, emphasizing popular sovereignty once again in order to win votes. Lincoln, in accordance with the custom of most candidates at that time, stayed home and allowed other people to seek support for him. During the campaign he acquired a colorful nickname when a Chicago newspaper cheered him as "Honest Abe." Republican women carried banners announcing:

> Westward the star of Empire takes its way,
> We link on to Lincoln, as our mothers did
>   to Clay.

The voting followed sectional lines. Lincoln picked up only 26,400 votes in the slave states. He received just 40 percent of the popular votes in the country as a whole, but carried every state in the North except New Jersey. He had a clear victory in the electoral college, however, winning 180 votes compared with 123 for his three opponents combined.

Lincoln gets ready to take office. Abraham Lincoln prepared purposefully for his great adventure and ordeal. No one knew the President-elect better than his law partner, Billy Herndon. As Lincoln started work on his inaugural address, he asked Herndon to obtain for him copies of the United States

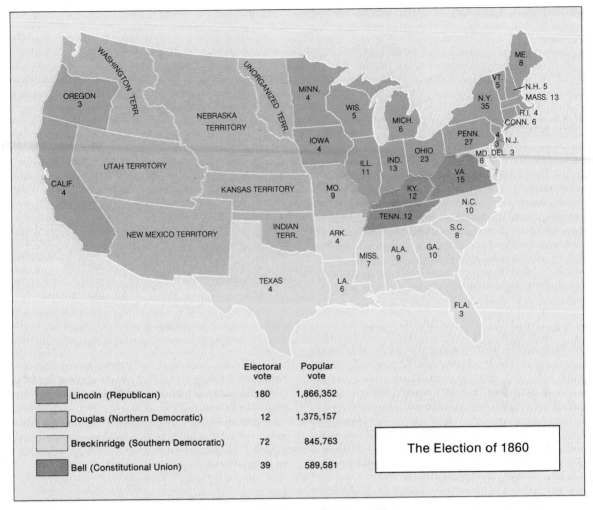

	Electoral vote	Popular vote
Lincoln (Republican)	180	1,866,352
Douglas (Northern Democratic)	12	1,375,157
Breckinridge (Southern Democratic)	72	845,763
Bell (Constitutional Union)	39	589,581

The Election of 1860

The combined vote of Lincoln's opponents topped his total by almost one million votes, but Lincoln won the presidency with a clear margin in the electoral college.

Constitution, Jackson's proclamation against nullification, Webster's reply to Hayne, and Clay's speech on the Compromise of 1850. Lincoln wanted history and eloquence at his side as he prepared to defend the Union. Herndon wrote of his friend, "When on [the subjects of] justice, right, liberty, the government and constitution, union, humanity, then you may all stand aside; he will rule then and no man can move him."

When the Lincolns were about to leave their home town for the nation's capital, the President-elect addressed his neighbors in a cold rain: "I leave now, not knowing when, or whether ever, I may return, with a task before me greater than that which rested upon Washington." So it was that Lincoln went forth to wrestle with the unknown. The time for words alone had passed.

SECTION REVIEW

1. (a) On what grounds did Dred Scott sue for his freedom? (b) What were the main points of the Supreme Court's decision?
2. (a) What was Senator Douglas's Freeport Doctrine? (b) What effect did the Freeport Doctrine have on his support in Illinois? (c) In the South?
3. (a) What was John Brown's purpose in the raid on Harpers Ferry? (b) How did the outcome influence public opinion?
4. (a) Who were the candidates for President in 1860? (b) What party won the election? Why?

Chapter 15 Review

Summary

The divisive question of slavery in the territories lurked beneath the surface of the election of 1848. Whigs and Democrats tried to keep the subject out of the campaign, but soon after his election as President, Zachary Taylor infuriated Southerners by urging California to press for admission to the Union as a free state.

In the Senate, Henry Clay offered a series of resolutions that came to be known as the Compromise of 1850. That plan called for the admission of California as a free state; popular sovereignty for the rest of the land acquired from Mexico; settlement of the Texas-New Mexico border dispute; abolition of the slave trade in the District of Columbia; and a stricter fugitive slave law. The furious debate over Clay's resolutions lasted six months.

The passage of the Compromise of 1850 turned out to be merely an armistice between the North and South. Failure by the North to enforce the Fugitive Slave Act, the wide circulation of *Uncle Tom's Cabin,* and Senator Douglas's Kansas-Nebraska Act (1854) inflamed public opinion on both sides. The Kansas-Nebraska Act, supported by President Pierce and by many Southerners, ignored the Missouri Compromise and asked for popular sovereignty in all the territories, setting the scene for the violence of "Bleeding Kansas."

By 1856, when James Buchanan became President, both major parties were losing their national base of support. Two new parties emerged: the Republicans, who opposed the expansion of slavery; and the Know-Nothings, who spoke of "protecting" the nation against immigrants and Catholics. The Republicans and their policies aroused fear in the South. Meanwhile, the Dred Scott decision (1857) caused outrage in the North. The Supreme Court had declared that slaves were property, under federal protection, and that the Missouri Compromise was unconstitutional.

Senator Douglas ran for re-election to the Senate in 1858 against Abraham Lincoln, a Republican who, in losing, attracted national attention with his eloquent opposition to the further spread of slavery. Douglas straddled the issue, losing support among southern Democrats for his presidential bid in 1860. In that fateful year the Democratic Party split in two. Southern Democrats bolted the regular party convention and sponsored their own candidate, John Breckinridge. Douglas became the candidate of the northern Democrats. Running against them were John Bell of the Constitutional Union Party and the Republicans' Abraham Lincoln. With the Democrats split, the Republicans won the election. Abraham Lincoln would become President in 1861.

Vocabulary and Important Terms

1. popular sovereignty
2. Free-Soil Party
3. Compromise of 1850
4. "Seventh of March" speech
5. *Uncle Tom's Cabin*
6. Kansas-Nebraska Act
7. Republican Party
8. Know-Nothing Party
9. "Bleeding Kansas"
10. Ostend Manifesto
11. Dred Scott case
12. Lincoln-Douglas debates
13. John Brown's raid
14. Constitutional Union Party

Discussion Questions

1. (a) What happened in 1849 to reopen the national debate over slavery? (b) What was the South's basic argument in that debate? (c) What position did many Northerners hold?

2. (a) Who were the leading statesmen in the Senate at the time of the debate over Henry Clay's compromise proposals? (b) What new congressional leaders were beginning to emerge?

3. Why was Millard Fillmore's succession to the presidency important to the enactment of the Compromise of 1850?

4. (a) Why was the Fugitive Slave Act important to the South? (b) How did Southerners view northern defiance of this law?

5. (a) Why did the introduction of the Kansas-Nebraska Act inflame sectional tensions? (b) How did Stephen A. Douglas respond to the charge that he was a traitor to the North?

6. (a) How did the competition for Kansas contribute to sectional differences? (b) What other evidence was there in the 1850's that sectional differences were becoming sharper?

7. How were sectional differences reflected in the formation of the Republican Party in 1854 and in the split in the Democratic Party in 1860?

8. (a) How did Northerners and Southerners react to the Supreme Court's ruling in the Dred Scott case? (b) What immediate effect did the Court's decision have on the Republican and Democratic parties?

9. What effect did the split in the Democratic Party have on the outcome of the election for President in 1860?

Relating Past to Present

The Lincoln-Douglas debates captured attention and affected public opinion throughout the nation. What debates between leading public figures today might have a similar effect? To what extent can a debate affect the outcome of a modern-day election? How are modern debates different from those that Lincoln and Douglas engaged in?

Studying Local History

Look at the map on page 353. What was the status of slavery in your state in 1854? If your state was still a territory in 1854, do research to find out what stand voters took on the slavery question.

Using History Skills

1. *Reading maps.* Study the map of the 1860 presidential election on page 363. (a) From what section of the country did John Breckinridge's electoral votes come? (b) What states did John Bell carry, and in what part of the country were those states located? (c) What state did Stephen Douglas carry? (d) What did the election results say about the appeal of the Republican Party?

2. *Organizing information.* Make a time line showing crucial events of the 1850's. On one side of your time line, list court decisions, legislative compromises, etc., that proslavery people welcomed. On the other side of the time line, do the same for the antislavery point of view.

3. *Reading sources.* Study the account of violence in the Kansas Territory on page 356. (a) Why did Victoria Clayton and her husband move to Kansas? (b) What was her opinion of John Brown's actions? (c) Is her description of Kansas in the late 1850's a complete one? What other information would help you understand the situation?

4. *Writing a report.* Do research on the admission of Kansas into the Union as a state. Prepare a short report on your findings.

WORLD SCENE

"Uncle Tom's Cabin" Abroad

The publication of *Uncle Tom's Cabin* in 1852 was a literary event of world importance. The book was eventually translated into 23 languages, including Siamese, Bengali, and Armenian.

The British response to "Uncle Tom's Cabin." The people outside America who responded most enthusiastically to *Uncle Tom's Cabin* needed no translation. Queen Victoria sent Harriet Beecher Stowe a note of congratulations and appreciation after the book's arrival in England. The Duchess of Sutherland sent Mrs. Stowe a gold bracelet in the form of a broken slave shackle. Half a million Englishwomen, inspired by the book, signed their names to a plea for abolition and sent a 26-volume petition to Mrs. Stowe.

The British were stirred by the book because, no less than the Americans, they were concerned over slavery. Antislavery advocates had brought an end to the institution in the British Empire in 1833. They continued their crusade thereafter, taking the lead in efforts to end the international slave trade. This evil commerce continued practically unchecked despite its prohibition by the major European nations. The abolitionists who kept this issue before the British public were helped by the popularity of *Uncle Tom's Cabin.*

At the invitation of British abolitionists, Mrs. Stowe and her husband, Calvin Ellis Stowe, in 1853 went to Britain. Crowds of admirers greeted Mrs. Stowe wherever she appeared; ordinary people and aristocrats alike paid her court. The Stowes, however, were not entirely pleased with their reception. Praise for *Uncle Tom's Cabin,* they found, often turned into denunciation of the United States for allowing slavery to continue.

One night, at a big meeting in London during which the audience hissed the name of President Pierce, Calvin Stowe's patience wore out. While thanking the assemblage for the honor being paid his wife, he charged that the British, as the chief consumers of cotton, shared the blame for the persistence of slavery in America. The audience listened in stunned silence as Stowe roared, "The receiver is as guilty as the thief!" The correspondent for the New York *Observer* sent word home that the exasperated Britons might have thrown the speaker "overboard" if he had not been the husband of the admired Harriet Beecher Stowe.

CHAPTER 16

The Agony of Civil War

1860 – 1865

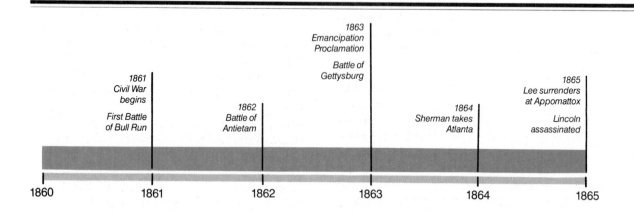

1861	
Civil War	
begins	

1863
Emancipation
Proclamation

Battle of
Gettysburg

1861
Civil War
begins

First Battle
of Bull Run

1862
Battle of
Antietam

1864
Sherman takes
Atlanta

1865
Lee surrenders
at Appomattox

Lincoln
assassinated

1860   1861   1862   1863   1864   1865

CHAPTER OUTLINE

1. The North and South take up arms.

2. The first blows are struck.

3. The fighting reaches its climax.

4. All-out war affects life behind the lines.

5. Fighting ends in victory for the North.

When news of Lincoln's election reached South Carolina, the Charleston *Mercury* proclaimed, "The tea has been thrown overboard. The revolution of 1860 has been initiated." The publisher of that newspaper was Robert Barnwell Rhett, long an advocate of secession from the Union. Comparing themselves to the Patriots of 1776, secessionists like Rhett called a convention that met on December 20, 1860, at Charleston. The gathering unanimously voted to secede from the Union.

Sentiment for disunion quickly swept the other cotton-growing states, overwhelming the pro-Union sympathy in many places. In the next two months six more states seceded: Mississippi, Florida, Alabama, Georgia, Louisiana, and Texas. In each state, the vote was overwhelmingly in favor of leaving the Union.

Delegates from the seven states gathered at Montgomery, Alabama, on February 4 to form a new government, the Confederate States of America. Within four days they had drawn up a constitution. Having completed this work, the convention next named Jefferson Davis of Mississippi as President of the Confederacy. Davis was inaugurated in Montgomery on February 18, 1861. As he appeared, a band struck up a rousing tune called "I Wish I Was in Dixie's Land." Davis took the oath of office on a Bible lying in a wreath of flowers which were red, white, and blue. The separation of the South from the Union was now complete.

1 The North and South Take Up Arms

Secession and the creation of the Confederacy had proceeded without significant response from the White House. James Buchanan, serving the last months of his term, seemed helpless. On hearing of South Carolina's secession, he said that he had "no authority to decide what shall be the relation between the federal government and South Carolina." Other Americans, meanwhile, cast about for a way to bring back the seceded states.

Last-minute compromises fail. On December 18, 1860, Senator John Crittenden of Kentucky — in the manner of his predecessor, Henry Clay — proposed a compromise. Crittenden suggested reviving the Missouri Compromise Line of 36°30' and extending it to the Pacific. North of the line, slavery would be prohibited; south of it, slavery would be protected by a constitutional amendment.

Abraham Lincoln advised his supporters to reject Crittenden's suggestion, and it failed to pass the Senate. The President-elect urged a friend, "Entertain no proposition for a compromise in regard to the extension of slavery. The instant you do, they have us under again." Still, Lincoln wanted to reassure Southerners that he would not interfere with slavery where it already existed. He wrote to Alexander H. Stephens, with whom he had served in the House and who shortly was elected Vice President of the Confederacy. Lincoln said, "You think slavery is *right* and ought to be extended; while we think it is *wrong* and ought to be restricted. That I suppose is the rub. It certainly is the only substantial difference between us." The difference, however, was proving difficult to overcome.

Into the breach came former President John Tyler. At the request of the Virginia legislature, Tyler presided over a "peace convention" held in Washington, D.C. The delegates, many of them formerly important government officials, devised a plan similar to the Crittenden compromise. The suggestions of this so-called "old gentlemen's convention" were, however, ignored by the Senate. Tyler himself soon became a secessionist and won election to the Confederate House of Representatives.[1]

Lincoln, meantime, was making his way to Washington from Illinois. The journey took twelve days. During that time he made a number of speeches. He spoke only in general terms, not wishing to arouse animosity before even taking the oath of

---

[1]Tyler died early in 1862 and was buried in the same Richmond, Virginia, cemetery as James Monroe.

Many soldiers, including these from Fond du Lac, Wisconsin, marched off to war. Less populous, the South had one third fewer troops than the North.

The flag that Lincoln raised in 1861 contained a star for the new free-soil state of Kansas.

office. In Philadelphia he stopped off at Independence Hall to unfurl the new United States flag, honoring the admission of Kansas to the Union.

Lincoln is inaugurated. On March 4, 1861, Lincoln dressed early for his inauguration, putting on a new black suit and freshly shined black boots. Clouds over the city were dark; it appeared that rain would fall at any minute. The somber scene matched the mood of the nation.

At the Capitol, where the oath-taking was to take place, a crowd of 25,000 people had assembled. Because rumors of an assassination plot were circulating, riflemen were stationed on rooftops, guarding the parade route. Soldiers, in addition, were ready to respond quickly if violence should break out.

Chief Justice Taney, now 84 years old, administered the oath of office. Taney had, in the Dred Scott decision, played a major part in bringing on the crisis. Senator Douglas, who had also helped stir up the trouble, sat on the platform with other northern Democrats. All of them were eager to show that they were lining up with the Republicans at this critical moment.

Lincoln had read his inaugural address privately to his family that morning. Now he delivered it in a voice that trembled a little from nervousness. He offered words of friendship to the states that had seceded. Slavery would be protected where it already existed, he said, but "no state, upon its own mere motion, can lawfully get out of the Union." Lincoln struck no note of retreat. "Physically speaking," he said, "we cannot separate." He did offer concessions, however. While the United States would continue to "hold, occupy, and possess" those forts in the South still in federal hands, "there will be no invasion, no using of force against or among the people anywhere." Nevertheless, he warned, "In your hands, my dissatisfied fellow countrymen, and not in mine, is the momentous issue of civil war. . . . You have no oath registered in Heaven to destroy the government, while I have the most solemn one to 'preserve, protect, and defend' it."

Lincoln chooses a Cabinet. People in the North praised Lincoln's speech. They could feel that energy had been restored to the government. While the country pondered Lincoln's eloquent words, the new President appointed his Cabinet. It included forceful men, among them candidates who recently had sought the presidential nomination. As Secretary of State, Lincoln named William H. Seward of New York (page 346), "the red-headed upstart" who was fiercely antislavery. Seward at first considered Lincoln a simple prairie lawyer whom *he* would have to teach, but shortly the Secretary was writing, "The President is the best of us." In time Lincoln came to think of Seward as a possible successor in the White House.

For Secretary of the Treasury, Lincoln selected an Ohio antislavery leader and former governor, Salmon P. Chase. It was Chase, a deeply religious man, who would have the words "In God We Trust" inscribed on the coins of the country. Arrogant and self-assured, he expected to be President himself one day. His daughter, Kate, whom he adored, was working determinedly to put him into the White House.

In the War Department was Simon Cameron, an important Pennsylvania politician. He was soon replaced by Edwin M. Stanton, a northern Democrat who favored preservation of the Union. The Secretary of the Navy was the incorruptible Gideon Welles of Connecticut. Welles, who had long before been a friend of Andrew Jackson, had helped found the Republican Party.

Federal authority is challenged at Fort Sumter. Meanwhile, the seceded states had been taking possession of federal forts and arsenals within their borders. Major Robert Anderson, who commanded United States troops at Charleston, South Carolina, had withdrawn his men to Fort Sumter, in Charleston harbor, because it could be more easily defended. Anderson, a regular army officer from Kentucky who sympathized with the Confederacy, had only a few weeks' supply of food for his soldiers. President Buchanan had tried to resupply the fort, but the unarmed relief ship had been driven off by Confederate fire. Lincoln, having promised in his inaugural to hold federal "property and places," could not now fail to send relief.

By this time Northerners, in general, were firmly against making any further

Virginia, Arkansas, Tennessee, and North Carolina joined the early secessionist states after Lincoln called up state militia following the attack on Fort Sumter. Part of Virginia remained in the Union and in 1863 became the state of West Virginia.

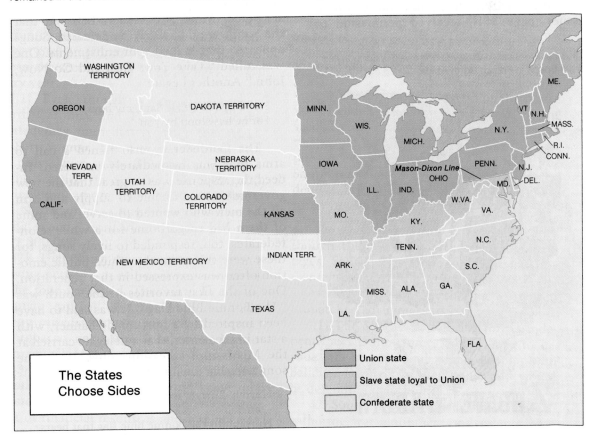

The States Choose Sides

Union state
Slave state loyal to Union
Confederate state

Although victorious at Bull Run, the Confederate forces could not follow up the advantage they had won. Defeated, the Union was spurred to greater effort.

uprisings as well as the continuing frontier conditions had long before created respect for the bearing of arms.

(3) The South had outstanding military leadership. Many southern youths, choosing to make the army their career, had attended West Point and other military schools. Like the Union, the Confederacy relied on West Pointers for its highest-ranking commanders. It would take the Union a long time, however, to find army leaders who could match those of the South.

The strategy of the war unfolds. Both sides quickly made long-range plans. Jefferson Davis expected to hold well-defended strong points along the Mason-Dixon Line west to the Ohio River and from there to the Mississippi River. Southerners doubted that Union troops would be able to smash their way into Confederate territory. They did concede that the Union navy would be able to blockade southern ports, for the South had limited seapower. But the result, Southerners believed, would be a shortage of cotton in Europe. When that happened, the Confederates expected Britain and France to send help. There was one exception to this defensive strategy. To bring the war to a speedy end, the Confederates intended to race northward, capture Washington, D.C., go through Maryland into central Pennsylvania, and divide the North in two.

Winfield Scott, general-in-chief of the United States Army and a public hero since the War of 1812, was now 75 years old. Suffering from a variety of infirmities, he was unable even to mount his horse without help. Still, he gave advice. His proposal was for an "anaconda plan," named after the snake that crushes its victims. The Union troops would capture Richmond, Virginia, which had been made the Confederate capital. The border states — Delaware, Maryland, Kentucky, and Missouri — would be held firmly under Union control. Naval forces, finally, would cut the Confederacy in two by taking control of the Mississippi River. Union ships would also blockade the chief ports along the coasts. When this iron grip had been placed on the Confederacy, the vast manpower of the North would be hurled against the South with overwhelming force.

Union troops are defeated at Bull Run. Shortly after the surrender at Fort Sumter, the cry "On to Richmond!" was heard in the North. General Scott finally yielded to the clamor. On July 16, 1861, he sent 30,000 men and boys in blue south toward Richmond under the command of General Irvin McDowell. The Southerners in gray waiting for them were under the command of General Pierre Beauregard. Beauregard and McDowell had been classmates at West Point. The face-off of these old friends — matched by many others like it — gave the war, in addition to its dreadfulness, the character of a school-boy competition.

On July 21, the two armies clashed at Manassas Junction, near a stream called Bull Run, about thirty miles south of Washington. McDowell was certain he could send the rebel army fleeing. Many people, including congressmen and their families, rode out to the battlefield to witness the expected northern victory. Victory indeed seemed within McDowell's grasp until Confederate General Joseph Johnston arrived with reinforcements. Moreover, southern troops under General Thomas Jackson held fast under heavy fire and probably prevented a Confederate rout. Jackson ever afterward was known as "Stonewall."

The Union troops, sent reeling, fled in panic toward Washington, along roads clogged by stunned sightseers. Fortunately for the North, the Confederates were too weary and disorganized to press forward. Lincoln, grimly watching the confusion in the streets from a White House window, began to get first-hand accounts of the Union disaster at Bull Run. Along with people throughout the North, he now realized that the war would not be over soon.

McClellan leads the Union forces. On the following day the President placed General George McClellan, then 34 years old, in charge of defending the capital. McClellan, a successful officer in the Mexican War, had left the army to be a railroad president. Now, back in uniform, he saw himself as the Union's savior. A splendid horseman, he cut a handsome figure as he dashed about Washington. He was also an excellent organizer. When General Scott retired in November, Lincoln named McClellan general-in-chief of the Union armies. "I can do it all," said McClellan. Still, he was strangely timid in moving his troops — the Army of the Potomac — into action.

Fighting begins in the West. While the North waited impatiently for McClellan to whip his army into shape, the Union drive had begun in the West. A force under General George Thomas, a West Pointer from Virginia, administered a defeat to the Confederates at Mill Springs, Kentucky, in January, 1862. A result was to open the way for an invasion of East Tennessee.

The western operations brought to the fore a general who proved equal to the task. He was Ulysses S. Grant, like McClellan a resident of Illinois. Grant had been an outstanding horseman at West Point and had also excelled in mathematics. He performed well in the Mexican War, but military life then lost its appeal for him. After the war he went from one occupation to another, unable to support his family satisfactorily. After the firing on Fort Sumter, Grant reentered the service as colonel of an Illinois regiment. His family was relieved. His father said, "You've got a good job now, Ulysses, don't lose it."

In early 1862 Grant sought to gain control of the Mississippi River by advancing first through Kentucky and Tennessee. Working with Commodore Andrew Foote, he captured Fort Henry, which guarded the Tennessee River. Most of the Confederate troops retreated to Fort Donelson, on the Cumberland River. When, after a brief battle, the Confederates prepared to surrender, General Simon Buckner asked for terms. Grant's reply was crisp and plain: "No terms except an unconditional and immediate surrender can be accepted." The initials of Grant's name took on new meaning as he was nicknamed "Unconditional Surrender" Grant. Meanwhile, Union forces scored a victory at Pea Ridge, Arkansas, driving the Confederates out of southern Missouri and northern Arkansas.

Grant completes the conquest of western Tennessee. After Grant had captured the two forts in Tennessee, Confederate forces under General Albert S. Johnston took up positions at Corinth, in northern Mississippi. Thirty miles to the northeast, Grant had pitched camp at Pittsburg Landing, a stopping place for boats on the Tennessee River. He did not expect an attack. As his men sat at breakfast on Sunday morning, April 6, 1862, Johnston's troops struck. The most exposed position, a little log church called Shiloh (SHY-loh), gave its name to the terrible battle that had now begun.

During the first day Grant's troops, including some raw recruits who did not even know how to use their muskets, took heavy

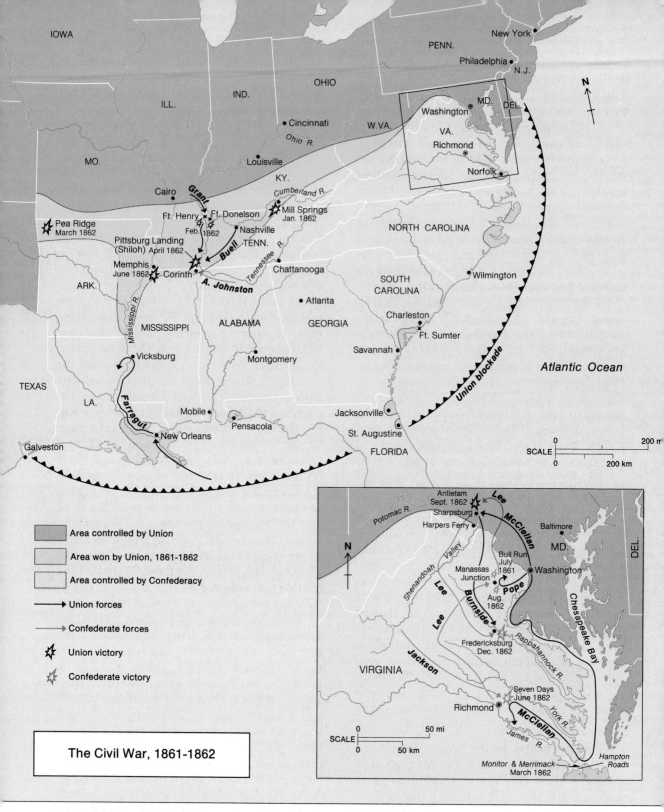

IOWA

ILL. IND. OHIO PENN. New York

Philadelphia

N.J.

Cincinnati W.VA. MD. DEL.

Washington

VA.

MO. Louisville Richmond

KY. Norfolk

Cairo *Grant*

Cumberland R.

Ft. Henry Ft. Donelson Mill Springs
Jan. 1862

Feb. 1862 Nashville NORTH CAROLINA

Pea Ridge
March 1862

Pittsburg Landing
(Shiloh) April 1862 *Buell* TENN. Tennessee R.

Memphis
June 1862 Corinth Chattanooga SOUTH
CAROLINA Wilmington

ARK. *A. Johnston*

Atlanta

MISSISSIPPI ALABAMA GEORGIA Charleston

Mississippi R. Montgomery Savannah Ft. Sumter

Vicksburg

TEXAS Atlantic Ocean

LA. *Farragut* Mobile

Galveston New Orleans Pensacola Jacksonville

St. Augustine

Union blockade

FLORIDA

SCALE

0   200 mi

0   200 km

Area controlled by Union

Area won by Union, 1861–1862

Area controlled by Confederacy

→ Union forces

→ Confederate forces

✮ Union victory

✮ Confederate victory

Antietam
Sept. 1862 *Lee*

Potomac R. Sharpsburg *McClellan*

Harpers Ferry Baltimore

Bull Run
July MD.
1861

N Manassas
Junction Washington DEL.

Lee *Pope*

Shenandoah Aug. Chesapeake Bay
1862

Burnside

Lee Rappahannock R.

Fredericksburg
Dec. 1862

Jackson

VIRGINIA Seven Days
June 1862

Richmond York R.

McClellan

SCALE James R.

0   50 mi Hampton
Roads
0   50 km

Monitor & Merrimack
March 1862

The Civil War, 1861–1862

Early in the war, Lincoln ordered a naval blockade of the South. While Farragut was
capturing New Orleans in early 1862, Grant and his troops were pressing southwest
from Tennessee toward the Mississippi River. In the East, McClellan, Pope, and
Burnside engaged Confederate forces around Washington and Richmond.

losses. The Battle of Shiloh, fought in part in a heavy rainstorm, appeared to be a Confederate victory by nightfall. Overnight, however, General Don Carlos Buell arrived with 25,000 fresh Union troops, giving Grant a decided edge in the struggle.

When the Confederates were finally driven into retreat, each side had suffered appalling casualties. For years to come, the words "bloody Shiloh" would make veterans on both sides shudder in horror as they recalled some of the costliest fighting of the war.

A few weeks earlier a magazine had published a poem called "The Battle Hymn of the Republic" by Julia Ward Howe, long an active abolitionist in Massachusetts. Northerners were gripped by the poem's haunting words. Shiloh seemed to be its very subject:

> Mine eyes have seen the glory of the
>   coming of the Lord;
> He is trampling out the vintage where the
>   grapes of wrath are stored;
> He hath loosed the fateful lightning of His
>   terrible, swift sword;
> His truth is marching on.

The North fights for control of the Mississippi. While Grant was fighting at Shiloh, Commodore David Farragut was preparing a fleet to capture New Orleans. The Confederates defended the city with heavy guns. Nevertheless, on April 26, 1862, New Orleans came into northern hands after Union naval forces bombarded the city. General Benjamin Butler, a political appointee and a military incompetent, soon arrived with 20,000 troops to occupy the city. His harsh administration earned him the label "Beast." Moreover, because of claims that his troops stole silver tableware, Southerners also called him "Spoons" Butler.

Upstream, Memphis surrendered in a naval battle on June 6. A northern attempt to take Vicksburg, Mississippi, by naval assault failed the same month, however. Troops were needed to hit the city from the east in a coordinated attack with vessels on the river, but thousands of northern soldiers were ill, and hundreds were dying of malaria, dysentery, and typhoid. The Confederate flag would fly over Vicksburg for another year.

SECTION REVIEW

1. (a) What were the major advantages of the North in the Civil War? (b) Of the South?
2. (a) What plans did the South make for winning the war? (b) What was the North's strategy?
3. What was the outcome and significance of the First Battle of Bull Run?
4. What steps did Union forces take to win control of the Mississippi River?

3 The Fighting Reaches Its Climax

While Union forces in the West were nearing their goal, those in the East enjoyed little success. Northern impatience with McClellan, who endlessly trained his army, was growing. Finally, Lincoln ordered "Little Mac" to attack Richmond by the end of February, 1862.

McClellan attacks Richmond. Despite prodding from the top, McClellan did not move south until late March. Lincoln had wanted McClellan to lead his 130,000 troops in a direct attack on Richmond. Regarding advice from civilians, including the President, as "sickening," McClellan took his own counsel. He decided to head for the Confederate capital by way of the lower Chesapeake Bay. He, therefore, directed a campaign in the marshy peninsular region lying between the York and James rivers (map, page 374).

The Confederates, in the meantime, had sent "Stonewall" Jackson into the Shenandoah Valley. With 18,000 men Jackson was pressing attacks on Union forces, hoping to make the Union generals fear for the safety of Washington. The strategy worked, as President Lincoln withheld large numbers of troops from McClellan's army in order to defend the capital.

Recognized by both North and South as a skilled leader and man of dignity, Lee resigned his army commission in loyalty to his home state but hoped he would never have to raise arms against the Union.

Richmond is defended. At the end of May, practically in sight of Richmond, McClellan came under a furious assault by the forces of General Joseph Johnston. When Johnston was wounded in the fighting, the command of the Confederate forces — the Army of Northern Virginia — fell to Robert E. Lee.

Lee, the son of Revolutionary hero "Light-Horse Harry" Lee, had been an outstanding soldier ever since his graduation from West Point in 1829. He served with distinction in the Mexican War and as Superintendent of West Point. He had freed his own slaves and was firmly opposed to secession. Still, when he was offered the command of the Union forces after Lincoln's call for troops, he refused it and resigned from the army. When his beloved Virginia seceded, Lee felt he must support it by putting on the Confederate uniform.

Taking over an enlarged Confederate army just outside of Richmond, Lee began a brutal struggle against McClellan. On June 26, 1862, the Confederates took the offensive, and in the fierce Seven Days' Battles succeeded in rolling back McClellan's army. Richmond still stood.

More losses discourage the North. Lincoln was beside himself with disappointment. He decided he needed new commanders, and appointed General Henry Halleck as general-in-chief. Halleck's nickname was "Old Brains," because he had been an exceptional cadet at the Military Academy. Northerners hoped he had not only intelligence but also the energy to end the war successfully. To command Union forces in Virginia, Lincoln chose General John Pope.

Northern politicians were now demanding a tougher prosecution of the war. When Pope was defeated disastrously by Lee at the Second Battle of Bull Run late in August, Lincoln was distraught. The 75,000 Union troops suffered almost twice as many casualties as the 50,000 Confederates. Moreover, the Union's supply depot at Manassas Junction had fallen into the hands of the rebels. Only a heavy rainstorm prevented Lee from marching on Washington.

In the face of these disheartening events, Lincoln restored McClellan to his command and issued a call for 300,000 volunteers. A poem written by a New York abolitionist, with the refrain "We are coming, Father Abraham, three hundred thousand more" and set to music by Stephen Foster, captured the popular fancy. The 300,000 men, however, did not quickly come forward. War weariness was slowly setting in upon the North. The Union was going to have to turn to a military draft.

Lee is checked at Antietam. Lee, meanwhile, pressed forward across the Potomac River. His plan was to invade Maryland and cut the northern railroad links to Washington. A bold victory now might bring diplomatic recognition — and possibly support — from France and Britain.

Luck at last came to McClellan's side in September, 1862, when a Union corporal happened upon a copy of Lee's orders. Lee's plans were so fully set forth that McClellan said, "Here is a paper with which, if I cannot whip Bobbie Lee, I will be willing to go home." In the ensuing battle at Sharpsburg

The Camera

Cameras revolutionized the way people perceived the world. The first photographs were one-of-a-kind images recorded directly on metal. The negative process made it possible to make many copies of an image. One of the first photographers in America was Mathew Brady, who opened a portrait studio in New York City in 1844. When the Civil War broke out, he realized that he could document that war using new techniques. Because the wet-plate process was time-consuming and required cumbersome materials — even an on-site darkroom — Brady could not take action shots. Still, he and his many associates could photograph wide-angle scenes such as Union encampments and battlefields.

near Antietam (an-TEE-tum) Creek, the landscape was turned red with blood. Both sides claimed victory: the North because the Confederates' northward advance had been halted; the South because their troops were able to slip back across the Potomac.

The Battle of Antietam had a powerful effect on Europe. The news that Union troops had forced the Confederates to retreat told leaders in Britain and France that the South might lose the war.

Antietam had produced the single bloodiest day of the war. In fact, more men were killed in that 24-hour period than on any other day in American history. What could Lincoln do to make such a sacrifice seem justified? He had already been making plans that would change the character of the war. Antietam gave him an opportunity to put them into effect.

Lincoln issues the Emancipation Proclamation. Lincoln had long known he would have to deal with slavery. He could see that the compelling power of antislavery feelings would have to be brought into support of the war. Fighting to save the Union alone would not be a sufficient goal to bring victory. Lincoln knew, however, that he would have to avoid talk of freeing the slaves if he hoped to keep the good will of northern Democrats and of border-state slave owners. Still, the antislavery Republicans were pressing him harder and harder to free the slaves. As Union casualties mounted, furthermore, Lincoln recognized that he must exact a higher price from Southerners than they yet had paid.

In July the President told his Cabinet that he intended to issue a proclamation that would *emancipate,* or set free, the slaves. First, however, he needed a military victory. Without it, as Seward cautioned, emancipation would sound like "our last shriek on the retreat" — a cry for help, not a measure to make nobler the purpose of the war. Lincoln never lost sight of that purpose, despite his desire to put an end to slavery. He explained: "If I could save the Union without freeing any slave, I would do it; and if I could save it by freeing all the slaves, I would do it; and if I could do it by freeing some and leaving others alone, I would also do that."

Five days after Antietam, on September 22, the President announced that beginning January 1, 1863, all slaves in areas still in rebellion against the United States "shall be then, thenceforward, and forever free." As the President signed the Emancipation Proclamation, he said to Seward, "If my name ever goes into history, it will be for this act, and my whole soul is in it." He wrote his name on it not "A. Lincoln," his usual style, but boldly, "Abraham Lincoln."

When news of the Proclamation was made public, the effect among black Americans was electric. They now foresaw the end of slavery. On the great day, Frederick Douglass (page 307) waited with friends at a telegraph station in Boston for news from Washington. Suddenly the instrument began to click and people streamed in, shouting, "It's coming! It's on the wires!"

Actually, the Proclamation did not immediately free a single slave. In the loyal border states it did not apply. In the Confederate states it could not be enforced. It was, rather, a military move designed to weaken the Southerners' war effort. Wherever Union armies now went, slaves flocked to their side. The Proclamation, furthermore, served notice on the entire country that the fate of slavery would no longer be left to the states. Henceforth it would be the business of the federal government. Emancipation brought new support to the Union cause from abroad. Charles Francis Adams, serving as United States minister to England, wrote that the Proclamation had put an end to "all effective sympathy in Great Britain with the rebellion."

Black Americans aid the northern cause. From the beginning of the war, blacks could see that a golden opportunity was at hand. In many places in the North they had tried to enlist in the Union army — only to be rebuffed at first. Beginning in the summer of 1862, however, the Department of War authorized their recruitment.

The first official black regiment was commanded by Thomas Wentworth Higginson of Boston, an abolitionist and an old

Black Soldiers in the Civil War

Lewis Douglass, son of the well-known abolitionist Frederick Douglass, was among the first black soldiers to enlist in the Union army. In a letter from a battlefield near Charleston, South Carolina, Lewis told his fiancée about the horror of battle and the valor of his fellow black recruits.

A black regiment

I have been in two fights, and am unhurt. I am about to go into another, I believe, tonight. Our men fought well on both occasions. The last was desperate. We charged that terrible battery at Fort Wagner, and were repulsed. Many of our friends are dead or wounded.

I escaped unhurt from amidst a perfect hail of shot and shell. It was terrible. I need not particularize, the papers will give a better account than I have time to give. My thoughts are often with you, you are as dear to me as ever. As I said before, we are on the eve of another fight and I am very busy and have just snatched a moment to write to you. Should I fall in the next fight killed or wounded, I hope I fall with my face to the foe.

This regiment has established its reputation as a fighting regiment, not a man flinched, though it was a trying time. Men fell all around me. A shell would explode and clear a space of twenty feet. Our men would close up again, but it was no use, we had to retreat, which was a very hazardous undertaking. How I got out of that fight alive I cannot tell, but here I am.

My dear girl, I hope again to see you. I must bid you farewell should I be killed. Remember, if I die I die in a good cause.

---

friend of John Brown. The unit was known as the First South Carolina Volunteers. Another black unit — one that saw heavy action — was the Fifty-Fourth Massachusetts Volunteers, under Robert G. Shaw, also a Boston abolitionist. Six weeks after the Fifty-Fourth had been authorized, only 100 volunteers had signed up. Black leaders sent out a call throughout the North. Within a short time 1,000 blacks representing every state in the Union were in training. Among them were Charles and Lewis Douglass, the sons of Frederick Douglass (page 307).

At first, blacks in the army received lower pay than whites, a fact that black and white abolitionists alike vigorously protested. At last, in June, 1864, Congress passed a law granting equal pay to all soldiers. Few black soldiers became officers,

partly because they lacked military experience and partly because of race prejudice.

By 1865 about 180,000 blacks had served in the Union army, with another 30,000 in the Union navy. Twenty-one earned the Congressional Medal of Honor for bravery. A white officer said with deep admiration that his black troops had proved themselves equal to "the grand historic moment which comes to a race only once in many centuries."

Lincoln searches for the right general. Emancipation could be made complete only by full victory. But how could Lincoln bring that about? The North was dismayed early in October, 1862, when J. E. B. Stuart's cavalry made a daring raid around the Union army, temporarily bringing Confederate

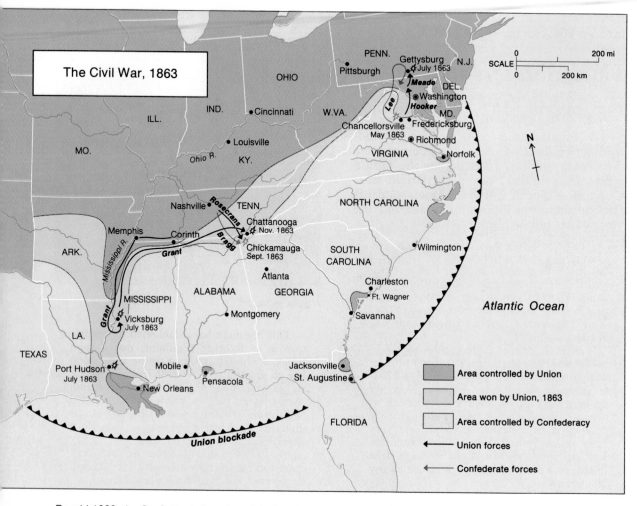

The Civil War, 1863

SCALE

Area controlled by Union

Area won by Union, 1863

Area controlled by Confederacy

Union forces

Confederate forces

By mid-1863, the Confederate invasion of the North had been repulsed, and by year-end the Union had succeeded in taking full control of the Mississippi River.

forces into Pennsylvania. McClellan explained that he could not move because his horses were tired. Lincoln sent him an angry telegram: "Will you pardon me for asking what the horses of your army have done since the Battle of Antietam that fatigues anything?" Lincoln removed McClellan and put General Ambrose E. Burnside in his place.

Burnside decided to lead the army across the Rappahannock River at Fredericksburg in December, 1862, and make a direct assault on Richmond from there. At Fredericksburg he found Lee's forces. In the deadly struggle that followed, 200,000 men were engaged, with the Confederates vastly outnumbered. Still, in the 48 hours of fighting, Union losses far exceeded those of the

Confederacy. Burnside finally withdrew across the river, badly defeated.

Once more Lincoln searched for a new general, this time turning to "Fighting Joe" Hooker. Hooker now prepared for his historic opportunity. He told his officers, "My plans are perfect, and when I start to carry them out, may God have mercy on General Lee, for I will have none."

Hooker soon discovered, however, that he had miscalculated. Like Burnside he went across the Rappahannock in search of the Confederates. When he caught up with them at Chancellorsville, Lee had divided his army in two, giving one part to "Stonewall" Jackson and leading the other himself. Lee drove at Hooker's left and center, Jackson at the right. After three days of fighting in early May, 1863, Hooker's forces had been sent sprawling across the river in defeat. Lincoln was devastated by the news of the disaster. "What will the country say?" he asked in anguish.

The South, too, was taking heavy losses. Among their 11,000 casualties at Chancellorsville was "Stonewall" Jackson, accidentally wounded by his own men. Lee said of the fallen general, whose arm had to be amputated, "He has lost his left arm; but I have lost my right arm." A few days later Jackson was dead.

Lee invades Pennsylvania. The South could ill afford the loss. It would need outstanding military talent for what lay ahead. Recognizing that the Confederates must carry the war into the North, Jefferson Davis, his Cabinet, and Lee decided on an invasion of Pennsylvania. Their chief aim was to cut the North in two and hasten the end of hostilities. The Confederates also hoped to arouse sentiment for peace in the North and, possibly, force Europeans again to consider openly aiding the Confederacy.

All during the month of June, 1863, Lee led his army northward. He missed Jackson badly, but with him were James Longstreet, Richard S. Ewell, and A. P. Hill. The Union army was now under the command of General George G. Meade. Although Meade had a bad temper (his troops called him "the old snapping turtle"), he had their respect. He rode with his hat pulled so low over his head that he looked like a medieval knight wearing a helmet.

Gettysburg marks a turning point. As Lee's army approached the town of Gettysburg, Pennsylvania, his advance force encountered Meade's troops. It was July 1, 1863, and the Battle of Gettysburg was about to begin. It would prove to be the bloodiest battle ever waged on the North American continent.

Lee hoped to overpower Meade's army, which had taken up positions on a series of hills and ridges near Gettysburg. After two and a half days of fighting, however, it became obvious that Meade's men were well dug in. Lee had no choice but to strike Meade head on.

The high point came on July 3. On Lee's orders, General George Pickett, a dandy who wore his hair in ringlets, daringly led his troops against Union forces on Cemetery Ridge. "Up, men, and to your posts!" Pickett cried. "Don't forget that you are from Old Virginia!" Forward swept 15,000 men, their regimental flags flying.

Pickett's charge was doomed to fail. As the brave soldiers came within range of the Union guns, they met a withering fire. Only a handful reached the top of Cemetery Ridge. When the firing ceased at last, not a single mounted officer was left. Three fourths of Pickett's troops had been killed or wounded. Lee in despair said to Pickett, "Your men have done all that men could do; the fault is entirely my own."

The Union's ability to reach and hold its position atop Cemetery Ridge was a key to its success at Gettysburg.

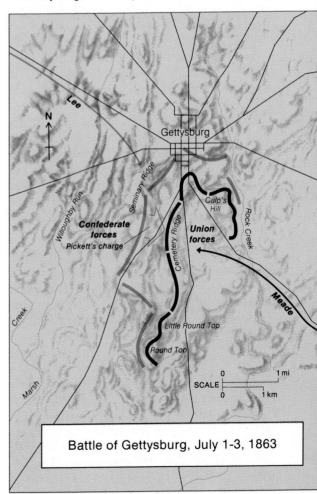

Battle of Gettysburg, July 1-3, 1863

The Battle of Gettysburg signaled a turning tide in favor of the Union, but losses were heavy — 23,000 Union soldiers and 20,000 Confederate.

The following day — the Fourth of July — Lee began his retreat in a drenching rain. Meade inexcusably allowed the Confederate army to escape. Where Meade was pleased with himself for having driven "the invaders from our soil," Lincoln was in despair. "Is that all?" he asked. Lincoln's associates had never before seen the President so discouraged. "We had only to stretch forth our hands and they were ours," he declared glumly. Still, many Northerners were now convinced that victory was near.

The fall of Vicksburg gives the North control of the Mississippi. In the West there was good news for the Union on the same Fourth of July. On that day Vicksburg surrendered to Grant after a siege lasting 47 days.

The Union victory had come about as a result of a notable series of events. In the spring of 1863, Grant had cut himself loose from his supply lines and had "lived off the country" below Vicksburg. During those months he won four battles against separate Confederate forces that together might have overwhelmed him. Then, penning the Confederates up in Vicksburg, he gradually tightened his grip, bombarding the city until it surrendered.

With the surrender a few days later of Port Hudson, the Mississippi was controlled entirely by the Union. Lincoln, much heartened, said that "the Father of Waters again goes unvexed to the sea." In gaining control of the Mississippi, the Union had cut off Arkansas, Louisiana, and Texas from the rest of the Confederacy.

The occupation of Tennessee is completed. After the fall of Vicksburg a Union army led by General William Rosecrans advanced south, pursuing Confederate forces under General Braxton Bragg. Bragg surprised "Rosy" — as he was called — at Chickamauga, Georgia, and the Union army was forced to flee. Lincoln later said that Rosecrans had acted "confused and stunned like a duck hit on the head." Rosecrans was saved from utter disaster, however, by the stand of Union troops commanded by General George Thomas. Thomas would be remembered ever afterward as the "Rock of Chickamauga." Even his family in Virginia, which had turned his picture to the wall when he decided to fight for the Union, was pleased to hear how well he had fought.

Chickamauga was a victory for the Confederates, and they soon had the Union army bottled up in nearby Chattanooga. General Grant and General William T. Sherman, however, came over from Vicksburg and succeeded in breaking the siege. In the battles of Lookout Mountain and Missionary Ridge, not far from Chattanooga, the combined Union forces defeated Bragg. By December 3, 1863, all of Tennessee, another link between the two parts of the Confederacy, was in the Union's hands.

SECTION REVIEW

1. Vocabulary: *emancipate*.
2. What reverses did Union forces suffer in early 1862?
3. (a) Why did Lee advance into Maryland? (b) Of what importance was the Battle of Antietam?
4. (a) Why did Lincoln issue the Emancipation Proclamation? (b) How did black Americans aid the Union cause?
5. Why were the battles of Gettysburg and Vicksburg turning points in the Civil War?
6. How did Union forces complete the occupation of Tennessee?

4 All-out War Affects Life Behind the Lines

The fighting went on relentlessly, even though the South's leaders knew now that the Confederacy was on a slippery downward slope. Both sides, meanwhile, struggled with the problems of supplying the troops, financing the war, and maintaining support on the home front.

The lack of southern industry is felt. A critical problem for the South throughout the Civil War was the shortage of manufactured goods. Even at the height of the fighting in 1863, the Confederacy was making its military uniforms by hand. The largest government warehouse employed 3,000 women who sewed endlessly. Whereas the North was using shoe-stitching machines to produce the millions of shoes its troops required, the South was turning out only 5,000 pairs a week — all handmade.

The South doggedly tried to provide its troops with adequate arms. It had the services of Josiah Gorgas, a former United States army officer who was an expert at designing and developing weapons. Gorgas established arsenals throughout the South. He was hampered, however, by the absence of a factory system and by insufficient railroad transportation. In 1862, when the North had tooled up to produce 5,000 rifles a day, the South was turning out only 300. Metals were so scarce that church bells were melted down to make cannon. Artillery batteries were sometimes named for the churches from which the iron for their guns had originated.

Inadequate railroads also gravely handicapped the Confederacy's operations. The 11 states of Dixie had 9,000 miles of roadbed; the North, comprising an equal area, had 20,000 miles of track. Moreover, the South's railroad lines were badly built, badly equipped, and badly run. Since the tracks of these roads were of different

Jefferson Davis brought a military background to his tasks as president of the Confederacy. He had fought in the Mexican War and had served as Secretary of War under President Pierce.

gauges (the gauge is the distance between the two rails of a railroad), it was virtually impossible to run trains from one part of a state to another, let alone from state to state. More important, no track was manufactured in the South during the war, making it necessary to take rails from branch lines or side tracks in order to repair main lines. Finally, because of local rivalries, the Confederacy was unable to coordinate the operation of the railroad lines. The food shortage that developed resulted at first mainly from the inability to move crops and animals where they were needed. Later on, as large areas were occupied by the federal armies and as slaves left the land, crop production fell off sharply.

The South suffers hard times. The shortages that developed in the South gradually drained the people's strength. Certain items were difficult to obtain. One was salt, necessary for preserving fish and meat. A sack of salt that cost 65 cents in 1861 sold for $20 four years later. A shortage of quinine, used in treating malaria, caused considerable suffering.

While some Southerners prospered during the war — especially those who got through the Union naval blockade and brought in scarce luxuries — most people experienced hardship. The fate of John Beauchamp Jones, a clerk in the War Department at Richmond, tells us something of life on the home front. In 1862 the family's income was $6,000 and they lived comfortably. By July, 1863, however, Jones wrote in his diary, "We are in a half-starved condition." Six months later he was writing, "With flour at $200 a barrel, meal $20 per bushel, and meat from $2 to $5 a pound, what income would suffice?" A year later his words were full of distress: "What I fear is starvation." Jones died the following year — likely of malnutrition.

The South has difficulty financing the war. The Confederacy also had to struggle with financial problems. When the fighting began, it had seized the gold, totaling less than $400,000, stored in the federal mint in New Orleans. It had, in addition, a $500,000 loan from the state of Alabama. With so little money on hand, the Confederate government had to borrow heavily from its citizens by issuing bonds. By the time of Gettysburg these securities had fallen in value because of growing doubts that they would ever be redeemed. A Georgian predicted, "An oak leaf will be worth just as much as the promise of the Confederate treasury to pay one dollar."

Day-to-day transactions were conducted with paper currency that rolled steadily off the printing presses. Some was issued by the central government, some by the states, some even by cities. By the end of the war more than a billion dollars in paper money was in circulation, most of it virtually worthless.

Slaves await a Union victory. The Confederacy was also handicapped by constant concern over the loyalty of the slaves. Slaves might have been put to work on public projects, such as repairing railroads or building fortifications. Owners steadfastly refused to allow their hands to be hired out, however, lest they be injured or run away. Furthermore, continuing to believe that cotton was the key to southern prosperity, most planters could not imagine their slaves doing anything but working in the fields.

The fear of uprisings made the idea of arming slaves and enlisting them in the army seem out of the question. Said Howell Cobb of Georgia, "If slaves will make good soldiers, our whole theory of slavery is wrong." When in the end the enlistment of blacks was authorized in the South, the war was almost over and none ever served in Confederate uniform.

Undoubtedly, southern blacks sensed that a Union victory would destroy the institution of slavery. Booker T. Washington, then a slave, recalled years later that his mother would kneel at his bedside "fervently praying that Lincoln and his armies might be successful and that one day she and her children might be free." Black people who heard Union soldiers singing "John Brown's Body" and "The Battle Cry of Freedom" did not have to think twice about the side they supported.

From St. George, Bermuda, blockade-runners sped rifles and needed supplies to Wilmington, North Carolina, and other southern ports.

The South fails to break the blockade. The South never overcame its lack of naval forces. In 1861 the Confederates seized a steam frigate called the *Merrimack*, covered it with iron plates, and rechristened it the *Virginia.* It succeeded in damaging wooden federal ships in Hampton Roads, Virginia. Then, in March, 1862, it met a Union ironclad, the *Monitor.* This first duel between two ironclad vessels ended in a draw, and the federal blockade was never seriously threatened.

The Confederacy lacks central authority. When delegates met early in 1861 to form the Confederate government, they quickly drew up a constitution — a task made easier by copying much of the United States Constitution. They made, nevertheless, a number of significant changes. The new frame of government, as expected, safeguarded states' rights and the institution of slavery (although it prohibited the importing of slaves). It also limited the President to a single six-year term and gave him the power to veto specific provisions in appropriation bills. It provided, furthermore, for a simpler process of amendment.

The deep faith in the principle of states' rights, embodied in the constitution, proved to be another serious handicap to the Confederate war effort. At first the goal of establishing a unified southern nation had been widely accepted. The movement never developed fully, however, despite the lip-service that people paid to "the cause." Resistance to the idea was mainly in the mountain areas of eastern Tennessee and in western Virginia (the part that in 1863 was admitted to the Union as the new state of West Virginia). Gradually, the seceded states themselves began to resist the Confederate government. Defiance showed up especially in North Carolina, South Carolina, and Georgia. The governors of those states placed obstacles in the way of the Richmond government when it sought to conscript the state militias. Few people in 1861 would have predicted that states' rights would be a flaw in the structure of the Confederacy and would help to destroy it.

The North is prepared to fight a modern war. The advantages that the North enjoyed (page 371) eventually proved themselves. From about 1800 on, the North had been

385

laying the basis for a modern nation. First the Federalists, then the Whigs, and then the Republicans had been friendly to the development of industry. The signs of their efforts were the railroads and factories of the North.

The railroads were a powerful weapon in the fighting. In being able to move troops and supplies from one part of the North to another, the Union forces had a flexibility that the South could not match.

Also helping bind the North together were telegraph lines. Two telegraph companies had become dominant by the time of the Civil War: the American Telegraph Company in the East, and the Western Union Company in the West. As business-minded people, Northerners had greater use for the telegraph than Southerners. Telegraph facilities, as a result, were more readily available in the North.

Similarly, express companies equipped to carry money, letters, and packages safely and rapidly had also appeared in the 1850's. The best known was Wells Fargo and Company. It, too, was busier in the North than in the South. By the 1860's, Wells Fargo had become indispensable for moving products and documents required in the Union war effort.

Northern industry booms. The North was producing more of its necessities every year, from vast quantities of manufactured goods to food of every description. A number of important inventions in addition to the telegraph became directly useful to the war effort. One was the process for vulcanizing rubber, discovered by Charles Goodyear in 1839. Through the use of chemicals and heat, rubber was toughened for new and unprecedented uses — for wagon and carriage tires, raincoats, and waterproof boots. It also made possible the inflated balloons from which Union troops observed Confederate positions.

Another invention was Elias Howe's sewing machine, patented in 1846. It opened the way for the mass production of clothing and shoes. By 1861 over 3,800 companies were manufacturing ready-made clothing. These factories were readily converted to the production of uniforms for "the boys in blue."

Yet another new process aided the Union cause. This was the canning of food — replacing the older method of preserving it with salt. An important pioneer in this field was Gail Borden, who in 1856 received a patent for his method of "evaporating milk in vacuum." On the eve of the Civil War he had opened a plant producing cans of evaporated milk. Since the milk could easily be transported to the battlefields, it became an important part of the soldiers' diet.

Nothing, finally, aided the northern war effort more than the mechanical grain reaper. The man chiefly responsible for it was Cyrus McCormick, a native Virginian, who in 1832 improved upon a model his father had built. McCormick built a plant in Chicago to manufacture his reapers. The use of these machines eliminated the need to detach units of men to help harvest the grain in the fall. The South had no comparable technological help.

New laws strengthen the northern economy. After the South left the Union, Congress was able to pass legislation long opposed by representatives from below the Mason-Dixon Line. The first of these laws was the Morrill Tariff of 1861, passed even before Lincoln took office. It provided for a sizable increase over the existing tariff rates. The following year tariff rates were raised even higher. The tariff enabled American factory owners to raise prices on their products. The profit gained could be used for plant expansion and other investments.

A second law was the Homestead Act of 1862. It provided a grant of 160 acres of free federal land as a *homestead* to anyone willing to live on it for five years. Southerners had long opposed such a law, recognizing it would benefit small farmers of the North, not plantation owners. Southerners had also foreseen that homesteading would result in more free states in the Union.

A third law, passed in 1863, was the National Bank Act, which gave central direction to American banking for the first time since Andrew Jackson's presidency.

The law empowered newly created national banks to issue bank notes, giving the country its first reliable national currency.

The federal government sells bonds. The ability of the North to thrive in the midst of a war showed the strength of the northern economy. To finance the war, the government readily sold more than two billion dollars' worth of bonds. For the daily business of the Union, Congress authorized the issuance of *greenbacks,* paper money which had to be accepted in payment of debts. Greenbacks were printing-press money, much like the currency issued by the South. The administration accompanied their issuance with heavy taxation which absorbed some of the inflation they created.

Lincoln reveals rare qualities of leadership. War always brings developments beyond control and predicting. During the Civil War the most notable surprise was Lincoln's genius as a leader. People who at first doubted that Lincoln was equal to the task of saving the Union began to appreciate the unique quality of his mind and character. In setting policies, he did not waste words or show his hand too soon. Billy Herndon, his law partner, called him the most "shut-mouthed" man who ever lived. When Lincoln acted, however, he acted decisively.

To do his work, Lincoln exercised greater power than any President before him. Despite the growing respect he earned, some of the steps he took were widely criticized as unconstitutional. He justified them on the ground that the rebellion had created an unprecedented emergency requiring extraordinary actions. For example, Lincoln unhesitatingly suspended some traditional civil liberties in suppressing opposition to the military effort. His target was southern sympathizers and the so-called Peace Democrats, who were for peace at any price. Altogether about 13,000 people were arrested for their activities.

The most extreme of the Peace Democrats, those who actually favored the South, were called Copperheads — after the deadly snake of that name. The most prominent Copperhead was Clement L. Vallandigham,

THE COPPERHEAD PARTY.—IN FAVOR OF *A VIGOROUS PROSECUTION OF PEACE!*

The leading spokesman for the Peace Democrats was C. L. Vallandigham, whose face is shown on the Copperheads that attack the Union in this cartoon.

a member of Congress from Ohio. Lincoln in time pardoned many of the people who were arrested, but he had Vallandigham banished to the Confederacy.

Both sides use a military draft. The long years of fighting brought about a certain war-weariness. As the numbers of volunteers fell off, both sides offered cash payments to attract recruits. They also found it necessary to pass draft laws. In April, 1862, the Confederacy had made all white males between the ages of 18 and 35 liable for service. (In 1864 the draft was extended to include white males between 17 and 50.) In March, 1863, the North also passed a draft law. On either side, however, a draftee could escape service by hiring a substitute. By paying $300 a Northerner could become exempt altogether.

The uneven operation of the draft law brought keen frustration in the North. Moreover, as the war dragged on and as rising prices were not matched by rising wages, many people felt resentful. On July 13, 1863, a week after the news from Gettysburg and Vicksburg, brutal draft riots broke out in New York City. Mobs roamed the streets, looting and burning and shouting "Down with the rich!" The disturbances, the worst in American history, cost

The Gettysburg Address (1863)

Four score and seven years ago our fathers brought forth on this continent, a new nation, conceived in liberty, and dedicated to the proposition that all men are created equal.

Now we are engaged in a great civil war, testing whether that nation or any nation so conceived and so dedicated, can long endure. We are met on a great battlefield of that war. We have come to dedicate a portion of that field, as a final resting place for those who here gave their lives that that nation might live. It is altogether fitting and proper that we should do this.

But, in a larger sense, we cannot dedicate — we cannot consecrate — we cannot hallow — this ground. The brave men, living and dead, who struggled here, have consecrated it, far above our poor power to add or detract. The world will little note, nor long remember what we say here, but it can never forget what they did here. It is for us the living, rather, to be dedicated here to the unfinished work which they who fought here have thus far so nobly advanced. It is rather for us to be here dedicated to the great task remaining before us — that from these honored dead we take increased devotion to that cause for which they gave the last full measure of devotion — that we here highly resolve that these dead shall not have died in vain — that this nation, under God, shall have a new birth of freedom — and that government of the people, by the people, for the people, shall not perish from the earth.

hundreds of lives. In the furor, gangs lynched a dozen blacks and set fire to the Colored Orphan Asylum. The ringleaders preached that freed blacks would soon be taking the jobs of whites. Some of General Meade's troops at Gettysburg had to be dispatched to help restore order.

Relations between the North and Europe are strained. People in European countries followed the news of events in America with lively interest. When the war broke out, many wealthy English people made known their sympathy for the South. Some of them envisioned a close tie between cotton-raising Southerners and cotton-manufacturing Britons. The truth proved to be, however, that Britain, and other countries in Europe, did not need cotton from the South as much as they needed wheat from the North.

A serious episode in Anglo-American relations occurred late in 1861. A Union naval vessel, commanded by Charles Wilkes (page 323), stopped the British mail-steamer *Trent* at sea and removed from it James

Mason and John Slidell, two Confederate diplomats bound for duty in Europe. Britain immediately claimed that its rights as a neutral had been violated. Lincoln was faced with a difficult decision. If he released the two Southerners, many Northerners would see him as a weakling. If he refused, he might have an additional war on his hands. In the end Lincoln ordered the two Confederates set free. As a face-saving gesture he expressed satisfaction that Britain had finally recognized that American arguments in 1812 about the rights of neutrals had been correct.

Other British activity was far more costly. Despite protests by the United States, English shipyards built three commerce raiders for the South. The most famous of these ships was the *Alabama*. Before the vessels ceased their raids, they had captured 140 northern merchant ships.[2]

[2]In 1871 Britain agreed to pay over $15 million as compensation for the damages — known as the *Alabama* claims — inflicted by Confederate cruisers.

Relations with France also produced moments of anxiety. The French in 1864 established as the puppet rulers of Mexico an Austrian archduke, Ferdinand Maximilian, and his wife Carlota, daughter of the king of Belgium. The United States viewed this action as a violation of the Monroe Doctrine and protested vigorously. The crisis was resolved in 1867 when the French withdrew their forces from Mexico. Without the support of the French, Maximilian was arrested and executed by his subjects.

Russia brought joy to the Union by sending two fleets on a goodwill visit to the United States in 1863. One anchored in New York, the other in San Francisco. Only later did Americans learn that the Russians had sent their vessels out of European waters in order to avoid being bottled up by the British navy in the event of war.

The abolition of slavery guarantees European neutrality. As it became clear that a northern victory would mean an end to slavery, people throughout Europe became more sympathetic to Lincoln's work. Millions of Europeans striving to obtain greater freedom for themselves understood that a Union triumph would advance democracy everywhere. The governments of Britain and France would never be willing to bring to the South the aid the Confederates had once counted on.

In November, 1863, Lincoln journeyed to Gettysburg to help dedicate a new National Soldiers' Cemetery on the battlefield there. Coffins awaiting burial could be seen wherever people in the huge crowd turned. The main speaker was Edward Everett, a distinguished Massachusetts statesman and former president of Harvard College. Everett droned on for two hours. Then came the President's turn. He spoke ten sentences. (He had promised that he would be "short, short, short.") Those sentences express better than anyone else ever has the ideals the republic stands for and that the Union was struggling to preserve. The Gettysburg Address (page 388) speaks as eloquently to the world today as on the day when Lincoln delivered it.

SECTION REVIEW

1. Vocabulary: *homestead, greenbacks.*
2. (a) How did the lack of industry in the South affect the Confederacy's war effort? (b) How did the South try to finance the war? (c) Why was the Confederacy reluctant to enlist slaves in its army?
3. (a) In what ways was the North better prepared for war than the South? (b) Why did northern industry boom during the war? (c) How did the North finance the war?
4. What qualities of leadership did Abraham Lincoln reveal during the Civil War?
5. (a) What episodes threatened relations between the North and Britain? (b) Between the North and France? (c) Why did the South fail to gain European support?

5 Fighting Ends in Victory for the North

Early in 1864 Lincoln decided to bring Grant east and make him general-in-chief. Grant, who now had the responsibility for ending the war, began to lay plans. He would move south toward Richmond and take on Lee's army. General Sherman, who had succeeded Grant in the West, would move from Chattanooga toward Atlanta.

Union forces open the Wilderness campaign. Grant's troops greatly outnumbered Lee's, but the marshy woodland of northern Virginia, known as The Wilderness, made pursuit of the Confederates difficult. In this terrain Grant first encountered Lee's forces on May 5, 1864. In the three-day battle that followed, the Union lost about 18,000 men and the Confederates about 10,000. Unlike his predecessors, however, Grant pressed forward, not back toward Washington. At Cold Harbor another costly battle took thousands of lives. An observer remembered the murderous, hand-to-hand combat: "Rank after rank was riddled by shot and shell and bayonet-thrusts, and finally sank, a mass of torn and mutilated corpses; then fresh troops rushed madly forward to replace the dead."

In the Wilderness campaign Clara Barton, a nurse who later founded the American Red Cross, gave merciful service. On the Confederate side Sally Tompkins was commissioned a captain of cavalry for her work, having set up a hospital at her own expense in Richmond. Wherever soldiers suffered, volunteers came forward to nurse them. Inadequate medical treatment, nevertheless, was the rule in both armies. It brought new terror to those wounded on the field of battle.

By early June, 1864, Grant was advancing on Richmond by way of Petersburg. His goal was to seize the railroad running from Petersburg to the Confederate capital. If he succeeded, he would cut Lee off from his supplies.

Lee now could only delay defeat. In one month of fighting Grant had lost more men than the total number of soldiers in Lee's army. Confederate losses were also heavy, however, and they could not be replaced.

Lincoln was often criticized for his extraordinary use of executive power in the Civil War, but his re-election in 1864 reflected the people's approval of his conduct of the war.

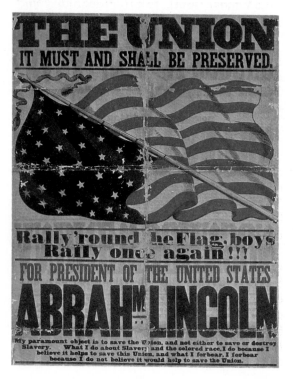

Sherman takes Atlanta. At about the same time that the Wilderness campaign was under way, a momentous operation was in progress farther south. Following the occupation of Chattanooga by northern troops, the way was open for an invasion of Georgia. Sherman's troops moved to capture Atlanta and then go north along the Atlantic coast to prevent Lee's army from retreating. Sherman took Atlanta on September 2, 1864, after a hard struggle against General John Hood's forces.

Lincoln is re-elected. The news from Georgia helped Lincoln in the presidential campaign of 1864. In June the Republicans and the War Democrats (northern Democrats who supported Lincoln's policies) had met at Baltimore. Calling themselves the National Union Party, they renominated the President. In tribute to the support from the War Democrats, the delegates nominated Andrew Johnson to be Vice President. Johnson, a Democrat from Tennessee, was the only Southerner still in the Senate.

The regular Democrats, who held their convention in Chicago, aimed to take advantage of the sentiment for peace that had set in. Their platform declared the war a failure and urged an end to hostilities. The party nominated General McClellan for President and George Pendleton of Ohio — a close friend of Clement Vallandigham, the Copperhead — for Vice President. McClellan accepted the nomination but rejected the party's platform. "I could not," he said, "look into the face of my gallant comrades and tell them that we have abandoned the Union for which we have so often periled our lives."

The fall of Atlanta delivered a mortal blow to the Democrats. A Republican newspaper ran a headline calling the Union victory "Old Abe's Reply to the Chicago Convention." Southerners, too, now knew that the North was not going to call a halt to the fighting. Lincoln won re-election with 212 electoral votes to McClellan's 21.

The President was inaugurated for a second time on March 4, 1865. As at his first inauguration, the sky was threatening —

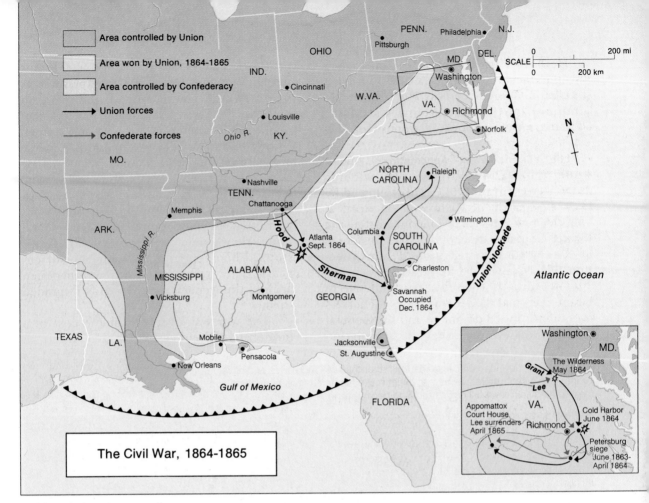

The final events of the war took place as General Grant moved to capture Richmond and as General Sherman advanced through Georgia in his "march to the sea."

but this time the sun suddenly appeared when the President stepped forward to speak. Lincoln's words showed he was thinking of the time of peace soon to come:

> With malice toward none; with charity for all; with firmness in the right as God gives us to see the right, let us strive on to finish the work we are in; to bind up the nation's wounds; to care for him who shall have borne the battle, and for his widow, and his orphan — to do all which may achieve and cherish a just and lasting peace among ourselves and with all nations.

Sherman divides the South. Shortly after the election, Sherman and his troops set out from Atlanta on a march to the sea. Sherman, who had once been head of a military college in Louisiana, knew and admired Southerners. He had even been offered a

high rank in the Confederate army. Now he was at the head of 60,000 northern troops with orders to lay waste to whatever they found of military value along a fifty-mile path through Georgia.

Some of Sherman's men, their discipline relaxed after so much constant danger, disobeyed orders, burning and looting at will. Each regiment daily sent a group of men into the countryside to forage for food. Living off the country in this fashion, they slaughtered livestock and carried off harvested crops. Still, much of the unauthorized destruction was done by civilian deserters (Confederate as well as Union), stragglers, and other army hangers-on. Some burning, moreover, had been done by Confederate cavalry under orders to leave behind nothing the Union could use.

Just before Christmas, Sherman reached Savannah, his destination. Behind him lay a stretch of Georgia completely ruined. He continued into South Carolina and North Carolina, meeting almost no opposition.

Lee surrenders at Appomattox. Meanwhile, the war in Virginia was winding down. Petersburg fell to Grant, followed by Lee's evacuation of Richmond on April 2, 1865. A few days later Lincoln visited the former Confederate capital. Black residents of Richmond gathered around him affectionately as he walked in the streets.

On April 9, 1865, Lee surrendered to Grant. Lee had said to an aide, "There is nothing for me to do but go and see General Grant, and I would rather die a thousand deaths." The exhausted Lee, astride his horse, Traveller, rode off to Appomattox Court House. The meeting of the two generals was correct but cordial, with Grant opening the conversation by saying simply, "I met you once before, General Lee, while we were serving in Mexico."

Grant offered Lee generous terms. The Confederate officers would be allowed to keep their side arms, while the troops were permitted to take home any horses and mules they would need for plowing. Grant stopped his men from cheering the surrender. "The rebels are our countrymen again," this general of few words reminded them.

The war was over, but at the cost of a million battlefield casualties. No American

Robert E. Lee surrendered at Appomattox rather than risk more lives and devastate the countryside. Grant offered terms that might make the defeat less humiliating and gave the southern soldiers a full day's rations to begin their journeys home.

Lincoln's funeral passed through New York City on its way to Springfield, Illinois. The nation mourned not only its President but also those killed in battle.

had been untouched by the struggle. The poet James Russell Lowell could have been speaking for all Americans when he learned of the news from Appomattox: "Bow down, dear Land, for thou hast found release!"

Lincoln is assassinated. On April 14, 1865, five days after Appomattox, the President and Mrs. Lincoln went to Ford's Theater in Washington to see a stage comedy. The performance was in progress when John Wilkes Booth, an actor grieving over the South's defeat, entered the President's box. He fired one shot, then jumped to the stage and escaped from the theater. (Booth was killed a few days later by soldiers sent to capture him.) The President, mortally wounded, was carried to a house across the street. There he died the next morning.

Lincoln's body, after lying in state at the White House, was carried in a black-draped railroad car on the long journey back to Springfield, Illinois. The train retraced the route by which Lincoln had come from the West four years earlier. The nation mourned as it had never mourned before. Only recently had it come to appreciate Lincoln's greatness.

On the day Lincoln was shot, another dramatic event had taken place — in the South. The Stars and Stripes had been raised once again over Fort Sumter. Lincoln had ordered that every gun-battery which had fired at Old Glory on that fateful day in 1861 must now be fired in a solemn salute of respect. The sound of the guns thundering across Charleston harbor deafened the onlookers. The restored Union, symbolized brilliantly in this touching scene, is Abraham Lincoln's memorial — the only one he had sought.

SECTION REVIEW

1. What was Grant's plan for ending the war?
2. (a) What candidate opposed Lincoln in 1864? (b) What event assured Lincoln's re-election?
3. What terms did Grant offer Lee at Appomattox?
4. When and by whom was President Lincoln assassinated?

Chapter 16 Review

Summary

After news of Abraham Lincoln's election reached the South, southern delegates gathered in February, 1861, to form the Confederate States of America. Neither President Buchanan nor any legislator could come up with a compromise plan to restore the seceded states to the Union. When Confederate shore batteries opened fire on Fort Sumter on April 12, 1861, all hope of avoiding bloodshed was lost. The Civil War had begun.

At first the North believed it could quickly defeat the South. With a larger population and superior resources, a vast network of railroads, plentiful capital, self-sufficiency in food production, and a growing factory system, the northern states had powerful advantages. The eleven Confederate states, on the other hand, also had advantages. Southerners were fighting for their independence and would be defending their homes against Union invasion. In addition, many southern youths had chosen to make the army their career and had been trained in military schools. The South, therefore, had formidable military leadership.

The Civil War was far longer and more catastrophic than either side envisioned. With the exception of General Ulysses S. Grant in the West, northern generals made no successful advances into southern territory. The Union army had its hands full trying to contain the advancing Confederate army, led by General Robert E. Lee.

The turning point in the war came in July, 1863, at Gettysburg, Pennsylvania. The bloody battle fought there cost each side tens of thousands of lives. In the end the Confederate army withdrew to the South, never to invade Union territory again.

In the final campaign of the war, General Grant relentlessly pushed south in pursuit of Lee's exhausted Confederate troops. Another section of the Union army, meanwhile, was making a devastating sweep through Georgia, taking Atlanta and then Savannah by Christmas, 1864. The South was now incapable of halting Union advances. Grant took Richmond on April 3, 1865, and accepted General Lee's surrender at Appomattox Court House six days later.

Celebration was short-lived for the North. On April 14, while enjoying a play at Ford's Theater in Washington, the President was assassinated. Abraham Lincoln was mourned by people in both sections who had come to recognize the remarkable role he had played.

Vocabulary and Important Terms

1. Confederacy
2. Crittenden compromise
3. Fort Sumter
4. "anaconda plan"
5. Antietam
6. emancipate
7. Emancipation Proclamation
8. National Bank Act
9. Vicksburg
10. Morrill Tariff
11. homestead
12. Homestead Act
13. Battle of Gettysburg
14. greenbacks
15. Copperhead
16. *Trent* affair
17. Appomattox

Discussion Questions

1. (a) What was the original goal of the North and of Lincoln in fighting the Civil War? (b) How did Lincoln at first reassure Southerners on the issue of slavery?

2. Taking into account the odds against the South, explain why the Confederacy was able to hold out for four years.

3. How did the North and the South raise armies during the course of the war?

4. (a) Why did Southerners believe they would receive help from Britain and France? (b) Why did the governments of Europe never bring to the South the aid Confederates expected?

5. Why did the South carry the fighting into the North on two separate occasions, and what was the significance of the battles at Gettysburg and at Antietam?

6. (a) To what extent had the North by war's end carried into effect the strategy outlined in the "anaconda plan"? (b) What key battles did the North win in carrying out this strategy?

7. (a) Why can it be said that Lincoln spent much of the war searching for a general? (b) Why did Lincoln bring Grant east and make him general-in-chief? (c) How did Grant differ from his predecessors in fighting the war?

8. (a) As the war continued, why did the South suffer hard times? (b) What industrial and technological help proved indispensable to the northern war effort?

9. (a) In what ways did black Americans aid the northern war cause? (b) Why were slaves not called upon to aid the South? (c) What contributions did women like Clara Barton and Sally Tompkins make during the course of the Civil War?

10. What rare qualities did Lincoln bring to the office of President?

Relating Past to Present

1. During the Civil War the roles of blacks and women in warfare were strictly limited. What part do blacks and women play in the nation's armed forces today?

2. To save the Union, Lincoln exercised extreme presidential powers, even suspending some civil liberties. Would the American people today tolerate the suspension of civil liberties (for example, freedom of speech) in the event of an emergency? Explain your answer.

Studying Local History

What Civil War battles, if any, took place in your state or locality? What effect, if any, did they have on the eventual outcome of the war? If no battles took place in your state, what individuals or fighting units from your locality distinguished themselves in battles fought elsewhere during the war?

Using History Skills

1. *Reading maps.* Study the map on page 380 showing the military situation in 1863. (a) In what three areas of the country did major campaigns take place? (b) What was the outcome of Lee's march into Pennsylvania? (c) Why was the Confederate surrender of Vicksburg so costly?

2. *Placing events in time.* Make a time line that shows some of the major events of the Civil War period. On that time line include the following events: (a) the secession of South Carolina, (b) the Battle of Antietam, (c) the fall of Vicksburg, (d) Lee's surrender at Appomattox, (e) the first inauguration of Lincoln, (f) the date the Emancipation Proclamation went into effect, (g) the second inauguration of Lincoln, (h) the firing on Fort Sumter, (i) the Battle of Gettysburg, and (j) the assassination of Lincoln.

3. *Comparing.* In what ways was the military strategy of the Confederates similar to that of the Patriots in 1776? In what ways was it different?

WORLD SCENE

Modern Warfare

In the nineteenth century new developments in weaponry changed the way wars were fought. At the same time, advances in medical care improved the chances of survival for sick and wounded soldiers.

New tools of war. A new rapid-firing weapon made available to the Union in 1862 was the Gatling gun, named after its inventor, Richard Gatling, a North Carolinian by birth. This weapon, capable of discharging bullets in a steady stream, was a forerunner of the machine gun. The Gatling gun was adopted by the United States Army in 1866. It was also used extensively in Africa and Asia by the expanding European nations during the 1880's and 1890's.

The first fully automatic machine gun was invented in 1884 by Hiram Maxim. Maxim, who had been born in Maine, moved to London as a young man and later became a British citizen. His weapon revolutionized battlefield tactics. A frontal assault by massed infantry and cavalry became suicidal when up against a battery of machine guns. Within a few years after its invention, the machine gun was being used by every major country in the world.

The famous engagement between the ironclads *Monitor* and *Merrimack* marked the beginning of a new type of naval warfare. Wooden sailing ships were now outmoded. Steam-powered, armor-plated vessels soon came into use. Another important innovation first installed on the *Monitor* was the rotating gun turret, making the vessel look like "a cheese box on a raft." The turret permitted large cannon to be fired in various directions.

Improved medical care. The British nurse Florence Nightingale was the central figure in bringing improved medical care to soldiers. As the head of a unit of British nurses during the Crimean War (1853–1856), she set procedures for sanitation and hygiene that substantially reduced deaths from infection among wounded soldiers. In 1860 she founded a school for training professional nurses. It became the standard the world over for modern nursing education.

In 1863 a voluntary relief service called the Red Cross was organized in Europe by the Swiss humanitarian Jean Henri Dunant (doo-NAHN). Dedicated to helping soldiers and victims of war, the Red Cross soon had chapters in many countries. More than any other organization, the Red Cross worked to establish international guidelines for the humane treatment of prisoners of war.

CHAPTER 17

Remaking the Union

1865 – 1877

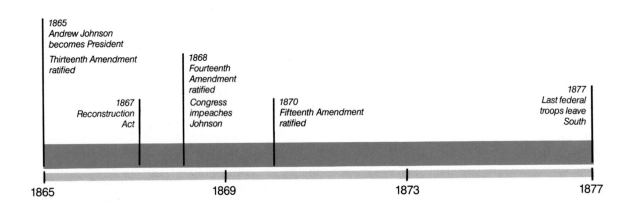

1865
Andrew Johnson
becomes President

Thirteenth Amendment
ratified

1867
Reconstruction
Act

1868
Fourteenth
Amendment
ratified

Congress
impeaches
Johnson

1870
Fifteenth Amendment
ratified

1877
Last federal
troops leave
South

1865   1869   1873   1877

CHAPTER OUTLINE

1. Different programs are offered for restoring the Union.

2. The Radicals take control.

3. Reconstruction comes to an end.

The Union, welded in the fire of war, would henceforth be "indivisible." Never again would people talk of secession. New and formidable topics, nevertheless, were now before the country. During the period of reconstruction, which lasted for about a decade, the nation faced the following questions: On what basis would the states of the Confederacy be allowed to conduct "business as usual" with the rest of the country? What price would former Confederates have to pay in order to be full-fledged citizens again? How would the civil and political rights of freed blacks be protected? To these difficult questions there could be no easy answers.

The immediate need of the South in 1865 was simply to begin the enormous task of rebuilding. The devastation of parts of the South would remain painfully apparent for years to come. An English traveler along the Tennessee River in 1870 described what he saw: "The trail of war is visible throughout the valley in burnt-up [buildings], ruined bridges, mills and factories . . . and in large tracts of once cultivated land stripped of every vestige of fencing. The roads, long neglected, in many places have become impassable; new 'tracks' have been made through the woods and fields without much respect to boundaries." Of Charleston, another observer wrote, "Luxury, refinement [and] happiness have fled . . . and poverty is enthroned there." The task of rebuilding would challenge the South for years to come.

1 Different Programs Are Offered for Restoring the Union

The deep emotions the Civil War aroused in both Northerners and Southerners were not easily stilled. A legacy of bitterness stood in the way of restoring the South to the Union.

The sections bind up their wounds. Many white Southerners found it hard to accept the fact that their old way of life was gone. In their minds they relived the past over and over as they mourned their young men sacrificed in the "Lost Cause." Many Northerners, on the other hand, would never again view the South as anything other than the land of treason. Busy building monuments to their war dead, they were constantly reminded of the price that had been paid to save the Union. They measured the cost in dollars too — billions of them.

In the South, nevertheless, some people were once again ready to think warmly of the Union. A war prisoner, recently released by Union troops, told how gratifying it was "for our people to see a government which was lately fighting us with fire, and guns, and shell, now generously feeding our poor and distressed." He might have added that rarely before had a defeated people been treated so open-handedly by the victors. Of all the people who created the Confederacy, only a few were imprisoned — and only for a brief time. No Confederate civil official was executed, and just one military figure was put to death. He was Henry Wirtz, commander of the infamous Andersonville prison where more than 12,000 Union soldiers died.

Lincoln offers conciliation to the South. The first work of restoring the Confederate states to the Union was political. Abraham Lincoln viewed this task as a duty for the President. Using his powers as commander-in-chief, he had, on December 8, 1863,

Large parts of the South suffered enormous destruction during the Civil War. Southern farms, towns and cities, and railroads and bridges had to be rebuilt or repaired.

issued a proclamation outlining a policy of conciliation toward the South. President Lincoln maintained that since a state could not leave the Union, the southern states had never lost their place in it. They were merely not in their proper relation to the Union.

Lincoln's plan provided **amnesty,** that is, official pardon, to all Confederates who would take an oath of loyalty to the United States.[1] For a state to be restored to the Union, at least ten percent of those who had voted in 1860 would have to take that oath. Finally, when the state also accepted emancipation, its political reconstruction would be complete.

Congress seeks to control reconstruction. At the same time that Lincoln presented his "ten percent plan," many Republicans were arguing that the task of reconstruction really belonged to Congress. A number of congressmen, known as Radical Republicans, had already been harshly critical of Lincoln and his conduct of the war. For one thing, they believed that Lincoln had moved much too slowly to free the slaves. In 1861, they had established a Joint Committee on the Conduct of the War, which more and more criticized the President's policies. In 1864, at the insistence of the Radicals, Congress refused to seat representatives and senators sent by Louisiana and Arkansas, then occupied by Union troops.

Senator Charles Sumner of Massachusetts insisted that the southern states, by seceding, had "committed suicide." Other congressmen held that the states of the South were "conquered provinces," to be dealt with as Congress saw fit. The issue was, therefore, more than a dispute between the executive and legislative branches of the government. It also meant a choice between a lenient and a harsh policy toward the states that had formerly been part of the Confederacy.

---

[1] Excluded from amnesty were civil, diplomatic, and high-ranking military officers of the Confederacy, officeholders who had resigned from positions in the United States government, and anyone who had mistreated black Union troops.

Congress passes the Wade-Davis Bill. In the summer of 1864 Congress gave a preview of its plans. It passed the Wade-Davis Bill, which would have granted Congress the authority to reconstruct the South. The bill required a *majority* of the white males in each conquered state to take a loyalty oath. Then a convention would be held to write a new state constitution, one which was required to abolish slavery, disfranchise former Confederate leaders, and **repudiate,** or refuse to pay, Confederate war debts. (In order to cast ballots for delegates to the convention, voters would have to take an additional oath that they had never voluntarily taken up arms against the United States.) When all these steps had been taken, the state would finally be readmitted to the Union.

Lincoln killed the Wade-Davis Bill with a **pocket veto** — that is, he refused to sign it within ten days after Congress had adjourned, thus preventing it from becoming law. Lincoln's veto provoked an angry attack from the bill's authors, Benjamin F. Wade of Ohio and Henry Winter Davis of Maryland. Their so-called Wade-Davis Manifesto, published in the New York *Tribune,* warned the President that "if he wishes our support, he must confine himself to his executive duties . . . to suppress by arms armed rebellion, and leave political reorganization to Congress."

Republicans in Congress fear loss of power. The motives of the Republicans were varied. With the southern states out of the Union, they had been able to dominate Congress. Many of them were now convinced that the continued existence of their party — only ten years old — was at stake. If southern representatives — all Democrats — returned to Congress, the Republicans could be consistently outvoted.

The problem, however, was not merely a question of who had a majority in Congress. Republicans were also afraid that important economic measures they had enacted during the war would be in danger. They had in mind the laws establishing a national banking system, raising the tariff,

Life After Emancipation

In the years immediately following the Civil War a writer from Scotland named David Macrae traveled throughout the South, talking to people from all walks of life. He was especially interested in the former slaves and in the progress they had made since emancipation.

A reconstruction school scene

I was glad to find the condition and prospects of the emancipated slaves better than the reports led me to expect. I was often told that they are poorer now and less happy than they were in slavery.

That many of the former slaves are poorer is beyond a doubt. But this was exactly what had to be looked for at first, even by those who fought for emancipation. In any country the subversion of the whole system of labor, especially if it meant the turning adrift of four million slaves unaccustomed to provide for themselves, would necessarily involve much confusion and distress.

The distress was so great that the government had to establish a bureau for the issue of supplies to keep many of the freed blacks from starving. But I was assured by the bureau officers that things were righting themselves. Mr. E. P. Smith, with whom I visited in North Carolina, said in his report for 1870, "I have seen unmistakable signs of improvement every year, but never more evidence of industry, thrift, and general prosperity than this season. On every hand there are tokens of steady progress."

All this talk about the black people being happier in slavery I heard amongst white Southerners, but rarely if ever amongst the former slaves themselves. Many of the poorest of them told me that they had to put up with coarse food in the meantime and poorer clothing than they used to have, and that they had a hard struggle even for that; but the usual wind-up was, "But, thank the Lord, we are free."

and instituting the distribution of free land. Before the war all these policies had been blocked by southern congressmen.

Moreover, many Republicans had long been active abolitionists. They believed that the freed slaves ought to be assured freedom, justice, and opportunity. One way to achieve these ends was to obtain for blacks the right to vote. The Republicans were determined that the South not be allowed to re-establish state governments run by whites only. Blacks, most Radicals believed, must be allowed full participation in the political life of the South.

Andrew Johnson succeeds Lincoln. At the time Lincoln was assassinated, in April, 1865, no one knew whether he planned more severe measures than the ones he had announced in 1863. His successor, Andrew

Johnson, would have awesome decisions to make on his own.

Johnson, born in poverty in North Carolina, had experienced a bleak childhood. Left fatherless at the age of three, he was apprenticed to a tailor when he was fourteen. When Johnson was eighteen, he moved to Tennessee, where he started his own tailor shop. Shortly he and Eliza McCardle, the daughter of a local shoemaker, were married. She taught him to read, write, and do arithmetic.

When he began to prosper, Johnson hired a man to read to him as he worked. Often the reading matter was the Constitution of the United States, which Johnson soon knew by heart. The tailor shop became a kind of political club, whose members wanted more voice in government. Johnson became their leader, and was elected in turn alderman, mayor, and state legislator. In 1843 he was elected as a Democrat to the House of Representatives, and in 1857 he became a senator. As we have seen (page 390), when the secession crisis came, he stood by the Union.

Johnson initially follows Lincoln's plan. At first the Radicals looked upon Johnson as the answer to their needs. Even as Lincoln's body lay in state at the White House, Benjamin Wade was saying to the new President, "Johnson, we have faith in you. By the gods, there will be no trouble now in running the government!" When he heard that Johnson intended to follow a policy of conciliation, however, Wade despaired. "If we follow such leadership," he declared, "we will be in the wilderness longer than the children of Israel under Moses."

In the early months of his presidency, Johnson was satisfied that reconstruction was going along smoothly. All the former Confederate states except Texas had met the conditions first set down by Lincoln and modified only slightly by Johnson. The President sent General Grant on a fact-finding trip through the South. After a five-day inspection, Grant reported that the Southerners were accepting their defeat. He advised that the fate of blacks be left to the "thinking people of the South."

Others, including many Southerners, did not think that Grant had made an accurate report. A prominent southern newspaperman wrote, "The war feeling here is like a burning bush with a wet blanket wrapped around it. Looked at from the outside, the fire seems quenched. But just peep under the blanket and there it is, all alive, and eating, eating in."

The South faces many problems. The truth was that the South could not quickly turn itself around. Plantation owners and many farmers were trying to remake their lives without their customary resources. The suffering of white Southerners was fearful during the summer and winter after Appomattox, as malnutrition took its toll.

The freed blacks suffered hard times too. Blacks responded to freedom in different ways, depending on their circumstances. Many of them fled the fields as soon as they could, their flight lending new meaning to the spiritual "Free at last, free at last." They drifted to the cities in search of work or traveled about looking for family members who had been sold to different owners. Others stayed on the land, eventually becoming *sharecroppers.* They would lease small plots to farm, turning over a share of the harvest to the landowner, who furnished the seed, livestock, and supplies. Thousands of other ex-slaves made their way westward, like many white Southerners, in search of a new life.

The Freedmen's Bureau is established. To help the newly freed blacks realize some of the benefits of emancipation, Congress created the Freedmen's Bureau in March, 1865. The Bureau's purpose was to distribute food and clothing to needy Southerners, provide shelter when necessary, establish schools, and find jobs for both blacks and whites.

The Freedmen's Bureau undoubtedly relieved the suffering of many Southerners displaced by the war. At times its officials were able to move people from crowded areas to other places where jobs were available. The Bureau also gave some public land to freed blacks, and in several states it set up facilities to care for the ailing and aged.

One of the most important contributions of the Bureau was to arrange labor contracts between black workers and their new employers. In addition, the Bureau placed more than 250,000 black children in over 4,000 schools by 1870.

The head of the Bureau was Oliver Otis Howard, who had commanded a wing of Sherman's army during its march from Atlanta to the sea (page 391). He was an astute man and good at managing people. Many of Howard's subordinates, however, were inefficient, corrupt, and careless with public funds. Most white Southerners came to regard the Bureau as a tool of the Republican Party, engaged not in the work of relief and rehabilitation, but in bringing benefits to blacks at the expense of white Southerners.

The South passes black codes. Even as the Freedmen's Bureau did its work, there was much evidence that many people in the South were undermining its purpose. They believed that somehow the former ways of doing things could be revived. Ex-Confederate leaders were elected to high positions in the "reconstructed states" and some were even sent to Congress. Alexander Stephens, the former Confederate Vice President, was elected by Georgia to the United States Senate — which indignantly refused to seat him.

Even more troubling, southern state legislatures, beginning in Mississippi, began to pass laws known as *black codes.* Designed to control and restrict the economic and social activities of blacks, the new laws were modeled on the old slave codes (page 311). The black codes extended a number of rights to freed blacks, including the right to hold property, make contracts, and sue in court. Nevertheless, important civil rights, such as the right to serve on juries, testify in court against whites, carry arms, or organize and attend meetings without whites present were denied black people. In many states black people could be arrested and fined as vagrants if they had no visible

Following emancipation, the former slaves wanted land of their own. Instead, most southern blacks became sharecroppers, working land owned by others.

means of support, and then be hired out by local sheriffs to work until they had earned enough money to pay the fine.

Black Southerners were often physically abused for violating the black codes, and many feared for their lives. Black schools, in addition, were sometimes burned to the ground.

Congress organizes its own reconstruction program. When Congress gathered in December, 1865, the Republicans — outraged by the black codes — were in a mood to take action. The freeing of the slaves had been their proudest achievement. Immediately after the war, they had introduced into Congress what became the Thirteenth Amendment to the Constitution. Its words carried a simple message — slavery was abolished in the United States forever.

The Thirteenth Amendment, duly ratified, had gone into effect just as Congress was convening. Determined to continue their work on behalf of black Americans, the Republicans saw Johnson as a major obstacle. Their frustration mounted when, in

This cartoon shows Andrew Johnson (left) and Thaddeus Stevens (right), rivals in the debate over reconstruction policy.

February, 1866, he vetoed a bill extending the life of the Freedmen's Bureau. Johnson insisted that the Constitution did not provide for a relief agency created by the federal government. White Southerners regarded the Bureau as a painful reminder of northern conquest and punishment. Johnson apparently supported this view.

In April, 1866, Congress passed a Civil Rights Act to protect blacks from such discriminatory legislation as the black codes. The act conferred citizenship on the former slaves, and declared that blacks were entitled to enjoy the same "full and equal benefit of all laws and proceedings for the security of person and property, as is enjoyed by white citizens." Johnson vetoed the bill. He argued that the granting of citizenship was up to the states, not the federal government. When Congress promptly passed the bill over his veto, a struggle was on between the President and Congress.

Leaders in Congress oppose Johnson's policies. Johnson's opponents were men of strong will, like himself. One of the leaders was Representative Thaddeus Stevens of Pennsylvania, a stern man of 74. Stevens owned an iron factory that had been damaged in the Battle of Gettysburg — a fact his enemies said made him especially angry at the South.

Stevens earnestly supported the equality of the races. "This is not a white man's government," he declared in a notable address. "This is a man's government; the government of all men alike." Stevens, furthermore, did not believe that freed blacks who talked of starting their own farms were only daydreaming. He insisted that unless freed blacks received help to make a living, freedom would be a useless prize. He proposed that the estates of the leading rebels be confiscated and a portion of the acreage distributed to the freed slaves. The remainder of the land, he suggested, should be sold in order to pay off the national debt incurred in fighting the war.

Two other important Radical leaders were Charles Sumner and Benjamin Wade. Stiff in manner, Sumner was a man who carried an air of superiority. Idealistic and incorruptible, he had as a young man delivered a fervent speech against war as a means of solving international disputes. Many of Sumner's opponents charged that his fierce support of justice for black people was in revenge for the beating he had received in the Senate in 1856 (page 355). Sumner believed sincerely, however, that the freed slaves must be able to take part in the government of the states in which they lived.

Ben Wade of Ohio, co-author of the Wade-Davis Bill, had long been an antislavery advocate. Now he was *president pro tem* of the Senate. Under the law then in effect he would become President if Johnson should die.

The Fourteenth Amendment is adopted. The confrontation between these figures and their colleagues, on the one hand, and the President, on the other hand, made 1866 the "critical year" of reconstruction. As the months passed, the break between Congress and the President widened. To make sure that the federal action regarding citizenship was constitutional, Congress passed the Fourteenth Amendment. In unmistakable language the amendment defined American citizenship for the first time: "All persons born or naturalized in the United States . . . are citizens of the United States and of the state wherein they reside." These words opened citizenship to all ex-slaves.

Another section of the amendment declared a penalty for any state denying suffrage to male adult citizens. The penalty would be a reduction in its representation in Congress. The Fourteenth Amendment also provided that former Confederate leaders could not hold office again unless pardoned by Congress. Yet another section of the amendment declared the Confederate debt invalid and forbade compensation to Southerners for the loss of their slaves.

The Fourteenth Amendment was submitted to the states for ratification. President Johnson, however, let it be known that he hoped the measure would be turned down. All of the former Confederate states followed his advice, except Tennessee, which ratified the amendment. Tennessee was readmitted to the Union.

When the Fourteenth Amendment failed (Kentucky and Delaware joined ten other states in opposing it), the halls of Congress rang with indignation. The blame was laid squarely on Johnson. One Radical predicted what lay ahead for the South: "They would not cooperate with us in rebuilding what they destroyed. We must remove the rubbish and rebuild from the bottom." The Radicals resolved to proceed on their own, ignoring the President and his views, and attacking him at will.

SECTION REVIEW

1. Vocabulary: *amnesty, repudiate, pocket veto, sharecropper, black codes.*
2. (a) What were the requirements for a state to be restored to the Union under President Lincoln's plan? (b) How did the Wade-Davis Bill differ from Lincoln's plan?
3. (a) What was Andrew Johnson's attitude toward reconstruction? (b) Why did it anger the Radical Republicans?
4. (a) What problems did the South face after the Civil War? (b) Why was the Freedmen's Bureau set up? (c) How was it regarded by most white Southerners?
5. (a) Why did southern state legislatures pass black codes? (b) What was the reaction of Congress?
6. What were the chief provisions of the Fourteenth Amendment?

2 The Radicals Take Control

To prepare for the congressional and state elections of 1866, a new Union Party, made up of Johnson's supporters, held a convention in Philadelphia. More Democrats than Republicans attended, among them many former Confederates.

The Republicans campaign aggressively. In the ensuing campaign, the Radicals continually reminded manufacturers and investors that their interests could be hurt if southern Democrats returned to Congress quickly. The Radicals also appealed to patriotism, repeating over and over that the Republican Party was the party that had saved the Union.

Johnson did not serve himself well with a speaking tour that brought him into the Midwest late in August. He called the eighteen-day journey, undertaken to defend his views, a "swing around the circle." Accompanying him, among other dignitaries, were General Grant and Admiral Farragut. Most of Johnson's speeches were of a rabble-rousing type that many people regarded as unworthy of a President of the United States. At some of the meetings hecklers, sympathetic to the Radicals, goaded him into making tactless and ill-tempered remarks. In Indianapolis a confrontation led to a riot in which one man was killed.

The Radicals, meanwhile, gained support from people who were outraged when white mobs in New Orleans killed or wounded hundreds of blacks in the spring and summer of 1866. In the North, Johnson and his policies were blamed for the shameful violence.

In the elections the Radical Republicans won sweeping victories. Every northern state chose a Republican governor. Moreover, in the House and Senate Johnson's opponents could now muster the two-thirds vote they might need to override his vetoes of their bills. The Republicans were ready to take over the work of reconstruction.

The Republicans enact their program. In March, 1867, the Radicals passed over Johnson's veto a series of bills that contained their plan of reconstruction (which came to be known as the Congressional Plan). Under the Reconstruction Act of 1867 the South was divided into five military districts, each with its own military commander. These commanders were under instructions to prepare the states in their districts for self-government by enrolling all male voters, including blacks. A state would be ready for readmission to the Union when it had taken several steps. First, a convention in each state would have to draw up a new constitution, ratified by the voters, that would create a state government acceptable to Congress. Second, the state legislature would have to ratify the Fourteenth Amendment. Even then a state would not automatically be readmitted. It would have

to wait until a sufficient number of states had ratified the Fourteenth Amendment to put it into effect. This provision was included in order to guarantee that blacks would not be denied suffrage by any state.

By the end of 1868 seven states — Alabama, Arkansas, Florida, Georgia, Louisiana, North Carolina, and South Carolina — had taken the steps required by the Reconstruction Act of 1867. Since this meant that the Fourteenth Amendment had been ratified, the states were readmitted to the Union. Virginia, Texas, and Mississippi still remained unreconstructed.

Congress confronts Johnson. Despite the passage of the Reconstruction Act, President Johnson still had vast power as commander-in-chief to block the Radicals' plans. As a result, a hostile Congress sought to reduce his ability to influence or control policy. In March, 1867, on the same day that the Radicals pushed through the Reconstruction Act, Congress also enacted two laws that severely reduced the powers of the President.

The first of these laws was the Tenure of Office Act. It provided that the Senate's consent would be required to remove from office any official whose appointment had originally been approved by the Senate. The purpose of the law was to prevent President Johnson from dismissing Secretary of War Edwin M. Stanton, a holdover from Lincoln's Cabinet, who was widely regarded as a Radical.

The second law passed by Congress was the Command of the Army Act, which was intended to reduce Johnson's power as commander-in-chief. It provided that the President could issue military orders through one person only, the general in charge of the army (in this case, General Grant). Grant had earlier approved a lenient reconstruction program. Now, appalled by the violence against blacks, he had become sympathetic to the Radicals.

The Radicals warned Johnson that they would watch him carefully to see that he carried out their reconstruction policies. He complied by appointing sympathizers of congressional policies to command the military districts in the South. Still, Johnson believed the Radical program to be unconstitutional, because it had been passed without the South being represented in Congress.

When Congress adjourned in the summer of 1867, Johnson decided to test the constitutionality of the Tenure of Office Act by asking Stanton to resign. When Stanton refused, Johnson suspended him and put Grant in his place. The Senate, convening again in December, refused to consent to Stanton's suspension. Grant, furthermore, immediately stepped aside, not wishing to be caught in a struggle between the President and Congress. He was already being mentioned as a candidate for President in 1868, and did not wish to be at the center of a storm that could damage his chances.

Frustrated, the President appointed another general, Lorenzo Thomas, to be Secretary of War. Stanton, however, also had his eye on the presidency and needed Radical support. He would not resign to allow Thomas to take office.

Congress impeaches President Johnson. The Radicals at last had a clear opening to attack the President. They had already placed restrictions on his powers, but now they were determined to remove him from office. Led by Thaddeus Stevens, the House impeached Johnson for "high crimes and misdemeanors."

Most of the charges dealt with Johnson's efforts to remove Stanton. The President was also accused of attempting "to bring into disgrace, ridicule, hatred, contempt, and reproach the Congress of the United States. . . ." This portion of the indictment was the work of Ben Butler (page 375), now a representative recently elected from Massachusetts. The supporting evidence for the charge consisted of extensive quotations from Johnson's speeches on his "swing around the circle."

The impeachment trial opened in the Senate on March 13, 1868, with Chief Justice Salmon P. Chase presiding. Stevens, so ill that he had to be carried into the chamber, was a dramatic figure as he leaned

Tickets were issued for Andrew Johnson's impeachment trial, which lasted from March 13 to May 26, 1868.

hard upon his cane. All his pent-up feelings were expressed in the words he addressed to Johnson, who was not present: "Unfortunate, unhappy man, behold your doom."

Among the newspaper reporters in the Senate gallery was a young Frenchman, Georges Clemenceau, destined one day to be the leader of France. The British author Charles Dickens, in Washington for a public appearance, wrote his friends that he was attentively following the convulsions of the republic.

The trial was an ordeal for the nation. Hanging in the balance was the nature of the American government. Was the President to be turned into a puppet who could be manipulated by Congress? Some people believed that if Johnson were removed from office, the United States would have a dictatorship run by Congress.

Johnson is acquitted. The Radicals in the Senate, confident of the outcome, were unprepared for the tense drama of the roll call when the vote to convict the President was taken. For weeks they had hounded fellow senators to line up support for removal. Nevertheless, at the final vote the Radicals were one short of the two-thirds majority needed to remove the President.

Seven of the "not guilty" votes came from Republicans. Heavy pressure was put on Edmund Ross, a Republican senator from Kansas. Ross often escaped the angry debate by taking refuge in a tiny room in the Capitol where Vinnie Ream, a young sculptor, was working on a bust of Lincoln. Vinnie Ream greatly admired President

A number of black leaders were elected to Congress during reconstruction. Here, Robert B. Elliot of South Carolina addresses the House of Representatives in 1874.

Johnson and often spoke of him to Ross. The Radicals tried very hard, without success, to get her to persuade Ross to change his mind. Yet Ross stood his ground, even though he knew he probably was committing political suicide. He later said of the moment when he voted, "I almost literally looked down into my open grave."

As tempers cooled, many of the Radicals were relieved that they had not removed the President after all. They had come to the conclusion that Benjamin Wade (page 403) might not have made a good President; nor would Wade's intended choice, Ben Butler, have made a good Secretary of State. None of the senators who had voted to acquit Johnson was re-elected. When Johnson's term as President was over, however, the voters of Tennessee returned him to Washington as senator.

Many blacks serve in government. Between 1868 and 1877, when the reconstruction governments were brought to an end, a number of blacks were elected to office in the South. Sixteen blacks at various times served in Congress — fourteen in the House (six from South Carolina) and two,

both from Mississippi, in the Senate. The senators were Hiram R. Revels and Blanche K. Bruce. Revels, born in North Carolina, had graduated from Knox College in Illinois. A minister, he served during the war as chaplain of a black regiment. The seat he won in the Senate in 1871 had last been held by Jefferson Davis.

Blanche Bruce was the outstanding black politician of his time. Bruce, who had escaped from slavery in Virginia, attended Oberlin College in Ohio and later became a successful planter in Mississippi. As a senator he offered a number of bills affecting black rights. He also devoted himself to other issues, including the treatment of Indians and government policy toward Chinese immigrants.

The black official who held the highest office in the South was Pinckney B. S. Pinchback. He served for a brief period as acting governor of Louisiana.

Reconstruction governments come under attack. The reconstruction governments were the target of much criticism. Stories of corruption and extravagance were widespread. In Florida in 1869, for example, the cost of government printing was said to be higher than the entire state budget in the last year before the war. In Louisiana the governor said simply, "Corruption [down here] is the fashion."

The dishonesty of many politicians in the South was much like what could be found throughout the country at that time. Part of the explanation lay in the general letdown of public morality after the war. In addition, state and local governments everywhere in the country were commencing new projects — building schools, roads, and other facilities. Some of this activity represented an effort to meet public needs that had been ignored for too long. Some of it grew out of new functions being taken on by governments, including the running of hospitals, orphanages, and asylums. The letting of construction contracts for the unprecedented number of new public buildings opened the way for bribery and other crooked dealings. These abuses were not confined to state governments. In the major cities of the North, millions of dollars of the taxpayers' money were embezzled during the postwar period.

The reconstruction governments shared, then, in the generally lower standard of official conduct. Some of them, furthermore, were saddled with responsibilities requiring heavy expenditures. Practically the entire South had to rebuild its physical facilities as a first step in reviving its economy. Eager to encourage industry, Southerners had to repair or reconstruct railroads. Schools had to be built and staffed — for white children as well as black. In 1868 South Carolina had about 30,000 pupils. Eight years later the enrollment was more than 120,000. The cost of building schools in the South was greater than elsewhere because the section had two systems, one for blacks and one for whites. During the reconstruction years, only Louisiana and South Carolina forbade segregated school facilities.

Carpetbaggers and scalawags participate in government. Most officeholders in the Radical state governments were white, including a good number who came from the North. The Northerners were called, with distaste, carpetbaggers, suggesting that they carried everything they owned in bags fashioned from carpeting, the style of the day. In fact, most of the carpetbaggers had arrived before 1867. They had come at a time when political careers were as yet far from their minds. Many were Union army officers who had stayed on after the war because they liked the climate or saw opportunity ahead. Others were teachers or ministers or workers in the Freedmen's Bureau. It is estimated that about two thirds of the carpetbaggers were trained as lawyers, doctors, or engineers.

The carpetbaggers brought far more than satchels to the South. Some brought capital to invest in new factories, railroads, and other businesses. They worked to help the South to recover physically and to modernize at the same time. Because they had arrived at an advantageous moment for themselves, however, and because of their alliance with blacks, they were often bitterly denounced.

Another group of whites making common cause with blacks in government were Southerners called scalawags. The word *scalawag* originally meant a rascal or a "no-good." Some of the scalawags may have been seeking personal advancement too, especially a chance to get rich quickly. Nevertheless, many of them were people who had remained loyal to the Union or who now recognized the new conditions and hoped to encourage cooperation with the North. One of the best-known scalawags was James Longstreet, the Confederate general who had been a southern hero at the First Battle of Bull Run and later commander of one of Lee's corps at Gettysburg. After surrendering at Appomattox, Longstreet went to New Orleans, where he founded an insurance business and became a partner in a cotton-trading firm. He joined the Republican Party because of his conviction that the Radicals' terms for peace had to be accepted.

Secret organizations oppose reconstruction policies. Opposition in the South to Radical policies was keen. Sometimes it was secret; sometimes it was out in the open. Whites

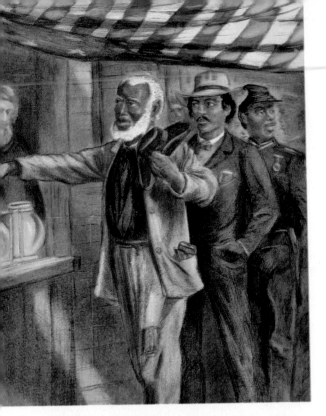

The promise of protecting black voting rights was not fulfilled. By a variety of means, the Ku Klux Klan and other terrorist groups eventually succeeded in keeping black voters from going to the polls.

who took part in the reconstruction governments were often jeered, even by neighbors and old friends. Beginning in 1867, thousands of white Southerners began to band together to frighten and bring pressure on black voters and officeholders — and their white supporters. The best known of the antiblack organizations was the Ku Klux Klan. The head of the Klan, its "Grand Wizard," was Nathan Bedford Forrest, a Confederate army hero. The Klan carried out a campaign of terror against blacks who did not "know their place." Its methods included tarring and feathering, beating, and murder — usually by hanging. The Klan also attacked Republican political leaders and white teachers in black schools.

The Fifteenth Amendment is ratified. The rise of the Klan and other groups in the South resulted in further efforts to protect black voting rights. Congress, in February, 1869, proposed another amendment to the Constitution. The Fifteenth Amendment,

ratified in 1870, provided that suffrage could not be denied because of "race, color, or previous condition of servitude." Congress added approval of this amendment to the list of steps that states now had to take to rejoin the Union. Mississippi, Texas, and Virginia were finally brought back into the Union in 1870, after complying with the new requirement. Georgia, readmitted earlier but then expelled for evicting blacks from its state legislature, also had to ratify this amendment to gain readmission.

In 1870 and 1871 Congress passed the Ku Klux Klan acts. These laws provided severe penalties for violations of the Fourteenth and Fifteenth amendments. The President was authorized to introduce martial law where the rights of blacks were considered endangered. Federal courts, moreover, rather than state courts, were given jurisdiction over cases arising under this legislation.

Within a short time the Klan and other such groups had been crippled by federal action. The Klan was later succeeded by semimilitary organizations known variously as White Leagues, Red Shirts, or by other names. Armed, and insisting they were only enforcing law and order, they succeeded in keeping black voters from the polls. Meanwhile, as more white voters regained the vote, white control in the South was being re-established.

SECTION REVIEW

1. (a) What were the results of the 1866 congressional elections? (b) What steps did the new Congress take in working out a plan of reconstruction?
2. (a) What steps did Congress take to prevent Johnson from carrying out his policies? (b) What was the outcome of the impeachment movement?
3. (a) What different groups held power in the reconstruction state governments? (b) What were the main challenges facing those governments?
4. Why did Congress propose the Fifteenth Amendment?
5. (a) Why were secret organizations, such as the Ku Klux Klan, formed in the South? (b) How did Congress try to stop them?

3 Reconstruction Comes to an End

As the 1868 presidential election approached, the Radicals were busy drumming up support for General Grant. Although he had made no public statements about the impeachment proceedings, Grant privately had supported President Johnson's removal. Regardless, Grant was the great man of the American republic, whose heroic deeds had kept all the states in the Union, all the stars in the flag.

GRANT AS PRESIDENT

The Republicans nominate Grant. The Republican convention met in Chicago, in Grant's home state. Grant easily won the nomination on the first ballot. His running mate was the Speaker of the House, Schuyler Colfax of Indiana, whose grandfather had been Washington's bodyguard during the Revolution. In his written statement accepting the nomination, Grant said, "Let us have peace" — words that reflected the same generosity he had shown General Lee. The Republican Party, however, was still belligerent and it quickly created a slogan to elect its hero: "Vote as you shot."

The Democrats selected as their candidate Horatio Seymour, twice governor of New York. Seymour tried to refuse the nomination, knowing that against Grant he had no chance. Finally, on the twenty-second ballot "the great decliner," as he was ever after called, reluctantly accepted.

Grant wins the presidency in 1868. During the campaign, the Republicans painted the Democrats as traitors who had brought on the Civil War and who, even now, were working to undo its results. (This style of campaigning, known as "waving the bloody shirt," persisted for many years.) The election outcome was as Seymour had anticipated. The most revered military figure since Jackson, Grant automatically brought to people's minds the Battle of Shiloh and the northern triumphs at Vicksburg and Appomattox. The Grand Army of the Republic, a powerful organization of Union veterans, gave Grant its complete support.

As the votes were being counted in November, Grant received the returns at a friend's house in Galena, Illinois. In the tradition of the times no women were present, and Julia Grant waited at home with the children, eager to hear the results. Although Grant's victory in the electoral college was overwhelming, his popular margin was only about 300,000 votes. His victory was assured by the 700,000 black voters in the South who went to the polls for the first time.

New figures emerge in Congress. Even as Grant was moving into the White House, a new group was rising to power in the Republican Party. These politicians opposed reform and reformers. Many of them were northern political bosses, commonly called spoilsmen. This was a word of contempt, used to describe politicians who believed that public office need not be conducted for the public good but could be treated rather as spoils of war. Some of the spoilsmen were in the pay of the new oil, coal, and iron interests, whose leaders hoped to arrange legislation to their liking. The spoilsmen were soon able to dominate the Republican Party because Grant seemed unwilling to oppose them.

Among the leading spoilsmen in Congress were Senators Oliver P. Morton of Indiana and Roscoe Conkling of New York. Morton had been wartime governor of his state, and had now become a master of "waving the bloody shirt." He exercised strong influence on Grant, frequently conferring with him alone in the White House. Conkling, a good talker, had close ties to powerful business interests in New York. He, too, became a close friend of the President, and Grant allowed him control of all federal appointments in that state.

Scandals erupt during Grant's first term. Grant's administration was stained by the low public standards of the day. Two scandals in Grant's first term offered a preview of things to come. In 1869 two unscrupu-

As President, Ulysses S. Grant showed few of the qualities of leadership that had distinguished him as commander of the Union armies.

lous speculators, Jay Gould and Jim Fisk, decided to corner, or monopolize, the market for gold. They schemed to buy up all the gold they could, and then make a huge profit by selling it at a high price. Fisk and Gould, through Grant's brother-in-law, gained access to the President. Their purpose was to convince him that it would be bad for the country if the Treasury Department sold gold, as it always had done from time to time. Grant, who was awed by rich people, at first seemed to go along with Fisk and Gould. When rumors reached the public that the Treasury had blocked further gold sales, its price went higher and higher. Grant, finally realizing that he had been made to seem a fool, ordered the Treasury to sell gold. Fisk and Gould no longer had a corner on the market. The price of gold dropped suddenly, causing a financial panic on September 24, 1869, a day since remembered as "Black Friday."

Another scandal, one that began before Grant became President, came to public at-

tention during his administration. The misdeeds occurred in the building of the first transcontinental railroad. The Union Pacific had chartered a company, the Crédit Mobilier, to do the actual work of constructing the railroad. Crédit Mobilier was owned by a small group of Union Pacific stockholders. Their purpose was to cheat the rest of the stockholders in that railroad company. The swindling company charged the line $73 million for work costing only $50 million.

To obtain favors from influential politicians, Crédit Mobilier sold them stock at ridiculously low prices. An investigation later showed that both Republicans and Democrats were involved, including Vice President Colfax and eight congressmen.

Corruption was extensive in state and local governments too. In New York City, for example, the Tweed Ring, headed by the political boss William Marcy Tweed, embezzled tens of millions of dollars of public funds through faked leases, padded bills, and kickbacks. Tweed was arrested and convicted in the fall of 1872.

Grant wins a second term. By 1872 a reaction to the scandals of Grant's administration was setting in. Grant's achievements as President were few, although he could take credit for the Treaty of Washington in 1871, which settled the *Alabama* claims (page 388). Meanwhile, a group of dissident Republicans and other foes of corruption in high places formed the Liberal Republican Party. Many leading journalists and several former members of Lincoln's Cabinet were prominent in the new party.

As their candidate for President the Liberal Republicans nominated Horace Greeley, the eccentric editor of the *New York Tribune*. Greeley was a flamboyant man who, over the years, had taken up many fads and attracted many enemies. The Democrats, afraid that a third candidate would guarantee the election of Grant, nominated Greeley too. In the campaign Greeley was attacked so hard that he later said, "I hardly knew whether I was running for the presidency or the penitentiary." Grant was reelected handily.

Grant's second term is a disappointment.
Shortly after Grant's second inauguration, the Panic of 1873 broke upon the country. The direct cause seemed to be the failure of the banking house of Jay Cooke and Company. Yet the Panic was really the result of excessive speculation and overexpansion, currency inflation, government waste, and an adverse trade balance. The unemployment resulting from the Panic caused much suffering throughout the nation.

Grant's second term, moreover, was tarnished by continued misbehavior and scandal. In the so-called Salary Grab Act of 1873, Congress retroactively doubled the pay of the President and raised that of congressmen by 50 percent. The Whiskey Ring, finally broken up in 1875, was a conspiracy of internal-revenue collectors and distillers. It had been formed for the purpose of cheating the government out of tax money in St. Louis, Chicago, and Milwaukee. Among the 238 people indicted was General Orville E. Babcock, Grant's private secretary. The following year the Secretary of War, William W. Belknap, was impeached for accepting bribes in connection with assigning trading posts in the Indian Territory.

RISE OF THE "NEW SOUTH"

Reconstruction ends. The era of reconstruction was gradually coming to an end. In many places it was over by 1872. A law passed that year gave amnesty to almost all former Confederates, allowing them to vote and to hold public office. At the same time, Congress allowed the Freedmen's Bureau to go out of existence.

A number of factors explain this change in Congress's attitude. First, the Radical leaders were leaving the scene. Stevens had died in 1868. Within a few years, Stanton and Chase were gone too. Charles Sumner died in 1874, his power by then having been broken in a struggle with Grant. Second, the abolitionists and others who hoped to improve the condition of black Americans had simply run out of steam. By the 1870's, the friends of blacks had exhausted themselves in the struggle. Third, many northern businessmen, eager to invest money in the enterprises the South needed so badly, regarded the reconstruction governments as unreliable.

Southerners recognize the need for industry.
As reconstruction came to an end, many Southerners realized that substantial economic change was needed for their region to compete with the North. Once dependent almost entirely on the growing of cotton, the South was desperately in need of a more diverse economy.

The South was rich in natural resources and had a large work force. The one element lacking was the money to finance the development of new factories. Once arrangements were made with northern bankers for funding, many southern businessmen quickly went to work.

The new industries that appeared in the South were usually tied to agriculture. Although many of the larger plantations had been broken up and sold to smaller farmers, the growing of cotton and tobacco remained the dominant occupation in the South. By the mid-1870's, cotton production equaled the prewar level of four million bales per year. Instead of shipping the raw cotton to the North or to Europe for processing, however, textile mills were now set up all over the South. In addition to textiles, a large industry developed around the processing of cottonseed oil, which was used in the manufacture of soap and cosmetics. The tobacco industry also made great strides, particularly in North Carolina through the initiative of James B. Duke.

In addition to industries based on agriculture, modern steel and iron plants were developed in the South. The availability of coal and iron ore in Alabama made steel production cheaper in that state than in Pennsylvania. So many steel and iron factories were built around Birmingham, Alabama, that soon it was being called the "Pittsburgh of the South."

Industry brings changes to southern life. Although most Southerners continued to live in rural areas, the growth of industry encouraged people to move to towns and cities. Older cities, including Nashville, New Orleans, Atlanta, and Savannah, grew in size; small villages, at the same time, became towns. Many of the towns, especially those built around textile mills, were known as "mill towns." Factory workers in these communities lived in company-owned houses and depended on company stores for most of their needs. The majority of the factory jobs were held by whites, since there was a conscious effort to keep black workers out of the mills.

Throughout the last quarter of the nineteenth century, the South made continued progress toward a more balanced economy. In the 1880's Henry Grady, editor of the Atlanta *Constitution*, coined a term to describe the changes taking place in the postwar South. He wrote about a "New South" emerging from the ashes of the Civil War.

A DISPUTED ELECTION

Hayes faces Tilden in 1876. The Democrats were confident they could win the presidency in the election of 1876. White rule was returning in the southern states,

In this cartoon, published during the 1876 presidential campaign, the Republican elephant tramples on the Democratic tiger.

and the unstable economic times and political scandals had lessened the appeal of Republicans.

The Democrats chose as their candidate Samuel J. Tilden, a reform governor of New York. Painfully shy, Tilden was known as "Whispering Sammy." He is said to have coined the phrase "See you later," to postpone making decisions. Tilden's fame rested on his role in smashing the Tweed Ring (page 410).

At their convention in Cincinnati, the Republicans nominated Rutherford B. Hayes, the governor of Ohio. Hayes had an outstanding war record and was known as an ardent reformer. But Henry Adams, the Harvard historian and a grandson of John Quincy Adams, wrote of Hayes, "A third-rate nonentity, whose only recommendation is that he is obnoxious to no one." Still, Hayes was a decent man. His wife was a temperance supporter. Although politicians snidely called her "Lemonade Lucy," the public saw the Hayeses as more satisfactory than the Grants, at whose table it was rumored — falsely — that too much alcohol was poured.

An election deadlock arises. The election returns reflected the fact that black voters had been kept away from the polls in the South, and that the Democrats throughout the region had returned to power. Tilden received 4,300,590 popular votes to 4,036,298 for Hayes. In the electoral college, however, where a total of 185 votes was required for victory, Tilden had 184 votes. In dispute were 20 votes, 19 of them in South Carolina, Florida, and Louisiana, states still under Radical governments in 1876.[2] In each of the three states there were rival boards of election officials — one Democratic, the other Republican. Both boards reported returns in each state. The Democratic boards declared that Tilden had won. The Republican boards named Hayes the winner.

The Constitution offered no guide for such a situation. To complicate matters, the

---

[2] A single disputed vote from Oregon was quickly settled in favor of Hayes.

Senate was dominated by Republicans and the House by Democrats. Only delicate diplomacy would break the deadlock.

Hayes is elected President. Congress appointed an Electoral Commission, consisting of seven Democrats and seven Republicans, to decide the election. The fifteenth member — who, it was assumed, would have to cast the deciding vote — was expected to be David Davis, a Supreme Court justice. Davis was thought to be as impartial as anyone could be. At the last moment, however, he accepted an appointment as senator from Illinois. Davis was replaced on the Commission by another Supreme Court justice, Joseph P. Bradley, a Republican from New Jersey. By a vote of 8 to 7, the Commission gave Hayes the disputed votes, allowing him to carry the electoral college by 185 to 184. A few weeks later Hayes took office. Democrats hooted from the sidelines, calling Hayes "Old 8 to 7" or simply "His Fraudulency."

Behind the scenes a bargain had been struck in order to bring about a peaceful end to the dispute. Called the Compromise of 1877, the deal consisted of a series of "understandings." In return for their acceptance of the Electoral Commission's verdict, Southerners were promised that all federal troops would finally be withdrawn from their section. The new President, in addition, promised to appoint a Southerner to the Cabinet and to make money available for railroad construction in the South.

Reconstruction had now come to a formal end. For the first time in a generation, peace existed between the North and the South. The ex-slaves, however, would have to fend for themselves. By 1889 Henry Grady reported, "The Negro as a political force has dropped out of serious consideration." Still, the Fourteenth and Fifteenth amendments were lasting results of Radical reconstruction. One day they would take on their full meaning.

———

The nation celebrated its one-hundredth anniversary in 1876. The Centennial Exposition at Philadelphia became an attraction for tourists from around the world. Presi-

Freedom's Torch, part of the Statue of Liberty, was shown at the Centennial Exposition at Philadelphia before the statue was erected in New York harbor.

dent Grant, after visiting the exhibits, proposed that they be brought to Washington and installed permanently in buildings there. Americans were especially delighted with the most powerful machine of the day, the Corliss Engine, being shown for the first time. Also on exhibition, and drawing huge crowds, was the gigantic upraised hand and torch of the Statue of Liberty (the body of which was still being constructed in France). The immense power of machines and the unmatchable spirit of liberty so dramatically revealed in these displays became symbols of America in the minds of people throughout the world.

SECTION REVIEW

1. (a) Who was elected President in 1868? (b) Who were the spoilsmen? (c) Why were they able to dominate the new President?
2. (a) What was "Black Friday"? (b) The Crédit Mobilier scandal?
3. (a) Why was the Liberal Republican Party formed in 1872? (b) What success did it have?
4. What kinds of industry were developed in the South after the Civil War?
5. (a) Why did the Democrats think they would win the presidency in 1876? (b) Why did they fail to win it? (c) What concessions to the South helped settle the election dispute?

413

Chapter 17 Review

Summary

During the Civil War, Abraham Lincoln had outlined a policy of conciliation to permit the former Confederates to rebuild their state and local governments. Congress, however, thought *it* should have the authority to plan a policy of reconstruction. After Lincoln's assassination there was continual tension between President Johnson, who supported Lincoln's moderate program, and the Radical Republicans in Congress, who demanded a harsher policy. The Republicans sought to aid the freed blacks, to punish white Southerners, and to keep power in the hands of their party.

Following the war, the South faced many problems as the people — whites and blacks alike — started to rebuild their lives. To help, Congress created the Freedmen's Bureau, which distributed food, provided jobs, and set up schools. White Southerners, viewing the Bureau as a tool of northern Republicans, responded by enacting black codes, which severely restricted the activities of the newly freed black people.

Congress convened in December, 1865, and proposed the Fourteenth Amendment to the Constitution, aimed at assuring citizenship to all black Americans. The Radicals, led by Charles Sumner and Thaddeus Stevens, continued to oppose Johnson and his policies. Congress finally impeached the President, but his trial, in March, 1868, brought acquittal.

The Radicals had been able to enact their own reconstruction program in March, 1867. They created five military districts in the South and specified strict requirements for states to be readmitted to the Union. Meanwhile, reconstruction governments were set up in the South. Many northern whites, or carpetbaggers, and southern whites, or scalawags, served alongside blacks in these reconstruction governments. Most white Southerners opposed these state governments, and secret organizations came into existence to prevent blacks from voting. In response Congress proposed the Fifteenth Amendment, intended to assure black men the right to vote.

In 1868 the Republicans actively "waved the bloody shirt" during the presidential campaign, and secured the election of the Civil War hero, Ulysses S. Grant. President Grant served for two terms that were marked by corruption, scandal, and worsening economic conditions.

By 1876 the Democrats saw a chance to recapture the White House. The contest between Rutherford B. Hayes and Samuel J. Tilden ended in a disputed vote in the electoral college. Hayes, the Republican, was finally able to obtain sufficient votes, but only after concessions had been made to the South formally ending the era of reconstruction.

Vocabulary and Important Terms

1. amnesty
2. "ten percent plan"
3. Radical Republicans
4. Wade-Davis Bill
5. repudiate
6. pocket veto
7. sharecropper
8. Freedmen's Bureau
9. black codes
10. Thirteenth Amendment
11. Civil Rights Act of 1866
12. Fourteenth Amendment
13. Reconstruction Act of 1867
14. impeach
15. carpetbagger
16. scalawag
17. Ku Klux Klan
18. Fifteenth Amendment
19. spoilsman
20. Tweed Ring
21. Crédit Mobilier
22. "New South"
23. Compromise of 1877

Discussion Questions

1. (a) What did Abraham Lincoln say was the status of the states that had seceded from the Union? (b) What was the view of Charles Sumner and other northern congressmen? (c) Why was this difference in viewpoints important?

2. (a) For what reasons did the Republicans in Congress want to control the terms under which southern states could rejoin the Union? (b) What evidence was there that many white Southerners wanted to return to the old prewar days?

3. (a) Why has 1866 been called the "critical year" of reconstruction? (b) What effect did the elections of 1866 have on the question of who would control reconstruction?

4. (a) In what ways did Congress try to ensure that blacks would be able to participate fully in the political life of the South? (b) How did blacks take part in reconstruction? (c) How did black voters affect the outcome of the presidential election of 1868?

5. (a) Why did the Radical Republicans blame Andrew Johnson for the initial failure of the Fourteenth Amendment to secure ratification? (b) How did Congress try to reduce Johnson's power?

6. (a) For what reasons did the House impeach Andrew Johnson? (b) How close did the Senate come to removing the President? (c) Why were many of the Radicals relieved that they had not removed the President after all?

7. What factors help explain the abuses in government in the period after the Civil War?

8. (a) Why had the congressional attitude toward reconstruction changed by the early 1870's? (b) How did reconstruction come to a formal end?

Relating Past to Present

Southern industry first began to take hold in the reconstruction period. What important industries are found in the South today? To what extent has southern agriculture remained important?

Studying Local History

1. Find out about the role, if any, that political leaders from your state played during reconstruction. Try to find out, for example, how your state's senators voted at the impeachment trial of Andrew Johnson.

2. If your state was a Confederate state, under what conditions and circumstances was it readmitted to the Union?

Using History Skills

1. *Reading source material.* Study David Macrae's description of the South on page 399. (a) What, according to Macrae, were the reasons for the poverty of black Southerners? (b) What different views did he hear on the subject of emancipation? (c) What might account for those differences?

2. *Classifying.* Make a chart with two columns. In one column list the accomplishments of Radical reconstruction policy and of reconstruction governments in the South. In the other column write the shortcomings or failures of reconstruction.

3. *Writing a report.* The Radical Republicans, in addition to trying to remove President Johnson from office, sought to reduce the Supreme Court's ability to influence reconstruction policy. Use an encyclopedia or books on the reconstruction period to find out how the Radicals tried to limit the power of the Supreme Court. Also find out how the Radicals made it impossible for Andrew Johnson to appoint anyone to the Court. Write a report based on the information you find.

WORLD SCENE

Unification

While the North and the South were reuniting after the American Civil War, other nations were achieving unification for the first time.

German unification. In the peace agreement of 1815 settling the Napoleonic Wars, a loose confederation of 38 German states had been created. It was dominated in the north by Prussia and in the south by Austria. The conquest of Germany by Napoleon had, however, awakened a sense of national spirit among the German people. In 1848 revolts aimed at unifying the states erupted throughout the German confederation. These nationalist revolts were put down, but in 1862 the cause was taken up again by the new prime minister of Prussia, Otto von Bismarck.

Bismarck was a crafty and aggressive leader who believed that only war — "blood and iron," he called it — would unite the Germans. His well-trained Prussian army crushed Austria in 1866 and then turned its sights on France. In 1870 Bismarck used an alleged insult to the Prussian king by the French ambassador to arouse nationalist feelings among the Germans. He thereupon declared war on France.

The war ended in victory for Bismarck and Prussia. Shortly afterward the German states were united into one nation and the Prussian king, Wilhelm I, was crowned its emperor.

The unification of Italy. For years, many Italian people looked forward to ridding the Italian peninsula of the foreign powers that dominated it. A leader in the struggle to unite the Italian states was Giuseppe Garibaldi. To avoid arrest in 1834 for revolutionary activities, Garibaldi escaped to South America and joined the fight for freedom in Brazil and Uruguay.

In 1848, when revolutions swept Europe, Garibaldi returned home to Sardinia and helped set up an Italian republic. Independence was short-lived, however, when France and Austria sent troops to re-establish control. This time Garibaldi fled to the United States. He worked for a time as a candle-maker in New York and became an American citizen.

Garibaldi slipped back into Italy and organized an army of patriots who dressed in red shirts. In 1860 the army of 1,000 Red Shirts conquered southern Italy. The prime minister of Sardinia, Count Camillo di Cavour, then succeeded in uniting most of Italy under the Sardinian king, Victor Emmanuel. By 1870 the goal of Italian unification was achieved.

UNIT 4 REVIEW

Important Dates

1836 Texas declares independence from Mexico.
1845 Texas becomes state.
1846 War with Mexico begins.
1848 Treaty of Guadalupe Hidalgo.
1850 Compromise of 1850.
1854 Kansas-Nebraska Act.
1857 Dred Scott decision.
1859 John Brown raids Harpers Ferry.
1860 Abraham Lincoln elected President.
1861 Civil War begins.
1863 Battle of Gettysburg.
1865 Lee surrenders at Appomattox.
       Lincoln assassinated.
       Thirteenth Amendment ratified.
1867 Reconstruction Act.
1868 Fourteenth Amendment ratified.
1870 Fifteenth Amendment ratified.
1877 Last federal troops leave South.

Review Questions

1. (a) What areas were added to the United States in the years 1845 to 1853? (b) How was each new area added, and to what extent did this expansion fulfill the concept of manifest destiny?

2. When President Polk asked Congress to declare war on Mexico, he argued that the war had been started "by the act of Mexico herself." On what basis did Polk make this argument?

3. (a) Why was the question of Texas's admission to the Union controversial? (b) How did the question of slavery in the territories continue to divide Northerners and Southerners in the years before the Civil War? (c) How did the Compromise of 1850 seek to settle that controversy? (d) What events after 1850 pushed the country beyond the point of compromise?

4. In his First Inaugural Address, Lincoln said that the basic reason for the breakup of the Union was that "One section of our country believes slavery is right, and ought to be extended, while the other believes it is wrong, and ought not to be extended." (a) What historical evidence supports Lincoln's conclusion? (b) What other conditions led to the outbreak of the Civil War?

5. (a) What advantages did each side have at the beginning of the Civil War? (b) What advantages ultimately meant victory for the North? (c) How was each section affected by the war?

6. The reconstruction era was a time of readjustment after the Civil War. What role did the Freedmen's Bureau, black codes, and carpetbaggers and scalawags play in the South during the reconstruction period?

7. In the years just after the Civil War three new amendments were added to the Constitution. Explain the significance of the Thirteenth, Fourteenth, and Fifteenth amendments.

8. Describe the changes in ways of living that took place in the South after the Civil War.

Projects

1. On an outline map of the United States, draw the routes of the Oregon Trail and the Santa Fe Trail. Mark the major stopping places along the way. On your map illustrate the traffic that followed these two trails by drawing pictures or attaching magazine illustrations. Include pictures that show the kinds of people who migrated westward.

2. Write a script for a debate between a supporter (Northerner) and an opponent (Southerner) of the Wilmot Proviso. In writing your script, try not to favor one side over the other.

3. Prepare a book report on Harriet Beecher Stowe's *Uncle Tom's Cabin*. In your report focus on the main characters. Analyze what these characters have to say about the institution of slavery.

4. Make a campaign poster for one of the four presidential candidates in the election of 1860. On your poster, be sure to include information that makes clear your candidate's stand on the major issues of the day. Use pictures and slogans where appropriate.

5. Write an essay on the topic "The Civil War could have been averted if the Democratic Party had not split in 1860." You may either agree or disagree with this statement, but be sure to include evidence to support your point of view.

6. Prepare a bulletin board display on one of the battles of the Civil War. Include such items as pictures, maps, newspaper articles, and songs.

7. Write an essay on one of the leading Radical Republicans during the reconstruction era. Find out about the person's background, his feelings about Southerners and freedmen, his role in the shaping of reconstruction policy and in the attempt to remove Johnson from office, and his life and career after reconstruction came to an end.

THE NATION TRANSFORMED

1860–1900

*Give me your tired, your poor, your huddled
masses yearning to breathe free, . . .
Send these, the homeless, the tempest-tossed, to me:
I lift my lamp beside the golden door.*

EMMA LAZARUS, "THE NEW COLOSSUS," 1886

18

The Last Great West

1860 – 1900

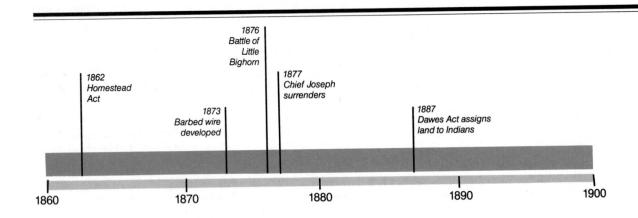

1876
Battle of
Little
Bighorn

1862
Homestead
Act

1877
Chief Joseph
surrenders

1873
Barbed wire
developed

1887
Dawes Act assigns
land to Indians

1860   1870   1880   1890   1900

CHAPTER OUTLINE

1. The Plains Indians lose their homelands.

2. Ranchers and miners penetrate the West.

3. Farmers settle the Great Plains.

Americans of the 1840's, venturing westward to Oregon and California from territories along the Mississippi, encountered a vast and varied region. The eastern part of the trans-Mississippi West, extending roughly from the present state of Minnesota south to Texas and west to the foothills of the Rockies, was characterized by a level surface or by low, rolling hills. This region — often called the Great Plains — received less rainfall than the eastern part of the country and became more arid the farther west pioneers traveled.

The second part of the trans-Mississippi West consisted of the Rocky Mountains, explored by Lewis and Clark, Pike, Frémont, and others. This imposing mountain system had long been a barrier to easy passage across the continent.

The third part of the region was the plateau lying west of the Rockies and extending to the Cascades and the Sierra Nevada. Much of this section, particularly its southern part, was a forbidding desert area.

For centuries, the trans-Mississippi West had been the home of Indian tribes. In the years following the Civil War, the arrival of ranchers, miners, and farmers brought far-reaching changes to the Indians' ways of living. This chapter tells the story of the conquest of the Indians and the settlement of the land west of the Mississippi.

1 The Plains Indians Lose Their Homelands

Throughout America's history, white settlers pushed the Indians out of their homes and hunting grounds. In the many battles between whites and Indians, the Indians were occasionally victorious. Never, however, were they able to stop the white settlers for long.

The Indian Territory is organized. In 1834 a region that included most of the present state of Oklahoma was set aside by Congress for the Indians of the Five Civilized Tribes (the Cherokee, Chickasaw, Choctaw, Creek, and Seminole). Known as the Indian Territory, this area became home to those tribes after they were forced to leave their lands east of the Mississippi (pages 266–269). Eventually, more than 75,000 Indians were living in the territory.

The Civil War, in part, changed the relationship between the United States and the resettled Indians. The tribespeople believed that under the treaties they had accepted, they had exchanged their historic independence for the protection of the United States. When war broke out between the North and South, however, the Union withdrew United States troops from Texas and Arkansas, convincing the Indians that they had been abandoned. Quickly the Confederacy annexed the Indian Territory and wooed the tribes to the rebel side. The Indians were guaranteed representation in the Confederate Congress and were also promised a state of their own if the South won. The alliance seemed logical, since many Indians were slaveholders and therefore sympathized with the South in the struggle.

After the introduction of the horse, the Plains Indians adopted new methods of pursuing buffalo, their source of food and clothing. Later, buffalo hunting became a sport for white settlers, whose coming greatly altered life on the Plains.

During the Civil War about 5,500 Indians fought on the Confederate side.[1] In fact, the last Confederate leader to surrender was General Stand Watie, a Cherokee chief who did not lay down his arms until a month after Appomattox.

The Indian wars begin. In the period before the Civil War, white settlers had bypassed the Indian Territory, making their way into the traditional hunting grounds of the Plains Indians. Soon, so many white settlers were living on the Plains that territories were organized. After the Kansas and Nebraska territories were created in 1854, other territories were formed one after another: Dakota, Montana, Wyoming, Idaho, and Colorado.

The Indians who had long made their home at the eastern edge of the Rockies soon felt the force of change. In 1858 gold was discovered in the vicinity of Pikes Peak. Almost immediately 100,000 miners entered the region. The local Indians — the Cheyenne and the Arapaho — having no place to go, chose to stand and fight. The ensuing struggle between whites and Indians gradually spread eastward onto the Plains. It was destined to last for thirty years.

The Indian warriors of this period, on horseback with feathered headdresses streaming in the wind, quickly became familiar figures to other Americans. They were celebrated in magazines and books and later in motion pictures. Even today the image of the Plains Indians is burned into people's minds as typical of *all* Indians.

Actually, when Coronado first came into contact with the Plains Indians in 1540, he found that they were generally peaceful people. Three centuries later, however, they had been radically changed by their contact with Europeans. The Indians of the South and West had acquired horses from the Spanish, and the Indian horse-frontier gradually spread up the Rio Grande Valley onto the Great Plains. In the meantime, Indians in the East had acquired guns from the British and later from the Americans. The gun-frontier reached the Plains about the time the Indian Territory was created and merged with the horse-frontier. As a result, mounted Indians armed with guns appeared for the first time, just when white settlers were beginning to settle the trans-Mississippi West.

For a considerable time, the Plains Indians had a decided advantage over their enemies. Then the Colt six-shooter was introduced into the United States Army in the 1850's. Invented by Samuel Colt and patented in 1836, it was the first firearm to have a revolving loading device. The six-shooter enabled soldiers to pursue their enemy without having to stop and reload their rifles after every shot.

The destruction of the buffalo signals an end to the Indians' ways of living. The superior weapons of the United States Army were not the only disadvantage the Indians faced. Their will to resist was also weakened by the destruction of the American buffalo herds. The huge beasts had once provided the nomadic tribes with food and materials for tools and shelter.

Perhaps fifteen million of the buffalo roamed the Plains when Coronado passed through the region. It was possible, Coronado reported, to see as many as 300,000 animals at one time. One of Coronado's men described in amazement what he had learned:

> The Indians live or sustain themselves entirely from the buffalo, for they neither grow nor harvest corn. With the skins they build their houses; with the skins they clothe and shoe themselves; from the skins they make rope and also obtain wool. With the sinews they make thread, with which they sew their clothes and also their tents. From the bones they shape awls [pointed tools for making holes].

The wiping out of the buffalo herds was begun by the Indians themselves. Since the time when Lewis and Clark crossed the Plains, the tribes had been killing off the animals at a rate that reduced their number each year. By the mid-1800's the Indians were selling about 100,000 buffalo hides annually to the American Fur Company.

---

[1]The North recruited Indians as well, and by the war's end some 4,000 Indians had fought for the Union.

"Born Upon the Prairie"

In October, 1867, the chiefs of many Indian tribes met with government commissioners in southern Kansas. Ten Bears, a Comanche chief from Texas, spoke to the gathering about the feelings of his people for their way of life on the open prairie and about their conflicts with white soldiers.

Chief Ten Bears

My people have never first drawn a bow or fired a gun against the whites. There has been trouble on the boundary between us, and my young men have danced a war dance. But fighting was not begun by us. It was you who sent out the first soldiers and we who sent out the second. Two years ago I came upon this road, following the buffalo. But the soldiers fired on us, and since that time there has been a noise like that of a thunderstorm, and we have not known which way to go.

The blue-dressed soldiers came out of the night when it was dark still, and for campfires they lit our lodges. So it was in Texas. They made sorrow come into our camps, and we went out like buffalo bulls when their cows are attacked. When we found white soldiers, we killed them. The Comanche are not weak and blind. They are strong and farsighted like horses.

But there are things which you have said to me which I do not like. You said that you wanted to put us upon a reservation. I do not want that. I was born upon the prairie, where the wind blew free and there was nothing to break the light of the sun. I was born where there were no enclosures and where everything drew a free breath. I want to die there and not within walls. I have hunted and lived like my fathers before me, and, like them, I lived happily. So, why do you ask us to leave the rivers, and the sun, and the wind, and live in houses?

The slaying of the buffalo became more highly organized after 1867. In that year the railroad penetrated the Plains. Hunters, like the experienced scout and Indian fighter William F. Cody, were hired to supply the construction crews with buffalo meat. Buffalo Bill, as Cody became known, slaughtered thousands of the animals.

Between 1871 and 1874 hunters killed about three million buffalo each year. Most of the skins were sold in the East, where owning a buffalo hide became a mark of elegance. The carcasses would be left to rot in the sun. When only the bones were left, they would be picked up and shipped to fertilizer factories in the East. In 1874 about 3,500 tons of bones were shipped out of Kansas and Colorado alone. By 1883 the animals had virtually disappeared. It is said that when the United States Mint in 1913 created a five-cent coin showing a buffalo, the artist had to go to the Bronx Zoo in New York to find a live specimen for a model!

The Indians fight a losing battle. Serious trouble between white settlers and Indians broke out in the Minnesota Territory in 1862. In the summer of that year the Sioux, led by Little Crow, went on the warpath, killing hundreds of settlers. Panic quickly spread and the governor sought aid from Washington. To restore order, President Lincoln put General John Pope in charge of a new Department of the Northwest, which included Minnesota and several other states

Fur traders who moved into Sioux country built outposts such as Fort Laramie in Wyoming.

and territories.[2] Pope's orders regarding the Sioux were clear: "They are to be treated as maniacs or wild beasts, and by no means as people with whom treaties or compromises can be made."

In the Minnesota campaign, the American soldiers showed no mercy. When many of the Sioux surrendered, there was an immediate cry for revenge from local whites. Pope favored condemning to death more than 300 of the 1,800 Sioux prisoners. President Lincoln intervened, however, and prevented the slaughter — although he authorized the hanging of 38 Indians. Pope continued his drive against the Sioux, finally succeeding in pushing them onto new lands in the Dakota Territory. Many of these Indians were reduced to starvation.

In the Colorado Territory the Cheyenne and Arapaho had been forced by the federal government in 1861 to give up their claims to land that had once been guaranteed to them. They were then resettled in eastern Colorado near Sand Creek. Some of the warriors, led by Chief Black Kettle, resisted

the removal by raiding mining camps and other settlements. In response, a force of local militia, commanded by Colonel J. M. Chivington, surprised 500 Cheyenne at Sand Creek. Attacking at daybreak, the militiamen killed 270 Indians — 200 women and children and 70 men.

Hardly had the struggle broken off in Colorado when warfare erupted again, this time on the northern Plains. There the Sioux tribes, who had been promised a permanent homeland, had become inflamed by the news of Sand Creek. They were also aroused when a wagon trail was built through their land and when the army sent troops to ensure the safety of white travelers. The Sioux, led by Crazy Horse and Red Cloud, proved a determined foe. Every wagon train came under attack.

The Indians are placed on reservations. Before the fighting ended in 1867, both sides had suffered heavy losses. By then it was clear that new steps would have to be taken to end Indian resistance.

Congress decided that only one solution was possible: all Indians must be settled on *reservations.* These were tracts of land set aside for the different tribes. The government expected the Indians to give up their hunting way of life and get food through government agents on the reservation or through farming.

In 1867, the government established two large reservations. One, located in the western part of the Dakota Territory, was to contain some 54,000 Indians. The other, forced on the Five Civilized Tribes as punishment for having supported the Confederacy, was carved out of the western part of the Indian Territory. It would be the home of 86,000 tribespeople. Both reservations were far from the new transcontinental railroads that were being built, and far, too, from any land that white settlers might want. Other small reservations were scattered throughout the West.

Some Indian chiefs were bribed and flattered into accepting the government's terms. Red Cloud, for one, had the fight taken out of him by the royal treatment he received in Washington when he visited

<hr />

[2]The Union defeat at the Second Battle of Bull Run (page 376) had led Lincoln to remove Pope from command of the Army of the Potomac, making necessary a new assignment for the defeated commander.

President Grant. Younger warriors, however, refused to accept retreat to reservations. Beginning in 1868, they waged relentless warfare against the advancing white settlers, ranging far and wide over the Plains from Texas to the Canadian border.

Indian resistance is crushed. The effort to suppress the Indian unrest resulted in many bloody encounters. The most severe was the Red River War of 1874–1875, during which 3,000 United States troops under Generals William T. Sherman and Philip H. Sheridan engaged the Comanche, Kiowa, Arapaho, and other tribes in battle. When that struggle was finally over, Indian resistance on the southern Plains had been broken.

Resistance on the northern Plains was another matter. In the early 1870's surveying parties of the Northern Pacific Railroad were working through the Yellowstone country under the protection of the Seventh United States Cavalry, a group of veteran Indian-fighters. The commanding officer was a handsome, long-haired lieutenant colonel named George Armstrong Custer. The great-grandson of a Hessian officer who had remained in America after surrendering with Burgoyne, Custer had graduated from

West Point just in time to take part in the First Battle of Bull Run. His gallantry and dashing manner drew favorable attention and assignments. After Appomattox, General Sheridan presented him with the Confederate flag of truce and the table on which Grant wrote the terms of surrender. Sheridan commented at that time, "I know of no one whose efforts have contributed more to this happy result than those of Custer."

Seeking even more glory, Custer was pleased to be assigned to Indian fighting. Soon the Indians recognized him as a formidable opponent. In 1868 he defeated the Cheyenne, led by Black Kettle, in a battle at the Washita River in the Indian Territory. In addition to killing more than 100 warriors (including Black Kettle), Custer's forces also killed 38 unarmed women and children.

In June, 1876, Custer prepared to surprise a large force of Sioux and Cheyenne who had gathered near the Little Bighorn River in Montana. When the Indians discovered his presence, however, Custer decided to make a frontal attack. To this day no one knows why Custer acted so recklessly. Possibly he thought the Indians were afraid to stand and fight; possibly he hoped

The Indians in the West were resettled on lands set aside as reservations, such as the Pine Ridge reservation in southwestern South Dakota.

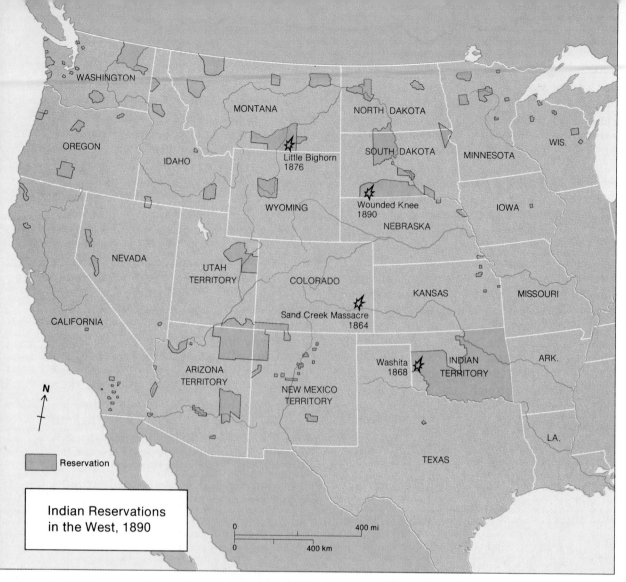

WASHINGTON

MONTANA

NORTH DAKOTA

WIS.

OREGON

IDAHO

★ Little Bighorn 1876

SOUTH DAKOTA

MINNESOTA

★ Wounded Knee 1890

NEBRASKA

IOWA

WYOMING

NEVADA

UTAH TERRITORY

COLORADO

KANSAS

MISSOURI

CALIFORNIA

★ Sand Creek Massacre 1864

ARIZONA TERRITORY

NEW MEXICO TERRITORY

★ Washita 1868

INDIAN TERRITORY

ARK.

N

TEXAS

LA.

Reservation

Indian Reservations in the West, 1890

| 0 | | 400 mi |

| 0 | | 400 km |

By 1890 the many efforts of the Indians to resist the encroachment of white settlers had ended, and most Indians had been confined to reservations.

to win everlasting fame. At any rate, he died along with his detachment of 264 troops. A Blackfoot chief later said that the rush of Indians toward Custer's column was "like a hurricane . . . like bees swarming out of a hive." The Battle of the Little Bighorn is remembered as "Custer's Last Stand."

The news of Custer's death raised to new heights the fury against the Indians. The nation, celebrating the centennial of its independence, demanded a swift end to further Indian resistance. Troops now relentlessly waged war against the outgunned Indians. By late 1876 fighting in the Dakota Territory had ended.

The Indian wars come to an end. Some Indians continued to resist in the next years, but without real hope. In the Pacific Northwest, Chief Joseph led the Nez Perce in a brilliant campaign against well-equipped army forces who were trying to force his people onto a reservation. His small band traveled more than 1,300 miles across Oregon and Idaho in 1877 before being forced to surrender in Montana. The last major resistance was offered by the Apache Indians in New Mexico. Indian warfare came to an end there in 1886 when the Apache leader, Geronimo, was captured.

The final tragic chapter in the long history of Indian warfare was written on the northern Plains in 1890. A religious revival had spread through the Sioux tribes, based on the belief that a Messiah was about to appear who would defeat the whites and restore the Indians' land. A practice of the religion was to hold long, exhausting dances, which put many of the participants into trances. Settlers, fearing the "Ghost Dance" religion, called in troops to disarm a group of Indians they thought posed a threat. At Wounded Knee Creek, in southwestern South Dakota, the tribespeople — 120 men and 230 women and children — were encamped, prepared to surrender their weapons. In a moment of confusion, someone fired a shot. The troops opened fire with rifles and with their new Gatling guns, the earliest type of machine gun. About 300 of the unprotected Sioux perished.

The government changes its Indian policy. Americans as a whole had long been blind to the question of Indian rights. By the early 1880's, however, after the cruel struggles were over, the public attitude started to change. Reformers began to take a different view of Indian affairs. One reformer was Helen Hunt Jackson. Her book *A Century of Dishonor*, published in 1881, drew national attention to the shameful treatment of the tribespeople. The book has been called "the Indians' *Uncle Tom's Cabin*."

Supporters of Indian rights were soon speaking out in Congress. Under the guiding hand of Henry L. Dawes, senator from Massachusetts, the Dawes Act was passed in 1887. It abolished most tribal organizations and authorized the President to divide up the reservations. Each head of an Indian family would be allotted 160 acres, while smaller tracts would be granted to unmarried men, women, and children. After 25 years, each landholder would receive title to his or her homestead and would be made a citizen of the United States. Any reservation land left over after the distribution would be sold by the government, the proceeds to be set aside for Indian education.

The Dawes Act is a failure. The speedy "Americanization" of the Indian was now the goal of the United States. The Dawes Act, as a government official said, would make the American Indian into an Indian American. However, the Dawes Act did not work as well as its author had hoped. Many Indians had no desire to give up their tribal organizations or to become farmers. The land they received, moreover, was rarely good for farming. Many Indians fell so heavily in debt that they had to sell their land as soon as they obtained title to it. Of the 150 million acres owned by Indians in 1880, about 60 percent was taken from them in one way or another.

The economic condition of the Indians declined steadily, and as their poverty deepened, their health and general well-being declined. By 1900 the situation was so critical that people began talking about the "vanishing" Indians. They noted that in 1900 the entire Native American population had fallen to a mere 237,000. The Indians, however, did not vanish. The twentieth century would see a resurgence of Indian population and culture.

SECTION REVIEW

1. Vocabulary: *reservation*.
2. (a) What was the Indian Territory? (b) Which side did the Indians in that territory choose during the Civil War?
3. What advantages did army troops have in their struggle with the western Indians?
4. Of what significance was the destruction of the buffalo herds?
5. (a) Why did the Indians resist white settlement? (b) Who were some of the Indians' leaders in that struggle? (c) What was the result of the Indian wars?
6. (a) How did the Dawes Act mark a change in the government's Indian policy? (b) How successful was it?

2 Ranchers and Miners Penetrate the West

The Great Plains, which had once been an obstacle to pioneers heading for Oregon or California, became a region of opportunity in the years after the Civil War. Beginning in the 1860's, a colorful new era opened: the day of the cattle rancher and the miner.

THE SPREAD OF RANCHING

Ranching begins in Texas. Soon after the Spanish had arrived in Mexico, they began to raise cattle. By the 1700's they had brought livestock into Texas. When Americans first moved there under Stephen Austin's leadership, they earned their living almost entirely from cattle raising. The San Antonio Valley — a diamond-shaped tract formed by the Gulf of Mexico and the Rio Grande on the south and the town of San Antonio at the north — proved ideal for the purpose. Animals known as Texas longhorns were developed there by crossbreeding English and Spanish cattle. By the 1830's about a million head of cattle roamed the Texas landscape, most of them untended. These animals were valued mainly for their hides.

Cowboys become part of the western scene. Already the cowboy as a distinctive type had appeared. The first cowboys were Mexican *vaqueros* (vah-KAIR-ohz).[3] The *vaqueros* taught the Americans how to handle the animals, how to rope them, trail them, and brand them. The Americans later anglicized the word *vaquero* to "buckaroo." In time other familiar words of the cowboy's trade were adapted from their Spanish forms: *lasso, lariat, chaps, stampede, rodeo,* and others. Some words were taken over unchanged: *corral, bronco, sombrero.*

Cowboys began tending large herds of cattle in the years after Texas won its independence in 1836. The cattle industry expanded, as beef-eating in the United States increased. The cowboys were already guiding small numbers of cattle northward along the Shawnee Trail into Missouri. Then the cattle were shipped to other parts of the country. In 1852 the first longhorns arrived in New York and were quickly acclaimed for the quality of their beef.

Cowboys became American heroes through popular fiction — at first through the dime novels dealing with "the West," then through Wild West shows that toured the country, and later through movies and television. The cowboy was made out to be larger than life, dealing bravely with cattle rustlers, stubborn Indians, evil sheriffs, and brutal outlaws. In reality cowboys were, as one of them said, "merely folks, just plain, every-day bowlegged humans." It is estimated that 5,000 of the cowboys were black. One of them, the rodeo star Bill Pickett, was the greatest of all bulldoggers.

A cowboy's work was hard, usually wearisome, and at times dangerous. The cowboy was almost constantly on horseback. Like the cattle themselves, the mustangs that cowboys rode came originally from Spain — no doubt brought there long before from North Africa. The mustang had what everybody agreed was "cow sense" and an instinctive ability to help the cowboy make the right move in difficult situations — a sudden stampede, a blinding blizzard, an unexpected downpour. Traveling incessantly in the saddle took its toll on the rider, and cowboys tended to wear out physically after a few years. When at the end of a drive cowboys had the relief of seeing a town and other human beings, they were not inclined to search for excitement. Mostly they wanted to rest from the tension and responsibility of their work.

Cow towns help develop a market for cattle. After the firing on Fort Sumter, many cowboys quickly found themselves in Confederate uniforms. The cattle were left untended once more, and most Americans soon forgot the taste of western beef.

When veterans from Texas returned home after Appomattox, however, they again took up cattle raising. Two important conditions had developed in the years the cowboys were away. One was the prosperity in the North, which had created a livelier market than ever for beef. The other was a discovery farmers in Missouri and Kansas had made. They had noticed that their own cattle fell ill from a disease called "Texas fever" shortly after coming into contact with the longhorns. Aiming to prevent the Texas animals from being driven into their region, farmers armed themselves. They began firing on animals and often stampeded herds.

---

[3] *Vaquero* is a Spanish word meaning "one who works with cows."

Cattle that bred and roamed on the open range were gathered in the spring roundup and branded with the distinctive mark of the owner.

The question of how to satisfy the public's hunger for beef without risking conflict — and heavy loss — was solved by Joseph McCoy, an Illinois businessman. McCoy picked out a small village in Kansas named Abilene, on the Kansas Pacific Railroad. The community had only a few log huts but was surrounded by luxuriant grassland. Within sixty days, beginning in July, 1867, McCoy had turned the little place into a beehive of activity — constructing stockyards, pens, and chutes for cattle, and a rooming house for cowhands. In selecting Abilene, McCoy ignored a Kansas law restricting the entry of Texas cattle, but the region was so thinly settled that nobody objected.

McCoy sent his associate, W. W. Sugg, to make contact with cattle ranchers, urging them to bring their herds into Abilene in order to get them to market. Sugg could assure the Texans that the trail to Abilene was far enough west to avoid protests and clashes. By the beginning of August, 7,000 cattle had been driven to Abilene. Early in September the first cattle train, consisting of twenty cars, chugged off for Chicago and its waiting stockyards. Before 1867 was over, at least 36,000 cattle — and possibly twice that number — had passed through Abilene.

The long drive is hard work. Reaching Abilene was the culmination of what came to be called the *long drive.* Herd after herd beat its dusty way north along such well-known routes as the Chisholm Trail. Each herd was led by two cowboys known as "pointers." These were experienced hands, some of them still in their teens, whose task was to guide the cattle and keep them from becoming mixed up with other herds. Behind the pointers rode the "swing riders," (or "flank riders"), who kept the herd from spreading out. Bringing up the rear were the "drag riders," who coaxed straggling cattle. The entire operation was directed by the trail boss, or foreman. He planned the daily

427

Chicago, the rail crossroads of America, became a center for livestock trade, as indicated by these stockyards, and for the meat-packing industry.

drive, found out ahead of time where water was available, and arranged for food and shelter along the way. As the railroads pushed westward, other cow towns developed in the same way as Abilene. After 1875, Dodge City, Kansas — on the Western Trail — became the busiest of them all.

Cattle are wintered on the open range. Hard times in 1873 caused a sharp drop in the price of beef. Cattle dealers decided not to ship the animals to slaughter but to have them spend the winter on the open range of the northern grasslands. Astonishingly, the cattle thrived despite the cold. Soon cattle were kept on the plains as a matter of course. By 1880, four million head of cattle had been driven north, many of them on the Pecos Trail that ran from Texas to Cheyenne, Wyoming, a distance of more than a thousand miles. Where the drive to Abilene took two or three months, the journey to Wyoming took somewhat longer. When the cattle industry spread even farther north, the drives to Montana or the Dakotas often took half a year.

The cattle business on the open range grew rapidly. Gradually better cattle were raised there, with scrawny longhorns being crossbred with stock like the Aberdeen Angus and Hereford.[4] The improved ani-

mals combined the stamina of the longhorn with the greater weight of the two more recently imported breeds.

Open-range cattle raising comes to an end. Many of the cattle barons of the 1880's found the open-range cattle industry profitable because their animals were allowed to graze on government-owned land and needed only limited attention from cowboys. For several reasons, however, the days of the long drive and the open range were numbered. First, the open range was rapidly becoming overstocked and the grass overgrazed. Second, destructive diseases were being passed from one animal to another on the open range, and regular inspection of the herds was impossible. Third, the purity of selectively bred animals could not be protected under the conditions of the long drive and the open range.

The year 1885 brought hard times to the open-range cattle industry. First, prices fell because of the enormous supply of animals. Then, the weather conspired against the industry. The winter of 1885–1886 was extremely severe. Snows covered the grass early in the season and froze, making it impossible for the animals to graze. By spring, 85 percent of the range cattle were dead.

The following summer a fearful drought was accompanied by withering heat. The temperature often reached 120 degrees in the shade — where there was any. Fighting

---

[4]Herefords had first been brought into the United States in 1817 by Henry Clay.

prairie fires kept the cowboys as busy as tending the animals did.

Weather in the following winter (1886–1887) again proved devastating. From December to mid-February the temperature hovered between 34 degrees and 60 degrees below zero. In late January came a brief *chinook,* or warm southern wind, that partly melted the snow, followed by a cold spell that seemed to turn everything to ice.

The cowboys struggled valiantly to save the animals. Their efforts, however, were mostly in vain, for the day of the open range was ending. By the end of the 1880's farmers began using fencing to enclose pastures on the range. They also began to raise hay on their property and to feed it to the animals during the winter. As one cowboy put it, "I tell you times have changed. You didn't hear the sound of a mowing machine in this country ten years ago." Before long, the sound of the threshing machine was also heard on the Great Plains, in fields where buffalo and cattle had once roamed.

MINING IN THE ROCKIES

Gold is discovered in Colorado and Nevada. Even as the cattle frontier was reaching the edge of the Rockies, the mountains themselves were the scene of another dramatic development: the miner's frontier. In 1859 gold was discovered in Colorado and Nevada almost simultaneously. Practically overnight, thousands of people rushed to the mountains, determined to make a lucky strike. Stories circulated that there were good "pickings" in the vicinity of Pikes Peak. Covered wagons known as "prairie schooners" were soon on their way west, emblazoned with the words "Pikes Peak or bust!" Most of them eventually returned, bearing the sad news "Pikes Peak and busted!"

Only a few prospectors — as in any gold strike — hit pay dirt. Among the luckiest were the shopkeeper H. A. W. Tabor and his wife, Augusta, who was the first white woman in the region. The Tabors had looked for treasure themselves without success. Two prospectors persuaded Tabor in 1878 to lend them money and supplies to go digging, in return for a third of whatever ore they might find. On an investment of just $50, Tabor earned $1 million for his portion of the successful strike made by the two prospectors. Enriched by this and other strikes, he built the Tabor Grand Opera House in Denver in 1879.[5]

The gold rush resulted in the growth of towns in Colorado. By 1860 Leadville — nicknamed Cloud City because it was situated more than 10,000 feet above sea level — had become the main center of activity for gold-seekers. Most of them were young men who knew nothing about mining. A new town, Ore City, flourished for only two years, then became a ghost town as the diggings were exhausted. Still, prospectors continued to sing:

> The gold is there, 'most anywhere,
> You can take it out rich, with an iron
> crowbar,
> And where it is thick, with a shovel and
> pick,
> You can pick it out in lumps as big as a
> brick.

The people who settled in the larger towns that sprang up — towns such as Denver, Boulder, and Canon City — made a living by supplying the miners. The first Colorado farmer to irrigate his land, David K. Wall, soon made money by supplying fresh vegetables to the miners.

Coloradans learned to persevere after the surface gold had been extracted. Crops failed, a grasshopper plague took its toll, and the first transcontinental railroad was built through Wyoming, not Colorado. Still, the region continued to grow. In 1876 Colorado came into the Union as the Centennial State.

The Comstock Lode attracts miners to Nevada. New mining "booms" continued for many years. Soon after the Colorado rush was over, the magnet for prospectors became Nevada, in that day a part of the Utah Territory. At first prospectors were drawn by their pursuit of gold. Soon it was silver that became the lure.

---

[5]Not until four years later did the Metropolitan Opera House open its doors in New York.

In western Nevada a band of miners in 1859 found the richest deposit of precious ores in history. It was named the Comstock Lode for Henry T. P. Comstock, the miner who claimed to have made the discovery. The nearby town of Virginia City was named, it is said, for Comstock's partner whose nickname was "Old Virginia."

The rush to the region defies description. By the end of 1860 — just before Lincoln took office — 154 businesses had been established in Virginia City to serve the miners. The drinking water, however, contained such harmful minerals that practi-cally everybody fell ill at some time during the next two years. Although the town had six doctors, hundreds of people died.

The Comstock mines yielded more than $500 million in silver and gold by the time they were worked out around 1880. One mine, the "Big Bonanza," netted about $200 million to four prospectors of Irish immigrant background. John W. Mackay, one of them, gave away half of his money to charities, always anonymously. Most new millionaires, however, showed off their riches. One mine owner shod his horses with silver. Another filled his water tank

Mining boom towns were situated along major railroads. Cattle trails ended at points on those same rail lines, which carried ore and beef to eastern markets.

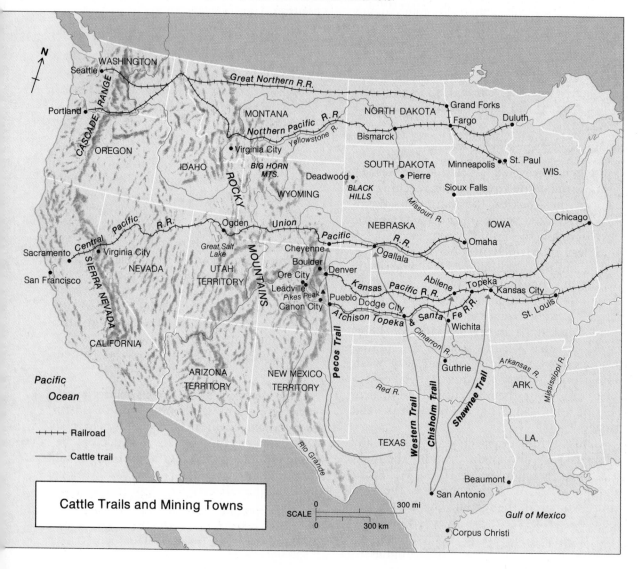

Cattle Trails and Mining Towns

+++++ Railroad

——— Cattle trail

SCALE

0 — 300 mi
0 — 300 km

with champagne in order to serve his wedding guests.

When the silver was exhausted, Nevada suffered economic depression. It was brought into the Union as a state in 1864, however, even though the territory did not meet the population requirement. President Lincoln, believing that one more free state might be needed to ratify an emancipation amendment, signed the proclamation of admission.

The mining rush speeds up the development of the mountain states. The mining frontier also left its mark on the Washington and Montana territories. Idaho on the eve of the Civil War was part of the Washington Territory (which in turn had been carved out of the Oregon Territory in 1853). Congress, yielding to Idaho miners, in 1863 organized the Idaho Territory, which included Montana and practically all of Wyoming.

Montana became the scene of a gold rush beginning in 1862. People here, like others on the mining frontier, were isolated from the rest of the world. Wrote one Montanan, "All the great battles of the season of 1862 — Antietam, Fredericksburg, Second Bull Run — all the exciting debates of Congress and the more exciting battles at sea, first became known to us on the arrival of the newspapers in the spring of 1863."

With the Montana gold rush, so many people filled the region that in 1864 Congress organized the Montana Territory, with another Virginia City as its territorial capital. For almost twenty years gold was found in the maze of gulches in the Rockies. When the surface outcroppings of gold were gone, however, mining became big business. Deep shafts were sunk and ore refineries built. These operations required large sums of money, usually provided by investors in the East.

The last of the mining rushes took place in the Black Hills of the Dakotas. The area, over two hundred miles from the nearest railroad, repeated the pattern of the early mining operations elsewhere. The colorful figures of the region — including Deadwood Dick (the nickname of an English-born frontiersman) and his friend Calamity Jane — were celebrated in the popular dime novels. Probably the most famous hero was Wild Bill Hickok, a soldier, Indian scout, Union spy, and United States marshal, who was slain by a shot in the back in a tavern brawl in the mining town of Deadwood.

The mining communities never had the glamor of the cow towns. They were filled with too much greed and too much squabbling over claims. Criminals were kept under control by *vigilantes.* Secret and outside the law, these citizen committees set out to provide law and order. Using intimidation and threats, the vigilantes insisted that they were the servants of justice, seeking only to put down lawlessness. At times, however, they were the instruments of vengeance and mob violence.

Constituted governments, in any event, quickly began to take control. North Dakota, South Dakota, Montana, and Washington received statehood in 1889, as the country marked the hundredth anniversary of George Washington's inauguration. The following year Idaho and Wyoming entered the Union as the forty-third and forty-fourth states.

SECTION REVIEW

1. Vocabulary: *long drive, vigilante.*
2. (a) Describe the origins of cattle ranching in Texas. (b) What role did cow towns play in the development of ranching?
3. Why did open-range cattle raising come to an end?
4. What part did prospectors play in opening up the Rocky Mountain area?

3 Farmers Settle the Great Plains

While ranchers and miners were staking their claims in the West, pioneer farmers, without drama or fanfare, were beginning to create an agricultural empire on the Great Plains. The movement of farmers into the region beyond the Mississippi River had started in 1862 with passage of the Homestead Act (page 386).

The settlers endure hardships. The Great Plains forced Americans to use all the ingenuity they could muster. The region had far less rainfall than farmers east of the Mississippi were accustomed to. It also lacked the usual building materials for houses and fences. Fences were essential because crops had to be protected from grazing herds of sheep and cattle. Moreover, nature seemed harsher on the Plains: high winds that fanned raging prairie fires; baking sun in summer; fierce blizzards in winter.

Insects plagued the farmers too. No one was prepared for the invasion of grasshoppers that began in 1874 and lasted for three years. The insects first appeared in the form of a giant cloud; then they descended and chewed up everything green. When no crops were left, they went to work on farm tools, broom handles, the walls of houses, and even harnesses. Falling into the wells, the 'hoppers ruined water supplies.

One of the greatest problems that Plains farmers faced was loneliness. Farm families lived many miles apart and felt their isolation keenly. Few pleasures relieved the hard work and drabness of farm life in the late 1800's.

Hamlin Garland, who wrote about rural life of that period, grew up on midwestern farms. Once, after a few years in the East, Garland returned for a visit and was struck by what he had never noticed before: "The lack of color, of charm in the lives of the people, anguished me. I wondered why I had never before perceived the futility of woman's life on a farm." He remembered the plight of his mother, worn out by years of unending toil: "I recalled her as she passed from the churn to the stove, from the stove to the bedchamber, and from the bedchamber back to the kitchen, day after day, year after year, rising at daylight or before, and going to her bed only after the evening dishes were washed and the stockings and clothing mended for the night."

Many a bride arrived at the new homestead to discover that "home" would be a dug-out or a sod house. A dug-out was a dwelling cut into the side of a hill or into a rise in the ground. A sod house was constructed of strips of sod sliced from the ground. Cut into blocks and fashioned into walls and roofing, the sod thus provided shelter until other materials became available. Some sod houses were carefully chinked with a kind of "native lime" made of sand and clay, which kept the chill wind out. Occasionally the interiors were whitewashed and attractively furnished. Many sod houses leaked when it rained, however, and sometimes collapsed without warning during a storm.

Many settlers who moved west did not take into account the expense of taming the Plains. First of all, it was estimated that the cost of putting a wooden fence around a 160-acre farm in 1870 was about $1,000 — a sum beyond the reach of almost all farmers. Second, getting water on the vast, nearly treeless Plains involved digging wells deeper than farmers had ever gone before — sometimes many hundreds of feet. The cost of digging such wells ran as high as $2 a foot — again a sum very few farmers could raise. Third, to bring water to the surface from such depths required power. The "old oaken bucket" would not answer the need. Windmills were needed to pump water that was deep in the ground, but like the wells themselves, most farmers could not afford them.

Inventions and new techniques help the Plains farmers. A number of inventions enabled the pioneers to cope with their new surroundings. In 1873 Joseph F. Glidden, a native of New Hampshire living in Illinois, developed a way of twisting wire so that it had a sharp barb every few inches, like a thorny hedge. By 1883 Glidden had built a factory that produced enough of the barbed wire each day to make 600 miles of fence. Within a few years mass production methods had lowered the price of 100 pounds of barbed wire to less than $4 — a price that brought decent fencing within the reach of all. This invention ranks with the cotton gin in its revolutionary impact on American agriculture.

If cheap fencing became available to most farmers fairly early, wells and wind-

A settler used the soil from about a half acre to build a typical sod house, a construction that was an adaptation of Indian winter dwellings.

mills were not generally affordable until about 1890. Meanwhile, farmers turned to a technique called *dry farming.* Actually dry farming is an ancient agricultural practice. In America the Anasazi people (page 34) had mastered the technique — as had the Arabs and Jews of the ancient Near East. White Americans, however, had never had need of the method before moving onto the Great Plains.

Dry farming requires rainfall of at least ten inches annually. The soil must be plowed to a depth of about ten inches before the arrival of winter rains and snow. The topsoil is cultivated after each rain to keep it loose. In that way the moisture that has soaked in is kept from evaporating.

The thick sod covering the Plains was a problem which had to be overcome even before new farming methods could be introduced. What was required was a plow strong enough to break the tough prairie grassland. John Deere, a native of Vermont, had made an effective steel plow in his Illinois blacksmith shop in the 1840's. Then, in 1868 James Oliver introduced a plow that could cut a smooth furrow in practi-

cally any kind of soil. Soon Oliver was turning out 200,000 plows a year in a plant he built in Indiana.

Many other machines also made their appearance, enabling relatively few people to work large farms. The innovations included grain drills for planting seeds in rows; plows that farmers could ride on; and threshing machines that separated the chaff from the wheat.

Railroads encourage settlement. Some of the early settlers broke under the strain of life on the Plains, never becoming accustomed to the loneliness and the relentless howl of the wind. No frontierspeople since the first settlers in Virginia and Massachusetts were so far removed from the daily conveniences they had earlier known. Nevertheless, the pioneers arrived in a ceaseless stream. Some at first were Civil War veterans adjusting to civilian life. Others were immigrants from western Europe seeking wider opportunity. Still others were the footloose adventurers and speculators who have been found on every frontier in American history.

The railroad was the means by which most people reached the Great Plains. After the Indian wars the influx of newcomers to Kansas followed the line of the Atchison, Topeka, and Santa Fe Railroad. The people who settled Nebraska set up farms along the route of the Union Pacific. (Nebraska joined the Union as the thirty-seventh state in 1867.) Ranchers trying to preserve the open range opposed the steady increase of homesteads in both Kansas and Nebraska. In the end, though, the farmers won. By 1880, for instance, the population of Kansas was 850,000 and that of Nebraska about 450,000.

Western population grows. The development of the Dakotas was hastened by the construction of the Northern Pacific Railroad as well as by the gold rush to the Black Hills. The area was the home of immense "bonanza" farms. The best-known bonanza farm was run by Oliver Dalrymple, a successful wheat farmer. Dalrymple was hired by the Northern Pacific to prove the fertility of the Red River valley. On 18 sections of land — each one mile square — he produced 600,000 bushels of wheat in 1861. By 1880 over 300 farms flourished in this rich river valley, averaging over 1,000 acres in size; a few were as large as 100,000 acres. While bonanza farms were not typical of the grain-growing region, they gave a hint of the scale on which crops would be raised in the future.

The Dakotas were boosted further by the Great Northern Railroad. Rails laid northwestward from St. Paul, Minnesota, reached Fargo and Grand Forks before heading west to Seattle, Washington. Thousands of European immigrants were drawn to the Dakotas, principally Scandinavians, Germans, and Czechs. Some of the newcomers worked on the bonanza farms, but most of them quickly acquired family holdings of their own. By 1885 all Dakota had been settled east of the Missouri River. The population of over 500,000 people was four times what it had been only five years earlier.

When the Dakotas were divided into two states in 1889, North Dakota's capital was named Bismarck in honor of Germany's chancellor — in hopes of attracting German investment. Once, Lewis and Clark had camped near its site; now it was a booming river port and supply center. South Dakota's capital was Pierre, but its largest city was Sioux Falls. Settled in 1856, Sioux Falls had been abandoned during the Indian troubles. Now its name remains as a reminder of the Indians who once dominated the area.

Wyoming and Montana were not reached by farmers until the 1880's. In both of these territories life for farmers was hard. Wyoming's settlers mainly engaged in ranching and its population grew only slowly, being less than 65,000 in 1890. Montana had 132,000 people in 1890, most of them miners.

A land rush takes place in Oklahoma. As white settlement grew larger on the Great Plains, the Indian Territory (page 419) also began to attract the attention of frontierspeople. In 1883, at Wichita, Kansas, an "Oklahoma Colony" of settlers called "boomers" began to call for the opening of Indian lands. The railroads also applied pressure. The particular areas the "boomers" had in mind were the as yet unsettled portions of central Oklahoma. Congress finally agreed to negotiate with the Indians, and land soon was purchased for white settlement.

At noon on April 22, 1889, central Oklahoma was opened for settlement. Some 50,000 people had gathered at the border, waiting for the pistol shot announcing that the "run" was on. (Already, many "sooners" had jumped the gun.) Upon hearing the signal, they surged forward by bicycle, wagon, carriage, on horseback, and on foot to stake out claims. How Guthrie, Oklahoma, was settled is described in this account:

Unlike Rome, the city of Guthrie was built in a day. To be strictly accurate in the matter, it might be said that it was built in an afternoon. At twelve o'clock on Monday, April 22nd, the resident population of Guthrie was nothing; before sundown it was at least ten thousand. In that time streets had been laid out, town lots staked off, and steps taken toward the formation of a municipal government. At twilight the camp-fires of ten thousand people gleamed on the grassy slopes of the Cimarron Valley, where, the night before, the coyote, the gray wolf, and the deer roamed undisturbed.

The population of the Oklahoma Territory grew rapidly, and in 1907 Oklahoma entered the Union as the forty-sixth state — 300 years after the founding of Jamestown.

Arizona and New Mexico join the Union. Other territories which became states as a result of the settling of the last great West were New Mexico and Arizona. In 1905 and 1906 Congress failed in its efforts to admit the two territories as a single state. The effort was unpopular because many New Mexicans feared the extinction of their proud Spanish heritage. Arizonians, for their part, sought to avoid domination by the far more numerous New Mexicans. In 1912 New Mexico and Arizona were admitted as separate states, giving the flag its forty-seventh and forty-eighth stars.

The settlement of the last frontier is completed. Stretching from ocean to ocean, the United States now contained 48 separate states, most of them concerned with problems that would hardly have been recognized by the people who started the original thirteen colonies. An era had ended. The land of America was still sparsely settled in many places, but maps no longer could show a line separating populated areas from unsettled land.

By 1900, a total of 500 million acres of public land had been distributed by the federal government in less than forty years — an achievement unmatched anywhere in the world. Of this total, eighty million acres had been taken by homesteaders. Much of the rest had been acquired by railroads, lumbering interests, and mining concerns. In addition, states had handed out under one arrangement or another millions of acres of their public land.

America was now a country of small farmers to a greater extent than ever before. In the years from 1860 to 1910 the number of American farms increased from 2 million

Many Scandinavian immigrants who arrived in the 1800's became farmers in the Plains states.

to 6.4 million. The number of acres under cultivation more than doubled — from about 400 million acres to more than 875 million acres. The production of wheat — not to mention other crops — rose from about 200 million bushels in 1860 to over 625 million bushels in 1910. Out of the mills and packing houses of Kansas City, Minneapolis, and Chicago flowed an abundance of relatively inexpensive food. Moreover, surplus food now entered the international market, where it could help feed people in other parts of the world.

The new farmers of America were, however, not the free spirits Thomas Jefferson had envisioned. Making the trans-Mississippi region suitable for farming had been the work not only of intrepid individuals but also of railroads, new technology, and complex machinery. The farmer had gradually become dependent on American industry and eastern businesspeople. The adjustment of farming people to this condition would raise concerns that those who had "tamed" the last West never imagined.

SECTION REVIEW

1. Vocabulary: *dry farming.*
2. (a) What hardships did settlers on the Great Plains encounter? (b) What innovations helped relieve the hardships?
3. What western states were admitted to the Union as a result of the influx of new settlers?

435

Chapter 18 Review

Summary

In the period from 1820 to 1842, eastern Indian tribes were forced to move to territories set aside for them west of the Mississippi River. Soon, white settlers began to move west too. They bypassed the Indian Territory, but settled on lands that had long been the hunting grounds of the Plains Indians. Faced with being pushed off their lands and having their traditional way of life destroyed, these powerful tribes attacked white settlers, miners, and soldiers.

From the 1850's to the 1880's many tribes, including the Sioux, Cheyenne, Arapaho, and Apache, fought fierce battles with the United States Army. The Indians, who faced overwhelming odds, suffered heavy losses before being subdued and forced onto reservations. Government policies attempted to integrate the remaining Indians into white society, but those policies were not successful and the tribes continued to suffer.

Beginning in the 1860's, meanwhile, cattle ranching became an important occupation in the West. Cattle had first been introduced into Texas by the early Spanish settlers. By the 1830's, about a million head of cattle roamed the Texas landscape. Having learned how to handle the animals from Mexican *vaqueros,* American cowboys rounded up the cattle and drove the herds hundreds of miles north to shipping points on railways in Missouri. As the railroads moved westward, cow towns such as Abilene, Dodge City, and Cheyenne grew up almost overnight. Cattle were later raised on the open range, but by the end of the 1800's the ranchers had begun to fence in their herds and grow hay to feed the animals.

Another attraction for thousands of newcomers at this time was mining. The discovery of precious metals in the mountains of Colorado, Nevada, Idaho, Montana, Wyoming, and the Dakotas produced great wealth for some people and led to the rapid development of these regions.

In the last decades of the nineteenth century, large numbers of pioneer farmers moved onto the Great Plains. Enduring a difficult environment, these hardy farmers learned to use new types of machinery and new techniques to make the fertile soil produce bountiful crops.

Vocabulary and Important Terms

1. Great Plains
2. Indian Territory
3. Sand Creek
4. reservation
5. Little Bighorn
6. Wounded Knee Creek
7. *A Century of Dishonor*
8. Dawes Act
9. *vaquero*
10. cow town
11. long drive
12. open range
13. Comstock Lode
14. vigilante
15. barbed wire
16. dry farming
17. bonanza farm

Discussion Questions

1. (a) How did the introduction of horses and guns affect the Plains Indians? (b) What part did the buffalo play in the lives of the Plains Indians?
2. (a) For what reasons did the Indian wars break out in the late 1850's? (b) What was the result of the Indian wars?
3. (a) Why did Congress decide to settle all Indians on reservations? (b) What was the reaction of many Indians?
4. (a) Why did the public attitude toward the problem of Indian rights begin to change in the early 1880's? (b) What was the goal of the Dawes Act? (c) Why did it not work as well as its author had hoped? (d) What was the situation of the Indians by 1900?
5. (a) Who were the first cowboys? (b) In what ways did the cowboy of legend differ from the real cowboy?
6. (a) What new conditions did the cattle industry face after the Civil War? (b) How did the cattle industry change in response to these conditions?
7. (a) What pattern of mining operations was repeated with each of the mining rushes in the trans-Mississippi West? (b) What was life like in a mining town?
8. (a) How did agricultural conditions on the Great Plains differ from conditions east of the Mississippi? (b) What inventions and new farming techniques helped farmers tame the Great Plains?
9. What role did railroads play in encouraging western settlement?
10. (a) To what extent was America by the early 1900's a land of small farmers? (b) How were American farmers different from the farmers Thomas Jefferson had once envisioned?

Relating Past to Present

1. How do farmers live on the Great Plains today? How have some of the hardships faced by pioneer farmers been eased? What difficulties still exist for today's farmers?

2. Where do Indians live in the United States today? In what ways has life changed for American Indians since 1900?

Studying Local History

1. In what way, if any, was your state affected by the settlement of the trans-Mississippi West? If your state is located in this region, what communities grew up as parts of the ranching, mining, and farming frontiers?
2. How important, if at all, is mining to the economy of your state or region?

Using History Skills

1. *Reading maps.* Study the map on page 430 showing cattle trails. (a) From which state did the cattle trails start? (b) Which trail ended in Abilene, Kansas? (c) Why did the trails run north-south?

2. *Reading source material.* Study Ten Bears' speech on page 421. (a) Why, according to Ten Bears, did fighting start between the Comanche and government soldiers? (b) What solution did the government commissioners offer? (c) What was Ten Bears' response? (d) Based on what you have read in this chapter, what might have been the outcome of this meeting?
3. *Analyzing evidence.* In 1890 the Census Bureau reported that settlement in the region west of the Mississippi had been so rapid that "there can hardly be said to be a frontier line." What evidence in this chapter supports the report of the Census Bureau?
4. *Writing a report.* Use an encyclopedia or a history of the trans-Mississippi West to find out about the removal of the Navajo Indians from their homeland to Fort Sumner, New Mexico, in 1864. It is an event the Navajo remember in their history as the "Long Walk."

WORLD SCENE

The New Breadbaskets

After 1865 many foreign families began settling the Great Plains of the United States and the grasslands of Argentina. The knowledge of farming brought by the immigrants helped develop these regions.

Mennonites and Russian wheat. Among the settlers of the Russian steppes were Mennonites, a religious group originally from Holland and Germany. Known to be good farmers, the Mennonites had been invited by Catherine the Great to develop farms in the part of southern Russia called the Ukraine. Before long, the Mennonites had turned the Ukraine into a prosperous wheat-producing area.

In 1871 the Russian czar ordered all men to report for military duty. The Mennonites, being pacifists, refused to serve. As a result, they had to leave Russia or face imprisonment. Enticed by an offer of land and a promise of exemption from military service, nearly 20,000 Mennonites immigrated to the United States, bringing with them seed for a variety of winter wheat known as Turkey Red. They settled on the Great Plains and planted the Turkey Red. It began to replace spring wheat as the nation's most widely raised crop, and in time made Kansas's reputation as the Wheat State.

The pampas of Argentina. Like the Great Plains, the Argentine pampas were transformed in the late nineteenth century from a sparsely populated grassland into a rich agricultural center. In the 1870's this region — between the Atlantic and the Andes — became accessible through the construction of railroads. At the same time, government-sponsored programs were encouraging Europeans to come and settle on it.

Between 1880 and 1890, more than a million men, women, and children — primarily from Spain and Italy — entered Argentina and started farming the pampas. New types of grains brought by the immigrant farmers grew well on this fertile land. As on the Great Plains, the new settlers also raised sheep and cattle.

In the 1880's the development of ships with refrigerated compartments stimulated the beef-cattle industry, since fresh meat could now be exported safely all the way to Europe. By the early 1900's Argentina had become the leading agricultural nation in South America.

CHAPTER 19

The Making of Big Business

1865 – 1900

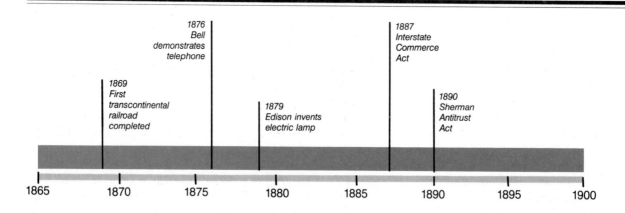

1876
Bell demonstrates telephone

1869
First transcontinental railroad completed

1879
Edison invents electric lamp

1887
Interstate Commerce Act

1890
Sherman Antitrust Act

1865   1870   1875   1880   1885   1890   1895   1900

CHAPTER OUTLINE

1. Many factors stimulate industrial growth.

2. Railroads tie the nation together.

3. Business leaders contribute to the growth of industry.

Even as ranchers, miners, and farmers were moving into the West, other Americans were making giant strides in business and manufacturing. Factory-made goods had already become commonplace by the 1840's, thanks to the pioneering work of such individuals as Samuel Slater and Eli Whitney. Now, the ability to produce unlimited quantities of consumer goods was looked upon as opening a new time of prosperity and opportunity for all Americans.

The creation of industries mobilized the entire country in a seeming frenzy of activity. Within one generation after Appomattox, Americans had opened up the continent's forest and mineral resources, assembled immense armies of workers, built a variety of manufacturing establishments, and laced the land with a mighty railroad system.

By the end of the century the United States had emerged as the world's leading industrial power. Between 1850 and 1900 the number of American factories soared from 123,000 to 205,000. In those same years the number of factory workers increased almost tenfold. By 1900 more than 60 percent of the American work force had nonagricultural jobs. The value of manufactured goods, furthermore, had long since exceeded the value of agricultural products. More truly than ever, Americans had become a nation. They were bound together by the sinews wrought in their factories and the common belief that a stream of undreamed-of products would help make tomorrow better than today.

1 Many Factors Stimulate Industrial Growth

Several factors help to explain the remarkable increase in America's industrial production in the years after the Civil War.

Inventors help the United States develop industry. Americans had long been said to have a special talent for invention. "Yankee ingenuity," as it was called, may have been stimulated by the constant need of isolated settlers to solve technical problems on the frontier. Widespread experimenting may have also flowed from the curiosity that could sometimes be aroused in people by the free schooling and literacy that most Americans enjoyed. Certainly, Americans were also spurred by the knowledge that industrial development in England was based on imaginative inventions. In the North, the need to save labor — almost always in short supply — also brought out creative ideas. Finally, the Constitution itself provided inventors with a powerful inducement when it gave Congress the power to enact patent laws. A *patent* enabled an inventor to have for a certain period of years the exclusive right to make, use, and sell his or her inventions. In 1836 Congress established the United States Patent Office to administer the patent laws.

A growing work force is available. In the years between 1860 and 1900 the population of the United States more than doubled, growing from 31 million to 76 million. The arrival of fourteen million immigrants during those years provided part of the increase. Although many immigrants took up farming, the bulk of them found jobs in the big cities of the North. There they applied their brawn and brains to the development of American industry. They were joined by thousands of native-born Americans who had left the land and joined the movement of people to the cities.

Resources are plentiful. In the richness and diversity of its resources, the United States was especially favored. All of the most important minerals required for heavy industry were abundant. These included coal, iron ore, oil, copper, zinc, and bauxite (from which aluminum is manufactured). Almost all of these resources had been discovered by the 1850's, and the means of extracting them were well developed. Moreover, magnificent forests provided lumber for the construction of buildings of every description.

Coal. Coal was the most important resource in the industrial development of the country. It was essential to the iron and steel industries and in powering factory machines of all kinds. Coal was at first mined

An improved steel-making process was recognized by the United States Patent Office in 1857. This and other inventions encouraged industrial growth in the late 1800's.

Gusher in the Oil Fields

As a reporter for the *Derrick*, a newspaper published in western Pennsylvania, Frank Taylor attended a demonstration of a new method for blasting through bedrock to reach trapped oil. He watched as a "torpedo" of explosives was dropped into a deep shaft and detonated. Taylor then wrote about the excitement of seeing a huge geyser shoot into the air, showering oil over the surrounding area.

A Pennsylvania oil well

On October 27, 1884, those who stood at the brick school house and telegraph office and saw the Semple, Boyd, and Armstrong No. 2 well torpedoed, gazed upon the grandest scene ever witnessed in oildom. When the shot took effect and the barren rock poured forth its torrent of oil, it was such a magnificent spectacle that no painter's brush or poet's pen could do it justice. Men familiar with the wonderful sights of the oil-country were struck dumb with astonishment, as they beheld that mighty display of nature's forces.

For over an hour that grand column of oil, rushing swifter than any torrent and straight as a mountain pine, united derrick floor and top. In a few moments the ground around the derrick was covered inches deep with petroleum. The branches of the oak trees were coated and a stream as large as a man's body ran down the hill to the road. Heavy clouds of gas, almost obscuring the derrick, hung low in the woods, and still that mighty rush continued. People packed up their household goods and fled to the hillsides. It was literally a flood of oil.

Several men volunteered to undertake the job of capping the largest well ever struck in the oil region. Three thousand pounds of weight were added before a cap was successfully fitted and the well put in operation. It was estimated that the production of that well later reached ten thousand barrels of oil a day.

---

chiefly in northeastern Pennsylvania, where the largest deposits in the world of the anthracite variety are located. By 1870 the bituminous fields lying in the Appalachian Mountains from Alabama to Pennsylvania were also being developed.[1]

---

[1] Anthracite coal, which burns with very little smoke, was used for home heating; bituminous coal, which produces heavy smoke, was used in smelters and other industrial operations.

Iron ore. A second indispensable mineral resource, iron ore, was the most widely found metal in the United States. It was first mined in quantity in the Lake Superior region, following its discovery in northern Michigan in 1844. The Soo Canal, joining Lake Superior and Lake Huron, was completed in 1855, enabling steamships to move ore to points on Lake Michigan and Lake Erie where it was refined. Farther west, a vast ore belt in the Mesabi (muh-

SAH-bee) Range of northeastern Minnesota was discovered by Leonidas Merritt, a Civil War veteran, and his brothers. The belt, more than 100 miles long and from one to three miles wide, proved to be one of the most extensive iron ore deposits in the world. Ore from the Mesabi Range was sent by rail to Duluth, Minnesota, which became the nation's chief ore-shipping port.

Oil. A third essential resource was oil. Unlike iron, which was important even in colonial times, oil was unfamiliar to most Americans until the 1860's. Indians had long skimmed it from the surface of streams and used it in medicine and for making paints. Some white Americans had also used it for medicinal purposes, believing it to be a cure for various ailments.

A New Yorker, George H. Bissell, long interested in oil chemistry, came up with the idea of drilling into the earth near a creek in western Pennsylvania on which oil had always floated. Bissell arranged with E. L. Drake, a conductor on the New Haven Railroad, to do the work. At a place later called Titusville, Drake began his task. Most people laughed at the project, and it quickly became known as Drake's Folly. Success rewarded Drake's efforts, however, and by August, 1859, he had a well that was producing 25 barrels of oil a day.

Within a short time an oil rush got under way in the region. The chief commercial product made from the petroleum was kerosene, refined at nearby plants. Kerosene lamps became the rage throughout the country, giving much better light than the candles and whale-oil lamps in common use. Oil as a source of mechanical energy awaited the invention of the internal-combustion engine and its application in automobiles, trucks, tractors, and airplanes. When that happened, a seemingly unlimited market opened for gasoline, another petroleum product obtained by refining.

Government interest encourages industrial expansion. The interest of the national government in promoting the growth of industry had been evident ever since the days when Alexander Hamilton had proposed tariff and bank legislation. Subsequent fed-eral assistance had taken many forms. Land grants had been offered to builders of canals and railroads. Scientific expeditions had been sent out not only to add to general knowledge but also to locate raw materials and find new markets. Rivers and harbors had been improved by the Army Corps of Engineers, and rights of way had been surveyed for railroads. The first telegraph line, between Baltimore and Washington, D.C., had been constructed in 1844 with a direct grant from Congress.

Capital helps the United States develop its industries. The stability of the American government and economy had long attracted Europeans eager to invest their *capital* for a profit. (Capital is wealth, in the form of money or property, that is owned by an individual or business organization.) In addition, these *capitalists* — that is, people with capital available for investment — noticed with much interest that the population

Oil was once used in small amounts chiefly for medicines. After the strike at Titusville, it was produced in abundance as fuel for lamps.

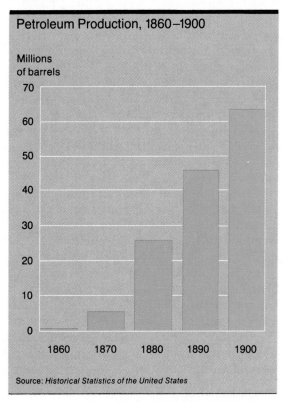

Petroleum Production, 1860–1900

Millions of barrels

Source: *Historical Statistics of the United States*

of the United States was growing rapidly, a strong indication of an expanding market for goods and services. Many Europeans, especially investors from Great Britain, put their money into American factories, mines, and railroads.

American capitalists, for their part, also invested money in the expansion of industry. Factory owners tended to put the capital they accumulated back into the companies they knew best — their own.

The Civil War stimulates business activity. The Civil War played a large role in speeding up the growth of industry. Nevertheless, the outbreak of hostilities, which disrupted the supplies of some raw materials, at first slowed production in many factories. Moreover, the rupture of normal economic ties between the North and South contributed to the failure of almost 7,000 northern businesses. For a time, people became reluctant to invest more money in industry.

By late 1862, however, business was reviving. The fighting had created an enormous government market for factory products, including iron goods, munitions, and clothing. Philadelphia, then the country's center of manufacturing, saw 58 new factories open in 1862, 57 the following year, and 65 in 1864. The large profits that industrialists earned enabled them to accumulate capital for further investment.

The absence of southern representatives in Congress during the war allowed the North to pass laws that the South had long opposed (page 386). These laws made it easier for people to accumulate capital. Tariffs were increased, for instance, helping the manufacturers of basic goods to make substantial profits and to use some of them to expand further. The Homestead Act, by encouraging the settlement of the western plains (page 386), created a powerful demand for railroad facilities and for other industrial products such as farm machines.

The Civil War significantly stimulated invention, as industry sought short-cuts in manufacturing. By 1865 Americans were even turning out many new devices unre-lated to war, among them passenger elevators and fountain pens. The war, moreover, gave many leaders in industry and government their first experience in organizing production on a large scale and distributing goods nationally.

Business leaders form corporations. As American industry grew bigger, more and more *corporations* were formed. Already, in the years before the Civil War, the corporate form of business organization had come into use. A corporation is created when three or more people are granted a charter, or license, by a state government. Such a charter permits the corporation to sell shares of stock (certificates of ownership) as a means of raising capital. The shareholders who buy the stock are the actual owners of the corporation and receive a portion of the corporation's profits, or *dividends.*

After 1860, corporations began replacing individual proprietorships (small businesses run by individuals or families) as the leading form of business organization. The corporation offered many advantages over the proprietorship. It provided businesses with an efficient way to raise the large amounts of money needed for expansion. The corporation gave investors the freedom to sell their stock whenever they wished. In the event that the corporation went bankrupt, the shareholders would only lose the money they had paid for the stock; they could not be held liable for any of the corporation's debts. Finally, because stock could be transferred from person to person and from one generation to the next, a corporation had permanent life. It could not be disrupted by the death or resignation of an owner.

SECTION REVIEW

1. Vocabulary: *patent, capital, capitalist, corporation, dividend.*
2. (a) Name five factors that played a part in the growth of American industry. (b) Explain why each was important.
3. What were the advantages of corporations as compared with individual proprietorships?

2 Railroads Tie the Nation Together

Conditions in post-Civil War America were ripe for the rapid expansion of large-scale production. Because railroads had kept pace with the growth of industry, the means were already at hand for carrying raw materials to manufacturing plants and for distributing finished products. Industry and the railroads each depended on the other, and the nation came to depend on both.

The railroads enjoy rapid growth. During the Civil War the importance of railroads had been well established. When the war ended, the demand for new railroad lines was heard throughout America. In 1865 the nation had slightly more than 35,000 miles of railroad track, most of it in the North and East. The railroads of the South, virtually destroyed in the war, had to be rebuilt. The lines between the Atlantic coast and the Mississippi Valley were too few to carry the goods of the country. Meat-packers in Chicago, oil prospectors in Pennsylvania, and grain growers in Iowa all complained about the shortage of rail facilities. In response, a new era of railroad construction swiftly got under way. By 1872 the nation's total railroad mileage had nearly doubled, and in the 1880's and 1890's almost 7,000 miles of track were laid every year. In 1900 the nation had nearly 200,000 miles of roadbed in use.

Along with this remarkable growth came improvements in the quality of train travel, as railroads became safer and more reliable. Brittle iron rails were replaced by steel ones able to sustain the weight of heavier trains. Huge iron bridges capable of bearing great loads were constructed, making possible the use of more powerful locomotives. Freight cars, each large enough to contain twenty tons of goods, were also put into operation. The use of a standard gauge allowed for the easy transfer of cars from one line to another. The chief effect was to speed up long-distance service.

As railroads crossed the nation, the depot became a familiar site at minor junctions and in larger cities, where it was often named "Union Station."

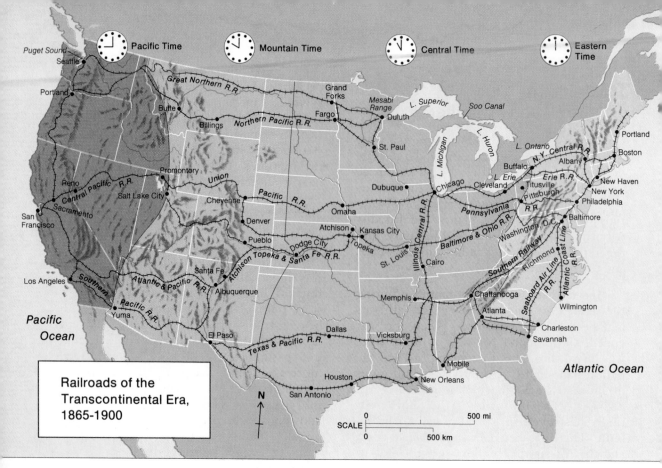

Map labels:

Pacific Time · Mountain Time · Central Time · Eastern Time

Puget Sound
Seattle
Portland
Butte
Billings
Great Northern R.R.
Grand Forks
Fargo
Mesabi Range
Northern Pacific R.R.
Duluth
L. Superior
Soo Canal
St. Paul
L. Michigan
L. Huron
L. Ontario
N.Y. Central R.R.
Portland
Boston
Buffalo
Albany
Promontory
Union Pacific R.R.
Reno
Central Pacific R.R.
Salt Lake City
Cheyenne
Dubuque
Chicago
Cleveland
L. Erie
Erie R.R.
Titusville
Pittsburgh
New Haven
New York
Philadelphia
Sacramento
San Francisco
Denver
Omaha
Pennsylvania R.R.
Atchison
Kansas City
Illinois Central R.R.
Baltimore & Ohio R.R.
Washington, D.C.
Baltimore
Pueblo
Topeka
Dodge City
Atchison Topeka & Santa Fe R.R.
St. Louis
Cairo
Southern Railway
Richmond
Seaboard Air Line R.R.
Atlantic Coast Line R.R.
Los Angeles
Santa Fe
Atlantic & Pacific R.R.
Albuquerque
Memphis
Chattanooga
Atlanta
Wilmington
Southern Pacific R.R.
Yuma
Charleston
Savannah
Pacific Ocean
El Paso
Dallas
Vicksburg
Texas & Pacific R.R.
Houston
San Antonio
Mobile
New Orleans
Atlantic Ocean

Railroads of the
Transcontinental Era,
1865-1900

N

SCALE
0   500 mi
0   500 km

By 1900, the United States had nearly 200,000 miles of railroad track, almost one third of the world's total railroad mileage.

Passenger service also improved. The accidents that for years had discouraged travel were significantly reduced after George Westinghouse's automatic air brakes came into use in 1869. All the cars of a train could now be stopped in an emergency. Passengers were also attracted by the introduction of the dining car. Travel was made more comfortable, too, when heating systems, drawing on steam from the locomotives, replaced the smoky wood-burning stoves of earlier days.

Great railroad systems are formed. At the same time that railroad construction was going on everywhere, an effort was under way to join together many small railroad lines into major routes, or *trunk lines.* A leader in this movement was Cornelius Vanderbilt, whose New York Central Railroad reached Chicago in 1869. It was now possible to travel from New York to Chicago without transferring from one railroad to another — eliminating the old need to change trains eight or ten times.

Other trunk lines quickly followed the lead of the New York Central in connecting Chicago with eastern cities. One was the Erie Railroad. Known for the unsavory financial dealings of its owner, Daniel Drew, it was the Central's chief rival. By 1869 it boasted: "1,400 miles under one management; 860 miles without change of cars."

Another trunk line was the Pennsylvania Railroad, a system linking Philadelphia to Chicago. The Pennsylvania also obtained a route to St. Louis, while shrewd deals gave it access to leading cities on the eastern seaboard as well. Not until 1910, however, when the line completed a tunnel under the Hudson River, did the Pennsylvania Railroad have access to a terminal in New York City.

A fourth major trunk line was the Baltimore and Ohio. Following the path of the old National Road (page 292), the line reached northward to Philadelphia and as far west as Chicago and St. Louis.

All of these trunk lines had their own depots in Chicago, and the constant arrival and departure of trains created a lively transportation business within the city. The first-class hotels of Chicago had towers from which local coach operators watched with telescopes for incoming trains. Once a train was sighted, carriages rushed out to meet it. Frank Parmelee started a service for transferring passengers between the various railroad stations. It became respected for the quality of its vehicles and the courtesy of the drivers. Later Parmelee organized the first commercial fleet of taxicabs.

Trunk lines are built in the South. In the years following the Civil War, railroad construction took place in the South at a pace faster than the national average. Between 1870 and 1873 alone, over 2,500 miles of new roads were built in the South. The Southern Railway was formed in 1894 by the financier J. P. Morgan, who joined several bankrupt lines. It eventually linked cities of the Mississippi Valley with Washington, D.C., and points south.

A competitor of the Southern was the Atlantic Coast Line Railroad, with connections linking important towns and cities between Richmond and Wilmington, North Carolina. The Illinois Central was yet another major line of the South, its tracks linking cities and towns from Chicago to Mobile. When the Illinois Central developed a connection with Savannah, it became a funnel through which the beef and grain of the Middle West found its way onto southern tables. Another line, the Seaboard Air Line Railroad, consisted of 4,000 miles of track, serving the same region as the Atlantic Coast Line.

A transcontinental railroad is proposed. West of the Mississippi the building of a transcontinental railroad became "the great work of the age." Some Americans predicted that a rail line connecting the east and west coasts would at last provide a "Northwest Passage," threaded through the heart of the United States itself. The lead-

ing advocate of such an iron highway had been a New Yorker named Asa Whitney. Beginning in the 1840's, he relentlessly pressed Congress to finance the construction of a transcontinental railroad. Whitney was convinced that trade with China would enrich America, and that a rail line to the Pacific was essential for that trade.

Congress had been unable to carry out Whitney's plan. The intense rivalry between the sections of the country was the main stumbling block, since it prevented agreement on the location of a route. Then a financial panic struck the nation in 1857, ending the immediate likelihood of constructing a transcontinental line.

Work begins on the first cross-country railroad. By 1862 the importance of railroads had become so obvious that Congress approved funds for a transcontinental line. The Union Pacific Company was established to build a road westward from Omaha, Nebraska, while the Central Pacific was formed to build eastward from Sacramento, California.

The federal government's contribution to the two companies was generous. In addition to the rights of way, the companies received large tracts of public land for each mile of track that was laid. The government also supplied some of the enormous amounts of timber and stone required in the immense task. For every mile of track, furthermore, the government paid a subsidy in the form of a thirty-year loan in United States bonds. The sum varied with the terrain: $16,000 per mile for the relatively level land across the plains east of the Rockies, $32,000 per mile in the plateau region, and $48,000 per mile across the mountains.

The building of the Union Pacific and Central Pacific railroads is one of the triumphant dramas of American history. The heroes were the laborers, numbering 20,000 at the height of the operation. Many of the workers, like the chief engineer of the Union Pacific, Grenville Dodge, were Civil War veterans. The railroads also hired thousands of young men recently arrived in the United States from Ireland and China.

Although the technique of track-laying varied according to local conditions, the procedure was always basically the same. Two gangs of workers, one on each side of the new tracks, walked ahead of a railroad car piled high with rails. The men would throw a pair of rails to the ground — one on each side of the roadbed, on which the wooden "sleepers" or ties were already in place. The rails would then be bolted to the ties, and the railroad car pulled forward. Over and over the process would be repeated. An observer described the action:

> The chief of the squad calls out "Down" in a tone that equals the "Forward" to any army. Every 30 seconds there came that brave "Down," "Down," on either side of the track. They were the pendulum beats of a mighty era; they marked the time of the march and its regulation beat.

The nation followed the progress of the first transcontinental with intense interest. People read accounts of workers facing the blistering heat of the plains in summer or the blizzards and freezing cold of the mountains in winter. At first, laying a mile of

These workers posed proudly at one of the mountain passes they helped to construct for the Northern Pacific Railroad, which was completed in 1887.

track a day was regarded as a good rate of progress. Then, even in the winter months with considerably less daylight, the crews were laying two miles a day. As the competition grew keener between the eastern and western companies, a record was set one day when nearly eight miles of track were put in place between sunrise and sunset. Soon the record was raised to ten miles.

The transcontinental railroad is completed. By the summer of 1868 the Central Pacific had laid tracks across California and was crossing Nevada. The Union Pacific, meanwhile, was pressing westward from Cheyenne, Wyoming.

The two competing companies had agreed that their lines would join at the tiny town of Promontory, Utah. By then the Union Pacific would have laid 1,086 miles of track, and the Central Pacific 689 miles. In an impressive ceremony on May 10, 1869, the junction was made. Two locomotives, as the author Bret Harte put it, were at last "facing on the single track, half a world behind each back." A golden spike was driven into place, completing the road, and Western Union flashed the news from Promontory all over the country. Every city in the Union heard the telegraph clicking the pre-arranged signal: "One, two, three — done!" Chimes rang in New York City, a huge parade got under way in Chicago, and in Philadelphia the Liberty Bell pealed once again. President Grant received a telegram sent from the scene announcing the festive "mountain wedding."

In a short time the high hopes of the original promoters of the transcontinental railroad seemed fulfilled. Along the route of the transcontinental, towns mushroomed, becoming centers of local business. Within a short time, scores of small communities were linked to the transcontinental "lifeline" by feeder tracks.

Other transcontinental lines are built. Even before the ceremony at Promontory, railroad companies were getting ready to build other transcontinental lines. One was the Northern Pacific, chartered by Congress to run from a point on Lake Superior to Portland, Oregon. Building it involved crossing some of the continent's most difficult terrain. Much of the money to accomplish the forbidding task was supplied by Jay Cooke, a Philadelphia banker. When Cooke's bank failed in 1873, the Northern Pacific found itself in financial trouble. The line was not completed until the 1880's, finally reaching Portland through the use of a local railroad's tracks.

Another transcontinental was the Southern Pacific. Started in 1864, it was developed out of a branch of the Central Pacific. In time the Southern Pacific extended as far north as Oregon, and to the south it connected New Orleans and Los Angeles.

The Atchison, Topeka, and Santa Fe, which followed the old Santa Fe Trail, was yet another transcontinental. A promoter of the Santa Fe — as the railroad was known — was a native of Pennsylvania named Cyrus Holliday. He had moved to Kansas in the 1850's and had helped make the state free soil. The construction of his road was begun in 1869 at Atchison, Kansas, and by 1872 the tracks had reached the cow town of Dodge City. Crossing the major cattle trails, the line soon made quick profits from the booming cattle business.

The railroads attract settlers. The managers of the transcontinental lines, recognizing that their profits would be increased if farm communities were built along their rights of way, successfully advertised in Europe for settlers. The Great Northern Railroad, running between Lake Superior and Puget Sound, was one line that actively encouraged settlers to move west. The Great Northern was the work of a railroad builder from Canada named James J. Hill. Hill settled in St. Paul, Minnesota, and began to build what turned out to be a railroad empire. He started by purchasing a small bankrupt line in 1873. Over the years, he built up his rolling stock — cars and locomotives — and began buying other railroad companies. Hill earnestly believed in the future of the region he was serving. He predicted that the northern Great Plains — and the region west, including the northern Rockies and Pacific Northwest — would one day be remarkably prosperous.

To attract settlers to the area, the Great Northern sent agents to Europe to publicize the virtues of what Americans were calling "Hill country." Hill held out the lure of free land under the Homestead Act. He also offered newcomers special arrangements that helped them get a start. He charged emigrants low fares from Chicago to any point on his line, and offered inexpensive freighting of household goods, farm animals, and equipment. He also supplied lumber, fence posts, and even trees and shrubs for the building and landscaping of new homes. Thousands of Europeans found his offer irresistible.

Railroads influence American life. The rapidly expanding railroad lines changed the face of America. Manufacturers were able to send their products into almost every part of the country, creating for the first time a truly national marketplace. Raw materials, moreover, could swiftly and conveniently be shipped to factories, even those located far away. Railroads, for instance, were able to bring iron ore from the Lake Superior region to the site of the coal supply in Pennsylvania for the production of iron and steel. Speeding up traffic from one part of the country to another, the railroads also strengthened contacts between people from different places.

Railroads at first had mostly a local impact. They tied a particular town to the "outside world." Soon, however, the effect of having railroads reaching *everywhere* changed the nation's behavior profoundly. Through railroads, both magazines and newspapers circulated nationally. Moreover, railroads helped to discipline the population in a new way. By establishing regular schedules, they made people be "on time." In addition to making people more punctual, railroads notably increased the tempo of American life. Henry David Thoreau, the poet and essayist, once asked: "Do [people] not talk and think faster in the depot than they did in the stage-office?"

Time zones are introduced. To make schedules easier to follow, the railroads put a system of standard time zones into effect on November 18, 1883. The country was divided into four time zones, known today as Eastern, Central, Mountain, and Pacific. The system replaced a crazy-quilt arrangement that had been based on local times. The terminal at Buffalo, New York, for example, had had three clocks, all showing slightly different times because they served railroad lines coming from different places. In Illinois there had been 27 local times and in Wisconsin 38! Congress formally adopted the time-zone system in 1918.

SECTION REVIEW

1. Vocabulary: *trunk line.*
2. What improvements were made in the quality of railroad travel in the years after the Civil War?
3. (a) Why did small railroads merge to form trunk lines? (b) What were some of the major trunk lines?
4. (a) What role did the federal government play in the building of the first transcontinental railroad? (b) What two companies built that railroad, and when was it completed?
5. Why did railroads encourage western settlement?
6. In what ways did railroads affect American life?

3 Business Leaders Contribute to the Growth of Industry

The forward march of American industry in the years after the Civil War opened new opportunities for people with boldness and energy. Among the business leaders were notable individuals who enlarged American production beyond imagination.

Andrew Carnegie organizes the steel industry. For centuries, people had made steel in small amounts by laboriously removing impurities from melted iron. Prized for its strength and toughness, steel was, nevertheless, too expensive to be manufactured in large quantities. Then, in the 1840's and 1850's, William Kelly in America and Henry Bessemer in England discovered independently that a blast of air directed at melted iron could remove the impurities.

The Bessemer process, as it was called, set the stage for the Age of Steel. In a short time steel rails became standard on all railroads. Before long, moreover, skyscrapers built with steel frames were transforming the look of American cities.

The steel industry came to be identified with the name of Andrew Carnegie. At the age of thirteen, Carnegie had been brought by his parents to America from Scotland. The impoverished Carnegies settled in Pennsylvania, where, after working briefly as a bobbin-boy in a cotton factory, Andrew got a job as a telegraph clerk in Pittsburgh. The young fellow had a keen instinct for opportunity, like successful business people of every era. Moreover, he was not afraid of hard work.

In the telegraph office Carnegie met the head of the Pittsburgh division of the Pennsylvania Railroad, Colonel Thomas A. Scott. Scott took a liking to the young man and decided to hire him as his private secretary. Through Scott, Carnegie met other business leaders, and from then on he advanced rapidly in the business community. He acquired interests in the iron business and in bridge building, and it was only a matter of time before he turned his attention to steel. After traveling in Europe and meeting Henry Bessemer, Carnegie decided to invest all his money in producing steel by the new air-blast method.

In 1873 Carnegie, already a multimillionaire, began building an immense steel plant just outside Pittsburgh. Shrewdly he named it the J. Edgar Thomson Works, after the president of the Pennsylvania Railroad. Carnegie hoped to get orders for rails from "the Pennsy," as people called it. He was not disappointed. Thomson helped make Carnegie the world's largest manufacturer of steel. By 1889 the United States passed Great Britain in the quantity of steel produced annually.

Carnegie was an astute investor. He also had a gift for finding the right people to be his associates. He once said, in jest, that he hoped his grave would be marked "Here lies the man who was able to surround himself with men far cleverer than himself."

448

The Carnegie organization gained a tight grip on companies that provided the services and supplies it required, including deposits of iron ore, limestone, and coal. Carnegie also established steamer lines on the Great Lakes to control the transportation of iron ore to Pittsburgh, and operated his own railways that carried raw materials to smelters and mills. By 1900, Carnegie controlled most of the steel production in America. When Carnegie finally sold his company to J. P. Morgan's newly created United States Steel Corporation in 1901, he received bonds with a face value of $250 million in payment.

In retirement Carnegie devoted his time to giving away much of his enormous wealth. His gifts included the establishment of public libraries in many American towns and cities. He also devoted himself to advancing the causes of world peace, education, and medical research. In all, Carnegie gave away more than $350 million.

John D. Rockefeller organizes the oil industry. Another master builder of industrial America was John D. Rockefeller. Born in New York State to a family of modest circumstances, Rockefeller eventually made a fortune in the nation's oil business. From his father, who earned a living by selling patent medicines, young John acquired an interest in business. From his mother, who was a stern woman deeply devoted to religion, he acquired self-discipline and a dedication to church affairs.

Born in 1839, Rockefeller was to live for 98 years, from the day of horsepower to the eve of the atomic age. Like Carnegie, Rockefeller kept his eyes open for opportunity — and like Carnegie, he came to maturity just when industry was beginning to revolutionize American life.

Rockefeller was fascinated by the rush to the Pennsylvania oil fields (page 441) and the growing market for petroleum products. He decided, however, that while the drilling for oil could be a wild gamble, the refining of it was practically a sure investment. At the age of 23, Rockefeller put his money into a small Cleveland refinery.

Andrew Carnegie built up the steel industry in America. By 1900, his corporation was providing nearly 75 percent of all United States output, and the nation had become the world's leading steel producer.

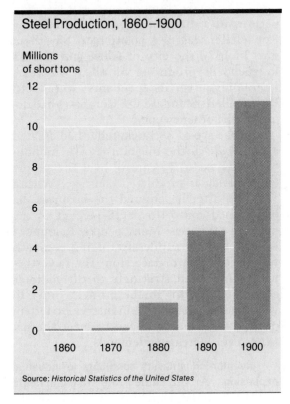

Steel Production, 1860–1900

Millions of short tons

Source: *Historical Statistics of the United States*

A stickler for detail, Rockefeller hated waste. In a short time, he was conducting a more efficient business than his rivals, steadily bringing down the cost of producing and selling kerosene. Success did not change Rockefeller's ways; he continued to reinvest his earnings. He advised his partners, "Take out what you [need] to live on, but leave the rest in. Don't buy new clothes and fast horses; let your wife wear her last year's bonnet. You can't find any place where money will earn what it does here."

Rockefeller developed a business that owned all the sources of most of its supplies. He saw to it that he and his partners controlled the pipelines and tank cars they required and the ships that carried their products. They even had their own plants for manufacturing barrels. Within a few years Rockefeller was pioneering in research. Such products as paraffin and insecticides were developed in his laboratories.

As early as 1867 Rockefeller reached an agreement with the railroads under which his companies were granted special freight rates. The lower shipping costs put his competitors at a disadvantage, and before long Rockefeller was in a position to buy them out. In 1870 the city of Cleveland had 25 independent producers of oil. Two years later only five independents were left: Rockefeller's Standard Oil Company had acquired the other twenty!

By the age of 38 Rockefeller had created a *monopoly* in the oil industry. (A monopoly is the exclusive control over the supply of a particular product or service.) Within 15 years after he entered the business, he had gained control over 95 percent of the nation's refineries. Many people denounced Rockefeller for ruthlessly forcing competitors to join him or face ruin. He, nevertheless, contributed strikingly to the nation's economic growth, for he brought order to what had been a chaotic industry. He left an oil industry well equipped to meet the nation's ever-increasing demands.

Inventor-industrialists contribute to industrial expansion. At the same time that Carnegie and Rockefeller were making their marks through the processing of natural resources, inventions were helping make possible entirely new industries. Among them was an industry built around an important new source of power — electricity.

For many years inventors had experimented with electricity. In an experiment with a kite, Benjamin Franklin had won international fame as "the man who captured lightning" by demonstrating that lightning and electricity are the same. In 1821 an English scientist, Michael Faraday, had shown that people could generate electricity by spinning a magnet around a wire. In making this discovery, he found a force that eventually would free America from its dependence on steam power.

Electricity was first put to work in a practical way in communication when Samuel F. B. Morse built a telegraph line running between Baltimore and Washington, D.C., in 1844. The first message tapped out by Morse's telegraph was a quotation from the Bible: "What hath God wrought!" Out of this modest beginning later developed the Western Union Company, whose lines helped bind the entire nation together.

Thomas Edison develops the light bulb. The man who dramatized the potential of electricity was Thomas Alva Edison. Edison, like Carnegie, had been trained to be a telegraph operator. His natural inclination, however, was inventing. Edison had a remarkable gift — and infinite patience — for applying to practical purposes ideas that others had put forward. Before he was 23, he had built an improved stock ticker. A few years later — in 1878 — he patented a phonograph able to "store" voices on tinfoil. This invention was Edison's most original work, although he would wait ten years before improving it.

Meanwhile, Edison devoted himself to his most spectacular creation: the electric light bulb. Early advances had taken place in England where Sir Joseph Wilson Swan had constructed a bulb with a carbon filament (the thread within the glass bulb). Edison tackled the problem of introducing a filament that would burn for more than a few hours. In October, 1879, he announced

The Telegraph

In 1836 Samuel F. B. Morse developed a telegraph that was capable of sending electrical impulses over copper wire. Later, Morse perfected two devices that made speedy communication practical: one clicked out a dot-dash code while the other relayed long-distance messages by means of switching mechanisms. The telegraph enabled newspapers to receive timely news by wire from all over the country. The telegraph was also valuable in scheduling the many trains that were crisscrossing the nation. In 1866 another achievement, after repeated failures, was the successful laying of a transatlantic cable. This engineering feat made communication by telegraph possible between Europe and the United States.

his success in getting a cotton thread covered with carbon to glow for forty hours. On the last day of 1879 he ran a special train to bring 3,000 people to his laboratory in New Jersey where he had hundreds of small lamps — all lighted by electricity.

Even before Edison perfected the light bulb, he had made plans for a central power plant from which underground cables would carry electrical current to homes and shops. He had to consider details no one had ever thought about previously: transmission cables, fittings of all kinds, electrical conductors, and switches. Most technicians did not believe that the turning on and off of lights — which would produce a constantly changing energy load — could be handled successfully. Edison solved the problem, however, and by 1882 had his system working in New York City. His company, the Edison Illuminating Company, eventually became Consolidated Edison and served as a model for power companies throughout the United States. Three separate manufacturing companies were established to produce electric light bulbs, generators, and cables. In a few years these companies were combined to form the Edison General Electric Company.

A significant improvement in Edison's system for distributing electric current was made by George Westinghouse, whose transformer enabled electricity to be transmitted as alternating current to far-away points. In 1885 the Westinghouse Electric Company came into existence as a manufacturer of transformers and alternating-current equipment.

The electrical industry — embracing companies selling electrical current and those selling appliances and equipment — had not existed before the Civil War. Now, as the twentieth century was dawning, the number of electric light bulbs in use was approaching 20,000,000. Power stations were also being built as fast as possible. In 1882 there were only 38 of them; by 1900 there were more than 3,000.

Alexander Graham Bell introduces the telephone. Another invention that gave rise to an important new industry was the tele-

phone. It was the work of Alexander Graham Bell, a speech teacher who had come to America from Scotland in 1871 to teach in a Boston school for the deaf. Besides teaching young people, Bell began work on a device he hoped to sell to Western Union. He was making an instrument for transmitting sound over a telegraph wire.

Bell's knowledge of acoustics — the science of sound — enabled him to build a telephone. Where the telegraph transmitted pulses of current translated into dots and dashes, the telephone required a continuous current. The current would vary in intensity exactly as the density of air varies when a given sound is made. As a result, the sound of a voice could be duplicated at the end of the wire.

The telephone was shown for the first time in Philadelphia at the Centennial Exposition of 1876, shortly after it was patented as an "improvement in telegraphy." Bell, then 29 years old, had the opportunity to demonstrate the telephone to the emperor of Brazil, Dom Pedro, who was visiting the exposition. "It talks!" shouted the emperor as he placed the instrument to his ear. Dom Pedro's interest brought the telephone to the attention of other visitors to the exposition. From that moment on, Bell's invention was a sensation.

Soon after the demonstration at Philadelphia, Bell and an assistant talked over a wire strung a distance of two miles between Boston and Cambridge, Massachusetts. In the years that followed, the number of telephone lines increased, and Bell continued to improve his invention. In 1877 a telephone was used for the first time to report a story to a newspaper. That same year the first switchboard was put into use. The first regularly employed operator was a man, in New Haven, Connecticut, who answered the phone "ahoy-ahoy" rather than "hello." Male operators soon were replaced by women, who were almost immediately nicknamed "hello girls."

The Bell Telephone Company was formed in 1877 by Gardiner G. Hubbard, a public-spirited man who in the 1850's had introduced gas for lighting purposes in Cambridge, Massachusetts. Hubbard had become interested in Bell's work because the Hubbards' daughter, Mabel, had been left completely deaf by an attack of scarlet fever. Two days before the Bell Company was formed, Mabel Hubbard, then eighteen years old, married Alexander Graham Bell.

Most of the money for the Bell Company came from Thomas Sanders, a Massachusetts horse-breeder and leather dealer. Sanders had had little faith at first in Bell's device for "talking by telegraph," but he had loaned the young Scotsman money for experimenting anyway. Sanders was grateful to Bell for teaching the Sanders' eldest child, who was deaf, how to read lips.

The Bell Company eventually became the giant American Telephone and Telegraph Company. Made up of various local companies, it enabled customers to make telephone calls from one end of the country to the other. Hubbard had keen business sense and he introduced a policy of renting, not selling, telephones to the public. In time the Bell system became one of the most reliable telephone networks in the world.

New forms of business organization are developed.
Throughout the late 1800's, corporations in the same business tended to join together to form large combinations. In so doing, they eliminated competition and reduced waste and the risk of losses.

Pools. One way many corporations acted in combination was by forming **pools.** The pool was an arrangement by which corporations in the same line of business agreed to control their output and divide up the available market. Sometimes business pools went so far as to place the profits of an industry in a joint treasury and later share them according to proportions agreed upon. More commonly, as for example among the railroads in a particular region, the managers would meet and decide what percentage of local business each would control. Such arrangements were finally outlawed in 1887 when the Interstate Commerce Act prohibited railroad pools. Pools might have died out anyway, since their agreements had no legal standing, were not enforceable, and were often violated by the participants.

The business trusts increasingly drew criticism. Published in a popular magazine, this cartoon characterized the trusts as birds of prey who grew fat by feeding upon the Senate.

Mergers. An answer to the shortcomings of the pool was the outright **merger** of rivals in the same industry. Usually the strongest in a group of competitors would buy out the others. The powerful New York Central Railroad came into existence in this way. Similarly, the Edison Electric Light Company merged with other companies to form the General Electric Company.

Trusts. A more common form of business combination was the **trust.** Under this arrangement stockholders deposited their stock certificates with a board of trustees and received trust certificates in exchange. Through the trust a number of companies actually united into one system.

The first trust was formed in 1882 when John D. Rockefeller organized the Standard Oil Company. This trust established a virtual monopoly of the nation's oil-refining facilities. Soon, other business leaders saw advantages in forming trusts. Competition in a particular industry could be practically eliminated and prices could be controlled. Unlike the pools, trusts were chartered by state legislatures.

By the 1890's, the nation had giant trusts in sugar, tobacco, lead, and whiskey. A large number of smaller trusts had also been organized. Soon the word *trust* was being used to describe any monopoly or near-monopoly.

Many Americans objected to the vast power that trusts could exercise. They pointed out that since its earliest days the United States had prospered under a *free enterprise system.* Free enterprise permits businesses to compete in the selling of goods and services to the largest possible number of people. It is a system, furthermore, in which private individuals have the responsibility for making economic decisions. The creation of trusts, critics charged, was an abuse of the free enterprise system. They pointed out that though business operators liked to say that "competition is the life of trade," in actuality they worked to reduce it as much as possible.

To try and restore some competition and prevent harmful monopolies, Congress passed the Sherman Antitrust Act in 1890. The new law made it illegal for businesses to set up monopolies. However, the Sherman Antitrust Act was vaguely worded and difficult to enforce.

Holding companies. After 1890 still newer forms of business consolidation were being organized. One was the *holding company.* In a holding company, a new corporation is formed and stock is issued. The money raised from the sale of the stock is then used to purchase the stock of other corporations. Without producing any goods or services, therefore, a holding company could control the corporations whose stocks it held.

Interlocking directorates. Another form of business consolidation was the *interlocking directorate.* Under this method, a group of directors of one company served as directors for several other companies. Consequently, they could develop a uniform policy for an entire industry or, for that matter, for several industries.

Finance capitalists provide funds for further investment. As American business continued to expand, a new kind of leader emerged — the *finance capitalist.* Finance capitalists were not usually qualified to provide technical know-how or to show how an industry could be made more productive. They did not deal in the products of an industry as such. Rather, they were bankers who exerted their influence through control of the bonds and stocks that corporations issued to raise money. A finance capitalist's center of activity was not the grimy atmosphere of the factory town but splendid offices in the financial district of a major city.

The most powerful of all finance capitalists was J. Pierpont Morgan. Born to wealth and college-educated — unlike practically all the other industrialists of his time — Morgan opened a branch office of the family banking firm in New York City in 1860. Turning to railroads, he took an important hand in ending stock speculation and in creating consolidated lines out of rival ones. By the end of the century he had helped finance the Hill system (page 447), as well as the New York Central and Pennsylvania systems.

Morgan's influence gradually extended throughout the nation's economy and included control over commercial banks, insurance companies, and a wide range of stock-market operations. The sums of money Morgan dealt in stagger the imagination. When Andrew Carnegie sold out his company to Morgan (page 449), Morgan's payment made Carnegie the richest man in the world. A year or two later the men met again, on shipboard. In the course of conversation, Carnegie said, "I made one mistake, Pierpont, when I sold out to you." "What was that?" asked Morgan. "I should have asked you for a hundred million more than I did," said Carnegie. "Well," replied Morgan, "you would have got it if you had."

In 1912 it was reported that Morgan and his banking associates held positions as directors in 112 corporations with assets of over $22 billion. This sum was said at the time to be three times greater than the assessed value of all the real estate in New York City.

Business leaders dominate American society. Successful business leaders like Morgan, Carnegie, and Rockefeller became well-known public figures. Where politicians had been popular idols in the early days of the republic, many industrialists and finance capitalists were now national heroes. Their dealings created jobs for thousands; they lived like wealthy monarchs; and they were actively changing the very look of America by the railroads they built, by the products they manufactured, and by the standard of living they helped raise. They acted decisively and boldly, and they had an air of authority that Americans found lacking in many of their elected leaders at that time.

Underlying the public's admiration of successful business leaders was a widespread conviction that it was possible for practically anybody to go from rags to riches. The son of an Irish immigrant who rose to prominence as a lawyer pointed out, "In worn-out king-ridden Europe, men must stay where they are born. But in America a man is accounted a failure, and certainly ought to be, who has not risen above his father's station in life."

The most influential children's books of the era, those of Horatio Alger, helped popularize the "rags-to-riches" theme. Alger's books, which poured from his pen in a steady stream, inspired youths who were eager to rise from poverty. Some of the titles tell of their contents: *Strive and Succeed, Brave and Bold, Strong and Steady, Slow and Sure, Try and Trust.* These books reinforced the belief in old sayings like "Genius thrives on adversity," and "There's always room at the top."

The new millionaires, for their part, believed in the theory of the "survival of the fittest," having concluded that they themselves were best suited to run American business. As to swallowing up their weaker competitors, was it not, they said, a law of nature that in the ocean big fish eat little fish, and that on land weak animals become prey to the strong? Rockefeller once summed up the industrialists' point of view about destroying their competitors by comparing the process to the cultivation of a rose. "The American Beauty rose," he said, "can be produced in the splendor and fragrance which bring cheer to its beholder only by sacrificing the early buds which grow up around it. This is not an evil tendency in business. It is merely the working-out of a law of nature and of God."

These thoughts were accompanied by another and kindlier point of view that many of the new millionaires advanced, one that Carnegie called "the gospel of wealth." Monied people, Carnegie said, must not gloat over their wealth. They should, rather, view themselves as guardians of it for the whole community. A rich person, he said, is simply "the agent and trustee for his poorer brethren, bringing to their service his superior wisdom, experience, and ability to administer, doing for them better than they would or could do for themselves." The gifts that Carnegie made (page 449) showed that he tried to live by what he preached.

In 1889, one hundred years after George Washington was sworn in as the nation's first Chief Executive, Benjamin Harrison of Indiana became President. The America he knew was worlds removed from the one in which Washington had made his mark. The new President observed proudly in his inaugural address that America now possessed "power and wealth beyond definition." But what would be their effect on the nation? The lofty principles of the United States faced a new time of testing.

SECTION REVIEW

1. Vocabulary: *monopoly, pool, merger, trust, free enterprise system, holding company, interlocking directorate, finance capitalist.*
2. What parts did Andrew Carnegie and John D. Rockefeller play in the expansion of American industry?
3. (a) Who were some of the leading American inventor-industrialists? (b) What new industries grew up as a result of their inventions?
4. (a) For what reasons did Americans look up to successful business leaders? (b) How did industrialists justify their business methods?

Chapter 19 Review

Summary

In the decades after the Civil War the United States experienced extraordinary economic growth, making it in time the world's leading industrial power. A number of factors contributed to this development. One was "Yankee ingenuity," which produced many of the inventions that spurred the growth of American industry. Another was the availability of an energetic and growing labor force required by large manufacturing concerns. Yet another was access at home to huge amounts of indispensable natural resources — including coal, iron ore, and oil. These factors were enhanced by the encouragement and assistance the federal government gave to industry and by the substantial investments made in America by wealthy European and American capitalists. The creation of the corporation facilitated the raising of money to finance industrial activity.

Hand in hand with industry went the development of an extensive railroad system. The railroads expanded rapidly after the Civil War, reaching a total of nearly 200,000 miles of track by 1900. Small railroads were merged to form trunk systems that linked the large cities of the East and the West. A transcontinental line was completed in 1869.

Railroads were essential to the settlement of the West. They brought thousands of European and American homesteaders to areas once remote. At the same time, they shipped east the products of the new western farms and ranches.

The expansion of industry created opportunities for enterprising individuals. Andrew Carnegie and John D. Rockefeller were two such people, rising from modest backgrounds to become millionaires and leaders of enormous industrial organizations. Carnegie made his reputation and fortune in the steel industry, while Rockefeller took advantage of the wealth to be made in the refining of oil.

Another group that acquired fame and fortune at this time were the inventor-industrialists. Among them were Thomas Edison, who contributed the phonograph and the electric light, and Alexander Graham Bell, who invented the telephone.

To control large manufacturing concerns and growing markets, business leaders devised various forms of business organizations. The pool, merger, trust, holding company, and interlocking directorate were all outgrowths of large industry. As the American economy continued to expand, banks became active in financing industrial growth. Finance capitalists such as J. Pierpont Morgan were powerful participants in all fields of business and industry.

Vocabulary and Important Terms

1. patent
2. capital
3. capitalist
4. corporation
5. stock
6. dividend
7. trunk line
8. "the gospel of wealth"
9. time zone
10. pool
11. monopoly
12. Bessemer process
13. merger
14. trust
15. free enterprise system
16. holding company
17. interlocking directorate
18. finance capitalist
19. Standard Oil Company
20. transcontinental railroad

Discussion Questions

1. (a) What role did inventors play in helping the United States develop industry? (b) For what reasons was a large work force available? (c) What resources were available? (d) How did the government promote the growth of industry?

2. (a) Why were both Europeans and Americans eager to invest their money in the expansion of industry? (b) How did the Civil War help to stimulate economic growth?

3. As American business continued to grow, what role did finance capitalists play in further industrial development?

4. (a) Why did the corporation become the leading form of American business organization after 1860? (b) Why did business corporations later join together to form large combinations?

5. (a) To what extent did railroads grow in the period after the Civil War? (b) Why was the development of railroads important to industrial growth?

6. (a) Why had a transcontinental railroad been proposed as early as the 1840's, and why had Congress been unable to carry out this proposal prior to the Civil War? (b) When did Congress agree to a transcontinental railroad? (c) To what extent were the hopes of the railroad's original promoters fulfilled?

7. (a) Who was James J. Hill? (b) What did he believe would be the future of the northern Great Plains? (c) How was he able to attract settlers to that area?

8. (a) How did Andrew Carnegie become the world's greatest manufacturer of steel? (b) Why in retirement did Carnegie give away much of his enormous wealth?

9. (a) What business practices enabled John D. Rockefeller to organize the Standard Oil Company?

(b) How did Rockefeller contribute to the nation's economic growth?

10. (a) What were some of Thomas Edison's creations? (b) What effects did the electrical industry have on American life?

11. (a) How did Horatio Alger's books popularize the "rags-to-riches" theme? (b) How did that theme contribute to the public's admiration of successful business leaders?

Relating Past to Present

1. One of the reasons for America's rapid industrial growth was the nation's abundance of minerals and other resources required for heavy industry. Which resources are still plentiful in the United States today? Which resources are not plentiful today?

2. New inventions during the period of great industrial growth improved transportation and communication. Among other things, these inventions helped bring people throughout the nation closer together. What are some modern-day inventions involving transportation and communication? How have they affected American life?

3. The "rags-to-riches" theme gained popularity in the late 1800's. Do the American people still believe that anyone can rise from "rags to riches"? Explain your answer.

Studying Local History

The rapidly expanding railroad lines in the period after the Civil War changed the face of America. What railroad building took place in your state between 1865 and 1900? How did this railroad expansion affect the growth of towns and cities in your state or region? In what other ways, if any, did the railroads affect life in your community?

Using History Skills

1. *Comparing graphs.* Study the graph on page 441 showing petroleum production and the graph on page 449 showing steel production. (a) Describe the gains made by the petroleum industry between 1860 and 1900. (b) Describe the gains made by the steel industry in those same years. (c) How does the upswing in production in these two industries correspond to the growth of heavy industry in the late 1800's?

2. *Placing events in time.* Make a time line that shows some events during the period that marked the rise of big business. On that time line include the following: (a) the completion of the first transcontinental railroad; (b) the invention of the telephone; (c) the organization of the Standard Oil Company; (d) the passage of the Sherman Antitrust Act.

WORLD SCENE

Capital for Railroads

Without capital from British, French, and German investors, the remarkable world-wide expansion of railroads during the 1800's could not have taken place so rapidly.

British investment in the Americas. During the 1700's the Industrial Revolution in Britain had led to the accumulation of large amounts of capital. The British, therefore, were in an especially good position to invest money required for railroad construction in other countries.

Helped by British investments, the expansion of railroads in North America was dramatic. In 1840 Canada and the United States had a total of 3,000 miles of track; by 1900 that total had increased to nearly 500,000 miles. In South America, where practically no railroads had existed in 1850, over 27,000 miles of track had been built by the end of the century.

Russian railroad expansion. In 1850 Russia was a sprawling land with only about 850

miles of railroad track. When the Russians lost the Crimean War in 1856, in part because they could not transport their army easily, they saw the importance of having a satisfactory railroad system.

Since Russia had neither the necessary funds nor the industrial strength for railway construction, the czars turned to Europe for help. The French, recognizing the diplomatic advantages in having Russia as a debtor, made substantial loans to finance Russian railroads. The emerging German nation, meanwhile, had an economy that was largely dependent on its iron and steel industries. Supplying Russia with thousands of miles of rails and hundreds of locomotives and railroad cars boosted German industry.

By the early 1900's Russia had been able to add 40,000 miles to its railroads, including the important Trans-Siberian line. This route, stretching across Asia for 4,000 miles, connected Moscow with the Pacific coast port of Vladivostok.

CHAPTER 20

An Urban Industrial Society

1865 – 1900

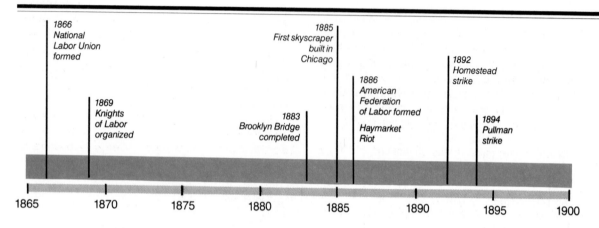

1866
National
Labor Union
formed

1869
Knights
of Labor
organized

1883
Brooklyn Bridge
completed

1885
First skyscraper
built in
Chicago

1886
American
Federation
of Labor formed

Haymarket
Riot

1892
Homestead
strike

1894
Pullman
strike

1865　1870　1875　1880　1885　1890　1895　1900

CHAPTER OUTLINE

1. Immigrants continue to move to the United States.

2. Cities grow rapidly after the Civil War.

3. Laborers organize to improve working conditions.

4. Organized labor faces strong opposition.

The opportunities offered by the expansion of American industry drew millions of immigrants to the United States. Most of them were young people unable or unlikely to make a go of it at home. They felt the force embodied in a song that the labor leader Samuel Gompers had learned as a child in Europe, and that Andrew Carnegie's father also once sang with hope. The tune begins:

> To the west, to the west, to the land of the free
> Where mighty Missouri rolls down to the sea,
> Where a man is a man if he's willing to toil,
> And the humblest may gather the fruits of the soil.

The immigrants helped make the wheels of American industry turn faster. Mostly from agricultural regions in their native lands, they went to work in the urban centers of the North and the Middle West, alongside native-born Americans also from the countryside.

As a result of the post-Civil War immigration, the ballooning cities became jumbles of ethnic neighborhoods. The city dwellers were forced to endure overcrowding, poor sanitation, and the threat of raging fires. Still, the combined labors of the millions of workers contributed to a higher standard of living year after year for everybody — including the workers themselves.

1 Immigrants Continue to Move to the United States

Between 1870 and 1900, more than eleven million immigrants entered the United States. Until the 1880's most immigrants came from western and northern Europe — from Great Britain, Ireland, Germany, and Scandinavia. On the eve of the Civil War, natives of Ireland, Germany, and Great Britain had made up 80 percent of America's foreign-born population. By 1890, however, the pattern of immigration had changed. Increasingly large numbers of people began arriving from southern and eastern Europe — from Italy, Greece, Russia (including Poland), and Austria-Hungary.

Most immigrants settle in cities. Unlike earlier immigrants, relatively few of those who came to America in the generation after the Civil War took up farming. Most of them settled in the large urban centers of the North. New York City was the principal point of entry for immigrants from Europe. Vast numbers of the newcomers remained there, finding shelter in neighborhoods filled with relatives or friends. In New York City, they could find familiar foods and also advice in their own language on how to get started in America. Many of the immigrants flowed into Connecticut and New Jersey, finding work in the factories there, or into Pennsylvania's mining and manufacturing towns. The city of Buffalo on Lake Erie became a center of Polish and Italian immigrant life. Many Slavs — people from central, southern, and eastern Europe speaking closely related languages — found work in the Pennsylvania coal fields. Thousands of Slavs also found work in Cleveland's iron

Immigrants gaze at the Statue of Liberty after arriving in New York. For these people, like millions of others, America seemed to be a land of golden opportunity.

and steel plants. Chicago, the hub of the nation's railroad network and the site of a variety of industries, rapidly acquired the largest number of Poles and Czechs in the country.

In New York as well as Philadelphia, Boston, and Cincinnati, German Jews established garment businesses and gave work to many fellow-newcomers. The growth of specialized labor had ended dressmaking at home for most Americans, and the market for mass-produced clothing seemed a likely place in which to make a living. The Irish also tended to settle in cities, and like other newcomers they were often recruited to work at building the railroads, bridges, and tunnels that the emerging industries required.

Reasons for immigration are unchanged. The basic reason for the flood tide of immigration — no matter from what part of the world — remained the same as in earlier decades. People regarded the United States

This graph shows immigration between 1820 and 1900. During that period, more than 19 million immigrants came to American shores.

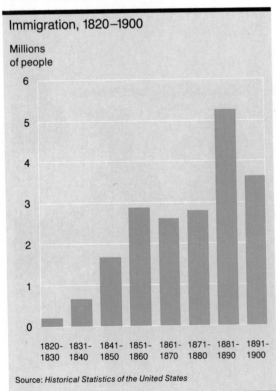

Immigration, 1820–1900

Millions of people

6
5
4
3
2
1
0

1820-1830 1831-1840 1841-1850 1851-1860 1861-1870 1871-1880 1881-1890 1891-1900

Source: *Historical Statistics of the United States*

as a "promised land" with bright opportunities for themselves and their children. The factors that motivated specific immigrant groups to move to America varied widely, however. The experiences of southern Italian farmers and eastern European Jews offer two illustrations.

Italian immigration. Agriculture in Italy was disastrously affected by events of the 1880's. The rising production of lemons and oranges in California and Florida was wiping out the American market for Italian citrus fruit. Moreover, the market in France for Italian wines was being cut severely by high French tariffs. On top of everything, severe epidemics of cholera had killed tens of thousands of Italians.

America beckoned to the survivors of these bad times. Up to 1879 there had never been a year in which as many as 5,000 Italians immigrated to the United States. Then, in 1880 it seemed as if the floodgates had opened. By the middle 1880's tens of thousands of Italians were arriving each year, with the figure reaching 100,000 in 1900, soaring to more than 230,000 in 1903, and peaking in 1914 at 284,000.

In their flight from poverty at home, the Italian immigrants were often at the mercy of employers who took advantage of their unfamiliarity with the English language. Hundreds of thousands of young Italian men were already in the hands of labor bosses by the time they set foot in the United States. At first the system worked this way: a *padrone* — an Italian American who could speak English and knew American ways — would recruit young men in the villages of southern Italy. He could promise them jobs because he already had made arrangements with American factory owners or construction contractors. The *padrone* paid for the ocean passage of the young immigrants and put them to work as soon as they landed. He made a good living by supplying gangs of workers to American industrialists. In fact, the workers' salaries were usually paid directly to the *padrone*, who deducted a commission for himself.

After 1890 so many Italians came to America on their own that it was no longer necessary to search the Italian countryside

Immigrants in America

Millions of immigrants left their homes for the promise of a better life in the United States. Many arrived carrying everything they owned. Adjusting to life in America included celebrating the holidays of their new country (above) and sending their children to school to learn English (left).

for workers. The *padrone* served simply as an employment agent whose ability to obtain housing for the newcomers made them dependent on him.

The Italians, like all immigrants, took jobs wherever they could find them. When they were able to escape backbreaking labor with the shovel, they opened barber shops, vegetable and fruit stores, ice and coal dealerships, bakeries, and restaurants. Many Italians spent their first years in America working and scrimping in order to send money to enable relatives to join them in the land of opportunity. As time went on, the Italian immigrants could take satisfaction that they were adding to the country's supply of goods and services.

Jewish immigration. Among the newer immigrants from eastern Europe were significant numbers of Jews. Jews, of course, had been present in the United States since colonial times. As late as 1877, however, they totaled only about 250,000 people. Then, by the 1880's, Jews started to arrive in large numbers. Of the more than two million Jewish immigrants who came to the United States between 1870 and 1900, most were from Russia. Relaxed emigration laws enabled them to flee from political and religious persecution in their homeland.

The uprooted Jews streamed into the poorest parts of New York, Philadelphia, and Chicago. Thousands of them found work with Jewish employers in the garment

461

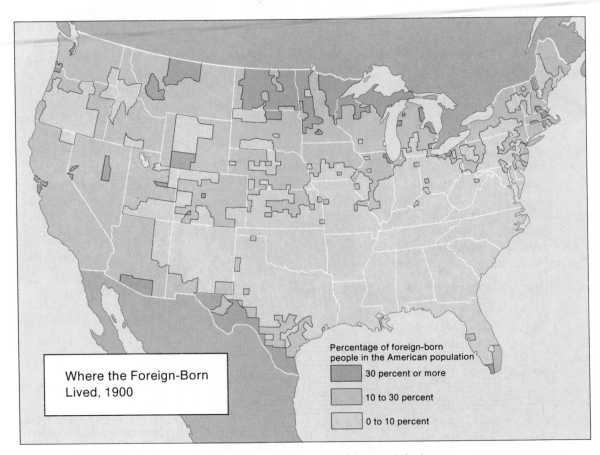

Where the Foreign-Born Lived, 1900

Percentage of foreign-born people in the American population

- 30 percent or more
- 10 to 30 percent
- 0 to 10 percent

In 1900 a number of states had areas where more than 30 percent of the people had been born in other countries.

industry. Others threw themselves into the variety of opportunities that urban living offered to all Americans. Like other immigrant groups, the Jews looked to their children to lift the whole family through economic and social success. Aided by habits of study and learning that had been deeply ingrained through the centuries, the young people quickly took advantage of educational facilities. Their study of science, medicine, and the law often led to brilliant achievement in the expanding society, which had large need for people with such training.

Calls for restriction of immigration are heard. Some native-born Americans, alarmed by the size of the post-Civil War immigration, began demanding restrictions on the number of newcomers. They pointed out

that during the period of the "old immigration" before the war, the largest number of people who had ever arrived in one year totaled only 400,000. Now, with the "new immigration," as many as 750,000 people were arriving every year. How could so many newcomers be absorbed into American life, they asked?

Critics of the traditional policy of unrestricted immigration offered a variety of arguments. Some of the newcomers, they said, were simply "birds of passage" — people who came to the United States planing to remain a short time and then go back to Europe, without becoming Americans. Indeed, many eastern Europeans immigrated simply to make enough money in order to live comfortably in the old country. It is said, for instance, that most Greek immigrants, deeply devoted to their native land, came to the United States without any intention of staying permanently. They were chiefly peasants forced by crop failures to seek opportunity overseas — temporarily, they assumed. The 500,000 Greeks who came to America in the years 1900 to 1925 represented about 10 percent of the entire Greek population.

Foreigners also aroused criticism because they appeared to be clannish — sticking together in their own well-defined neighborhoods in the cities and factory towns. Most big cities had a "little Italy" or a "little Rumania" or a "little Armenia," as the case might be. Actually, in these neighborhoods the newcomers found the friendship and security they needed to survive in a new country.

Immigrants came under criticism, too, for working in low-paying jobs. Many unions opposed further immigration, maintaining that newcomers were undercutting American labor. In truth, people newly arrived in the United States took jobs at low pay not because they wanted to but because they had no choice. Furthermore, the jobs they took often were the least desirable ones, jobs they would shun in a few years.

Religious prejudice also often lay behind sentiment to restrict immigration. It was more polite to be anti-immigrant than to be anti-Semitic or anti-Catholic, and the effect could be the same. Jews had long felt the barbs of discrimination. In one well-remembered incident in 1877, Joseph Seligman, a financier and long-time friend of President Grant, was turned away from the Grand Union Hotel at Saratoga, New York. The owner had decided to exclude "Israelites as a class" from his establishment. Now, as Jews became more numerous, the ancient shameful prejudice against them often became evident. At many places of employment the sign "No Jews" was familiar by the beginning of the 1900's.

The sign "No Catholics need apply" was also seen — a tragic, bigoted response to the fact that the majority of new immigrants were Roman Catholics. The American Protective Association, an anti-Catholic organization founded in Iowa in 1887,

spread from its rural stronghold to the big cities in the 1890's. This and other similar groups beat the drums for limiting the suffrage to native-born Americans. In this way, they insisted, America could protect itself from the Roman Catholic Church which, they alleged, instructed its members on how to vote. A professor at Columbia College in New York, supporting the restriction of immigration, said that newcomers should not have the suffrage until the "power of American life has had time to loosen the bonds of priestly authority."

Immigration from China is restricted. The first significant steps to restrict immigration were taken against the Chinese. Many Americans had once heartily welcomed the Chinese, who began to arrive in California in the 1850's. A journalist there, watching Chinese people parade in celebration of Washington's Birthday, once called them "our most orderly and industrious citizens." Then, when the Panic of 1873 struck and bad times followed, the competition for jobs became intense. The cry, "The Chinese must go!" was suddenly heard, and anti-Chinese riots broke out in California.

Under a treaty with China in 1868, Chinese immigrants had been formally granted the right to enter the United States in unlimited numbers. Before long, however, a new treaty was negotiated, giving the United States the right to "regulate, limit or suspend" but not "absolutely prohibit" the immigration of Chinese workers. Finally, in 1882 Congress suspended all immigration from China for a period of ten years. This Chinese Exclusion Act was extended several times and remained in effect until World War II. The passage of the law was the first change in the traditional American policy of "come one, come all."

SECTION REVIEW

1. (a) What changes took place in patterns of immigration after the Civil War? (b) Why did most immigrants settle in cities?
2. (a) Why did some Americans call for restrictions on immigration? (b) What restrictive measure was enacted?

2 Cities Grow Rapidly After the Civil War

A phenomenal growth of cities accompanied the development of American industry. Factories and mills were built in or near urban communities in order to attract immigrants and native-born Americans looking for work. Houses, consisting at first mostly of ramshackle shanties, were quickly thrown up to accommodate the workers and their families.

As street after street filled up, America was on its way to becoming "a nation of cities." In the years between 1870 and 1900, the number of people living in cities of 100,000 or more increased from four million to fourteen million. Only one city — New York — had a million people in 1870. By 1900 Chicago and Philadelphia had also passed the million mark.

Cities face new problems. The rapid growth of urban America brought about problems not quickly solved. The most pressing need was the supplying of safe drinking water. As late as 1878, only 600 communities had reliable sources of water and modern systems to distribute it. The high rate of typhoid fever in cities lacking proper water-supply systems dramatized the need.

The quest for safe water supplies was stimulated by the growing acceptance of the germ theory of disease, which grew out of the work of the French biologist Louis Pasteur. Still, urban public health, closely related to the purity of drinking water, lagged behind that of rural America. As late as 1890, a baby born in a large American city could expect to live only 44 years — ten years less than a child born on a farm.

The disposal of wastes was another problem. While New York, Boston, and a few other places had some sewer lines, they were inadequate for the needs of the expanding population. Most cities simply drained their sewage into nearby rivers and lakes. Chicago's sewage was dumped into Lake Michigan, from which the city also drew its drinking water. Philadelphia poured its wastes into the Delaware River.

Memphis began to build a modern sewer system in 1880 (following a frightening yellow-fever epidemic wrongly blamed on improper waste disposal). Soon, other cities followed suit and built plants to dispose of sewage satisfactorily.

Cities expand in area. Until the 1850's cities and towns were compactly arranged, built in many instances on a waterfront. Commercial activities were carried on along the docks. Close by were warehouses, various manufacturing establishments, and shipping offices. Not far away were banks, churches, shops, and the city or town hall. Scattered among these structures were the dwellings. In the best locations — as, for instance, on the top of a hill — lived the wealthier people. Nearby, however, would

Ten Largest Cities in the United States		
1860	1880	1900
1. New York 813,669	New York 1,206,299	New York 3,437,202
2. Philadelphia 565,529	Philadelphia 847,170	Chicago 1,698,575
3. Baltimore 212,418	Chicago 503,185	Philadelphia 1,293,697
4. Boston 177,840	Boston 362,839	St. Louis 575,238
5. New Orleans 168,675	St. Louis 350,518	Boston 560,892
6. Cincinnati 161,044	Baltimore 332,313	Baltimore 508,957
7. St. Louis 160,773	Cincinnati 255,139	Cleveland 381,768
8. Chicago 109,260	San Francisco 233,959	Buffalo 352,387
9. Buffalo 81,129	New Orleans 216,090	San Francisco 342,782
10. Newark 71,941	Washington 177,624	Cincinnati 325,902

Source: *Twelfth Census of the U.S., 1900*

Advances in transportation and communication contributed to the rapid growth of cities after the Civil War. This 1892 painting shows a busy street in Indianapolis.

be people of lesser means. Rich and poor, immigrant and native-born, lived in close proximity to one another.

The need for everything to be within walking distance of everything else controlled the physical size of these cities. One effect, however, was that they became crowded. Even before big factories, the density of urban population was startling. By 1850 an acre in New York City contained on average 135 people; in Boston and Philadelphia, around 80.

These "walking cities" began to disappear by the time of the Civil War. Bridges and ferries enabled some people to move to nearby towns and villages while still holding jobs in the cities. What broke the limited size of cities and allowed them to sprawl, however, was the development of new systems of urban transportation.

Advances are made in urban transportation. Some experimenting in transportation had already been carried on by enterprising individuals. Omnibuses — long, horse-drawn vehicles with two decks — had operated on the streets of major cities since the 1830's. The first omnibus (copied from a French version) was actually a stagecoach that ran on Broadway in New York City in the time of Andrew Jackson. The omnibus driver rode up and down the thoroughfare, picking up passengers and taking them where they wanted to go. Before long, the system became regular, and the idea behind it spread to other cities.

An improvement on the horse-drawn omnibus was the horse-drawn streetcar which ran on rails. The first one, built by John Stevenson of Philadelphia, was put into service by the New York and Harlem Railway in 1832. Running the vehicle on tracks helped provide a smoother, faster ride. Streetcars, which could hold thirty passengers, were divided into three compartments with ten seats each. Within a few years much bigger vehicles were being constructed, capable of transporting substantially more people.

Despite much experimentation, not until the 1880's did electrically operated streetcars come upon the scene. The first electric streetcar was put into use in 1886 in Montgomery, Alabama. This vehicle, looking much like the horse-drawn streetcar, had a motor at the front powered by a cable attached to a wire strung overhead along the right of way.

The electric streetcar was perfected by Frank Sprague, a young graduate of the Naval Academy who had worked with Thomas Edison. Sprague became an expert builder of motors, and his genius lay in adapting his "constant speed" motor to street-railway service. He completed the first street railway system in Richmond, Virginia, in 1888. This triumph was remarkable because of the many steep grades and sharp curves the cars had to negotiate in Richmond. For the transmission of electric current to his vehicles, Sprague relied on a troller — a wheeled device that moved along on an overhead wire. Soon the word troller became "trolley," and trolley-car lines were being built in every city of substantial size.

Some of the largest cities dealt with local transportation by constructing elevated railways. The first of them appeared in New York in the 1870's. These "els" allowed more street room than even the trolley cars. Still, they were unsightly and noisy, and created barriers to air and light for people who lived along their path. As an alternative to "els," major cities such as Boston (1897) and New York (1904) began to build subways or "undergrounds."

Improved transportation helps make suburbs possible. The development of transportation systems had an almost immediate effect on the larger cities and their surrounding communities. Take, for example, the city of Boston. In 1850 Boston was still a walking city with a diameter of four miles. By 1873 the city's limits had been extended half a mile, and another mile and a half was added by the end of the 1880's. The edge of settlement by then was about four miles from City Hall. In the 1890's, the distance to the city line from City Hall had become six miles. Trolleys — accompanied shortly by electric commuter trains — then made their appearance. Now people could travel many miles to the city from out of town, and return at night. When that happened, the first true suburbs came into existence.

Advances in architecture help cities adapt to the growth of population. Devising ways of moving people through and under city streets was made possible by engineering know-how that only an industrial nation develops. Another by-product of advanced technology was the ability to construct taller buildings than ever before.

From the 1850's to the early 1880's cast iron was widely used to erect tall buildings — as high as five stories. The man who first used cast iron in the construction of urban commercial buildings was a New Yorker, James Bogardus. Cast iron — hard, brittle, and heavy — can be inexpensively produced and can support great weight. In the major cities cast iron was first used in constructing department stores. These popular institutions for displaying and selling large amounts of consumer goods were yet another result of industrial growth and response to urban life.

Bogardus's achievement produced a need to be able to transport people safely between floors in a tall building. Elisha G. Otis, a native of New England, answered the need. Otis invented the first elevator with an automatic safety device. If the cables broke, the device kept the elevator from falling. Otis's first elevator was installed in a New York City department store in 1857. Frank Sprague, the trolley-car pioneer, made improvements in elevator motors, and the first electric elevator began operation in 1889. Sprague's elevator business was later taken over by the Otis Company.

Soon, architects and engineers found ways to erect taller and taller buildings. They assembled gigantic steel frames to support structures of many stories. The first skyscraper, completed in 1885, was the Home Insurance Building in Chicago, ten stories high. In the next few years, even taller buildings went up, primarily in New York and Chicago.

The pace of activity in major cities was constantly stimulated by the traffic that new bridges helped deliver. These bridges linked the parts of urban communities separated by rivers. The completion in 1883 of the Brooklyn Bridge, connecting Brooklyn

Until the completion of the Manhattan Bridge, shown here under construction, ferries in New York City connected the boroughs of Manhattan and Brooklyn.

and the island of Manhattan, gave New York a structure of rare beauty. Designed by John A. Roebling, it was also an engineering marvel, the longest suspension bridge in the world.

Only a few years earlier the Eads Bridge, a steel and masonry structure, had been built over the Mississippi River at St. Louis, Missouri. During the late 1800's Boston bridged the Charles River; Pittsburgh, the Allegheny; and St. Paul and Minneapolis, the Mississippi.

The need for city housing is great. As urban transportation systems permitted cities to expand physically, "downtown" in large cities became a distinct place. It was the scene of bustle, crowded roadways, and more and more tall buildings making canyons of the narrow streets and allowing little sunlight to fall upon them. People who could not afford better accommodations were forced to live in run-down dwellings in the shadow of these buildings. Working people who were somewhat better off lived a distance away in buildings known as *tenements.* The word *tenement* originally referred to any dwelling containing room for more than three families. New York's first

tenements, built in 1850, were designed as an improvement for poor people who had been living in cellars and even flimsy shacks. The tenements contained "railroad flats," that is, apartments laid out with rooms leading one to another in a straight line.

New York's Tenement House Law of 1879 was regarded as providing a major improvement in tenement construction. The law required the construction of the so-called "dumbbell" tenement — named after the shape of its floor plan. The buildings, five or six stories high, contained on each floor fourteen rooms in two three-room and two four-room apartments. The arrangement satisfied the legal requirement that every room in the new tenements have a window. In the hall were two toilets to serve the needs of four families.

Ideal for New York's standard lot size of 25 by 100 feet, a dumbbell tenement also provided an air shaft on each side because of the indention in the middle of the building. These shafts gave some light and ventilation to the interior rooms. The airshafts were a curse, however, if fire broke out, because they insured the rapid spread of the flames.

467

Following the opening of the Metropolitan Museum of Art in 1880, New Yorkers could enjoy looking at paintings once held in private collections.

Ten tenements to a city block meant that as many as 4,000 people were jammed together under conditions constantly exposing them to disease and vermin as well as fire. So many people died of tuberculosis on one block of New York's Lower East Side that it was known as "lung block." These slum areas were home to thousands of poor people, most of them immigrants, in the nation's teeming cities.

Significant tenement-house reform came only slowly. In 1901 New York passed a law requiring a more open courtyard for each building and a separate toilet for each apartment. Many slum dwellers, however, could not afford to rent a flat, or apartment, in the new buildings. Attempts to limit the number of people who could live in a flat, moreover, were resisted by the very people reformers hoped to help. One of the few ways most slum dwellers could eke out a living was by taking in boarders.

Cities provide cultural and educational opportunities. If the nation's rapidly growing cities suffered from problems, they also presented advantages. City people had more cultural facilities than did people in rural areas. The larger the population, the easier it was for men and women eager to pursue particular interests to find like-minded people. The Metropolitan Museum of Art in New York, as an example, was opened in 1880. It placed on view some of the artistic treasures of the world. In time, almost every major city had museums.

Music, too, became available for more than a mere few. In 1873 Cincinnati established the May Music Festival, which became an annual civic highlight. A number of large cities also had symphony orchestras which came to be compared favorably with some of the best in the world. Practically every city supported a public library system out of tax revenues.

People were able to find in the cities many other ways to fill their leisure time. They could attend sport events or theaters or simply visit relatives and friends elsewhere in town. They could also have the pleasure of shopping in the multitude of retail stores that lined the principal avenues and side streets.

The department store became an important place for browsing as well as for shopping. R. H. Macy and Company, which had opened in New York in 1858, was one of the first. Later, some of the many types of goods that department stores could provide were made available to isolated farm communities by mail-order houses. The firm of Montgomery Ward, which began operation in Chicago in 1872, pioneered in distributing a catalog of goods for sale by mail. Such catalogs helped to spread city styles to rural areas and thus make those styles national.

Cities also provided educational opportunities not available elsewhere. Large schools, characteristic of the cities, could have a more varied course of study than the small ones found in villages and towns. Moreover, city schools could be more readily supervised. Standards were, therefore, more easily set and maintained than in country schoolhouses. The bigger communities, furthermore, had the means for enforcing laws making attendance in school compulsory.

SECTION REVIEW

1. Vocabulary: *tenement.*
2. (a) What problems arose from the rapid growth of cities after the Civil War? (b) What efforts were made to find solutions to those problems?
3. How did advances in urban transportation and architecture contribute to the growth of cities?
4. What cultural and educational opportunities did cities provide?

3 Laborers Organize to Improve Working Conditions

Although the expansion of manufacturing provided jobs for millions of people, industrialization also had unwelcome effects. Working people looked for ways to deal with problems that concerned them.

Factory work is monotonous. The most noticeable fact about factory work was that working people using machines were doing the same task over and over again, making the workday boring and monotonous. The massing of large numbers of people in factories, moreover, made many workers feel that they were mere cogs in a giant system, that they were individuals no longer.

Workers also came to recognize that, like machine parts, they themselves were replaceable parts in industrial America. With so many people competing for jobs, some factory operators felt little concern over the wages and working conditions of their help. An employee who complained could be replaced overnight.

Workers fear loss of jobs. Among the most troubling effects of industrial growth was periodic unemployment. One kind of unemployment was seasonal, resulting from the regular closing down of factories (usually to conform with the ups and downs of the market or the availability of raw materials). The other kind of unemployment was called structural unemployment. It occurred — and still occurs — during hard times, when plants shut down for an indefinite period because of a lack of demand for their products.

Workers in the garment industry were in the forefront of the movement to organize American laborers into unions.

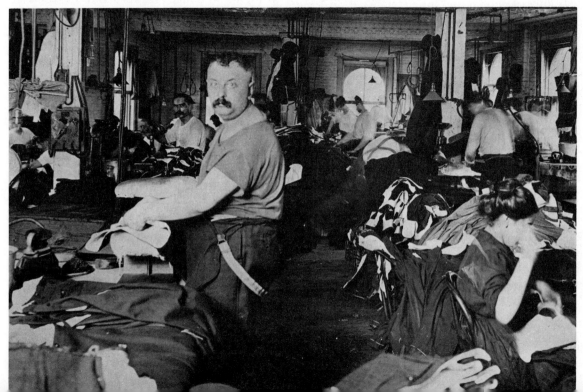

The industrial world also produced periodic panics and depressions, resulting in widespread general joblessness. Before the Civil War, unemployment had not been as devastating to most workers as it would be later on. In the earlier days many of the laid-off people could return to the family farm and wait until things improved. After the Civil War, however, millions of people had permanently moved to the big cities. Now a lay-off could be a calamity. For immigrants especially there was no way to "return to the farm." At best the unemployed could rely on the good will of more fortunate neighbors, or possibly on handouts from local charities. No government agency existed to offer assistance.

Factory work is dangerous. Yet another distressing fact was that many workers were laboring at machines that could maim or kill. The hazards grew worse as new, faster equipment was introduced. Workers' safety was often neglected when employers went forward with plans to speed up production.

New relations exist between worker and employer. Many working people who read about the new millionaires no doubt envied them. Working people still remembered that rich men had been able to buy their way out of the Civil War draft (page 387). Workers never forgot, either, that the increase in prices of consumer goods during the war had not been accompanied by a comparable rise in wages. Added to the old resentments was a particular new one: factory workers rarely experienced the close contact with their employers that had once been common in small workshops. Unable to have ready contact with their employers, working people found it practically impossible to complain about their conditions of work — except among themselves.

William Sylvis organizes the National Labor Union. By the time the Civil War ended, there was fertile ground for organizing factory workers into unions. Labor unions were not new in the United States. Circumstances now presented fresh opportunity,

however, for imaginative labor leaders to do their work.

One of the first able organizers was William Sylvis of Pennsylvania. A leader in the iron-molders union in Philadelphia, Sylvis had been instrumental in 1859 in bringing together representatives from eighteen locals to form the Iron Molders International Union. By 1865 Sylvis's union was the strongest labor organization in the country, boasting 53 locals and a total membership of 7,000.

A persuasive speaker, Sylvis was hostile to the new capitalist leaders, denouncing them as "a monied aristocracy — proud and dishonest, blasting and withering everything it comes in contact with." In 1866 Sylvis organized the National Labor Union in Baltimore. Two years later he became its president, bringing to the role his inexhaustible energy. He would say of the union, "I hold it more dear than I do my family or my life."

Sylvis and the other founders of the National Labor Union hoped to combine in "one big family" farmers and workers — skilled and unskilled — all across the United States. The union would seek, too, to improve the conditions of "the sewing-women and daughters of toil in this land." In 1868 the union accepted delegates from women's suffrage groups, and in 1869 it seated black delegates. In an era when most employees worked ten or twelve hours a day, the National Labor Union was calling for an eight-hour working day. It also advocated tenement-house reform, the establishment of reading rooms and educational facilities for working people, and the transfer of public land to genuine settlers only and not to speculators.

The National Labor Union collapses. At the height of its power, the National Labor Union had 600,000 members. However, Sylvis's death after just a year in office was a blow from which the National Labor Union could not recover. The union later tried to turn itself into a political organization — the National Labor Reform Party — but in the presidential election of 1872 it made a very poor showing and collapsed shortly afterward.

The movement for an eight-hour day continues. Union leaders did not give up the fight for an eight-hour work day. A leading spokesman for this reform was Ira Steward, a Bostonian. At the age of nineteen he had served an apprenticeship as a machinist and was forced to work twelve hours a day. His insistence on shorter hours cost him his job. He was dismissed for holding "peculiar views." Steward persisted in his crusade so earnestly that he became known as "the eight-hour monomaniac." He formed the Grand Eight-Hour League of Massachusetts, which soon was copied in many states.

Steward believed that workers should be paid no less for an eight-hour day than for a longer one. A popular jingle that Steward's wife wrote helped make the idea clear:

> Whether you work by the piece or work by
>   the day
> Decreasing the hours increases the pay.

Steward contended that if working people had a shorter workday, they would have time to enjoy the use of more goods, including possibly those they themselves were making. In that way, as Steward saw it, employers no less than employees would benefit from a shortening of the hours of work, because the factory products would find a larger market. By 1867 six states had passed eight-hour-day laws, but they contained too many loopholes to have the desired effect.

The labor movement endures hard times. The depression of 1873 set back further efforts to organize laboring people. The mere hint that a worker wanted to join a union could mean instant unemployment. Between 1873 and 1878 total union membership dropped from 300,000 to about 50,000. Where there had once been thirty national craft unions, only seven remained. Labor's prospects seemed grim.

One union that flourished even in the hard times of the mid-1870's was the Knights of St. Crispin, an organization of shoemakers. The leader of the union was Charles Litchman of Massachusetts. The

Union leaders urged the labeling of union-made goods, believing it would assure the American people of high-quality products.

Knights of St. Crispin felt the competition of non-union labor so keenly that Litchman opened a campaign to have a label placed on union-made products to identify them as such. The union label came to stand for quality workmanship performed under satisfactory conditions.

Violence breaks out in Pennsylvania labor disputes. The depression of 1873 produced for the first time large numbers of homeless, jobless, hungry people. The unemployed held mass meetings in the leading industrial cities, considerably alarming the general public. The police did not hesitate to break up these gatherings of protest. In the coal mines of Pennsylvania the struggle was tragic. The work was hard and dangerous, and the wages low. The miner who was fully employed was fortunate; most miners averaged only 130 days of work in a year.

To go on strike would be fatal, however, because management could readily find strike-breakers — men just as desperate for work as those they replaced. As Jay Gould had once cynically observed, "I can hire one half of the working class to kill the other half."

Nevertheless, the miners did strike. Late in 1874, the coal operators cut wages below the minimum that they had earlier agreed to in conversations with miners' organizations. In anguish and outrage, workers walked off the job. The operators promptly hired replacements and brought in armed guards to protect them. There were pitiful scenes as sheriffs' posses evicted the striking miners and their families from homes owned by the coal companies. Women — alongside the men — vainly tried to stand off the sheriffs' deputies with sticks and rocks. In the end the strike was broken.

A number of Pennsylvania miners belonged to a secret society known as the "Molly Maguires," which aimed to spread terror among mineowners. The name of the society was taken from an organization of anti-landlord agitators in Ireland in the 1840's led by one Molly Maguire. Since most of the miners came from Ireland, they were likening their troubles in America to their former situation in the old country. The Mollies intimidated and even murdered uncooperative mine bosses and supervisors.

In 1874 the president of the Philadelphia Coal and Iron Company decided to take steps to destroy the Mollies. He hired a private detective, James McParlan, who worked his way into the inner circle of the terrorist organization, posing as a counterfeiter and killer. As a result of McParlan's testimony, 24 Mollies were convicted of crimes, and 10 of them were hanged for murder. Union-organizing in the coalfields suffered a very serious setback, as a result, from which it did not recover for 25 years.

Federal troops break a railroad strike. Labor unrest also reached the railroads. In July, 1877, following an announcement of a wage cut, employees of the Baltimore and Ohio went out on strike. As the strike spread to other lines, riots broke out in a number of cities, including Baltimore, Pittsburgh, Chicago, and St. Louis. The outburst of violence in Baltimore lasted four days and cost fifty lives. This uprising led many people to believe that as in Paris a few years earlier, a workers' revolution was at hand. The *New York Tribune*, nonetheless, stated that public opinion was "almost everywhere in sympathy with the insurrection."

Later that month, striking railroad workers seized control of trains in Pittsburgh. Because of long-standing resentment over the power of the Pennsylvania Railroad in the state, local authorities tended to sympathize with the strikers. To quell the violence, state militiamen had to be dispatched from Philadelphia. When the soldiers arrived, they fired at the strikers, killing 25 men and wounding many others. Enraged, the strikers rushed to neighborhood gun shops, armed themselves, and drove the soldiers out of town. Joined by others who were unemployed, the strikers took over railroad property. Vandals among them set fire to the freight yards, creating a wall of flame three miles long. Order was not restored until President Hayes sent in federal troops — the first time since Andrew Jackson had called up troops to quell a strike of canal laborers. The trouble subsided and by August, 1877, the men had gone back to work.

Labor violence provokes strong opposition. The leaders of industry were dismayed by the bloody strife. They denounced unions, whatever the kind, and became determined to crush them. Many leading people endorsed the hostile sentiment regarding workers that had been expressed by the preacher Henry Ward Beecher: "God intended the great to be great and the little to be little." Many states revived conspiracy laws that permitted the prosecution of labor unions. Some communities built new armories to prepare for future uprisings.

The Knights of Labor is organized. Laboring people had also learned from their disappointments. They were beginning to see that they must organize more effectively. But how? The leaders who had formed the

Sweatshop Work

At the turn of the century, a young Polish girl named Sadie Frowne arrived in New York with her mother. As immigrants they were fortunate to have relatives who helped them find employment. Sadie Frowne later described her first few years in America.

A factory worker

Mother and I came on a steamship. Aunt Fanny and her husband met us at the gate of this country and were very good to us. Soon I had a position as a servant, while my mother got work in a factory making white goods.

I was only a little over thirteen and a greenhorn, so I received nine dollars a month and room and board, which I thought was doing well. Mother made nine dollars a week.

Mother caught a bad cold and coughed and coughed. She tried to keep on working, but it was no use. She had not the strength. At last she died and I was left alone.

After mother died, I thought I would try to learn a trade. Then I could go to school at night and learn to speak the English language well. So I went to work in what is called a sweatshop, making shirts by machine. I was new at the work, and the foreman scolded me a great deal. I did not know at first that you must not look around and talk, and I made many mistakes with the sewing. But I made four dollars by working six days a week.

After a while I got another job in a factory making skirts. I am earning five dollars and fifty cents a week now. The factory is on the third floor of a brick building. It is a room twenty feet long and fifteen wide.

Often I get to the factory soon after six o'clock and do not leave until six at night. At seven o'clock we all sit down at our machines and the boss brings to each one the pile of work that he or she is to finish during the day. The machines go like mad all day, because the faster you work the more money you get. The machines are all run by foot power, and at the end of the day one feels so weak that there is the temptation to lie right down and sleep.

We have just finished a strike in our business. It spread all over and the United Brotherhood of Garment Workers was in it. We struck for shorter hours, and after being out four weeks won the fight. We only have to work nine and a half hours a day and we get the same pay.

Noble Order of the Knights of Labor in 1869 believed that they had found the formula. At their head was a garment cutter from Philadelphia named Uriah S. Stephens. Having once studied to be a preacher, Stephens was an accomplished public speaker.

Stephens and the six men with whom he founded the Knights decided to permit the admission of all workers — skilled and un-skilled, immigrant and native-born, men and women, blacks and whites. The only people barred from joining were doctors, liquor dealers, lawyers, bankers, professional gamblers, and stockbrokers. Stephens created elaborate titles and rituals for the Knights. Officials had names like "Inside Esquire" and "Venerable Sage." As head of the Knights, Stephens enjoyed being called

The nation's leading union in the 1880's, the Knights of Labor provided a way for black and white workers to join together for labor reform.

the "Grand Master Workman." He invented a secret initiation ceremony, a secret password, and a secret handshake.

The secrecy of the Knights of Labor seems excessive today — even foolish. In that day, however, workers were usually safer if their employers did not know that they belonged to a union. The Knights did not begin to drop their secret practices until 1881. By then a strong sense of unity among the members had been established.

The Knights become the nation's leading union. The Knights bluntly attacked the "unjust accumulation" of wealth, arguing that it would lead to poverty for all working people. Many of the demands of the Knights of Labor were familiar to labor movements of the era: an eight-hour day, the distribution of public lands to actual settlers only, "equal pay for equal work" for men and women, and an end to convict and child labor. Later the Knights called for government ownership of the railroads and telegraph lines, and a graduated income tax — that is, one providing for higher rates on larger incomes than on smaller incomes. Because Stephens preached a message of mu-

tual respect between employer and worker, the Knights opposed strikes as a means of achieving their goals.

Like many other labor groups of the time, the Knights believed strongly in *cooperatives.* These were businesses owned and operated by the workers themselves. Among a variety of ventures, the Knights had a coal mine and a shoe-manufacturing plant.

The Knights of Labor grew slowly in the early 1880's. Then, after the organization ceased being secret in 1881, its rolls expanded rapidly. In that year its membership was 19,000; three years later the number had passed 100,000. Ironically a victory in a notable railroad strike in the West — notwithstanding the stated opposition to strikes — raised the Knights' prestige and helped swell their ranks. Within a few months after the 1885 strike, membership had reached 700,000. This figure included some 60,000 black members.

The Knights owed much of their success to the work of Terence V. Powderly, a machinist by trade who had succeeded Stephens as Grand Master Workman in 1879. Powderly, then only thirty years old, had strong ideas. Handsome, impeccably dressed, and displaying formal manners, he did not appear at first glance — as a writer who knew him said — to be "the leader of a million of the sons of toil." Like Stephens, he disapproved of strikes and insisted that working men and women should establish cooperatives.

The popularity of the Knights declines. The Knights were badly hurt by unauthorized strikes, which the organization felt forced to support despite its official anti-strike position. The failure of some of the cooperative ventures also damaged the Knights. In addition, many union people were beginning to dispute the Knights' idea that skilled and unskilled workers belonged in the same organization. Common sense seemed to show that the two segments of the working population had divergent needs and goals. The lofty legislative goals of the Knights, moreover, seemed extravagant to working people primarily interested in a shorter day and higher wages. Many workers had come to the conclusion that employers would respond only to the pressure of strikes, and that unions must sponsor them.

The Haymarket Riot destroys the Knights. The year 1886 proved bad for the Knights. There were strikes in almost every industrial region. Although only a few of them involved the Knights, the public tended to blame all of them on the Order. Worst of all, the Knights received a terrible blow from an event in Chicago that was not of their making.

A number of unions in Chicago had gone on strike for an eight-hour day — against the wishes of the Knights' leaders. The strikers quickly had the support of a group of *anarchists*, people advocating the abolition of all forms of government. The anarchists found an opportunity to spread their views when four strikers were killed in an encounter between strikers and police at the McCormick harvester works.

To protest the slayings, the anarchists held a rally in Chicago's Haymarket Square, in May, 1886. Near the end of the meeting, which was breaking up because of threatening skies, the police arrived. Suddenly a bomb was hurled, killing seven police officers and injuring many other people.

A wave of hysteria swept the city. Although the identity of the culprit was never established, eight anarchists were arrested and tried for the crime. They were all found guilty. Four of them were hanged, one committed suicide, and the rest were sentenced to life in prison. A few years later, the surviving three were pardoned by Illinois governor John P. Altgeld, a friend of labor who declared that the trial had been a miscarriage of justice.

One of those executed was Albert Parsons, who had been a member of the Knights. Powderly repudiated him, saying, "Honest labor is not to be found in the ranks of those who march under the red flag of anarchy, which is the emblem of blood and destruction." Nevertheless, many people linked the Knights to the Haymarket affair. Said the *New York Sun*, "Five men in this country control the chief interests of five hundred thousand workingmen, and can at any moment [by calling a strike] take the means of livelihood from two and a half million souls. These men compose the executive board of the noble order of the Knights of Labor." The membership in the Knights melted away, from 700,000 in mid-1886 to 200,000 only two years later.

Powderly himself, far from being the dictator some people said he was, was exhausted by the problems associated with his organization. Dejectedly he said, "The position I hold is too big for any ten men. It is certainly too big for me." Lacking forceful leadership, the Knights soon became only a memory. By 1893, another year of depression, the number of members had fallen to 75,000. Soon thereafter the organization died out.

SECTION REVIEW

1. Vocabulary: *cooperative, anarchist.*
2. For what reasons did working people seek to organize unions in the years after the Civil War?
3. (a) What was the National Labor Union? (b) The Knights of Labor? (c) Why did each fail?

4 Organized Labor Faces Strong Opposition

At the time that the Knights of Labor were declining, some labor leaders began organizing separate unions for skilled workers in different trades or crafts. They believed, for example, that carpenters or hatmakers or steamfitters would be better served if they each had a union of their own. In 1881 a number of these trade unions joined to form a federation. Five years later the organization became known as the American Federation of Labor (AFL). It did not enroll individual members. A worker could join only through being a member of an affiliated craft union.

Samuel Gompers leads the American Federation of Labor. One of the guiding spirits in establishing the AFL was Samuel Gompers, president of the International Cigarmakers Union. Gompers had long enjoyed success as head of the cigarmakers. He had put his union on what he called a "business basis." He meant by the phrase that the union collected dues, restricted membership, and made only such demands on employers as seemed reasonable. The union established sickness and death benefits and arranged its finances so that the stronger locals sometimes supplied funds to weaker ones.

Of Dutch-Jewish background, Samuel Gompers had been born in England in 1850 and immigrated to New York at the age of thirteen. As a young man sitting at a worktable rolling cigars, Gompers listened attentively to the older hands discussing politics. Sometimes the workers paid one of their number to read to them. Gompers often had this assignment. Frequently the reading material contained radical ideas for solving some of labor's problems. Gompers did not believe such revolutionary proposals were desirable. He was convinced that "pure and simple" trade unionism was the answer to

Under the direction of Samuel Gompers, shown here at the time of a union drive in West Virginia, the AFL became the nation's leading labor organization.

labor's needs. Later, as president of the AFL he never sought to change the capitalist system. He merely hoped to obtain a fair share of its benefits for working people. Once, at a Senate committee hearing, a senator asked Gompers about the aims of the AFL. Gompers replied straightforwardly, "We have no ultimate ends. We are going on from day to day. We fight only for immediate objects — objects that can be realized in a few years."

The AFL gains popularity. The AFL did not hesitate to support strikes but tried as much as possible to avoid them. It insisted that employers sign binding agreements, or contracts, with their unions. These contracts fixed for a stated period the conditions of work, including wages and hours. Through the efforts of the AFL, the slogan "No contract, no work" became a familiar saying of working people. Contracts had existed as early as 1866 in the iron-and-steel industry, but in the 1890's the AFL made them a symbol of the labor movement.

For a brief time there was rivalry between the Knights of Labor and the AFL. Most skilled workers agreed, however, that the strike and the contract were sensible instruments for advancing labor's interests. By 1904 the AFL, with 1,750,000 members, had become the nation's leading union. The AFL continued to restrict its membership, barring unskilled workers. In addition, reflecting some of the prejudice of the time, the AFL excluded women and blacks.

The AFL faced difficulties and frustrations, for business leaders were as hostile to it as they had been to the Knights. Nevertheless, the dignified Gompers, who with the exception of one year remained president of the AFL until 1924, earned the respect of his opponents. He became a familiar figure before state and congressional legislative committees, pleading the cause of labor. Gompers never forgot the people for whom he spoke, even when he was present at social gatherings with business and banking leaders.

Some labor leaders advocate violence. Scorn for the accommodating methods of the AFL led to the establishment in 1905 of the Industrial Workers of the World (IWW). Its founders hoped to organize unions that would gain control of industry and overthrow capitalism. Under the leadership of Vincent St. John and William ("Wild Bill") Haywood, the Wobblies, as the IWW came to be nicknamed, had about 70,000 members at its peak in 1913. Open to everybody regardless of race, sex, or nationality, the IWW was most active among western miners, lumbermen, and migrant farm workers. When the United States went to war in 1917, many IWW leaders were arrested, indicted, and convicted on charges of sedition and espionage.

Business opposes unions. Business, meanwhile, developed new methods for opposing the efforts of working people to organize unions. A method already familiar was to plant a spy among employees to eavesdrop on their plans. A man who specialized in spying on industrial workers was Allan Pinkerton, a detective who had gained fame for uncovering a plot to assassinate Abraham Lincoln in 1861. Pinkerton's services were advertised in this way: "Corporations or individuals desirous of ascertaining the feelings of their employees, and whether they are likely to engage in strikes or are joining any secret labor organizations . . . , can obtain a detective suitable to associate with their employees and obtain this information." Pinkerton also was in the business of providing employers with forces of strikebreakers.

A second method of intimidating employees was the *blacklist.* Workers who joined unions or went out on strike found they could not get another job in the same town. Their names would be circulated among all local employers. These blacklists closed the door to "troublemakers."

As unions became more powerful, employers devised a third method of controlling union activity: the *yellow dog contract.* This was an agreement that new workers were forced to sign. In it they swore that they were not members of a union, and they pledged not to join one.

Business people also sometimes resorted to seeking an *injunction,* or court order. By

obtaining an injunction from a judge, an employer facing labor problems was able to enlist the power of the government in forbidding a strike or a boycott or picketing.

Labor suffers defeat in the Homestead strike. Well-organized and growing bigger, business held the advantage in its struggle with labor. The balance became more uneven after the failure of two major strikes in the 1890's.

The first of these strikes began in 1892 when workers at the Carnegie Steel Company at Homestead, Pennsylvania, refused to accept new wage cuts. Henry Clay Frick, Andrew Carnegie's right-hand man, thereupon shut down the plant and surrounded it with special guards to protect the property. The guards, however, were soon run out of town by infuriated workers who realized that Frick intended to reopen the plant with strikebreakers.

Frick was glad to take up the challenge to the company's authority because he believed he now had a chance to destroy the union once and for all. On July 6, two river barges filled with 300 hired Pinkerton detectives were towed up the Monongahela River toward Homestead. As the detectives came ashore, armed workers fired on them from behind barricades, and the battle was on. After a thirteen-hour struggle, the Pinkertons finally raised a white flag of truce, laid down their arms, and surrendered. In the fighting, ten men had been killed and dozens wounded.

The Carnegie Company then persuaded the governor of Pennsylvania to provide help, and in short order the state militia was summoned to restore peace. Meanwhile, the company began bringing in strikebreakers to replace workers who had walked off the job. Of the original 4,000 employees at the plant, only 800 were rehired. Many of the leaders of the strike were prosecuted in court for rioting and murder. The steel workers' union was destroyed. Forty years would pass before union organizers once again operated in the steel industry.

While some members of Congress were sympathetic to the Homestead strikers, the public in general was not. The working per-

WORKMEN CANNONADING THE BARGES.

SOLDIERS IN CAMP.

WORKMEN ATTACKING THE BARGES.

GREAT BATTLE OF HOMESTEAD.
Defeat and Capture of the
PINKERTON INVADERS
July 6th 1892.

The artist who drew these pictures of the Homestead strike sympathized with the steel workers. The public, however, disapproved of the strikers' actions.

son, it was widely asserted, must remain free to sell his or her services as an individual and not through a union. Furthermore, many people held that the right to work was sacred. They insisted that union organizers had no business interfering with employees willing to accept whatever terms the company offered. The readiness of the federal government to enter disputes on the side of business, therefore, was firmly supported by people throughout the United States.

Government action breaks the Pullman strike. No event showed better the role of government in labor disputes than did the Pullman strike of 1894. George Pullman, whose sleeping car had revolutionized overnight rail travel, had built for his employees what was widely hailed as a model company town, near Chicago. All the houses, schools, stores, and churches in the town of Pullman were owned by the Pullman Company. Rents in Pullman ran about 25 percent

higher than in neighboring towns. George Pullman bought water from Chicago at four cents a thousand gallons and sold it at ten cents a thousand to the consumers in his town. Employees were not obliged to live in Pullman, but those who did not were likely to lose their jobs.

In 1893 the nation was faced with another financial depression. During the hard times, Pullman cut wages an average of 25 percent without making a comparable cut in rent or in the cost of services. The pastor of a church in Pullman declared that "after deducting rent the men invariably had only from one to six dollars or so on which to live for two weeks."

Into the picture stepped the American Railway Union, a nation-wide organization of all railway workers — skilled or unskilled. By 1894 the union had a membership of 150,000, including some Pullman workers. At its head was Eugene V. Debs, who had made the well-being of working people the passion of his life.

A gentle man, Debs instructed union members at Pullman to avoid violence. On May 11, 1894, however, about 4,000 Pullman employees went on strike, and events were soon out of control.

The strike, up to now local, became national when the American Railway Union instructed its members not to handle trains with Pullman cars attached. By the end of June, 1894, railroad traffic throughout the western United States had come to a standstill. Before much longer every part of the country was affected.

The railroad owners now decided to attach Pullman cars to trains carrying mail. Any attempt to interfere with such trains would be an interference with the mails — a federal crime. The strikers, however, refused to handle these trains. At this point the railroads persuaded the Attorney General, Richard Olney, to hire an army of special deputies — actually in the pay of the railroads — to help keep the trains moving.

Violence broke out as the deputies came under attack from striking workers. President Cleveland ordered federal troops to Chicago to restore order. Governor Altgeld insisted that troops were not needed, but Cleveland sent them anyhow. He is supposed to have said, "If it takes every dollar in the Treasury and every soldier in the United States to deliver a postal card in Chicago, that postal card should be delivered."

When the strike continued to paralyze transportation, the railroads obtained an injunction against the American Railway Union, forbidding it to interfere in any way with their operations. Debs, quickly judged to be in violation of the injunction, was sent to prison for six months. The strike was virtually over; the union had been smashed. By the middle of July, train service was returning to normal. Almost forty years would pass before legislation was enacted preventing strikes from being so readily broken by an injunction.

———

The America that was being forged in the factories and cities was as dependent as ever on the variety and ingenuity of the people. Once again, finding common goals

Eugene Debs gained national attention for his role in the Pullman strike. Some Americans, like this cartoonist, criticized Debs for bringing the nation's railroad traffic to a halt.

for everybody — worker or industrialist, urban dweller or farmer, native or immigrant — became a national requirement. Would the American "melting pot" — a phrase coined by an English journalist, Israel Zangwill — fuse the people into one great whole? Would the physical landscape, changing into a scene of cities and factories, continue to allow Americans to pursue happiness as well as economic progress? Would America continue to offer opportunity for all? "I lift my lamp beside the golden door," were words inscribed on the base of the Statue of Liberty, which was unveiled in New York harbor in 1886. Fulfilling the promise was the duty all Americans assumed, as the nineteenth century completed its course.

SECTION REVIEW

1. Vocabulary: *blacklist, yellow dog contract, injunction.*
2. (a) What were Samuel Gompers's goals for the American Federation of Labor? (b) How successful was the AFL?
3. What methods did business use to try to prevent the forming of unions?
4. What effects did the Homestead and Pullman strikes have on the labor movement?

Chapter 20 Review

Summary

The population of the United States changed dramatically by the end of the nineteenth century. In the generation after the Civil War millions upon millions of immigrants arrived in the United States — many of them from southern and eastern Europe — and settled, for the most part, in northern cities.

Like most previous immigrants, the new ones came to America to improve their lives and make a future for themselves and their families. They faced, however, ethnic and religious prejudices. Demands were heard among some native-born Americans for laws to restrict the number of newcomers.

The expansion of industry stimulated urban America in the decades after the Civil War. The unprecedented growth of cities put severe strains on their basic facilities. Water service, sewer lines, and housing were everywhere inadequate, making living conditions difficult and unhealthful for many city dwellers.

Working people, in addition to finding fresh opportunities, suffered some disadvantages. Factory work often was monotonous and dangerous. Moreover, lay-offs could be unexpected and long. Usually having no direct contact with their employer, workers in big plants organized unions with the aim of making their voices heard. In 1866 the National Labor Union was founded. It advocated improved working conditions and an eight-hour work day, but lasted only a short time. Following the economic depression of 1873, union membership in general fell off. Moreover, violent confrontations during mining and railroad strikes damaged the reputation of unions and set back their cause.

Another attempt to create a national labor union was made by the Knights of Labor. This union admitted practically all workers — regardless of race, color, sex, national origin, or degree of skill — and by the mid-1880's had a membership of over 700,000. The Knights disapproved of strikes, advocating instead negotiations with employers for improved conditions. Once again violent labor strife, this time in Chicago in 1886, led to public fear of unions and to a decline in union strength. The depression of 1893 dealt the final blow to the Knights of Labor.

Just as the Knights of Labor disappeared, a federation of craft unions was created under a dynamic labor leader named Samuel Gompers. The organization, known as the American Federation of Labor, accepted the idea of the strike but only as a last resort. In its place, the AFL encouraged the signing of contracts that specified wages, hours, and working conditions. By the early 1900's, the AFL had become the nation's leading union.

Vocabulary and Important Terms

1. *padrone*
2. American Protective Association
3. Chinese Exclusion Act
4. "walking city"
5. omnibus
6. streetcar
7. suburb
8. tenement
9. National Labor Union
10. eight-hour day
11. "Molly Maguires"
12. Knights of Labor
13. cooperative
14. anarchist
15. Haymarket Riot
16. American Federation of Labor
17. Industrial Workers of the World
18. blacklist
19. yellow dog contract
20. injunction
21. Homestead strike
22. Pullman strike

Discussion Questions

1. (a) What was the basic reason for immigration after the Civil War? (b) How did the post-Civil War "new immigration" differ from the "old immigration," both in terms of national origin and numbers of immigrants? (c) What specific factors motivated Italian immigrants and Jews from eastern Europe to move to America?

2. (a) How were Chinese immigrants originally received when they began to arrive in California? (b) Why did the attitude toward Chinese immigrants change? (c) What was the result of this change in attitude?

3. Describe the relationship between the rapid expansion of American industry and the growth of American cities.

4. (a) How did tenements provide an answer to the problem of urban housing? (b) What kinds of problems were created by tenements? (c) What attempts at housing reform were undertaken? (d) How successful were those attempts?

5. (a) What kinds of periodic unemployment were created by the development of the factory system? (b) Why did unemployment become a more serious problem after the Civil War than it once had been?

6. How did the factory system affect relations between worker and employer?

7. (a) What were some of the demands of labor unions in the years after the Civil War? (b) How did working people try to win their demands? (c) How successful was the labor movement in this period?

8. (a) In what ways were the Knights of Labor and the American Federation of Labor similar? (b) In what ways were they different? (c) Why was the American Federation of Labor the more successful organization?

Relating Past to Present

1. As American cities grew, they underwent many changes, in part as a result of advances in transportation. How do the transportation systems of today's cities compare with those that were developed in post-Civil War America? Explain the similarities and differences.
2. By 1900 three American cities had population of over one million. How many American cities today have more than a million people?

Studying Local History

1. What cities in your state or region grew larger as a result of the rise of industry? What kinds of factories were developed in those cities? What groups of immigrants, if any, were drawn to them?
2. Study the map on page 462. Did your state have a large or small percentage of foreign-born people in 1900? What percentage of your state's population today is foreign-born?

Using History Skills

1. *Reading source material.* Study Sadie Frowne's description of sweatshop work on page 473. (a) Why did Sadie Frowne go to work in a sweatshop? (b) What hardships did she encounter on the job? (c) Do you think she felt optimistic or pessimistic about the future? Give reasons for your answer.
2. *Using the index.* In the index find the entry for unions. On what pages in your book are labor unions mentioned or discussed? Look up each of those references. Based on the information you find, write a brief account of the history of the American labor movement.

WORLD SCENE

The Spread of Industry

During the last decades of the nineteenth century, manufacturing developed rapidly in a number of countries. In addition to the United States, Germany and Japan were emerging as industrial powers.

German industry. From 1870 to 1900 Germany experienced extraordinary industrial expansion. The political unification of Germany sparked this extraordinary expansion. At last, Germany's abundant resources of coal and iron ore and highly motivated labor could be brought together efficiently.

Government policies did much to encourage new German industries. High tariffs were instituted, offering protection from foreign competition. Monopolies, furthermore, were allowed in heavy industry, giving large companies tight control over production and distribution.

The most dramatic example of German industrial growth was in the manufacture of steel. Dominated by companies such as Krupp and Thyssen, the German output of steel rose from 1.5 million tons in 1880 to 7.4 million in 1900. The talent of its scientists and inventors also gave Germany a running start in the development of new industries. The nation became a leader in the manufacture of chemical and electrical products.

Manufacturing in Japan. At the same time, on the other side of the world, Japan was laying the foundation for becoming a major industrial power. In 1868 a new Japanese government embarked on a program of modernization that would transform the country.

Opening up Japan for the first time to the influence of western technology, the government raised taxes to pay for the construction of railroads, telegraph lines, shipyards, mines, and factories. A banking system was organized along western lines. Japanese students were sent abroad to schools, and foreign advisers were invited to Japan. A national education system emphasizing technical training was created within a few years.

A result of these changes in Japanese society was the growth of large companies, especially for the manufacture of textiles, glass, and weapons. By 1900 production of industrial goods had increased twenty times over that of 1868. In three decades the Japanese had established the industrial base of what would become one of the most impressive economies in the world.

Politicians and Protest

1865 – 1900

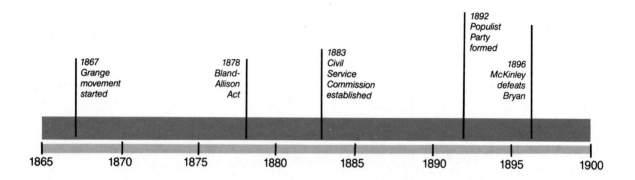

| 1867 Grange movement started | 1878 Bland- Allison Act | 1883 Civil Service Commission established | 1892 Populist Party formed | 1896 McKinley defeats Bryan |

1865　1870　1875　1880　1885　1890　1895　1900

CHAPTER OUTLINE

1. Corruption marks party politics.

2. Efforts at reform continue.

3. Farmers begin to join together.

4. The Populists propose far-reaching reforms.

The rapid economic and social changes that the United States underwent in the years after the Civil War put severe strains on the nation's political institutions. Politicians had had no experience — nor had anyone else — in dealing with industrial problems. No national officeholders, for instance, had ever before had to think about railroad strikes, or industrial unemployment, or the pollution of the environment. The Presidents continued to come from farms or small-town America. They were unfamiliar with slums and the world of the immigrant, because all of them had grown to adulthood far from such concerns. The vast majority of congressmen had similar backgrounds. Since most seats in Congress were filled by representatives from rural districts, urban matters were seldom discussed.

The Presidents of the post-Civil War period, moreover, did not think that Chief Executives should produce new ideas and programs in government. The public, as a whole, agreed. Some of the worst suffering in the history of the United States took place during the depression of 1873. The hard times were seen as inevitable, for the most part, and the federal government was not inclined to adopt measures that might assist the victims of economic disaster. Some voices, however, called for reform, most notably among labor organizations, associations of farmers, and the new political parties that were appearing.

1 Corruption Marks Party Politics

What posed a threat to the American political system was not the transformation that big business and big cities were bringing about, but unprecedented graft and corruption in government. Nationally it made no difference which party controlled Congress. Members of both parties were guilty of wrongdoing. A change of party after an election brought new faces before the public but had little effect on how politics was conducted.

Corrupt lobbyists wield influence. During the post-Civil War period, Congress had fallen into the habit of passing out special favors to powerful groups that had the means to hire lobbyists. The best-known lobbyist was Sam Ward — elder brother of Julia Ward Howe (page 375). He was called "King of the Lobby" in tribute to his efforts on behalf of financiers. There were hundreds of men like Ward, operating not only in Washington but also in state capitals throughout the country.

The method of lobbyists was to offer public officials bribes in the form of expensive gifts. In return, the lobbyists obtained for their clients some desired governmental action. State legislatures were often honeycombed with members who had been "bought" by big-business magnates. A magazine sadly complained in 1876, "Legislative bribery and its satellite, lobbying, have become the most grievous political evil of the country."

Many business leaders had concluded that bribery was an appropriate way to deal with government officials. Collis Huntington, one of the owners of the Southern Pacific Railroad, candidly told an aide, "If you have to pay money to have the right thing done, it is only just and fair to do it." The Crédit Mobilier affair (page 410) was a perfect example of corruption at work in the national government. It was unusual only in that the public learned about it.

By the mid-1870's, some people had recognized that the sale of political favors was

In his painting "Electioneering," artist E. L. Henry portrays townspeople gathering around to hear a candidate discuss the issues of the day.

a danger to the well-being of the republic. Representative government could not exist if the men conducting it were dishonorable and unscrupulous. Reform became a lively topic for discussion in a few circles, but the public at large continued to be indifferent to the subject. People were distracted by the intense campaigns waged for office, seeing them as a form of entertainment.

The parties avoid major issues. Neither of the major parties took much interest in reform. Each party represented a wide variety of interests, and each sought to avoid taking clear positions on most issues.

The two parties were fairly evenly matched. The Republican Party — which called itself the "Grand Old Party" (GOP) — almost always saw its candidate elected President in the postwar years. Its supporters included the industrialists of the East and the grain-growing farmers of the Middle West. In addition, most laborers in the industrial cities followed the lead of their employers and voted Republican. The Republicans also had the backing of the war veterans and of their organization, the Grand Army of the Republic (GAR), because the veterans credited the party with having saved the Union.

Thousands of Americans in every part of the country voted Republican out of respect for the memory of Lincoln. Still others, never forgetting the idealism with which the Republican organization had begun in 1854, supported it as the humanitarian party. Black people, understandably, revered it as the party of emancipation.

The Democratic Party relied heavily on the support of voters in the South. After 1876, the former Confederate states always voted Democratic, producing the expression "the solid South." In cities throughout the country the Democrats were strong and in political control. Immigrants — particularly the Irish — tended to vote Democratic. They were attracted by the Democrats' traditional support for easy naturalization of newcomers. Business leaders and their employees who opposed the tariff also voted for the Democrats, who since Jackson's time had advocated a low tariff.

For many years after 1865, the Democrats insisted on keeping the Civil War issues alive. They opposed suffrage for blacks; they continued to argue for states' rights; and they identified themselves generally with the lost cause of the Confederacy. Thoughtful Democrats, however, realized that the party could not continue to live in the past. Ironically, it was Clement Vallandigham, the former Copperhead (page 387), who in 1871 urged the Democrats to shift to new issues, to take, as he said, a "New Departure." In 1872, when they nominated the reformer Horace Greeley for President, however, the Democrats were soundly defeated by General Grant (page 410).

Hayes breaks with the party bosses. After the disclosures of corruption in the Grant administration, the Republicans knew that to hold the White House they must elect a man of undoubted integrity and good sense. Moreover, they knew the country required such a President, for the Democrats too had established a sad reputation for being corrupt. A leading Republican, striking hard at them, bellowed extravagantly: "That party never had but two objects — grand and petty larceny."

The Republicans believed that in Rutherford B. Hayes of Ohio they had found a figure the people could admire. When Hayes came to the White House in 1877 (page 413), he was known as someone interested in reform. His motto was, "He serves his party best who serves his country best."

The new President's choice of Cabinet officers made the party bosses indignant. Hayes named William M. Evarts to be Secretary of State. Evarts was well-remembered for his role as chief counsel to Andrew Johnson during the impeachment trial. Another of Hayes's appointments also angered party regulars. David M. Key, a former Confederate from Tennessee, was named to be Postmaster General. This apparent gesture of reconciliation with the South was part of the Compromise of 1877 (page 413).

To be Secretary of the Interior, Hayes selected Carl Schurz (pronounced SHIRTS). Schurz had come to the United States from

"Who stole the people's money?" was the caption of this cartoon, one of many drawn by Thomas Nast to expose the activities of the Tweed ring. The Hayes administration sought reforms to stop such political corruption.

Germany in 1852. Briefly the United States minister to Spain and then a general in the Civil War, he had helped organize the Liberal Republican Party in 1872. Schurz had a fervor for honesty in government. In the Hayes Cabinet, he came to be noted also for his fair dealings with the Indians and for his support of reform.

Hayes begins the fight for civil service reform. A decent man of high intelligence, Hayes made Congress recognize again the dignity of the presidency — badly damaged by Johnson and Grant. Early in his administration, the new President decided to make changes in the way public officeholders were appointed.

Hayes detested the spoils system, which had been widely used ever since the days of Andrew Jackson (page 264). He believed that appointments to government positions should be made on the basis of ability and experience, not as a reward for political support. He favored use of a *merit system* as a basis for government appointments. Under the proposed system, jobs would go to those applicants scoring highest on competitive examinations. The movement to establish the merit system was called civil service reform.

Hayes faces a difficult situation. Few people in Congress shared Hayes's enthusiasm for civil service reform and little was done about it during his administration. Meanwhile, Hayes had four difficult years in the White House. His role in calling on federal troops to bring order in the Baltimore and Ohio Railroad dispute angered working people (page 472). In addition, many farmers had come to the conclusion that the high-tariff policy of the Republican Party was placing too heavy a burden on them. Farmers deeply resented the fact that they had to buy household goods and farm equipment that were protected from foreign competition, while having to sell their crops in a market totally unprotected. Why, they asked, should they not receive prices for their produce comparable to prices they were forced to pay for manufactured items?

The parties select candidates for the 1880 election. When he was nominated in 1876, Hayes had stated that he would not run a second time. The Republican Party did not try to make him change his mind. The Republican convention in 1880, which met in Chicago, was one of the stormiest ever held. The party had become split between two factions. The Stalwarts, led by Senator Roscoe Conkling of New York, were enemies of reform and of the President. The Half-Breeds, on the other hand, were followers of the President. Their leader was James G. Blaine of Maine, one of the most influential members of the Senate.

Hayes had been an enemy of Conkling's ever since 1877, when he had directly challenged the senator's power in New York. In that year, the President sought the resignation of Chester Arthur, a Conkling appointee who was Collector of the New York Custom House and who had been accused of cheating the government. Conkling, who strutted like a peacock in the Senate, often wearing white flannel trousers and brightly colored vests, raged at the President. "Parties are not built up by deportment," he shouted, "or by ladies' magazines, or gush!" Parties, he said, would die if "the faithful" could not be rewarded with jobs. Conkling was able to block the confirmation of Arthur's successor for three years. The fight, however, was far from settled.

Conkling and the Stalwarts were intent upon bringing General Grant back for a third presidential term, but Blaine, who could not obtain the nomination for himself, was able to prevent Grant from receiving it. The convention turned instead to a dark-horse candidate, James A. Garfield of Ohio. To appease the Stalwarts, Chester Arthur was nominated to be Vice President.

Garfield, who had served in the House and in the Senate, had been a Civil War general too. Earlier he had been head of Hiram College in Ohio. A pious man, he was an outstanding debater and preacher. To make him seem a "man of the people," the Republicans publicized him as a former canal boy, since he had once worked on a barge. "From the tow path to the White House" was the theme of the Republican campaign.

The Democrats, meeting at Cincinnati, also selected a Civil War veteran, General Winfield Scott Hancock of Pennsylvania. Hancock was remembered as a hero of the Battle of Gettysburg. His nomination, it was hoped, would quiet those people who continued to view the Democrats as the party of former Confederates and their sympathizers. Although inexperienced in politics, Hancock was once described as "a good man, weighing 250 pounds with a record as stainless as his sword."

Garfield is elected President. The Democrats waged a lackluster campaign in 1880, mainly denouncing Garfield for having received a dividend check of $329 on Crédit Mobilier stock. Again and again audiences jeered, "Three twenty-nine!" Although the campaign was without issues, Hancock was long remembered for a remark he made to a newspaper reporter: "The tariff question is a local question." Manufacturers who regarded the tariff as an important national issue thought the statement foolish.

In the election, out of nine million ballots cast, Garfield led by fewer than 10,000 votes. He carried the key states, however, and scored an impressive victory in the electoral college.

Garfield and the Stalwarts clash. As soon as Garfield was inaugurated, the battle between the Stalwarts and the Half-Breeds was resumed. Blaine, who had been appointed Secretary of State, tried to use his influence to limit Senator Conkling's power. He had Garfield nominate one of Conkling's foes in New York to be Collector of the New York Custom House. Conkling was furious. Once more he had been challenged.

In a dramatic gesture, Conkling and the other senator from New York, Thomas

Platt, resigned their Senate seats. At that time (before the Seventeenth Amendment to the Constitution went into effect) senators were elected not by popular vote but by their state legislatures. Conkling, therefore, expected the legislature at Albany, the state capital, to restore him and Platt to their places in the Senate — thus rebuking the President. To their astonishment, the legislature refused to reseat them, despite a humiliating trip Vice President Arthur made to Albany on their behalf. They had violated an unwritten rule of politics: politicians must never level an attack on a President from their own party. Those who do suffer the consequences.

Garfield is assassinated. During Garfield's brief administration, he was hounded day and night by people trying to obtain political appointments in the civil service. Garfield had written in his diary, "My day is frittered away with the personal seeking of people when it ought to be given to the great problems which concern the whole country."

Then tragedy struck. On July 2, 1881, Garfield left the White House for a trip to New England, intending to show his two sons Williams College, where he had been educated. As the President stood in the Washington, D.C., railway station, he was shot in the back by one Charles Guiteau, a disappointed office-seeker. Garfield lingered through the summer while the nation prayed for his recovery. When James Garfield died on September 19, Chester Arthur became President.

SECTION REVIEW

1. Vocabulary: *merit system.*
2. (a) What dangers confronted America's political institutions during the 1870's? (b) What was the response of the public? (c) Of the two major parties?
3. (a) What were the views of President Hayes on civil service reform? (b) What problems did Hayes face during his administration?
4. (a) Who were the Stalwarts? (b) Who were the Half-Breeds? (c) Why did James Garfield clash with the Stalwarts during his very short time as President?

2 Efforts at Reform Continue

The assassination of President Garfield opened the door wider on the burning issue of civil service reform. The shocked nation was now more aware than ever of the abuses of the old spoils system.

The movement for political reform gains strength. In the years after the Civil War, government at every level had become more complex, requiring officials in the various bureaus to have specialized knowledge. People recognized that it was no longer acceptable for appointees to have as their main qualification the fact that they knew the "right" politician.

The leading voices in the movement for civil service reform were two magazine editors — George W. Curtis of *Harper's Weekly* and E. L. Godkin of *The Nation.* Many of the people who joined them in the movement came from old New England families. The reformers were also often men and women who had been working to secure civil rights for the freed slaves.

The reformers' opponents, the bosses who defended the old system of providing jobs for political supporters, were not evil people. The spoils system, after all, had grown out of democracy itself. In order to win voters and "get out the vote" on Election Day, politicians had built local "machines." These machines consisted of local, state, and federal employees whose jobs depended on victory for "the boss." In large cities, bosses often enlarged their base of support by the favors they could dispense through friends in government. A political boss could arrange for an ailing father to be put into a hospital; he could rescue a wayward boy from the clutches of the court; he could find a job for the daughter of a poor family. All that the boss demanded for running this private social security system were votes. Although the boss system worked unevenly and unfairly, it filled a need not being met in any other way.

The city machines continued to function in many parts of the country, but the idea of appointing people to civil service positions on the basis of merit took hold following Garfield's assassination. Declared *The Nation*, "We do not think we have taken up a newspaper during the last ten days which has not in some manner made the [assassination] the product of 'the spoils system.'"

The Pendleton Act is passed. Ironically, it was Chester Arthur, the Stalwart, who presided over the beginning of reform. In his first annual message to Congress, Arthur strongly endorsed civil service reform. In January, 1883, he signed into law a bill introduced by Senator George H. Pendleton, a Democrat from Ohio. The law created a Civil Service Commission empowered to hold examinations and make appointments on a merit basis. Broadened from time to time, the Pendleton Act eventually ended the spoils system in the federal government.

President Arthur supports reforms. Chester Arthur was a widower when he came to the White House. He looked impressive, for he was such a stylish dresser that some people called him "the Dude President." Mrs. Blaine, who kept close tabs on the White House, said in 1882 that Arthur had bought 25 new coats that year. Arthur's interests were not limited to clothes, however. An honors graduate of Union College in New York, he had become a lawyer. In one of his first cases, he won $500 in damages for a black woman who had been forced off a street car because of her race. Black people in New York thereafter had received better treatment on public transportation.

Arthur proved to be a better President than most people expected, conducting the affairs of the country honestly and effectively. For instance, he vigorously prosecuted criminals when irregularities were discovered in the operation of the Post Office. Some of the culprits included high-ranking figures in his own party.

Arthur was fortunate that there was a surplus in the United States Treasury, owing to substantial tariff and tax yields. Determined that the money should not be wasted on the rash schemes of congressmen, Arthur proposed restoring the United States Navy to strength. Of late it had fallen into a deplorable condition. Under Arthur's direction, the navy began to construct modern ships. Within a short time America's naval vessels could be favorably compared with those of Great Britain and France.

The Democrats win the presidency in 1884. Although an effective President, Arthur's endorsement of civil service reform had cost him the support of Republican bosses. In 1884 they denied him the nomination for a presidential term in his own right. Arthur thus joined John Tyler, Millard Fillmore, and Andrew Johnson — the previous "accidental Presidents" who also had failed to receive their party's highest honor.

In 1884 the Republicans finally turned to James G. Blaine — "the Plumed Knight," as admirers called him. The Stalwarts, however, refused to support Blaine. Asked to deliver a speech on behalf of the candidate, Roscoe Conkling replied, "I am not engaged in criminal practice." Reform Republicans who were called Mugwumps (from an Indian word meaning "big shot") also withheld their support from Blaine because of political favors he had once done for a railroad in Arkansas. They hoped that, in the expression of the day, they could "go in for" the Democratic choice. It turned out that they could.

The Democrats' nominee was the big, burly governor of New York, Grover Cleveland. Earlier elected mayor of Buffalo, New York, Cleveland had aroused admiration for his political courage and honesty. As governor, he had battled Tammany Hall (the Democratic machine in New York City) and endeared himself to reformers.

The campaign of 1884 raised no social or economic question on which the candidates had to express opinions. Both parties resorted to mudslinging. The Republicans spread gossip about Cleveland's personal life. The Democrats harped on Blaine's political past. One of their taunts went:

Blaine, Blaine, James G. Blaine
Continental liar from the state of Maine!

The campaign was also enlivened by the candidacy of Belva Lockwood. A lawyer,

Belva Lockwood was the first woman to plead a case before the United States Supreme Court. Nominated by the National Equal Rights Party as a candidate for President, she ran on a ticket urging voting rights for women.

The outcome of the 1884 election may have been determined a few days before Election Day. A minister in New York City made a speech at a meeting of Protestant clergymen referring to the Democrats as the party of "rum, Romanism, and rebellion." Blaine, who was present, allowed this insult to Catholics to go unanswered. His failure to respond may have cost him votes.

Cleveland won the popular vote in a close race, receiving only 29,000 more votes than Blaine. In the electoral college, however, Cleveland's margin was more substantial: 219 to 182. Minor parties, including the National Equal Rights Party, failed to make a significant showing.

Grover Cleveland occupies the White House. The election of Cleveland brought the first Democratic President to the White House since Buchanan left it in 1861. Cleveland's inaugural ball was one of the most lavish in history — and the first ever lighted by electricity. Two years later, Cleveland celebrated another important event. At the age of 49, he became the first President to be married in the White House. His bride was Frances Folsom, then 21 years old. The young First Lady adopted a policy of holding receptions in the White House on Saturday afternoons. Her aim was to greet young women who worked during the week. Sometimes she welcomed as many as 8,000 visitors on one day — a tribute not only to public curiosity but to the increasing number of working women.

Cleveland hoped to live by his motto: "A public office is a public trust." Still, he had little imagination or sensitivity to social injustice. He said he was in favor of civil service reform. Nevertheless, he yielded to the pressure of his party, so long out of power, in dismissing thousands of jobholders simply in order to put Democrats in their place. The Mugwumps were dismayed.

President Cleveland signed nearly 1,500 private pension bills but is known for his unprecedented veto of many such bills, which litter the floor in this cartoon.

Cleveland vetoes pension bills. Cleveland, though, could also show backbone. He vetoed a bill, for example, that would have given a pension to any Union army veteran who had served at least ninety days. Cleveland also unhesitatingly vetoed the pension bills that members of Congress introduced on behalf of favored veterans in their home districts. One family, for instance, sought a pension for the service of a son who had drowned in a canal — after deserting from the army! No previous President had vetoed pension bills. In the northern states, former soldiers were exasperated, especially because Cleveland had not himself served in the armed forces.

Cleveland further angered Union veterans by ordering the return of captured Civil War flags — Union and Confederate alike — to the various states. The commanding officer of the GAR, Lucius Fairchild, turned a wrathful tongue on the President: "May God palsy the hand that wrote that order. May God palsy the brain that conceived it, and may God palsy the tongue that dictated it." Despite Fairchild's outburst, Cleveland had helped to put the Civil War in the past.

Cleveland takes other firm stands. Cleveland's vetoes of the pension bills were in keeping with his view of the presidency. He believed it was the President's job to be an impartial "umpire," making sure that no individual or group was either granted special favors or deprived of their rights.

Cleveland also vetoed a bill which would have provided federal assistance to Texas farmers who had suffered losses in a drought. The President expressed the dominant view of the time in his message: "I do not believe that the power and duty of the general government ought to be extended to the relief of individual suffering which is in no manner properly related to the public service or benefit." The President stated a principle: "Though the people support the government, the government should not support the people."

Cleveland, however, did not oppose other kinds of intervention by government. In 1887 he signed into law the Interstate Commerce Act to regulate railroad rates. This act provided for the creation of an Interstate Commerce Commission (ICC), the first of a long series of regulatory agencies that involved the federal government directly in the lives of individuals.

In addition to accepting regulation of the railroads, many Americans had concluded that the tariff on manufactured goods was too high. Cleveland agreed with this view. The tariff, he had come to believe, was bringing unnecessarily large returns to business at the expense of consumers. Most Democrats supported him when, in an unheard-of step, he devoted one entire annual message to Congress to his call for a reduction in tariff rates.

Cleveland knew he might be hurting his chances for re-election by his strong stand, but he was determined to do what he thought right. He told one of his advisers, "What is the use of being elected or re-elected, unless you stand for something?"

To his intense disappointment, a bill providing for lower tariff rates failed to pass Congress.

The Republicans win the election of 1888. Cleveland was enthusiastically renominated by the Democratic Party in 1888. His opponent was Benjamin Harrison of Indiana. Harrison's great-grandfather, also named Benjamin Harrison, had signed the Declaration of Independence. His grandfather was "Old Tippecanoe," President William Henry Harrison. A forbidding person, Benjamin Harrison earned the nickname "Old Ice Water."

Although Cleveland won about 100,000 more popular votes than Harrison, the Republican candidate carried the electoral college. It seems clear that fraudulent returns in New York, Rhode Island, Ohio, and Indiana gave those states to Harrison. Harrison was a devout man who regularly studied the Bible and held a prayer service in his library daily. When told of his victory by Matt Quay, chairman of the Republican Party, Harrison said, "Providence has given us the victory." Quay, who knew how the votes had been counted in the doubtful states, repeated Harrison's words to a friend in private and commented, "Think of the man. He ought to know that Providence hadn't a thing to do with it."

Cleveland's policies are reversed. Harrison was content to follow the advice of party leaders during his years in office. James Blaine, who had played a key role in getting Harrison the nomination, was again named Secretary of State. John Wanamaker, a wealthy dry-goods merchant from Philadelphia, was appointed Postmaster General. So many prominent businessmen were in the new official family that people called it "The Millionaire's Cabinet." The Cabinet members quickly followed traditional practices. Wanamaker, for instance, fired some 30,000 Democrats in his department and replaced them with Republicans.

From its start, the Harrison administration came under heavy pressure from interest groups seeking favorable treatment. Aided by the Speaker of the House, Thomas

Grover Cleveland's re-election in 1892 is celebrated in this painting with great triumph and fanfare. In actuality, the campaign had been a lackluster one.

B. Reed, appropriation bills — most of them "pork-barrel" proposals[1] — were sent in a steady stream to the White House for signature. Among the bills was one entitling all Union veterans to pensions.

The highest tariff ever passed to date also went through Congress. The man who worked hardest for it — and who gave his name to the bill — was Representative William McKinley of Ohio. To aid American sugar refiners, the McKinley Tariff removed the levy on raw sugar. It protected American sugar growers, however, by paying them a bounty of two cents a pound for their crop. On imported manufactured goods, it set duties so high that western farmers, traditional supporters of Republican Presidents, were infuriated. They could see the cost of the factory products they would buy going higher than ever.

The farmers' criticism of the Republicans was quieted temporarily by the passage in 1890 of two laws named for Senator John

Sherman of Ohio. The Sherman Silver Purchase Act increased the amount of silver the government purchased annually and allowed for the printing of paper money backed by silver. Farmers believed that these steps would increase the amount of money in circulation and make it easier for them to repay their financial obligations. The Sherman Antitrust Act (page 454) made illegal the creation of any "combination . . . or conspiracy" that produced a monopoly "in restraint of trade."

The Democrats regain the White House in 1892. By the time of the 1892 election, the clamor for reform was rising again. A new political organization, the Populist Party, had been formed by distressed farmers. Attracting strength from other discontented people, it nominated a candidate for President and expected to make a good showing in the election.

The Republicans renominated Harrison, while the Democrats once again chose Grover Cleveland to be their standard-bearer. The campaign was dull. There were few torchlight parades or huge rallies. Possibly the ordeal of the Homestead strike (page 477) and other unrest contributed to the

---

[1]*Pork-barrel* is a slang term applied to legislation that chiefly benefits the locale of the legislator obtaining it. The expression originated in the pre-Civil War practice of distributing pork to plantation slaves from huge barrels.

lack of spirit. At any rate, the Democrats won, with Cleveland achieving the most overwhelming presidential victory at the polls since Lincoln's in 1864. The strength of the Populist candidate, James Weaver, surprised the country. He polled over a million popular votes and took 22 electoral votes. The Populists were the first *third party* to win electoral votes since 1860. (A third party is any party organized in opposition to the two major parties.)

The depression of 1893 hits the country. Cleveland's new term in the White House opened just as hard times — the depression of 1893 — struck the country. Economic conditions remained bad for the four years Cleveland was in office. Thousands of businesses failed, and farm prices gradually fell to new lows. One fifth of all the country's factory workers lost their jobs. Some Democrats blamed the depression on the McKinley Tariff which, they said, had reduced the demand for foreign goods and consequently produced a decline in customs revenue.

Cleveland was not prepared to give aid to the victims of the depression. In the four years between his two terms, Cleveland had practiced law in New York City. The experience had made him even more sympathetic to the concerns and interests of eastern bankers and businessmen. In truth, the leading politicians of *both* parties seemed blind and deaf to the needs of farmers and working people.

A sign of the hard times was a march on Washington of protesting citizen groups from many parts of the country. The most publicized of these "armies" was one led by Jacob S. Coxey, a successful Ohio businessman. A reformer by instinct, Coxey favored a massive road-building program financed by the federal government. He also supported a public-works program for unemployed people in the cities.

The orderly little ragtag army that Coxey led from Ohio to Washington numbered about 500. The men traveled about fifteen miles a day, slept under a circus tent, and relied for food on handouts from local authorities and union people. The marchers' goal was to dramatize the plight of the jobless. When Coxey reached Washington, he was arrested and sent to jail for twenty days for walking on the grass at the Capitol. Coxey's army soon broke up, and nothing came of his proposals.

The Sherman Silver Purchase Act is repealed. Cleveland believed that prosperity would return only if Americans had confidence in the backing of their paper currency. Ever since the passage of the Sherman Silver Purchase Act (page 491) in 1890, Cleveland believed that the people's faith in the nation's currency had been destroyed. He argued that basing paper money on both silver and gold as provided in the law was a mistake. People were using silver to obtain paper money, turning it in for gold and then hoarding it. By 1893 the hoarding of gold — both by banks and individuals — was threatening the nation's gold reserves. Cleveland maintained that for a healthy economic climate, *a gold standard,* or currency based solely on gold, was necessary. He succeeded in persuading Congress to repeal the Sherman Silver Purchase Act in 1893, much to the dismay of the silver-producing states and of farmers.

In the face of the dwindling supply of gold in the Treasury, Cleveland also concluded what people came to call the "Morgan bond deal." A group of bankers, headed by J. P. Morgan, agreed to pay $62 million in gold for government bonds. Because Morgan profited handsomely from the transaction, many people believed that Cleveland was himself in league with the "money trust." By showing that leading bankers were supporting the government, however, Cleveland stopped the flow of gold and re-established confidence in United States currency.

Congress approves the Wilson-Gorman Tariff. Cleveland continued to put his faith in tariff reduction. Through his efforts, Congress in 1894 passed the Wilson-Gorman Tariff. In its orginal form, the bill provided for overall lower tariff rates. During the Senate debate on the bill, however, hundreds of amendments were added to protect special interests. In the version passed by Congress, the Wilson-Gorman Act was nearly as protectionist as the McKinley Tariff.

The Wilson-Gorman Tariff finally became law without the President's signature. Among the many amendments to the bill was an income-tax provision. The Supreme Court, however, declared the income tax unconstitutional in 1895. The Court ruled that the income tax, being a direct tax, was contrary to the Constitution since it was not apportioned according to population.[2]

SECTION REVIEW

1. Vocabulary: *third party, gold standard.*
2. (a) What was the Pendleton Act? (b) Why was it enacted?
3. (a) Why did Chester Arthur fail to gain the Republican nomination for President in 1884? (b) What factors led to Grover Cleveland's victory in that election?
4. What stand did President Cleveland take on each of the following? (a) Pension bills (b) Federal assistance to farmers (c) Railroad regulation (d) Tariff rates
5. What tariff policy did Benjamin Harrison follow after he won the presidency in 1888?
6. (a) What was the Sherman Silver Purchase Act? (b) Why did Grover Cleveland support the effort to repeal it after he was re-elected President?

3 Farmers Begin to Join Together

Although the United States had become, as Speaker Reed said, "a billion-dollar country," signs of unrest showed that many people felt left out of the benefits. Southern and western farmers, particularly, had long been struggling to organize and to seek answers to the problems they confronted.

Farmers join the Grange. The first significant organization of farmers was founded in 1867. Called the National Grange of the Patrons of Husbandry, it was the brain child

---

[2]The Sixteenth Amendment to the Constitution, which went into effect in 1913, removed the constitutional barrier to this kind of tax.

Women as well as men were admitted to the Grange. At meetings like this one in Illinois, Grangers met to exchange ideas and solve common problems.

of Oliver H. Kelley, a clerk in the Department of Agriculture. A man of boundless energy, Kelley planned to bring farmers together in intellectual and social activities. He recognized that one of the results of settling the Great Plains was the loneliness imposed on people by the immense distances between settled places. He understood, too, that farmers needed a place where they could discuss ways of improving farming. Kelley planned that each local unit, or Grange, would have among its officers a "lecturer" who would at each meeting present a report on some topic of general interest.

Kelley talked over his plans with his niece, Carrie Hall, who convinced him that if his organization were to attain its goals, it would have to include women. Kelley soon began conducting a drive for members, and by the early 1870's was having incredible success. Said Kelley of the Grange, "It must be advertised as vigorously as if it were a patent medicine." By 1873, 20,000 local Granges had sprung up, located in all but four states (though concentrated mainly in the South and West). These locals contained about 800,000 members.

Like the Knights of Labor, the Grangers started cooperative enterprises, the aim being to eliminate middle agents and

Farmers and the Grange

The writer Hamlin Garland (page 432) grew up on midwestern farms in the 1860's and 1870's. He moved from Wisconsin to Iowa, and then to the Dakotas, and later wrote about life in rural America.

> Many of our social affairs were now connected with "the Grange." During these years on the new farm, while we were busy with fencing and raising wheat, there had been growing up among the farmers of the west a social organization officially known as The Patrons of Husbandry.
>
> My father was an early and enthusiastic member of the order, and during the seventies its meetings became very important dates on our calendar. In winter "oyster suppers" with debates, songs, and essays drew us all to Burr Oak Grove schoolhouse, and each spring the Grange picnic was a grand "turn out." It was almost as well attended as the circus.
>
> The central place of meetings was usually in some grove along the river to the west and south of us. Early on the appointed day the various lodges of our region came together one by one at convenient places, each one moving in procession and led by great banners on which the women had blazoned the motto of their home lodge. Some of the columns had bands and came preceded by far faint strains of music, with marshals in red sashes galloping to and fro in fine assumption of military command.
>
> It was grand, it was inspiring to us, to see those long lines of carriages winding down the lanes, joining one another at the

A poster depicting agricultural life

> crossroads till at last all the Granges from the northern end of the county were united in one mighty column advancing on the picnic ground, where orators awaited our approach with calm dignity and high resolve. Nothing more picturesque, more delightful, has ever risen out of American rural life. Each of these assemblies was a most grateful relief from the loneliness of the farm.

thereby make prices lower. The most successful cooperatives were grain elevators — buildings equipped to load, unload, clean, and store grain. Many farmers had become convinced that elevators owned by the railroads were overcharging for their use.

The Supreme Court upholds Granger laws. The Grange also turned to politics, urging that railroad and warehouse rates be regulated. Between 1869 and 1874, so-called Granger laws were passed by legislatures in Illinois, Iowa, Wisconsin, and Minnesota. These laws were designed to fix maximum freight and storage charges. In a number of states, official commissions were appointed to help enforce the legislation.

The railroads strongly opposed the Granger laws and in some instances appealed to the courts. In 1877 the United States Supreme Court acted on a number of cases, which came to be called the "Granger cases." The main question the Court had to deal with can be summarized: Has a state the right to regulate a private corporation on grounds that the business involved affects the public welfare?

In the best known of the cases, *Munn v. Illinois*, the Supreme Court held that states have the power to regulate private property when it is "clothed with a public interest." In other words, a state did indeed have grounds for regulating private property devoted to public use. The Court modified the decision somewhat in 1886, however, when it held in a case called *Wabash, St. Louis and Pacific Railroad Company v. Illinois* that a state could regulate a railroad only within the state's own borders.

Since most railroads ran between states, clearly only the federal government was in a position to regulate them. The Interstate Commerce Act, passed in Cleveland's first term (page 490), had provided the beginning of an answer to the problem of railroad abuse. This momentous law forbade pools, rebates, and the setting of high rates for short hauls. Railroads were required to post their rates and to make them "reasonable and just." The Interstate Commerce Act was a monument to the work begun by the Grangers.

Grange membership declines. For all its success in bringing farmers together, the Grange was, like the Knights of Labor, ultimately the wrong *kind* of organization. By concentrating on cooperatives — which often failed — the Grangers proved incapable of solving the farmers' specific problems. During the 1880's, membership fell off. Still, the Grange had proved to farmers the advantages of political action.

The Greenback Party is formed. Many farmers were heavily burdened by debts contracted during the Civil War. At that time the market for grain had been good, and money for buying more land had been easy to borrow. When the price of grain declined, these debts were more difficult to pay off. The harder the farmers worked, the larger the crops they produced. This abundance forced prices lower.

Some farmers began to be attracted by the program of the Greenback Party. This group had organized for the purpose of convincing the federal government to keep in circulation the large amounts of greenbacks issued during the Civil War (page 387). The members also believed that if additional paper money without backing were added to the money supply, farm prices would rise. Farmers would then be better able to pay off their debts. After a financial panic struck the nation in 1873, Greenback parties arose independently in a number of states. A national organization was formed at Indianapolis in 1876, and Peter Cooper of New York, then 85 years old, was nominated for President. In 1880 the Greenback candidate for President was James Weaver. In those presidential elections, however, neither Cooper nor Weaver received a significant number of votes.

The Greenbackers ran the eccentric Ben Butler for President in 1884, but they had long since gone into decline. The party never recovered from a decision by Congress in 1875 to redeem all greenbacks in gold and retire them. This Resumption Act deeply disappointed farmers and other "cheap money" advocates who had hoped that the issuing of *more* greenbacks would solve their problems.

The Farmers' Alliances appear. By the beginning of the 1880's, farmers were once again seeking reform through politics. They began establishing pressure groups called Farmers' Alliances. The goals of the Alliances included more paper money in circulation, the unlimited coinage of silver, government ownership of the railroads, and the return to the federal government of the public land the railroads had received.

Step by step the alliances came into existence. Farmers first banded together locally, then the locals became state-wide; afterward, state units came together in regional organizations. Eventually there were two major sectional voices of farming people: the Southern Alliance and the Northwestern Alliance. The Southern Alliance became highly influential, with three million white members and one million black members in an affiliated Colored Farmers' Alliance.

Although idealized in this painting of harvest time, the lives of farmers in the late 1800's were strained by devastating weather, high costs, and fluctuating prices.

In 1889 an effort was made to link the Southern and Northwestern Alliances. Representatives of labor were also invited to participate in order to join together "the organized tillers and the organized toilers." There were, however, serious obstacles to such unity. The Southern Alliance, for one thing, insisted upon separate white and black lodges, a proposal the Northwestern Alliance rejected.

In the election of 1890, the Southern Alliance, tying itself to the Democratic Party, captured four governorships, forty-four seats in the House of Representatives, three seats in the Senate, and control of eight state legislatures. On the Plains, the Northwestern Alliance was able to send six representatives to Congress from Kansas and Nebraska.

The considerable time it took farmers to begin running their own candidates for political office can be accounted for by the relative slowness with which people communicated in this period. The telephone had not yet entered the lives of most farmers. Furthermore, the ferocity of the Civil War had tied farmers — like all people — to the traditional political parties. The ties were based on sentiment as well as interest. To northern farmers, forsaking the Republicans seemed a betrayal of the party that had saved the Union. To white farmers of the South, forsaking the Democratic Party was unthinkable.

Farmers face complex new problems. By the end of the 1880's, however, hard times had loosened old political loyalties. Farmers confronted a combination of falling prices, unusually bad weather, and above all, heavy *mortgages.* (A mortgage is a pledge of property to a creditor — often a bank — usually against the repayment of a money loan.)

The increase in the population of the western states had been so sudden and substantial that the region had become a powerful magnet for eastern investors with money to lend. The number of people in Kansas and Nebraska between 1880 and 1890, for instance, went from 1,448,000 to almost 2,500,000. In those same years, the population of North and South Dakota jumped from 135,000 to 511,000. Most of these people could not have survived without borrowing money. They required it to put up houses and farm buildings and to purchase equipment, fencing, and seed grain. To obtain the money they needed, many farmers mortgaged their property, often beyond what they could readily afford. Meeting the payment on the mortgages was a heavy burden. It became a severe problem when things turned sour at the end of the 1880's. By 1887 the number of mortgages in Kansas was three times greater than in 1880. Half the farmers of Kansas and North Dakota had taken mortgages, most of them heavy.

Nature played a cruel hand in the calamity that followed. The terrible weather from 1885 to 1887 that had devastated the cattle industry (page 428) also ravaged the grain growers. Within a short time, thousands of farmers were unable to pay the installments due on their mortgages. Soon they lost their farms as creditors took them over. It was said that if the farms covered by the failed mortgages were laid end to end, they would form a tract of land thirty miles wide and ninety miles long.

The farmers who survived knew they must pay back the money they owed. But how? They had always noticed that when railroads went bankrupt, they were reorganized under court orders. This meant that the debts of the railroads were cut down, but that the trains continued to run. As a result of such practices, many farmers considered railroad managers, judges, and eastern bankers to be "the enemy." The editor of a farm journal expressed it this way:

There are three great crops raised in Nebraska. One is a crop of corn, one a crop of freight rates, and one a crop of interest. One is produced by farmers who by sweat and toil farm the land. The other two are produced by men who sit in their offices and behind their bank counters and farm the farmers.

Farmers began to leave the Plains states in droves. Many a covered wagon departed bearing a sign that read: "In God We Trusted, In Kansas We Busted." Some farmers held on for a while by borrowing from "loan sharks" at exorbitant interest rates. In the end they were defeated too.

As farmers tried to understand what had gone wrong, they began to accept the simple idea that not enough money was available to do what they called "the money work." The reasoning appeared logical enough. At the time of the Civil War the country had about $1 billion in circulation. Twenty-five years later the population had

almost doubled, but the money in circulation had increased only slightly. No wonder that farm prices were so low, said the farmers. There were too few dollars on hand to buy the increased amount of farm products. It took $1.20, for example, to buy a bushel of wheat in 1871; in 1892 the same amount of money could buy two bushels. Farmers thought the solution was to inflate the currency, that is, to somehow get more money into circulation. Few of them gave thought to the rise in the price of manufactured goods that would surely follow putting the idea into practice.

The coinage of silver becomes a political issue. The failure of the Greenback Party, which had advocated expanding the currency, had keenly disappointed many farmers. In the same years, however, rich veins of silver were being discovered in the mountains of the West. These silver strikes suggested another solution. Why not freely issue silver coins?

The struggle to put more silver into circulation had grown out of earlier developments. During most of the nation's history, both gold and silver coins had circulated. Both were legal tender, which meant that a person who was owed money *had* to accept either gold or silver in repayment of the debt. Silver and gold had been valued for coinage purposes in 1834 at a ratio of 16 to 1. In other words, 16 ounces of silver were equal in value to 1 ounce of gold. To put it another way, there was sixteen times as much silver in a silver dollar as there was gold in a gold dollar.

After the discovery of gold in California in 1849, the metal became more plentiful and its value in relation to silver fell. Still, the old ratio of 16 to 1 remained the official relationship between the two precious metals. People soon were aware that the silver in a silver dollar was worth more than the gold in a gold dollar. A silversmith making silver jewelry, umbrella handles, snuffboxes, silver comb-and-brush sets, and hundreds of other items would pay more for the metal than would the United States Mint. Consequently, so little silver was brought to the Mint for coinage that in

1873 Congress removed the silver dollar from the list of standard coins. At the time, the decision attracted almost no attention.

By the end of the 1870's, however, the increased silver production in the West was having a noticeable effect. The value of silver in relation to gold was declining sharply. By 1875, as the price of silver at the silversmiths' shops fell lower and lower, silver producers were denouncing Congress for having committed the "Crime of '73!" They called for the coinage of silver once again. "Give us back the dollar of our daddies," they pleaded.

The silver controversy continues. The mine owners raised this cry, of course, hoping to induce the government to buy the total output of the silver mines. The interests of the silver producer and the farmer — the one in disposing profitably of the ore, the other in enlarging the currency — came together. Congress responded to the clamor in 1878 with the Bland-Allison Act. It provided for the Secretary of the Treasury to purchase not less than $2 million and not more than $4 million worth of silver each month.

The law satisfied neither the silver producers nor the farmers, and both groups pressed hard for even larger purchases of silver by the government. The admission to the Union in 1889 and 1890 of several silver-producing states increased the pressure on Congress. Finally yielding, Congress in 1890 passed the Sherman Silver Purchase Act (page 491). In spite of expectations, however, the operation of the law did not dramatically increase the amount of money in circulation.

New farm leaders attract national attention. The farmers were interested in more than currency reform. Meeting in St. Louis in 1889, representatives of the Alliances adopted a wide-ranging political platform. It called for a graduated income tax, government ownership of railroads, and an end to national banks.

Leaders of the Alliances had, by this time, become nationally recognized names. Among them was "Pitchfork Ben" Tillman of South Carolina. Once, when Tillman was running for the Senate, he told an audience,

"send me to Washington and I'll stick my pitchfork into [President Cleveland's] old ribs." Another notable was Tom Watson of Georgia. Like Tillman, Watson had special affection for the nation's poor farmers, and he became a dogged spokesman for them in the House of Representatives.

From Kansas came the fiery Mary Elizabeth Lease. Those who admired Mrs. Lease called her a "Patrick Henry in petticoats." Another impressive advocate of immediate action was Annie Diggs of Kansas, an editor and political organizer. Yet another influential figure from Kansas was "Sockless Jerry" Simpson. He had earned the nickname after claiming that a political rival — a banker — wore silk socks. A newspaper reporter twisted the statement to mean that Simpson wore none!

Possibly the most persuasive orator among all the farm politicians was Ignatius Donnelly of Minnesota. He cultivated many interests. He believed, for instance, that he had proved Francis Bacon was actually the author of the plays of Shakespeare. The figure known to the public the longest was James Weaver. As the Greenback candidate for President in 1880 (page 495), Weaver, a Civil War general from Iowa, had spoken to crowds in towns and villages from one end of the country to another. With his white hair and earnest manner, he seemed a fatherly figure to his admirers and had earned respect.

Through the work of these people, the farmers' concerns were brought to the attention of all Americans. In the next few years, those concerns would have an extraordinary impact on national politics.

SECTION REVIEW

1. Vocabulary: *mortgage.*
2. (a) What was the Grange? (b) What kinds of laws did it support? (c) What was the significance of *Munn v. Illinois*?
3. (a) What program did the Greenback Party offer? (b) Why did it attract the support of farmers?
4. (a) What were some of the serious problems faced by farmers in the late 1800's? (b) What solutions to those problems did the Alliances propose?

4 The Populists Propose Far-Reaching Reforms

By 1890 many farmers were talking about forming a new political party. Alliance members, Grangers, Greenbackers, Knights of Labor, and many other reformers met in St. Louis in February, 1892, for that purpose. The convention adopted the name "People's Party," though in time the new organization became known as the Populist Party. The excitement created by the Populists swiftly gained momentum.

The Populists call for a new direction. Meeting at Omaha in July, 1892, the Populists adopted a platform that embraced proposals farmers and union members had advocated for years. The planks included a call for legislation to tighten control over the railroads, the free and unlimited coinage of silver at a ratio of 16 to 1, and a graduated income tax. The extensive platform also contained pleas for the secret ballot in elections and liberal pensions for Union veterans. It also proposed the direct election of senators and a one-term limit for the President and the Vice President. Reaching out for labor's support, the platform advocated the eight-hour day and condemned the use of Pinkerton detectives in labor disputes.

The Populists get off to an encouraging start. The enthusiasm that greeted the adoption of the platform had the air of a religious revival meeting. The Populists nominated James Weaver to be their presidential candidate. When the 1892 election returns came in (page 492), the Populists had a right to be encouraged. Immediately, they began making plans for 1896. Weaver predicted, "The Republican Party is as dead as the Whig Party was after the Scott campaign of 1852, and from this time forward will diminish in every state of the Union and cannot make another campaign."

The Populists were overestimating their strength. In the congressional elections of 1894, only 12 states gave more than 30 percent of their votes to Populist candidates. Still, the Populists were confident that they would carry the day in 1896. They assumed

A PARTY OF PATCHES.
Grand Balloon Ascension—Cincinnati, May 20th, 1891.

Satirized as a patchwork of interests, the Populists had their own presidential candidate by 1892.

that the Democrats and the Republicans would reject the free-silver issue. Then *they* would use it to win the support of the silverites in both major parties. The result, they hoped, would be a widened base of support for their own program of reform.

The Republicans prepare for the election of 1896. In June, the Republicans gathered in St. Louis for their convention. The dominant figure was Mark Hanna, a wealthy industrialist from Ohio and the very symbol of the "enemy" the Populists had in mind. Hanna began lining up delegates to make William McKinley — a Civil War veteran who had twice been elected governor of Ohio — the party's nominee. The naming of McKinley on the first ballot was assured even before the delegates arrived.

The Republican platform, denouncing the idea of free silver, stated firmly that "the existing gold standard must be maintained." McKinley's own views on the matter were less solid. Some people tagged him "Wobbly Willie." He would often speak out for "sound money" (meaning the gold standard) and sometimes in favor of bi-metallism (meaning money based on gold *and* silver). He understood, however, that the Republican platform could win him votes in the East from big businessmen and from people afraid that a shift to silver might endanger business and eventually their jobs. Moreover, being an advocate of a high tariff (page 491), he counted on the backing of working people who saw tariffs as necessary to keeping wages up. McKinley knew, too, that many workers would support him because he had once defended in court a group of strikers arrested in a riot.

The Democrats nominate Bryan.

The Democrats gathered in Chicago for their convention early in July. Already they had been weakened by six years of the Populist onslaught that drew supporters away from their ranks. Party leaders saw that the silver issue could be theirs now that the Republicans had passed it by. Silver Democrats were calling for a rejection of the "gold Democrats" and sought to make the issue a weapon for victory.

The Democrats' platform showed who was in charge. The most important plank was a clear call for "the free and unlimited coinage of both gold and silver at the . . . ratio of sixteen to one." The huge audience cheered when Ben Tillman denounced Grover Cleveland — the party's own sitting President — as a "tool of Wall Street."

One of the delegates who had spoken in favor of the party platform was William Jennings Bryan, a handsome, broad-shouldered, 36-year-old Nebraskan. A brilliant orator with a melodious voice that carried to the farthest corners of the hall, he hypnotized the crowd with his speech. When he reached his final words, the people were on their feet, cheering wildly. He concluded: "You shall not press down upon the brow of labor this crown of thorns; you shall not crucify mankind upon a cross of gold."

The Democrats had found their new leader. On the fifth ballot they made Bryan the party's choice for President. He was destined to be the dominant figure of the Democratic Party for the next sixteen years.

The Populists support Bryan.

The Populists were in deep gloom when they came together in St. Louis two weeks later. Should they too make Bryan their candidate? He was not in sympathy with many of the Populist proposals. Yet a separate candidate would only assure a victory for the Republicans. Many Populists resisted the idea of being joined with the Democrats. Tom Watson, deeply distressed, said that the Democrats wanted the Populists to "play Jonah while they play the whale."

In the end the Populists decided they had no choice but to nominate Bryan. Still, they balked at taking Bryan's running mate, Arthur Sewall of Maine. A shipyard owner, Sewall was also a bank president and a railroad director. The Populists nominated their favorite, Tom Watson, for the vice presidency.

McKinley wins the 1896 election.

Bryan waged a fiery and strenuous crusade for the White House. In so doing he introduced the modern presidential campaign, one in which candidates themselves play the chief part. Sometimes making as many as six speeches a day, Bryan was greeted everywhere by brass bands and hoopla. He tried to persuade the faithful that he represented "the people" in their mighty struggle with "Wall Street."

The Republicans campaigned along traditional lines. McKinley, a devoted husband, refused to be away from his ailing wife for any length of time. He conducted his campaign from the front porch of his house in Ohio. Week after week he greeted thousands of people, who came from all parts of the country to hear him speak. McKinley kept in touch by telephone with politicians throughout the country, thus becoming the first presidential nominee to use the phone extensively for campaigning.

On Election Day, McKinley won convincingly. He carried not only the nation's industrial areas — where employers had threatened mass dismissals if Bryan won — but also the important farming states of Iowa, Minnesota, and North Dakota. Many farmers, possibly influenced by a slight rise in wheat prices at the end of the summer, had decided to vote Republican, as they always had. Many working people also

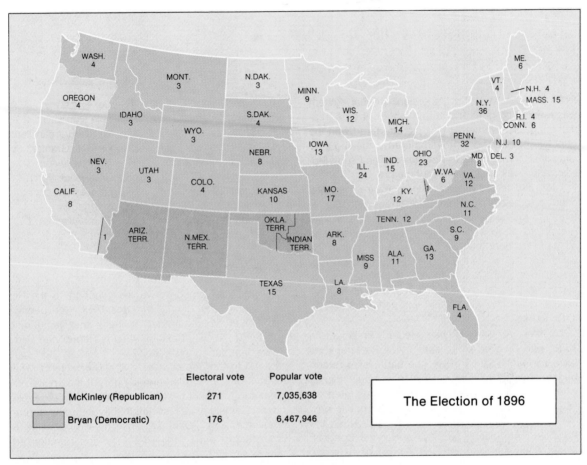

	Electoral vote	Popular vote
McKinley (Republican)	271	7,035,638
Bryan (Democratic)	176	6,467,946

The Election of 1896

Bryan's nationwide speeches in 1896 and the well-financed campaign of McKinley resulted in the largest popular vote in any presidential election to date.

voted for McKinley, not so much out of fear for their jobs but out of fear that Bryan's proposals could lead to cheap dollars and inflation that would hurt wage earners. To the silverites, Bryan's defeat was a deep disappointment; to the Populists, it was an unrelieved disaster.

The gold standard is formally established. The silver issue soon disappeared. When gold was discovered in western Canada and in Alaska shortly after the election, the supply of money began to increase rapidly. The United States went on the gold standard in 1900, and the silver question faded from public interest.

The Populist legacy was mixed. Some of the party's suggestions were eventually enacted into law, including the graduated income tax and the direct election of senators.

After a generation of protest, however, the batteries of reform had run down. Meanwhile, the country was looking abroad for new opportunities. Suddenly, domestic affairs were pushed into the background as foreign issues took center stage. Within two years, William Jennings Bryan was in a colonel's uniform training troops in the state of Nebraska. Tom Watson would write, "The blare of the bugle drowned the voice of the reformer."

SECTION REVIEW

1. (a) Who were the Populists? (b) What did the Populists call for in their platform of 1892?
2. (a) Who won the Republican and Democratic nominations for President in 1896? (b) Which candidate did the Populists support? (c) What was the outcome of the election?

Chapter 21 Review

Summary

After the Civil War, the American political system was marked by graft and corruption. Lobbyists, representing special interest groups, interfered with the effective functioning of government by seeking special favors through the use of bribes. The Crédit Mobilier affair was characteristic of the era.

In 1876 the Republicans were aware that they needed to select a candidate of unquestionable integrity to run for President. The man they chose was Rutherford B. Hayes of Ohio. When Hayes was elected President, he tried to change the method by which public officeholders were appointed. Opposed to the spoils system, Hayes favored a merit system as a basis for government appointment. Civil service reform, however, met with little enthusiasm in Congress.

James A. Garfield was elected President in 1880, with Chester Arthur as his Vice President. As soon as Garfield took office, the battle over reform began again. The issue came to a tragic climax when Garfield was assassinated by a frustrated office-seeker. Shocked by this event, the public now demanded immediate action. In January, 1883, the Pendleton Act established a Civil Service Commission to make appointments on the basis of merit.

In 1884 Grover Cleveland won the presidency, becoming the first Democrat to occupy the White House since 1861. Cleveland tackled two particularly sensitive issues: the pension bills and tariff rates. Possibly because of Cleveland's forthrightness, Republicans once again were able to take over the presidency in 1889 with the inauguration of Benjamin Harrison.

Cleveland returned to the White House in 1893, just as a devastating depression was about to begin. Lasting for four years, the hard economic times caused the failure of numerous businesses, and thousands of Americans suffered keenly.

One group that felt victimized by economic fluctuations were the farmers. To deal more effectively with their situation, farmers began to join together. In 1867 the National Grange was formed. Then, in the 1880's farmers formed organizations called Farmers' Alliances. By 1892, Alliance members, Grangers, and other farmers and workers joined together to form the Populist Party. In the 1896 election, the Populists backed William Jennings Bryan, the Democratic candidate for President, who was running on a free-silver platform. Republican candidate William McKinley won, however, and his election was a victory for the gold standard.

Vocabulary and Important Terms

1. "solid South"
2. merit system
3. Stalwarts
4. Half-Breeds
5. Pendleton Act
6. Mugwumps
7. Interstate Commerce Act
8. McKinley Tariff
9. third party
10. Coxey's army
11. gold standard
12. Wilson-Gorman Tariff
13. National Grange
14. *Munn v. Illinois*
15. Greenback Party
16. Farmers' Alliances
17. mortgage
18. Bland-Allison Act
19. Populist Party

Discussion Questions

1. (a) What groups gave their support to the Republican Party during the post-Civil War period? (b) Which voters tended to back the Democratic Party? (c) To what extent was the Republican Party dominant during this period?

2. (a) In the debate over civil service reform, what arguments were offered in support of the spoils system and the merit system? (b) What effect did President Garfield's assassination have on the reform movement? (c) What setbacks did civil service reform suffer during the Cleveland and Harrison administrations?

3. (a) Why did many farmers oppose high tariffs? (b) What stand did President Cleveland take on the tariff question? (c) Why did he not sign the Wilson-Gorman Tariff?

4. (a) What effect did the depression of 1893 have on the country? (b) What did President Cleveland believe to be the cause of the depression? (c) What step did he take as a result?

5. In what sense was the Interstate Commerce Act a monument to the efforts of the Grangers?

6. (a) Why were farmers slow to organize their own political parties and run candidates for office? (b) Why, by the end of the 1880's, had old political loyalties begun to loosen?

7. (a) Why, in the 1870's, did mine owners and farmers call for government coinage of silver? (b) How did Congress respond to these demands? (c) Why were neither silver producers nor farmers satisfied with the laws passed? (d) What part did the silver issue play in the election of 1896? (e) What happened to the silver issue after that election?

8. (a) What groups joined together in 1892 to form the organization known as the Populist Party? (b) What proposals were made in the Populist platform of 1892? (c) What electoral successes did the Populists enjoy? (d) What was the Populist legacy?

Relating Past and Present

The late 1800's saw the rise of a number of third parties. What third parties have been formed in recent years? What platforms have they adopted? What successes have they had? In what ways, if any, have these third parties affected the major parties and the outcome of recent elections?

Studying Local History

Find out about the history of the Granger movement in your state or region. How popular was the Grange? What Granger laws, if any, were passed in your state? What social and educational activities did the Grange sponsor? What activities does the Grange carry on in your state or region today?

Using History Skills

1. *Reading maps.* Study the map on page 501 showing the election results of 1896. (a) What sections of the country supported McKinley? (b) What sections supported Bryan? (c) What divisions in national politics are revealed in the map?
2. *Reading source material.* Study Hamlin Garland's description of the Grange on page 494. (a) What social activities did the Grange sponsor in Hamlin Garland's county? (b) Where were regional Grange meetings held? (c) How does Garland's account convey the importance of the Grange to rural Americans?
3. *Making connections.* List the planks of the Populist Party (page 499). Then do research to find out which planks were later enacted into law.

WORLD SCENE

Citizen Participation

The period from 1865 to 1900 saw efforts in many countries to bring about some degree of citizen representation in government.

The Third French Republic. The collapse of the French army and the capture of Emperor Napoleon III at the end of the Franco-Prussian War (1870) gave groups in Paris favoring the establishment of a republic an opportunity to take over the government of France. The new government was named the Third Republic (previous republics had been created in 1792 and 1848), and national elections were held to choose an assembly.

The election returns of 1870 showed that rural areas had chosen representatives who wished to restore the monarchy in France. Radical groups, adamantly opposed to the return to any form of monarchy, quickly set up their own independent government in the city of Paris. Known as the Paris Commune, this revolutionary government was crushed within two months by the French army.

A coalition of monarchist groups governed France until 1875. In that year republicans gained control of the National Assembly and wrote a new constitution which provided for a more representative government. The Third Republic lasted well into the twentieth century, but it was unstable because competing interests in France, all of them represented in the assembly, were unable to work together effectively.

Self-government in Canada. By the end of the American Revolution, thousands of Loyalists had moved to Canada, most of them settling around the Great Lakes. This influx of English-speaking people led in 1791 to the division of the old province of Quebec into two parts. The region occupied by the Loyalists became Upper Canada (present-day Ontario), while the French-speaking area became Lower Canada (present-day Quebec).

In the late 1830's rebellions against British rule erupted in both parts of Canada. These uprisings were quickly subdued, but the British government, deeply concerned, sent Lord Durham to investigate the troubles. The Durham Report, submitted in 1839, was a document of considerable insight. It recommended that to keep Canada loyal to the British Crown, Parliament should grant the Canadian people self-government. Soon after Lord Durham made his suggestions, Upper and Lower Canada were united in a single province under one governor. It was several years before Britain granted Canada self-government.

In 1864 Canadian representatives, meeting in Quebec, produced the basis for a constitution and outlined a plan for the political union of the various provinces. The plan was accepted by the British, and in 1867 Parliament passed the British North America Act. The new union, calling itself the Dominion of Canada, became the first self-governing nation within the British Empire.

UNIT 5 REVIEW

Important Dates

1862 Homestead Act.
1866 National Labor Union formed.
1867 Grange movement started.
1869 First transcontinental railroad completed.
      Knights of Labor organized.
1876 Battle of Little Bighorn.
      Bell invents telephone.
1877 *Munn v. Illinois.*
1879 Edison invents electric lamp.
1882 John D. Rockefeller organizes Standard Oil Company.
1883 Pendleton Act signed into law.
1886 Haymarket Riot.
      American Federation of Labor formed.
1887 Interstate Commerce Act.
      Dawes Act assigns land to Indians.
1890 Sherman Antitrust Act.
      Sherman Silver Purchase Act.
1892 Homestead strike.
      Populist Party formed.
1893 Sherman Silver Purchase Act repealed.
1894 Pullman strike.
1900 United States goes on gold standard.

Review Questions

1. (a) Why was the trans-Mississippi West the last region of the continental United States to be opened to white settlement? (b) What different groups moved into that region during the 1800's? (c) What conditions attracted each group?

2. (a) Why were the Indians who lived in the Great Plains unable to stem the tide of white settlers? (b) What Indian policies did the federal government enact in the years after the Civil War? (c) What was the effect of those policies on the Indians?

3. (a) What factors contributed to the rapid industrial growth experienced by the United States after the Civil War? (b) How did the business activities of Andrew Carnegie and John D. Rockefeller reflect some of the changes in the ways Americans conducted business during this period? (c) What effect did industrial growth have on America's cities?

4. (a) What factors contributed to the building of America's railroads? (b) Why were railroads important to industrialists? (c) To average citizens?

5. How did inventions in the post-Civil War period play a part in the growth of American industry?

6. (a) Why did an increasing number of immigrants come to the United States after the Civil War? (b) Why and how did some native-born Americans oppose this "new" immigration? (c) To what extent was immigration restricted during this period?

7. (a) With the rise of big business, what new relationship grew up between workers and their employers? (b) In what ways did working people seek to change their working conditions, and what changes did they demand? (c) What obstacles did labor unions encounter?

8. (a) Why did civil service reform, tariff reduction, and free silver become important national issues in the period after the Civil War? (b) What was the fate of each of those issues by 1900?

9. (a) What problems did farmers face in the late 1800's? (b) What actions did farmers take to solve those problems? (c) How successful were they?

Projects

1. On an outline map of the United States write in the date of admission for those states that joined the Union as a result of the settlement of the trans-Mississippi West. Also, illustrate what brought settlers into each new state after the Civil War.

2. Find out more about life on the Great Plains in general and about the role of pioneer women in particular by reading the writings of one or more of the following authors: (a) Hamlin Garland, (b) O. E. Rölvaag, (c) Willa Cather, (d) Laura Ingalls Wilder. Select one or more descriptive passages to read to the class. Tell how this and other passages have contributed to your understanding of ways of living on the Plains.

3. Submit an imaginary application to the United States Patent Office for a patent on one of the inventions described in this unit. On the application form name the invention and how it works. Also briefly describe the usefulness of the invention and its anticipated effect on American life. Read your patent application to the class.

4. Write an essay on the topic "The post-Civil War period was a time of political corruption, ignored issues, and hard times for most Americans." You may either agree or disagree with this statement, but be sure to support your position with evidence.

5. Create a set of five handbills in which you illustrate some of the demands of farmers in the late 1800's. On these handbills include pictures, slogans, and other information that shows the determination of farmers to solve their problems.

6. Make a bulletin-board display that depicts American society in the year 1900. Your display should illustrate significant changes in American ways of living and working in the period after the Civil War.

CRUSADING AT HOME AND ABROAD

1865 – 1920

We must make up our minds that, whether we like it or not, we are a great people and must play a great part in the world.

THEODORE ROOSEVELT, 1910

CHAPTER 22

A Force in the World

1865 – 1900

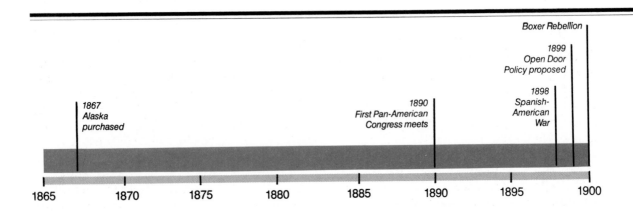

1867
Alaska
purchased

1890
First Pan-American
Congress meets

1898
Spanish-
American
War

1899
Open Door
Policy proposed

Boxer Rebellion

1865 1870 1875 1880 1885 1890 1895 1900

CHAPTER OUTLINE

1. Americans begin to look beyond their borders.

2. Interest in expansion grows.

3. The United States fights a war with Spain.

During the 1870's and 1880's, most Americans had little interest in foreign affairs. They were absorbed with such domestic matters as reconstruction, the dazzling changes in the look and behavior of the nation, and the boundless physical exertion required in developing the West. The Presidents, furthermore, reflected the habit Americans had acquired of knowing little about other countries. From Lincoln until the end of the century, no Chief Executive who came to office had ever traveled abroad.

America, nevertheless, was being drawn slowly into world politics. The Atlantic cable, made permanent in 1866, enabled news from Europe to be transmitted instantaneously. To follow the course of diplomatic and military events no longer required waiting for the next ship to arrive. Moreover, there was no escaping the fact that the world was growing smaller. Steamships, which had begun crossing the Atlantic in the unheard-of time of ten days in 1850, were coming across the water in the 1880's in seven days. By 1900, they made the trip in five and a half days.

The United States finally began to recognize its interest in helping maintain peace among nations. Not only did foreign trade depend upon world peace, but shortened distances were putting Europe's international troubles — and shortly those of other continents — close to America's backyard. By the 1890's, Americans would look "outward" and the United States would become active in foreign affairs.

1 Americans Begin to Look Beyond Their Borders

Even though Americans as a whole gave little thought to the world outside, the United States was involved continually in diplomacy abroad. Immediately following the Civil War, it carried on delicate negotiations that resulted in overseas expansion.

THE BEGINNINGS OF EXPANSION

The United States seeks to buy islands in the Caribbean. The acts of marauding Confederate cruisers during the Civil War had convinced many officials that the United States should have naval bases in the Caribbean. As a result, Secretary of State William H. Seward in 1865 asked Denmark to sell the United States the Danish West Indies. Following a favorable vote by the inhabitants of the islands, Denmark agreed to terms.

The treaty had scarcely been signed when the islands were ravaged in rapid succession by an earthquake, a hurricane, and a tidal wave. Seward was roundly assailed for having made such a foolish deal. The navy, furthermore, had by now fallen into disuse, and it had no need for bases outside the country. The House of Representatives humiliated Seward by refusing to vote the money to complete the sale. When General Grant became President, he put the treaty aside. The islands would remain Denmark's until 1917 when a new set of circumstances led to their purchase by the United States.

Seward was also eager to obtain Samaná Bay in the Dominican Republic, offering in 1868 to pay $2 million for it. The Dominican government replied by inviting the United States to buy the entire island! Although President Johnson recommended that Congress accept the offer, it was rejected. Later, President Grant wished to go ahead with the arrangement, but his Secretary of State, Hamilton Fish, opposed it. Still, a treaty of annexation was submitted to the Senate. It ran into unshakeable opposition from the chairman of the Senate Foreign Relations Committee, Charles Sumner. To Sumner, the deal looked like a scheme to

Ships from the United States Navy paraded on the Hudson River in 1899. Naval strength was instrumental in the spread of American influence in the late 1800's.

enrich some of Grant's White House staff and various corrupt Dominican politicians. In Sumner's view, the United States would do better by backing a free confederation of the West Indian islands, where the "black race should predominate" under American protection. After the treaty failed, Grant was so angry — he had once believed he had Sumner's support — that for a long time whenever he passed Sumner's house in Washington, he shook his fist at it.

Seward purchases Alaska. Seward's expansionist ideas were grand in scope. The Secretary envisioned the annexation of Haiti, as well as of various Spanish and French islands in the Caribbean. As his gaze swept further, he could see the United States purchasing Iceland and Greenland and annexing Hawaii.

Seward's ambitious ideas would never be fully realized, but in 1867 he seized an opportunity to extend America's frontiers by purchasing Alaska from Russia. The Russians had feared that if war ever broke out in Europe, Britain might use the opportunity to take over this territory, then known as Russian America. Only a few years earlier, furthermore, the governor of Siberia (the Russian domain in Asia) had warned the czar, "The ultimate rule of the United States over the whole of [North] America is so natural that we will sooner or later have to pull back from there." When the Russians let it be known that they were interested in selling Alaska, Seward was eager to negotiate. He drew up a treaty by which the United States agreed to pay Russia $7,200,000 for the vast territory. Word that Russia had accepted Seward's terms arrived on the newly laid Atlantic cable.

Alaska contained almost 600,000 square miles — twice the size of Texas. Many people ignorantly regarded the territory as worthless. Some members of Congress ridiculed the proposed purchase as "Seward's Folly" and, more playfully, as "Frigidia" and "Walrussia." Charles Sumner, however, came to Seward's side. Sumner argued that Alaska's rich resources were necessary for America's future development. Believing that the purchase of Alaska could be compared with the purchase of Louisiana, Sumner saw the following significance: "One by one they have retired, first France, then Spain, then France again; and now Russia; all giving way to the absorbing unity which is declared in the national motto, *E Pluribus Unum*."[1] The treaty transferring Alaska was ratified by the Senate on April 9, 1867, by a vote of 37 to 2.

The United States watches the situation in Cuba. The Spanish colony of Cuba was high on Seward's list of places to be acquired. Because slavery still existed there, however, the Radical Republicans in control of Congress would not hear of any scheme to take it over. Still, because France and Britain had an active interest in Cuba as the "world's sugar bowl," the United States felt it must keep a watchful eye on the island. Located on an approach to the Gulf of Mexico, Cuba could become a threatening base if it fell into the wrong hands.

In 1868, when a rebellion broke out in Cuba, the Grant administration was tempted to intervene, but held back. In the course of the uprising, a Spanish naval vessel captured a rebel ship, the *Virginius*, off the Cuban coast. Fifty-three passengers, some of them United States citizens, were taken ashore and shot as "pirates." The American outcry could have led to war, but the United States accepted an apology and a money indemnity. A few years later, Spain put down the rebellion, and abolished slavery. Cuba, nevertheless, remained a potential trouble spot in the Caribbean, for Spain's presence was a standing invitation to Americans to intervene there.

The United States becomes interested in Asia and the Pacific islands. Americans had long sought a toehold in Asia too. The annexation of Alaska, bordering on the northern Pacific, gave fresh life to the notion of expanded trade with Asian peoples. Japan, for instance, had fascinated American merchants and seafarers ever since 1852, when Commodore Matthew C. Perry had set out

---

[1]This Latin phrase, meaning "out of many, one," appears on the seal of the United States.

with a naval expedition for the "Land of the Rising Sun." For two centuries, the rulers of this ancient empire had forbidden its people to have contact with foreigners. Received hesitantly by Japanese officials, Perry persuaded them in 1854 to sign a treaty highly favorable to the United States. The treaty ended Japan's seclusion by giving American traders access to Japanese ports.

Other Pacific islands also attracted American attention. In 1867, the year of the Alaska purchase, the United States annexed Midway Island (map, page 523), discovered a few years earlier by Americans. In 1878, the United States acquired a coaling station, Pago Pago, on Tutuila, one of the Samoa Islands. Germany and Great Britain were also active in Samoa and their rivalry led to serious squabbling. Finally, in 1899 the two European powers entered into an agreement with the United States. Germany received the islands of Western Samoa and the United States acquired what became known as American Samoa (map, page 523).

Interest in Hawaii develops. Hawaii's strategic importance had long been clear to Americans hoping for influence in the Pacific. As early as 1842, Daniel Webster, then Secretary of State, declared that the United States would not permit any other country to take over those islands, then independent. In 1849, French forces seized Honolulu but quickly pulled out when the United States protested.

Hawaii's place in American thinking loomed larger in the 1880's. The United States was engaged in rebuilding and modernizing its navy and expanding the range of naval operations. In 1887, America acquired from the Hawaiian monarchy the right to establish a coaling and repair station at Pearl Harbor, the magnificent land-locked harbor on the southern coast of the island of Oahu. The agreement was especially satisfying to American sugar planters, traders, and missionaries, already influential on the islands. This new tie with the United States strengthened the hope of

American interests in Hawaii included pineapple and sugar plantations. Owners of these plantations sought annexation in 1893 and finally won it in 1898.

these Americans that Hawaii would soon come under United States protection.

Hawaii is annexed. Matters came to a head in 1891 when Liliuokalani (lee-LEE-oo-oh-kah-LAH-nee) became queen of Hawaii. A forthright person, she was generally unfriendly to the American planters on the islands. Those settlers were already in an angry mood over the McKinley Tariff (page 491), which permitted *all* foreign sugar — not just sugar from Hawaii — to enter the United States duty-free.

Early in 1893, fearing that Queen "Lil" might rid the government of American influence, the planters staged a revolt against her. They toppled the queen from her throne and then quickly formed a provisional government.

Less than a month of Benjamin Harrison's administration was left when the President sent the Senate a treaty providing for the annexation of Hawaii. The treaty was still in the Senate when Grover Cleveland came to the White House. Cleveland was, in general, against the acquisition of colonies, and his sense of justice led him to withdraw the treaty. He declared himself "unalterably opposed to stealing territory, or of annexing a people against their consent." Moreover, he said, "The people of Hawaii do not favor annexation." Still, the only way to put the queen back in power was to use force against the Americans who had helped depose her. Democrats disappointed by Cleveland's position pointed out sarcastically that it was not their party's tradition to restore monarchs to their thrones.

Cleveland, unwilling to send troops, turned the Hawaiian question over to Congress, which did nothing about it for the next few years. Not until the United States went to war with Spain in 1898 did Congress approve a resolution annexing Hawaii.

STRENGTHENING THE MONROE DOCTRINE

The United States promotes Pan-Americanism. Ever since it was proclaimed in 1823, the Monroe Doctrine had been the cornerstone of American foreign policy. The United States had already invoked the Doctrine when France tried to install Maximilian in Mexico during the Civil War (page 389). Another kind of challenge to the Doctrine developed during the presidency of Rutherford B. Hayes. At that time a private French company was attempting — unsuccessfully, it proved — to build a canal across the Isthmus of Panama. Many Americans were made uneasy by the enterprise, fearing that the French government itself might become involved in the Americas.

By the 1880's the United States was taking an even more active role in the Western Hemisphere. It tried to promote *Pan-Americanism* — that is, the spirit of economic and political cooperation among all American nations. The individual who deserves much credit for furthering this movement was Secretary of State James G. Blaine. Like most Americans of his era, Blaine knew little about international relations. He came to office at a time when the United States was just beginning to recognize the need for a trained corps of diplomats. His achievements, nonetheless, were impressive.

In Blaine's few months as Secretary under President Garfield in 1881, he made arrangements for a conference of representatives from all the American nations. The plans were canceled, however, after Garfield's assassination. When Blaine returned to the Department of State under President Harrison in 1889, the idea of a Pan-American Congress was renewed, and representatives of the American nations met in Washington, D.C., in 1890.

Blaine made a number of proposals at the conference. While he had general concern for the peace of Latin America, he also worried about the growth of European influence in that region. He was particularly troubled that British manufactured goods were widely sold there and that products from the United States often were not given a chance to compete. Blaine hoped to remedy the situation by a program to foster the unity of the Western Hemisphere. He called for an inter-American customs union, better transportation between North and South America, a uniform system of weights and measures, and even a common silver coin to be used in all the Americas.

Uncle Sam reminds European powers of the United States' policy by pointing to the Monroe Doctrine in this cartoon and warning, "That's a live wire, gentlemen."

The Pan-American Union is established. At the 1890 meeting, the delegates agreed to establish the Pan-American Union. The purpose of this organization was to encourage the exchange of information about the customs, laws, and trade of American countries. It also aimed to encourage economic, social, and cultural cooperation. Although few other concrete decisions came from the Pan-American gathering, some observers were optimistic that the Monroe Doctrine had passed "into a stage of higher development." They could foresee that Pan-Americanism would extend the principles of the Monroe Doctrine. Maintaining the peace and security of the hemisphere would become a shared responsibility. Most Latin American nations, however, remained distrustful of the United States.

The United States becomes involved in a boundary dispute. A dramatic example of the defense of the Monroe Doctrine was provided by the Venezuela boundary dispute of 1895. Ever since 1840 there had been disagreement over the dividing line between Venezuela and British Guiana (map, page 543). When Britain seemed to be extending its territorial claims in the mid-1880's, the United States, no less than Venezuela, was concerned. Was Britain violating the Monroe Doctrine as well as infringing on a neighbor's territory?

Anti-British feeling in the United States was especially high. Irish-Americans were helping keep it stirred up. Also, many people believed that British trade practices had caused the depression of 1893.

The Monroe Doctrine, it appeared, would have to be defended. Early in 1895, Congress asked President Cleveland to urge the British and Venezuelan governments to submit their boundary dispute to **arbitration,** that is, to have the dispute settled by a board of fair-minded, neutral persons. At the same time, a pamphlet entitled *British Aggression in Venezuela, or the Monroe Doctrine on Trial* was circulating in Washington and having noticeable influence. The title suggests its inflammatory contents.

Not long after the publication appeared, Cleveland appointed Richard Olney to be Secretary of State. A brusque, no-nonsense man, Olney took action. He sent a message to London in which he declared that if Britain seized the disputed territory by force, it would be violating the Monroe Doctrine. Olney assured the British that the United States would not sit idly by and watch the violation of a neighbor in the hemisphere. He recommended that they give up British Guiana altogether. Then Olney added words that infuriated not only Britons but most Latin Americans as well: "Today the United States is practically sovereign [supreme] on this continent." (By "this continent" he meant both of the Americas.) Olney's startling assertion of power was followed by an equally bold explanation. Said the Secretary, the United States' "infinite resources combined with its isolated position render it master of the situation and practically invulnerable as against any or all other powers."

Cleveland threatens war over Venezuela. The British rejected this assertion of American authority. They had never accepted the Monroe Doctrine in the first place. Now they said that even if they had accepted the Doctrine, it did not apply in this case. They could not see, furthermore, why they must entrust their interests in the Venezuela dispute to the United States.

President Cleveland was infuriated by the British response, describing himself as "mad clear through." Politically, he could not afford this type of rebuff, for Irish-Americans were staunch supporters of the Democratic Party. He believed, moreover, that Britain was not only violating the Monroe Doctrine but also bullying Venezuela — something that offended his sense of decency. Unless Britain accepted arbitration in the dispute, Cleveland said, the United States would use "every means in its power" to protect Venezuelan territory. Because the British were having even more serious difficulties in South Africa and because they feared that in a war with the United States they might lose Canada, they finally agreed to cooperate. The dispute was settled by arbitration in 1899.

The episode undoubtedly strengthened the Monroe Doctrine. The peaceful solution also marked the end of sniping between the United States and Great Britain. Never again would the British challenge America's dominant position in the Caribbean region.

SECTION REVIEW

1. Vocabulary: *Pan-Americanism, arbitration.*
2. (a) What efforts did William Seward make to buy islands in the Caribbean? (b) What were the results? (c) How did the United States purchase Alaska?
3. (a) What was the *Virginius* affair? (b) How was it resolved?
4. (a) Why did Americans become interested in Asia and the Pacific islands? (b) What Pacific islands did the United States acquire?
5. (a) What proposals did Blaine make to the first Pan-American Congress? (b) What was the outcome?
6. (a) What was the cause of the dispute between Britain and Venezuela in the 1890's? (b) How was the issue settled?

2 Interest in Expansion Grows

In spite of prodding by Seward and a handful of other expansionists, the United States, as we have seen, did not readily seize opportunities to acquire overseas territories. The celebration of the nation's one-hundredth birthday in 1876 had reminded the nation anew of how much they prized their independence. Most thinking Americans held political liberty to be so sacred that they believed it should not be denied to any people. Nevertheless, a number of factors were leading to an active interest in taking over territories far from home.

European powers set an example. The most important cause for the change in Americans' attitudes was the example Europe was providing. Since the 1870's the major countries there had been engaged in establishing overseas colonies. By the end of the century, European countries had taken control of much of Asia and Africa and most of the islands of the Pacific. Because Britain's colonies were situated on every continent and in time zones all around the world, its people boasted that "The sun never sets on the British Empire." Germans, deeply envious, believed they could explain the success of the British: "The Lord wouldn't trust them in the dark!"

Many Americans wanted to join in the lively competition for colonies in order to have a place among the mighty nations of the earth. Said Henry Cabot Lodge, a senator from Massachusetts and a leader of the American expansionists, "As one of the great nations of the world, the United States must not fall out of the line of march."

The United States reaches for new markets. The nation's industrial and agricultural growth also helped arouse interest in acquiring possessions. American industrialists and farmers were beginning to seek overseas markets for their products. Senator Albert J. Beveridge of Indiana recognized the economic profits that could be gained abroad. In a speech in 1898, he said:

> American factories are making more than the American people can use; American soil is producing more than they can consume. Fate has written our policy for us; the trade of the world must and shall be ours. We will establish trading posts throughout the world as distributing points for American products. We will cover the ocean with our merchant marine. We will build a navy to the measure of our greatness. Great colonies governing themselves, flying our flag and trading with us, will grow about our posts of trade.

New ideas gain popularity. Additional support for expansion came from writers and professors who believed in the racial superiority of white America. One of them was a historian, John Fiske, who taught at Harvard College. Another was a Congregational minister, Josiah Strong. Both of them wrote popular books in which they argued that among all living things there is a ceaseless "struggle for existence." Both believed that the principle of the "survival of the fittest," which biologists claimed to have found in the world of nature, also applied to the world of international politics.

In the competition among nations, Fiske and Strong asserted that the "English

In this cartoon, Uncle Sam is obviously pleased with United States expansion overseas, which many Americans in 1898 viewed as almost an obligation.

race" (by which they meant white, English-speaking peoples) had moral, intellectual, and technological superiority. Wrote Fiske, "The two great branches of the English race have the common mission of establishing throughout the larger part of the earth a higher civilization and more permanent political order than any that has gone before."

In his book *Our Country*, Strong wrote in 1885 of what the United States specifically could contribute to this task of dominating other peoples. The American nation, he was convinced, had inherited from Britain the energy and perseverance required "to spread itself over the earth." Other writers quickly added to this idea the notion that the United States had a divine obligation to hasten the fulfillment of its destiny as a colonizing power.

One of the most influential of the men who accepted this belief was John W. Burgess, a professor at Columbia College in New York. Burgess found it deplorable that "by far the larger part of the surface of the globe is inhabited by populations which have not succeeded in establishing civilized states." America, he believed, had a vital role to play in correcting this situation. He argued that the United States should acquire colonies in order to train people in the art of self-government. Failure to do so, he asserted, would be a "disregard of duty."

Theodore Roosevelt was influenced by Alfred T. Mahan's writings on naval power. In 1897, Roosevelt became Assistant Secretary of the Navy.

A new generation of political leaders urges expansion. A group of striving political leaders also spoke out for colonies. The most powerful of these advocates were Theodore Roosevelt of New York and two friends and associates — Senator Lodge and John Hay. They were men with deep roots in the nation's past, who claimed to speak for the future. Roosevelt belonged to the seventh generation of Roosevelts living in New York City. Lodge could relate how a grandfather of his as a young boy hid under a sideboard at home in order to watch George Washington, a guest of the family, eat breakfast. Hay, at the age of 23, had gone to Washington, D.C., from Indiana in 1861 to be a private secretary to Abraham Lincoln.

These up-and-coming leaders claimed to be irritated by both the industrialists' single-minded concern with making money and the ordinary politicians' careless disregard of public honor. They considered themselves, on the other hand, to be "well-born and intelligent men" who would direct the nation's attention toward noble ends. High on their list of goals were a clash of arms and the acquisition of colonies. Roosevelt wrote in 1895, "This country needs a war." He dismissed people willing to have "peace at any price"; with exasperation he identified them as "bankers, brokers, and Anglo-maniacs [lovers of England]." Hay, also favoring a "large policy" — which meant the conquest of distant peoples and territory — wrote to President McKinley that "the greatest destiny the world ever knew is ours."

Mahan favors a strong navy. Yet another person strongly urging the necessity of colonies was Captain Alfred Thayer Mahan. A magnetic teacher and a writer of rare gift, he preached that Americans needed colonies because the country had reached the limit of expansion. "In our infancy," Mahan wrote, "we bordered upon the Atlantic only; our youth carried our boundary to the Gulf of Mexico; today maturity sees us upon the Pacific." Regarding expansion as something needed by every vigorous country, he insisted that "whether they will it or no, Americans must now begin to look outward." Mahan called for a strong navy, a canal across the Isthmus of Panama, and the establishment of coaling stations and naval bases in the Caribbean and the Pacific.

Politicians took up Mahan's call. Lodge proclaimed in the Senate, "It is sea power which is essential to every splendid people." He added, "We have too great an inheritance to be trifled with. . . . It is ours to guard and extend." Acting on Mahan's advice and with broad support in Congress, administrations during the 1890's brought into being a modern navy. By 1900 the United States had the third largest fleet in the world.

A revolt breaks out in Cuba. The growing interest in foreign affairs and expansion could be seen in 1895 when a rebellion against Spanish rule broke out in Cuba. Steadily worsening economic conditions had made Cuba ripe for trouble. The island suffered badly in the depression of 1893. Then the tariff of 1894 had placed such a high duty on raw sugar that Cuba's ability to sell it in the United States was substantially reduced.

Many of the leaders of the Cuban revolt had lived or traveled in the United States. Because they admired America, they hoped to turn their homeland into a republic too. Their rallying cry was *"Cuba Libre!"* (meaning "A Free Cuba!").

The rebels, lacking sufficient arms to fight openly against the Spanish troops, resorted to guerrilla tactics. They set fire to villages, raided sugar plantations, and disrupted railroad lines. They reserved their harshest treatment for people who supported the Spanish authorities, not hesitating to execute them. Deep down, the Cuban revolutionaries did not believe they could oust the Spanish from the island. They hoped, rather, to win concessions by causing so much damage that the island's plantations and trade would be paralyzed.

To counter the insurgents, the Spanish adopted what they called a reconcentration policy, which meant forcing thousands of people out of their homes and into camps enclosed by barbed wire. Through this program, the rebels in the countryside were cut off from their civilian supporters. The reconcentration camps became places of unimaginable torment, with starvation and disease widespread. As many as 200,000 people had died in these camps by 1898.

Americans watched the events in Cuba with interest — and with increasing dismay. The desperate situation called forth their humanitarian instincts. They also sympathized with the effort to establish an independent republic. Some Americans, furthermore, had never forgotten the *Virginius* incident (page 508).

Newspapers inflame public opinion. The Cuban struggle was made to order for American newspapers. Catering to the tastes of their growing number of readers, the papers had become more and more sensational. In their columns, journalists could blow up the slightest international incident into a life-or-death crisis. The invention of the Linotype machine had made it possible to "break open" the front page of a newspaper and quickly replace a story with a new one fresh off the telegraph wire or cable. Improved methods of reproducing pictures made it possible to illustrate even ordinary stories and make them vivid and intimate.

Interest in the latest news was heightened by the keen competition for circulation among New York newspapers, which were widely copied throughout the country. The chief rivals were Joseph Pulitzer's New York *World* and William Randolph Hearst's New York *Morning Journal.* Both of these newspapers practiced what came to be called "yellow journalism." This meant that they casually took liberties with the truth and felt no need to provide balanced reporting. Yellow newspapers did not hesitate to fake the "news," either. Nevertheless, the theatrical character of yellow journalism — including exaggerated headlines, melodramatic cartoons and sketches, and gruesome crime stories — appealed to millions of readers.

In the Cuban struggle, Hearst early advocated American intervention on the side of the rebels. He also quickly saw the insurrection as useful in his contest with Pulitzer. Pulitzer, too, saw he could put the struggle to profitable use. Soon, the newspapers were vying with each other in presenting accounts of atrocities said to have been carried out by Spanish authorities. A favorite villain was Spain's commander in Cuba, General Weyler (or, as he came to be called in the press, "Butcher" Weyler).

In a short time, the newspapers were acting as if they had government authority. They sent "commissions" to meet with insurgent leaders and sometimes even to carry official messages from rebels in Cuba to those in the United States. They also assigned correspondents to the island to search out stories. Some of the reporters sent dispatches without ever visiting the areas they described. Hearst once sent the artist Frederic Remington to sketch the scenes of a battle. Remington, finding things quiet, wired the home office for instructions. Hearst is reported to have replied, "You furnish the pictures and I'll furnish the war."

McKinley tries to avoid war. President McKinley, who had personally known the horror of the American Civil War, was unwilling to become involved in the Cuban tangle. He expressed his hope that a new government in Spain would make the changes necessary to end the rebellion in Cuba. Throughout 1897 he practiced patience. He was pleased when Spain removed General Weyler and began a policy that was expected to bring peace to the island.

The New York newspapers, nevertheless, kept up their calls for American intervention. Hearst excited the country with the touching story of Evangelina Cisneros, a young Cuban who had voluntarily accompanied her father, a rebel, into imprisonment. Eventually she, too, was charged by the Spanish with antigovernment activities. The *Journal* reported, however, that her sole crime had been to resist the advances of a Spanish officer and that she was about to be shipped to a prison colony in Africa. The word went out from Hearst, "Enlist the women of America!" Well-known women responded swiftly. Mrs. Jefferson Davis appealed to the queen of Spain to release Evangelina Cisneros and turn her over to American women. Julia Ward Howe implored Pope Leo XIII to use his influence to make Spain show mercy. A petition to the Spanish government signed by 20,000 American women included many famous names: Julia Dent Grant, General Grant's widow; Nancy McKinley, the President's mother; and Mrs. Mark Hanna. The Spanish would have liked to release Miss Cisneros and silence the distressed Americans. To do so, however, would have seemed a surrender to pressure.

The *Journal*, displaying its impatience, sent one of its adventurous reporters to Cuba to rescue the young woman. He snatched her out of her cell by reaching down from a next-door rooftop, and rushed her to a waiting ship. She was soon in the United States, a heroine of the insurrection. The *Journal's* headline trumpeted: AN AMERICAN NEWSPAPER ACCOMPLISHES AT A SINGLE STROKE WHAT THE BEST EFFORTS OF DIPLOMACY FAILED UTTERLY TO BRING ABOUT IN MANY MONTHS. As congratulations poured in, the governor of Missouri

suggested to Hearst that he send 500 reporters to Cuba and liberate the island!

The De Lôme letter angers Americans. On February 9, 1898, the *Journal* published another scoop, a letter that the Spanish minister to the United States, Dupuy de Lôme, had sent a friend in Cuba. Intercepted by a rebel spy in the Havana post office, it was delivered to the *Journal* in New York.

The De Lôme letter created a fresh sensation. In it, the minister described McKinley as "a would-be politician who tries to leave a door open behind himself while keeping on good terms with the jingoes [war advocates] of his party." The *Journal's* headline exaggerated wildly the importance of the diplomat's unwise comment: THE WORST INSULT TO THE UNITED STATES IN ITS HISTORY. When De Lôme promptly resigned his post, the *Journal* published a cartoon showing an irate Uncle Sam snarling at the crestfallen Spaniard, "Git!" That the letter had been stolen and that much worse was being said about McKinley in the daily press were points few Americans seemed to recognize.

The "Maine" sinks. Six days after the De Lôme letter was published, a truly momentous event occurred. The battleship *Maine*, which had been sent by the United States to Havana harbor to protect American lives and property, was torn apart there by an explosion. In the inferno, 260 sailors perished, and many others were injured. The destruction of the *Maine* stunned the American people. The actual cause of the disaster will likely never be known. Recent investigations have concluded that in all probability the *Maine* was destroyed by an accident which took place inside the vessel.

From the start, most of the American press and public charged Spain with responsibility for the loss of the vessel. In the tidal wave of national anguish, the *World* screamed in a headline that it was sending its own divers to Havana to find out if the explosion had been caused by a bomb or a torpedo. The *Journal* already had an explanation: THE WARSHIP "MAINE" WAS SPLIT IN TWO BY AN ENEMY'S SECRET INFERNAL

Calls for American intervention in the Cuban revolt became more intense after the mysterious explosion of the United States battleship *Maine* in Havana harbor.

MACHINE. A popular song expressed the common judgment:

> Spain, Spain, Spain!
> You ought to be ashamed
> For doing such a thing
> As blowing up the *Maine.*

A new slogan — "Remember the Maine!" — swept the country.

The United States moves closer to war. The expansionists were for going to war against Spain. The most active of them was Theodore Roosevelt, now Assistant Secretary of the Navy. He was more and more irritated by McKinley's apparent reluctance to fight. Roosevelt wrote, "I would give anything if President McKinley would order the fleet to Havana tomorrow."

Roosevelt was using his boundless energy to make preparations for a war he was sure was coming. One day in February,

1898, when Secretary of the Navy John D. Long took the afternoon off, Roosevelt acted as if he were responsible for the Department of the Navy. He put himself in touch with important senior naval officers, redistributed the vessels of the fleet, and placed orders for ammunition. Moreover, Long later wrote, the Assistant Secretary sent "messages to Congress for immediate legislation authorizing the enlistment of an unlimited number of seamen." To Commodore George Dewey, commander of the Pacific fleet (then based in Hong Kong), Roosevelt sent a fateful cable. In the event of war, Roosevelt ordered, Dewey's duty would be to sail to the Philippine Islands, a possession of Spain, and see to it that the Spanish naval squadron did not get away.

President McKinley was in the painful position of having a war forced upon him that he did not want. He called in a group

On April 12, 1898, the *Examiner*, a San Francisco newspaper, urged Congress to declare war on Spain.

of congressmen and told them, "I must have money to get ready for war. I am doing everything possible to prevent war, but it must come and we are not prepared for war." Early in March, Congress unanimously passed a bill providing $50 million for "national defense."

The news of the congressional action took the Spanish by surprise. It also intimidated them. As the United States minister there reported, "To appropriate fifty millions out of money in the Treasury, without borrowing a cent, demonstrates wealth and power. Even Spain can see this."

The United States declares war on Spain. On April 9, 1898, the Spanish, under extreme pressure from the United States, agreed to an armistice in Cuba. In Washington, the ambassadors of six European powers called upon President McKinley to halt the preparations for war. In spite of the news of the armistice, McKinley finally asked Congress to declare war on Spain. He had spent many a sleepless night in coming to his decision, but the pressure to declare

war was too great. Roosevelt, fretful over what he considered to be foot-dragging, told a friend that McKinley had actually prepared two messages for Congress — "one for war and one for peace, and he doesn't know which one to send in!"

The United States formally declared war on Spain on April 25, 1898. A few days earlier, Congress had recognized Cuba's independence and had given McKinley the authority to use force to drive the Spanish from the island. An amendment to the war resolution was proposed by Senator Henry M. Teller of Colorado. Approved by Congress, the Teller Amendment stated that when the fighting in Cuba was over, the United States would "leave the government and control of the island to its people."

SECTION REVIEW

1. (a) Why did interest in overseas expansion grow in the late 1800's? (b) How did this attitude affect the navy?
2. (a) Why was the Cuban revolt of interest to Americans? (b) What role did newspapers take in the debate over American intervention?
3. (a) What events led to the outbreak of war between the United States and Spain? (b) What was the Teller Amendment?

3 The United States Fights a War with Spain

The long-awaited war with Spain was fought with purpose and bravery — and not a little awkwardness resulting from inexperience. The navy was ready to move swiftly, but the army was unprepared for war.

Dewey defeats the Spanish fleet at Manila. In accordance with instructions, Commodore Dewey had been waiting in Hong Kong for news of the war declaration. On April 27, he received orders to proceed to the Philippines. British officers whom Dewey knew believed that the Americans were headed toward certain defeat. Their view, Dewey later wrote, was that the Americans were "a fine set of fellows, but unhappily we shall never see them again."

Dewey at Manila Bay

The naval battle at Manila Bay in 1898 made Commodore George Dewey a national hero and proved the worth of America's navy. In this passage from his autobiography, Dewey described the victory at Manila Bay, including the issuing of his famous order to Charles Gridley, captain of the flagship *Olympia.*

Commodore Dewey

The misty haze of the tropical dawn had hardly risen when at 5:15, at long range, the Spanish forts and squadron opened fire. Our course was not one leading directly toward the enemy, but a converging one, keeping him on our starboard bow. Our speed was eight knots and our converging course and ever-varying position must have confused the Spanish gunners. My assumption that the Spanish fire would be hasty and inaccurate proved correct.

So far as I could see, none of our ships was suffering any damage, while, in view of my limited ammunition supply, it was my plan not to open fire until we were within effective range, and then to fire as rapidly as possible with all our guns.

At 5:40, when we were within a distance of 5,000 yards (two and one half miles), I turned to Captain Gridley and said: "You may fire when you are ready, Gridley."

. . . Gridley took his station . . . and gave the order to the battery. The very first gun to speak was an 8-inch from the forward turret of the *Olympia,* and this was the signal for all other ships to join the action. . . .

There was no cessation in the rapidity of fire maintained by our whole squadron, and the effect of its concentration, owing to the fact that our ships were kept so close together, was smothering, particularly upon the two largest [Spanish] ships, the *Reina Cristina* and *Castilla.* . . .

Victory was ours, though we did not know it. Owing to the smoke over the Spanish squadron, there was no visible signs of the execution wrought by our guns. . . . It was a most anxious moment for me. So far as I could see, the Spanish squadron was as intact as ours. I had reason to believe that their supply of ammunition was as ample as ours was limited.

Therefore, I decided to withdraw temporarily from action for a redistribution of ammunition if necessary. . . . But even as we were steaming out of range, the distress of the Spanish ships became evident. Some of them were perceived to be on fire and others were seeking protection behind a point. . . . Moreover, the Spanish fire, with the exception of the Manila batteries, to which we had paid little attention, had ceased entirely. It was clear that we did not need a very large supply of ammunition to finish our morning's task.

At midnight on April 30, 1898, Dewey's ships sailed into Manila harbor. For unexplained reasons, the Spanish allowed them to pass unchallenged. As the sun rose, Dewey confronted the Spanish fleet. Less than two hours later, the entire Spanish naval force of ten ships had been sunk or destroyed, and the American squadron was pounding the Spanish shore batteries. By sunset, Dewey's ships were anchored off the city of Manila as safely as if it were peacetime. Their brass bands played "the usual evening concert."

When news of the victory at Manila arrived in Washington, the nation went wild with joy. Dewey became an instant hero. A popular poem went:

> Oh, Dewey was the morning
> Upon the first of May,
> And Dewey was the admiral
> Down in Manila Bay. . . .

To take the city itself, Dewey waited for help from an American army unit. Late in July a force of 11,000 troops under General Lesley Merritt arrived. By the middle of August, after light resistance, Spanish forces had surrendered Manila to the Americans and to Filipino guerrillas led by Emilio Aguinaldo (ah-gwee-NAHL-doh).

The American fleet blockades Santiago. Meanwhile, the war was also being fought in the Caribbean. Before troops could be sent to Cuba, the American navy was given the task of controlling the seas. Its orders were to find and destroy the Spanish fleet of Admiral Cervera (sair-VAY-rah), which had left the Cape Verde Islands for Cuba soon after the declaration of war. Many Americans living along the Atlantic coast were in a panic, fearing that they were about to be hammered by Cervera's guns. Rear Admiral William T. Sampson, commander of the American Atlantic fleet, lay in wait for Cervera in the Caribbean. Off the coast of Virginia, Commodore Winfield Scott Schley patroled with an American squadron, ready to cut off the Spaniards if they came into his path.

The Spanish fleet managed to slip past the Americans and sail safely into the Cuban port of Santiago. Admiral Sampson, however, quickly bottled up Cervera by blockading the harbor.

Land forces are sent to Cuba. Meanwhile, an American expeditionary force of 17,000 regulars and volunteers had been assembled at Tampa, Florida. These troops were under the overall command of General William R. Shafter. Shafter weighed 300 pounds — not perfect condition for fighting a demanding campaign in tropical heat, but made to order for mischievous cartoonists.

Included among Shafter's officers was General Joseph ("Fighting Joe") Wheeler. Now 61 years old, the former Confederate cavalry commander was wearing once again the Union blue — a symbol of the reconciliation between the North and South. Also among Shafter's troops was a volunteer unit known as the Rough Riders. Although led by Colonel Leonard Wood, the Rough Riders' second-in-command drew far more attention than Wood. He was Lieutenant Colonel Theodore Roosevelt, who had left Washington for the thick of the battle.

The training of the American land forces had been inadequate and their embarkation from Tampa was a model of confusion. The single railroad line to the docks at Tampa was insuffient for handling a modern army. Black troops suffered the additional indignity of being refused service in local restaurants. They would have remained unfed if they had not been able to buy food from street vendors.

On June 14, 1898, the troops, including the Rough Riders, set sail for Cuba. Wearing woolen uniforms, they were ill-clad for a war in the tropics. The broiling heat on the five-and-a-half-day sea journey to Cuba added to their discomfort. Still, they were eager to fight. They sang a favorite tune, "Hot Time in the Old Town Tonight," which Theodore Roosevelt would later turn into a political campaign song.

The United States defeats Spain in the Caribbean. Landing just east of Santiago, the American troops went into action almost immediately. Their goal was to capture that city, install guns on the heights overlooking the harbor, and pound Cervera's fleet below. On the morning of June 24, the land battle began.

Two fortified positions outside of Santiago blocked the Americans' advance. One was at the village of El Caney. Spanish sharpshooters had set themselves up in the church where Cortés was said to have prayed the night he went forth to conquer Mexico. Only after a savage, eight-hour battle did the Americans gain control of El Caney.

The volunteers known as the Rough Riders charge up San Juan Hill in this famous painting by Frederic Remington, who was sent to Cuba by newspaperman Hearst.

After El Caney fell, the Americans pushed on to San Juan Hill. Again, the outnumbered Spanish forces put up stiff resistance. Their sharpshooters pinned down 8,000 Americans for hours. At one point a force of Rough Riders under Colonel Roosevelt found itself under heavy fire. Roosevelt's men, aided by two regiments of black soldiers, worked their way through tall grass to the top of San Juan Hill. Roosevelt fought with a bravado equal to his warlike words before the war. Barely able to see without his glasses, he went into battle with a dozen pairs sewn to the lining of his hat — in case a few should get shot off!

The victories at El Caney and San Juan Hill were later described by a young lieutenant named John J. Pershing: "White regiments, black regiments, regulars and Rough Riders, representing the young manhood of the North and the South, fought shoulder to shoulder, unmindful of color, . . . and mindful only of their common duty as Americans." Having taken the heights dominating Santiago, the Americans could now bring the city and the Spanish fleet under direct fire from strategic artillery positions.

Two days after San Juan Hill fell to the Americans, Admiral Cervera, under instructions not to surrender his ships, made a desperate attempt to escape into the open sea. July 3 was a Sunday, and the church bells were sounding when Cervera ordered the bugle blown for the beginning of the battle. Cervera guessed the outcome, for he nodded knowingly when an aide whispered "Poor Spain!" as the grave gamble began.

In a battle lasting just four hours, the technical superiority of the American fleet asserted itself. The Spanish ships were destroyed. Admiral Sampson cabled Washington, "The fleet under my command offers the nation as a Fourth of July present the whole of Cervera's fleet." Unable without their ships to reinforce their troops in Cuba, the Spanish realized they had been defeated. Santiago surrendered on July 17, 1898. The Spanish flag — first brought to the city in 1513 — was hauled down for the last time. Spanish resistance in Cuba was now at an end.

After the surrender of Santiago, General Nelson A. Miles led an American force to the Spanish island of Puerto Rico. The

General Miles and his forces met little resistance as they crossed Puerto Rico. Their march ended when an armistice was signed on August 12, 1898.

troops took Puerto Rico without significant opposition. Meanwhile, as America celebrated its victory over Cervera, a small detachment from the Philippines landed on Wake Island, which the United States formally occupied in 1899.

Peace brings the United States new responsibilities. After its defeats in the Caribbean and the Pacific, Spain sued for peace. On August 12, 1898, the day before Manila fell, an armistice was arranged.

As the Spanish withdrew from their possessions in the Caribbean and the Pacific, the world recognized that the United States had become a great power. A French politician could see that America had been transformed. He explained, "When a people have interests everywhere, they are called upon to involve themselves in everything. The United States intervenes thus in the affairs of the universe. It is seated at the table where the great game is played, and it cannot leave it."

Under the terms of the Treaty of Paris, signed on December 10, 1898, Spain granted Cuba its independence and ceded the Philippine Islands, Guam, and Puerto Rico to the United States. The United States agreed to pay $20 million to Spain for the Philippines.

Annexation of the Philippines presents a problem. Following the peace treaty, the United States faced the question of what to do with the new possessions. President McKinley admitted that when he first heard of the Philippines, he could not have said within 2,000 miles where they were located. Now he had to decide whether to keep the islands or not.

McKinley agonized over the fateful decision on the Philippines. At one point he said, "If old Dewey had just sailed away when he smashed the Spanish fleet, what a lot of trouble he would have saved us." Finally the President decided, as he told a group of clergymen, that the United States must take control of the islands in order "to educate the Filipinos, and uplift and civilize and Christianize them."[2] Most members of Congress supported the decision and, indeed, would have resisted efforts to abandon the islands. Senator Beveridge spoke for the new generation of national leaders: "We cannot fly from our world duties. . . . We cannot retreat from any soil where Providence has unfurled our banner; it is ours to save that soil for liberty and civilization."

---

[2]McKinley apparently did not know that most Filipinos were Roman Catholics.

Filipinos resist American rule. In spite of the high motives of McKinley and Beveridge, many Filipinos were not satisfied to exchange Spanish domination for American rule. A revolutionary group had arisen earlier in the Philippines under the leadership of Emilio Aguinaldo. At the time that he had joined his forces with the Americans to defeat Spain (page 520), Aguinaldo believed he had assurances that the United States would not claim the Philippines at the end of the struggle. When the United States decided to keep the islands, a second war broke out — in February, 1899. Called the Philippine Insurrection, it did not formally end until July 4, 1902. United States soldiers suffered over 7,000 casualties, while Aguinaldo's forces lost between 16,000 and 20,000 men. Possibly a quarter of a million civilians also died in the struggle. Many were victims of disease and starvation as well as of violence.

By 1900, American expansionists had succeeded in extending United States influence beyond the boundaries of the continent. American possessions included Puerto Rico and many islands in the Pacific Ocean.

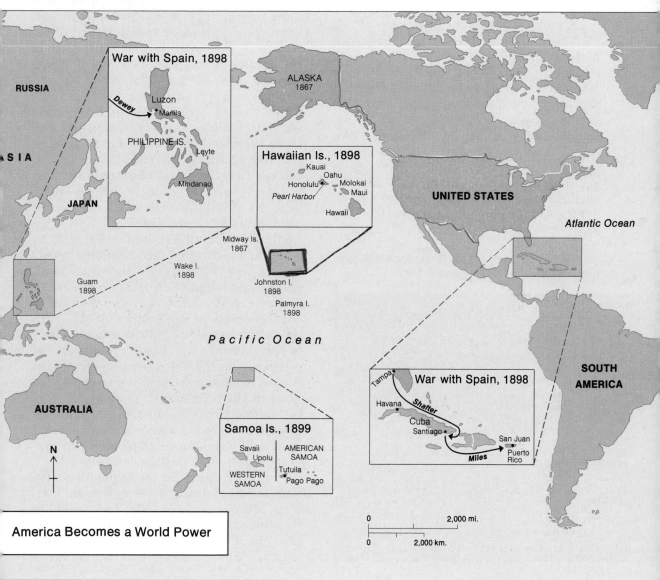

America Becomes a World Power

Imperialism becomes a campaign issue in 1900. Americans who had opposed annexing the Philippines pointed to the insurrection on the islands as one of the dangers of following a policy of *imperialism* — the establishment of political or economic control over other peoples. William Jennings Bryan told an audience in Omaha, "Our guns destroyed a Spanish fleet but can they destroy that self-evident truth, that governments derive their just powers, not from superior force, but from the consent of the governed?" Many Americans agreed with these thoughts, contending that the highest ideals of the nation had been violated when it decided to have an empire.

A group opposing the possession of colonies formed the Anti-Imperialist League in Boston in 1898. By 1900 the League claimed to have 30,000 members and over 500,000 contributors. Its chief financial supporter was Andrew Carnegie. Members of the League also included Carl Schurz, Samuel Gompers, and Jane Addams. "We regret," the League declared, "that it has become necessary in the land of Washington and Lincoln to reaffirm that all men, of whatever race or color, are entitled to life, liberty, and the pursuit of happiness."

Troops bearing the colors of the United States helped to end the Boxer Rebellion that raged in China.

In 1900, Bryan, again nominated for the presidency by the Democrats, made an issue of anti-imperialism. The party platform, in words echoing Lincoln's, stated, "No nation can long endure half republic and half empire." The Republicans renominated McKinley, now a victorious war President. His running mate was Theodore Roosevelt, recently elected governor of New York. The Republican ticket won overwhelmingly, mostly because McKinley was a symbol of the triumph over Spain, but also because he promised to maintain "the full dinner pail" for every worker.

The United States urges equal treatment in China. Once the United States had taken control of territory in the western Pacific, American diplomats became embroiled in the politics of that part of the world. China was the focus of much diplomatic activity. Crushed in a war with Japan in 1894–1895, China seemed unable to defend itself. After the defeat, China had been forced to give Japan the island of Formosa and to agree to the independence of Korea. Recognizing China's weakness, the European powers began to force the Chinese to grant them "spheres of influence" in which they would have special trade privileges.

The British were deeply alarmed by what they considered the impending break-up of China. They disliked the policy of allowing special rights for major powers in Chinese port cities, advocating instead equal commercial opportunity for all. When the British asked the United States in 1898 to join them in a statement opposing special privileges in China, the offer reminded American diplomats of Canning's offer to Rush in 1823 (page 241). Once again — as in Monroe's time — the United States decided it preferred to act alone, knowing that eventually Britain would be obliged to support the American position.

In 1899, Secretary of State John Hay sent almost identical notes to Britain, Germany, Russia, France, Italy, and Japan. In them he set forth what became known as the Open Door Policy. Hay asked the other nations for assurances that all countries would "enjoy perfect equality of treatment for their commerce and navigation" in China. Although most of the answers were noncommittal, Hay went ahead and announced that the major powers had approved the Open Door Policy.

The Chinese rebel against foreign interference. The Chinese people understandably resented the efforts of foreign powers to carve up their country. A patriotic organization called the "Society of the Righteous and Harmonious Fists" (shortened, by Westerners, to "Boxers") began a movement to drive all foreigners from China. In a campaign of violence in 1900, the Boxers attacked western missionaries and then seized parts of Peking, the capital city. Foreigners took refuge in the British legation there.

Widespread fear existed in the West that all foreigners in Peking would be killed. At the same time, the United States was afraid that if the European countries sent troops to crush the rebellion, they might also take over more Chinese territory. Concerned, Hay in July, 1900, sent a new note to the powers of Europe. In it, he declared that America supported a policy of seeking to preserve China's territorial unity. The nations replied that they accepted this position of the United States as desirable.

In the end, the siege of Peking was lifted by a joint expedition of western troops — 2,500 of whom were American. The expedition freed the foreigners and forced the Chinese government to pay large sums of money for damages caused by the uprising.

———

As the nineteenth century passed into history, Americans were sure they stood on the threshold of such progress and prosperity as no people had ever enjoyed. The *New York Times* was pleased to point out that the United States was helping to bring "the regenerating forces of popular government to the uttermost parts of the earth." Few people could have guessed, however, that

China's government in the late 1800's was too weak to resist foreign powers. The Open Door Policy was the American diplomatic response to this situation.

the energies unleashed by the Spanish-American War could also be harnessed for a peaceful remaking of life at home.

SECTION REVIEW

1. Vocabulary: *imperialism.*
2. (a) Where did fighting take place during the Spanish-American War? (b) What were the results of the fighting?
3. What territory did the United States gain in 1898 as a result of the Treaty of Paris?
4. (a) What arguments were put forward by Americans who supported annexation of the Philippines? (b) What arguments were put forward by opponents? (c) What was the reaction on the part of many Filipinos? (d) How did the election of 1900 reveal the thinking of American voters on the subject of expansion?
5. (a) Why did the United States propose the Open Door Policy in China? (b) What was the Boxer Rebellion? (c) How was it suppressed?

Chapter 22 Review

Summary

In the years after the Civil War, the United States gradually took on new international responsibilities. The change began slowly when Congress, in 1867, approved a treaty purchasing the vast territory of Alaska from Russia. Midway Island was annexed in that same year, while a coaling station on Tutuila was acquired in 1878. The influence of American traders, sugar planters, and missionaries on Hawaii, meanwhile, had been growing steadily. In 1893 a group of these Americans staged a revolt against the Hawaiian queen. The islands were annexed by the United States in 1898.

To enhance the role of the United States in the Western Hemisphere, Secretary of State James Blaine sponsored a congress of American nations. At that meeting, held in 1890, the delegates agreed to create the Pan-American Union as a means of promoting inter-American unity. United States commitment to the Monroe Doctrine was tested in 1895, when President Cleveland rose to the defense of Venezuela in a boundary dispute with Britain.

Throughout the late nineteenth century, the nations of Europe were engaged in sharp competition for colonies. Many Americans, recognizing the need for foreign markets, believed the United States also should possess colonies. These expansionists were influenced, furthermore, by popular ideas about American superiority.

In 1895 a rebellion broke out against Spanish rule in Cuba, arousing deep concern in the United States. President McKinley tried to avoid American involvement in the revolt. Nevertheless, the publication of the De Lôme letter and the destruction of the battleship Maine aroused Americans, and led to a declaration of war against Spain.

The war was quick and decisive. By the end of July, 1898, the navy had destroyed Spanish fleets in the Caribbean and the Pacific. The United States Army, meanwhile, had captured the Philippines, Cuba, Puerto Rico, and Guam. On December 10, 1898, the Treaty of Paris was signed. Cuba was granted independence, while Spain ceded the Philippines, Puerto Rico, and Guam to the United States.

The annexation of the Philippines was opposed by the Anti-Imperialist League, formed in 1898 to protest the acquisition of overseas possessions. American voters seemed to approve of the nation's new foreign policy, however, when they gave President McKinley a decisive majority over William Jennings Bryan in the election of 1900.

Vocabulary and Important Terms

1. "Seward's Folly"
2. *Virginius* incident
3. Pan-Americanism
4. Pan-American Union
5. arbitration
6. yellow journalism
7. De Lôme letter
8. Teller Amendment
9. Rough Riders
10. Treaty of Paris (1898)
11. Philippine Insurrection
12. imperialism
13. Anti-Imperialist League
14. Open Door Policy
15. Boxer Rebellion

Discussion Questions

1. (a) What plans for expansion did Secretary of State William H. Seward make? (b) Which of Seward's goals were realized?
2. (a) Why did Hawaii begin to interest Americans in the 1880's? (b) Describe the steps by which Hawaii was annexed.
3. (a) On what occasions in the 1860's and 1870's was the Monroe Doctrine invoked? (b) How did the United States expand its role in the Western Hemisphere during the 1880's and 1890's? (c) What was the position of the United States in the dispute over the boundary between Venezuela and British Guiana? (d) What was the significance of the peaceful settlement of the boundary dispute?
4. (a) Why, in the years immediately following the Civil War, did the United States not readily seize the opportunity to own overseas territories? (b) For what reasons did public opinion shift on the question of overseas expansion by the 1880's?
5. (a) Who were the leading American spokesmen for expansion? (b) What were some of the arguments used by the expansionists?
6. (a) Why were American newspapers increasingly influential in shaping public opinion? (b) What role did those newspapers play in helping push the United States toward war with Spain?
7. What was the state of American preparedness at the start of the Spanish-American War?
8. (a) What did the victory of the United States over Spain indicate to the rest of the world? (b) What question did the United States face as a result of its acquisition of new territory? (c) How did imperialism become a political issue in 1900?

Relating Past to Present

1. The sensational measures used by newspapers in the late 1800's often influenced public opinion.

How influential are newspapers in shaping opinion today? What other sources of news are available?

2. Arbitration led to a peaceful settlement of the Venezuelan boundary dispute in the late 1890's. What are some recent examples of international disputes that have been settled by arbitration?

3. Secretary of State Blaine promoted Pan-Americanism at a meeting in 1890. What organization exists today as a result of those first efforts of cooperation among all American nations?

Studying Local History

Find out if the newspapers of your state or region played a part in helping push the United States into the Spanish-American War. What evidence is there that they did or did not follow the lead of the Hearst and Pulitzer newspapers?

Using History Skills

1. *Reading maps.* Study the map on page 523 showing America's rise to world power. (a) What island possessions had the United States gained by 1900? (b) What strategic advantages did each of those possessions offer the United States?

2. *Reading source material.* Study Senator Beveridge's statement on page 513. What are the chief characteristics of the colonial empire described by Beveridge?

3. *Writing a summary.* Use the information presented in this chapter to write a short summary explaining American expansion in the late 1800's. Explain how the United States became interested in acquiring new territory, what new territories the United States acquired, and what new responsibilities and involvement in world affairs resulted.

WORLD SCENE

European Imperialism

European imperialism reached its height in the last half of the nineteenth century as nations competed with one another to establish overseas empires.

The French in Indochina. In the late 1700's French missionaries and traders began arriving in what is now Vietnam. When rulers hostile to Christianity came to power after 1820, the French decided to intervene. French forces were sent to Southeast Asia in 1858. Eventually they forced the local ruler to hand over territory around the city of Saigon to France and to allow the free exercise of the Catholic faith.

French imperialists soon persuaded their government to expand from this base and claim more and more of Southeast Asia. Cambodia was made a French protectorate in 1863, and all of what is today Vietnam was occupied by French forces by 1885. In 1887 the French joined these provinces into a colonial possession they called Indochina, with a governor-general in charge. Laos became part of the confederation in 1893.

Indochina was a lush and productive region that the French quickly developed. Mining operations were undertaken in the north, while in the south large plantations were established for the production of rubber and rice.

The division of Africa. Africa was the last major land area to be colonized by European nations. Over the centuries footholds had been established along the coasts, but by 1880 only about 10 percent of the African continent had been claimed by European colonial powers. During the next two decades, however, the map of Africa changed drastically. Eager to acquire overseas territories to improve their access to raw materials and dependable markets, Britain, France, Germany, Italy, Portugal, Spain, and Belgium vied for colonies.

The British, in particular, had grandiose ambitions in Africa. By the early 1880's they controlled Capetown in southern Africa and Egypt in the north. They hoped to expand their influence on the continent. British colonies stretching from the Cape to Cairo would give them dominance in Africa — a situation which other nations opposed.

As tensions increased over colonial claims in Africa, Otto von Bismarck, the chancellor of Germany, arranged a meeting of all interested countries. Fourteen nations, including the United States, sent delegates to the Berlin Conference in 1884. In a short time the Europeans divided nearly all of Africa among themselves. By 1900 the only African nations that had escaped becoming part of a colonial empire were Liberia and Ethiopia.

CHAPTER 23

The Progressive Presidents

1900 – 1920

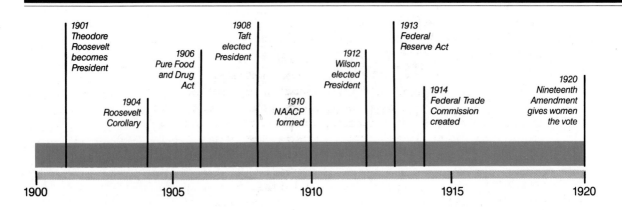

| 1901 Theodore Roosevelt becomes President | 1906 Pure Food and Drug Act | 1908 Taft elected President | 1912 Wilson elected President | 1913 Federal Reserve Act | 1920 Nineteenth Amendment gives women the vote |

1904 Roosevelt Corollary — 1910 NAACP formed — 1914 Federal Trade Commission created

1900 — 1905 — 1910 — 1915 — 1920

CHAPTER OUTLINE

1. The progressives call for reform.

2. Reform begins at the city and state levels.

3. Theodore Roosevelt offers Americans a "Square Deal."

4. The United States strengthens its interests in the Caribbean and Asia.

5. Taft tries to follow in Roosevelt's footsteps.

6. The Progressive Era draws to a close.

On September 5, 1901, President McKinley delivered a speech at the Pan-American Exposition in Buffalo, New York. He spoke optimistically about the nation's future and about peace among nations. He also offered what was at that time a new idea: "Isolation is no longer possible or desirable," he said. "God and man have linked the nations together." The following day, as the President stood in a receiving line to greet the public, a 28-year-old anarchist stepped up to him and fired two bullets. Early in the morning of September 14, McKinley died, and Theodore Roosevelt took the oath of office as President.

Theodore Roosevelt's powerful personality and considerable popularity would soon make a strong impression. A patriot who loved American history, he saw himself as helping to mold the future. He believed it his mission as President "to look ahead and plan out the right kind of civilization."

By the time Roosevelt became President, many deep-seated problems caused by the rapid growth of industry and cities had aroused nationwide concern. In many states and cities attempts were made to solve some of these problems through legislation. Gradually, the interest of Congress was enlisted, as the movement to find solutions attracted support from middle-class Americans. The effort at reform taken as a whole has come to be known as the Progressive Movement.

1 The Progressives Call for Reform

During the late 1800's a number of people had spoken out against political corruption, industrial monopolies, and the inequities faced by farmers and workers. By 1900 a new generation of reformers — the progressives — were getting ready to face these nagging issues.

Progressivism has its roots in earlier political movements. The Progressive Movement resulted from a number of political ideas and movements that came together as the new century opened. The first was that of populism, which had called not only for good government but also for specific reforms in American economic and social life. Most of the people who became progressive reformers, ironically, had been opposed to the rural-based Populists. The progressives, mostly city people, could never accept the Populists' hostility to business or their radical proposals that included government ownership of the railroads. Nevertheless, the new reformers took over the Populist idea that government must work to ensure the public's economic well-being. They also approved of the Populist idea that the average citizen must be allowed to play a more direct role in politics.

Progressives are disturbed by inequalities. Another element nourishing a new era of reform was the growth of a well-educated urban middle class. It included professors and teachers, lawyers, social workers, small business operators, and rising numbers of women who had leisure time. These people were offended that the advantages of America were not being distributed more widely. Possessed of a keen sense of justice, these people had developed a fuller consciousness of the conditions of life borne by so many fellow Americans. They turned a spotlight on many blemishes of society, and sometimes they saw more of them than they could readily remove: hazardous sweatshops and cruelty to children, fire-trap slums and unhealthful food, infant mortality and ineffective schools.

Writers awaken public opinion. Still another element in shaping the Progressive Movement was the so-called "mugwump literature." Appearing in the late 1800's, these books had fostered a desire for laws

Despite prosperous times, reflected in this painting of New York's Central Park, many Americans called for reform in the early 1900's.

that would make government more responsive to the needs of the people. Henry George's *Progress and Poverty*, for example, which appeared in 1879, was widely read. In it, George argued that any increase in national wealth always brings with it a matching increase in poverty. He sought to explain this seemingly impossible connection. He concluded that it resulted from the steady increase in the value of land, which he called "unfair." He maintained that the increase enriched a mere handful of people, even though it was made possible only by the existence of the entire community. He proposed a single tax to replace the existing variety of taxes. The single tax would be based on what he labeled the "unearned" increase in the value of land.

Another popular writer was Edward Bellamy. His fame stemmed from his novel *Looking Backward, 2000–1887*, published in 1888. Describing an imaginary society of the future, Bellamy painted a vivid picture of a world no longer burdened by the shortcomings he found in the America of his day. Read by millions, *Looking Backward* stirred readers to imagine the possibilities of social and economic change.

Still another influential author was Henry Demarest Lloyd, who was greatly distressed over the growth of monopoly. His *Wealth Against Commonwealth*, which came out in 1894, made a fierce attack on the Standard Oil Company. Lloyd was not able to provide a solution to the question of how to regulate trusts. Nevertheless, he piled fact upon fact so convincingly that a reader felt a powerful urge to do *something* about the situation.

One of the first books to deal with a specific urban problem was *How the Other Half Lives*, published in 1890 by Jacob Riis (REES), an immigrant from Denmark. A description of life in the slums of New York, the book shocked its readers and helped launch a crusade for improved housing.

The muckrakers expose social problems. Lloyd and Riis were the first of a group of writers and editors who came to be called *muckrakers.* The name was coined by Theodore Roosevelt in 1906. Highly critical of sensationalism in the press, Roosevelt said that people who wrote such articles reminded him of the man in John Bunyan's *A Pilgrim's Progress* (1678) who "could look no way but downward with a muckrake in his hand." Despite Roosevelt's barb, the name *muckraker* became a badge of distinction. Through magazine articles and novels, the muckrakers drew attention to abuses that had crept into American life.

During the early 1900's, muckraking magazines, having picked up some tricks from yellow journalism, gained large circulations, some of them in the hundreds of thousands. The articles dealt with political graft, street crime, fraudulent advertising of patent medicines, and other topics.

The first notable muckraking magazine began under the inspiration of S. S. McClure. As an immigrant youth from Ireland, he had started his career in the 1880's, publishing a magazine devoted to bicycling, a craze beginning to sweep the country. Among those writing for *McClure's* was Ida M. Tarbell, a trained historian, who in 1903 wrote a series of articles describing the excesses of the Standard Oil Company. Her articles became a model for other muckrakers. Lincoln Steffens, for instance, produced a series on municipal corruption called "The Shame of the Cities." In yet another series, Ray Stannard Baker wrote about railroad abuses.

Magazines all over the country copied *McClure's.* For *Everybody's,* Thomas W. Lawson in 1905 and 1906 attacked the "money kings" in a number of articles. David Graham Phillips's account of bribery in high places, "The Treason of the Senate," ran as a serial in *Cosmopolitan* in 1906.

Other writers criticize American life. A number of muckraking books also became best-sellers. The most important was Upton Sinclair's novel *The Jungle* (1906), which revealed the unsanitary conditions in Chicago's large meat-packing plants. Other influential novels were written by Frank Norris on what he called "the epic of wheat." The first was *The Octopus* (1901), a recounting of the struggle in California between wheat farmers and the railroads. Another, *The Pit* (1903), examined business transactions on the Chicago wheat exchange. Two wealthy sisters-in-law, Marie and Bessie Van Vorst, published in 1903 a startling book called *The Woman Who Toils*. They had gathered their material on women in industry by disguising themselves as workers. A persuasive book on still another problem was *The Bitter Cry of the Children* by John Spargo, an Englishman. Appearing in 1906, it provided a heart-rending account of boys and girls at work in sweatshops.

The progressives seek legislative solutions. Muckrakers provided ammunition for the progressive reformers. But what could be done to rectify specific situations?

The progressives assumed that once the evils of society were revealed, proper laws could be framed to deal with them. The progressives, in fact, were sure that through legislation America could eventually achieve "social justice" for all.

The progressives were not radicals. They opposed the call of **Socialists** for government ownership of the means of production. The progressives, it is true, were willing to enlarge the power of the federal government. They saw the things that were wrong simply as flaws, however, capable of being remedied without significantly altering institutions or upsetting society.

Most progressives believed that the federal government should be a referee in what they saw as the contest between big business and "the people." They believed, too, that people in small businesses needed help against larger competitors. The progressives regarded the accumulation of wealth in fewer and fewer hands as a particularly serious danger to the republic. They concluded, therefore, that monopoly — of all kinds — must be their prime target.

Individuals recognize the need for reform. As the spirit of progressivism spread, people from many walks of life became crusaders in the work of improving social

Ida Tarbell contributed to *McClure's*, one of the mass-circulation magazines that was responsible for uncovering abuses in government and in business.

conditions. An outstanding figure was Jane Addams, the daughter of a well-to-do miller in rural Illinois. She gave up the idea she had once had of becoming a doctor, and instead became a "doctor" to the troubled cities. She created Hull House in the heart of Chicago's tenement district in 1889 to help the underprivileged of the neighborhood. Hull House was a settlement house, a community center offering a wide range of services to people of all ages, many of them immigrants recently arrived in America.

Jane Addams's example inspired reformers elsewhere. A wealthy young woman named Lillian Wald organized the Henry Street Settlement on the Lower East Side of New York. Lillian Wald, who had once started training to be a nurse, also established a pioneering visiting nurse service for the needy.

SECTION REVIEW

1. Vocabulary: *muckraker, Socialist.*
2. (a) What ideas did the Progressive Movement draw from the Populists? (b) How were the progressives influenced by "mugwump literature"?
3. What were some of the problems exposed by the muckrakers?
4. How did the progressives seek to remedy social evils?

2 Reform Begins at the City and State Levels

The progressive crusade took to heart the observation of James Bryce, a noted English observer of the United States, that city government was the nation's greatest single failure. People in many cities went to work on the problem.

Reformers attack municipal problems. Municipal reform soon had a number of heroes. Toledo, Ohio, for example, benefited from the election to city hall of a businessman named Samuel "Golden Rule" Jones.[1] First elected in 1897, Jones spent the next seven years as mayor fighting dishonesty and political corruption. His most important action was the establishment of the merit system for civil servants in city departments. He also set up the city's first kindergarten and public playgrounds. Jones's successor, Brand Whitlock, became a national figure in the work of reforming city government.

In Cleveland, Mayor Tom L. Johnson was a leader of reform. Johnson had achieved success in business through his control of street-railway systems in Indiana and Ohio. Henry George's writings had greatly influenced him. As mayor of Cleveland, he gathered together a group of bright young advisers who helped him make their city the best-governed in the United States. Johnson worked hard to establish public ownership of electric power plants and the street railway system.

New forms of city government are introduced. In attempting to adapt to modern needs, some cities began experimenting with new types of government. One arrangement, known as the "Des Moines idea," provided for a commission to run the city. Under this system, five commissioners were selected in a nonpartisan election. Another arrangement was the city-manager form of government. The city manager, hired under contract, was responsible to a commission or to a city council. By 1923, some 300 cities had city managers.

Reforms are instituted on the state level. State government also came under the influence of progressive ideas. A memorable figure at the state level was Robert La Follette of Wisconsin, known as "Fighting Bob." As governor of his state from 1901 to 1906 and United States senator for the next nineteen years, La Follette gained a national reputation as a reformer. In 1903, Wisconsin adopted the *direct primary.* This allowed for candidates for state office to be chosen by the people in preliminary, or primary, elections rather than by party bosses. Within the next ten years, almost every state had a similar law. The ambitious program that La Follette pushed through was known as the "Wisconsin idea." In addition to primary elections, it introduced the merit system in the state civil service and regulation and taxation of the railroads.

Other states also enacted reforms intended to give the people tighter control of government. The *referendum* was widely adopted. Under this plan, the people were allowed to vote directly on proposed bills. The *initiative* — a process by which citizens propose legislation or constitutional amendments — also gained popularity. First adopted in South Dakota in 1898, it spread from there to other parts of the country. The *recall* — a process enabling voters to dismiss public officials before the end of their terms — was adopted by the city of Los Angeles in 1903. Oregon put a provision for recall into its constitution in 1908, and a number of other states quickly followed suit.

Progressives also supported the adoption of the *secret ballot* (sometimes called the Australian ballot). Until the early 1890's, political parties had printed their ballots in distinctive colors. How a person voted, therefore, was easy for all to see. Placing the names of all candidates on a single ballot and allowing voters to make their choices in secret put an end to open voting and to the abuses it brought.

---

[1] Jones had acquired his nickname after posting a card bearing the golden rule as a guide for the treatment of employees in his machinery-manufacturing plant.

The Seventeenth Amendment is ratified. The progressives took up, in addition, the old Populist call for the direct election of United States senators. The pressure became so great that by 1912 Congress passed the Seventeenth Amendment. Ratified the following year, it took from the state legislatures, and gave to the people, the right to elect United States senators.

Women gain the right to vote. The progressives' desire to widen the people's role in politics helped advance the cause of women's suffrage. Ever since the Seneca Falls Convention in 1848 (page 286), the question of voting rights for women had been debated. For many years, Susan B. Anthony and Elizabeth Cady Stanton, leaders of the National Woman Suffrage Association, carried on the campaign, often in the face of unbending opposition. The dam began to break in 1869 when Wyoming Territory gave women over 21 the right to vote. When Wyoming came into the Union in 1890, its constitution retained suffrage for women.

In the next few years, the movement for women's voting rights grew stronger. By 1900, Colorado, Utah, and Idaho had joined Wyoming in granting women the ballot. Then, as the impulse to reform generally took hold, the movement gained victories in other states. By 1919, women had acquired equal suffrage in fifteen states, and a number of other states were allowing partial suffrage (map, page 533).

The work of Carrie Chapman Catt, Alice Paul, and Lucy Burns — and many other dedicated women's rights advocates — led finally to the ratification in 1920 of

Around 1900, women's groups, chiefly in the Midwest, were working to secure female suffrage in individual states and localities. In 1914, Alice Paul formed a national organization to champion women's right to vote.

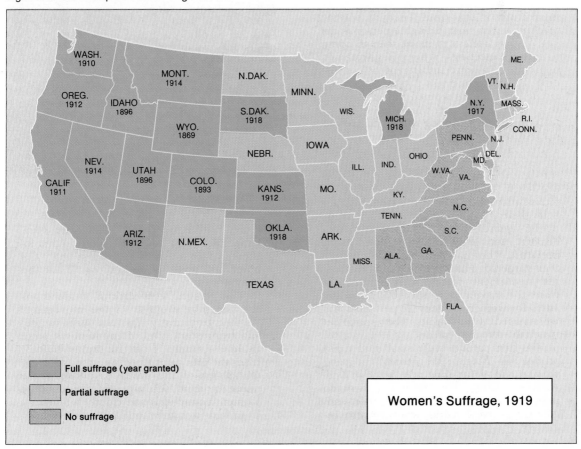

Women's Suffrage, 1919

- Full suffrage (year granted)
- Partial suffrage
- No suffrage

the Nineteenth Amendment to the Constitution. It prohibited the denial of the vote to anyone "on account of sex." Women continued to face discrimination in seeking entry into many jobs and professions. Still, the new amendment was a springboard to fuller rights that women would win in the years ahead.

Reform affects other aspects of American life. The work of the progressives cannot be measured only by the reforms they undertook. Part of what they accomplished was to help reshape important American attitudes. To a greater degree than ever before, people focused attention on individual hygiene and public health. Moreover, they

---

EYEWITNESS TO HISTORY

Suffragist Tactics

Gertrude Foster Brown left a career in music to devote herself to the suffragist cause. As president of the New York State Suffrage Association from 1913 to 1915, she helped plan strategies to convince the public of the injustice done to women by denying them the right to vote. In this passage Gertrude Foster Brown described how attention was drawn to the suffrage issue.

A suffragist rally

> There were no radios and no effective talking pictures at that time. The only way of reaching voters was through a personal appeal. It was useless to invite men to come to suffrage meetings. Where they were not opposed, they were indifferent or considered the whole business a joke. Since they would not come to women, suffragists had to go to them wherever they were.
>
> In the days of trailing skirts and picture hats, to see a woman mount a soap box on a street corner, or stand on the back seat of an automobile and begin to orate, was so startling that men could not help but stop and listen. The street meetings were so effective that soon, all over the state, women held their meetings on street corners or public squares, wherever the traffic was heaviest, with [colorful] banners and much literature. They haunted every place where men gathered. His clubs, his conventions, his amusement places, were never safe from the danger of a speech demanding votes for women. Vaudeville performances were staged by suffragists. They spoke between the acts in theaters.
>
> The first parades were small and timid affairs. In May, 1911, three thousand women and eighty-nine men were in line. A year later, ten thousand women marched, and, in 1915, forty thousand. Always in New York, women were received with respect. Not so the men sympathizers. Jeers and scurrilous remarks showered on them. The mildest was "Go home and wash the dishes" or "Rock the baby."
>
> The parades were striking evidence of the sweeping progress of the movement. Women from every class and walk of life, and from every kind of employment were in line. Women from luxurious homes, from the tenement districts, girls from the workshops of the lower East Side, trade union women, teachers and professional women, young girls and elderly women — all united for a common cause.

began to make a virtue of looking and "staying" young. The boyish President Roosevelt and his family were the very symbols of this new attitude.

The concern over cleanliness accompanied a growing awareness that germs can cause disease. Major cities established departments of public health. Some of them set up child-care "stations," offering free milk and medical examinations to needy children. In many parts of the country, laws were passed requiring the vaccination of school children against smallpox and diphtheria.

The worth of outdoor living in promoting health took hold too. Leading cities had started in 1885 to build public playgrounds. Still, young people seemed to require more organized activities. As one answer, the Boy Scouts of America were established in 1910, followed two years later by the Girl Scouts and the Camp Fire Girls. Progressives believed that scouting would help make citizens stronger — mentally and physically. President Roosevelt was especially interested in the scout movement.

Reform does not touch the lives of all Americans. Most progressives were white, middle-class city dwellers whose reforming instincts went only so far. Immigrants during the Progressive Era found themselves scorned as "the foreign element" or talked-down to as "our foreigners." Even Irish-American Catholics, who controlled many a city hall and sometimes a state house, frequently were excluded from business and professional opportunities. Although Oscar S. Straus, who served under Theodore Roosevelt as Secretary of Commerce and Labor, was the first Jew appointed to a Cabinet office, prejudice against Jews in general was widespread.

Black Americans fight discrimination. Blacks benefited very little from progressive reforms. In the decades after the Civil War, black Americans had advanced economically. Many black people owned their own homes or farms and ran businesses. However, after the last federal troops were removed from the South in 1877 (page 413),

People imitated the fashions and lifestyles made popular by the magazines of the day. In this formal portrait, Alice Roosevelt presents a good example of what was known as the "Gibson Girl" — upswept hairdo, large hat, elegant clothes, and an air of sophistication.

state laws had been passed restricting the rights of black citizens. These *Jim Crow laws,* as they were known, forced black Southerners by 1890 to use separate restaurants, hospitals, railroads, and streetcars. Through the introduction of literacy tests and poll taxes, furthermore, many southern states prevented blacks from voting.

Although some black people went to court to challenge the Jim Crow laws, the courts usually upheld the state laws. The worst defeat for blacks came in 1896, when the Supreme Court ruled in *Plessy v. Ferguson* that "separate but equal" transportation facilities were legal. The Court offered the following explanation: "If one race be inferior to the other socially, the Constitution of the United States cannot put them upon the same plane." For more than fifty years, "separate-but-equal" laws were in effect in the South. Despite the Fourteenth

Amendment (page 403), blacks were second-class citizens.

Discrimination, unofficial and only a little more subtle, was practiced in the North. Ray Stannard Baker wrote a revealing account of discrimination in his muckraking book *Following the Color Line* (1908). In it, he spared neither the North nor the South.

Blacks responded in various ways to the obstacles they faced. The educator Booker T. Washington was the best-known black leader of the late 1800's and early 1900's. He preached that blacks must accommodate themselves to their circumstances and make the best of the situation. In a speech in Atlanta in 1895 he made public his acceptance of the separation of the races, declaring, as he held up his hand with the fingers spread wide, "In all things that are purely social we can be separate as the fingers, yet one as the hand in all things essential to mutual progress." Washington pressed upon his people the value of vocational education. Tuskegee Institute in Alabama, which he established, became famous as a training place for young black people. Privately, Washington hoped for equality of the races. He emphasized in his speeches, however, that this could only be a long-term objective.

Many black critics of Washington insisted that Jim Crow laws must be overturned immediately. One of these voices was W. E. B. Du Bois (doo-BOYS), for many years a professor at Atlanta University. Du Bois delivered a blistering attack on Washington, accusing him of urging black people to do only menial work. In his book *The Souls of Black Folks* (1903), Du Bois argued that only through political agitation could blacks put an end to segregation. In 1905 he brought together a group of black leaders at Niagara Falls to protest the steady curtailment of the civil and political rights of black people. Five years later, along with sixty other prominent Americans, Du Bois helped organize the National Association for the Advancement of Colored People (NAACP). Lawyers for the NAACP took the fight against discrimination to the courts.

SECTION REVIEW

1. Vocabulary: *direct primary, referendum, initiative, recall, secret ballot, Jim Crow laws.*
2. (a) What new forms of city government were introduced during the Progressive Era? (b) What political reforms were introduced at the state level?
3. (a) How did the Seventeenth Amendment change the way United States senators were selected? (b) What steps led to passage of the Nineteenth Amendment?
4. (a) How were the rights of black Americans restricted in the late 1800's? (b) What was the Supreme Court's decision in *Plessy v. Ferguson*? (c) How did the NAACP fight discrimination?

3 Theodore Roosevelt Offers Americans a "Square Deal"

Theodore Roosevelt's exuberance and energy made many progressives regard him as their leader. His feeling that people deserved a "Square Deal" from their government made him one of the nation's most popular Presidents.

Theodore Roosevelt is an inspiring leader. Theodore Roosevelt was born to wealthy parents in 1858 in New York City. Frail and weak, he suffered from asthma, and only his father, Theodore Roosevelt, Sr., could comfort him when he battled for breath. Then, as his health began to improve, "Teedy," as his brothers and sisters called him, took up boxing and began to lead the "strenuous life."

A man of great vigor, Roosevelt turned his energy to the field of government soon after his graduation from Harvard College in 1880. He served for three years as a member of the New York state legislature. Then for two years he took up ranching in what is now North Dakota, spending time shooting big game in the Rockies. He wrote about his experiences and also penned several volumes of history and biography. When he returned to New York in 1886, he made an unsuccessful run for mayor. President Harrison shortly made him a member of the United States Civil Service Commission, on which Roosevelt served until he became head of New York City's board of police commissioners. In 1897 President McKinley appointed him Assistant Secretary of the Navy. From there on, his career was a stirring adventure — first as a Rough Rider in the Spanish-American War and then as a hero elected to the governorship of New York. In 1900 he was elected Vice President. By September, 1901, Roosevelt was President and people were calling him Teddy[2] or TR, with affection.

The Roosevelt family filled the White House with a joyfulness it had not recently known. There were six children. The eldest was Alice, who was seventeen years old in 1901; the youngest was Quentin, not yet turned four. Theodore Roosevelt imparted to his children his own burning love of action. As they grew up, they tried to live by his standard of public duty.

Roosevelt could inspire unmatchable admiration in other people too. William Allen White, a famous Kansas newspaper editor, wrote of his first meeting with the President: "He overcame me. And in the hour or two we spent that day . . . he poured into my heart such visions, such ideals, such hopes, such a new attitude toward life and patriotism and the meaning of things, as I never dreamt men had."

Roosevelt made the office of the President the center of news and public attention. He understood that his personal popularity readily made him spokesman for the poor as well as the rich, factory owners as well as working people. The White House, he believed, must be a "bully pulpit" for defining national obligations and pointing to possible ways of meeting them.

Roosevelt settles a coal strike. Roosevelt's sympathy for working people was tested during a strike in the anthracite coal mines in 1902. Over 150,000 men had walked off

Theodore Roosevelt's family was energetic and much in the public eye while they lived in the White House. Alice Roosevelt (middle) was married there in 1906.

their jobs in May. Led by John Mitchell of the United Mine Workers, they demanded a pay increase, a shorter work day, and recognition of their union. The mine owners refused to meet any of these demands.

After the dispute had dragged into autumn, the President called union and company leaders to a conference in Washington. At the meeting, the mine owners refused to budge, calling the strikers "a set of outlaws." In an unprecedented action, Roosevelt threatened to send 10,000 troops into the mines to get production started again. The operators finally yielded and agreed to submit the issues to arbitration.

In the settlement, the miners received a wage increase — about half of what they had sought. More important in the long run, Roosevelt earned national esteem for taking steps to get coal for the public. Laboring people were delighted that he had appeared to side with the workers — an extraordinary departure from the government's usual support of management.

Roosevelt tackles the trusts. Theodore Roosevelt had a knack for assuming leadership of a cause as if he had discovered the cause himself. One such issue of growing

[2]In a joking reference to Roosevelt's love of big-game hunting, the cartoonist of the *Washington Evening Star*, Clifford K. Berryman, drew the first teddy bear in 1902. Within a few years, teddy bears were helping to enrich childhood everywhere.

concern to the public was the spread of trusts. During the late 1890's, new combinations had been formed, greatly alarming the public. Roosevelt was not opposed to big business in general. Instead, he applied his own yardstick to decide which businesses were good and which were bad. He believed that certain trusts ought to be brought under the regulation of the government. Roosevelt was determined that trusts be responsive to the public interest. He later observed, "We drew the line against misconduct, not against wealth."

In an important trust-busting action, Roosevelt took on the Northern Securities Company, a corporation that had created a railroad monopoly in the Pacific Northwest. The organization included some of the leading names of railroading and finance: James J. Hill, J. P. Morgan, Edward H. Harriman, and, indirectly, John D. Rockefeller. The government brought suit against this formidable company for violation of the Sherman Antitrust Act (page 454). Public opinion was on the govern-

ment's side. Roosevelt reported that J. P. Morgan had said to him, "If we have done anything wrong, send your man [meaning the Attorney-General] to my man [referring to one of his lawyers] and they can fix it up." The President was outraged that Morgan arrogantly considered him to be simply, as Roosevelt said, "a big rival operator."

In 1904 the Supreme Court ruled that the Northern Securities Company should be broken up. Roosevelt was overjoyed at the news. "The most powerful men in this country were held to accountability before the law," he declared. The public cheered him on.

Through the creation of the Bureau of Corporations in 1903, the government was able to gather facts that enabled it to keep watch on big businesses. Using evidence collected by the bureau, Roosevelt brought cases against Standard Oil, the American Tobacco Company, and some forty other trusts. Roosevelt used these cases and the Northern Securities case to enhance his reputation as a "trust-buster."

Roosevelt wins the election of 1904. As the 1904 presidential race neared, business interests in the Republican Party talked about replacing Roosevelt with Senator Mark Hanna, William McKinley's old friend. Hanna, however, died early in 1904. In any event, Theodore Roosevelt had gained control of the Republican Party machinery through shrewd appointments. When he sought the Republican nomination, therefore, he had virtually no opposition. He became the first "accidental" Chief Executive to be nominated for the presidency in his own right.

Roosevelt's Democratic opponent in 1904 was a colorless New York judge, Alton B. Parker. Remaining on the bench but fearing he would no longer seem impartial, Parker did not campaign purposefully. A third candidate was Eugene Debs (page 478), who ran on the Socialist ticket.

Roosevelt easily defeated his opponents. On the eve of his inauguration, he blustered, "Tomorrow I shall come into my office in my own right. Then watch out for me!"

Roosevelt's image as a "trust-buster" is featured in this cartoon as he vigorously washes the American eagle with "anti-trust soap."

New railroad regulations are imposed.
Roosevelt believed that a call for reform was now sweeping the country, and he was determined to be at its head. He made railroad rate abuse a particular object of his attention.

Roosevelt had already persuaded Congress in 1903 to begin to deal with the railroad question by passing the Elkins Act. This law, which expanded the powers of the Interstate Commerce Commission, made it illegal for railroad officials and shippers to give rebates (discounts) to favored customers. Three years later, Roosevelt oversaw the passage of a stronger law, the Hepburn Act. This law broadened the authority of the Commission over railroad rates, even allowing it to reduce objectionable rates — subject to court approval. Moreover, the Hepburn Act gave the Commission power to regulate sleeping car companies, oil pipelines, ferries, bridges, and railroad terminals.

Regulations curb the sale of harmful products. Other federal legislation was aimed at protecting the public from the sale of harmful products. In 1906, the very year that Upton Sinclair published *The Jungle* (page 530), Congress passed the Pure Food and Drug Act. It provided for the elimination of abuses in the processing of food and the manufacturing of patent medicines. Enforcement of this law was up to Dr. Harvey W. Wiley, for many years the chief chemist in the Department of Agriculture. Wiley sent inspectors throughout the country to check on methods of preparing foods and medicines.

Another law passed in 1906 was the Meat Inspection Act. This law made compulsory the federal inspection of all meat sold in interstate commerce to see that it came from healthy animals and was packed under sanitary conditions.

Serious efforts at conservation are begun.
In the conservation of natural resources, Roosevelt also made an original and lasting contribution. He believed that America's natural resources belonged to *all* of the people. His passion for conservation grew out of a deep love of America's West and the incomparable beauty he had first encountered there as a youth. The President's affection for the great outdoors was matched by his intimate knowledge of nature.

The need to protect the nation's timber resources had been a growing concern for many years. The first step in preserving them had been taken in 1828 when President John Quincy Adams set aside 30,000 acres of oak forest in Florida for the use of the navy. Yellowstone National Park was created in 1872, and Yosemite in 1891. Nevertheless, because of the indiscriminate cutting of trees without replanting, the nation's forests were rapidly disappearing.

Beginning in 1891, Congress authorized the Presidents to withdraw timber land from public sale. Benjamin Harrison set aside seventeen million acres as national forest reserves, and succeeding Presidents followed his example. By the time Theodore Roosevelt left office in 1909, over 230 million acres of forest land had been set aside for future use — almost five times the acreage in 1900.

Roosevelt also helped bring about passage of the Newlands Act in 1902. Under this law, money received from the sale of public lands in sixteen western states was set aside to pay for the irrigation of wasteland. Through the Newlands Act, millions of acres of arid land were brought under cultivation.

In 1903 the first wildlife refuge was established. By 1909 there were 51 such refuges. The Antiquities Act of 1906 put under federal protection land of historic or scientific interest. This law helped protect such locations as New York's Niagara Falls, Arizona's Grand Canyon and Petrified Forest, Oregon's Crater Lake, Colorado's Mesa Verde, California's Muir Woods, and Wyoming's Devils Tower.

The Inland Waterways Commission was established in 1907 to create a comprehensive plan for improving and controlling the nation's rivers. Plans were also made for protecting lowlands from floods, improving navigation on rivers and streams, and increasing water supplies.

HUMBER & CO LTD
32. HOLBORN VIADUCT. LONDON. E.C.

Leisure and Recreation

The game of tennis was sweeping the country in 1900, and by 1908 there were 115 tennis clubs. The bicycle remained a favorite means of recreation. Vacationing Americans flocked to the national parks, four of which were created during Theodore Roosevelt's presidency.

The administration deals with the Panic of 1907. Near the end of his presidency, Roosevelt suffered a disappointment. Following a slump on Wall Street in the summer of 1907, a number of banks and businesses failed. Roosevelt said he believed that the "malefactors of great wealth" were to blame for the economic downturn. Nev-ertheless, in dealing with the Panic of 1907, the trust-busting President was put into the embarrassing position of approving an increase in the power of United States Steel — organized by J. P. Morgan in 1901. The President had been told that he could prevent a stock-market collapse by allowing the giant steel company to purchase its largest competitor, the Tennessee Coal and Iron Company. Roosevelt gave Morgan advance assurance that United States Steel would not be prosecuted under antitrust laws if the deal went through.

The Panic of 1907, fortunately, was not followed by a prolonged depression. As a result, Roosevelt's popularity remained high.

SECTION REVIEW

1. (a) Describe Theodore Roosevelt's concept of the presidency. (b) What was his attitude toward the coal strike? (c) Toward the trusts?
2. (a) What reforms were advanced by the Elkins Act? (b) The Hepburn Act? (c) The Pure Food and Drug Act? (d) The Meat Inspection Act? (e) The Newlands Act? (f) The Inland Waterways Commission?

4 The United States Strengthens Its Interests in the Caribbean and Asia

Theodore Roosevelt's reputation as a man of energy and action was strengthened by his handling of foreign affairs. In dealing with other countries he claimed to be guided by an old West African proverb: "Speak softly and carry a big stick, and you will go far." He did not always speak softly, but he sometimes used "a big stick" to get what he wanted.

Plans for a canal across Central America are revived. The United States had long been interested in building a canal across the Isthmus of Panama (map, page 543). An episode during the Spanish-American War had dramatized the need for a waterway between the Caribbean and the Pacific. After the *Maine* blew up in Havana harbor (page 516), orders were sent to the battleship *Oregon*, then in San Francisco, to sail to the Caribbean. The nation waited anxiously while the ship took nearly 70 days to make the 14,000-mile journey. For weeks, its location and progress were unknown. The "matchless race of the *Oregon*" — as a popular poem called it — made Americans deter-

mined never again to endure such a nerve-tingling time.

When Roosevelt became President, he announced that he intended to get busy on a canal project. Immediately, he faced the diplomatic obstacle of the Clayton-Bulwer Treaty, which had been agreed to in 1850. Under that treaty, the United States and Great Britain had agreed that neither country would exercise exclusive control over a Central American canal. By the beginning of the new century, however, the British had become alarmed over Germany's growing power and were beginning to appreciate the value of a friendly America. Britain was willing to reduce its fleet in the Caribbean and recognize the United States as the primary power in the region. Britain was also willing to permit the United States to construct, own, and defend a canal alone.

A route across Panama is chosen. Roosevelt now had to answer a difficult question: should the canal be constructed through Nicaragua or through Panama? The Panama route would be shorter but more difficult to build. A Nicaraguan canal would be longer but, being entirely at sea level, it would be easier to construct and operate.

In 1879 a French company had started to build a canal across Panama — at that time ruled by Colombia — but had abandoned the project. The French company offered to sell the United States its right of way, equipment, and agreement with Colombia. The United States decided that the asking price was too high and turned its attention to building across Nicaragua.

The chief agent of the French company, a crafty lobbyist named Philippe Bunau-Varilla (boo-NOH vah-ree-YAH), grew concerned. He dropped the company's price for its Panama interests from $109 million to $40 million. He also warned Americans about recent volcanic activity in Nicaragua. Luck was on the side of the French company. In May, 1902, Mount Pelée, a volcano on the Caribbean island of Martinique, erupted with devastating effect, killing more than 30,000 people. A few days later a volcano in Nicaragua began to rumble. Astutely, Bunau-Varilla sent to every United

The Panama Canal, shown here under construction in 1907, uses a system of locks to enable ocean vessels to pass between the Pacific Ocean and the Atlantic.

States senator a copy of a Nicaraguan postage stamp depicting a smoking volcano. Accompanying the picture was the Frenchman's note: "An official witness of the volcanic activity in Nicaragua." The senators were persuaded. In June, Congress enacted a bill providing for the construction of a *Panama* canal.

The consent of Colombia was now required. In 1903 Secretary of State John Hay reached an agreement with Tomás Herrán, the Colombian representative in Washington. The Hay-Herrán Treaty provided that the United States would lease a six-mile-wide strip of land across Panama for a lump sum of $10 million in gold and a yearly rental of $250,000. However, when the treaty was sent for ratification to Bogotá, the Colombian capital, the government responded that the sums agreed to were unacceptable. The Colombians, hoping to win better terms, were blocking the project.

Panama revolts against Colombia. A small group of Panamanians, fearing that the

United States might build its waterway across Nicaragua and deprive them of this important artery, took steps to break away from Colombia. They soon had the active cooperation and assistance of the United States. In fact, details of the revolt were worked out in Room 1162 of the Hotel Waldorf-Astoria in New York City. The principal planner was Philippe Bunau-Varilla! Roosevelt and Secretary of State Hay were aware of the scheme, although they did not encourage it. Still, Roosevelt let it be known that the warship U.S.S. *Nashville* would be sent to Panama. Its mission would be to maintain "free and uninterrupted transit" across the isthmus in accordance with an 1846 treaty between the United States and Colombia.

On November 3, 1903, the day after the *Nashville* arrived in Panama, the revolt broke out. Panama City quickly fell under rebel control. Some 400 Colombian troops had already been landed at Colón, but marines from the *Nashville* prevented them from marching across the isthmus to Panama City (map, page 543). The success of the revolution was thus guaranteed.

The United States gains a right of way through Panama. Within three days the United States recognized the independent Republic of Panama. Revolutionary leader Manuel Guerrero became the nation's first president. Philippe Bunau-Varilla, although a French citizen, was named as the first Panamanian minister to the United States. Already Panama's first flag had been designed and fashioned by Madame Bunau-Varilla! On November 18, 1903, Bunau-Varilla and Secretary Hay agreed to a treaty satisfactory to both sides. The Hay-Bunau-Varilla Treaty was the same as the Hay-Herrán Treaty, except that the zone of land across the isthmus was widened to ten miles and granted "in perpetuity" (meaning forever).

Early in 1904 the Senate ratified the treaty. Roosevelt had assured Congress that the acquisition of the Canal Zone had been conducted in the most ethical way, but later he boasted, "I took Panama." Many Americans felt guilty and angry about the methods used to acquire the Canal Zone.

Latin Americans were outraged by Roosevelt's "big stick" method. In 1921, two years after Roosevelt's death, the United States gave $25 million to Colombia. Observers regarded the gift as a diplomatic way of apologizing to that country.

The Panama Canal is constructed. The building of the Panama Canal, begun in 1904, was the stiffest challenge to the nation's engineers since the construction of the first transcontinental railroad a generation earlier. The workers who labored on the "big ditch" risked disease and injury. They were directed by Colonel George W. Goethals (GOH-thalz), who gave the undertaking a quality of leadership that the French company had never known. Goethals was assisted by Colonel William C. Gorgas, surgeon-general of the army, who worked valiantly to wipe out the threat of yellow fever. The Panama Canal, fifty miles long, was opened on August 15, 1914. The feat of building it had involved removing about 240 million cubic yards of rock and earth and setting in place a complicated system of canal locks.

Within a short time the canal was playing a major part in world commerce. Travel between New York and San Francisco was now 7,000 miles shorter. The canal also enhanced the nation's naval strength by making possible a quick move of ships from one ocean to another.

The Panama Canal affects American foreign policy. The construction of the Panama Canal gave the United States important new interests in the Caribbean. The need to protect the canal also provided the President with new opportunities to wield the big stick in the region.

United States interest in the entire Caribbean region was heightened after the completion of the Panama Canal, whose strategic importance is shown on this map.

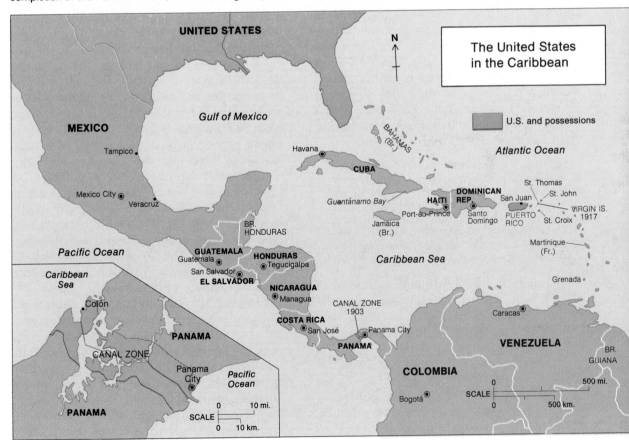

Political instability had long been characteristic of many of the Latin American republics. The persistent gulf separating rich and poor people had created arrogance on one side and envy on the other. Moreover, the lack of easy contact between people living along the coasts and those in the interior prevented the rise of strong national feeling in many of these countries. Government in practically all the Latin American lands remained under the control of a handful of people and was often passed around from one faction to another.

The United States had already felt forced to intervene in Latin American countries to prevent interference from abroad. In 1902 Germany, Britain, and Italy sent warships to blockade Venezuelan ports in order to force the payment of debts. The United States objected strenuously to the naval blockade. The Department of State persuaded Venezuela to accept arbitration in order to end the episode peacefully.

Theodore Roosevelt issues the Roosevelt Corollary. To avoid any such incidents in the future, the United States took a new stand. If a Latin American nation did not repay its debts, then the United States claimed a right to intervene. In his annual message to Congress in 1904, President Roosevelt announced the bold policy. His words, now famous, are known as the Roosevelt Corollary to the Monroe Doctrine:

> Chronic wrongdoing . . . may in America, as elsewhere, ultimately require intervention by some civilized nation, and in the Western Hemisphere the adherence of the United States to the Monroe Doctrine may force the United States, however reluctantly, . . . to the exercise of an international police power.

Acting on these principles, American troops were sent to the Dominican Republic in 1905 and to Cuba in 1906. The United States, in short, had taken on the role of "policing" the Caribbean. Because the United States had appointed itself for this task, many Latin Americans were gravely offended. Still, unlike Europeans who were continuing to seek new colonies, the United States showed no desire to annex more territory. On the subject of the Dominican Republic, Roosevelt once said, "As for annexing the island, I have about the same desire to annex it as a gorged boa constrictor might have to swallow a porcupine the wrong end to."

"Dollar diplomacy" extends American influence. After Roosevelt left the White House in 1909, his foreign policies were maintained by other Presidents. His immediate successor, William Howard Taft, adopted a stance known as "dollar diplomacy." Under this policy, American banks and businesses were encouraged to invest in Latin America. If the investments were endangered by defaults or by failure to make interest payments, the United States would intervene.

Taft applied dollar diplomacy to several Latin American countries. In 1912, for example, he sent troops to Nicaragua to put down an insurrection and restore order.

American influence in Asia grows stronger. United States policy toward Asia also was aimed at protecting American interests, now expected to grow. One goal was to maintain the stability of China.

China's problems had not ended with the crushing of the Boxer Rebellion (page 525). At the beginning of the century Russia had begun to take over Manchuria (map, page 524), a move that alarmed American policy makers. China's territorial integrity, it seemed, was being threatened by Russia.

Because of concern over China, the United States watched approvingly when Japan struck at Russia in a surprise attack in 1904. A modest victory for Japan, many Americans believed, would blunt Russia's aggressiveness. The Japanese did so well in the Russo-Japanese War that they threatened the balance of power in the region.

Hoping to avoid such an outcome, Roosevelt invited delegates from Russia and Japan to meet with him in a peace conference at Portsmouth, New Hampshire, in August, 1905. The resulting Treaty of Portsmouth considerably strengthened Japan's position on the Asian continent. Still, Roosevelt had been able to prevent Japan from humiliating Russia. As a result, he may have saved China from being dominated by either power. For his work at Portsmouth, Roosevelt was awarded the Nobel Peace Prize in 1906 — the first American to be so honored.

Relations between Japan and America are strained. Many Japanese, who expected a better settlement at Portsmouth, felt that Roosevelt had let them down. American-Japanese relations were further strained when San Francisco school authorities insisted that Japanese-American children attend a separate school. The President succeeded in getting the school order reversed. In return, however, he promised Californians that he would seek to halt further Japanese immigration.

In 1907 Roosevelt concluded what came to be known as the Gentlemen's Agreement with Japan. The agreement, which remained in force until 1924, effectively ended Japanese immigration to the United States.

The Great White Fleet circles the globe. Roosevelt expected the anti-American sentiment in Japan to pass. Tensions on both sides of the Pacific reached a point, however, where there was even talk of war. Suddenly Roosevelt decided upon the dramatic step of sending the entire United States fleet around the world. Behind the decision lay several motives. Most important, the President wanted to impress the Japanese with America's naval power. He also wanted to demonstrate to Germany — then expanding its navy — that the United States had the means to enforce its will in the Western Hemisphere. Finally, he was eager to persuade what he regarded as a penny-pinching Congress to support a new ship-building program.

The ships departed from a Virginia port just before Christmas, 1907, as the bands played "The Girl I Left Behind Me." Many young men had left school in order to sign on with the Great White Fleet — so-called because the vessels were painted white.

The journey was enormously successful and the war fever abated. In Japan thousands of school children turned out to sing "The Star-Spangled Banner." The ships returned to American waters on Washington's Birthday, 1909. It became Theodore Roosevelt's firm belief that the sending of the fleet around the world was "the most important service I rendered to peace."

In a demonstration of national strength, the sixteen ships of the Great White Fleet visited all the inhabited continents and paused twice for military maneuvers.

The United States supports plans for world peace. Part of the reforming spirit of the progressives was seen in their support of efforts to promote world peace. The fledgling peace movement was encouraged by two conferences that met at The Hague in the Netherlands in 1899 and 1907. At the first Hague Conference, 26 nations agreed to outlaw poison gas, the dropping of bombs, and the use of explosive bullets. The delegates also created a Permanent Court of International Arbitration. Countries involved in a dispute could bring their quarrels to this Court for settlement. The second Hague Conference was unable to do anything beyond extending the agreements made eight years earlier.

The United States gave arbitration a boost by helping to call the Algeciras (al-jeh-SEER-us) Conference in Spain in 1906. The purpose of the gathering was to settle differences between France and Germany that had arisen over the North African state of Morocco. The Senate condemned the President's support of the conference, arguing that it represented a departure from the pledge in the Monroe Doctrine to stay out of European affairs. Nevertheless, many people were proud that an American President had taken a hand in protecting the peace of the world.

SECTION REVIEW

1. (a) Why was American interest in building a canal across Central America revived following the Spanish-American War? (b) Why was a route across Panama chosen?
2. (a) How were the Panamanians helped in their revolt against Colombia by the United States? (b) What was the Hay-Bunau-Varilla Treaty? (c) How did the Panama Canal affect American foreign policy?
3. (a) What was the Roosevelt Corollary? (b) How was it applied? (c) What was "dollar diplomacy"?
4. (a) Why did the United States mediate an end to the Russo-Japanese War? (b) What were the causes of tension between Japan and the United States? (c) Why was the Great White Fleet sent around the globe?
5. (a) What was the purpose of the two conferences held at The Hague in 1899 and 1907? (b) What was achieved at those conferences?

5 Taft Tries to Follow in Roosevelt's Footsteps

Theodore Roosevelt's popularity was so commanding that he was able to dictate to the Republicans his successor in 1908. The man he chose was William Howard Taft of Ohio — experienced, affable, and weighing over 300 pounds.

Taft is elected President. In 1904 Taft had joined Roosevelt's Cabinet as Secretary of War. Earlier, he had been a federal judge and had served as the first governor of the Philippines. Roosevelt enjoyed Taft's company and admired his achievements. One night early in 1908, the Roosevelts had invited the Tafts to the White House for dinner. After the meal the two families went to the library to talk. There, in the sing-song fashion of a fortune-teller, the President made believe he could foretell the future: "I see a man standing before me weighing about 350 pounds. There is something hanging over his head. I cannot make out what it is; it is hanging by a slender thread. At one time it looks like the presidency — then again it looks like the chief justiceship."

With great enthusiasm, Mrs. Taft shouted, "Make it the presidency!"

"Make it the chief justiceship," said Taft in a quiet voice.

Taft was sincere about what he wanted, and so was Mrs. Taft. She soon had her wish. In the election that year she became First Lady as her husband decisively defeated William Jennings Bryan, the Democrats' candidate for the third time. Years later, Taft was appointed Chief Justice — becoming the only person who has ever held the two highest offices in the land.

Mounting troubles mark Taft's presidency. On his own, Taft was much like Martin Van Buren: a brilliant lieutenant unable to fill a famous predecessor's shoes. Taft once said that whenever he heard the words "Mr. President," he turned around expecting Roosevelt to be there. Roosevelt, for his part, was certain that "Taft will carry on the work substantially as I have. He will do all in his power to further the great causes for which I have fought." Taft, however, could see problems ahead. "There's no use trying to be William Howard Taft with Roosevelt's ways," he said. "Our ways are different."

As Taft's term began, Roosevelt retired from the scene and sailed for Africa to hunt big game. "Health to the lions!" was said to be the toast offered by political enemies as he departed. However, Roosevelt was not off the scene for long.

In his years in office, Taft pleased many progressives with his record of accomplishments. He continued Roosevelt's trust-busting program and strengthened the Interstate Commerce Commission. He tried to lower the tariff substantially and extended federal control over public lands. He saw to it, finally, that New Mexico and Arizona were admitted to the Union in 1912, completing the continental base of 48 states.

In spite of these accomplishments, Taft's years in office were marked by conflict with fellow Republicans. One faction, which included Senator La Follette, considered themselves insurgents — that is, politicians opposed to the policies of their own party. The insurgents believed that Taft had not worked hard enough for tariff reduction, which western farmers supported in order to bring down the cost of manufactured goods.

During Roosevelt's absence, Taft wrote him, "I have been conscientiously trying to carry out your policies, but my method of doing so has not worked smoothly." Roosevelt was soon home again and could see for himself the trouble Taft was in. For one thing, Taft was involved in a bruising fight with Gifford Pinchot, a well-known conservationist whom Roosevelt had appointed Chief Forester. Taft finally fired Pinchot, an action that made the President seem opposed to conservation. Then, in 1910 when insurgents in Congress succeeded in stripping Speaker of the House Joseph Cannon of some of his powers, Taft failed to take a clear-cut stand on the issue. He thus gave the impression that he was opposed to what was termed the "Revolution of 1910," and many progressives were infuriated.

President Taft posed with his family in 1911. Sons Charles and Robert both later held public office.

Roosevelt re-enters politics. Roosevelt believed that he had been let down by Taft. Still ambitious and vigorous, Roosevelt decided to enter political life again — as if he had ever left it. Late in the summer of 1910, he delivered a speech in Kansas, asserting that "property shall be the servant and not the master" of the people. The speech showed the influence of a new book, *The Promise of American Life*, written by Herbert Croly. Croly, a superb writer, was the son of Jane Cunningham Croly, the first widely read female newspaper correspondent. Croly's book issued a clear call for social planning by the federal government as a way to promote prosperity and happiness. Roosevelt adopted this viewpoint as his own, calling his program the "New Nationalism." Said he, "The New Nationalism regards the executive power as the steward of the public welfare."

By late 1911 Roosevelt was openly supporting the insurgent Republicans. The insurgents had hoped to nominate La Follette for President, but Roosevelt had his eye on the White House again. Taft said privately, "If you were to remove Roosevelt's skull now, you would find written on his brain '1912.'" After La Follette collapsed while making a speech early in 1912, Roosevelt announced, "My hat is in the ring."

President Taft decided to resist his old friend's campaign for the nomination.

Taft told his military aide, Archibald Butt, "It is hard, very hard, Archie, to see a devoted friendship going to pieces like a rope of sand." It would be some time before Taft and Roosevelt spoke to each other again.

The Republicans are split in 1912. Taft's friends controlled the Republican convention of 1912, and only allowed the seating of nineteen progressive delegates. Angered, Roosevelt's backers refused to have anything to do with the convention. The remaining delegates then nominated Taft on the first ballot.

The Roosevelt people quickly held their own convention, choosing the old Rough Rider in a tumultuous gathering. With religious fervor, Roosevelt told his followers, "We stand at Armageddon, and we battle for the Lord." Thus, the Progressive Party was launched, sometimes nicknamed the Bull Moose Party.[3] The Progressive platform called for the adoption in all states of the initiative, referendum, and recall, and backed a corrupt-practices act to guard against election fraud. It also contained a call for women's suffrage, federal aid to agriculture, laws to protect women in industry, an end to child labor, and minimum-wage and maximum-hour legislation.

In spite of the enthusiasm of his Progressive backers, Roosevelt must have

---

[3]The name grew out of a Roosevelt remark, "I am as strong as a bull moose."

The Democrats and Woodrow Wilson won an easy presidential victory in 1912 because the Progressive faction, with Theodore Roosevelt as its candidate, split the Republican ranks. The Democrats also won majorities in both the Senate and the House.

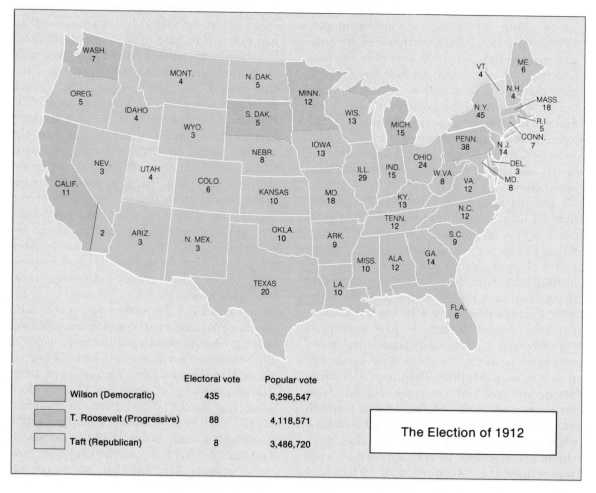

	Electoral vote	Popular vote
Wilson (Democratic)	435	6,296,547
T. Roosevelt (Progressive)	88	4,118,571
Taft (Republican)	8	3,486,720

The Election of 1912

known that he and Taft would split the Republican vote and open the way to victory for the Democrats. In the words of a prominent New Yorker, "The only question now is which corpse gets the most flowers."

Woodrow Wilson leads the Democrats to victory. In the Democratic Party, William Jennings Bryan worked hard for the nomination once again. When the convention became deadlocked, however, he threw his support to Woodrow Wilson, the reform governor of New Jersey. Finally, on the forty-sixth ballot, Wilson won the party's nomination.

Wilson's campaign for President had one leading idea — that the country needed new laws to protect people in small businesses. Wilson was eager to restore free economic competition and put an end to trusts. He knew that no one could turn back the clock to the days before the trusts. He hoped, however, that some of the spirit of that time could be revived — that the "curse of bigness" in business could be eliminated. Wilson called his program the "New Freedom."

Taft ran a listless campaign, acting long before Election Day as if he had already been defeated. Roosevelt directed his campaign to his old admirers, who saw him as a fighter-hero re-entering the battlefield. On one occasion Roosevelt refused to cancel a scheduled speaking date even though he had just been shot by a would-be assassin. He told his audience, "I am going to ask you to be very quiet and please excuse me from making a long speech. I'll do the best I can but there is a bullet in my body. I have a message to deliver and will deliver it as long as there is life in my body."

Wilson was a brilliant speaker, but it was the split in Republican ranks that assured his election. He won only 42 percent of the vote. In the three-way race it was sufficient, however, to give him 435 electoral votes and carry him to victory. Roosevelt was second in the popular and electoral votes, and Taft was third (map, page 548). The Progressive Era was entering a new stage — one that would be its final stage.

SECTION REVIEW

1. (a) What progressive legislation was passed during Taft's years as President? (b) What political problems did Taft encounter?
2. (a) Why did Theodore Roosevelt re-enter politics? (b) What was the "New Nationalism"?
3. (a) What caused a split in Republican ranks in the election of 1912? (b) What was the result of that election?

6 The Progressive Era Draws to a Close

The 1912 election had been a clear-cut victory for progressives. When he came to the White House, Woodrow Wilson could count on widespread public support for his "New Freedom" program.

Wilson brings strong leadership to the presidency. Woodrow Wilson was the most scholarly man to occupy the White House since John Quincy Adams. Born in Virginia in 1856, Wilson had begun his career as a lawyer, but very early he decided to make his mark in politics. Receiving a Ph.D. in political science, he became one of the most stimulating college professors of his time. He wrote influential books and articles on government and in 1902 became president of Princeton University. As an academic man, however, he felt he could not fulfill his keen "longing to do immortal work." In 1910 he ran for the governorship of New Jersey, convinced that all his reading and training had prepared him for high public office. He had the support of the state Democratic Party bosses, who thought he would only be a figurehead governor. Once in office, however, he proved to be beyond their control. He quickly transformed the state into a model of reform as he drove out corrupt officials. Two years later, he was elected President.

Wilson had come to admire Theodore Roosevelt's aggressive use of the power of the presidency, and he intended to be a strong Chief Executive too. He even revived the practice, broken by Jefferson, of presenting his messages personally to Congress. The purpose, Wilson said, was to show that the President "is a human being trying to cooperate with other human beings in a common service." With confidence he presented his programs, and his energetic leadership brought practical results.

Tariffs are reduced. One of President Wilson's first steps was to seek a reduction in tariff rates. After publicly denouncing lobbyists who opposed tariff reform, Wilson encouraged Congress to pass the Underwood Tariff Act of 1913. Rates were lowered on almost 1,000 items. To make up for the anticipated loss of revenue, the Underwood Tariff included a provision for an income tax. Wilson proudly said, "I have had the accomplishment of something like this at heart ever since I was a boy."

The Federal Reserve System is set up. Wilson also sought reforms in the nation's banking system. Along with other progressives, he argued that a handful of private

Legislation passed during Wilson's administration sought to curb the increasing concentration of money and credit in the hands of the "money trust."

investment firms in the East controlled the existing banks. Wilson's views were reminiscent of Andrew Jackson's. Whereas Jackson had wanted to get the government out of banking, however, Wilson supported a government-controlled system that would be able to provide an elastic currency. In other words, the volume of currency could be increased or decreased according to the changing needs of the economy, thus providing greater stability for the banking structure of the country.

After intricate negotiations with Congress, Wilson agreed to sign the Federal Reserve Act into law in 1913. The act divided the United States into twelve banking districts, each with a Federal Reserve Bank. All national banks had to become members of the Federal Reserve System, while all state banks were invited to join. The Federal Reserve Banks were strictly "banker's banks," with considerable power over the money and credit policies of member banks. A central Federal Reserve Board directed the whole system.

Wilson deals with the trusts. Another goal of Wilson's "New Freedom" program was stricter control of the trusts. The Clayton Antitrust Act, passed in 1914, strengthened the Sherman Act (page 454) by defining unfair business practices. It prohibited a company from acquiring the stock of another company for the purpose of forming a monopoly. It made interlocking directorships illegal. The new law also seemed, for the first time, to exempt labor and farm organizations from being prosecuted as conspiracies in restraint of trade. The Clayton Act brought union people to the side of the Democrats. In 1917 Wilson became the first President to address a convention of the American Federation of Labor.

At the President's request, Congress also created the Federal Trade Commission in 1914 to deal with the trust problem. The purpose of the Commission was to keep an eye on big corporations and to issue "cease and desist" orders — subject to court review — whenever antitrust laws were violated. The act creating the Commission also outlawed certain unfair methods of competition in interstate commerce.

Other progressive laws are passed. During his years in office, Wilson could claim credit for several other laws. The La Follette Seamen's Act of 1915 gave merchant seamen improved working conditions. The Federal Farm Loan Act of 1916 provided farmers with long-term credit. The Adamson Act, also passed in 1916, established an eight-hour workday for railroad employees.

Still, the work of the progressives, many leaders believed, remained incomplete. The laws that Wilson and his associates advocated were not as far-reaching as those that some progressives supported. Wilson, furthermore, remained blind to the situation of black people. Many people, in fact, blamed him for the increase in Jim Crow regulations in the city of Washington during his presidency. W. E. B. Du Bois had supported Wilson in 1912 and had urged other black leaders to do likewise. Once in office, however, Wilson would not budge from his belief that segregation was the best policy for both races. Even Booker T. Washington was saying, as Wilson's term went on, that he had never seen black people "so discouraged and bitter as they are at the present time."

The Progressive Movement brings important changes in American life. By the time Woodrow Wilson won election to a second term of office (Chapter 24), the Progressive Movement had run its course. Its accomplishments, nevertheless, were noteworthy. It had enlisted the leaders of the urban communities in attacking problems that had earlier been ignored. It had made an effort to root out privilege and monopoly. It had established the principle that big business must exercise public responsibility. Much remained to do, but even Wilson believed that to remake America would require "a generation or two."

Meanwhile, the constant revelations of what was wrong with American life had brought a reaction: people gradually became inattentive to them. Moreover, fresh pride

President Wilson was deeply saddened when his first wife, Ellen, died in 1914. The next year he met Edith Bolling Galt, shown with him here, and they were married in December, 1915.

in the nation, generated by the completion of the Panama Canal, was drowning out the chorus of complaints.

The next era of history was being glimpsed too. Already the automobile was on the scene: the Ford Motor Company had been organized in 1903. Already airplanes were flying: the first powered flight had taken place in that same year as the Wright Brothers kept their four-cylinder machine aloft for twelve seconds. Theodore Roosevelt in 1902 had become the first President to ride in an automobile and in 1910 the first to ride in an airplane.

The engines of Europe's military machines were beginning to whir too. Few Americans could hear them. Still, those sounds from abroad were not lost on Wilson. He had written just before taking the train to his inauguration in 1913, "It would be the irony of fate if my administration had to deal chiefly with foreign affairs."

SECTION REVIEW

1. How did Woodrow Wilson view the role of the President?
2. (a) Why did Wilson support passage of the Underwood Tariff Act? (b) The Federal Reserve Act? (c) The Clayton Act?
3. (a) What were some of the progressives' chief accomplishments? (b) For what reasons did the Progressive Movement slow down?

Chapter 23 Review

Summary

At the beginning of the twentieth century a spirit of reform, known as the Progressive Movement, swept the nation. The movement was stimulated by the growth of a well-educated middle class which objected to corruption in government and to unfair practices in the world of business. Many of the shortcomings of government and of monopolistic businesses were brought to light by a crusading group of writers and journalists.

One goal of the progressives was to reform municipal government. Programs carried out by such mayors as Samuel Jones in Toledo and Tom Johnson in Cleveland were copied by other cities. On the state level, Robert La Follette of Wisconsin led the way with a sweeping program of reform. The direct primary, the secret ballot, the direct election of senators, women's suffrage, and the referendum, initiative, and recall were adopted during the Progressive Era. The progressives made little progress, however, in alleviating resentment toward foreign immigrants or in ending discrimination against blacks.

When Theodore Roosevelt became President in 1901, he brought to the White House a spirit of enthusiasm. He was sympathetic to the Progressive Movement and undertook a program of antitrust suits. He also persuaded Congress to pass laws to regulate railroad rates, limit the sale of harmful products, and conserve national resources.

Theodore Roosevelt took an active role in strengthening America's interests in the Caribbean and Asia. One of the most dramatic projects during his presidency was the construction of the Panama Canal. Roosevelt acquired for the United States a right of way across the Isthmus of Panama and immediately organized the building of a canal to connect the Pacific with the Atlantic Ocean. To reaffirm the Monroe Doctrine, Roosevelt issued a statement of policy — known as the Roosevelt Corollary — under which the United States claimed the right to intervene in Latin American countries to prevent intervention by European powers. In Asian affairs, Roosevelt negotiated a peace between Russia and Japan and won a Nobel Peace Prize for his efforts. To impress the world with America's military strength, Roosevelt sent the United States fleet around the world in 1907–1909.

William Howard Taft, hand-picked by Roosevelt as his successor, was elected President in 1908 but ran into trouble trying to fill his predecessor's shoes. Disillusioned with Taft's policies, Roosevelt re-entered politics in 1912 and split the Republican Party when he ran as a candidate of the newly formed Progressive Party. This division assured the election of the Democratic candidate, Woodrow Wilson. A scholarly, accomplished man, Wilson brought strong leadership to the White House and continued the reforms begun by Roosevelt.

Vocabulary and Important Terms

1. Progressive Movement
2. "mugwump literature"
3. muckraker
4. Socialist
5. direct primary
6. "Wisconsin idea"
7. referendum
8. initiative
9. recall
10. secret ballot
11. Seventeenth Amendment
12. Nineteenth Amendment
13. Jim Crow laws
14. *Plessy v. Ferguson*
15. Northern Securities Company case
16. Hepburn Act
17. Pure Food and Drug Act
18. Meat Inspection Act
19. Hay-Bunau-Varilla Treaty
20. Roosevelt Corollary
21. "dollar diplomacy"
22. Treaty of Portsmouth
23. Great White Fleet
24. Underwood Tariff Act
25. Federal Reserve Act
26. Clayton Act
27. Federal Trade Commission

Discussion Questions

1. (a) When did the Progressive Movement get its start, and what were its roots? (b) What kinds of problems were the progressive reformers seeking to correct?

2. (a) What, according to the progressives, was the proper role of the federal government in the world of business? (b) What progressive measures at the local, state, and national levels gave people increased participation in government?

3. (a) Why did many progressives regard Theodore Roosevelt as their leader? (b) How did Roosevelt display his conviction about right and wrong in handling the coal strike? (c) In dealing with big business? (d) In acquiring the Panama Canal? (e) In settling the Russo-Japanese War?

4. (a) How did Roosevelt interpret his election victory in 1904? (b) What steps did he take as a result? (c) What contributions did Roosevelt make to the conservation of natural resources?

5. (a) Why did the United States take an active interest in building a canal across the Isthmus of Pan-

ama? (b) How did the Panama Canal affect American foreign policy? (c) What role did the United States assume for itself in Latin America? (d) In what countries did the United States intervene during the Roosevelt and Taft administrations?

6. (a) Who were the three major candidates for President in 1912? (c) Why did Wilson win?

7. What progressive legislation was passed during Woodrow Wilson's years in office?

Relating Past and Present

In the eyes of today's reformers, what aspects of American society need attention? Are today's reformers more likely to be active at the local, state, or national levels? What do they see as the most effective methods of achieving reform?

Studying Local History

1. The Progressive Movement began at the local and state levels. Which progressive reforms, if any, affected your state? For example, does your state have a direct primary? Initiative? Referendum? Re-

call? If so, to what extent have they been used?

2. Study the map on page 533 showing women's suffrage. What voting rights had women gained in your state by 1919?

Using History Skills

1. *Reading source material.* Study Gertrude Foster Brown's description of suffragist tactics on page 534. (a) Why did the suffragists find it necessary to take their appeals directly to men? (b) How did they go about doing so? (c) How were the suffragist parades "striking evidence of the sweeping progress of the movement"?

2. *Writing a report.* Choose one of the following American authors, all of whom are classified as muckrakers, and report on him or her to the class. Tell what abuses the author uncovered and what reforms, if any, resulted from the author's writings: (a) Ida M. Tarbell, (b) Lincoln Steffens, (c) Ray Stannard Baker, (d) Upton Sinclair, (e) Frank Norris.

3. *Comparing.* What personal characteristics and accomplishments made Theodore Roosevelt and Woodrow Wilson outstanding Presidents?

WORLD SCENE

Political Reform

In the early 1900's the spirit of reform prompted people in many parts of the world to demand more responsive governments.

The Russian Revolution of 1905. For many years there had been dissatisfaction with the inept rule of Czar Nicholas II and criticism of the corruption of the Russian government. The humiliating Russian defeat in the Russo-Japanese War of 1904–1905 contributed to unrest among the Russian people.

On a Sunday in January, 1905, thousands of workers assembled peacefully in front of the imperial palace in St. Petersburg. They intended to present a petition seeking improved working conditions and a representative assembly. Without warning, the palace guards fired on the protesters, killing and wounding hundreds. "Bloody Sunday," as the incident came to be called, triggered upheaval throughout Russia.

To head off full-scale revolution, Nicholas agreed to certain reforms. He authorized the establishment of an elected assembly and permitted freedom of speech and other basic liberties for the Russian people. Once order had been restored, however, Nicholas took away

many of the concessions he had been forced to make.

Revolution in China. By 1900 the Chinese government was on the verge of collapse. Pressure was mounting from Britain, France, and Russia for increased trading rights. There was pressure, too, from many young people filled with a desire to "Westernize" their country.

In a desperate effort to modernize the government, the young Manchu emperor, Kuang Hsü, began extensive reforms in 1898. These measures were seen as a threat by many traditional Chinese, and after only a few months Kuang Hsü was dethroned. He was succeeded by his aunt, Tz'u Hsi, then 62 years old. Although she gradually made important reforms, the Manchus were unable to control the revolutionary groups active throughout China.

In 1911 a spontaneous uprising led to a revolution that finally toppled the dynasty. An exiled Chinese revolutionary, Sun Yat-sen, was in America when he heard news that the Manchus had fallen. Quickly returning to China, he helped establish a Chinese republic and was chosen its first president.

24

Defending Democracy

1910 – 1920

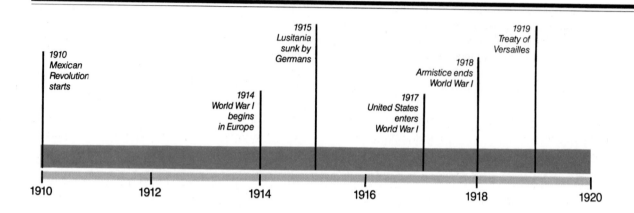

1910	1912	1914	1916	1918	1920

1910 Mexican Revolution starts

1914 World War I begins in Europe

1915 Lusitania sunk by Germans

1917 United States enters World War I

1918 Armistice ends World War I

1919 Treaty of Versailles

CHAPTER OUTLINE

1. Latin American policy remains unchanged.

2. World War I begins.

3. The United States enters the war.

4. The United States helps win the war.

5. The United States rejects world leadership.

Although Woodrow Wilson had had no experience in foreign relations, fate thrust him into the role of international leader. The perplexing issues of the day caught him, as they did the nation, by surprise. In dealing with them he could not even turn to trained people in the Department of State, for there were none. His Secretary of State, William Jennings Bryan, knew practically nothing about the world outside America, and he was an amateur in diplomacy.

Wilson, for his part, took as a guide in facing his duties the moral instruction that he had received as a boy. His father, a Presbyterian minister, had instilled in the youth the idea that knowing right from wrong meant fighting for the right at whatever the cost. From his adoring mother, Wilson acquired a belief that he was superior in mind and morality to his associates. As President, living up to his parents' teaching made him feel keenly that wrong in the world could be made right through the will of the United States.

If, then, the path of international politics was for Wilson unknown territory, he was confident he could make his way on it successfully. He believed, furthermore, that he understood the place of the United States in the world. He once said, "My dream is that as the years go on and the world knows more and more of America . . . that America will come into the full light of day when all shall know that she puts human rights above all other rights, and that the flag is the flag not only of America, but of humanity."

1 Latin American Policy Remains Unchanged

President Wilson had hoped to complete his program of domestic reform. Foreign affairs, nonetheless, became his consuming concern. Eager to help remodel American life at home, he was quickly caught up in helping shape international politics.

Wilson continues the policy of intervening in Latin America. Shortly after he became President, Wilson declared himself to be firmly set against imperialism. In an unprecedented pledge in October, 1913, he said, "the United States will never again seek one additional foot of territory by conquest. She will devote herself to showing that she knows how to make honorable and fruitful use of the territory she has."

Wilson's words were reassuring, especially to Latin Americans who had grown deeply distrustful of their powerful neighbor to the north. Still, Wilson carried out more armed intervention in Latin America than any of his predecessors. He sent marines to Haiti in 1915 to insure the payment of debts, and in 1916 installed an American government that remained for eight years in the Dominican Republic. America extended its influence in the Caribbean, furthermore, with the purchase in 1917 of the Danish West Indies (now called the Virgin Islands) for $25 million (page 507).

Fighting breaks out in Mexico. Relations with Mexico proved most serious during Wilson's presidency. In 1911 the dictator of Mexico, Porfirio Díaz, who had ruled with an iron hand for almost all of the preceding 34 years, fell from power in a sudden upheaval. Mexico under Díaz had been a country controlled by a small privileged class. The vast majority of Mexicans were peons, or peasants, who did not own the land they worked. Díaz had sold about 75 percent of Mexico's mineral resources to foreign interests and had disposed of millions of acres of land to his friends.

Textile workers draped their factory with a huge flag. President Wilson hoped that the flag of the United States would symbolize freedom and human rights for all people.

Díaz's successor was Francisco Madero, a democratic idealist who had led the revolution. Madero was too inexperienced, however, to put into effect the reforms he had planned. His followers, moreover, were badly divided. One group was led by General Victoriano Huerta (WEHR-tah), a former supporter of Díaz, who secretly plotted against the new president and finally drove him out of office. The counter-revolution reached its climax when Madero was assassinated — a deed most people blamed on Huerta himself.

Wilson follows a policy of "watchful waiting." When Wilson moved into the White House, he inherited the knotty problem of whether or not to recognize "the unspeakable Huerta," as he called the general. Wilson decided he would have nothing to do with Huerta. His hope was for a "tranquil and righteous government in Mexico." He desired it also to be democratic.

Many Americans were made uncomfortable by Wilson's refusal to extend diplomatic recognition to Huerta. A prominent editor asked, "What legal or moral right has a President of the United States to say who shall or shall not be President of Mexico?" Actually, Wilson was expressing a novel point of view: that the United States would only establish diplomatic relations with governments chosen in free elections. The policy of the United States had long been to recognize governments regardless of how they had come into existence.

Wilson decided to follow a policy of "watchful waiting," that is, of sitting by until the Huerta regime was toppled. The President was dismayed, however, when the Huerta government hung on. He had already cut off the shipment of arms to Mexico. In 1914 he lifted the embargo so that weapons and ammunition would flow to Huerta's chief opponents, Venustiano Carranza and Francisco ("Pancho") Villa (VEE-yah). Still, Wilson would go no further. He did not wish to endanger the investments — totaling nearly a billion dollars — that Americans had made in Mexican enterprises. These included ranches, oilfields, railroads, mines, and public utilities. Wilson feared, furthermore, for the safety of the 50,000 Americans living in Mexico.

American troops occupy Veracruz. Eventually, though, the President decided he had to try stronger methods. Following an incident involving American sailors in Tampico, Mexico, the President asked Congress for the authority to use force against Huerta's government. American naval units pounded the Mexican port of Veracruz, and marines and sailors went ashore to occupy the city. Wilson had expected the operation to be carried out without loss of life. Cadets of the Mexican Naval Academy resisted the attackers, however, taking heavy losses.

Wilson felt frustrated and quickly accepted an offer of the ABC countries (Argentina, Brazil, and Chile) to mediate the dispute. Under intense pressure, Huerta finally resigned in July and fled the country. Carranza became Mexico's new president.

American forces pursue Pancho Villa. Wilson, who believed that the Mexican Revolution could now go forward, was appalled when civil war broke out. Carranza was beset by troops under Pancho Villa. Villa, who had been angered by American aid given Carranza, crossed the United States border in March, 1916, and raided a town in New Mexico, killing nineteen inhabitants. The American public was outraged. Wilson felt he must act decisively.

The President sent Brigadier General John J. Pershing into Mexico on an expedition to find Villa and punish him. Villa cleverly eluded Pershing, however, and the Americans eventually clashed with Carranza's forces, who resented American soldiers on Mexican soil. When Carranza demanded their withdrawal, Wilson sent more troops to the border.

Tension mounted alarmingly. Still, Wilson shunned the idea of waging war against people struggling for freedom. In the end, he accepted Carranza's proposal that a joint Mexican-American commission try to settle the difficulties. The commission produced no solution, but Carranza soon destroyed Villa's forces, enabling Wilson to withdraw Pershing and his troops.

Brigadier General John J. Pershing and his troops crossed into Mexico in pursuit of Pancho Villa.

In spite of the frustrating events, the President remained friendly to the lofty goals of the Mexican Revolution. His actions had not led to the democratic Mexican government he had hoped for. He was satisfied, nevertheless, that Carranza had wide popular backing.

———

Wilson's diplomacy seemed sufficiently successful in Mexico to try it on a larger scale. Indeed, the opportunity came to him to preach democracy to the entire world. The occasion was war in Europe — long-threatened and long-anticipated.

SECTION REVIEW

1. Why may it be said that President Woodrow Wilson carried on the Latin American policy of his predecessors?
2. (a) Why did the Mexican people overthrow Díaz? (b) What was the policy of "watchful waiting"? (c) What circumstances led Wilson to follow that policy?
3. (a) What actions did Wilson take against the Huerta regime? (b) Why did he send General Pershing into Mexico? (c) What was the outcome of the dispute with Mexico?

2 World War I Begins

On June 28, 1914, Archduke Francis Ferdinand, heir to the throne of Austria-Hungary, and his wife Sophie were shot and killed in the city of Sarajevo, capital of the province of Bosnia (map, page 572). The assassinations were the work of conspirators from Serbia,[1] a neighboring country angered by Austria-Hungary's recent annexation of Bosnia, which it claimed as its own. Austria-Hungary, backed by Germany, its main ally, decided to use the incident as an excuse for crushing Serbia. On July 28, 1914, Austria-Hungary declared war on Serbia.

Within a week the war had spread with astonishing speed, as Europe's two mighty alliance systems found themselves locked in combat. In one camp were the *Central Powers*, led by Germany and including Austria-Hungary and the Ottoman Empire (Turkey). In the other camp were the *Allies*, consisting of Great Britain, France, Russia, Serbia, and, from 1915 on, Italy.

What were the causes of World War I? The rivalries of the powers of Europe were deeply rooted. The rise of the German Empire in the years following Germany's victory over France in the Franco-Prussian War in 1871 had greatly alarmed Britain and France. The Germans quickly made a virtue of military life and developed an aggressive foreign policy. With their formidable army and navy, they entered into competition with Britain and France to set up colonies in Africa and in the Pacific.

Situated in central Europe, Germany had fear of having one day to fight a "two-front" war, that is, a war on its eastern and western borders at the same time. To assure itself of some security, Germany signed a secret treaty of friendship with Austria-Hungary in 1879. The Ottoman Empire, fearing Russian designs on its port city of Constantinople (now Istanbul), had moved steadily closer to Germany by 1914.

Britain, France, and Russia were afraid that Germany and its allies might be able to

---

[1]Serbia is today part of Yugoslavia.

Citizens of Paris welcomed France's mobilization against Germany in 1914. As the "great war" broke out in Europe, the United States maintained neutrality.

control the continent of Europe. France and Russia put aside their old feuds and became allies in 1894. Britain and France, long-time enemies, resolved their differences by signing a treaty in 1904. When Russia joined England in an agreement in 1907, the three countries were linked together in a pledge to assist one another in the event of war. They hoped their combined strength would counterbalance that of the Central Powers.

Throughout Europe the international rivalry was fueled by an uncontrolled arms race that reinforced overheated national feelings. The huge armies of the European nations consisted of millions of men, expensively equipped and distinctively attired. The senior officers' dress uniforms were adorned with yards of gold braid. Their hats, trimmed with feathers or fur, seemed worthy headgear for gods. When these armies marched on parade, the civil-ian populations swelled with pride at the show of *their* troops, *their* flag, *their* national strength.

The United States follows a policy of neutrality. Despite these ominous developments in Europe, Americans felt removed from any possible danger. Few people regarded European affairs as the business of the United States. On the whole, Americans continued to think that the Atlantic and Pacific oceans protected the United States from dangers outside — in much the way that moats once protected medieval castles.

Americans were astounded when the war broke out in 1914. They followed the news from Europe with fascination. Most people assumed that the hostilities would be over quickly. No one imagined the prophetic truth uttered by Edward Grey, Britain's foreign secretary: "The lamps are going out all over Europe; we shall not see them lit again in our lifetime." A new world was in the making.

Wilson was personally stunned by the news of war. He was especially dismayed when Germany marched against France through Belgium, a neutral country. He regarded the assault on the Belgians as lawless and uncivilized. Still, he issued a statement proclaiming America's neutrality. He urged all Americans to be "neutral in fact as well as in name . . . impartial in thought as well as in action."

Most Americans favor the Allies. To be neutral "in thought as well as in action" was not easy. Americans regarded the British and French as friends. The United States, it is true, had fought two wars against the British, and the millions of Irish immigrants who had come to America helped keep alive the feeling of hostility and distrust. By the late 1800's, however, relations between America and Great Britain had at last become friendly. The two nations were drawn closer by their common concern over Germany's commercial and military strength.

The revived feeling of kinship with the English came easily to Americans. The two nations shared the same language, the same faith in representative government, and the same view of personal freedom. American laws and customs were based on English traditions. Practically every American was familiar with the novels of Charles Dickens, the adventures of Sherlock Holmes, and the works of William Shakespeare. Millions of Americans who had never visited England knew its famous place names: Trafalgar Square, Windsor Castle, the Tower of London, and countless others.

United States relations with France were also cordial. Any American who had studied history could recall with gratitude the aid France had given during the War for Independence. Americans applauded the thought expressed in a poem penned soon after the outbreak of hostilities:

Forget us, God, if we forget
The sacred sword of Lafayette.

At first, few Americans felt hostility or even irritation toward Germany or Austria-Hungary. Germany was a comparatively new nation with which America had had little experience. Austria-Hungary also was only a name. A mention of Vienna, its capital, might bring to mind the lilting music of Johann Strauss, the "waltz king," who had lived there.

Trade with the Allies is important. The fighting in Europe gradually changed American feelings. One observer said that public opinion became, "Sure I'm neutral. I don't care who licks the Hun." ("Hun" was hostile slang for "the Germans.")

The people's sympathy with the Allied cause grew as American prosperity seemed more and more dependent on trade with the Allies. Being a neutral nation the United States could sell supplies, including munitions, to either or both sides in the struggle. At first, Americans sold only a little more than usual to Britain and France. As the war heated up, however, the trickle of goods to those countries became a mighty Niagara. Because the British navy controlled the seas and had clamped a blockade on Germany's coastlines, the Central Powers could not readily obtain products from America.[2]

Americans also lent money to the Allies to help them purchase food and war equipment. By the end of 1916, the Allies had borrowed about $2.3 billion in the United States, compared with Germany's modest $20 million. Plainly the eventual recovery of their money gave Americans a heavy stake in an Allied victory. The outcome was by no means certain, however, for the war had already taken unpredicted turns.

Germany devises a strategy for attacking France. The war planning of the major European powers had been under way since the beginning of the century. The French and the Germans both viewed Belgium as

---

[2]Despite the much-publicized build-up of naval forces before the war, the only important naval engagement was the Battle of Jutland, fought off the west coast of Denmark in 1916. Although the British took heavy losses, the German fleet was forced to return to its home base and remain there during the rest of the war.

the highway each would have to use in order to strike at the other. In 1905 the Germans had adopted as their strategy the plan of Count Alfred von Schlieffen (SHLEEF-un), the chief of the German general staff. Schlieffen's strategy called for sending his best troops in a wide, wheeling movement through Belgium into northeastern France. In a gigantic hammer blow the troops would sweep down upon Paris, entrapping the French armies and destroying them. Meanwhile, a defensive war would contain the slow-moving Russians in the east. Then, after Paris had fallen, German troops would be dispatched to the Eastern Front to deal with the enemy there.

Schlieffen had said that everything depended on keeping strong the right wing of the attacking German army. Moreover, he wanted that right wing to travel in an arc that would take it as far west as possible. "When you march into France," he had said, "let the last man on the right brush the [English] Channel with his sleeve."

These Allied soldiers were entrenched in northeastern France. By one estimate, the trenches of the Allied and the Central Powers totaled 25,000 miles.

The surprises that war inevitably produces defeated the plan. Schlieffen's successor as chief of staff, Helmuth von Moltke (MOLT-kuh), grew alarmed when three things went wrong: (1) the Belgians, led by Albert, their king, resisted the Germans fiercely; (2) the supposedly inefficient Russians were able to get their troops to the front much earlier than expected; and (3) Britain sprang swiftly to the defense of Belgium. Moltke, in panic, weakened the right wing of the German army by detaching units of his army and sending them east to help stem the Russian advance.

The German advance is stopped. Germany's plan for a quick victory, therefore, was shattered. French forces stopped the Germans just north of Paris early in September, 1914, at the First Battle of the Marne. The French were aided by troops hurriedly brought to the front from Paris in 1,200 taxicabs — the first time troops had ever been moved into battle by motor vehicle. The Germans now tried to reach the English Channel, extending their lines as far west as they could. Determined to win this "race to the sea," the Allied armies — British, French, and Belgian — slugged it out with the Germans at Ypres (EE-pruh) during October and November. In the carnage, the British Expeditionary Force of 100,000 men was reduced by more than half.

Both sides use trench warfare and new types of weapons. A tragic stalemate soon developed. The armies, constantly reinforced with new conscripts, burrowed into trenches running from Belgium across northern France and southward to the border of Switzerland. The troops held fixed positions that for the next three years never shifted more than a few miles forward or backward.

The machine gun became the war's supreme firearm. It was ideal for trench warfare. When troops went "over the top," seeking to advance across "no man's land," they faced the withering fire of these diabolical weapons. A frontal assault on enemy trenches inevitably produced a hideous number of casualties.

In 1915 the war was made even more horrible by the introduction of poison gas by the Germans. Then, in 1916 at the Battle of the Somme, the British unveiled still another new weapon — the tank.

Fighting takes place on other fronts. On the Eastern Front, the Russians, having been rolled back from East Prussia, recovered to prevent the Germans from taking the Polish capital of Warsaw. By the fall of 1915, after a year of invasions and counterinvasions, neither side was making progress.

A British-French fleet, meanwhile, sought to attack Constantinople. The effort failed, and the scheme to isolate Turkey from the other Central Powers was foiled.

Germany uses its submarines. During 1914 and 1915 both sides tried to observe the rights of neutrals, which meant the rights chiefly of the United States. Nevertheless, by 1915 Britain and Germany had become like two huge bloody giants blindly battling each other to the death. The mounting casualties and the search for a means to bring the war to a victorious conclusion made both sides bolder. The British declared that food was essential to the war effort and, therefore, subject to seizure if found on a neutral vessel bound for Germany. They began to halt American ships on the high seas. Sometimes the British took American vessels into port and held them so long that the cargoes rotted. To fool German submarines, British ships occasionally displayed the American flag — also a violation of international law.

Still, British actions affected only property. Claims for damages could be adjusted after the war. German actions produced loss of life because they employed a relatively new naval weapon: the submarine, also called the U-boat (from the German word *Unterseeboot*).

The submarine changed the nature of warfare at sea. Formerly a neutral ship that had been stopped at sea would have been boarded and searched; passengers and crew would have been removed before sinking the vessel. Submarines, however, had thin metal hulls easily pierced by the guns of enemy ships. Submarines were obliged to fire their torpedoes and flee.

Early in the war, Germany made known its plan to torpedo, without warning, enemy or neutral merchant vessels sailing in the waters around the British Isles. The Wilson administration responded to the German announcement with a stern warning. If Germany's new policy — clearly a violation of international law — led to a loss of American lives or property, Germany would be held "to a strict accountability." Nevertheless, the notice to the Germans neither defined the threat nor dealt with the question of what would happen if American lives were lost aboard an Allied, not an American, vessel.

The "Lusitania" is sunk. The German government instructed its U-boats to avoid attacks on American ships. Still, the conduct of any war has a way of slipping out of control, almost as if it has a life of its own. An American was killed when a British merchant vessel was torpedoed in March, 1915, and an American tanker was sunk on May 1, with the loss of two American lives. The United States had not yet decided how to respond to these German actions when a great turning point occurred on May 7: a U-boat torpedoed the British liner *Lusitania* within sight of the Irish shore. The liner sank within a few minutes. Almost 1,200 people perished, including 128 Americans.

Chance, always a factor in war, had played a part in the disaster. The U-boat commander had been disappointed over his assignment to the vulnerable little vessel. During his time at sea, moreover, he had seen nothing exciting to aim at. Running out of fuel and other supplies, he had decided to head home when suddenly the *Lusitania* loomed in his periscope. He did not know that it was carrying a cargo of munitions. The *Lusitania*, furthermore, would not have been in the U-boat's range of fire if its captain had followed orders to pursue a zig-zag course across the Atlantic from New York, in order to avoid submarines. He had placed such supreme confidence in his luxurious "Lucy" and especially in its speed that he had sailed a straight path.

An undated German recruiting poster bears remarkable resemblance to the British poster of 1914. More and more enlistments were needed to fill the ranks of those killed.

Wilson reacts to the crisis. Americans were outraged by the sinking of the *Lusitania.* Theodore Roosevelt denounced the attack as "piracy on a vaster scale of murder than old-time pirates ever practiced." The Wilson administration sent a series of stern diplomatic notes to Germany, insisting upon an apology, compensation for the losses, and a pledge to stop attacking unarmed merchant ships.

The position of the United States had now been made clear. Americans claimed the right to travel anywhere — even on Allied merchant ships and regardless of what cargoes those ships might be carrying. The United States, in short, would protect its citizens, even when they were sailing under a foreign flag. The United States remained committed, nevertheless, to a policy of neutrality toward the warring nations. In response to those critics who called for war with Germany, Wilson declared, "There is

such a thing as a man being too proud to fight. There is such a thing as a nation being so right that it does not need to convince others by force that it is right."

Germany issues the "Arabic" and "Sussex" pledges. While the American public was still inflamed over the *Lusitania* incident, further distressing news arrived: On August 19, 1915, a U-boat had sunk the British steamer *Arabic,* causing the loss of two American lives. Eager to avoid further trouble with the United States, the German ambassador to Washington issued the so-called *Arabic* pledge. Germany promised not to sink unarmed vessels without warning, unless they tried to escape. The *Arabic* pledge was short-lived. In March, 1916, a U-boat torpedoed the unarmed French passenger ship *Sussex* in the English Channel. The German commander had assumed, he said, that the *Sussex* was laying mines.

When President Wilson learned that several Americans aboard the *Sussex* had been injured, he was furious. He warned the German government that if it did not "immediately declare and effect an abandonment of its present methods of submarine warfare against passenger and freight-carrying vessels, the government of the United States can have no choice but to sever diplomatic relations with the German Empire altogether." When Germany's ruler, Kaiser Wilhelm II, read the note from the United States, he was furious. He scribbled on it what he considered to be his sad choices: "Either starve at England's bidding or face war with America!" In what became known as the *Sussex* pledge, however, Germany renewed its promise not to sink unarmed ships without warning. Germany added the condition, however, that the United States must persuade the British government to give up its blockade.

Wilson wins the election of 1916. Wilson's desire to keep the United States at peace was a barrier to his making preparations for the possibility of going to war. Nevertheless, a program to strengthen the armed forces was begun in 1916. The regular army was doubled in size and the National Guard was vastly increased and strengthened. The navy began a building program aimed at giving the United States the largest fleet in the world by 1920.

Since most Americans still favored neutrality, the President's slowness stood him in good stead in the 1916 presidential campaign. The Democrats' slogan, "He kept us out of war," made a favorable impression upon peace-loving Americans. Wilson was proud to explain, moreover, that he had maintained "peace with honor." In the big industrial cities, laboring people regarded the President as a friend whose policies they valued. Election posters showing a worker's family bore the caption, "He has protected me and mine." The Republicans, making an issue of America's alleged lack of preparedness, issued placards showing the widow of a drowned American and her children with the words, "He has neglected me and mine."

In 1916, President Wilson campaigned on his policy of neutrality, although the aggressive attacks of German U-boats were drawing the United States closer to war.

Many Republicans believed they could win in 1916 if they nominated Theodore Roosevelt once again. He was eager to make the race, but important party leaders could not accept the man who had deserted them four years earlier (page 548). Besides, they wanted a "safer" candidate. They found him in Charles Evans Hughes of New York. Stately and handsome, Hughes had gained fame as a reform governor of New York, a position he resigned when President Taft named him to the Supreme Court in 1910. Now he stepped down from the Court in order to accept the Republican nomination.

Hughes's slogan was "America first and America efficient." Hughes earnestly courted the so-called "hyphenate vote," especially the Irish-Americans and the German-Americans. Many people assumed that Wilson's apparently pro-Britain and anti-Germany stance had already cost him the support of those people.

On election night, Hughes appeared to have won. Many of the Bull Moosers of four years earlier were back in the Republican Party again, and they had given Hughes their support. It was said of the Democrats receiving the returns at the Hotel Biltmore in New York that never was there "such a morgue-like entertainment in the annals of time." Hughes went to sleep believing he would be the next President.

The following day, however, the returns from California came in, making Wilson the victor after all. For the first time since the days of Andrew Jackson, a Democrat had been elected for a second consecutive term in the White House.

SECTION REVIEW

1. (a) What incident touched off the First World War? (b) What were the underlying causes of that conflict?
2. (a) What policy did the United States follow at the beginning of World War I? (b) Which side did most Americans favor? Why?
3. (a) How successful were Germany's plans for scoring a quick victory? (b) Why did both Britain and Germany try to restrict American shipping? (c) What methods did each use?
4. (a) What was the effect on American public opinion of the sinking of the *Lusitania*? (b) Why did Germany issue the *Arabic* and *Sussex* pledges?
5. (a) What steps did President Wilson take to prepare the United States for war? (b) What slogan did he use in his successful bid for re-election in 1916?

3 The United States Enters the War

As 1916 drew to a close, things were looking up for Germany. German forces had been victorious on the Eastern Front and were on the verge of forcing Russia out of the war. Germany had also won an impressive victory over Rumania, which had recently entered the war on the Allied side. Perhaps the Germans could defeat *all* their enemies.

Wilson urges negotiations. Meanwhile, Wilson had been working to end the war. In 1915 he had sent abroad his close friend and adviser, Colonel Edward M. House, to discuss possible peace terms. Both sides were still convinced they could win, however, so the efforts of House came to nothing. In early 1916, Wilson again sent House to Europe for a round of talks. German leaders were eager for Wilson to call a peace conference. They hoped a settlement would reflect the military situation, which favored the Central Powers. The Allies, of course, were afraid to negotiate until their military position had improved. Again the peace effort failed.

In December, 1916, Wilson asked each side to state privately its terms for peace, aiming to mediate an end to the fighting. The answers were so extravagant that they offered no possibility for successful negotiation. Wilson knew that Germany would now try to end the war by resuming unrestricted submarine warfare. In that event, he might not be able to keep the United States from being drawn into the struggle.

Germany gambles on a quick victory. On January 31, 1917, the German ambassador in Washington informed the American government that all ships found in the war zone would be subject to submarine attack. Germany, in other words, had gone back on its *Sussex* pledge and was about to resume unrestricted submarine warfare. Three days later the United States broke off diplomatic relations with Germany. Despite the opposition of a handful of senators, whom Wilson called "a little group of willful men," the President announced that American merchant vessels would now be armed with naval guns. The country had moved from "strict neutrality" to armed neutrality.

The "Zimmermann telegram" pushes the United States closer to war. The German government further shocked Americans by proposing an alliance between Germany and Mexico if Germany and the United States went to war. In return, Germany would help Mexico recover Texas, New Mexico, and Arizona. The message containing this secret proposal was sent by Foreign Minister Arthur Zimmermann to the German minister in Mexico City. Transmitted in code, it was intercepted and decoded by British intelligence officers. The British government passed on the message to authorities in Washington, knowing the effect it would have.

Made public, the Zimmermann telegram created a sensation. In the Southwest, where the issues of the war had not aroused much excitement, people were aghast. Wilson had more support than ever for the strong stand he was taking against Germany's decision to return to unrestricted submarine warfare.

Wilson still hoped that somehow there could be "a peace without victory," as he told Congress early in 1917. "Only a peace between equals can last," he declared. Fundamentally, he hated the idea of war, believing that it might weaken democracy in America and turn the country into an armed camp. Still, he spoke of Germany privately as "a madman that should be curbed." He was becoming convinced that a victory for Germany would mean the triumph of militarism in the world, and that America's free way of life could be a casualty of such an outcome.

The United States goes to war. From March 12 to March 19, 1917, Wilson was confined to the White House by illness. During that time he seems to have pondered deeply the choice he felt he must make: war with Germany or a continuing effort to defend neutral rights through diplomacy and armed neutrality. During that week, submarines sank three American merchant vessels as the Germans pressed relentless attacks against shipping in the waters around the British Isles, France, and Italy.

During those days also, the czar of Russia, Nicholas II, was forced to give up his throne. Military reverses and incompetent leadership had brought to the surface a long-smouldering hostility to the Russian royal family. Russian revolutionaries quickly set up a provisional government that aimed to carry on the war. Headed by Alexander Kerensky, the new government offered hope that Russia might create a parliamentary regime. A democratic Russia fighting on the Allied side would make Germany stand out even more as a repressive country dominated by its "military masters."

When the week was over, Wilson was sure of what he must do — absolutely sure, it appeared. He issued a call for Congress to assemble on April 2, 1917. Standing before its members, he asked them to recognize the state of war that Germany had forced upon the United States. "The present German submarine warfare against commerce is a warfare against mankind," he declared. "[We] will not choose the path of submission and suffer the most sacred rights of our nation and our people to be ignored or violated," he went on. Then the President abruptly shifted gears — from defending American rights to asserting that as long as the existing German government was in power "there can be no assured security for the democratic governments of the world." He added a sentence that became America's rallying cry: "The world must be made safe for democracy." Suddenly Wilson was transformed from being a man "too proud to fight" into a man willing to wage war for a lofty end.

Wilson may still have had doubts that he had done right in asking for war. That night, when he was alone with his secretary in the White House, he recalled the cheering of the crowd that had greeted him as he rode to Capitol Hill. "My message today," the President said softly, "was a message of death for our young men. How strange it seems to applaud that." He then put his head on the table and wept.

The public approved overwhelmingly of the war resolution that Congress voted on April 6, 1917. Being joined with England and France — now underdogs in the fighting — satisfied millions of Americans who believed that the Allies embodied the same democratic ideals as the United States. Americans were also reassured by the idea that winning the war would ensure permanent world peace. Many people itched for the troops to be sent to Europe in order to get on with the task. A popular song was

Your Song—My Song—Our Boys' Song

OVER THERE

With Both English and
French Text as sung by
ENRICO
CARUSO

WORDS AND MUSIC BY
GEORGE M. COHAN

LEO. FEIST — NEW YORK

Many artists contributed their talents in support of the war. Norman Rockwell illustrated this sheet-music cover.

the rousing "Over There," written by a stage star, George M. Cohan:

> Over there — over there —
> Send the word, send the word over there —
> That the Yanks are coming, the Yanks are coming,
> The drums rum-tumming ev'rywhere. . . .

The armed forces are strengthened. With America's entry into the struggle, Allied representatives began to arrive in the United States, pleading for quick assistance to save their nations from defeat. The United States, however, was not yet prepared for heavy military participation. It did not have a single complete army division. The navy was ill-equipped. The air force, simply a section of the army, consisted of 35 pilots and 50 aging planes.

Still, a crusading spirit developed. The nation mobilized with lightning speed, astonishing the world and especially Germany. The Germans had concluded that

American troops would not arrive in Europe in time to affect the fighting.

Because the Defense Act of 1916 had provided for a regular army of only 175,000 men, Wilson turned to a military draft to provide a force large enough for the nation's needs. The Selective Service Act, which went into effect in May, 1917, aroused opposition among people who feared that it would cause the nation to glorify military life. The Speaker of the House, "Champ" Clark, said he could see "precious little difference between a conscript and a convict." In general, however, the public accepted the draft. The Selective Service Act eventually made all men between the ages of 18 and 45 subject to induction. By the end of the war, almost five million men had served in the armed forces.

Among the troops who served in the armed forces were some 370,000 black Americans. Blacks served in every branch of the army. They were not allowed to enlist in the Marine Corps, however, and the navy took them solely for noncombat duties. Only through much agitating, moreover, was a school established for the training of black army officers. Blacks, nevertheless, distinguished themselves. The first Allied unit to break through to the Rhine River was the 369th, an all-black regiment.

Convoys protect American shipping. United States naval forces in the Atlantic were under the command of Rear Admiral William S. Sims, who helped devise a way of outfoxing the U-boats: the convoy system. The vulnerable merchant ships would travel the Atlantic surrounded by a convoy (an escort of destroyers and cruisers). As a result, despite the presence of German submarines, the United States Navy did not lose a single troopship sent abroad. Moreover, the navy shipped about five million tons of essential supplies to Europe.

Government agencies expand their operations. President Wilson understood from the beginning that the fighting front depended on the well-organized support of people at home. Through sweeping powers granted him by Congress, he set about making this possible. The daily life of Americans was soon regulated by dozens of government committees, boards, and councils. These bureaus greatly expanded the role of the federal government. Many Americans for the first time began to complain that Wilson had instituted a **bureaucracy,** that is, a government run by rules and regulations made by unelected officials.

The War Industries Board placed centralized controls on the nation's economy. The Board's chief work was to obtain supplies for the United States military forces and for the Allies. It also managed the distribution of raw materials at home and abroad. The chairman was Bernard M. Baruch, a successful financier. Baruch persuaded many business executives to give up well-paid positions in private business and become "dollar-a-year men," donating their talent to the war effort.

In 1917 the President chose Herbert C. Hoover, a California mining engineer and businessman, to head the Food Administration. Hoover had earlier demonstrated rare ability in distributing food in war-torn Belgium. Hoover and the volunteers who worked with him toured the United States urging the public to conserve food. The government proclaimed wheatless and meatless days and preached "the gospel of the clean plate." "To Hooverize" became a popular verb meaning "to save food."

The President also appointed a fuel administrator to see that the public conserved coal for the war effort. "Gasless Sundays" and "heatless Mondays" were introduced to dramatize the need.

The government took over the management and operation of the nation's railroads. To supervise the Railroad Administration, Wilson named his son-in-law, Secretary of the Treasury William Gibbs McAdoo. Meanwhile, the United States Shipping Board was placed in charge of an accelerated program of shipbuilding. In one day — July 4, 1918 — 95 vessels were launched. A sign in many shipyards read, "Three ships a week or bust."

Support for the war effort by laboring people was important to the nation's military success. The National War Labor Board was created in April, 1918. It sat as the final judge in labor disputes. One of its chairmen was former President Taft.

Money is raised to help finance the war. About a third of the war's cost was met through increased taxation. The remainder was raised through the sale to the public of Liberty Bonds, long-term bonds with face values as low as $50. The series of five issues — including a final "Victory" Loan — brought in more than $21 billion. Actors and actresses, sports figures, and government officials helped to sell the bonds at meetings, in theaters, hotel lobbies, and in restaurants. In all, over twenty million Americans purchased Liberty Bonds.

The war provides new opportunities for women. As men answered the call of the draft and left their jobs, women found they were welcome in many fields previously closed to them. Soon they were making ammunition, running elevators, collecting fares on streetcars, and doing many other indispensable tasks. When the navy found it was short of clerks, the Secretary of the Navy, Josephus Daniels, asked, "Is there

This college student earned credit for her work on an American farm during the war.

any law that says a yeoman must be a man?" He quickly answered his own question by putting more than 10,000 women into uniform. Some women eventually served with the troops as nurses, Red Cross and Salvation Army workers, ambulance drivers, and canteen hostesses.

Black migration from the South gathers force. Black Americans also found fresh opportunities. For the first time in the nation's history, blacks were invited to participate in a great national undertaking. The beckoning jobs in war factories lured many black people northward and westward. Blacks could find jobs in all the war industries, mainly doing heavy work such as riveting the hulls of ships, cutting coal in the mines, and butchering cattle in the slaughterhouses. Still, the *Christian Recorder*, a black church paper, said in 1917 that the job openings the war created were the best thing that had happened to blacks "since the Emancipation Proclamation."

In the cities of the North, where blacks had traditionally lived in white neighborhoods, large, exclusively black "ghettos" quickly developed. In New York there was Harlem; in Chicago, the South Side; in Cleveland, the Hough section; and so forth. The National Urban League, organized in New York in 1911 with the help of concerned whites, played a significant role in helping southern blacks shift from rural to big-city life. The League shortly had branches throughout the country.

Public opinion is mobilized. Despite strong support for the war effort, some Americans had been against Wilson's declaration of war. Opposition came from some Americans of German and Irish extraction. It also came from pacifists opposed to war, whatever the purpose, as well as from radical groups who regarded the struggle solely as a means of defending capitalism.

To counter the voices of opposition, the government took positive steps. It established the Committe on Public Information to "sell" the war to the people. George Creel, a successful journalist, was named to head the Committee. He so dominated it that it became known as the Creel Commit-

tee. To whip up public enthusiasm, the Creel Committee enlisted poster artists, college professors, and novelists. An army of 75,000 lecturers delivered "Four-Minute Speeches" — in theaters, at church gatherings, at union meetings — on such topics as "Why We Are Fighting" and "The Meaning of America."

Critics charged that the Creel Committee was attempting for the first time in American history to manipulate public opinion. Creel stirred up much hatred of Germans, suggesting that German spies were everywhere. Still, those Americans who agreed with Wilson that a better world would come from the struggle, admired Creel's work in publicizing at home and abroad the President's stirring speeches.

A climate of intolerance is fostered. Just before the United States entered the conflict, President Wilson expressed his concern to an editor. "Lead this people into war," he said, "and they'll forget there ever was such a thing as tolerance." The dire prophecy was partly fulfilled when Congress made stern arrangements for dealing with disloyal individuals. The Espionage Act (1917) provided severe punishment for people engaging in spying, sabotage, or obstruction of the war effort. The Sedition Act (1918) extended these penalties to individuals who made disloyal remarks. In time, over 1,500 people were arrested for sedition. Eugene Debs (page 478), who expressed pacifist sentiments, was sent to prison for violation of the Espionage Act. (He received a presidential pardon in 1921.)

Local vigilante committees sometimes took things into their own hands. In one midwestern town, a minister who had been forbidden to use German was caught speaking it as he comforted a dying woman who spoke only German. Local anti-German feeling was so great that he was tarred, feathered, and run out of town. In many places throughout the country, schools dropped the teaching of German. The playing of music by German composers was commonly banned. On menus everywhere sauerkraut became "liberty cabbage" and hamburgers became "Salisbury steak."

The Fourteen Points (1917)

Open covenants of peace, openly arrived at, after which there shall be no private international understandings of any kind, but diplomacy shall proceed always frankly and in public view.

Absolute freedom of navigation upon the seas . . . in peace and in war. . . .

The removal, so far as possible, of all economic barriers and the establishment of an equality of trade conditions among all the nations. . . .

Adequate guarantees given and taken that national armaments will be reduced. . . .

A free, open-minded, and absolutely impartial adjustment of all colonial claims, based upon . . . the principle that . . . the interests of the populations concerned must have equal weight with the . . . claims of the government whose title is to be determined.

A general association of nations must be formed under specific covenants for the purpose of affording mutual guarantees of political independence and territorial integrity to great and small states alike.

Wilson issues the Fourteen Points. Still, the war aroused high-mindedness in Americans too. Millions found inspiration in Wilson's public addresses. In them he put on display his idealism, his vision, and his gift of language. None of them was more influential than the statement of war aims that became known as the "Fourteen Points." He delivered it before Congress on January 8, 1918.

In the speech — the main parts of which are summarized above — the President tried to appeal to thinking people everywhere. He set forth fourteen "points" or proposals for helping to reduce the risk of war in the future. The first five were general in scope. They called for an end to secret diplomacy; the establishment of freedom of the seas; the removal of economic barriers to international trade; the reduction of arms; and a readjustment of "all colonial claims, based upon . . . the interests of the populations concerned. . . ." The eight points that followed called for specific territorial changes to relieve the distress of various peoples living under foreign domination. In recommending, for example, independence for Poland, Wilson was advancing the principle of "national self-determination," an end being pursued by a number of nationalities in Europe.

The fourteenth point expressed Wilson's chief goal for the postwar world: the creation of a League of Nations. Wilson, a year earlier, in the "peace without victory" speech, had stated his belief that the United States would willingly join a "League for Peace." Such an organization, Wilson was convinced, would help guarantee the political independence and territorial security of all countries, small as well as great.

SECTION REVIEW

1. Vocabulary: *bureaucracy.*
2. Why were Wilson's efforts to end the war in Europe unsuccessful?
3. What events led the United States to declare war against Germany?
4. (a) How did the United States strengthen its armed forces? (b) What agencies administered the war effort on the home front? (c) What steps were taken to finance the war?
5. (a) What opportunities did the war create for women? (b) For black Americans?
6. (a) How was public opinion mobilized? (b) What were the Espionage and Sedition acts?
7. What were the Fourteen Points?

569

4 The United States Helps Win the War

By early 1918 the war had reached a decisive stage. The Germans, in control of most of Belgium and northern France, were attempting once again to take Paris. The Allies' situation seemed desperate. To make matters worse, at the end of 1917 Italy had been decisively defeated by Austrian troops at the Battle of Caporetto, losing 300,000 men and 30,000 pieces of artillery.

A new government comes to power in Russia. Adding to the Allies' woes, Russia was about to leave the war. The Kerensky government (page 565) had been driven from power in November, 1917, by a small party called the Bolsheviks. The Russian people, tired and exhausted, had lost their heart for fighting. They responded to the slogan of the Bolsheviks: "Peace, Land, Bread." They were enticed, too, by the Bolsheviks' announced plan to create a government of workers, soldiers, and peasants.

The new regime signed a humiliating peace treaty with Germany at the city of Brest-Litovsk. The Germans were now free to transfer to the Western Front the huge armies on duty in the east. The Bolsheviks, meanwhile, established a Communist dictatorship in Russia, doing away with private ownership of property and allowing no opposition parties, no free elections, and no freedom of the press, speech, or religion.[3]

American forces arrive in Europe. Upon entering the war, the United States had speedily organized an American Expeditionary Force, called the AEF for short. Its commander was John J. Pershing, now 57 years old and a major general. Pershing had made the headlines in 1906 when President Roosevelt "jumped" him in rank from captain to brigadier general. He became a national name in 1916 by his pursuit of Pancho Villa (page 556). Because he had commanded black troops early in his career, he had acquired the nickname "Black Jack."

The American soldiers, "Yanks" as they were known,[4] were untried but enthusiastic. Their arrival on French soil, beginning in June, 1917, heartened the Allies and shook the morale of the Germans. France's Marshal Ferdinand Foch (FOHSH), the supreme commander of the Allied forces, was impressed by the quality of the Americans. He hoped to use them to fill in the badly mauled ranks of the Allies. Reluctantly, he honored Pershing's instructions from Washington that the United States forces must fight as a separate unit.

The Germans quickly discovered the fighting ability of the Yanks. In the first offensive in which Americans were engaged, they captured from the Germans the key town of Cantigny (kahn-tee-NYEE) on the road to Paris.

Germany launches an offensive. At the beginning of June, 1918, the Germans had fought to within about fifty miles of the French capital. They now knew they must deliver a knockout blow before more Amer-

United States Army pilots first downed German aircraft in April, 1918. The excitement of air combat contrasted greatly with the grimness of trench warfare.

---

[3]In 1922 the Bolsheviks changed the official name of Russia to the Union of Soviet Socialist Republics. It is often referred to as the Soviet Union or the USSR.
[4]They also were called "doughboys." The word probably originated from the white dust of the adobe soil in the Southwest that covered mounted troops. From early days, the Spanish had applied the word *adobe* to all military people. The step from there to "dobie" and then to "doughboy" was short.

Americans to the Front

An American war correspondent and writer, Frederick Palmer, was with the United States forces when they landed in France in 1917. In his book *America in France*, he described the scene as the first American troops took their place alongside the French in the front-line trenches.

We were moved into the trenches with all the care of father teaching son to swim. The French are thorough people. They believe in no short cuts to learning, but in gradual process.

Our battalions, three at a time, were to be placed between French battalions in the line in what was to be distinctly considered as another step in our course of training. Every American battery was to be paired off with a French battery. The French regulated the amount of our artillery fire and their observers named our targets.

The artillery moved up on the night of October 22nd. Battery C, of the Sixth Field Artillery, wanted the honor of firing the first shot of the war. Without waiting to go into position at the time set, the men dragged a gun forward in the early morning and sent a shell at the enemy. There was no particular target. The aim was in the general direction of Berlin.

The night of October 23rd, when our infantry left their barracks for the trenches, was chill and rainy. Down the street you heard a sturdy rhythmic tread; and then a moving shadow, taking form in the darkness, developed into a column of soldiers with their faces much alike in the gloom. For all they knew they might be going into violent action. They had been drilled and drilled and schooled and lectured, warned

An American doughboy

by their veteran instructors what a tremendous, formidable enemy, with all his preparation and experience, the German was in the complicated techniques of trench warfare, with its sudden surprises of raid and artillery concentration.

There was nothing downhearted about their mood. They were worried lest they should make a mistake and not remember all their training in case of a crisis. It did not matter so much to them that they might be killed as they might be killed in a manner that was contrary to instruction. If they had been told to charge machine guns then and there, I think that they would have let out the cry of hounds off the leash.

ican divisions were put into action. In this crucial moment for the Allies, doughboys were pressed into action in the Battle of Chateau-Thierry (shah-TOH tyeh-REE), where they helped the French halt the enemy advance.

Substantial numbers of Americans also took part in recapturing Belleau Wood from the Germans — west of Chateau-Thierry and on the path to Paris too. In the struggle,

United States marines obeyed their orders: "We dig no trenches to fall back on. The marines will hold where they stand."

An Allied counteroffensive helps win the war. By the end of July, the German offensive had finally been slowed. Then, in the Second Battle of the Marne, the Allies, reinforced by 85,000 Americans, halted the Germans. The tide of the war was turning.

571

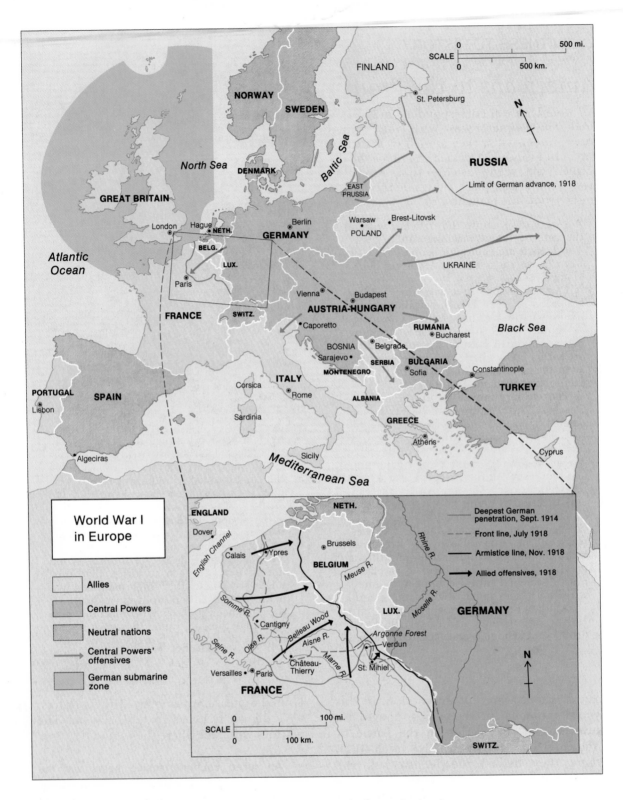

World War I in Europe

Legend:
- Allies
- Central Powers
- Neutral nations
- Central Powers' offensives
- German submarine zone

Inset map legend:
- Deepest German penetration, Sept. 1914
- Front line, July 1918
- Armistice line, Nov. 1918
- Allied offensives, 1918

In the east, Germany achieved relatively easy victories over Russia's disorganized and ill-equipped forces. In the west, the Allied powers defended their positions in northern France. The inset map shows that the line of deepest German penetration in 1914 was barely a hundred miles from the line of armistice four years later.

The Allies began to force the Germans into retreat on a line from the Aisne (AYN) River to the Marne (map, page 572). About 270,000 United States troops participated in this mighty effort.

The first major United States offensive took place in September, 1918, as part of the final stages of the war. The Americans were assigned the task of driving the Germans out of the St. Mihiel (SAN mee-YEL) area, which had been held by the enemy since 1914. After four days of bloody fighting that cost 7,000 American lives, St. Mihiel came under American control.

The troops in the St. Mihiel offensive were aided by airplanes that strafed the enemy and helped spot artillery positions. This was the first significant use of air support in the history of warfare. The planes were English or French, but many of the fliers were American. Most of them were members of the Lafayette Escadrille, under the command of Colonel "Billy" Mitchell. The Escadrille was a group of devil-may-care young men who had originally entered the French air service and had only recently transferred to the United States forces. Because they expected their lives to be short, they flew without parachutes. The first of them killed in action was a 21-year-old New Yorker named Edmond Genêt, the great-great grandson of Citizen Genêt (page 184). Some of the pilots became public heroes — like Eddie Rickenbacker, who was eventually credited with shooting down 26 German planes.

American forces were now sent to the area between the Meuse River and the Argonne Forest. The attack, launched on September 26, 1918, was part of a general Allied offensive.

Over a million Americans were engaged in the Meuse-Argonne operation. In the densely wooded Argonne Forest, the troops often could not see more than a few yards ahead. The Yanks crawled inch by inch over barbed wire covered by heavy undergrowth. The setting was made to order for German machine-gunners. Before the battle was over, the Americans had sustained 120,000 casualties. They had, nevertheless, severely weakened the German military position. In

These American troops waited at St. Mihiel. Under General Pershing, they would soon begin their rigorous drive against the German lines of defense.

this campaign, Alvin C. York of Tennessee became a household name for his exploit of single-handedly taking on an enemy platoon. He captured more than 100 prisoners before the shooting was over.

An artillery captain who earned a reputation for effective leadership in the Argonne campaign was a peppery Missourian named Harry Truman. For brave generalship, Douglas MacArthur won a promotion and a decoration. For his craft in maneuvering troops, Colonel George C. Marshall won the admiration of the Germans as well as of his own superiors. A generation later, these men's lives would again be intertwined in common purpose.

SECTION REVIEW

1. (a) Describe the military situation facing the Allies by the end of 1917. (b) Why did Russia sign a peace treaty with Germany?
2. What part did American troops play in the Allied drive that finally ended the war?

5 The United States Rejects World Leadership

On November 11, 1918, an armistice finally silenced the guns. In the sudden stillness the nations could take stock. The total casualties staggered the imagination: 8.5 million soldiers had been killed on both sides, while an equal number of civilians had lost their lives. The United States had suffered a small number of casualties by comparison with other nations. Still, America had had a preview of what the rest of the twentieth century might be like.

Wilson decides to go to Europe. With the signing of the armistice, Wilson was in excellent spirits. Said one of his Cabinet officers, "He is certainly in splendid humor. And why shouldn't he be, for the world is at his feet, eating out of his hand! No Caesar ever had such a triumph!"

Wilson saw his role as that of peacemaker and shaper of a new order for people everywhere. Domestic politics, however, had set the stage for disappointment. The first blow was delivered by the congressional elections of 1918. Wilson asked for a "vote of confidence" from the voters, that is, for a new Democratic Congress. The American people, for a variety of reasons mostly unconnected with the war, turned him down, as they elected a Republican House and Senate. Many Europeans, and some Americans, wondered how Wilson could speak for the world's people now that he had been rejected at home.

A second blow was the growing anger of Republicans. Wilson had decided to attend the peace conference in Europe personally. Some Americans believed it was wrong for him to leave the country, because no President had ever done so. Others were dismayed because no Republicans were being included in the official American peace delegation. Americans of both parties had backed the war effort, Wilson's critics pointed out. Was the fashioning of the peace to be an honor for *Democrats* only? Former President Taft charged that Wilson simply wanted "to hog the whole show."

The weakened support at home did not seem to concern Wilson as he set forth for Paris early in December, 1918. He was certain that he could bring back a peace treaty that the Senate would not dare reject. His reception in Europe would show his critics at home that the world expected him to have his way.

He was right about the fervor with which Europeans greeted him. In Paris his motorcade proceeded under banners reading "Honour to Wilson the Just." Hundreds of thousands of French people cheered him deliriously. The cry "Vive Wilson! Vive Wilson! [Long live Wilson!]" rolled across Paris like a tidal wave. In other countries he was welcomed with similar frenzy. Wounded soldiers in Italy even reached to touch him in hope of being miraculously healed.

The Allies disagree over terms of peace. Wilson's colleagues among the Allied leaders did not share the popular enthusiasm for the American President; nor did they share Wilson's idealism. French premier Georges Clemenceau (kleh-mahn-SOH), "the tiger of France," was 77 years old. Clemenceau had seen his country overrun by German troops in 1870 and again in 1914. Now he wanted no visionary peace, but a harsh one that would keep Germany from invading his country a third time. David Lloyd George, prime minister of Great Britain, also had little patience for Wilson's high-flown goals. He and Clemenceau privately made sarcastic comments about the Fourteen Points, with Clemenceau calling them "the Fourteen Commandments" and adding that "even the Almighty had only Ten." The Italian premier, also at Paris, was Vittorio Orlando. His chief aim was to acquire the territories that the other Allies had secretly promised Italy in return for entering the war in 1915. Of the Big Four leaders, then, President Wilson often stood alone against Clemenceau, Lloyd George, and Orlando.

Peace treaties are written. Representatives from 27 nations attended the peace conference held in Paris, but matters were

574

The Treaty of Versailles officially ended the First World War. The treaty was signed on June 28, 1919, in the elegant Hall of Mirrors at the Palace of Versailles, near Paris. In this painting Woodrow Wilson, Georges Clemenceau, and David Lloyd George (seated center, left to right) look on as the German representatives sign.

decided by the Big Four. For instance, in treaties signed with the Central Powers, they redrew the boundary lines of eastern Europe to create new, independent countries. These countries were formed out of the defeated German, Austro-Hungarian, Russian, and Turkish empires. The new countries were Poland, Czechoslovakia, Finland, Yugoslavia, Estonia, Latvia, and Lithuania. In addition, Austria and Hungary became separate states (map, page 577).

Despite Wilson's earlier call for a "peace without victory," the Versailles Treaty (vehr-SIGH),[5] in the end, forced harsh peace terms on Germany. The treaty made Germany accept responsibility for having started the war. Germany had to agree to remain disarmed. It was deprived of its colonies. The new German government was saddled with staggering *repara-*

tions — the bill for war damages. Germany ultimately was assessed $33 billion.

The Covenant of the League of Nations establishes a world organization. Although the Versailles Treaty was harsher than Wilson had wished, he was able to have some of his ideas incorporated in it. To him the most important of these was the Covenant (terms of agreement) of the League of Nations. The Covenant provided for a League of Nations which had the task of keeping peace in the world. The "heart" of the Covenant was Article X, which made the members of the League promise to defend one another's territory against aggression. The League would have a permanent Secretariat (that is, an administrative and secretarial staff), an Assembly, and a Council. The Assembly would consist of representatives from the member nations of the League, each having one vote. The Council, composed of delegates from the United States, Great Britain,

---

[5]The treaty was signed at the Palace of Versailles, just outside the city of Paris.

France, Italy, Japan, and four non-permanent members chosen by the Assembly, would be given the duty of mediating disputes between members and devising plans for bringing about disarmament.

The League was Wilson's proudest effort in behalf of world peace. Still, he gave his attention to other matters, for he aimed to be remembered as the architect of a world without war. Believing that imperialism had been a powerful cause of the struggle just ended, he succeeded in preventing the former colonies of Germany and Turkey from being handed over to the Allies. Instead, on his suggestion, they were made part of a **mandate system.** Under this system, specially named countries, answerable to the League, were assigned the task of preparing the colonies for self-government.

Opposition to the League arises in the Senate. When Wilson eloquently presented the Versailles Treaty to the Senate in July, 1919, opposition to it had already been organized. (Two senators failed even to rise out of courtesy to the President when he entered the chamber.) A few months earlier, more than a third of the senators had signed a statement asserting that the treaty was not acceptable in the form then proposed.

The critics' chief objection was to the League Covenant, which Wilson insisted was indispensable to the treaty. Opponents of the League concentrated their attack on Article X. They maintained that if the United States joined the League, the Monroe Doctrine and the nation's power to declare war and peace would be destroyed. Some people even argued that the United States would be drawn into wars to save the British Empire. One angry senator denounced the President as "Britain's tool — a dodger and a cheater." Another said the President's words were mere "soap bubbles of oratory." Wilson replied that the nation must "follow the vision" of world leadership. As the battle over ratification proceeded, Wilson said of the hostile senators, "They have poisoned the wells of public sentiment."

The senators who opposed the treaty were divided into two main groups. One,

known as the "irreconcilables," or "bitter-enders," included Hiram Johnson of California, William E. Borah of Idaho, and Robert M. La Follette of Wisconsin. They were determined to battle to the bitter end against acceptance of the treaty with the League under any conditions.

A second group, called "reservationists," was led by Henry Cabot Lodge of Massachusetts. Lodge's followers favored participation in the League, provided certain reservations (limiting conditions) were agreed to that would protect American national interests. Lodge drew up a list of fourteen such reservations. Many people were sure that Lodge, who envied and disliked Wilson, was spitefully mocking the President's Fourteen Points.

Wilson appeals to the American people. In the face of senatorial opposition, Wilson grew stubborn and uncompromising. The series of mild strokes he apparently had suffered beginning in the 1890's may have begun affecting his personality. Gone was the gracious manner he often displayed. Now, when urged to accept the Lodge reservations, he shouted, "Accept the treaty with the *Lodge* reservations? Never! Never!"

In September, against the counsel of his advisers, Wilson set out on a speaking tour of the Middle West and West to win public support. Even a much younger man in excellent health would have been taxed by Wilson's exhausting schedule. With his usual eloquence, Wilson spoke of his glowing dream. He told an audience in Ohio, "When this treaty is accepted, men in khaki will not have to cross the seas again." He seemed to be making progress among his listeners. However, the traveling and speaking were wearing him out — and he seemed near collapse.

After addressing an audience in Colorado on September 25, 1919, Wilson spent a distressful night. His doctor and his wife appealed to him to break off the tour. He was concerned that his opponents would call him a quitter, but he agreed to return to the White House. There, on the night of October 2, he suffered a stroke that paralyzed his left side.

Wilson's advisers tried to keep from the public the severity of the President's illness. Mrs. Wilson carefully screened her husband's visitors and even dealt with official documents. Still, when she urged him to compromise on the League issue, he would not yield. "Little girl, don't you desert me; that I cannot stand," he pleaded.

The treaty is defeated. The original favorable sentiment toward the League began to wane. Other issues seemed more pressing: the world-wide epidemic of "Spanish flu," which cost half a million lives in the United States alone; labor disputes in the coal mines and the steel mills; a fear of radicalism after the Bolshevik Revolution in Russia; and the question of how to dispose of the railroads (which were still in government hands). The public was more interested in reading about the exploits of a young heavyweight boxer named Jack Dempsey and a Boston Red Sox player named Babe Ruth, who was attracting crowds with his home-run hitting.

When the Senate voted on the Versailles Treaty on November 19, 1919, with the Lodge reservations, a combination of Wilson Democrats and "irreconcilables" defeated it. A vote on the treaty *without* the Lodge reservations also failed. Upon hearing the news, Wilson said quietly, "They have shamed us in the eyes of the world." Soon afterward, Congress passed a resolution declaring the war with Germany ended. Wilson, never angrier, vetoed it, calling it a "stain upon the gallantry and honor of the United States." (In 1921, a new President signed a similar resolution and the war with Germany was officially over.)

As his administration drew to a close, Wilson, now only a shadow of his former self, waited hopefully for the election of 1920. He was confident the Democrats would win handsomely and that a Democratic-controlled Senate would ratify the Versailles Treaty. In the meantime, Wilson was satisfied with the fight he had waged — although he had never been a good loser. "I would rather fail in a cause that will ultimately triumph than triumph in a cause that will ultimately fail," he said.

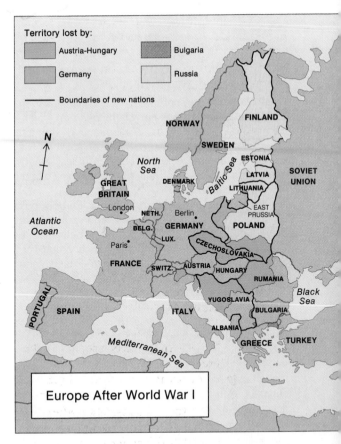

Europe After World War I

The map of eastern Europe, altered by treaties in 1919, looked vastly different than it did before the war.

When Wilson returned from Paris after the peace conference, a newspaper had commented sarcastically: "Just think, we are going to have a President all by ourselves from now on." Many Americans must have shared this sentiment by 1920. They wanted to go back to "the good old days." The zeal to crusade abroad had vanished.

SECTION REVIEW

1. Vocabulary: *reparations, mandate system.*
2. (a) What evidence was there of weakened support at home for Wilson's peace plans? (b) What were the positions of France, Great Britain, and Italy concerning a peace treaty? (c) What were the terms of the Versailles Treaty?
3. (a) Describe the organization of the League of Nations. (b) For what reasons did opposition to the League arise in Congress? (c) What was the fate of the Versailles Treaty in the Senate?

577

Chapter 24 Review

Summary

When Woodrow Wilson entered the White House in 1913, the nation's attention was focused on American responsibilities in the Caribbean. Wilson followed the interventionist policies established by earlier Presidents. During his years in office, American troops were sent to Haiti, the Dominican Republic, and then to Mexico.

In 1914 the outbreak of fighting in Europe took Americans by surprise. Rivalries among the great powers of Europe had finally led to war between the Central Powers (Germany, Austria-Hungary, and Turkey) and the Allies (France, Britain, Russia, and Italy). Although President Wilson declared that the United States would remain neutral, most Americans strongly favored the Allies. During the conflict, Germany ordered its submarines to prevent American supplies from reaching Britain and France. When American lives were lost with the sinking of the *Lusitania* and other ships, Wilson's protests brought a temporary halt to the submarine attacks. The resumption of unrestricted submarine warfare in 1917 finally brought the United States into the conflict on the side of the Allies.

Following the declaration of war, the nation's armed forces were strengthened by a draft, and industry was placed under central control. Support for the war was mobilized by the Creel Committee, while the Espionage and Sedition acts were passed to control dissent. Wilson made clear his administration's war aims when he issued the Fourteen Points.

Although the first American fighting units arrived in France in June, 1917, they did not become engaged in heavy combat until the following spring. At that time they helped turn back the last offensive staged by Germany. An Allied counteroffensive in the summer of 1918, in which over one million American troops took part, led to Germany's call for an armistice on November 11, 1918.

President Wilson went to Europe for the peace conference and was hailed as a hero by the European people. Disagreement over the terms of the peace treaty arose, however, with Wilson trying to impose his Fourteen Points on the other Allied leaders. He did succeed in getting the Covenant of the League of Nations accepted as part of the peace settlement, and returned home to present the Versailles Treaty to the Senate for ratification. There he was greeted by intense opposition from senators who objected to American involvement in an international organization. The President toured the country to encourage support for the League but suffered a stroke during his journey. The treaty was defeated, and Wilson left office a disappointed man.

Vocabulary and Important Terms

1. "watchful waiting"
2. Central Powers
3. Allies
4. Schlieffen plan
5. U-boat
6. *Sussex* pledge
7. *Arabic* pledge
8. Zimmermann telegram
9. Selective Service Act
10. convoy
11. bureaucracy
12. Liberty Bonds
13. National Urban League
14. Creel Committee
15. Espionage Act
16. Sedition Act
17. Fourteen Points
18. Bolsheviks
19. Treaty of Versailles
20. reparations
21. League of Nations
22. mandate system

Discussion Questions

1. (a) Why did President Wilson try to influence events in Mexico? (b) What steps did he take?
2. (a) What was the reaction of most Americans to the news of war in Europe? (b) Why did the American people's sympathy with the Allied cause grow as the war progressed?
3. (a) According to international law, to what rights was the United States entitled as a neutral nation? (b) How did the United States respond to Germany's announcement early in the war that it would sink all vessels in waters around the British Isles? (c) On what occasions prior to entering the war did the United States restate its position on German submarine warfare? (d) Why did Germany decide in early 1917 to resume unrestricted submarine warfare, and what was the result of this decision?
4. (a) In his war message to Congress, what did President Wilson say were the main reasons for going to war against Germany? (b) What phrase became America's rallying cry? (c) What was the attitude of the public regarding United States entry into the war? (d) What did Americans believe the war would accomplish?
5. (a) What was the state of American preparedness when the United States entered the war? (b) Why did the military situation in Europe make it essential that the United States mobilize its armed forces quickly? (c) In what areas of American life was the role of the federal government expanded during the war years?

6. (a) What contributions did the United States make to the Allied war effort? (b) In what battles did American troops play a key role?

7. (a) Why did Woodrow Wilson decide to go to Europe when the war was over? (b) What feelings at home and among Allied leaders frustrated Wilson's goal of becoming a peacemaker? (c) In what ways did the Versailles Treaty favor the Allies?

8. (a) What two groups of senators opposed the Versailles Treaty? (b) How did Wilson respond to senatorial opposition? (c) What action did the Senate finally take concerning the Versailles Treaty?

9. (a) What did Woodrow Wilson believe were his main accomplishments? (b) How had the outlook of the American people changed by 1920?

Relating Past to Present

1. What opportunities are there for American Presidents to play the role of peacemaker in the world today? What recent Presidents have tried to serve as peacemaker? What successes have they had?

2. What is the present-day status of each of the countries created at the end of World War I (page 577)?

Studying Local History

What contributions did people in your community make to the American war effort during World War I? What memorials of the First World War are in or near your community?

Using History Skills

1. *Comparing maps.* Compare the map of Europe during World War I (page 572) with the map of Europe as it was redrawn after the war (page 577). (a) Which countries gained territory at the end of the war? (b) Which countries lost territory? (c) What new nations were established? (d) Which country was divided in two?

2. *Reading source material.* Study Frederick Palmer's description of action in World War I on page 571. (a) What was the relationship between the French troops and the Americans? (b) What was the mood of the American troops as they took their positions in the trenches? (c) What was their main worry? (d) How extensive was the cooperation between the French and American forces? Explain your answer.

WORLD SCENE

The World at War

Hostilities during the First World War were not confined to Europe. The war also spread to the colonial empires.

Fighting in the Middle East. A leading concern of the British throughout the First World War was the protection of their interests in Egypt. In particular, Britain was determined to keep the Suez Canal out of German hands. When the Ottoman Turks, who controlled much of the Middle East, allied themselves with Germany, they presented a formidable threat to Egypt. To prepare for a campaign to drive the Turkish and German forces out of the Middle East, the British constructed roads and a railroad leading from the Nile to the Sinai Peninsula.

The British launched their attack in November, 1916, but were stalled by a Turkish-German force at Gaza in April, 1917. A magnetic young British colonel named T. E. Lawrence, now remembered as Lawrence of Arabia, succeeded, however, in persuading Arab chieftains to help the British defeat the Turks. With Arab help, Britain was able to drive the Turks out of Palestine and Syria, and then force Turkey to withdraw from the war. The defeat of the Turks ended their four-centuries-old grip on the Middle East.

Fighting in East Africa. At the outbreak of the First World War, the German colony of East Africa had for its defense the warship *Königsburg* and an army consisting of 260 German soldiers and 4,600 African troops. This force was led by Colonel Paul von Lettow-Vorbeck. The British moved quickly to seize Germany's African possessions, but Lettow-Vorbeck and his men put up a spirited defense.

The little German army led the British on a never-ending chase through swamps and forests and across mountains. Lettow-Vorbeck used hit-and-run tactics to disrupt British supply lines and communications.

Lettow-Vorbeck's men eluded the British for four years. Only when the general received news of the armistice in November, 1918, did he surrender. In Germany, he was recognized as a national hero.

UNIT 6 REVIEW

Important Dates

1867   Alaska purchased.
1889   Jane Addams founds Hull House.
1890   First Pan-American Congress meets.
1895   Venezuelan boundary dispute.
1896   *Plessy v. Ferguson.*
1898   Spanish-American War.
          Hawaii annexed.
1899   Open Door Policy in China announced.
1900   Boxer Rebellion.
1901   Theodore Roosevelt becomes President.
1903   Right of way through Panama acquired.
1904   Roosevelt Corollary.
1905   Treaty of Portsmouth ends
          Russo-Japanese War.
1906   Pure Food and Drug Act.
1910   NAACP formed.
1911   National Urban League organized.
1912   Wilson elected President.
1913   Federal Reserve Act.
1914   Panama Canal opened.
          World War I begins in Europe.
1915   The *Lusitania* sunk.
1916   Border campaign against Villa.
1917   United States enters World War I.
1918   Armistice ends World War I.
1919   Treaty of Versailles.

Review Questions

1.   (a) Why did the views of some Americans regarding overseas territories change between the end of the Civil War and the beginning of the twentieth century? (b) What territories did the United States acquire during those years?

2.   (a) Why did the United States begin to take an interest in the Far East in the late 1800's? (b) In what ways did the United States become involved with China and Japan in the late nineteenth and early twentieth centuries?

3.   (a) In what ways did the United States seek to expand its role in Latin America during the post-Civil War period? (b) During the administrations of Roosevelt, Taft, and Wilson?

4.   (a) What political reforms did the progressives bring about at the local, state, and national levels? (b) How did those reforms enable citizens to participate more directly in the affairs of government?

5.   (a) What obstacles did black Americans face during the late nineteenth and early twentieth centuries? (b) How did black leaders differ in their response to the situation? (c) What progress did blacks make within American society, especially during the First World War?

6.   (a) What activities helped to bring about national suffrage for women? (b) When the United States entered World War I, what contributions did women make to the effort?

7.   (a) Before 1917, to what extent were the American people "neutral in fact as well as in name" when it came to favoring sides in World War I? (b) Why did the United States finally enter the war? (c) What contributions did America make to the Allied victory?

8.   (a) What were Wilson's goals at the time the United States entered World War I? (b) At the end of the war, what opposition to his plans did he encounter both at home and abroad? (c) Which of his goals were accomplished, and which were not?

Projects

1.   On an outline map of the world, indicate the territories that were gained by the United States between 1867 and 1917. Give the date each became an American possession, and tell how each territory was acquired.

2.   Create a set of three handbills, one each for the candidacies of William Howard Taft, Woodrow Wilson, and Theodore Roosevelt in the election of 1912. On these handbills include pictures, slogans, and other information that illustrate the political positions of each of the three presidential candidates and his respective party.

3.   Make a model of one of the new weapons introduced during World War I. Your model might be of a submarine, an airplane, a tank, or of some other World War I innovation. Show your model to the class and explain how it affected warfare.

4.   Find out more about the shaping of public opinion at home during World War I by reading the words to songs that encouraged the Allied war effort and by locating posters that encouraged Americans to buy Liberty Bonds, to conserve food and fuel, to enlist in the armed forces, to aid wartime agencies, and to support in all other ways the American war effort. Share this information with the class.

5.   Participate in a classroom debate on the question of whether the United States should have ratified the Versailles Treaty and entered the League of Nations. One group should argue for American participation in the League of Nations, while the other group should argue against membership in the League.

GOOD TIMES, HARD TIMES, AND WAR
1919 – 1945

This generation of Americans has a rendezvous with destiny.

FRANKLIN D. ROOSEVELT, 1936

A Roaring Decade

1919 – 1929

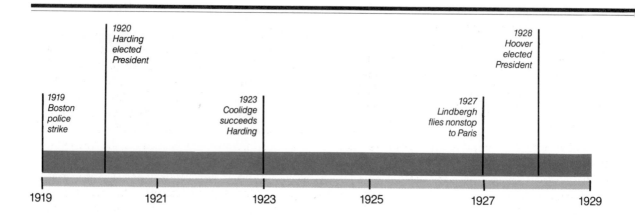

CHAPTER OUTLINE

1. The postwar years are marked by political and economic unrest.

2. The Republicans provide presidential leadership during the 1920's.

3. American society undergoes rapid change.

When the "doughboys" returned from Europe in 1919, Americans felt satisfaction and relief. The United States had been tested in battle overseas and had triumphed. Millions of citizens were convinced that the war had truly been the "war to end war." Now they looked forward to better and calmer days. They also hoped for a return to more familiar times. They were tired of Wilson's idealistic struggle for peace in the world and reform at home.

Nevertheless, in the postwar era the nation underwent rapid change. Some of it resulted from the economic downturn of the early 1920's, marked by distress among farmers and by labor unrest. Some of it came from the continued growth of cities at the expense of rural America. As the decade wore on, change produced conflict and confusion. Many older people were shocked by what they saw: the boldness of young people; open disrespect for the law; and the many new ways of working, living, and thinking.

Although times were hard for farmers and some other groups, most Americans were prosperous during the 1920's. The majority of Americans were now living in cities. The air was filled with the sounds of factories, radios, telephones, phonographs, automobiles, "talking" pictures, crowds of cheering sports fans, airplanes, electrical appliances — and occasionally a raucous mob or a gangster's machine gun. This noisy, fast-paced decade has been called the "Roaring Twenties."

1 The Postwar Years Are Marked by Political and Economic Unrest

Within a few months after the armistice ended the First World War, over three million Americans were discharged from the armed forces. In the same period, hundreds of thousands of wartime workers were cut from the payrolls of government and industry. Unemployment suddenly became a serious problem. Farmers, meanwhile, were confronted with sharply falling crop prices. Wheat, which sold for over $2 a bushel in 1919, was selling for 52 cents in 1921. The nation was entering a period of economic and political unrest.

Labor troubles break out. Workers had taken a no-strike pledge when the United States went to war. Since the nation was in a state of emergency, laboring people had agreed not to force their demands until the conflict had ended. Now, with the return of peace, working people had become increasingly discontented. The cost of living had almost doubled since 1916, while in many industries wages lagged behind. Also, factory workers were no longer willing to endure wartime working conditions — which, in the steel industry, consisted of a 69-hour, 7-day work week. They were ready to fight for improvements in their standard of living and in their working conditions. In 1919 there were almost 4,000 strikes, many of them violent.

One of the most dramatic incidents took place when the Boston police went on strike for higher wages and improved working conditions. With the police off the scene, looters had a field day, smashing shop windows and stealing merchandise. The mayor of Boston finally called for troops, and Governor Calvin Coolidge responded by sending the National Guard. Meanwhile, a volunteer corps, largely made up of Harvard students and recently returned veterans, patrolled the streets of the city. Coolidge had moved slowly in the

Many developments in the 1920's had lasting impact. Assembly-line production, particularly in the automobile industry, created new jobs and spurred demand for additional mass-produced items.

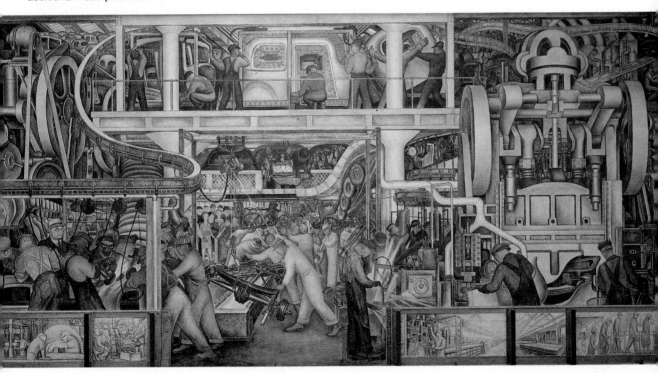

crisis but nevertheless gained a national reputation as a strong leader. He condemned the strike in blunt words: "There is no right to strike against the public safety by anybody, any time, anywhere." President Wilson congratulated the governor on a "victory for law and order."

The trouble in Boston had scarcely ended when two disruptive industrial strikes broke out. The first was called at a plant of the United States Steel Corporation in Indiana. The second, under the shrewd leadership of John L. Lewis, head of the United Mine Workers, was directed against the operators of soft-coal mines.

The steel strike, aimed at organizing the workers in a union, ended in failure. Before it was broken, the strike had involved more than 350,000 workers. The coal strike was halted by a federal court injunction ordering the workers back to their jobs.[1]

The "Red scare" begins. Many Americans had been deeply disturbed by the Bolshevik victory in the Russian Revolution of 1917 (page 570) and the subsequent spread of communism. German Communists were able to hold the city of Berlin for a few days in 1919. For five months Communists ruled Hungary, which had regained its independence from Austria following the First World War. Communist sympathizers in the United States and western Europe seemed to many people to have great power. The labor turmoil alarmed people who feared that America, too, was turning radical.

During the First World War, moreover, people had been made suspicious of anything "un-American." Those old suspicions were now revived, this time with Communists in mind. For instance, the chief speaker for the coal operators declared, without any evidence, that the coal strike was financed by Bolshevik gold on direct orders of the Russian leaders. This feverish suspicion of Communist revolutionaries became known as the "Red scare."

Americans were further distressed by a number of acts of terrorism. One involved Mayor Ole Hanson of Seattle. Hanson had gained nationwide publicity when he had called in troops to break up a strike of shipyard workers in February, 1919. Soon afterward he received a bomb in the mail. Fortunately, the bomb was found before anyone was hurt.

Other terrorist incidents followed. Senator Thomas Hartwick of Georgia, a well-known anti-Communist, received in the mail a bomb that did explode, injuring the maid who opened the package. Another bomb destroyed the home of Attorney General A. Mitchell Palmer. During the spring and summer of 1919, postal authorities discovered more than thirty bombs addressed to citizens known to be opposed to organized labor or unrestricted immigration.

The high point of tension came on September 16, 1920, when a bomb exploded on Wall Street at noon, killing more than thirty people and injuring hundreds of others. Palmer's opinion that Communists were preparing "to rise up and destroy the government at one fell swoop" was widely accepted as true.

Beginning in the fall of 1919, Palmer, a zealous man, led law-enforcement agencies in a series of raids against suspected Communists. Over 6,000 people were arrested, and about 550 of them were deported. During the "Red scare," even governmental officials were not immune from attacks on their civil liberties. In New York in 1920, five Socialists who had been legally elected were denied their seats in the state legislature.

The effects of the "Red scare" linger. Many Americans became concerned about violations of constitutional rights. They said that claims about the dangers of radicalism had proved to be wildly exaggerated. The strong emotions sparked by the national debate over radicalism, nevertheless, lingered throughout the decade. Nowhere was this seen more clearly than in the case of Sacco and Vanzetti.

Nicola Sacco and Bartolomeo Vanzetti, two anarchists, were arrested in 1921. They

---

[1]Although the strikes were failures, the mine workers received a wage increase through arbitration, and a few years later the steel companies agreed to establish an eight-hour workday.

The bombing of Wall Street in 1920 took place near the offices of the financier J. P. Morgan. The terrorist who threw the bomb was never identified.

were charged with the slaying of two uniformed guards in a payroll robbery at a shoe factory near Boston. In a widely publicized trial, the two men were found guilty and condemned to death. After mass demonstrations at home and abroad in protest of the death sentence, they were executed in 1927.

Americans were deeply aroused by the Sacco-Vanzetti case. Many legal experts insisted that there was no solid evidence against the convicted men and that they had been convicted because of their political beliefs. Others were convinced that justice had been done.

New demands are heard for the restriction of immigration. At the same time that Americans debated the dangers of radicalism, the movement to restrict immigration into the United States gained new force. Old values had been rudely shaken by the great wave of immigrants from southern and eastern Europe who poured into American cities from the 1890's until the First World War. As the war industries shut down, scores of factory workers found themselves unemployed. Many were convinced that foreigners, who were so numerous, were occupying jobs that otherwise would be filled by native-born Americans. When disappointment with the outcome of the war set in — for the world had not been made "safe for democracy" — they found it easy to blame foreigners. After all, they asserted, foreigners had caused the war in the first place.

The "Red scare," moreover, had planted the belief that radical ideas were being brought into the country by aliens. Further, because many of the new immigrants were Catholic or Jewish, it was convenient to turn anti-Catholicism and anti-Semitism into "antiforeignism," which was less embarrassing to express. Also, rural people, fearing the spread of urban influence, could show their concern by opposing immigration. They could sense that the newcomers were an important source of strength to the cities. Finally, economic conditions were so discouraging in so many countries that, it was said, "the whole world is preparing to move to the United States."

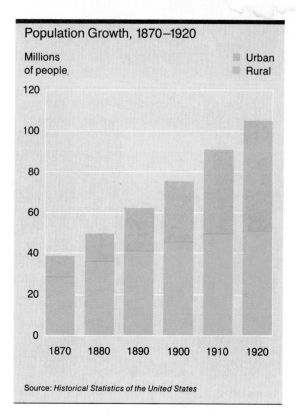

Population Growth, 1870–1920

Millions of people

■ Urban
■ Rural

Source: *Historical Statistics of the United States*

By 1920, an increasing proportion of the American population was living in urban areas.

The first attempt to limit immigration had already been taken. This was the passage of a bill requiring that people seeking to enter the country pass a literacy test. The bill had been vetoed by President Taft in 1913 and by President Wilson in 1915 and again in 1917. Congress, however, enacted it over Wilson's second veto.

Congress establishes immigration quotas. In response to public pressure, Congress passed the Emergency Quota Act of 1921, which restricted the admission of foreigners to 3 percent of the number of each nationality living in the United States in 1910. It also limited the total number of immigrants to about 350,000 a year.

Many considered this law unsatisfactory. The year 1910 was the wrong one to choose, they argued, because by then millions of eastern and southern Europeans had entered the country. The critics insisted that northern and western Europeans made more desirable Americans. Therefore, they

said, the year 1890 was a better year to use because the country had relatively few eastern or southern Europeans at that time. As a result, the National Origins Act was passed in 1924, with the base year set at 1890. The quota was reduced from 3 percent to 2 percent. The law forbade all immigration from Asia — which caused Japan to hold a day of national mourning and anger. The act did not, however, restrict immigration from Canada or Latin America. In 1927 the number of immigrants allowed to enter the country each year was reduced to 150,000.

Black Americans face hostility. During the war years, hundreds of thousands of southern black workers had moved north to find jobs in war industries. Many thousands more served with the American army in Europe. Black veterans, many of them treated as heroes in France, returned home with a sense of pride and with hope for the future. Nevertheless, the demands of blacks for better jobs, housing, and fair treatment were resisted by many whites, who feared the competition of black workers for jobs. Racial tension rose.

The summer of 1919 witnessed more than 25 race riots. In Washington, D.C., Omaha, Chicago, and other cities hundreds of people were injured and dozens were killed. The worst riot was touched off by an incident at a public beach in Chicago. For three days violence raged. By the time it ended, 38 people had been killed and more than 100 injured. Moreover, a vast amount of property had been destroyed.

Black music, art, and literature are recognized. In spite of the obstacles they faced, many black Americans made brilliant contributions to music, poetry, drama, and painting during the 1920's. For the first time in American history, large numbers of black literary and artistic people were recognized for their work by the nation as a whole. Because so many creative blacks lived in the Harlem section of New York City, their outpouring of work was called the "Harlem Renaissance."

The literature of the Harlem Renaissance brought new pride to black people. In 1925, Alain Locke, a professor of philosophy at Howard University, published a collection of poems, stories, and essays entitled *The New Negro.* The "New Negroes" represented in Locke's book were young writers — penetrating, assertive, and imaginative. Locke, through his work, helped bring the literary output of black writers to the attention of the nation at large. The poets Langston Hughes, Claude McKay, and Countee Cullen also contributed significantly to American literature as a whole with works about the treatment of blacks. Along with the historians Carter G. Woodson and W. E. B. Du Bois, these writers and poets explored the story of blacks in America, as well as reminding readers of the African heritage of black people.

A leading spokesman of the new feeling of black pride was Marcus Garvey, a Jamaican who captured the imagination of large numbers of black Americans. He preached in his weekly paper, *Negro World,* that blacks should leave America and build a country of their own in Africa. A splendid organizer, he created the Universal Black Cross Nurses and the Black Star Steamship Line to advance the cause of black nationalism. He also declared himself president of the Empire of Africa and gave impressive titles to the most faithful of his 500,000 followers. Garvey, however, never realized his dream of founding a black homeland. He had, nevertheless, helped awaken among many black people a sense of cultural pride.

The Ku Klux Klan is revived. The race consciousness of the day also produced intolerance. The most flagrant example was the organization of a new Ku Klux Klan. It had no formal connection with the infamous Klan that had flourished during Reconstruction (page 408), but it adopted many of the methods of its predecessor. It revived the

Many black musicians moved from New Orleans to cities like Chicago and New York City in the 1920's. Their new and spontaneous music was a blend of blues, spirituals, and West African rhythms and was called jazz. Louis Armstrong and his band, shown here, recorded some of the finest music of the period.

secret rituals, the white-hooded robes, and the burning of crosses.

A goal of the Ku Klux Klan was to preserve America for white Protestants. Although it resumed the antiblack campaign of the old Klan, the new organization also carried out campaigns of violence against Catholics, Jews, and immigrants.

By the mid-1920's, the Klan claimed a membership of between four and five million Americans. Especially active in the small towns of the South and Midwest, the Klan also had branches in such far-flung states as New York and Oregon. Its power was so extensive that at one point five United States senators and four governors were members. Klan influence, however, faded rapidly after 1925. A scandal involving a powerful Indiana Klan leader, as well as publicity about corruption within the organization, dealt the Klan heavy blows.

The Eighteenth Amendment is added to the Constitution. Nothing better illustrates the clash of values in American society during the 1920's than the national debate over *prohibition* — the effort to eliminate the sale and consumption of alcoholic beverages. The prohibition movement had begun in earnest during the middle of the nineteenth century when the first prohibition legislation was passed in Maine. The early prohibitionists had believed that persuasion through individual contact alone would end the drinking of alcoholic beverages. The work became more systematic in 1874 when the Woman's Christian Temperance Union (WCTU) was organized in an attempt to bring the Protestant churches into the effort. Before long, some of the energy that Protestant ministers had only a few years earlier put into the antislavery crusade was being marshaled against "Demon Rum." The new crusade did not become truly effective, however, until the Anti-Saloon League was established in 1893. The League's lobbying effort was so successful that by 1917, 24 states had passed local-option laws, which allowed individual counties to adopt prohibition. In addition, Michigan, Montana, Nebraska, South Da-

kota, and Utah established prohibition on a state-wide basis.

By the time the United States entered the First World War in 1917, the Anti-Saloon League was lobbying Congress for a constitutional amendment that would forbid the sale of liquor anywhere in the country. The sense of high moral purpose created by entering the war was an advantage for the movement.

On December 18, 1917, Congress approved the Eighteenth Amendment, which prohibited the manufacture, transportation, and sale of beverages containing more than one half of one percent alcohol. By January 16, 1919, two thirds of the states had ratified the amendment, and it went into effect a year later. The Volstead Act was passed in October, 1919, to provide the government with the power to carry out the intent of the amendment.

Prohibition proves hard to enforce. Enforcing prohibition became an enormous and expensive battle. Many otherwise law-abiding Americans violated the Volstead Act. Others who respected the new law themselves refused to help enforce it by reporting people who broke it. In the face of the public's attitude, the enforcement of prohibition became impossible.

By the middle of the 1920's "bootlegging" — the illegal manufacture and sale of liquor — had become big business. Liquor was smuggled into the country from Canada and Mexico or from rum-running vessels lying off the coasts. In place of saloons, "speakeasies" sprang up. In speakeasies, drinks were served to those who were known to the proprietor or who had been sent by other customers.

Criminal gangs are organized. The disregard of prohibition weakened respect for laws in general. Meanwhile, violating the liquor laws was immensely profitable. Gangs of criminals, busily engaged in transporting liquor across state lines, came to be linked together.

The gangs that controlled the liquor traffic were as well-organized as the law-enforcement agencies. The gangsters, moreover, were ruthless in their operations. Violence, including murder, was their method of maintaining discipline in the ranks. Between 1920 and 1929, more than 500 gang-style killings took place in the city of Chicago alone.

The best-known criminal in the prohibition era was Al Capone. He controlled the flow of "bootleg" whiskey into Chicago's 10,000 speakeasies. By 1925 Capone had even gained control of the town government of the Chicago suburb of Cicero.

The task of combating organized crime fell to the Federal Bureau of Investigation, a division of the United States Department of Justice. In 1924 the FBI was placed under the leadership of J. Edgar Hoover, a young lawyer. Eventually, FBI agents worked their way into Capone's gang and collected enough evidence to send him to prison — for income tax evasion.

Despite widespread dissatisfaction with prohibition, few people believed that a movement that had been eighty years in the making would ever be called off. Besides, prohibition had been written into the Constitution. No amendment had ever been removed. A senator said in 1930, "There is as much chance of repealing the Eighteenth Amendment as there is for a hummingbird to fly to the planet Mars with the Washington Monument tied to its tail." The issue, nevertheless, was by no means settled.

SECTION REVIEW

1. Vocabulary: *prohibition*.
2. (a) Why were there labor troubles in the years immediately following the First World War? (b) What major strikes were called in 1919? (c) What was the outcome of each?
3. (a) What was the "Red scare"? (b) What actions were taken against suspected Communists?
4. What steps were taken to restrict immigration during the 1920's?
5. (a) What obstacles did black Americans face after the First World War? (b) What was the Harlem Renaissance?
6. (a) How did the Eighteenth Amendment come to be passed? (b) Why did it prove to be difficult to enforce?

2 The Republicans Provide Presidential Leadership During the 1920's

Throughout the 1920's Republican Presidents occupied the White House. In 1920 the party's candidate was Warren G. Harding, an Ohio senator and newspaper publisher. Many people doubted that Harding would be equal to the job. By comparison with his predecessors — Wilson, Taft, and Roosevelt — Harding appeared to be an uninspired choice for the White House.

Harding is elected President in 1920. Harding selected as his running mate Calvin Coolidge, the governor of Massachusetts who had become a national hero through his handling of the Boston police strike. The Democrats' candidate for President was another Ohio newspaper publisher, James M. Cox. For Vice President the Democrats chose the former Assistant Secretary of the Navy, Franklin D. Roosevelt of New York.

President Harding, shown throwing the first pitch at a baseball game, won the election in 1920 with more than 60 percent of the vote.

589

Personally a genial man, Harding was eager to get along with people. He loved to be among people in a "folksy" way, to shake their hands, and to make long speeches — "bloviating" he called it. He conducted his campaign from the front porch of his home in Ohio. There he met visitors who flocked to catch a glimpse of him. "Keep Warren at home," said a leading Republican politician. "Don't let him make any speeches. If he goes out on tour, somebody's sure to ask him questions, and Warren's just the sort of fool that'll try to answer them."

Handsome and distinguished in appearance, Harding looked every inch a President. He was, furthermore, made-to-order for the nation's new mood. The public seemed tired of the Democrats and all that Wilson represented: internationalism, idealism, and do-goodism. Where Cox and Roosevelt supported United States entry into the League of Nations, Harding called the organization a fraud. He called for a "return to normalcy," meaning, it was assumed, a return to what were considered the calmer days of before the war. When it came to the regulation of big business, Harding promised he would "put less government in business and more business in government."

The election results suggested that Harding had correctly interpreted the public's mood. He received sixteen million votes compared to just nine million for Cox. The Republicans also increased their margins in the House and Senate.

Harding chooses a Cabinet. Harding was not prepared by training or temperament for the tasks he would face in the presidency. Indeed, early in his administration he told a visitor to the White House, "I knew that this job would be too much for me." There was still the peace treaty to be taken care of; unemployment was growing; agriculture demanded help; relations with Latin America, Asia, and Russia had to be restudied; and the problem of war debts needed attention.

Harding knew his limitations and said he would choose some of the "best minds" to help him govern the nation. He appointed to his Cabinet some of the ablest men in his party. Charles Evans Hughes, the Republican presidential candidate in 1916, was appointed Secretary of State. Andrew Mellon, a millionaire and reputed financial wizard, became Secretary of the Treasury, while Henry C. Wallace, a distinguished Iowan, was named Secretary of Agriculture. Herbert Hoover, famous for his relief work during World War I (page 567), was made Secretary of Commerce. Mellon and Hoover set in motion a program to balance the federal budget. They also promoted economy in government and trade opportunities abroad for American manufacturers.

Some of Harding's other appointees were totally wrong for the job. They eventually made his administration the most corrupt since Grant's. Harding had been unable to resist placing many unqualified friends — who became known as the "Ohio gang" — in important government positions. He soon was confessing to a reporter, "I can take care of my enemies. But my friends. . . . They're the ones that keep me walking the floors nights!"

President Harding dies in office. Although troubled and worried by the dishonesty of many of those around him, the exhausted Harding went on a fact-finding trip to the Pacific Northwest and Alaska in 1923. He was visibly ill upon his return from Alaska. Then, on August 2, 1923, he died suddenly in San Francisco of a heart attack.

At the time of Harding's death, Calvin Coolidge was vacationing at his father's home in Vermont. His father, a justice of the peace, administered the oath of office by the light of a kerosene lamp.

Coolidge's coming to the White House may well have saved the Republicans from political disaster. The new President was a man of integrity and character. He was a symbol of the old-fashioned, thrifty, small-town American. Coolidge helped to restore people's faith in the high office.

The nation learns of the Harding scandals. Immediately after his death, Warren Harding was praised by a friend as "one of the knightliest, gentlest, truest men who ever lived in the White House." Disclosures soon showed how wrong that judgment was. The Harding administration had been riddled with the misconduct of important officials. Harding, who was weak but honest himself, had permitted dishonest, self-seeking politicians to occupy positions of trust in the national government.

The most shocking case concerned the leasing of two oil fields. When oil replaced coal as fuel for most of the navy's warships around 1912, oil deposits became vital to national defense. By 1919, the navy was using seven million barrels a year. Still, Secretary of the Interior Albert B. Fall persuaded Harding to transfer from the Department of the Navy to the Department of the Interior certain reserve oil fields in California and Wyoming. Fall then secretly leased the Elk Hills Reserve in California to an oil company controlled by Edward L. Doheny. He also leased the Teapot Dome Reserve in Wyoming to Harry F. Sinclair, another wealthy oilman. For his cooperation, Fall received $100,000 from Doheny for Elk Hills and $300,000 from Sinclair for Teapot Dome. He was also given expensive gifts, including a herd of cattle. After a long trial, Fall was convicted in 1929 of accepting a bribe. He was fined $100,000 and sentenced to a year in prison — the first Cabinet member ever so punished.

Other revelations about the "Ohio gang" now followed. The head of the Office of Alien Property, Jess Smith, and the director of the Veterans' Bureau, Colonel Charles Forbes, had both accepted bribes. Smith busily sold pardons and paroles to criminals as well as performing other "favors." He at times was heard to mutter, "My, how the money rolls in!" In return for payoffs, Forbes systematically sold off government supplies badly needed by former soldiers. His swindling is said to have cost the taxpayers $200 million. Attorney General Daugherty, personally involved in these scandals, was tried twice for accepting bribes. Each time, however, the jury failed to reach a decision, and he went free.

Coolidge is elected President. In 1924 the Republicans nominated "Silent Cal" as

After being informed that President Harding had died, Calvin Coolidge was sworn in by his father, a justice of the peace.

their candidate for President. He ran on the simple slogan "Keep cool with Coolidge."

The Democrats, on the other hand, had a hard time settling on a candidate. They battled fiercely for seventeen days in the sweltering heat of summer at their convention in New York. The struggle centered on William Gibbs McAdoo of California, a former Secretary of the Treasury (page 567), and on Alfred E. Smith, the popular governor of New York.

The conflict reflected the national debate over the changes America was undergoing. Smith, a Roman Catholic, represented the nation's emerging urban centers. He had been born in a slum on New York City's Lower East Side. He was a "wet" — that is, he was opposed to prohibition — and he denounced the Ku Klux Klan without hesitation. McAdoo, on the other hand, was a Protestant. He was a "dry," supported mainly by southern and western delegates who favored prohibition.

After three weeks of deliberation, the exhausted delegates chose John W. Davis of West Virginia on the 103rd ballot. A former member of Congress and ambassador to Great Britain, Davis was a capable man. However, he had no popular following.

Both major parties had turned their backs firmly on the progressivism that had marked their recent past. The voters who

The Farm Tractor

The development of the internal-combustion farm tractor was of great significance for American farmers in the early 1900's. By replacing a team of horses with a tractor, a farmer had the capacity to do many times more work in a fraction of the time once required. With the invention in 1918 of a device called a power takeoff, the tractor could be used to drive many kinds of attachments. This improved, multi-purpose tractor could not only pull a plow and cultivator but also run planters, harvesters, loaders, winches, and even post-hole diggers. The need for draft animals on a farm was greatly reduced. By 1920, there were nearly a quarter million tractors in operation in the United States, and farm families were relieved of the worst drudgery of farming. These gasoline-powered vehicles revolutionized American agriculture and farm life.

continued to seek reform found a champion in Robert M. La Follette who ran on the ticket of the Progressive Party, a new third party. Still, the Progressives, who favored union activity and government ownership of railroads, seemed out of touch with the views of most Americans.

Coolidge was easily elected, carrying 35 of the 48 states. The Republicans also retained control of Congress. The Progressive Party polled nearly five million votes, more than any third party in American history, but carried only La Follette's home state of Wisconsin.

Farmers suffer hard times. Much of the success of Republican candidates during the 1920's can be explained by the booming economy and the rise in the standard of living. The market for industrial and consumer products seemed unlimited, especially as Europe recovered from the war and sought American goods. Business profits were high, and the future of American industry seemed rosy. Millions of Americans felt prosperous.

This prosperity, though, rested on a shaky foundation. Many working people did not have the means to buy the consumer goods that were well advertised and much desired. Nor could most blacks, Mexican Americans, or Indians afford them. Excluded, too, from the general prosperity were the nation's farmers.

In 1920 agriculture slipped into a depression from which it did not emerge for many years. During World War I, the high price of wheat had led farmers to overextend their operations. Then, as European nations resumed production, the price of wheat and other farm crops fell dramatically. Total net income from farming dropped from $9 billion in 1919 to $3.4 billion in 1921. This collapse came just when young men were returning to the farms from the army. Many of the veterans returned to find that the mortgage on the family homestead had been foreclosed.

In 1921, members of Congress from the farm states organized themselves into what was called the farm bloc. The farm bloc had enough votes to hold a commanding posi-

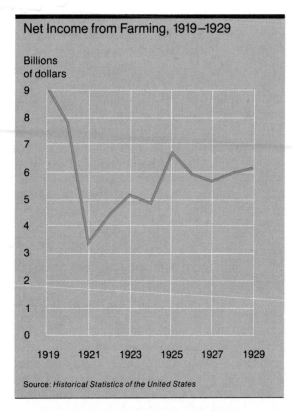

Net Income from Farming, 1919–1929

Billions of dollars

Source: *Historical Statistics of the United States*

The income of farmers plummeted in the 1920's, and they sought legislation to alleviate their difficulties.

tion in Congress and proposed a number of solutions to the farmers' problems. Farmers complained, for instance, that the importation of Canadian foodstuffs had forced down the price of the crops they sold. Attempting to satisfy them, Congress passed an "emergency" tariff on May 27, 1921, that placed duties on wool, sugar, meat, wheat, and corn. This act was replaced the following year by the Fordney-McCumber Act, which raised tariffs generally to the level where they had been during the Taft administration.

The farm bloc succeeded in enacting other important laws. One was the Grain Futures Trading Act, which gave the Secretary of Agriculture broad control over the farm commodity markets, or grain exchanges. A second was a law exempting farm cooperatives from the operation of the antitrust laws. A third was the Agricultural Credits Act of 1923, which made it easier for farmers to obtain loans.

The huge annual crop surpluses, however, remained the biggest problem for farmers. The McNary-Haugen Farm Relief Bill of 1924 sought to raise the domestic price of farm products by setting up a federal farm board that would buy surpluses and then sell them on the world market. Twice President Coolidge vetoed the proposal, objecting to it as government price-fixing. He expressed a general feeling when he said, "Farmers have never made much money. I don't believe we can do much about it."

Signs of economic trouble appear. The farmers were not alone in their difficulties. By 1927 the coal and textile industries were depressed. In 1928 the oil industry, owing to a glut of its products, faced a sharp slump in prices. By late 1929 the construction industry was 25 percent below the performance of the previous year.

The nation as a whole, however, accepted the view of President Coolidge: "The business of America is business." People believed that business would expand and all would be well. In any event, the stock market was regarded as the *real* index of business activity, and it was going up, up, up.

In many fields, corporations made substantial profits, so the price of their stock was high. Some companies, instead of borrowing the money they needed, simply sold new shares of stock. With the additional funds, they enlarged their plants and produced more goods. Again, profits went up and so did stock prices. The cycle then repeated itself. But what would happen if the goods could not be sold because the market for them suddenly collapsed? Also, what would happen if the stock market suddenly fell sharply and stayed down?

A couple of times in 1928 stock prices broke sharply, but each time they rebounded quickly. Nobody seemed to regard these events as indications of things to come. Indeed, twice in 1928 President Coolidge reassuringly declared that stocks were "cheap at current prices."

Herbert Hoover is elected President. Calvin Coolidge's name had become a synonym for the prosperity that many Americans were enjoying. Most people believed he would run for re-election, but in the summer of 1927 he calmly announced, "I do not choose to run for President in 1928." He may have had a feeling that serious economic troubles were about to occur. Indeed, Grace Coolidge, the First Lady, referring to the President, said casually to a friend, "Papa thinks a depression is coming."

Republican eyes turned to Herbert Hoover. Although he lacked a sparkling personality, Hoover was well-regarded for his work as Secretary of Commerce under Harding and Coolidge. He represented big business, rural America, Protestantism, and prohibition.

Born in Iowa in 1874, Hoover had been orphaned at eight and went to live with an uncle in Oregon. In time he became independently wealthy as a mining engineer and business promoter. At the Republican convention in 1928, Hoover was nominated on the first ballot.

Having lost his bid for the Democratic nomination in 1924, Al Smith again drew support from those who championed the interests of the cities. His big-city manner, combined with his religion and his opposition to prohibition, made him popular in many urban areas. An accomplished reformer in New York, Smith seemed the ideal choice for the Democrats. His name was placed in nomination by Franklin Roosevelt, who labeled him the "happy warrior." Smith easily won the nomination on the first ballot.

It was a fierce campaign, with prohibition and Smith's Catholicism as the main issues. Only rarely, however, has the party controlling the White House been defeated when economic conditions have appeared to be good. Herbert Hoover won an overwhelming victory in 1928, receiving 444 electoral votes to Smith's 87.

For the first time since reconstruction days, the Republicans had carried five states in the formerly solid South. Still, the twelve largest cities in the country, carried by the Republicans in 1924, were now in the Democratic column. The Democrats, in other words, had made major gains in the Republican North. If the trend continued, the

Democrats next time might become the nation's majority party.

But why should such a trend continue? During the campaign, Hoover had stated, "We in America today are nearer to the final triumph over poverty than ever before in the history of any land. The poorhouse is vanishing from among us." As Hoover took the oath of office on March 4, 1929, the outlook for the nation seemed bright.

SECTION REVIEW

1. (a) Why was Harding elected President in 1920? (b) What scandals marred his presidency? (c) Who succeeded him in office?
2. (a) Who were the leading candidates for President in 1924? (b) Who won the election?
3. (a) Why did farmers suffer hard times after World War I? (b) What was the farm bloc? (c) How did it try to help farmers?
4. (a) Who was elected President in 1928? (b) Why did most people look to the future with optimism? (c) What signs of coming trouble were appearing?

3 American Society Undergoes Rapid Change

During the 1920's a number of new technological developments transformed American society. None was more important than the automobile. The automobile had already seized the imagination of the American people. Early in his term, President Taft had converted the White House stables into a garage and startled many people by riding around Washington in a "horseless carriage." His chauffeur was under strict orders never to run the machine faster than 20 miles per hour. Warren Harding in 1921 was the first President to ride to his inauguration in an automobile. The day of the elegant horse-drawn carriage for state occasions was over.

Henry Ford puts America on wheels. America, with its wide-open spaces and great distances, was made to order for the automobile. The potential market for car sales was almost unlimited. Any manufacturer who could produce an efficient, easily maintained, and inexpensive car could count on success.

Such a man was Henry Ford. His Model T, eventually the most famous car ever built, was the most revolutionary invention of the young century. The impact of Ford's automobile was comparable in American history to that of the cotton gin.

Ford was a mechanical genius who believed he could make a car that practically everybody could afford. After long experimentation with various designs, he produced the first Model T in 1908. The high-sitting, ungraceful vehicle was practical if not elegant. It soon found a huge market. By 1913 Ford was producing over 500 cars a day, and two years later his one-millionth car was on the road.

Car production grows rapidly. The amazing increase in car production was made possible by the use of the *assembly line.* The assembly line was Henry Ford's most important contribution to American industry. Under this system, the hundreds of parts used in an automobile were manufactured by specialized machines. The parts were then placed on a conveyor belt which passed from worker to worker. As the belt moved along, each worker performed a single operation: fastening mudguard brackets

Henry Ford's Model T was produced in mass volume at low cost, enabling many Americans to buy one.

or installing the engine or simply putting in place a bolt on which the next worker would place a nut. The production of an automobile at Ford's plant was accomplished in 45 such operations. On operation 44 the radiator was filled, and on operation 45 the car was driven off the line. By 1925 Ford had so perfected the process that a car came off the assembly line every ten seconds.

Tourists came to the Ford plant and watched in awe as these cars "for the great multitude" — to use Ford's phrase — rolled in a steady stream from the assembly line. Because Ford cut his price almost every year (the lowest price was $290 in 1924), sales kept rising. He became the most successful manufacturer in history.

Henry Ford had established a minimum wage for his factory employees in 1914: $5 a day, at a time when the national average for unskilled workers was $1 a day and for skilled workers $2.50. This rate of pay seemed excessively high to many of Ford's critics. Ford argued, however, that unless his employees were paid well, they would never be able to buy Ford cars. If some people thought Ford had made a mistake, they were soon surprised. Ford's profits raced even higher. By 1926 he was paying his workers $10 a day.

Powerful competitors of Ford, including Chrysler, Packard, and Studebaker, also achieved remarkable success. General Motors' Chevrolet was making friends too. In addition to being an inexpensive car, the Chevy — as it was popularly called — had a "refined" look copied from high-priced cars like the Cadillac.

Ford himself saw the change in taste and in 1927 ended production of the Model T. The following year he put the Model A on the market to compete with the Chevy.

By 1920 there were about 8 million cars on the road. Ten years later, Americans owned over 23 million cars, and the automotive industry had become the nation's biggest business. General Motors developed the system of introducing a new model each year. Owning an automobile became a mark of personal success. By the late 1920's, having "two cars in every garage" seemed a worthy goal for every American family.

The automobile brings many changes. The automobile made it possible for Americans to travel more widely. Families with automobiles could enjoy picnics and vacations in distant places. This new mobility also meant that people could commute greater distances to their jobs. It meant, too, that young people were beginning to spend less time at home. Many of them, driving their own "tin lizzies," enjoyed more personal freedom than any previous generation of youth. Their new-found freedom led to social changes. The idea, for instance, that a young woman needed a chaperone on a date vanished.

The wide use of the automobile resulted in a doubling of the number of miles of paved roads during the 1920's. At the same time, traffic jams and accidents became common. By 1930 more than half the accidental deaths in the country were caused by auto crashes.

Americans were on wheels to stay. Whereas most people a few years earlier lived and died only a few miles from where they had been born, now they had new choices as to where they would make their home. The automobile produced a boom in the development of suburbs, which created thousands of jobs in the construction industry as homes, schools, libraries, churches, stores, motels, service stations, garages, and post offices were built. By 1930 one out of nine workers had jobs in glass, steel, rubber, or other industries related to automobile production.

Accompanying the rise of the automobile was the development of the trucking industry, which more and more competed with the railroads in the shipment of goods. There were only a million trucks in 1920, but more than three times that number in 1930. Furthermore, in the same decade, the number of buses went from about 18,000 to almost 41,000.

The automobile brought increased demands for petroleum products, and people constantly searched for new oil fields. The modern oil industry had its beginnings at the turn of the century when a huge oil field was found in eastern Texas, just south of Beaumont. For most of his life a Texan named Pattillo Higgins had been convinced that the land in that area contained oil. Sometimes he would take his Sunday school classes to a place named Spindletop, near Beaumont. With a cane he would poke holes in the ground there and light the natural gas as it escaped. Fascinated by the underground gas, he finally bought the land at Spindletop and, along with an Austrian-born mining engineer named Anthony Lucas, began drilling on it.

The determination of the men paid off. On January 10, 1901, a deafening roar shook the earth as oil gushed to the surface. Spindletop was the biggest oil strike that had ever been made. Soon the field was producing between 85,000 and 100,000 barrels of oil daily, and an oil boom was on. Prospectors crowded into Texas, searching for more Spindletops. New fields were found, and soon Texas was the nation's leading oil-producing state.

Mass media creates mass markets. To sell automobiles and all the other products pouring out of America's factories, advertising itself became big business. Advertising created new tastes and persuaded people that they had new needs. More and more Americans measured their status in society by their ability to buy new and more intriguing goods.

The use of advertising slogans and alluring models had started at the turn of the century. As ads whetted the nation's appetites for consumer goods, new customers were also created by the introduction of the installment plan. By selling "on time," merchants expanded the ready market for expensive products such as automobiles, radios, refrigerators, and typewriters.

Movies set the style. The motion-picture industry, also new, played a large part in fastening the mass-production economy on the country. Movie audiences saw their heroes driving up-to-date models of cars, wearing the latest style of clothing, dancing the newest step, and singing the newest tune. Thousands of people imitated what they saw on the motion-picture screen.

In this way the film industry contributed to raising the expectations of average

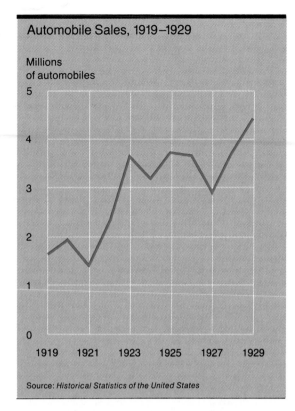

During the 1920's, sales of automobiles more than doubled.

people — and increasing their dissatisfactions. How shabby one's own house seemed in comparison to those in the movies! How carefree the characters appeared, living in mansions without visible means of support and enjoying boundless luxury! Millions of people began to follow the lead of the "stars" in their demands for pleasure, leisure, and material goods. Where people once saved their money for a rainy day — a time of need — they now saved for a sunny day — a time of vacation.

The motion-picture industry had produced its first screen story, *The Great Train Robbery*, in 1903. Soon afterward, a promoter in Pittsburgh set up facilities in a warehouse for projecting one-reel shows, charging five cents admission. These "nickelodeons" spread quickly to other cities. By 1907 nearly every city had a movie theater, and more were being built every year.

The actors and actresses of the screen were constantly in the public eye: the Gish sisters, Charlie Chaplin, Mary Pickford,

Douglas Fairbanks, and many others. Some of their names and even the stories about their lives were made up by promoters — all a part of the make-believe that movies were fostering. Clara Bow, known as the "It" girl, dramatized her glamour daily. She liked to draw attention by driving on the streets of Hollywood in an open convertible, accompanied by seven chow dogs whose color matched her flaming-red hair.

In 1922, forty million movie tickets were being sold each week; by the end of the decade the figure had doubled. The production of motion pictures had quickly become big business.

The radio serves America. The beginning of commercial radio broadcasting went hand-in-hand with the movies in changing American tastes and use of leisure time. In millions of homes, families gathered around the radio to hear Paul Whiteman's orchestra or long-running serials like the Goldbergs with Molly Berg. Others enjoyed hearing songs by the A&P Gypsies or the Connecticut Yankees.

The first commercial radio station was KDKA in Pittsburgh which, on November 2, 1920, broadcast the presidential election returns. In 1922 the White House acquired its first radio. Within a few years the radio was a familiar item in American life.

Radio seemed to speed up American life. The regular broadcasting of news reports gave listeners immediate access to what was going on. People not only knew what their leaders looked like — an element added to political life in the 1880's with the invention of quick methods of reproducing pictures. Now they knew what their leaders sounded like too.

Women have new opportunities. The 1920's also saw the rise of the "new woman." As the decade progressed, women began to experience new freedom and opportunity. Many women who had taken jobs outside the home during the First World War continued to be gainfully employed. Furthermore, the number of fields open to women gradually increased, however slowly.

A giant step toward a new era for women was the ratification in 1920 of the Nineteenth Amendment (page 533). After almost a century of effort, women had at last gained the right to vote. Soon, organizations such as the League of Women Voters were formed to help women participate more fully in political life.

Equally important for many women was the introduction of new labor-saving devices, freeing them from age-old drudgery. Much of this new freedom came from the

New movie theaters opened in every American city. Broadway in New York City was so brightly lighted by movie marquees that it became known as the Great White Way.

A Working Woman

In 1924 a team of sociologists began a pioneering study of life in a typical Midwestern city. In 1929 Robert and Helen Lynd published their work in a book entitled *Middletown: A Study in American Culture.* The following statement was made by a married woman who had two sons and worked six days a week outside her home.

I began to work during the war when everyone else did; we had to meet payments on our house and everything else was getting so high. The mister objected at first, but now he [does not] mind. I'd rather keep on working so my boys can play football and basketball and have spending money their father can't give them. We've built our own home, a nice brown and white bungalow, by a building and loan like every one else does. We have it almost all paid off and it's worth about $6,000.

No, I don't lose out with my neighbors because I work; some of them have jobs and those who don't [have jobs] envy us who do. I have felt better since I worked than ever before in my life. I get up at five-thirty. My husband takes a dinner and the boys buy theirs uptown and I cook supper. We have an electric washing machine, electric iron, and vacuum sweeper. I don't even have to ask my husband any more because I buy these things with my own money. I bought an icebox last year — a big one that holds 125 pounds; most of the time I don't fill it, but we have our folks visit us from back East, and then I do.

We own a $1,200 Studebaker with a nice California top, semi-enclosed. Last

An office worker

summer we all spent our vacation going back to Pennsylvania — taking in Niagara Falls on the way. The two boys want to go to college, and I want them to. I graduated from high school myself, but I feel if I can't give my boys a little more, all my work will have been useless.

---

widespread use of electrical appliances. Nowhere were the effects clearer than in homes equipped with electric irons, refrigerators, vacuum cleaners, and washing machines.

Many women showed how free they were by shortening their skirts and even rolling their stockings to below their knees. In so doing they earned the admiring nickname "flappers." A fashion editor wrote in 1920 that "the American woman . . . has lifted her skirt far beyond any modest limi-

tations." The hem was then nine inches from the ground. It soon reached the knee. Lipstick and rouge, once seen only on actresses, were now used by millions. Many women also decided that hair worn in braids or in a bun was a thing of the past. When a popular dancer named Irene Castle "bobbed" her hair — that is, cut it short — millions of women imitated her.

Fads and sports capture the public imagination. As life speeded up, the nation became

599

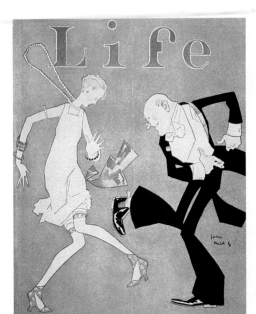

Fads and Spectacles

Americans danced the Charleston in the 1920's, solved crossword puzzles, and cheered when Helen Wills won tennis championships. Pole-sitting drew much attention but was not widely practiced!

more than ever addicted to fads — popular crazes that lasted for a season or two and then faded out. For a time, millions of Americans were caught up in the cross-word-puzzle fad and then in the game of *mah jongg*. The opening in 1922 of the tomb of the Pharaoh Tutankhamen in Egypt led to the popularity of clothing with a "King Tut" motif.

The search for leisure-time activities had much to do with the popularity of organized sports. A reflection of the growing size of cities was the increasing interest in spectator sports. Professional baseball, which had started in 1869, grew in popularity in the 1920's. Yankee Stadium, opened in 1922, became a showcase for Babe Ruth's dramatic home-run hitting. Ruth revolutionized a game that had previously concentrated on base-running and crafty pitching. Professional football and hockey were also introduced in the 1920's, but baseball remained "the national sport."

Other sports also produced popular idols: Bobby Jones in golf, Bill Tilden and Helen Wills in tennis, and Jack Dempsey and Gene Tunney in boxing. In 1926 Gertrude Ederle, the daughter of a New York butcher, became the first American and the first woman to swim the English Channel. New York City lauded her with a homecoming parade upon her return.

The airplane comes of age. The greatest hero of the 1920's, however, was Charles A. Lindbergh, who received the public's acclaim for his solo flight across the Atlantic in 1927. His extraordinary achievement grew out of a series of events that took place early in the twentieth century.

The airplane industry, which was American in origin, had its beginnings in 1903. In that year Orville and Wilbur Wright made a successful flight at Kitty Hawk, North Carolina. During the First World War, airplanes were at first assigned to the signal corps for use in observing enemy movements. By the end of the fighting, however, they were being used in combat.

The first regular airmail route was opened in 1918 between Washington, D.C., and New York. The service was extended within a few years to routes between New York, Chicago, and San Francisco. The planes were owned by the Post Office Department. Beginning in 1925, Congress started the practice, already common in Europe, of subsidizing private airlines to carry the mail.

Commercial air travel began in 1926. In that year 18 lines carried more than 5,000 passengers. Innovators soon dotted the scene. One was 26-year-old Juan Trippe, who combined his love of flying with skill in obtaining the financial backing necessary to make commercial flying a success. In 1927 he and his friends launched Pan American Airways. Another innovator was William Boeing, an airplane designer and manufacturer who helped start United Airlines. Still another was Eddie Rickenbacker, an air ace of World War I (page 573), who later became head of Eastern Airlines. Auxiliary industries were also established. Frederick B. Rentschler, the son of a German immigrant iron maker, helped establish Pratt and Whitney Aircraft, an engine manufacturer. Within a few years Rentschler had turned his original cash investment of $253 into over $35 million.

Lindbergh crosses the Atlantic. The drama and the risk of flying created constant news. The United States Navy seaplane NC–4 in 1919 had become the first to fly across the Atlantic. The most sensational flight, however, would be a nonstop journey from New York to Paris.

In 1919 a New York hotel owner offered a prize of $25,000 to the first pilot who succeeded in such an undertaking. On May 20, 1927, from a muddy field on Long Island, Charles A. Lindbergh took off in his plane, *The Spirit of St. Louis,* on one of the most memorable flights in history. He had planned the flight with infinite care. Half the weight of the plane was fuel. Some of the fuel was carried in tanks in front of Lindbergh's seat, blocking his forward view. His few personal supplies included a canteen of water and a brown bag containing five sandwiches.

On the way, Lindbergh battled sleet, snow, and sleep. Thirty-three and a half hours after takeoff, he put his plane down at Le Bourget airfield near Paris. "Well, I made it," he said modestly.

"Lucky Lindy," as he was quickly dubbed, became an instant international hero. He was an unassuming young man who had dared to reach for an "impossible" goal. When he refused to cash in on his sensational journey by signing testimonials and accepting movie contracts, Americans were both astonished and pleased. One newspaper called him "the fair-haired boy that every man would like to have been." In Lindbergh, who had now opened the era of intercontinental flight, Americans saw a reminder of days now gone forever. He was an American frontiersman in an increasingly urban time.

SECTION REVIEW

1. Vocabulary: *assembly line.*
2. (a) What economic and social changes were brought about by the introduction of the automobile? (b) By movies? (c) By the radio?
3. How did the role of American women change during the 1920's?
4. What fads and sports held the attention of the American public during the 1920's?
5. (a) Who were some of the individuals responsible for the development of commercial air travel? (b) How did Charles Lindbergh capture the imagination of the American people?

601

Chapter 25 Review

Summary

The years immediately following World War I were unsettled ones for the United States. The adjustment from a wartime economy to normal operations was not entirely smooth. Prices during the war had increased dramatically, and workers in every sector now demanded higher wages. Police officers in Boston, steel workers in Indiana, and miners in the soft-coal fields were just three groups who went out on strike over salary demands.

News from Europe about Communist uprisings combined with the labor unrest to frighten many Americans. People became suspicious that outsiders were threatening American society. Increased demands for restrictions on immigration were one consequence of these fears of foreign influence.

Black Americans who had served in the armed forces or worked in war industries looked forward to greater opportunities after the war. Competition with white workers for jobs, however, resulted in tension, and in the summer of 1919 race riots took place in many cities. Still, black creativity flourished during the 1920's, producing a wealth of music, art, and literature.

The movement to prohibit the sale and consumption of alcohol gathered strength during the war, resulting in the ratification of the Eighteenth Amendment in 1919. Measures to enforce prohibition, however, were ineffective.

In the presidential contest of 1920, the Republican candidate, Warren G. Harding, emerged victorious. After Harding died in 1923, numerous scandals involving members of his Cabinet came to light. Calvin Coolidge finished Harding's term and was elected President himself in 1924. During Coolidge's administration much of the American economy boomed. Foreign imports and huge farm surpluses caused agricultural prices to fall sharply, however, and slumps in the coal, textile, and construction industries by the end of the decade foretold economic problems ahead. When Coolidge decided not to run again, his Secretary of Commerce, Herbert Hoover, received the Republican nomination for the presidency and then won the election of 1928.

The decade after the First World War brought profound changes to American life. The automobile, thanks in large part to Henry Ford, became available to millions of Americans. Motion pictures, the radio, and professional sports provided new entertainment. Commercial air travel began and Charles A. Lindbergh became a national hero by flying nonstop from New York to Paris.

Vocabulary and Important Terms

1. "Red scare"
2. quota
3. National Origins Act
4. Harlem Renaissance
5. prohibition
6. Volstead Act
7. Federal Bureau of Investigation
8. "Ohio gang"
9. farm bloc
10. McNary-Haugen Bill
11. Model T
12. assembly line

Discussion Questions

1. (a) Immediately after World War I, what difficulties did the nation's economy face? (b) Why were many workers discontented?
2. (a) Why did Congress establish immigration quotas in the 1920's? (b) Why did those who supported immigration restriction insist that 1890 was the best year on which to base quotas?
3. (a) What effects did the general disregard for prohibition have on American society? (b) Why did few people believe prohibition would be repealed?
4. (a) How did the presidential election of 1920 reflect the national debate over America's involvement in international affairs? (b) What was the outcome of that election? (c) Why was Coolidge's succession to the presidency important both for the Republican Party and for the American people?
5. (a) Why are the 1920's remembered as a time of prosperity? (b) What groups did not share in that prosperity? (c) What evidence was there that the prosperity rested on a shaky foundation?
6. (a) What were the main issues in the presidential campaign of 1928? (b) Why did Herbert Hoover win the election? (c) What new voting trends were revealed by the 1928 election?
7. (a) Why was Henry Ford's Model T a revolutionary invention? (b) Why might Ford's treatment of factory workers also be considered "revolutionary"?
8. How did advertising, movies, radio, and consumer credit help create mass markets for the vast outpouring of products from America's factories?
9. What were some of the ways in which Americans spent their newly created leisure time during the 1920's?

Relating Past and Present

1. Al Smith's religion was a major issue in his race for the presidency in 1928. What Catholics have run for President in recent years? Was their religion an issue?

2. What fads and sports have captured the imagination of the American public in recent years? Besides participating in organized sports, in what other ways do Americans fill their leisure time?

Studying Local History

1. Find out which candidate received your state's electoral votes in the presidential elections of 1920, 1924, and 1928. Then try to explain *why* your state voted as it did.
2. The radio station KDKA began operation in 1920. Find out when the first commercial radio station began in your local area. What kinds of programs were popular?

Using History Skills

1. *Reading source material.* Study the account of the working woman on page 599. (a) When did this woman first find a job? (b) What was the reaction of her husband? (c) For what reasons did she enjoy working outside the home?
2. *Reading graphs.* Study the graph showing farm income on page 593. How does the graph help explain the difficulties that American farmers faced during the 1920's?
3. *Using the dictionary.* Find the word *normalcy* in the dictionary. (a) What part of speech is *normalcy*? (b) From what word is it derived? (c) What did President Harding have in mind when he called for a "return to normalcy"?
4. *Writing a report.* Choose one of the following American authors and write a report based on his or her life: (a) F. Scott Fitzgerald, (b) Ernest Hemingway, (c) Willa Cather, (d) Sinclair Lewis, (e) Eugene O'Neill. In your report describe the impact the author had on literature during the 1920's. What were some of the settings of the author's works?

WORLD SCENE

The Collapse of Empires

The impact of the First World War was far-reaching. Centuries-old empires had collapsed, and new nations arose in their place.

The breakup of the Ottoman Empire. The decision of the Ottoman Turks to side with Germany in World War I proved costly. The Ottoman Empire, badly defeated, was stripped of much of its territory. The new nations of Palestine, Trans-Jordan, Syria, Lebanon, and Iraq, all of which were created out of former Ottoman territory, were placed under the supervision of either Britain or France.

A nationalist group known as the Young Turks had forced reforms on the Ottomans before the war. They now organized an army to challenge the Ottoman sultan. By the end of 1922 the Young Turks had abolished the office of sultan and had even persuaded the Allies to negotiate a new, less harsh peace treaty for their country.

In October, 1923, a democratic republic was proclaimed in Turkey, and the leader of the nationalist movement, Mustafa Kemal, was elected president. A resourceful and resolute man, Kemal believed his nation could not prosper without rapid modernization. He initiated sweeping changes — Western dress, the Roman alphabet, and the Christian calendar were adopted, as was a law requiring all Turks to choose a surname, in the European style. Kemal himself became Kemal Atatürk, meaning "father of the Turks."

The new state of Czechoslovakia. Czechoslovakia was one of the nations created following the breakup of Austria-Hungary in 1918. The new state was fortunate in inheriting the most valuable industrial areas of the old empire. Czechoslovakia was also fortunate in the leadership that guided its new constitutional government. The first president was Tomás Masaryk, a widely respected statesman and scholar. Married to an American, Masaryk was well known in the United States, where he had many friends.

Masaryk had the difficult task of mediating the often-conflicting interests of the country's ethnic groups. Czechoslovakia was largely made up of two Slavic elements — the Czechs, constituting 60 percent of the people, and the Slovaks, constituting 30 percent. The remaining 10 percent of the population consisted of Germans, Poles, and Hungarians. Tomás Masaryk, who greatly admired Thomas Jefferson's achievements, helped mold Czechoslovakia into a democracy by the end of the 1920's.

26

Fashioning the New Deal

1929 – 1940

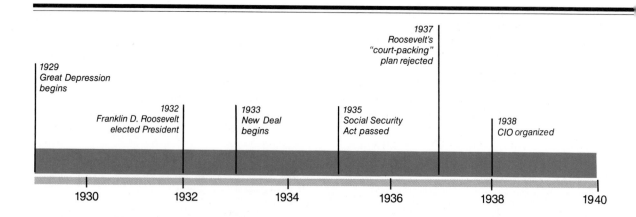

1929
Great Depression
begins

1932
Franklin D. Roosevelt
elected President

1933
New Deal
begins

1935
Social Security
Act passed

1937
Roosevelt's
"court-packing"
plan rejected

1938
CIO organized

1930   1932   1934   1936   1938   1940

CHAPTER OUTLINE

1. The Great Depression begins.

2. The New Deal takes shape.

3. The second New Deal introduces reforms.

4. The New Deal comes to an end.

Herbert Hoover was sworn in as President in an atmosphere of high optimism. Although March 4, 1929, was a rainy day, Hoover's words were sunny: "Ours is a land rich in resources . . . blessed with comfort and opportunity. In no nation are the fruits of accomplishment more secure. . . . I have no fear for the future of the country."

If Hoover had misgivings, they included one that he confided to a newspaper editor. The public, Hoover had observed, considered him "a sort of superman, that no problem is beyond my capacity. . . . If some unprecedented calamity should come upon the nation, I would be sacrificed to the unreasoning disappointment of a people who expected too much." The calamity came soon enough — the deepest economic depression the nation had ever experienced. It put Hoover on the defensive throughout his presidency and paved the way for the election of Franklin Delano Roosevelt in 1932.

Franklin Roosevelt had grown up in the time of Theodore Roosevelt and Woodrow Wilson. From them he acquired his admiration for strong and active leadership. He showed clearly that he enjoyed the exercise of power and responsibility. He also demonstrated a willingness to use his office to propose a seemingly endless series of measures to restore the nation's economic health. Deeply rooted in American history, he considered himself a conservative man guided by the motto "Reform, if you would preserve."

1 The Great Depression Begins

In 1929 Americans everywhere were buying shares of stock and creating a record boom on Wall Street. The average price of common stock in 1926 had been below $100 a share; by late summer in 1929, the average price had climbed to over $216. The Secretary of the Treasury, Andrew W. Mellon, answered those who urged caution: "There is no cause to worry. The high tide of prosperity will continue."

Warning signs appear. Words, however, could not alter facts. By the middle of 1929 consumer spending had slackened noticeably, a slowdown in new construction was setting in, and the boom in automobile sales had come to an end. A potential source of trouble was the large amount of money — running into billions of dollars — that people had borrowed to buy stocks on margin. (Buying on margin is a method by which investors put up only a fraction of the purchase price for stock shares and borrow the remainder from their brokers.) Despite warnings that stock prices were too high, more and more Americans invested in stocks.

The Federal Reserve Board (page 550), which had inflated the money supply during the 1920's, may have helped set the stage for disaster. The easy-money policy probably stimulated the public's urge to speculate. Recognizing the danger of over-speculation, the "Fed" finally warned its member banks not to lend money for speculative purposes.

By 1930 the nation was faced with the worst depression it had ever known. Factories stood idle, farms were abandoned, and millions of people were out of work.

The stock market crashes. Disaster struck on October 23, 1929, when stock prices dropped sharply. The trend continued the following day — which has ever since been remembered as Black Thursday. Stock shares began to be sold in huge quantities and the bottom fell out of the market. Orders from thousands of people desperate to sell their stock jammed the wires from every part of the country.

A group of bankers gathered on Black Thursday, amid much publicity, at the office of J. P. Morgan and Company. After a short meeting they announced they were going to support the market by buying stocks — with millions of dollars supplied by their banks. Prices rallied somewhat, and for a few days a measure of confidence returned. The words of President Hoover were reassuring too: "The fundamental business of the country — that is, the production and distribution of goods and services — is on a sound and prosperous basis."

Actually, the business of the country was *not* soundly based. Some economists pointed out that the prosperity of the previous years had been unevenly spread. Factories, as a result, were producing more goods than workers and other consumers could afford to buy.

The pattern of American international trade also contributed to economic weakness. The United States had emerged from the First World War as a creditor nation, with other countries owing Americans billions of dollars. The debtor nations could repay their obligations — and continue to buy American products — only by selling goods in the United States. High tariffs, however, prevented this. Consequently, foreigners borrowed more and more money from the United States. When the foreigners could not repay what they had borrowed, American investors were hurt. After the stock market began to slide, the flow of dollars abroad was reduced to a mere trickle. Foreign markets for American goods dried up, causing American factories to shut down.

On Tuesday, October 29, the stock market began to sink again with another big sell-off. More than sixteen million shares were sold that day. In the weeks that followed, stock prices moved steadily downward. By the middle of November it was apparent that stock prices were not going to "bounce back" quickly. In fact, for the next two and a half years the market continued to drift lower and lower.

Prosperity comes to an end. The stock market "crash" was the first stage of the disastrous Great Depression. Stock market losses from mid-October to mid-November, 1929, amounted to $30 billion, wiping out the resources of millions of Americans. People began to cut down on their purchases. As more and more factories closed or went on part-time operation, thousands upon thousands of jobs simply disappeared. Construction of new homes and buildings ground to a halt, throwing more people out of work. By the autumn of 1931, eight million people were unemployed.

The Depression spreads. It is impossible today to imagine the fear and anxiety that came into countless homes. The wages of those fortunate enough to have jobs were slashed again and again as the business collapse deepened. The average yearly income of a working person fell from $703 in 1929 to only $375 in 1933. People with savings, meanwhile, quickly used them up. Credit companies reclaimed furniture, automobiles, radios, refrigerators — even clothing — that had been purchased on the installment plan. Millions of families, unable to make mortgage payments, lost their homes. In the cities, families that could not pay the rent were forced out of their apartments. Sometimes people would sit on the street with all their possessions, hoping that a friend or neighbor would give them a helping hand.

Farm conditions grew worse as the Depression settled in. Farm income, which had been $6 billion in 1929, dropped to $2 billion in 1932. When farmers tried to increase their return by raising more crops, prices slipped even lower. To add to the problem, large parts of the nation were beset by drought beginning in 1930. In a short time, so many dust storms had struck

Drought and wind turned much of the Great Plains into a "Dust Bowl" during the Depression years. Here an Oklahoma family struggles against a raging dust storm.

the entire area from Texas to the Dakotas that it came to be labeled the "Dust Bowl." The scope of the disaster is suggested by the grim joke told by a Nebraska farmer during one such storm: "I'm counting the Kansas farms as they go by."

Industrial workers and farmers were not the only Americans affected by the Depression. Middle-class people were also badly hurt by hard times. Few jobs were available to a laid-off school teacher, or a clergyman whose salary was not being paid, or a lawyer unable to collect fees. The effect on morale was devastating, as people like these went door to door shining shoes or selling newspapers.

People tried to keep up their courage. They struggled to assure themselves that "prosperity was just around the corner." In Cincinnati someone distributed thousands of buttons that read "I'm sold on America. I won't talk depression." There was a kind of cheerfulness in a popular song of 1931, "Life is Just a Bowl of Cherries." As things grew worse, however, optimism faded, and in 1932 people began singing a gloomier tune, "Brother, Can You Spare a Dime?"

Hoover urges voluntary action. Because the Republicans had claimed credit for the pros-

perity of the 1920's, they could not escape blame for the nation's predicament. In the White House, Herbert Hoover was filled with anguish. Many people, mistaking his unsmiling face for hard-heartedness, jeered him in public. Soon, the homeless unemployed had given the name "Hoover blankets" to the newspapers they covered themselves with at night. The shanties in which these unfortunates huddled became known as "Hoovervilles." An empty pocket turned inside out was called a "Hoover flag."

Hoover did not believe that extraordinary measures were required. He firmly insisted that voluntary activities would bring the nation out of its doldrums. He urged people, for instance, to be more generous than usual in donating money to charity. He opened a Give-A-Job campaign in which job-holding Americans were encouraged to provide a day's work to their unemployed neighbors, allowing them, for instance, to clean out a cellar or whitewash a fence. Most people were embarrassed to offer such work to someone they knew. Many people who needed help were too proud to ask the family next door for assistance. Hoover, meanwhile, turned a deaf ear on an idea being discussed in many quarters — that

607

"Broken Hopes and Dreams"

Mahalia Jackson, who later became a world-famous singer, was a young woman in 1928 when she moved from the South to live with her aunt in Chicago. In the hard times that began soon afterwards, she observed what happened to people around her. She wrote about the period in her autobiography *Movin' On Up.*

When the Depression hit Chicago, the life the Negroes had built up for themselves in Chicago fell apart. On the South Side it was as if somebody had pulled a switch and everything had stopped running. Every day another big mill or factory would lay off all its colored help. Suddenly the streets were full of men and women who'd been put out of their jobs. . . . Banks all over the South Side locked their doors, and I'll never forget seeing the long lines of people outside them crying in the streets over their lost savings and falling on their knees and praying.

The Depression was much harder on the city Negroes up North than it was on the Negroes down South because it cost them all the gains they had struggled for. Many of the Negroes in the South didn't feel the Depression too much. Some of them could hardly tell the difference from prosperity. They never had had much for themselves and still had their little vegetable gardens and their chickens and maybe a pig or two, so they could still get enough to eat.

But in Chicago the Depression made the South Side a place of broken hopes and dreams. It was so sad that it would break your heart to think about it.

The big fine cars disappeared from the streets. People's clothes began to look more and more shabby, and families began to pile in together to save rent money. . . .

Mahalia Jackson

The city parks were full of people living in shanties made out of tin and wood scraps. All over the city, people were lining up to eat at bread lines and soup kitchens. If you earned a dollar, you felt guilty about spending it on yourself. I remember one day I earned $1.75 washing clothes, and on the way home I had to pass the people standing in one of those bread lines. I fished the money out of my pocket and told those people to follow me. We bought a sack of potatoes and a mess of smoked ribs . . . with that money and took it all back to my place and had one big supper.

the federal government assist the unemployed by giving them relief through direct payments. To Hoover the idea of a government "hand-out" was not permissible under a system of free enterprise.

City governments tried as best they could to relieve the suffering, but by 1932 many of them could not provide any more help. When city governments ran out of money, the states lent a hand. New York

State, under Governor Franklin D. Roosevelt, took the lead in giving direct assistance to the unemployed. Before long, other states were doing likewise.

Even as they agonized over their condition, most Americans retained confidence in capitalism as a system of production and distribution of goods. Moreover, although there was widespread discontent, it produced little violence. The public, accustomed to self-discipline, did not destroy property — even to get food or obtain shelter. Some hunger marches took place, and on occasion people prevented bank agents from foreclosing farms. In general, however, the orderly processes of public life went on as usual.

Hoover tries to stop the downward trend. In spite of his desire to keep the government out of the economy, Hoover early accepted the idea that the government would have to take on certain responsibilities. In 1929, for instance, the Hoover administration supported passage of the Agricultural Marketing Act. The measure set up a Federal Farm Board, which had a special fund of $500 million to stabilize farm prices and discourage the growing of surplus crops. Farm cooperatives could borrow money from the fund to pay for the costs of storing produce until prices were higher. The Agricultural Marketing Act was the first instance where federal funds were used in an attempt to regulate farm prices. It failed, however, to stop the fall in farm prices or to prevent the continued growth of surpluses.

Hoover strongly believed that if business could somehow be revived, the rest of the country would share in the benefits. Following the failure of a number of banks in 1931, therefore, he called for the establishment of the Reconstruction Finance Corporation (RFC). Set up by Congress in 1932, the RFC was granted the authority to lend money to banks, railroads, and other institutions in financial trouble. Some critics denounced the RFC as "a federal breadline for business." At any rate, despite advancing nearly $2 billion in loans during Hoover's years in office, the RFC proved unable to restore prosperity.

When President and Mrs. Hoover moved into the White House in 1929, there were few indications of the trouble that lay ahead.

Hoover also recommended a cut in income taxes. The effect, he hoped, would be to put additional money in circulation so that people could purchase more consumer goods. The results were modest, however, because millions of Americans had no income at all.

The "Bonus Army" marches on Washington. Nothing dramatized the agony of the times better than the march of the "Bonus Army" on Washington, D.C., in 1932. Made up of 15,000 veterans of World War I, the "Army" consisted of marchers from many parts of the country. Their purpose was to petition Congress for immediate payment of a bonus for wartime service. The bonus was not scheduled to be distributed until 1945.

Congress rejected the petition of the Bonus Army but offered to pay their fare home. All of them departed except about 2,000 die-hards, who had set up a camp of shacks and tents on the banks of the Potomac. Following a scuffle between a band of veterans and the police, the government of the District of Columbia declared itself unable to maintain order. On July 28, 1932, Hoover finally called in the army to disperse the holdouts. Soldiers led by the Chief of Staff, General Douglas MacArthur, set fire to the camp and scattered the occupants with bayonets and tear gas.

SECTION REVIEW

1. What were some of the advance signs of economic trouble in 1929?
2. Describe the effects of the stock market crash.
3. (a) What was President Hoover's attitude toward government relief projects? (b) What programs did he institute in an effort to halt the Depression?
4. (a) Why did the "Bonus Army" march on Washington? (b) What happened to the "Bonus Army"?

2 The New Deal Takes Shape

In 1932 the Republicans nominated Herbert Hoover for a second term as President. Only the most optimistic members of the party believed, however, that he could be re-elected. Most voters felt certain that *anybody* the Democratic Party named would win the election. Interest, therefore, centered on the struggle among the Democratic hopefuls.

The Democrats nominate Franklin Roosevelt. Al Smith longed for a second nomination, but most Democratic leaders, remembering the religious issue in 1928 (page 594), did not want to see it raised again. An eager contender with a magical last name was Franklin Delano Roosevelt, who had been re-elected governor of New York in 1930. Roosevelt had a winning smile and a warm public manner. Still, he had no clearly thought-out program for dealing with the problems the Depression had brought. As a practiced politician, he, of course, found it an advantage not to be in favor of any specific plan of action.

In a victory mood, the Democrats gathered in Chicago in late June, 1932, and on the fourth ballot nominated Roosevelt for President. John Nance Garner of Texas, Speaker of the House of Representatives, was named as their candidate for Vice President. The Democratic platform called for reduced government spending, a sound currency, aid to agriculture, and repeal of the prohibition amendment.

Roosevelt had been born in 1882 at Hyde Park, New York, in a mansion overlooking the Hudson River. Young Roosevelt grew up in a protected world of wealth and leisure. His father, James, who was 52 years old at the time of the boy's birth, was a gentleman farmer, who had known Sam Houston. The mother, Sara Delano, half her husband's age, came from a family that had made its money in the trade with China.

Educated by private tutors until he was fourteen years old, Roosevelt received a good background in French and German. As a youth, he traveled abroad more widely than any President since John Quincy Adams. After graduating from Harvard College in 1904, he entered the Columbia University Law School. The following year he married his distant cousin, the gifted and energetic Anna Eleanor Roosevelt. Her "Uncle Ted," then President of the United States, traveled to New York for the ceremony.

After serving in the New York State legislature, Roosevelt was named by Woodrow Wilson to be Assistant Secretary of the Navy. In 1920 Roosevelt became well-known nationally when he ran unsuccessfully for Vice President. Then, in 1921, a personal tragedy struck. While vacationing with his family in Canada, he was stricken with polio and his legs became paralyzed. With the encouragement of his wife and family, he gradually regained his strength. Still, he would never again be able to stand or walk without assistance.

Roosevelt, spurred by his wife and many friends, remained active in politics. His rousing nominating speech for Al Smith at the Democratic convention in 1924 brought him public acclaim. In 1928, he was elected governor of New York. To silence opponents during the campaign who whispered about Roosevelt's paralysis, Smith had had an answer: "We do not elect [a governor] for his ability to do a double back flip or a handspring." By the time the Depression struck, FDR, as people referred to him, was becoming a symbol of an afflicted nation determined to stir and be itself again. In millions of people, he inspired fresh confidence that determination and hard work could bring triumph over adversity.

Roosevelt promises a New Deal. Ignoring the custom that a candidate must wait for formal notification of his nomination, Roosevelt flew to Chicago in June, 1932, to address the Democratic convention. In his speech, he pledged that he would provide a "new deal for the American people." Roosevelt did not — because he could not — say in detail what he meant. Still, people could hear in the phrase "New Deal" an echo of the earlier Roosevelt's "Square Deal." The ring of familiarity hinted that whatever changes took place would be in keeping with tradition.

The Democrats win the election. The Democrats' theme song, "Happy Days Are Here Again," held promise for millions of people laid low by the Depression. They ignored Hoover's assertion that if Roosevelt became President, "grass will grow in the streets of a hundred cities."

On Election Day, Roosevelt carried 42 of the 48 states, receiving 23 million votes in contrast to Hoover's 16 million. The electoral vote was 472 for Roosevelt and 59 for Hoover. The landslide signaled the beginning of the longest hold on power of any politician in American history.

Prohibition is repealed. Responding to the election results, Congress in February, 1933,[1] approved an amendment that would bring an end to prohibition. Later that year, the Twenty-First Amendment became effec-

Franklin Roosevelt refused to let a severe disability destroy his political career. In 1932 the voters elected him President, believing he could bring the Depression to an end.

tive, repealing the Eighteenth Amendment. The controversial experiment of national prohibition was over.

The crisis deepens. In the months between November, 1932, and March, 1933, economic conditions had greatly deteriorated. Banks closed at a faster rate than ever before, wiping out the savings and deposits of millions of people. As panic spread, so many people withdrew their money that

---

[1]Until it was abolished in 1933 by the Twentieth Amendment, a "lame duck" session of Congress was held from the December following a presidential election to March 4, when the new President was inaugurated.

Franklin D. Roosevelt's First Inaugural Address (1933)

This is pre-eminently the time to speak the truth, the whole truth, frankly and boldly. Nor need we shrink from honestly facing conditions in our country today. This great nation will endure as it has endured, will revive and will prosper.

So first of all let me assert my firm belief that the only thing we have to fear is fear itself — nameless, unreasoning, unjustified terror which paralyzes needed efforts to convert retreat into advance. . . .

Our greatest primary task is to put people to work. This is no unsolvable problem if we face it wisely and courageously.

It can be accomplished in part by direct recruiting by the government itself, treating the task as we would treat the emergency of a war, but at the same time, through this employment, accomplishing greatly needed projects to stimulate and reorganize the use of our national resources. . . .

I am prepared under my constitutional duty to recommend the measures that a stricken nation in the midst of a stricken world may require.

These measures, or such other measures as the Congress may build out of its experience and wisdom, I shall seek, within my constitutional authority, to bring to speedy adoption. . . .

even banks with sound management faced disaster.

Some angry farmers began taking the law into their own hands. In the Midwest, the National Farmers' Holiday Association refused to permit any crops to reach market until prices were boosted. Farmers even dumped milk on highways in order to reduce supplies and, presumably, lift prices. Charles M. Schwab, chairman of the board of Bethlehem Steel, confessed, "I'm afraid; every man is afraid." As Hoover prepared to attend the swearing-in of his successor, he said grimly, "We are at the end of our string."

Roosevelt seeks to restore the nation's confidence. On Inauguration Day, Roosevelt addressed the stricken country with words of reassurance. The speech, portions of which appear on this page, electrified the country. Hundreds of thousands of people wrote to the President, applauding his words and offering support. Their backing encouraged him as he began his administration.

A Cabinet is named. Roosevelt's Cabinet consisted of strong personalities also ready to try new ways. In the Department of State was Cordell Hull, a long-time senator from Tennessee, eager to batter down the tariff walls between nations. In charge of the Department of Agriculture, Roosevelt put Henry A. Wallace of Iowa, an agricultural economist who was well-known for developing a hybrid corn. The Secretary of the Interior was Harold L. Ickes of Illinois, a former Progressive, an outspoken foe of business interests, and a devoted conservationist. As Secretary of Labor, the President appointed Frances Perkins, who had been Industrial Commissioner in New York in the late 1920's. Once a worker at Hull House (page 531), she was the first woman ever to serve in a President's Cabinet.

The "brain trust" advises Roosevelt. Roosevelt also depended on the suggestions of a group of advisers affectionately labeled the "brain trust." In the group were several Columbia University professors. They included Raymond Moley, a political scientist; Rexford G. Tugwell, a specialist in agricultural affairs; and Adolf A. Berle, an expert in corporate finance. Other consultants included William Green, president of the AFL, and Bernard Baruch, a well-known financier.

The First Lady, Eleanor Roosevelt, provided her husband with an extra set of eyes and ears. Restless and untiring, Eleanor Roosevelt traveled incessantly and, upon returning to the White House, reported to the President on a variety of subjects. Her interests included areas of American life that had been long ignored — poverty in coal-mining communities, the plight of black people and other minorities, and the violation of civil liberties. She later wrote that she became a better observer as the years went by and as she came to anticipate her husband's wide-ranging questions.

A "bank holiday" is declared. Upon taking office, Roosevelt immediately declared a "bank holiday," a four-day period during which all the nation's banks were closed. The banks were allowed to reopen only after government inspectors had examined their records and confirmed their soundness. Roosevelt then told the nation over the radio, "I can assure you that it is safer to keep your money in a reopened bank than under the mattress." Roosevelt's move brought an end to bank failures resulting from the withdrawal of savings by frightened depositors.

The New Deal is inaugurated. From March 9 through June 16, 1933, Congress met in

When Roosevelt took office, many of the nation's banks were on the verge of collapse. Scenes like the one below were commonplace, as rumors of bank failures created panic and sent depositors rushing to withdraw their savings.

special session. Its members were eager to follow the leadership of the White House. The legislation they passed during the "Hundred Days" profoundly changed American life. The new laws fell into three categories: *relief* measures for emergency assistance; *recovery* measures to try to bring an end to the Depression; and *reform* measures to provide a means of solving or preventing the recurrence of long-standing problems.

Relief is provided for the unemployed. The most urgent problem facing the President after the banking crisis was the situation of millions of unemployed Americans. To provide them with immediate help, the administration moved quickly. Congress, through a much-publicized measure, established the Civilian Conservation Corps — generally called the CCC. It dealt on a massive scale

The Civilian Conservation Corps combined work relief for unemployed men between the ages of 18 and 25 with badly needed conservation projects. This corpsman is learning how to survey land.

with the problem of unemployment. The law eventually put some 2,500,000 young men to work constructing dams, clearing beaches and camp sites, and planting trees. Most CCC members were allowed to keep only a small part of the meager wages they were paid. The balance was sent home to their needy families. The law was generally popular because the work done under its terms aided in protecting the natural environment — and because so many young people now could escape the need to stand in breadlines.

A second relief measure authorized the setting up of the Federal Emergency Relief Administration (FERA). Congress provided the agency with funds — $500 million at first and, later, $3 billion more. These funds were to be distributed to the states for direct relief to the unemployed.

The FERA was a departure in American history, and it was not a success. Direct relief seemed like an undeserved gift to many recipients, who were embarrassed to receive it. Harry Hopkins, administrator of the FERA, persuaded Roosevelt that the country needed a program to provide people with work. As a result, the Civil Works Administration was established before 1933 ended, with Hopkins at its head. The CWA swiftly provided four million jobs, most of them "make-work" projects with little permanent value, like raking leaves. (Cynics were soon calling these jobs "boondoggles" — a word once applied to the trivial chores cowboys performed when they were not managing their herds.)

The sale of stocks and bonds is regulated. A step to restore trust in financial institutions was embodied in the Federal Securities Act, passed in May, 1933. This law required corporations offering new stock or bonds to register them with the Federal Trade Commission and to disclose accurate information on them. The aim was to prevent fraud and misrepresentation. This new measure appealed especially to investors who believed, rightly or wrongly, that they had been cheated by brokers during the stock market boom of the late 1920's.

In 1934 Congress went further by establishing the Securities and Exchange Commission. The SEC — an independent commission appointed by the President — was given broad powers to regulate the stock exchanges in order to weed out unscrupulous operators.

Legislation is passed to promote recovery. To launch the nation's recovery, Roosevelt moved to assist various segments of the population. The names of the agencies he established told of their functions. The Home Owners Loan Corporation (HOLC) was created in 1933 to help people avoid the loss of their homes through the foreclosure of mortgages. The law eventually lent a total of $3 billion to more than a million homeowners, enabling them to save their dwellings.

Suitable housing, a vital factor in restoring public morale, was often on the President's mind. In 1934 the Federal Housing Administration (FHA) began to offer federally guaranteed loans to middle-income families who wanted to repair an old house or build a new one. In the six years after its passage, the law made possible 554,000 loans totaling $2.3 billion for the construction of new housing.

In an effort to help farmers recover economic health, Congress passed the Agricultural Adjustment Act (AAA). This law provided for direct payments to farmers who reduced the production of such crops as wheat, corn, rice, and tobacco. The subsidies were made possible through a processing tax placed on industries — flour mills and slaughterhouses, for instance — that prepared products for market. The tax, of course, was passed on to consumers through higher prices.

For a time the most widely discussed recovery law was the National Industrial Recovery Act (NIRA), the crowning law of the "Hundred Days." It provided that each industry — with the aid of the National Recovery Administration (NRA) — would cooperate in preparing "codes of fair competition" to establish standard prices, wages, and hours in their businesses. Sec-

Following passage of the National Industrial Recovery Act in 1933, manufacturers and retailers proudly displayed the NRA poster in store windows, on factory doors, and on delivery trucks.

tion 7a of the law also guaranteed labor's right to organize unions and to bargain collectively with employers through agents of their own choosing.

The NRA was inaugurated with high hopes and much publicity. A likeness of an eagle with the slogan "We Do Our Part" was made the symbol of the NRA and exhibited in store windows and on factory walls throughout the country. The presence of an eagle poster was evidence that the company displaying it had promised to abide by the code of fair competition established in that industry.

The NRA act also created the Public Works Administration (PWA) with an appropriation of $3.3 million to stimulate the construction industry. In addition to providing jobs on public works, PWA projects were intended to help revive the economy through the sale of building materials such as steel, cement, and lumber.

The United States goes off the gold standard. Roosevelt did not believe that worldwide remedies for the Depression would be effective, so he felt free to take independent steps. For example, he decided that inflation was needed to raise prices. He therefore took the country off the gold standard. This meant that the nation's currency would no longer be redeemable in gold. The President expected that the cheaper dollars would lead to a rise in prices. Business profits would also rise, he believed, followed soon by higher wages and substantial re-employment.

Critics predicted that going off the gold standard would lead to catastrophe. Bernard Baruch bluntly commented, "Maybe the country doesn't know it yet, but I think we may find that we've been in a revolution more drastic than the French Revolution." For a brief period in 1933, prices and production did indeed rise. Wages, however, lagged behind, and ordinary people were unable to buy the consumer goods that had begun to pour from the factories. By late summer, business activity was in the doldrums again.

Congress increases banking security. No one could say how long the recovery measures would be required, nor when the tinkering with the economy would end. The New Deal's reform measures, however, were meant to be a permanent part of American life.

A step to reform the banking business was the Glass-Steagall Act that Congress

Heeding President Roosevelt's proposal that the government undertake the development of the Tennessee River valley, Congress established the Tennessee Valley Authority in 1933.

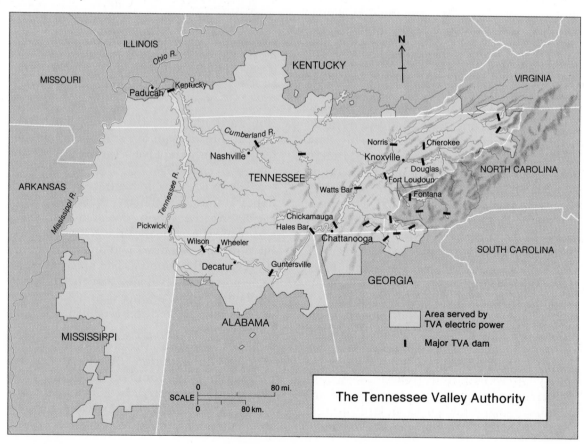

The Tennessee Valley Authority

passed in 1933. It provided for the separation of commercial banking and investment banking. In short, it prohibited banks from speculating in stocks and bonds with the money of depositors. The act also established the Federal Deposit Insurance Corporation — the FDIC. Its function was to insure customers' deposits, up to a certain amount. Americans as a whole quickly regained confidence in the banking system.

The TVA is a new kind of experiment. One reform measure of the early New Deal that raised controversy was the development of the Tennessee Valley, a region that had been plagued for years by floods and erosion. In 1933, Congress established the Tennessee Valley Authority (TVA). This vast project had a number of purposes — flood control, improved river navigation, irrigation, and the generation of hydroelectric power. All in all, the TVA was an enormous effort to develop and rehabilitate the entire region drained by the Tennessee River. The undertaking affected parts of Tennessee, Kentucky, North Carolina, Virginia, Mississippi, Alabama, and Georgia — a 41,000-square-mile region containing three million people.

By 1944, scores of dams had been constructed on the Tennessee River and its major tributaries. The dams made possible the construction of an inland waterway system with a nine-foot channel extending 650 miles from Knoxville, Tennessee, to Paducah, Kentucky. In time, the TVA acquired facilities that gave it control over the production and sale of electricity throughout the Tennessee Valley.

Run as an independent public corporation by a board of three directors, the TVA had as its goal the economic and social well-being of the entire region. The agency and its work became a model for similar river projects throughout the world. In addition to the improvements brought about by better management of the land, the region benefited from the electrification of millions of homes.

Nonetheless, the TVA had many critics, some of whom argued that the program seemed like government interference with private enterprise. Utility companies pointed out, moreover, that the TVA could charge low rates for electricity because, as a government agency, it was exempt from paying taxes. Opponents of the TVA were able to prevent similar projects — such as a proposal for an "MVA" in the Missouri River valley — from being started.

Other conservation measures are proposed. The TVA was just one of the New Deal's conservation programs. Boulder Dam on the Colorado River (begun in the Hoover Administration and later called Hoover Dam) was completed in 1936. The Bonneville and Grand Coulee dams, started under Roosevelt, were constructed on the Columbia River. Like the TVA dams, these immense triumphs of American engineering aided flood control, improved the navigation of the affected rivers, made irrigation of the land more efficient, and produced enormous amounts of electric power.

Land conservation was another area in which the Roosevelt administration had a deep interest. To deal with the "Dust Bowl" (page 607), the President ordered the planting of a vast belt of trees on the Great Plains. The aim was to break the stiff winds there, anchor the soil, and hold moisture. Today the millions of trees planted during the 1930's are mighty reminders of a far-sighted policy.

SECTION REVIEW

1. (a) Who were the candidates in the 1932 presidential election? (b) What were the main issues? (c) What was the outcome of the election?
2. For what reason was the Twenty-First Amendment adopted?
3. (a) What was the nation's mood when Franklin Roosevelt was sworn in as President? (b) What steps did Roosevelt take to restore confidence in the nation's banks?
4. (a) What steps were taken to help unemployed Americans? (b) Homeowners? (c) Farmers? (d) Business? (e) Labor?
5. (a) What was the TVA? (b) What did it achieve? (c) On what grounds was it criticized? (d) What other conservation measures did the New Deal take?

3 The Second New Deal Introduces Reforms

By the beginning of 1934, some Roosevelt opponents — mostly Republicans but also dissatisfied Democrats like Al Smith and John W. Davis — joined together and formed the Liberty League. They charged that the country was being destroyed through overspending and the pampering of jobless people. In the 1934 elections, however, the Democrats gained even more seats in both houses of Congress.

Hard times continue despite New Deal efforts. Most of Roosevelt's opponents accused him of conducting a "give-away" government. A number of other critics, though, attracted attention by charging that the government was too tight-fisted. Senator Huey P. Long of Louisiana, making himself a spokesman for poor people, advocated a "share-our-wealth" program that would have entitled every family in the nation to a yearly income of $2,500. Another figure who drew crowds was Dr. Francis E. Townsend of California, who organized a national movement calling for a monthly pension of $200 for every person over sixty years of age. Yet another man with a ready solution was Father Charles E. Coughlin, a Roman Catholic priest who advocated government ownership of banks, public utilities, and natural resources.

Roosevelt was well aware of the strong appeal of these seemingly easy solutions to hard times. Moreover, the Depression was by no means over. The jobless still numbered more than eleven million at the end of 1934, about 22 percent of the labor force. (To be sure, the figures were an improvement over early 1933, when more than thirteen million people had been out of work.) In the view of many Democratic leaders it was time to seek further reforms, for recovery had not taken place as anticipated.

The second New Deal begins. The President's annual message to Congress on January 4, 1935, marked the beginning of what is now known as the second New Deal.[2] The major theme of the address was that the federal government had to take greater responsibility for the economic well-being of the American people. The administration had broad new goals: better housing, and protection from the effects of old age, unemployment, and disability. Roosevelt proposed to treat the economy as a tree that had to be watered at the roots. He would help the victims of the Depression increase their ability to buy consumer goods and lift their standard of living, thereby stimulating production and bringing about economic recovery.

The Social Security Act is passed. The most far-reaching law adopted by the new Congress was the Social Security Act, passed in August, 1935. It established benefits for retired workers, unemployment insurance, and a health and child-welfare program. The old-age benefits would be paid out of an insurance fund to which both employers and employees would contribute. The unemployment insurance would be paid for by a compulsory payroll tax on employers. Federal grants matched by state grants would aid widows, dependent children, blind people, and certain other handicapped persons. A number of classes of employees were not eligible for social security coverage: agricultural workers, domestic servants, civil servants, and most professional people, including doctors and lawyers.

Herbert Hoover denounced the measure. He maintained that "social security, [must be built] upon a cult of work, not a cult of leisure." Many other Americans agreed. Some critics insisted that the Social Security bill would destroy the freedom of the American people by substituting government control for free enterprise.

Work relief programs are continued. The driving force of the second New Deal was

---

[2]The idea that there were "two New Deals" is merely a convenience for studying the period. Roosevelt himself did not differentiate between a first and a second New Deal.

Newspaper cartoonists often poked fun at the multitude of federal agencies, designated by initials, created by the New Deal.

the Emergency Relief Administration Act, passed by Congress in April, 1935. It enabled Roosevelt to take strong measures to cope with unemployment. Under the act, the President established by executive order the Works Progress Administration (WPA) and appointed Harry Hopkins to be its head. The CWA, which Hopkins had administered (page 614), had been terminated in 1934, when Roosevelt had become concerned over its cost and over rumors of corruption in its management. As a result, the United States had once more returned to direct relief for the unemployed. By the end of 1935 approximately twenty million Americans were receiving some form of public assistance.

The WPA had an initial appropriation of $5 billion — the largest that had ever

been made in peacetime in America. The aim of the WPA was to give people work as soon as possible. People in WPA jobs, administration officials hoped, would feel once again the dignity that comes from working purposefully.

Projects had to be found that had public usefulness and local sponsors. Moreover, the projects had to be planned so that they did not call for excessive amounts of equipment and supplies. As much as possible, the available funds were to be spent on wages. Also, projects had to be completed in one year since Congress made only annual appropriations.

By 1941 the WPA had an average of over two million people on its payroll each month. WPA workers constructed more than a hundred airports throughout the country, built or rebuilt over a hundred thousand public buildings, laid half a million sewer lines and 650,000 miles of roads, and improved thousands of parks and school grounds. A WPA project was built in almost every town and city in the nation: a new swimming pool, or hospital, or post office, or bridge.

The WPA also broke fresh ground in the realm of the arts. The Federal Theater, organized under its auspices, presented plays in parts of the country that had never previously seen live stage performances. For the first time the lobbies of public buildings were adorned with colorful murals. They were the work of artists who would not otherwise have had a showplace for their talent.

Still, many WPA undertakings were a waste of time and money, for the ways of putting people to work were often far-fetched. John Steinbeck, the author, was once assigned as a WPA worker to take a census of dogs in a California community. Furthermore, on construction projects many WPA workers loafed shamefully, knowing they would not be fired. Another problem was that the WPA was sometimes used for partisan purposes. Some politicians found it easy to corral the votes of people so dependent on the Democratic Party's remaining in office.

Congress created a "junior" WPA for young people — the National Youth Administration (NYA) — in June, 1935. During the eight years the NYA was in existence, it created jobs for over 1,500,000 high school students and 600,000 college students. The work consisted of helping in laboratories, libraries, and school and college offices. The small salaries that went with the jobs enabled many young people to stay in school. The NYA funds were distributed through the states. One of the most energetic state administrators was a future President, Lyndon B. Johnson of Texas.

The Works Progress Administration was the first federal agency to give jobs to artists. This WPA-financed mural glorifies American workers.

The second New Deal passes more reform measures. The administration's experiments made the White House a constant source of news and excitement. One such undertaking was the establishment of the Rural Electrification Administration (REA) in 1935. Its goal was to bring electricity to the rural areas of the country. Whereas power lines had reached only 4 percent of America's farms in 1925, they reached 25 percent by 1940.

A less successful experiment was the Resettlement Administration, created in 1935. This agency was given funds to buy up poor and infertile land occupied by destitute farmers, tenants, sharecroppers, or migrant workers, and to resettle the people in more promising places. The RA eventually purchased about nine million undesirable acres and removed them from cultivation. The RA also created so-called "greenbelt towns" — planned suburban communities outside Milwaukee, Cincinnati, and Washington, D.C. The degree of federal involvement that this type of activity required, however, received little public support.

Another controversial measure was a tax bill passed by Congress in August, 1935. It was directed at eliminating what Roosevelt considered "an unjust concentration of wealth and economic power" in the hands of a small fraction of the population. The bill provided for a significant increase in individual and corporate income taxes. The proposal boosted the inheritance tax. To prevent evasion of that levy, the gift tax, too, was increased. Opponents labeled the measure a "soak-the-rich" scheme.

Organized labor makes gains under the Wagner Act. In July, 1935, Congress passed the National Labor Relations Act. The guiding spirit behind it was Senator Robert F. Wagner of New York. The law — often called the Wagner Act — made stronger the provisions of Section 7a of the NRA (page 615). It guaranteed the right of workers to organize and to bargain with employers for better wages and working conditions. The act was to be enforced by a National Labor Relations Board. The NLRB was authorized to hear testimony about unfair labor practices by employers. Such practices included forcing workers to join company unions and preventing them from joining unions of their choice. The NLRB could issue binding orders compelling companies to stop these practices.

Perhaps no piece of legislation aroused so much controversy as the Wagner Act. Employers insisted that it unfairly tied their hands while giving unions a free rein.

The CIO is formed. As the second New Deal proceeded, the strengthened labor movement became more forceful. The AFL had remained true to its traditional reliance on organization by craft unions (page 475). Some AFL members, however, regarded this outlook as stodgy and old-fashioned. The AFL's policy, moreover, irritated the hundreds of thousands of noncraft workers — mostly unskilled — who remained unorganized. Now, encouraged by the pro-labor legislation of the New Deal, these workers began seeking ways to organize unions.

Some labor leaders set about organizing unions for workers in the mass-production industries (automobile, rubber, steel, cement, radio). An important figure in this movement was John L. Lewis, head of the United Mine Workers. Lewis knew the labor movement from the inside out. His father had been a member of the Knights of Labor, and he himself had gone into the coal pits to work at the age of twelve. Joined by Sidney Hillman and David Dubinsky of the garment workers' unions, Lewis in November, 1935, formed the Committee for Industrial Organization — the CIO — and began trying to organize entire industries into one union. Lewis became the Committee's chairman. When the AFL suspended the members of the Committee in 1938, the CIO turned itself into a separate organization. It kept its initials and adopted the name Congress of Industrial Organizations. At once the CIO began to organize industrial unions that included unskilled as well as skilled members.

Labor violence breaks out. The attempt to organize the steel industry in 1936 and the

In 1937 industrial workers began making use of a new weapon in their drive to organize unions—the sit-down strike. Here, workers in a Flint, Michigan, auto plant refuse to leave their posts.

automobile industry in the following year resulted in some of the angriest labor strife in American history. In the steel industry, ten men were killed in 1937 during a labor disturbance at a Chicago plant of the Republic Steel Company. In that same year, however, the giant United States Steel Corporation recognized the CIO steelworkers' union. Four years later, the National Labor Relations Board forced several smaller steel companies to recognize the CIO union as the employees' representative.

In the automobile industry, workers made use of the "sit-down strike," simply refusing to leave their posts until their unions had won recognition from management. Even when plant managers turned off the heat in the dead of winter, the strikers remained in the factories.

The AFL disclaimed responsibility for the sit-down strikes, and the CIO never gave them official approval. Opinion polls showed overwhelming public opposition to labor's new-found weapon. In any event, as the NLRB continued its work, elections were held to name collective bargaining units, and the sit-downs no longer served a purpose.

By the end of 1937 the CIO had done a remarkable job of organizing unskilled workers. Unions in the mining, automobile, steel, textile, and garment industries all had hundreds of thousands of members. In addition, the CIO brought into the ranks of organized labor more women, blacks, and immigrants than ever before. For the first time in the heavy industries, working people were union members, able to bargain effectively with management. Because the New Deal had hastened this development, Roosevelt was widely regarded as labor's best friend. Labor became a powerful source of New Deal support.

The Supreme Court declares New Deal legislation unconstitutional. Critics in Congress, frustrated by their inability to prevent passage of New Deal legislation, sometimes called Roosevelt's program the "Raw Deal." Nonetheless, the only effective roadblock to Roosevelt's programs, as it turned out, was the Supreme Court. In 1935, decisions in two important cases struck hard at important New Deal measures.

The first of the cases was *Schechter v. United States.* These were the facts: A Brooklyn, New York, poultry company had violated its industry's "code of fair competition" by paying wages below the minimum and by selling unhealthful chicken. The company argued that it was not engaged in interstate commerce and that, therefore, the code did not apply to it.[3]

The Court, in a unanimous decision handed down on May 27, 1935, held that the NRA was unconstitutional. The Court ruled that if the federal government could regulate *everything* affecting interstate commerce, then "there would be virtually no limit to federal power." The Court declared also that in giving the NRA control over wages and hours, Congress had improperly delegated legislative authority to the executive branch.

---

[3]Congress, which had created the NRA, had taken the position that anything affecting interstate commerce — even commerce conducted entirely within a state's borders — was subject to national legislative control.

Franklin Roosevelt frequently took to the radio airwaves during his years in office to speak directly to the American people.

Roosevelt, angered by the decision, denounced the Supreme Court for using a "horse-and-buggy definition of interstate commerce." He knew, nevertheless, that the NRA had probably outlived its usefulness. It was badly run, and many small businesses had been hurt by its operation, because the "codes of fair competition" usually favored bigger companies. Some labor leaders, furthermore, were calling the NRA a failure and were even referring to it as the "National Run-Around."

On January 6, 1936, the Supreme Court wiped out another recovery law. In the case of *United States v. Butler*, the Court declared the Agricultural Adjustment Act unconstitutional. The justices held that the processing tax established by that act (page 615) was invalid because it took "money from one group" of citizens for the "benefit of another."

The administration quickly obtained passage of laws allowing it to salvage useful parts of the legislation the courts had knocked down. For example, to get around the decision on NRA, Congress in August, 1935, passed the Bituminous Coal Conser-vation Act. It established standards for regulating wages and working conditions in the soft-coal industry. The provisions of the AAA that paid farmers to reduce the size of their crops, moreover, were revived in a new way. Under the Soil Conservation and Domestic Allotment Act, passed in February, 1936, farmers were compensated for planting grasses and other soil-holding plants instead of cash crops like tobacco, corn, and wheat. Farmers, therefore, were being paid for aiding in soil conservation, not for reducing production.

Further Court decisions weaken the New Deal. In the late spring of 1936, the Supreme Court delivered two decisions that shook the Roosevelt administration to its foundations. In the first ruling, the Court struck down the Coal Conservation Act as unconstitutional. Roosevelt and his advisers were stunned by the Court's view that the federal government could not regulate hours and wages. They concluded that the people would have to rely on the state governments to do this work. That idea, too, was shattered when on June 1, 1936, the

Supreme Court declared unconstitutional New York State's minimum wage law. The law, passed in 1933, had been designed to protect working women and children. The Court maintained that by establishing a minimum wage for women, New York was denying people the freedom, guaranteed by the Fourteenth Amendment, to make contracts. Roosevelt — and reformers in both parties — were appalled by the decision. At a press conference, the President asserted that there was now a no-man's land where neither the state *nor* the federal government could act.

Some groups denounced the decision and made proposals that would have altered the Court's power of judicial review. Because a number of the important recent decisions had been by a 5 to 4 vote, some people suggested that a vote on the Court of at least six to three ought to be required to overturn a law. Other people proposed giving Congress the power through a constitutional amendment to override decisions of the Court by a two-thirds vote. Still other commentators maintained that Congress should forbid judicial review altogether. Whatever the answer, the New Deal seemed at an impasse.

Roosevelt runs for re-election. The presidential campaign of 1936, meanwhile, was about to begin. Roosevelt felt he needed a new mandate from the people to go forward with the New Deal.

The President's renomination was certain. Meeting at Philadelphia, the Democrats in wild enthusiasm named him and Vice President Garner without a formal ballot. The party platform contained a bold promise to seek a constitutional amendment if the Supreme Court should continue to declare New Deal legislation unconstitutional.

The Republicans gathered in Cleveland to nominate a candidate. Herbert Hoover was hoping for a new nomination — and personal vindication. The party turned, however, to Governor Alfred M. Landon of Kansas, who had been a Bull Moose Republican in 1912. Landon had gained national attention for balancing his state's budget at a time when state and federal deficits had become commonplace. Landon's running mate was Colonel Frank Knox, a Chicago newspaper publisher who had fought as a Rough Rider in the Spanish-American War. The convention sang a parody of "O Susanna." It began:

> If Roos-e-velt would have his way
> We'd all be in his grip,
> And soon he'd change the ship of state
> To his dictatorship.

In spite of their scorn for Roosevelt, the Republicans adopted a platform endorsing

Auto license tags like this one urged Roosevelt's re-election in 1936. The Democrats won the contest in a landslide.

624

many New Deal measures, including unemployment insurance, old-age pensions, and benefit payments for farmers. The Republicans maintained that they could run these programs better than the Democrats.

The Democrats are returned to office. Roosevelt understood the issue of the campaign: "It's myself, and people must be either for me or against me." On Election Day, 1936, Roosevelt swamped the hapless Landon. Roosevelt, who won the electoral votes of every state except Maine and Vermont, was now at the height of his popularity. He had received 61 percent of the popular vote. No President since Monroe in 1820 had won such a sweeping victory.

SECTION REVIEW

1. What were some of the criticisms of the New Deal offered by Roosevelt's opponents?
2. What programs were provided in the Social Security Act?
3. (a) Why was the WPA established? (b) The National Youth Administration?
4. (a) How did the Wagner Act help organized labor? (b) Why was the CIO formed?
5. What New Deal programs did the Supreme Court declare unconstitutional?
6. (a) Who were the candidates in the 1936 election? (b) What was the outcome?

4 The New Deal Comes to an End

Seeing his re-election as a ringing endorsement of the second New Deal, President Roosevelt set about extending his programs. He could proceed without delay, for he became the first President to be inaugurated in the month of January, in accordance with the Twentieth Amendment, ratified in 1933 (page 611).

The President attacks the Supreme Court. Roosevelt had declared in his campaign that the nation was on the road to recovery. But how far did it still have to go? In his second inaugural address he spoke of the work ahead: "I see one third of a nation ill-housed, ill-clad, ill-nourished. It is not in despair that I paint you that picture. I paint it for you in hope — because the nation, seeing and understanding the injustice in it, proposes to paint it out. . . . "

At the same time that Roosevelt considered new programs, he felt concern that the Supreme Court might now invalidate some of the administration's reform measures as well. He was particularly fearful about the fate of the Wagner Act and the Social Security Act. In 1937 he proposed that a new justice be appointed for each one who did not retire upon reaching his seventieth birthday. (The total membership of the Court, however, was not to exceed fifteen.) At the time, six of the nine justices were seventy or older. Under Roosevelt's scheme, therefore, six new justices would be appointed. This would be more than enough to establish a pro-New Deal majority on the Supreme Court.

The Court issue weakens the New Deal. The response to Roosevelt's "court-packing" plan, as it was soon called, was generally unfavorable. Many members of the President's own party were dismayed at his attack on the "Nine Old Men," as the Court was sometimes called. After a long battle and seemingly endless discussion of the proposal in the newspapers, Congress would not go along with it.

While Congress was debating the Court plan, decisions handed down in the spring of 1937 upheld the Wagner Act and the unemployment-insurance tax provision of the Social Security Act. Soon afterward the Court upheld a minimum-wage law passed by the state of Washington, reversing the decision in the New York case of two years earlier (page 624). Some people had a clever explanation for the Court's new opinions: "A switch in time saves nine." In any case, a number of retirements from the Court soon enabled Roosevelt to appoint justices who supported New Deal legislation. Roosevelt could claim that he had lost a battle but won the war.

By now, however, the President's political support was noticeably weaker. Many

THAT COMPASS
DOESN'T POINT THE WAY
I WANT TO GO.
CHANGE IT.
NOW!

Roosevelt's "court-packing" plan cost him support. One cartoonist compared the President to an admiral trying to change a basic law of nature.

Americans felt less comfortable with his policies. They complained that the federal government had grown too large in size and power, and that labor unions had acquired too much influence in the Democratic Party. The attack on the Court, furthermore, had cost Roosevelt much popular support.

Another cause of popular dissatisfaction with the New Deal was its unconventional attitude toward government finances. Some of Roosevelt's advisers had been influenced by the English economist John Maynard Keynes (pronounced CANES). Keynes had argued that it is acceptable for the government to use monetary and fiscal policies to stimulate the economy. Millions of people were aghast, however, as the administration began to spend more than it took in through taxes. The national debt rose every year during Roosevelt's term of office. Standing at $22.5 billion in 1933, it had almost doubled by 1940.

Business slumps in 1937. Roosevelt was concerned about the unbalanced budget and in 1937 insisted on a sharp cut in government spending, including the outlays for relief. His aim was to assure Americans that he was working to keep expenditures from exceeding income. Unfortunately, private business was not yet strong enough to offer jobs to people dropped from the relief rolls. At the same time, industrial output was slowing down because the Federal Reserve Board had raised interest rates. Higher Social Security taxes, in addition, were taking a bigger bite of business profits. As a result, by the fall of 1937 Democrats had to admit that the country was in a *recession* (a moderate slump in business). Republicans, on the other hand, spoke of "Roosevelt's depression."

Roosevelt soon asked for a large "lend-spend" program for public works and other projects. Meanwhile, he searched for other ways to reduce unemployment, which in 1938 still stood at ten million. Critics charged that the immense number of people who still had no jobs after five years of the New Deal demonstrated the failure of Roosevelt's policies.

More New Deal legislation is passed. By 1938 the New Deal had lost its momentum. Only a few more important New Deal measures were put on the books. The Farm Security Administration, set up in 1937, was designed to enable tenant farmers to borrow money at low interest rates so that they could buy the land they worked. The United States Housing Authority was also formed in 1937. Its function was to lend money to state and local agencies for the purpose of clearing slums and building housing for the poor.

In 1938 Congress passed a second Agricultural Adjustment Act. The measure was aimed, as the first one had been (page 615), at reducing crop production. This time, however, subsidies would be provided by the Treasury itself, rather than through a tax. Farmers would be paid to store surplus quantities of wheat, corn, cotton, rice, and tobacco in warehouses. The deposited surpluses would help establish an "ever-normal granary" for use in years of scarcity.

Congress in 1938 also passed a Fair Labor Standards Act which affected all companies engaged in interstate commerce. The law provided eventually for a maximum workweek of forty hours and a minimum wage of forty cents an hour. The act also prohibited the employment of children under sixteen years of age.

Minority groups receive little attention. Despite his wide range of concerns, Roosevelt gave little attention to the subject of minority rights. He regarded those issues as politically unimportant. The plight of minorities, consequently, never became a significant concern for officials in the Roosevelt administration.

The Depression was a dreadful time for most black Americans. In the South, black tenant farmers and sharecroppers suffered terribly from the sharp drop in agricultural prices and from the persistent drought that blighted the region in the early thirties. In the North, many blacks who had started their own businesses during the 1920's saw their enterprises go bankrupt. Black industrial workers became victims of the "last hired, first fired" practice. At the depth of the Depression, over two thirds of all black Americans working in industry had lost their jobs.

Assistance and employment from such New Deal programs as the WPA helped thousands of black Americans survive the bad times. By 1939, only agriculture and domestic service provided more jobs for

Mary McLeod Bethune, shown here with Eleanor Roosevelt, supervised the administration's job-training program for minority youth.

black Americans than did the WPA. In all the New Deal programs, however, blacks usually had to accept lower wages than white workers.

Roosevelt slowly began to place blacks in significant federal positions. Practically every New Deal agency appointed an adviser on black affairs. By 1936 these people were being called the President's "black cabinet." Noteworthy members of the black cabinet included Mary McLeod Bethune, a college president who was named director of the Division of Negro Affairs of the National Youth Administration; Robert L. Vann, who was appointed Special Assistant to the United States Attorney General; and Robert C. Weaver, who served as a lawyer in the Interior Department. In addition, some black architects, engineers, and other professionals found work in government positions that had never before been open to black people. In 1937, Roosevelt appointed William Hastie, the dean of Howard University's law school, to be a judge in the Virgin Islands — the first black to sit on the federal bench.

Out of gratitude for what was provided by the Roosevelt programs, black voters began to leave the party of Lincoln and shift to the Democratic Party. This trend was apparent in the 1936 election, and by the end of the decade black Americans were giving Democratic candidates solid support at the polls.

Mexican Americans felt the force of the Depression as keenly as any other disadvantaged group. During the years of the Mexican Revolution (page 555), thousands of people had crossed the border from Mexico into the United States searching for work. The barrier of language and lack of education forced most newly arrived Mexicans to take low-paying jobs in agriculture, mining, or railroad construction. By the 1930's, over a million Mexicans had come to the United States — seeking a chance to improve their lives.

At the time the Depression took hold, most Mexican Americans were employed as migrant laborers, going from farm to farm harvesting crops. As a result, they were rarely affected by New Deal programs. To make matters worse, established labor groups often resented the migrant workers for accepting substandard wages — not recognizing that the newcomers were doing so out of necessity. Ill will reached such a level during the Depression that the United States and Mexico agreed on a program that would encourage migrants to return to Mexico. Some American officials went further, urging a policy of deportation. The resettlement program never accomplished its goals. Many people who went back to Mexico vowed they would one day live in the United States again.

American Indians were already in a state of economic and social disorder by the time the Depression set in. The Dawes Act of 1887 (page 425) had caused great confusion and distress among the tribes. The few non-Indians who bothered to inform themselves about the plight of the tribespeople regarded the Dawes Act as a failure. New programs and policies were considered, but the only positive result came in 1924 when Indians were granted citizenship.

In 1933, Roosevelt appointed John Collier to be Commissioner of Indian Affairs. Under Collier's guidance, the Indian Reorganization Act was passed by Congress in 1934. The act halted the allotment of land to individuals and re-established tribal ownership. It also provided for local tribal government, made loans available for businesses owned by Indians, and recognized the need for programs to teach new methods of farming, irrigation, and land development. Of no less significance to American Indians was a provision encouraging efforts to reintroduce traditional customs, beliefs, and crafts to the communal life of the tribes.

Efforts at reform come to an end. The President continued to believe that new measures of reform were required to restore prosperity to America. As international events took more and more of his time, however, the steam went out of domestic efforts. In 1939 Roosevelt proposed to Congress no new major legislation. The need, he said, was "to preserve our reforms." The New Deal was coming to an end.[4]

How effective was the New Deal? Roosevelt's domestic policies aroused in people either blind devotion or burning distrust. Few could be neutral about FDR. Even today Americans disagree in assessing his role in the nation's history. Still, the legacy of the New Deal shows itself most prominently in the idea that people in the United States are a national resource. The belief that no individual should ever want for the necessities of life became firmly rooted in the American mind. A companion of this view is that government, far from being the master of the people, must be its servant — and a reliable friend in time of need.

New Deal programs, furthermore, transformed the physical condition of the country. The thousands of WPA projects, the TVA complex, and many other enterprises remain visible reminders of the remarkable era in which they burst upon the scene.

Nevertheless, the New Deal failed to end large-scale unemployment and thus cure the Depression. Nor did Roosevelt make even a dent in the hard-core poverty afflicting many people, both urban and rural. Moreover, during his time in office the federal bureaucracy swelled from 600,000 employees to 3,800,000, turning government into big business. The new federal agencies in which these civil servants worked often created rules and regulations that business people found a discouraging obstruction to private enterprise.

Roosevelt sometimes seemed to foster governmental activity for its own sake. He counted on the unshakable loyalty of his followers to make whatever he tried seem necessary and right. He saw himself, though, as working in a noble purpose with fellow-citizens, whom he often spoke to informally on the radio in what he called "fire-

---

[4]Roosevelt never lost his exuberance for breaking fresh ground. He enjoyed being the first President ever to appear on television — at an experimental telecast at the 1939 New York World's Fair.

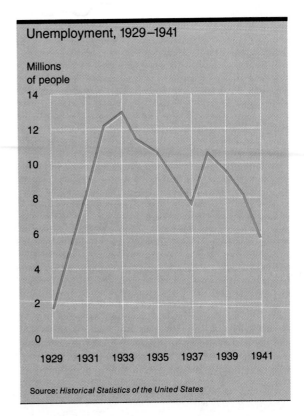

Unemployment, 1929–1941

Millions of people

Source: *Historical Statistics of the United States*

The unemployment rate, at a record level when Roosevelt was inaugurated in 1933, remained high throughout the decade.

side chats." The aim was to renew and restore the nation's flagging spirit. Will Rogers, a beloved humorist of the day, once visited the White House and asked Mrs. Roosevelt, "Where is the President?" She replied, "Wherever you hear the laugh." Even though Roosevelt was so disabled that he had to lock his legs into heavy steel braces before he could be helped to stand, he taught Americans to laugh again. It was the laugh of a people whose confidence was reviving and who could believe that once more the nation was on the way.

SECTION REVIEW

1. Vocabulary: *recession*.
2. (a) What was Roosevelt's "court-packing" plan? (b) What was the outcome?
3. (a) What New Deal measures were passed in 1937 and 1938? (b) Why did the reform program come to an end after 1938?

Chapter 26 Review

Summary

When Herbert Hoover became President in March, 1929, Americans looked forward to a prosperous future. Before the year was out, however, the United States was entering the worst economic depression in its history. As the Great Depression deepened, it affected every sector of society. Unemployment soared to record levels, and thousands of families lost their homes and possessions. Farmers suffered not only from falling crop prices but also from a severe drought that turned part of the country into a "dust bowl."

President Hoover believed that the road to recovery lay chiefly in voluntary actions. By 1932, however, voters responded to Franklin Delano Roosevelt's promise of a "new deal." Immediately upon taking office as President, Roosevelt recommended new laws to provide emergency relief. He also backed recovery measures intended to end the Depression, and reform measures that he hoped would solve long-standing economic problems.

The key pieces of New Deal legislation extended the power of the federal government and created a series of agencies to administer relief and recovery programs. Direct relief was distributed to the unemployed, while millions of young men were put to work in special relief projects. Farmers were given payments to reduce production of certain crops in order to raise prices. Industry was asked to cooperate in setting fair prices and wages. The Tennessee Valley Authority built dams, irrigation systems, and hydroelectric plants on a scale never before attempted by the government. Laws were also passed to protect bank depositors and to regulate the sale of stocks and bonds.

Early in 1935, Roosevelt proposed legislation that called for government to assume far-reaching responsibility for the well-being of its citizens. The Social Security Act and the Wagner Labor Relations Act were the principal pieces of new legislation.

After his re-election in 1936, Roosevelt attacked the Supreme Court, which had declared important New Deal measures unconstitutional. His plan to "pack" the Court was criticized by many Americans, however, and was defeated in Congress. By 1939 all the major New Deal laws had been passed.

New Deal legislation never brought an end to large-scale unemployment. Still, Franklin Roosevelt's place in American history is secure. His influence restored the faith of Americans in the power of representative government to deal with its problems, boldly and imaginatively.

Vocabulary and Important Terms

1. margin
2. Dust Bowl
3. Agricultural Marketing Act
4. Reconstruction Finance Corporation
5. Bonus Army
6. brain trust
7. Civilian Conservation Corps
8. Agricultural Adjustment Act
9. National Industrial Recovery Act
10. Tennessee Valley Authority
11. Liberty League
12. Social Security Act
13. Works Progress Administration
14. Wagner Act
15. recession
16. Indian Reorganization Act

Discussion Questions

1. (a) What was the first stage of the Great Depression? (b) As the Depression got under way, what did Hoover believe to be the cure for the nation's economic problems?

2. (a) How well-defined was Franklin Roosevelt's pledge to provide a "new deal for the American people"? (b) What did the words "new deal" suggest?

3. (a) Describe the banking crisis that Roosevelt faced when he took office. (b) What steps did he take to meet the crisis?

4. (a) What was the "Hundred Days"? (b) Into what three categories did the laws of the New Deal fall?

5. (a) What was the second New Deal? (b) How was the responsibility of government expanded under the second New Deal?

6. How did each of the following criticize the New Deal? (a) Liberty League (b) Huey Long (c) Francis Townsend (d) Father Coughlin (e) Herbert Hoover

7. (a) Why was the Roosevelt administration regarded as being friendly to labor unions? (b) How did labor repay Roosevelt?

8. (a) Why did Roosevelt see the Supreme Court as a major barrier to the success of the second New Deal? (b) How did his "court-packing" plan actually play into the hands of New Deal opponents?

9. (a) Describe the problems faced by blacks, Mexican Americans, and American Indians during the Depression. (b) How was each group affected by New Deal programs and measures?

Relating Past and Present

1. The passage of the Social Security Act marked an important change in America's economic and so-

cial life. What is the status of the Social Security System today? What concerns do the American people have about it? What changes have been proposed to ensure that the system is on a sound footing?

2. Which of the programs initiated by the Roosevelt administration has had lasting significance? Explain why in each case.

3. Union membership grew steadily during Roosevelt's years in office, reaching almost 36 percent of the work force in 1945. Find out what percentage of the American work force belongs to labor unions today. What factors help explain the change in percentage?

Studying Local History

Find out if any buildings, parks, or roads were built in your community as part of a New Deal program. If so, find out what kind of project it was and if it is still in use today.

Using History Skills

1. *Reading source material.* Study Mahalia Jackson's recollections of the Depression on page 608. (a) What, according to Mahalia Jackson, was the effect of the Depression on black people in Chicago? (b) Was that effect sudden or gradual? (c) Why did she believe that the Depression hit northern blacks harder than southern blacks?

2. *Reading graphs.* Study the graph on page 629 showing unemployment figures. (a) Approximately how many million people were out of work in 1931? (b) In 1939? (c) How would a critic of the New Deal interpret the information contained in this graph?

3. *Organizing information.* Turn to the list of Presidents at the back of the book. Which Presidents were defeated when they ran for re-election? Then, using the index to locate the appropriate pages in your book, find out the reason for the defeat of each of those Presidents. Explain these reasons in a sentence or two.

WORLD SCENE

International Transportation

In the 1920's and 1930's developments in ocean and air transportation significantly reduced the time of travel from one part of the world to another. Journeys that once took weeks could now be made in days or even hours.

Commercial aviation. After the First World War hundreds of American military aircraft were fitted out for civilian use. By the mid-1920's these planes were flying everywhere, seemingly shrinking the distances between the continents. The popularity of air travel grew rapidly: a total of only 18,000 people flew in 1927; that number had reached 3,500,000 by 1938.

In 1928 Germany inaugurated transatlantic flights to North and South America. The Germans used huge, lighter-than-air craft called Zeppelins — in honor of Count Zeppelin, who had designed them. These airships carried up to fifty passengers in plush accommodations. Zeppelins were slow and expensive, however, and flights were often delayed by bad weather. When the *Hindenburg* exploded while landing in New Jersey in 1937, the day of the airship was suddenly over.

Ocean liners. The vast majority of travelers in the 1920's and 1930's crossed the Atlantic in fast, luxurious, passenger liners. Many of these giant ships could make the voyage to North America in just over four days.

The French liner *Ile de France* was launched in 1926 and was the first modern ocean liner built for speed as well as comfort. France stayed in the forefront of transatlantic passenger service with the launching of the *Normandie* in 1932.

The British Cunard Line, whose *Lusitania* had been one of the fastest liners before the First World War, decided to challenge French dominance of the North Atlantic passenger trade. Cunard built the *Queen Mary* and the *Queen Elizabeth*, both of which rivaled the French liners in speed and luxury.

The ocean liners were floating palaces. Passengers could feast in elegant dining rooms, dance in ballrooms to the music of famous orchestras, lounge around huge swimming pools, or enjoy the latest movies in the ships' theaters. By the late 1940's, however, airplanes were flying daily to Europe in a fraction of the time and at about half the cost of traveling by ship. As more and more people chose to fly, the age of the luxurious liners came to a close.

From Isolation to Involvement

1920 – 1941

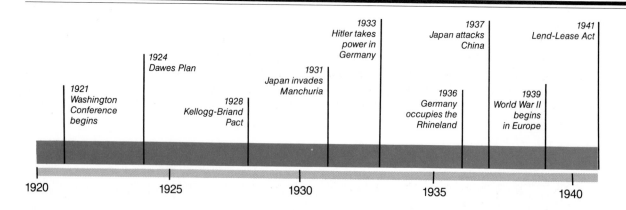

1921
Washington
Conference
begins

1924
Dawes Plan

1928
Kellogg-Briand
Pact

1931
Japan invades
Manchuria

1933
Hitler takes
power in
Germany

1936
Germany
occupies the
Rhineland

1937
Japan attacks
China

1939
World War II
begins
in Europe

1941
Lend-Lease Act

1920   1925   1930   1935   1940

CHAPTER OUTLINE

1. The United States plays a limited role in world affairs during the 1920's.

2. The United States governs its possessions.

3. Dictators menace world peace.

4. World War II begins.

With the end of the First World War, Americans could see that the United States had the most powerful economy in the world. Woodrow Wilson spoke exuberantly of the future: "The financial leadership will be ours. The industrial primacy will be ours. The commercial advantage will be ours. The other countries of the world are looking to us for leadership and direction."

By 1920 the picture of American economic power was awesome. The United States was pumping nearly 70 percent of the world's petroleum and digging 40 percent of the world's coal. The nation lacked supplies of some raw materials, but in general it was more nearly economically independent of the rest of the world than any other country.

Americans were making serious inroads, furthermore, in markets formerly dominated by Europeans. American automobiles, especially, were on the shopping list of many wealthy foreigners. The center of world banking and finance, moreover, had shifted from London to New York.

A comparable shift in world political authority was also taking place. Though the United States had not joined the League of Nations, its voice was a weighty factor in foreign affairs. That voice was, nevertheless, uncertain. Masters of industrial production, Americans were still only apprentices in conducting international relations. Their education, which could no longer be postponed, would come during decades that were fateful for all humanity.

1 The United States Plays a Limited Role in World Affairs During the 1920's

The First World War had a far-reaching effect on the world's economic situation: it changed the United States from a debtor to a creditor nation. By 1919, European governments owed the United States more than $10 billion.

WAR DEBTS AND TARIFFS

The question of war debts divides the Allies. By the end of the war, the bankrupt nations of Europe had no idea how they could pay off their debts to the United States. The British and French, who owed the most money, assumed that they could use reparations payments collected from Germany (page 575) to repay their war debts to the United States. Germany, however, was in the midst of a severe economic crisis and soon fell behind in its payments.

A number of Europeans suggested solutions to the problem. The proposal heard most often was that both the German reparations and the war debts be scaled down. There were also suggestions that the debtors be permitted to pay their obligations in industrial goods — an idea that no American manufacturer wished to hear. Some Europeans went so far as to advocate the outright cancellation of all war debts. It was only fair, went the argument, that the

The United States was the world's leading industrial power by the time the artist Charles Sheeler painted *American Landscape* in 1930.

United States bear this burden because the European allies had fought much longer than the Americans and had also suffered heavier losses in life and property. Spokesmen from France, moreover, did not hesitate to point out that the French had never been reimbursed for their military assistance during the War for Independence. The United States, they maintained, should absorb the war debts, just as France had once borne the cost of its aid to America.

Woodrow Wilson and his successors in the White House refused to accept the arguments against full repayment. Calvin Coolidge expressed a view shared by most Americans: "They hired the money, didn't they?" There were other sound reasons for saying no. One was that the arguments of the debtors surely did not apply to the substantial loans that had been made in the years following the war. (During the 1920's, American bankers lent Europe nearly $5 billion.) Futhermore, American military sacrifices in the war had been substantial too. Finally, it was not the United States that had insisted on reparations from the defeated Central Powers, but the Allies themselves. In addition, the United States had neither sought nor received territory from the defeated countries, as the other victors had.

The war debts are never repaid. Despite its unwillingness to connect the payment of reparations to war debts, the United States government lent its support to various plans devised to help Germany meet its payments — originally set at $33 billion. Charles G. Dawes, a Chicago banker, came up with a plan in 1924 that was readily adopted. It called for American and Allied bankers to lend Germany millions of dollars for the purpose of boosting industrial recovery and making the German currency stable. In 1928 the Young Plan — the work of Owen D. Young, an American industrialist — cut down Germany's annual payments and limited them to 59 years. In return, the Allies agreed to end their occupation of German territory and to end their controls on the German economy.

These plans strengthened the confidence of American investors who were buying German government and corporation bonds. When the worldwide economic collapse began in 1929, however, the American investments ended, and the reparations could no longer be paid. The European nations agreed in 1932 to accept cancellation of Germany's reparations payments. Then, in the following year, all the governments that owed war debts (except Finland) defaulted on their payments. In all, Germany paid about $4.5 billion in reparations. The Allies, in turn, paid off about $2.5 billion in war debts to the United States.

The United States raises tariff rates. America's mostly unsuccessful attempts to collect war debts caused resentment in Europe. So, too, did America's tariff policy. Many European countries had looked forward after the war to being able to sell their products in the United States. The sale of such products, these countries assumed, would enable them to pay off their obligations. Soon after the war, however, the leading industrial nations were battling one another with a new weapon: tariffs. In the United States the Fordney-McCumber Tariff Act of 1922, for example, increased import duties on hundreds of items.

During the 1920's, many Americans believed the protective tariff to be the basis of prosperity. Indeed, the idea was so well accepted that in response to the onset of the Great Depression, Congress in 1930 passed the Hawley-Smoot Tariff, raising rates yet again. After first protesting the enactment of this tariff, one foreign nation after another put into effect self-protecting tariffs aimed at the United States. Many American businesses and farms were thus deprived of needed markets.

NEW ROADS TO SECURITY

Debate over the League of Nations continues. In the years after the First World War, many people remained gravely concerned over the failure of the United States to join the League of Nations. To be formally linked with other nations, these people said, could provide *collective security* — the mutual protection that becomes possible when countries stand together against peace-breakers. John H. Clarke, a Democrat who had recently retired from the Supreme Court, was in favor of the United States entering the League. He insisted, "If we remain out of it, the next war will come as the last one did, without our having any opportunity to prevent it and with only the privilege of fighting our way out of it."

Arguments on the other side were no less passionate. Proponents of remaining out of the League maintained that the United States must not be burdened with permanent obligations. These people were not shunning the rest of the world. They were simply arguing that the United States must keep itself free to work on behalf of justice wherever help might be required.

The United States cooperates with the League. Although the United States had no formal association with the League of Nations, it cooperated with the League's nonpolitical agencies. It participated in world health programs, in the control of international drug traffic, and in efforts to improve the conditions of labor. It may be said that United States policy, which began as "nonrecognition," gave way to "unofficial cooperation." By 1931 there were five permanent American representatives at Geneva, Switzerland — the headquarters of the League — to monitor issues that concerned the United States.

It is pointless to guess whether international problems would have been more satisfactorily handled if the United States had joined the League of Nations. Americans came quickly to see that the United States would have to cooperate with other nations for its own well-being. The Harding administration, soon after taking power, was seeking ways to accomplish this goal. It focused attention on *disarmament* (a reduction in the size of military forces).

A disarmament conference is held in Washington. Even before the First World War ended, an intense naval race had developed involving the United States, Great Britain,

and Japan. After the peace, Japan began building naval bases on Pacific islands that had come under its control. Many people, remembering how the arms race in Europe before 1914 had led finally to war, feared that a naval armaments contest might lead to a similar outcome.

Since most Americans wished to avoid such a competition, not to mention a war with Japan, the time seemed ripe to take steps. The task of finding a solution to the problem was undertaken by Senator William E. Borah. Borah had taken a leading part in keeping the United States out of the League of Nations. Now he felt forced to find a substitute arrangement for the nation's security.

In the spring of 1921, Borah proposed that the United States invite Great Britain and Japan to a conference in Washington, D.C., for the purpose of discussing naval disarmament. Both houses of Congress approved the proposal. President Harding then sent invitations to the nine major powers having interests in Asian affairs.

The conference, held in Washington's Memorial Continental Hall, pleased many Americans, who continued to think that Wilson should never have traveled to Europe in 1918. A well-known journalist wrote of his feelings as he entered the simple meeting chamber, whose chief adornments were portraits of George and Martha Washington: "How infinitely more beautiful is this room than the glaring red and gold of the room at Paris where the Peace Conference was held."

The sessions began on November 12, 1921. The delegates had been deeply moved the day before — the third anniversary of the armistice — when the Unknown Soldier was buried with the highest military honors at Arlington National Cemetery in nearby Virginia. The representatives had had an opportunity to reflect on the terrible cost of war. Only a few people knew about the startling proposal Secretary of State Charles Evans Hughes was about to present.

Hughes entered the hall with an air of confidence. Newspaper reporters liked to say they could tell the state of American foreign relations by the condition of Hughes' beard. This day, an observer wrote, "every hair was at a satisfactory upward angle." Within minutes of beginning his speech, Hughes surprised his audience. He suggested that the major powers set limits on the number of battleships in their navies. This meant the scrapping of ships already built or under construction. Hughes also called for a ten-year "holiday" in the construction of all capital ships (that is, battleships and heavy cruisers).

The British and the Japanese were stunned by Hughes's proposal. An English military commentator said that the Secretary was proposing to sink "in 35 minutes more ships than all the admirals of the world have sunk in a cycle of centuries." When the conference reassembled after a weekend to think over the American proposal, however, world opinion seemed to be firmly behind it.

Subsequent negotiations produced a number of agreements. The first and most dramatic of these was the Five-Power Treaty, so called because the signers were the five great sea powers. Signed in February, 1922, it provided for a ten-year "holiday" in naval shipbuilding that would bring the capital-ship strength of the United States, Britain, and Japan into a ratio of 5:5:3. France and Italy were each to have a ratio of 1.67 to the other powers. Some Japanese diplomats were displeased with the treaty. Still, the arrangement was advantageous to Japan, because the United States and Britain also agreed not to fortify further their possessions in the western Pacific — including the Philippines and Hong Kong.

The Washington Conference seeks international cooperation in Asia. A second agreement reached that year at Washington was the Four-Power Pact, entered into by the United States, Great Britain, Japan, and France. The nations signing the pact agreed to respect one another's possessions in the Pacific. What made the treaty remarkable was that it rested upon the word and pledge of the signing nations — not on a specific military commitment or international organization. A third agreement signed by all the delegates at the conference, and known as the Nine-Power Treaty, guaranteed the independence and territorial unity of China. For the first time, an international gathering had recognized the doctrine of the Open Door (page 525).

Later disarmament conferences are held. Most Americans applauded the results of the Washington Conference (1921–1922), and the Senate gave its approval to the three treaties. In the years that followed, however, concern grew over a new naval competition in the construction of smaller vessels (submarines and destroyers). In 1927 President Coolidge invited all the nations that had signed the Five-Power Treaty to meet at Geneva. Only Britain and Japan accepted the invitation, and the conference was a failure. Seemingly more successful was another meeting held in London in 1930. It produced an agreement among Great Britain, the United States, and Japan to extend the naval holiday for five more years. It also set limitations on the building of smaller vessels. In 1935, however, a year before that treaty was set to expire, Japan demanded naval equality with the United States and Great Britain. When this demand was refused, Japan withdrew from the treaty.

An attempt is made to outlaw war. While the United States was participating in the naval disarmament movement, it also took the lead in an effort to outlaw war. The intriguing proposal to declare war illegal was first made by a Chicago lawyer named Salmon O. Levinson. Levinson captivated Senator Borah with the idea. Another group that eventually supported the proposal were backers of American entry into the League of Nations. They believed that if all nations renounced war, the League would become the agency of enforcement.

The movement was getting nowhere when a Columbia University professor named James T. Shotwell persuaded the French foreign minister, Aristide Briand (bree-AHN), that the United States and France ought to conclude a "pact of perpetual friendship." On April 6, 1927, the tenth anniversary of America's entry into World

War I, Briand made such a proposal. He called, in addition, for an agreement between the United States and France to outlaw war between the two countries. The French saw such a treaty as possible protection against any revival of German military power.

Not enthusiastic about Briand's proposal, Secretary of State Frank B. Kellogg was slow in responding. The public, however, still imagining a world without war, supported the French suggestion. On August 27, 1928, the United States and France, joined by thirteen other nations (all of the major countries except the Soviet Union) signed the Pact of Paris — sometimes called the Kellogg-Briand Pact. They solemnly renounced war "as an instrument of national policy" in their relations with one another. In time the treaty was signed by more than sixty nations.

There were critics of the Pact. One of them called it "an international kiss." Senator Carter Glass of Virginia hoped, he said, that the people of his state did not think he considered the treaty "worth a postage stamp." Many Americans, along with people everywhere, could see that the treaty said nothing about enforcement. Nor did it exclude wars fought in self-defense — a label that even aggressors could apply to their adventuring.

RELATIONS WITH LATIN AMERICA

Diplomacy repairs relations with Latin America. In the days of Roosevelt, Taft, and Wilson, the United States had periodically intervened in Latin American countries, in part to keep out meddling European powers. After the armistice ending the world war, no European nation dared challenge United States military and naval authority in the Western Hemisphere. As a result, there were signs that the United States was modifying the Roosevelt Corollary (page 544). Secretary Hughes, for instance, allowed marines stationed in the Dominican Republic in 1916 to leave in 1924 after a constitutional regime was established there.

Under the terms of the Kellogg-Briand Pact, signed in Paris in 1928, more than sixty countries agreed to ban war as an instrument of national policy.

Efforts to pull American troops out of Nicaragua were more halting. Marines had been sent to that country in 1912 to monitor a government deeply in debt. They were withdrawn in 1925 after the financial situation improved. Civil war soon broke out, however, as rebels sought to oust the government, and in 1927 President Coolidge sent troops to Nicaragua once more.

In the United States there was so much opposition to Coolidge's action that he sent Colonel Henry L. Stimson (who had been Secretary of War under Taft) to Nicaragua to seek a settlement between the competing groups. Stimson succeeded in bringing to power the Nicaraguan rebels, and they quickly received United States support. As relations between the Americans and the Nicaraguans improved, the United States gradually pulled out its troops — the last of them in 1933. Almost immediately Anastasio Somoza began to rise to power. He and his family would rule Nicaragua for the next 45 years.

Relations with Mexico improve. Tension between the United States and Mexico had been high ever since the withdrawal of American troops from Mexican soil in 1917 (page 556). The key to the dispute was a provision in the Mexican constitution of 1917 giving the Mexican people control over all oil and mineral resources. An unanswered question was whether or not the provision applied to mineral and oil properties acquired by Americans before 1917. In 1923 Mexico agreed not to interfere with those rights. Then, in 1924 an ardent nationalist, Plutarco Calles (KAH-yays), became president of Mexico. He made clear that he intended to abandon the arrangement of 1923 in favor of a new one.

A desire on both sides for a peaceful resolution of the dispute led President Coolidge in the summer of 1927 to send his Amherst College classmate, Dwight W. Morrow, to Mexico City as United States ambassador. Morrow was uncommonly successful. His warm personality attracted the good will of the rough and ready Calles. The two men worked out a compromise on American rights to Mexican oil and minerals. Companies that had begun to work their subsoil holdings before 1917 would be permitted to keep them. Meanwhile, the Mexican public's view of America was greatly helped by a good-will flight late in 1927 from Washington to Mexico City by Charles A. Lindbergh, fresh from his conquest of the Atlantic (page 601) and soon to become Morrow's son-in-law.

Hoover travels to Latin America. Stimson and Morrow had contributed notably to the idea that the Roosevelt Corollary was now out of date. Shortly after Herbert Hoover was inaugurated President, he went on a tour of the Latin American republics. In his speeches he emphasized America's desire "to maintain not only the cordial relations of governments with each other but the relations of good neighbors."

Nothing helped to demonstrate America's change in policy better than a memorandum written by Undersecretary of State J. Reuben Clark in 1928 and made public in 1930. "The Monroe Doctrine," said the Clark Memorandum, "states a case of the United States vs. Europe, not of the United States vs. Latin America." The Doctrine could not be used, therefore, as justification for American intervention in the internal affairs of its neighbors. Clark's statement was unofficial — and was even treated as unimportant by President Hoover — but it helped somewhat to clear the air in United States-Latin American relations.

SECTION REVIEW

1. Vocabulary: *collective security, disarmament.*
2. (a) What problem arose when Germany failed to make its reparations payments? (b) Why did the United States reject the suggestion that the Allies' war debts be reduced or canceled?
3. In what ways did the United States cooperate with the League of Nations?
4. (a) What conditions led to the Washington Conference of 1921–1922? (b) What agreements were reached concerning disarmament? (c) Concerning cooperation in Asia? (d) Why did Japan later withdraw from the treaty?
5. (a) What was the Kellogg-Briand Pact? (b) Why was it hailed by some and criticized by others?
6. (a) Why did relations with Latin America improve in the years after World War I? (b) What was the Clark Memorandum?

2 The United States Governs Its Possessions

Throughout the 1920's and 1930's the United States prepared its major possessions for self-government and eventual independence. The mood of the late nineteenth century, when so many voices had been lifted in favor of having colonies, had passed. Americans were finding that they had no enthusiasm for ruling other peoples. Moreover, they had learned that it is more difficult and expensive to manage possessions than to acquire them.

The constitutional status of the territories is fixed. A difficult question for Americans from the time they first acquired possessions was whether or not the people living in the territories were entitled to the rights

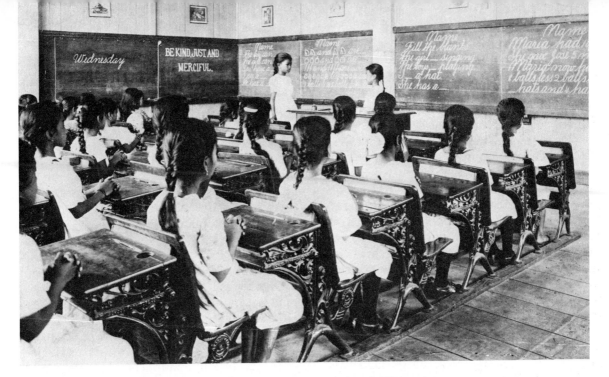

The United States established public schools in the Philippines to help train Filipinos in the ways of self-government.

and privileges of American citizens. The question was often stated this way, "Does the Constitution follow the flag?"

A number of Supreme Court cases, known as the Insular Cases, answered this question and related ones. Beginning in 1901 the Supreme Court ruled that there were two kinds of possessions to be considered — incorporated and unincorporated. The Court went on to say that in the incorporated possessions — those which were destined for statehood — inhabitants could enjoy the fundamental rights guaranteed by the Constitution. In the unincorporated possessions — those which were *not* destined for statehood — the inhabitants would enjoy life, liberty, and the right of property. They would not, however, be entitled to all constitutional guarantees.

The United States sets up territorial governments. Having had no experience in governing colonies, Americans invented their methods as they went along. After 1900, for instance, Hawaii was under the rule of a governor and a territorial legislature — the way American territories had always been governed. The Department of the Interior was responsible for Hawaii (and for Alaska).

Being primarily naval stations, the Virgin Islands, Guam, Tutuila, and Wake Island (map, page 523) were placed under the jurisdiction of the Department of the Navy. The Philippines, and a few years later the Panama Canal Zone, were put under the control of the Department of War. This department also took over responsibility for Puerto Rico after 1901.

In 1931 a Division of Territories and Island Possessions was organized in the Department of the Interior. This body became responsible for all of America's possessions except Guam, American Samoa, Wake Island, the Virgin Islands, and the Canal Zone. The three Pacific islands and the Virgin Islands remained under the Department of the Navy; the Canal Zone remained under the Department of War.

Guam in 1950 and American Samoa in 1951 were transferred from the Department of the Navy to the Department of the Interior. In 1950 Congress granted United States citizenship to the residents of Guam, along with the right to send a nonvoting representative to Congress. Guam has a governor and a legislature, who, since 1970, have been popularly elected. American Samoa, meanwhile, elected its first governor in

1977 and also sends a nonvoting representative to Congress. The Virgin Islands have elected their own governor since 1970. The residents of the Virgin Islands have been United States citizens since 1927.

The Panama Canal, beginning in 1951, has been operated by a federal agency, the Panama Canal Company. The governor of the Zone, chosen by the President, also serves as president of the company. A treaty signed by the United States and Panama in 1978 was designed to provide for the future of the Canal Zone. Under the treaty, the United States agreed to give Panama full control over the canal at the end of 1999.

American influence remains strong in Cuba. In accordance with the Teller Amendment (page 518), the United States promised to leave Cuba after the island had won its independence from Spain. The American government expected, however, to exercise some control over the new republic. In 1901, therefore, Congress set forth in the so-called Platt Amendment certain conditions that it insisted be incorporated in the Cuban constitution. Cuba's treaty-making powers and its right to borrow money were restricted. Cuba, furthermore, could not refuse to sell or lease lands to the United States for coaling or naval stations. (Accordingly, in 1903 the United States acquired the land around Guantánamo Bay for the construction of a naval base.) Lastly, the United States retained the right to intervene in Cuba "for the protection of life, property, and individual liberty." During the next decades the United States frequently intervened in Cuban affairs, aiming to protect American interests there. The Platt Amendment remained a bone of contention until it was canceled in 1934.

Puerto Rico gains some self-government. When Puerto Rico was acquired by the United States (page 522), General Miles had assured the people that they would receive "the guarantees and blessings of the liberal institutions of our government." Many Puerto Ricans, however, were disappointed in the civil government set up under the terms of the Foraker Act of 1900. Under that law, Puerto Rico was granted a House of Delegates elected by popular vote. Legislation passed by the House of Delegates had to be approved by the governor, who was appointed by the President of the United States. The President also appointed the members of the upper house, which was known as the Executive Council. The United States Congress, furthermore, had the power to overturn any law passed by the House of Delegates. The Foraker Act declared the island's people to be citizens of Puerto Rico, not of the United States. Puerto Ricans were represented in Washington by a resident commissioner with a seat, but no voice or vote, in the United States House of Representatives. Many Puerto Ricans were offended because under Spanish rule they had been equal in status to citizens residing in Spain. They had also been represented in the Spanish parliament.

Puerto Ricans soon began to seek a larger role in their own political destiny. In 1910 Luis Muñoz Rivera became Puerto Rico's resident commissioner in Washington. Muñoz Rivera had led Puerto Rico's movement for self-government in the last days of Spanish rule. Now he directed his energies toward gaining from the United States more rights for his people.

Muñoz Rivera's efforts began to bear fruit in 1917 when Congress passed the Jones Act. Under this law, citizens of Puerto Rico were granted United States citizenship. (Some Puerto Ricans objected on the ground that the island's people had not been formally consulted about their wishes in the matter.) A senate to be elected by Puerto Ricans was also established. The governor of the island, however, continued to be an appointee of the President. Congress, furthermore, reserved the right to annul or amend any act passed by the island's legislature.

The Jones Act failed to satisfy most Puerto Ricans. The continued campaign of the islanders for more self-government was rewarded in 1947 when Congress passed a law enabling them to elect their own governor. The governor, whose term would be four years, was also empowered to appoint the heads of the executive departments, with the consent of the island's senate. (Judges of Puerto Rico's highest court continued to be appointed by the President of the United States.)

Puerto Rico becomes a commonwealth. In 1948 the leading candidate for governor was Luis Muñoz Marin, son of the revered Muñoz Rivera. Muñoz Marin was the most popular politician on the island and he was easily elected. He then proposed a new status for the island.

In 1952 a new constitution was approved by Congress and by the voters of Puerto Rico. It made the island a self-governing commonwealth under United States protection. As residents of a commonwealth, Puerto Ricans would pay no federal income taxes and would be able to move to the mainland without being subject to immigration restrictions.

For the first time, the islanders had voted on their own relationship to the United States. It was understood, furthermore, that no future alteration in the status of Puerto Rico would be made without the express consent of the Puerto Ricans.

The Filipinos seek independence. The Philippines were the most distant and most populous of American possessions. In 1901 William Howard Taft was named the first governor of the islands. In the following year, Congress passed an act declaring the inhabitants to be citizens of the Philippine Islands "entitled to the protection of the United States." A law enacted in 1907 provided for a two-house legislative assembly, the lower house to be elected every two years. The upper house would consist of members of a commission appointed by the President.

In 1912 the Democratic platform contained a pledge to set the Philippine Islands free as soon as practicable. President Wilson sought to fulfill this promise with passage of the Jones Act of 1916 (not to be confused with the Jones Act of 1917 regarding Puerto Rico). Under this law an elective senate replaced the commission as the upper house of the Philippine legislature. The Jones Act

Luis Muñoz Marin, the first elected governor of Puerto Rico, helped make his island a self-governing commonwealth.

promised independence "as soon as a stable government can be established."

During the 1920's the Filipinos made repeated requests for independence. Finally, in 1934 the Tydings-McDuffie Act provided for complete independence for the Philippines, following a transition period of ten years. The outbreak of World War II interrupted that period, delaying fulfillment of the promise. On July 4, 1946, independence came to the islands, and the Republic of the Philippines was born.

SECTION REVIEW

1. According to the Supreme Court, what was the difference between incorporated and unincorporated possessions?
2. How is each of the following possessions governed? (a) Guam (b) American Samoa (c) Virgin Islands (d) Canal Zone
3. (a) Describe the government set up in Puerto Rico under the Foraker Act. (b) What rights did Puerto Ricans gain in 1917? (c) What rights did they gain in 1947? (d) What step did the voters of Puerto Rico take in 1952?
4. Describe the steps by which the Philippines gained independence.

3 Dictators Menace World Peace

While the United States was making adjustments in the governing of its territorial holdings, the long shadow of a possible new war dominated relations with Europe. By the mid-1930's, changed conditions were upsetting the structure of peace that had been established in Paris in 1919.

Dictators come to power in Europe. In central and eastern Europe, governments seeking democratic reforms had arisen after the First World War, replacing the defeated monarchies. Few democratic governments, however, lasted long. They were too weak and inexperienced to cope with the chaos that war and hard times had left behind. People began to heed the promises offered by demagogues — leaders who appeal to emotion and to prejudice.

In a number of countries *totalitarian* regimes were set up, so named because a single leader and his close supporters exercised absolute control over all spheres of life. Opposition parties were not tolerated. Indeed, all opposition was cruelly suppressed. In ad-

Adolf Hitler, shown reviewing troops, set up a totalitarian regime in Germany.

dition, traditional freedoms were not allowed: every individual had to bow to the will of the state. Meanwhile, arms industries were expanded and the military spirit was glorified.

The first of the totalitarian governments had been established in the Soviet Union after the Bolsheviks seized power in 1917 (page 570). The Bolsheviks' use of a single-party system, of secret police, and of murder as a political tool provided a model for similar brutality in other countries. By the mid-1920's the Soviet Union had come under the control of Joseph Stalin. Through systematic "liquidation" of his political opponents, Stalin made his dictatorship unchallengeable in the Soviet Union. The reign of terror he let loose on his own people was unmatched in history.

By the early 1930's, concern in the West over developments in Russia was overshadowed by events in Germany. There, under the direction of Adolf Hitler and his Nazi Party subordinates, Germany made bold plans for the future.

Shortly after World War I (in which he had served as a corporal in the German army) Hitler began plotting to overthrow the republican government of Germany. While serving a prison term in 1923 for political activities, Hitler wrote *Mein Kampf* ("My Struggle"). The book, ferociously anti-democratic as well as anti-Semitic, gradually became the guide to the future for disillusioned Germans. By 1933 Hitler had attracted millions of followers and was named to the high office of chancellor. Within the next few years he gained control of all branches of the Germany government. Meanwhile, he was making plans to restore Germany's military power.

In Italy, too, plans were being laid to carry out military adventures. Benito Mussolini had made himself Italy's dictator in 1922. In the next few years, with the aid of his Fascist Party, he wiped out the republican institutions of his country. By the 1930's he had made the very word *fascism*, the name of his dictatorial system, a synonym for anti-democracy. Mussolini's announced goal in foreign affairs was to convert the Mediterranean Sea into an Italian lake by taking control of neighboring territory. Mussolini saw himself as belonging in the company of the Roman emperors of old, whose glories he wanted to revive. His enemies regarded his grandiose schemes with contempt, dubbing him the "sawdust Caesar."

Japanese expansion threatens world peace. In Asia, too, aggressive military planners were menacing world peace. Japan had been steadily expanding since the 1870's. It had taken over the Kurile Islands in 1875 and Taiwan (Formosa) in 1895. After the Russo-Japanese War (page 544) Japan had acquired control of the southern half of the island of Sakhalin. As one of the victorious Allies in the First World War, it had been granted control of a number of Germany's Pacific islands.

In 1931 China became a target of Japan's aggressive appetite. In a short time the Japanese swallowed up the rich province of Manchuria and created a puppet government there. In the presence of this serious threat to peace, the League of Nations proved powerless. When the League condemned the Japanese action in Manchuria, Japan responded by withdrawing from membership in the organization. In messages that Secretary of State Henry L. Stimson sent to China and Japan on behalf of the Hoover administration, he set forth America's position. It has come to be known as the Stimson Doctrine. The United States, Stimson said, would refuse to recognize any territorial change brought about as a result of aggression.

Isolationists gain strength in the United States. Words alone, however, could not stop nations from attacking their neighbors. The United States and other peace-loving countries faced the painful truth that no sure force stood in the way of the aggressor nations. In devising foreign policy, however, American statesmen had to take into consideration a number of facts. The most important was that throughout the country many people were determined that the United States should stay out of future wars — at all costs. Known as *isolationists,* they maintained that the United States should

avoid foreign entanglements and concentrate on the problems of the Depression. Some isolationists in Congress feared that the New Deal reforms would be endangered if the United States took action against the aggressor nations.

The United States recognizes the Soviet Union. The burden of countering Japan's aggression seemed increasingly to be falling to the United States. A step that some Americans believed could help blunt Japanese military moves was to raise the prestige of the Soviet Union, a natural rival of Japan. This end, they said, could be accomplished by granting diplomatic recognition to the Soviet Union. Other Americans optimistically believed that recognition might open fresh markets for American products and possibly reduce unemployment.

Throughout the 1920's, the United States had refused to recognize the Communist government of the Soviet Union. One reason for withholding recognition was that upon assuming power the Bolshevik revolutionists had refused to pay the debts owed to the United States by the czars. Moreover, the new Communist government had confiscated millions of dollars' worth of American property. A third reason for withholding recognition was the continued effort by the Soviet Union to subvert institutions of the United States in the interest of world communism. The Secretary of State had pointed out that even Soviet diplomatic representatives could be regarded as "agitators of dangerous revolt."

In the negotiations over diplomatic recognition, the Soviet Union agreed to discontinue Communist propaganda in the United States. Any discussion of the debts and other claims, however, was postponed. Late in 1933, President Roosevelt announced that diplomatic recognition of the Soviet Union had been granted.

Many Americans soon came to see recognition of the Soviet Union as a blunder. The anticipated trade never materialized, and Communist propaganda continued. Later, when Soviet leaders were refused a loan by the United States, they broke off discussion of the debts and other claims.

Tensions mount in Europe. In Europe, threats to world peace developed with increasing frequency. In March, 1935, Hitler renounced the clauses of the Versailles Treaty which had stipulated that Germany must be disarmed. Britain and France did not lift a finger to hold Germany to this obligation.

Within a few months, Mussolini made a move. No doubt motivated by the German action and by the display of British and French weakness, he attacked the East African kingdom of Ethiopia in October, 1935. Lacking the weapons to resist, Ethiopia was defeated in eight months. The League of Nations passed a resolution calling Italy an aggressor and imposed economic sanctions on Italy. Oil, however, which was indispensable to Mussolini's armies, was left off the list of products that could not be sold to Italy. Britain and France were afraid to push Italy too hard, fearful of bringing on unwanted hostilities. Moreover, the peace-loving nations were concerned that they might force Mussolini to seek an alliance with Germany.

Roosevelt, ever watchful not to offend isolationists, would not officially associate the United States with the League's action. Some American oil-producers placed a voluntary embargo on shipments of oil to Italy, but it had little effect.

Further breaches of the peace took a variety of forms. In 1936 civil war broke out in Spain. By the time it had ended three years later, General Francisco Franco, a dictator backed with arms and troops sent by Hitler and Mussolini, had come to power.

Meanwhile, the Germans continued to make menacing moves. In 1936, again defying the Treaty of Versailles, Germany sent troops into the Rhineland, an area along the French border that had been demilitarized after the First World War. In that same year Germany and Italy formed the Axis alliance, sometimes known as the Rome-Berlin Axis. (In 1940 Japan joined, making it the Tripartite Pact, sometimes known as the Rome-Berlin-Tokyo Axis.)

The United States adopts a Neutrality Act. Italy's attack on Ethiopia in 1935 prompted the United States to pass neutrality legislation. The supporters of these laws hoped to avoid the kinds of events that many people believed had brought about United States involvement in the First World War.

The first Neutrality Act — signed by Roosevelt in August, 1935 — required the President to prohibit the shipment of arms to belligerents (that is, nations engaged in war). The President, at his discretion, could forbid American citizens to travel on the ships of warring powers, except at their own risk. Clearly, America was hoping to avoid an incident like the *Lusitania* disaster (page 651).

Six months later the Neutrality Act was extended, and restrictions were laid on the granting of loans or credits to nations at war. This law satisfied people who maintained that the war loans to Britain and France made by American bankers had drawn the United States into the struggle in 1917.

The neutrality legislation left the United States almost powerless to restrain Mussolini or Hitler by force. As Roosevelt watched the rising tide of aggression abroad, he was deeply concerned over the ability of isolationists to influence national policy. Still, he did not believe he could defeat them in a showdown. During the presidential campaign of 1936, he made only one reference to foreign affairs. When he did — in a speech in New York State — he unreservedly satisfied the isolationists: "We shun political commitments which might entangle us in foreign wars. . . . I have seen war on land and sea. . . . I have seen the agony of mothers and wives. I hate war."

Congress passes a second Neutrality Act. On May 1, 1937, in response to the Spanish Civil War, Congress passed a second Neutrality Act. By a joint resolution it retained the restrictions against loans and arms sales made in the earlier act and prohibited travel aboard the vessels of warring nations. A new feature was included in this Neutrality Act — a "cash-and-carry" plan. Nonmilitary goods could be sold only to belligerents who sent their own ships for them and paid in cash.

The neutrality legislation was, in truth, *un*neutral. First, it failed to distinguish between aggressor and victim — a fact that offended many Americans. Second, Germany, Italy, and Japan already had large stockpiles of arms and did not require such supplies from the United States. Third, the cash-and-carry program gave an advantage to nations that had both money and vessels.

Japan wages war on China. Almost as soon as the second neutrality law went into effect, Japan resumed large-scale fighting against China. The Chinese, under the leadership of Chiang Kai-shek (jee-AHNG KYE-SHEK), refused to give in. Yet they lacked sufficient arms to keep Japanese forces from capturing coastal ports and from pushing inland up river valleys. Roosevelt, eager to help China, decided not to recognize that a war existed, since that would have forced him to invoke the neutrality law. The President also relied on the fact that Japan referred to its operations not as hostilities, but as an "incident."

Roosevelt offers his "quarantine speech." Roosevelt was in a predicament. He wanted to support political leaders in Britain, France, and China who were seeking to stand up to aggression. But how? In October, 1937, he tried to alert the country to the dangers that loomed and to suggest a principle for dealing with them. He put his warning and proposal in a speech he delivered in Chicago — a stronghold of isolationist sentiment. In the address, he declared that "the epidemic of world lawlessness" was spreading. Countries that loved peace, he said, would have to organize "a concerted effort to uphold laws and principles on which alone peace can rest secure." They would have to do this, he went on, the way a community faced by an epidemic disease "joins in a quarantine of the patients in order to protect the health of the community. . . ."

The "quarantine speech," an effort to test whether public opinion was changing, was not well received. The people were not yet ready to see the threats to peace abroad as threats to America itself.

Germany becomes an aggressor. Meanwhile, Germany had built up a powerful army and had begun to threaten its neighbors. In early 1938, Hitler's forces occupied Austria. Joining Austria to Germany had always been a Nazi aim. By threats amounting to an ultimatum, Hitler forced his small neighbor to surrender its independence.

After Hitler had annexed Austria, he began to menace the neighboring democratic nation of Czechoslovakia. He demanded that Czechoslovakia give up the Sudetenland, an area with a large German-speaking population. Once that happened, he pledged, there would be "no further territorial problems in Europe."

As the situation grew tense, the leaders of Britain and France agreed to meet with Hitler at Munich, Germany, in September, 1938, to find a solution. There the British prime minister, Neville Chamberlain, and the French premier, Edouard Daladier, consented to the separation of the Sudetenland from Czechoslovakia. Chamberlain claimed that through this surrender to Hitler he had obtained "peace for our time." Many people, however, were shocked by this example of *appeasement* (granting concessions to a potential enemy in order to maintain

The failure of the appeasement policy was made clear when German troops completed their take-over of Czechoslovakia in March, 1939, less than six months after the Munich Conference.

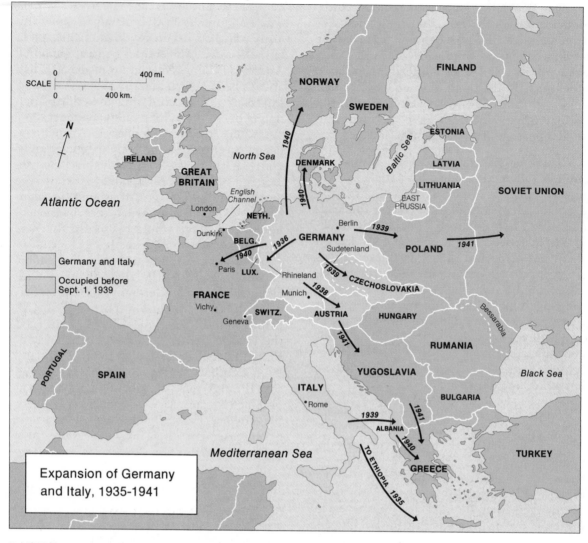

By 1939 Germany and Italy had seized strategic territory in Europe. In the years that followed, Axis attacks spread across the continent.

peace). In any event, Hitler soon ignored his promise to make no more territorial demands, and in March, 1939, seized the rest of Czechoslovakia. Within weeks, Mussolini, made bold by Hitler's success, followed his example and took over Albania (map, above).

Observing these moves with growing anxiety, Britain and France began to see the foolishness of relying on a policy of appeasement, and they hastened to build up their armed forces. They also pledged to defend the independence of Poland, a country which Hitler was now starting to threaten. In addition, Britain and France tried to per-

suade the Soviet Union to join with them in resisting further German aggression. While waiting hopefully for a favorable response, they were shocked on August 23, 1939, to learn that the Soviet Union had signed a nonaggression pact with Germany. The Nazis and Communists had long been rivals. The fact that they were now linked together stunned the world. The public did not yet know that Germany and the Soviet Union had agreed secretly to divide Poland. The pact also made clear that Germany would not oppose Soviet moves to take Finland, Estonia, Latvia, Lithuania, and Bessarabia (in Rumania).

The United States formulates the Good Neighbor Policy. Roosevelt, in view of the dismaying events abroad, had long seen the need to cultivate the friendship of countries in the Western Hemisphere. In his inaugural address in 1933, he had declared, "In the field of foreign relations I would dedicate this nation to the policy of the good neighbor." Late in 1933, a Pan-American conference held at Montevideo, Uruguay, adopted a "Convention on the Rights and Duties of States," which was heartily supported by the United States. This agreement proclaimed the equality of all nations in their right to be free of outside interference. Before the year ended, Roosevelt announced that henceforth it would be United States policy to oppose armed intervention in Latin American countries.

The Good Neighbor Policy having been launched, the United States showed it would adhere to it despite provocation. For instance, when the government of Cuba was overthrown in 1933, the United States refrained from sending troops there. Indeed, it was in this period that the United States canceled the Platt Amendment (page 640), which had troubled relations with Cuba for years. As further evidence of the Good Neighbor Policy, the last marines were brought home from Haiti in 1934.

For the purpose of increasing trade with Latin America, Roosevelt backed passage of the Trade Agreements Act of 1934. This law, which passed Congress after much debate, empowered the President to reduce tariff rates by as much as 50 percent, in return for similar concessions from other nations. Soon, tariff rates among the nations of the Western Hemisphere had been lowered, paving the way for the desired increase in trade.

Another milestone was reached in December, 1936, when Roosevelt traveled to Buenos Aires, Argentina, to attend an inter-American conference for the maintenance of peace. The American nations pledged to consult with one another in the event of threats to peace in the Western Hemisphere. Then, at Lima, Peru, in December, 1938, the capstone of the Good Neighbor Policy was set in place. There, at the eighth Pan-American Conference, the American republics pledged to defend themselves from any outside threat. The transformation of the Monroe Doctrine was completed at Mexico City in 1945. By the Act of Chapultepec, the American nations accepted the principle that an attack from abroad on one of them was to be considered an attack upon them all. The Monroe Doctrine was no longer the policy of the United States alone; it had become a shield to be used in time of need by all the American republics.

SECTION REVIEW

1. Vocabulary: *totalitarian, isolationist, appeasement.*
2. (a) Why did dictators come to power in Europe in the years after World War I? (b) What methods did those dictators use?
3. (a) How did Japan threaten world peace in 1931? (b) What was the response of the League of Nations?
4. (a) How did Italy take over Ethiopia? (b) Why did Italy's attack lead to passage in Congress of neutrality legislation?
5. How did Hitler take over Austria and the Sudetenland?
6. (a) What was Roosevelt's Good Neighbor Policy? (b) How was the policy put into effect?

4 World War II Begins

On September 1, 1939, with dive bombers wailing overhead, Hitler's troops stormed into Poland. Having promised to aid the Poles, Britain and France declared war on Germany — slightly more than 25 years after the beginning of World War I.

The outbreak of war affects American neutrality. Immediately upon the eruption of hostilities, President Roosevelt issued a declaration of American neutrality. He called Congress into special session, nevertheless, to bring about a repeal of the embargo on arms. The debate in Congress was furious as isolationists declared that in the end, as Senator Borah put it, the United States "would be sending armies as well as arms." In a radio address, the President responded: "The simple truth is that no person . . . has ever suggested ... the remotest possibility of sending the boys of American mothers to fight on the battlefields of Europe." In November, 1939, Congress lifted the embargo, and arms and munitions began to flow freely to Britain and France on a cash-and-carry basis.

By then, Poland, invaded in the west by Germany and in the east by the Soviet Union, had been crushed. Winter now closed in, and the war settled into a period of inactivity. Taking advantage of the lull, Roosevelt sent Undersecretary of State Sumner Welles to Europe to see if a peace conference could be organized. The effort failed. The President knew now that the immediate future was dark. He warned the American people that they could not expect to remain untouched if the war destroyed European civilization.

The war spreads over western Europe. In the spring of 1940, Hitler's war machine went into high gear. In April, Nazi forces overran and occupied Norway and Denmark. In May, just as the tulips were blooming, the Netherlands, Belgium, and Luxembourg fell. Before the month was out, France's armies had been sent reeling into

retreat. A British expeditionary force of 350,000 troops, which had been rushed to France to help, was pushed back to the French port of Dunkirk on the English Channel. Hundreds upon hundreds of vessels — some simply pleasure craft manned by civilians — slipped across the Channel under the protection of the Royal Air Force to rescue the beleaguered troops. By June 4, the troops had been evacuated in one of the memorable actions of British naval history.

Within a few weeks of the Dunkirk evacuation, France had signed an armistice with Hitler, yielding half the country to German occupation forces. The rest of France would be run from Vichy (VEE-she) by a French government under Marshal Henri Philippe Pétain, who was willing to obey Hitler's orders.

On June 10, just before the French laid down their arms, Italy declared war on France. Roosevelt was infuriated. He said of Italy's action, "The hand that held the dagger has struck it into the back of its neighbor."

The United States aids Great Britain. More and more, Americans were beginning to understand the Fascist threat. A widely re-

After German armies swept into northern France in 1940, the British expeditionary force and other Allied soldiers were evacuated from the port of Dunkirk.

Report from London

In September, 1940, Hitler ordered the German air force to concentrate its attacks on the city of London. Hoping to break the morale of the British people, German bombers unmercifully pounded Britain's capital city. In radio broadcasts to the United States, an American commentator, Edward R. Murrow, reported on the German raids.

Edward R. Murrow

This is London at 3:30 in the morning. This has been what might be called a "routine night" — air-raid alarm at about nine o'clock and intermittent bombing ever since. I had the impression that more high explosives and less incendiaries [fire bombs] have been used tonight. Only two small fires can be seen on the horizon. Again the Germans have been sending in their bombers singly or in pairs. The anti-aircraft barrage has been fierce, but sometimes there have been periods of twenty minutes when London has been silent. Then the big red buses would start up and move on till the guns started working again.

That silence is almost hard to bear. One becomes accustomed to rattling windows and the distant sound of bombs, then there comes a silence that can be felt. You know the sound will return, you wait, and then it starts again. That waiting is bad. It gives you a chance to imagine things.

I have been walking tonight — there is a full moon, and the dirty-grey buildings appear white. The stars, the empty windows, are hidden. It's a beautiful and lonesome city where men and women and children are trying to snatch a few hours' sleep underground [in bomb shelters].

---

spected journalist, Walter Lippmann, cautioned that the United States must prepare for the worst: "Before the snow flies again, we may stand alone and isolated, the last great democracy on earth."

Hitler now was menacing Great Britain. In May, 1940, Winston Churchill had become prime minister. Churchill had vehemently opposed his nation's appeasement policies. Now he had finally been called to power. He promised the British people only "blood, tears, toil, and sweat" as they made ready for the expected German onslaught.

As the summer of 1940 drew on, the British Isles were subjected to a daily pounding by Nazi bombers. The Battle of Britain was under way. Opinion polls now showed that more than half of all Americans were willing to aid Britain, even at the risk of war. Roosevelt released planes and arms and ammunition for use by the British. The public was unprepared, however, for the boldness of the President's announcement on September 3, 1940. Roosevelt reported that he had concluded a deal with Great Britain, swapping 50 over-age destroyers for 99-year leases on air and naval bases in Bermuda, Newfoundland, and the Caribbean. The British needed the destroyers — small, speedy vessels — to fight off German submarines and keep open the shipping lanes to the United States. The

United States required the bases to strengthen the defenses of the Western Hemisphere.

Roosevelt called the destroyer deal the most important contribution to the national defense since the Louisiana Purchase. Many Republicans, while applauding the arrangement, were distressed that the President had made it through an executive agreement,[1] rather than by a treaty. Clearly, neutrality was ended.

The United States strengthens its defenses. In September, 1940, Congress passed a Selective Service Act. It created the first peacetime draft of men in American history, calling for the registration of all males between the ages of 21 and 35. The draftees would be subject to one year's military training, but they were not liable for service outside the Western Hemisphere.

As a result of the draft, the military services, which had fewer than 500,000 men in uniform in 1940, had 1,800,000 by the end of 1941. Congress, more and more responsive to the President's view of the dangers to America, increased its appropriations for military defense from $1.7 billion in 1940 to over $6 billion the following year.

The United States was linking its fate to that of other democracies standing against aggression. But how far would the United States go? Roosevelt had an answer for the American people: "I have said this before, but I shall say it again and again and again. Your boys are not going to be sent into any foreign wars." Previously, Roosevelt had always added "except in case of attack." He explained the omission: "If we're attacked, it's no longer a foreign war."

Roosevelt wins a third term. At this juncture the American people were preparing to vote in the 1940 presidential election. Roosevelt had for a time been uncertain whether or not he should seek a third term. Everything, he stated, cried out to him to go back to his home on the Hudson. Then, in May — as France was on the verge of surrender — he announced that he would run again. By so doing, Roosevelt was breaking the tradition established by George Washington that a President serve no more than two terms. Renominated at the Democratic convention in Chicago, Roosevelt dropped Vice President Garner from his ticket and replaced him with Henry A. Wallace, the Secretary of Agriculture and an ardent New Dealer.

The Republicans nominated Wendell L. Willkie, formerly of Indiana and now a Wall Street lawyer. A powerfully built man with tousled hair, he appealed to Americans as a person without pretense. He made his main campaign issue Roosevelt's quest for a third term. A typical Republican campaign button read: "I'm against the third term. Washington wouldn't. Grant couldn't. Roosevelt shouldn't." On international affairs, however, Willkie and the President saw eye to eye. Like Roosevelt, Willkie favored all possible aid to Britain — short of joining in the fighting.

Clearly the outcome of the election would be influenced by the course of the war. A Republican member of the House put it this way: "Franklin Roosevelt is not running against Wendell Willkie. He's running against Adolf Hitler."

The public followed the news from Europe with growing alarm. An invasion of the British Isles seemed next on the Nazis' timetable. As the German air assaults over Britain grew more intense, opinion polls showed the President's popularity rising. Roosevelt, not Willkie, would know what to do if the situation grew even grimmer, people seemed to be saying.

On Election Day, 1940, Roosevelt won easily. He received over 27 million votes compared to somewhat more than 22 million for Willkie. The triumph in the electoral college was overpowering: 449 votes to 82. Willkie had carried only ten states. Nevertheless, the popular vote was the closest in a presidential election since 1916.

The Lend-Lease Act is passed. Soon after the election, the President received a momentous letter from Churchill. The prime minister informed Roosevelt that Britain

---

[1]Executive agreements do not require the approval of the Senate. They do not bind future Chief Executives, who may or may not choose to keep them in force.

had virtually run out of cash. Soon the British would no longer be able to buy munitions in the United States and thus would be unable to conduct offensive operations against the Nazi forces. Roosevelt's response was quick. The United States, he said, would lend or lease to Great Britain the equipment and supplies required to make "our common cause" succeed. "We must be the great arsenal of democracy," the President told the nation.

The Lend-Lease Act, introduced in Congress early in 1941, was passed after extensive debate. Under this law the President was granted the authority to rent, sell, exchange, lease, or even give war materials to any country whose security he regarded as necessary to America's defense. Roosevelt explained that goods lent would be returned or replaced at the end of the war — in the way a neighbor returns a hose borrowed to put out a fire. Congress appropriated $7 billion to carry out the law's intent.

The United States moves closer to war. Shortly after the Lend-Lease bill passed, Roosevelt said, "Ours is not a partial effort. It is a total effort. . . . Our country is going to play its full part." In order to guarantee the safe delivery of aid to Britain, the United States started providing naval convoys to escort merchant ships. Meanwhile, American troops began setting up air and naval bases in Greenland in April, 1941. Then, in May the President proclaimed a state of "unlimited national emergency," putting into operation some 99 laws giving him broad special powers. Included was the power to repel "acts or threats of aggression directed against any part of the Western Hemisphere." In July, American troops landed on Iceland to prevent that island from being occupied by German forces.

Germany's attention, at that time, was riveted elsewhere. In June, 1941, despite the nonaggression pact signed by the two countries less than two years earlier, Germany had suddenly invaded the Soviet Union. Hitler explained to his generals his startling decision to turn on his ally: "We have the chance to smash Russia while our own back is free. That chance will not come

Following passage of the Lend-Lease Act in 1941, the United States began providing the Allies with arms, munitions, and equipment. Here, lend-lease supplies are loaded for shipment to Europe.

again soon." He was confident he would defeat the Russians in two or three months, thus making Germany master of the European continent. Then he would dispose of Britain and be ready to take on the United States.

For many Americans, Hitler had already stated the issue clearly: "Two worlds are in conflict; one of these worlds must break asunder." Roosevelt, profoundly worried over what might lie ahead, called upon Americans in early 1941 to heed the fate of the nations the Nazis had conquered. The lesson to be learned was simple: "It would be suicide to wait until they are in our front yard." Then he added, "Our Bunker Hill of tomorrow may be several thousand miles from Boston."

SECTION REVIEW

1. (a) What effect did Germany's invasion of Poland have on Britain and France? (b) How did the United States react?
2. (a) What European countries did Germany conquer in 1940? (b) How did the United States help Great Britain?
3. (a) What was the main campaign issue in the presidential election of 1940? (b) What was the result of that election?
4. (a) What was the Lend-Lease Act? (b) How did the United States move closer to war?

Chapter 27 Review

Summary

As a consequence of the First World War, the United States was owed large sums of money, especially by Great Britain and France. The British and French counted on reparations from Germany to help pay their war debts, but a severe economic crisis in Germany caused this scheme to fail. During the 1920's, the United States devised plans to help Germany pay its reparations. The economic collapse of 1929, however, frustrated efforts to collect either the reparations or the war debts.

Throughout the 1920's, American Presidents concerned themselves with creating a system of worldwide collective security. Disarmament conferences, held in Washington in 1921 and in London in 1930, limited the number of warships built by the major world powers. In 1928 the United States, France, and twelve other nations signed the Kellogg-Briand Pact, which outlawed war as an instrument of national policy.

After the First World War, efforts were made by the United States to improve relations with Mexico and the nations of Central and South America. The Clark Memorandum, made public in 1930, declared that the Monroe Doctrine did not give the United States the right to interfere in the internal affairs of its neighbors.

Overseas possessions were a new responsibility for the United States and required special attention. Supervision of these territories was divided among the Departments of Navy, War, and the Interior. Various plans were devised to help prepare the territories for statehood, self-government, or independence.

In the 1920's and 1930's totalitarian governments took control of Italy and Germany, creating a dangerous situation in Europe. In Asia, meanwhile, Japan became an aggressive military power. Following Italy's invasion of Ethiopia in 1935, President Roosevelt issued the first Neutrality Act, forbidding the sale of arms or the granting of loans to warring nations. In 1936 world tension increased as civil war broke out in Spain, as Germany occupied the Rhineland, and as Japan resumed its attacks on China.

After 1937, as war in Europe seemed more likely, the United States moved away from a policy of strict neutrality. Once war had broken out in September, 1939, Congress permitted the sale of war supplies to Britain and France.

By the summer of 1940, most of Europe had fallen to Germany. Expecting the worst, the United States increased its aid to Britain, and President Roosevelt ordered the strengthening of American military forces.

Vocabulary and Important Terms

1. Hawley-Smoot Tariff
2. collective security
3. disarmament
4. Washington Conference
5. Kellogg-Briand Pact
6. Clark Memorandum
7. Insular Cases
8. Platt Amendment
9. Stimson Doctrine
10. commonwealth
11. totalitarian
12. isolationist
13. Axis alliance
14. appeasement
15. Good Neighbor Policy
16. Battle of Britain
17. Selective Service Act
18. Lend-Lease Act

Discussion Questions

1. (a) Why did American efforts to collect war debts after World War I cause resentment in Europe? (b) Why was United States tariff policy another source of friction?

2. (a) To what extent was the United States willing to cooperate with the League of Nations? (b) What role did the United States play in the disarmament movement? (c) What role did it play in the quest for world peace?

3. (a) Why did the United States deliberately prepare its major possessions for independence? (b) Which possession became independent, and under what circumstances did it gain its independence? (c) Which possessions remained under United States control?

4. (a) What nations threatened world peace in the 1930's? (b) What expansionist activities did they carry out?

5. (a) Why did many Americans in the 1920's and 1930's want the United States to keep out of foreign entanglements? (b) What effect did isolationist sentiment have on the actions of the Roosevelt administration?

6. (a) What were the provisions of the neutrality acts of 1935 and 1937? (b) What effect did those acts have on the ability of the Roosevelt administration to restrain the aggressor nations? Explain your answer.

7. (a) In what ways did President Roosevelt try to move the United States away from isolationism and neutrality? (b) What effect did the outbreak of war in Europe have on American foreign policy?

8. (a) By 1941 what was the relationship of the United States to its Latin American neighbors? (b) To Great Britain? (c) To Germany and Japan?

Relating Past to Present

1. In the period between the two world wars, the United States sought to improve relations with Latin America through the Good Neighbor policy. What is the state of relations between the United States and Latin America today?
2. Are there Americans today who believe the United States should isolate itself from involvement in world affairs? What arguments for isolationism might be offered today? What might be the arguments against isolationism?
3. After the First World War the United States tried to collect the money it had lent its wartime allies, thereby causing resentment in Europe. Find out what countries owe the United States money today and the circumstances under which they contracted their debts. Should the United States insist on the repayment of those debts? Explain your answer.

Studying Local History

Choose one of the following world events: Mussolini's invasion of Ethiopia; Hitler's takeover of Austria; the Munich conference; the Dunkirk evacuation; or the Battle of Britain. Then do research to find out how newspapers in your state or community covered the event.

Using History Skills

1. *Reading source material.* Study Edward R. Murrow's description of the German attack on London on page 649. (a) What, according to Murrow, was a "routine night"? (b) What defense did the British have against the air attacks? (c) Suppose you were in the United States listening to Murrow's broadcast. What words would you use to describe the people of London? Explain your answer.
2. *Placing events in time.* Look back through the chapter and find five important events that led to the outbreak of World War II. Make a time line showing those events.

WORLD SCENE

New Tools of War

From 1919 to 1939, military theorists analyzed the new weaponry that had been introduced in the First World War. They focused on the airplane and the tank in contemplating future battlefield tactics.

Air power. One of the first to write about the potential of air power in warfare was an Italian army officer named Giulio Douhet. In a book published in 1921, Douhet described how the airplane could be used to break enemy morale. He argued that if a nation took control of the air at the outbreak of war and attacked enemy cities, factories, and military installations, a quick victory would be assured.

Another advocate of air power was an American general named Billy Mitchell. As commander of United States aircraft in the First World War, Mitchell knew how potent a weapon the airplane could be. He pleaded with the War Department and with members of Congress to allocate funds for a large independent air force. When his recommendations fell on deaf ears, he publicly criticized the nation's military leaders. Charged with insubordination, he was court-martialed and suspended from the army.

Tank warfare. The British introduced tanks during the First World War. Difficult to maneuver and extremely slow-moving, these early armored vehicles were the cause of much debate.

In the 1920's two British military experts — J. F. C. Fuller and B. H. Liddell Hart — made startling predictions about the use of tanks on the battlefield. They believed that massed armored units could be used to penetrate enemy lines and then push rapidly forward. The confusion that the tanks would create among the enemy would allow the infantry to move in to do its work.

Despite those arguments, the British government paid little attention to developing tank warfare. The German army, on the other hand, took keen interest in the writings of Fuller and Liddell Hart. General Heinz Guderian, commander of Germany's tank corps, studied the idea of massed armored units. Guderian emphasized that "not a drizzle, but a downpour" of tanks was needed to invade enemy territory and create terror among the populace. Beginning in 1939, Germany combined this tactic with the use of air power to seize control of much of Europe.

Global War

1941 – 1945

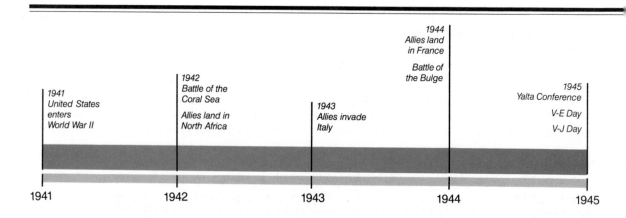

1944
Allies land
in France

Battle of
the Bulge

1942
Battle of the
Coral Sea

Allies land in
North Africa

1941
United States
enters
World War II

1943
Allies invade
Italy

1945
Yalta Conference

V-E Day

V-J Day

| 1941 | 1942 | 1943 | 1944 | 1945 |

In August, 1941, President Roosevelt and Prime Minister Churchill met aboard the British battleship *Prince of Wales* off the coast of Newfoundland. The two men recognized the symbolic importance of their meeting. Each wanted the world to know that the English-speaking nations would stand shoulder to shoulder against the enemy who meant to destroy them.

Roosevelt was the senior partner in the close friendship that existed between the two leaders. Churchill had admired Roosevelt for many years. He deferred to the President because Roosevelt had been in office longer than he, and because the United States was much more powerful than Great Britain. Roosevelt, for his part, admired Churchill's eloquence and determination. He once wrote his friend, "It is fun to be in the same decade with you." The relationship between the two men led to a degree of military cooperation unparalleled in modern history.

Out of the discussions held on shipboard came a statement of principles, known as the Atlantic Charter, on which the two nations rested their hopes for the future. The principles included the right of all people to self-government; economic cooperation among all nations; free access of all nations to trade and raw materials; freedom of the seas; and an abandonment of the use of force in settling international disputes. A world shaped by the attainment of such goals, however, was only a distant dream in August, 1941.

1 The United States Enters the War

One weighty question hung in the air in August, 1941. Would the United States extend more than moral and financial support to the Allies? Most Americans opposed the commitment of United States troops, although many people feared that the chances of staying out of the fighting were slim.

Relations with Japan deteriorate. Germany, policy-makers assumed, would likely provide the occasion for American entry into the war. Still, Japan's behavior was a constant concern. Japan's decision to join the Axis in 1940 (page 644) had left no doubt that the Land of the Rising Sun was solidly in the camp of the aggressors. Japan continued to fight in China, while the United States stepped up its aid to the forces of Chiang Kai-shek. At the same time, Japan sought to take advantage of the situation in Europe by seizing French, British, and Dutch possessions in Asia.

In July, 1941, Japanese troops occupied French Indochina. Alarmed by this move, and fearing that the Japanese intended further aggression to the south, Roosevelt froze Japanese assets in the United States and placed an embargo on oil, steel, and other essential war supplies that American firms had been selling to Japan. He then issued a stern warning to the Japanese: if they seized any more territory, the United States would take "any and all steps" necessary to protect its national interests.

At a shipboard meeting off the coast of Newfoundland in August, 1941, President Roosevelt and Prime Minister Churchill drew up the historic Atlantic Charter.

Japan began to make plans to attack Pacific possessions of the United States, Great Britain, and the Netherlands, but in the meantime it continued to take part in peace negotiations. In November, 1941, the Japanese government sent a special ambassador, Saburo Kurusu, to Washington, D.C., to assist in talks with the Americans, which had been going on since early in the year. The Japanese were demanding that the United States recognize Japanese conquests in China and Indochina, stop aid to China, unfreeze Japanese assets, and supply Japan with oil. The United States, in turn, was demanding that Japan withdraw from China and Indochina, recognize the Nationalist regime of Chiang Kai-shek as the only government of China, and sign a nonaggression pact with other Pacific nations. Although the Japanese rejected these proposals, they demanded that the negotiations be continued. The chief American negotiator, Secretary of State Cordell Hull, told Secretary of War Henry L. Stimson late in November, "I have washed my hands of [the Japanese situation], and it is now in the hands of . . . the Army and Navy."

Hull was pessimistic because he had special information. American intelligence agents had broken the Japanese code and knew, from the radio messages being exchanged among Japanese diplomats around the world, that the Japanese were planning something. What that plan was, however, the Americans did not know. They knew only that the Japanese negotiators had received word from Tokyo that if no settlement was reached by November 29, "things are automatically going to happen." The United States was not aware that, on November 25, a Japanese fleet had left home waters on a deadly mission to Hawaii.

Pearl Harbor, shown in this photograph before the Japanese attack, was the home base of America's Pacific fleet.

Roosevelt's War Message to Congress (1941)

Yesterday, December 7, 1941 — a date which will live in infamy — the United States was suddenly and deliberately attacked by naval and air forces of the Empire of Japan. . . .

The attack yesterday on the Hawaiian Islands has caused severe damage to American naval and military forces. Very many American lives have been lost. In addition American ships have been reported torpedoed on the high seas between San Francisco and Honolulu.

Yesterday the Japanese Government also launched an attack against Malaya. Last night Japanese forces attacked Hong Kong. Last night Japanese forces attacked Guam. Last night Japanese forces attacked the Philippine Islands. Last night the Japanese attacked Wake Island. This morning the Japanese attacked Midway Island.

Japan has, therefore, undertaken a surprise offensive extending throughout the Pacific area. The facts of yesterday speak for themselves. The people of the United States have already formed their opinion and well understand the implications to the very life and safety of our nation.

As Commander-in-Chief of the Army and Navy, I have directed that all measures be taken for our defense. . . .

No matter how long it may take us to overcome this premeditated invasion, the American people in their righteous might will win through to absolute victory. . . .

I ask that the Congress declare that since the unprovoked and dastardly attack by Japan on Sunday, December seventh, a state of war has existed between the United States and the Japanese Empire.

War comes at Pearl Harbor. Japanese naval officers had long considered the possibility of one day attacking the powerful American naval base at Pearl Harbor in Hawaii. Always the idea had been discarded as impossible. Admiral Isoroku Yamamoto, however, believed that such an attack could deal a fatal blow to American power in the Pacific. In December, 1940, he began to plan in earnest. Yamamoto possessed, said a close colleague, "a gambler's heart."

On December 7, 1941, a clear Sunday morning, a wave of 183 Japanese dive-bombers zoomed in to strike Pearl Harbor. The American fleet was riding at anchor along Battleship Row, the ships lined up like ducks on a pond. The surprise was complete. A bomb pierced the armor of the *Arizona*, setting afire its powder magazine, which exploded with such force that the vessel split in two and settled into the deep. In all, eight battleships were sunk or badly damaged, and eleven other vessels were put out of action. An eyewitness later said, "It was awful, for great ships were dying before my eyes! Strangely enough, at first I didn't realize that men were dying too." More than 2,300 Americans were killed; almost 1,200 others were wounded.

In Washington, D.C., it was 1:50 P.M. when the first news arrived from Hawaii: AIR RAID PEARL HARBOR. THIS IS NO DRILL. Reading it, Secretary of the Navy Knox exclaimed, "This can't be true; they must mean the Philippines!" American leaders could hardly bring themselves to believe that the Japanese had outfoxed them in this way. In any case, the wrangling and uncertainty in the United States were now over. The nation was united as never before.

On December 8, the President asked Congress to recognize that a state of war existed between the United States and Japan. Roosevelt, who had a keen sense of history, had invited Mrs. Woodrow Wilson to be present in the hushed House chamber where he spoke. Calling December 7 "a date which will live in infamy," he calmly promised to avenge Pearl Harbor. "Always," he said, "will we remember the character of the onslaught against us. No matter how long it may take . . . , the American people in their righteous might will win through to absolute victory." The approval of the President's proposal was one vote short of unanimous. The single no vote was cast by Representative Jeannette Rankin of Montana, who had also voted against United States entry into the First World War in 1917. The first woman to serve in Congress, she said that on principle *someone* ought to vote no, and that it ought to be a woman.

Germany and Italy declare war on the United States. Hitler was not obliged under the Tripartite Pact (page 644) to assist Japan now that it had made war. Yet on December 11, he declared war on the United States. Why?

Hitler may have decided he had had great good luck, that the United States would be tied up in the Pacific so thoroughly that it could not be further involved in the war in Europe. Possibly he also had a romantic view of how his country ought to behave in the embarrassing situation Japan had created. At any rate, he declared his country to be at war with the United States. "A great power like Germany declares war itself," he said, "and does not wait for war to be declared on it." That same day Italy, too, declared war on the United States. The United States thus found itself arrayed against the Axis powers on the side of Great Britain, China, and the Soviet Union, who were known as the Allies.[1]

The war in Europe takes priority. The Roosevelt administration had already decided that if war came the United States would concentrate on defeating Germany. Many Americans were upset when the administration went ahead with a "Europe-

---

[1] By the end of the war the Allies numbered 49 nations.

first" strategy. They were more eager to strike back at the Japanese than to defeat the Germans and Italians. Still, most people could see that the more immediate danger was in Europe.

Japanese aggression continues. Despite the decision to give priority to the struggle in Europe, the United States was not idle in the Pacific, and the fighting there was intense. The Japanese boasted of having reduced the United States to the status of a third-rate power. The statement was absurd, but the damage to American naval and air power in the Pacific had been substantial. The Japanese took quick advantage of their success not only in knocking out the battle fleet at Pearl Harbor and most of America's heavy bombers at Manila, the Philippine capital, but also in wrecking the British battle squadron at Singapore. Before the end of December, 1941, Japan had captured Guam, Wake Island, and the British colony of Hong Kong. In February, Japanese forces overran the Malay Peninsula and the British naval base at Singapore. By the end of March the Dutch East Indies were also in Japanese hands. Meanwhile, a battle was being fought for possession of the Philippine Islands.

The Philippines are conquered. In January, 1942, Japanese forces occupied Manila. American and Filipino troops, under the command of General Douglas MacArthur, withdrew to the Bataan Peninsula. There, against overwhelming odds, they continued to fight, hoping to hold out until reinforcements could arrive. Lacking air and sea support, and with no help forthcoming, the defenders surrendered in April. A remnant of the forces escaped to the nearby island of Corregidor. Now under the command of General Jonathan Wainwright, they, too, surrendered — on May 6. General MacArthur, who had been evacuated by submarine to Australia in February, declared solemnly upon his arrival, "I came through and I shall return."

The Japanese forced the defeated garrison of Americans and Filipinos to march 85 miles to board a train for internment in a prisoner-of-war camp. The overland journey proved to be a death march for thousands of the men. They were beaten, starved, and tortured by their captors. As word drifted back to America of this episode, Americans resolved that they would have revenge. MacArthur's words, "I shall return," became a battle cry, a pledge the United States intended to redeem.

American forces achieve victories in the Pacific. In the spring of 1942 — the low point of American fortunes, as it turned out — many people believed that Australia, too, would soon fall to the enemy. Two American victories at sea, however, encouraged the Allies. The surviving American fleet in the Pacific was under the command of Admiral Chester W. Nimitz. On May 7 and 8, 1942, immediately following the surrender of Corregidor, the United States Navy battered a Japanese force heading for New Guinea, thus ending the immediate threat to Australia. This encounter, known as the Battle of the Coral Sea, was the first instance in which the Allies had succeeded in blocking Japan's lightning-like progress.

The following month, American naval forces again won a mighty victory, this time at the Battle of Midway. The encounter was a turning point in the war because it ended the possibility of a Japanese occupation of Hawaii.

These victories, combined with the first American air raid on Tokyo and other Japanese cities in April, 1942, lifted American spirits. The situation, nevertheless, remained grim. By May, 1942, six months after Pearl Harbor, the Japanese had under their flag an area extending eastward to the Aleutian Islands, south almost to Australia, and west to the borders of India (map, page 676). To root the enemy out of their strongpoints would require savage fighting, some of it hand-to-hand. Furthermore, much of the fighting would take place on almost impenetrable jungle terrain, or on bleak coral or volcanic islands that provided no natural shelter or means of concealment.

The Japanese advance is halted at Guadalcanal. The Japanese, bent on controlling the South Pacific, began building an air base on Guadalcanal (one of the Solomon Islands) in

The scene of heavy fighting, Guadalcanal was freed from Japanese occupation early in 1943. Here, Japanese ships burn following an American air strike.

Erwin Rommel, shown here during the North African campaign, was one of Germany's most brilliant generals. Later implicated in a plot to kill Hitler, Rommel chose to commit suicide rather than face certain execution.

of all United States forces in Europe. Born in Texas and reared in Kansas, Eisenhower had an open manner and an infectious grin. A descendant of Germans who had settled in Pennsylvania in the 1730's, he was raised to respect pacifism. For some years he had served on the staff of General MacArthur in the Philippines. By the time of the attack on Pearl Harbor, General George C. Marshall, the Chief of Staff, had already identified Eisenhower as deserving of a high command.

The men of Rommel's famed Afrika Korps put up tremendous resistance, but they were doomed to failure. Cut off from their supply lines by Allied sea and air power, they were caught between the advancing armies of Eisenhower from the west and those of Montgomery from the east. On May 12, 1943, after seven months of intense fighting, the last of Rommel's forces laid down their arms. The 55,000 men who surrendered that day in Tunisia were some of the enemy's best fighting men. By their defeat the Axis had lost control of North Africa and the Mediterranean. Now what Winston Churchill termed "the soft underbelly of Europe" lay open to an Allied attack.

SECTION REVIEW

1. (a) What steps taken by Japan in 1940–1941 alarmed the United States? (b) What demands did the United States and Japan make on each other? (c) What action brought the United States into World War II?
2. (a) What attacks did Japan make following United States entry into the war? (b) What was the significance of the Allied victories in the Coral Sea, off Midway, and at Guadalcanal?
3. How did the Allies check German submarine warfare?
4. How were the Russians able to stop the German invasion?
5. (a) What threat did the Axis pose in North Africa? (b) How did the British and Americans defeat the Axis in that region?

2 The United States Mobilizes for War

In the United States people had closed ranks after the attack on Pearl Harbor. Now that war had come, said Charles A. Lindbergh, a former isolationist critic of the President's views on foreign policy, "we must meet it as united Americans regardless of our attitude in the past. . . . "

Fifteen million people serve in the armed forces. American military forces were vastly expanded immediately following the attack on Pearl Harbor. The mustering of troops from civilian ranks, an American tradition, depended on the Selective Service System. The draft was administered by local boards under the supervision of Major General Lewis B. Hershey. Most of the draftees were single men under the age of 30, but all men between the ages of 18 and 45 were eligible for military service, and all men between 18 and 64 were required to register with their draft boards. About ten million men were drafted in the course of the war. Five million other Americans — men and women alike — volunteered to serve.[2]

For the first time the armed forces established women's branches. Women volunteered for military service so that men would be free to go to the front. Over a quarter of a million women served the country in uniform as ambulance drivers, mechanics, pilots, radio operators, clerical workers — as everything but actual combatants. Many other women served in the armed forces as nurses.

United States industry gears up for war. In January, 1942, President Roosevelt created the War Production Board to mobilize the economy. The Board supervised American industry to ensure that the country would meet the needs of the Allied troops. The en-

tire automobile industry, for example, switched to the production of tanks, airplanes, trucks, and other military vehicles. Other industries made similar changeovers. The Board decided on the distribution of government contracts and on the allocation of scarce resources. Certain consumer goods, such as new automobiles, became unavailable. Other goods were in short supply — including sugar, coffee, meat, gasoline, fats and oils, butter, cheese, and shoes — and were rationed by means of stamps distributed through local rationing boards.

The government demands sacrifices from the American people. Taxes were heavy during the war years. By 1945, 42 million citizens were subject to income taxes — ten times the number that had been required to pay them in 1939. In order to ensure that these taxes were collected, the government introduced the practice of withholding income taxes. Employers were required, under this plan, to deduct employees' taxes from their paychecks and turn the money over directly to the government. Still, only 40 percent of the cost of the war was met by taxation. The remainder was raised by heavy borrowing. As a result, between 1941 and 1945 the national debt rose from $50 billion to $250 billion.

One way the government borrowed money was through the sale of war bonds. Millions of workers at home and soldiers in the field purchased bonds through a vigorously promoted payroll-deduction plan. Movies, for instance, invariably closed with "The End — Buy War Bonds." From 1941 to 1946 bond sales totaled over $61 billion.

Americans were also constantly urged to conserve resources. Doing little things helped many civilians to feel the pride of participating in the war effort. To save material, women wore straight skirts, instead of full or pleated ones. Families also planted "victory gardens" to help increase the available food. Communities contributed by collecting scrap metal of all kinds.

Shortages caused increases in the prices of most goods, and the government took

---

[2]The citizen-soldiers were quickly dubbed "GI's" — the initials standing for "government issue," an old phrase applied to equipment distributed by army supply depots.

The Home Front

During the Second World War, Ray Hartman was a student in Chicago. In this account, he remembers how his school helped the American war effort.

A war bond

Everybody was campaigning to sell war bonds. The school set a goal. They were selling stamps. Each kid would buy stamps and try to fill books to get an $18.75 bond. We were using our allowances and paper drives and whatever way we could to get money to purchase the stamps. In those days we were going around selling war stamps similar to the way children now sell chances on raffles. We'd go door-to-door and ask people to contribute dimes and quarters and fill up a book of stamps and buy the bonds.

The goal of the school, I believe, was somewhere in the $79,000 to $80,000 range, and we were told that this would be sufficient money to purchase a P–38 fighter plane. We reached the goal. I was the student chairman of the drive, and after probably eight or nine months of work, we were successful, and there was a P–38 named after the school. Alphonsus was the name of the school, and they named the plane "The Spirit of Saint Al's." We went to the Douglas Aircraft Company where they painted the name on the plane, more or less christened it, and took pictures. I was thrilled, being the chairman of the student drive. I did the ribbon cutting or something like that. We received a letter of commendation from a general for the school.

measures to control inflation. The Office of Price Administration — the OPA — was established early in the war to keep a lid on the prices of a large number of commodities. Ceilings were also placed on rents. These controls did not eliminate inflation, but they kept it from reaching disastrous levels. In late 1942 the Wage Stabilization Act empowered the government to control wages.

For the most part, Americans accepted these sacrifices without grumbling, remembering the men at the front and the stakes for which they were fighting. Gradually, people realized that the war was disposing of a long-standing problem. As factories geared up for maximum production — many working around the clock — the unemployment that had plagued the country for a decade disappeared. Farm production rose too, and farmers' incomes almost doubled. The Great Depression had ended at last.

Japanese Americans are interned. A blot on the country's record during the war was its treatment of Americans of Japanese ancestry. After the attack on Pearl Harbor, many people feared that there might be some Japanese Americans — perhaps many — whose loyalty lay with Japan rather than the United States. People on the West Coast, which was regarded as a potential target of Japanese invasion, were especially alarmed at the prospect of sabotage. Although no such activity was ever discovered, the President was convinced that the Japanese Americans were a threat to the nation's security. In February, 1942, he authorized the forcible relocation of 100,000 people of Japanese ancestry, about two thirds of whom were American citizens. With little warning, these people had to leave their houses and businesses, suffering heavy financial losses. They were then moved to isolated camps and held there for the duration of the war.

Despite this harsh treatment, Japanese Americans remained loyal to the Allied cause. Not a single Japanese American was convicted of espionage. When given the opportunity to enlist in the armed forces, more than 1,200 of the interned men volunteered to fight for the United States. The 442nd Regimental Combat Team served valiantly in the campaign against Italy, along with another Japanese American unit from Hawaii.

Black Americans make advances during the war. The effect of the war on black Americans was felt even before Pearl Harbor. Black leaders had long pointed out the contradiction in opposing unjust governments abroad while tolerating racial discrimination and segregation at home. Many Americans were more and more troubled by this argument.

In 1941, before the United States entered the war, A. Philip Randolph, president of the Brotherhood of Sleeping Car Porters, threatened to lead a march on Washington, D.C., unless the President took steps to give black workers access to jobs in defense industries. As a result, Roosevelt issued an executive order forbidding racial discrimination by defense contractors. A Committee on Fair Employment Practices was also established. By the end of the war, the work of the Committee, helped by the general shortage of labor, had opened doors previously closed to black people.

In the armed forces, barriers to black advancement also began to break down. About one million black men and women were in uniform, serving in all branches of the military and in every campaign of the war. At the beginning, they served under white officers, but by the end of the war even the navy, which had traditionally taken blacks only as mess workers and porters, had started to commission black officers.

In the army the walls of discrimination came down somewhat faster. At the height of the war in 1944, black officers were being commissioned at the rate of about 200 a month. Benjamin O. Davis, whose military service had begun in the Spanish-American War, was promoted to Brigadier General in 1940 — the first black ever to hold that rank. His son, Colonel Benjamin O. Davis, Jr., who had graduated from West Point in 1936, commanded a black unit, the 332nd Fighter Group in Italy, which played a key role in the Mediterranean campaign. In the South Pacific an outstanding black unit was the 93rd Combat Division, which

Colonel Benjamin O. Davis, Jr., commanded a unit which destroyed over 200 enemy planes. Davis later became America's first black major general.

SAVE FREEDOM OF SPEECH

BUY WAR BONDS

LIFE IN AMERICA

The Arsenal of Democracy

Following the attack on Pearl Harbor, Americans worked day and night to provide needed war materials. Women filled vital jobs in defense factories, citizens bought bonds to finance the war effort, and drives were held to collect rubber.

SCRAP RUBBER JUNE 15TH TO 30TH WANTED

TIRES-TUBES-GLOVES SHEETING-PADS-MATTING RAINCOATS-HEELS TO WIN THIS WAR

SCRAP-RUBBER JUNE 15 TO 30 TO WIN THIS WAR

saw heavy action beginning with the landings in the Solomon Islands in 1942.

Despite such progress, black soldiers fighting for their country still faced serious discrimination. Most units continued to be racially segregated. Most blacks, furthermore, remained in the lowest ranks, and in many parts of the nation black military personnel confronted strict social segregation in camp as well as in nearby towns.

Mexican Americans experience both opportunities and problems. Mexican Americans also benefited from the shortage of labor the war produced. Many industrial jobs in the American Southwest became available to Mexican Americans for the first time during the war. The need to step up food production to feed the army created new agricultural jobs as well.

Mexican Americans found, however, that these new opportunities created tension with the larger community. As they competed with other groups for housing and jobs, ill will often showed itself. In Los Angeles in 1943 resentment exploded as a brawl between servicemen and Mexican American youths touched off a week of rioting.

Many women enter the labor force. The war opened many new opportunities for American women too. Not only did women serve in the military for the first time, but they became an important part of the civilian labor force. Immediately after the attack on Pearl Harbor, women quickly moved into jobs as truck drivers, lumberjacks, welders, chemists, and mechanics. Without their contribution, the "arsenal of democracy" could not have performed the miracles of production needed to bring victory. By August, 1945, women constituted over a third of the labor force in the United States. About 18,000,000 women who had not previously worked now held jobs.

Roosevelt wins a fourth term. In the summer of 1944, as the fighting raged in Europe, Americans held their presidential nominating conventions as usual. Though ailing and tired, Roosevelt consented to run again — for an unprecedented fourth term. He was virtually unopposed within the Democratic Party. As his running mate, the party named Senator Harry S. Truman of Missouri. The Republicans nominated Thomas E. Dewey, the governor of New York, for President, and Governor John W. Bricker of Ohio for Vice President.

Not surprisingly, the war was the chief issue on the minds of the voters. Some Republicans privately condemned "Roosevelt's war" and whispered about the President's failing health. Dewey, however, confined himself to criticizing the administration's handling of military matters. In the end, people were convinced that this was no time to elect a President inexperienced in the management of foreign affairs. In November, Roosevelt was re-elected, winning 53 percent of the popular vote and 432 of the 531 votes in the electoral college. The drama of a democratic election held during wartime — the first such in the United States since 1864 — was an inspiration to people everywhere who loved freedom.

SECTION REVIEW

1. (a) How did the United States expand its armed forces following its entry into World War II? (b) By what means was industrial production mobilized?
2. (a) Why were Japanese Americans living in the West Coast interned during the war? (b) How did wartime conditions affect black Americans? (c) Mexican Americans? (d) American women?

3 The Allies Win the War in Europe

By the end of 1942, the terrifying successes of Germany and Japan had ceased, and the Allies were ready to go on the offensive.

Churchill and Roosevelt confer at Casablanca. In January, 1943, while the fighting for North Africa was still going on in Tunisia, Churchill and Roosevelt met at Casablanca, Morocco, to discuss their next moves. Stalin had been invited to attend but did not, to the annoyance of FDR and Churchill. No American President had ever before left the country during wartime, but Roosevelt was convinced that it was essential for him to see his commanders and troops. He was also fascinated by the idea of making a trip to places he had never before visited.[3]

---

[3]In traveling by airplane on this occasion, Roosevelt became the first Chief Executive to fly while in office. Nine years earlier Mrs. Roosevelt, visiting lands in the Caribbean, traveled by plane, the first wife of a President to do so.

The two English-speaking leaders reached conclusions on three crucial matters at their Casablanca meeting. First, they decided that as soon as the fighting in Africa had ended, the Allies would invade Italy. Second, the two leaders decided that it was time to send enough men and supplies to the Pacific to allow General Mac-Arthur and Admiral Nimitz to launch an offensive against the Japanese. Third, and most important, they decided to accept nothing less than unconditional surrender from the enemy. The two men were determined that politicians in the Axis countries would never be able to claim that their soldiers had been "stabbed in the back" by a government eager to make peace. (Hitler had used this argument to explain Germany's defeat in 1918.) They also sought to reassure Stalin that they had no intention of making a separate peace with Hitler.

The Allies invade Italy. In July, 1943, two months after the fighting ended in Africa, a combined American and British force of 160,000 men landed on the Italian island of Sicily. By mid-August, they had secured the island. The loss of Sicily led to the overthrow of Mussolini. As the first of the enemy leaders fell from power, American newspapers trumpeted: ONE DOWN AND TWO TO GO! A new Italian government ordered the arrest of the would-be "Caesar." Two months later, a daring German rescue party freed Mussolini and took him to northern Italy where he was put in charge of a puppet Italian government.

On September 3, the Allies set forth from Sicily to conquer the rest of Italy. The Germans, suspecting that the Italians were about to give up, had occupied most of the country. The Allies now faced veteran Nazi troops determined to hold Italy.

President Roosevelt shares a jeep with General Eisenhower in North Africa. Eisenhower had just been given command of the operation to launch an invasion of France.

To take Italy, Allied troops were forced to fight a long and costly campaign, as they slowly drove the Germans northward. By October 1, the G.I.'s under General Mark W. Clark entered Naples. Attempting to outflank the Germans, they landed at Anzio, south of Rome. They ran into a relentless German defense, however, and suffered heavy casualties. It was June, 1944, before Allied forces, led by Clark, entered Rome. Even then, months of hard fighting lay ahead. Not until May, 1945, did the Germans finally surrender their hold on Italy. A few weeks earlier, Mussolini had been captured and executed by anti-Fascist Italians.

Plans are made to invade France. The Italian campaign gave the Russians some relief by pinning down German troops who otherwise could have been transferred to Eastern Europe. Nevertheless, the long-awaited second front in France was about to be opened. Germany would be caught in the middle as Soviet forces pressed westward and the Americans and British pressed eastward.

In the greatest secrecy, Allied strategists laid their plans — the most elaborate in the history of warfare. The Supreme Commander of Operation Overlord — the code name for the invasion of France — was General Eisenhower. Over two million British, American, and other Allied troops were mobilized and given special training in the British Isles. Allied planes, meanwhile, bombarded the French coast, attempting to destroy Nazi lines of communication and transportation. Having held France for four years, the Germans were well-entrenched there. Expecting an invasion, they had tried to make their defenses invincible.

The Allies also took care to mislead the enemy as to the precise place they intended to land. They set up dummy installations in the British Isles and used false radio signals to convince the Nazis that plans were being made to invade France at Calais. Even the strategic bombing of northern France throughout early 1944 was designed to keep secret the planned site of invasion: the Normandy coast.

By the late spring of 1944, the invading forces were ready. As the troops waited anxiously for orders, "Axis Sally," a notorious Nazi propagandist who made English-language broadcasts, played a popular wartime tune called "I Double Dare You." Now she had new words for it, including the jeering lines:

> I double dare you to venture a raid.
> I double dare you to try and invade. . . .
> I double dare you to come over here.
> I double dare you.

France is liberated. Shortly after midnight on June 6, 1944 — D-Day — the mighty invasion began. Three divisions of paratroopers dropped silently behind German lines to sabotage transportation and communication systems. At 3:30 A.M., Eisenhower's Order of the Day was broadcast to the troops of the expeditionary force: "You are about to embark upon a great crusade. . . . " it said. "The hopes and prayers of liberty-loving people everywhere go with you." The Allied ground forces were under the command of General Omar Bradley. Superb at devising tactics, Bradley came to be called with affection "the G.I.'s general."

Although casualties on the Normandy beaches were high, the Allies succeeded in establishing five beachheads where they could land more men and supplies. These footholds were gradually linked together and then widened. Illustrating the surprises that war can produce despite planning, the toughest fighting took place on a landing area called Omaha Beach. There the Allies encountered a German division that by luck was in the vicinity on maneuvers.

By nightfall of D-Day about 155,000 men were ashore. Within a month, a million Allied troops had been landed in Normandy, along with 172,000 vehicles and more than half a million tons of supplies. The invasion was a success. Now the troops began to fan out over French soil, pressing toward Paris. On August 25, 1944, after less than three months of fighting, Allied troops moved into the French capital.

Meanwhile, on August 15 a combined force of American, British, and French

Having broken through German defenses at the town of Saint Lo in Normandy, American forces were ready to advance toward Paris.

COURTESY TIME-LIFE BOOKS INC.

soldiers had landed at Toulon on the southern coast of France and was racing northward along the Rhone Valley. At the same time, General George S. Patton, in command of the United States Third Army, was spearheading with his armored units a spectacular advance from Normandy through Brittany and northern France. By November the Germans had been cleared out of France.

The Germans launch their final offensive. As planned, Stalin's troops had launched an offensive to coincide with the British and American push through Western Europe. The Russians marched west, retaking the Ukraine, the Crimea, White Russia, eastern Poland, and most of Lithuania. By October, 1944, the Red Army had moved into Rumania, Bulgaria, Hungary, and Yugoslavia.

At this point, Hitler personally directed one last, desperate counteroffensive. On December 16, 1944, taking the Allies off guard, the Nazis attacked along a fifty-mile front in the thinly held area around the Ardennes Forest in Belgium. Hitler hoped to cut the Allied forces in two, leaving the northern half without supplies. The Allies were driven back some 65 miles, creating an enormous bulge in their line of defense. The attack thus became known as the Battle of the Bulge.

After their initial retreat, Allied troops stood their ground at the town of Bastogne in the freezing winter weather. Surrounded by Nazi troops, the place was held by an airborne division commanded by a young brigadier general, Anthony C. McAuliffe. To a demand that he surrender, McAuliffe fired back a one-word answer: "Nuts!" His division dug in bravely until it was rescued.

By the end of January, the Germans had lost every inch of territory they had retaken, and 120,000 men besides. The American price for wiping out the bulge was 77,000 casualties. The Germans had only delayed the outcome of the war. By the beginning of 1945, Allied troops were converging on Germany.

The Allies confer at Yalta. In early February, 1945, President Roosevelt traveled to Yalta, in the Crimea, to meet with Churchill and Stalin. Victory over Germany appearing certain, the leaders had come together to discuss strategy for ending the war and to agree on postwar settlements.

The Big Three, as these leaders were called, concluded plans for the unconditional surrender of Germany. They agreed that Germany would be divided into three zones, to be occupied separately by the victorious Allies. (France would be given a zone out of the territory assigned to the United States and Great Britain.) The city of Berlin, deep inside the Soviet zone, would also be split into three zones. East Prussia would be divided between Poland and the Soviet Union. The Big Three also announced that a meeting would be held at San Francisco to establish a new organization for keeping world peace.

At the Yalta conference, Stalin made several commitments. He restated his

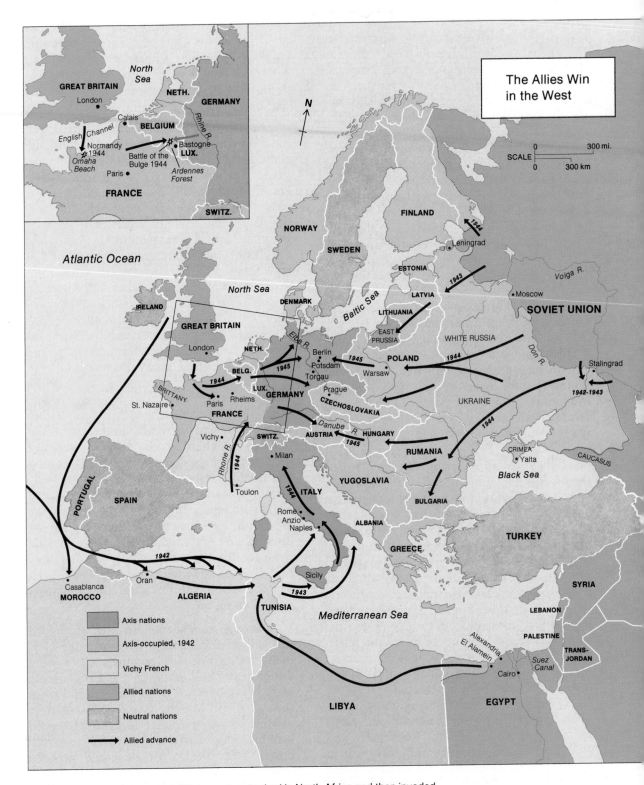

The Allies Win in the West

Inset map labels:
North Sea
GREAT BRITAIN
London
Calais
NETH.
GERMANY
English Channel
BELGIUM
Rhine R.
Normandy
1944
Omaha Beach
Battle of the Bulge 1944
Bastogne
LUX.
Ardennes Forest
Paris
FRANCE
SWITZ.

SCALE
0   300 mi.
0   300 km

Main map labels:
N
Atlantic Ocean
North Sea
NORWAY
SWEDEN
FINLAND
Leningrad
1944
ESTONIA
Volga R.
1943
LATVIA
Moscow
LITHUANIA
SOVIET UNION
IRELAND
GREAT BRITAIN
London
DENMARK
Baltic Sea
EAST PRUSSIA
WHITE RUSSIA
Don R.
NETH.
Elbe R.
Berlin
1945
POLAND
1944
Stalingrad
BELG.
1944
1945
Potsdam
Torgau
Warsaw
BRITTANY
LUX.
Prague
1942-1943
St. Nazaire
Paris
Rheims
GERMANY
CZECHOSLOVAKIA
UKRAINE
FRANCE
1944
Vichy
Danube R.
HUNGARY
1944
SWITZ.
AUSTRIA
1945
CRIMEA
Yalta
CAUCASUS
Rhone R.
1944
Milan
RUMANIA
Black Sea
PORTUGAL
SPAIN
Toulon
1944
ITALY
YUGOSLAVIA
BULGARIA
TURKEY
Rome
Anzio
Naples
ALBANIA
GREECE
SYRIA
1942
Casablanca
Oran
Sicily
1943
LEBANON
MOROCCO
ALGERIA
TUNISIA
Mediterranean Sea
PALESTINE
Alexandria
El Alamein
TRANS-JORDAN
Suez Canal
Cairo
LIBYA
EGYPT

Legend:
Axis nations
Axis-occupied, 1942
Vichy French
Allied nations
Neutral nations
→ Allied advance

To defeat the Axis, the western Allies counterattacked in North Africa and then invaded Italy and France. In the East, meanwhile, Russian armies advanced westward toward Germany. Following the death of Hitler and the fall of Berlin, Germany surrendered to the Allies on May 7, 1945.

671

promise to declare war on Japan within three months after Germany surrendered. He agreed with Roosevelt and Churchill that Poland and other Eastern European countries that were wholly or partially occupied by Russian troops would have "free elections." These would lead, it was understood, to governments "responsible to the will of the people" and "broadly representative of all democratic elements." He promised, finally, that he would sign a "pact of friendship and alliance" with the Chinese government of Chiang Kai-shek.

In return for these pledges, Stalin won concessions from Roosevelt and Churchill. First, the Russians would gain control of several important Japanese islands off the Pacific coast of the Soviet Union. The Russians would also be allowed to occupy Outer Mongolia, a portion of Central Asia that bordered on the Soviet Union. Second, despite an earlier promise that Roosevelt had made to Chiang Kai-shek, the Soviet Union would have special privileges in Manchuria. Third, the Soviet Union would receive half of any war reparations Germany would be forced to pay.

The Yalta agreements were at first greeted with enthusiasm in the United States. By the end of the war, however, many Americans were deeply concerned, believing that the West had given away more than it had received from Stalin. Some critics said that Roosevelt and Churchill had been foolish to trust Stalin. They pointed out that in August, 1944, when the Poles had risen in revolt against the Nazis in Warsaw, the Soviet army stationed nearby had done nothing to help. The Russians had seemed willing to allow the rebellious Poles to be wiped out, making it easier for the Soviet Union to take control of Poland once Germany was defeated.

Defenders of the Yalta agreements argued that Stalin had held most of the cards at that meeting. First, Roosevelt and Churchill expected a long and costly war in the Pacific in which they would have found the help of the Soviet Union indispensable. It was reasonable to make concessions in order to spare their own troops. Second, Stalin's forces were already in possession of Eastern Europe and stationed on the border of China at the time of the Yalta meeting. Short of war, there was little Churchill and Roosevelt could have done to assure freedom to the peoples of these occupied lands.

President Roosevelt dies. When Roosevelt returned from Yalta, he was exhausted. For the first time, he remained seated while he addressed Congress. In April, he traveled to Warm Springs, Georgia, for a rest. There, on April 12, 1945, he died suddenly of a stroke. Mrs. Roosevelt cabled her sons serving in the battle zones: "Darlings: Pa slept away this afternoon. He did his job to the end as he would want you to do." Churchill later said that he sat speechless for five minutes after hearing the news. "I felt," he said, "as if I had been struck a physical blow." In a eulogy to Parliament he called Roosevelt "the greatest champion of human freedom who has ever brought help and comfort from the New World to the Old."

Roosevelt had occupied the White House for twelve years — longer than any other President. The new President, Harry S. Truman, was virtually unknown. A policeman on guard at the Capitol who had seen many Presidents commented sourly, "Truman's only a Coolidge with eyeglasses." Many people shared this view at first, wondering if Truman was up to the job. Truman himself confessed to having doubts. The day after taking office he said modestly to the press corps, "When they told me yesterday what had happened, I felt like the moon, the stars and all the planets had fallen on me."

Germany surrenders. In the spring of 1945, the Allied armies were bringing Germany to its knees. Germany's cities were under heavy bombardment, and its borders were being overrun from the east and from the west. In March, General Eisenhower was faced with a crucial decision. He could lead his troops eastward as quickly as possible to seize Berlin, or he could proceed slowly, wiping out all Nazi resistance in the territory he occupied.

Churchill had urged that the Western Allies take territory as far to the east as possible, especially the capital cities of Berlin

Thousands of mourners lined the streets of Washington, D.C., to honor Franklin Roosevelt. The President died on April 12, 1945, while vacationing at Warm Springs, Georgia. He was buried at his home in Hyde Park, New York.

and Prague. The more Eastern European territory the West held, he believed, the more power it would have to force Stalin to live up to his promise of free elections for the countries in that region. Eisenhower, backed first by Roosevelt and then by Truman, decided not to follow Churchill's advice. On April 27, American forces linked up with the Russian army at the town of Torgau, on the Elbe River — sixty miles south of Berlin.

Germany was in chaos, its leaders holed up in an underground bunker in the capital, its people dazed and dispirited. Hitler, finally recognizing the certainty of defeat, died by his own hand on April 30, 1945. Berlin fell to the Russians two days later. On May 7, at Eisenhower's headquarters in Rheims, France, a German field marshal signed an unconditional surrender. The war in Europe ended the next day (V-E Day).

Nazi atrocities are revealed. During the war, word of unspeakable crimes committed by the Nazis had reached America, but it was not until Allied troops entered German territory that the extent of those horrors came to light. The Nazis had set up enormous concentration camps for the purpose of murdering their political enemies, including the entire Jewish population of Europe. The world, stunned and sickened by this program of extermination, called it the Holocaust. The Nazis had systematically killed millions of men, women, and children in these camps. Among their number were six million Jews.

Throughout his political career Hitler had made the Jewish people his particular scapegoat. Building on the long-standing, unreasoning hostility to Jews, Hitler had come to power partly on the legend that Germany had been defeated in 1918 because of the disloyalty of Jews on the home front. The Nazi leader, maintaining that the Germans were a superior race, succeeded in driving his people into a frenzy against the German Jews as a domestic enemy.

Hitler's campaign against the Jews went through a number of increasingly brutal stages. The first stage came in 1933 when gangs of Nazis, prodded by the government, looted and boycotted shops and other businesses owned by Jews. The second stage was the enactment of laws a few years later that disfranchised all people who had "Jewish blood" — which included anybody with at least one Jewish grandparent. The third stage began in 1939 with mass arrests of Jews, soon followed by the establishment of concentration camps. In these wretched places Jews were kept on the verge of starvation and forced to labor like slaves. The fourth stage began in 1941 after Hitler had sent his armies into the Soviet Union. He ordered that some of the concentration camps be converted into extermination camps. In these camps, the Nazis operated gas chambers and crematoriums to carry on the mass murders "efficiently." Even near the end of the war, German energies were systematically devoted to rounding up Jews and shipping them to their destruction.

Although recognizing that nothing could atone for the atrocities of the Nazi regime, people of the Allied nations demanded that those responsible for committing them be brought to justice. In 1945 and 1946, Allied courts tried Germans accused of these war crimes. Hundreds were executed; many thousands of others received lesser punishments.

SECTION REVIEW

1. (a) What agreements did Roosevelt and Churchill reach at Casablanca in 1943? (b) Why did the Allies invade Italy? (c) What were the results?
2. (a) How did the Allies strike at Germany from the west? (b) How did the Germans try to counter the Allied advance? (c) What were the results?
3. (a) What agreements were reached at Yalta? (b) For what reasons were those agreements controversial?
4. (a) How did the war in Germany come to an end? (b) Why were war-crime trials held?

4 The War in the Pacific Is Won

By 1943 the Allies had taken the offensive in the Pacific. Their task was forbidding, because in the early years of the war Japanese troops had occupied many islands in the Pacific. As defenders of these islands the Japanese were fearsome enemies. They considered surrender a disgrace — even when no possibility of victory remained. Grimly, the Allies prepared to fight the Japanese to the bitter end.

The Allies prepare the way for the invasion of Japan. Allied strategy in the Pacific had three main objectives: to recapture the Philippines; to cut Japanese lines of transportation and communication; and to set up bases from which Japan itself could eventually be attacked. These objectives were to be accomplished through a strategy called "island-hopping." Instead of clearing the enemy out of every island on the route north toward Japan, Allied troops would capture only certain strategic ones. The others, cut off from reinforcements and supplies, would cease to pose a threat.

There were two major lines of Allied advance. The first, assigned to Admiral Nimitz's forces, was to move on Japan from the central Pacific, taking the Gilbert, Marshall, Caroline, and Mariana Islands as they went. From airbases on these islands, the Japanese had been attacking Allied troops under General MacArthur, who was leading the second Allied advance by way of New Guinea.

Allied forces under Admiral Nimitz succeeded in taking key islands in the central Pacific, capturing, in the summer of 1944, Guam and Saipan in the Marianas. These victories placed Allied troops within striking distance of Japan. As soon as the islands were cleared of resistance, enormous airfields were built and B–29 bombers were turned loose in strikes against Japan.

The Philippines are liberated. In October, 1944, General MacArthur fulfilled his long-standing promise to liberate the Philippine Islands. He declared dramatically, "People of the Philippines! I have returned. . . . Rally to me." After two years of slogging their way up from New Guinea and fighting one bloody engagement after another, his men went ashore on Leyte (LAY-tay), in the central Philippines. In the ensuing clash of navies known as the Battle of Leyte Gulf — the greatest naval engagement of all time — the Allies smashed the Japanese fleet once and for all. The way was now clear for Allied troops to move on to the main Philippine island of Luzon, where the capital city of Manila is located. Japanese forces offered stiff resistance. Finally, on March 9, 1945, after three months of struggle, the Japanese troops on Luzon surrendered to the Americans.

American troops advance toward Japan. While MacArthur's troops battled for control of the Philippines, Nimitz's powerful units moved even nearer to the Japanese homeland. A fleet under the command of Admiral William F. ("Bull") Halsey was beginning to roam at will along the coasts of Japan, pounding what remained of enemy shipping. In February, 1945, American marines landed on the tiny island of Iwo Jima. This desolate spot had been selected because it was close enough to Japan to be a base for stepped-up bombing of Japanese cities. Using flamethrowers and dynamite, the marines rooted out the Japanese defenders on the way to the island's highpoint, Mt. Suribachi. At its top, the marines succeeded in planting a pole bearing the Stars and Stripes.

From Iwo Jima, American forces pushed on toward the large and strategically important island of Okinawa, less than 400 miles from Japan. On April 1, 1945, 100,000 American soldiers and marines began to go ashore, backed by an armada of 1,300 ships of all kinds. In a last-ditch gesture, Japanese pilots flew suicide missions against American vessels, crashing their planes on the decks of the ships in order to deliver the bomb loads.[4] Nearly 200 American ships were damaged or destroyed by these tactics.

---

[4]The Japanese airmen were known as *kamikazes*, a word meaning "divine wind."

General MacArthur fulfilled his promise to return to the Philippines when he waded ashore at Leyte, 948 days after he had left the islands.

By the time the G.I.'s had gained control of Okinawa, in June, 1945, they had suffered almost 50,000 casualties. The Japanese, too, had suffered fearsome losses, but they showed no sign of weakened resolve.

Scientists develop the atomic bomb. Ever since 1938, scientists had known that it was possible to split the atom, once regarded as the smallest particle of matter. This procedure, they believed, would release the enormous energy at the atom's nucleus or core. In August, 1939, Albert Einstein, acknowledged to be the most brilliant scientist of the century and recently arrived in the United States as a refugee from Nazi Germany, wrote President Roosevelt a fateful letter. In it Einstein stated that the ability to unlock the nucleus of the atom could be used to create "extremely powerful bombs."

Acting on Einstein's suggestion, Roosevelt in 1940 ordered a top-secret project to begin work on an atomic weapon. He knew it was necessary to beat out the Germans and the Japanese, who were working — in separate undertakings — on similar projects. In early 1943 the Manhattan Project, as the American research effort was

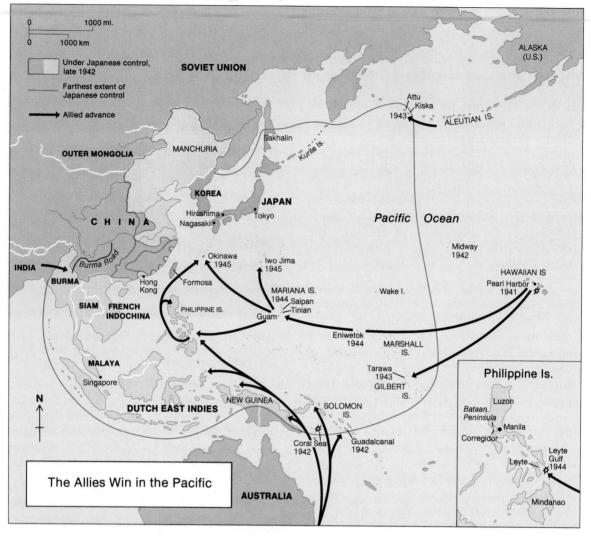

The Allies Win in the Pacific

American naval victories in the Coral Sea and off Midway marked turning points in the war in the Pacific. Allied forces then began their advance on Japan.

called, was established at Los Alamos, New Mexico, where its work could be carried on in total secrecy. On June 16, 1945, the first atomic bomb was tested in the New Mexican desert.

President Truman was conferring with other Allied leaders in Potsdam, Germany, when news of the successful explosion reached him. He told Stalin only that the United States had a new weapon capable of vast destruction. (Stalin, through espionage agents, already knew about the Manhattan Project.) Then, on July 26, 1945, the Allied leaders issued this warning to Japan: "The alternative to surrender is prompt and utter destruction." The Japanese decided to ignore the ultimatum.

Truman was thoroughly convinced that the Japanese military forces would never surrender unless American troops actually invaded and conquered their homeland. American military strategists estimated that such an operation could not be accomplished in less than eighteen months and without the loss of a million Allied lives. Truman therefore ordered that the new bomb be dropped on a Japanese city. He used it, he explained, "in order to save the lives of thousands and thousands of young Americans."

As Americans celebrated Japan's formal surrender, held aboard the *Missouri*, President Truman addressed the nation on radio. "It was the spirit of liberty," he said, "which gave us our armed strength and which made our men invincible in victory."

Atomic weapons end the war. On August 6 a B–29 carrying an atomic bomb took off from Tinian Island in the Marianas and headed for Hiroshima, one of the few Japanese cities so far spared by Allied bombers. At 8:00 A.M. the plane dropped its awesome new weapon. The bomb exploded with the force of 20,000 tons of TNT. The city was leveled. Almost 78,000 people were killed and 70,000 were wounded.

In spite of the fearful destruction, the Japanese still did not give up. On August 8 the Soviet Union declared war on Japan and invaded Manchuria. The next day, the Allies dropped another atomic bomb, this time on the city of Nagasaki. Finally, on August 14, the emperor of Japan ordered his military leaders to surrender unconditionally.

The war ended formally on September 2 (V-J Day) in Tokyo Bay. General MacArthur was in charge of the surrender ceremonies, held aboard the American battleship *Missouri*. Among the high-ranking Allied military and naval officers present was General Wainwright (page 658), recently released from a Japanese prison camp. From the foremast of the *Missouri* floated the same American flag that had flown over the Capitol in Washington, D.C., on December 7, 1941. Near it was flying the 31-starred flag that Commodore Perry had brought to Tokyo Bay nearly a century earlier. As the proceedings ended, MacArthur spoke solemnly: "Let us pray for peace . . . and that God will preserve it always." In the moment of joyful relief that the war was over, people could not forget that in this most destructive combat in human history as many as fifty million lives had been lost.

No one knew, that day, whether the terrible memory of the Second World War would prevent future wars. No one knew, either, whether the Allies, who had worked together so magnificently, would be able to sustain their close relationship in peacetime. Of one fact, however, there was no doubt: the United States was now the world's most powerful country, to which free people and those yearning for freedom everywhere looked for leadership.

SECTION REVIEW

1. (a) What were the Allies' main objectives in the Pacific campaign? (b) Why was the "island-hopping" strategy used?
2. What islands did Allied forces capture as they moved closer to Japan in 1944–1945?
3. Why did the Japanese finally agree to an unconditional surrender?

677

Chapter 28 Review

Summary

When Roosevelt and Churchill met in the summer of 1941, they pledged mutual support against totalitarian aggression. At this time, Japan was making clear its intention of dominating Asia. Relations between the United States and Japan deteriorated, and on the morning of December 7, 1941, Japanese planes attacked the American naval base at Pearl Harbor, Hawaii. In the following days the United States recognized the existence of a state of war with Japan; Germany and Italy, in turn, declared war on the United States.

Japan moved quickly to consolidate its position in the Pacific. Guam, Wake Island, Hong Kong, Singapore, and the Philippines fell to the Japanese. American victories in the battles of the Coral Sea, Midway Island, and Guadalcanal finally contained Japanese expansion.

The first priority for the United States was to help control the advance of German armies in Europe and North Africa. In the winter of 1941–1942 the Russians fought the German army to a standstill. After an Allied force defeated the German army in North Africa during the spring of 1943, Roosevelt and Churchill turned their attention to an invasion of Europe.

On the home front, the country quickly mobilized for war. The military was expanded through the Selective Service System, and industry was organized for war production. Increased taxes and the sale of war bonds helped finance the American war effort.

Allied forces landed in Sicily in July, 1943, and for the next year fought their way northward to Rome. Italy surrendered in September, 1943, but the German army continued to hold most of northern Italy. Plans to invade France, meanwhile, were made with great care. On June 6, 1944, an Allied army under the command of General Dwight D. Eisenhower landed on the beaches of Normandy. By August, Allied troops liberated Paris and then began to close in on Germany itself. Hitler ordered one last desperate offensive in December, but Allied soldiers held their ground and repulsed the German advance. The war ended in Europe when Germany surrendered on May 7, 1945.

In 1944 and 1945 the Allies used a strategy of "island-hopping" as they made their way toward Japan. With America now in possession of the atomic bomb, Japan was asked in July, 1945, to surrender or face destruction. When the Japanese ignored this warning, President Truman ordered atomic bombs to be dropped on Japan. On September 2, 1945, Japan formally surrendered — ending the Second World War.

Vocabulary and Important Terms

1. Allies
2. Battle of the Coral Sea
3. Battle of Midway
4. War Production Board
5. war bond
6. D-Day
7. Committee on Fair Employment Practices
8. Battle of the Bulge
9. Yalta agreements
10. V-E Day
11. Holocaust
12. Manhattan Project
13. V-J Day

Discussion Questions

1. (a) Following the entry of the United States into World War II, why did the Roosevelt administration adopt a "Europe-first" strategy? (b) What fighting, nevertheless, took place in the Pacific? (c) How large an area had come under Japanese control by mid-1942?

2. (a) Why was winning the Battle of the Atlantic so critical to the Allies? (b) Why was Hitler unable to defeat the Russians? (c) What effect did Hitler's losses in the Soviet Union have on the outcome of the war?

3. (a) Why were American and British troops sent to Morocco and Algeria in 1942? (b) How did the decision to send troops to North Africa reflect a division in Allied thinking on the question of how best to prosecute the war?

4. (a) What role did the United States government play in the mobilization of resources during the war? (b) What impact did the war have on the American economy?

5. (a) What did the holding of elections in 1944 show about the American system of government? (b) Why were Japanese Americans relocated during the war?

6. (a) Why did Allied leaders decide to demand the unconditional surrender of their enemies? (b) When, and under what conditions, did Italy, Germany, and Japan surrender?

7. (a) Why did the United States develop the atomic bomb? (b) Why did the United States use the bomb against Japan? (c) What effect did the use of the atomic bomb have on the outcome of World War II?

Relating Past to Present

1. Under what circumstances do world leaders meet today and make decisions that potentially have long-lasting effects? Are these decisions as important as those reached by Allied leaders during World War II? Why or why not?
2. Scientists began work in 1940 on the top-secret Manhattan Project. How do the results of their research affect all people today?

Studying Local History

1. Find out how the war effort affected your community. Were there armed forces facilities or military camps in your region? What contributions did high school students make to the war effort? How did your community honor those who died in the war?
2. Study the headlines and editorials of newspapers published in your community in December, 1941. Find out the reaction of people to the news of Japan's attack on Pearl Harbor. What do subsequent newspaper stories tell you about early wartime mobilization efforts in your community?

Using History Skills

1. *Reading source material.* Study Ray Hartman's description of the student war bond drive on page 664. (a) How did the students in Ray Hartman's school raise money for the war effort? (b) What did the school buy with the money the students had collected? (c) Would you infer from this passage that Ray Hartman was an effective leader? Explain your answer.
2. *Comparing.* Compare the role of the federal government during the First World War and the Second World War. How was American industry mobilized during each conflict? What efforts were taken to control public opinion? What opportunities were opened to women and to members of minority groups?
3. *Reading Maps.* Study the map on page 676 showing the Pacific campaign during World War II. (a) How does the map indicate the farthest extent of Japanese control? (b) From what directions did Allied forces advance on Japan? (c) Explain how the strategy of "island-hopping" enabled Allied forces to advance across the Pacific.

WORLD SCENE

Naval Warfare

Advances in the design and construction of warships brought changes in naval warfare during the Second World War.

German pocket battleships. Germany had created in the early 1930's a new classification of warship, the "pocket battleship." Not a true battleship as measured in size or armament, it was equipped with eleven-inch turret cannon and could travel extremely fast.

At the outbreak of war in 1939, the Germans had three pocket battleships. One, the *Graf Spee*, was at sea when the fighting began. Immediately, it began to sink Allied ships in the South Atlantic. British and French task forces were sent to hunt down the *Graf Spee*. In December a British squadron located it off the coast of Uruguay. After a fierce two-hour battle, in which both sides suffered heavy damage, the *Graf Spee* broke off the action and took refuge in the harbor of Montevideo.

In the days that followed, British diplomats stationed in the port spread rumors that additional Allied ships had arrived and were in position outside the port. Rather than subject his crew to what he thought would be a hope-less battle, the German captain ordered the *Graf Spee* to be blown up. The sinking of the *Graf Spee* was a stirring victory for the Allies.

Japanese and American aircraft carriers. No development since the coming of ironclads had a greater impact on warfare at sea than the introduction of aircraft carriers. With aircraft carriers, naval forces could launch squadrons of torpedo bombers to seek out and destroy enemy ships.

In the months after Pearl Harbor, Japanese and American task forces assembled in the South Pacific and carefully stalked one another. Then, in May, 1942, the Battle of the Coral Sea was fought, marking the first time in naval history that two fleets were engaged in battle without ever coming in sight of each other. The entire battle consisted of a duel between airplanes that took off from the carriers.

This battle, in which the Americans emerged victorious, changed the way nations organized their naval task forces. No battle group could be without at least one aircraft carrier, and all ships were now outfitted with antiaircraft weapons and thicker armor.

UNIT 7 REVIEW

Important Dates

1920 First American radio broadcasting station.
Harding elected President.
1921 Washington Conference begins.
1924 National Origins Act passed.
Coolidge elected President.
1927 Lindbergh flies nonstop to Paris.
1928 Kellogg-Briand Pact.
Hoover elected President.
1929 Great Depression begins.
1931 Japan invades Manchuria.
1932 Franklin Roosevelt elected President.
1933 New Deal begins.
Hitler takes power in Germany.
1934 Indian Reorganization Act passed.
1935 Social Security Act passed.
1936 Supreme Court declares AAA unconstitutional.
1937 Roosevelt's "court-packing" plan rejected.
1938 CIO separates from AFL.
1939 World War II begins in Europe.
1941 Lend-Lease Act.
United States enters World War II.
1944 Allies land in France.
1945 World War II ends.

Review Questions

1. (a) To what extent were the years after the First World War marked by political and economic unrest? (b) Why was immigration policy a matter of concern to many Americans? (c) What major changes were made in American immigration laws?
2. (a) Why are the 1920's often remembered as a time of prosperity? (b) How was the Great Depression a consequence of some of the economic conditions present in the United States during the 1920's? (c) How was the Great Depression influenced by economic conditions outside the United States?
3. (a) Why was Hoover unwilling to use the powers of the national government to end the depression? (b) To what extent did Roosevelt's attitude differ?
4. (a) How successful was Roosevelt in ending the Depression? (b) What New Deal measures were especially controversial? (c) In each case explain why.
5. (a) Describe the situation minority groups faced during the 1920's and 1930's. (b) How did the role of American women change in the 1920's and 1930's?
6. (a) To what extent did the United States involve itself in world affairs during the 1920's and 1930's?

(b) What changes took place in relations between the United States and its possessions? (c) What changes took place in the nation's Latin American policy?
7. (a) In what ways was world peace threatened during the 1930's? (b) What was the attitude of the United States? (c) Why did this country enter World War II?
8. How did each of the following countries contribute to the defeat of the Axis powers in World War II? (a) The United States (b) The Soviet Union (c) Great Britain

Projects

1. Make a display featuring American society in the 1920's. Your display should illustrate some of the significant changes in ways of living that took place during that decade.
2. Create a set of three handbills on which you indicate either support or criticism of the Agricultural Adjustment Act, the National Industrial Recovery Act, and the Tennessee Valley Authority. On your handbills include pictures, slogans, and other information to back up your point of view.
3. Simulate key aspects of a debate over the effectiveness of the New Deal by re-enacting the roles of supporters and critics. Roles should include (a) supporters of Roosevelt and the New Deal; (b) critics who charged Roosevelt with doing too much; and (c) critics who accused Roosevelt of doing too little (including representatives of the philosophies of Huey Long, Francis Townsend, and Father Coughlin).
4. On an outline map of the world indicate the possessions of the United States. Then list the acts of Congress passed for each territory between 1900 and 1952 and the dates of those acts. Also state the current status of each territory.
5. Write an essay on the topic "The neutrality legislation of the 1930's was a proper response by the United States to the growing threat of another world war." You may either agree or disagree with this statement, but be sure to include evidence to support your point of view.
6. Do research to find out what songs were popular during the Second World War. Present your findings in class.
7. On an outline map of the world indicate the key battles of World War II. Include both sea and land battles. On the back of the map briefly state why each battle was important and what effect, if any, it had on the outcome of the war.

8

CONFIDENCE AND CONCERN

1945–1968

If we falter in our leadership, we may endanger the peace of the world — and we shall surely endanger the welfare of our own nation.

HARRY S. TRUMAN, 1947

Cold War and Hot

1945 – 1952

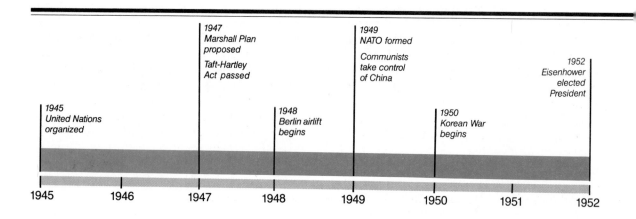

1947
Marshall Plan
proposed

Taft-Hartley
Act passed

1949
NATO formed

Communists
take control
of China

1952
Eisenhower
elected
President

1945
United Nations
organized

1948
Berlin airlift
begins

1950
Korean War
begins

1945   1946   1947   1948   1949   1950   1951   1952

CHAPTER OUTLINE

1. The nation returns to peacetime pursuits.

2. The cold war begins.

3. The cold war leads to a hot war in Korea.

The opening of the postwar era coincided with the beginning of Harry Truman's time in the White House. An able politician and a popular member of the Senate, Truman had been chosen to run with President Roosevelt in 1944. Less than three months after inauguration day in 1945, Roosevelt died and Truman was on his own. Like all "accidental" Presidents, he promised to continue the policies of his predecessor. Problems soon arose, however, for which there were no clear answers.

Truman proved a match for his responsibilities. He was not awed by the people with whom he would have to deal. He wrote his mother after meeting Churchill for the first time, "We had a most pleasant conversation. . . . He gave me a lot of hooey about . . . how he loved Roosevelt and how he intended to love me, etc., etc. . . . I am sure we can get along if he doesn't try to give me too much soft soap." When the new President met the Soviet foreign minister, Vyacheslav Molotov in May, 1945, he severely scolded him for Russia's failure to honor its pledges in Poland. Molotov, livid, responded that no one had ever talked to him that way. Truman retorted, "Carry out your agreements, and you won't get talked to like that!"

The leader of the wartime alliance had been Roosevelt; the cement had been the struggle against Hitler. With both now gone, a new international scene had opened.

1 The Nation Returns to Peacetime Pursuits

Americans in 1945 greeted the end of the war with relief and anticipation. Most people — as after all wars — hoped to return to their old patterns of living. Much, however, would never be the same.

The armed forces return home. Almost immediately President Truman faced demands to "bring the boys home." Although he would have preferred to demobilize the armed forces gradually in order to ease the burden on civilian society, he bowed to the public's wishes to get the troops out of uniform as quickly as possible. By August, 1946, a year after the war ended, the number of troops had been reduced from twelve million to three million.

To ease the transition of discharged military personnel back to civilian life, Congress had passed the Servicemen's Readjustment Act in 1944. Known as the "GI Bill of Rights," this legislation provided veterans with a variety of benefits. In addition to priority for many jobs, veterans were guaranteed wide-ranging educational and financial assistance. The GI Bill's popularity rested in large part on the fact that it enabled millions of young Americans to start over again — if that was what they wanted — with better schooling or in a better job or in better housing than they had known previously. The GI Bill helped wipe out the handicaps resulting from lack of opportunity that the Depression had imposed on so many young people. Nearly eight million veterans were assisted in obtaining education and training — at a cost of about $13.5 billion. The Veterans' Administra-

Servicemen are welcomed home in a victory parade. The GI Bill of Rights helped ease the transition of veterans to peacetime conditions.

The DC-3

The most widely used aircraft in aviation history was the DC-3. When it appeared in 1936, the DC-3 was the first plane to meet the essential requirements of commercial flight—speed, safety, and economy. Operated by a crew of three and able to hold up to 36 passengers, the DC-3 had a pressurized cabin for high-altitude flying. It could maintain a cruising speed of 170 miles per hour. Many DC-3's flew 70,000 hours without major repair.

During World War II the DC-3 was converted to military use and became America's standard medium-range transport and cargo plane. Following the return of peace in 1945, the amazingly dependable and durable DC-3 was put back into commercial use as more and more Americans began to travel by air.

tion, which administered the GI Bill, guaranteed more than $16.5 billion worth of loans to veterans for homes, farms, and businesses. Those generous benefits to the returned veterans aided them enormously in adjusting once again to civilian life.

The economy converts to peacetime. Truman recognized the importance of taking steps to head off the kinds of economic problems that had plagued the country after previous wars. He struggled hard for passage of a full employment bill in 1945, calling for the creation of sixty million jobs — with the understanding that if private business could not provide jobs the government would use all its resources to guarantee full employment. Congress, however, refused to pass the bill.

In general, unemployment did not turn out to be a major problem after the war. Inflation, however, quickly became one of Truman's chief concerns. In 1946, when wartime price controls were removed, prices immediately shot up, increasing nearly 25 percent during 1946–1947. The pent-up demand for goods after four years of austerity was astounding. There was a waiting market for practically every type of consumer product — from automobiles to washing machines, from pots and pans to tables and chairs. A headline in the New York *Daily News* referred to the rising cost of meat:

PRICES SOAR, BUYERS SORE
STEERS JUMP OVER THE MOON

Inflation leads to labor unrest. Working people felt the squeeze of rising prices keenly. The end of the war had put a stop to Sunday, holiday, and overtime work in most branches of industry. For many people, the result was a reduction in take-home pay. In order to catch up with current prices, unions sought substantial wage increases. The problem was that higher wages would increase the cost of manufactured goods, forcing consumer prices higher in an endless upward spiral.

At the end of 1945, automobile workers, electrical workers, and steelworkers took part in crippling strikes.

Many of these walk-outs ended with significant wage increases — soon followed by higher prices for the goods the industries produced. In the spring of 1946 a long coal strike came to an end only when Truman had the government seize the mines.

An even more ominous development came when union members threatened to shut down the nation's railroads. To head off this possibility, Truman called for government operation of the lines. When union leaders went ahead with the strike anyhow, the President sought authority from Congress to draft the strikers. Truman ignored the advice of the Attorney General that such action would be unconstitutional. "We'll draft 'em first," he said, "and think about the law later." Many members of Congress were shocked by the President's stand. The day was saved when, even as the President was speaking, word was handed to him that the labor unions had agreed to settle the strike.

The Taft-Hartley Act is passed. Many Americans blamed the Democratic administration for the strikes and inflation of 1946. Campaigning with a simple but pointed slogan — "Had Enough?" — Republicans swept the congressional elections that year. For the first time since 1928 they won control of both houses of Congress. Among the new members of the House of Representatives were John F. Kennedy from Massachusetts and Richard M. Nixon from California — both destined to be President in the 1960's.

Republican leaders interpreted their victory as a sign of the public's desire for stricter government regulation of organized labor. In June, 1947, Congress passed the Labor-Management Relations Act, also known as the Taft-Hartley Act. The law affirmed labor's right to bargain collectively, and it authorized the continuance of the National Labor Relations Board. Nevertheless, it changed the ground rules for labor-management relations in several respects:

(1) It required a "cooling-off period" of sixty days before a contract could be ended by either an employer or a union. If the Attorney General believed that an impending

As reflected in this cartoon, President Truman vainly hoped for public rejection of the Taft-Hartley Act.

strike or lock-out would threaten the national health or safety, he could obtain an injunction postponing that action for eighty days.

(2) The law forbade the closed shop (in which only workers who were already union members could be hired), allowing instead the union shop (in which workers were required to join a union immediately upon being hired) if the majority of workers voted for it.

(3) State governments were authorized to pass *right-to-work laws.* Such laws allow workers to obtain and keep jobs without joining a labor union at all.

(4) Unions were prohibited from making contributions to political campaigns, establishing secondary boycotts (boycotts against a firm other than the one being struck), putting pressure on nonunion workers to join the union, or charging unusually high initiation or membership fees.

(5) Both employers and unions were permitted to sue for damages resulting from breach of contract.

(6) Union officials were required to sign affidavits saying that they were not Communists and did not advocate the violent overthrow of the United States government.

Supporters of the Taft-Hartley Act argued that it restored the balance of power between labor and management that had been upset (in favor of labor) by the Wagner Act (page 621). To the delight of union members and their leaders, who had only recently been denouncing him as anti-labor, Truman vetoed the bill. Congress, however, overrode the veto. Despite dire predictions, tension between labor and management lessened in the years after the Taft-Hartley Act went into effect.

The Republican Congress passes other measures. Another piece of legislation enacted over Truman's veto was a $5 billion tax cut. Republicans argued that wartime tax increases had been excessive, and especially unfair to wealthy Americans. In 1948 Congress cut taxes across the board, giving special consideration to people in upper-income brackets.

The Republican Congress also expressed disapproval of Franklin Roosevelt's long tenure in office by passing the Twenty-Second Amendment, limiting future Presidents to two terms in office. This Amendment was ratified and became part of the Constitution in 1951. In addition, Congress changed the order of presidential succession. An act adopted in 1947 made the Speaker of the House and the President *pro tempore* of the Senate (instead of Cabinet members) the first and second officials in line after the Vice President.

Truman proposes new social legislation. In the tradition of Franklin Roosevelt, Harry Truman wanted the federal government to take an active role in solving the nation's domestic problems. In addition to guaranteed full employment, his goals included an extension of Social Security benefits, a national health insurance program, federal aid to education, and an enlarged public-housing and slum-clearance effort. Despite his determination, Truman had little success in pushing his program through Congress.

Black Americans find new opportunities.
Along with these proposed reforms, President Truman backed steps to end discrimination against black Americans. Truman seemed to many observers to be the ideal person to bring the issue of civil rights to national attention. Truman had a good sense of the country's mood. He knew that many Americans were troubled by the toleration of racial segregation and discrimination at home while standing as champions of freedom and justice abroad. He believed that people would be receptive to efforts to end racial injustice.

In some areas of American life, racial barriers were already beginning to fall. For the first time, for instance, black athletes began to enter organized baseball. The man who broke the "color bar," as it was called, was Jackie Robinson, who was signed by the Brooklyn Dodgers in the fall of 1945. After a year in the minor leagues, he became the first black man to play major league baseball. Elected as the National League's Rookie of the Year in 1947, he was Most Valuable Player in 1949.

Robinson's success on the baseball diamond helped open the door to black athletes in all professional sports. The color bar in professional football was broken in 1946, tennis in 1949, and basketball in 1950.

Discrimination against black people in other fields was also ending. In 1945 Todd Duncan became the first black man to join a major American opera company. The following year, Camilla Williams became the first black woman to break the color bar in opera when she appeared in the title role of *Madama Butterfly*. Both of these performers were members of the New York City Center Opera Company. In 1955 Marian Anderson became the first black member of the Metropolitan Opera Company.

Parallel with these developments was a movement calling for the end of segregation in the nation's armed forces. In June, 1948, A. Philip Randolph (page 665) organized the League for Nonviolent Civil Disobedience Against Military Segregation. Randolph threatened to urge blacks to resist induction into the armed forces unless segregation and racial discrimination were ended. In

Harry Truman was the first President to address a convention of the NAACP. At this meeting, held in 1947, he endorsed the association's views.

July, Truman issued Executive Order 9981, forbidding segregation in military facilities.

The issuance of Executive Order 9981 was not merely the result of pressure from black leaders like A. Philip Randolph. Truman had been pressing for civil rights legislation since he came into office, though with little success. In February, 1948, he had taken the unprecedented step of sending Congress a special message on civil rights. In it he called for an anti-lynching law, an anti-poll tax law,[1] a permanent Fair Employment Practices Commission, and a permanent Commission on Civil Rights. Truman was seeking, he said, "modern, comprehensive civil rights laws, adequate to the needs of the day and demonstrating our continuing faith in the free way of life."

Truman's re-election chances look slim.
When the Democrats looked ahead to the 1948 presidential election, many members of the party agreed with the assessment of the *New York Times* that "the President's influence is weaker than any President's has been in modern history." The Republicans

---

[1]The payment of a poll tax as a requirement for voting was used by some states as a means of discouraging black people — and poor white people — from going to the polls.

were jubilantly expecting to take over the White House. Clare Boothe Luce, a former Republican congresswoman from Connecticut, said simply, "Mr. Truman's time is short; his situation is hopeless. He is a gone goose." The Republicans again turned to Thomas E. Dewey (page 667) as their candidate for President. Earl Warren of California was nominated for Vice President.

Two splits in the Democratic Party made Republican victory seem certain. The first split came when a group of southern delegates, known as Dixiecrats, formed the States' Rights Democratic Party and named Governor J. Strom Thurmond of South Carolina as their candidate for President. The principal argument of the Dixiecrats was that, in pressing for federal civil rights legislation, the Democrats were violating state sovereignty.

The other dissident group called itself the Progressive Party. The new Progressives advocated sweeping social reforms and cooperation with the Soviet Union. They chose as their candidate former Vice President Henry A. Wallace.

Truman was not discouraged. In a rousing acceptance speech at the Democratic convention in Philadelphia, he issued a challenge to the Republicans. He was going to call the Republican-dominated Congress back in session, he declared, so that it could enact the promises of domestic reform included in the Republican platform. When nothing came of this session, Truman made the 80th Congress a campaign issue. He traveled the length and breadth of the country by train on what he called a "whistle-stop tour." Tens of thousands of people turned out to hear Truman deliver folksy, sometimes rambling, attacks on the Republicans. Dewey, meanwhile, gave lofty addresses, treating the campaign as a formality that would soon be over. The major public-opinion polls predicted that Dewey would win easily.

Truman wins a surprise victory. On election night, the nation awaited a Dewey landslide. By 10 P.M. newsboys in Chicago were hawking an "extra" edition of the *Tribune* bearing the following headline: DEWEY DEFEATS TRUMAN. The President later said, "Of course, he *wished* he had, but he didn't and that's all there was to it." In the astounding upset, Truman polled 24 million votes, two million more than Dewey. Moreover, the Democrats won a majority in both houses of Congress.

Congress rejects Truman's programs. At his inauguration in January, 1949, a confident Truman was accompanied by an honor guard from his old World War I outfit, Battery D. In his inaugural address he dedicated himself and his administration to obtaining a "fair deal" for the American people. He restated the goals he had worked for during his first term.

Despite the election returns, the 81st Congress, like the 80th Congress, showed little interest in passing Truman's Fair Deal legislation. It refused to pass civil rights legislation or a program of national health insurance. It did, however, increase and extend Social Security benefits, raise the minimum wage from 40 to 75 cents an hour, and appropriate money for the construction of low-income housing.

The government investigates internal security. Truman's presidential years from the beginning were marred by a nagging concern over loyalty in government. The issue had come to public attention in 1946, when a Soviet defector revealed that a spy ring in Canada had conspired to steal atomic secrets and hand them over to the Russians. Although he himself did not believe there were any disloyal people in the United States government, President Truman bowed to public pressure and in 1947 created the Loyalty Review Board. The Board's task was to judge whether government workers considered by the FBI to be security risks should be kept on the job. During the rest of Truman's term of office, some 300 government employees were dismissed as the result of the Board's investigations.

Some of these people, like other Americans, had been drawn into the Communist Party in the 1930's during the terrible suf-

Celebrating his stunning victory in the 1948 presidential contest, Harry Truman displays an early edition of the *Chicago Tribune*, which mistakenly announced Dewey's victory.

fering caused by the Great Depression. At that time, Communist promises of universal brotherhood and equality had seemed to some people to offer a possible solution to the harsh realities of the Depression. The terrible repression of Stalin's regime in the Soviet Union was ignored. Some of the men and women who became Communists in the 1930's were well-educated and later gained positions of responsibility in American society and government. By the time of the Second World War, many of these people had become disillusioned with the Soviet Union. Others, however, had not.

Charges of Communist espionage startle the nation. In 1948 the House Un-American Activities Committee (HUAC) revealed that charges of espionage had been brought against a trusted State Department official. Alger Hiss, who had been in the delegation that accompanied Roosevelt to Yalta, was accused by Whittaker Chambers, an editor of *Time* magazine and a former Communist agent, of handing over important secret documents to the Russians during the 1930's. Despite vigorous denials by Hiss and expressions of disbelief by his friends, Chambers could not be shaken in his story. In 1950 Hiss was convicted of perjury (for lying under oath in court about his relationship with Chambers) and sent to prison.

Public anxiety was heightened after the Soviet Union successfully tested its first atomic bomb in September, 1949. This disturbing development was soon followed by the shocking charge that Americans had apparently aided the Soviet Union in developing nuclear weaponry. In 1950 Klaus Fuchs, a British physicist who had worked at Los Alamos (page 676), confessed to being a Soviet agent. As a result of his confession, an

American couple, Julius and Ethel Rosenberg, were arrested and charged with having passed atomic secrets to the Soviet Union. A jury found them guilty, and they were executed in 1953.

These two cases convinced many Americans that there was good reason for concern over internal security and that President Truman had been seriously mistaken in believing that there were no disloyal people in the government. In 1950, Congress passed the McCarran Internal Security Act, which required Communist organizations to register with the Attorney General's office and to furnish membership lists and financial statements. Truman strongly opposed the law, believing it unconstitutional. Congress passed the McCarran Act over his veto.

SECTION REVIEW

1. Vocabulary: *right-to-work laws.*
2. (a) What benefits were provided veterans after the Second World War? (b) What was the chief economic problem facing the nation? (c) Why was there labor trouble?
3. (a) What was the Taft-Hartley Act? (b) What were its main provisions?
4. (a) How did Congress show its disapproval of reforms advocated by Truman? (b) Why did it pass the Twenty-Second Amendment?
5. What gains did black Americans make during the Truman years?
6. (a) What splits developed in the Democratic Party in 1948? (b) What candidates ran for office in 1948? (c) What was the outcome?
7. (a) How did the question of loyalty in government become a concern? (b) Why was the McCarran Internal Security Act passed?

2 The Cold War Begins

Even before the end of the Second World War, tension had begun to appear in relations between the Western powers and the Soviet Union. Already Soviet leaders were insisting on putting into power in Poland and Rumania governments under Russian control. The Red Army was also removing vast amounts of industrial equipment from Germany and was violating the arrangements for reparations agreed to at Yalta. Many Americans were becoming convinced that Roosevelt had been wrong in counting on Russia's cooperation in the postwar world. Senator Robert A. Taft, the son of a former President and himself known as "Mr. Republican," said that Roosevelt had been basing his policy "on the delightful theory that Mr. Stalin in the end will turn out to have an angelic nature."

The United Nations is formed. The drama of establishing the United Nations Organization at San Francisco on the very day, April 25, 1945, that American and Soviet troops were meeting on the Elbe (page 673) covered over the ill will that was developing between Russia and its allies. The UN, founded to promote peace and security for all people in the postwar world, had officially come into being the previous October. Its creation was the result of years of planning by leaders of the Allied nations.

The United Nations Charter, adopted by delegates from 46 nations at the San Francisco Conference, contained a preamble modeled on the preamble to the Constitution of the United States. It expressed the high-minded spirit in which the founding members formed the organization:

> We the peoples of the United Nations, determined to save succeeding generations from the scourge of war . . . to reaffirm faith in fundamental human rights . . . to promote social progress . . . and to ensure that armed force shall not be used, save in the common interest, . . . have resolved to combine our efforts to accomplish these aims.

The Charter included the following provisions:

(1) Each member nation would have one vote in a General Assembly, which was authorized to discuss any matter within the scope of the UN Charter. Although the Assembly had no power to compel action by any government, it could make recommendations that, it was hoped, would carry moral authority.

Delegate to the United Nations

In January, 1946, when the first meeting of the United Nations General Assembly was held in London, President Truman asked Eleanor Roosevelt to serve as a member of the United Nations delegation. Mrs. Roosevelt recorded her experiences at that historic assembly in this passage from her autobiography, *On My Own*.

Eleanor Roosevelt

I drove to the first session of the General Assembly in London with Mr. Stettinius, who was then Assistant Secretary of State, accompanied by Mr. Sandifer and two younger advisers. We drove slowly through the streets, past the Parliament buildings and the impressive statue of Abraham Lincoln that stands nearby, to the doors of the big auditorium where huge crowds of spectators had gathered to see the delegates of many nations arrive. The people were very hospitable and there was quite a lot of cheering, probably because people who had just survived a terrible war were desperately eager for the world's statesmen to find some better way to solve international problems. . . .

I might point out here that during the entire London session of the Assembly, I walked on eggs. I knew that as the only woman on the delegation I was not very welcome. Moreover, if I failed to be a useful member, it would not be considered merely that I as an individual had failed, but that all women had failed, and there would be little chance for others to serve in the near future.

I tried to think of small ways in which I might be more helpful. There were not too many women on the other delegations, and as soon as I got to know some of them, I invited them to tea in my sitting room at the hotel. . . . The party was so successful that I asked them again on other occasions, either as a group or a few at a time. I discovered that in such informal sessions we sometimes made more progress in reaching an understanding on some question before the United Nations than we had been able to achieve in the formal work of our committees.

(2) A Security Council was to be made up of representatives from the "Big Five" — the United States, Great Britain, France, China, and the Soviet Union — plus six (later ten) nonpermanent members who would be elected to two-year terms by the General Assembly. The Security Council would be authorized to investigate disputes between nations, foster their peaceful settlement, and take military action against peace-breakers. Decisions on substantive issues could be made only with the assent of all five permanent member nations. A veto by any of the permanent members could prevent action by the Council.

(3) An Economic and Social Council, responsible to the General Assembly and not subject to veto by the Security Council,

691

would be established to seek solutions to social and economic problems.

(4) An International Court of Justice would be established to pass judgment on the legal aspects of international disputes.

(5) A Trusteeship Council would advise the UN on the government of territories held in trust by the organization.

(6) A Secretariat would carry out the day-to-day work of the UN. The organization's chief administrator was to be called the Secretary-General.

The state of Israel is founded. The first major problem facing the United Nations was that of the conflicting claims of Jews and Arabs to the area of the Middle East known as Palestine. Hundreds of thousands of Jewish refugees from Europe were seeking to enter Palestine. The British, who had ruled the area since the First World War, had pledged support to a Jewish national home in Palestine with the understanding that the rights of non-Jewish peoples in the region would be protected.

In early 1947, Britain turned over the Palestine question to the United Nations. In November the United Nations voted to divide Palestine into two states: one for Jews and one for Arabs. Jewish leaders agreed to this solution, but the Arab

For his work in the Middle East, Ralph Bunche was awarded the Nobel Peace Prize in 1950, the first black person thus honored.

spokesmen refused to accept it, insisting that all of Palestine was rightfully theirs.

On May 14, 1948, the independence of the new state of Israel was proclaimed. Within a few minutes of the announcement, President Truman granted Israel formal recognition. The next day, Israel was invaded by Arab armies from Syria, Lebanon, Trans-Jordan, Iraq, Saudi Arabia, Yemen, and Egypt. The Arab League, as these nations called themselves, refused to recognize the legitimacy of the partition of Palestine and were determined to bring about the destruction of Israel. The League's armies were unable to defeat the Israelis, however, and in 1950 an American diplomat, Ralph Bunche, working for the United Nations, was able to arrange an armistice. Despite Bunche's success, the peace was an uneasy one because the basic problem remained: the refusal of the Arab nations to accept Israel's very existence.

Friction develops over the fate of Germany. Meanwhile, the German question was troubling Europe. The trials of Nazi war criminals in 1945 and 1946 (page 674) had been conducted by the former Allies. On other matters concerning the handling of Germany, however, the Western leaders were at odds with Stalin.

As had been planned at Yalta and Potsdam, Germany was divided into four zones that were administered by the United States, Great Britain, France, and the Soviet Union respectively. Problems arose, however, over the way the Soviet Union was handling its zone. In addition to dismantling entire German factories and sending them back to the Soviet Union, the Russians were shipping home food and other goods that they had earlier agreed to deliver to the Western zones. Moreover, the Russians set up a Communist government in their part of the divided country. This was a violation of the promise Stalin had made at Potsdam to help rebuild Germany as a democracy.

Gradually it became clear to Western leaders that the Soviet Union had no intention of giving up control over the German territory it had occupied. This, too, was a violation of promises Stalin had made at Potsdam, where it had been agreed that military occupation of Germany would be only temporary and that, after the occupation, the country would be reunited. Russian behavior caused the prewar distrust of Stalin to come alive again.

Stalin rules with an iron hand. Stalin had consolidated his despotic power in the mid-1930's through a campaign of violence and terror conducted against his own people. On every side, Stalin imagined conspiracies being hatched against him. Between 1936 and 1938 he carried out purges of the Communist Party, ordering the execution of perhaps 800,000 members. Among them were scores of party officials and several hundred senior army commanders, including many leaders of the Bolshevik revolution. Countless others also died. The total number of Stalin's victims has been estimated in the millions.

After the war Stalin became even more autocratic. Having made common cause with the democracies in order to prevent conquest by the Nazis, he now seemed fearful that further cooperation would weaken his control. He was no doubt strengthened in this view as he saw thousands of Soviet citizens and members of the armed forces defect to the West when the fortunes of war gave them the opportunity. Captured Russian soldiers who were returned to the Soviet Union after the peace were thrown into concentration camps — the dreaded *gulags*, cesspools of cruelty and deprivation. Thousands upon thousands of the former prisoners of war were put to death, the fact that they had surrendered to the enemy being "proof" that they were traitors. As he turned his country into a vast prison dominated by his secret police, Stalin felt secure only with a frightened populace.

The Soviet Union sets up a Communist government in Poland. At Yalta, Stalin had agreed to allow free elections in Poland after the war. No such elections were ever held. Truman pointed out at Potsdam how important a free election reported by a free Polish press would be to Americans of Polish heritage.

The majority of Poles were staunch anti-Communists who recalled the role of the Soviet Union in the invasion of their country in 1939 (page 648). The Polish people also recalled the discovery in 1943 of the mass graves of some 14,000 Polish officers who had been prisoners of war in Russian hands. Memories of the Katyn Forest massacre led many Poles to resist Communist domination.

Polish resistance to the Soviet Union, however, was quickly stamped out, and in 1945 a Soviet-backed government was installed. Two years later, when elections were finally held, the opposition to Soviet control had been so completely suppressed in Poland that the Communists polled 90 percent of the vote. Western protests to Stalin fell on deaf ears.

The Soviet Union takes permanent control of Eastern Europe. Because the Red Army had helped roll back the enemy and had then occupied Hungary, Rumania, Bulgaria, Czechoslovakia, and Yugoslavia, the Soviet Union had great power in Eastern Europe. Events in those countries followed a pattern similar to that in Poland. First, Russian-backed Communist groups worked to set up coalition regimes (governments in which various parties were represented). Then they ousted the non-Communist parties and suppressed all political opposition. In the Baltic Sea region three small countries — Latvia, Lithuania, and Estonia — had simply been absorbed into the Soviet Union after the arrival of Russian troops. The countries of Eastern Europe remained independent in name, but in fact they were, by the late 1940's, completely dominated by the Soviet Union.[2] They became known as Russian *satellites.*

In all these lands, people's lives were tightly controlled by their government. No book, magazine, or newspaper critical of

---

[2]Yugoslavia, although a Communist country, was able through the leadership of Marshal Tito to claim a measure of independence from Moscow after 1948.

In an eloquent speech delivered in 1946 at Fulton, Missouri, Winston Churchill described the Soviet threat to Europe.

countries they could control and to maintain a large standing army ever on the alert.

Churchill calls for a policy of strength. The West was alarmed by these developments. In March, 1946, former Prime Minister Winston Churchill was invited by President Truman to speak at Westminster College in Fulton, Missouri. In his address, Churchill said, "A shadow has fallen upon the scenes so lately lighted by Allied victory . . . an iron curtain has descended across the Continent. Behind that line lie all of the capitals of the ancient states of Central and Eastern Europe." The phrase "iron curtain" caught people's imagination; it gave people an image of the world divided in two, with the Soviet-dominated half living in self-imposed isolation. Churchill had helped Americans understand that the United States was involved in a "cold war" with Communist totalitarianism and that the danger of the war years was by no means over.[3]

American policy-makers decide on containment. Many American officials shared the view expressed by Churchill that the expansion of Russian influence was a serious threat to world peace. As early as February, 1946, George F. Kennan, a leading State Department expert on Russia, pointed out that the Soviet Union was growing increasingly hostile to the United States. Kennan argued that the Soviet empire would have to be contained, or restricted, within existing limits. People who favored a policy of *containment* agreed with Churchill's assessment of the Soviet Union's goals: "I do not believe," he had said, "that Soviet Russia desires war. What they want is the fruits of war and the indefinite expansion of their power and doctrines." Backers of the containment policy believed that the Russians were aggressive, but cautious — that the Soviet Union would expand only where its leaders thought they could do so without risking war. American policy-makers be-

the Soviet Union or of communism could be published. There was no freedom of speech, assembly, or petition. Those who dared to criticize their rulers risked imprisonment, exile, and even execution. Religion was seen as a harmful influence, so houses of worship were strictly regulated. In all of the satellites, the borders were tightly guarded so that people could not flee to the West and so that non-Communist Westerners could not readily visit, lest they bring with them unwelcome ideas.

The Soviet Union explained its actions on the grounds of self-defense. The Second World War had cost twenty million Russian lives. Russian leaders maintained that from the war they had learned that they must never let down their guard again. They were determined to surround themselves with

---

[3]Immediately after the speech, Truman suggested to Stalin that he respond to Churchill's words from the same platform. Stalin turned down the opportunity.

lieved, with Churchill, that if earlier Western leaders had stood up to Hitler's expansionist aggression in the 1930's, the Second World War might never have taken place, and they drew a parallel to the present. They concluded that the United States must resist Soviet expansion wherever it occurred.

The Truman Doctrine is announced. In the fall of 1946, the government of Greece, which had been receiving aid from Great Britain, came under attack from Communist rebels, who were financed by neighboring Soviet satellite countries. Early in 1947, Britain sent word to the United States that it could no longer afford to support the Greek government's war against the rebels. Neither did it have the means to help Turkey resist Russian demands for a naval base in its territory.

The Truman administration acted quickly. Secretary of State George Marshall worked out an arrangement for sending military and economic aid to the two embattled countries. The President then asked Congress for $400 million to finance Marshall's aid program. Thus was born what became known as the Truman Doctrine. "I believe it must be the policy of the United States," Truman stated, "to support free peoples who are resisting attempted subjugation by armed minorities or by outside pressures." As a result of American aid, both Greece and Turkey were able eventually to withstand the threatened Communist take-overs.

The Marshall Plan aids Europe's recovery. Great Britain's inability to help Greece and Turkey was a symptom of the economic decline into which the Second World War had plunged Europe. Not only were European nations deeply in debt, but they had suffered enormous destruction during the war.

Compassion for the people of Europe, combined with the recognition that a healthy European economy was necessary to the security and prosperity of the United States, led to the adoption of a massive aid program. The Marshall Plan, as it was called, was proposed by Secretary of State Marshall in an address at Harvard University in June, 1947. Under the Marshall Plan, the governments of all the European nations, including Russia, were invited to decide among themselves what aid they would need from the United States in order to restore their economic well-being and stability. "Our policy," said Marshall, "is directed not against any country or doctrine but against hunger, poverty, desperation, and chaos. . . . Any government that is willing to assist in the task of recovery will find full cooperation . . . on the part of the United States government."

The Marshall Plan was vigorously debated in Congress. Most critics argued that the United States could not afford to rebuild Europe. Some people, including former Vice President Henry Wallace, denounced it as somehow aimed against the Soviet Union — indeed, as a "Martial Plan." Following the Communist take-over of democratic Czechoslovakia in February, 1948, however, opposition to the Plan started to fade.

On April 2, 1948, Congress passed an act creating the Economic Cooperation Administration to manage and distribute funds for the European Recovery Program — the official name of the Marshall Plan. Over the next three years, the United States sent $12 billion in assistance to Europe, mostly to Britain, France, and Germany. Poland and Czechoslovakia wished to take part in the Plan, but the Soviet Union stood in the way, refusing to allow them to accept United States aid. In the end, only Western European nations received help. As the economy of Europe improved, a leading British publication said it was plain to see that the Marshall Plan was "the most straightforward generous thing that any country has ever done for others." By 1951 the countries of Western Europe were well on their way to recovery.[4]

---

[4]For his efforts on behalf of the economic reconstruction of Europe, Marshall was awarded the Nobel Peace Prize in 1953.

Berliners watch an American transport plane come in for a landing during the 1948-1949 airlift. Such flights kept West Berlin supplied with food and fuel during the Soviet blockade of land routes.

The effort to reunify Germany strains East-West relations. In apparent resentment at the brightened scene in Western Europe, Soviet leaders became increasingly stubborn when discussing plans for the reunification of Germany. The Soviet Union, moreover, gradually ceased to cooperate with its former allies in the administration of occupied Germany. In the spring of 1948, therefore, France, Britain, and the United States announced plans to join their zones together. By so doing, they brought into existence what became the Federal Republic of Germany, or simply West Germany.[5]

The Russian response, on June 24, 1948, was to shut off all land and water routes through the Soviet zone to Berlin. (Berlin, like the rest of Germany, had been divided among the Allied countries after the war, but the city lay deep inside the Soviet zone.) The Russians hoped that their blockade would drive the Western powers out of West Berlin and force residents to choose between starvation and Communist rule.

President Truman realized that if the Western powers pulled out of the former German capital, they would be handing the Russians a uniquely symbolic prize. Truman stated the West's intention tersely: "We are going to stay, period."

President Truman might have used military force to open the routes to the city. Instead, he chose to try a peaceful way of making the Russians back down. In no time, a gigantic airlift was organized to overcome the Berlin blockade. Day after day an awesome fleet of C–54 Skymasters landed in West Berlin with food and fuel for two million people. At the height of the

---

[5]Shortly the Russians turned their zone into the German Democratic Republic, usually called East Germany.

airlift's operation an average of between four and five thousand tons of supplies, including coal, were being flown daily into the beleaguered city. When the weather prevented flights, it was said, Berlin held its breath, and when the roar was heard overhead again "a hundred thousand sighs of relief" rose from the city.

Finally, after 321 days, Soviet leaders recognized that the Western powers would not be driven out of Berlin. As a result, they finally decided to reopen rail lines, canals, and highways to Berlin on May 12, 1949. The blockade was over.

The airlift had backfired on the Soviet Union. Western nations, now convinced that Russia's activities were a threat to world peace, had been spurred to strengthen their armed forces. They recognized that even more serious military measures might be required to halt Soviet aggression.

NATO is formed. On April 4, 1949, while the Berlin blockade was under way, the United States signed the North Atlantic Treaty with Britain, France, Belgium, the Netherlands, Luxembourg, Italy, Portugal, Denmark, Iceland, Norway, and Canada. (In 1952 Greece and Turkey joined, and in 1954 so did West Germany.) Under the terms of the treaty, an armed attack against one country would be considered an armed attack against all. Moreover, a combined military force would be administered by the North Atlantic Treaty Organization (NATO). The United States, by far the richest of the member-nations, assumed the chief responsibility for NATO's expenses.

Following World War II the Soviet Union imposed Communist governments on neighboring Eastern European countries. To resist Soviet domination of the continent, the United States and Canada joined Western European nations in forming NATO.

Europe After World War II

Not since 1800, when the alliance with France from revolutionary days had been terminated, had the United States belonged to an alliance in peacetime outside the Americas. Americans had learned, said Secretary of State Dean Acheson, that "if free nations do not stand together, they will fall one by one." The threat of Soviet aggression had, in a short time, profoundly altered American foreign policy. First, it had led to the Truman Doctrine, which modified the Monroe Doctrine's pledge not to intervene in Europe's affairs. Now, in the North Atlantic Treaty, it had broken a long-standing policy of having "no entangling alliances" in time of peace.

SECTION REVIEW

1. Vocabulary: *satellite, containment.*
2. (a) For what reason was the United Nations formed? (b) What are the main bodies of the United Nations? (c) What role did the United Nations play in the founding of Israel?
3. (a) How did the Soviet Union take control of Eastern Europe? (b) What were the Truman Doctrine and the Marshall Plan? (c) Why was each proposed?
4. (a) What was the response of the United States to the blockade of West Berlin? (b) For what reason was the North Atlantic Treaty Organization formed? (c) What nations became members of NATO?

3 The Cold War Leads to a Hot War in Korea

The United States and the Soviet Union were also in contention in Asia, as the Russians aimed to advance communism in that part of the world too. The three main areas of contention were Japan, China, and Korea.

The United States occupies Japan. The competition was mildest in Japan. America's war allies had only an advisory role in the occupation of Japan. Authority lay almost entirely with the United States, represented by General Douglas MacArthur.

Under MacArthur's supervision, Japanese society experienced drastic change. The emperor was stripped of his political role and his claim to divinity; a new constitution was put into effect providing for representative government; the power of the traditional ruling class was weakened through educational and economic reforms; and many laws and customs that discriminated against women were abolished. The purpose of these reforms was to bring democracy to Japan and ensure that the military would never again gain control of the government as it had in the 1930's. The Japanese armed forces were disbanded after 1945 and not allowed to exist again until 1951, when the United States ended its occupation and signed a treaty of peace. Even then, only a small defensive force was authorized.

For decades, Japan had been the most powerful nation in East Asia. When it surrendered to the Allies in 1945, the balance of power in the region shifted, affecting many countries. Two countries that felt this shift most keenly were China, portions of which had spent many years under Japanese occupation, and Korea, which had been governed by Japan.

Communists come to power in China. The Chinese Nationalist government of Chiang Kai-shek had, since the early 1930's, been forced to divide its energies between fighting Japanese invaders and Chinese Communist rebels. During the Second World War, the rebels, led by Mao Tse-tung, joined in the struggle against Japan.

For most Americans and millions of people everywhere, however, Chiang and his sophisticated wife symbolized China and its hopes for the future. When Madame Chiang, a graduate of Wellesley College in Massachusetts, addressed Congress in 1943, she thrilled the audience with her eloquent presentation of China's cause.

After the war, with the Japanese threat gone, civil war again broke out in China. The United States attempted to mediate, urging a Nationalist-dominated coalition government, but negotiators found both sides uncooperative.

As Chinese Communist forces closed in on Nationalist-held Shanghai in 1948, thousands of sampan dwellers sought refuge in the center of the city.

In an attempt to prevent a Communist take-over, the United States sent more than $3 billion in aid to Chiang Kai-shek between 1945 and 1949. Meanwhile, the Soviet Union, which had occupied Manchuria at the end of the war, aided Mao's Communist forces. By the end of 1949, Mao had succeeded in gaining control of the entire Chinese mainland. Chiang and large numbers of his loyal supporters fled to the island of Formosa.

The victory of the Chinese Communists set off a fierce argument in the United States. Critics denounced the Truman administration, accusing it of having betrayed the Nationalists. Truman, they said, had let himself become preoccupied with events in Europe and had ignored the threat to America's former ally in Asia. More aid, they maintained, would have allowed the Nationalists to overcome their foes. Truman's defenders insisted that Chiang's downfall

had been the Chinese leader's own doing. He had permitted corruption to become rampant, they said, and had refused to abolish abuses in his government that would have allowed him to compete with the Communists for popular support. The Nationalists, according to Truman's supporters, had simply lost the will to defeat the Communists, and no amount of money would have saved them from defeat.

The United States continued to grant diplomatic recognition only to the Nationalists on Formosa, saying that they were the legitimate government of all of China. In the United Nations, too, the United States used its veto to ensure that China was represented by the Nationalist government and that the Communists were denied China's seat in the Security Council (page 691).

Korea is divided. China's neighbor, Korea, was also a trouble spot. Long under

Chinese domination, Korea had been annexed by the Japanese in 1910. When Japan surrendered to the Allies in 1945, Russian troops occupied the northern half of Korea, while American troops occupied the southern half. The division of the country was expected to be temporary, because Allied leaders had agreed in 1943 that Korea would be made a unified, independent nation after the surrender of Japan. To that end, the United Nations organized elections in Korea in 1948, but the Russians refused to allow the north to participate. The elections established the Republic of Korea and placed its capital at Seoul (SOHL), just south of the 38th parallel of latitude, which divided the country.

The United Nations and many of its individual members recognized the Republic of Korea as the legitimate government of all Korea. At the same time, in the north, the Communists called their territory the People's Republic of Korea and claimed that it was the only legitimate government of Korea. By June, 1949, both the United States and the Soviet Union had withdrawn their occupation forces, leaving North and South Korea (as the two nations were commonly called) to defend their own territories.

North Korea invades South Korea. On June 25, 1950, without advance warning, the Communist army of North Korea invaded South Korea. The attack put Truman's policy of containment (page 694) to the test. Secretary of State Acheson warned that the attack was more than an attack on the authority of the United Nations. It was, he declared, "a challenge to the whole system of collective security."

Acheson, at Truman's request, brought the issue before an emergency meeting of the United Nations Security Council. The Security Council promptly passed a resolution ordering the North Koreans to withdraw their forces from south of the 38th parallel. The Soviet Union no doubt would have vetoed this resolution, but its representatives had walked out six months earlier in protest against the United Nations' refusal to recognize the Communist government in China. The North Korean troops, ignoring the order of the Security Council, continued to move south.

On June 27 the Security Council called on UN members to aid South Korea in repelling the invading forces. The United Nations did not have troops of its own, but it invited member nations to take part in a joint "police action" under the command of General MacArthur. Sixteen nations contributed troops to the UN forces, but the

For three years, fighting between Communist and United Nations forces raged back and forth across the Korean peninsula.

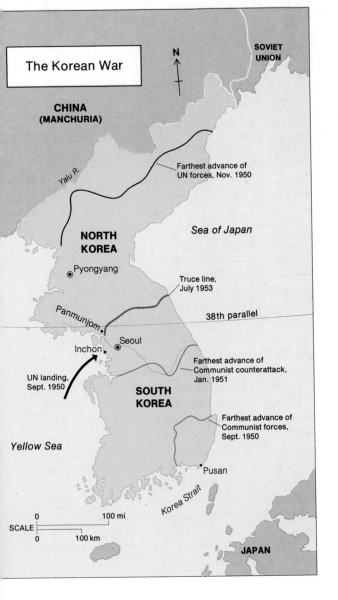

The Korean War

SOVIET UNION

CHINA (MANCHURIA)

Yalu R.

Farthest advance of UN forces, Nov. 1950

NORTH KOREA

Sea of Japan

Pyongyang

Truce line, July 1953

Panmunjom

38th parallel

Inchon

Seoul

UN landing, Sept. 1950

Farthest advance of Communist counterattack, Jan. 1951

SOUTH KOREA

Farthest advance of Communist forces, Sept. 1950

Yellow Sea

Pusan

Korea Strait

SCALE

0   100 mi

0   100 km

JAPAN

majority of the men who took part in the military action were South Koreans and Americans.

During the summer of 1950, the North Koreans were on the offensive. The outnumbered American and South Korean forces gradually retreated south. They were determined to defend their last foothold, the port of Pusan. Then, on September 15 the course of the war turned when MacArthur daringly landed troops behind North Korean lines at Inchon. Shortly, UN forces recaptured Seoul. By October they had driven the North Koreans back to the 38th parallel.

The objectives of the war change. At this point, the original purpose of the UN forces had been accomplished. The General Assembly now debated whether to order its troops into North Korea. On October 8, UN troops, in accordance with the decision of the General Assembly, crossed the 38th parallel. By November, MacArthur's troops had taken over almost all of North Korea.

The Chinese Communists had warned that they would aid the North Koreans if MacArthur's troops moved north of the 38th parallel. MacArthur assured Truman that there was little possibility of such an intervention. Suddenly, late in November, 1951, Chinese forces struck the UN army with devastating power. Greatly outnumbered and overextended, the UN forces were quickly pushed back below the 38th parallel, sustaining heavy casualties and losing the South Korean capital as they retreated.

MacArthur's troops, the general now said, were in "an entirely new war." He demanded that the United States blockade the Chinese coast, bomb China's supply bases in Manchuria, and use Chiang Kai-shek's troops to invade mainland China. General Omar Bradley, chairman of the Joint Chiefs of Staff, argued that to strike China would be to have "the wrong war, in the wrong place, at the wrong time, and with the wrong enemy." President Truman agreed with him and ordered MacArthur to continue to fight a *limited* war aimed only at freeing South Korea from the invaders.

American troops fought in rugged terrain to help repel the Communist invasion of South Korea.

MacArthur denounced the idea of fighting a war with "one hand tied behind our back." Even as the UN forces recovered and began to make plans for a counterattack, MacArthur publicly defied his superiors by calling for an offensive against mainland China. "There is no substitute for victory," he insisted.

Truman dismisses MacArthur. On April 11, 1951, the world was astonished to learn that Truman had dismissed MacArthur for failing to give wholehearted support to United States policy. Truman explained to a friend, "I will undoubtedly create a great furor, but under the circumstances I could do nothing else and still be President of the United States. Even the Chiefs of Staff came to the conclusion that civilian control of the military was at stake, and I didn't let it stay at stake very long." The new commander in Korea was General Matthew B. Ridgway, another distinguished hero of the Second World War.

Following his return to the United States, MacArthur was given triumphal receptions by his supporters. In an address to a joint session of Congress, he ended a moving speech by quoting from a barracks-room tune of his youth: " 'Old soldiers never die, they just fade away.' And like the old soldier of that ballad, I now close my military career and just fade away, an old soldier who tried to do his duty as God gave him the light to see that duty."

Truce talks begin in Korea. Under the new leadership of General Ridgway, UN troops fought a limited war in Korea, in which neither side made much headway. In June, 1951, the Russian ambassador to the UN suggested that a settlement in Korea was possible. Truce talks began in July.

A particularly difficult question arose over the many Chinese and North Korean prisoners of war who did not want to be returned to their homelands to live under communism. Agreement on a cease-fire line and on a means of enforcing the truce also proved difficult to reach. As the talks dragged on, sporadic fighting continued. The American people, who were paying most of the costs of the war, became impatient, and the conflict became an issue in the 1952 presidential election.

Eisenhower is elected President. As the 1952 elections drew near, there was widespread dissatisfaction with the Truman administration. First, the country seemed mired in an expensive war. Second, the public was alarmed by charges that Communist agents had been able to infiltrate the government because of laxness on the part of the Democratic administration. Third, the public was soured by accusations of corruption and influence-peddling among some of the President's friends. In March, 1952, Truman took himself out of the running. The President said, in his characteristically crisp language, "I shall not accept a renomination. I do not feel that it is my duty to spend another four years in the White House."

On the Republican side, Dwight D. Eisenhower, freshly returned from his duties as commander of NATO forces, beat out Senator Taft for the presidential nomination. At the party's convention in Chicago the galleries cheered wildly, "We like Ike!" The general's running mate was Senator Richard M. Nixon of California, who had won national attention through his role in the investigation of Alger Hiss (page 689). Accurately judging the national mood, the Republicans campaigned on the themes of "Korea, communism, and corruption."

The Democrats nominated Governor Adlai E. Stevenson of Illinois, a candidate who had President Truman's strong backing. Stevenson, an eloquent and witty man, bore the same name as his grandfather, who had been Vice President under Grover Cleveland. At first reluctant to seek the presidency, Stevenson was not well-known outside his home state at the beginning of the campaign. As time went on, his effective speeches and agreeable personal style won him heavy support among intellectuals and leaders of organized labor.

In spite of Stevenson's impressive performance, Eisenhower's fame and popularity made his election a certainty. His campaign speeches were often bland and repetitious (causing reporters to joke, "He's crossing the 38th platitude again"). Nevertheless, he displayed a warmth and devotion to traditional values that millions of people found comforting and reassuring. In addition, shortly before the election, Eisenhower made headlines by declaring, "I shall go to Korea." The country took his words to mean that he would end the war.

Eisenhower won by a landslide, the first Republican to break the Democrats' hold on the Solid South since 1928. The victory was proof of Eisenhower's magnetism but not of the drawing power of the Republican Party as a whole. Republicans gained control of Congress, though only by a slim margin.

Along with their wives, Dwight Eisenhower and Richard Nixon celebrate their nominations as Republican candidates for President and Vice President in 1952.

Truman leaves office. As Truman prepared to return to private life, he delivered a farewell address on television. In it he said, "I suppose that history will remember my term in office as the years when the 'cold war' began to overshadow our lives. I have hardly had a day in office that has not been dominated by this all-embracing struggle . . . and always in the background there has been the atomic bomb."

By the time of Eisenhower's inauguration, Truman and Ike were barely talking to each other. Their strained relations grew out of a clash of personalities. Still, the good of the nation came first. When Eisenhower sat at his desk in the Oval Office on his first day as President, he found one drawer locked. Calling for a key, he opened the drawer and there found a folder of confidential memoranda from Truman on immediate pressing problems. The cold war had been transferred to fresh hands.

SECTION REVIEW

1. (a) What changes were brought about by the American occupation of Japan? (b) What change in power took place in China? (c) What was the reaction in the United States to the news from China?
2. (a) How did war break out in Korea? (b) What was the response of the United Nations? (c) Why did President Truman dismiss General MacArthur in 1951?
3. (a) Who were the candidates for President in 1952? (b) What issues did the Republicans stress? (c) What was the outcome?

Chapter 29 Review

Summary

Thrust into the presidency by Franklin Roosevelt's death, Harry Truman led the nation in the years immediately following the Second World War. At home, the American people were adjusting to peacetime. Programs such as the GI Bill of Rights had been initiated to help veterans. The wartime economy, meanwhile, was quickly converted to peacetime production. The ending of price controls in mid-1946, combined with the pent-up demand for all kinds of consumer goods, caused prices to increase rapidly. Workers, in turn, demanded pay raises, and labor disputes took place in many industries. After a series of crippling strikes, Congress passed the Taft-Hartley Act in June, 1947. This legislation established new rules for collective bargaining.

During his presidency, Harry Truman backed efforts to eliminate racial discrimination. He ordered an end to segregation in the nation's armed forces and asked Congress to create a Commission on Civil Rights.

During the postwar years, problems with the Soviet Union occupied the President's attention. The Russians imposed Communist governments on the nations of Eastern Europe and created what Winston Churchill called an "iron curtain" across Europe. Russian threats against Greece and Turkey prompted Truman to send aid to those countries and to declare a policy that was based on the containment of Soviet expansion. In June, 1947, the Marshall Plan was announced, offering American assistance in rebuilding the war-damaged economies of European countries.

Efforts to reunify Germany led to continued friction between the Soviet Union and its former Allies, as did the unsuccessful Russian attempt to blockade West Berlin. To counter the aggressive actions of the Soviet Union, the North Atlantic Treaty Organization was formed in April, 1949.

In the summer of 1950, the Communist forces of North Korea staged a surprise invasion of South Korea. This action caused the United Nations to take a stand against Communist aggression. The bulk of the fighting during the Korean War fell to the American forces, led by General Douglas MacArthur. Disagreement with Truman over how the war should be fought led to MacArthur's dismissal. Truce talks began in July, 1951, but dragged on into late 1952 with no end to the fighting in sight. The frustrating news from Korea, combined with fear of Communist infiltration into the government, caused voters to turn away from the Democrats. Dwight Eisenhower was elected President in 1952, thus bringing to an end twenty years of Democratic control of the presidency.

Vocabulary and Important Terms

1. GI Bill of Rights
2. Taft-Hartley Act
3. right-to-work laws
4. Twenty-Second Amendment
5. McCarran Internal Security Act
6. Dixiecrats
7. Loyalty Review Board
8. Executive Order 9981
9. Security Council
10. General Assembly
11. satellite
12. "iron curtain"
13. containment
14. Truman Doctrine
15. Marshall Plan
16. Berlin airlift
17. North Atlantic Treaty Organization (NATO)

Discussion Questions

1. (a) After the Second World War, what economic problems beset the country? (b) Why did labor leaders issue calls for strikes? (c) Why did Congress pass the Taft-Hartley Act?
2. (a) What gains were made by black Americans in the years immediately following the Second World War? (b) What actions did President Truman take to end segregation?
3. Compare and contrast the elections of 1948 and 1952. (a) Who were the candidates in each election? (b) What were the main campaign themes? (c) What were the results?
4. (a) What factors and events contributed to concern about internal security in the American government during the postwar era? (b) What was the response of Congress and President Truman to this concern?
5. (a) What were the goals of the United Nations? (b) What responsibilities were assigned to the Security Council? (c) How were the Security Council's actions limited?
6. (a) What steps did the Soviet Union take in Eastern Europe during the postwar era? (b) How did Soviet leaders justify their actions? (c) What was life like for people behind the "iron curtain"?
7. What effect did Soviet aggression have on American foreign policy?
8. (a) To what extent did the United States involve itself in Asian affairs immediately after the Second

World War? (b) After North Korea invaded South Korea in 1950, what role did the United States play in the Korean conflict? (c) What happened after UN forces invaded North Korea?

Relating Past and Present

1. To what extent does the containment of communism remain a major concern of American foreign policy? Have American-Soviet relations fundamentally changed in the years since Truman's presidency? Explain your answer.
2. In 1948 there was a split in the Democratic Party because of differing viewpoints concerning civil rights and American-Soviet relations. What issues have the potential for dividing political parties today? Explain your answer.

Studying Local History

Find out how your state voted in the election of 1948. Then locate a local newspaper story or editorial that contains comments on Truman's surprise victory. What is the tone of the newspaper commentary? What explanation for Truman's victory does the newspaper offer?

Using History Skills

1. *Reading maps.* Study the map on page 697 showing Europe after World War II. (a) What European countries were members of NATO? (b) What countries were behind the "iron curtain"? (c) How does the location of Berlin help explain the Soviet decision to blockade that city?
2. *Reading source material.* Study Eleanor Roosevelt's description on page 691 of the United Nations meeting. How does she convey the high hopes felt by people in 1946 that the United Nations would be able to promote world peace?
3. *Placing events in time.* Look back through the chapter and find five important events of the cold war period. Make a time line showing those events.

WORLD SCENE

Independence in Asia

Many Asians had sought independence for their nations in the years prior to the Second World War. Immediately after the war, patriots in the Philippines and in India achieved their goal.

The Philippine Republic. Preparations for Philippine independence from the United States were interrupted by the Japanese invasion in 1942. After the war the move toward independence was resumed. Elections were held, and Manuel Roxas won the office of president. On July 4, 1946, the Philippines became a republic.

When Roxas died in 1948, his vice president, Elpidio Quirino, succeeded him. Quirino was immediately faced with a challenge to his government from a group of Communist-led rebels. Known as the Huks, the rebels fought a guerrilla war against the Philippine army for several years and were not defeated until the mid-1950's.

Gandhi and the independence of India. One of the leading figures of the twentieth century was Mohandas Gandhi of India. Beginning in 1915, Gandhi led a movement to persuade the British to grant India its independence. His insistence on nonviolent tactics set an example that was adopted by oppressed groups in many other nations. The protests organized by Gandhi took the form of widespread boycotts and acts of civil disobedience (protests in which British laws were openly defied). British officials repeatedly imprisoned Gandhi but were powerless to halt the unrest.

At the end of the Second World War in 1945, the British government agreed to give India its independence. The British withdrawal, however, was complicated by the demands of the Muslim minority for a separate Islamic state. Gandhi tried to persuade the Muslim leaders to share power with the Hindus in a united India but to no avail. When independence finally came in 1947, two new nations were created: India and the Islamic state of Pakistan. Gandhi, who continued to oppose partition of India, was assassinated in 1948 by a Hindu fanatic infuriated by Gandhi's willingness to cooperate with Muslims.

CHAPTER 30

Tensions Amid Affluence

1953 – 1963

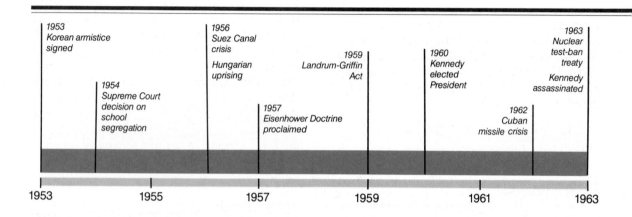

1953
Korean armistice
signed

1954
Supreme Court
decision on
school
segregation

1956
Suez Canal
crisis

Hungarian
uprising

1957
Eisenhower Doctrine
proclaimed

1959
Landrum-Griffin
Act

1960
Kennedy
elected
President

1962
Cuban
missile crisis

1963
Nuclear
test-ban
treaty

Kennedy
assassinated

1953   1955   1957   1959   1961   1963

CHAPTER OUTLINE

1. Cold-war tensions remain high.

2. The nation prospers under Eisenhower.

3. The Democrats regain the White House.

When Dwight Eisenhower became President, he may have been the most widely admired new Chief Executive since George Washington. Fellow Americans believed they saw in Ike a man who stood above politics — a fatherly figure whose sole interest was the good of the country. They knew and admired the fact that he had grown up in a humble home in Abilene, Kansas, and had risen to walk with kings and queens. They also respected him for his patriotism and devotion to service. As a youth, Ike had attended West Point. He later described the feeling that came over him as he took the cadets' oath and uttered the words "the United States of America." "From here on," he said, "it would be the nation I would be serving, not myself. Suddenly the flag itself meant something. I haven't heard other officers speak of their memories of that moment but mine have never left me."

Eisenhower was followed in office by John Kennedy. At his inauguration in 1961, Kennedy proclaimed that "the torch has been passed to a new generation of Americans." By so doing, he helped create the impression that a sharp change was taking place in national life. In fact, the time Eisenhower and Kennedy spent in office may be regarded as a single period. It was a time characterized by general prosperity, public confidence in the judgment of national leaders, and faith in the future.

1 Cold-War Tensions Remain High

At the end of the Korean War, both the Soviet Union and the United States came under new leadership. Joseph Stalin, the ruthless Soviet dictator who had ruled for almost a quarter of a century, died in 1953. His political heirs were vying for power and it was as yet unclear who would emerge the winner. Meanwhile, in the United States, the election of President Eisenhower had ended twenty years of uninterrupted Democratic leadership in the White House. People watched intently to see what effect these changes would have.

The Korean War ends. Eisenhower's first important business as President was to bring the Korean War to a close. In December, 1952, while he was still only President-elect, he had carried out his campaign pledge to go to Korea to seek an end to the hostilities. His trip had no immediate results. The negotiations dragged on for seven more months.

Finally, in July, 1953, an armistice was signed. The negotiators also established a demilitarized zone about two and a half miles wide between the two Koreas. A committee was set up to settle the fate of the Korean prisoners of war who did not wish to return to their home countries, and a military commission was formed to supervise other terms of the armistice. North Korea wound up with about 1,500 fewer square miles of territory than before the war. The United States and South Korea shortly signed a mutual-security treaty,

A symbol of the cold war, the Brandenburg Gate stands at the boundary between East and West Berlin. The sign warns, "Attention! You are leaving West Berlin."

Dwight Eisenhower, shown here at his desk in the White House, fulfilled a promise made during the 1952 presidential campaign by achieving a negotiated settlement to the Korean conflict.

pledging to consult with each other in case of threatened attack.

The Americans and their UN allies had accomplished their objective. Through prompt military action they had turned back Soviet-supported aggression, thus saving the South Koreans from being swallowed up by the Communist world. Still, Americans found it hard to rejoice. The Korean War had taken the lives of over 33,000 American servicemen, and more than 100,000 had been wounded.

The cold war continues. Although the hot war was over, the cold war went on. The new Secretary of State, John Foster Dulles, was a man of definite ideas. Under his guidance, the incoming administration decided it must no longer wait for Communist aggression to occur before trying to contain it. The resulting "brush-fire wars" — like the one in Korea — were too costly. The Eisenhower-Dulles position was that in order to discourage Communist aggression, the United States must make clear its determination to retaliate directly against the Soviet Union.

The new American military strategy was known as *massive retaliation.* Dulles boldly declared, moreover, that his diplomatic method was "to get to the verge without getting into war." Critics of this policy called it *brinkmanship,* charging that Dulles's apparent willingness to bring the United States to the brink of war could, through some misunderstanding, lead to war itself. Brinkmanship, they said, was especially unsuitable now that both the United States and the Soviet Union had developed hydrogen bombs. These weapons had been successfully tested by the United States in 1952 and by the Russians less than a year later. They had thousands of times more explosive force than the atomic bombs that had been dropped on Japan in the final days of World War II.

President Eisenhower also expressed concern about the development of these powerful weapons. Speaking at the United Nations in 1953, he said, "Let no one think that the expenditure of vast sums for weapons and systems of defense can guarantee absolute safety. . . . The awful arithmetic of the atomic bomb does not permit of any such easy solution." In this address, known as the Atoms for Peace speech, Eisenhower offered to talk to Soviet leaders, "to seek an acceptable solution to the atomic armaments race, which overshadows not only the peace but the very life of the world."

The Eisenhower administration, meanwhile, did not neglect conventional weapons or defense systems. During the 1950's the United States continued to work closely with its NATO allies to build up military strength sufficient to deter a Russian invasion of Western Europe. It was also decided that the rearming of West Germany was central to the defense of Europe. For this reason, Germany was admitted to NATO in 1955 and allowed to build up an army of half a million men.

The French withdraw from Indochina. Only months after the Korean War was brought to an end, another military crisis arose in Asia. It was destined to have lasting significance for the United States.

Indochina, a French colony in Southeast Asia, was torn by civil war. Rebels, known as Viet Minh, were fighting to drive the French out of the country and to establish a Communist government. The insurgents had the backing of China and the Soviet Union. The United States gave aid to the French and their anti-Communist Indochinese allies, but by 1954 it was clear that the Viet Minh were winning. Late that spring, after suffering defeat in the fierce Battle of Dien Bien Phu, the French decided to pull out of Southeast Asia.

An international conference met at Geneva, Switzerland, to decide the political fate of Indochina. Negotiations led to a political settlement under which the independence of Laos and Cambodia were guaranteed. Vietnam was temporarily divided at the 17th parallel, with the Communists given control of the northern portion. The anti-communist government of President Ngo Dinh Diem (noh din ZEE-em), meanwhile, was given control of the southern portion. Elections were to be held in 1956 with the aim of reuniting the country under one government. The United States participated in the conference but refused to sign the agreements, in protest against the concessions made to the Communists.

A crisis develops in the Middle East. The American public grew accustomed to seeing the focus of the cold war shift constantly from one part of the world to another. The Middle East entered the spotlight in 1956 in an unexpected way. Two years earlier, a nationalist leader named Gamal Abdel Nasser had come to power in Egypt. To obtain Nasser's good will, Secretary of State Dulles offered American help in building a large dam at Aswan, on the Nile River. At the same time, the Soviet Union, bent on wooing Nasser, also held out an offer of a loan for the big project. The Russians, meanwhile, entered into an agreement to trade weapons for Egyptian cotton. Egypt soon used the arms to carry out raids against Israel, which Nasser had pledged to destroy.

In July, 1956, angered by Nasser's dealings with the Soviet Union, Dulles abruptly withdrew the offer of American aid. Nasser lashed back by seizing the Suez Canal, which ran through Egyptian territory but was owned by an international company. He then announced that Israeli ships would no longer be allowed to use the waterway. Britain and France feared that they, too, might soon be denied access to it. They appealed to the United States to join them in taking action against Egypt, but Eisenhower and Dulles were earnestly opposed to military intervention.

The tense situation was heightened when, on October 29, 1956, Israel launched a strike against Egypt. Two days later, without having informed the United States of their intentions, Britain and France joined Israel. When the Soviet Union threatened to send "volunteers" to Egypt to aid Nasser, the world seemed on the threshold of war. Eisenhower decided to place the issue before the United Nations, which quickly passed a resolution calling for the withdrawal of all invading forces. Furious with the United States for its lack of support, Britain, France, and Israel nevertheless complied with the UN resolution.

American commitments grow. One outcome of the 1956 war was a further extension of United States military commitments. In a special message to Congress in January, 1957, the President announced what became known as the Eisenhower Doctrine. He obtained from Congress a resolution permitting him to send troops to any Middle East country whose rulers considered themselves threatened by "international communism."

Three months later, when Egypt's Nasser tried to topple King Hussein of Jordan, the United States Navy was sent to the Mediterranean in a show of force. Then, in July, when the pro-Western government of Lebanon seemed about to be overthrown, Eisenhower sent a contingent of marines to

Hungarians burned pictures of Stalin during the revolt of 1956. Soviet troops soon put down the uprising, crushing hopes for freedom.

restore order in the country. The use of troops in this instance was, however, unusual. The administration mostly relied on the sale of arms and on the distribution of economic aid to maintain its influence in the region.

New crises arise in Europe. At precisely the same time that the world seemed near war in the Middle East, a revolution broke out in Hungary. On October 23, 1956, popular discontent exploded into street fighting in Budapest, the nation's capital. A crowd toppled the immense statue of Stalin that stood in the center of the city and was a hated symbol of Russian domination. The revolution spread quickly throughout the country, with freedom fighters demanding

that Soviet troops be withdrawn and that the Hungarian people be allowed to organize a democratic government.

The Soviet Union moved quickly to quell the Hungarian uprising. While about 200,000 refugees managed to make their way across the Austrian border to freedom, within two weeks the revolution had been crushed by Soviet tanks. In the operation, thousands of people were killed. Once the fighting had ended, the new government, a puppet of the USSR, rounded up all known rebels and imprisoned them, either in Hungary or in the Soviet Union. The inability of the Eisenhower administration to act on a promise it had earlier given to liberate Eastern Europe produced frustration in the United States and disappointment abroad.

Two years after the Hungarian uprising, another crisis arose in Eastern Europe. In November, 1958, Nikita Khrushchev (nih-KEE-tah kroosh-CHOFF), who had emerged as Stalin's successor in the Soviet Union, demanded that the Western powers withdraw from Berlin. Khrushchev threatened that unless they yielded to his demand within six months, he would sign a peace treaty with East Germany and cut off Western access to Berlin. The United States, Britain, and France made it clear that they had no intention of abandoning the city. Meanwhile, thousands of refugees continued to flock to West Berlin to escape the harsh repression in East Germany.

Cold-war tensions are eased. Early in 1959, Khrushchev seemed to back down, saying that he would extend the Berlin deadline if Western leaders agreed to a summit conference. Negotiations to arrange such a meeting began, but no firm agreement was reached. Still, tensions relaxed enough for Vice President Nixon to visit Poland and the Soviet Union during the summer of 1959. That fall, Khrushchev visited the United States and conferred with Eisenhower at Camp David, the presidential retreat in Maryland. The two leaders concluded their meetings by issuing a joint statement in which they said that they would settle all existing disagreements through negotiation. They also said they would soon hold a summit conference that would include European leaders.

Khrushchev cancels the summit conference. In early May, 1960, just as the long-awaited summit conference was about to open, cold-war tensions again took over. Khrushchev announced that on May 1 the Russians had shot down an American U–2 reconnaissance plane flying over their territory. He insisted that the United States apologize, punish those responsible, and promise that such flights would cease. At first, the administration denied that the U–2 had been engaged in spying, but soon the government acknowledged the truth of the Soviet charges. Eisenhower accepted full responsibility for the incident and promised that U–2 flights over Russia would be halted.

He refused, however, to apologize. Other Western leaders supported Eisenhower in his firm stance. Khrushchev would not remain at the summit conference without an apology. He flew back to Moscow, and the summit conference collapsed.

After the U–2 incident, relations between the United States and the Soviet Union seemed to worsen. Khrushchev canceled an invitation he had extended to Eisenhower to visit Russia, and continued to insist that the American President apologize. Eisenhower stood his ground, but nevertheless continued his efforts to reduce tensions. His labors, however, were unsuccessful. Khrushchev continued to denounce American "aggression." In 1960, at a session of the UN in New York, the Soviet leader both alarmed and amused the Western world by taking off his shoe and pounding the table with it to demonstrate his outrage at the United States.

SECTION REVIEW

1. Vocabulary: *massive retaliation, brinkmanship.*
2. (a) What were the terms of the armistice signed in Korea in 1953? (b) How did the Eisenhower administration modify the containment policy? (c) What was the result of the French defeat in Southeast Asia?
3. (a) What factors contributed to the Suez crisis? (b) How was the situation resolved? (c) What was the Eisenhower Doctrine? (d) How was it tested in Lebanon?
4. (a) What was the response of the Soviet Union to the Hungarian uprising? (b) What demands did Nikita Khrushchev make concerning Berlin? (c) Why did he cancel the 1960 Paris summit conference?

2 The Nation Prospers Under Eisenhower

When Dwight Eisenhower later described his election to the presidency, he modestly wrote, "The homely old [saying] had proved to be true: in the United States, any boy *can* grow up to be President." In domestic matters Eisenhower depended upon his forthrightness and his ability, learned during his

Overproduction was the basic problem facing American farmers during the 1950's. Crop output climbed, while farm income declined.

long army career, to work through a trusted staff. He gave his subordinates much leeway. He liked to say, "You do not lead by hitting people over the head."

DOMESTIC POLICIES

The Republicans try to reduce the size of government. Eisenhower had taken office promising to balance the budget. He found it difficult, however, to reduce national expenditures. Eisenhower tried to cut government spending, even allowing about 100,000 civil service jobs to remain unfilled. Still, when a business recession came at the end of his first year in office, the administration resorted to methods formerly used by the Democrats. It cut taxes, increased Social Security payments, and extended unemployment compensation. All of Eisenhower's annual budgets, furthermore, were larger than any of Truman's.

The size of the budgets reflected, in part, the fact that Eisenhower made no attempt to tamper with the main body of social reforms enacted in the previous administrations. Most people probably agreed with Eisenhower's assertion that the path for the nation to take was "down the middle."

Farm problems continue. Notably fewer disputes on domestic economic issues arose during Eisenhower's years in office than in recent administrations. Many farmers, however, were distressed by the proposals of Secretary of Agriculture Ezra Taft Benson.

On American farms overproduction had continued to be a problem. Improvements in all aspects of agriculture — better seed, better cultivation, better storage facilities — had increased the production of crops far beyond national need. As a result, farm prices were dismally low, and many farmers were forced off the land.

Under the existing farm program, the government bought surplus crops from farmers if prices dropped below a certain level. Secretary Benson argued that these fixed payments actually encouraged farmers to overproduce. The solution he proposed was to make price supports flexible. This program was passed by Congress, but it was no more successful than earlier arrangements in reducing farm surpluses.

In 1956 the government made a further attempt to halt overproduction by offering to pay farmers who agreed to cut back their planting. Price-support payments, it was hoped, could be reduced. At the same time, by keeping the soil idle its fertility would be maintained. Even this program, however, failed to prevent mounting farm surpluses.

Americans express concern over internal security. Worry over the loyalty of people employed by the federal government had become widespread during Truman's years in the White House. The same concern confronted Eisenhower when he took office in 1953. In response, he supported strict internal-security laws that provided for the suspension of any government employee accused of being a security risk. He also backed laws that allowed the death penalty for espionage.

The Senate, at this time, was investigating the extent of Communist infiltration into the federal government. A leader of the investigation was Senator Joseph R. McCarthy of Wisconsin. In February, 1950, McCarthy had brought himself to national attention by charging, without substantiation, that the State Department employed more than 200 Communists. The Senate promptly appointed a subcommittee to investigate these and similar accusations. From his position on this subcommittee, McCarthy became one of the most powerful politicians in the country.

The turning point in Senator McCarthy's career came in 1954, when he publicly insisted that there were Communists in the ranks of the United States Army. The Army countercharged that McCarthy was attempting to gain special favors for the recently drafted son of a friend. A special Senate committee held televised hearings on the matter in April and May of 1954. Many supporters, seeing McCarthy in action, turned against him. His manner struck viewers as rude and bullying, and his reckless use of unfounded accusation offended their sense of fair play. From then on, McCarthy's support eroded. In December, 1954, his Senate colleagues formally condemned him for "conduct unbecoming a member." McCarthy's political career never recovered from this blow.

Eisenhower is re-elected. President Eisenhower's remarkable popularity continued undiminished through his first term. His reelection in 1956 seemed sure. The only uncertainty was his health. In September, 1955, he had suffered a heart attack, and less than a year later he underwent abdominal surgery. In each case, however, his recovery was swift and complete.

In running for a second term in 1956, Eisenhower did almost no campaigning. Still, there was little that the Democrats could do. Adlai Stevenson, nominated for a second campaign against Eisenhower, was buried in a Republican landslide. The President won with 35,600,000 votes to slightly over 26,000,000 for Stevenson. In the electoral college the results were even more decisive: 457 votes to 73. In carrying 41 states, the President had won the most overwhelming victory since Roosevelt crushed Landon in 1936. The Democrats had, however, retained control of both houses of Congress. For all his political strength, Eisenhower was unable to transfer his own popularity to his party.

Organized labor faces new problems. As his second term got under way, Eisenhower confronted fresh issues already forming. In 1955 the American Federation of Labor (AFL) and the Congress of Industrial Organizations (CIO), once deadly rivals, had come together in a unified labor organization. At the time of unification, the AFL-CIO represented over fifteen million workers. George Meany of the AFL was named president and Walter Reuther of the CIO became vice president.

The major long-term problem union leaders faced was *automation* — the manufacture of goods by machines controlled electronically rather than by hand. New technology was making it possible for whole factories to be run with only a handful of workers present. The challenge unions faced was how best to serve their members, now subject to loss of jobs owing to technological change rather than economic conditions.

A further problem confronting labor unions during the late 1950's was the corruption of some union leaders. A Senate investigation of the Teamsters, the single largest union in the AFL-CIO, showed that the organization's pension and welfare funds had been used for questionable purposes. The probe also revealed that some Teamster leaders had ties to organized crime and that a large amount of money entrusted to the leadership was missing. Dave Beck, the president of the union, was charged with misappropriating union funds, and eventually he went to jail. When the Teamsters replaced Beck with Jimmy Hoffa, who had also been implicated in criminal activity during the investigation, the AFL-CIO decided to expel the Teamsters from its ranks.

In 1959 Congress passed the Landrum-Griffin Act, the first major piece of labor legislation since the Taft-Hartley Act of 1947 (page 685). The new law was designed to clean up corruption in organized labor. It prohibited Communists and recently convicted felons from serving as union officials; required union elections to be held by secret ballot at least once every five years; and called for union officials to provide the Secretary of Labor with detailed information on the handling of union funds.

Two new states join the Union. In 1959 Alaska and Hawaii, each of which had become United States territories in the nineteenth century, became the 49th and 50th states. They were the first new states to join the Union since New Mexico and Arizona were admitted in 1912. They also shared the distinction of being the first states that did not have a common border with any other state.

THE AFFLUENT SOCIETY

Americans enjoy widespread prosperity. Eisenhower's terms as President coincided with an economic boom unparalleled in the nation's history. The war years had been the launching pad for this unprecedented growth. Between 1949 and 1960, the *gross national product* (the nation's total output of goods and services) nearly doubled. The accompanying good times brought a higher standard of living to most Americans. An economist named John Kenneth Galbraith published an influential book in 1958 that described this prosperity and gave the American scene a name. The book was called *The Affluent Society.*

After enduring the uncertainties of the Depression and the sacrifices of the war years, Americans seemed bent on enjoying their new-found abundance. Countless appliances altered ways of living for practically everybody. Automatic washing machines and clothes driers, for example, simplified one of the oldest household tasks; electric can openers eliminated another nuisance; coffee makers operating on electric timers made preparing breakfast more convenient; power lawn mowers gave countless youths freer weekends; home freezers reduced trips to the store.

The television set was a symbol of the prosperous 1950's. The technology for TV had been known for many years, and experimentation had brought about one improvement after another by the beginning of the Second World War. After the war, commercial television burst on the scene. Suddenly, Americans were viewing everything from Cabinet meetings to World Series games, from religious services to grand opera, from surgical operations to underwater exploration. For the first time, people by the millions were able to watch the same program simultaneously, producing common subjects of conversation in schools, factories, and offices. The advertising that paid for the "free" television served even further to blur local differences in taste as people all across the nation bought the latest gadget or food product shown on the television screen.

Population increases rapidly. While television and other media helped greatly to stimulate consumption, the tremendous leap in population also played a major part. Between 1950 and 1960, the number of Americans increased by more than 18 percent.

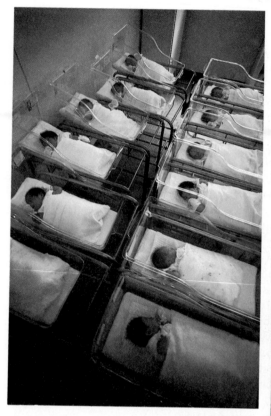

LIFE IN AMERICA

The Prosperous 1950's
Economic advances in the 1950's allowed most Americans to raise their standard of living. Many families moved into suburban houses as soon as they were built and bought their first television sets. Population grew rapidly, partially as the result of a baby boom.

The cause of this increase was the trend toward earlier marriages and larger families, which produced a baby boom during the postwar years. At the same time, advances in medical science had a role in increasing the population by helping people to live longer. By 1960 the average life expectancy was seventy years. A third factor in the population explosion was the arrival in the United States of 2.5 million immigrants.

The United States experiences shifts in population. Along with the growth in population, major changes took place in the geographical distribution of people during the 1950's. The West grew faster than any other part of the country, and by the mid-1960's California had become the most populous state in the Union.

A second major shift in population in the postwar era was the mass migration of middle-class Americans to the suburbs. People who could afford to move began leaving the central cities. Suburban communities were said to offer the best possible setting in which to raise a family — safe streets and open spaces, modern schools and clean air. These were precisely the things that most cities lacked.

The suburbs that grew up in the 1950's were different from those of the 1920's, which had remained dependent on the central city. The newer suburbs were largely self-sufficient communities. They maintained their own school systems, police and fire departments, hospitals, and public health and sanitation services. Many suburban people commuted into the city to work, but increasingly the suburbs themselves were creating local economic opportunities.

Advances in transportation change the way Americans live. One factor shaping the new, emerging society was the widespread ownership of automobiles. Reflecting this fact, the nation began to build a network of highways extending from one end of the country to another. Unlike public transportation, which is bound to fixed schedules and routes, the private automobile gave its users a sense of personal freedom to come and go at will. One effect was to change shopping habits. The central city, convenient to trains and buses, was no longer the only possible location for major department stores. Branches of downtown stores could now be built outside the cities. Soon, many of these were situated in "shopping centers" that transformed the suburban landscape. Surrounded by acres of parking lots and accessible by highways, shopping centers vastly stimulated consumer spending even as they made shopping more attractive and convenient. Entertainment facilities in the suburbs also began to rival those in the cities as movie theaters, bowling alleys, roller-skating rinks, and restaurants sprang up along the local roadways.

Travel and commuting patterns throughout the United States were affected by the construction of superhighways.

The lives of Americans were also affected by the growth of commercial airline travel. The introduction of commercial jet airliners in the late 1950's added comfort and speed to air travel that propeller-driven planes could not provide. For many people it now became routine to fly to other parts of the country to visit relatives or take a vacation. American business, too, was speeded up by advances in aviation technology. Business meetings to which participants had to travel could now be planned with confidence. Since most airplane passengers were people on business, their needs stimulated a motel-building boom as well as the creation of car-rental agencies.

THE FIGHT AGAINST DISCRIMINATION

The civil rights movement wins an important victory. For black Americans the affluent 1950's was a period both of frustration and dramatic accomplishment. Obstacles to the goal of full civil rights included the continued existence of Jim Crow laws (page 535) and of *de facto* discrimination — discrimination established not by law but by custom and practice.

During the Truman and Eisenhower administrations, civil rights lawyers took a number of cases to the Supreme Court. The most important ruling came in 1954, in a case concerning segregation in primary and secondary schools. Dealing with the issue firmly, the Supreme Court handed down a landmark decision in *Brown v. Board of Education of Topeka.* The unanimous finding of the justices would prove to be a turning point for all Americans, black and white.

In the *Brown* decision, the Court held that state or local laws requiring racial segregation in public schools were unconstitutional. Chief Justice Earl Warren, who wrote the opinion, based it on the Fourteenth Amendment, which says that no state may "deny to any person within its jurisdiction the equal protection of the laws." Fifty-eight years earlier, in *Plessy v. Ferguson* (page 535), the Court had declared that segregation did not violate the Fourteenth Amendment as long as the separate facilities were equal. Now the Court was saying, in effect, that in education the doctrine of "separate but equal" was unconstitutional. Declared Warren, "in the field of public education the doctrine of 'separate but equal' has no place. Separate educational facilities are inherently unequal." In a later decision, the Court ordered local authorities to proceed "with all deliberate speed" to desegregate their schools.

The "Brown" decision meets resistance. Supporters of the civil rights movement were delighted, but they recognized that such an enormous change in society could not be brought about easily. School desegregation was accomplished with relative ease in Washington, D.C., and in some of the border states, but elsewhere public resistance was strong. In Little Rock, Arkansas, opposition to school desegregation was so intense that President Eisenhower sent in federal troops to maintain order while the law was carried out. Under armed guard, nine black students enrolled at Little Rock Central High School in the fall of 1957.

In response to growing protests that black citizens were being denied full rights, Congress in 1957 passed the first civil rights law since Reconstruction. This Civil Rights Act set up a federal Commission on Civil Rights. Its duty was to investigate cases where voting rights were being denied, to examine the effects of federal laws and policies on Americans' civil rights, and to conduct studies on related issues.

The Montgomery bus boycott draws attention. Meanwhile, other developments advanced the movement for civil rights. On December 1, 1955, a seamstress named Rosa Parks took a courageous and fateful step. Her home town, Montgomery, Alabama, was one of the nation's most rigidly segregated cities. Black passengers were required to sit at the back of city buses and were expected to give up their seats to white passengers if a bus was too crowded for everyone to sit down. Mrs. Parks defied this custom. When she refused to give up her place to a white man, she was arrested and jailed. The next day the 50,000 black

Rosa Parks's refusal to give up her seat to a white passenger led to the Montgomery bus boycott of 1955.

citizens of Montgomery began a boycott of the city's buses, choosing to walk rather than ride under humiliating conditions.

The boycott was led by a young Baptist minister named Martin Luther King, Jr. In advocating a policy of passive resistance and nonviolent direct action, King was deeply influenced by the thoughts of two men whose writings he had studied: the Indian nationalist leader Mohandas Gandhi, and the nineteenth-century American philosopher Henry David Thoreau. No matter what violence was done to them, King preached to his followers, they must not fight back, and they must be willing to go to jail for their disobedience of unjust laws. If his people followed this method, he assured them, they would win the attention and sympathy of fellow Americans.

Despite great inconvenience and hardship, the black citizens of Montgomery kept up the boycott for over a year, bringing the bus company close to bankruptcy. In the end, however, it was another court decision that settled the matter. The Supreme Court ruled, late in 1956, that segregation on buses was unconstitutional. The issue had finally been settled. In riding city buses, blacks and whites would at last be treated equally.

Civil rights leaders take direct action. King and other civil rights leaders, encouraged by the boycott and its outcome, formed the Southern Christian Leadership Conference (SCLC) early in 1957. They pledged that they would use nonviolent methods to fight racial discrimination, not only in the South but throughout the United States.

In this spirit, a new desegregation campaign began. On February 1, 1960, in Greensboro, North Carolina, four black students from a local college sat down at a lunch counter in a downtown store. Upon being refused service, they remained seated in protest. Every day, they returned to the lunch counter and sat, their silent presence an eloquent protest against the store's refusal to serve black people. Throughout the country, sympathizers staged demonstrations on behalf of the Greensboro protesters. Finally, in July, the store announced its decision to integrate the lunch counter.

Following the success of the Greensboro "sit-in," thousands of demonstrators, black and white alike, engaged in similar protests — in restaurants, theaters, libraries, churches, and at swimming pools, beaches, and other public places that excluded blacks. This kind of direct action helped bring down the walls of segregation.

SECTION REVIEW

1. Vocabulary: *automation, gross national product.*
2. (a) What were Eisenhower's views about the scope of the federal government's operations? (b) How did his administration tackle the problem of overproduction by the nation's farmers? (c) How successful was the farm policy?
3. (a) Who were the candidates in the 1956 presidential election? (b) What was the outcome?
4. (a) What problems did labor unions face during the 1950's? (b) What was the Landrum-Griffin Act, and what were its main provisions?
5. (a) What evidence was there that by the 1950's the United States had become an affluent society? (b) Describe the major changes in population distribution during the decade. (c) What effect did advances in transportation have on the way Americans lived?
6. (a) What was the importance of the *Brown* decision? (b) What reactions did it provoke? (c) How were nonviolent tactics used in the civil rights movement?

3 The Democrats Regain the White House

In July, 1960, the Democrats held their convention in Los Angeles. As their candidate for President, the delegates chose John Fitzgerald Kennedy, a senator from Massachusetts. His running mate was Senator Lyndon B. Johnson of Texas. Kennedy set lofty national goals in his acceptance speech, when he pledged to help conquer a "New Frontier" that consisted of "uncharted areas of science and space, unsolved problems of peace and war, unconquered pockets of ignorance and prejudice, unanswered questions of poverty and surplus."

A NEW PRESIDENT

Kennedy is elected President. At first, the odds seemed to be against Kennedy. For one thing, he faced a formidable Republican opponent — Richard M. Nixon. Nixon was the first Vice President since 1836 to be chosen by his party to succeed his chief. Nixon's running mate was Henry Cabot Lodge, Jr., of Massachusetts, the United States ambassador to the United Nations. Nixon, recognizing the advantage of his connection with Eisenhower, campaigned on the record of the previous eight years. The country was enjoying unprecedented prosperity, peace, and, he insisted, military superiority over its enemies. He offered the nation stability, promising to build on the strong foundations Eisenhower had laid.

Some Democrats feared that Kennedy's youth and religion would prove to be handicaps to his candidacy. Kennedy was the youngest man ever to win his party's nomination for President. Only 43 years old, he had considerably less political experience than his opponent. He was a Roman Catholic as well, and many political observers believed, based on Al Smith's disastrous showing in 1928 (page 514), that a Catholic could not win the presidency. Kennedy

The first President born in the twentieth century, John F. Kennedy won election by a narrow margin. Here, Kennedy greets voters during the 1960 campaign.

faced the religious issue squarely, which proved effective in overcoming concern. "I refuse to believe," he said, "that I was denied the right to be President on the day I was baptized."

The race was extremely close, but the tide turned in Kennedy's favor following a series of four televised debates held late in the campaign. The broadcasts gave voters a chance to see the two candidates side by side and form judgments about them. Many viewers who had previously known little about Kennedy came away from their television sets favorably impressed by him.

On Election Day, a record number of voters went to the polls. Kennedy triumphed with the smallest margin of any President since 1884. Out of a total of 68 million votes, Kennedy won by only 118,000. In the electoral college, he won by 303 to 219.

Kennedy takes office. In his inaugural address, delivered in front of the snow-covered Capitol on January 20, 1961, Kennedy challenged Americans to follow his lead. "Of those to whom much is given, much is required," he declared. ". . . And so, my fellow Americans, ask not what your country can do for you; ask what you can do for your country."

Kennedy was the first American President born in the twentieth century. His youth, thought to be a handicap during the campaign, became an asset to him in office. The public was fascinated by news reports about his young children and his family's zeal for athletics and the out-of-doors. His personal grace and bright wit, moreover, stamped him as an admirable model to copy — especially for young people. The word frequently used to describe the image he projected was "style" — a term suggesting that he was different from his predecessors in the White House, that he was an innovator ready to break loose from established ways without being a radical reformer. John Kennedy and his beautiful wife Jacqueline served French food, wore elegant clothing, and invited leading artists to attend lavish evenings at the White House. The President appreciated the role of intellectuals and serious writers in American life. He once sponsored a dinner for Nobel Prize winners, welcoming them as "the most extraordinary collection of talent, of human knowledge, that has ever been gathered together at the White House, with the possible exception of when Thomas Jefferson dined alone."

New programs are started. The idealism that seemed to accompany Kennedy into office was quickly translated into action. The new administration proposed the establishment of the Peace Corps, an organization designed to provide help for impoverished countries. Peace Corps volunteers — thousands of them — were quickly recruited to serve as teachers, medical aides, agricultural advisers, and technicians in Asia, Africa, and Latin America. Their endeavors and enthusiasm made many fast friends for the United States.

Through a program he called the Alliance for Progress, Kennedy hoped to create in Latin America some of the warm feeling toward the United States that the Good Neighbor Policy had once generated. Under the Alliance, aid was distributed to Latin American countries. It was hoped that this program would raise standards of living, promote economic growth, and help stabilize democratic governments. The results, however, proved to be disappointing. The Alliance did not meet its economic goals. Moreover, the governments of Honduras, Ecuador, and Peru were taken over by military leaders.

COLD-WAR TENSIONS

Communists come to power in Cuba. From the beginning, the Kennedy administration was tied down by the demands of the cold war, which continued unabated. Cuba was a particularly troublesome subject. In 1959, while Eisenhower was President, Cuban rebels had overthrown the dictatorial regime of Fulgencio Batista. At first, most Americans welcomed the new government formed by Fidel Castro, which promised to institute reforms. Their enthusiasm, however, quickly faded. Instead of allowing his people greater liberty than they had known under Batista, Castro declared publicly that

On Assignment with the Peace Corps

Beginning in the early 1960's, the Peace Corps sent volunteers to help teach and train people in countries requesting assistance. The following passage is from a letter written by a Peace Corps volunteer after several months on assignment in the West African nation of Sierra Leone.

A Peace Corps volunteer

For what should Peace Corps volunteers be prepared? They should be prepared for a delightful, warm, friendly, appreciative, and fun-loving people, and for the nerve-racking frustration that arises out of lack of understanding and consistent failure. They should be prepared for a rewarding experience which will live with them as long as they are on the earth.

I know that I have come upon a situation which has caused me to stop and completely re-evaluate myself, my ideas about education, and my ideas about a person's basic relationship with his culture. I have always held that there is a certain "oneness" about humanity which no amount of difference in skin coloring or cultural uniqueness could hide. The last five months in West Africa have done nothing to alter that view, except to strengthen it.

The need for education in Sierra Leone is desperate, and the appreciation we have been getting from people on all levels is no less than astounding. Some are a little hesitant to believe that we would give up the luxuries of America — the good job, the money, and the conveniences — for that which West Africa has to offer, but they are nonetheless glad to have us. One student said to me, "I really don't understand why you would want to do this, but welcome."

The question "Why did you join the Peace Corps?" that has plagued us all from the beginning becomes increasingly less and less difficult to answer. One no longer has to resort to abstract philosophical arguments, for I now find myself in the midst of the answer, surrounded by a situation which cries out in self-explanation. The poverty, the illiteracy, the substandard educational opportunities which are widespread in this as well as many other countries, are reasons enough for anyone to want to extend his hand and heart in order that these blights might be at least partially erased.

he was a Communist and banned opposition parties, censored the press, refused to hold elections, and murdered or jailed thousands who spoke out against him. In addition, he nationalized the holdings of American companies operating in Cuba and became generally hostile in dealing with the United States.

In 1960, Castro signed a trade agreement with the Soviet Union. The Eisenhower administration responded by suspending American purchases of sugar, Cuba's main export. By the time Kennedy took office, the United States had broken diplomatic relations with Cuba, which was now firmly in the Soviet camp.

The United States aids anti-Castro rebels.
This state of affairs disturbed Kennedy, as it had distressed Eisenhower before him. Would Cuba try to export revolution to other Latin American countries? Would it provide the Soviet Union with military bases? When Kennedy came into the White House, he learned of the existence of a secret program begun under Eisenhower to train and equip anti-Castro exiles whose goal was the invasion of Cuba. The new President decided to continue the project.

On April 17, 1961, only three months after Kennedy had taken office, the planned invasion of Cuba was launched. It ended quickly in utter disaster. The little army of

More than three million East Germans fled to West Berlin before Communist authorities ordered the building of the Berlin Wall in 1961.

1,400 men, lacking air cover, was overwhelmed by Castro's forces as it tried to land at a place called the Bay of Pigs. The President, gravely disappointed and dejected, said of the failed scheme, "How could everybody involved have thought such a plan would succeed? I don't know the answer."

Kennedy meets Khrushchev. The costly and humiliating Bay of Pigs episode made the Soviet Union bolder. Russian leaders wondered if the young President would hesitate to resort to force in future crises. In June, 1961, Kennedy flew to Vienna to hold talks with Nikita Khrushchev. The President was stunned when the Soviet premier spoke boldly of ending the United States presence in Berlin. Kennedy made clear his unshakable determination to keep West Berlin from falling into Russian hands. As he left Khrushchev, Kennedy told him bluntly, "It will be a cold winter." Both men returned home ready to seek a build-up of arms. Before long, thousands of Americans were constructing air-raid shelters, and schools and factories were conducting air-raid drills.

A crisis develops in Berlin. In the meantime, as they had since 1945, East Germans continued to risk their lives to flee to West Berlin. This steady exodus was an embarrassment to the Soviet Union. In August, 1961, in order to prevent further loss of population — and prestige — the East German government began constructing a wall across the city. The West quickly dubbed this symbol of Communist repression "the wall of shame."

To help assure the security of West Berlin and to make certain that Western rights were defended, President Kennedy sent additional troops to West Berlin. In the end, the Russians ceased pressuring the United States to pull out.

Kennedy quarantines Cuba. Cuba continued to be a hot spot of anxiety for the United States. During the fall of 1962, American airplanes flying over the island discovered a massive military build-up in

Cuba. Reconnaissance photographs showed that the Soviet Union was equipping Cuba with offensive missiles capable of firing nuclear warheads at most of the major cities in North America.

After a week of secret deliberations with his advisers, Kennedy told the public on October 22, 1962, about the alarming situation in Cuba. He announced, furthermore, his decision to "quarantine," or blockade, Cuba to prevent the importation of more Soviet weapons. He also demanded that the Soviet Union dismantle and remove the missile installations. To underscore the American determination, he placed United States military forces on full alert.

The world held its breath as Russian ships continued to sail toward Cuba and as American ships took up stations to enforce the blockade. On October 24, having reached American-patrolled waters, the Russian ships suddenly stopped dead in the water or simply circled in place. There would be no shoot-out. Secretary of State Dean Rusk observed, "It's eyeball to eyeball, and I think the other fellow just blinked." Four days later, Khrushchev announced that he had ordered the removal of the offending missiles.

A nuclear test-ban treaty is signed. Like his immediate predecessors, Kennedy tried to find a solution to the growing threat of nuclear weapons. Since 1958, the United States and the Soviet Union had informally agreed to halt the testing of atomic weapons in the atmosphere. In 1961, however, the Soviet Union resumed atmospheric testing. Reluctantly, Kennedy authorized the United States to follow suit.

Two years later, in a sudden about-face, the Soviet Union decided to accept a Western offer to ban nuclear testing in the atmosphere, in space, and under water. Representatives of the United States, Britain, and the Soviet Union, meeting in Moscow in July, 1963, signed a treaty embodying this agreement. The good-will between the two superpowers also led to the establishment of a "hot line" — an emergency channel of communication — between the White House and the Kremlin, aimed at preventing an accidental war.

The United States is drawn into conflict in Vietnam. Southeast Asia became another area of concern for President Kennedy. The situation there had its roots in the withdrawal of French forces from Indochina in 1954 (page 709). At the conference which ended French involvement in Indochina, the participants had agreed that Vietnam would be reunited in 1956 through a national election. The election was never held. The South Vietnamese government of Ngo Dinh Diem argued that South Vietnam had not been fairly represented at the conference. In addition, Diem pointed out that the North Vietnamese government had already broken the agreement by building up its armed forces. When the date for the elections passed, the North Vietnamese, along with sympathizers in the south (called the Viet Cong), began to wage guerrilla warfare against the government of South Vietnam. Their aim was to unify Vietnam.

During his last years in office, President Eisenhower had become increasingly concerned about the mounting pressure on South Vietnam. He warned that it was necessary to stop Communist aggression in Southeast Asia. Victory for North Vietnam, he argued, would eventually mean a Communist take-over in every country in that region. This view became known as the "domino theory." Eisenhower explained: "You have a row of dominos set up. You knock over the first one, and what will happen to the last one is the certainty that it will go over very quickly."

By the time Kennedy took office in 1961, the United States had already sent nearly 800 military advisers to South Vietnam. America was also bearing most of the cost of that country's military effort and was helping run Diem's government. Kennedy, who agreed with Eisenhower that South Vietnam must not be allowed to fall to the Communists, decided to send more American military personnel and equipment. Within a year, the number of Americans in Vietnam had increased to 2,700.

Diem is assassinated. Diem, meanwhile, was losing support in his own country. Instead of carrying out reforms, as proposed by his American advisers, he persecuted his political opponents. In 1963, Buddhist monks responded by staging public demonstrations. Then, late in 1963, a group of South Vietnamese generals, displeased by Diem's policies and the corruption in his government, plotted to overthrow Diem. On November 1, 1963, military officers took over the government of South Vietnam, and Diem was assassinated.

Before the year was out, about 17,000 United States military advisers were in Vietnam. Still, most Americans who thought about the war at all regarded it as a matter primarily for the Vietnamese themselves to settle.

DOMESTIC PROGRAMS

Kennedy proposes reform legislation. Kennedy's domestic program was in the tradition of his Democratic predecessors, Truman and Roosevelt. Not having great interest in the legislative process, however, Kennedy never developed a reliable technique for dealing with Congress. Administration members, moreover, were not comfortable with Vice President Johnson, a master of the legislative process, and they never drew significantly on his experience to accomplish domestic goals. An unsympathetic coalition of opponents in Congress defeated many of Kennedy's proposals, including federal aid to public schools, health insurance for the elderly, and the creation of a Department of Urban Affairs. Congress also turned down his proposal for a tax cut and gave him less money for foreign aid than he sought, maintaining that the federal government was too deeply in debt.

Kennedy commits the nation to a massive space program. Kennedy, nevertheless, offered some proposals that met with congressional approval. The Housing Act of 1961 authorized the spending of large sums of money on urban-renewal projects. Public works and job training programs were started in order to aid the unemployed. In addition, minimum wages were raised by 25 percent.

The administration also set a dramatic new goal for the nation: to place an American on the moon before the end of the 1960's. Competition between the United States and the Soviet Union in space exploration had already begun during Eisenhower's second term. In October, 1957, Soviet scientists launched the first space satellite, called *Sputnik*, which circled the earth for three months. Less than four years later, a Soviet air force officer, Yuri Gagarin, became the first human to travel in space.

The United States, meantime, was developing its own space program. In May, 1961, Alan Shepard became the first American launched into space. The first American to orbit the earth was John Glenn, on February 20, 1962. The American people were confident that further successes would follow and that the United States would overtake the Soviet Union's lead in space.

The civil rights movement gains momentum. Kennedy had been elected on a platform containing a strong pledge to end racial discrimination. He did not propose any civil rights legislation, however, until 1963. He had concluded that he could not persuade Congress to follow him, and he feared dividing the country.

Kennedy did issue a number of executive orders to insure equal justice for black Americans. In November, 1962, he signed an executive order prohibiting racial or religious discrimination in housing financed by the federal government. In addition, the President created the Commission on Equal Employment Opportunities, which sought to persuade firms holding government contracts to follow nondiscriminatory hiring practices. Another action taken during his administration was the Interstate Commerce Commission's banning of discrimination on all interstate buses, trains, and airlines. Kennedy also placed a number of black leaders in important positions. Thurgood Marshall was made a judge of the

United States Court of Appeals; Robert Weaver became Home Finance Administrator; Carl Rowan was named ambassador to Finland; and Andrew Hatcher was appointed Kennedy's associate press secretary.

The civil rights movement, meanwhile, was acquiring a momentum of its own. In September, 1962, for example, a black air force veteran named James Meredith tried to enroll at the all-white University of Mississippi. Supreme Court Justice Hugo Black ruled that Meredith had to be admitted. When the governor of the state announced that he would go to jail, if necessary, to prevent Meredith (or any other black student) from attending the university, Kennedy ordered federal marshals to escort Meredith to class. Rioting broke out, and Kennedy sent in 5,000 federal troops to restore order. Meredith was admitted to the University of Mississippi and later became the school's first black graduate.

The ratification of two new amendments to the Constitution was applauded by black Americans. The Twenty-Third Amendment, ratified in 1961, made it possible for residents of the District of Columbia, most of them black, to vote in presidential elections. The Twenty-Fourth Amendment, approved by Congress in 1962, prohibited any state from requiring voters to pay a poll tax in order to participate in federal elections. This amendment became part of the Constitution in 1964.

On May 5, 1961, astronaut Alan Shepard became the first American launched into space. Millions of television viewers watched the dramatic moment of recovery as his capsule was hauled out of the sea after the fifteen-minute, suborbital journey.

Martin Luther King, Jr.'s
"I Have a Dream" Speech (1963)

. . . I say to you today, my friends, that in spite of the difficulties and frustrations of the moment, I still have a dream. It is a dream deeply rooted in the American dream. I have a dream that one day this nation will rise up and live out the true meaning of its creed: "We hold these truths to be self-evident: that all men are created equal. . . . "

I have a dream that one day on the red hills of Georgia the sons of former slaves and the sons of former slaveowners will be able to sit down together at the table of brotherhood. . . .

I have a dream that my four children will one day live in a nation where they will not be judged by the color of their skin but by the content of their character. I have a dream today.

I have a dream that one day . . . little black boys and black girls will be able to join hands with little white boys and white girls as sisters and brothers.

I have a dream today. . . .

From every mountainside, let freedom ring. And when we allow freedom to ring, when we let it ring from every village, from every hamlet, from every state and every city, we will be able to speed up the day when all God's children, black men and white men, Jews and Gentiles, Protestants and Catholics, will be able to join hands and sing in the word of the old Negro spiritual: "Free at last! Free at last! Thank God almighty, we are free at last!"

Black Americans make political gains. In 1963, the hundredth anniversary of the Emancipation Proclamation, American civil rights leaders called for a renewal of nonviolent public protest against segregation and against the obstacles faced by black voters in many states. During that year, the nation witnessed scores of demonstrations against racial discrimination.

The peaceful and dignified behavior of most of the demonstrators contrasted favorably with the violence with which their efforts were sometimes met. During a series of demonstrations against segregation in Birmingham, Alabama, for example, a bomb was thrown into a black church, killing 4 children and injuring 21 other people. In Jackson, Mississippi, a civil rights leader, Medgar Evers, was shot to death in front of his home.

By June, 1963, public opinion in many parts of the country had swung sharply in favor of the civil rights demonstrators. Kennedy seized the moment to recommend the passage of strong new civil rights legislation, saying, "We are confronted primarily with a moral issue. . . . The heart of the question is whether all Americans are to be afforded equal rights and equal opportunities." The civil rights legislation Kennedy proposed would (1) prohibit segregation in any public place; (2) ban discrimination in hiring practices; (3) speed school integration; and (4) provide job training for unskilled black workers.

Martin Luther King, Jr., now the undisputed leader of the civil rights movement, called for a "March on Washington" to demonstrate public support for the President's proposed legislation. On August 28, 1963, close to a quarter of a million black and white citizens from all over the country converged on Washington. The enormous demonstration listened as Mahalia Jackson (page 608) sang soaring spirituals and as Martin Luther King delivered an unforgettable speech (page 726). The voice of the crowd then swelled in a heartfelt rendering of the mighty theme song of the civil rights movement: "We Shall Overcome."

Kennedy is assassinated. The Kennedy administration had only a little longer to run. On November 22, 1963, President Kennedy arrived in Dallas, Texas, on a trip designed to build support for his re-election. Kennedy, Vice President Johnson, and Governor John Connally of Texas, accompanied by their wives, rode in open limousines through the downtown area, waving to the large, cheering crowds. Suddenly, shots rang out. The President, struck in the head and neck, was rushed to a hospital where he was shortly pronounced dead. That afternoon, aboard the plane that would carry the President's body back to Washington, United States District Judge Sara T. Hughes administered the presidential oath of office to Lyndon Baines Johnson.

Meanwhile, Dallas police combed the city to find the President's assassin. Within an hour and a half of the shooting, they arrested Lee Harvey Oswald in a Dallas theater. Oswald, a former marine who had once tried to become a Russian citizen, was taken to the city jail. He denied any knowledge of the shootings, but the evidence against him was overwhelming.

Two days later, television cameras were rolling as Oswald was led out of the city jail to be transferred to another facility. Suddenly a local nightclub owner named Jack Ruby stepped forward from the crowd and shot Oswald dead. Millions of Americans witnessed the killing on television.

In Washington, Kennedy's body lay in state at the Capitol rotunda. Hundreds of thousands of people filed past the casket to pay their respects. On Monday, November 25, Kennedy was buried at Arlington National Cemetery in Virginia after a funeral attended by foreign leaders from many parts of the world. They represented grieving people everywhere who had felt the hope for a better tomorrow that the youthful President had inspired in his thousand days in office.

With Mrs. Kennedy on his left and Mrs. Johnson on his right, Lyndon Johnson took the oath of office aboard Air Force One shortly after the assassination of President Kennedy.

SECTION REVIEW

1. (a) Why did the odds seem to be against John Kennedy in the 1960 presidential campaign? (b) When did the tide turn in his favor? (c) What were the results of the election?

2. (a) Why was the Peace Corps established? (b) What was the purpose of the Alliance for Progress?

3. What was the outcome of each of the following? (a) The Bay of Pigs invasion (b) The Berlin crisis (c) The quarantine of Cuba

4. (a) What was the "domino theory"? (b) To what extent had the United States become involved in Vietnam by the end of 1963?

5. (a) Which of President Kennedy's domestic proposals were blocked by Congress? (b) Which of his proposals were passed? (c) What success did the American space program enjoy during the Kennedy administration?

6. (a) What steps were taken by Kennedy in support of civil rights? (b) What civil rights legislation did he propose in 1963? (c) Why was the "March on Washington" organized?

727

Chapter 30 Review

Summary

President Eisenhower's first goal upon taking office in 1953 was to end the war in Korea. After months of negotiations, an armistice was signed in July, 1953, dividing North and South Korea at the 38th parallel.

Although the Korean War was concluded, cold war tensions continued. Eisenhower's Secretary of State, John Foster Dulles, took a firm stand against the Soviet Union and formulated a policy of massive retaliation to deter Communist aggression. The NATO alliance was strengthened in the 1950's, and when the French withdrew from Indochina in 1954 the United States offered to help South Vietnam.

In 1956 a conflict between Egypt and the forces of Israel, Great Britain, and France created an international crisis that led to strained relations between the United States and its Western allies. Cold-war tensions also flared in Europe in 1956 when a Hungarian revolt against Soviet domination was brutally crushed. Two years later the Soviet leader, Nikita Khrushchev, demanded that the city of Berlin be turned over to the Communists. When the Western powers took a strong stand against such an action, Khrushchev backed down and agreed to a summit conference. Tensions increased again in 1960, when a United States reconnaissance plane was shot down over Soviet territory.

The Eisenhower presidency was a time of unprecedented prosperity and change in America. The population grew dramatically and millions of Americans moved from the eastern states to the West. Meanwhile, thousands of families abandoned the cities for homes in suburban communities.

At the same time, the growth of the civil rights movement was bringing hope to black Americans. The Supreme Court ruled against school segregation in 1954, and a new Civil Rights Act was passed in 1957. Civil rights leaders began organizing boycotts and demonstrations to protest racial discrimination.

The presidential election of 1960 brought John F. Kennedy to the White House. This new President was soon confronted with cold war realities when an American-backed invasion of Cuba ended in failure. The presence of Soviet missiles on the island led to another confrontation — this one with the Soviet Union in 1962. In Europe, tensions over Berlin flared once again; in Southeast Asia, guerrilla war in South Vietnam led to increased American involvement.

At home, Kennedy was largely unsuccessful in his efforts to get legislation through Congress. The government did become more active, however, in safeguarding the rights of all Americans. Tragically, an assassin's bullet ended Kennedy's presidency in November, 1963.

Vocabulary and Important Terms

1. massive retaliation
2. brinkmanship
3. Battle of Dien Bien Phu
4. Eisenhower Doctrine
5. automation
6. Landrum-Griffin Act
7. gross national product
8. baby boom
9. *Brown v. Board of Education of Topeka*
10. Civil Rights Act of 1957
11. Southern Christian Leadership Conference
12. Peace Corps
13. Alliance for Progress
14. Bay of Pigs invasion
15. Cuban missile crisis
16. domino theory

Discussion Questions

1. (a) What incidents contributed to tension between the United States and the Soviet Union during the Eisenhower and Kennedy administrations? (b) What steps were taken to improve relations between the two nations?

2. (a) Why did the Eisenhower administration adopt a policy of massive retaliation? (b) How, at the same time, did President Eisenhower show his concern about the build-up of nuclear weapons?

3. (a) What was the general economic condition of the United States during Eisenhower's presidency? (b) What special problem did farmers face?

4. (a) Why did many Americans move to suburbs during the 1950's? (b) How were those suburbs different from the suburbs of the 1920's?

5. (a) How did the *Brown* decision differ from the *Plessy v. Ferguson* ruling? (b) Why was ratification of the Twenty-Third and Twenty-Fourth amendments important for black Americans? (c) Describe various actions taken by civil rights leaders to fight discrimination. (d) How effective were those actions?

6. (a) What problem did Cuba pose for the United States during the Eisenhower and Kennedy years? (b) What successes and failures did Kennedy have in dealing with Cuba? (c) What step did he take to improve United States relations with Latin America?

7. (a) How did United States involvement in Vietnam begin? (b) What was the extent of this involvement at the end of Eisenhower's presidency? (c) At the time of Kennedy's assassination?

Relating Past and Present

1. Dwight Eisenhower remained highly popular throughout his eight years as President. Could a President maintain a similar degree of popularity today? Explain your answer.

2. John Kennedy's age and religion were considered liabilities when he began campaigning for the presidency. Is either age or religion a characteristic that the American people consider important in presidential candidates today? What other personal characteristics might be considered either assets or liabilities for a modern-day presidential candidate?

Studying Local History

1. The government-funded road construction program of the 1950's resulted in the building of over 40,000 miles of four-lane highways. What highways, if any, were built in your region as part of this program? What impact did these highways have on your community?

2. The 1960 presidential election was one of the closest contests in American history. Which candidate captured the electoral votes of your state? Try to find out the reasons for that candidate's popularity among your state's voters.

Using History Skills

1. *Reading source material.* Study the description of Peace Corps service on page 721. If you were to consider joining the Peace Corps, would you find the letter encouraging or discouraging? Explain your answer.

2. *Analyzing evidence.* Belief in the domino theory contributed to United States involvement in Vietnam. Do research to find out the political status of the countries of Southeast Asia today. To what extent has the domino theory come true?

WORLD SCENE

New Nations in Africa

In the 1950's and 1960's new nations began to emerge from the African colonial empires.

Ghanaian independence. The movement for African independence got its start in the Gold Coast, a British colony in West Africa. The organizer was Kwame Nkrumah (KWAH-mee en-KROO-mah). As a young man, Nkrumah had studied Western political systems in the United States and Britain. When he returned to the Gold Coast in 1949, he founded a political party dedicated to seeking self-government for his homeland.

After the Second World War, Britain developed a plan to free its African colonies gradually. Britain's timetable, however, was too slow for Nkrumah and his nationalist party. In 1950, inspired by the example of Gandhi in India, he organized a campaign of civil disobedience in the Gold Coast.

Full independence was finally granted in 1957. At that time the former colony was renamed Ghana (after an ancient African kingdom) and Nkrumah was elected president. Some leading black Americans, including W. E. B. Du Bois, later moved to Ghana to show their support for the new country.

Algerian independence. In the hundred years that France had controlled Algeria, the colony became the home of over a million settlers of European descent. The settlers controlled much of the wealth and property in Algeria, which had a Muslim majority.

When widespread demonstrations broke out against French rule in 1945, troops killed more than a thousand Algerians in an effort to restore order. To appease the Muslim population, the French government in 1947 made Algeria formally a part of France and extended French citizenship to all Algerians.

This tactic only briefly restored calm. In 1954, nationalists led another uprising. When European settlers became the target of terrorist attacks, France sent 500,000 troops to Algeria to stop the violence. A ferocious civil war followed.

Dissatisfaction with the government's conduct of the war led French settlers and some army officers to take control of Algeria in 1958 — an action which constituted rebellion against France. The resulting crisis brought General Charles de Gaulle to power in France. De Gaulle moved swiftly to suppress the rebellion and negotiate an end to the war. Peace talks began in 1961, and a year later Algeria was granted independence. This conclusion to the years of struggle was followed by an exodus of the vast majority of Europeans from Algeria.

CHAPTER 31

The Turbulent Johnson Years

1963 – 1968

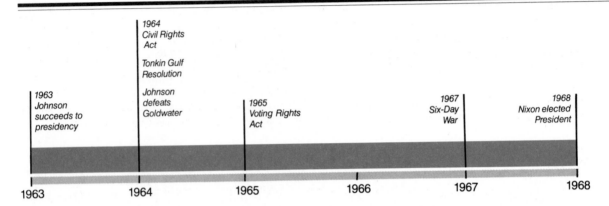

1964
Civil Rights
Act

Tonkin Gulf
Resolution

1963
Johnson
succeeds to
presidency

Johnson
defeats
Goldwater

1965
Voting Rights
Act

1967
Six-Day
War

1968
Nixon elected
President

1963   1964   1965   1966   1967   1968

CHAPTER OUTLINE

1. Johnson becomes President.

2. The United States confronts problems abroad.

3. The nation elects a new President.

The torch of national leadership had now passed to Lyndon Baines Johnson. "All I have I would have given gladly not to be standing here today," he said in his first address to Congress, five days after the assassination. He pledged to carry out President Kennedy's policies. Where Kennedy had earlier said, as he listed his goals, "Let us begin," Johnson now said, "Let us continue."

The new President, born in 1908 in Texas, had greater experience as a legislator than any previous Chief Executive. His father, a schoolteacher and a farmer, had also served as a state legislator. As a boy, Johnson fell in love with politics, often sitting at his father's side in the Texas House.

Lyndon Johnson was first elected to Congress in a special election in 1937, campaigning as an ardent supporter of Franklin Roosevelt. In 1948 he ran for the Senate and won by 87 votes, thus acquiring the teasing nickname "Landslide Lyndon." Quickly making his mark in the Senate, he was named Democratic whip (assistant leader) while still serving his freshman term.

Johnson became known for his skill at lobbying members and for his ability in getting bills passed. If anyone could obtain passage of Kennedy's domestic legislation, people commented, surely it was Johnson. LBJ's unmatched knowledge of government in general, and of Congress in particular, were reassuring to the grief-stricken American people.

1 Johnson Becomes President

Lyndon Johnson's legislative ability had won him the respect of colleagues in both parties. Now the new President turned to Congress, which responded in the next few months by passing the most far-ranging social programs since those of the New Deal.

The Warren Commission investigates the Kennedy assassination. One of Johnson's first steps was to appoint a special commission to investigate the circumstances of the Kennedy assassination. Chief Justice Earl Warren headed the panel, which examined more than 500 witnesses and reviewed the reports of the FBI and other law-enforcement agencies. The Warren Commission, as the panel came to be called, concluded that Lee Harvey Oswald had assassinated Kennedy and that there was no conspiracy behind either the assassination or the murder of Oswald by Jack Ruby (page 727).

The commission's work was almost immediately criticized and questioned. According to opinion polls, many Americans believed that the full story behind the assassination was not yet known. Public suspicion that there had been some sort of conspiracy behind the assassination remained widespread. In 1979 the investigation was reopened. A House committee found evidence to support charges that more than one assassin had fired at Kennedy. The committee did not, however, draw any conclusions about who the other assassin or assassins might have been.

Lyndon Johnson, assuming leadership after the assassination of President Kennedy, moved with poise and confidence to pull the shocked nation together.

Johnson tackles the nation's economic problems. The unfinished business of the Kennedy administration included a proposed tax cut which had been opposed as inflationary by influential members of Congress. Where Kennedy had failed to bring about its passage, Johnson succeeded. Called the Revenue Act of 1964, it reduced tax rates, giving the economy an important boost. Under its impact, the nation continued to enjoy the long period of economic growth that had begun after the Second World War.

In trying to control inflation, Johnson, like Kennedy, took an interest in the union contracts of the nation's major industries. He tried to talk leaders of business and labor into keeping prices and wages from rising rapidly. In addition, he urged the Federal Reserve Board to limit the loans it made to member banks. Johnson hoped this measure would also help to keep inflation in check.

Congress passes the Civil Rights Act of 1964. One of the most significant laws

A skilled political leader, Johnson persuaded Congress to approve many of the programs Kennedy had proposed, as well as legislation of his own. Some Americans questioned the rapid changes taking place.

"Hope I know where we're goin'."

passed under Johnson's leadership was the Civil Rights Act of 1964. This legislation had been proposed by Kennedy the year before (page 726) but had not yet been taken up by Congress at the time of his death. In his first address to Congress, Johnson urged its passage. "We have talked long enough in this country about equal rights," he said. "We have talked for a hundred years or more. It is time now to write the next chapter — and to write it in the books of law."

The civil rights bill passed the House of Representatives easily, but it ran into trouble in the Senate. Making use of the Senate's traditional policy of allowing unlimited debate on any topic, a number of southern senators attempted to kill the bill by dragging out the debate so long that the supporters of civil rights legislation would give up trying to bring the measure to a vote. This tactic is called a *filibuster.* Opponents of the bill kept up the filibuster for 83 days. By the end of that time, Johnson and his backers in Congress had managed, through tireless effort, to convince the necessary two thirds of the Senate to close debate by imposing *cloture.* The cloture rule, rarely used, limits debate on a matter under consideration. Once administration supporters succeeded in applying cloture, they were able to get a vote on the bill within days. It passed by a wide margin. "Stronger than all the armies," observed Illinois Senator Everett Dirksen, "is an idea whose time has come."

The Civil Rights Act of 1964 was one of the most far-reaching laws ever passed by Congress. Among its most important provisions, it (1) prohibited discrimination in public places such as theaters, restaurants, and hotels; (2) insisted on identical voting requirements for blacks and whites in all states; and (3) prohibited discrimination on the basis of race or sex by all employers, unions, and employment agencies engaged in interstate commerce. The new law also offered financial aid to school districts that needed help in beginning desegregation programs and required that federal funds be denied to districts practicing segregation.

Johnson calls for a war on poverty. In addition to pressing for civil rights, President Johnson sought to bring about yet another social revolution — the elimination of poverty in the United States. In his first State of the Union address, delivered to Congress on January 8, 1964, the President announced, "This administration today, here and now, declares unconditional war on poverty in America." One part of this "war" was an economic policy designed to stimulate growth in the nation's economy as a whole. Johnson also asked Congress to pass legislation aimed at providing direct help to impoverished Americans. "Our task," he said, "is to help replace their despair with opportunity."

The Economic Opportunity Act of 1964, passed by Congress at the President's urging, established an Office of Economic Opportunity to administer a billion-dollar social spending program. The act provided for the creation of the Job Corps, an agency charged with training and finding employment for young people aged sixteen through twenty-one. The act also organized Project Head Start, an effort to provide preschool educational opportunities for disadvantaged children. Other programs instituted under the Economic Opportunity Act included VISTA (Volunteers in Service to America), which created a domestic Peace Corps, and the Community Action Program, which provided federal grants to states and localities for antipoverty programs of their own design. As he signed the act into law, the President declared that "for the first time in all the history of the human race, a great nation is able to make, and is willing to make, a commitment to eradicate poverty." A food-stamp program, designed both to provide food for the needy and to make use of the agricultural surpluses, was also enacted in 1964.

Johnson is elected President. While the administration's efforts to eliminate racial discrimination and poverty were applauded by many Americans, the programs also aroused strong opposition. In July, 1964, one of Johnson's chief critics in Congress

In 1964, Congress set up the Head Start program to provide preschool children with rewarding play and learning activities.

won the Republican presidential nomination. Senator Barry Goldwater of Arizona was chosen on the first ballot and selected as his running mate William Miller, a congressman from New York.

Goldwater opposed Johnson's domestic policies on the ground that the federal government had no constitutional right to undertake social programs like the war on poverty or to enact civil rights laws. Such programs, he argued, if they were undertaken at all, should be the concern of state and local goverments. Furthermore, Goldwater maintained that most of the Democrats' social programs were infringements on individual liberty. He criticized what he called the "me-tooism" of many members of his own party — people who, in his view, were practically indistinguishable from the Democrats. He promised to offer the American people "a choice, not an echo."

In August the Democrats, meeting in Atlantic City, quickly nominated Lyndon Johnson. His running mate was Senator Hubert H. Humphrey of Minnesota. Humphrey had first come to national attention during the Democratic convention of 1948, when he fought for a civil rights plank in the party platform. The 1964 convention adopted a platform endorsing the policies of Kennedy and Johnson, and saluted the President for the notable legislative victories of his nine months in office.

Goldwater could not overcome the belief, held by many people, that he was an extremist. He had proclaimed in his acceptance speech, "Extremism in defense of lib-

erty is no vice. And . . . moderation in pursuit of justice is no virtue." There was a widespread perception also that if elected, Goldwater might be too likely to rely on military force, even on the use of nuclear weapons. To the Republican slogan, "In Your Heart, You Know He's Right," the Democrats retorted, "In Your Heart, You Know He Might."

In November, Johnson swamped Goldwater, capturing 61 percent of the popular vote. In the electoral college Johnson received 486 votes compared to Goldwater's 52. The senator carried only his home state and five southern states.

Swept into office with the Johnson landslide was the most lopsidedly Democratic Congress since the days of the New Deal. Democrats outnumbered Republicans by 155 in the House and 38 in the Senate. Johnson interpreted the election results as a "mandate for unity" as well as for his vision of a strong federal government.

Barry Goldwater, defeated in the 1964 race for President, later returned to the United States Senate where he served with distinction.

On the Campaign Trail

The political journalist Theodore H. White won wide acclaim for his book on the 1960 presidential campaign. White also covered the 1964 presidential race, and in the following account describes an exciting day in the campaign of Lyndon Johnson.

Lyndon Johnson campaigning

In every campaign, as politicians know, there can come an unexplained . . . jump of attention when the crowds surge into the streets to cheer their candidate and give him love. It happened to Eisenhower in late September of 1952. It happened to Kennedy the first week in October of 1960. It happened to Lyndon Johnson on Monday, September 18, 1964. His crowds, as I say, had been good and growing throughout September. But on the last weekend of September the Warren Commission issued its massive report. On Sunday afternoon the great television networks devoted hours to it; Monday-morning papers throughout the nation bannered the report, tearing open the scarcely healed wounds in the emotions of the American people. . . . It was as if the nation hungered to see a President, real, live, healthy, in the flesh — as much as the President hungered to see them.

Lyndon Johnson had read the report himself on his ranch in Texas on Saturday and Sunday, September 26th and 27th; had flown back to Washington that night; and had risen early on Monday, September 28th, to give a day to campaigning in New England.

He arrived at the airfield in Providence, Rhode Island, at 9:30 A.M. on a cool fall day, and already some 3,000 people were at the airport, surging against the wire fence,

girls squealing, children crying in the crush, babies held aloft, and boys chanting the particularly New England chant of "Two-four-six-eight, Who-do-we-appreciate?" The President's face suddenly illuminated. It was as if someone had turned the current on in the house. He paused only briefly to hug ninety-seven-year-old ex-Senator Theodore Green . . . and then strode directly to the wire fences. On the trip up, he had complained to the newsmen about their reporting of crowd reaction. Now he hailed them . . . as he grabbed hands . . . and said, "How's that for crowd reaction?"

Johnson launches the Great Society. On Inauguration Day, Lady Bird Johnson, the President's wife, held the Bible as her husband took the oath of office — the first time a woman had participated in the swearing-in ceremony. In his address, President Johnson asked Congress to pass legislation to implement his plan for what he termed the Great Society — a phrase he had introduced the previous year. He had said,

"We have the opportunity to move not only toward the rich society and the powerful society, but upward to the Great Society." The goals of Johnson's crusade went beyond efforts to eradicate poverty and racial discrimination. They also included medical insurance for elderly Americans, immigration reform, federal assistance to education, urban housing projects, and the elimination of pollution.

With Johnson's active urging, Congress approved vast new and expanded undertakings. (1) Over $3 billion was appropriated for aid to the nation's public and parochial schools and for colleges and universities. (2) The Medicare bill, which provided medical insurance for people over 65, was passed, and Social Security taxes were increased to cover the cost. (3) The nation's immigration policy, which had, since 1924, favored immigrants from northern Europe, was replaced by a system that treated all nations equally. Under the new policy, immigration from countries in the Western Hemisphere was restricted for the first time. (4) Over $7 billion was set aside to finance urban-renewal and public-housing programs. The President appointed Robert C. Weaver, the first black American to hold a Cabinet position, as head of the newly created Department of Housing and Urban Development. (5) The amount of money to be spent on federal antipoverty programs was doubled.

This graph shows immigration from 1900 to 1980. During which decade did immigration reach a peak?

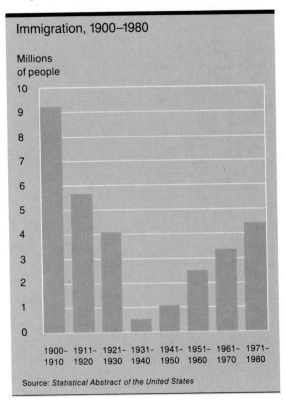

Immigration, 1900–1980

Millions of people

Source: *Statistical Abstract of the United States*

Johnson attained one legislative goal after another: a highway-beautification program (of special interest to Mrs. Johnson); traffic- and highway-safety programs; anti-pollution programs; a model-cities program (to rejuvenate urban communities); and others. The Speaker of the House, John McCormack of Massachusetts, who had been an early New Dealer, said he saw the outpouring of new laws as "realized dreams" of long ago.

The Voting Rights Act of 1965 is passed. One of the most pressing civil rights issues was the denial of suffrage to black voters in some areas of the South. Civil rights legislation had been passed in 1957 and 1960 to protect the right to vote. The procedures specified in those laws had proved too cumbersome, however, to be effective. Another measure removing an impediment to black suffrage — and to that of poor white people — was the ratification in 1964 of the Twenty-Fourth Amendment (page 725).

Recognizing the power of the vote as a key to advancing civil rights, Martin Luther King, Jr., announced his intention of launching a voter-registration drive in the South. King, awarded the 1964 Nobel Peace Prize for his work in promoting nonviolent social change, now had additional prestige. He chose to begin his work in Selma, Alabama, a city in which blacks formed a majority of the population but only a tiny percentage of registered voters. When they met violent resistance, King and his followers decided to march from Selma to Montgomery, the state capital, in protest against this violation of their rights.

To assure the safety of the marchers, President Johnson placed the Alabama National Guard under federal authority and charged it with the responsibility of keeping the peace. On that same evening, March 15, 1965, Johnson addressed a joint session of Congress and lent the full weight of the White House to the Alabama marchers. He appealed to the nation to "overcome the crippling legacy of bigotry and injustice," and asked Congress to pass legislation that became the Voting Rights Act of 1965.

Martin Luther King, Jr., recognized as the leading figure in the civil rights movement, is shown greeting supporters. In his efforts to end segregation and discrimination, King was a devoted advocate of nonviolent methods.

No less than the 1964 Civil Rights Act, the new law had far-reaching effects. It authorized the United States Attorney General to suspend discriminatory voter-registration tests in districts where less than half of the adult population had registered to vote in the 1964 election. It also empowered the Department of Justice to send federal agents to monitor elections and to register qualified black voters in those districts.

After passage of the Voting Rights Act, a wave of enthusiastic voter-registration drives swept across the South. The number of black voters on the rolls increased substantially, and in the next few years black candidates began to be elected to local and state offices. The Voting Rights Act, which originally applied for five years, was renewed by later Congresses and became a powerful symbol of the federal government's determination to protect the civil rights of all Americans.

Riots cause alarm. Although black Americans had made substantial progress by the mid-1960's, they still faced formidable hurdles. Many black people lived in the decaying neighborhoods of the inner city, where good jobs were hard to find. The high unemployment rates angered and discouraged many blacks, who came to believe that they had no chance of escaping poverty.

In the late summer of 1965, only days after the Voting Rights Act was signed into law, resentment and despair erupted into violence in the mostly black area of Los Angeles known as Watts. Rioting and looting raged for six days. Fifteen thousand troops from the National Guard were sent in to quell the uprising, but by the time order was restored 34 people had been killed and 850 wounded. Property damage was estimated to be more than $30 million.

Some Americans were inclined to blame the havoc in Watts on a new generation of black leaders beginning to gain prominence.

Exasperated at what they believed was the slow pace of improvement in American race relations, these leaders had begun to call for fresh ways of achieving better conditions for blacks. They also warned that unless reforms took place, the black ghettos would be breeding grounds for turbulence.

An influential leader in the early 1960's was Malcolm X, born in Omaha, Nebraska. He was an evangelist of the Nation of Islam, a black religious group (commonly known as the Black Muslims) which advocated the separation of the races. A magnetic speaker, Malcolm X preached discipline, self-help, cultural pride, and complete separation from white society. In the last year of his life, Malcolm X changed his mind about black separatism. He began to work with groups favoring integration, but he did not change his insistence that black people must meet violence with violence (not with the passive resistance urged by Martin Luther King and his followers). In February, 1965, Malcolm X was assassinated in a public auditorium in New York City.

The black-power movement attracts attention. Malcolm X was killed before the black militants became prominent in the United States, but he influenced many younger blacks who became leaders of what was called the black-power movement. "Black power" meant different things to different people but, in general, it included the argument that blacks should organize the people in their own communities for political action and should build their own schools and businesses in those communities. There was also a strong feeling that blacks should feel pleasure and satisfaction in their own cultural heritage. Some black militants moved to much more extreme positions, however, advocating the use of violence to achieve their ends and rejecting the goal of racial integration.

Many black leaders opposed the tactics and goals of the black-power movement. They sought to establish a harmonious and "color-blind" society. Martin Luther King and his followers believed that such a society could be established only through non-

violent tactics. Supporters of King's point of view criticized the black-power movement, saying that it stirred up racial hatred, fed people's fears, and threatened to destroy the progress the civil rights movement had made. The vast majority of black Americans supported this more moderate stand. Like the rest of the country, they were shocked by the civil turmoil that broke out in major cities, including Newark, Detroit, Cleveland, Baltimore, and Washington, D.C., in 1966 and 1967.

Republicans do well in the 1966 election. The Democrats' stunning victory in the election of 1964 had been seen by many political observers as a permanent setback for the Republican Party, one from which it might never recover. The mid-term elections of 1966 proved these predictions wrong.

During the campaign, Republican candidates sharply attacked the methods, if not the goals, of the Great Society programs. The Johnson administration, said the critics, was making the federal government too powerful and intrusive. One example often cited was the President's attempt to pass a federal housing law, which would have banned discrimination in the sale or rental of houses and apartments. Many Republicans in Congress opposed the measure, saying that it interfered with people's property rights. Americans, they said, should be able to dispose of their property in any way they saw fit. (Many Democrats agreed with them, and the bill was defeated.)[1] Republican candidates in the 1966 election generally criticized the administration's social programs as ineffective, poorly run, and too expensive.

In November the Republican Party gained 8 new governorships, 47 new seats in the House of Representatives, and 3 new seats in the Senate (including that won by Edward Brooke of Massachusetts, the first black senator since reconstruction). The Democrats did not lose their majority in either the House or the Senate, but President

---

[1]Not until passage of the Civil Rights Act of 1968 was discrimination in the sale and rental of housing prohibited.

The Saturn V Rocket

During the course of Lyndon Johnson's presidency, American scientists at the National Aeronautics and Space Administration (NASA) developed the Saturn rocket. This large multi-stage launch vehicle, they believed, would enable them to meet the goal of the Apollo space program — to land astronauts on the moon before the end of the decade. The first Saturn rocket was successfully tested in 1964 and was used to place unmanned capsules in orbit around the earth. The improved Saturn IB was introduced soon thereafter, and it launched several manned Apollo spacecraft. The last rocket of the Saturn series — the powerful Saturn V — was ready for testing in 1967. The three-stage Saturn V was designed to lift a manned spacecraft into orbit around the earth and then propel it into a trajectory to the moon. The Saturn V soon made it possible for American astronauts to accomplish the extraordinary feat of exploring the surface of the moon.

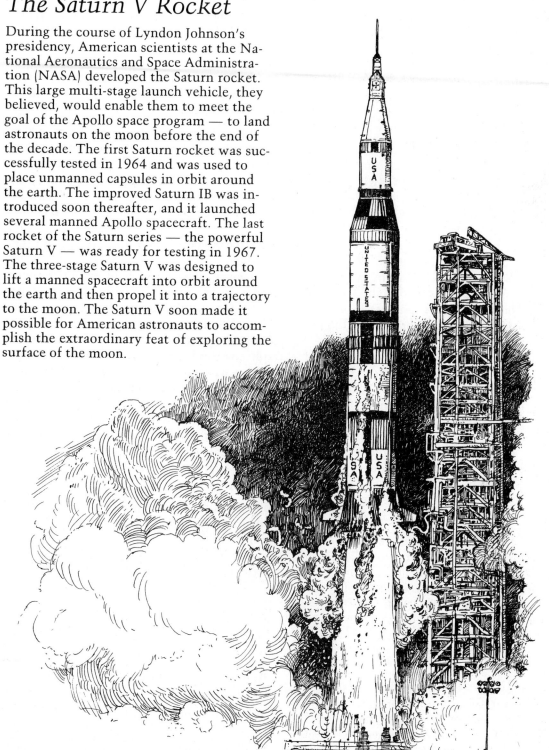

Johnson no longer had the wide margin that had allowed his Great Society programs to pass so easily during the previous term.

The youth movement gains national attention. Another concern facing President Johnson during his last years in office was the growth of dissatisfaction among the country's youth. Only a small minority of young people were involved, but their concerns seemed to reveal something amiss in the land. One part of the movement was made up of those who turned their backs on mainstream American culture. Some of these young people moved to remote rural areas to set up utopian communities; others lived in New York's Greenwich Village, San Francisco's Haight-Ashbury district, and similar places elsewhere. In general, they shared certain ideas, including pacifism, the ideal of universal brotherhood, and an aversion to what they saw as Americans' addiction to material possessions and consumerism. They were not politically active, though most were sympathetic with the political protests of the 1960's.

The more politically significant part of the youth movement was centered on the nation's college and university campuses. Beginning with student involvement in the civil rights movement of the early 1960's, protests grew to include demonstrations against American higher education, the arms race, and what these students considered to be America's failure to live up to its ideals at home and abroad. Increasingly, student protests focused on the conflict in Vietnam.

SECTION REVIEW

1. Vocabulary: *filibuster, cloture.*
2. (a) Why was the Civil Rights Act of 1964 such a significant law? (b) What were the provisions of the Economic Opportunity Act of 1964?
3. (a) Who were the candidates in the presidential election of 1964? (b) What was the outcome of the election?
4. (a) What new social legislation was passed by the 89th Congress? (b) What were the provisions of the Voting Rights Act of 1965?
5. (a) What was the black-power movement? (b) Why did many black leaders oppose this movement?

2 The United States Confronts Problems Abroad

Every aspect of the nation's foreign policy — as well as much of domestic policy — eventually was overshadowed by the issue of American involvement in Vietnam. Even as the Vietnam War grew wider, however, dramatic events elsewhere also occupied national attention.

China breaks with the Soviet Union. A remarkable and unheralded turn in world affairs during the 1960's was the growing strain between the Soviet Union and China, the major Communist powers. The two nations had been allied since China's revolution in 1949, and China had accepted massive economic and military aid from the Russians. By the early 1960's, however, the two nations were publicly criticizing each other — the Chinese charging that the Soviet Union had drawn too close to the United States, the Russians denouncing the Chinese as brutal Stalinists. The Sino-Soviet split, as the break between these two countries was called, was of enormous importance because it weakened the Soviet Union's domination of the Communist world and gave the United States the chance to play off one Communist power against the other.

France withdraws its military forces from NATO. At the same time that this promising opportunity came up, tension also developed among the Western powers. This tension placed a strain on the Atlantic alliance, which had been the basis of American foreign policy since the late 1940's.

In 1958, General Charles de Gaulle came to power in France. An ardent nationalist, De Gaulle resented American and British domination of the NATO alliance and sought to increase the power and prestige of his own country. In 1964, France established diplomatic relations with China and broke with the United States and Great Britain over many of the policies they advocated in the United Nations. De Gaulle also strongly criticized the American presence in Vietnam. In 1966, he withdrew French

The Six-Day War of 1967 resulted in a decisive Israeli victory. Israel's fighter-bombers quickly established mastery of the air.

forces from NATO and insisted that NATO military installations be removed from French soil.

The United States intervenes in the Dominican Republic.

During the Johnson years, relations between the United States and the Soviet Union were somewhat more relaxed than in the recent past. Nevertheless, a concern of the United States was the possibility of communism taking hold in Latin America. American leaders were determined to block efforts of the Soviet Union — or its ally, Cuba — to sow the seeds for Communist revolution in the Western Hemisphere.

In April, 1965, a revolt broke out in the Dominican Republic, a Caribbean island nation. Fearing that Communists might seize power if the Dominican Republic were left in chaos, Johnson sent more than 22,000 marines to restore order there. Soon afterward, a peacekeeping force established by the Organization of American States brought about a ceasefire and the election of a government in June, 1966.

Johnson's intervention in the Dominican Republic was denounced as highhanded by many people in the United States as well as in Latin America. They insisted that the United States had deprived the Dominican Republic of its right to determine its own form of government.

War breaks out in the Middle East.

World tensions increased in 1967 with the third Arab-Israeli war in twenty years. In the spring of 1967, Egypt demanded that United Nations peacekeeping troops be withdrawn from its border with Israel. The Egyptians also closed the vital Gulf of Aqaba to Israeli ships.

On June 5, Israel launched a surprise attack on the airfields of Egypt, Syria, and Jordan, almost completely destroying those nations' air forces. The United States announced that it did not intend to enter the hostilities, but President Johnson immediately placed military forces on alert in case Soviet intervention on the side of the Arab nations made American action necessary. For the first time, the "hot line" — the direct telephone link between Moscow and Washington — was used as Johnson and the Soviet leaders assured each other that they did not wish to enter the war.

By June 10, Israel had defeated the Arab nations, occupying Egyptian, Syrian, and Jordanian territory. The conflict became known as the Six-Day War. Its swift and decisive conclusion, however, was not the end of the strife between Israel and its Arab neighbors. The humiliating defeat only made the Arab world more determined than ever to destroy Israel, which America felt bound to defend.

Communists threaten South Vietnam. All the while, the conflict in Vietnam was increasingly occupying the attention of administration officials. When Johnson took office, there were about 17,000 American military advisers in Vietnam. Reports from South Vietnam suggested that if United States participation were not substantially increased, the Communists would certainly win. Johnson's top advisers, including Secretary of State Dean Rusk and Secretary of Defense Robert S. McNamara, urged him not to abandon the South Vietnamese. Convinced that the domino theory was sound (page 723), they believed America must show its willingness to stop Communist aggression. They were also concerned that if the United States pulled out of Vietnam, the American reputation for reliability as an ally would suffer, seriously affecting the country's foreign policy all over the world.

Many people in the United States and elsewhere called on Johnson to end the war by supporting the establishment of a coalition government in South Vietnam. In such a regime, they said, Vietnam's disagreements could be settled politically rather than by force. The President, however, recalling the history of Eastern Europe after World War II, was concerned that such an arrangement might quickly end in a Communist-dominated government for South Vietnam. He therefore rejected the idea.

Johnson became more and more convinced that further military assistance to South Vietnam was necessary, but he wanted popular and bipartisan support for this commitment. He waited for the right moment, and in the summer of 1964 the time came, just as the presidential election campaign was opening.

Congress passes the Tonkin Gulf Resolution. On August 4, two United States destroyers were attacked by North Vietnamese gunboats in the Gulf of Tonkin, off the coast of North Vietnam. That evening, President Johnson reported the incident on national television. He announced that retaliatory air strikes would be conducted against North Vietnam and called on Congress to authorize him to take whatever further action might be required. His handling of the incident met with broad public support. Johnson did not reveal that South Vietnamese patrol boats, assisted by the United States, had attacked North Vietnamese coastal islands only hours before the American destroyers were hit.

On August 7, 1964, Congress passed the Tonkin Gulf Resolution, which empowered the President to take "all necessary measures to repel any armed attack against the forces of the United States and to prevent further aggression." The vote on the meas-

This map shows the countries of Southeast Asia at the time of the Vietnam War.

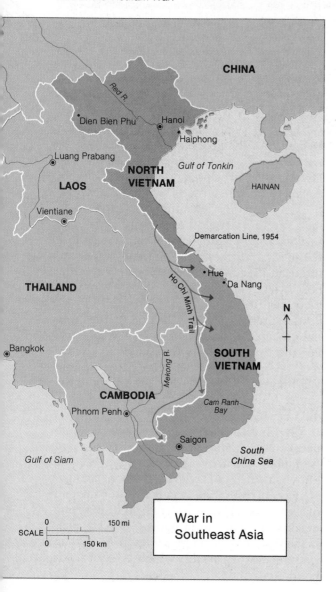

War in Southeast Asia

At Tuesday lunch meetings, President Johnson and his top advisers — the "Tuesday Cabinet" — discussed the situation in Vietnam.

ure was overwhelming — 416–0 in the House and 88–2 in the Senate. Thus, the President was authorized to continue America's military effort in Vietnam.

American involvement in Vietnam grows. During the 1964 presidential campaign, Lyndon Johnson made it clear that he did not wish to broaden the war. He said, "We are not about to send American boys nine or ten thousand miles from home to do what Asian boys ought to be doing for themselves." Shortly after the election, however, Communist gains in South Vietnam caused him to expand the role of the United States. The number of American advisers in the country was increased, reaching 23,000 by the end of 1964. In February, 1965, following Viet Cong attacks on American barracks, Johnson ordered bombing raids against North Vietnamese supply routes and military installations. Shortly, American ground combat troops were sent into action.

American military strategists expected that the escalation of United States military involvement and the heavy bombing of North Vietnam would not only hurt the enemy militarily but destroy the country's morale. That expectation proved false. By mid-1966, 265,000 American troops were on duty in South Vietnam, and the North had endured heavy bombing for over a year. Secretary of Defense McNamara, returning from a visit to Vietnam, reported to the President that the determination of the highly disciplined Communists seemed only to have increased.

Many Americans question Johnson's Vietnam policies. At the time of the Tonkin Gulf Resolution, there was widespread support for Johnson's handling of the Vietnam situation. As the country became more deeply enmeshed in Vietnam, however, criticism of administration policy began to grow. Some people became convinced that the United States had no right to be intervening

By the end of President Johnson's term of office, nearly half a million American soldiers were stationed in South Vietnam. Here, American helicopters remove Vietnamese civilians from a combat zone.

in what they said was a civil war. The Vietnamese, they argued, should be left to settle their conflict themselves. Other critics pointed to the corruption and apparent unpopularity of the South Vietnamese government or to the difficulty of judging progress in a guerrilla war. Still others noted that the rising cost of the war was diverting money away from Great Society programs and fueling inflation at home.

Many people, on the other hand, criticized Johnson's handling of the war because they believed the administration was not pressing hard enough for victory. If the full military might of the United States were turned on North Vietnam, they insisted, the Communists could be brought quickly to the bargaining table and the killing would be over. Johnson, calling these critics "hawks," feared that such a policy might

lead to war with China — as had happened during the Korean conflict (page 701).

The administration tried in a number of ways to end the fighting. Although Johnson had rejected the idea of allowing South Vietnam to be ruled by a coalition government, he sought to negotiate a settlement with the North Vietnamese. At Christmastime, 1965, he announced that he was mounting a "peace offensive." As a goodwill gesture, he called a halt to the bombing of the North and announced that the United States would work to find a means to begin peace talks. After more than a month, there was no response from the North Vietnamese, and the bombing was resumed.

Another peace effort in February, 1967, met with no greater success. The North Vietnamese refused to negotiate as long as

American troops remained in Vietnam, and the United States government regarded this condition as unreasonable. The North Vietnamese also turned down Johnson's offer of an enormous aid program for Southeast Asia. The fighting, meanwhile, went on. By the end of 1967, almost half a million Americans were on duty in Vietnam.

The Tet offensive is a turning point. In an attempt to strengthen support for the anti-Communist government of South Vietnam both at home and abroad, the United States pressed for elections to establish a representative form of government. In September, 1967, voters in South Vietnam approved a new constitution and elected a new president, General Nguyen Van Thieu (nuh-WIN van TYOO).

Despite increasing opposition at home, Johnson and most of his advisers believed at this point that the war could be won. With the combination of a government that gave an image of democracy and with continued American military aid, they maintained, the South Vietnamese would have both the morale and the strength to defeat their Communist opponents.

The administration's optimism stemmed, in part, from reports that were being sent by General William Westmoreland, the American commander in Vietnam. These reports were passed along to the American public, with the assurance that there was "light at the end of the tunnel." The hope was shattered early in 1968, when the Communists launched the strongest offensive of the war.

During the Vietnamese New Year holiday, called Tet, a truce had traditionally been observed by both sides. For this reason, American and South Vietnamese troops had their guard down when, in January, 1968, the Communists launched surprise attacks on some thirty South Vietnamese cities. The Communists paid dearly for the Tet offensive and soon lost the areas they had taken. The costly battles, nevertheless, had a tremendous psychological impact on the American people.

Military and government leaders were shocked and embarrassed by this demonstration of the Communists' ability to mount a sustained, coordinated assault. General Westmoreland, responsible for the optimistic reports that had recently flowed from his headquarters in Saigon, was soon relieved of his command. In March, 1968, the Senate Foreign Relations Committee held televised hearings on the war, examining closely its conduct and purpose. The President himself was beginning to conclude that the United States would have to find some way of withdrawing its forces from Vietnam.

SECTION REVIEW

1. Describe the significance for the United States of the split between the Soviet Union and China.
2. (a) What steps led to the outbreak of the Six-Day War? (b) Which nations took part in the war? (c) What was the outcome?
3. (a) Why did President Johnson's top advisers urge him to keep American troops in Vietnam? (b) Why did the Johnson administration reject calls for the establishment of a coalition government in South Vietnam? (c) What was the Tonkin Gulf Resolution?
4. What reasons did administration critics give for their belief that the United States should withdraw from Vietnam?
5. (a) What was the Tet offensive? (b) What effects did it have?

3 The Nation Elects a New President

The year 1968, which began so violently in Vietnam, would prove to be the stormiest of a stormy decade. Amid the agony of a foreign war and growing domestic unrest, a presidential election was being conducted at home.

Johnson is challenged in the presidential primaries. Early in January, 1968, Eugene McCarthy, a Democratic senator from Minnesota, announced that he was a candidate for the presidency. To try to take the nomination from a President of one's own party, as the senator was doing, was almost unheard of. An outspoken foe of Johnson's Vietnam policy, McCarthy entered the New Hampshire presidential primary and won an astounding 42 percent of the vote. President Johnson, who had not yet announced his candidacy and had not campaigned, actually won the primary with about 48 percent of the vote. Nonetheless, McCarthy's showing was read by almost everyone as a defeat for the President. A challenge to Johnson's renomination clearly had a chance of success. A few days later, Robert F. Kennedy, brother of the slain President and now a senator from New York, also declared his candidacy for the Democratic nomination. Like McCarthy, Kennedy criticized the President's conduct of the war in Vietnam.

Johnson withdraws from the presidential race. Following the Tet offensive, Johnson had asked his advisers for a full-scale review of American policy in Vietnam. The conclu-

sions they drew were very different from those on which Johnson had earlier based his policy decisions. Far from being close to victory, he now was told, the United States could not hope to gain its objectives in the war without sending another 206,000 American troops to Vietnam. To fail to send them could result in military reverses or in an indefinite continuation of the agonizing struggle. To provide the men, however, would require mobilizing reserve units and making heavy new demands on the public just when protests against the war were becoming more heated.

Johnson reached a momentous decision: the United States must find a way to wind down the war. He would aim again to open negotiations with the North Vietnamese, although he emphasized that the outcome must not be "peace at any price."

On the night of March 31, 1968, Johnson went on national television to announce that as a prelude to peace negotiations, the bombing of North Viet-

Eugene McCarthy's surprise showing in the New Hampshire primary helped persuade President Johnson not to run for re-election in 1968.

nam was to be stopped (except in any area where the enemy was continuing to build up its troops and supplies). Then, in grim tones, he announced his decision to withdraw, for the good of the country, from the presidential race. "I have concluded," he said, "that I should not permit the presidency to become involved in the partisan divisions that are developing in this political year. Accordingly, I shall not seek, and I will not accept, the nomination of my party for another term as President."

Johnson stepped out of the race to help emphasize the sincerity of his wish to end the war. No doubt he also hoped to contribute to restoring an atmosphere of harmony in the country. Possibly he was influenced too by opinion polls suggesting he might not be able to win renomination. Later, he wrote that he had long before decided not to seek re-election. Having suffered a heart attack in 1955, he had a constant fear of being incapacitated in office. He confided, "Whenever I walked through the Red Room and saw the portrait of Woodrow Wilson hanging there, I thought of him stretched out upstairs in the White House, powerless to move, with the machinery of the American government in disarray around him."

Martin Luther King is assassinated. Shortly after Johnson's announcement that he would not run for re-election, the nation was stunned by the assassination of Martin Luther King, Jr., the revered civil rights leader. On the evening of April 4, 1968, he was fatally shot while standing on the balcony of a motel room in Memphis, Tennessee. News that King had been slain touched off rioting in many cities across the country. National leaders pleaded with black rioters not to turn to violence and destruction, but for a time the appeals went unheeded. The rioting continued for a week, at one point coming within two blocks of the White House.

The widespread disorders of the 1960's had led President Johnson in 1967 to appoint a presidential commission, headed by Illinois governor Otto D. Kerner, to investi-

Thurgood Marshall became the first black member of the Supreme Court in 1967. A lawyer best known for winning the *Brown* case (page 717), Marshall served as Solicitor General before being named to the Court.

gate the root causes of urban rioting. The Kerner Commission warned in its report, issued in 1968, that the United States was becoming two societies — one black, one white — "separate and unequal." The Commission proposed increased funding for antipoverty programs as a solution to the festering problem. Many Americans, however, rejected the findings of the Kerner Commission. They believed that tougher law enforcement, not more spending on social programs, was required. The question of how to deal with unrest in America became an important issue as the Democrats and Republicans looked ahead to the 1968 presidential campaign.

Democrats vie for the party's nomination. In late April, Vice President Hubert Humphrey joined the race for the Democratic presidential nomination. He entered too late to participate in the primaries, but his strong support in party organizations at the local level won him delegates in states that did not have primaries. Robert Kennedy and

McCarthy, meanwhile, battled it out in those states that held presidential primaries, moving toward a decisive showdown in California.

Kennedy won the California primary by a 46 to 42 percent margin. As he was leaving a hotel after his victory speech, he was shot. His assassin was Sirhan Sirhan, a Jordanian immigrant who hated Kennedy for his pro-Israel position. The next morning, Kennedy was dead — another shock in a year of shocks for the American people.

After Kennedy's death, some of his supporters decided to support McCarthy while others promoted the candidacy of Senator George McGovern of South Dakota. Neither of these candidates, however, had strong backing at the party convention, which was held in Chicago in late August.

Discord plagues the Democrats. Vice President Humphrey, who had the confidence of most party leaders, easily won the Democratic nomination. He chose as his running mate Senator Edmund Muskie of Maine. The domestic planks of the Democratic platform, basically an endorsement of Great Society programs, caused little discussion within the party.

The most controversial issue at the convention was the party's position on Vietnam. Antiwar delegates, most of whom backed McCarthy or McGovern, sought a platform plank calling for the withdrawal of American troops from Vietnam and the establishment of a coalition government there. Humphrey delegates, on the other hand, supported a platform advocating the holding of peace talks. They argued that the United States could not responsibly withdraw from South Vietnam if the North Vietnamese did not do so at the same time. In the end, the Humphrey position was endorsed by a majority. Nonetheless, the fact that 40 percent of the delegates had voted against it demonstrated the sharp disagreements within the party over Vietnam.

The division in the Democratic Party was reflected in the country as a whole, nowhere more violently than just outside the convention hall, in the streets and parks of Chicago. There, thousands of antiwar protestors had assembled. Irate at the certainty of Humphrey's nomination, some became unruly, taunting the police who were standing guard. Pelted with bricks and bottles, the police struck back, and rioting broke out. Americans watching the convention proceedings on television could hardly believe that the scenes of violence were real. Many people concluded that the police had overreacted; others blamed the demonstrators for having started the fighting. Whatever their opinions about the causes of the rioting, most Americans were deeply concerned about the direction the nation seemed to be taking.

The Republicans nominate Richard Nixon. The chief beneficiary of the divisions within the Democratic Party was the Republican nominee, former Vice President Richard M. Nixon. Nixon had gained the Republican nomination on the first ballot at

This poster from the 1968 presidential campaign urged the election of Republican candidate Richard Nixon.

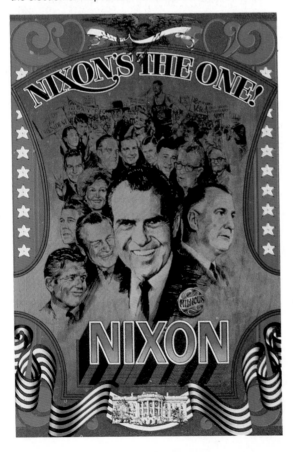

the party's convention in Miami, defeating his chief competitors, governors Ronald Reagan of California and Nelson Rockefeller of New York. The apparent peacefulness and unity of the gathering in Florida contrasted sharply and favorably with the scene at Chicago. The picture of calm gave Nixon and his running mate, Governor Spiro T. Agnew of Maryland, an initial advantage that was revealed by their substantial lead in the early opinion polls.

Nixon campaigned as the candidate who could bring the country together again. He called upon those who longed for restoration of American prestige abroad and harmony at home to vote Republicans into office. Nixon argued that many of Johnson's social programs had been expensive failures. He pledged to take personal charge of a law-enforcement campaign to end the street crime and violence that terrified many citizens. Furthermore, he said, he had a plan to end the war in Vietnam honorably. He refused, however, to reveal any specifics, saying that he did not want to upset the peace negotiations then in progress.

The peace talks had opened in Paris in May, 1968, but quickly went nowhere. The North Vietnamese insisted that the United States cease all acts of war, although they themselves were continuing to press the battle against South Vietnam. Some political observers believed that North Vietnam was holding off serious discussions until after the election, hoping that a new President would be easier to deal with.

George Wallace runs as a third-party candidate. A third candidate for the presidency in 1968 was George C. Wallace, an ex-governor of Alabama, who organized his own American Independent Party. Wallace, who had first gained national attention through his opposition to the desegregation of the University of Alabama, campaigned on a states' rights platform. He hoped to benefit from an expected backlash against urban riots, crime, political protest, and the growth of federal social programs.

Nixon is elected President. As the date for the 1968 election approached, Nixon saw his lead in the opinion polls begin to slip. Humphrey greatly helped his prospects when he broke with the Johnson policy by calling for an end to the bombing of North Vietnam. A month later, only a week before the election, Johnson announced a halt to all air, naval, and artillery bombardment of North Vietnam, adding further impetus to Humphrey's surge.

Nixon, however, held on at the finish. Although he received only 43.4 percent of the popular vote to Humphrey's 42.7, his victory in the electoral college was decisive: 301 to 191. Wallace received 13.5 percent of the popular vote, carrying five states in the Deep South. The narrowness of Nixon's victory was underscored by the fact that the Republicans had failed to win a majority in either house of Congress.

As Lyndon Johnson prepared to return to Texas, he spoke of his pride that a hundred years hence he would be remembered as the "civil rights President" for having placed the nation on the road to racial justice. That he had not been able to attain his goals in Vietnam was a tormenting disappointment to him, denying him a place among America's most admired Chief Executives. He later wrote that every President, deep down, knows that "no living mortal has ever possessed all the required qualifications" to lead the nation. As for his own presidency, "I had given it everything that was in me."

SECTION REVIEW

1. (a) What candidates challenged President Johnson in the 1968 presidential primaries? (b) Who won the Democratic presidential and vice-presidential nominations in 1968? (c) What disagreements arose over the party's official position on Vietnam?
2. (a) Who were the Republican presidential and vice-presidential candidates in 1968? (b) On what issues did the Republican candidates campaign?
3. (a) What was the outcome of the 1968 presidential election? (b) Which party won a majority in both houses of Congress?

Chapter 31 Review

Summary

When Lyndon Johnson succeeded to the presidency in 1963, he took up the unfinished business of the Kennedy administration. A skillful politician, Johnson was able to secure passage of many far-reaching pieces of legislation, including a tax-cut bill and a new civil rights law.

Johnson's landslide victory over Barry Goldwater in the 1964 election provided the President with an opportunity to implement an ambitious program of social legislation. Johnson's goals, in addition to reducing poverty and discrimination, were to provide medical insurance for the elderly, clean up the environment, and improve American education.

The passage of the Voting Rights Act in 1965 was of particular importance to black Americans. This law enabled thousands of black Southerners to register to vote. No law, however, could immediately solve the problems faced by families living in urban slums across the country. The nation was shocked by rioting that broke out in urban ghettos from 1965 to 1967.

At the same time that Johnson was trying to persuade Congress to enact his Great Society program, foreign-policy problems demanded his attention. In Europe, President Charles de Gaulle pulled French forces out of the NATO alliance. In the spring of 1965, Johnson sent American forces to the Dominican Republic to restore order after an outbreak of rioting. When war broke out in the Middle East in June, 1967, United States forces were put on alert.

The most demanding issue that Johnson had to face was American policy in Vietnam. Convinced that the defense of South Vietnam was vital to all of Southeast Asia, Johnson sent large numbers of American combat troops to that nation to try to prevent a Communist take-over. American involvement in Vietnam led to heated debate at home. The presidential election of 1968 provided a forum for opposition to the administration's Vietnam policies. Johnson, faced with challenges for the Democratic nomination by senators Eugene McCarthy and Robert Kennedy, surprised the nation by announcing in March, 1968, that he would not seek re-election.

In the next few months, the nation was shocked by the assassinations of Martin Luther King, Jr., and Robert Kennedy. Vice President Hubert Humphrey won the Democratic presidential nomination, but discord within the party contributed to the victory of the Republican candidate, Richard Nixon, in the 1968 election.

Vocabulary and Important Terms

1. Warren Commission
2. Revenue Act of 1964
3. Civil Rights Act of 1964
4. filibuster
5. cloture
6. Great Society
7. Medicare
8. Voting Rights Act of 1965
9. black power
10. youth movement
11. Sino-Soviet split
12. Six-Day War
13. Tonkin Gulf Resolution
14. Tet offensive
15. Kerner Commission

Discussion Questions

1. (a) What unfinished business did Lyndon Johnson inherit from the Kennedy administration? (b) Which of Kennedy's legislative goals were enacted under Johnson?
2. (a) Through what programs did the Johnson administration attempt to wage war on poverty? (b) On what grounds did Barry Goldwater and other Republican leaders criticize the domestic policies proposed by Lyndon Johnson?
3. (a) Describe the situation of the Republican Party after the 1964 election. (b) To what extent had the Republicans recovered by 1966? (c) What was their standing following the 1968 election?
4. (a) What were the goals of Johnson's Great Society? (b) What social legislation did Congress enact at Johnson's urging?
5. What attempts were made in the 1960's to guarantee the voting rights of black Americans?
6. (a) What obstacles did black Americans face in the mid-1960's? (b) How did the new generation of black leaders differ from earlier civil rights leaders in their efforts to achieve better conditions?
7. (a) During Lyndon Johnson's presidency, what problems did the United States confront in Europe? (b) What problems arose in Latin America? (c) In the Middle East?
8. (a) What factors led to increased American involvement in Vietnam during Johnson's presidency? (b) In what ways was Johnson's handling of the war in Vietnam criticized, and what alternatives did the critics recommend?
9. (a) Why was the Tet offensive regarded as a turning point of the Vietnam War? (b) How had Johnson's perception of American involvement in Vietnam changed by 1968? (c) How did the argument over Vietnam affect the Democratic Party and the election of 1968?

Relating Past and Present

1. By the early 1960's a split had developed between China and the Soviet Union. What is the current status of Sino-Soviet relations? What effect does the relationship between China and the Soviet Union have on the United States today?

2. President Johnson's policies regarding South Vietnam drew criticism both from those who felt the commitment was too great and from those who felt the commitment was not great enough. In what parts of the world does the United States have commitments today, and in what ways, if any, are those commitments criticized by some Americans?

Studying Local History

Find out how the people of your state voted in the presidential election of 1968. What policies of the Johnson administration were widely discussed in your state during the 1968 campaign? Which issues seemed to affect the outcome of the election in your state?

Using History Skills

1. *Reading graphs.* Study the graph on page 736 showing immigration to the United States. (a) Approximately how many people immigrated to the United States in the period from 1970 to 1980? (b) In which decade was immigration at a low point? (c) What factors might explain that decline?

2. *Reading source material.* Study Theodore White's description of the 1964 campaign on page 735. (a) What words would you use to describe Johnson's reception in Rhode Island? (b) What other information would you need to determine accurately Johnson's popularity in that state? (c) What evidence does the account provide concerning President Johnson's relations with reporters?

WORLD SCENE

Communist Repression

In the 1960's the repressive nature of communism was revealed by events in Europe and in Asia.

The invasion of Czechoslovakia. In the decades after World War II, Czechoslovakia had become a satellite of the Soviet Union. The Soviet leadership exercised firm control over the Czech government and used Czechoslovakia's extensive industries to build up the economic strength of the Communist bloc.

Czech discontent grew, and in 1968 reformers managed to install Alexander Dubcek (DOOB-chek) as the party secretary. From his post, Dubcek introduced reforms that promised the Czech people more civil liberties and greater political independence from the Soviet Union. Dubcek did not plan to abandon Communist rule in Czechoslovakia, but he hoped his government could practice what he called "socialism with a human face."

These developments were viewed with alarm by the Soviet rulers in Moscow. When Dubcek refused to curtail his program of reform, the Soviet Union sent an army of 200,000 troops into Czechoslovakia in August, 1968. By the middle of 1969, the Soviet Union had removed Dubcek from office and re-established a tight grip on the Czech Communist Party. For the people of Czechoslovakia, hopes for reform had ended.

The Cultural Revolution in China. The take-over of China by Communist forces in 1949 made Mao Tse-tung the undisputed ruler of that vast land. Mao believed that the Chinese Communist revolution would result in a classless society. Toward that end, and aiming to keep revolutionary fervor high, he devised several economic-development programs. Under one plan, devised in 1958 and known as the Great Leap Forward, the Chinese people were called upon to double industrial production, especially in such key industries as iron- and steel-manufacturing. Hundreds of thousands of small industrial plants requiring substantial hand labor were set up throughout China, but the scheme was a disastrous failure. Workers could not meet production requirements, and the quality of the products was poor.

Influential opponents of the Great Leap Forward denounced Mao's policies. He struck back in 1966 by launching what was called the Cultural Revolution. As part of this movement, Mao unleashed groups of students organized in Red Guards. The Red Guards marched across China, pledging support for Mao's ideas and publicly disgracing officials who were thought to lack proper revolutionary enthusiasm. The resulting turmoil lasted until 1968, when Mao finally called a halt to Red Guard activities.

UNIT 8 REVIEW

Important Dates

1945 United Nations organized.
1947 Marshall Plan adopted.
          Taft-Hartley Act passed.
1949 NATO formed.
          Communists take control of China.
1950 Korean War begins.
1952 Eisenhower elected President.
1953 Korean armistice signed.
1954 Supreme Court decision on school
          segregation.
1955 AFL-CIO formed.
1956 Suez Canal crisis.
          Hungarian uprising.
1957 Eisenhower Doctrine proclaimed.
1959 Landrum-Griffin Act passed.
          Alaska and Hawaii become states.
1960 Kennedy elected President.
1962 Cuban missile crisis.
1963 Nuclear test-ban treaty signed.
          Kennedy assassinated.
1964 Tonkin Gulf Resolution passed.
          Johnson wins presidential election.
1965 Voting Rights Act passed.
1966 France withdraws military forces from NATO.
1967 Six-Day War.
1968 Tet offensive.
          Nixon elected President.

Review Questions

1. (a) What was Truman's containment policy? (b) Through what programs did the Truman administration attempt to carry out containment? (c) Which efforts at containment proved most successful, and why?

2. (a) Why were there many labor strikes in the years immediately following World War II? (b) What labor legislation was passed during the Truman and Eisenhower administrations? (c) What effect did this legislation have on unions? (d) What new problems did organized labor encounter during the 1950's?

3. What was the response of the United States to each of the following? (a) The creation of Israel (b) The struggle between Nationalist and Communist forces in China (c) The Soviet blockade of Berlin (d) The Suez crisis

4. (a) What similarities were there among the domestic proposals put forth by the Truman, Kennedy, and Johnson administrations? (b) What major social programs were enacted during each administration? (c) What criticism was there of these programs?

5. (a) How did Dwight Eisenhower's foreign and domestic policies differ from those of the Democratic Presidents who preceded and followed him? (b) What were the major characteristics of American society during the Eisenhower years?

6. (a) What was the extent of American involvement in Vietnam during the Eisenhower, Kennedy, and Johnson administrations? (b) Why, by 1968, had the Johnson administration begun to reassess America's role in Vietnam? (c) How did the war affect American society?

7. (a) What civil rights legislation was enacted during the 1950's and 1960's? (b) What court decisions and executive orders also advanced the civil rights movement, and in what ways?

Projects

1. Form a committee to find out more about the Eastern European countries that fell under the control of the Soviet Union after World War II. Each member of the committee might choose one country to study. Use the library to find out how that country came under Soviet domination and the degree to which Soviet domination exists there today. Report your findings to the class.

2. Recreate some of the sights and sounds of the 1940's and 1950's. Begin by finding out more about the music, literature, and other aspects of American society in the period after World War II. Share the information with the class by describing trends in music, reading aloud some of the literature, or telling the class about some of the other ways of living that distinguished American society in the period.

3. Write an essay on this topic: "The civil rights movement of the 1950's and 1960's fulfilled the promise of equality found in the Declaration of Independence." You may either agree or disagree with this statement, but be sure to include evidence to support your point of view.

4. President Johnson prided himself on having "out-Roosevelted Roosevelt" in obtaining social-welfare laws from Congress. Write a report in which you compare the domestic legislation enacted during Franklin Roosevelt's and Lyndon Johnson's administrations. Conclude by stating whether you agree or disagree with Johnson's statement and explain why.

5. Relate past and present by discussing as a class the state of American-Soviet relations today. Recall the reasons why relations between the United States and the Soviet Union were strained after World War II and the degree to which those relations have changed in recent years.

9

UNIT

TOWARD A
NEW CENTURY

1969 – 1980's

*We are a powerful force for good. With faith
and courage, we can perform great deeds and take
freedom's next step.*

RONALD REAGAN, *STATE OF THE UNION MESSAGE,* 1984

CHAPTER 32

Crisis in the Presidency

1969 – 1976

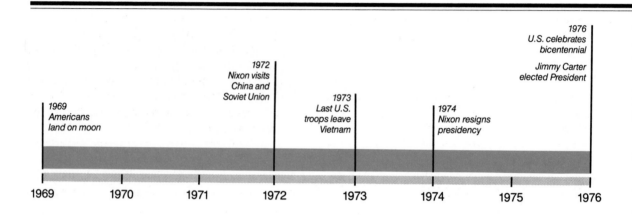

1969
Americans
land on moon

1972
Nixon visits
China and
Soviet Union

1973
Last U.S.
troops leave
Vietnam

1974
Nixon resigns
presidency

1976
U.S. celebrates
bicentennial

Jimmy Carter
elected President

| 1969 | 1970 | 1971 | 1972 | 1973 | 1974 | 1975 | 1976 |

On January 20, 1969, Richard Nixon was inaugurated as the nation's thirty-seventh President. No one in recent American politics had worked harder toward this goal. Born in 1913 in California, Nixon had long been climbing the political ladder. He had long been climbing life's ladder too, for his Quaker parents had struggled constantly to make ends meet for their family of five sons. As a twelve-year-old, Nixon was fascinated and repelled by the corruption of the Harding administration. Nixon's mother remembered the boy's resolve at that time to play a part in public affairs. "I will be an old-fashioned kind of lawyer," he vowed, "a lawyer who can't be bought."

Elected to the House of Representatives in 1946, Nixon attracted national attention soon afterward during the investigation of Alger Hiss. Nixon was elected to the Senate in 1950, and shortly became Vice President, winning on the Republican ticket as Dwight Eisenhower's running mate in 1952 and again in 1956.

An obvious choice as Eisenhower's successor, Nixon was narrowly defeated in the 1960 election by John F. Kennedy. He lost again (more decisively) in a bid for the California governorship in 1962. His political career seemingly over, he moved to New York City to practice law. The allure of politics, however, proved too strong to resist. By 1966, Nixon was making plans that would ultimately bring him to the White House, in a remarkable political comeback.

1 Nixon Tackles Foreign Policy Issues

President Nixon had concluded, as he said in his inaugural, that after the tumultuous presidencies of Kennedy and Johnson, America was suffering from "a fever of words." He declared, "We cannot learn from one another, until we stop shouting at one another." The principal way to lower the national voice appeared to be by finding a solution to the war in Vietnam.

THE VIETNAM WAR

Nixon announces a plan to end the war. Nixon, who had first made his national reputation as a strong anti-Communist, had supported the escalation of United States involvement in Vietnam under Presidents Kennedy and Johnson. By 1968 he believed, however, that the United States was being torn apart by the war and that American troops must be withdrawn. He worked closely with his chief foreign policy adviser, Henry A. Kissinger, a political scientist from Harvard University, to find a way to end the war. Nixon and Kissinger were determined to make an "honorable peace" in Vietnam. The terms under which the United States left Vietnam must not, they maintained, damage America's reputation as a trustworthy ally.

Soon after taking office, Nixon announced his plan for ending American involvement in the war. The United States would pull out its combat forces while South Vietnamese troops would be trained to take over the duties Americans had been performing. This plan came to be called "Vietnamization."

During the next three years, hundreds of thousands of American troops were brought home. By 1972, only 139,000 Americans remained in Vietnam — compared

Richard Nixon took the oath of office as the nation's thirty-seventh President on January 20, 1969. His major goal was settlement of the Vietnam War.

with over 500,000 stationed there when Johnson left office. Nixon also sought to reduce American casualties by ordering United States troops to fight only when under attack or facing the threat of attack.

Vietnamization, nevertheless, presented problems for the Nixon administration. For one thing, the policy did not satisfy those in the United States who demanded the immediate withdrawal of all American troops. In addition, the South Vietnamese were hardpressed to replace the departing American troops. In order to relieve the pressure on the Saigon government, Nixon ordered intensive bombing raids against the Communist forces, which were gradually extending their control over the South Vietnamese countryside.

Cambodia is invaded. American strategists were becoming increasingly worried about the fate of South Vietnam once United States forces were withdrawn. They feared that as the United States reduced its presence, the enemy would become bolder and less willing to negotiate. Nixon decided to take vigorous action. He would seek to cripple the North Vietnamese by striking at their military sanctuaries.

The Vietnamese Communists' presence in neutral Cambodia (map, page 742) had long concerned American and South Vietnamese policy-makers. Communist troops routinely assaulted South Vietnamese targets from Cambodia and then retreated across the border.

In late April, 1970, President Nixon announced that American and South Vietnamese troops had crossed into Cambodia. Their mission was to destroy enemy camps and supply depots. Nixon explained his belief that this action would shorten the war and save American lives, and he promised to withdraw United States troops within two months.

Most Americans supported the President's decision in this matter, but administration critics charged that instead of ending the war, Nixon was now expanding it. During the next month, antiwar demonstrations were held in a number of cities and on college campuses. At Kent State University, in Ohio, student protests ended in tragic violence. The National Guard, sent to the campus to restore order, fired without warning into a crowd of students on May 4 and killed four people. Violence also erupted at Jackson State College in Mississippi, where two students were killed in a clash with state troopers.

Diplomacy and military force are used in efforts to end the war. Throughout this period the United States, North Vietnam, South Vietnam, and the Viet Cong carried on peace talks in Paris, but made little progress toward reaching an agreement. In the spring of 1972, the Communists attempted to break the stalemate by launching a major offensive in the South. The United States responded with massive bombing raids on enemy positions, a naval blockade of North Vietnam, and the mining of Haiphong harbor. By the end of the summer, the Communist invasion had been halted.

At this point, there was some progress in the negotiations. The North Vietnamese seemed to conclude, as a result of the costly offensive, that the time had come to make concessions at the bargaining table. Beginning in late September, 1972, Henry Kissinger and Le Duc Tho (lee duk TOH), the North Vietnamese negotiator, met in Paris for several weeks. In October an agreement seemed imminent, and Kissinger confidently told reporters, "Peace is at hand."

The announcement proved to be premature. Kissinger had not counted on the strong resistance of South Vietnamese President Thieu, who refused to accept the proposed settlement. Thieu objected to provisions permitting North Vietnamese troops to remain in South Vietnam after a cease-fire had been signed. He objected also to the projected establishment of a coalition government in South Vietnam. Thieu feared that creating such a regime would simply be a prelude to a take-over by the Communists. Talks were again suspended, and the fighting went on.

Following Nixon's re-election in November, 1972, negotiations resumed once more in Paris. In mid-December, however, they again broke down, and a decision was reached to bomb Hanoi and Haiphong in order to force the North Vietnamese back to the bargaining table. This was the first time the United States had bombed North Vietnam since 1968. After absorbing enormous destruction, the Communists agreed to resume the talks, and Nixon ordered the bombing raids halted.

A settlement is reached. Meetings resumed in Paris early in January, 1973. It now took only a short time to reach a final settlement. On January 27, the parties agreed to (1) a cease-fire effective immediately and supervised by an international commission; (2) the withdrawal of all American military personnel from Vietnam within sixty days; and (3) the release of all American prisoners. It was also understood that North Vietnamese forces could remain in South Vietnam, and that the United States would continue to supply the Saigon government with economic and military assistance.

Americans count the costs of the war. Thus ended American participation in the longest and most divisive war in the nation's history. Over 56,000 Americans had died in Vietnam, and more than 300,000 others had been wounded. There was widespread feeling in the country that the war had not been handled correctly but no consensus about what alternative policy should have been followed. There was also no ready agreement on how to deal with the thousands of military deserters or with the young men who had left the United States to avoid being drafted.

One immediate result of the Vietnamese conflict was the enactment of the War Powers Act of 1973, passed over President Nixon's veto. The measure was an attempt by Congress to ensure that it would participate in any future commitment of American troops. The act provides that the President, upon deploying American forces abroad, must notify Congress of the action within 48 hours. If within sixty days Con-

Peace negotiators Le Duc Tho and Henry Kissinger shake hands early in 1973 after the United States and North Vietnam agreed on terms to bring the Vietnam conflict to an end.

gress does not approve the deployment, the troops must be withdrawn.

Vietnam falls to the Communists. As it turned out, the Paris peace treaty did not end the war. Both sides in Vietnam expected the fighting to continue after the American forces were withdrawn, and both sides sought to build up their strength. Then, in the early spring of 1975, North Vietnam launched a powerful military offensive. Meeting only weak resistance from the South Vietnamese armed forces and seeing no threat of renewed United States intervention, the North Vietnamese pushed for final victory.

Gerald R. Ford, the new American President, urged Congress to increase military aid to South Vietnam. (American aid to South Vietnam had fallen from $2.3 billion in 1973 to approximately a billion in 1974.) Congress rejected the President's request, regarding the cause as hopeless. It agreed, however, to appropriate $300 million for "humanitarian" aid.

Late in April, as Communist troops approached Saigon, President Ford ordered a pull-out of all Americans still in South Vietnam. American ships and planes were able also to evacuate approximately 130,000 Vietnamese, most of whom came to live in the United States. On May 1, 1975, Viet Cong soldiers raised their flag over Saigon. After decades of fighting, Vietnam became a single nation under a Communist government. Neighboring Laos and Cambodia also came under Communist control.

CHANGES IN FOREIGN POLICY

President Nixon visits China. Even as the Vietnam War was winding down, the Nixon administration was looking for ways to reduce world tensions. The President and Henry Kissinger (who became Secretary of State in 1973) saw the quarrel between the Soviet Union and China (page 740) as an opportunity for the United States to win concessions from both countries. The chief fear of each of the Communist giants, American leaders reasoned, was that the other would draw closer to the United States, leaving one of them dangerously isolated. The Nixon administration decided to open negotiations with both countries. It began using a new word to describe its policy of bringing peace to the world: *détente* (day-TAHNT), a French word that means the relaxing of tensions.

The first phase of the administration's policy of détente was the establishment of diplomatic contact with Communist China. In July, 1971, Kissinger secretly flew to China and met with Premier Chou En-lai. Less than a week later, President Nixon astonished the world by announcing that he

Richard Nixon surprised the world by visiting China in 1972. After being greeted upon his arrival by Premier Chou En-lai, the President inspected Chinese troops.

had accepted an invitation to visit China. "I have taken this action," he said, "because of my profound conviction that all nations will gain from a reduction of tensions and a better relationship between the United States and the People's Republic of China."

President and Mrs. Nixon flew to China early in 1972. On February 27, 1972, after a week of meetings in Peking, President Nixon and Premier Chou issued a joint statement. They had agreed to establish trade relations between their two countries and to allow cultural and scientific exchanges. Because of continuing disagreements over the status of the Nationalist government on Taiwan, the establishment of full diplomatic relations between China and the United States was delayed. Clearly, however, a new era in international relations had begun.

Agreements are reached with the Soviet Union. As Nixon and Kissinger had expected, the Soviet Union was alarmed by the prospect of friendship between the United States and China. To reassure the Russians, Nixon announced that he would fly to the Soviet Union in May, 1972, for a summit conference with Leonid Brezhnev, the Soviet premier.

At the conclusion of their talks, Nixon and Brezhnev signed a number of agreements, the most important of them concerning arms limitations. For a five-year period, the two superpowers would freeze the level of offensive missiles and limit the deployment of defensive missiles to two sites in each country. This agreement was the culmination of the Strategic Arms Limitation Talks (SALT) that had been started in November, 1969. The two leaders also agreed to cooperate on various cultural and scientific projects and to establish closer economic ties.

In June, 1973, Brezhnev came to the United States for further talks with Nixon. The two leaders pledged to continue the SALT talks and reaffirmed earlier agreements. This summit meeting was chiefly symbolic, indicating a continuing commitment to détente. Tension between the United States and the Soviet Union appeared to be lower than at any time since the beginning of the cold war.

The Yom Kippur War threatens world peace. Just when the United States was adjusting to the idea of détente, the world was again catapulted into crisis by events in the Middle East. The uneasy peace that had settled over the region after the Six-Day War (page 741) was shattered on October 6, 1973, when Egyptian and Syrian forces attacked Israeli-held territory. The attacks took place on the eve of Yom Kippur, the holiest day in the Hebrew calendar. The Israelis, taken by surprise, fought stubbornly to defend their country and suffered heavy casualties at first. By mid-October, however, they were on the offensive, pushing back the Syrians in the north and crossing the Suez Canal in the south.

Alarmed at the prospect of another Arab defeat in the Middle East, the Soviet Union threatened to intervene. To counter the threat, Nixon placed American military forces on alert throughout the world. Within 24 hours, the Russians backed down, agreeing to the establishment of a United Nations peacekeeping force in the region. Once again, the fighting in the Middle East had been halted, but still no solution had been found to the long-standing antagonism between Israel and its Arab neighbors.

Arab nations impose an oil embargo. The Arab countries were furious with the United States for giving support to Israel during the Yom Kippur War. In retaliation, Saudi Arabia announced in late October, 1973, that it would no longer sell oil to the United States. The other Arab members of the Organization of Petroleum Exporting Countries (OPEC) quickly followed suit.

The United States, dependent on the Middle East for about 12 percent of its oil, suffered from the oil embargo. Fuel prices rose sharply, and long lines of automobiles formed at service stations, waiting for the limited supplies of gasoline.

The oil embargo was not lifted until March, 1974. In the meantime, the American people began making efforts to reduce the country's dependence on Middle East

759

The Alaska pipeline, built in response to the fuel crisis, carries oil about 800 miles across the state.

2 Nixon Faces Domestic Concerns

During most of his presidency, Richard Nixon was forced to concentrate on international relations. There were, however, absorbing matters on the home front — among them a shining triumph for America's space program.

Americans land on the moon. Early in Nixon's term, the centuries-old dream of reaching the moon became a reality. President Kennedy's pledge that America would put a man on the moon before 1970 was fulfilled. Apollo 11 was launched on July 16, 1969, with Neil Armstrong, Edwin E. "Buzz" Aldrin, Jr., and Michael Collins aboard. Four days later, the lunar landing ship touched down on the moon. As Armstrong stepped onto the moon's surface, he said, "That's one small step for a man, one giant leap for mankind." Aldrin soon joined him. Perhaps a billion people watched the live telecast of the extraordinary event. They saw the Americans plant the Stars and Stripes and leave a plaque reading: "Here men from planet earth first set foot upon the moon, July 1969, A.D. We came in peace for all mankind."

Nixon appoints four Supreme Court justices. During his campaign in 1968, Nixon had made the Supreme Court an issue, charging that several of its rulings in criminal cases had protected the rights of accused persons at the expense of society at large. In June, 1969, Chief Justice Earl Warren retired. To replace him, Nixon appointed Warren E. Burger of Minnesota, who had publicly supported the President's criticisms of the Warren Court. Burger won quick confirmation by the Senate.

In seeking to fill a second vacancy on the Court, however, the President ran into trouble. The Senate refused to approve the first two men he nominated. The President's third choice, Harry A. Blackmun, also a Minnesotan, won unanimous approval in the Senate.

Later in his term, further vacancies enabled Nixon to put Lewis F. Powell, Jr., of

oil. Conservation measures were introduced, new oil reserves were sought, and research was stepped up on finding alternative forms of energy. Energy prices, however, never returned to former levels.

SECTION REVIEW

1. Vocabulary: *détente*.
2. (a) What did Nixon hope to achieve by his Vietnamization policy? (b) Why was that policy difficult to carry out?
3. (a) What steps led to the signing of a settlement ending American involvement in Vietnam? (b) Describe what happened to South Vietnam after American troops were withdrawn.
4. (a) Why did Nixon travel to China in 1972? (b) What agreements did the United States and the Soviet Union reach shortly thereafter?
5. (a) What was the Yom Kippur War? (b) Why did the oil-producing countries of the Middle East impose an oil embargo on the United States?

After landing on the moon, Neil Armstrong and Edwin Aldrin installed scientific instruments, collected moon rocks, and snapped hundreds of photographs.

Virginia and Assistant Attorney General William H. Rehnquist of Arizona on the Supreme Court. These four appointments led to a significant, though by no means drastic, change in the Court's decisions. The Burger Court did not reverse the decisions of the Warren Court, but it tended to interpret the Constitution more strictly, especially on the issue of the rights of persons accused of crimes.

Americans take steps to end pollution. During the Nixon years, a number of steps were taken that would help reshape American life. None was more important than the fight against pollution.

By the late 1960's, environmental issues had become matters of widespread concern in the United States. The majority of Americans now lived close together in cities and suburbs, and there had been harmful effects on the nation's air, water, and land. As people became aware of pollution problems, local, state, and federal governments began to take measures to clean up the environment. In 1970, President Nixon created the Environmental Protection Agency. The EPA had the responsibility of enforcing the growing number of laws to protect the environment.

Amendments to the Constitution are proposed. Another development during Nixon's presidency was a formal recognition of the role young people were playing in American society. The Twenty-Sixth Amendment to the Constitution was ratified in 1971, lowering the voting age to eighteen in all state and federal elections.

In 1972, Congress passed and then sent to the states a proposed Twenty-Seventh Amendment, which came to be called the Equal Rights Amendment, or ERA. Its first and principal article read, "Equality of rights under the law shall not be denied or abridged by the United States or by any state on account of sex." Unlike the Twenty-Sixth Amendment, the ERA met strong opposition. By the end of Nixon's presidency, it had not been ratified by the required three fourths of the states.

Nixon tries to slow down inflation. As always, most domestic problems did not have easy solutions. One of the most troubling problems was that of inflation. The increases in government spending under the Johnson administration — to finance both Great Society programs and the military effort in Vietnam — had created upward pressure on prices.

In 1970, Congress authorized the President to regulate wages and prices if he thought it necessary. This step had never been taken in peacetime, and Nixon opposed it as incompatible with the free enterprise system. By mid-1971, however, the inflation rate had risen to over 6 percent and showed no sign of slowing down. The President faced increasing pressure to take action. On August 15, 1971, he surprised the nation by announcing a ninety-day freeze on wages, prices, and rents. This step became known as Phase I of the President's economic plan. He also proposed tax reductions designed to stimulate the economy.

The second stage in the President's economic plan went into effect late in 1971. Phase II permitted wage and price increases if they were no greater than the increase in productivity, that is, the stepped-up creation of goods and services. Immediately, however, problems arose. In its very first decision, the federal board overseeing wages authorized a 15 percent boost for coal miners. The price board shortly made similar exceptions, and the floodgates of inflation were reopened.

McGovern challenges Nixon in 1972. In July, 1972, the Democratic National Convention gathered in Miami. The party was badly divided, as it had been since 1968. The major candidates for the nomination were former Vice President Hubert Humphrey, Senator Edmund Muskie of Maine, and Senator George McGovern of South Dakota. Alabama governor George Wallace, who had also been a contender, had withdrawn from the campaign in May

after an assassination attempt left him paralyzed from the waist down.

Owing to changes in party rules, the mix of Democratic delegates had changed significantly since the 1968 convention. For the first time, large numbers of women, blacks, and young people served as delegates. The chief beneficiary of the change was George McGovern, a candidate closely identified with the antiwar movement. McGovern was nominated on the first ballot and chose as his running mate Senator Thomas Eagleton of Missouri. The Democratic platform called for the immediate withdrawal of American troops from Vietnam, amnesty for draft resisters, tax reform, and cuts in military spending.

Doubts about McGovern's ability to lead the nation arose when, only two weeks after the convention, his choice of a running mate was called into question. At that time, Senator Eagleton revealed that he had once been hospitalized for emotional illness. McGovern at first insisted that he was "1,000 percent" behind Eagleton. Within a week, however, McGovern changed his mind and asked Eagleton to step down. He then chose R. Sargent Shriver, former director of the Peace Corps, to be the candidate for Vice President. The episode hurt McGovern, because it led many people to conclude that he was indecisive.

Nixon is re-elected. Nixon easily won renomination at the Republican convention, which was also held in Miami. Confident of victory, he did little personal campaigning, allowing Vice President Agnew and Cabinet officers to make public appearances in his place. Throughout the campaign, he maintained a large lead over McGovern in the opinion polls.

In November, Nixon was re-elected in a landslide. He won 60 percent of the popular vote to McGovern's 37 percent, carrying 49 of the 50 states and winning 520 electoral votes to McGovern's 17. It was the best showing ever made by a Republican presidential candidate. The triumph, however, was a personal one, for the Democrats retained control of both the Senate and the House of Representatives.

The Watergate affair begins to unfold. A seemingly minor campaign event, which attracted only limited attention at the time, soon became the center of a political scandal unmatched in American history. On June 17, 1972, five burglars were arrested at the headquarters of the Democratic National Committee in Washington's Watergate office complex. They had been placing electronic listening devices and were busy copying documents from files. It was later revealed that they were working for officials in Nixon's campaign organization, the Committee to Re-elect the President. At the time, however, the head of the committee, former Attorney General John Mitchell, denied that the burglars had been acting under orders from anyone in the organization. White House officials dismissed the event as a "third-rate burglary."

By early 1973 there was growing suspicion that responsibility for the Watergate break-in did not end with the individuals charged with the crime. Many people believed that officials in the Nixon administration had authorized the burglary and other illegal activities that they were now trying to cover up. Possibly, it was rumored, even the President himself was involved. In response to these suspicions, the Senate voted unanimously to set up a special committee to investigate the matter. Sam J. Ervin, a senator from North Carolina, was appointed chairman of the bipartisan panel, which held televised proceedings in the summer of 1973.

The fight over the tapes begins. On July 16, 1973, testimony was given before the Ervin Committee that, in the end, would undo the President. A White House official, in response to committee questioning, revealed that conversations in Nixon's office had routinely been tape-recorded. This information was important because it meant that the question of whether or not the President was involved in the Watergate cover-up might easily be resolved.

The Senate Select Committee on Watergate was headed by Sam J. Ervin. The televised hearings made the senator from North Carolina a popular figure.

Both the Ervin Committee and Archibald Cox, a Harvard law professor who had been named by the Attorney General as Special Prosecutor in the case, asked to listen to the tapes. The President, however, denied their requests. He argued on the grounds of "executive privilege" that these officials had no constitutional power to force him to reveal the contents of private conversations. To hand over the tapes, he asserted, would forever weaken the presidency. They persisted, however, and went to court to obtain the tapes.

After almost two months of court proceedings, Nixon offered a compromise. He agreed to supply the Special Prosecutor with summaries of the recorded conversations if Cox would seek no more presidential documents. Cox refused the offer on the grounds that summaries were not admissible evidence in courts of law and were therefore of no use to him. Angered by the refusal, Nixon ordered Attorney General Elliot Richardson to fire Cox. Richardson resigned rather than carry out this order. Deputy Attorney General William Ruckelshaus followed suit. Solicitor General Robert Bork, who became acting Attorney General, finally fired Cox. The resignations and the firing took place on the evening of Saturday, October 20, 1973. Known as "the Saturday Night Massacre," the affair prompted public outcry and added to the suspicion that the President had something to hide.

Vice President Agnew resigns. Meanwhile, in the fall of 1973, a separate investigation involving Vice President Agnew was under way. A federal grand jury in Baltimore was examining charges that Agnew, first as governor of Maryland and then as Vice President, had received illegal payments from private firms seeking favored treatment in the awarding of government contracts. Agnew resigned as Vice President on October 10, after pleading *nolo contendere* ("no contest") to a reduced charge of income tax evasion. In return, the court agreed not to sentence him to prison and not to prosecute him for any of the other crimes with which he was charged.

Under the terms of the Twenty-Fifth Amendment, ratified in 1967, President Nixon was empowered to appoint a new Vice President to fill the vacancy in that office. He nominated Congressman Gerald R. Ford of Michigan to replace Agnew as Vice President. Ford, well-liked by his colleagues in Congress, was quickly confirmed by the Senate.

The storm gathers. All the while, the Watergate affair was increasing its hold on the nation's attention. On October 30, 1973, as a result of the firing of Cox, the House Judiciary Committee began preliminary investigations to decide whether President Nixon should be impeached. Two days later, Leon Jaworski, a Houston attorney, was appointed to replace Cox as Special Prosecutor. Both Jaworski and the Judiciary Committee asked the President to supply them with recordings that contained discussions relating to Watergate. The President again refused on the grounds of executive privilege. As a result, in April, 1974, both the Judiciary Committee and the Special Prosecutor issued court orders requesting the White House tapes. Under increasing public pressure, Nixon decided, late in April, to release heavily edited transcripts of 46 tape-recorded conversations. The transcripts were quickly published in the nation's newspapers and in book form.

The release of the transcripts did not improve the President's position. Although they were edited, they contained much embarrassing material. Instead of satisfying public curiosity, the transcripts led to renewed demands for full disclosure and further investigation.

The President resigns. Events moved toward a climax in the last weeks of July, 1974. Jaworski, frustrated by delays in the investigation, asked the Supreme Court to decide, once and for all, whether Nixon could be forced to turn over tapes that had been requested by a federal court. On July 24, the Court unanimously ruled against the President. The decision was written by Chief Justice Burger, who argued that the President could not legally withhold evi-

Newspaper headlines on August 9, 1974, announced that Richard Nixon had resigned from office.

gate break-in. The transcripts clearly showed that Nixon had been a participant in the cover-up effort almost from the beginning. At this point, the calls for his resignation became widespread. It had become clear that, if he did not resign, the Senate would almost certainly remove him from office.

On the evening of August 8, the President announced his decision to leave office. The following day his letter of resignation was delivered to Secretary of State Henry Kissinger. Nixon became the first President to yield his office before the end of his term for any reason other than death. Less than an hour later, Chief Justice Burger administered the oath of office to the new President, Gerald R. Ford.

SECTION REVIEW

1. What success did America's space program enjoy in 1969?
2. (a) What promise did Richard Nixon make during the 1968 campaign concerning the Supreme Court? (b) How successful was he in carrying out that promise?
3. (a) Describe the steps President Nixon took to slow down inflation. (b) What success did he have?
4. (a) What were the results of the 1972 presidential election? (b) What events led to Richard Nixon's resignation?

dence needed in a criminal trial. Within hours, Nixon announced that he would hand over the tapes.

The President's position was further eroded by the action of the House Judiciary Committee. After days of nationally televised debate and discussion, the committee voted to recommend Nixon's impeachment. Republicans as well as Democrats supported the recommendation, prompting observers to predict that the full House would vote to impeach the President. He would then, under the provisions of the Constitution, be tried by the Senate. If found guilty, he would be removed from office.

Despite these severe setbacks, Nixon retained some backing in Congress. On August 5, however, most of this support collapsed. On that day, Nixon released transcripts of three conversations that had taken place only five days after the Water-

3 Ford Completes Nixon's Second Term

Until he became Vice President, Gerald Ford had represented Michigan's Fifth Congressional District for almost a quarter of a century. Minority leader in the House of Representatives since 1965, he once said that his highest ambition in life was to serve as Speaker of the House. Now, through a series of unparalled events, he had become President of the United States — the first person in the nation's history to become Chief Executive without having been elected President or Vice President.

Ford takes office. Keenly aware of the need to restore public confidence in the national government, President Ford pledged that his administration would be characterized by openness and candor. As his Vice President he quickly nominated Nelson Rockefeller, a four-term governor of New York and a political figure well known to the public. Ford also urged Americans to recognize that the Watergate affair — which he called "our long national nightmare" — had demonstrated the country's strength. "Our Constitution works," he said. "Our great republic is a government of laws and not of men."

Ford seemed to many people to be just the kind of leader the nation needed after the events of the previous two years. The first President to have been an Eagle Scout, he had played center on the University of Michigan football team in the 1930's and had served in the Pacific during the Second World War. Appreciating his unpretentious manner and conciliatory words, Americans rallied around the new Chief Executive.

Nixon is pardoned. On September 8, 1974, a month after Nixon's resignation, Ford made a controversial announcement. He had decided, he said, to grant Richard Nixon a "full, free, and absolute" pardon for all crimes that Nixon "committed or may have committed or taken part in."

Critics of the new President's decision argued that Ford had denied the American people the opportunity to find out, by means of a public trial, the full truth about what the former President had done. Some critics even charged that a deal had been struck — that Ford had guaranteed Nixon a pardon in return for his resignation.

Ford strongly denied these charges. He answered that bringing the former President to trial would create dissension among the American people, who were just beginning to put Watergate behind them. Nonetheless, Ford's popularity declined, and some people never forgave him for the decision to issue the pardon. In the 1974 congressional elections, possibly as a result of Ford's actions, the Democrats scored large gains.

Gerald Ford was sworn in as President shortly after Nixon's resignation. Mrs. Betty Ford watched as Chief Justice Warren Burger administered the oath of office.

Delegations headed by Gerald Ford (right) and Soviet leader Brezhnev (left) met in Helsinki in 1975 to negotiate a treaty that fixed the national boundaries of Europe.

The nation faces economic problems. Another reason for the Democrats' congressional victory in 1974 was the slump in the nation's economy. Convinced that inflation was the nation's chief economic problem, Ford advocated keeping a lid on federal spending and supported a tight monetary policy by the Federal Reserve. He also established a Council on Wage and Price Stability, which had the responsibility of exposing inflationary wage and price increases. Despite these measures, a recession that had begun in the fall of 1973 worsened, and by the spring of 1975 over 9 percent of the nation's workers were unemployed. At the same time, a four-fold increase in oil prices announced by OPEC in early 1974 was putting strong upward pressure on the inflation rate. During 1974 the inflation rate rose to 11 percent; in 1975 it was still above 9 percent.

Ford carries on Nixon's foreign policy. In dealing with other nations, Ford relied on the advice of Secretary of State Kissinger, who kept his Cabinet post in the new administration. As a result, there was a large degree of continuity in the foreign policy of the Nixon and Ford administrations.

In 1975, President Ford and representatives from 34 other countries, including the Soviet Union, gathered in Helsinki, Finland. The outcome was a treaty recognizing the existing boundaries of Europe as permanent and unalterable. The participating nations also pledged to respect and promote basic human rights. Supporters of the treaty saw it as another step in the lessening of tensions between the superpowers. Critics maintained that Western nations, in signing the treaty, were approving of the Soviet Union's domination of Eastern Europe. They also pointed out that, despite the

Impressions of the Bicentennial

The occasion of America's two-hundredth birthday was celebrated in many ways across the nation. The editors of *The New Yorker* magazine published the following account of what they observed in New York City on July 4, 1976.

A bicentennial celebration in New York City

The Fourth of July, 1976, was unlike any other day we can remember. It was as if a day had descended upon our nation from somewhere else. Yet it was ours. It couldn't be mistaken for anything but an American day. People had been talking about it for months in advance, but when it came, it came unannounced. No one had foreseen this particular day. It had an unplanned, unarranged quality — homemade, do-it-yourself. Government officials took their modest place in the background. Public-relations and promotion people bowed out altogether. Television and press people became self-effacing. People normally drawn to the limelight lay low. And the country's citizens, on their own, took to celebrating a birthday they all shared and suddenly understood. The idea of freedom hung in the air; and the idea of peace. We were at peace with the world, we were at peace with each other, and, unaccountably, we seemed at peace within ourselves. No one was telling us what to think, how to feel, where to go. Mostly, we went outdoors — into the streets, into the parks, down to the riverbanks — just in order to be with one another; and we thought our individual thoughts (thankful ones, very likely) and we felt good. Political rhetoric was held at a minimum, but the words we did hear sounded true. There was little flag-waving, but the flag was once more recognizable and thrilling. Our parades were weak on firepower and strong on high-school bands. It was a blithe day, a gentle day, a curiously lighthearted day. It was a holiday.

promises made in the treaty, the governments of Eastern Europe and the Soviet Union continued to violate the human rights of their citizens.

The nation celebrates the bicentennial. On July 4, 1976, President Ford led the nation in celebrating the two-hundredth anniversary of its declaration of independence. The disappointments and disagreeable events of recent years were still on people's minds. Nevertheless, in every corner of the land the bicentennial brought satisfaction that the freest country on earth, living under the oldest continuous government in the world, had safely weathered fierce storms.

The parties choose their presidential nominees. In 1976, Gerald Ford decided to seek election to a full term as President. He had a difficult time, however, winning his party's nomination. His challenger in the primaries was Ronald Reagan, who had served two terms as governor of California.

At the Republican convention in Kansas City, Missouri, Ford narrowly defeated Reagan for the party's nomination. As his running mate, Ford chose Senator Robert Dole of Kansas.

Republican fortunes were at a low point in 1976 because of the recession and the lingering effects of the Watergate affair. Many prominent Democrats, therefore, sought their party's nomination, believing it would be a sure ticket to the White House. Instead of a familiar name, however, a newcomer to national politics gained a first-ballot victory at the July convention in New York City. He was Jimmy Carter.

Carter, a graduate of the United States Naval Academy, was a peanut farmer and businessman who had served one term as governor of Georgia. He had begun planning to run for the presidency as early as 1972, and with excellent organizational work and tireless campaigning was able to score well in the first events of the 1976 presidential campaign. By winning the Iowa caucuses and the New Hampshire primary he attracted wide attention, leading to his victory in New York.

Jimmy Carter is elected President. Immediately after the Democratic convention, Carter and his running mate, Senator Walter Mondale of Minnesota, held a substantial lead over their Republican rivals. As the campaign shifted into full gear, however, the gap between the two candidates narrowed considerably. Ford and his fellow Republicans argued that Carter lacked the necessary experience to be President and that his positions on particular issues were difficult to pin down. Carter, on the other hand, charged that Ford's policies had failed to end the recession. He promised to boost the economy through increased government spending, to streamline the federal bureaucracy, and to develop alternative sources of energy to reduce dependence on foreign oil. As Election Day neared, neither candidate had a significant lead in the opinion polls.

By a narrow margin, the voters favored the outsider. Carter won 51 percent of the vote to Ford's 48 percent and carried the

Jimmy Carter, a newcomer to national politics, defeated Gerald Ford in the presidential election of 1976.

electoral college by a margin of 297 to 241. The Democrats once again maintained control of both houses of Congress.

As President Ford prepared to leave the White House after less than two and a half years in office, he was satisfied with the historic role he had played. He would be remembered for having helped the nation put behind it two of its most distressing experiences: the war in Vietnam and the Watergate affair.

SECTION REVIEW

1. (a) Why did President Ford pardon Richard Nixon? (b) On what grounds was Ford's decision criticized?
2. (a) What steps did Ford take to fight inflation? (b) How effective were they?
3. How did Ford carry on the Nixon administration's policy of détente?
4. (a) Who were the nominees for President in the 1976 election? (b) What issues were debated in that campaign? (c) What was the outcome?

Chapter 32 Review

Summary

Richard Nixon's overriding concern upon taking office as President in 1969 was to end American involvement in the Vietnam War. With the aid of his foreign policy adviser, Henry Kissinger, Nixon formulated a plan to withdraw American combat forces and train Vietnamese troops to take over the fighting. A peace settlement was finally reached in January, 1973, but not before Nixon ordered an invasion of Cambodia, renewed the bombing of North Vietnam, and witnessed bitter antiwar demonstrations at home.

At the same time that American involvement in the Vietnam War was being concluded, Nixon was pursuing other means of easing international tensions. In a historic move, he journeyed to China early in 1972 and established trade and cultural ties. In May, 1972, Nixon visited the Soviet Union and met with Soviet leader Leonid Brezhnev to work out an arms-limitation agreement.

Although Nixon concentrated on foreign policy, domestic issues also demanded his attention. During his presidency, Nixon had the opportunity to appoint four justices to the Supreme Court. Nixon addressed the growing concern over pollution by creating the Environmental Protection Agency. The agency's duty was to enforce laws designed to protect the environment. The pressing issue of inflation prompted Nixon to regulate wages and prices, an effort that was largely unsuccessful.

Nixon easily defeated George McGovern in the 1972 presidential election, but an incident during the campaign set in motion a sequence of events that proved to be the President's undoing. Men associated with the Committee to Re-elect the President were arrested during a break-in at Democratic Party headquarters in Washington. Evidence of White House involvement in a cover-up of the so-called "Watergate affair" was eventually disclosed by a congressional investigation. Faced with impeachment proceedings, Nixon chose to resign, leaving office on August 9, 1974. Vice President Gerald Ford was sworn in as President and completed Nixon's second term.

One of Ford's first acts as President was to issue a pardon freeing Nixon from any possible criminal prosecution, growing out of the Watergate affair. Ford continued Nixon's foreign-policy initiatives, while at home he faced increases in the inflation and unemployment rates. In the 1976 presidential election, the Democratic candidate, Jimmy Carter, defeated Ford by a narrow margin.

Vocabulary and Important Terms

1. Vietnamization
2. War Powers Act
3. détente
4. Strategic Arms Limitation Talks
5. Yom Kippur War
6. Environmental Protection Agency
7. Twenty-Fifth Amendment
8. Twenty-Sixth Amendment
9. Equal Rights Amendment
10. Watergate affair
11. "Saturday Night Massacre"
12. Council on Wage and Price Stability
13. bicentennial

Discussion Questions

1. (a) What was President Nixon's plan for ending American involvement in the Vietnam War? (b) Why did Nixon send troops into Cambodia? (c) What was the reaction at home? (d) Why did the Paris peace treaty not end the war? (e) How did the Vietnamese conflict spill over into the Ford administration, and what was the eventual fate not only of Vietnam but also of Laos and Cambodia?

2. (a) What were the costs of the Vietnam War for the United States? (b) What aspects of the war did Americans continue to debate even after the conflict had ended?

3. (a) What steps did President Nixon take as part of his détente policy? (b) To what extent was the United States committed to détente during Gerald Ford's tenure as President?

4. (a) What were some of the most pressing domestic issues facing the nation during Nixon's presidency, and what steps were taken to deal with those issues? (b) What factors contributed to Nixon's landslide victory in the election of 1972?

5. (a) What caused inflation to be a major domestic problem for both the Nixon and Ford administrations? (b) How similar were their proposed solutions to the problem? (c) To what extent was either successful in bringing inflation under control?

6. (a) During the Watergate investigation, on what grounds did Nixon argue that neither members of Congress nor the special prosecutors should have access to the White House tapes? (b) How did the Supreme Court respond to the President's argument? (c) What happened when the transcripts of the tapes were released?

7. (a) What political experience and personal qualities did Gerald Ford bring to the presidency? (b) How did he try to restore public confidence?

8. What factors contributed to Jimmy Carter's election as President in 1972?

Relating Past and Present

1. One of the most pressing concerns of the Nixon administration was the effort to halt pollution. To what extent is pollution a problem today? What other environmental concerns receive attention today?
2. What is the state of American-Soviet relations today compared to the relations that existed during the Nixon administration? What factors have caused American-Soviet relations to change? What has happened to the policy of détente?

Studying Local History

1. How did your community respond to the concern about environmental issues in the late 1960's? What measures, if any, did your local and state governments take to deal with air, water, and land pollution and with other environmental concerns? What measures are being taken today?
2. Find out how your community celebrated the bicentennial and report on it to the class.

Using History Skills

1. *Using the index.* In the index find the entry for Vietnam. On what pages of your book is Vietnam mentioned or discussed? Look up each of these references. Based on the information you find, write a brief history of American involvement in Vietnam from its beginnings to the withdrawal of the last American troops.
2. *Comparing.* Compare the resignations of Vice President Spiro Agnew and Vice President John Calhoun. Why did each resign? How similar were the reasons for their resignations?

WORLD SCENE

Political Changes in Europe

In the early 1970's, the long-established authoritarian regimes of Spain and Portugal came to an end. Both countries gained new, democratic governments.

A constitutional monarchy in Spain. In 1939, General Francisco Franco led his forces to victory in the Spanish Civil War. With the backing of the army, Franco set up a dictatorship and established himself as Spain's all-powerful leader.

Franco's economic reforms in the 1950's and 1960's brought industry to Spain and provided a higher standard of living for most of the Spanish people. By the end of the 1960's, Franco began to ease some of his restrictions on personal freedom. Soon, protests against his rule broke out. Student demonstrations forced the closing of several universities in 1969, and labor strikes in the early 1970's were further proof of the extent of popular dissatisfaction.

Franco managed to retain power until his death in 1975. When Prince Juan Carlos succeeded Franco, he announced that Spain would become a constitutional monarchy. Elections were held two years later to select a parliament. These were the first free elections held in Spain in more than forty years.

A new Portuguese republic. In 1926 military leaders overthrew Portugal's democratic government. To deal with severe economic problems, an economics professor named Antonio Salazar was appointed minister of finance. Before long, Salazar extended his influence beyond economic matters and took control of the Portuguese government.

Salazar ruled Portugal as a dictator. He remained in power for nearly forty years with the help of a powerful secret-police organization which assured obedience to his repressive laws. During Salazar's rule, little improvement took place in the living standards of the people, and Portugal remained the poorest country in Western Europe.

Inspired by memories of past Portuguese empires, Salazar was determined to maintain his nation's hold on its African colonies. In the 1960's, when rebellions erupted in Angola, Mozambique, and Portuguese Guinea, Salazar sent large numbers of troops to deal with the trouble.

Salazar fell seriously ill in 1968 and was forced to retire. His followers tried to maintain the dictatorship, but young army officers overthrew the hated regime in 1974. Reforms were rapidly introduced that abolished the secret police, restored civil liberties, and allowed the formation of political parties. Arrangements were made to grant Portugal's African possessions their independence, and in 1976 elections led to the formation of a new Portuguese republic.

Challenging Years

1977 – 1980's

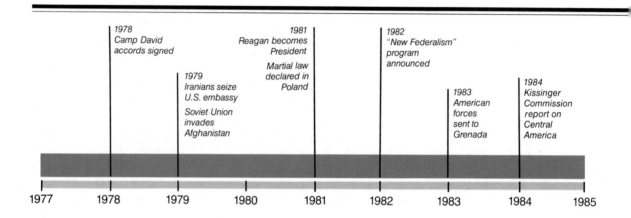

| | 1978 Camp David accords signed | 1979 Iranians seize U.S. embassy; Soviet Union invades Afghanistan | 1981 Reagan becomes President; Martial law declared in Poland | 1982 "New Federalism" program announced | 1983 American forces sent to Grenada | 1984 Kissinger Commission report on Central America |

1977 1978 1979 1980 1981 1982 1983 1984 1985

The 1976 election was the first presidential contest following the Watergate affair. Many voters, distrustful of politicians whose base was Washington, D.C., seemed ready to accept a candidate whose service was not associated with the capital. The Democrats had emphasized that Jimmy Carter was an outsider to Washington, whose political know-how came from state rather than federal experience. Carter thought of himself as a citizen who was reviving the ideal of plain goodness in national politics. He pledged: "I'll never tell a lie." At his inauguration, Carter presented himself as an ordinary man by wearing a business suit rather than the traditional formal attire. Instead of the usual limousine ride back to the White House from the Capitol, he chose to walk the route with his wife and children.

Ronald Reagan, the Republican candidate who ran against Carter in the 1980 presidential campaign, also adopted an anti-Washington stance. Reagan, long a motion-picture and television star, was a familiar name and face to millions of Americans. Twice elected governor of California, he had never held national office. An admirer of Franklin D. Roosevelt, Reagan had once been a Democrat. He changed his mind, however, as he grew older. "I didn't desert my party," he liked to explain. "It deserted me." His campaign promise to reduce the federal government's involvement in many areas of American life appealed to voters.

1 Jimmy Carter Faces Critical Problems

When Jimmy Carter came to office, he announced that he was eager to usher in "a new national spirit of unity and trust." One of his first official acts was to issue an unconditional pardon to all draft resisters from the Vietnam War period. He hoped that this measure would help erase some of the resentfulness the war had aroused and allow the country to face the future with a clean slate.

CONCERNS AT HOME

The administration proposes an energy program. A major problem requiring attention when President Carter took office was the country's dependence on imported oil. Ever since the Arab oil embargo of 1973 (page 759), Americans had been well aware of the danger of this kind of dependence. Even though conservation measures had been instituted, the proportion of the country's oil needs filled by imported supplies had actually increased during the 1970's.

Carter began his efforts to solve the energy problem by creating the Department of Energy. The department's duty was to develop and coordinate national energy programs and policies. Next, Carter proposed new legislation that he believed would reduce — and, ultimately, eliminate — America's dependence on foreign oil. His program sought to increase the prices of domestically produced oil and natural gas by removing federal controls from the price of these fuels. He also called for additional taxes on gasoline to discourage its wasteful use. Revenue from the new taxes would be used to support research on the development of alternative sources of energy.

Not until 1978 did Congress pass a modified version of Carter's energy pro-

Washington, D.C., is not only the capital of the United States but also a symbol of the nation's unity, history, and traditions.

gram. The legislation encouraged some industries to use coal as a fuel despite the likely adverse effect on the environment. Government controls over natural gas prices were relaxed, and new taxes were passed to encourage conservation.

Relations with Congress are strained. The prolonged debate over President Carter's energy program was typical of his relations with Congress, which often were rocky, especially on domestic issues. After the events of the Vietnam War and Watergate, Congress was mistrustful of the executive branch of government. One effect was that a President could no longer count on near-automatic support of his programs from members of his own party. Party loyalty, too, had declined. In running for office, many candidates relied heavily on personal television advertising, leading some of them to conclude that they had been elected on their own, rather than through identification with a particular party.

Carter's lack of experience in Washington's ways soon was viewed by many Americans as a handicap. Members of Congress complained that the White House was ignoring their concerns. A number of minor controversies reinforced this impression. Early in his administration, for instance, the President vowed to fight what he considered to be "pork-barrel" public works projects. He neglected, however, to consult with members of Congress in whose districts those projects were to be located. The result, almost from the beginning, was strained relations between the executive and legislative branches.

Although the administration worked at improving relations with Congress, the effort was only moderately successful. Many members of Congress — even fellow-Democrats — never forgave Carter and his staff for those early mistakes.

Economic problems continue. When Carter took office, unemployment was on the upswing. Approximately seven million Americans were out of work. The new President's economic program, designed to create jobs, included proposals to reduce government spending, initiate public works projects, and cut taxes. By the end of 1978, the unemployment rate was on the way down. Inflation, however, had become a serious problem. In January, 1977, the inflation rate was running at 4.8 percent annually. By the fall of 1978, it had climbed to 10 percent.

In October, the administration announced the establishment of voluntary wage and price guidelines as part of an anti-inflation program. A Council on Wage and Price Stability was created to monitor compliance with these guidelines. The administration announced that businesses failing to follow the guidelines would be ineligible for government contracts. Overall, however, the necessary strong incentives for compliance were lacking, and the guidelines were not widely followed.

Owing partly to domestic causes and partly to enormous increases in the price of oil, inflation continued to soar. By 1979 the rate had reached 11.3 percent. The alarming rise in inflation became a major political liability for the President as the 1980 election drew near.

Carter's popularity declines. By the spring of 1979, administration officials were uneasy about Carter's prospects for re-election. The administration laid much of the blame for the President's difficulties on Congress, which had failed to pass many of Carter's legislative proposals. The overriding issue for Americans, however, continued to be oil. During the early months of 1979, political turmoil in the Middle East had resulted in reduced oil supplies and an OPEC price hike. Once again, Americans were lining up to pay high prices for gasoline, and many people, in their irritation, held the White House responsible.

On July 4, 1979, the President abruptly canceled a planned television address on the subject of energy and journeyed to the presidential retreat at Camp David in Maryland. There, for the next ten days, more than a hundred American leaders from various fields met with Carter and his top advisers, suggesting ways of increasing the administration's effectiveness.

Following the Camp David meetings, Carter addressed the country. He admitted that he had made mistakes and promised to provide stronger leadership. He also warned of a national "crisis of confidence" and passionately repeated his calls for the enactment of a massive federal energy program. Two days later, the President announced that the resignations of a number of Cabinet officers had been accepted.

The dramatic "crisis-of-confidence" speech and the Cabinet shuffle did not achieve the desired goal of restoring public faith in the Carter presidency. In the following months, the President's prospects for re-election seemed bleaker than ever.

FOREIGN POLICY

Carter supports human rights. In foreign affairs, President Carter made human rights a cornerstone of his foreign policy. He declared in his inaugural address that he would work to guarantee "the basic right of every human to be free of poverty, disease, and political repression." He criticized nations that denied these rights to their people, and he encouraged people living under repression to speak out against it. He even tried to persuade American allies in Asia, Africa, and South America to cease their violations of human rights. In some cases, Carter threatened to withdraw American aid if such offenses continued.

Carter mediates an agreement between Israel and Egypt. Like his predecessors, Carter worked hard to reduce tension in the Middle East. Taking advantage of startling new developments, he was able to play the role of peacemaker.

The Egyptian president, Anwar Sadat, had stunned the world by flying to Jerusalem in November, 1977, to meet with the Israeli prime minister, Menachem Begin. Up to that time, no Arab leader had ever visited Israel or even formally recognized its existence. Addressing the Israeli parliament, Sadat called for the normalization of Egyptian-Israeli relations, the negotiation of a peace treaty, and the withdrawal of Israeli forces from all occupied Arab lands.

President Carter's mediation of an agreement between President Sadat of Egypt (left) and Prime Minister Begin of Israel (right) boosted hopes for peace in the Middle East.

American diplomats, delighted with this turn of events, redoubled their efforts to bring about peace in the Middle East. When the talks between Sadat and Begin seemed to be at a stalemate, President Carter intervened, inviting the two leaders to meet with him in the United States.

Early in September, 1978, the three leaders went into seclusion at Camp David. Carter started by holding individual sessions with Sadat and Begin in order to probe their positions. When he brought them together, however, the meetings proved unproductive, and the two foreign leaders were soon barely talking to each other. Carter thereupon resumed the one-on-one arrangement, going back and forth between the two men, slowly nudging them off their fixed stands.

After twelve tense days Carter produced a diplomatic "miracle" — the Camp David accords. Under the accords, signed in a dramatic ceremony at the White House on September 17, 1978, an Israeli-Egyptian peace treaty was to be drawn up, and Israel would withdraw from Egyptian territories it had occupied. The Camp David accords included arrangements to discuss self-government for other occupied territories and Palestinian representation in later stages of the peace talks.

Sadat paid a high price for what he had done. Other Arab leaders denounced him for "selling out" the cause of the Palestinian Arabs, and they immediately subjected Egypt to a diplomatic and economic boycott. For Israel, removing its forces from the Sinai Peninsula was also a hard concession to make. Many Israelis criticized Begin, fearing that a withdrawal from the occupied territory would endanger their country's security.

The formal treaty was signed at the White House in March, 1979. Although little progress was made in later discussions on the other territories or on the Palestinian question, the "spirit of Camp David" generated hope for eventual peace between Israel and the Arab world. For President Carter,

his success as a mediator boosted the public's confidence in his leadership.

The United States establishes formal relations with China. American recognition of the People's Republic of China was another milestone of the Carter administration. The United States took this action on January 1, 1979, having received informal assurances from the mainland Chinese that they would not invade Taiwan, the offshore island which remained under Nationalist control (page 759).

In 1980 the United States and China signed a trade agreement. Soon, American commerce with the Chinese, especially in agricultural produce, outstripped trade with Russia. The continuation of American arms sales to Taiwan, however, remained a point of controversy between the United States and China.

Following the establishment of formal relations between the United States and China, Deputy Chairman Deng Xiaoping visited Washington, D.C. After talks with President Carter, the two leaders attended a theater performance with their families.

Massive demonstrations forced the shah to leave Iran in 1979 and led to the return from exile of the Ayatollah Khomeini, a fiercely anti-American religious leader.

A pro-Western government is overthrown in Iran. United States relations with Iran were close when Carter came to office. In an unlikely way, however, they became so strained that they eventually undermined Carter's presidency. Iran had long been of interest to the West because of its strategic location between Russia and the oil fields of Saudi Arabia and because of its own important oil deposits. The Iranian monarch, Shah Mohammed Reza Pahlevi, who had come to the throne in 1941, was closely allied with the United States. His program of modernization, which included land reform and greater freedom for women, won praise from many quarters. In the 1970's, however, the shah faced increasing opposition from his subjects. Many Iranians who supported modernization criticized the shah's harsh repression of political dissent. Muslim extremists, on the other hand, opposed modernization, claiming that it violated sacred religious rules. This group, which grew rapidly during the late 1970's, advocated the installation of a government that would strictly enforce Islamic law.

Successive waves of angry protest forced the shah to leave Iran in January, 1979. Soon a religious leader, the Ayatollah Khomeini (AH-yah-tol-ah koh-MAY-nee), took over the government. His followers demanded that the shah, who had sought asylum in a number of countries, be returned to Iran for trial. They were outraged when President Carter allowed the former ruler to enter the United States in October, 1979, to undergo medical treatment at a New York hospital.

The American embassy is seized. On November 4, 1979, in an apparent attempt to force the United States to return the shah, an Iranian mob stormed the American embassy in Tehran, the Iranian capital, and took hostage Americans who worked there. Even though the United Nations Security Council and the International Court of Justice unanimously demanded the immediate release of the hostages, the Khomeini government, which had announced its support of the embassy take-over, remained unmoved.

In deciding what action to take, Carter placed the highest value on the safety of the hostages. For this reason, he said, he would order no military action against Iran. He instead pursued a variety of avenues in seeking the hostages' release, including

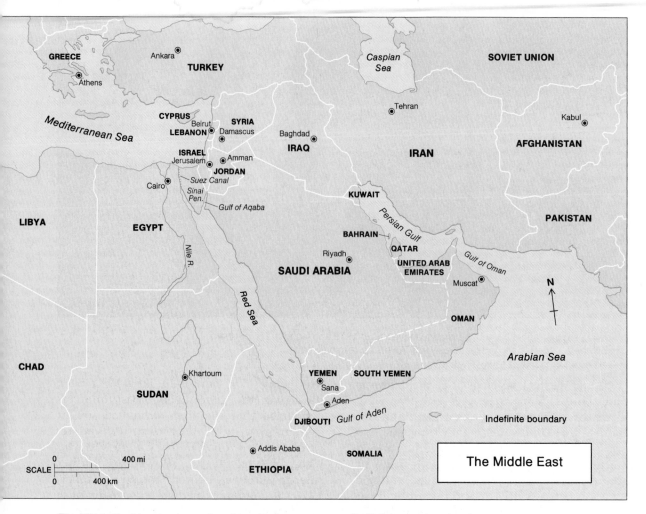

The Middle East has been a region of tension in recent years. Strife between Israel and its Arab neighbors continues, while events in Iran and Afghanistan have posed threats to world peace.

economic sanctions, diplomatic pressure, and secret negotiations.

As the months of frustration dragged on, Carter came under intense pressure to resolve the crisis. Five months after the embassy seizure, he ordered a secret military mission to rescue the hostages. Eight helicopters left an American aircraft carrier in the Gulf of Oman and headed for a desert area of Iran. From the desert, they were to proceed to Tehran. Mechanical difficulties in the desert, however, caused the operation to be canceled. As the American forces began their pull-out, a helicopter collided with a transport plane, killing eight servicemen and wounding five others.

The hostages are released. After the failure of the rescue mission, the United States renewed its efforts to gain the release of the hostages through negotiation. Again, months passed without significant progress. Even the death of the shah, who was then in exile in Egypt, brought no change in the Iranian position.

Finally, late in 1980, the Algerian government helped the two sides reach a settlement. The United States agreed not to interfere in Iranian affairs. The United States also promised to release most of the Iranian funds that President Carter had "frozen" in American banks in November, 1979, and agreed to drop financial claims

Homecoming for the Hostages

On January 20, 1981, the American hostages in Iran were released and began their journey back to the United States. Ed Magnuson, a writer for *Time*, described how people throughout the country reacted to the return of the hostages.

America's joy pealed from church belfries, rippled from flagstaffs, and wrapped itself in a million miles of yellow ribbon, tied around trees, car antennas, and even the 32-story Foshay Tower in Minneapolis. Barbara Deffley, wife of the Methodist minister in Holmer, Illinois, rang the church bell 444 times, once for each day of captivity. "At about 200 pulls, I thought I'd never make it," she gasped. "Then at about 300 pulls, I got my second wind and kept going all the way." Massachusetts House Speaker Thomas W. McGee, 56, was too impatient to wait for a ladder, so he shinnied ten feet up a pole to . . . hoist the U.S. flag over the statehouse in Boston. In Mountain Home, Idaho, some 200 townspeople staged an impromptu parade, driving their cars three abreast, headlights on and horns blaring. Patrolman Joseph McDermott coasted his cruiser to the side of a street in Rochester, New Hampshire, fighting back tears. Said he: "I am overjoyed. I feel proud again."

Joy at the restoration of pride to a nation that had been humbled for so long by [Iran] was but one of the many reactions of Americans to the release of the 52 U.S.

The American hostages are welcomed home.

hostages last week. There was a sense of relief too. And scorn for Iran. But above all the initial dominant mood was one of continuing celebration, from the moment the first plane carrying the former captives cleared Iranian airspace to the climactic touchdown on U.S. soil . . . at Stewart Airport, 50 miles north of New York City. There in privacy that not even the longest lens of press and TV cameras could penetrate, the returnees from Iran at long last were tearfully reunited with their families. . . .

against Iran. On January 21, 1981, just as Ronald Reagan was taking the oath of office, a plane containing the hostages left Tehran, bringing the Americans back to a hero's welcome.

The United States responds to the Russian invasion of Afghanistan. Late in 1979, while the American negotiations with Iran were still under way, the Soviet Union alarmed the world by sending troops southward into Afghanistan. The Soviet troops were or-

dered to support Afghanistan's Communist government, which was under attack from Muslim guerrillas. Within days, the Soviet forces had taken control of the capital city of Kabul and set about crushing resistance in the countryside.

President Carter, concerned that the Soviet Union might invade Iran as well, decided that immediate action was necessary. Declaring that "aggression unopposed becomes a contagious disease," the President announced sanctions against the Soviet

Union. A major arms-limitation treaty (SALT II) was withdrawn from consideration by the Senate; an embargo was placed on sales of grain to the Soviet Union; and the United States announced that it would boycott the 1980 Olympic Games, which were to be held in Moscow. In addition, the President asked Congress to enact a new draft-registration law which would enable the armed forces to mobilize quickly in the event of war. Congress complied.

Other nations were unwilling to join in economic sanctions against the Soviet Union, but international disapproval of the Soviet invasion was widespread. Both the United Nations Security Council and the General Assembly condemned the Soviet action and demanded the immediate withdrawal of the Red Army. Such protests, however, had no apparent effect. Instead of withdrawing, the Soviet Union built up its troop strength in Afghanistan. There, Soviet forces faced continuing resistance from anti-Communist guerrillas.

For Americans, the invasion of Afghanistan aroused fresh concern over Soviet aggression. In combination with the failure of the American rescue mission in Iran, it led many Americans to place renewed emphasis on the need for strong national defenses.

THE 1980 ELECTION

Carter is challenged by fellow Democrats. The crises in Iran and Afghanistan coincided with the 1980 presidential campaign. President Carter found himself under attack not only from the Republicans but from members of his own party as well.

On November 7, 1979 — just three days after the seizure of the American embassy in Tehran — Senator Edward Kennedy of Massachusetts, youngest brother of President Kennedy, announced his decision to challenge Carter for the Democratic presidential nomination. The governor of California, Jerry Brown, soon entered the race too. In their quest for support, Kennedy and Brown both argued that the United States faced difficult problems and that Carter had

been unable to exert the strong leadership the country required.

Carter did not actively campaign during the first four months of the year because, he maintained, the hostage crisis made it necessary for him to remain in Washington. His Democratic opponents scornfully condemned his behavior. They charged that he was using the episode in Iran as an excuse to avoid the political risks of campaigning and open debate.

As the incumbent, the President had an advantage over Kennedy and Brown. Many Democrats, furthermore, were convinced that neither Kennedy nor Brown could win the support of the majority of the American people. In addition, the crises in Iran and Afghanistan had caused many Americans to rally around the President, regarding his restraint during the early months of 1980 as worthy of support.

By the end of the primary season, Carter had won more than enough delegates to capture the party's nomination. At the Democratic National Convention in New York City, the Carter-Mondale team was again chosen to face the Republicans in the November election. The party platform, which had been heavily influenced by Kennedy and his supporters, called for an expanded federal jobs program, opposition to any anti-inflation measure that would tend to increase unemployment, détente with the Soviet Union, and extensive revamping of the nation's armed forces.

Ronald Reagan wins the Republican nomination. At the beginning of 1980, Ronald Reagan appeared to be the leading Republican contender for the presidential nomination. Reagan's main rival was George Bush, who had served as a congressman from Texas, ambassador to the United Nations, director of the Central Intelligence Agency, and diplomatic representative to China. Bush ran a strong campaign, but by the end of May, Reagan clearly had locked up enough delegates to gain the Republican nomination. At that point, Bush withdrew from the race, asking his delegates to support Reagan.

At the Republican convention, which was held in Detroit, the major question centered around the vice-presidential nomination. There was speculation that former President Gerald Ford might accept the spot. Many Republicans believed that Reagan and Ford would make an unbeatable combination — a "dream ticket." In the end, however, Ford decided not to seek the nomination. Reagan then announced that he had chosen George Bush as his running mate.

The Republican platform reflected Reagan's views. On economic matters, the platform called for a major tax cut, limits on federal spending, and a reduction in government regulation of American business. In foreign policy, it called for increased emphasis on national defense and a firm policy toward the Soviet Union.

John Anderson runs as an independent. Polls showed that a significant number of Americans were disappointed in the nominees of both major parties. It was to this group of voters that Representative John Anderson of Illinois attempted to appeal. Having lost his bid for the Republican nomination, Anderson ran as an independent candidate for President. Despite some interest in Anderson as a new man in the race, significant support for his candidacy failed to materialize.

Reagan wins by a landslide. The contest between Carter and Reagan was widely considered to be close. Polls were inconclusive — some giving a slight edge to Carter, some to Reagan. In the final weeks of the campaign, each candidate tried to concentrate on what he believed to be his opponent's major weakness. Reagan emphasized what he called the nation's "misery index" — the combination of high unemployment and double-digit inflation that had plagued the country under the Carter administration. Carter, on the other hand, pointed to his foreign-policy achievements — especially the Camp David agreements — saying that his administration had succeeded in reducing world tensions. He argued that the

Ronald Reagan stands before the delegates at the 1980 Republican convention, having just won his party's nomination for President.

hard-line foreign policy advocated by Reagan and the Republicans might lead the country into war.

Late in October, an audience of over 100 million people watched as the two candidates met in a televised debate. In the course of his exchanges with the President, Reagan displayed his personal warmth and did much to defuse the Democrats' charges that he was a dangerous extremist.

On Election Day, the American voters chose Reagan in a landslide — defying the predictions of a close race. The vote was the most sweeping repudiation of an incumbent President since Hoover's loss to Roosevelt in 1932 (page 611). Reagan won 51 percent of the popular vote compared to Carter's 41 percent. In the electoral college, Reagan's triumph was even more overwhelming: 489 votes to 49. Anderson, who captured less than 7 percent of the popular vote, received no electoral votes.

In winning so convincingly, Reagan carried many other Republican candidates into office. For the first time since 1952, the Republicans emerged with a majority in the Senate. They also gained 32 seats in the House, which remained under Democratic control but by a significantly narrower margin. In addition, Republicans won four new governorships.

SECTION REVIEW

1. (a) For what reason did Carter propose a new energy program? (b) What steps did he take?
2. Why did Carter find it difficult to work with Congress?
3. (a) How did Carter try to combat unemployment and inflation? (b) How effective were his efforts?
4. (a) What were the Camp David accords? (b) Why were they important?
5. (a) What problem developed as the result of the seizure of the American embassy in Tehran? (b) What steps did Carter take to secure the release of the American hostages? (c) On what terms were the hostages released?
6. (a) Why did the Soviet Union send troops to Afghanistan? (b) What was the reaction of the United States?
7. (a) Who were the candidates in the 1980 election? (b) What were their main campaign themes? (c) What was the election result?

2 New Patterns of Population Growth Affect Ways of Living

As it has done at the start of each decade since 1790, the United States government took an inventory of the nation's population in 1980. The statistics tabulated from the 1980 census showed that some 226 million people lived in the United States. The census also provided new insights into the nature of the American population.

Population growth slows down. One of the most notable findings of the Census Bureau was that the rate of population growth in the 1970's was the lowest it had been since the Great Depression. A major cause for this slowdown was the increase in the proportion of Americans aged 65 and older. The 1980 census found that there were 25 million Americans in this category. During the 1970's this group grew twice as fast as the rest of the population and in the future seemed likely to continue growing at a similar rate.

The "graying of America" can be attributed in part to the simple fact that more people in the United States are living longer. Medical advances have raised the average lifetime in the United States from 70.8 years in 1970 to 73.8 in 1980. This greater longevity produced a large constituency of elderly Americans whose concerns about health care, housing, and social security make them a powerful political force. In the 1980 presidential election, for example, one third of those who voted were 55 years old or older.

The population of America continues to shift. The results of the 1980 census also reconfirmed a trend that had begun after World War II. This trend had to do with where Americans preferred to live. Many people, seeking to escape the harsh winter weather and high heating bills of the North, moved to the *sunbelt,* a region stretching across the country from the southeastern Atlantic coast to southern California. Industries also relocated to the sunbelt, prompting people unable to find jobs in the Northeast and Upper Midwest to flock to this region in search of employment.

Statistics from the census showed a sharp contrast between population growth in the South and West as compared with the Northeast and Upper Midwest. Nearly 90 percent of the increase in population in the 1970's took place in the South and West, with many states in those regions growing at a rate of over 20 percent. The population of most states in the Northeast and Upper Midwest, on the other hand, grew by only about 2 percent. By 1980 more than half of all Americans lived in the South and West.

New Trends

The 1980 census revealed that although population growth in general had slowed, minority groups had rapidly increased in size. The census also reported on employment trends, finding that more and more Americans were employed in service occupations — such as computer operations and programming — and that large numbers of women were entering the work force.

The shifting of population had important political consequences because the census is used to determine the number of members a state sends to the House of Representatives. After the 1980 census, 17 congressional seats were lost by northern and midwestern states to states in the sunbelt.

The 98th Congress, which was elected in 1982, was the first in American history to have a majority of its members come from the South and West.

Urban centers lose population. Another trend revealed by the 1980 census was the

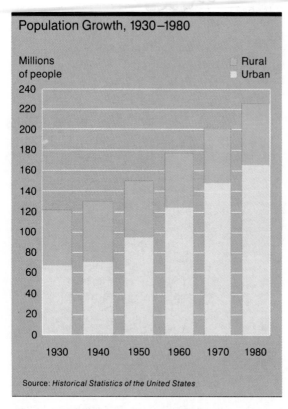

Population Growth, 1930–1980

Millions of people

☐ Rural
▨ Urban

Source: *Historical Statistics of the United States*

Population growth from 1930 to 1980 is shown in this graph. The 1980 census indicated that the United States population has passed the 225-million mark.

large-scale migration out of older urban areas. This was an historic shift because for well over a century most Americans had preferred to live in or near large metropolitan centers. In the 1970's, rural areas and small towns, which for years had been losing population, grew at a rate of approximately 15 percent.

The older cities of the Northeast and Upper Midwest suffered the greatest loss of population. Between 1970 and 1980, for instance, the New York metropolitan area lost over 850,000 inhabitants. During those same years, the population of the Cleveland metropolitan area declined by nearly 200,000. Of the 32 urban centers that suffered decreases in population during the 1970's, all but two were in the Northeast and Upper Midwest. The loss of population led to a reduction in tax revenues, severely hurting urban areas.

Minority groups gain in population. Due to improved methods of gathering population figures, the Census Bureau in 1980 was able to tabulate the growth of minorities in the United States more accurately than ever before. The results showed that the percentage of Hispanics, black Americans, Asian Americans, and American Indians was increasing dramatically.

The Hispanic population was the fastest-growing segment of American society. People of Spanish origin had increased nearly 60 percent since 1970 and by 1980 made up over 6 percent of the total population of the United States. Increases in immigration contributed to this rapid rise. At the time of the census, the great majority of Spanish-speaking people was concentrated in California, Texas, New York, and Florida. The Census Bureau predicted that before the end of the decade Hispanic Americans would be the largest minority group in the United States.

The number of black Americans increased by 17 percent in the 1970's and by 1980 constituted 11.7 percent of the national population, up from 11.1 percent in 1970. One notable fact brought to light by the census was that for the first time since the Civil War the number of black Americans moving to the South equalled the number of those moving to the North. This was another indication that northern industrial cities were no longer providing the employment opportunities that once had attracted millions of workers, both black and white.

The continent from which the largest number of immigrants arrived during the 1970's was Asia. Nearly two million Asian immigrants came to the United States. Many were fleeing the unrest that was convulsing the Southeast Asian countries of Vietnam, Laos, and Cambodia, while others were leaving the Philippines, Korea, and Taiwan. Three fourths of all Asian Americans made their homes in the following seven states: California, Hawaii, New York, Illinois, Texas, Washington, and New Jersey.

The size of households decreases. Another finding of the 1980 census was that the average size of households in the United States was becoming considerably smaller. Even though the number of households increased by nearly 30 percent between 1970 and 1980, the number of people living in households grew by only 12 percent. As a result, the average household fell in size from 3.11 people in 1970 to 2.75 in 1980. The sharp decline reflected changes in the way Americans lived — more divorces, fewer marriages, couples having only one child or none at all, and more elderly people living alone.

The nature of work changes. Over the decades, the types of jobs Americans have held have changed dramatically. At first an agricultural nation and then an industrial one, the United States by the late twentieth century was experiencing yet another transformation in the nature of the work its citizens do. This change was in the growth of service occupations. Instead of working in mills and factories, where they produced goods, more and more Americans were employed as teachers, salespeople, lawyers, writers, computer operators, government workers, restaurant and hotel personnel, repair workers, and so on. By 1980 more than half of all American jobholders were working in what is called the service sector, and the probable trend was for that number to continue to increase.

During the 1970's an increasing number of women in the United States were seeking employment outside the home. Compared with 1950, when only about 30 percent of women held jobs, the figure in 1980 had risen to nearly 50 percent.

As more and more women found work outside the home, the campaign for women's rights was renewed. Women demanded equal treatment in business, education, and in other professions. National groups were also formed to get more women elected to public office. Among these groups was the National Organization of Women (NOW), formed in 1966. By

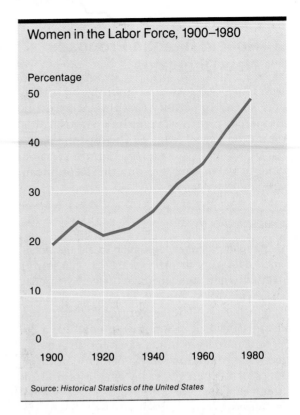

Women in the Labor Force, 1900–1980

Percentage

Source: *Historical Statistics of the United States*

In the 1960's and 1970's women entered the work force in large numbers and were employed in nearly every occupation. By 1980 almost 50 percent of American women held jobs outside the home.

1975, 4 percent of all the elected officials in the United States were women; just six years later that figure had risen to nearly 10 percent.

SECTION REVIEW

1. Vocabulary: *sunbelt.*
2. (a) What information did the 1980 census provide concerning the rate of population growth? (b) What information did it provide concerning the number of Americans aged 65 and over? (c) The shift of population distribution? (d) The population of urban centers?
3. (a) What was the fastest growing minority group in the United States during the 1970's? (b) From what continent did the largest number of immigrants come in that same decade?
4. (a) What changes took place in the nature of work in the United States? (b) In the number of women in the work force?

3 Ronald Reagan Proposes New Directions

President Reagan's first months in office were so full of activity that they were often compared with Franklin Roosevelt's "Hundred Days" (page 614). With the backing of Congress, the new administration went to work carrying out the Republican campaign pledges.

DOMESTIC POLICY

Reagan proposes legislation to aid the economy. The top priority was the economy, plagued when Reagan took office by unemployment, high interest rates, and double-digit inflation. The centerpiece of the new administration's program was a call for a 30 percent reduction in tax rates for all Americans. The reduction was to be made in three stages of 10 percent each, over a period of three years.

The President's program was based on the idea that, by stimulating investment and productivity, a reduction in taxes would actually result in an increase in tax revenues. Critics of the bill argued that a tax cut would not stimulate enough new economic activity to yield such revenues. They feared that the tax reduction would lead to a shortage of funds for government programs they regarded as indispensable. Many critics, opposed to what they called "Reaganomics," also charged that the tax cuts unfairly favored those in higher income brackets. Economists who supported the Reagan proposal responded by saying that tax cuts for wealthier people were essential to economic recovery. They claimed that from these reductions would come the capital for new investments which, in turn, would make new jobs.

Early in 1981 the nation's attention was diverted from the administration's economic proposals by an attempt on the President's life. On March 30, as he left a Washington hotel, Reagan was wounded by a would-be assassin's bullet. He was rushed to a nearby hospital to undergo emergency surgery. Reagan's courage won him widespread sympathy and admiration. Two weeks later, he was back in the White House on the road to complete recovery.

Congress approves the President's legislation. Late in July, Reagan's tax-cut bill — slightly modified — was passed by Congress. In its final form, the bill called for a reduction of federal revenues by an estimated $750 billion over a five-year period. The proposed 30 percent reduction in tax rates wound up as 25 percent, the first 5 percent coming in October, 1981, to be followed by successive 10 percent reductions in 1982 and 1983. Congress also approved the President's plan to cut back government spending by eliminating or reducing appropriations for certain domestic programs.

Economic troubles worsen. In the fall of 1981 the nation entered a recession marked by a sharp increase in the unemployment rate. By April, 1982, the unemployment rate had reached 9.4 percent — the highest it had been in the postwar era. The recession placed enormous demands on the federal budget. Government outlays for many so-called "entitlement programs," such as those for unemployment insurance and welfare benefits, could not be limited to any dollar amount. Payments to individuals were made automatically to all who qualified. Because of the hardships caused by the recession, large numbers of people were eligible for federal aid.

In addition to causing these unexpectedly high outlays, the recession contributed to a budgetary crisis by decreasing the government's tax receipts. Many American businesses were cutting back production, closing down plants, and even declaring bankruptcy. Individuals, too, had less income because of lay-offs and pay cuts. As their incomes decreased, they paid less in taxes. If it could not cut its spending, the government had only two choices: to increase taxes or go deeper into debt.

The administration proposes a new budget. In February, 1982, the Reagan administration presented its 1983 budget to Congress.

President and Mrs. Reagan appear at a Texas campaign rally for congressional supporters of the administration's economic program.

The budget called for new cuts in domestic spending, increased military spending, and no tax increases. It projected a deficit of $91.5 billion.

The proposed budget met with criticism from all sides. Many critics were concerned with the size of the deficit. To reduce the government's debt, some wanted further cuts in spending. Others wanted a tax increase. Republicans in Congress warned the President that his budget could not be passed in its original form, and they urged him to reconsider his demands.

Negotiations between administration officials and members of Congress finally produced a compromise package. This compromise, which Reagan accepted, called for further reductions in both defense and social-welfare spending and for a tax increase. President Reagan and Speaker of the House Thomas P. O'Neill joined in an unusual bipartisan effort to secure passage of the new tax bill. The bill, which approved a three-year round of tax increases totalling $98.3 billion, was passed by a narrow margin, and President Reagan signed it into law.

The inflation rate drops rapidly. The recession created many problems, but it also helped to solve one. Inflation, which had been running at well over 10 percent in 1980, had dropped by mid-1982 to an annual rate of about 5 percent. In the next year, it fell even lower. One effect was a desired leveling-off of the cost of living. Another restraining influence on the cost of living was the "tight-money" policy of the Federal Reserve Board. By controlling the amount of money available for private loans, the Federal Reserve forced interest rates to rise, which decreased demand for goods and services. The drop in demand resulted in lower prices.

Democrats make gains in the mid-term elections. Inflation continued to decline at a much faster pace than most observers had expected, and even interest rates began to fall. Unemployment, nevertheless, continued to be a serious problem and was a handicap for the Republicans in the 1982 elections. In October, 1982, the Labor Department announced that the unemploy-

Industrial Robots

Advances in electronic technology have made robots available for use in industry. These self-operating mechanical units, directed by microcomputer "brains," perform a wide range of manufacturing operations. Depending on how they are programmed, or instructed, industrial robots can use their claw-like "hands" to weld, drill, rivet, paint, assemble, inspect, and load.

The development of robots for industry holds out the promise of increased efficiency and greater productivity. At the same time, jobs will be created for highly skilled workers to build, program, and service these devices. To insure that the United States remains competitive in the world economy, robots have already been introduced in the automobile industry, where they have demonstrated their many capabilities and have proved their value in reducing operating costs.

ment rate had climbed to 10.1 percent. Democrats blamed the administration's economic policies for the recession. The President and his allies, on the other hand, asked the public to "stay the course," arguing that the new policies had not had time to prove their worth. In November, the Republicans lost 26 seats in the House of Representatives — about the average loss the party in power suffers in a mid-term election. They maintained control of the Senate.

Economic recovery begins. In November, 1982, the recession reached what proved to be its bottom, and an economic recovery began. Production indexes rose, and inflation remained under control. The unemployment rate held steady and within a few months began to drop. With the recovery under way, the President remarked of his critics, "They don't call it 'Reaganomics' any more."

Meanwhile, Reagan proposed other solutions to long-standing domestic concerns. The President's major new domestic pro-

gram became known as the "New Federalism." This plan called for a reduction in the size, power, and cost of running the federal government by gradually turning over responsibility for many of its social programs to state and local governments. In return, the federal government would assume full responsibility for Medicaid, a health-care program for needy Americans.

The President argued that his plan would make government more responsive to the needs of citizens by allowing programs to be tailored to the needs of each locality. State and local governments, on the other hand, were wary of accepting responsibility for funding more programs, especially in the midst of a recession. As a result, the New Federalism program did not win significant support.

The space shuttle is a success. A major domestic achievement in space exploration brightened the early days of the Reagan administration. In April, 1981, the spaceship *Columbia* completed 36 orbits of the earth

Having completed a successful mission, the space shuttle *Columbia* is placed aboard a jumbo jet for the flight back to the Kennedy Space Center in Florida.

and made a perfect landing at Edwards Air Force Base in California. The remarkable *Columbia* was the world's first reusable spacecraft. Whereas every previous space flight had required the enormous expense of building a new craft and new launching equipment, the *Columbia* could be used over and over. The comparatively frequent flights would make it possible for private industry to lease room on the shuttle to conduct experiments, which, it was predicted, would lead to advances in industrial technology. Successive flights of the *Columbia* began to fulfill the expectations of the planners that shuttle flights would play a part in America's future.

The Equal Rights Amendment fails to be ratified. For a number of years the Equal Rights Amendment (page 761) had been the focus of national attention. Supporters argued

Sandra Day O'Connor, shown with Chief Justice Warren Burger, was named by President Reagan to serve on the Supreme Court.

that the amendment was necessary to halt what they said was flagrant discrimination against women in areas such as taxation, insurance, marriage law, and Social Security. Opponents of ERA, who included President Reagan in their ranks, countered that the amendment was unnecessary because the Constitution and existing federal laws already guaranteed equal rights. The ERA, opponents maintained, would abolish many benefits enjoyed by women, such as alimony and child-support laws.

In June, 1982, time ran out for ERA. Only 35 of the required 38 state legislatures had ratified the amendment — and five of those states had later voted to reverse their decision. Pro-ERA forces immediately reintroduced the amendment in Congress, but in 1983 it failed to pass in the House of Representatives.

Women's rights leaders, though angered by the President's opposition to the ERA, had applauded his appointment in 1981 of Sandra Day O'Connor to the Supreme Court. Following her unanimous confirmation by the Senate, Mrs. O'Connor, a former Arizona state senator and judge, became the first woman member of the Supreme Court.

FOREIGN AFFAIRS

The United States strengthens its armed forces. During the 1980 campaign, Reagan had argued that because of the Soviet Union's threat to world peace, American foreign policy needed to be based on a strong national defense. Under his administration, the nation expanded the arms build-up that had been started in the last year of Carter's presidency. Reagan's concern about America's defense systems was clearly demonstrated in his budget proposals. While recommending cuts in spending in nearly all other sectors of government, Reagan asked for large increases in expenditures for the defense budget.

Reagan responds to a crisis in Poland. In addition to an arms build-up, the President relied on diplomatic and economic pressure to influence the actions of the Soviet government. In Soviet-dominated Poland, a

World tensions mounted in 1981 when Polish officials declared a state of martial law and suspended the operations of the independent trade union Solidarity.

crisis arose late in 1981. Polish workers had, the year before, formed a labor union called Solidarity, and had begun to demand a voice in government policy-making. They had wide support from the Polish people, who resented the Soviet Union's strangle hold on their country.

In December, 1981, Solidarity leaders called for a national referendum on whether Poland should continue its alliance with the Soviet Union and whether Poland itself should maintain a Communist form of government. In response, the Polish government declared martial law. The Soviet Union, claiming that its own security was being threatened by the Polish crisis, began to build up troop strength along the Polish border.

Western leaders feared that the Red Army would invade Poland to put an end to demands for reform. Through diplomatic channels and in public, the Reagan administration warned the Soviet Union not to interfere in Poland. Blaming the Soviet Union for the repression of Solidarity, Reagan also announced a number of sanctions. He placed an embargo on the sale of electronic equipment to the Soviet Union; postponed

discussions on the lifting of the Carter grain embargo (page 780); suspended American landing rights for Aeroflot, the Soviet airline; and halted the sale of American equipment that was to have been used in constructing a natural-gas pipeline between the Soviet Union and Western Europe.

The Soviet Union did not invade Poland, but the Communist government of Poland did not relax its political repression either. Even the minimal civil liberties granted to citizens under the Polish constitution were suspended. Private meetings were banned, identity papers had to be carried at all times, and a curfew was strictly enforced. Many Poles, furthermore, were jailed for their support of Solidarity. Among these was the immensely popular leader of the movement, Lech Walesa, who was imprisoned for eleven months. For his efforts on behalf of the Polish people, Walesa was awarded the Nobel Peace Prize in 1983.

Many of America's European allies, meanwhile, objected to President Reagan's efforts to halt construction of the gas pipeline. They complained that they had not been consulted on the equipment embargo and that contracts for construction of the pipeline, which had been signed long before the Polish crisis, could not legally be broken. As a result of the protests, the Reagan administration afterwards decided to lift the embargo.

The arms race stirs controversy. During the Carter presidency, the Soviet Union had installed hundreds of long-range missiles in Eastern Europe, aimed at targets in Western Europe. In response, the United States and its NATO allies moved ahead with the production of new weapons designed to counter the Soviet missiles. At the same time, they sought an arms-limitation agreement with the Soviet Union.

As the new missiles went into production, public concern that the arms race might lead to nuclear war was heightened. In Western Europe and the United States, a movement arose that demanded a "freeze" in the existing levels of nuclear weapons possessed by both the United States and the Soviet Union. Advocates of a nuclear freeze saw it as a first step in bringing the arms race under control, to be followed by negotiations leading to further reductions in armaments. Reagan administration officials favored arms-reduction talks but opposed an immediate freeze. Two sets of arms-limitations talks proceeded simultaneously in Geneva, Switzerland — the strategic arms reduction talks (START), which involved intercontinental missiles, and the intermediate-range nuclear forces talks (INF), which focused on the missiles being placed in Europe. As these negotiations went on, so did planning for deployment of the new NATO missiles. The first of those missiles were put in place late in 1983.

The Soviet air force shoots down a Korean plane. Tension between the United States and the Soviet Union was heightened in September, 1983, when a South Korean commercial airliner was shot down over Soviet territory. In the incident, 269 people were killed — 61 of them American. World reaction was highly critical, especially because Soviet leaders refused at first even to admit that their pilots had shot down the

plane and later because of their claims that they had been within their rights to do so. Investigations eventually revealed that the Soviet pilot had erred in destroying the jetliner, apparently having mistaken it for an American reconnaissance plane. Nevertheless, the Soviet Union did not take responsibility for the tragedy.

The United States seeks peace in the Middle East. The Middle East offered the Reagan administration perhaps its greatest challenge in foreign policy. The framework of the administration's efforts to achieve a lasting peace in the region was the Camp David accords (page 775). The durability of these agreements was called into question in October, 1981, when President Sadat of Egypt was assassinated by extremists.

Relations between the United States and Israel, meanwhile, were strained in December, 1981, when Israel annexed the Golan Heights, strategically located on its border with Syria. Israel defended its action as necessary to its security. The United States, on the other hand, charged that the annexation was a direct violation of the Camp David agreements.

Israel invades Lebanon. In 1982 the focus of trouble in the Middle East shifted to Lebanon. The Palestine Liberation Organization (PLO), a terrorist group pledged to the destruction of Israel, had long used southern Lebanon as a base for attacks on Israel. Israel appealed to the Lebanese government to put a stop to these assaults, but the government, plagued by years of civil strife, was unable to control the PLO guerrillas.

Determined to rid themselves of the constant harassment and loss of life, Israeli forces invaded Lebanon early in June, 1982. The Israelis quickly moved northward, and within a week they had pushed the PLO back to Lebanon's capital city of Beirut (bay-ROOT). There the guerrillas mingled with the civilian population, while continuing to fire on the Israeli troops that surrounded the city.

More than any previous incident, the invasion of Lebanon strained Israeli-American relations. The United States attempted to persuade Israel to withdraw from Lebanon, but the Israelis, clearly victorious, refused to withdraw before certain security conditions were met. The most important of these were the withdrawal of the PLO and of Syrian forces that had occupied parts of Lebanon since 1976; the introduction of a strong, multinational peacekeeping force; and the creation of a government sympathetic to Israel's concerns. Through the tireless efforts of United States diplomats, Israel's conditions were largely met, and in August, 1982, units of troops from the United States, France, and Italy arrived in Beirut to supervise the evacuation of the PLO guerrillas.

Reagan proposes a new Middle East peace plan. Responding to these events and sensing an opportunity, President Reagan in a major speech on September 1, 1982, made public a new plan for ending the strife in the Middle East. Linking his proposals directly to the recently halted war in Lebanon, he called for the cooperation of all parties to make a fresh start toward the achievement of a lasting peace not only in Lebanon but throughout the region. First, he called on the international community to help in the rebuilding of Lebanon, which had been devastated by years of warfare. Second, he called on Israel to reverse its policy of building new settlements in the occupied territories of the West Bank and the Gaza Strip, which had been won in the 1967 war. In return, he called upon Arab and Palestinian leaders to recognize Israel's right to exist and to begin peace negotiations. Finally, as a solution to the problem of the Palestinians' demands for a homeland, he proposed a five-year transition period after which the Palestinians on the West Bank and in the Gaza Strip would be granted self-government under the supervision of Jordan.

Tanks and armored personnel carriers spearheaded the Israeli drive into Lebanon in 1982, as Israel sought to destroy Palestine Liberation Organization strongholds.

Following the withdrawal of Israeli forces from Beirut, American warships moved into position just off the Lebanese coast.

Reaction to the President's plan was mixed. Before it was thoroughly debated, however, events in Lebanon again chilled hopes for peace in the Middle East. Just two weeks after Reagan's speech, the president-elect of Lebanon was assassinated. Shortly thereafter, there was more shocking news, this time of mass killings in two Palestinian refugee camps in Beirut. As a result of these incidents, the Lebanese government asked for the return of the peacekeeping force (which had left the city following the evacuation of the PLO).

During the next months, sporadic fighting continued among the Israelis, the Syrians, and the many Lebanese factions that had developed during years of civil war. Meanwhile, agreement was finally reached on the withdrawal of Israeli troops from their positions around Beirut to fortified positions in southern Lebanon. As the time for their departure approached, however, fighting among various Lebanese groups intensified. Each group sought to gain control of the areas the Israelis were about to abandon. Twice, the Israelis agreed to postpone their pullback in order to give the Lebanese army more time to arrange a cease-fire with rebel groups, but these efforts failed. When the Israelis finally departed, Lebanon seemed to be on the brink of full-scale civil war.

The search for peace in the Middle East continues. The peacekeeping force stationed in Beirut faced a dangerous assignment. They constantly found themselves under sniper fire. Then, on October 23, 1983, a terrorist drove a truck filled with explosives into barracks that were used for housing American marines. The massive explosion left 241 dead and more than 80 wounded. A similar attack on French barracks resulted in 56 dead and 15 wounded.

Shortly, there was another disturbing event in the troubled region. An American navy reconnaissance plane was shot down while flying over Syrian positions in Lebanon. The pilot was killed and the navigator, Robert Goodman, was captured and held by the Syrians as a prisoner of war.

When negotiations failed to obtain Goodman's speedy release, Jesse Jackson, a Democratic candidate for President in 1984, flew to Damascus to confer with the Syrian president, Hafez al-Assad. After three days of discussions, Assad agreed to release Goodman, who returned home to a hero's welcome. Observers hoped that the good will arising from Goodman's release might lead to further progress in achieving peace in the Middle East. Soon, however, the situation in Lebanon deteriorated into a chaotic, bloody struggle between Muslim militiamen and the shaky Lebanese army. Early in 1984 the multinational peacekeeping force withdrew from Beirut.

War in the Falklands strains relations with Latin America. Reagan was confronted with problems not only in Europe, Asia, and the Middle East but in the Western Hemisphere as well. Early in his administration the United States was caught in the middle of a dispute between two of its allies — Argentina and Great Britain. In April, 1982, Argentina seized the Falkland Islands, a British possession lying 300 miles off the Argentine coast. Outraged, the British government sent naval forces to retake the islands.

The United States wanted to avoid angering either party in the dispute, but neutrality proved to be impossible. Because Argentina had been the aggressor in the incident, Secretary of State Alexander Haig announced that the United States was backing Britain. Along with a number of European countries, the United States imposed economic sanctions on Argentina. This action angered many Latin Americans who, while disapproving of Argentina's resort to force, believed its claim to the islands to be legitimate.

By mid-June, British forces had defeated the Argentinians and retaken the Falklands.

Relations between the United States and Latin America, however, had been severely strained.

Unrest in Central America causes concern. The ire felt by many Latin Americans was soon fed by events in Central America. Communist-backed revolutionaries had come to power in Nicaragua in 1979. Nicaraguan officials, assuming a harsh anti-American position, seemed to be moving relentlessly toward the establishment of a one-party Marxist state. They were also, the Reagan administration had concluded, mounting a major Soviet-backed arms build-up and supplying arms and ammunition to guerrillas who were trying to overthrow the government of neighboring El Salvador.

In light of this situation, administration officials sought to remove the immediate threat to El Salvador by sending military aid and by trying to halt the flow of arms to the rebels. They also attempted to address the underlying causes of popular discontent in Central America by pressing for economic and political reforms in countries receiving American assistance.

The flow of American arms to El Salvador gave rise to controversy in the United States. Opponents of the administration's policy argued that the role of outsiders in the civil war there was being exaggerated and that the causes of the war were internal. In addition, they criticized the Salvadorian government for serious human-rights violations, including political killings.

To answer the criticism, the President appointed a commission, headed by former Secretary of State Henry Kissinger, to analyze United States policy in Central America. In its report, issued early in 1984, the National Bipartisan Commission on Central America strongly endorsed administration policies. It asserted that the Soviet-Cuban backing of Nicaragua posed a threat to the security of the region, and it insisted on changes toward democracy in Nicaragua. It also proposed that the United States provide Central America with $8 billion in economic aid from 1985 to 1989.

Reagan sends American troops to Grenada.
The Caribbean island of Grenada was the setting for another crisis for the United States. American and various Latin American and Caribbean officials had been watching for months the involvement of Cuba and other Soviet allies in Grenadian life. The Marxist government of Grenada was constructing an international airport with Cuban money and hundreds of Cuban workers. American observers believed that the airport was to be used as a staging point for Cuban and Soviet military aircraft.

On October 20, 1983, the Grenadian prime minister was assassinated. His slayers, acting for a hard-line Marxist faction in the government, immediately took full control of the island and enforced a shoot-on-sight curfew.

Three days later, leaders of several Caribbean nations asked President Reagan for American assistance in restoring order and democracy to Grenada. The President, who shared their concern about the situation on the island, also wanted to ensure the safety of Americans living in Grenada. On October 25, military forces from the United States and six Caribbean nations landed on Grenada. They quickly secured their military objectives and safely evacuated all the Americans who wanted to leave. In the course of the fighting, they discovered supplies of Soviet-made weapons and a number of Communist-bloc "advisers." The weapons were confiscated and the foreign nationals were allowed to return home.

In the United States, reaction to this incident was overwhelmingly on the President's side. Within a few days, all reports indicated clearly that the Grenadians had welcomed the international force that had rid them of an unwanted dictator. Moreover, the enthusiastic gratitude of the rescued American nationals was enough to persuade the majority of Americans that Reagan had made the right decision.

Within a few weeks of restoring order in Grenada, American combat troops were withdrawn from the island.

THE ELECTION OF 1984

The 1984 presidential campaign gets under way. Confident that the American people were feeling more prosperous and optimistic than four years earlier, President Reagan announced that he would seek re-election in 1984. Again he chose George Bush to be his Vice President. As their candidate, the Democrats nominated former Vice President Walter Mondale, who won out at the party's convention in San Francisco over a field that included Senator Gary Hart of Colorado and Jesse Jackson (page 795).

Mondale selected Congresswoman Geraldine A. Ferraro of New York as his vice-presidential running mate. The choice of a woman to share for the first time the leadership of a major-party ticket stirred the nation. The Democrats apparently hoped to influence women voters, who in 1980 had cast six million more votes than men. Mondale, however, explained simply, "I looked for the best Vice President and I found her in Gerry Ferraro."

During the campaign the Democratic standard-bearer denounced the President for failing to sit down with Soviet leaders to discuss nuclear-arms control — a charge that lost force when Reagan met with the Soviet foreign minister shortly before the election. Mondale also declared that, if elected, he would raise taxes in order to reduce the enormous federal budget deficit of $175 billion — the largest in the nation's history. Reagan derided Mondale's proposal. "Why raise our taxes when we can raise our sights?" he said, as he pointed to the booming American economy and the sharp reduction in the rate of inflation.

Reagan wins re-election. Two televised debates between the candidates resulted in much discussion of the President's age (Reagan was 73 years old), and whether he had full command of the details of government. The voters gave a resounding judgment. On Election Day, 1984, Reagan swept 49 states, giving him 525 electoral votes, the highest total in history. He had captured 59 percent of the popular vote. Mondale, with 41 percent of the vote, carried only his home state of Minnesota and the District of Columbia. The Republicans retained control of the Senate, although the Democrats still held a majority in the House of Representatives. Ronald Reagan's overwhelming personal triumph marked the first time a presidential candidate had won two landslide victories in a row since Dwight D. Eisenhower.

In setting a course for tomorrow, nations gaze backward as well as forward. They search in their history for guidelines, if not for directions. Americans have the satisfaction of finding in their past, for instruction and inspiration, an incomparable story of high achievement and steady devotion to the ideal of freedom for all. Each succeeding generation of the Glorious Republic takes on the obligation to write a bright new chapter in this grandest of unfinished epics. Every patriotic voice — young and old alike — echoes the poet's proud salute penned long ago:

> . . . Sail on, O Ship of State!
> Sail on, O Union, strong and great!
> Humanity with all its fears,
> With all the hopes of future years,
> Is hanging breathless on thy fate!

SECTION REVIEW

1. (a) What economic problems did the nation face when Ronald Reagan took office? (b) How did Reagan attempt to solve those problems? (c) What were the results?
2. (a) What happened to the Equal Rights Amendment? (b) What historic appointment did President Reagan make?
3. (a) How did Reagan respond to the crackdown on Solidarity in Poland? (b) What caused the nuclear-freeze movement to gain strength? (c) What was the reaction of the Reagan administration?
4. (a) What events in the Middle East upset the progress toward peace that had earlier been made at Camp David? (b) Why did Israel invade Lebanon? (c) What role has the United States played in the Middle East in recent years?
5. (a) Why did the Reagan administration send aid to El Salvador? (b) Why were American troops sent to Grenada?

Chapter 33 Review

Summary

When Jimmy Carter took the oath of office as President in 1977, he faced many challenges. To try to heal the disunity caused by the Vietnam War, he granted an amnesty to all Vietnam-era draft resisters. In an attempt to ensure that there would be no repeat of the 1973 energy crisis, Carter introduced a comprehensive energy program designed to develop American independence from foreign energy sources. Alarming rates of unemployment and inflation also confronted the Carter administration, and efforts were made to stabilize wages and prices as well as reduce the jobless rate.

Carter's greatest achievement was to bring Israel's Menachem Begin and Egypt's Anwar Sadat together at Camp David to mediate agreements that were seen as a first step toward peace in the Middle East. His most difficult challenge came after Iranians seized the American embassy in Tehran and made hostages of the embassy staff. Unable to negotiate a release of the hostages, Carter authorized a military rescue mission that ended in failure. The hostages were finally released early in 1981, on the last day of Carter's presidency.

In the presidential campaign of 1980, Carter again won the Democratic nomination, while Ronald Reagan became the Republican candidate. The election resulted in an overwhelming victory for Reagan, and the Republican Party gained control of the Senate for the first time since 1952.

The 1980 census provided the American people with an opportunity to examine a number of trends that had been developing in their country. The population growth rate was slowing considerably, while the average age of the nation's citizens was steadily increasing. Minority population in the United States grew rapidly during the 1970's, while many people continued to leave the Northeast and the Upper Midwest for the sunbelt.

The most pressing issue facing Ronald Reagan when he came to office in 1981 was the state of the economy. High unemployment and inflation were crippling the nation. Reagan proposed legislation designed to stimulate the economy through a series of tax cuts. By the end of 1982 the economy had begun to recover, and the rate of inflation had notably declined.

Reagan's main position in foreign affairs was to take a firm stand against the Soviet Union by building up America's military power. Tension between the two superpowers heated up following unrest in Poland, the installation of new Soviet missiles in Eastern Europe, and the shooting down of a Korean airliner that strayed over Soviet territory. Reagan showed his readiness to display strength by sending advisers and arms to Central America, stationing a contingent of marines in Lebanon, and sending troops to the Caribbean island of Grenada.

Vocabulary and Important Terms

1. Department of Energy
2. Council on Wage and Price Stability
3. "crisis-of-confidence" speech
4. human rights
5. Camp David accords
6. sunbelt
7. New Federalism
8. *Columbia*
9. Solidarity

Discussion Questions

1. (a) To what extent were inflation and unemployment problems during the Carter administration? (b) During the Reagan administration? (c) How did Carter and Reagan differ in their proposals to aid the economy, and what successes, if any, did each have?

2. (a) What role did Carter play in helping Israel and Egypt reach a peaceful agreement? (b) What events after the Camp David accords strained relations between the United States and Israel? (c) How did Reagan propose to bring peace to the Middle East? (d) What happened to Reagan's peace plan, and why?

3. (a) On what grounds was Carter challenged for the Democratic presidential nomination in 1980? (b) Why were the challenges of his Democratic opponents unsuccessful? (c) What factors contributed to Carter's defeat in the election?

4. (a) What events caused a deterioration in American-Soviet relations during Carter's presidency? (b) During Reagan's years in office? (c) How did this deterioration in relations affect the arms race?

5. (a) What areas of the country have experienced the fastest rate of growth in recent years? (b) How has the percentage of elderly Americans changed? (c) What factor helps explain that change?

6. (a) Why did the Falklands War strain relations between Latin America and the United States? (b) What was the Reagan administration's policy regarding El Salvador? (c) Why did that policy give rise to controversy? (d) Why did Reagan send American troops to Grenada? (e) What was the reaction of the American people?

Relating Past and Present

1. Unrest in Central America in the early 1980's caused concern among Reagan administration officials. Does unrest in Central America continue to be a problem for the United States? What is the current policy regarding Central America?
2. What economic problems does the United States face today? To what extent are inflation, unemployment, and deficit spending cause for concern, and what is the current economic policy?

Studying Local History

Find out what shifts in population occurred in your region during the 1970's. Account for any local population gains or losses. Explain how shifts in population affected your region.

Using History Skills

1. *Using reference books.* Find the population figures for the 1980 census in library reference books. (a) Which regions of the United States showed the greatest gains in population between 1970 and 1980? (b) Which regions showed the smallest gains? (c) What were the ten largest states by 1980, and by what percentages did their population change between 1970 and 1980? (d) Which states actually lost population during that same decade, and by what percentages?
2. *Reading graphs.* Study the graph on page 785 showing the percentage of women in the labor force. (a) Approximately what percentage of women worked outside the home in 1900? (b) In 1940? (c) In 1980? (d) What factors help explain the growing percentage of working women?

WORLD SCENE

The Quest for Human Rights

The right of individuals to express their opinions is a fundamental freedom for which people throughout history have fought. In many nations today, the struggle to gain this freedom continues.

Soviet dissidents. The Communist government of the Soviet Union demands absolute obedience and loyalty from its citizens. Dissidents who defy the government by speaking out against injustice are considered by Soviet officials to be traitors who threaten the security of the state.

Opposition to Communist rule comes from various sectors of Soviet society. Many dissidents are intellectuals who oppose control of what they may write and teach; others represent religious and ethnic minorities who resist government efforts to deny them freedom to worship and live as they desire; still others are individuals who object to the Soviet Union's participation in the nuclear arms build-up.

All opposition to official policy is regarded by Soviet authorities as criminal activity. The notorious KGB, the Soviet secret police, harasses dissidents and their families. Many Soviet dissidents have been sentenced to years in forced-labor camps. Some dissidents have been confined to mental hospitals and treated as if they were ill. A number of dissidents have been forced into exile.

Novelist Alexander Solzhenitsyn (sohl-zhuh-NEET-sihn) was one well-known Soviet dissident. After being forced to spend years in labor camps and mental hospitals, Solzhenitsyn wrote about his experiences in books that were eventually published in Europe and the United States. Solzhenitsyn's novels and insistent calls for greater freedom in the Soviet Union led to even more trouble with Communist authorities. Shortly after receiving the Nobel Prize for literature in 1970, Solzhenitsyn and his family were forced to leave the Soviet Union. They finally settled in the United States, where he continued to write about the denial of freedom in Communist Russia.

Another prominent dissident was Andrei Sakharov. A highly honored scientist who had helped develop the Soviet Union's hydrogen bomb, Sakharov publicly challenged his government's human-rights violations. He also organized a movement in the Soviet Union to protest the deployment of nuclear missiles. For his courageous efforts, Sakharov was awarded the Nobel Peace Prize in 1975.

Sakharov was arrested in 1980 on the charge that he was a threat to the security of the state. His Soviet honors were revoked, and he was exiled to the remote city of Gorky. His banishment caused governments and civil-liberties groups around the world to protest this outrage.

UNIT 9 REVIEW

Important Dates

1969 Americans land on moon.
1970 Environmental Protection Agency created.
1972 Nixon visits China and Soviet Union.
Watergate break-in.
1973 Last American troops leave Vietnam.
Yom Kippur War.
Ervin Committee investigates
Watergate affair.
1974 Nixon resigns presidency.
Ford pardons Nixon.
1976 Carter elected President.
1978 Camp David accords signed.
1979 American embassy in Iran seized.
Soviet Union invades Afghanistan.
1980 United States boycotts Olympic Games.
Reagan elected President.
1981 American hostages released by Iran.
American space shuttle completes first
successful flight.
First woman named to Supreme Court.
1982 Falklands War.
Israel invades Lebanon.
1983 American forces sent to Grenada.

Review Questions

1. (a) Upon taking office, every President faces important challenges. What, in your opinion, were the most important challenges facing President Nixon, Ford, Carter, and Reagan? (b) How successful was each at achieving his goal? Explain your answer.
2. (a) What have been the major economic concerns of recent years? (b) What proposals have various administrations made to solve those economic problems?
3. (a) What events led to President Nixon's resignation? (b) Why did Gerald Ford pardon Nixon? (c) Why did some Americans criticize that action?
4. (a) What factors contributed to the defeat at the polls of Presidents Ford and Carter? (b) In what ways were the reasons for each incumbent's defeat similar? (c) How were they different?
5. (a) What were America's notable achievements in space during the 1970's and 1980's? (b) Why were these achievements important?
6. (a) What was the state of relations between the United States and Soviet Union during the Nixon administration? (b) What actions by the United States brought about this relationship?
7. (a) What events affected American-Soviet relations during the Carter and Reagan administrations?

(b) What effect did these events have on American defense spending and on the arms race? (c) During the same span of years, what changes took place in United States relations with China?
8. (a) How did the Yom Kippur War of 1973 threaten world peace? (b) What approach did the Camp David accords of 1978 take in laying the foundation for peace in the Middle East? (c) What factors contributed to a renewal of tension in that region?

Projects

1. Play the part of a newspaper editor whose job it was to write headlines regarding the end of American involvement in Vietnam. Your first headline should announce Nixon's Vietnamization policy. Your subsequent headlines should focus on American diplomatic and military efforts to end the war. Your final headline should indicate what happened to Vietnam once American troops were withdrawn.
2. Make a model of one of the spacecraft that projected the United States into the forefront of the space race. You might make a model of an Apollo command module, an Apollo lunar module, the space shuttle, or some other American contribution to space exploration. Include a brief description of how the innovation represented by your model helped advance space exploration.
3. Form a committee to find out more about the impact of pollution on the nation's environment. Each member of the committee might choose one type of pollution (air, water, or land pollution) and use the library and other resources to find information about it. Report your findings to the class.
4. Participate in a classroom panel discussion of the current situation in the Middle East. The panel should identify the countries that are located in the Middle East, the ways in which these countries interact with one another, and the extent of American and Soviet involvement in that area of the world. Panel members might also discuss possible solutions to the issues that divide the countries of the Middle East.
5. Write an essay relating United States concern over Central America during the 1980's to the concern expressed in 1823 when the Monroe Doctrine was proclaimed. First, review the circumstances under which the Monroe Doctrine was issued and the steps by which it became the cornerstone of American foreign policy. Then, write a paragraph or two in which you discuss whether or not United States concern about Central America today is an application of the Monroe Doctrine.

ATLAS AND REFERENCE SECTION

THE UNITED STATES
Cities and States

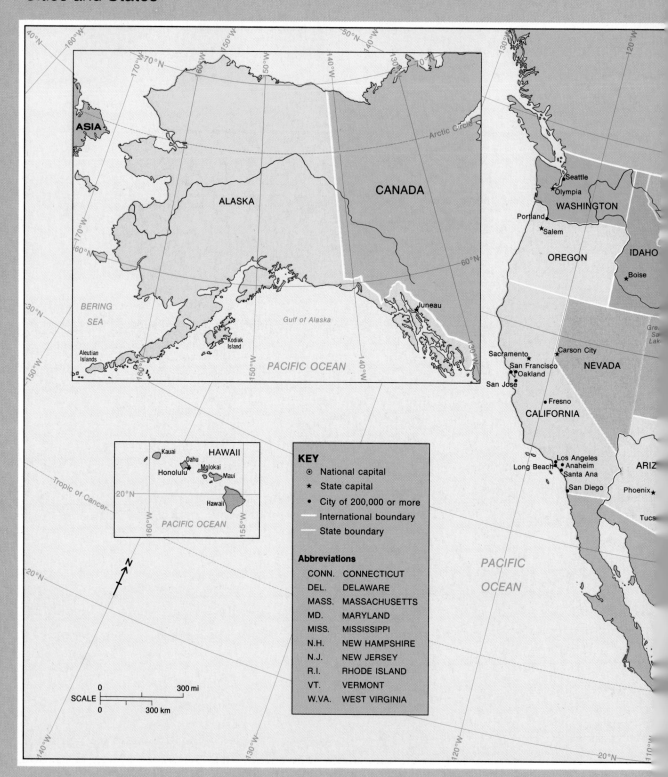

KEY

- ⊙ National capital
- ★ State capital
- • City of 200,000 or more
- — International boundary
- — State boundary

Abbreviations

CONN.	CONNECTICUT
DEL.	DELAWARE
MASS.	MASSACHUSETTS
MD.	MARYLAND
MISS.	MISSISSIPPI
N.H.	NEW HAMPSHIRE
N.J.	NEW JERSEY
R.I.	RHODE ISLAND
VT.	VERMONT
W.VA.	WEST VIRGINIA

SCALE

0 — 300 mi

0 — 300 km

Hudson Bay

CANADA

MONTANA

NORTH DAKOTA
★ Bismarck

MINNESOTA

Lake Superior

MAINE
★ Augusta

Montpelier ★
N.H.
NEW
YORK
VT.
★ Concord
Albany ★
★ Boston
MASS.
Hartford
Providence
R.I.
CONN.

WYOMING

SOUTH DAKOTA
★ Pierre

Minneapolis ★ St. Paul

WISCONSIN

Madison ★

Lake Michigan

MICHIGAN

Lansing ★

Lake Huron

Lake Ontario

Rochester

Buffalo

Milwaukee

Detroit

Lake Erie

Cleveland

Jersey City
New York
Newark

NEBRASKA

Cheyenne ★

Denver ★
COLORADO
Colorado
Springs

IOWA
★ Des Moines

Omaha ★
Lincoln ★

Chicago ★

ILLINOIS

INDIANA

Indianapolis ★

Toledo

Akron

Dayton

Cincinnati

OHIO

Columbus ★

Pittsburgh

PENNSYLVANIA

Harrisburg ★

Washington, D.C. ⊙

Philadelphia
N.J.
Trenton
DEL.
Dover
Baltimore
Annapolis
MD.

Santa Fe ★
Albuquerque

NEW MEXICO

El Paso ★

KANSAS

Topeka ★

Kansas
City

Jefferson
City

St. Louis

MISSOURI

Wichita ★

Tulsa ★

Oklahoma
City ★

OKLAHOMA

Little
Rock ★

ARKANSAS

Springfield ★

Louisville

Frankfort ★
Lexington

KENTUCKY

W.VA.

Charleston ★

Richmond ★

VIRGINIA

Norfolk
Virginia
Beach

ATLANTIC
OCEAN

Nashville ★

TENNESSEE

Memphis ★

Raleigh ★

Charlotte ★

NORTH CAROLINA

SOUTH
CAROLINA

Columbia ★

Fort Worth ★ ★ Dallas

Shreveport ★

Jackson ★

MISS.

Birmingham ★

Montgomery ★

ALABAMA

Atlanta ★

GEORGIA

Austin ★

TEXAS

San Antonio ★

Houston ★

LOUISIANA

Baton
Rouge ★
New Orleans

Mobile ★

Tallahassee ★

Jacksonville ★

FLORIDA

Tampa ★
St. Petersburg ★

Miami ★

BAHAMAS

Corpus Christi ★

Gulf of Mexico

MEXICO

Tropic of Cancer

CUBA

50°N
40°N
30°N
20°N
110°W
100°W
90°W
80°W
70°W

THE UNITED STATES
Physical Features

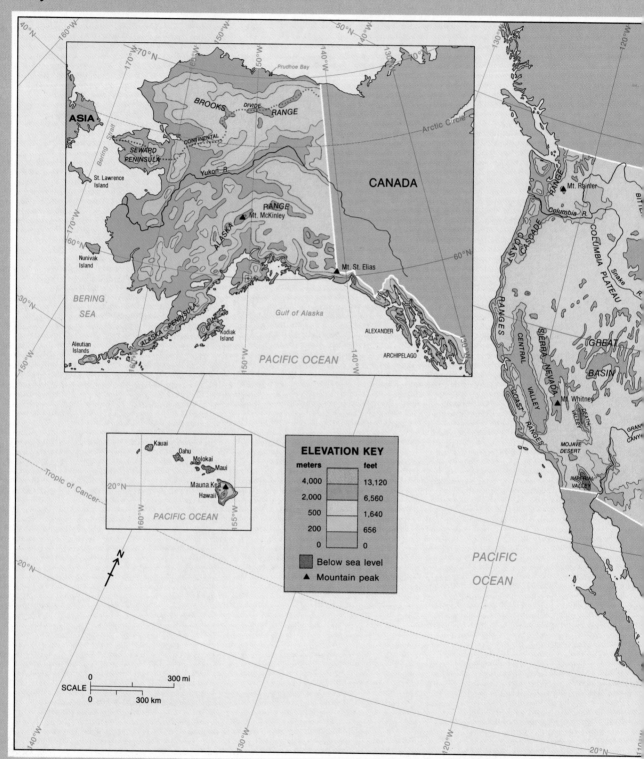

ASIA

Prudhoe Bay

BROOKS   DIVIDE   RANGE

CONTINENTAL

SEWARD
PENINSULA

St. Lawrence
Island

Yukon R.

CANADA

Arctic Circle

ALASKA   RANGE   Mt. McKinley

Nunivak
Island

Mt. St. Elias

BERING
SEA

Gulf of Alaska

Aleutian
Islands   ALASKA PENINSULA   Kodiak
Island

ALEXANDER

PACIFIC OCEAN   ARCHIPELAGO

Bering Strait

Mt. Rainier

Columbia R.

CASCADE   RANGE

COLUMBIA
PLATEAU

BITTER

Snake R.

RANGES

COAST   CENTRAL
RANGES   VALLEY

SIERRA NEVADA   DEATH
VALLEY   Mt. Whitney

GREAT

BASIN

GRAN
CANY

MOJAVE
DESERT

IMPERIAL
VALLEY

Kauai

Oahu

Molokai   Maui

Mauna Kea
Hawaii

Tropic of Cancer

PACIFIC OCEAN

ELEVATION KEY

meters		feet
4,000		13,120
2,000		6,560
500		1,640
200		656
0		0

Below sea level

▲ Mountain peak

PACIFIC

OCEAN

N

SCALE

0		300 mi
0		300 km

Hudson Bay

CANADA

ROCKY

Missouri R.

GREAT

BLACK
HILLS

CONTINENTAL DIVIDE

Mt. Elbert

Pikes Peak

ORADO

TEAU

MOUNTAINS

PLAINS

Platte R.

Missouri R.

Arkansas R.

LLANO
ESTACADO

Red R.

Rio Grande

EDWARDS
PLATEAU

MESABI
RANGE

Lake Superior

Mississippi R.

INTERIOR
PLAINS

OZARK PLATEAU

OUACHITA MTS.

Mississippi R.

GULF

COASTAL

MISSISSIPPI
DELTA

Lake Huron

Lake Michigan

Lake Ontario

Lake Erie

Ohio R.

CUMBERLAND PLATEAU

APPALACHIAN

BLUE RIDGE MTS.

PLAIN

ATLANTIC COASTAL PLAIN

St. Lawrence R.

WHITE
MTS.

ADIRONDACK
MTS.

GREEN MTS.

CATSKILL
MTS.

MOUNTAINS

CAPE
COD

Long Island

bay

ATLANTIC

OCEAN

CAPE
HATTERAS

CAPE
CANAVERAL

EVERGLADES

FLORIDA KEYS

BAHAMAS

MEXICO

Gulf of Mexico

Tropic of Cancer

CUBA

50°N

40°N

30°N

20°N

110°W

100°W

90°W

80°W

70°W

805

THE AMERICAN PEOPLE

It is now nearly 500 years since Columbus first reached the Americas. In those five centuries — as colonies were established and as the United States emerged as a mighty nation — millions of people immigrated to these shores. Every American today, in fact, is an immigrant or a descendant of an immigrant. As President Franklin D. Roosevelt once said, "Remember, remember always, that all of us . . . are descended from immigrants. . . ."

The following maps and graphs will tell you various things about the American people. They will also reinforce many of the themes you have read about in your study of American history. The map below, for example, shows the population density of the fifty states at the time of the 1980 census. The map also shows the nation's largest cities.

The bar graph at the top of the next page provides information about the national backgrounds of immigrants who have come to this country since 1820. It helps demonstrate the fact that in spite of recent changes in sources of immigration, the largest numbers of immigrants in the period since 1820 have come from Europe. Another graph on the next page shows the American population by age group. In recent years the group aged eighteen years and younger has been declining as a percentage of the population, while the two older age groups have been growing larger. One reason for the aging of the population is the rise in average life expectancy, the subject of the third graph on the next page. On average, an American baby born in 1980 can expect to live almost thirty years longer than could a baby born in 1900.

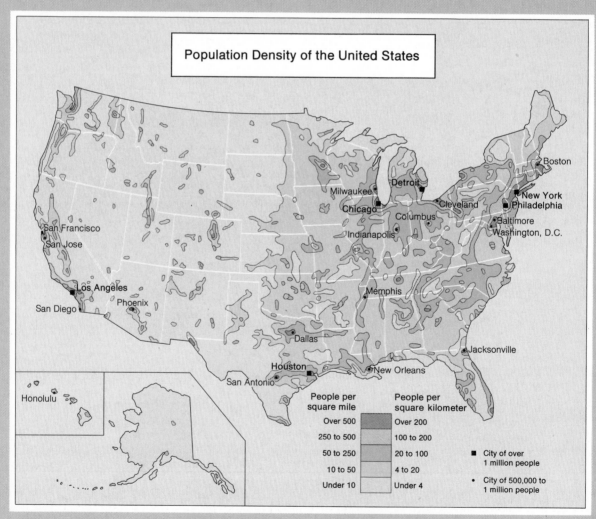

Population Density of the United States

People per square mile	People per square kilometer
Over 500	Over 200
250 to 500	100 to 200
50 to 250	20 to 100
10 to 50	4 to 20
Under 10	Under 4

■ City of over 1 million people

• City of 500,000 to 1 million people

Immigration by Country of Origin, 1820–1979

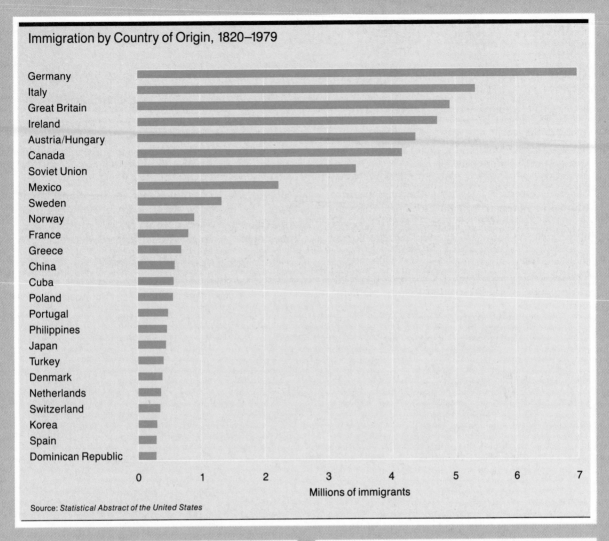

Country	Millions of immigrants
Germany	
Italy	
Great Britain	
Ireland	
Austria/Hungary	
Canada	
Soviet Union	
Mexico	
Sweden	
Norway	
France	
Greece	
China	
Cuba	
Poland	
Portugal	
Philippines	
Japan	
Turkey	
Denmark	
Netherlands	
Switzerland	
Korea	
Spain	
Dominican Republic	

Millions of immigrants

Source: *Statistical Abstract of the United States*

Population by Age Distribution, 1960–1980

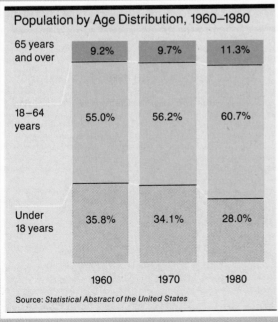

Age group	1960	1970	1980
65 years and over	9.2%	9.7%	11.3%
18–64 years	55.0%	56.2%	60.7%
Under 18 years	35.8%	34.1%	28.0%

Source: *Statistical Abstract of the United States*

Life Expectancy at Birth, 1900–1980

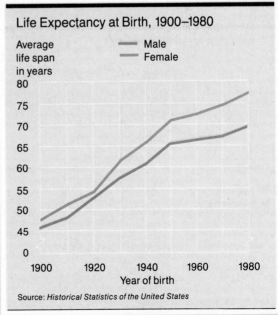

Average life span in years

— Male
— Female

Year of birth

Source: *Historical Statistics of the United States*

POPULATION TRENDS

The Constitution of the United States provides that a census be taken every ten years, primarily to establish a basis for the apportionment of members in the House of Representatives. The Bureau of the Census is responsible for counting the American people and also for compiling statistics on other subjects.

Among the trends revealed by the 1980 census was the continued decline in the percentage of Americans living in central cities. At the same time, the percentage of elderly Americans was on the rise. As shown in the table at the bottom of this page, in 1980 there were more than 25 million Americans aged 65 and over. Another trend had to do with the movement of Americans to the sunbelt. This shift in population, which started in the 1950's, has continued to gather force. Of the states that showed either a decline in population or low population growth in the 1970's, almost all were in the Northeast or Middle West. Many states in the South and West, on the other hand, enjoyed rapid population growth. As a consequence, adjustments have been made in congressional representation.

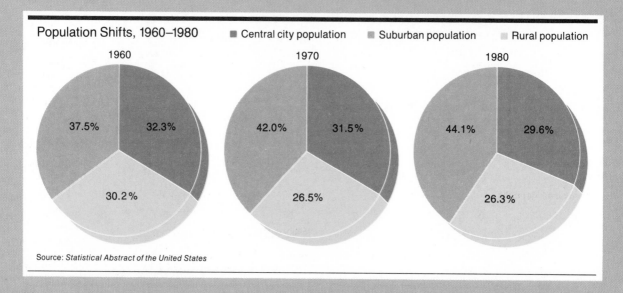

Population Shifts, 1960–1980 ■ Central city population ■ Suburban population ■ Rural population

1960
37.5% 32.3%
30.2%

1970
42.0% 31.5%
26.5%

1980
44.1% 29.6%
26.3%

Source: *Statistical Abstract of the United States*

Americans Aged 65 and Over

	1900	1920	1940	1960	1980	2000*
Millions of persons	3.1	4.9	9.0	16.7	25.5	31.8
As percentage of total population	4.1	4.6	6.8	9.2	11.3	12.2
As percentage of population 21 and older	7.6	8.0	10.7	15.3	17.2	17.7
Percentage of elderly who are 75 or older	29.0	29.8	29.3	33.6	39.0	45.2

Source: U.S. Bureau of the Census   *Projected

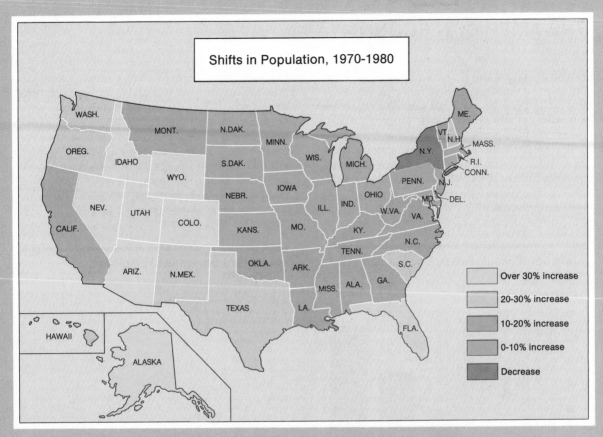

Shifts in Population, 1970-1980

Legend:
- Over 30% increase
- 20-30% increase
- 10-20% increase
- 0-10% increase
- Decrease

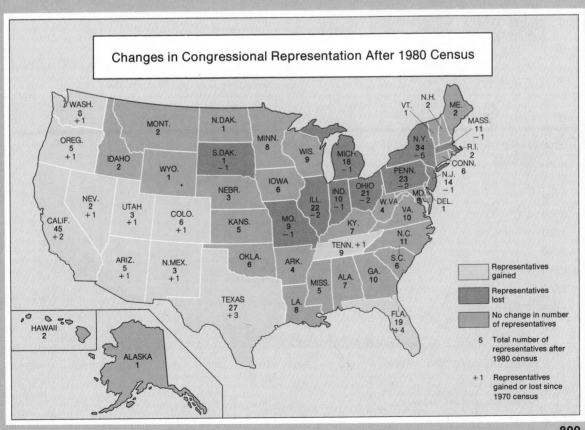

Changes in Congressional Representation After 1980 Census

State	Total	Change
WASH.	8	+1
OREG.	5	+1
MONT.	2	
IDAHO	2	
N.DAK.	1	
MINN.	8	
WIS.	9	
MICH.	18	−1
VT.	1	
N.H.	2	
ME.	2	
MASS.	11	−1
N.Y.	34	−5
R.I.	2	
CONN.	6	
WYO.	1	
S.DAK.	1	−1
IOWA	6	
ILL.	22	−2
IND.	10	−1
OHIO	21	−2
PENN.	23	−2
N.J.	14	−1
MD.	8	
DEL.	1	
NEV.	2	+1
UTAH	3	+1
COLO.	6	+1
NEBR.	3	
KANS.	5	
MO.	9	−1
KY.	7	
W.VA.	4	
VA.	10	
N.C.	11	
CALIF.	45	+2
ARIZ.	5	+1
N.MEX.	3	+1
OKLA.	6	
ARK.	4	
TENN.	9	+1
S.C.	6	
GA.	10	
MISS.	5	
ALA.	7	
TEXAS	27	+3
LA.	8	
FLA.	19	+4
HAWAII	2	
ALASKA	1	

Legend:
- Representatives gained
- Representatives lost
- No change in number of representatives
- 5   Total number of representatives after 1980 census
- +1 Representatives gained or lost since 1970 census

THE AMERICAN ECONOMY

America's rich natural resources, its hardworking population, and the ingenuity of its inventors and scientists have all contributed to the growth of the United States economy. These pages provide information about that growth.

The chief measure of economic activity is the gross national product (GNP). Throughout the nation's history the GNP has shown remarkable growth, indicating that millions of people have found employment and that capital and natural resources have been put to good use. Another measure of economic activity is productivity. The average American farmer, for example, now produces enough food for 66 people, compared to 26 people in 1960 and only 11 people in 1940. Meanwhile, as the economy has grown, so too has the number of government workers. Federal, state, and local governments have all hired more employees to help them meet responsibilities in such vital areas as defense and education.

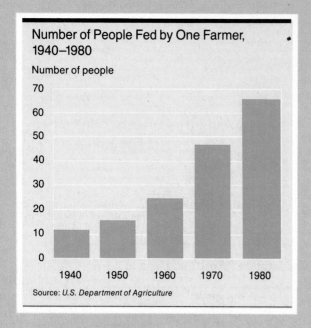

Number of People Fed by One Farmer, 1940–1980

Number of people

Source: U.S. Department of Agriculture

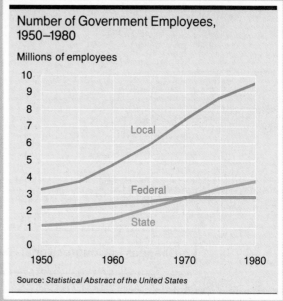

Number of Government Employees, 1950–1980

Millions of employees

Source: Statistical Abstract of the United States

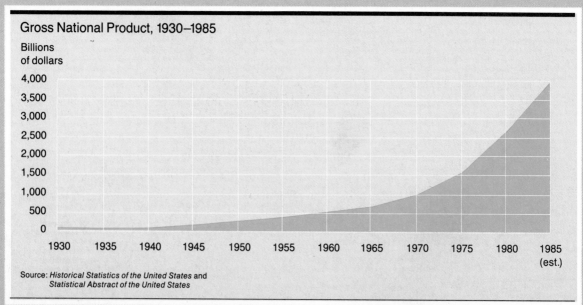

Gross National Product, 1930–1985

Billions of dollars

Source: Historical Statistics of the United States and Statistical Abstract of the United States

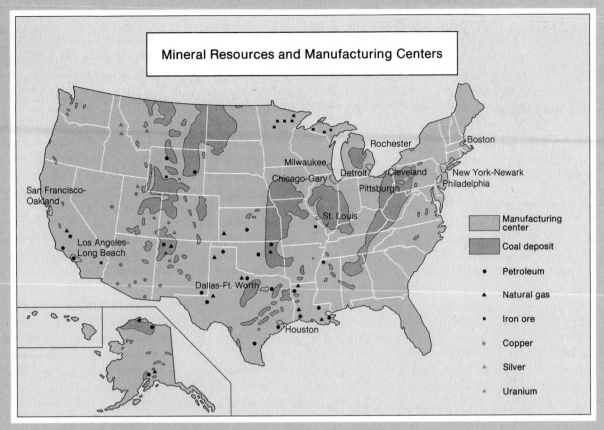

Mineral Resources and Manufacturing Centers

Rochester
Boston
Milwaukee
Detroit
Cleveland
New York-Newark
Chicago-Gary
Philadelphia
Pittsburgh
San Francisco-Oakland
St. Louis
Los Angeles-Long Beach
Dallas-Ft. Worth
Houston

- Manufacturing center
- Coal deposit
- Petroleum
- Natural gas
- Iron ore
- Copper
- Silver
- Uranium

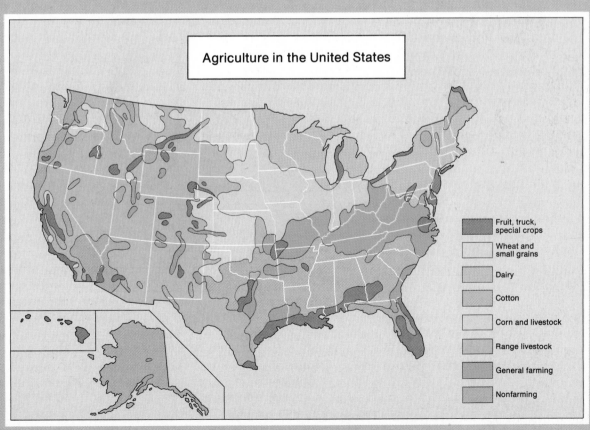

Agriculture in the United States

- Fruit, truck, special crops
- Wheat and small grains
- Dairy
- Cotton
- Corn and livestock
- Range livestock
- General farming
- Nonfarming

NATIONS OF THE WORLD

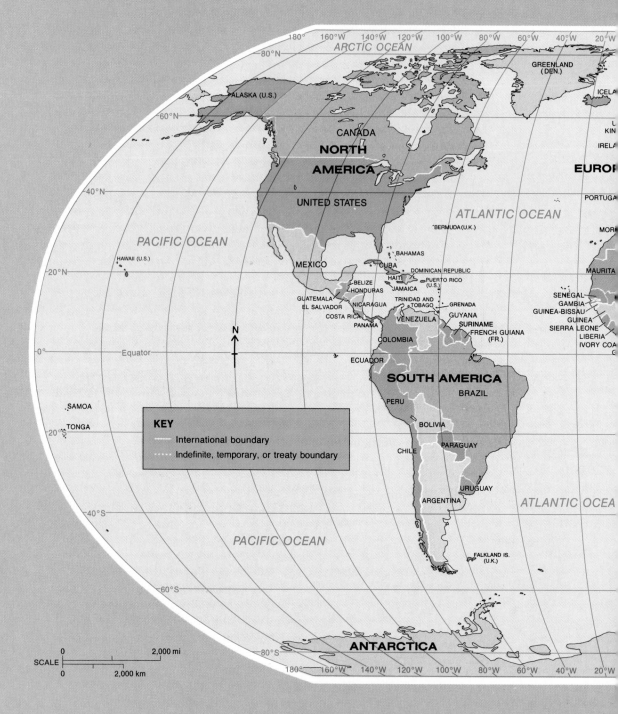

ARCTIC OCEAN

GREENLAND (DEN.)

ICELA

ALASKA (U.S.)

CANADA

NORTH AMERICA

UNITED STATES

EUROP

KIN

IRELA

PORTUGA

ATLANTIC OCEAN

PACIFIC OCEAN

BERMUDA (U.K.)

MOR

HAWAII (U.S.)

MEXICO

CUBA

BAHAMAS

DOMINICAN REPUBLIC

HAITI

PUERTO RICO (U.S.)

BELIZE

HONDURAS

JAMAICA

GUATEMALA

EL SALVADOR

NICARAGUA

COSTA RICA

PANAMA

TRINIDAD AND TOBAGO

GRENADA

VENEZUELA

GUYANA

SURINAME

FRENCH GUIANA (FR.)

COLOMBIA

ECUADOR

SOUTH AMERICA

BRAZIL

PERU

BOLIVIA

MAURITA

SENEGAL

GAMBIA

GUINEA-BISSAU

GUINEA

SIERRA LEONE

LIBERIA

IVORY COA

N

KEY

—— International boundary

········ Indefinite, temporary, or treaty boundary

SAMOA

TONGA

CHILE

PARAGUAY

URUGUAY

ARGENTINA

ATLANTIC OCEA

PACIFIC OCEAN

FALKLAND IS. (U.K.)

ANTARCTICA

SCALE

0 ——— 2,000 mi

0 ——— 2,000 km

Equator

ABBREVIATIONS

ALB. Albania
AUST. Austria
BEL. Belgium
C.AF.REP. Central African Republic

CZECH. Czechoslovakia
DEN. Denmark
E.GER. East Germany
EQ.GUINEA Equatorial Guinea

SWEDEN
FINLAND

ARCTIC OCEAN

80°N

60°N

UNION OF SOVIET SOCIALIST REPUBLICS

ASIA

GER. POLAND
CZECH
AUST.
HUNG
SWITZ.
YUGO
ITALY
ALB.
GREECE
MALTA
CYPRUS
TUNISIA
LEBANON
ISRAEL
JORDAN

BULGARIA

TURKEY

SYRIA
IRAQ
KUWAIT
QATAR
U. ARAB EMIR.

MONGOLIA

40°N

N. KOREA
S. KOREA
JAPAN

PEOPLE'S REPUBLIC
OF CHINA

IRAN

AFGHANISTAN

PAKISTAN

NEPAL
BHUTAN

LIBYA

EGYPT

SAUDI
ARABIA

INDIA

LAOS

TAIWAN

20°N

OMAN

BANGLADESH BURMA

GER.
CHAD
SUDAN

YEMEN
YEMEN (P.D.R.)

VIETNAM

AFRICA

DJIBOUTI

THAILAND

PHILIPPINES

PACIFIC OCEAN

RIA

C.AF.REP.

ETHIOPIA

SRI LANKA

KAMPUCHEA

CAMEROON

UGANDA

SOMALIA

MALDIVES

MALAYSIA

GABON

RWANDA
BURUNDI
ZAÏRE

KENYA

SINGAPORE

INDONESIA

Equator

NAURU

0°

ME
CONGO

TANZANIA

SEYCHELLES

PAPUA
NEW GUINEA

SOLOMON
ISLANDS

ANGOLA

MALAWI

COMOROS

ZAMBIA

MOZAMBIQUE

INDIAN OCEAN

FIJI

ZIMBABWE

MADAGASCAR

20°S

NAMIBIA

MAURITIUS

BOTSWANA

AUSTRALIA

SOUTH
AFRICA

SWAZILAND
LESOTHO

NEW
ZEALAND

40°S

60°S

ANTARCTICA

80°S

20°E
40°E
60°E
80°E
100°E
120°E
140°E
160°E
180°

HUNG. Hungary
NETH. Netherlands
SWITZ. Switzerland
U.ARAB EMIR. United Arab Emirates

U.K. United Kingdom
W.GER. West Germany
YEMEN (P.D.R.) People's Democratic Republic of Yemen
YUGO. Yugoslavia

The Presidents

	President	Dates	Years in Office	Party	Elected From
1	George Washington	1732–1799	1789–1797	None	Virginia
2	John Adams	1735–1826	1797–1801	Federalist	Massachusetts
3	Thomas Jefferson	1743–1826	1801–1809	Democratic–Republican	Virginia
4	James Madison	1751–1836	1809–1817	Democratic–Republican	Virginia
5	James Monroe	1758–1831	1817–1825	Democratic–Republican	Virginia
6	John Quincy Adams	1767–1848	1825–1829	National–Republican	Massachusetts
7	Andrew Jackson	1767–1845	1829–1837	Democratic	Tennessee
8	Martin Van Buren	1782–1862	1837–1841	Democratic	New York
9	William H. Harrison	1773–1841	1841	Whig	Ohio
10	John Tyler	1790–1862	1841–1845	Whig	Virginia
11	James K. Polk	1795–1849	1845–1849	Democratic	Tennessee
12	Zachary Taylor	1784–1850	1849–1850	Whig	Louisiana
13	Millard Fillmore	1800–1874	1850–1853	Whig	New York
14	Franklin Pierce	1804–1869	1853–1857	Democratic	New Hampshire
15	James Buchanan	1791–1868	1857–1861	Democratic	Pennsylvania
16	Abraham Lincoln	1809–1865	1861–1865	Republican	Illinois
17	Andrew Johnson	1808–1875	1865–1869	Republican	Tennessee
18	Ulysses S. Grant	1822–1885	1869–1877	Republican	Illinois
19	Rutherford B. Hayes	1822–1893	1877–1881	Republican	Ohio
20	James A. Garfield	1831–1881	1881	Republican	Ohio
21	Chester A. Arthur	1830–1886	1881–1885	Republican	New York
22	Grover Cleveland	1837–1908	1885–1889	Democratic	New York
23	Benjamin Harrison	1833–1901	1889–1893	Republican	Indiana
24	Grover Cleveland	1837–1908	1893–1897	Democratic	New York
25	William McKinley	1843–1901	1897–1901	Republican	Ohio
26	Theodore Roosevelt	1858–1919	1901–1909	Republican	New York
27	William H. Taft	1857–1930	1909–1913	Republican	Ohio
28	Woodrow Wilson	1856–1924	1913–1921	Democratic	New Jersey
29	Warren G. Harding	1865–1923	1921–1923	Republican	Ohio
30	Calvin Coolidge	1872–1933	1923–1929	Republican	Massachusetts
31	Herbert Hoover	1874–1964	1929–1933	Republican	California
32	Franklin D. Roosevelt	1882–1945	1933–1945	Democratic	New York
33	Harry S. Truman	1884–1972	1945–1953	Democratic	Missouri
34	Dwight D. Eisenhower	1890–1969	1953–1961	Republican	New York
35	John F. Kennedy	1917–1963	1961–1963	Democratic	Massachusetts
36	Lyndon B. Johnson	1908–1973	1963–1969	Democratic	Texas
37	Richard M. Nixon	1913–	1969–1974	Republican	New York
38	Gerald R. Ford	1913–	1974–1977	Republican	Michigan
39	Jimmy Carter	1924–	1977–1981	Democratic	Georgia
40	Ronald Reagan	1911–	1981–	Republican	California

The States

	State Name	Date of Admission	Population	Number of Representatives	Capital
1	Delaware	1787	595,225	1	Dover
2	Pennsylvania	1787	11,866,728	23	Harrisburg
3	New Jersey	1787	7,364,158	14	Trenton
4	Georgia	1788	5,464,265	10	Atlanta
5	Connecticut	1788	3,107,576	6	Hartford
6	Massachusetts	1788	5,737,037	11	Boston
7	Maryland	1788	4,216,446	8	Annapolis
8	South Carolina	1788	3,119,208	6	Columbia
9	New Hampshire	1788	920,610	2	Concord
10	Virginia	1788	5,346,279	10	Richmond
11	New York	1788	17,557,288	34	Albany
12	North Carolina	1789	5,874,429	11	Raleigh
13	Rhode Island	1790	947,154	2	Providence
14	Vermont	1791	511,456	1	Montpelier
15	Kentucky	1792	3,661,433	7	Frankfort
16	Tennessee	1796	4,590,750	9	Nashville
17	Ohio	1803	10,797,419	21	Columbus
18	Louisiana	1812	4,203,972	8	Baton Rouge
19	Indiana	1816	5,490,179	10	Indianapolis
20	Mississippi	1817	2,520,638	5	Jackson
21	Illinois	1818	11,418,461	22	Springfield
22	Alabama	1819	3,890,061	7	Montgomery
23	Maine	1820	1,124,660	2	Augusta
24	Missouri	1821	4,917,444	9	Jefferson City
25	Arkansas	1836	2,285,513	4	Little Rock
26	Michigan	1837	9,258,344	18	Lansing
27	Florida	1845	9,739,992	19	Tallahassee
28	Texas	1845	14,228,383	27	Austin
29	Iowa	1846	2,913,387	6	Des Moines
30	Wisconsin	1848	4,705,335	9	Madison
31	California	1850	23,668,562	45	Sacramento
32	Minnesota	1858	4,077,148	8	St. Paul
33	Oregon	1859	2,632,663	5	Salem
34	Kansas	1861	2,363,208	5	Topeka
35	West Virginia	1863	1,949,644	4	Charleston
36	Nevada	1864	799,184	2	Carson City
37	Nebraska	1867	1,570,006	3	Lincoln
38	Colorado	1876	2,888,834	6	Denver
39	North Dakota	1889	652,695	1	Bismarck
40	South Dakota	1889	690,178	1	Pierre
41	Montana	1889	786,690	2	Helena
42	Washington	1889	4,130,163	8	Olympia
43	Idaho	1890	943,935	2	Boise
44	Wyoming	1890	470,816	1	Cheyenne
45	Utah	1896	1,461,037	3	Salt Lake City
46	Oklahoma	1907	3,025,266	6	Oklahoma City
47	New Mexico	1912	1,299,968	3	Santa Fe
48	Arizona	1912	2,717,866	5	Phoenix
49	Alaska	1959	400,481	1	Juneau
50	Hawaii	1959	965,000	2	Honolulu
	District of Columbia		637,651	1 (non-voting)	
			226,504,825	435	

The Declaration of Independence

When in the Course of human events, it becomes necessary for one people to dissolve the political bands which have connected them with another, and to assume among the powers of the earth, the separate and equal station to which the Laws of Nature and of Nature's God entitle them, a decent respect to the opinions of mankind requires that they should declare the causes which impel them to the separation.*

New Principles of Government

We hold these truths to be self-evident, that all men are created equal, that they are endowed by their Creator with certain unalienable Rights, that among these are Life, Liberty and the pursuit of Happiness. That to secure these rights, Governments are instituted among Men, deriving their just powers from the consent of the governed, That whenever any Form of Government becomes destructive of these ends, it is the Right of the People to alter or to abolish it, and to institute new Government, laying its foundation on such principles and organizing its powers in such form, as to them shall seem most likely to effect their Safety and Happiness. Prudence, indeed, will dictate that Governments long established should not be changed for light and transient causes; and accordingly all experience hath shown, that mankind are more disposed to suffer, while evils are sufferable, than to right themselves by abolishing the forms to which they are accustomed. But when a long train of abuses and usurpations, pursuing invariably the same Object evinces a design to reduce them under absolute Despotism, it is their right, it is their duty, to throw off such Government, and to provide new Guards for their future security. Such has been the patient sufferance of these Colonies; and such is now the necessity which con-

strains them to alter their former Systems of Government. The history of the present King of Great Britain is a history of repeated injuries and usurpations, all having in direct object the establishment of an absolute Tyranny over these States. To prove this, let Facts be submitted to a candid world.

Tyrannical Acts of the British King

He has refused his Assent to Laws, the most wholesome and necessary for the public good.

He has forbidden his Governors to pass Laws of immediate and pressing importance, unless suspended in their operation till his Assent should be obtained; and when so suspended, he has utterly neglected to attend to them.

He has refused to pass other Laws for the accommodation of large districts of people, unless those people would relinquish the right of Representation in the Legislature, a right inestimable to them and formidable to tyrants only.

He has called together legislative bodies at places unusual, uncomfortable, and distant from the depository of their Public Records, for the sole purpose of fatiguing them into compliance with his measures.

He has dissolved Representative Houses repeatedly, for opposing with manly firmness his invasions on the rights of the people.

He has refused for a long time, after such dissolutions, to cause others to be elected; whereby the Legislative powers, incapable of Annihilation, have returned to the People at large for their exercise; the State remaining in the mean time exposed to all the dangers of invasion from without, and convulsions within.

He has endeavoured to prevent the population of these States; for that purpose obstructing the Laws for Naturalization of Foreigners; refusing to pass others to encourage their migrations hither, and raising the conditions of new Appropriations of Lands.

---

* In punctuation and capitalization the text of the Declaration follows accepted sources.

816

He has obstructed the Administration of Justice, by refusing his Assent to Laws for establishing Judiciary powers.

He has made Judges dependent on his Will alone, for the tenure of their offices, and the amount and payment of their salaries.

He has erected a multitude of New Offices, and sent hither swarms of Officers to harass our People, and eat out their substance.

He has kept among us, in times of peace, Standing Armies without the Consent of our legislatures.

He has affected to render the military independent of and superior to the Civil power.

He has combined with others to subject us to a jurisdiction foreign to our constitution, and unacknowledged by our laws; giving his Assent to their Acts of pretended Legislation:

For quartering large bodies of armed troops among us:

For protecting them, by a mock Trial, from Punishment for any Murders which they should commit on the Inhabitants of these States:

For cutting off our Trade with all parts of the world:

For imposing Taxes on us without our Consent:

For depriving us in many cases, of the benefits of Trial by Jury:

For transporting us beyond Seas to be tried for pretended offenses:

For abolishing the free System of English Laws in a neighbouring Province, establishing therein an Arbitrary government, and enlarging its Boundaries so as to render it at once an example and fit instrument for introducing the same absolute rule into these Colonies:

For taking away our Charters, abolishing our most valuable Laws, and altering fundamentally the Forms of our Governments:

For suspending our own Legislatures, and declaring themselves invested with power to legislate for us in all cases whatsoever.

He has abdicated Government here, by declaring us out of his Protection and waging War against us.

He has plundered our seas, ravaged our Coasts, burnt our towns, and destroyed the lives of our people.

He is at this time transporting large Armies of foreign Mercenaries to compleat the works of death, desolation and tyranny, already begun with circumstances of Cruelty & perfidy scarcely paralleled in the most barbarous ages, and totally unworthy the Head of a civilized nation.

He has constrained our fellow Citizens taken Captive on the high Seas to bear Arms against their Country, to become the executioners of their friends and Brethren, or to fall themselves by their Hands.

He has excited domestic insurrections amongst us, and has endeavoured to bring on the inhabitants of our frontiers, the merciless Indian Savages, whose known rule of warfare, is an indistinguished destruction of all ages, sexes and conditions.

Efforts of the Colonies to Avoid Separation

In every stage of these Oppressions We have Petitioned for Redress in the most humble terms: Our repeated Petitions have been answered only by repeated injury. A Prince, whose character is thus marked by every act which may define a Tyrant, is unfit to be the ruler of a free people.

Nor have We been wanting in attentions to our British brethren. We have warned them from time to time of attempts by their legislature to extend an unwarrantable jurisdiction over us. We have reminded them of the circumstances of our emigration and settlement here. We have appealed to their native justice and magnanimity, and we have conjured them by the ties of our common kindred to disavow these usurpations, which, would inevitably interrupt our connections and correspondence. They too have been deaf to the voice of justice and of consanguinity. We must, therefore, acquiesce in the necessity, which denounces our Separation, and hold them, as we hold the rest of mankind, Enemies in War, in Peace Friends.

The Colonies Are Declared Independent

We, therefore, the Representatives of the united States of America, in General Congress, Assembled, appealing to the Supreme Judge of the world for the rectitude of our intentions, do, in the Name, and by Authority of the good People of these Colonies, solemnly publish and declare, That these United Colonies are, and of Right ought to be Free and Independent States; that they are Absolved from all Allegiance to the British Crown, and that all political connection between them and the State of Great Britain, is and ought to be totally dissolved; and that as Free and Independent States, they have full Power to Levy War, conclude Peace, contract Alliances, establish Commerce, and to do all other Acts and Things which Independent States may of right do. And for the support of this Declaration, with a firm reliance on the protection of divine Providence, we mutually pledge to each other our Lives, our Fortunes and our sacred Honor.

The Constitution of the United States

Starting on this page is the complete text of the Constitution of the United States. The actual text of the Constitution appears in the column that is printed on a colored background. In the other column you will find explanations of each part of the Constitution.

Headings and subheadings have been added to help you identify the various parts of the Constitution. The portions of the original document that are no longer in effect are printed in italics.

The Preamble states the purposes for which the Constitution was written: (1) to form a union of states that will benefit all, (2) to make laws and establish courts that are fair, (3) to maintain peace within the country, (4) to defend the nation against attack, (5) to help the people lead happy and useful lives, and (6) to make sure that this nation's people and their descendants remain free.

The opening words of the Constitution make clear that it is the people themselves who have the power to establish a government or change it.

All national laws must be made by Congress. But Congress can make no laws except those permitted under the Constitution. Congress is made up of two houses—the Senate and the House of Representatives.

a. Members of the House of Representatives are elected in each state every two years. Any person who has the right to vote for representatives to the state legislature has the right to vote for the state's representatives in the House of Representatives. This is the only qualification for voting listed in the original Constitution. It made sure that the House would be elected by the people themselves.

b. A representative must be at least 25 years old, a United States citizen for at least seven years, and a resident of the state from which he or she is elected. (By custom, a representative must also live in the congressional district from which he or she is elected.)

PREAMBLE

We the people of the United States, in order to form a more perfect union, establish justice, insure domestic tranquillity, provide for the common defense, promote the general welfare, and secure the blessings of liberty to ourselves and our posterity, do ordain and establish this Constitution for the United States of America.

ARTICLE I / LEGISLATIVE BRANCH

SECTION 1 Congress

All legislative powers herein granted shall be vested in a Congress of the United States, which shall consist of a Senate and House of Representatives.

SECTION 2 The House of Representatives

a. Election and term of members. The House of Representatives shall be composed of members chosen every second year by the people of the several states, and the electors in each state shall have the qualifications requisite for electors of the most numerous branch of the state legislature.

b. Qualification of members. No person shall be a representative who shall not have attained to the age of twenty-five years, and been seven years a citizen of the United States, and who shall not, when elected, be an inhabitant of that state in which he shall be chosen.

c. Appointment of representatives and of direct taxes. Representatives *and direct taxes* shall be apportioned among the several states which may be included within this Union, according to their respective numbers, *which shall be determined by adding to the whole number of free persons, including those bound to service for a term of years, and excluding Indians not taxed, three fifths of all other persons.* The actual enumeration shall be made within three years after the first meeting of the Congress of the United States, and within every subsequent term of ten years, in such manner as they shall by law direct. The number of representatives shall not exceed one for every thirty thousand, but each state shall have at least one representative; *and until such enumeration shall be made, the State of New Hampshire shall be entitled to choose three; Massachusetts, eight; Rhode Island and Providence Plantations, one; Connecticut, five; New York, six; New Jersey, four; Pennsylvania, eight; Delaware, one; Maryland, six; Virginia, ten; North Carolina, five; South Carolina, five; and Georgia, three.*

d. Filling vacancies. When vacancies happen in the representation from any state, the executive authority thereof shall issue writs of election to fill such vacancies.

e. Officers; impeachment. The House of Representatives shall choose their Speaker and other officers; and shall have the sole power of impeachment.

SECTION 3 The Senate

a. Number and election of members. The Senate of the United States shall be composed of two senators from each state, chosen *by the legislature thereof,* for six years; and each senator shall have one vote.

b. Choosing senators. Immediately after they shall be assembled in consequence of the first election, they shall be divided as equally as may be into three classes. *The seats of the senators of the first class shall be vacated at the expiration of the second year, of the second class at the expiration of the fourth year, and of the third class at the expiration of the sixth year,* so that one third may be chosen every second year; *and if vacancies happen by resignation, or otherwise, during the recess of the legislature of any state, the executive thereof may make temporary appointments until the next meeting of the legislature, which shall then fill such vacancies.*

c. Qualifications of members. No person shall be a senator who shall not have attained to the age of thirty years, and been nine years a citizen of the United States, and who shall not, when elected, be an inhabitant of that state for which he shall be chosen.

c. The number of representatives each state has is determined by the state's population. Direct taxes are to be collected from the states according to the number of people living in each state. (Amendment 16 made the income tax an exception to this rule.) A direct tax is one paid to the government by the person who is taxed. Since there now are no slaves or indentured servants in the United States and Indians are citizens, all the people of a state are counted in determining the number of representatives a state shall have. Congress decides how the population is to be counted, but a census must be taken every ten years. The House of Representatives cannot have more than one member for every 30,000 persons in the nation. But each state is entitled to one representative, no matter how small its population. In 1910 Congress limited the number of representatives to 435.

d. When a state does not have all the representatives to which it is entitled—for example, when a representative resigns or dies—the governor of that state must call an election to fill the vacancy.

e. The House of Representatives elects its presiding officer (the Speaker) and other officers such as the chaplain. Only the House has the right to impeach, that is, to bring charges of misdeeds in office against an official of the United States.

a. The Senate is made up of two senators from each state. Senators are no longer chosen by the legislatures of their states. Amendment 17 states that they are to be elected by the people. A senator serves a six-year term.

b. Senators were divided into three groups so that their terms would not all end at the same time. Today all senators are elected for six-year terms, but only one third are elected in any election year. The provision for filling vacancies in the Senate was changed by Amendment 17.

c. A senator must be at least thirty years old, a United States citizen for nine years, and a resident of the state from which he or she is elected.

d. The Vice President serves as the president of the Senate, but cannot vote except in case of a tie. This is the only duty assigned to the Vice President. In recent years the Vice President has been given more responsibilities by the President.

e. The Senate chooses its other officers, including a President pro tempore. *Pro tempore* means "for the time being." The President pro tempore presides in the Senate when the Vice President is absent or serving as President.

f. The Senate tries the case when a federal official is impeached by the House of Representatives. The Senators must formally declare that they will be honest and just. If the President of the United States is tried, the Chief Justice presides over the Senate. Two thirds of the senators present must agree that the charge is true for the impeached person to be found guilty.

g. If the Senate finds an impeached official guilty, it may only punish that official by keeping him or her from ever holding a government job again. Once out of office, however, the former official may be tried in a regular court and, if found guilty, punished like any other person.

a. The legislature of each state has the right to determine how, when, and where senators and representatives are elected, but Congress may pass election laws which the states must follow. For example, a federal law requires that secret ballots be used.

b. Congress must meet at least once a year. Amendment 20 made January 3 the day for beginning a regular session of Congress.

a. Each house of Congress has the right to decide whether its members are qualified and fairly elected. Either house may by a majority vote refuse to seat a newly elected member. A *quorum* is the number of members which must be present for official business to be carried on. The Constitution states that a majority—half the members plus one —is a quorum in either the Senate or the House.

b. Each house of Congress has the right to make rules to follow in its work. Over the years many rules have grown up concerning the procedures used in conducting business. Each house may punish its members for wrongdoing or even expel them by a two-thirds vote.

d. President of Senate. The Vice President of the United States shall be President of the Senate, but shall have no vote, unless they be equally divided.

e. Other officers. The Senate shall choose their other officers, and also a President pro tempore, in the absence of the Vice President, or when he shall exercise the office of President of the United States.

f. Trials of impeachment. The Senate shall have the sole power to try all impeachments. When sitting for that purpose, they shall be on oath or affirmation. When the President of the United States is tried, the Chief Justice shall preside; and no person shall be convicted without the concurrence of two thirds of the members present.

g. Punishment. Judgment in cases of impeachment shall not exceed further than to removal from office, and disqualification to hold and enjoy any office of honor, trust, or profit under the United States; but the party convicted shall nevertheless be liable and subject to indictment, trial, judgment, and punishment, according to law.

SECTION 4   Elections and Meetings of Congress

a. Method of holding elections. The times, places, and manner of holding elections for senators and representatives shall be prescribed in each state by the legislature thereof; but the Congress may at any time by law make or alter such regulations, *except as to the places of choosing senators.*

b. Meeting of Congress. The Congress shall assemble at least once in every year, *and such meeting shall be on the first Monday in December, unless they shall by law appoint a different day.*

SECTION 5   Organization and Rules of Each House

a. Organization. Each house shall be the judge of the elections, returns, and qualifications of its own members, and a majority of each shall constitute a quorum to do business; but a smaller number may adjourn from day to day, and may be authorized to compel the attendance of absent members, in such manner, and under such penalties as each house may provide.

b. Rules. Each house may determine the rules of its proceedings, punish its members for disorderly behavior, and with the concurrence of two thirds, expel a member.

c. Journal. Each house shall keep a journal of its proceedings, and from time to time publish the same, excepting such parts as may in their judgment require secrecy; and the yeas and nays of the members of either house on any question shall, at the desire of one fifth of those present, be entered on the journal.

d. Adjournment. Neither house, during the session of Congress, shall without the consent of the other adjourn for more than three days, nor to any other place than that in which the two houses shall be sitting.

SECTION 6 Privileges and Restrictions

a. Pay and privileges of members. The senators and representatives shall receive a compensation for their services, to be ascertained by law, and paid out of the Treasury of the United States. They shall in all cases, except treason, felony, and breach of the peace, be privileged from arrest during their attendance at the session of their respective houses and in going to and returning from the same; and for any speech or debate in either house, they shall not be questioned in any other place.

b. Holding other offices prohibited. No senator or representative shall, during the time for which he was elected, be appointed to any civil office under the authority of the United States which shall have been created, or the emoluments whereof shall have been increased during such time; and no person holding any office under the United States shall be a member of either house during his continuance in office.

SECTION 7 Method of Passing Laws

a. Revenue bills. All bills for raising revenue shall originate in the House of Representatives; but the Senate may propose or concur with amendments as on other bills.

b. How bills become laws. Every bill which shall have passed the House of Representatives and the Senate shall, before it become a law, be presented to the President of the United States; if he approves he shall sign it, but if not he shall return it, with his objections, to that house in which it shall have originated, who shall enter the objections at large on their journal, and proceed to reconsider it. If after such reconsideration two thirds of that house shall agree to pass the bill, it shall be sent, together with the objections, to the other house, by which it shall likewise be reconsidered, and

c. Each house of Congress must keep a record of what goes on at its meetings and must publish the record. The *Congressional Record* is issued daily during sessions of Congress. Parts of the record that the members of Congress believe should be kept secret may be withheld. How members of either house vote on a question may be entered in the record if one fifth of those present in that house wish this to be done.

d. When Congress is meeting, neither house may stop work for more than three days without the consent of the other house. Neither house is allowed to hold its sessions in another city without the consent of the other house.

a. Senators and representatives are paid out of the United States Treasury. Their salary is determined by law passed by Congress. At the present time the salary is $60,662 annually, plus allowances for travel, office staff, stationery, and other expenses. Members of Congress also enjoy the *franking privilege*, that is, the right to send free any official mail stamped with their name. Members of Congress may not be arrested at meetings of Congress or while going to or from such meetings unless they are suspected of treason, other serious crimes, or disturbing the peace. They may not be punished for anything they say in Congress, except by the house of which they are a member.

b. Until after their terms have ended, senators or representatives may not hold offices created by the Congress of which they are members. The same restriction applies to jobs for which Congress has voted increased pay. No person may be a member of Congress without first giving up any other federal office he or she may hold.

a. Bills for raising money for the federal government must start in the House of Representatives, but the Senate may make changes in such bills. Actually, the Senate has as much influence over revenue bills as does the House.

b. A bill (except one for raising revenue) may start in either the Senate or the House of Representatives. However, exactly the same bill must be passed by a majority vote in both houses of Congress. Differences are usually ironed out in a conference committee made up of members of both houses. When both the Senate and House have voted in favor of the bill, it is sent to the President. The President can then do one of three things: sign the bill; veto it; or return it to the house where it began. If the bill is returned, it may then be discussed again in Congress. If two thirds of both houses of Congress vote for the bill after reconsidering it, the bill becomes law without the President's signing it. In such cases, the vote of each member of Congress is recorded.

The President has ten days (not counting Sundays) to study any bill. If the President keeps a bill more than ten days without signing or vetoing it and Congress continues to meet, the bill becomes a law. But if Congress adjourns before the ten-day period ends and the President does not sign it, the bill is dead. This is known as a "pocket veto."

if approved by two thirds of that house, it shall become a law. But in all such cases the votes of both houses shall be determined by yeas and nays, and the names of the persons voting for and against the bill shall be entered on the journal of each house respectively. If any bill shall not be returned by the President within ten days (Sundays excepted) after it shall have been presented to him, the same shall be a law, in like manner as if he had signed it, unless the Congress by their adjournment prevent its return, in which case it shall not be a law.

c. Other acts which require approval of both houses of Congress take effect only if they are signed by the President or passed over a presidential veto by a two-thirds vote of both houses. However, a vote to adjourn Congress requires only a majority vote of both houses.

c. Approval or disapproval by the President. Every order, resolution, or vote to which the concurrence of the Senate and House of Representatives may be necessary (except on a question of adjournment) shall be presented to the President of the United States; and before the same shall take effect, shall be approved by him, or being disapproved by him, shall be repassed by two thirds of the Senate and House of Representatives, according to the rules and limitations prescribed in the case of a bill.

SECTION 8   Powers Granted to Congress
The Congress shall have power

a. Congress may pass laws for collecting various kinds of taxes. All federal taxes must be the same in all parts of the nation.

a. To lay and collect taxes, duties, imposts, and excises; to pay the debts and provide for the common defense and general welfare of the United States; but all duties, imposts, and excises shall be uniform throughout the United States;

b. Congress has the power to borrow money that the federal government may need and to promise to repay this money. Borrowing is generally done by issuing government bonds or certificates of indebtedness.

b. To borrow money on the credit of the United States;

c. Congress has the power to pass laws concerning trade between this country and foreign countries and between one state and another state.

c. To regulate commerce with foreign nations, and among the several states, and with the Indian tribes;

d. Congress has the power to make laws determining how citizens of other countries may become citizens of the United States. Congress also has the power to make laws regulating bankruptcy. Such laws must be the same throughout the country.

d. To establish a uniform rule of naturalization, and uniform laws on the subject of bankruptcies throughout the United States;

e. Congress controls the minting of money and decides how much each coin is worth. And it may determine the value of foreign coins used in the United States. Congress also sets up standards for measuring weight and distance.

e. To coin money, regulate the value thereof and of foreign coin, and fix the standard of weights and measures;

f. Congress passes laws punishing people who make counterfeit money and government bonds.

f. To provide for the punishment of counterfeiting the securities and current coin of the United States;

g. Congress provides for a postal system and may build and maintain roads over which the mail is carried.

g. To establish post offices and post roads;

h. To promote the progress of science and useful arts by securing for limited times to authors and inventors the exclusive right to their respective writings and discoveries;

i. To constitute tribunals inferior to the Supreme Court;

j. To define and punish piracies and felonies committed on the high seas and offenses against the law of nations;

k. To declare war, grant letters of marque and reprisal, and make rules concerning captures on land and water;

l. To raise and support armies, but no appropriation of money to that use shall be for a longer term than two years;

m. To provide and maintain a navy;

n. To make rules for the government and regulation of land and naval forces;

o. To provide for calling forth the militia to execute the laws of the Union, suppress insurrections, and repel invasions;

p. To provide for organizing, arming, and disciplining the militia, and for governing such part of them as may be employed in the service of the United States, reserving to the states respectively the appointment of the officers and the authority of training the militia, according to the discipline prescribed by Congress;

q. To exercise exclusive legislation in all cases whatsoever over such district (not exceeding ten miles square) as may, by cession of particular states and the acceptance of Congress, become the seat of the government of the United States, and to exercise like authority over all places purchased by the consent of the legislature of the state in which the same shall be for the erection of forts, magazines, arsenals, dock-yards, and other needful buildings; and

r. To make all laws which shall be necessary and proper for carrying into execution the foregoing powers, and all other powers vested by this Constitution in the government of the United States, or in any department or officer thereof.

h. Congress encourages art, science, and invention by passing laws which protect artists and inventors. Copyright and patent laws make it illegal for a person to use the work of an artist, musician, author, or inventor without permission.

i. Congress has the power to establish federal courts other than the Supreme Court.

j. Congress may specifiy what acts committed on American ships are crimes. The accused will stand trial in a federal court when the ship returns to port.

k. Congress alone has the power to declare war. *Letters of marque and reprisal* are government licenses authorizing the holders to fit out armed ships for use in capturing enemy merchant ships. This power to commission privateers to prey upon enemy commerce was used extensively in the War of 1812. The practice is no longer followed.

l. Congress may create an army for the United States. But Congress may not vote the money to support the armed forces for more than two years in advance.

m. Congress may create a navy for the United States and vote the money necessary to operate it.

n. Congress may make rules for our armed forces. While on active duty, members of the armed forces are under military law rather than civil law.

o. Congress may determine when and how the militia, the citizen soldiers of the various states, may be called into the service of the national government. The militia may be used to enforce law, to put an end to rebellion, and to drive back an invasion of the country.

p. Congress provides for organizing, arming, and disciplining the militia. The states appoint the officers and train the militia under the regulations set up by Congress. When called out by the national government, however, the militia is part of the national armed forces.

q. Congress has the power to make laws for the District of Columbia. Because it contains the national capital, the District of Columbia is not under the control of any state. Congress also makes laws regulating the use of all other property belonging to the national government—forts, arsenals, etc.

r. Congress also has the power to pass all laws needed to carry out the responsibilities assigned it by the Constitution. This provision is called the "elastic clause." It can be stretched to meet the changing needs of the nation. It is the basis for much legislation not authorized in any other provision of the Constitution.

a. In 1808 Congress prohibited further importation of slaves.

b. Congress may not take away a person's right to the writ of habeas corpus except in time of great national danger. (A *writ of habeas corpus* is a court order directing that a prisoner be given a hearing so that the court can decide whether that person should be released or held and charged with a crime.)

c. Congress may not pass a bill of attainder. (A *bill of attainder* is a legislative act which condemns a person without a trial in court.) Neither can Congress pass an *ex post facto* law. Such a law makes an act a crime after the act has been committed.

d. Congress may not levy a direct tax that is not the same for all persons taxed. Amendment 16 provides an exception in the case of the income tax.

e. Congress may not tax goods sent from one state to another or goods sent to other countries.

f. In laws concerning commerce, Congress may not favor one port over other ports. Congress must not tax goods being sent by water from one state to another state.

g. Money can be paid out of the Treasury only if Congress has voted the appropriation. (An *appropriation* is money granted for a given purpose.) An account of money received and money spent must be published from time to time.

h. The United States may not grant a title of nobility. Federal officials may not accept titles, gifts, or honors from any foreign ruler or government unless Congress gives its permission.

a. States may not make treaties, enter into agreements with foreign countries, or grant their citizens the right to make war. States cannot issue their own money or declare that any money other than that of the United States can be used as legal money.

The states are forbidden to punish people without giving them a trial or to pass laws that would punish people for acts that were not against the law at the time they were committed. State governments must not pass any laws that would make contracts or other legal agreements less binding on the people who agreed to them.

SECTION 9   Powers Denied to the Federal Government

a. *The migration or importation of such persons as any of the states now existing shall think proper to admit shall not be prohibited by the Congress prior to the year one thousand eight hundred and eight, but a tax or duty may be imposed on such importation, not exceeding ten dollars for each person.*

b. The privilege of the writ of habeas corpus shall not be suspended, unless when in cases of rebellion or invasion the public safety may require it.

c. No bill of attainder or ex post facto law shall be passed.

d. No capitation or other direct tax shall be laid, unless in proportion to the census or enumeration herein before directed to be taken.

e. No tax or duty shall be laid on articles exported from any state.

f. No preference shall be given by any regulation of commerce or revenue to the ports of one state over those of another; nor shall vessels bound to or from one state be obliged to enter, clear, or pay duties in another.

g. No money shall be drawn from the treasury, but in consequence of appropriations made by law; and a regular statement and account of the receipts and expenditures of all public money shall be published from time to time.

h. No title of nobility shall be granted by the United States; and no person holding any office of profit or trust under them shall, without the consent of Congress, accept of any present, emolument, office, or title, of any kind whatever, from any king, prince, or foreign state.

SECTION 10   Powers Denied to the States

a. No state shall enter into any treaty, alliance, or confederation; grant letters of marque and reprisal; coin money; emit bills of credit; make any thing but gold and silver coin a tender in payment of debts; pass any bill of attainder, ex post facto law, or law impairing the obligation of contracts; or grant any title of nobility.

b. No state shall, without the consent of the Congress, lay any imposts or duties on imports or exports, except what may be absolutely necessary for executing its inspection laws; and the net produce of all duties and imposts, laid by any state on imports or exports, shall be for the use of the treasury of the United States; and all such laws shall be subject to the revision and control of the Congress.

b. States may not tax goods leaving or entering their territory. However, they may charge fees to cover the costs of inspection. Any profit from such inspection fees must be turned over to the United States Treasury. Congress has the power to change the inspection laws of a state.

c. No state shall, without the consent of Congress, lay any duty of tonnage; keep troops or ships of war in time of peace; enter into any agreement or compact with another state or with a foreign power; or engage in war, unless actually invaded or in such imminent danger as will not admit of delay.

c. Unless Congress gives permission, a state may not tax ships entering its ports, keep an army or navy—except the militia—in time of peace, make treaties with other states or foreign countries, or make war except when it is invaded.

ARTICLE II / EXECUTIVE BRANCH

SECTION 1   President and Vice President

a. Term of office.   The executive power shall be vested in a President of the United States of America. He shall hold his office during the term of four years, and, together with the Vice President chosen for the same term, be elected as follows:

a. The President of the United States enforces or executes the nation's laws and is elected, as is the Vice President, for a four-year term.

b. Electors.   Each state shall appoint, in such manner as the legislature thereof may direct, a number of electors, equal to the whole number of senators and representatives to which the state may be entitled in the Congress; but no senator or representative, or person holding an office of trust or profit under the United States, shall be appointed an elector.

The electors shall meet in their respective states and vote by ballot for two persons, of whom one at least shall not be an inhabitant of the same state with themselves. And they shall make a list of all the persons voted for and of the number of votes for each; which list they shall sign and certify, and transmit sealed to the seat of government of the United States, directed to the President of the Senate. The President of the Senate shall, in the presence of the Senate and House of Representatives, open all the certificates, and the votes shall then be counted. The person having the greatest number of votes shall be the President, if such number be a majority of the whole number of electors appointed; and if there be more than one who have such majority, and have an equal number of votes, then the House of Representatives shall immediately choose by ballot one of them for President; and if no person have a majority, then from the five highest on the list the said house shall in like manner choose the President. But in choosing the President the votes shall be taken by states, the representation from each state having one vote; a quorum for this purpose shall consist of a member or members from two thirds of the states, and a majority of all the

b. The President and Vice President are elected by electors chosen by the states according to rules established by the legislatures. Each state has as many electors as it has senators and representatives in Congress. No senator or representative or other person holding a federal job may be an elector. Today electors usually are important party members whose votes are pledged to a given candidate.

   This clause did not work well in practice and was changed by Amendment 12.

states shall be necessary to a choice. In every case, after the choice of the President, the person having the greatest number of votes of the electors shall be the Vice President. But if there should remain two or more who have equal votes, the Senate shall choose from them by ballot the Vice President.

c. Congress determines when electors are chosen and when they vote. The day is the same throughout the United States. The popular vote for electors takes place on the Tuesday after the first Monday of November in each "leap year." In mid-December the electors meet in their state capitals and cast their electoral votes.

c. Time of elections. The Congress may determine the time of choosing the electors, and the day on which they shall give their votes; which day shall be the same throughout the United States.

d. To be President, a person must be a citizen of the United States by birth, at least 35 years old, and a resident of the United States for at least 14 years.

d. Qualifications for President. No person except a natural-born citizen, *or a citizen of the United States, at the time of the adoption of this Constitution,* shall be eligible to the office of President; neither shall any person be eligible to that office who shall not have attained the age of thirty-five years, and been fourteen years a resident within the United States.

e. If the presidency becomes vacant, the Vice President becomes the President of the United States. If neither the President nor the Vice President is able to serve, Congress has the right to decide which government official shall act as President. Amendment 25 practically assures that there always will be a Vice President to succeed to the presidency.

e. Vacancy. In case of the removal of the President from office or of his death, resignation, or inability to discharge the powers and duties of the said office, the same shall devolve on the Vice President; and the Congress may by law provide for the case of removal, death, resignation, or inability, both of the President and Vice President, declaring what officer shall then act as President; and such officer shall act accordingly, until the disability be removed or a President shall be elected.

f. The President is paid a salary fixed by Congress. That salary may not be increased or decreased during the term of office. The President may not receive any other salary from the United States or from one of the states. The salary of the President is now $200,000 a year, plus additional amounts for expenses.

f. The President's salary. The President shall, at stated times, receive for his services a compensation, which shall neither be increased nor diminished during the period for which he shall have been elected, and he shall not receive within that period any other emolument from the United States, or any of them.

g. In taking the oath of office, the President promises to preserve, protect, and defend the Constitution of the United States.

g. Oath of office. Before he enter on the execution of his office, he shall take the following oath or affirmation: "I do solemnly swear (or affirm) that I will faithfully execute the office of President of the United States, and will to the best of my ability, preserve, protect, and defend the Constitution of the United States."

SECTION 2 Powers of the President

a. The President is commander-in-chief of the armed forces and of the militia when it is called out by the national government. As commander-in-chief, the President has great power, especially in time of war. The President may ask the heads of the executive departments for advice and for reports on the work of the various departments. No provision is made in the Constitution for the Cabinet or for Cabinet meetings, but the existence of executive departments is implied here.

a. Military powers; reprieves and pardons. The President shall be Commander-in-Chief of the Army and Navy of the United States, and of the militia of the several states, when called into the actual service of the United States. He may require the opinion, in writing, of the principal officer in each of the executive departments, upon any subject relating to the duties of their respective offices, and he shall have power to grant reprieves and pardons for offenses against the United States, except in cases of impeachment.

b. Treaties and appointments. He shall have power, by and with the advice and consent of the Senate, to make treaties, provided two thirds of the senators present concur; and he shall nominate and, by and with the advice and consent of the Senate, shall appoint ambassadors, other public ministers and consuls, judges of the Supreme Court, and all other officers of the United States, whose appointments are not herein otherwise provided for, and which shall be established by law; but the Congress may by law vest the appointment of such inferior officers as they think proper in the President alone, in the courts of law, or in the heads of departments.

b. The President may make treaties, but all treaties must be approved in the Senate by a two-thirds vote of the senators present. The President may also appoint important government officials. Such appointments must be approved in the Senate by a majority of the senators present. Congress may, however, pass laws giving the President, the courts, or the heads of departments power to appoint less important officials without the consent of the Senate.

c. Filling vacancies. The President shall have power to fill up all vacancies that may happen during the recess of the Senate, by granting commissions which shall expire at the end of their next session.

c. If the Senate is not meeting, the President may make temporary appointments to fill vacancies. These appointments end at the close of the next session of Congress unless the Senate approves them. Congress, with the approval of the President, has given the Civil Service Commission responsibility for determining the fitness of job applicants and for ranking them on civil service lists from which appointments to many federal positions are made.

SECTION 3 Duties of the President

He shall from time to time give to the Congress information of the state of the Union, and recommend to their consideration such measures as he shall judge necessary and expedient; he may, on extraordinary occasions, convene both houses, or either of them, and in case of disagreement between them with respect to the time of adjournment he may adjourn them to such time as he shall think proper; he shall receive ambassadors and other public ministers; he shall take care that the laws be faithfully executed, and shall commission all the officers of the United States.

The President must report to Congress from time to time on conditions within the United States. The President may also suggest that Congress act to pass certain laws or to solve problems facing the nation. The President may call a special session of Congress if a situation arises which requires action by Congress when that body is not in regular session. In case the Senate and House cannot agree when to end a session, the President may adjourn Congress. The President receives representatives of foreign nations, sees that the laws of the nation are enforced, and commissions officers in the armed services.

SECTION 4 Impeachment

The President, Vice President and all civil officers of the United States shall be removed from office on impeachment for, and conviction of, treason, bribery, or other high crimes and misdemeanors.

The President, Vice President, and other important government officials may be removed from office if impeached and found guilty of treason, bribery, or other serious crimes.

ARTICLE III / JUDICIAL BRANCH

SECTION 1 The Federal Courts

The judicial power of the United States shall be vested in one Supreme Court and in such inferior courts as the Congress may from time to time ordain and establish. The judges, both of the Supreme and inferior courts, shall hold their offices during good behavior and shall, at stated times, receive for their services a compensation which shall not be diminished during their continuance in office.

The power to interpret the laws of the United States belongs to the Supreme Court and the other federal courts established by Congress. District courts and courts of appeal are now part of the regular court system. Federal judges are appointed by the President with the approval of the Senate. They hold office as long as they live, unless they retire, resign, or are impeached and found guilty.

a. Federal courts may try cases concerning (1) the Constitution and federal laws and treaties, (2) representatives of foreign nations, (3) laws governing ships and sailors, (4) disputes between the United States and a person or another government, (5) disputes between states, (6) disputes between citizens of different states, (7) disputes in which citizens of the same state claim lands granted by different states, and (8) disputes between a state or its citizens and a foreign state or its citizens.

b. Any case involving a representative of a foreign country or one of the states is first tried in the Supreme Court. Any other case is first tried in a lower court, but the Supreme Court may hear a case from a lower court on appeal. Since the Supreme Court is the highest court in the land, its decision cannot be appealed.

c. Except in cases of impeachment, the accused has a right to a trial by jury in the state in which the crime was committed. If the crime did not take place within a state, a law passed by Congress determines where the trial is to be held.

a. A citizen who makes war on the United States or aids this country's enemies is guilty of treason. To be judged guilty of treason, one must confess in court or be convicted by the testimony of two or more persons.

b. Congress decides what the punishment for treason will be. But the family or descendants of a guilty person may not be punished.

The records and court decisions of one state must be accepted in all states. Congress has the power to see that this is done.

SECTION 2 Jurisdiction of the Federal Courts

a. Federal courts in general. The judicial power shall extend to all cases, in law and equity, arising under this Constitution, the laws of the United States, and treaties made, or which shall be made, under their authority; to all cases affecting ambassadors, other public ministers, and consuls; to all cases of admiralty and maritime jurisdiction; to controversies to which the United States shall be a party; to controversies between two or more states; *between a state and citizens of another state;* between citizens of different states; between citizens of the same state claiming lands under grants of different states, and between a state, or the citizens thereof, and foreign states, citizens, or subjects.

b. Supreme Court. In all cases affecting ambassadors, other public ministers, and consuls, and those in which a state shall be a party, the Supreme Court shall have original jurisdiction. In all the other cases before mentioned, the Supreme Court shall have appellate jurisdiction, both as to law and fact, with such exceptions and under such regulations as the Congress shall make.

c. Rules respecting trials. The trial of all crimes, except in cases of impeachment, shall be by jury; and such trial shall be held in the state where the said crimes shall have been committed; but when not committed within any state, the trial shall be at such place or places as the Congress may by law have directed.

SECTION 3 Treason

a. Definition of treason. Treason against the United States shall consist only in levying war against them or in adhering to their enemies, giving them aid and comfort. No person shall be convicted of treason unless on the testimony of two witnesses to the same overt act, or on confession in open court.

b. Punishment for treason. The Congress shall have power to declare the punishment of treason, but no attainder of treason shall work corruption of blood, or forfeiture except during the life of the person attainted.

ARTICLE IV / THE STATES AND THE FEDERAL GOVERNMENT

SECTION 1 State Records

Full faith and credit shall be given in each state to the public acts, records, and judicial proceedings of every other state. And the Congress may by general laws prescribe the manner in which such acts, records, and proceedings shall be proved, and the effect thereof.

SECTION 2   Privileges and Immunities of Citizens

a. Privileges. The citizens of each state shall be entitled to all privileges and immunities of citizens in the several states.

a. The citizens of all states have in a given state the rights and privileges granted to the citizens of that state. For example, a citizen of Oregon going into California would be entitled to all the privileges of citizens of California.

b. Extradition. A person charged in any state with treason, felony, or other crime who shall flee from justice and be found in another state shall, on demand of the executive authority of the state from which he fled, be delivered up, to be removed to the state having jurisdiction of the crime.

b. If the governor makes the request, a person charged with a crime in one state may be returned from another state to stand trial. Such action is called *extradition*. A request for extradition may be denied, however.

c. Fugitive workers. *No person held to service or labor in one state, under the laws thereof, escaping into another shall, in consequence of any law or regulation therein, be discharged from such service or labor, but shall be delivered upon claim of the party to whom such service or labor may be due.*

c. This clause referred to slaves. Amendment 13 abolished slavery.

SECTION 3   New States and Territories

a. Admission of new states. New states may be admitted by the Congress into this Union; but no new state shall be formed or erected within the jurisdiction of any other state; nor any state be formed by the junction of two or more states, or parts of states, without the consent of the legislatures of the states concerned, as well as of the Congress.

a. Congress has the power to add new states to the Union. However, no state can have some of its territory taken away without its consent as well as the consent of Congress.

b. National territory. The Congress shall have power to dispose of and make all needful rules and regulations respecting the territory or other property belonging to the United States; and nothing in this Constitution shall be so construed as to prejudice any claims of the United States, or of any particular state.

b. Congress has the power to make rules and regulations concerning the property and the territory of the United States.

SECTION 4   Guarantees to the States

The United States shall guarantee to every state in this Union a republican form of government, and shall protect each of them against invasion; and on application of the legislature, or of the executive (when the legislature cannot be convened), against domestic violence.

It is the duty of the federal government to see that each state (1) has a republican form of government, (2) is protected from invasion, and (3) receives help to put down riots and other disorders when such help is requested by the legislature or the governor of the state.

The Constitution may be changed by amendment. An amendment may be proposed by a two-thirds vote of both houses of Congress or by a convention called at the request of the legislatures of two thirds of the states. Proposed amendments must be approved by the legislatures of three fourths of the states or by conventions called in three fourths of the states. When an amendment is approved, it becomes part of the Constitution. However, no amendment may take away equal state representation in the Senate.

a. The framers of the Constitution agreed that the United States would be responsible for all debts contracted by the Confederation government.

b. The Constitution and the laws and treaties of the United States are the supreme law of the nation. If state law is in conflict with national law, it is the national law that must be obeyed.

c. All government officials, federal and state, must take an oath to support the Constitution. But no religious test can ever be required for an official to hold office.

The Constitution went into effect when nine states voted to accept it.

ARTICLE V / AMENDING THE CONSTITUTION

The Congress, whenever two thirds of both houses shall deem it necessary, shall propose amendments to this Constitution, or, on the application of the legislatures of two thirds of the several states, shall call a convention for proposing amendments, which, in either case, shall be valid to all intents and purposes, as part of this Constitution, when ratified by the legislatures of three fourths of the several states or by conventions in three fourths thereof, as the one or the other mode of ratification may be proposed by the Congress; provided that *no amendments which may be made prior to the year one thousand eight hundred and eight shall in any manner affect the first and fourth clauses in the ninth section of the first article; and that* no state, without its consent, shall be deprived of its equal suffrage in the Senate.

ARTICLE VI / SUPREMACY OF FEDERAL LAWS

a. Public debt.   All debts contracted and engagements entered into, before the adoption of this Constitution, shall be as valid against the United States under this Constitution as under the Confederation.

b. Supremacy of the Constitution.   This Constitution, and the laws of the United States which shall be made in pursuance thereof, and all treaties made, or which shall be made, under the authority of the United States, shall be the supreme law of the land; and the judges in every state shall be bound thereby, anything in the Constitution or laws of any state to the contrary notwithstanding.

c. Oath of office; no religious test.   The senators and representatives before mentioned, and the members of the several state legislatures, and all executive and judicial officers, both of the United States and of the several states, shall be bound by oath or affirmation to support this Constitution; but no religious test shall ever be required as a qualification to any office or public trust under the United States.

ARTICLE VII / RATIFICATION OF THE CONSTITUTION

The ratification of the conventions of nine states shall be sufficient for the establishment of this Constitution between the states so ratifying the same.

The Amendments

AMENDMENT 1 / FREEDOM OF RELIGION, SPEECH, PRESS, ASSEMBLY, AND PETITION (1791)

Congress shall make no law respecting an establishment of religion or prohibiting the free exercise thereof; or abridging the freedom of speech, or of the press; or the right of the people peaceably to assemble, and to petition the government for a redress of grievances.

This amendment protects the five basic rights of a citizen: (1) Congress must not pass laws that stop people from worshiping as they see fit. (2) Congress cannot stop people from voicing their views in private and public, as long as they do not slander or libel others or urge violent overthrow of the government. (3) Congress must respect the right of newspapers, books, and other media to express ideas and opinions, provided that no libelous or slanderous statements are made. (4) Congress must not take away the people's right to meet together for any lawful purpose, provided they do not interfere with the rights of others. (5) Congress must not take away the people's right to ask the government to correct grievances or abuses.

AMENDMENT 2 / RIGHT TO BEAR ARMS (1791)

A well-regulated militia being necessary to the security of a free state, the right of the people to keep and bear arms shall not be infringed.

Amendment 2 guarantees that the federal government cannot deny states the right to enlist citizens in the militia and to provide them with training in the use of weapons.

AMENDMENT 3 / QUARTERING OF SOLDIERS (1791)

No soldier shall, in time of peace, be quartered in any house without the consent of the owner, nor in time of war, but in a manner to be prescribed by law.

Amendment 3 was included because of the troubles caused when the British sought to quarter and supply their troops in colonists' homes. The amendment guarantees that in time of peace the federal government may not force people to have soldiers live in their homes. Even in time of war, people cannot be compelled to do this unless Congress passes a law requiring it.

AMENDMENT 4 / SEARCH AND SEIZURE (1791)

The right of the people to be secure in their persons, houses, papers, and effects, against unreasonable searches and seizures, shall not be violated, and no warrants shall issue but upon probable cause, supported by oath or affirmation and particularly describing the place to be searched and the persons or things to be seized.

This amendment extends the people's right to privacy and security by stating that the government may not search a home or arrest a person without good cause and then only after the official who makes the search or arrest has obtained a *warrant* —an official order from a judge. Judges may not issue warrants unless they believe such action is necessary to enforce the law.

AMENDMENT 5 / RIGHTS OF ACCUSED PERSONS (1791)

No person shall be held to answer for a capital or otherwise infamous crime, unless on a presentment or indictment of a grand jury, except in cases arising in

Amendment 5 says that no person may be tried in a federal court unless a grand jury decides that the person ought to be tried. (Members of the armed forces, however, may be tried in military court under military law.) People who have been tried for a crime and judged innocent cannot be tried again for the same crime. Neither can they be forced to give evidence against themselves. And no person may be executed, imprisoned, or fined except as punishment after a fair trial. A person's private property may not be taken for public use without a fair price being paid for it.

This amendment lists additional rights of an individual accused of a crime. A person accused of a crime is entitled to a prompt public trial before an impartial jury. The trial is held in the district where the crime took place. The accused must be told what the charge is. The accused must be present when witnesses give their testimony. The government must help the accused bring into court friendly witnesses. The accused must be provided a lawyer.

This amendment states that if a lawsuit involves property or settlement worth more than twenty dollars, the case may be tried before a jury. Today, cases involving lawsuits are not tried before federal courts unless large sums of money are involved.

Amendment 8 provides that persons accused of crimes may in most cases be released from jail if they or someone else posts bail. This is called "being out on bail." Bail, fines, and punishments must be reasonable.

This amendment was included because of the impossibility of listing in the Constitution all the rights of the people. The mention of certain rights does not mean that people do not have other fundamental rights, which the government must respect.

This is called the "reserved-power" amendment. It states that the powers which the Constitution does not give to the United States and does not deny to the states belong to the states and to the people.

the land or naval forces, or in the militia, when in actual service in time of war or public danger; nor shall any person be subject for the same offense to be twice put in jeopardy of life or limb; nor shall be compelled in any criminal case to be a witness against himself, nor be deprived of life, liberty, or property, without due process of law; nor shall private property be taken for public use without just compensation.

AMENDMENT 6 / JURY TRIAL IN CRIMINAL CASES (1791)

In all criminal prosecutions, the accused shall enjoy the right to a speedy and public trial by an impartial jury of the state and district wherein the crime shall have been committed, which district shall have been previously ascertained by law, and to be informed of the nature and cause of the accusation; to be confronted with the witnesses against him; to have compulsory process for obtaining witnesses in his favor; and to have the assistance of counsel for his defense.

AMENDMENT 7 / RULES OF COMMON LAW (1791)

In suits at common law, where the value in controversy shall exceed twenty dollars, the right of trial by jury shall be preserved, and no fact tried by a jury shall be otherwise re-examined in any court of the United States than according to the rules of common law.

AMENDMENT 8 / PROTECTION FROM EXCESSIVE PENALTIES (1791)

Excessive bail shall not be required, nor excessive fines imposed, nor cruel and unusual punishments inflicted.

AMENDMENT 9 / OTHER RIGHTS OF THE PEOPLE (1791)

The enumeration in the Constitution of certain rights shall not be construed to deny or disparage others retained by the people.

AMENDMENT 10 / POWERS KEPT BY STATES AND THE PEOPLE (1791)

The powers not delegated to the United States by the Constitution, nor prohibited by it to the states, are reserved to the states respectively, or to the people.

AMENDMENT 11 / SUITS AGAINST A STATE (1798)

The judicial power of the United States shall not be construed to extend to any suit in law or equity commenced or prosecuted against one of the United States by citizens of another state or by citizens or subjects of any foreign state.

This amendment was the first that was enacted to override a Supreme Court decision. It confirms that no federal court may try a case in which a state is being sued by a citizen of another state or of a foreign country. Amendment 11 changes a provision of Article III, Section 2, Clause "a."

AMENDMENT 12 / ELECTION OF PRESIDENT AND VICE PRESIDENT (1804)

The electors shall meet in their respective states and vote by ballot for President and Vice President, one of whom, at least, shall not be an inhabitant of the same state with themselves; they shall name in their ballots the person voted for as President, and in distinct ballots the person voted for as Vice President, and they shall make distinct lists of all persons voted for as President, and of all persons voted for as Vice President, and of the number of votes for each, which lists they shall sign and certify, and transmit sealed to the seat of the government of the United States, directed to the President of the Senate; the President of the Senate shall, in the presence of the Senate and House of Representatives, open all the certificates and the votes shall then be counted; the person having the greatest number of votes for President shall be the President, if such number be a majority of the whole number of electors appointed; and if no person have such majority, then from the persons having the highest numbers not exceeding three on the list of those voted for as President, the House of Representatives shall choose immediately, by ballot, the President. But in choosing the President, the votes shall be taken by states, the representation from each state having one vote; a quorum for this purpose shall consist of a member or members from two thirds of the states, and a majority of all the states shall be necessary to a choice. And if the House of Representatives shall not choose a President whenever the right of choice shall devolve upon them, *before the fourth day of March next following,* then the Vice President shall act as President, as in the case of the death or other constitutional disability of the President. The person having the greatest number of votes as Vice President shall be the Vice President, if such number be a majority of the whole number of electors appointed, and if no person have a majority, then from the two highest numbers on the list, the Senate shall choose the Vice President; a quorum for the purpose shall consist of two thirds of the whole number of senators, and a majority of the whole number shall be necessary to a choice. But no person constitutionally ineligible to the office of President shall be eligible to that of Vice President of the United States.

Amendment 12 describes the present-day procedure in the electoral college. The most important change made by this amendment was that the presidential electors would vote for President and Vice President on separate ballots. In 1800, when only one ballot was used, Thomas Jefferson and Aaron Burr received the same number of votes, and the election had to be decided by the House of Representatives. To guard against this possibility in the future, Amendment 12 calls for separate ballots.

The electors meet in their state capitals and cast their separate ballots for President and Vice President. They send them to the President of the Senate, showing the votes for each candidate. They are opened, and the electoral votes for President are counted in the presence of both houses. The candidate having a majority is declared elected. If no candidate for President receives a majority, the election goes to the House. The members of the House then vote by state for the three highest candidates. Each state casts one vote. A quorum consists of at least one member from two thirds of the states. The candidate who receives a majority of the votes of the states is elected President. If the House fails to elect a President, the Vice President acts as President.

The electoral votes for Vice President are also counted in the presence of both houses. The candidate having a majority is declared elected. If no candidate for Vice President receives a majority, the Senate chooses a Vice President from the two highest candidates. For this purpose, a quorum consists of two thirds of the total membership of the Senate. A majority of the whole number of the Senate is necessary to elect a Vice President. No person can be Vice President who does not meet the qualifications for President.

Amendment 13 is the first of three amendments that were a consequence of the Civil War. It states that slavery must end in the United States and its territories. The amendment was deemed necessary because the Supreme Court, in the Dred Scott decision, declared that ownership of slaves as a form of property was constitutional throughout the United States and its territories.

Congress may pass whatever laws are necessary to enforce Amendment 13. This statement is called an *enabling act*. Many amendments include an enabling act.

By the definition of citizenship in Amendment 14, black Americans were granted citizenship. The first section provides that all persons born or naturalized in the United States and subject to this country's laws are citizens of the United States and of the state in which they live. No state may take away the rights of citizens or take any person's life, liberty, or property except according to law. All state laws must apply equally to everyone in the state.

This section abolished the provision in Article 1, Section 2, Clause "c," which said that only three fifths of the slaves should be counted as population.

Section 3 dealt with persons who held appointive or elective offices or commissions in the armed forces which required an oath to support the Constitution of the United States and who had violated that oath by taking up arms against the United States. These officials were barred from holding any office which would again require them to take such an oath. This provision was designed to bar leaders of the Confederacy from holding federal office.

AMENDMENT 13 / SLAVERY ABOLISHED (1865)

SECTION 1. Abolition of slavery. Neither slavery nor involuntary servitude, except as a punishment for crime whereof the party shall have been duly convicted, shall exist within the United States or any place subject to their jurisdiction.

SECTION 2. Enforcement. Congress shall have the power to enforce this article by appropriate legislation.

AMENDMENT 14 / CIVIL RIGHTS GUARANTEED (1868)

SECTION 1. Definition of citizenship. All persons born or naturalized in the United States, and subject to the jurisdiction thereof, are citizens of the United States and of the state wherein they reside. No state shall make or enforce any law which shall abridge the privileges or immunities of citizens of the United States; nor shall any state deprive any person of life, liberty, or property, without due process of law; nor deny to any person within its jurisdiction the equal protection of the laws.

SECTION 2. Apportionment of representatives. Representatives shall be apportioned among the several states according to their respective numbers, counting the whole number of persons in each state, *excluding Indians not taxed.* But when the right to vote at any election for the choice of electors for President and Vice President of the United States, representatives in Congress, the executive and judicial officers of a state, or the members of the legislature thereof, is denied to any of the *male* inhabitants of such state, *being twenty-one years of age* and citizens of the United States, or in any way abridged, except for participation in rebellion, or other crime, the basis of representation therein shall be reduced in the proportion which the number of such *male* citizens shall bear to the whole number of *male* citizens *twenty-one years of age* in such state.

SECTION 3. Restrictions on public office. No person shall be a senator or representative in Congress, or elector of President and Vice President, or hold any office, civil or military, under the United States, or under any state, who, having previously taken an oath as a member of Congress, or as an officer of the United States, or as a member of any state legislature, or as an executive or judicial officer of any state, to support the Constitution of the United States, shall have engaged in insurrection or rebellion against the same, or given aid or comfort to the enemies thereof. But Congress may by vote of two thirds of each house remove such disability.

SECTION 4. Public debt of the United States valid; Confederate debt void. The validity of the public debt of the United States, authorized by law, including debts incurred for payment of pensions and bounties for services in suppressing insurrection or rebellion, shall not be questioned. But neither the United States nor any state shall assume or pay any debt or obligation incurred in aid of insurrection or rebellion against the United States, or any claim for the loss or emancipation of any slave; but all such debts, obligations, and claims shall be held illegal and void.

This section was included to settle the question of debts incurred during the Civil War. All debts contracted by the United States were to be paid. Neither the United States nor any state government, however, was to pay the debts of the Confederacy. Moreover, no payment was to be made to former slave owners as compensation for slaves who were set free.

SECTION 5. Enforcement. The Congress shall have power to enforce by appropriate legislation the provisions of this article.

AMENDMENT 15 / RIGHT TO VOTE (1870)

SECTION 1. The right of citizens of the United States to vote shall not be denied or abridged by the United States or by any state on account of race, color, or previous condition of servitude.

SECTION 2. The Congress shall have power to enforce this article by appropriate legislation.

Amendment 15 sought to protect the right of citizens to vote in federal and state elections. It states that citizens cannot be kept from voting because of their race or color or because they had once been slaves. After ratification of this amendment, states successfully kept black Americans from voting by the use of such impediments as literacy tests and poll taxes. Beginning in 1957, a series of federal civil rights acts sought to end such discrimination.

AMENDMENT 16 / INCOME TAX (1913)

The Congress shall have power to lay and collect taxes on incomes, from whatever source derived, without apportionment among the several states and without regard to any census or enumeration.

Amendment 16 authorizes Congress to tax incomes. An amendment was necessary because in 1895 the Supreme Court had decided that an income tax law, passed by Congress a year earlier, was unconstitutional.

AMENDMENT 17 / DIRECT ELECTION OF SENATORS (1913)

a. Election by the people. The Senate of the United States shall be composed of two senators from each state, elected by the people thereof, for six years; and each senator shall have one vote. The electors in each state shall have the qualifications requisite for electors of the most numerous branch of the state legislatures.

a. The Constitution originally provided that senators were to be elected by the state legislatures. Amendment 17 changed that provision to election by popular vote. Anyone qualified to vote for a state representative may vote for United States senators.

b. Vacancies. When vacancies happen in the representation of any state in the Senate, the executive authority of such state shall issue writs of election to fill such vacancies: provided that the legislature of any state may empower the executive thereof to make temporary appointments until the people fill the vacancies by election as the legislature may direct.

b. If a vacancy occurs in the United States Senate, the governor of the state affected may call a special election to fill the vacancy. The state legislature, however, may permit the governor to appoint someone to fill the vacancy until an election is held.

c. Senators chosen by state legislatures before Amendment 17 was added to the Constitution could complete their terms.

Amendment 18 forbade the manufacture, sale, or shipment of intoxicating beverages within the United States. The importation or exportation of such beverages was also forbidden. Amendment 18 was later repealed by Amendment 21.

Amendment 19 provides that a citizen who is a woman may not be denied the right to vote in a federal or state election.

When the Constitution first went into effect, means of transportation and communication were slow. There was a long period, therefore, between the President's election (November) and inauguration (March). One purpose of Amendment 20 was to shorten that waiting period. The amendment established that the terms of the President and Vice President end at noon on January 20 following a presidential election. The terms of one third of the senators and of all representatives, meanwhile, end at noon on January 3 in years ending in odd numbers. The new terms begin when the old terms end.

Section 2 provides that Congress must meet at least once a year, with the regular session beginning on January 3 unless Congress sets a different day.

c. Not retroactive. This amendment shall not be so construed as to affect the election or term of any senator chosen before it becomes valid as part of the Constitution.

AMENDMENT 18 / PROHIBITION (1919)

SECTION 1. *After one year from the ratification of this article the manufacture, sale, or transportation of intoxicating liquors within, the importation thereof into, or the exportation thereof from the United States and all territory subject to the jurisdiction thereof for beverage purposes is hereby prohibited.*

SECTION 2. *The Congress and the several states shall have concurrent power to enforce this article by appropriate legislation.*

SECTION 3. *This article shall be inoperative unless it shall have been ratified as an amendment to the Constitution by the legislatures of the several states, as provided in the Constitution, within seven years from the date of the submission hereof to the states by the Congress.*

AMENDMENT 19 / WOMEN'S VOTING RIGHTS (1920)

SECTION 1. The right of citizens of the United States to vote shall not be denied or abridged by the United States or by any state on account of sex.

SECTION 2. The Congress shall have power to enforce this article by appropriate legislation.

AMENDMENT 20 / TERMS OF OFFICE (1933)

SECTION 1. Terms of President, Vice President, and Congress. The terms of the President and Vice President shall end at noon on the 20th day of January, and the terms of senators and representatives at noon on the 3rd day of January, of the years in which such terms would have ended if this article had not been ratified; and the terms of their successors shall then begin.

SECTION 2. Sessions of Congress. The Congress shall assemble at least once in every year, and such meeting shall begin at noon on the 3rd day of January, unless they shall by law appoint a different day.

SECTION 3. Presidential succession. If, at the time fixed for the beginning of the term of the President, the President-elect shall have died, the Vice President-elect shall become President. If a President shall not have been chosen before the time fixed for the beginning of his term, or if the President-elect shall have failed to qualify, then the Vice President-elect shall act as President until a President shall have qualified; and the Congress may by law provide for the case wherein neither a President-elect nor a Vice President-elect shall have qualified, declaring who shall then act as President, or the manner in which one who is to act shall be selected, and such person shall act accordingly until a President or a Vice President shall have qualified.

Section 3 states that if the President-elect dies before being sworn in, the Vice President-elect becomes President. If the President-elect has not been chosen or does not qualify for office, the Vice President-elect acts as President until a President is chosen or qualifies. If neither the President-elect nor Vice President-elect qualifies to hold office, Congress decides who shall act as President until a President or Vice President is chosen or qualifies.

SECTION 4. Choice of President by the House. The Congress may by law provide for the case of the death of any of the persons from whom the House of Representatives may choose a President whenever the right of choice shall have devolved upon them, and for the case of the death of any of the persons from whom the Senate may choose a Vice President whenever the right of choice shall have devolved upon them.

Section 4 states that in cases in which the election is thrown into Congress because no candidate for either President or Vice President receives a majority of the electoral votes, Congress may make a law to decide what to do if one of the candidates dies.

SECTION 5. Date effective. Sections 1 and 2 shall take effect on the fifteenth day of October following the ratification of this article.

Section 5 set the date on which the first two sections of Amendment 20 were to take effect after the amendment had been approved by the states.

SECTION 6. Limited time for ratification. *This article shall be inoperative unless it shall have been ratified as an amendment to the Constitution by the legislatures of three fourths of the several states within seven years from the date of its submission.*

To become a part of the Constitution, Amendment 20 had to be approved within seven years.

AMENDMENT 21 / REPEAL OF PROHIBITION (1933)

SECTION 1. Repeal of Amendment 18. The eighteenth article of amendment to the Constitution of the United States is hereby repealed.

Amendment 21 repealed the Eighteenth Amendment, putting an end to the nationwide ban on the manufacture, sale, and shipment of alcoholic beverages. It was the only amendment submitted to special ratifying conventions instead of state legislatures.

SECTION 2. States protected. The transportation or importation into any state, territory, or possession of the United States for delivery or use therein of intoxicating liquors, in violation of the laws thereof, is hereby prohibited.

This section made it clear that intoxicating liquors may not be transported or imported into any state or territory of the United States if the laws of that state or territory prohibit the sale of liquor.

SECTION 3. Limited time for ratification. *This article shall be inoperative unless it shall have been ratified as an amendment to the Constitution by conventions in the several states, as provided in the Constitution, within seven years from the date of the submission hereof to the states by the Congress.*

Amendment 22 declares that no person may be elected President more than twice. A person who has served more than two years in the place of an elected President may be elected President only once. This limitation did not apply to President Truman, who was in office when Amendment 22 was proposed. Before this amendment was added, the Constitution placed no limit on the number of terms a President might serve. Presidents Washington, Jefferson, and Madison, however, limited themselves to two terms in office. Although Ulysses S. Grant and Theodore Roosevelt sought third terms, the precedent was not broken until 1940, when Franklin D. Roosevelt was elected for a third term.

This amendment gave the residents of the District of Columbia the right to vote in presidential elections. They may choose as many electors as does the state with the smallest population. Before this amendment was adopted, residents of the District of Columbia had not voted for President and Vice President because the Constitution provided that only states should choose presidential electors.

Amendment 24 prohibited the loss of voting rights in federal elections through failure to pay a poll tax or any other tax. The poll tax was a device used in some southern states to keep black voters from the polls. The poll tax was usually a cumulative tax.

AMENDMENT 22 / TWO-TERM LIMITATION ON PRESIDENCY (1951)

SECTION 1. Definition of limitation. No person shall be elected to the office of the President more than twice, and no person who has held the office of President, or acted as President, for more than two years of a term to which some other person was elected President shall be elected to the office of the President more than once. *But this article shall not apply to any person holding the office of President when this article was proposed by the Congress, and shall not prevent any person who may be holding the office of President, or acting as President, during the term within which this article becomes operative from holding the office of President, or acting as President during the remainder of such term.*

SECTION 2. Limited time for ratification. *This article shall be inoperative unless it shall have been ratified as an amendment to the Constitution by the legislatures of three fourths of the several states within seven years from the date of its submission to the states by the Congress.*

AMENDMENT 23 / VOTING IN THE DISTRICT OF COLUMBIA (1961)

SECTION 1. The District constituting the seat of government of the United States shall appoint, in such manner as the Congress may direct:

A number of electors of President and Vice President equal to the whole number of senators and representatives in Congress to which the District would be entitled if it were a state, but in no event more than the least populous state; they shall be in addition to those appointed by the states, but they shall be considered, for the purposes of the election of President and Vice President, to be electors appointed by a state; and they shall meet in the District and perform such duties as provided by the twelfth article of amendment.

SECTION 2. The Congress shall have power to enforce this article by appropriate legislation.

AMENDMENT 24 / POLL TAX PROHIBITION (1964)

SECTION 1. The right of citizens of the United States to vote in any primary or other election for President or Vice President, for electors for President or Vice President, or for senator or representative in Congress, shall not be denied or abridged by the United States or any state by reason of failure to pay any poll tax or other tax.

SECTION 2. The Congress shall have power to enforce this article by appropriate legislation.

AMENDMENT 25 / PRESIDENTIAL DISABILITY (1967)

SECTION 1. Accession of the Vice President. In case of the removal of the President from office or of his death or resignation, the Vice President shall become President.

SECTION 2. Replacing the Vice President. Whenever there is a vacancy in the office of the Vice President, the President shall nominate a Vice President who shall take office upon confirmation by a majority vote of both Houses of Congress.

SECTION 3. Vice President as Acting President. Whenever the President transmits to the President pro tempore of the Senate and the Speaker of the House of Representatives his written declaration that he is unable to discharge the powers and duties of his office, and until he transmits to them a written declaration to the contrary, such powers and duties shall be discharged by the Vice President as Acting President.

SECTION 4. Determining presidential disability. Whenever the Vice President and a majority of either the principal officers of the executive departments or of such other body as Congress may by law provide, transmit to the President pro tempore of the Senate and the Speaker of the House of Representatives their written declaration that the President is unable to discharge the powers and duties of his office, the Vice President shall immediately assume the powers and duties of the office as Acting President.

Thereafter, when the President transmits to the President pro tempore of the Senate and the Speaker of the House of Representatives his written declaration that no inability exists, he shall resume the powers and duties of his office unless the Vice President and a majority of either the principal officers of the executive department or of such other body as Congress may by law provide, transmit within four days to the President pro tempore of the Senate and the Speaker of the House of Representatives their written declaration that the President is unable to discharge the powers and duties of his office. Thereupon, Congress shall decide the issue, assembling within forty-eight hours for that purpose, if not in session. If

This meant that to register to vote a citizen had to pay all the back taxes for the years since coming of voting age. In 1966, the Supreme Court ruled that payment of poll taxes was also an unconstitutional precondition for voting in state and local elections.

Amendment 25 clarifies Article 2, Section 1, Clause "e," which deals with filling vacancies in the presidency. It also establishes procedures to follow when the President is too ill to serve. Section 1 states clearly that if the President dies or resigns, the Vice President becomes President.

Section 2 seeks to keep the office of Vice President filled so that there will always be an immediate successor to the President. It states that when there is a vacancy in the office of Vice President, the President may appoint a person to be Vice President.

Section 3 deals with the difficult problem of presidential disability. It declares that a President who is ill or unable to carry out official duties may assign those duties to the Vice President by notifying the Speaker of the House and the President pro tempore of the Senate. The Vice President then acts as President until the President is again able to serve.

Section 4 provides that when it is determined that the President is ill or unable for other reasons to carry out official duties and is unable or unwilling to assign those duties to the Vice President, the Vice President and a majority of the Cabinet must notify the Speaker of the House and the President pro tempore of the Senate. The Vice President then acts as President. The President cannot again assume official duties unless the Vice President and a majority of the Cabinet agree that he is fit to do so. If the Vice President and a majority of the Cabinet do not believe that the President is fit, Congress must meet and make a decision within 21 days. If two thirds of both houses of Congress vote that the President is unable to carry out the duties of his office, the Vice President continues to act as President. Otherwise, the President again takes over the duties of the presidency.

the Congress, within twenty-one days after receipt of the latter written declaration, or, if Congress is not in session, within twenty-one days after Congress is required to assemble, determines by two-thirds vote of both Houses that the President is unable to discharge the powers and duties of his office, the Vice President shall continue to discharge the same as Acting President; otherwise, the President shall resume the powers and duties of his office.

AMENDMENT 26 / VOTING AGE (1971)

SECTION 1. The right of citizens of the United States who are eighteen years of age or older to vote shall not be denied or abridged by the United States or by any state on account of age.

SECTION 2. The Congress shall have power to enforce this article by appropriate legislation.

Amendment 26 grants citizens 18 years of age or older the right to vote in federal and state elections. Prior to its ratification, most states limited the vote to citizens 21 years of age or older. In the Voting Rights Act of 1970, Congress lowered the minimum age to 18 in both federal and state elections. When the Supreme Court limited this law to federal elections, Congress proposed Amendment 26.

Thinking About Careers

During this school year you learned that in the early days of the American republic, most people earned a living by farming. By 1920, manufacturing had replaced agriculture as the nation's major economic activity. Then, forty years later, a second major shift began to take place. Manufacturing started being replaced by high-technology and service industries. Since 1970, jobs in manufacturing have declined, while those in high-technology and service industries have expanded. Three out of every four new jobs will be created in service industries.

YOUR INTERESTS, VALUES, AND SKILLS

Before you begin to consider a career, you should think about your interests, values, and skills. You can determine your interests by examining the kinds of things you like to do. Do you prefer group activities? Or would you rather spend your time working on your own? Do you prefer working with words or with your hands, with ideas or with things? Answering questions like these will help you identify your interests.

Your values indicate what you consider important in life. Is acquiring wealth important to you? Would you want to stay in your home community, or would you prefer to live elsewhere? How many years are you willing to invest in training for a career? Is job security important to you? Or would you be willing to take risks in the hope of achieving greater returns? Your values will affect your choice of a career.

Many skills can be learned, but most people find certain skills easier to master than others. Different career fields, furthermore, have different skill requirements. For example, good eyesight and quick reflexes are more important for a police officer than for a social worker. You should choose a career that matches your skills.

LEARNING MORE ABOUT CAREERS

There are many sources of information that can help you explore a career field. Government agencies, business firms, trade associations, labor unions, fraternal and patriotic groups, and educational institutions all publish a great deal of useful material. You might start with the *Dictionary of Occupational Titles,* put out by the Department of Labor. It describes about 20,000 different kinds of jobs. Another good government source is the *Occupational Outlook Handbook,* published every two years by the Bureau of Labor Statistics. In addition to information about job requirements and earnings, it predicts which industries will grow and which will shrink over the next few years. You can probably find both titles in your school or local library.

Another good source of career information is your school counselor or adviser. Counselors can discuss with you what your interests, values, and skills are and arrange for you to take tests that will help you assess these factors. They know the curriculum and costs of various schools and training programs. They are also familiar with the job market.

In recent years, various agencies have begun providing career information for special groups. For example, women's centers run by community organizations or local colleges offer suggestions about jobs. Vocational-rehabilitation agencies provide information aimed at the handicapped. Specialized magazines such as *The Black Collegian* and *Minority Engineer* deal with problems that members of minority groups may face.

The way you choose to earn your living is important not only to you but also to our nation. To meet future challenges, the United States needs skillful citizens.

Suggested Reading

General List

American Heritage Book of Indians. American Heritage. A beautifully illustrated history of the Indians of North America.

American Heritage Pictorial Atlas of United States History. American Heritage. A basic source.

Barzman, Sol. *The First Ladies.* Cowles. Brief but reflective biographies of the Presidents' wives from Martha Washington to Pat Nixon.

Brinton, Crane. *The Anatomy of Revolution.* Peter Smith. A famous comparative analysis of the American, French, and Russian revolutions.

A Cartoon History of United States Foreign Policy. Foreign Policy Association. A lively way of examining America's relations with other nations.

Commager, Henry Steele, ed. *Documents of American History.* Appleton-Century-Crofts. A basic collection.

Dinnerstein, Leonard, and David Reimers. *Ethnic Americans: A History of Immigration and Assimilation.* Harper and Row. A concise treatment of this stirring theme.

Dulles, Foster R. *America Learns to Play.* Peter Smith. Popular recreation traced from 1607 to the eve of World War II.

Franklin, John Hope. *From Slavery to Freedom,* 5th ed. Alfred A. Knopf. An award-winning history of black Americans.

Graff, Henry F., ed. *The Presidents: A Reference History.* Charles Scribner's Sons. Noted historians examine the Chief Executives in individual essays on their terms of office.

Hofstadter, Richard. *The American Political Tradition and the Men Who Made It.* Alfred A. Knopf. A collection of provocative and informative essays on political leaders.

Hughes, Langston; Milton Meltzer; and C. Eric Lincoln, eds. *A Pictorial History of Black-Americans.* Crown. An illustrated account of black people in American society.

Lingeman, Richard. *Small Town America.* Houghton Mifflin. A history of small-town life, from 1620 to the present.

Morris, Richard B., and Jeffrey B. Morris, eds. *Encyclopedia of American History.* Harper and Row. A standard reference work.

Ryan, William, and Desmond Guinness. *The White House.* McGraw-Hill. The first complete biography of America's most famou home. Profusely and handsomely illustrated.

Wertheimer, Barbara M. *We Were There.* Pantheon. The story of working women in the United States.

Unit One: Beginnings

Caffrey, Kate. *The Mayflower.* Stein and Day. The story of Plymouth from the European background of the *Mayflower's* passengers through their settlement in America.

Eaton, Jeanette. *Lone Journey: The Life of Roger Williams.* Harcourt Brace Jovanovich. A biography of the founder of Rhode Island.

Hertzberg, Hazel W. *The Great Tree and the Longhouse.* Macmillan. A classic description of Iroquois culture.

Lockridge, Kenneth A. *A New England Town: The First Hundred Years.* W. W. Norton. A combination of social history and geography that portrays the development of Dedham, Massachusetts, from 1636 to 1736.

Morison, Samuel Eliot. *The European Discovery of America: The Northern Voyages, A.D. 500–1600* and *The European Discovery of America: The Southern Voyages, A.D. 1492–1616.* Oxford University Press. A detailed account of the early explorers and the dangers and excitement of their adventures. The author personally retraced many of the routes.

Pease, Catherine Owens. *William Penn.* Holt, Rinehart and Winston. A life of the founder of Pennsylvania.

Scott, John Anthony. *Settlers on the Eastern Shore, 1607–1750.* Alfred A. Knopf. A description, with many primary sources, of life in the thirteen English colonies, the difficulties the people faced, and the issues that concerned them.

Smith, E. Brooks, and Robert Meredith, eds. *Pilgrim Courage.* Little, Brown. An adaptation of William Bradford's history of Plymouth.

Tourtellot, Arthur B. *Benjamin Franklin: The Shaping of Genius, The Boston Years.* Doubleday. A work of social and cultural history that carries its subject to his seventeenth year.

Tunis, Edwin. *Colonial Craftsmen.* T. Y. Crowell. An illustrated account of the beginnings of American industry and enterprise.

Williams, Selma R. *Demeter's Daughters: The Women Who Founded America.* Atheneum. An account of notable colonial women from 1587 to 1792.

Unit Two: A New People

Berkin, Carol. *Women in the American Revolution*. Viking Press. A description of the broad range of women's activities.

Butterfield, L. H.; Marc Friedlaender; and Mary-Jo Kline, eds. *The Book of Abigail and John: Selected Letters of the Adams Family, 1762–1784*. Harvard University Press. An intimate view of John and Abigail Adams and their perspectives on themselves, their friends, and the times in which they lived.

Canfield, Cass. *Samuel Adams's Revolution, 1765–1776*. Harper and Row. A fast-moving account of one man's influence on the coming of independence.

Crouse, Anne. *Alexander Hamilton and Aaron Burr*. Random House. A double biography of two Revolutionary leaders whose lives were politically and personally connected.

Davis, Burke. *Black Heroes of the American Revolution*. Harcourt Brace Jovanovich. Collective biographies of black Americans who aided the nation's fight for independence.

Flexner, James T. *Washington: The Indispensable Man*. Little, Brown. A leading biography of our first President.

Gelfaund, Ravina. *Freedom of Religion in America*. Lerner Publications. The question of religious freedom throughout America's history.

Kenyon, Cecilia, ed. *The Antifederalists*. Bobbs-Merrill. A collection of primary sources presenting arguments against ratification of the Constitution.

Lancaster, Bruce. *The American Heritage Book of the Revolution*. American Heritage. A profusely illustrated and well-written account.

Lieberman, Jethro K. *Free Speech, Free Press, and the Law*. Lothrop, Lee and Shepard. A detailed presentation of two of the freedoms protected by the First Amendment.

Morris, Richard B. *Seven Who Shaped Our Destiny*. Harper. Fascinating essays on Franklin, Washington, John Adams, Jefferson, Jay, Madison, and Hamilton.

Paine, Thomas. *Common Sense*. Doubleday. The classic political work that swung colonial public opinion in favor of independence.

Rossiter, Clinton. *1787: The Grand Convention*. The scene in Philadelphia as the Constitution was being written.

Unit Three: A Nation of Sections

Baker, Leonard. *John Marshall: A Life in Law*. Macmillan. A thoughtful biography of an outstanding Chief Justice.

Bealer, Alex W. *Only the Names Remain: The Cherokees and the Trail of Tears*. Little, Brown. An account of the Cherokee people and culture before Europeans arrived, their attempts to adjust to the newcomers, and their eventual forced removal to the West.

Clemens, Samuel. *Life on the Mississippi*. Harper and Row. A description of life in a river town during the 1830's and 1840's and of the changes brought about by the steamboat; also recounts the author's often hilarious experiences in learning to be a steamboat pilot.

De Voto, Bernard. *Across the Wide Missouri*. Houghton Mifflin. A portrayal of the lives of Indians, mountain men, and fur trappers in the West during the 1820's and 1830's.

Dodd, William E. *The Cotton Kingdom: A Chronicle of the Old South*. United States Publishers. A revealing description of the culture that revolved around a single product.

Graff, Henry F. *Thomas Jefferson*. Silver Burdett. Combines narrative with a picture portfolio and samples of Jefferson's own words.

Green, Constance. *Eli Whitney and the Birth of American Technology*. Little, Brown. An account of the effects of Whitney's inventions on the industrialization of the United States.

Gurko, Miriam. *The Ladies of Seneca Falls*. Macmillan. A description of the birth of the women's rights movement.

Haverstock, Mary Sayer. *Indian Gallery: The Story of George Catlin*. Four Winds Press. An illustrated biography of the well-known painter of Indian life.

Hoehling, Mary. *Yankee in the White House: John Quincy Adams*. Julian Messner. A biography of the sixth President.

Lord, Walter. *The Dawn's Early Light*. W. W. Norton. A stirring history of the War of 1812.

Macaulay, David. *Mill*. Houghton Mifflin. An illustrated history of a New England mill.

Perkins, Dexter. *A History of the Monroe Doctrine*. Little, Brown. An account of one of the foundation stones of American foreign policy.

Remini, Robert V. *The Revolutionary Age of Andrew Jackson*. Harper and Row. A favorable interpretation of the seventh President.

Taylor, George R. *The Transportation Revolution, 1815–1860*. M. E. Sharpe. The standard work on the railroads, canals, and other means of transportation that changed the face of our nation.

Unit Four: Union and Disunion

Billington, Ray Allen. *Westward Expansion: A History of the American Frontier*. Macmillan. A comprehensive study of the frontier.

Bishop, Curtis. *Lone Star Leader, Sam Houston*. Julian Messner. A biography of the Texas leader who supported the Union in the Civil War.

Bishop, Jim. *The Day Lincoln Was Shot*. Harper and Row. A detailed, absorbing chronicle of the events of April 14, 1865.

Chittenden, Elizabeth F. *Profiles in Black and White*. Charles Scribner's Sons. Biographies of people who opposed slavery.

Commager, Henry S., and Lynd Ward. *America's Robert E. Lee.* Houghton Mifflin. A biography of a man admired and respected by friends and enemies alike.

Crane, Stephen. *The Red Badge of Courage.* Dodd, Mead. The classic novel of a young soldier facing battle for the first time in the Civil War.

Douglass, Frederick. *Narrative of the Life of Frederick Douglass, An American Slave.* Belknap Press. The classic account of what slavery was like, written by a famous fugitive.

Gerson, Noel B. *The Trial of Andrew Johnson.* Nelson Bros. A dramatic telling of the nation's only presidential impeachment trial.

Holliday, J. S. *The World Rushed In.* Simon and Schuster. The story of the California gold rush, based on an eyewitness account.

Meltzer, Milton. *Bound for the Rio Grande.* Alfred A. Knopf. A lively account of the clash with Mexico; includes many primary sources.

Meltzer, Milton. *Thaddeus Stevens and the Fight for Negro Rights.* T. Y. Crowell. A biography of one of the most remarkable and controversial figures in American politics.

Meredith, Roy. *Mr. Lincoln's Cameraman: Mathew S. Brady.* Dover. A biography that also depicts the birth of photography.

Oates, Stephen B. *With Malice Toward None.* Harper. The best one-volume biography of Lincoln.

Scott, John Anthony. *Woman Against Slavery: The Story of Harriet Beecher Stowe.* T. Y. Crowell. A biography that does much to correct misconceptions about Mrs. Stowe's famous book.

Stampp, Kenneth. *The Era of Reconstruction, 1865–1877.* Alfred A. Knopf. A classic account of this controversial period.

Sterling, Dorothy, ed. *The Trouble They Seen.* Doubleday. A collection of primary sources about the black experience during reconstruction.

Wiley, Bell Irvin. *Confederate Women.* Greenwood Press. Collective biographies of southern women based on letters and diaries.

Wiley, Bell Irvin. *The Life of Johnny Reb: The Common Soldier of the Confederacy* and *The Life of Billy Yank: The Common Soldier of the Union.* Louisiana State University Press. Excellent depictions of the reality of the battlefront.

Unit Five: The Nation Transformed

American Heritage History of the Confident Years. American Heritage. A survey of the period from 1865 to 1914; combines pictures, narrative, and primary sources.

Brown, Dee. *Bury My Heart at Wounded Knee.* Holt, Rinehart and Winston. The westward expansion of the United States told from the viewpoint of Native Americans.

Callow, Alexander B., Jr. *The Tweed Ring.* Oxford. A close look at the famous political machine.

Garbedian, H. Gordon. *Thomas Alva Edison.* Julian Messner. A biography of the nation's most celebrated inventor.

Glad, Paul W. *McKinley, Bryan, and the People.* J. B. Lippincott. An analysis of the individuals and issues that shaped the 1896 election.

Handlin, Oscar. *The Uprooted.* Grosset & Dunlap. The classic study of late nineteenth-century immigration.

Harlow, Alvin. *Andrew Carnegie.* Julian Messner. A biography of the prototypical "rags-to-riches" American.

Josephson, Matthew. *Politicos.* Harcourt Brace Jovanovich. An overview of national politics in the post-Civil War years, with intimate accounts of the chief participants.

Katz, William Loren. *The Black West.* Doubleday. An account of black cowboys, cavalrymen, ranchers, and farmers in the West.

McCullough, David. *The Great Bridge.* Simon and Schuster. An account of the construction of the Brooklyn Bridge.

Maddow, Ben. *A Sunday Between Wars: The Course of American Life from 1865–1917.* W. W. Norton. A presentation of nineteenth-century life from the ordinary American's point of view.

Meltzer, Milton. *Bread and Roses.* Alfred A. Knopf. A history of the American labor movement from 1865 to 1915.

O'Connor, Edwin. *The Last Hurrah.* Atlantic-Little, Brown. A novel about the final campaign of an urban political boss.

Riis, Jacob. *How the Other Half Lives.* Harvard University Press. The classic work that focused attention on the nature of slum-dwelling.

Schlissel, Lillian. *Women's Diaries of the Westward Journey.* Schocken Books. A stirring portrayal of the westward adventure from the viewpoint of women.

Stiller, Richard. *Queen of Populists: The Story of Mary Elizabeth Lease.* T. Y. Crowell. A biography of one of the most colorful Populist leaders.

Strasser, Susan. *Never Done: A History of American Housework.* Pantheon. A lively, eye-opening account of the relationship between an industrializing economy and the household.

Thorndike, Joseph J., Jr. *The Very Rich.* American Heritage. A well-illustrated portrayal of rich families and their ways of life in the late 1800's.

Unit Six: Crusading at Home and Abroad

Addams, Jane. *Twenty Years at Hull-House.* Macmillan. The autobiography of one of the leaders of the settlement-house movement.

Archer, Jules. *World Citizen: Woodrow Wilson.* Julian Messner. A biography of the twenty-eighth President, with emphasis on his fight for the League of Nations.

Beale, Howard. *Theodore Roosevelt and the Rise of America to World Power.* Johns Hopkins University Press. An analysis of Roosevelt's influence on the nation's foreign policies.

Fleming, Alice. *Ida Tarbell.* T. Y. Crowell. A biography of the journalist who exposed the pricing tactics of the Standard Oil Company.

Flexner, Eleanor. *Century of Struggle.* Belknap Press. A history of the first hundred years of the fight for women's rights.

Garraty, John A. *Theodore Roosevelt: The Strenuous Life.* American Heritage. A study that shows how Roosevelt's belief in action expressed itself in both his personal and political life.

Ginger, Ray. *Eugene V. Debs.* Macmillan. A biography of the labor leader and presidential candidate who was a leading opponent of American involvement in World War I.

Jantzen, Steven. *Hooray for Peace, Hurrah for War.* Alfred A. Knopf. A description of World War I that uses such primary sources as letters, diaries, drawings, speeches, and songs.

La Follette, Robert M. *Autobiography.* University of Wisconsin Press. The autobiography of a leading progressive.

McCullough, David C. *The Path Between the Seas.* Simon and Schuster. The best presentation of the complex story of the construction of the Panama Canal.

May, Ernest R. *The Progressive Era.* Time-Life Books. A well-illustrated account of the politics and personalities of the period.

Reeder, Red. *The Story of the Spanish-American War.* Duell, Sloane. A good overall history.

Rouveral, Jean. *Pancho Villa: A Biography.* Doubleday. A biography of the controversial Mexican leader.

Sinclair, Upton. *The Jungle.* Airmont Publishing. The novel whose description of the meat-packing industry helped bring about passage of the Pure Food and Drugs Act.

Swanberg, W. A. *Citizen Hearst.* Charles Scribner's Sons. A biography of the newspaper publisher whose drive for higher circulation helped encourage American war fever in 1898.

Tuchman, Barbara. *The Guns of August.* Macmillan. A suspenseful account of the early days of World War I.

Unit Seven: Good Times, Hard Times, and War

Allen, Frederick Lewis. *Lords of Creation.* Harper and Row. Biographies of financial leaders of the United States.

Alsop, Joseph. *FDR: A Centenary Remembrance.* Viking. A combination of biographical essay, memoir, and history.

Ambrose, Stephen E. *Ike from Abilene to Berlin.* Harper and Row. A biography of Dwight D. Eisenhower from his childhood through victory in Europe.

Anderson, Jervis. *This Was Harlem.* Farrar, Straus & Giroux. A portrait of the writers, musicians, and artists of the Harlem Renaissance.

Buchanan, A. Russell. *The United States and World War II.* Harper and Row. A full account of the military history of World War II.

Burner, David. *Herbert Hoover: The Public Life.* Alfred A. Knopf. The most authoritative biography of the thirty-first President.

Burns, James M. *Roosevelt: The Lion and the Fox.* Harcourt Brace Jovanovich. A study of Roosevelt as a political leader.

Considine, Bob, and Ted Lawson. *Thirty Seconds Over Tokyo.* Random House. The gripping story of the first American air strikes on Japan's capital.

Handlin, Oscar. *Al Smith and His America.* Little, Brown. A biography that offers considerable insight into urban politics.

Houston, Jeanne Wakatsuka, and James D. Houston. *Farewell to Manzanar.* Houghton Mifflin. The poignant experiences of a Japanese-American girl who lived in an internment camp during World War II.

Kennan, George F. *American Diplomacy, 1900–1950.* University of Chicago Press. A thoughtful survey of the principles of American foreign policy.

Lord, Walter. *Day of Infamy.* Holt, Rinehart and Winston. A highly readable account of the Japanese attack on Pearl Harbor and the American response.

Marling, Karal Ann. *Wall-to-Wall America.* University of Minnesota Press. An account of the social and political significance of the murals painted under federal patronage during the Great Depression; well-illustrated.

Meltzer, Milton. *Brother, Can You Spare a Dime?* Alfred A. Knopf. The story of the Great Depression from the stock market crash to the New Deal, with numerous primary sources.

Meltzer, Milton. *Never to Forget: The Jews of the Holocaust.* Harper and Row. A searing account of the historical background of German anti-Semitism, Hitler's rise to power, and the Nazi death camps, combined with the recorded experiences of individual Jews.

Sherwood, Robert E. *Roosevelt and Hopkins.* Harper and Row. An intimate account of the President's relationship with his chief associate.

Sward, Keith. *The Legend of Henry Ford.* Russell and Russell. A biography of the man who revolutionized both American industry and the American way of life.

Williams, T. Harry. *Huey Long.* Vintage Books. A well-balanced biography of the Louisiana political leader.

Unit Eight: Confidence and Concern

Carter, Paul. *Another Part of the Fifties.* Columbia University Press. A fresh look at the 1950's.

Daniels, Jonathan. *The Man of Independence.* Kennikat. An illuminating biography of Harry S. Truman.

Ewald, William B. *Eisenhower the President: Crucial Days.* Prentice-Hall. An account of the eight years in office of the thirty-fourth President.

Goulden, Joseph C. *Korea: The Untold Story of the War.* Times Books. A well-documented portrayal of the individuals and events of the Korean War.

King, Martin Luther, Jr. *Stride Toward Freedom.* Harper and Row. A vivid account of the Montgomery bus boycott that led to the desegregation of public transportation.

Lewis, Anthony. *Gideon's Trumpet.* Random House. An account of the Supreme Court decision that poor people are entitled to legal counsel in criminal cases.

Nixon, Richard. *Six Crises.* Warner Books. Recounts the author's role in several controversial issues that arose in his career before he was President.

O'Neill, William L. *Coming Apart: An Informal History of America in the 1960's.* Quadrangle. An account of the political and social protests that marked the decade.

Robinson, Jackie. *I Never Had It Made.* G. P. Putnam's Sons. The autobiography of the first player to break the color bar in major league baseball.

Ross, Lillian. *Adlai Stevenson.* J. B. Lippincott. A biography of the able Democratic candidate for the presidency who lost to Eisenhower twice.

Schechter, Betty. *The Peaceable Revolution.* Houghton Mifflin. The development of nonviolent resistance in America from Thoreau to King.

Schwartz, Bernard. *Super Chief: Earl Warren and His Supreme Court — A Judicial Biography.* New York University Press. A biography that explains how Earl Warren guided the Court into issuing numerous landmark decisions in the area of individual rights.

Walton, Richard J. *America and the Cold War.* Seabury. A well-balanced analysis by a United Nations correspondent for the Voice of America.

White, Theodore H. *The Making of the President, 1960* and *The Making of the President, 1964.* Atheneum. Inside views of the campaigns by a leading political journalist.

Wicker, Tom. *JFK and LBJ.* Penguin. A comparison of the two Presidents, their personalities, and their administrations.

Unit Nine: Toward a New Century

Amrine, Michael. *The Great Decision.* G. P. Putnam's Sons. A gripping history of the development of the atomic bomb.

Bernstein, Carl, and Bob Woodward. *All the President's Men.* Simon and Schuster. The step-by-step story of Watergate as told by the reporters most responsible for uncovering the scandal.

Cohen, Warren I. *America's Response to China.* John Wiley. A significant examination of Sino-American relations.

Dean, John. *Blind Ambition.* Pocket Books. The story of Watergate as told by a presidential adviser who tried to balance moral values against a drive for success.

Gaddis, John L. *Russia, the Soviet Union, and the United States.* John Wiley. An outstanding examination of the subject reduced to its essentials.

Greenstein, Fred, ed. *The Reagan Presidency: An Early Assessment.* Johns Hopkins University Press. Scholars and policy-makers attempt to judge Reagan in four major policy areas — fiscal, foreign, defense, and domestic.

Grose, Peter. *Israel in the Mind of America.* Alfred A. Knopf. An account of the role of the United States in the re-establishment of a Jewish homeland.

Handlin, Oscar, ed. *Children of the Uprooted.* George Braziller. How the descendants of turn-of-the-century immigrants from eastern and southern Europe have fared in America.

Herring, George C. *America's Longest War.* John Wiley. A balanced overview of the conflict in Vietnam.

McGinniss, Joe. *The Selling of the President, 1968.* Pocket Books. A study of the role of image-making in presidential elections.

Meier, Matt S., and Feliciano Rivera. *The Chicanos: A History of Mexican-Americans.* Hill and Wang. A valuable primer on the subject.

Pierce, Neal, and Jerry Hagstrom. *The Book of America: Inside 50 States Today.* W. W. Norton. Detailed information about each of the states.

Sale, Kirkpatrick. *Power Shift.* Random House. The movement of population, industry, and political power from the Northeast to the South and West since the end of World War II.

Sitkoff, Harvard. *The Struggle for Black Equality: 1954–1981.* Hill and Wang. A leading survey of the civil-rights movement.

Important Dates

1000 Vikings cross Atlantic.
1487 Dias rounds Cape of Good Hope.
1492 Columbus reaches America.
1493 Line of Demarcation.
1498 Da Gama reaches India.
1513 Balboa reaches Pacific Ocean.
1519 Magellan begins voyage around world.
1521 Cortés conquers Aztecs.
1535 Cartier explores St. Lawrence River.
1541 De Soto reaches Mississippi River.
1565 Spanish settle St. Augustine.
1580 Drake circumnavigates world.
1607 Jamestown settled.
1608 Champlain founds Quebec.
1609 Santa Fe settled.
1619 Virginia House of Burgesses first meets.
1620 Pilgrims settle Plymouth.
1625 Dutch settle New Amsterdam.
1630 Puritans establish Massachusetts Bay Colony.
1634 Maryland founded.
1636 Roger Williams settles Providence.
1639 Fundamental Orders of Connecticut.
1649 Maryland Toleration Act.
1663 Carolina charter granted.
1664 English capture New Amsterdam.
1673 Marquette and Joliet explore Mississippi River.
1679 New Hampshire receives charter.
1681 Pennsylvania charter granted.
1682 La Salle reaches mouth of Mississippi River.
1733 Georgia founded.
1754 French and Indian War starts.
1759 British capture Quebec.
1765 Stamp Act.
1767 Townshend Acts.
1770 Boston Massacre.
1773 Boston Tea Party.
1774 Intolerable Acts.
     First Continental Congress meets.

1775 Battles of Lexington and Concord.
     Second Continental Congress meets.
     Battle of Bunker Hill.
1776 British evacuate Boston.
     American colonies declare independence.
1777 Burgoyne surrenders at Saratoga.
1778 Treaty of alliance signed with France.
1779 George Rogers Clark captures Vincennes.
1781 Cornwallis surrenders at Yorktown.
     Articles of Confederation go into effect.
1783 Treaty of Paris signed.
1785 Land Ordinance passed.
1786 Shays's Rebellion.
1787 Northwest Ordinance.
1788 Constitution ratified.
1789 George Washington becomes President.
1790 First American textile mill.
1791 Bill of Rights added to Constitution.
1793 Whitney invents cotton gin.
1794 Whiskey Rebellion.
1797 John Adams becomes President.
     XYZ Affair.
1798 Alien and Sedition Acts.
1801 Thomas Jefferson becomes President.
     Marbury v. Madison decision.
1803 Louisiana Purchase.
1804 Lewis and Clark expedition begins.
1807 Chesapeake Affair.
     Embargo Act.
1809 James Madison becomes President.
1811 Battle of Tippecanoe.
1812 War with Britain begins.
1814 Treaty of Ghent.
1817 James Monroe becomes President.
1819 Adams-Onís Treaty.
1820 Missouri Compromise.

1821 First public high school (Boston).
1822 Americans settle in Texas.
1823 Monroe Doctrine proclaimed.
1825 John Quincy Adams becomes President.
     Erie Canal completed.
1829 Andrew Jackson becomes President.
1830 Webster-Hayne debate.
     Indian Removal Act.
1831 Nat Turner organizes slave revolt.
1832 Jackson vetoes Bank Bill.
1833 Compromise tariff.
1834 Whig Party organized.
     National Trades Union formed.
1836 Texas declares independence from Mexico.
     Battle of the Alamo.
1837 Martin Van Buren becomes President.
     Oberlin College accepts women students.
     Panic of 1837.
1838 Cherokee forced west.
1841 William Henry Harrison becomes President.
     John Tyler becomes President on Harrison's death (April).
1842 Webster-Ashburton Treaty.
1845 James K. Polk becomes President.
     Texas and Florida become states.
1846 War with Mexico starts.
1847 Mormons settle in Utah.
1848 Treaty of Guadalupe-Hidalgo.
     Women's rights convention at Seneca Falls.
1849 Zachary Taylor becomes President.
1850 Millard Fillmore becomes President on Taylor's death (July).
     Compromise of 1850.
1852 *Uncle Tom's Cabin* published.
1853 Franklin Pierce becomes President.
     Gadsden Purchase.

1854 Kansas-Nebraska Act.
Republican Party formed.
Ostend Manifesto.
1857 James Buchanan becomes President.
Dred Scott decision.
1859 John Brown raids Harpers Ferry.
1861 Abraham Lincoln becomes President.
Civil War begins.
First Battle of Bull Run.
1862 Battle of Antietam.
Homestead Act.
1863 Emancipation Proclamation.
Battle of Gettysburg.
1864 Sherman takes Atlanta.
1865 Lee surrenders at Appomattox.
1865 Andrew Johnson becomes President on Lincoln's assassination (April).
Thirteenth Amendment abolishes slavery.
1866 National Labor Union formed.
1867 Reconstruction Act of 1867.
Alaska purchased.
Grange movement started.
1868 Congress impeaches Johnson.
Fourteenth Amendment defines American citizenship.
1869 Ulysses S. Grant becomes President.
First transcontinental railroad completed.
Knights of Labor formed.
1870 Fifteenth Amendment states voters' rights.
1873 Barbed wire developed.
1876 Battle of Little Bighorn.
Bell demonstrates telephone.
1877 Rutherford B. Hayes becomes President.
Chief Joseph surrenders.
Munn v. Illinois decision.
Last federal troops leave South.
1878 Bland-Allison Act.
1879 Edison invents electric light.
1881 James A. Garfield becomes President.
Chester A. Arthur becomes President on Garfield's assassination (September).
1882 John D. Rockefeller organizes Standard Oil Company.
1883 Civil Service Commission established.
Brooklyn Bridge completed.
1885 Grover Cleveland becomes President.
First skyscraper built in Chicago.

1886 Haymarket Riot.
American Federation of Labor formed.
1887 Interstate Commerce Act.
Dawes Act assigns land to Indians.
1889 Benjamin Harrison becomes President.
Jane Addams founds Hull House.
1890 First Pan-American Congress meets.
Sherman Antitrust Act.
Sherman Silver Purchase Act.
1892 Homestead strike.
1893 Grover Cleveland becomes President for second time.
Sherman Silver Purchase Act repealed.
1894 Pullman strike.
1896 *Plessy v. Ferguson* decision.
1897 William McKinley becomes President.
1898 Spanish-American War: U.S. acquires Philippines, Puerto Rico, Guam; frees Cuba.
Hawaii annexed.
1899 Open Door Policy proposed.
U.S. acquires American Samoa.
1900 Gold Standard Act.
Boxer Rebellion.
1901 Theodore Roosevelt becomes President on McKinley's assassination (September).
1903 U.S. leases Canal Zone in Panama.
Wright brothers make first successful airplane flight.
1904 Roosevelt Corollary.
1905 Treaty of Portsmouth ends Russo-Japanese War.
1906 Pure Food and Drug Act.
1909 William H. Taft becomes President.
1910 Mexican Revolution starts.
NAACP formed.
1911 National Urban League organized.
1913 Woodrow Wilson becomes President.
Sixteenth Amendment makes income tax legal.
Seventeenth Amendment provides for election of senators by voters.
Federal Reserve Act.
1914 World War I begins in Europe.
Federal Trade Commission created.
1915 *Lusitania* sunk by Germans.
1916 Border campaign against Villa.

1917 Virgin Islands purchased from Denmark.
U.S. enters World War I.
Communists seize power in Russia.
1918 Signing of armistice ends World War I.
1919 Eighteenth Amendment establishes prohibition.
Treaty of Versailles.
Boston police strike.
1920 Nineteenth Amendment gives women the vote.
First American radio broadcasting station.
1921 Warren G. Harding becomes President.
Washington Conference begins.
1923 Calvin Coolidge becomes President on Harding's death (August).
1924 Dawes Plan.
1927 Lindbergh flies nonstop to Paris.
1928 Kellogg-Briand Pact.
1929 Herbert Hoover becomes President.
Great Depression begins.
1931 Japan invades Manchuria.
1933 Twentieth Amendment provides that presidential and congressional terms begin earlier.
1933 Franklin D. Roosevelt becomes President.
New Deal begins.
Roosevelt pledges Good Neighbor Policy.
Hitler takes power in Germany.
Twenty-First Amendment repeals prohibition.
1934 Indian Reorganization Act.
1935 Wagner Act.
Social Security Act.
Italy attacks Ethiopia.
1936 Supreme Court declares AAA unconstitutional.
Germany occupies Rhineland.
Hoover Dam completed.
1937 Roosevelt's "court-packing" plan rejected.
Japan invades China.
1938 CIO organized.
1939 World War II begins in Europe.
1941 Lend-Lease Act.
United States enters World War II.
1942 Battle of the Coral Sea.
Allies land in North Africa.
1943 Allies invade Italy.

1944 Allies land in France.
Battle of the Bulge.
1945 Yalta Conference.
1945 *Harry S. Truman becomes President on Roosevelt's death* (April).
Germany surrenders (V-E Day).
Japan surrenders (V-J Day).
United Nations organized.
1947 Marshall Plan proposed.
Taft-Hartley Act.
1948 Berlin airlift begins.
1949 NATO formed.
Communists take control of China.
1950 Korean War begins.
1951 Twenty-Second Amendment puts two-term limit on presidency.
1952 Puerto Rico becomes self-governing commonwealth.
1953 *Dwight D. Eisenhower becomes President.*
Korean armistice signed.
1954 Supreme Court decision on school segregation.
1955 AFL-CIO merger.
1956 Suez Canal crisis.
Hungarian uprising.
1957 Eisenhower Doctrine proclaimed.
Soviet Union launches first Sputnik.
1959 Castro leads Cuban revolt.
Landrum-Griffin Act.
1960 Summit meeting canceled over U-2 incident.

1961 *John F. Kennedy becomes President.*
Peace Corps formed.
Twenty-Third Amendment allows D.C. residents to vote for President.
Berlin Wall built.
1962 Cuban missile crisis.
First U.S. manned orbital space flight.
1963 Nuclear test-ban treaty.
1963 *Lyndon Johnson becomes President on Kennedy's assassination* (November).
1964 Twenty-Fourth Amendment abolishes poll tax.
Civil Rights Act.
Gulf of Tonkin Resolution.
Johnson defeats Goldwater.
1965 Voting Rights Act.
Immigration quota system ended.
1967 Twenty-Fifth Amendment establishes procedures in case of presidential disability.
Six-Day War in Middle East.
1968 Martin Luther King, Jr., and Robert Kennedy assassinated.
1969 *Richard M. Nixon becomes President.*
American astronauts land on moon.
1971 Twenty-Sixth Amendment lowers voting age to eighteen years.
1972 Nixon visits China and Soviet Union.
Watergate break-in.

1973 Last American troops leave Vietnam.
Yom Kippur War in Middle East.
1974 *Gerald R. Ford becomes President on resignation of Richard Nixon* (August).
1975 South Vietnam falls to Communists.
1976 U.S. celebrates two-hundredth birthday.
1977 *Jimmy Carter becomes President.*
1978 Camp David accords signed.
1979 Iranians seize U.S. embassy and take hostages.
Soviet Union invades Afghanistan.
1981 *Ronald Reagan becomes President.*
American hostages released by Iran.
First woman appointed to Supreme Court.
1982 Reagan announces "New Federalism."
1983 American forces sent to Grenada.
1984 Kissinger Commission issues report on Central America.

Glossary

The glossary defines important words and terms used in this book. Remember that many words have more than one meaning. The definitions given here are the ones that will be most helpful in your reading of this book.

abolitionist: a person who worked in the movement to do away with slavery.

amnesty: a general pardon by a government for political offenses.

anarchist: a person who favors abolishing all forms of government.

annex: to incorporate territory into an existing country or state.

appeasement: the granting of concessions to a potential enemy in order to maintain peace.

apprentice: a youth who is bound to a skilled person in order to learn a trade.

arbitration: a process by which the parties to a dispute submit their differences to the judgment of an impartial party.

assembly line: a line of factory workers and equipment along which work being assembled passes from one operation to the next until completion.

automation: the automatic operation of manufacturing processes.

black codes: state laws that restricted the activities of southern blacks in the years after the Civil War.

blacklist: a list of workers whom employers refuse to hire because of their union activities.

blockade: to close off an area by the use of naval or other forces.

bond: a certificate issued by a corporation or a government in exchange for a loan of money.

borderlands: in the days of the conquistadors, the region across northern Mexico embracing what are now the states of Florida, Texas, New Mexico, Arizona, and California.

bounty: a reward or payment, especially one given by a government for acts beneficial to the state.

boycott: to express protest by refusing to deal with a certain party.

brinkmanship: a strategy by which a nation displays its willingness to risk war in order to make an adversary back down.

bureaucracy: administration of a government, chiefly by unelected officials.

Cabinet: the executive department heads who advise the President.

capital: wealth, in the form of money or property, that is owned by an individual or a business organization.

capitalist: a person who invests money in business in order to make a profit.

charter: a written grant issued by a ruler or government that gives the holder the right to establish a colony; a document creating a corporation.

checks and balances: a system that allows each branch of government to limit the power of the other branches.

cloture: a parliamentary procedure by which debate may be limited and a vote taken on the matter under discussion.

collective bargaining: discussions carried on between a union and an employer to determine such things as wages, hours, and working conditions.

collective security: the increased protection gained when nations stand together against aggression.

containment: a policy aimed at checking the expansion of a hostile power by diplomatic, economic, or military means.

cooperative: a business owned and operated by its workers.

corporation: a business chartered by a state and owned by shareholding investors.

craft union: an organization of workers in which all members practice the same trade.

culture area: a region in which various groups of people have similar ways of living.

democracy: a philosophy of government that recognizes the people's right to take part directly or indirectly in controlling their political institutions; the practices of society as a whole that enlarge opportunities for people and place emphasis on the dignity of the individual.

depression: a period of drastic decline in business activity accompanied by rising unemployment.

détente: a relaxing of tensions between nations.

direct primary: a preliminary election in which a political party's candidates are chosen by popular vote.

disarmament: the reduction or abolition of weapons and military forces.

dividend: the portion of a corporation's profits paid to a shareholder.

dry farming: a method of farming in arid areas without irrigation.

duty: a tax on imported goods.

elector: a person chosen by a state to cast one of its votes in a presidential election.

emancipate: to set free from bondage or oppression.

enumerated goods: in colonial days, items that had to be shipped to England before they could be sold elsewhere.

excise tax: a tax on certain goods produced, sold, or used within a country.

fall line: the imaginary line between the piedmont and the Atlantic coastal plain.

federal system: a system of government in which states that retain their local powers are united under a strong central government.

filibuster: the use of certain tactics, such as the making of prolonged speeches, for the purpose of delaying legislative action.

finance capitalist: a banker who invests in businesses and helps them obtain capital and credit.

forty-niner: one of the prospectors who sought gold in California in 1849.

free enterprise system: the economic system of private ownership of farms, factories, and other businesses; capitalism.

freeman: a male church member of early New England who enjoyed the right to hold office and vote for elected officials.

gold standard: the valuing of currency on the basis of gold.

greenbacks: paper money that was authorized by Congress in 1862 and was not backed by a gold or silver reserve.

gross national product: the total value of all goods and services produced by a nation.

holding company: a corporation formed to gain control of another corporation by buying its stock.

homestead: free federal land claimed by settlers under the Homestead Act of 1862.

impeach: to accuse a public official before a proper tribunal of misconduct in office.

imperialism: a national policy of extending political or economic control over other countries.

impress: to compel a person by force to give military service.

indenture system: a system under which people, in exchange for passage to America, were bound to service for a specified number of years.

inflation: a continuing increase in prices resulting from an abnormal rise in the amount of money and credit in circulation in proportion to the goods available.

initiative: a process by which citizens may propose legislation and have it submitted to the voters.

injunction: a court order forbidding a specific action.

interchangeable parts: identical parts that can be substituted for one another in the manufacturing or repair of a given product.

interlocking directorate: a means of controlling an industry by having the same people serve as directors for several companies.

internal improvements: a pre-Civil War name for roads and canals constructed with government funds under government sponsorship.

irrigation: the use of ditches, channels, or pipes to bring water to dry farmland.

isolationist: a person who favors a national policy of avoiding foreign entanglements.

Jim Crow laws: laws introduced following reconstruction that imposed or enforced segregation.

joint-stock company: a form of business organization developed in England to finance overseas undertakings by pooling the funds of many investors.

judicial review: the power of the courts to declare unconstitutional acts of Congress or of state legislatures.

long drive: the annual herding of cattle from Texas to railroad towns farther north.

loose construction: an interpretation of the Constitution holding that the federal government has broad powers.

mandate system: an arrangement by which the victorious Allies at the close of World War I were given the responsibility of preparing the former colonies of Germany and Turkey for independence.

massive retaliation: a strategy calling for swift, all-out military action against a nation committing aggression against a neighboring country.

mercenary: a soldier who serves in a foreign army for pay.

merger: the union of two or more companies.

merit system: a government employment system based on competitive examinations.

mesa: a flat-topped hill common in the Southwest.

minister: a representative of a government, next in rank to an ambassador.

minuteman: a colonial militiaman, ready to fight on short notice.

mission: a settlement, founded by priests, usually consisting of a church, a village, a fort, and farmland.

monopoly: exclusive control over the supply of a particular product or service.

mortgage: a pledge of property to a lender as security for a loan.

muckraker: a writer in the Progressive Era who exposed social and political evils.

nationalism: devotion to one's nation; the belief that national interests are more important than international considerations.

navigation: the science of charting the course of a ship or aircraft.

neutral: not favoring either side, as in a war.

nullification: the doctrine that a state may refuse to enforce a federal law it deems unconstitutional.

Pan-Americanism: a movement to promote economic and political cooperation among the nations of the Western Hemisphere.

patent: a government document that grants an inventor for a period of time the sole right to build and sell his or her invention.

piedmont: the region in the eastern United States extending eastward from the Appalachians to the fall line.

pocket veto: a President's indirect veto of a bill, exercised by retaining the bill unsigned until Congress adjourns.

pool: an arrangement among businesses in the same industry for the purpose of establishing control over prices and production.

popular sovereignty: the principle that the voters who lived in a territory should decide for themselves whether to permit slavery.

preamble: an opening statement explaining the purpose of a document.

privateer: a privately owned ship authorized by the government to attack enemy vessels.

prohibition: a ban on the manufacture, sale, and distribution of alcoholic beverages.

proprietary colony: a colony established on land granted to an individual or group of individuals by the Crown.

proprietor: an individual who received governing rights of a colony from the English monarch.

proviso: a conditional clause in a document.

ratification: official approval of a constitution or a treaty.

recall: the procedure by which a public official may be voted out of office before his or her term is ended.

recession: a moderate slump in business activity.

referendum: a process by which citizens may vote on a proposed law or other public measure.

reparations: compensation required from a defeated nation for war damages.

republic: a form of government controlled by the people through elected representatives.

repudiate: to refuse to recognize or pay.

reservation: a tract of land set aside for permanent settlement by a specific Indian tribe.

right-to-work laws: laws that allow workers to obtain and keep jobs without being required to join a union.

satellite: a nation dominated politically by another.

secede: to withdraw formally from membership in an alliance or organization.

secret ballot: a method of voting by which voters mark and cast their ballots in secrecy.

segregation: the separation of one race (or class) from another.

separation of powers: the division of government power into executive, legislative, and judicial branches.

sharecropper: a farm tenant who pays the landlord a share of the crops as rent.

slave codes: laws passed in the slave states before the Civil War to restrict the conduct and activities of slaves.

Socialist: an advocate of government ownership of the means of production.

spoils system: the practice of giving government jobs to party supporters after an election victory.

states' rights: the principle that upholds the powers of the states as opposed to the powers of the federal government.

stock: a certificate representing ownership in a corporation.

strict construction: an interpretation of the Constitution holding that the powers of the federal government are strictly defined.

strike: a work stoppage by employees.

suffrage: the right to vote; also, the exercise of that right.

sunbelt: the part of the United States that stretches from the southeastern Atlantic coast to southern California.

tariff: a tax on imported goods.

temperance movement: a campaign against the consumption of alcoholic beverages.

tenement: a crowded slum dwelling.

third party: a party organized in opposition to the two major political parties.

tidewater: a flat, coastal plain.

totalitarian: designating a policy by which a government's main characteristic is its absolute control over citizens' lives.

town meeting: a meeting of all the people of a town, assembled to discuss public issues and to elect officials.

township system: the system in colonial New England of land ownership and use.

triangular trade: a three-sided pattern of trade that developed during the colonial era; for example, trade between the West Indies, Boston, and Africa in molasses, rum, and slaves.

trunk line: the main line of a transportation or communication system, to which subsidiary lines are connected.

trust: a form of business uniting several companies into one system, often creating a monopoly.

turnpike: a highway on which users pay tolls.

utopian: ideal; applied to communities formed by people who sought to create a perfect society.

viceroy: a governor of a Spanish colony, ruling as the representative of the sovereign.

viceroyalty: a district or territory ruled by a viceroy.

vigilante: a member of a citizens' group operating to enforce the law, without authority.

writs of assistance: warrants that gave British colonial officials unrestricted rights to search for illegal goods.

yellow dog contract: an employment agreement, now illegal, in which working people promised not to join a union.

Acknowledgments

Text Credits

Grateful acknowledgment is made to authors, publishers, and other copyright holders for permission to reprint (and in some selections to adapt slightly) copyright material listed below.

Page 28: From *Original Narratives of Early American History — the Voyages of Columbus and of John Cabot* edited by Edward Gaylord Bourne. Charles Scribner's Sons, 1906. **Page 46:** From *Don Juan de Oñate: Colonizer of New Mexico* by George Hammond and Agapito Rey. Copyright © 1980, The University of New Mexico Press. Reprinted by permission of The University of New Mexico Press. **Pages 75, 421:** From *I Have Spoken: American History Through the Voice of the Indians* compiled by Virginia Irving Armstrong. Copyright © 1971, Virginia Irving Armstrong. Reprinted by permission of the Ohio University Press. **Page 81:** From *Eliza Pinckney* by Harriott Horry Ravenel. Charles Scribner's Sons, 1896. **Page 119:** From *Letters of Mrs. Adams* edited by Charles Francis Adams. Charles C. Little and James Brown, 1840. **Page 138:** From *The Revolution Remembered: Eyewitness Accounts of the War for Independence* edited by John C. Dann. Copyright © 1980, The University of Chicago. Reprinted by permission of The University of Chicago Press. **Page 160:** From *Retrospectives of America 1797–1811* by John Bernard. Harper and Brothers, 1887. **Page 191:** From *Recollections of a Lifetime, Men and Things I Have Seen* by Samuel G. Goodrich. Miller, Orton, and Mulligan, 1856. **Page 226:** From *Journals of Two Cruises Aboard the American Privateer Yankee* by A. Wanderer. Copyright © 1967, William Veazie Pratt. Reprinted by permission of Macmillan Publishing Company. **Page 237:** From *Letters From the South and West* by Arthur Singleton. Richardson and Lord, 1824. **Page 267:** From *Davy Crockett's Own Story* by Davy Crockett. Copyright © 1955, Citadel Press. Reprinted by permission of Lyle Stuart, Inc. **Page 277:** From *The Lowell Offering* edited by Benita Eisler. Harper & Row, Publishers, Inc., 1977. **Page 308:** From *Incidents in the Life of a Slave Girl* by Linda Brent, 1861. **Page 329:** From *Commerce of the Prairie* by Josiah Gregg, edited by Max L. Moorhead. Copyright © 1954, the University of Oklahoma Press. Reprinted by permission of the University of Oklahoma Press. **Page 350:** From "Ichabod" by John Greenleaf Whittier, 1850. **Page 356:** From *White and Black Under the Old Regime* by Victoria Clayton. The Young Churchmen Company, 1899. **Page 379:** From *Negroes in American Life* edited by Richard C. Wade. Houghton Mifflin Company, 1970. **Page 399:** From *The Americans at Home: Pen-and-Ink Sketches of American Men, Manners, and Institutions*, Vol. II by David Macrae. Edmonaton and Douglas, 1870. **Page 440:** From *Sketches In Crude-Oil* by John J. McLavrin, 1896. **Page 473:** From "The Story of a Sweatshop Girl" by Sadie Frowne. *The Independent*, Sept. 25, 1902. **Page 494:** From *A Son of The Middle Border* by Hamlin Garland. Copyright © 1917, Hamlin Garland, renewed 1945 by Mary I. Lord and Constance G. Williams. Reprinted by permission of Macmillan Publishing Company. **Page 519:** From the *Autobiography of George Dewey*. Charles Scribner's Sons, 1913. **Page 534:** From *Victory: How Women Won It* by The National American Women Suffrage Association. Copyright © 1940, The H. W. Wilson Company. Reprinted by permission of the H. W. Wilson Company. **Page 566:** From "Over There" by George M. Cohan. Copyright © 1917, renewed 1945 Leo Feist Inc., New York.

Page 571: From *American in France* by Major Frederick Palmer. Copyright © 1918 Dodd, Mead and Company. Reprinted by permission of Dodd, Mead and Company, Inc. **Page 599:** From *Middletown, A Study in American Culture* by Robert S. and Helen M. Lynd. Copyright © 1929 Harcourt, Brace & Jovanovich, Inc., renewed 1957 by Robert S. and Helen M. Lynd. Reprinted by permission of Harcourt, Brace & Jovanovich, Inc. **Page 608:** From *Movin' On Up* by Mahalia Jackson. Copyright © 1966 Mahalia Jackson and Evan McLeod Wylie. Reprinted by permission of E. P. Dutton, Inc. **Page 649:** From *In Search of Light: The Broadcasts of Edward R. Murrow 1938–1961* by Edward R. Murrow, edited by Edward Bliss, Jr. Copyright © 1967 the Estate of Edward R. Murrow. Reprinted by permission of Alfred A. Knopf, Inc. **Page 664:** From *Americans Remember the Home Front* by Ray Hoopes. Copyright © 1977 Ray Hoopes. Reprinted by permission of the author. **Page 669:** From the song "I Double Dare You" by Terry Shand and Jimmy Eaton. Copyright © 1937, renewed by Shapiro, Bernstein & Company, Inc. Reprinted by permission of Shapiro, Bernstein & Company, Inc. **Page 691:** From *On My Own* by Eleanor Roosevelt. Copyright © 1958 the Estate of Eleanor Roosevelt. Reprinted by permission of Franklin Roosevelt, Jr. **Page 721:** From *Letters From the Peace Corps* edited by Iris Luce. Copyright © 1964 Robert B. Luce, Inc. Reprinted by permission of Robert B. Luce, Inc. **Page 726:** From "I Have A Dream" by Martin Luther King, Jr. Copyright © 1963 Martin Luther King, Jr. Reprinted by permission of Joan Daves. **Page 735:** From *The Making of the President — 1964* by Theodore H. White. Copyright © 1965 Theodore H. White. Reprinted by permission of Atheneum Publishers. **Page 768:** From "Notes and Comment," *The New Yorker* magazine, July 19, 1976. Copyright © 1976 The New Yorker Magazine, Inc. Reprinted by permission of the New Yorker Magazine, Inc. **Page 779:** From "An End to a Long Ordeal" by Ed Magnuson, *Time* magazine, February 2, 1981. Copyright © 1981 Time Inc. Reprinted by permission of *Time*. **Page 797:** From "The Building of the Ship" by Henry Wadsworth Longfellow, 1849.

Art Credits

Cover: Concept by Ligature Publishing Services, Inc. Eagle watercolor rendering by Elizabeth Moutal, 1938, of wood carving by John Haley Bellamy, late 19th century. Coll: Index of American Design, National Gallery of Art, Washington, D.C.

Half-title: Eagle watercolor rendering by Alfred H. Smith, of wood carving by William Beal, 19th century. Coll: Index of American Design, National Gallery of Art, Washington, D.C.

Frontispiece: "Genesee Scenery," by Thomas Cole. Coll: Museum of Art, Rhode Island School of Design, Jesse Metcalf Fund.

Maps: All maps pages 29–778, 806, 809, 811 by Dick Sanderson. All maps pages 802–805, 812–813 by Donnelley Cartographic Services (pages 812–813, Robinson Projection).

Time lines by Gary Shellehamer.

Graphs and diagrams by Omnigraphics, Inc.

"Achievements in Technology" art by John D. Dawson.

The following abbreviations are used for some sources from which several illustrations were obtained:

ASKB — Ann S. K. Brown Military Collection **BA** — Bettmann Archive. **BB** — Brown Brothers. **CHS** — Chicago Historical Society. **CP** — Culver Pictures. **FDRL** — Franklin D. Roosevelt Library. **GC** — Granger Collection. **HSP** — Historical Society of Pennsylvania. **IWM** — Trustees of the Imperial War Museum. **LC** — Library of Congress. **MMA** — Metropolitan Museum of Art. **NA** — National Archives. **NGA** — National Gallery of Art, Washington, D.C. **NPG** — National Portrait Gallery, Washington, D.C. **NYHS** — New-York Historical Society. **NYPL** — New York Public Library. **RISD** — Museum of Art, Rhode Island School of Design. **SI** — Smithsonian Institution. **UPI** — United Press International. **WHHA** — White House Historical Association. **WM** — Henry duPont Francis Winterthur Museum. **WW** — Wide World. **YU** — Yale University Art Gallery.

7 "Explorers," by Theodore de Bry. Coll: Rare Books and Manuscripts Division, NYPL, Astor, Lenox, and Tilden Foundations. 8 "Spirit of '76" (detail), by Archibald M. Willard. Coll: Board of Selectmen, Abbot Hall, Marblehead, Massachusetts. 9 "The Bay and Harbor of New York" (detail), by Samuel Waugh, 1855. Coll: Museum of the City of New York. 10 Poster printed by Poole Brothers, c. 1885. Coll: CHS. 11 "Flags, Fourth of July, 1916," by Childe Hassam. Coll: Mr. and Mrs. Frank Sinatra. Photo: Hirschl & Adler Galleries. 12 "Iwo Jima," by Tom Lovell. Coll: U.S. Marine Corps Art Collection, History and Museums Division. 13 Gerald Davis/ Woodfin Camp and Associates. 15 Map of North and South America, 1596 (detail), by Theodore de Bry. Coll: National Map Collection, Public Archives of Canada. 18 Courtesy of The Boston Athenaeum. Photo: Charles Hogg.

23 "Vue de Lisbonne" (detail, modified version), 17th century. Coll: Museu Nacional de Arte Antiga-Lisboa. 25 Seal of the City of Bergen, Norway, c. 1280. Coll: Riksarkivet, National Archives of Norway. 28 "Christopher Columbus," by Sebastiano del Piombo, 1519. Coll: MMA, gift of J. Pierpont Morgan, 1900. 30 "Route of Magellan," from Baptista Agnese's Atlas, HM 25, ff. 12v–13r. Coll: Huntington Library, San Marino, California. 33 Harald Sund. 34 "Mih Tutta Hangkusch, A Mandan Village" (detail), by Karl Bodmer. Coll: Thomas Gilcrease Institute of American History and Art, Tulsa, Oklahoma. 36 Hans Namuth/Photo Researchers. 41 "The Arrival of Cortés at Veracruz." Coll: In the Ownership of Miss M. L. A. Strickland, York, England, On Loan to the Government Art Collection, London. 46 "Calvary Uniform of New Spain" (detail), anonymous. Coll: Archivo de Indias, Seville, Spain. Photo: Bradley Smith. 48 The Cerro Rico from Potosí Atlas of Sea Charts 1584. Coll: Library of the Hispanic Society of America, N.Y. 53 "Portage Around The Falls of Niagara. January 22, 1679" (detail), by George Catlin. Coll: Paul Mellon Collection, NGA. 54 "Queen Elizabeth I in Procession" (detail), by Marcus Gheeraerts The Younger. Coll: Simon Wingfield Digby, M. P. Dorset, England. 61 "The Marketplace at Jamestown," by Sidney King, 1957. Coll: Jamestown-Yorktown Foundation, Williamsburg, Virginia. 63 "First Legislature in the New World" (detail), by Jack Clifton, c. 1968. Coll: Virginia State Library, Richmond, Virginia. 64 From F. W. Fairholt, *Tobacco: Its History and Associations*, London, 1859. Coll: NYPL. 66 "The Mayflower" (detail), by Halsall. Coll: The Pilgrim Society, Plymouth, Massachusetts. 68 Plimoth Plantation. 69 "John Winthrop" (detail), by Charles Osgood, 19th century, after original by unknown artist. Coll: Massachusetts Historical Society. 72 Mike Mazzaschi/Stock, Boston. 73 "Hooker and Company Journeying Through the Wilderness from Plymouth to Hartford, in 1636" (detail), by Frederic Edwin Church, 1846. Coll: Wadsworth Atheneum. 74 "Indian Bible," by John Eliot. Coll: British Museum. 75 "Ninigret II, Son of Ninigret I Chief of the Ninantic Indians" (detail), c. 1681. Coll: RISD, gift of Mr. Robert Winthrop. 79 "Early Baltimore" (detail), after John

Moale view, aquatint, 1752. Coll: Stokes Collection, NYPL. 81 "The Plantation," c. 1825. Coll: MMA, gift of Edgar William and Bernice Chrysler Garbisch, 1963. 82 "Trustees of Georgia" (detail), by William Verelst. Coll: WM. 88 "Fairman's Mansion and Treaty Tree" (detail), engraving by Serz after Brittan. Coll: Library Company of Philadelphia. 91 "African Slave, Cinque" (detail), by Nathaniel Jocelyn, 1839. Coll: New Haven Historical Society, gift of Dr. Charles B. Purvis, 1898. 92 "The Marriage of Washington to Martha Custis" (detail), by Junius Brutus Stearns. Coll: Virginia Museum, gift of Col. & Mrs. Edgar W. Garbisch. 93 "Old Bruton Parish Church," by Wordsworth Thompson. Coll: MMA. 95 (left) "The Pewterers Flag" (detail), painted silk banner, 1788. Coll: NYHS. (right) Wool embroidery on linen. Coll: WM.

103 "The Reduction of Cape Breton" (detail). Coll: New Brunswick Museum. 105 "Colonel George Washington," by Charles Wilson Peale. Coll: Washington/Custis/Lee Collection, Washington and Lee University, Virginia. 110 "Patrick Henry Arguing the Parson's Cause" (detail), attributed to George Cooke, c. 1830. Coll: Virginia Historical Society. 111 "Chief Pontiac," by John Mix Stanley. Coll: Burton Historical Collection, Detroit Public Library. Photo: Nemo Warr. 114 "John Hancock and His Wife" (detail), by Edward Savage. Coll: Corcoran Gallery of Art, bequest of Woodbury Blair. 116 "Destruction of Tea in Boston Harbor" (detail), by Duris Cobb. Coll: Ancient and Honorable Artillery Company of Massachusetts. Photo: Hillel Burger. 119 Lexington Minuteman Statue, by Daniel Chester French, detail of bronze sculpture. Photo: Stuart Cohen/Stock, Boston. 121 "Paul Revere" (detail), by John Quidor. Coll: Oliver B. James Collection of American Art, Arizona State University Art Collections, Tempe. 125 "Attack on Bunker's Hill, With the Burning of Charles Town" (detail), anonymous. Coll: NGA, gift of Edgar William and Bernice Chrysler Garbisch. 130 "Congress Voting Independence," by Pine and Savage. Coll: HSP 132 "The Gathering of the Overmountain Men," by Lloyd Branson, 1915. Coll: Tennessee State Museum. Photo: Stephen D. Cox. 134 "Mrs. Schuyler Burning Her Wheat Fields on the Approach of the British" (detail), by Emanuel Leutze, 1852. Coll: Los Angeles County Museum of Art; Bicentennial gift of Mr. and Mrs. J. M. Schaef, Mr. and Mrs. William D. Witherspoon, Mr. and Mrs. Charles C. Shoemaker, and Mr. and Mrs. Julian Ganz, Jr. 137 "Battle of Princeton," by William Mercer. Coll: HSP. 138 "Fortifying Breed's Hill in the Night June 16th 1775." Coll: LC, #USZ62-19664. 140 "John Paul Jones" (detail), attributed to Ferdinand De Braekeleer. Coll: Collection of Hugh S. Watson, Jr., Yorktown Victory Center. 141 "The March to Valley Forge," by William B. T. Trego, 1883. Coll: Valley Forge Historical Society. Photo: Charles Mills and Son. 149 "Reverend Lemuel Haynes in the Pulpit," painted tray. Coll: RISD. 155 "Cincinnati 1800" (detail), after painting by A. J. Swing, c. 1880. Coll: Cincinnati Historical Society. 157 "China, Canton Factories" (detail), oil on glass. Coll: Peabody Museum of Salem. Photo: Mark Sexton. 160 "Thomas Hughes" (detail), anonymous, 1847. Coll: Joseph Dis Devar Collection, West Virginia Department of Culture and History. 162 "A View of Mount Vernon the Seat of General Washington" (detail). Coll: NGA. 164 "Second Street North From Market Street West Christ Church, Philadelphia" (detail), by Thomas Birch, c. 1800. Coll: HSP. 169 GC. 170 "James Madison" (detail), by Frothingham after Stuart. Coll: NPG. 171 GC. 175 "First in War, First in Peace, First in the Hearts of His Countrymen" (detail), by Montbaron and Gautschi, 1789. Coll: NYHS. 176 "Martha Dandridge Custis Washington" (detail), by Eliphalet F. Andrews after Gilbert Stuart, 1878. Coll: WHHA. Photo: National Geographic Society. 177 "First Cabinet." Coll: NYPL. 178 "He That Tilleth His Land Shall be Satisfied," c. 1850. Coll: Philadelphia Museum of Art, The Edgar William and Bernice Chrysler Garbisch Collection. 179 "Alexander Hamilton" (detail), by John Trumbull. Coll: YU. Photo: Joseph Szaszfai. 181 "Washington, D.C. 1801" (detail). Coll: LC, #USZC4-530. 182 "Washington Reviewing the Western Army at Fort Cumberland, Maryland," by Frederick Kemmelmeyer. Coll: MMA, gift of

Edgar William and Bernice Chrysler Garbisch. **185** "Edmond Genêt" (detail), by Ezra Ames. Coll: Albany Institute of History and Art. **186** "The Treaty of Greenville" (detail), anonymous, 1795. Coll: CHS. **189** "Abigail Adams and Grand-Daughter Suzannah Supervise as a Servant Hangs Wash in the East Room," by Gordon Phillips, 1966. Coll: WHHA. Photo: National Geographic Society. **190** "Shipbuilding" (detail), by William Birch. Coll: Stokes Collection, NYPL. **191** "The American Star"(detail), by Frederick Kemmelmeyer. Coll: MMA, gift of Edgar William and Bernice Chrysler Garbisch. **193** Coll: NYHS.

211 "Monticello Home of Thomas Jefferson 1743–1826," by Vail. Coll: Musée de la Coopération Franco-Américaine, Château de Blérancourt. Photo: Edimedia. **212** "Thomas Jefferson" (detail), by John Trumbull. Coll: MMA, bequest of Cornelia Cruger. **216** "A View of New Orleans Taken From the Plantation of Marigny, November 1803" (detail), by Boqueto de Woiserie. Coll: CHS. **217** "Toussaint L'Ouverture," by Pierre Dominique. Coll: Historical Pictures Service. **218** "Lewis and Clark on the Lower Columbia" (detail), by C. M. Russell, 1905. Coll: Amon Carter Museum. **220** "Fur Trappers" (detail), by Karl Bodmer. Coll: Rare Book Division, NYPL, Astor, Lenox and Tilden Foundations. **222** "Boarding The Chesapeake," by Thomas Hemy, 1895. Coll: The Honorable Mrs. H. M. Llewellyn. **226** "Abaellino, Brig Escaping from H. B. M. Brig Paulina off Sicily, 4 March 1815," by M. McPherson. Coll: Peabody Museum of Salem. Photo: Mark Sexton. **229** "Capture of City of Washington," from *History of England* by Rapin, c. 1815. Coll: ASKB. **235** "Fourth of July Parade" (detail), by Alfred Cornelius Howland, c. 1886. Coll: High Museum of Art. **237** "View of the Capitol, Washington, D. C. 1824" (detail), by Charles Burton. Coll: MMA, bequest of Joseph Pulitzer. **243** "The Old House of Representatives" (detail), by Samuel F. B. Morse. Coll: Corcoran Gallery of Art. **247** "Opposition blown sky high, sir, sky high" (detail), by P. Desobry. Coll: The Old Print Shop. **248** "John Quincy Adams" (detail), by Stuart and Thomas Sully. Coll: Fogg Art Museum, bequest of Ward Nicholas Boylston. **253** "Andrew Jackson at the Battle of New Orleans" (detail), by Alonzo Chappel. Coll: CHS. **254** "Rachel Jackson" (detail), by Earl. Coll: Ladies Hermitage Society. Photo: Roloc Color Slides. **255** "John Caldwell Calhoun" (detail), attributed to Charles Bird King. Coll: NPG, gift of Andrew W. Mellon. **256** "Webster's Reply to Senator Hayne" (detail), by G. P. A. Healy, 1851. Coll: City of Boston Art Commission, Faneuil Hall. Photo: Richard Cheek. **258** "Nicholas Biddle," by Henry Inman. Coll: Brig. Gen. Nicholas Biddle, Ret. **265** "Canvassing for a Vote" (detail), by George Caleb Bingham. Coll: Nelson-Atkins Museum, copyright 1978 W. R. Nelson Trust. **266** Coll: NYPL. **267** "Davy Crockett," by J. G. Chapman. Coll: The Alamo. Photo: J. D. Torres. **270** CP. **275** "Old Slater's Mill" (detail), by J. Reuben Smith. Coll: SI. **277** "Progress of Cotton (#9 Reading or Drawing In)" (detail), by Barfoot for Darton. Coll: YU, The Mabel Grady Garvan Collection. **279** "Chariot of Fame" (clipper ship), by Duncan McFarlane, 1854. Coll: Peabody Museum of Salem. Photo: Mark Sexton. **280** "The Wheelwright's Shop," by E. T. Billings, from Private Collection. **284** "Methodist Camp Meeting" (detail), by Clay. Coll: NYHS. **285** "The Country School, 1871," by Winslow Homer. Coll: St. Louis Art Museum. **287** "Oberlin College Class of 1855." Coll: Oberlin College Archives. **288** Coll: American Antiquarian Society. **290** "Vue de New York" (detail), by Hypolyte Sebron. Coll: Musée de la Coopération Franco-Américaine, Château de Blérancourt. Photo: Edimedia. **294** (top) "Views on the Erie Canal" (detail), by J. W. Hill. Coll: Prints Division, NYPL, Astor, Lenox and Tilden Foundations. (bottom) "Knickerbocker Line, The Coach '76' of the Knickerbocker Line Brooklyn" (detail), by Henry Boese, c. 1850. Coll: Museum of the City of New York. **301** "Cotton Plantation" (detail), by C. Giroux. Coll: Museum of Fine Arts Boston. **302** "Eli Whitney," by Samuel F. B. Morse. Coll: YU, gift of George Hoadley. **306** "Mississippi River Boat With Cotton, Baton Rouge, Louisiana" (detail). Coll: LC. **307** "Julius Meyenberg's Farm, Bluff/William's Creek/Settlement by La Grange, Fayette County, Texas," by Louis Hoppe. Coll: San Antonio Museum

Association. **308** Sketch (detail) by William H. Townsend. Coll: Beinecke Rare Book and Manuscript Library, Yale University. **309** "A Ride For Liberty — The Fugitive Slaves" (detail), by Eastman Johnson, c. 1862. Coll: Brooklyn Museum. **310** Charleston Museum. **311** "American Slave Market," by Taylor, 1852. Coll: CHS. **312** LC. **314** "Louisville Waterfront, 1856." Coll: Filson Club.

321 "The Oregon Trail" (detail), by Albert Bierstadt, 1869. Coll: Butler Institute of American Art. **325** "Winter Quarters (on the Missouri River)" (detail), by Carl Christian Anthon Christensen. Coll: Brigham Young University Art Museum Collection. **328** (left) "Padron" (detail), by James Walker. Coll: Bancroft Library, University of California, Berkeley. (right) Mission San Fernando by Norman Neuerburg. (bottom) "Mission San Carlos Del Rio Carmelo" (detail), by Oriana Day. Coll: Fine Arts Museums of San Francisco, M. H. de Young Memorial Museum. **329** "Moonlight and Shadows" (detail), by Olaf Wieghorst. Copyright Olaf Wieghorst Productions, Inc. From the collection of Senator and Mrs. Barry Goldwater. **331** "Fall of the Alamo" (detail). Coll: LC, #28237 262 745 A. **332** "Sam Houston," by George Catlin, c. 1838. Coll: R. W. Norton Art Gallery. **337** "Battle of Molino del Rey," by C. Nebel. Coll: Arts of the Book Collection, Sterling Memorial Library, Yale University. **341** Coll: Carl Sheafer Dentzel. Photo: J. R. Eyerman. **345** "Washington, D. C. 1851," by E. Sachse. Coll: LC, #USZC4-771. **351** BA. **354** "Battle of Hickory Point." Coll: ASKB. **356** "The Marais des Cynes Massacre, Kansas, May 19th 1858." Coll: NYPL. **359** "Lincoln-Douglas Debate" (detail), by Robert M. Root. Coll: Illinois State Historical Society. **360** "Trial of John Brown" (detail), from *Taylor Sketch Book*. Coll: Western Reserve Historical Society. **361** (right) BB. (left) Concord Free Public Library. (middle) "Nathaniel Hawthorne," by Emanuel Gottlieb Leutze. Coll: NPG, transfer from the NGA; gift of Andrew W. Mellon. (bottom right) "Harriet Beecher Stowe," by Alanson Fisher, 1853. Coll: NPG. **367** "Fond Du Lac, Wisconsin," by Louis Kurz and Henry Seifert after Louis Kurz, c. 1861. Coll: Stokes Collection, NYPL. **368** "Lincoln Raising the Flag at Independence Hall," by J. L. G. Ferris. Coll: Archives of 76. **370** "Zouave Cadets." Coll: ASKB. **372** "General Burnside's Brigade at the Battle of Bull Run." Coll: ASKB. **376** "Faithful Troops Cheer General Lee," by N. C. Wyeth. Coll: U.S. Naval Academy Museum. Photo: Dermott Hickey. **379** "Come and Join Us Brothers," printed by P. S. Duval & Son. Coll: CHS. **382** "Battle of Gettysburg," by Paul Philippoteaux. Coll: Gettysburg Cyclorama. Photo: Lane Studio. **383** "Jefferson Davis," by John Robertson, c. 1863. Coll: Museum of the Confederacy. **385** "Blockade Runners in Port . . . ," by William Torgerson. Coll: CHS. **387** GC. **390** Coll: NYHS. **392** "The Surrender of General Lee to General Grant, April 9, 1865," by Louis M. D. Guillaume. Coll: Appomattox Court House National Historical Park. Photo: David Muench. **393** "The Funeral of President Lincoln, New York, April 25th, 1865," by Currier and Ives, 1865. Coll: ASKB. **397** Bradley Smith/Photo Researchers. **399** Coll: Penn Community Services. **401** LC, #J713-1148. **405** GC. **406** "The Broken Shackle — By The Genius of Freedom," by E. Sachse & Co., 1874. Coll: CHS. **408** "The First Vote," by A. R. Waud, 1867. Photo: BA. **410** "President Grant," by Henry Ulke. Coll: WHHA. **412** Cartoon by Thomas Nast. Photo: GC. **413** Coll: HSP. Photo: Charles Mills & Son.

419 "Hunting Buffalo," by Alfred Jacob Miller. Coll: Stark Museum of Art. **421** "Ten Bears-Comanche Chief" (detail). Coll: SI. **422** "Interior of Fort Laramie," by Alfred Jacob Miller. Coll: Walters Art Gallery. **423** LC, #747 162 19725. **427** "The Roundup" (detail), by Charles M. Russell, 1913. Coll: MacKay Collection, Montana Historical Society. **428** CHS. **433** Solomon D. Butcher Collection, Nebraska State Historical Society. **435** Kansas State Historical Society. **439** "Bessemer Converter" (detail), by S. B. Shiley, 1895. Coll: Bethlehem Steel Corporation. **440** NYPL. **443** "Night Scene at an American Railway Junction," by Currier and Ives. Coll: LC, #3652. **446** University of Washington, Henry Art Gallery, Special Collections. **449** Coll: NPG. Photo: Rolland G. White. **453** "The Vultures' Roost," by E. W. Kemble.

Coll: LC, #4235 262 630634.   **459** BB.   **461** *(left)* Courtesy American Heritage Publishing Co., Inc. *(right)* LC, #USZ62-36986. *(bottom)* Photo by Jacob A. Riis, from Jacob A. Riis Collection, Museum of the City of New York.   **465** "Washington Street, Indianapolis at Dusk," by Theodore Groll, 1892. Coll: Indianapolis Museum of Art, gift of a couple of old Hoosiers.   **467** Photo by Irving Underhill, from LC, #USZ62-24063.   **468** MMA.   **469** Photo by Byron, from The Byron Collection, Museum of the City of New York.   **471** New York University, Tamiment Collection.   **473** Photo by Lewis Hine, from International Museum of Photography, George Eastman House.   **474** "Virginia-Tenth Annual Convention of the Knights of Labor at Richmond," by Joseph Becker. Photo: CP.   **476** Coll: George Meany Memorial Archives.   **478** "Great Battle of Homestead, Defeat and Capture of the Pinkerton Invaders July 6, 1892." Coll: LC.   **479** "King Debs," by W. A. Rogers. Coll: LC, #USZ62-2115.   **483** "Electioneering," by Edward Lamson Henry. Coll: Kennedy Galleries.   **485** Cartoon by Thomas Nast. Coll: NYPL.   **489** Cartoon by Thomas Nast. Photo: GC.   **491** "The Lost Bet," by Joseph Klir, 1892. Coll: CHS.   **493** LC.   **494** "Gift for the Grangers" *(detail)*. Coll: LC.   **496** "Harvest Time," by William Hahn. Coll: Fine Arts Museum of San Francisco, gift of Mrs. Harold McKinnon and Mrs. Harry L. Brown.   **499** GC.

507 "The Naval Parade, 1899," by Fred Pansing. Coll: Museum of the City of New York.   **509** Bishop Museum.   **511** From *New York Herald Tribune*. Coll: NYPL, Special Collections.   **514** Theodore Roosevelt Collection, Harvard College Library.   **517** "Destruction of the U.S. Battleship Maine in Havana Harbor, Feb. 15, 1898." Coll: CHS.   **518** *San Francisco Examiner*, April 12, 1898. Photo: Bell and Howell Labs.   **519** "Commodore George Dewey" *(detail)*, by N. M. Miller. Coll: U. S. Naval Academy. Photo: Dermott Hickey.   **521** "Charge of the Rough Riders Up San Juan Hill," by Frederic Remington. Coll: Remington Art Museum.   **522** "Surrender of Puerto Rico" *(detail)*, anonymous. Coll: CHS.   **524** "The Boxer Rebellion" *(detail)*. Coll: LC.   **529** "Central Park, 1901," by Maurice Prendergast. Coll: Whitney Museum of American Art. Photo: Geoffrey Clements.   **531** The Ida M. Tarbell Collection, Pelletier Library, Allegheny College.   **534** CHS.   **535** BB.   **537** BA.   **538** CP.   **540** *(left)* Coll: Museo Civico, "L. Bailo," Commune Di Treviso. *(right)* Staten Island Historical Society. *(bottom)* "Looking Down at Yosemite Valley from Glacier Point," by William Hahn, 1874. Coll: California Historical Society.   **542** NA.   **545** "The Great White Fleet" *(detail)*, by Henry Reuterdahl. Coll: U. S. Naval Academy Museum. Photo: Dermott Hickey.   **547** GC.   **550** "Reading the Death Warrant," by C. R. Macauley, 1913. Photo: GC.   **551** WW.   **555** Photo by Harlan Marshall, from Manchester Historical Association.   **557** GC.   **558** "Guerre 14/18: La Mobilisation sur les Boulevards," by A. Leveille. Coll: Musée de la Guerre. Photo: Edimedia/SNARK.   **560** BB.   **562** *(left)* Coll: Staatsgalerie Stuttgart. *(right)* Poster by A. Leete. Coll: IWM.   **563** Princeton University Library.   **566** "Over There" by George M. Cohan. © 1917 (Renewed 1945) LEO FEIST, INC. All Rights of LEO FEIST, INC. Assigned to CBS CATALOGUE PARTNERSHIP. All Rights Controlled by CBS FEIST CATALOG. International Copyright Secured. All Rights Reserved. Used by Permission. Song sheet illustration copyright F. B. Rockwell.   **567** BBC Hulton Picture Library/BA.   **570** "Douglas Campbell-World War I Pilot," by John T. McCoy, Jr. Coll: Aviation Americana.   **571** "Doughboy" *(detail)*, by Captain Harvey Dunn. Coll: SI.   **573** "Troops at Saint-Mihiel," anonymous. Coll: SI.   **575** "Signing of the Peace" *(detail)*, by W. Orpen. Coll: IWM.

583 "Detroit Industry," south wall *(detail)*, by Diego Rivera, 1932-1933. Coll: Detroit Institute of Arts, Founders Society, purchase, Edsel B. Ford Fund and gift of Edsel B. Ford.   **585**

WW.   **587** Frank Driggs Collection.   **589, 591** LC.   **595** CP.   **598** "The Great White Way — Times Square New York City" *(detail)*, by Howard Thain, 1925. Coll: NYHS.   **599** Photo by Lewis W. Hine, from International Museum of Photography at George Eastman House.   **600** *(top left)* "Teaching Old Dogs," by John Held Jr. Photo: GC. *(bottom left)* UPI. *(middle)* CP. *(right)* Baltimore Sun Papers.   **605** "Employment Agency" *(detail)*, by Isaac Soyer, 1937. Coll: Whitney Museum. Photo: Geoffrey Clements.   **607** LC.   **608** Springer/BA.   **609** Herbert Hoover Presidential Library/AP.   **611** FDRL, AP.   **613** BB.   **614** NA.   **615** BA.   **619** Cartoon by William Gropper. Coll: VANITY FAIR copyright 1935 (renewed 1963) by The Conde Nast Publications. Photo: Boston Public Library.   **620** "Construction of a Dam" *(detail)*, by William Gropper. Coll: U.S. Dept. of the Interior.   **622** LC.   **623** UPI.   **624** FDRL.   **626** Cartoon by J. N. "Ding" Darling. Coll: J. N. "Ding" Darling Conservation Foundation, Des Moines.   **627** FDRL.   **633** "American Landscape," by Charles Sheeler, 1930. Coll: Museum of Modern Art, gift of Abby Aldrich Rockefeller.   **637** BB.   **639** BA.   **641** Coll: Office of the Governor, Puerto Rico.   **642, 645** BA.   **648** "Battle of Dunkirk" *(detail)*, by Charles Cundall. Coll: IWM.   **649** UPI.   **651** Coll: IWM.   **655** FDR and Churchill by Raymond P. R. Neilson, 1941. Coll: FDRL.   **656** NA.   **659** NA #80-a-30517.   **661** Pictorial Parade.   **662** NA #242-GAP-181A-4.   **664** Bureau of the Public Debt.   **665** U. S. Air Force.   **666** *(left)* "Calship Burner," by Edna Reindel, 1943. Coll: Life Collection of World War II Art. Photo: U. S. Army. *(right)* Poster by Norman Rockwell. Coll: National Infantry Museum. *(bottom)* BA.   **668** FDRL.   **670** "Tank Break-Through at St. Lo," by Ogden Pleissner. Coll: City Commission of Detroit. Photo: *The Life History of the United States: New Deal and Global War*, Time-Life Books, Inc., Publisher © 1964 Time Inc.   **673** U.S. Army.   **675** UPI.   **677** U. S. Army.

683 BB.   **686** "Pre-Fourth Fizzle," by Edward Keukes from *The Plain Dealer*.   **687** WW.   **689** UPI.   **691** FDRL.   **692** Werner Wolf/Black Star.   **694** UPI.   **696** Walter Sanders, LIFE Magazine © 1948 Time Inc.   **699** WW.   **701** UPI.   **703** George Skadding, LIFE Magazine © 1952 Time Inc.   **707** Herman J. Kokojan/Black Star.   **708** Dwight D. Eisenhower Library.   **710** Lessing/Magnum.   **712** Thomas Hovland/Grant Heilman.   **715** *(left)* Farrell Grehan/Photo Researchers. *(right)* J.R. Eyerman, LIFE Magazine © 1953 Time Inc. *(bottom)* BB.   **716** John Launois/Black Star.   **718** UPI.   **719** Cornell Capa/Magnum.   **721** Marc and Evelyne Bernheim/Woodfin Camp and Associates.   **722** Berlin Bild/Black Star.   **725** NASA, courtesy LIFE MAGAZINE, © Time, Inc.   **727** Cecil Stoughton/Lyndon B. Johnson Library.   **731** Fred Ward/Black Star.   **732** "Hope I Know Where We're Goin'," by Shanks, *The Buffalo Evening News*.   **733** Bruce Roberts/Photo Researchers.   **734** Max Scheber-Stern/Black Star.   **735** Popperfoto.   **737** Leonard Freed/Magnum.   **741** WW.   **743** Lyndon B. Johnson Library.   **744** H. Kubota/Magnum.   **746** Ted Rozumalski/Black Star.   **747** UPI.   **748** SI.

755 WW.   **757** Sven Simon.   **758** Wally McNamee/Woodfin Camp and Associates.   **760** Doug Wilson/Black Star.   **761** Pictorial Parade.   **763** Fred Ward/Black Star.   **765** Alex Webb/Magnum.   **766** UPI.   **767** Dennis Brack/Black Star.   **768** Peter B. Kaplan/Photo Researchers.   **769** Dennis Brack/Black Star.   **773** Robert Llewellyn.   **775, 776** Wally McNamee/Woodfin Camp and Associates.   **777** Ledru/Sygma.   **779** Laffont/Sygma.   **781** Michael Evans/Sygma.   **783** *(left)* Jim Pickerell. *(right)* Billy E. Barnes/Uniphoto. *(center)* U. S. Bureau of Census. *(bottom)* Owen Franken/Stock, Boston.   **787** Uniphoto.   **789** Larry Dale Gordon/Image Bank.   **790** UPI.   **791** M. Philippot/Sygma.   **793** A. Keler/Sygma.   **794** Eli Reed/Magnum.   **796** Alex Webb/Magnum.

Index

This index includes references not only to the text but to pictures (p), charts (c), graphs (g) and maps (m) as well. Page numbers that are marked n. refer to footnotes.

Communism, in Russia, 570, 643, 646, 693; fear of, 584, 686, 708, 741; in U.S., 686, 688–689; and internal security, 689–690, 702, 713, 714; in East Germany, 692; in China, 698–699; in Korea, 700; in Vietnam, 709, 723, 742, 743, 745; in Cuba, 720–721

Comstock, Henry T. P.; Comstock Lode, 430

Concentration camps, 673, 674, 693

Concord, Battle of, 120, m 120, 121, 134

Confederate States of America, 366, m 369, 370, g 371, 371–372, m 374, 379–385; m 380, m 381, 385, 387, 389–390, m 391, 391–392. See also South

Confederation (under Articles), 152–154; weakness of, 156–161

Congress, powers of, 165, 166, 181, 238, 245; and reconstruction, 398–399, 402–403; impeachment struggle with Johnson, 403–404. See also specific acts and legislation

Congress of Industrial Organizations (CIO), 621, 622; joins AFL, 713

Conkling, Roscoe, 409, 486, 487, 488

Connecticut, 65, m 71, 72–73, m 86, 118, 164; education in, 94, 284; whaling in, 95; western land claims of, 117, m 153, 154; ratifies Constitution, 169; immigration to, 459; m 803

Conquistadors, 41–43, 44–46, p 46

"Conscience" Whigs, 346

Conservation, 539, 617, 623, 663, 759–760

Constitution, writing of, 164–168; preamble, 167; opposition to, 168–169; ratified, 168–170; Bill of Rights added, 170–171; strict and loose construction of, 181, 217, 244, 761; text of, 818–840; Amendments: First, 192; Twelfth, 193 n.; 247; Thirteenth, 289, 402; Fourteenth, 403, 404, 413, 624, 717; Fifteenth, 408, 413; Sixteenth, 93 n.; Seventeenth, 533; Eighteenth, 588, 611; Nineteenth, 534, 598; Twentieth, 611 n., 625; Twenty-First, 611; Twenty-Second, 686; Twenty-Third, 725; Twenty-Fourth, 725, 736; Twenty-Fifth, 764; Twenty-Sixth, 761

Constitution (ship), 228

Constitutional Convention, 163–168, 169

Constitutional Union Party, 362

Continental Army, 126, 127, 128, 131–133, 136–139, 140–143, 144

Continental Congress, First, 118–119, 125; Second, 125, 126, 128, p 130, 133, 151; draws up Articles of Confederation, 152–154; under Articles, 158; revises Articles, 162

Convention of 1818, 240

Cook, James, 173

Cooke, Jay, 447

Coolidge, Calvin, 583–584, 589; as President, 590, 591–593, 594, 636, 637, 638; takes oath, p 591; quoted, 584, 594, 633

Coolidge, Grace, 594

Cooper, Peter, 295, 495

Cooperatives, business, 474; farm, 493–494, 495, 593, 609

Copperheads, 484

Coral Sea, Battle of, 659, m 676, 679

Corinth, Miss., 373, m 374, m 380

Cornish, Samuel, 289

Cornwallis, Charles, 137, 141, 142–143, 145; surrender of, 143–144

Coronado, Francisco de, m 44, 45, 50, 420

Corporations, 238, 442; acting in combination, 453–454; regulation of, 495; Bureau of, 538; in 1920's, 594

Corpus Christi, Tex., m 336

Corregidor, 658, 659, m 676

Cortés, Hernando, p 41, 42–43, m 43, 520

Cotton, 302; importance of, 1820–1860, g 303; and southern economy, 303–304, m 304, 315, 411; and plantation system, 306–307, 317

Cotton gin, p 302, 303

Coughlin, Charles E., 618

Council Bluffs, Iowa, m 322, 325

Council for New England, 65, 69, 72, 73

Court system, 165–166; "midnight judges," 212–213; and judicial review, 213. See also Supreme Court

Cowboys, 426–428

Cowpens, Battle of, 142, m 142

Cow towns, 427–428, 447

Cox, Archibald, 764

Cox, James M., 589, 590

Coxey, Jacob S.; Coxey's march on Washington, 492

Crawford, William H., 247

Crazy Horse, 422

Crédit Mobilier affair, 410, 483, 486

Creek Indians, m 35, 36, 231, 239, m 268, 419

Creel, George; Creel Committee, 568

Crisis, The (Paine), 129

Crockett, Davy, p 267, 331; quoted, 262, 267

Crown Point, m 106, 107, 126, m 128

Cuba, 28, 29, m 29, 42, m 43, m 44, 107, 356, 647; revolts from Spain, 508, 514–515, 522; U.S. interest in, 508, 640; sinking of the Maine in, 516; and Spanish-American War, 518–521, 522, m 523; U.S. intervention in, 544, 640; naval base in, 640; communism in, 720–721; Bay of Pigs invasion, 722; blockade of, 722–723; and Grenada, 796

Cullen, Countee, 587

Cumberland Road, 292, m 293

Curtis, George W., 487

Custer, George Armstrong, 423–424

Czechoslovakia, 575, m 577, 603; immigrants from, 434, 460; Nazi take-over of, p 645, 645–646, m 646; Soviet control of, 693, 695; after World War II, m 697, 751

Da Gama, Vasco, 24, 30, m 32

Dakotas, 434. See also North Dakota; South Dakota

Dakota Territory, m 369, 420, 422, 424

Dallas, Tex., m 444, 727

Dalrymple, Oliver, 434

Dana, Richard Henry, 327

Daniels, Josephus, quoted, 567–568

Danish West Indies, 507, 555

Dare, Virginia, 57

Dartmouth College v. Woodward, 238

Daugherty, Harry M., 591

Daughters of Liberty, 113

Davis, Benjamin O., 665

Davis, Benjamin O., Jr., 665, p 665

Davis, Jefferson, 338, 352, 366, 372, 381, p 383

Davis, Mrs. Jefferson, 516

Davis, John W., 591, 618

Dawes, Charles G., 634

Dawes, Henry L., 425

Dawes Act, 425, 628

Deadwood, S.D., m 430, 431

Dearborn, Henry, 227, 228

Debs, Eugene V., 478–479, 538, 568

Decatur, Stephen, 214, 228

Declaration of Independence, 129–131, 149, 151, 242; text of, 816–817

Declaration of Rights (Texas), 333

Declaratory Act, 113

Deere, John, 433

De Gaulle, Charles, 740

Delaware, m 86, 87, 164; ratifies Constitution, 169; m 803

Delaware, Lord, 61

Delaware Indians, m 35, 88

De Lôme, Dupuy; De Lôme letter, 516

Democracy, extension of, 264, 269; Jacksonian, 264–266

Manassas Junction, 373, *m* 374, 376
Mandan Indians, *m* 35, 218; village, *p* 34
Manhattan Project, 675–676
Manifest destiny, 320, 332, 357, 370
Mann, Horace, 284
Manufacturing, beginning of, in England, 54–55; Hamilton's report on, 183; and protective tariff, 183, 243–244, 246; in North, 275–279, 386; slave labor in, 308; in South, 308, 315; growth of, 438, 442; in cities, 464; of automobiles, 595–596; automation in, 713. *See also* Factories; Industry
Mao Tse-tung, 698, 699, 751
Marbury v. Madison, 213, 237
Marion, Francis, 143
Marne River, Battles of, 560, 571 *m* 572, 573
Marquette, Jacques, *m* 51, 52
Marshall, George C., in World War I, 573; in World War II, 662; as Secretary of State, 695; awarded Nobel Prize, 695 n.; quoted, 695
Marshall, James, 340
Marshall, John, 170, 189; as Chief Justice, 213, 221, 236–238, 269; quoted, 238, 239
Marshall, Thurgood, 724–725, *p* 747
Marshall Plan, 695
Martineau, Harriet, 266
Martin v. Hunter's Lessee, 238
Maryland, 79–80, *m* 86, 87; slavery in, 91; education in, 94; surrenders western lands, 154; and Annapolis Convention, 162; and ratification of Constitution, 168, 170; and McCulloch case, 238; plantations in, 301; *m* 803
Mason, George, 170
Mason, James, 349, 388
Mason-Dixon Line, *m* 86, 87, 372
Massachusetts, 70, 74, *m* 86; education in, 94, 284; protests in, before Revolution, 109; in Revolutionary War, 113, 114–115, 116–117, 118, 120–121; and land claims, 117, *m* 153; Bank of, 158; and ratification of Constitution, 169–170; early manufacturing in, 244, 276, 278; recognizes unions, 282–283; and treatment of mentally ill, 287; *m* 803
Massachusetts Bay Colony, 65, 69, 70, 71, *m* 71, 74 n.
Maximilian, 389, 510
Mayas, *m* 35, 36, 43, *m* 43
Mayflower, *p* 66, 67
Mayflower Compact, 67
Meade, George G., 381, 382
Meany, George, 713
Medicare, 736

Mellon, Andrew W., 590, 605
Melville, Herman, 292
Memphis, growth of, 315; in Civil War, *m* 374, 375, *m* 380, 391; sewage disposal in, 464; Martin Luther King assassinated in, 747
Mendoza, Antonio de, 45
Mennonites, 437
Menomini Indians, 35, *m* 35
Meredith, James, 725
Merrimack, *m* 374, 385, 395
Merritt, Lesley, 520
Mesabi Range, 440–441, *m* 444
Metropolitan Museum of Art, New York, 468, *p* 468
Meuse River, *m* 572, 573
Mexican Cession, *m* 338, 339
Mexican War, 335–339, *m* 336
Mexico, 42, *m* 43, *m* 242; Indians of, *m* 35, 36, 43, *m* 43; as Spanish colony, 47, *m* 47; gains independence, 241, 251, 326; slaves freed in, 289; relations with U.S., 327, 637; and Texas revolution, 330–331; in war with U.S., 334, 335–339, *m* 336; French puppet ruler in, 389, 510; Revolution in, 555–556, 628; Wilson and, 556, 557; and resettlement program, 628; constitution of, 637
Mexico City, *m* 43, 44, 47, *m* 47, 326, *m* 336, 339, 638, 647
Miami, Fla., 749, 762, *m* 803
Miami Indians, *m* 35, *m* 268
Michigan, 295–297, 440, 588, *m* 803
Middle Colonies, settlement of, 83–90, *m* 86; education in, 94; trade in, 95; and Proclamation Line, 111–112
Middle East, Arab-Israeli conflict in, 692, 709–710, 741, 759, 775–776, *m* 778, 792–794; and oil embargo, 759–760
Midway, annexation of, 509, *m* 523; Battle of, 659, *m* 676
Mifflin, Thomas, 152
Miles, Nelson A., 521, 640
Miller, William, 733
Milwaukee, 291, 621, *m* 803
Mining, 429–431, 439–440, 584, 622
Minneapolis, *m* 430, 435
Minnesota, 297, 441, 494, 500
Minnesota Territory, 421–422
Minuit, Peter, 84, 85
Miranda, Francisco de, 147
Missions, missionaries, 46, 49, 94, 323, 324, 326, *m* 327
Mississippi, 236, 303, 370, 373 408, 617, 725, 756, *m* 803
Mississippi River, 45, *m* 51, 52, 53, 219, *m* 219, 315; as U.S. boundary, 145; navigation rights on, 158, 188; steamboats on, 236; in Civil War, 373, *m* 374, 375, 382; cities along, 445; bridges across, 467

Missouri, admitted, 244–246, 303; Mormons in, 324; slavery issue in, 354; Dred Scott case in, 357–358; and cattle industry, 426; *m* 803
Missouri Compromise, *m* 245 245–246, 352, 357, 358, 367
Missouri River, 218, 219, *m* 219, *m* 322
Missouri Synod, 291
Mitchell, Billy, 573, 653
Mobile, Ala., 135, *m* 142, 305, 315, *m* 444, 445
Moby Dick (Melville), 292
Mohawk Indians, 35, *m* 35, 85
Mohegan Indians, *m* 35, 74
Molasses Act, 110
"Molly Maguires," 478
Mondale, Walter, 769
Money, printed by states, 151; problems of, after Revolution, 152, 179–183; for War of 1812, 227; in South, in Civil War, 384; greenbacks, 387, 495; capital investments, 441–442; finance capitalists, 454, 455; silver-backed paper, 491–492; borrowing of, 497, 605, 609, 663, 685; gold and silver, ratio of, 497–498, 500; increased supply of, 501; for World War I, 559, 567; increased protection of, 617; and Keynes's theory, 626
Monitor, *m* 374, 385, 395
Monmouth, Battle of, 141, *m* 142
Monroe, James, in American Revolution, 137; supports French Revolution, 189; as envoy to Paris, 216; as President, 234, 236, 239, 240, 241, 246, 266, 328, 329; re-elected, 246; as governor of Virginia, 310; quoted, 245
Monroe Doctrine, 242, 389, 647; strengthened, 510–512; Roosevelt Corollary to, 544, 637, 638
Monrovia, Liberia, 245
Montana, 431, 434, 588, *m* 802–803
Montana Territory, 420, 431
Montcalm, Louis, 107
Monterey, Calif., *m* 322, *m* 327, *m* 336, 337, 346
Monterrey, Mexico, *m* 336, 337
Montgomery, Ala., 366, *m* 374, 465, 717–718, 736
Montgomery, Richard, 127
Monticello, 177, *p* 211
Montreal, 50, *m* 51, 52, *m* 106, 107, 127, *m* 128, *m* 139
Moody, Paul, 276
Moore's Creek, N.C., 127, *m* 128
Moravian Town, Battle of, *m* 227, 228
Morgan, Daniel, 142
Morgan, J. Pierpont, 445, 449, 454, 492, 540; quoted, 538
Mormons, 324–325
Mormon Trail, *m* 322

Niña, 27

Nixon, Richard M., in House of Representatives, 685; as Vice President, 702, 711, 719; at 1952 convention, *p* 703; visits Poland and Soviet Union, 711; in 1968 election, 748–749; as President, 749, 755–756, 757, 758–759, 760–765; at first inauguration, *p* 755; and Vietnam War, 755–756; re-elected, 756, 762; visits China and Soviet Union, *p* 758, 758–759; and Watergate, 763–764, 765; resignation of, 765; pardoned by Ford, 766; quoted, 754, 755, 759

Non-Intercourse Act, 223, 224

Normandy, 669, *m* 671

Norris, Frank, 530

North, Lord, 120, 139, 144, 145

North, steps toward abolishing slavery in, 151; early manufacturing and trade in, 275–279; reform movement in, 283–289; abolition movement in, 288–289; immigration to, 291, 292; united by better transportation, 293–297; Underground Railroad to, 312; relations of South and, 315; defies Fugitive Slave Act, 351; and Kansas-Nebraska Act, 352; in Civil War, *m* 369, 369–370, 371, 372–383, *m* 374, *m* 380, *m* 381, 385–390, *m* 391, 391–392; resources of, 371, *g* 371, 385–387; railroads of, 383, 386; discrimination in, 536; black ghettos in, 568; depression in, for blacks, 628

North Africa, English trade with, 55; Barbary pirates of, *m* 214, 214; in World War II, 660–662

North America, explorations of, *m* 32, *m* 43, *m* 44, *m* 51; in 1763, *m* 108; in 1783, *m* 144

North Atlantic Treaty Organization (NATO), 697–698, *m* 697, 708

North Carolina, 56, 81, *m* 86, 170 n., in Revolution, 127, *m* 128, *p* 132, 142, *m* 142; Loyalists in, 133; discrimination against women in, 150; western lands claimed by, *m* 153, 154; state university in, 285; plantations in, 301, 303; free blacks in, 306; slave revolts in, 310; secedes, 371; defies Confederate government, 385; in Civil War, 392; readmitted, 404; and TVA, 617; *m* 803

North Dakota, 218, 431, 434, 496, 497, 500, *m* 803

Northern Pacific Railroad, 423, *m* 430, 434, *m* 444, 446–447

North Korea, 700, 701, *m* 701, 708

North Vietnam, 709, 723, 742, *m* 742, 743, 744–745, 748, 749, 756, 757

Northwest, Indian wars in 185–186, 224–225, 424; and War of 1812, 228

Northwest Ordinance, 155–156

Northwest Territory, *m* 153, 154, 155, 158

Norway, *m* 646, 648, *m* 671, 697

Nuclear test-ban treaty, 723

Nuclear weapons, 675–676, 677, 689, 708

Nueces River, *m* 330, 335

Nullification, 255, 257

Oberlin College, 287, *p* 287

O'Connor, Sandra Day, 790, *p* 790

Oglethorpe, James, 82–83

Ohio, 236, 287, 324, 756, *m* 803

Ohio Company, 104

Ohio River (Valley), 104, 105, *m* 106, 292, *m* 293

Oil, 441, 449–450, 453; production, 1860–1900, *g* 441; and automobiles, 596–597; Arab embargo on, 759; conservation of, 759–760; increased prices for, 767; in Carter energy program, 773, 774

Okinawa, 675, *m* 676

Oklahoma, 45, 419; land rush to, 434–435; admitted, 435; *m* 803

Olive Branch Petition, 125–126

Oliver, Andrew, 113

Oliver, James, 433

Olney, Richard, 479, 511–512; quoted, 512

Omaha, Neb., *m* 444, 445, 499, 586

Omaha Beach, 669, *m* 671

Oñate, Juan de, *m* 44, 45, 46

O'Neale, Peggy (Mrs. John H. Eaton), 254

Oneida Indians, 35, *m* 35

O'Neill, Thomas P., 787

Onondaga Indians, 35, *m* 35

Open Door Policy, 525, 636

Orders in Council (British), 222, 225, 226

Ordinances of 1784 and 1785, 154–155, *c* 155

Oregon, 334, 412 n., 532, *m* 802

Oregon Country, *m* 219, 240, 321–324, *m* 322

Oregon Territory, *m* 338, 431

Oregon Trail, *p* 321, *m* 322, 323

Organization of American States (OAS), 741

Organization of Petroleum Exporting Countries (OPEC), 759, 767

Oriskany, Battle of, 137, *m* 139

Osceola, 268

Ostend Manifesto, 356–357

Oswald, Lee Harvey, 727, 731

Otis, Elisha G., 466

Otis, James, 109–110, 112, 113

Ottawa Indians, *m* 35, 186, *m* 268

Owen, Robert, 283

Owen, Robert Dale, 283, 285

Pacific Ocean, Magellan crosses, 31, *m* 32; sighted by Balboa, 42; U.S. interests in, 509–510, 524; Japanese expansion in, 643; World War II in, 655, 657–660, 674–677, *m* 676, 679

Pact of Paris (Kellogg-Briand), 636–637

Paine, Thomas, 129; quoted, 101, 129, 136

Palmer, A. Mitchell, 584

Panama, canal across, 541, *p* 542, 542–543, *m* 543; independence of, from Colombia, 542; to assume control of Canal, 640

Pan-American Conferences, 647

Pan-American Union, 510

Panic, of 1837, 262, 280, 282, 284, 294, 323, 324; of 1857, 445; of 1869, 410; of 1873, 411, 463, 495; of 1907, 540, 541. *See also* Depression

Paris, Treaty of (1783), 145; Lindbergh lands at, 601; Pact of, 636–637; liberation of, 669; peace talks in, 756, 757

Paris Peace Conference, 635

Parker, Alton B., 538

Parker, John, 121

Parker, Peter, 127

Parks, Rosa, 717, *p* 718

Parmelee, Frank, 445

Parsons, Albert, 475

Parsons, William, 92

Parson's Cause, 109

Patents; U.S. Patent Office, 439

Patriots, 114, 115, 116–117, 118–119, 120–121, 126–128, 129, 131–133, 151

Patton, George S., 670

Paul, Alice, 533

Pawnee Indians, 34, *m* 35

Pawtucket, R.I., 275

Peace Corps, 720, 721

Pea Ridge, Battle of, 373, *m* 374

Pearl Harbor, 509, *m* 523; in World War II, 657, 658, *m* 676

Pendleton, George H., 390, 488

Pendleton Act, 488

Penn, William, 87, 88, *p* 88

Pennsylvania, *m* 86, 87–90, 118; western land claims of, 117; Loyalists in, 133; in Revolution, 134, *m* 142; wage and price regulation in, 151; opposes Constitution, 169; Whiskey Rebellion in, 182; canals in, *m* 293, 294; in Civil War, 380, *m* 380, *m* 381, 381–382; oil in, 441; immigration to, 459; labor violence in, 471–472, 477; *m* 803

Pennsylvania Railroad, 295, *m* 297, 444, *m* 444, 454, 472

Pensacola, Fla., 135, *m* 142, 239, *m* 240

West, *m* 297, 420, 423, 434, 447; southern, 315, 443, 445; transcontinental, 352, 410, 429, *m* 444, 445–447; in Civil War, 371, 383–384, 386; cattle shipped by, 427; mileage, by 1900, 443; trunk lines, 444–445; influence of, on American life, 447; and time zones, 447–448; capital for, 457; strikes on, 472, 474, 478–479; regulations of, 490, 539; and Granger laws, 494–495; government operation of, 567, 685; discrimination forbidden on, 724

Raleigh, Walter, 56, 57, 59

Ranching, 425–429, 434

Randolph, A. Philip, 665, 687

Randolph, Edmund, 164, 177

Randolph, John, 248, 302

Rankin, Jeannette, 658

Rappahannock River, *m* 62, 63, *m* 374, 380

Rationing, in World War II, 663

Reagan, Ronald, as governor of California, 749; in 1976 election, 768, 769; in 1980 election, 780–782, *p* 781; as President, 779, 786–796, *p* 787; quoted, 753

Reconstruction, after Civil War, 398–399, 400–403, 404–405, 406–408, 411, 413

Reconstruction Act, 404

Reconstruction Finance Corporation (RFC), 609

Recovery legislation, 614, 615–617

Red Cloud, 412

Red River War, 423

"Red scare," 584

Reed, Thomas B., 490–491

Reform movement, 283–289, 491, 492, 495; working conditions, 281, 283; religion and, 284; education, 284–285; women's rights, 285–287; care of mentally ill, 287; temperance, 287–288; abolition of slavery, 288–289; Indian rights, 425; housing, 468; political corruption, 484, 485, 487–488, 549; civil service, 485, 487–488; progressivism, 529–531, 532–535; municipal and state, 532; peace movement, 546; New Deal and, 614, 616–617, 618, 621, 627. *See also* Progressive movement

Religion, in Europe, 54; freedom of, 71, 72, 80, 82, 87, 88, 150–151; and education, 94; separation of state and, 150; evangelical, spread of, 284; camp meeting, *p* 284; and treatment of women, 285; immigration of religious leaders, 291; and slave issue, 302; Indian, 425; in Communist world, 694

Republican Party, of Jefferson, 183, 184, 186, 187, 190, 191, 192, 211, 212, 213, 215, 243, 244, 247; National Republicans, 249; in 1831, 264; new, formed in 1854, 354–355, 357, 369; and Missouri Compromise, 358; and Lincoln, 378; and industry, 386; after Civil War, 398–399, 400, 402–407, 409, 410, 411, 412, 413; Liberal Republicans, 410, 485; dominance of, 484; Mugwumps, 488, 489; and farm vote, 496; and peace delegation, 574; and tax cut, 686; South returns to, 702

Reservations, Indian, 422–423, *p* 423, *m* 424

Resettlement Administration, 621

Resumption Act, 495

Reuther, Walter, 713

Revels, Hiram R., 406

Revere, Paul, 120, 121, *p* 121; route of, *m* 120

Revolutionary War, beginnings, *m* 120–121, *m* 126, 126–128, *m* 128; setbacks, 131–132; opposition to, 133; Patriots' advantages, 133–134; women and blacks in, 134–135, 141; foreign aid in, 135, 139, 143, 147; campaigns in late 1776 and 1777, 136–139, *m* 139; at sea, 139–140; on the frontier, 140; campaigns of 1778–1781, 140–143, *m* 142; in the South, 141–143, *m* 142, *m* 143; surrender at Yorktown, *m* 143, 143–144; Treaty of Paris, 144–145; and southern economy, 301

Reza Pahlevi, Mohammed, 777, 778

Rheims, France, *m* 671, 673

Rhett, Robert Barnwell, 366

Rhineland, 644, *m* 646

Rhode Island, *m* 71, 72, *m* 86, 163; joins Union, 170 n.; education in, 284; *m* 803

Rice, 80, 81, 301, 304, *m* 304, 306

Richmond, Va., 308, 351, 466; and slave revolt, 309–310; in Civil War, *m* 374, 375–376, 380, *m* 380, *m* 391, 392; rail service to, *m* 444, 445

Rickenbacker, Eddie, 573, 601

Ridgway, Matthew B., 702

Right of deposit, 188, 215, 216

Right-to-work laws, 686

Riis, Jacob, 530

Rio Grande, *m* 330, 331, 335, 336, 337

Ripon, Wis., *m* 297, 354

Roads, post roads, 236; surfacing of, 290, 293; improved, *m* 293; expanded system of, 716; beautification and safety of, 736

Roanoke Island, 56–57, *m* 56, *m* 62

Robinson, Jackie, 687

Robinson, John, 66

Rochambeau, Count de, 143

Rockefeller, John D., 449–450, 453, 538; quoted, 450, 455

Rockefeller, Nelson, 749, 766

Rockingham, Lord, 113

Rocky Mountains, 219, *m* 219, 220, 418, *m* 430; mining in, 429–431

Roebling, John A., 467

Rogers, Will, 629

Rolfe, John, 63, 65

Roman Catholics. *See* Catholics

Rome, Italy, 669, *m* 671

Rommel, Erwin, 660, 661, 662, *p* 662

Romney (ship), 113

Roosevelt, Alice, *p* 535, 537

Roosevelt, Eleanor, 610, 613, *p* 627, 629, 667 n., 672, *p* 691

Roosevelt, Franklin D., 589, 590, 594, 604, 610, *p* 611, 686; as governor of New York, 608, 610; as Assistant Secretary of the Navy, 610; First Inaugural Address, 612; "brain trust" of, 612–613; and banks, 613; recovery program, 615; and gold standard, 616; and conservation, 617; public assistance programs, 618, 628; and income tax, 621; and labor, 622; and NRA, 622–623; broadcasting, *p* 623; and Supreme Court, 624, 625; re-elected, 624, 625, 628, 650, 667; and minorities, 627, 628; recognizes Soviet Union, 643; imposes arms embargo, 644; "quarantine speech," 645; and Good Neighbor Policy, 647; lifts arms embargo, 647–648; and aid to Britain, 649–650; and Atlantic Charter, 654; war message to Congress, 657; in World War II, 657–658, 661, 663, 664, 665, *p* 668; at Casablanca, 667–668; at Yalta, 670–672; death of, 672; and atomic bomb, 675; quoted, 625, 644, 645, 647–648, 650, 651, 658

Roosevelt, Theodore, 514, 528, 536–537, 563; as Assistant Secretary of the Navy, *p* 514, 517, 537; in Spanish-American War, 520, 521; as Vice President, 524, 537; as President, 535, 538–541, 542–543, 544, 545, 546, 551, 610; and coal strike, 537; and family, *p* 537; and trusts, 537–538; and railroad regulation, 539; and conservation, 539; and foreign affairs, 541–546; awarded Nobel Prize, 545; re-enters politics, 547, 548, 549; quoted, 505, 517, 518, 530, 538, 546–547, 549, 562

Roosevelt Corollary, 544, 637, 638

Spoils system, 264, 485, 487, 488, 489, 490
Sprague, Frank, 466
Springfield, Ill., 393
Sputnik, 724
Squanto, 68
Square Deal, 536, 611
Stalin, Joseph, 642, 667, 676, 689, 694 n.; in World War II, 662, 670, 673; at Yalta and Potsdam, 670–672, 693; purges by, 693; death of, 707
Stalwarts (Republican wing), 486, 488
Stamp Act, 112–113
Stamp Act Congress, 113
Standard Oil Company, 450, 453, 530, 538
Standish, Miles, 67, 68
Stanton, Edwin M., 289, 369, 404, 405, 411
Stanton, Elizabeth Cady, 286, 533
States' rights, 192, 239, 255–257, 261, 749; in Confederate constitution, 385
States' Rights Democratic Party, 688
Statue of Liberty, 413, p 413, p 459, 479
Statute of Religious Freedom, 150
Steamboat, 236, 238, 278, 279, 315, 332, 449
Steam locomotive, p 294, 295
Steam power for manufacturing, 302
Steel industry, 448–449; in South, 411; 1860–1900, g 449; strikes in, 477, 584, 622; and unions, 622
Steel plow, 433
Steffens, Lincoln, 530
Stephens, Alexander H., 348, 367, 401
Stephens, Uriah S., 473–474
Stephenson, George, 295
Steuben, Baron von, 135, 141, 161
Stevens, Thaddeus, 404, 405, 411; quoted, 402
Stevenson, Adlai E., 702, 713
Stevenson, John, 465
Steward, Ira, 471
Stimson, Henry L., 637, 638, 643; quoted, 656
Stimson Doctrine, 643
Stock market, 594; crash of, 606
Stocks, stockholders, 55, 57, 70, 442, 453, 410, 605
Stockton, Richard, 137
Stockton, Robert, 337
Stowe, Harriet Beecher, 289, 351, p 361, 365
Strait of Magellan, 31, m 32
Strategic Arms Limitation Talks (SALT), 759, 780
Straus, Oscar S., 535
Streetcars, 465–466
Strikes, 281, 282, 474, 475, 478–479; in 1860, p 282; coal, 471–472, 537, 584, 685; steel, 477, 584, 622; after World War I, 583–584; after World War II, 685
Strong, Josiah, 513
Stuart, J.E.B., 379
Stuart, Robert, 220
Stuyvesant, Peter, 85, 86, 87
Submarines, 561, 562, 564, 565, 566, 660
Suburbs, 466, 596, 716
Subways, 466
Sudetenland, 645, m 646
Suez Canal, 660, 661, m 671, 709, m 778
Suffrage. *See* Voting
Sugar, m 304, 306, 309, 491, 514
Sugar Act, 110–111
Sugg, W. W., 427
Sullivan, John, 140
Sumner, Charles, 355, 398, 402–403, 411, 507–508
Sunbelt, 782–783
Supreme Court, established, 166–167; and judicial review, 213; acquits Burr, 221; interprets Constitution, 236–238; and Indian removal, 269; Dred Scott decision, 357–358, 359, 368; first woman before, 489; and income tax, 493; and Granger laws, 494–495; and "separate-but-equal" principle, 535, 717; and Northern Securities case, 538; and New Deal, 622–624, 625; Roosevelt and, 624, 625; and Insular Cases, 639; on civil rights, 717, 718; Nixon and, 760–761, 764; O'Connor appointment, 790
Sussex pledge, 562–563
Sutter, John, 327, 340
Sutter's Fort, m 322
Swedish colonies, 85, m 86
Sylvis, William, 470
Syms, Benjamin, 94
Syria, 692, 741, 759, m 778, 793

Taft, Robert A., 702; quoted, 690
Taft, William Howard, as Chief Justice, 546; and dollar diplomacy, 544; as President, 546–547, 549, 586, 595; as governor of Philippines, 641; quoted, 547, 548
Taft, Mrs. William Howard, 546
Taft-Hartley Act, 685–686
Taiwan, 643, 759, 776
Tallmadge, James, 244
Tammany Hall, 488
Tampa, Fla., 520
Tampico, Mexico, m 336, 556
Taney, Roger B., 259, 357–358, 368
Tarbell, Ida M., 530, p 531
Tariff, 182, 183, 442, 490; of 1816, 243–244; of 1824, 246; Tariff of Abominations, 249, 255, 257; and nullification, 255, 257; Compromise, 257; of 1832, 257, 271; of 1842, 271; Morrill, 386; McKinley, 491, 492, 493, 510; Wilson-Gorman (1894), 492–493, 514; resented by farmers, 495–496; reduced, 547, 647; Underwood, 550; Fordney-McCumber, 593, 634; high, and foreign trade, 606; Harley-Smoot, 634
Taxes, imposed by Britain, 110–111, 112, 113, 114; without representation, 112–113; state, 152; export, import, 165; Hamilton's plan for, 182; under Jefferson, 213; for education, 284–285; in Civil War, 387; single tax, 530; income, 550, 609, 621, 663; processing, 615; inheritance, 621; Social Security, 626, 736; in World War II, 663; poll, 687 n.; cuts in, 732; Reagan program, 786
Taylor, Augustine, 290
Taylor, Margaret Smith, 346
Taylor, Zachary, 335, 336–337, 345, 346–347, 350, 351
Tea Act, 115–116; and Boston Tea Party, 116–117
Teapot Dome scandal, 591
Technological advances, 236, 290, 386, 413, p 592, 595–598, 713–714. *See also* Inventions
Tecumseh, 225, 228
Tehran, 776, m 778
Telegraph, 386, 441, 446, 450, 452; railroad office, p 451
Telephone, 452–453, 500
Television, 629 n., 703, 714, 720, 727, 760
Teller Amendment, 518, 640
Temperance movement, 287–288, 289
Tenements, 467–468, 531; Tenement House Law, 467
Tennessee, admitted, 236; and issue of slavery, 302; agriculture in, 303, m 304; joins Confederacy, 371; in Civil War, 373–375, 382–383, 385; readmitted, 403; Johnson as senator from, 406; m 803
Tennessee River, 373, m 374, m 616
Tennessee Valley Authority (TVA), m 616, 617, 629
Tenochtitlán, 36, m 43
Tenure of Office Act, 404, 405
Territories, constitutional status of, 638–639; government of, 639–640
Tet offensive, 745
Texas, 240, 400, 404; admitted, 303, 334; farming in, p 307; Americans settle in, 329–330; independence for, 330–331, 332; debate over acquiring,

Van Buren, Martin, 346; as Secretary of State, 253, 254, 259; as President, 261-263, 270, 332, 333, 338; and Independent Treasury, 262; and *Caroline* affair, 262-263
Vancouver Island, 321, *m* 322
Vanderbilt, Cornelius, 444
Vann, Robert L., 628
Van Rensselaer, Kiliaen, 84, 228
Van Rensselaer, Stephen, 228, 248
Van Vorst, Marie and Bessie, 531
Vanzetti, Bartolomeo, 584-585
V-E Day, 673
Venezuela, 147, 511-512, 544
Venice, Italy, 25, *m* 32
Veracruz, Battle of, *m* 336, 337, 338; U.S. occupation of, 556
Vermont, *m* 153, 158, 236 n., *m* 803
Verrazano, Giovanni da, 49-50, *m* 51
Versailles Treaty, 575, 576, 577, 644
Vesey, Denmark, 310
Vespucci, Amerigo, 30, *m* 32
Veterans' Administration, 683-685
Veterans' organizations, 409
Vichy government, France, 648, 661
Vicksburg, Battle of, *m* 374, 375, *m* 380, 382, *m* 391
Viet Cong, 723, 743, 756, 758
Viet Minh, 709
Vietnam, as French colony, 527; division of, 709; U.S. involvement in, 723, 724, 740, 742-745, 755, 756, 757, 758
Vietnam War, 740, *m* 742, 742-745, 755-758; opposition to, 742, 743-745, 746, 748, 749; Vietnamization of, 755, 756; costs of, 757
Vikings, 24-25, *m* 29; ship, *p* 25
Villa, Francisco ("Pancho"), 556
Vinland, 25
Violence, against blacks, Catholics, Jews, immigrants, 402, 404, 408, 586, 588, 736; in labor disputes, 471-472, 475, 477-479, 583, 622; prohibition and, 589; antiwar protest, 748, 756
Virginia, *m* 86, 104, 109, 404; colonial, 56-57, 61-65, *m* 62, 112; slavery in, 91, 151; education in, 94; in French and Indian War, 105; House of Burgesses, 109, 112, 118; western lands claimed by, 117, *m* 153, 154; in Revolution, 143, *m* 143; Statute of Religious Freedom, 150; and Annapolis Convention, 162; ratifies Constitution, 170; agriculture in, 301, *m* 304; debates abolition, 302; and slave uprisings, 310; manufacturing in, 315; secession of, 371; in Civil War, 375-376, 380-381, 385,

389-390, *m* 391; readmitted, 408; and TVA, 617; *m* 803
Virginia (Merrimack) (ship), 385
Virginia City, Mont., *m* 430, 431
Virginia City, Nev., 430, *m* 430
Virginia Company, 57, 61, 62, 67
Virginia Plan, 164
Virginia Resolution, 192
Virgin Islands, *m* 543, 555, 639, 640
Virginius incident, 508, 515
VISTA (Volunteers in Service to America), 733
V-J Day, 677
Volstead Act, 588
Voting, requirements for, 149, 264, 761; for women, 286, 533-534, 599; for blacks, secured by 15th Amendment, 408; blacks denied right of, 535, 687 n.; direct primary, 532; secret ballot, 532; extended to D.C. residents, 725; voter-registration drives, 736, 737
Voting Rights Act, 736-737

Wade, Benjamin F., 402, 403, 406; quoted, 400
Wade-Davis Bill, 398
Wage and Price Stability, Council on, 767
Wages, and Henry Ford, 596; minimum wage laws, 624, 625, 627, 688; controlled, 664, 762, 767; and payroll-deduction plan, 663; increasing, 685, 724
Wage Stabilization Act, 664
Wagner, Robert F., 621
Wagner Act, 625, 686
Wainwright, Jonathan, 658
Wake Island, 522, *m* 523, 639, 658, *m* 676
Wald, Lillian, 531
Walden (Thoreau), 295
Walesa, Lech, 791
Walker, Joseph, 327
Wallace, George C., 749, 762
Wallace, Henry A., 612, 650, 688, 695
Wallace, Henry C., 590
Walpole, Horace, quoted, 107, 108
Waltham, Mass.; Waltham System, 276, 278, 280
Walther, Carl F. W., 291
Wampanoag Indians, *m* 35, 68, 75
Wanamaker, John, 490
War bonds, 663
War Democrats, 390
War Department, 176, 177
War Hawks, 225
War Powers Act, 757
Ward, Sam, 483
War of 1812, 224, 225-230, *m* 227, 292
War Industries Board, 567
War Production Board, 663
Warren, Earl, 731, 760; quoted, 717

Warren Commission, 731
Washington, Booker T., 551; quoted, 384, 536
Washington (state), 431, 625, *m* 802
Washington, D.C., *p* 181, 193, *m* 227, *p* 773; White House in, 193, 211, 212; in War of 1812, *p* 229, 229-230; Capitol, *p* 237, *p* 243, 246; issue of slave trade in, 347, 348; "peace convention" in, 367; Lincoln assassinated in, 393; and telegraph, 441, 450; rail service to, *m* 444, 445; Coxey's march on, 492; Pan-American conference in, 510; Jim Crow regulations in, 551; race riots in, 586, 738; airmail to, 601; "Bonus Army" in, 609-610; "greenbelt" towns around, 621; disarmament conference in, 635-636; school desegregation in, 717; citizens of, allowed to vote, 725; civil rights march on, 726-727
Washington, George, 99, 105, *p* 105, 111, 170, 302; at Continental Congress, 118; in Revolution, 126, 127, 128, 133-134, 135, 136, 137, 138, 140, 141, 143, 144; on Shays's Rebellion, 161; and Mount Vernon conference, 162; at Constitutional Convention, 163-164; as President, 171, 212; inauguration of, *p* 175, 175-176; Cabinet of, 176-177, *p* 177, 178; and Hamilton's bank plan, 181; and Whiskey Rebellion, 182, *p* 182; re-elected, 183; and French Revolution, 184, 185; and Jay's Treaty, 187; Farewell Address, 187, 188; retirement of, 188; death of, 191, *p* 191; quoted, 134, 145, 161, 187
Washington, Martha, 141, 175, *p* 176
Washington, Tex., *m* 330, 331
Washington Territory, 431
Washita, Battle of, 423, *m* 424
Watergate, 763-764, 766
Waterloo, Battle of, 229
Watertown, Mass., 70, *m* 71
Watson, Tom, 498, 500, 501
Wayne, "Mad Anthony," 186
Weapons, Civil War, 395; Gatling gun, 395, 425; Colt six-shooter, 420; machine gun, 560; poison gas, torpedoes, 561; tanks, 561, 653; nuclear, 675-676, 677, 708
Weaver, James, 493, 495, 499
Weaver, Robert C., 628, 725, 736
Webster, Daniel, 85, 259, 261, 270, 271, 347, *p* 347, 509; in debate with Hayne, 255-256, *p* 256; and Webster-Ashburton Treaty, 263; opposes Mexican War, 335-336; and Compromise of 1850, 348, 349-350;